Canadian Politics
CRITICAL APPROACHES

Canadian Politics
CRITICAL APPROACHES

Sixth Edition

RAND DYCK
Carleton University

NELSON / EDUCATION

NELSON / EDUCATION

Canadian Politics: Critical Approaches, Sixth Edition

by Rand Dyck

**Vice President,
Editorial Director:**
Evelyn Veitch

**Editor-in-Chief,
Higher Education:**
Anne Williams

Acquisitions Editor:
Anne-Marie Taylor

Marketing Manager:
Ann Byford

Senior Developmental Editor:
Linda Sparks

Photo Researcher:
Melody Tolson

Permissions Coordinator:
Melody Tolson

Content Production Manager:
Christine Gilbert

Production Service:
MPS Limited, A Macmillan
Company

Copy Editor:
Jessie Coffey

Proofreader:
Dianne Fowlie

Indexer:
Maura Brown

Manufacturing Coordinator:
Loretta Lee

Design Director:
Ken Phipps

Managing Designer:
Franca Amore

Interior Design:
Katherine Strain

Cover Design:
Jennifer Leung

Cover Image:
Kate Leblanc/GetStock.com

Compositor:
MPS Limited, A Macmillan
Company

Printer:
Edwards Brothers

Library and Archives Canada
Cataloguing in Publication

Dyck, Rand, 1943-Canadian politics:
critical approaches/Rand Dyck. —
6th ed.

Includes bibliographical references
and index.
ISBN 978-0-17-650165-5

1. Canada–Politics and
government–Textbooks. I. Title.

JL75.D93 2010 320.971
C2009-906597-5

ISBN-13: 978-0-17-650165-5
ISBN-10: 0-17-650165-7

To the faculty, staff, and students of the Carleton University Department of Political Science, who gave me a new lease on life!

For updated material, such as new election results from 2010 onward, please go to the text's website at http://www. canadianpolitics6e.nelson.com

Brief Contents

Preface   xx

PART 1   INTRODUCTION   **1**
Chapter 1   The Study of Politics   3
Chapter 2   Institutional Foundations and the Evolution of the State   27

PART 2   THE SOCIETAL CONTEXT: CLEAVAGES AND IDENTITIES   **47**
Chapter 3   Regionalism   51
Chapter 4   Aboriginal Peoples   77
Chapter 5   French Canada and the Quebec Question   103
Chapter 6   Ethnocultural Minorities   127
Chapter 7   Gender   147
Chapter 8   Class   169
Chapter 9   Other Cleavages and Identities: Urban/Rural Location,
            Religion, and Age   197
Chapter 10 Canada's External Environment: The United States and
            the World   217

PART 3   LINKING PEOPLE TO GOVERNMENT   **247**
Chapter 11 The Canadian Political Culture   249
Chapter 12 Political Socialization, the Mass Media, and Public
            Opinion Polls   281
Chapter 13 Elections and the Electoral System   313
Chapter 14 Political Parties and the Party System   337
Chapter 15 Parties, Voting, and the Election Campaign   371
Chapter 16 Advocacy Groups, Social Movements, and Lobbying   395

PART 4   THE CONSTITUTIONAL CONTEXT   **425**
Chapter 17 The Canadian Constitution and Constitutional
            Change   427
Chapter 18 The Provinces and the Federal System   455
Chapter 19 The Charter of Rights and Freedoms   491

PART 5   GOVERNING   **523**
Chapter 20 The Policymaking Process and Policy Instruments   525
Chapter 21 The Executive: Crown, Prime Minister, and
            Cabinet   545
Chapter 22 The Bureaucracy   583
Chapter 23 Parliament   617
Chapter 24 The Judiciary   659

Glossary   685
Index   709

Web Appendix A Constitution Act, 1867 (excerpts)   A-1
Web Appendix B Constitution Act, 1982   A-2

Contents

Preface   xx

PART 1 INTRODUCTION   1
Chapter 1 The Study of Politics   3
The Political System   3
Approaches to the Study of Politics   10
The Pluralist Approach   11
The Public Choice Approach   14
The Class Analysis Approach   16
The State-Centred Approach   19
Globalization   22
Conclusion   24
Discussion Questions   25
Notes   25
Further Readings   26

Chapter 2 Institutional Foundations and the Evolution of the State   27
Early Settlement and Political Institutions   27
The Road to Confederation   30
The British Parliamentary System Compared with the American
Congressional System   32
Canadian and American Federalism   35
Principles of the Canadian Constitution   37
The Road to Canadian Sovereignty   38
The Changing Role of the State   41
Conclusion   44
Discussion Questions   45
Notes   45
Further Readings   46

PART 2 THE SOCIETAL CONTEXT: CLEAVAGES AND IDENTITIES   47
Chapter 3 Regionalism   51
Theoretical Considerations   51
Geography   53
Physiographic Regions   53
Transportation and Communications Systems   53
Population Distribution   56
Economy   58
The Atlantic Region   58
Quebec   59
Ontario   60
The Prairie Region   60

British Columbia 61
The North 61
Regional Economic Demands 62
Historic Regional Conflicts 62
Ownership of Natural Resources 62
Tariffs 63
Transportation 63
Banking 63
The Atlantic Provinces 65
Recent Regional Conflicts 65
Taxation and Regulation of Natural Resources 65
Other Regional Economic Conflicts 65
Regional Economic Disparities 67
Regional Identities 70
Conclusion 73
Discussion Questions 75
Notes 75
Further Reading 76

Chapter 4   Aboriginal Peoples 77
Theoretical Considerations 77
Colonialism, Identities, and Changing Terminology 77
Theoretical Models 78
Aboriginal Demographic Profile Today 79
Historical Evolution 82
Aboriginal Political Issues Since 1970 85
Land Issues 86
Governance Issues 89
Recent Aboriginal Issues 95
Conclusion 97
Discussion Questions 99
Notes 99
Further Reading 102

Chapter 5   French Canada and the Quebec Question 103
The French–English Demographic Profile in Canada Today 103
Theoretical Considerations 105
Identities and Quebec Nationalism 105
Different Conceptions of French Canada 106
Historical Overview of French–English Relations 107
Pre-Confederation Developments 107
Ethnic/Linguistic Conflicts, 1867–1960 108
The Quiet Revolution: Quebec in the 1960s 110
Quebec and French Canada Since 1970 113
The 1970s 113
The 1980s 114
The 1990s 116
Developments in Other Provinces and Territories 117
Contemporary Issues 119
Conclusion 121

Discussion Questions 123
Notes 124
Further Reading 125

Chapter 6   Ethnocultural Minorities   127
A Profile of Ethnocultural Minorities in Canada Today 128
Theoretical Considerations 129
History of Canadian Immigration 130
Racial Discrimination 132
Overcoming Discrimination: Multiculturalism, Equity, and
Inclusiveness 134
Backtracking in the 1990s 137
Current Ethnocultural Issues 139
Conclusion 142
Discussion Questions 144
Notes 144
Further Reading 146

Chapter 7   Gender   147
Theoretical Considerations 147
Evolution of Women's Rights to 1970 148
The Women's Movement After 1970 152
Representation in Politics and Government 152
Employment Issues 155
Constitutional, Legal, and Aboriginal Women's Issues 156
Reproduction, Sexuality, Health, and Violence Issues 158
The Feminization of Poverty and Child Care 160
Women's Centres and Women's Groups 160
Gay, Lesbian, Bisexual, and Transgendered Issues and Identities 162
Conclusion 163
Discussion Questions 165
Notes 165
Further Reading 167

Chapter 8   Class   169
Theoretical Considerations 169
A Profile of Class Divisions in Canada Today 172
The Upper Class 172
Identifying the Corporate Elite 172
Demands of the Corporate Elite and Results 175
The Middle Class 178
The Working Class 180
The Poor 183
The Rise of the Social Safety Net 186
The Demise of Social Programs 187
Conclusion 190
Discussion Questions 192
Notes 192
Further Reading 195

Chapter 9   Other Cleavages and Identities: Urban/Rural Location, Religion, and Age   **197**

Theoretical Considerations   197
Urban/Rural Location   198
Religion   203
Separate Schools   *203*
Other Religious Issues   *205*
Current Religious Issues   *207*
Age   209
Earlier Struggles   *209*
Population Projections   *210*
Current and Future Issues   *212*
Conclusion   213
Discussion Questions   215
Notes   215
Further Reading   216

Chapter 10   Canada's External Environment: The United States and the World   **217**

The Global Setting   218
Foreign Governments   *218*
International Organizations   *218*
International Agreements   *220*
Transnational Corporations and Globalization   *221*
International Terrorism   *222*
Global Influences in Defence, Foreign, and Border Policies   223
Defence Policy   *223*
Foreign Policy   *225*
Border Policy   *226*
Global Economic Influences on Canada   227
Foreign Investment   *227*
Trade   *231*
The Environment   *234*
Energy   *235*
Trade Unions   *236*
The Canadian Economy in an Age of Globalization   *236*
Global Influences on Canadian Culture   237
Television   *237*
Magazines   *238*
Film and Video   *239*
Publishing   *240*
Newspapers, Radio, and Sound Recordings   *240*
Other Cultural Industries   *240*
Canadian Cultural Industries in an Age of Globalization   *241*
Global Influences on Other Aspects of Canadian Political Life   241
Conclusion   242
Discussion Questions   243
Notes   244
Further Reading   246

PART 3   LINKING PEOPLE TO GOVERNMENT   247
Chapter 11   **The Canadian Political Culture**   249
Theoretical Considerations   250
The Traditional Canadian Political Culture   251
Democracy   *251*
Distinguishing between Canadian and American Values   *255*
Other Basic Values   *262*
Canada's Changing Political Culture   263
"Limited Identities": Subcultures in Canada   267
Regional and Provincial/Territorial Subcultures   *267*
Ethnic Subcultures   *268*
Other Subcultures   *269*
Political Participation   269
Electoral Participation   *269*
Nonelectoral Participation   *272*
Conclusion   273
Discussion Questions   275
Notes   275
Further Reading   278

Chapter 12   **Political Socialization, the Mass Media, and Public Opinion Polls**   **281**
Theoretical Considerations   281
Political Socialization   282
The Family   *282*
The School   *282*
Peers   *284*
The Mass Media   *284*
Other Agents of Political Socialization   *284*
The Mass Media   286
Newspapers   *287*
Broadcasting   *289*
The Changing Media World   *292*
The Internet   *293*
The Media and the Public   *294*
The Media and the Politicians   *297*
Public Opinion Polls   299
Measuring Public Opinion   *299*
The Importance of Polls in Elections   *301*
Impact of Polls on the Authorities   *303*
Conclusion   304
Discussion Questions   307
Notes   307
Further Reading   310

Chapter 13   **Elections and the Electoral System**   313
Theoretical Considerations   313
Drawing the Electoral Map   314
Distribution of Seats among Provinces   *314*

Drawing Constituency Boundaries *315*
The Official Election Machinery 317
Setting the Date *317*
Election Officials *318*
The Voters' List *318*
Nomination *319*
Election Day *319*
The Ballot *320*
The Franchise *320*
The Proportionality of the Electoral System 322
Discrepancies between Seats and Votes: National Level *323*
Discrepancies between Seats and Votes: By Province *324*
Remedies *325*
Financing Elections 327
Pre-1974 *327*
Federal Election Finance Law and Its Results, 1974–2003 *328*
Federal Election Finance Law after 2003 *329*
Third-Party Advertising and the Royal Commission on Electoral Reform and Party Financing *331*
Conclusion 332
Discussion Questions 334
Notes 334
Further Reading 335

Chapter 14 Political Parties and the Party System **337**
Theoretical Considerations 337
Historical Evolution of Canadian Parties 339
The First Party System, 1867–1921 *339*
The Second Party System, 1921–1957 *341*
The Third Party System, 1957–1993 *342*
The Fourth Party System, 1993– *344*
Interpretations of the Canadian Party System 346
The Broker System *346*
Ideological or Class-Based Parties *347*
Other Interpretations *348*
Party Ideology 351
Party Organization 355
Party Membership *355*
Party Leadership *356*
Party Policymaking *359*
General Structures and Operations *360*
Conclusion 363
Discussion Questions 365
Notes 366
Further Reading 369

Chapter 15 Parties, Voting, and the Election Campaign **371**
Theoretical Considerations 371
The National Party Campaign 372
Party Headquarters and Pre-Writ Preparations *372*
Election Strategy *373*

Election Platform 373
The Leader's Tour 374
Media Coverage 374
National Media Advertising 375
The Leaders' Debates 377
The 2004, 2006, and 2008 Election Campaigns 378
The Local Candidate Campaign 380
Nomination 380
The Local Campaign 381
Explaining Canadian Voting Behaviour 382
Sociodemographic Bases of Party Support 382
Core Values and Beliefs 385
Party Identification 386
The Economy, the Issues, and the Government's Performance 386
Leadership 388
Strategic Voting 388
The Absent Mandate 388
Conclusion 389
Discussion Questions 390
Notes 391
Further Reading 393

Chapter 16 Advocacy Groups, Social Movements, and Lobbying **395**
Theoretical Considerations 396
The Array of Canadian Advocacy Groups 397
Business Groups 399
Nonbusiness Groups 400
Other Categorizations of Advocacy Groups 400
Social Movements 402
Advocacy Group Structures 403
Targets and Methods of Advocacy Group Activity 404
Policy Communities and Policy Networks 404
The Bureaucracy 405
The Prime Minister, the Cabinet, and Ministers 406
Parliament 407
Other Targets 408
Group Resources and Determinants of Success 410
Lobbying in Canada 412
Emergence of Modern Lobbying 413
Legalizing Lobbying: The Registration System 413
Lobbying under the Chrétien, Martin, and Harper Governments 415
Conclusion 418
Discussion Questions 420
Notes 421
Further Reading 423

PART 4 THE CONSTITUTIONAL CONTEXT **425**
Chapter 17 The Canadian Constitution and Constitutional Change **427**
Components of the Canadian Constitution 427
The Constitution Act, 1867 428
Amendments to the Constitution Act, 1867 429

British Statutes and Orders in Council 429
Organic Canadian Statutes 430
Constitution Act, 1982 430
Judicial Decisions 431
Constitutional Conventions 431
The Quest for Constitutional Change 432
A Domestic Constitutional Amending Formula 433
A Constitutional Charter of Rights 435
The Quiet Revolution in Quebec 436
The Victoria Charter 437
The Constitution Act, 1982 437
The Meech Lake Accord 440
The Charlottetown Accord 442
The 1992 Referendum 444
Post-Charlottetown Constitutional Developments 445
Future Constitutional Change? 448
Conclusion 449
Discussion Questions 451
Notes 451
Further Reading 453

Chapter 18 The Provinces and the Federal System **455**
The Provincial Political Systems 456
The Confederation Settlement 459
Evolution of Canadian Federalism 461
Division of Powers 461
Federal–Provincial Finance 466
Federal Controls 472
Phases of Canadian Federalism 473
Canadian Federalism, 1867–1945 473
Executive Federalism, 1945–1984 474
Canadian Federalism, 1984–2000 476
Canadian Federalism in the 21st Century 477
Active Areas of Federal–Provincial Interaction 478
Stephen Harper's Conservatives 482
Conclusion 483
Discussion Questions 486
Notes 486
Further Reading 489

Chapter 19 The Charter of Rights and Freedoms **491**
Defining and Protecting Rights and Freedoms 492
En Route to the Charter 492
The Charter of Rights and Freedoms 495
The Reasonable Limits Clause 496
Fundamental Freedoms 496
Democratic Rights 499
Mobility Rights 499
Legal Rights 500
Equality Rights 504

Official Languages of Canada 506
Minority-Language Education Rights 507
Enforcement 507
General Provisions 508
Application of the Charter 509
The Notwithstanding Clause 509
Implications of Constitutionalizing the Charter of Rights 510
Conclusion 515
Discussion Questions 516
Notes 517
Further Reading 522

PART 5   GOVERNING **523**
Chapter 20   The Policymaking Process and Policy Instruments **525**
Government in the 21st Century 525
The Policymaking Process 527
Initiation 528
Priority Setting 530
Policy Formulation 530
Legitimation 530
Implementation 531
Interpretation 531
Policy Communities and Policy Networks Revisited 532
Policy Instruments 535
Privatization 535
Symbolic Response 535
Exhortation 536
Tax Expenditures 536
Public Expenditures 537
Regulation 537
Taxation 538
Public Ownership 538
State of Emergency 539
The Environment as a Case Study 539
Conclusion 540
Discussion Questions 542
Notes 542
Further Reading 543

Chapter 21   The Executive: Crown, Prime Minister, and Cabinet **545**
The Crown 545
The Governor General 547
Powers of the Crown 547
Other Functions of the Crown 551
Advantages and Disadvantages of the Monarchy 551
The Prime Minister and Cabinet 552
Powers of the Prime Minister and Cabinet 552
The Prime Minister 554
Composition of the Cabinet 561
Operation of the Cabinet 565

Central Agencies	571
Conclusion	575
Discussion Questions	577
Notes	578
Further Reading	582
Chapter 22 The Bureaucracy	**583**
Functions and Powers of the Bureaucracy	583
Government Departments	585
Number, Structure, and Size	585
Responsibility and Accountability at the Top of the Department	586
Exempt Staff	587
The Rest of the Department	588
Relations with Other Departments and Central Agencies	589
The Merit Principle and a Representative Bureaucracy	590
The Estimates System	592
Departmental Interaction with Provinces and the Public	594
Crown Corporations	595
Administrative Agencies	598
Controlling the Bureaucracy	600
Prime Minister, Ministers, and Cabinet	601
Bureaucrats Controlling Bureaucrats	601
House of Commons	601
The Judiciary	602
Watchdog Agencies	602
Dysfunctions and Reform of the Bureaucracy	604
Dysfunctions of the Bureaucracy	604
Reform of the Bureaucracy	605
Sponsorship, Gomery, Responsibility, and Accountability Revisited	608
Conclusion	609
Discussion Questions	612
Notes	612
Further Reading	615
Chapter 23 Parliament	**617**
Functions and Powers of the House of Commons	618
Composition of the House of Commons	619
The Parliamentary Timetable	620
The Typical Session	621
The Typical Week	622
Party Discipline	624
Caucus Meetings	626
Stages and Kinds of Legislation	627
Organization and Officers of the Commons	630
The Speaker	630
House Leaders, Party Whips, and Clerk	632
Voting	632
Speeches	633
The Committee System	633
Members' Services and Ethics	637

Roles of Members of Parliament 638
The Government–Opposition Balance 640
Minority Government 640
Reform of the House of Commons 643
Purposes and Powers of the Senate 644
Composition of the Senate 645
Operation of the Senate 646
Senate Reform 651
Conclusion 652
Discussion Questions 654
Notes 655
Further Reading 658

Chapter 24   The Judiciary 659
The Function of Adjudication 659
Access to and Costs of Justice 661
Categories of Laws 662
Structure of the Courts 663
Provincial Courts 664
The Superior Trial Court 665
Provincial and Territorial Courts of Appeal 666
The Federal Court of Canada 666
The Supreme Court of Canada 667
The Appointment of Judges 672
Retirement, Removal, and Independence of Judges 676
Conclusion 678
Discussion Questions 680
Notes 680
Further Reading 683

Glossary 685

Index 709

Web Appendix A Constitution Act, 1867 (excerpts) A-1
Web Appendix B Constitution Act, 1982 A-2

Preface

This sixth edition of *Canadian Politics: Critical Approaches* seeks to preserve the merits of its predecessors while updating political developments and strengthening certain features of the book. It continues to present the reality of Canadian government and politics in a comprehensive yet lean and readable manner. Although it is principally designed as a textbook, I hope it is also useful and enjoyable for general readers.

This text divides almost equally between the two parts of the Canadian political system: its "environment" and its institutions. It can thus be used for courses in either half of the subject or for full courses that cover both parts. In the former case, the book gives much emphasis to the societal setting of the political system, with discussions of regionalism, Aboriginal peoples, the French–English cleavage, ethnocultural groups, gender, class, age, religion, urban/rural location, and the global environment. Student interest in the subject is therefore stimulated by observing the clash of interests from which political activity stems. In the latter case, it includes chapters on all the institutions of Canadian government, including the constitution, federalism, the Charter of Rights and Freedoms, the executive, bureaucracy, Parliament, and the judiciary, institutions which also feature exciting daily happenings. Part 3, which includes equally fascinating topics—political culture, the mass media, elections, parties, and advocacy groups—can be fit into either half of the subject.

Beyond that comprehensive scope, the book provides five analytical models with which to view the subject matter: the pluralist, public choice, class analysis, and state-centred approaches, plus the impact of globalization. The text refers to these approaches wherever appropriate. It especially emphasizes, from public choice theory, the constant priority of those in power to enhance their chances of re-election; from class analysis, the inequality of political power, and the pervasiveness of capitalist values; from pluralism, the predominant influence in a contest of floating coalitions of groups and interests of business pressure groups; from the state-centred model, the overwhelming presence of the bureaucracy; and then places the whole subject in the context of globalization.

Although the Canadian political system functions better than most others around the world, it is far from perfect and certainly embodies a huge "democratic deficit;" thus, no account could be completely satisfied with the status quo. This book therefore points out aspects of the political and governmental operations of the country that are not working as well as they might, and suggests possible reforms and alternative arrangements, sometimes drawing on the experience of other countries. Without being ideological, the book is a critical account and seeks to make informed critics of its readers.

For those familiar with previous editions of the book, let me briefly outline what is different about this new edition. First, of course, it has been updated to early 2010. This allowed me to include many interesting developments emanating from four years' experience with the Stephen Harper government. Some of these included the 2006 and 2008 elections, election finance reforms, a new administration in the United States, the 2008–09 worldwide economic meltdown with its dramatic impact on government finances, the change in the Liberal leadership, battles over equalization payments and the status of Quebec, Aboriginal issues, real and alleged terrorists, changes in the mass media and the increased importance of the Internet, the controversial position of the governor general in late 2008, new Charter decisions, the troubled relations between the government and the public service, and an increasingly dominant prime minister. Second, I have given the environment more attention than ever before. Third, I have added a more theoretical background to the chapters in the first half of the book, developing them beyond basic factual presentations.

I really hope that readers will also take advantage of the book's website, http://www .canadianpolitics6e.nelson.com. That is where you will find numerous Web Links for each chapter, in addition to quiz questions for students and PowerPoint® slides and an Instructor's Manual for professors. Of vital concern to me are the text updates that I will post there on a regular basis to keep the book current.

Introducing the Nelson Education Testing Advantage (NETA) Test Banks. In most college and university courses, a large percentage of student assessment is based on multiple choice testing. But many instructors use multiple choice reluctantly, believing that it is a methodology best used for teaching what a student remembers rather than what she or he has learned. Furthermore, the quality of publisher-supplied test banks can vary.

Nelson Education Ltd. believes that a good-quality multiple choice test bank can test not just what students remember, but higher-level thinking skills as well. Recognizing the importance of multiple choice testing in today's classroom, Nelson has created the Nelson Education Testing Advantage program to ensure the high quality of our test banks.

The test bank for *Canadian Politics: Critical Approaches* was developed under the Nelson Education Testing Advantage. NETA was created in partnership with David DiBattista, a 3M National Teaching Fellow and professor of psychology at Brock University. NETA ensures that test bank authors have had training in two areas: developing clear multiple choice test questions while avoiding common errors in construction, and creating multiple choice test questions that "get beyond remembering" to assess higher-level thinking.

The outcome of NETA development is that as you select multiple choice questions from your Nelson test bank for inclusion in tests, you can easily identify whether items are memory-based or require your students to engage in higher-level thinking. By making your selections appropriately, you can construct tests that contain the proportion of recall and higher-level questions that reflects your personal instructional goals.

All NETA test banks are accompanied by David DiBattista's guide for instructors, "Multiple Choice Tests: Getting Beyond Remembering." This guide has been designed to assist you in using Nelson test banks to achieve your desired outcomes in the classroom.

The NETA test materials are presented in two formats:

1.   *Test Bank.* The Test Bank includes multiple choice, completion, true/false, and short essay questions. A proofreader checked all questions, including the new or revised questions created for the Sixth Edition. Each question is categorized by difficulty level, type of question, and text page reference. Files are provided in rich text format for easy editing and printing with all common word-processing formats.

2.   *ExamView.* All Test Bank questions are included in the ExamView computerized version. The easy-to-use software is compatible with Microsoft Windows and Mac. Create tests by selecting questions from the question bank, modifying these questions as desired, and adding new questions you write yourself. You can administer quizzes online and export tests to WebCT, Blackboard, and other formats.

The preparation of this sixth edition gave me the opportunity to peruse a great deal of scholarly writing on various aspects of Canadian government and politics and to communicate with a large number of people "on the Hill" who provided me with valuable information on the workings of different parts of the political system. I also relied on the impressive, informative, and accessible websites now maintained by federal government departments and agencies and most other political actors. In preparing this edition, I had the luxury of living in Ottawa, thanks to my appointment as Adjunct Professor at Carleton University, which gave me the advantage of personal observation of the operation of many institutions and processes discussed in the book.

The book is immensely better for having been reviewed, in now six editions, by a large number of helpful academics recruited by the publisher, as well as those who contacted me directly. For this particular edition, the reviewers included Scott Matthews, Queen's University; Dennis Pilon, University of Victoria; Marc Poulin, Concordia University College of Alberta; and John Soroski, Grant McEwan University. I would be happy to receive further feedback—even questions—via e-mail at Rand_Dyck@carleton.ca. The book is made more readable, too, for being punctuated with the work of some of Canada's leading editorial cartoonists and political photographers.

The people at Nelson Education Ltd. have become an important part of my life. Their ability to transform a nondescript manuscript into a beautiful book never fails to astound me. This edition was guided to publication by the talents and dedication of Linda Sparks, Lenore Taylor-Atkins, Anne-Marie Taylor, and Christine Gilbert, along with many others.

I also wish to thank all those in the Department of Political Science at Carleton University who welcomed me into their midst, supported me at every turn, and helped with this specific project.

I hope the book contributes to a better informed and more involved Canadian citizenry.

Rand Dyck

PART 1

Introduction

Part 1 consists of two chapters. The first provides a general framework on which the rest of the book is built and outlines a number of different approaches to the study of politics. These approaches reveal that the subject matter of political science is not all cut-and-dried factual material and that the same topic can be viewed from different perspectives. The second chapter explores the historical context of Canadian politics and sketches its institutional foundations. These are examined in more depth in Parts 4 and 5, but a general knowledge of Canadian governmental institutions is advisable before embarking on Parts 2 and 3. In particular, Chapter 2 deals with the aspects of the British and U.S. models that Canada chose as the basis for its own, establishes the institutional differences between the Canadian and U.S. systems of government, and traces the evolution of government in Canada.

Chapter 1

THE STUDY OF
Politics

Anyone reading this book is probably already open to the excitement and importance of the subject of politics and government in Canada. How a whole society makes collective, public decisions is a fascinating question. Political personalities are often as interesting as movie stars, and the conflicts between them and their respective teams are as hard-fought as any hockey game. Politics often brings out the worst in human nature—ambition, selfishness, greed, and the will to control—but it is also sometimes characterized by the best—an altruistic desire to serve the public interest and to improve the lives of the less fortunate. Politics and government are the only means of solving many societal problems, and may well be the best way to solve some of your own!

THE POLITICAL SYSTEM

Perhaps it is best to begin with the 34 million individuals who inhabit the territory called Canada. All of these individuals have an array of needs that they attempt to satisfy, ranging from water and food through security and friendship to self-esteem and self-fulfillment. Some of these needs are felt individually, while others are shared with people of similar position or characteristics, in small or large groups. These needs have been ranked by the psychologist Abraham Maslow into a hierarchy, some being more basic than others.[1] Political science often lumps such needs together with interests, preferences, opinions, motivations, expectations, and beliefs. It is quite obvious that most of us spend much of our time trying to satisfy such needs and concerns.

We may first try to meet our needs by our own efforts, in pairs, in families, in organizations of all kinds, at work, and at play. It could be said that we begin by operating in the **private or voluntary sectors**, those parts of society and the economy that function separately from government. At some point, however, we may begin to feel that the satisfaction of these needs is beyond such personal, interpersonal, family, or group capacity and conclude that the government should step in to help us. When we express the opinion that the government should take some action (or desist from an action that it is already taking), we are converting a need into a "demand" and crossing the threshold to the **public sector**. We can therefore say that a demand is the expression of opinion that some government action be taken. What governments do is to make and execute decisions for a society or formulate and enforce social or public policies. However, governments do not necessarily wait for demands to be articulated; they often seek out the expectations of the electorate, and they sometimes make decisions that are primarily based on the values and preferences of the people in authoritative positions. With the worldwide economic collapse of 2008–09, and the meltdown of the private sector, most people turned to government in a desperate hope that the public sector could provide some kind of lifeline.

The first fundamental question that arises in politics and government is therefore whether people should "solve their own problems" or whether they should ask the government or the state to intervene. Almost everyone agrees that the government should provide certain security measures, such as police services and armed forces. Most people also support public highways and a public education system. The population may be more divided, however, on the extent to which the government should provide such programs as social assistance, social housing, public pensions, and universal health care. One of the main reasons for such divisions of opinion is that government intervention normally costs money and usually relies on taxes of one kind or another. People also disagree on which areas of life the state should *regulate* and how much regulation is appropriate.

The largest group of people reading this book will be young students, some of whom have probably not yet given too much attention to the role of government in their lives. But if you do, you will find many interesting questions come to mind. To what extent should you be expected to pay for your postsecondary education, and to what extent should it be financed by the state? Why do tuition fees keep increasing, and what form and level of student assistance is most appropriate? In travelling to school or work, should the state (provincial or municipal) provide a transit system or subsidize bus or subway fares? Should the state (federal or provincial) intervene to regulate the price of gasoline? If living away from home, should students' housing needs be supplied by private property owners, should the province regulate the rental market, or should the municipality, university, or college provide public housing? For those who work, should there be a minimum wage, and if so, what is an appropriate rate? Should all colleges and universities be public institutions, or is private postsecondary education a good idea?

Then think of other political questions that go beyond your status as a student. For example, should affluent people be able to get quicker medical attention because they can pay for such health care, or should Canada maintain a universal system where no one can "jump the queue"? Should the public health care system be extended to pharmaceutical drugs and dental care? Should federal and provincial/territorial governments cooperate in providing a universal daycare program, or, as an alternative, should the government give parents of young children a monthly cheque and let them use it to arrange their own child care?

Should the state put more restrictions on greenhouse gasses and other environmental hazards, or should companies be unrestricted in pollution emissions in the interest of providing jobs or oil and gas? How far should the state go in prohibiting discrimination in the workplace? Should it engage in employment equity programs to enhance the employment prospects of those discriminated against in the past? Should those who enjoy pornographic materials be able to do so, or should these be censored by the state? Such a list of questions barely scratches the surface of potential government action, but it serves to demonstrate the relevance of government to our daily lives. Of course, it is generally true that the more we rely on government, the more money it will have to raise through taxation to finance its operations.

We are thus introduced to the concept of **government**, which can be defined as the set of institutions that make and enforce collective, public decisions for a society. Those who control the government can make appointments, spend money, extract taxes, enact regulations, and generally impose their will on society. This capacity invites a discussion of the concept of **power**. Power is often defined in political science as the ability of one actor to impose its will on another, to get its own way, to do or get what it wants. Moreover, backed up by armed forces, police, and punishments, if necessary, government possesses a particular kind of power called **coercion**. That is, the government has the ability to impose its will on us by means of sanctions or penalties. Indeed, as a general rule, *only* the government is allowed to use force or coercive power in society. But if we (or our ancestors) had a hand in the creation of such a government apparatus, as well as in the selection of the current governors, then we have in a sense agreed to be bound by its decisions, and we have cloaked it with "legitimacy." Such legitimate power is often called "authority," and a synonym for government is "the authorities." To some extent, we obey the government because of the threat or expectation of penalties if we do not, but we also obey because we accept government decisions to be binding on us and necessary for the general good. Think of stopping at a red light as an example.

Who are these authorities? As can be seen in the diagram of the political system in Figure 1.1, we usually divide them into four branches of government: the legislature, the executive, the bureaucracy, and the judiciary. The authoritative decision that a demand seeks can sometimes be made by a single branch of government. If the demand requires the adoption of a new or amended law, an action of the legislative branch will be necessary. If an individual desires a patronage appointment or if a corporation wants a large monetary grant, a decision of the political executive or Cabinet will be required. If the demand is for the provision of routine government services, such as disability benefits under the Canada Pension Plan, or for changes in technical regulations, a bureaucratic act will probably

Figure 1.1 A Model of the Political System

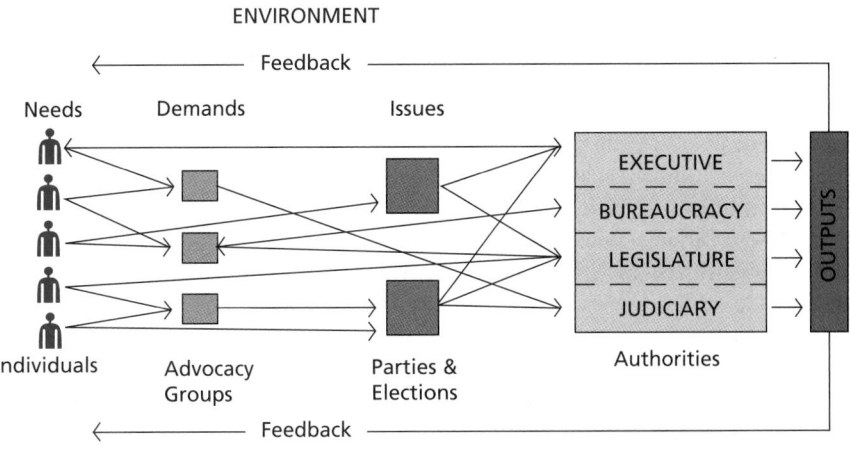

suffice. Finally, if the demand can be settled only by judicial interpretation or adjudication, it should be addressed to the courts.

In many instances, however, the demand will require combined actions of any two of the executive, legislative, and bureaucratic branches, or even all three working together, such as in the formulation, passage, and implementation of a new law. The courts normally stand somewhat apart from the other three organs of government, operating on the principle of the independence of the judiciary. Judicial decisions usually follow authoritative actions in other branches of government, such as when the Supreme Court overturned the abortion provisions of the Criminal Code. But judicial decisions may also lead to subsequent legislative action, as when the government enacted an amendment to reverse a Supreme Court ruling that had permitted an extreme state of intoxication to serve as an excuse for committing sexual assault.

Authoritative decisions take many forms—laws, regulations, appointments, grants, contracts, services, and judgments—and can collectively be referred to as the "outputs" of the political system. Authoritative decisions are also made in the provinces and territories and in an assortment of regional and local councils and boards, and they often require the agreement of two or more levels of government. Federal and provincial decisions and policies can sometimes be in conflict, such as when the two levels pursue different strategies in dealing with the reduction of greenhouse gases, waiting lists for health care, or stimulating the economy.

Having encountered demands and authorities as two main parts of the political system, we must now discover how demands are transmitted from individuals to the government, as indicated in the model of the political system. This can be done on a personal basis, by means of a letter, fax, telephone call, e-mail, or face-to-face encounter. Sometimes such directly transmitted demands will achieve their desired result, but very often they will not. If not, it may be time to consider some kind of group action, since, as a general rule, the authorities are more likely to respond to a demand coming from a group than from a single individual. Canadian society is replete with groups and social movements, and it is quite likely that a group already exists to articulate the individual's concern. If not, it may be worthwhile to create one. Such groups are usually called "interest groups," "pressure groups," or "advocacy groups," and they constitute an important part of Canadian political activity. The Canadian Chamber of Commerce and the Canadian Labour Congress are two prominent examples. Corporations and other institutions also make demands, either individually or in groups.

A special kind of group that is even more overtly political is the *political party*, and this instrument can also be used to transmit demands to the authorities. People join a political party or support it financially and try to get it to recognize their concerns in its platform or policies. If the party forms the government, it can incorporate the demand into its decisions and government policy; if the party is in opposition, it may be able to bring the problem to national attention through mass media coverage of parliamentary proceedings. Parties are particularly responsive to such demands during an election campaign, when they want to attract the support of large numbers of individuals and groups by promising them the actions they seek. Those dissatisfied with the manner in which existing parties are responding to their demands can create new parties, such as the Canadian Alliance or the Bloc Québécois, which arrived on the scene in the 1990s.

Another means of transmitting the demand to the authorities is, as suggested above, through the mass media of communication. The media are usually eager to publicize controversial issues and often delight in pointing out problems that the government has failed to resolve. The media give attention to individual and group concerns on a regular basis, cover political party activities, and are especially active in election campaigns. But the media are much more important than that. In providing the electorate with most of its information about politics and government, they tend to shape the whole nature and quality of political discourse in Canada.

We have assumed thus far that all demands expressed actually reach the authorities. In fact, however, relatively few have any impact. Those demands that do not concern very many people or those that call for action that is contrary to the values of the authorities of the day may be ignored. Governments have historically been much more sensitive to the views of the business community, for example, than to the concerns of Aboriginal peoples. Since the number of demands under serious consideration at any given time is such a small proportion of the total number being made, it is sometimes useful to distinguish between demands and "issues," the latter including only those that the authorities have taken under serious consideration.

The authorities are thus bombarded by demands, no matter what means are used to transmit them. What is more striking than the vast quantity of demands, however, is that intense conflict usually exists among them. The essence of politics and government, therefore, lies not only in making and executing decisions for society, but in having to choose among competing demands, in trying to resolve conflict, or in making social choices in the midst of social conflict. **Politics**, therefore, is said to originate in conflict, and is often defined as the struggle for power and the management of conflict. Here, let us say that politics is an activity in which conflicting interests struggle for advantage or dominance in the making and execution of public policies. It should also be added that the authorities can make their own demands, which may well carry more weight than those arising from the wider society.

Besides promoting their own interests, governments put increasing effort into seeking out the views of the public. There are several reasons for this development, which is indicated in Figure 1.1 by arrows going from the authorities back into society. One is that advances in technology, such as polling and communications, make it possible for government to solicit such views; another is that after a decade or more of downsizing government, the authorities were left with fewer policy analysis resources of their own; a third is that more think tanks and policy advocacy organizations exist than ever before. In some cases, these reasons are supplemented by the view that governments *should* increase the opportunities for citizen involvement in the policymaking process. It is therefore now common to identify the "third" or "voluntary" sector consisting of nonprofit groups in distinction to the profit-oriented private sector and the public sector or government. The Canadian government even signed an accord with the voluntary sector in 2001 that committed it to increased interaction with such organizations.

Demands are only one of two kinds of "inputs" in the system. The other is the concept of "support." This is not as concrete a phenomenon, but it is also fairly evident. Support can be defined as a positive orientation toward something; as used in this context, three different parts of the system can be objects of support. First, you can support the government of the day—that is, the party and Cabinet that currently occupy the authoritative political positions (for example, the Harper Conservative government). Second, you can support the whole decision-making apparatus, or the constitutional principles and arrangements according to which decisions are being made. In this case, you might not support the government of the day but still feel positively about the general decision-making process. Most Canadians fall into this category most of the time. Third, you can support the political community called

Canada. Again, you can do so without supporting the current government, or even the institutions it occupies. For example, an Albertan obsessed with Senate reform to articulate regional interests in federal institutions might support the political community without supporting the existing policymaking structures. Conversely, a Quebec separatist would not support the political community of Canada.

Support is a more passive concept than demands, and it usually exists in the realm of feelings and orientations rather than in action. Of course, action is involved in voting for one party or another on election day—in demonstrating support for the incumbent government or an opposition party. The act of voting is also a subtle indication of support for the decision-making structure and for the political community. But apart from voting (or standing at attention for the national anthem), support is mostly demonstrable in terms of such feelings as trust, efficacy, pride, and patriotism. The accompanying cartoon of Canada's political system reflects a humorous cynicism about Canadian politics and politicians that is very widespread. This text will help you to develop informed opinions about whether such negative feelings are justified.

Whatever the type of output, it usually sparks a reaction in the rest of the system. This leads us to the concept of "feedback"—that is, a communication of the outputs back into the system, in response to which the pattern of demands and support is altered. If an output

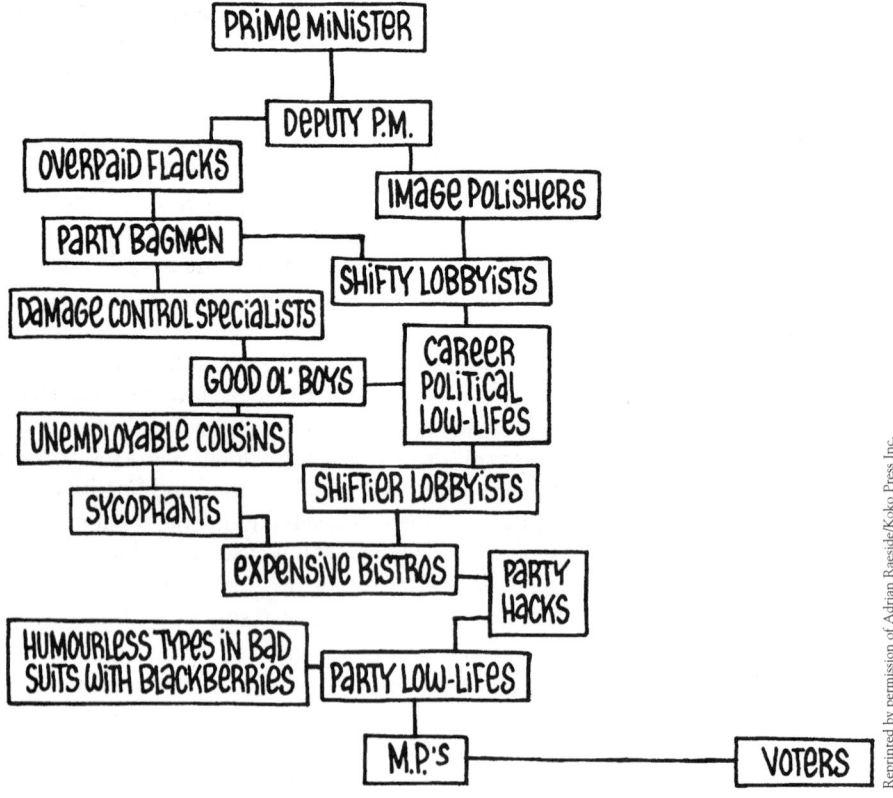

Reprinted by permission of Adrian Raeside/Koko Press Inc.

satisfies a particular demand, then that demand will no longer have to be articulated. Think of the Official Languages Act silencing the demands for bilingualism in the federal government. But the bilingualism issue also shows that the satisfaction of one demand may lead those involved to expect even more along the same lines, such as French-language services at the provincial/territorial level as well. However, a backlash may result: the Official Languages Act also promoted the articulation of contrary demands—protection for unilingual public servants, for example. Similarly, outputs affect support. Gratitude for the satisfaction of a demand will likely lead to increased levels of support, whether for the governing party, the decision-making apparatus, or the country. Conversely, those opposed to such an output will probably have less confidence in the authorities and the system, and their level of support will decline, such as the alienation of Western Canada in response to the Trudeau government's National Energy Program. The authorities will then respond in one way or another to this new pattern of demands and support.

By now we have established that the political system is a dynamic, circular, never-ending process in which the authorities, in addition to imposing their own priorities, react to demands and support, seek out public sentiment, convert some of the demands into outputs, and then respond in turn to whatever changes in the pattern of inputs have resulted from the feedback from such outputs. Individuals and groups raise conflicting demands, but because a consensus exists on the legitimacy of the government, people generally abide by its authoritative decisions, even when they disagree with them. It is sometimes said, therefore, that politics and government are characterized by both conflict and consensus. Although the conflict is usually more evident, it normally operates within an underlying consensus about the decision-making apparatus and about remaining together as part of a united political community. Moreover, the authorities usually seek to develop some kind of consensus out of the conflicting demands.

One more part that must be added to the model we are constructing is the "environment" of the political system. This is an even more abstract concept than those encountered thus far and can be defined as everything surrounding the political system. If the political system within a society is made up of all those actions and interactions concerned with the making of public policy, the same society contains a geographic system (physical and human), an economic system, a social system, and perhaps many others. These other systems constitute the domestic environment of the Canadian political system.

Most of these systems are characterized by internal divisions, and from these divisions springs the concept of "cleavages." A cleavage, in political science terms, is a deep and persistent division in society that has significant implications for the political system. The cleavages in Canadian society that most readily come to mind are between the geographic regions; among English, French, Aboriginal, and other ethnocultural and linguistic groups; and between various socioeconomic classes. Others are related to gender, religion, age, and rural/urban location. The relative importance and nature of these cleavages change over time. Although such cleavages are part of the environment of the political system, they can also be seen as the source of many of the demands expressed. In other words, demands can be said to originate from cleavages in the internal environment.

There is also an external or global environment consisting of a huge number of international, multinational, transnational, and supranational factors, such as other states, international organizations, international agreements, transnational corporations, and nongovernmental organizations (NGOs). In fact, in this age of **globalization**, such actors in the external environment increasingly serve both as the source of demands on national political systems and as constraints on domestic policymaking. Not a day goes by without the government of Canada having to factor such external influences into its decisions. The North American Free Trade Agreement (NAFTA) among Canada, the United States, and Mexico is perhaps of greatest impact, and an even broader international coalition tried to coordinate a response to the worldwide economic recession of 2008–09.

. . . .

APPROACHES TO THE STUDY OF POLITICS

The model of the political system just described and illustrated in Figure 1.1 is designed to provide a framework for the study of government and politics in Canada. It is a simplified version of systems analysis, largely the work of Canadian political scientist David Easton,[2] which many of his colleagues find useful for organizing and explaining political phenomena. Nevertheless, a few complications should probably be added to the model.

It is perhaps more common today to talk about "identities" rather than cleavages. Each of us has many identities—male or female, Newfoundlander or Albertan, Roman Catholic or Muslim, francophone or Aboriginal, young or old, rich or poor. Our identities evolve from those characteristics and experiences that are most important to us as individuals and groups. Canada is replete with regional identities, ethnic and linguistic identities, religious identities, class identities, and gender and sexual identities, to mention only a few. Whether a person articulates a demand in the political system based on any such identities will depend on whether he or she is conscious of such characteristics and experiences and considers them salient—to be an important part of their being. Thus, the "politics of identity" is an increasingly evident phenomenon.

A further complication that many contemporary political scientists point out is that such identities are not necessarily automatic, voluntary, individualistic choices. While what one wants is a product of who one understands oneself to be, the social environment exercises much influence on the individual in constructing his or her identity. "Structural" analysts emphasize the role of social structures—traditions, customs, practices, and institutions—which largely determine how individual members of a society behave. They influence our behaviour and contribute to our identities, whether we realize it or not. They also help explain why we have multiple identities, decide which ones to emphasize, and change them over time.[3] The basic point is that we are not as autonomous as we think we are in choosing our identities: we operate within a powerful set of pre-existing societal norms. Structural analysis is particularly appealing to those identity groups who feel they have been subject to social, political, and economic exclusion in the past.

In this connection, let us also add the concept of "hegemony." This is the general idea that we all operate within the context of the dominant values and expectations of society. It is not only definitions of identity that are determined by the social environment; to a large extent the actions we take in the political system are ones that have been historically considered to be "normal." We accept the way things are done because they have always been done that way; we accept the roles of different actors in the system because they have always acted that way: it only makes common sense. We are so accustomed to think and act in traditional ways that we rarely think "outside the box." But who has determined the dominant values and expectations that have produced such patterns of behaviour?

It is those who have always been in power—the elite, whether political, economic, bureaucratic, religious, cultural, media, or otherwise. If the dominant class can lead us to share its assumptions about how society should operate and if it can manipulate our understanding of things political so that we consent to what is actually in *its* interests, it will not have to resort to more coercive measures.[4]

Even with these complications, the model of the political system does not exhaust the possible analytical approaches that can be applied to Canadian politics. Any one of a number of other theoretical approaches can be used alongside it. Such models and approaches provide a guide in selecting significant and relevant facts, as well as in putting the facts together in a meaningful way. They direct our attention to different aspects of social reality and emphasize different relationships within the same population and territory. Before getting into the substance of our subject, therefore, we will outline five other approaches that political scientists have found useful in illuminating aspects of the Canadian political system: the pluralist, public choice, class analysis, state-centred, and globalization approaches. They focus on such crucial questions as how widely power and influence are shared, which political actors in society are most important, which government institutions are most powerful, how politicians seek and maintain power, and how much government actions are affected by external factors. It should be added that many alternative approaches could also be mentioned.

These approaches can be divided between those that are society-centred and those that focus on the autonomy of the government and the state. The pluralist, public choice, and class approaches maintain that the authorities respond to various demands emanating from societal forces or are concerned to discover what the wider population wants, while the state-centred approach is based on the assumption that those in government do what *they* think is best. Another distinction is that the pluralist and public choice approaches contend that power is derived from the population at large and that the authorities respond to the influence of the masses. The class and state-centred approaches, conversely, argue that power is concentrated in the corporate and state elites, respectively, an "elite" being defined as a small group with a disproportionate amount of power. There are other elites in society, of course, and they often interact in their collective dominance of the political system, but here we emphasize these two. The fifth approach—globalization—is somewhat different in its emphasis on external rather than internal forces.

The Pluralist Approach

Pluralism is the analytical framework closest to the democratic ideal. It postulates that power is widely dispersed among many interests in society, rather than tightly controlled by one or more groups or elites, and that the political system is characterized by much openness or "slack." In particular, the pluralist approach suggests that individuals can make use of many different resources in their political participation, that those sharing a demand are free to join together to seek a governmental response, that such group action is the norm of political activity, and that the authorities are open to pressure from a wide variety of such interests. Pluralism does not necessarily expect everyone to be equally interested and involved, or for everyone or all groups to be equally influential; indeed, it makes much of most individuals' political "inertia." But the theory argues that a feeling of being overlooked by government will lead a group to mobilize and activate its resources, that the authorities can be moved by

THE CANADIAN PRESS/Toronto Star/Steve Russell

The Canadian Federation of Students demonstrates against rising tuition fees.

the articulation of demands by different groups in different policy areas, and that the policies adopted are usually the result of compromises among competing group demands. The term "brokerage politics" is sometimes used in this connection because in a pluralist system the authorities engage in wheeling and dealing with the various groups in an effort to keep them all content. A pioneer of the pluralist approach was political scientist Robert Dahl's book *Pluralist Democracy in the United States*, and many accounts of Canadian politics assume a basic pluralist perspective, even if they do not say so.

Pluralism assumes that group action is more common and more effective than individual political activity, and it puts particular stress on the role of pressure or advocacy groups in both the making and the execution of public policy. Political scientists generally agree that as society becomes increasingly specialized, the number of groups grows, and as political issues become more complex, political parties and politicians may be less and less capable of dealing with them. In these ways, at least, the significance of advocacy groups rises, and no one doubts their contemporary importance. Paul Pross has explicitly emphasized the group approach in his work on Canadian politics, such as *Group Politics and Public Policy*. Business-oriented groups in particular have attracted much scholarly attention.[5]

The pluralist approach can be summarized as follows:

- Power is widely dispersed in the political system and not monopolized by any state or corporate elite.
- Individuals are free to employ a variety of resources at their disposal and to organize whatever groups they want in order to back their demands to the authorities.
- The authorities make decisions that are basically compromises among the various competing interests that articulate their demands.

- Different policy areas are characterized by different individuals and groups making demands on different authorities.
- Advocacy group activity is increasingly replacing individual and party activity in the political system.

There are several reasons to think that the pluralist approach is appropriate to the Canadian political system. First, Canada has always been a diversified society, given its regional, provincial/territorial, ethnic, class, religious, gender, age, and other divisions. But today, it is even more pluralistic, especially in terms of ethnic and religious diversity. Pluralism is also of growing relevance because various groups and interests are becoming more self-conscious and self-confident. Women, French Canadians, Aboriginals, minority ethnocultural groups, and non-Christian religious groups are challenging the elitism of the past. Greater diversity than ever before also exists among individuals who compose the institutions of government. Such interests, sometimes in the form of identities and subcultures, are part of the very political culture of the country, and are even succeeding in changing provisions in the Constitution to protect themselves. But the pluralist approach goes beyond the mere existence of a pluralist society and claims that a certain amount of equality among interests is possible.

Certain aspects of the Canadian political system are particularly appropriate to the pluralist approach. The broker system used by political parties as they design their election platforms is certainly one; so are the efforts of those who seek to strengthen the provinces and territories in the operation of Canadian federalism. The limitation of authority that is provided when political institutions have checks on one another is a hallmark of this approach, and, in that sense, federal–provincial conflict and the power of the courts to overrule both federal and provincial governments by means of the Charter of Rights and Freedoms are relevant.

Most Canadians have unfortunately been true to that part of the pluralist model that suggests people do not usually take advantage of opportunities to be active political participants. However, citizens' desire to be heard is probably on the rise, and all kinds of organizations, including government itself, are asking for their views in public opinion polls. Canada has hundreds of interest groups, and many are active in the political process. If pluralism means that much government activity is a response to the influence of advocacy groups and that they are displacing parties in many respects, then it is probably correct, as it is in emphasizing that government decisions are made in a diversity of specialized policy communities.

Others would argue that the pluralist approach is not such a perfect fit for the Canadian political system; indeed, the other approaches outlined below are largely critiques of an ideal pluralist system. First, a pluralist society does not necessarily mean that pluralism is the operating principle of that society. As mentioned, the pluralist approach requires an element of equality of the different interests in society, and many observers do not find that to be the case here.

Second, where such interests take the form of organized groups, they have great disparities in the influence or resources among them. Only a handful of groups speak for the poor and the working class, for example, and the middle class has no collective voice at all. Meanwhile, every imaginable business interest has organized a pressure group, and several peak business associations are better endowed than national political parties. Two other aspects of Canadian society that do not mesh with the pluralist approach are the original centralized framework of Canadian federalism, which proved to be inappropriate in such a diversified society, and the rigid party discipline in the House of Commons, which has sometimes been identified as dysfunctional.

To take a practical example of a policy issue that reflects the relevance of the pluralist approach, let us return to the concerns of postsecondary students mentioned above, concentrating on tuition fees. As expected, national and regional student advocacy groups have been formed to try to exert their influence on this issue in particular, especially the **Canadian Federation of Students**, and the resulting level of tuition fees is at least partly a result of federal and provincial governments balancing such student demands against those that want higher tuition (often universities themselves, along with business groups) or those that prefer government funding go to other areas entirely. The pluralist argument would continue, however, that if student organizations were larger and stronger, and if student identities led them to take a more aggressive part in the political system, they might have greater success.

The Public Choice Approach

The public choice approach also begins with the assumption that Canada is a democracy. It postulates that rational, self-interested voters support the party whose policies are of greatest utility to themselves, and that politicians seeking re-election adopt policies that will most likely keep them in power. This approach emphasizes bargaining between politicians and voters and takes its inspiration from the economic system, its pioneer being Anthony Downs in his book *An Economic Theory of Democracy*.[6] It is sometimes bears the "rational choice" label.

At first sight, in a democracy, the largest groups are the most influential because they represent the greatest numbers of voters. This is only true, however, if the members of such groups are conscious of their common interests and have a group identity. Furthermore, since the authorities do not have to worry about the support of their committed voters, and since they are unlikely to win over those who are hostile, the usual recipe for political success is to concentrate on marginal, undecided voters or voters in strategically located constituencies, rather than on the will of the electorate as a whole.

Politicians will go to great lengths to keep themselves in power. They take credit for popular policies or the strength of the economy but blame others (international forces, provincial/territorial governments, the courts, and so on) for unpopular policies or economic decline. They give popular policies maximum publicity but try to conceal those that are bound to be unpopular; they exaggerate the benefits of their policies and understate the costs. They make disagreeable decisions early in their term and unveil popular programs just before the next election.

The public choice approach can be summarized as follows:

- Politics is a bargaining process in which both politicians and voters act in a rational, self-interested, utility-maximizing fashion; politicians make promises in return for votes.
- Politicians and parties generally adopt policies that will get themselves elected, and, other things being equal, they respond to those interests representing the largest number of votes.
- Since it is a waste of effort to appeal to committed supporters or opponents, politicians concentrate on marginal, undecided, or strategically located voters.
- Politicians try to maximize publicity of their successes and minimize their failures, take credit for good things and blame others for the bad, and manipulate the timing of positive and negative decisions.

- A similar rational, self-serving bargaining process also goes on at other points in the political system, where it is more often called "rational choice," such as between politicians and the bureaucracy, the authorities and advocacy groups, and the authorities and the media.

In practice, the public choice approach can be seen at many points in the Canadian political system, especially in the relationship between politicians and voters in the formulation of election platforms and in the citizen's decision of how to vote. The operation of the House of Commons is also central to this approach because observing the partisan exchanges in that chamber helps voters to make up their minds about which party will best satisfy their demands. Public choice is relevant, too, to the operations of the Cabinet as that body calculates which interests it will have to placate to ensure re-election. In this calculation, the role of public opinion polls is crucial, as governments, parties, the media, and other organizations seek to identify the basic concerns of different groups within the electorate. Governments rarely do what is in the long-term interest of the country if it conflicts with short-term electoral advantage. The public choice approach is confirmed on a daily basis when it emphasizes the ways in which the authorities portray their performance in the most favourable light, such as in timing, packaging, exaggerating benefits, and downplaying costs.

The public choice approach gives particular attention to marginal voters. In regional terms, the party preferences of a majority of Quebeckers (Liberal) and Westerners (Conservative) could historically be taken for granted, so that parties focused their campaigns in Ontario, which had the largest number of flexible voters. Quebeckers abandoned their Liberal roots in 1984 and since that time have also provided a great pool of marginal voters; indeed, the threat of separation only heightened the attention that parties and politicians paid to Quebec.

Not everything about the public choice approach is appropriate to the Canadian political system, however. When it comes to manipulating or "spinning" their message, for example, the level of sophistication of the authorities far exceeds that of the average voter, and the public choice model probably overstates the extent to which voters are rational and well informed. The lack of class-consciousness among all but the upper classes and the delayed political consciousness of women and certain other groups in society all attest to the skill of authorities and parties in persuading voters to support platforms that were not necessarily in their own interests. It would take an alert, informed, and skeptical electorate to see through the authorities' attempts to manipulate the "public choice." Public choice theory may therefore go too far if it expects that individuals in the political marketplace are always as rational and well informed as they may be in their economic transactions.

How would the public choice approach apply to the range of public policy concerns of postsecondary students? It assumes that students are rational, self-interested, and well informed, that their identity as students is foremost in their minds, and that they vote for parties and politicians that will provide them with the most favourable policies. It notes that students compose a relatively large segment of the electorate and constitute a significant body of voters in particular constituencies where postsecondary educational institutions are located (possibly helping to explain the NDP victory in Edmonton-Strathcona in the 2008 election). Box 1.1 illustrates the public choice approach in the government's spending spree just before the 2006 election.

BOX 1.1   Government Spending Spree

From November 3rd to November 25th, the Canadian Taxpayers Federation (CTF) tracked 145 pre-election spending announcements totalling $24.5 billion made by Paul Martin's government. . . . Most of the spending is being announced in swing ridings where the Liberals are vulnerable and where the electoral battles are tight between government members and the opposition parties. . . . The federal government has embarked on the largest pre-election spending spree in Canadian history.

Source: John Williamson. Canadian Taxpayers Federation, Budget Archives. *Liberal Government's Pre-Election Spending Bender.* Found at http://www.taxes.ca/blog/archives/budget/index.php (Accessed March 21, 2006)

The Class Analysis Approach

A third approach to the study of Canadian government and politics—class analysis—emphasizes socioeconomic classes.[7] This approach is sometimes called neo-Marxism because to some extent it is based on the writings of Karl Marx. It is neither possible nor appropriate to deal with that analysis in any depth here, but the demise of Marxist-Leninism as a state-sponsored ideology in Eastern Europe does not necessarily make this critique obsolete. Suffice it to say that in Marxist eyes political activity is determined by economic relationships, particularly in the production process. In a capitalist system, Marx saw these relationships primarily in terms of a class struggle between the "proletariat" (the working class) and the "bourgeoisie" (the capitalist class). He emphasized that the latter would exploit the former until the proletariat engaged in an eventual revolution. Many modern observers see much truth in what Marx wrote more than 100 years ago, but most would modify his analysis to some extent in the light of subsequent developments, which is why the term "class analysis" is a preferable label.

In this approach, the political elite normally take orders from the capitalist elite, and the state is an instrument of bourgeois domination. Capitalism generally prefers to minimize the role of the state in order to allow "free market" forces to have full play, and such capitalist forces were influential in reducing the size of the state in the 1990s in particular. Nevertheless, class analysts point out that the bourgeoisie will tolerate collective, public activity to some extent, but only to further its own interests in the accumulation of capital. Public policies advocated by the capitalist elite include, for example, the assumption by the public purse of many of the costs of capitalist development, such as education, health care, electricity, and transportation. Although a degree of fragmentation may exist within the bourgeoisie, such as between manufacturers and resource industries, this approach sees the state pursuing policies that seek to create or maintain the conditions in which capitalists can maximize their wealth, in what is called the "accumulation" function. Given today's universal franchise, however, most modern, democratic governments find it politically advantageous to disguise much of this activity on behalf of capital, and other, more numerous, classes *can* influence events if they act as a class.

The Toronto skyline is dominated by the head offices of Canadian banks, the heart of the capitalist system.

Many political observers who do not necessarily claim the validity of class analysis would nevertheless agree that the state gives priority to the demands of big business.[8] In part this is because the bourgeoisie provides personnel for public offices, organizes powerful pressure groups, finances political parties (at least in the past), and generally shapes societal values (note the earlier discussion of hegemony), particularly through its ownership of the media. Another reason for the predominance of the corporate elite is that the state depends on the capitalist system for the provision of jobs, economic growth, and a portion of tax revenues.

Class analysis recognizes that modern society is composed of more than just the bourgeoisie and the proletariat, and it generally inserts between them the traditional "petite bourgeoisie" (farmers, small-business people, and self-employed professionals) and the "new middle class" (civil servants, teachers, and other salaried professionals). The increasing size of the middle class and the enfranchisement of the working class give such groups considerable significance today. Class analysts refer to the use of the state to benefit the middle or working classes as "legitimation." They still emphasize, however, that by humanizing and legitimizing the capitalist system and by disguising support for it, the authorities continue to enable the bourgeoisie to pursue the basic accumulation function.

If legitimation is not effective in facilitating capital accumulation, the government may have to resort to a third function, that of "coercion." This involves adopting penalizing policies or measures to impose order, such as legislation to end strikes or the intervention of the police to quell demonstrations. Coercion is more often imposed on labour, student, and other subordinate groups than on those with greater political and economic clout.[9]

Another central theme of class analysis is the influence of the external environment on the political system. The role of transnational corporations as sources of investment in Canada and the policies of dominant capitalist countries, especially the United States, are particularly important in this regard. So too are the actions of such organizations as the International Monetary Fund (IMF), the World Bank, and the World Trade Organization (WTO).

The class analysis literature in Canadian politics and economics is voluminous. Indeed, the whole "political economy" school of scholarship that goes back many decades and emphasizes the connection between politics and economics has been taken over by such writers. A list of such sources is contained at the end of Chapter 8, including the journal *Studies in Political Economy* and the publications of the Canadian Centre for Policy Alternatives.

The class analysis approach can be summarized as follows:

- The corporate elite or bourgeoisie not only control the private sector of the economy but also largely determine the shape of public policies and ensure that these policies are designed to facilitate its accumulation of wealth.
- This predominant influence of the bourgeoisie is the result of providing personnel for public offices and funds for political parties, shaping societal values, and organizing pressure groups; it also results from the dependence of the state on the capitalist system for the provision of jobs and economic growth.
- The petite bourgeoisie, the new middle class, and even the working class must be accommodated to some extent by public policies that legitimate the capitalist system, and these elements can influence events if they act as a class.
- If these classes are not satisfied by legitimation, the government may have to resort to coercion.
- Especially in an era of globalization, modern states must also contend with powerful transnational corporations and international agreements that states have signed on their behalf.

Class analysts ironically find practical confirmation of their approach in the widespread definition of politics by the media, politicians, pressure groups, and other participants and observers in terms of regionalism, ethnicity, and gender, rather than class. Such definitions serve the interests of these apologists of capitalism—to disguise the underlying class conflict—as does the concern with government deficits and debts at the expense of essential public services to the have-not segments of society. Until recently, the Liberal and Conservative parties were heavily financed by major corporations, and they rewarded such contributions in their general policies as well as in specific favours once in power. The most prominent pressure groups are those representing big business, while individual companies also lobby for government handouts. Individuals frequently serve as Cabinet ministers between stints in the corporate sector, and some senators represent corporate interests in their parliamentary work. Large corporations control most of the media and influence public opinion with carefully selected images that portray the ease and desirability of material success.

Class analysts point out that a close scrutiny of policy instruments reveals how the authorities choose more intrusive instruments and apply them more coercively when dealing with the working class or with students than with the corporate elite. This could be seen at the 1997 APEC summit in Vancouver and the Summit of the Americas in Quebec in 2000. Class analysts demonstrate how governments disguise their routine servitude to the corporate sector with occasional legitimating measures for the working class. "Snitch lines" send welfare recipients to jail while corporate income tax evasion is rampant. And these analysts remind us of incidents in which the full force of the law has been brought down on strikers or demonstrators but not on corporate executives who allow pollution of the environment, who make employees work in hazardous conditions, or who abuse their position to become wealthy at the expense of their shareholders. As critical as they are of politicians' actions, such analysts are equally suspicious of the courts. Given the expense and elitist personnel involved, they do not expect judicially imposed limitations on the other branches of government to benefit the working classes. Moreover, class analysts are critical of U.S. transnationals operating in Canada and of efforts by the U.S. government to have Canada follow its policy lead. On the world stage, class analysts often support nongovernmental organizations (NGOs) as an antidote to transnational corporations.

For most observers, however, it is too extreme to say that accumulation and coercion tempered by legitimation explain everything political in Canada. Since all classes are now enfranchised, politicians obviously have to accommodate the demands of people other than those at the very top, and they cannot completely mislead the wider electorate into thinking that they are being better cared for than they actually are.

How does class analysis apply to the postsecondary educational population? It would first examine the class composition of the postsecondary educational cohort—in particular, what proportion of such students come from the less affluent levels of society? Do high tuition fees and inadequate financial assistance programs keep lower-income students out? Second, much depends on whether the bourgeoisie believe that the state should pursue student-friendly policies. Well-educated students are an asset to the corporate elite, and if they can be hired fully trained, it will save corporations money. Since corporations provide much employment for this group as well as others, grateful politicians will be responsive to their concerns on these as well as other issues. Third, attitudes toward student concerns on the part of the population as a whole, as well as of many students themselves, will have been influenced by the way such issues are portrayed in the corporate-owned media. Fourth, student protestors, especially on such wider issues as globalization or poverty, may well be victims of coercive actions on the part of the police, but students can influence the system if they work together.

The State-Centred Approach

Public choice theory, class analysis, and pluralism all see the state as responding to societal forces. The state-centred approach, conversely, views the state—those individuals endowed with the authority to formulate and implement public policies—as basically autonomous from the rest of society. Public policies are made by the authorities without much reference to the demands flowing in from the public, and often despite them. Since the authorities try to direct the development of society, the French word *dirigiste* is sometimes used to describe their activity. The executive and bureaucracy do what they think is best for the country or act in pursuit of their own preferences and priorities, regardless of anyone else's interests or opinions. Such state actors seek to enhance their autonomy by generating internally the information needed to pursue their objectives and by maximizing their jurisdiction, discretionary power, and fiscal resources. In this approach, it is possible to single out either the political executive or the bureaucracy or to see them as acting together in making such decisions. Individually or in tandem, they try to persuade the public of their wisdom or, failing that, resort to coercion, the main point being that government operations are quite divorced from public input. The originator of this approach was Eric Nordlinger, who wrote in his book *On the Anatomy of*

The Parliament Buildings, Ottawa—the seat of the Government of Canada.

THE CANADIAN PRESS/Peter Bregg

the Democratic State that "the preferences of the state are at least as important as those of civil society in accounting for what the democratic state does and does not do."[10]

Although the political executive (the prime minister and Cabinet in Canada) have the right to make major governmental decisions, subject to some kind of accountability to Parliament, some theorists prefer to emphasize the influence of the bureaucracy within the apparatus of the state. They see the bureaucracy as the most important part of the policymaking process because neither legislators nor Cabinet ministers can understand the details of complex modern issues and are therefore content to be advised by their experts. Politicians may still have a role to play in identifying problems and determining priorities, but once that is done, they are in the hands of their advisers in finding ways to proceed.

The following points summarize the state-centred approach:

- The state is largely autonomous from societal forces.
- The authorities decide what is good for society and design policies to fulfill their vision of the public interest.
- The politicians rely heavily on the bureaucracy for advice.
- The authorities seek to enhance their autonomy by the internal generation of information and by maximizing their discretion, jurisdiction, and financial resources.
- If necessary, the authorities resort to the manipulation of information or coercion to persuade the public of their wisdom, or seek the support of the most relevant societal interest.

A variant of the state-centred approach is that of institutionalism or neo-institutionalism. This approach essentially argues that the institutions that make up the state should be the principal focus of attention in political science. Like the state-centred approach, institutionalism downplays the importance of societal forces and contends that institutions affect societal forces as much as the reverse. Institutionalism is particularly relevant to Canada because so much of our political debate is about governmental institutions, and because many societal forces—French, English, Aboriginal, and so on—are actually in conflict over institutional change. Institutionalism has always been an integral part of the political science discipline in this country, but neo-institutionalism is a reaction to an emphasis on broader social, cultural, and economic forces in recent years. Taking a neo-institutional approach, the third edition of *Parameters of Power* argued that institutions help to determine who has standing in the political process, structure the interactions of the players, are often the very things at stake in politics, and shape the interests at play in the political system.[11]

The state-centred approach is anchored in the traditional Canadian political culture—in the values of deference to authority, elitism, and collectivism—and, at least in the past, Canadians have generally welcomed state intervention and trusted the authorities who intervened.

Politicians and bureaucrats naturally took advantage of this invitation to function in such an autonomous fashion. This approach is related to the low level of political participation in Canada, to the minimal effort of most political parties to develop policy within their own ranks, and to the consequent lack of policy differences among the parties in election campaigns. Governing parties have changed policy directions so frequently after achieving power that doing so no longer causes particular criticism.

The state is not equally autonomous from societal forces in all policy areas. At least in the past, foreign policy was one traditionally autonomous field because relatively few citizens felt deeply about it; the constitution and federalism were other such state-centred sectors. Pierre Trudeau's policy of official bilingualism and Brian Mulroney's policies of privatization, deregulation, and deficit reduction were all imposed from the top rather than being demanded by the grassroots at the time. So, too, were the Goods and Services Tax (GST) and the Canada–U.S. Free Trade Agreement. These latter cases provide good examples of what the authorities do when they encounter public criticism of state-centred policies: they resort to public relations campaigns and manipulation of public opinion via the media at public expense.

Other state-centred policies bear the mark of bureaucratic inspiration, although the bureaucracy contributes a great deal even to those that do originate with the political executive. In this advisory capacity, the bureaucracy does not always act in its own interest alone; sometimes bureaucrats promote policies that they genuinely believe to be in the public interest. Cases of government (both politicians and bureaucrats) actually creating advocacy organizations to demand or support what the authorities themselves want to do have also been documented.[12]

It should be added that the state, large as it is, is not without internal conflicts. Moreover, to maximize their influence and protect themselves, state forces are often wiser to develop functional links with certain private or voluntary sector interests, especially advocacy groups, than to try to act in total isolation. Thus, the concept of "policy communities" is often helpful in this discussion.[13] The state is composed of a conglomeration of specialized policy processes, each of which nurtures support from the most relevant interest in society. Not only that, but with a weakened bureaucracy as a result of downsizing governments in the 1990s, the state is increasingly turning to think tanks for advice, as well as using other innovative means of soliciting the views of its citizens. Box 1.2 illustrates the state-centred approach with respect to gun control policy.

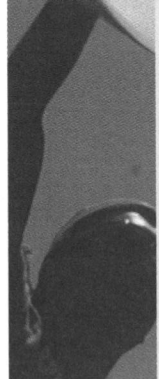

BOX 1.2	Gun Control

Although there was much demand for the government to register firearms, especially after the 1989 Montreal massacre, public opinion was seriously divided on this highly emotional issue. In such a situation, politicians often try to avoid taking action. In this case, however, Justice Minister Alan Rock and Prime Minister Jean Chrétien made it their personal mission to push through tougher gun laws, and "the federal government remained the leading advocate for comprehensive gun controls throughout the debate. . . ."

Source: Samuel A. Bottomley. *Locked and Loaded: Gun Control Policy in Canada.* From *The Real Worlds of Canadian Politics,* 4th ed. Robert M. Campbell, Michael Howlett, and Leslie A. Pal, eds. Broadview Press. 2004

Globalization

As mentioned in the discussion of the model of the political system, governments have always been subject to external influences. The 21st century, however, has witnessed a quantum leap in the extent to which the government of any state—Canada included—has had to contend with external forces. It is no longer the case that "the external environment" can be confined to a single part of this book: such global influences must be considered in almost every chapter.

Although the concept of globalization is extremely prominent in current discussions of public affairs, it means different things to different people. One of the most negative views of globalization is the claim that multinational corporations have become so large and powerful in the modern world that they often force governments to make decisions in the corporations' interests alone. In a sense this is a kind of class analysis extended to corporations operating beyond the state. The claim continues that because of the pressure of such corporations or of the governments of the countries in which they originate (especially the United States), states have joined organizations and signed international agreements that allow domestic government decisions to be overturned by supra-state authorities. Stephen Clarkson has suggested that such international organizations and agreements constitute a kind of "external constitution" that constrains government actions just as much as the internal constitution.[14]

A more neutral perspective on globalization is that it represents an intensification of global movements and interactions that have always been evident, whether we speak of human travel and migration, international trade (which has usually been the domain of corporations), or relations among states. Globalization reduces many limits on the interactions between individuals and communities once imposed by physical location; it involves the growth of "supraterritorial relations" among people; it is a complex set of connections that now binds our practices, our experiences, and our political, economic, and environmental fates together across the modern world.[15] In this view, globalization is a fact of modern life, with both positive and negative consequences, the latter including a serious challenge to democratic accountability and control.

Some also argue that globalization is a positive, liberating development. If it represents a more efficient operation of the world economy, for example, it means that more goods and services are available for all. If it involves exposure to a greater range of cultural experiences, it enriches the lives of all who participate. If it allows people who share attributes or interests across state boundaries to communicate more easily with one another, they can organize to protect and promote their causes.

Given these diverse perspectives on globalization, we can be on the lookout for the following phenomena throughout this book:

- The government must increasingly respond to demands from external actors to take certain actions or to refrain from actions already being taken.
- The government is constrained from acting as it otherwise would by the rules of international organizations it has joined or international agreements it has signed.
- Those branches of government most closely involved with external relations have become more active and significant than those dealing with purely domestic issues.
- Actors in the political system at the citizen level increasingly interact with counterparts in other states to protect and promote their common interests.

- Political ideas and ideologies and their transmission are increasingly globalized and less distinctive to individual states; indeed, the ideology of neoliberalism became influential almost everywhere, although its heyday may have passed.

Few aspects of Canadian government and politics have not been affected by the forces of globalization. Of course, for this country, globalization continues to be centred on the influence of the United States on Canadian public policies, including such sectors as defence, foreign policy, the economy, and culture. Because of Canada's military contribution to Afghanistan, developments in that country are of daily concern to both the government and the Canadian public. Globalization also relates in important ways to the rules of such multinational agreements and organizations as the North American Free Trade Agreement (NAFTA) and the World Trade Organization. The significance of globalization can also be seen in the prime minister's agenda, in the prominence of certain Cabinet ministers and departments, and in the mass media (including the Internet), to which Canadians turn for information and entertainment. But practically all groups and organizations in society have more international links than they used to—for example, women, Aboriginals, labour organizations, and universities. There may be only one main area where Canada is more actually autonomous than previously—in being able to enact our own constitutional amendments without going to Britain; however, judges who interpret laws, charters of rights, and constitutions increasingly refer to one another's decisions across state boundaries. Thus, all the approaches outlined above must be understood in the context of an abundance of external forces having an increasing impact on the constellation of domestic political actors.

The other side of this question is that individual governments still have a great deal of discretion in dealing with domestic demands. It may be increasingly feasible to consider foreign models, but government options in making public policies are not as limited as is often claimed. Moreover, a foreign state may have progressive policies that Canadians would like to emulate; U.S. President Barack Obama's environmental policies come to mind.

One respect in which this approach is relevant to postsecondary education is in the very student protests against the pressures of globalization. More positively, globalization would also suggest that ideas and ideologies relevant to postsecondary education flow readily across state borders. This flow might increase Canadian students' awareness of European countries' policies where postsecondary education is free! Box 1.3 illustrates how this approach is relevant to the long-standing softwood lumber dispute between Canada and the United States.

BOX 1.3	Softwood Lumber

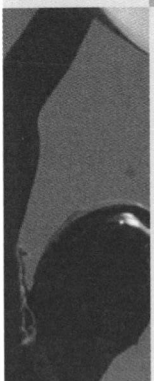

The issue of fair trade in softwood lumber between the U.S. and Canada has been a recurrent problem in the trade regimes of the two countries. . . . The U.S. lumber producers continue to demand that softwood imports from Canada be artificially capped since structural differences between the two economies cyclically bring Canadian market share to a level where it directly threatens them.

Source: Robert M. Campbell, Leslie A. Pal, and Andrea Migone. *Speaking Loudly and Carrying a Very Large Stick: Hardball Politics and Softwood Lumber.* From *The Real Worlds of Canadian Politics,* 4th ed. Robert M. Campbell, Michael Howlett, and Leslie A. Pal, eds. Broadview Press. 2004.

. . . .

CONCLUSION

This book suggests that each of the approaches outlined above offers useful perspectives that enhance our understanding of Canadian government and politics. Accordingly, the approaches have been applied to the subject matter of each chapter wherever relevant and are identified in the conclusion of each chapter by their respective symbols. It should be added that these approaches do not necessarily constitute competitive explanations and, in fact, often overlap. They point to the multidimensional character of politics and are useful whenever they add insight to the explanation of aspects of the political system.

Although the book takes the position that the Canadian political system is too variable and complex to be explained in any single, simple fashion, we can extract and combine aspects of these approaches to construct a coherent, general framework. Five central themes of this book are (1) the predominant influence of business pressure groups, (2) the pervasive influence of capitalist values, (3) the government's attempt to present itself to the electorate in the most favourable light, and (4) the persistent influence of the bureaucracy, (5) all of which are increasingly subject to the forces of globalization.

Two variations on this theme should also be mentioned. The first is the concept of **elite accommodation**.[16] This theory refers to the interaction of various elites, either within government circles or in both the public and the private sectors, in order to work out policies in their own mutual interests. Although they are seriously divided in some ways, the elites of various ethnic, regional, and other groupings have certain common background characteristics and values that enable them to come to agreement. Specific individuals have often come to know each other before occupying elite positions or have shared educational and social institutions and experiences in their youth. It is sometimes argued that the mass members of any group have such confidence in their own group leaders that they will abide by whatever decisions have been arrived at in the interaction of their group leaders with other elites. It is even hypothesized that elite accommodation is a means of contributing to national unity in a country like Canada, which is characterized by so many cleavages. In other words, the mass members of various ethnic, religious, regional, or class groupings may find themselves in conflict with the mass members of other groups, but if their leaders can arrive at compromises with the leaders of other groups, the mass members will accept them. The foremost advocate of elite accommodation, Robert Presthus, applies it primarily to interaction among the political, bureaucratic, and economic elites, an approach that is quite compatible with what is outlined above.

Another variation on the combined approach is that of the **embedded state**.[17] This is the idea that although the political and bureaucratic elites can sometimes function quite independently of societal forces, the state is so embedded in society that the elites cannot operate with total autonomy. Instead, because of this fusion of state and society or web of state–society interdependence, they interact with whatever societal elites are most relevant to their operations. Close interaction occurs between specialized governmental elites and the advocacy groups that constitute their principal clienteles.

DISCUSSION QUESTIONS

1. Give examples from Canadian politics that support the pluralist approach.

2. What advocacy groups are you aware of or do you belong to?

3. Do you agree that business groups have more influence than other groups? Why or why not?

4. What examples from Canadian politics support the public choice approach?

5. Give examples from Canadian politics that support class analysis.

6. Can you think of examples from Canadian politics that support the state-centred approach?

7. Can you think of recent examples of government decisions that resulted from external forces?

8. What can postsecondary students do to increase their influence on the Canadian political system?

NOTES

1. In *Canada: A Socio-Political Report* (Toronto: McGraw-Hill Ryerson, 1974), ch. 1, Ronald Manzer has linked these needs to the traditional political science concerns about security, liberty, equality, and fraternity.
2. David Easton, *A Systems Analysis of Political Life* (New York: John Wiley & Sons, 1965).
3. A relatively straightforward account of this perspective can be found in Leslie Paul Thiel, *Thinking Politics: Perspectives in Ancient, Modern, and Postmodern Political Theory* (Chatham, N.J.: Chatham House Publishers, Inc., 1997).
4. This is a simplified amalgam of ideas from Antonio Gramsci and Michel Foucault.
5. Stephen Brooks and Andrew Stritch, *Business and Government in Canada* (Scarborough: Prentice-Hall Canada, 1991); William Coleman, *Business and Politics* (Montreal: McGill-Queen's University Press, 1988); W.T. Stanbury, *Business–Government Relations in Canada* (Toronto: Methuen, 1986); and Geoffrey Hale, *The Uneasy Partnership: Politics of Business and Government in Canada* (Peterborough: Broadview Press, 2006). Pluralism and the group approach are increasingly viewed in combination with the state-centred approach in terms of "policy communities." See William Coleman and Grace Skogstad, eds., *Policy Communities and Public Policy in Canada* (Mississauga: Copp Clark Pitman, 1991).
6. Canadian applications include D.G. Hartle, *A Theory of the Expenditure Budgetary Process* (Toronto: University of Toronto Press, 1976); M.J. Trebilcock, D. Hartle, R. Prichard, and D. Dewees, *The Choice of Governing Instrument* (Ottawa: Economic Council of Canada, 1982); M.J. Trebilcock, *The Prospects for Reinventing Government* (Toronto: C.D. Howe Institute, 1994); Stanbury, *Business–Government Relations in Canada*, ch. 4; Mark Sproule-Jones, "Institutions, Constitutions, and Public Policies: A Public Choice Overview," in Michael Atkinson and Marsha Chandler, eds., *The Politics of Canadian Public Policy* (Toronto: University of Toronto Press, 1983); and Réjean Landry, "Biases in the Supply of Public Policies to Organized Interests," in Coleman and Skogstad, eds., *Policy Communities and Public Policy in Canada*. See also Thomas Flanagan, *Game Theory and Canadian Politics* (Toronto: University of Toronto Press, 1998).
7. See, for example, Leo Panitch, "Elites, Classes, and Power in Canada," in Michael S. Whittington and Glen Williams, eds., *Canadian Politics in the 1990s*, 4th ed. (Scarborough: Nelson Canada, 1995); and Tony Clarke, *Silent Coup: Confronting the Big Business Takeover of Canada* (Toronto: Lorimer, 1997).

8. Coleman, *Business and Politics*; Brooks and Stritch, *Business and Government in Canada*; and Robert Dahl and Charles Lindblom, *Politics, Economics and Welfare* (Chicago: University of Chicago Press, 1976).

9. Nicolas Baxter-Moore, "Policy Implementation and the Role of the State: A Revised Approach to the Study of Policy Instruments," in Robert Jackson, Doreen Jackson, and Nicolas Baxter-Moore, eds., *Contemporary Canadian Politics* (Scarborough: Prentice-Hall Canada, 1987).

10. Canadian applications include Elizabeth Riddell-Dixon, "State Autonomy and Canadian Foreign Policy: The Case of Deep Seabed Mining," *Canadian Journal of Political Science* (June 1988), pp. 297–317; Leslie Pal, "Relative Autonomy Revisited: The Origins of Canadian Unemployment Insurance," *Canadian Journal of Political Science* (March 1986), pp. 71–102; Leslie Pal, *State, Class and Bureaucracy: Canadian Unemployment Insurance and Public Policy* (Montreal: McGill-Queen's University Press, 1987); K.R. Nossal, *The Politics of Canadian Foreign Policy*, 3rd ed. (Scarborough: Prentice-Hall Canada, 1997); and R. Brian Howe and David Johnson, "Variations in Enforcing Equality: A Study of Provincial Human Rights Funding," *Canadian Public Administration* (Summer 1995).

11. Keith Archer, Roger Gibbins, Rainer Knopff, Heather MacIvor, and Leslie Pal, *Parameters of Power: Canada's Political Institutions*, 3rd ed. (Scarborough: Nelson, 2002). Interestingly enough, the fourth edition of this book found it necessary to bring societal forces into the picture.

12. Leslie Pal, *Interests of State: The Politics of Language, Multiculturalism, and Feminism in Canada* (Montreal: McGill-Queen's University Press, 1993).

13. Paul Pross, *Group Politics and Public Policy* (Toronto: Oxford University Press, 1986); and Coleman and Skogstad, *Policy Communities and Public Policy in Canada*.

14. Stephen Clarkson, *Uncle Sam and Us: Globalization, Neoconservatism, and the Canadian State* (Toronto: University of Toronto Press, 2002).

15. William D. Coleman, "The Politics of Globalization," in Rand Dyck, ed., *Studying Politics: An Introduction to Political Science*, 3rd ed. (Toronto: Nelson Education, 2009).

16. Robert Presthus, *Elite Accommodation in Canada* (Toronto: Macmillan, 1973).

17. Alan C. Cairns, "The Embedded State: State–Society Relations in Canada," in Alan C. Cairns, *Reconfigurations: Canadian Citizenship and Constitutional Change* (Toronto: McClelland and Stewart, 1995).

· ·

FURTHER READINGS

Charlton, Mark, and Paul Barker, eds. *Crosscurrents: Contemporary Political Issues*, 6th ed. Toronto: Nelson Education, 2009.

Clarke, Tony. *Silent Coup: Confronting the Big Business Takeover of Canada*. Toronto: Lorimer, 1997.

Clarkson, Stephen. *Uncle Sam and Us: Globalization, Neoconservatism, and the Canadian State*. Toronto: University of Toronto Press, 2002.

Coleman, William, and Grace Skogstad. *Policy Communities and Public Policy in Canada*. Mississauga: Copp Clark Pitman, 1991.

MacIvor, Heather. *Parameters of Power: Canada's Political Institutions*, 5th ed. Toronto: Nelson Education, 2010.

McMenemy, John. *The Language of Canadian Politics: A Guide to Important Terms and Concepts*, 4th ed. Waterloo: University of Waterloo Press, 2006.

Pal, Leslie. *Interests of State: The Politics of Language, Multiculturalism, and Feminism in Canada*. Montreal: McGill-Queen's University Press, 1993.

Panitch, Leo. "Elites, Classes, and Power in Canada." In Michael S. Whittington and Glen Williams, eds., *Canadian Politics in the 1990s*, 4th ed. Scarborough: Nelson Canada, 1995.

Whittington, Michael, and Glen Williams, eds. *Canadian Politics in the 21st Century*, 7th ed. Toronto: Thomson Nelson, 2008.

Chapter 2

Institutional Foundations and
THE EVOLUTION
of the State

How much violence occurred during Canada's constitutional development? How did the new British conquerors treat the almost completely French colony of Quebec? How much of the new government structure in 1867 was based on that of Britain, and how much on that of the United States? What were the key points in the move toward the achievement of Canadian sovereignty? How has the role of the state changed over the past 140 or so years?

This chapter sketches the historical context within which the Canadian political system operates and outlines the basic institutional foundations of that system. It surveys the institutions established in the colonial period, focuses on the great fusion in 1867 of the British parliamentary system with a variation on American federalism, enumerates the main principles of the Canadian Constitution, and discusses the evolution of Canada from a British colony to a sovereign state. It concludes with a brief overview of the changing nature of the state.

The developments discussed in this chapter are not of mere historical interest; in many respects they continue to frame contemporary political issues and often lead to strong and conflicting feelings about them. To a large extent, these historical precedents determined modern-day French-language rights, federal–provincial relations, the relationship between parliament and the courts, and the connection between the prime minister and Cabinet on the one hand and the House of Commons on the other.

EARLY SETTLEMENT AND POLITICAL INSTITUTIONS

The territory that is now called Canada was first occupied by self-governing Aboriginal peoples. France and Britain colonized parts of this territory in the 1500s and 1600s, interacted with the Aboriginals in a variety of ways, and periodically fought each other over North American claims for nearly 200 years. France established permanent settlement in Quebec or New France in the early 1600s, the British Hudson's Bay Company took possession of Rupert's Land around Hudson Bay, and Britain gained control of Nova Scotia and Newfoundland by the 1713 Treaty of Utrecht. Britain's conquest of Quebec in the 1759 Battle of the Plains of Abraham profoundly changed the history of the colony and led to Quebec's continuing struggle to retain its distinctive character. That battle was part of the Seven Years' War between these traditional European rivals, and in addition to Quebec, Britain gained Prince Edward Island, Cape Breton, and New Brunswick by the 1763 Treaty of Paris. This reduced France's North American holdings to the islands of Saint Pierre and Miquelon.

The **Royal Proclamation of 1763**, the first distinctively Canadian constitutional document, created the British colony of Quebec[1] and purported to protect the interests of Aboriginal peoples. As far as ex-Europeans were concerned, Quebec was largely made up of French-speaking farmers, clergy, and seigneurs, but the British-appointed government was English speaking, and the non-agricultural economy increasingly came under British control. However, British governors resisted the idea of imposing the English language and Protestant religion on such a homogeneous French-Catholic population. The accompanying time line highlights constitutional developments between 1759 and 1867.

. . . .

TIME LINE

Constitutional Developments, 1758–1867

"Canada"	*"Maritimes"*
	1758 Nova Scotia assembly
1759 British conquest of Quebec	
1763 Royal Proclamation	
	1773 Prince Edward Island assembly
1774 Quebec Act	
	1784 New Brunswick assembly
1791 Constitutional Act	
1837 Rebellions	
1840 Act of Union	
1848 Responsible government	1848 Responsible government (NS and NB)

1867 British North America Act (Constitution Act, 1867)

In 1774, the **Quebec Act** provided for a new set of government institutions. It established a council to advise the Governor of the colony but no elected assembly. Roman Catholics were allowed freedom of religion and could be appointed to the council, while the colony combined British criminal law with French civil law. Meanwhile, the first elected assembly in the "Canadian" part of British North America was summoned in Nova Scotia in 1758, followed by Prince Edward Island in 1773.

In 1776, the residents of the 13 "American" colonies declared their independence from British rule. French Canadians essentially remained neutral in this dispute, and because little anti-British sentiment existed in the "Canadian" colonies, thousands of ex-Americans loyal to Britain—the United Empire Loyalists—migrated to "Canada." Many settled in modern-day New Brunswick, leading to the severing of that colony from Nova Scotia in 1784, together with the creation of its own assembly. Then, in response to pressure from those Loyalists who moved into what is now Ontario and who were already accustomed to operating with an elected assembly, Britain passed the **Constitutional Act of 1791**. This gesture also served to reward the loyalty of the French for not joining the American Revolution. The act divided the colony in two—Upper and Lower Canada—each with a governor, an executive council, an appointed legislative council, and a locally elected assembly. In the case of Lower Canada, the appointed councils were primarily composed of Anglophones, and the assembly, of francophones. In Upper Canada, which was almost exclusively English, the Constitutional Act provided for British, rather than French, civil law. The executive council gradually evolved into the Cabinet, while the legislative council was the forerunner of the Senate. Thus, by 1791, all the colonies had achieved **representative government**—that is, a set of political institutions that included an elected legislative assembly. (See Figure 2.1 to trace the evolution of the political institutions.)

While the colonies welcomed this advance, they soon discovered that it left much to be desired. In fact, subsequent discord in the Canadian colonies was not so much between them and Britain as between the local assembly and the executive, comprising the governor and his appointed advisory executive council. The elected assembly represented and articulated the views of the people but had no real power over the appointed councils. This situation was complicated by the cultural division in Lower Canada, where Lord Durham found "two nations warring in the bosom of a single state."[2] Reformers demanded **responsible government**, in which advisers to the governor would be both chosen from and reflect the views of the elected assembly. This presented a problem in the colonies, however, because on many subjects Britain wanted the governor to do its will, not that of the local assembly. As a result, rebellions erupted in 1837 in both Upper and Lower Canada, led by William Lyon Mackenzie and Louis-Joseph Papineau respectively, and forced the British government to appoint Lord Durham to investigate the situation.

The 1839 **Durham Report** provided a blueprint for solving the problems of assembly–executive relations, recommending that the principle of responsible government be implemented with respect to local affairs, so that the executive branch would govern only as long as it retained the confidence of the elected assembly. Durham outlined a division of powers between local and imperial authorities such that in local matters the governor would follow the advice of colonial authorities, but in matters of imperial concern he would act as an agent of the British government. Responsible government came to Nova Scotia, New

. . . .

Figure 2.1 Evolution of Canadian Pre-Confederation Political Institutions

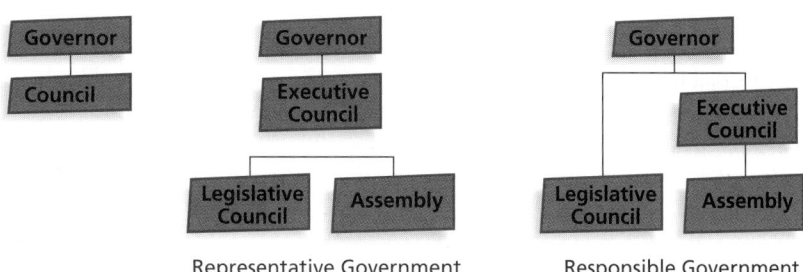

Representative Government   Responsible Government

Brunswick, and the colony of Canada in 1848, and three years later to Prince Edward Island. In other words, all these pre-Confederation British colonies now operated on the basis that the Governor chose the Cabinet or executive council from the assembly and it had to resign if it lost the confidence of the elected members. British Columbia acquired responsible government when it joined Confederation, as did the other provinces as they were created. Responsible government remains a sacred principle of Canadian government and is usually expressed as follows: a form of government in which the political executive must retain the confidence of the elected legislature and must resign or call an election if and when it is defeated on a vote of nonconfidence. At this period of time, of course, the government remained otherwise undemocratic in the sense that the vote for the assembly was limited to privileged white men.

Durham also recommended that Upper and Lower Canada be united into a single colony of Canada, partly as one last attempt to submerge and assimilate the French. Thus, to this day, Durham is reviled by many French-Canadians. The colonies were amalgamated by the 1840 **Act of Union** (which came into effect in 1841), but English did not remain the sole language of government operations for long. When it became clear that assimilation of French Canadians would not be achieved, French was also recognized as an official language of the legislature. Moreover, most governments of the period were headed by a combination of English and French leaders.

. . . .

THE ROAD TO CONFEDERATION

Shortly after achieving responsible government, the individual British North American colonies began to think of uniting. The colonies were driven to consider such a union because of economic, political, and military factors.[3] Since the British had discontinued colonial trading preferences, and because a reciprocity treaty with the United States had expired, the colonies hoped to establish a new free trade area among themselves. This large internal market would be enhanced by a railway link between the Maritimes and central Canada, which in turn would provide the latter with a winter Atlantic port. The future prospect of annexing and developing the West was also seen as a source of economic prosperity.

Meanwhile, the colony of Canada had experienced political deadlock between its two parts, then called Canada East (Quebec) and Canada West (Ontario), as well as between the French and English component groups. Public decisions had to be made in one large, combined set of governmental institutions, yet the needs and demands of the two parts were often quite different. This led to the practice of requiring a "double majority" (a majority of members from each part of the colony) for the passage of bills. Confederation would allow greater autonomy to the two parts because while a central government would deal with problems that all the colonies had in common, provincial governments would handle distinctive internal matters on their own. Such a two-tier structure also appealed to the Maritime provinces, which did not feel like turning all decisions over to a distant central government.

The individual colonies also felt vulnerable militarily. The United States had a powerful army on their doorstep, and prominent Americans could be heard to advocate the takeover of the existing colonies and the vast territories to the west. Moreover, the British government was no longer interested in providing military protection to the colonies. By joining together, the colonies would make American military aggression more difficult and provide a stronger force to resist its appetite for the "Canadian" West.

Confederation was thus precipitated by economic, political, and military problems and seemed to most colonial leaders to be a means of solving them. But it also held out the hope that the new country would one day become a prosperous, transcontinental nation similar to its southern neighbour.

In the 1860s, Nova Scotia, New Brunswick, and Prince Edward Island began to consider forming a Maritime union, and they called the Charlottetown Conference for this purpose in 1864. When the self-invited delegates from the colony of Canada arrived, however, the idea of a larger union was put up for debate. Discussions continued at the Quebec Conference later that year, where the essentials of the Confederation scheme were agreed on. The London Conference of 1866 fine-tuned the agreement, leaving Prince Edward Island (and Newfoundland) temporarily on the sidelines. While retaining their individual identities, Nova Scotia, New Brunswick, and the colony of Canada—now divided between Ontario and Quebec—were officially united on July 1, 1867, by the **British North America Act**, later renamed the **Constitution Act, 1867**. Figure 2.2 is a map of Canada in 1867.

. . . .

Figure 2.2 Canada at Confederation, 1867

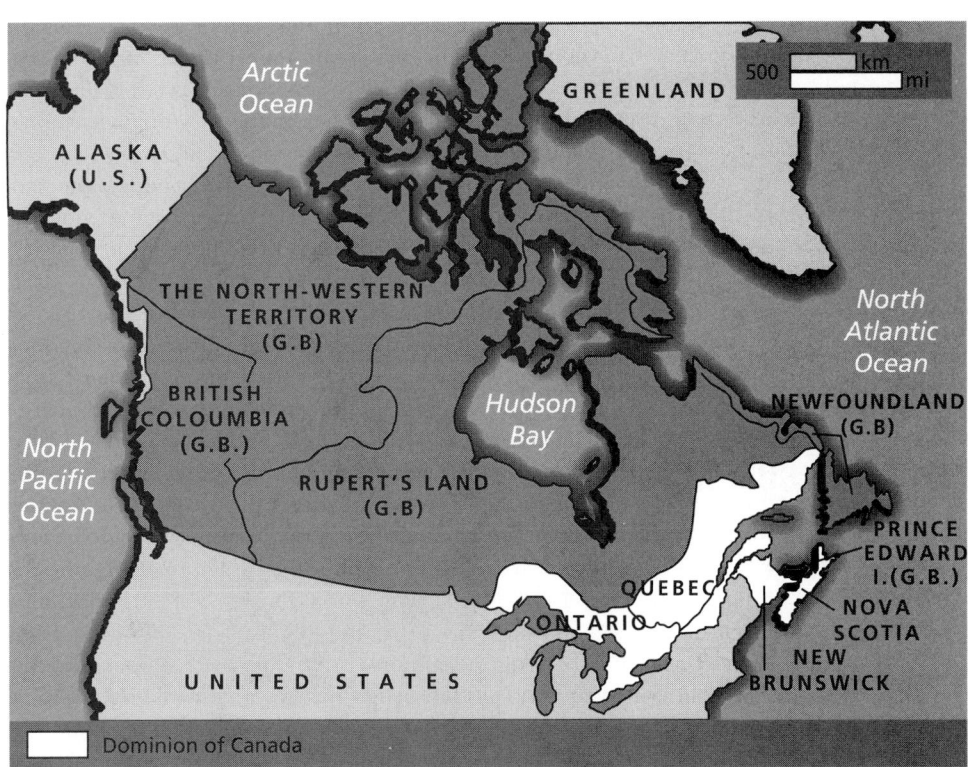

· ·

Figure 2.3   Date of Entry or Creation of Provinces and Territories

It did not take long for the country to grow. Inspired by Louis Riel, Canada acquired Rupert's Land from the Hudson's Bay Company, and Manitoba was added as a fifth province in 1870, to be followed by British Columbia in 1871, and Prince Edward Island in 1873. In 1905, Alberta and Saskatchewan were carved out of the Northwest Territories, and Newfoundland was added in 1949. Besides these 10 provinces, Canada now consists of three semi-autonomous territories: Yukon, Northwest Territories, and Nunavut. Figure 2.3 shows the map of Canada in 2010, and changes over this period can be found at http://atlas.nrcan. gc.ca/site/english/maps/historical/territorialevolution.

· ·

THE BRITISH PARLIAMENTARY SYSTEM COMPARED WITH THE AMERICAN CONGRESSIONAL SYSTEM

Within the new central government (often called the "federal government," to make things more confusing), the British parliamentary system provided the institutional foundations. This system is based on the periodic popular election of the members of the House of Commons. Parliament also has a second or "upper" chamber; in Britain, this was the hereditary House of Lords. Canada lacked the historic landed nobility found in Britain, however, so it was decided that the members of the Canadian Senate would be appointed by the prime minister. The third part of the British Parliament is the monarch or the Crown, and approval of all three parts is necessary for the passage of legislation and certain other authoritative decisions. Canada would, of course, continue to be a monarchy and automatically shared the widely esteemed British monarch of the day, Queen Victoria. On a practical, daily basis, however, the governor general would exercise the functions of the Crown.

Although the British system is called parliamentary government, and although it is said to operate on the principle of the **supremacy of Parliament**, such labels and descriptions are somewhat misleading. The core of the parliamentary system, even in 1867, was the prime minister and the Cabinet. Although they must be members of Parliament, they are such an important part of Parliament that they often relegate both the monarch and the other members of the House of Commons and Senate (or House of Lords) to a position of insignificance. To the prime minister and Cabinet are conferred the powers to lead the country and make the most important decisions in the political system. But the principle of responsible government holds that they retain their position and their powers only as long as they are supported by a majority in Parliament. If the House of Commons declares a lack of confidence in the prime minister and Cabinet, they must either resign and make way for another group to take their place, or call an election, the latter option being the most common. Because the prime minister and Cabinet ministers have seats in the legislative branch, mostly the House of Commons, and because they are the source of most legislation, the system is often termed a "fusion of powers"—that is, it involves a combination of legislative and executive powers.

In the British parliamentary system, then, the prime minister and Cabinet ministers, who have seats in Parliament, are given the power to introduce most legislation and the right to control most of the time of the legislature. They also have the exclusive power to introduce legislation of a financial nature—laws either to raise or spend money. They have wide powers to make appointments, to draft subordinate legislation under the authority of laws, to conduct international affairs, and essentially all the powers necessary to provide effective political leadership for the country. The parliamentary system is executive-dominated, and because the British Parliament operates in the Palace of Westminster, this system is sometimes called the **Westminster model**. Other members of Parliament (MPs) may criticize and propose amendments, the monarch (or governor general) may advise and warn, but the prime minister and Cabinet almost always get their way. This is because a majority of the members of Parliament normally belong to the same political party as the prime minister and Cabinet, and together they constitute a **majority government**. Even more in Canada than in contemporary Britain, the prime minister and Cabinet impose rigid party discipline on their MPs to support their every move. The prime minister and Cabinet have less control in a **minority government** situation, where their supporters are outnumbered by opposition MPs, as has usually been the case in recent years.

It should be added that although government was small and simple at the time of Confederation, it has gradually developed another important branch: the bureaucracy or public service. The bureaucracy essentially advises the prime minister and Cabinet on their decisions and then carries out whatever government programs have been authorized. The current Canadian bureaucracy consists of about 250 000 "core" public servants in departments and agencies, and another 150 000 in the armed forces, RCMP, and Crown corporations.

The significance of the Senate has declined since Confederation because its appointed, rather than elected, base diminishes its members' legitimacy in a democratic age. While the powers of the Senate have remained virtually equal to those of the House of Commons (unlike those of the British House of Lords, whose powers have been curtailed), senators have rarely felt it proper to exercise them. Moreover, independent behaviour has usually been discouraged by the fact that the party with a majority in the Senate has usually been the same one as had a majority in the Commons. If for any reason the Senate should ultimately defeat a government bill, it does not affect the constitutional standing of the prime minister and Cabinet. In

The British Parliament, housed in the Palace of Westminster.

other words, the principle of responsible government in the Westminster model, whether in Britain or Canada, does not apply to upper chambers. The model outlined above is also operational in each of the provinces, except that they now all possess one-chamber, or unicameral, legislatures.

The British parliamentary system also incorporates the principle of **judicial independence**. Although courts are established by acts of Parliament and judges are appointed by the prime minister and Cabinet or attorney general, the whole judicial system is then expected to operate independently of the executive and legislative branches of government. In the case of Britain itself, the judges have considerable discretion in interpreting laws but lack the power of **judicial review**—that is, the power to declare laws invalid. The Canadian judiciary soon appropriated to itself the power to invalidate laws that violated the federal–provincial division of powers but were otherwise quite restrained. Figure 2.4 outlines the Canadian political institutions.

The British parliamentary system is distinct in many ways from the U.S. presidential–congressional system. There, the president and the two houses of the legislature are independently elected, and no one is permitted to sit in more than one branch of government. The "separation of powers" means that executive, legislative, and judicial powers are distributed to three separate branches of government: the president, Congress, and the courts, respectively. Moreover, the U.S. system is also characterized by "checks and balances" designed to ensure that the actions of any one branch of government are subject to veto by another.

· ·

Figure 2.4   An Outline of Canadian Political Institutions

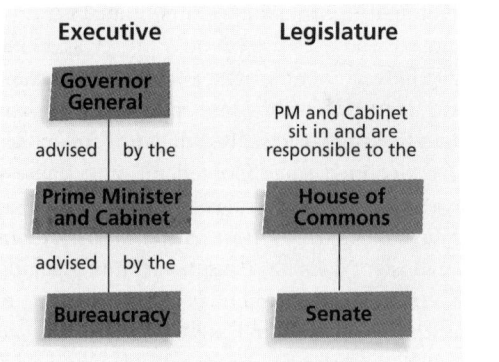

Figure 2.5 U.S. System of Separation of Powers and Checks and Balances

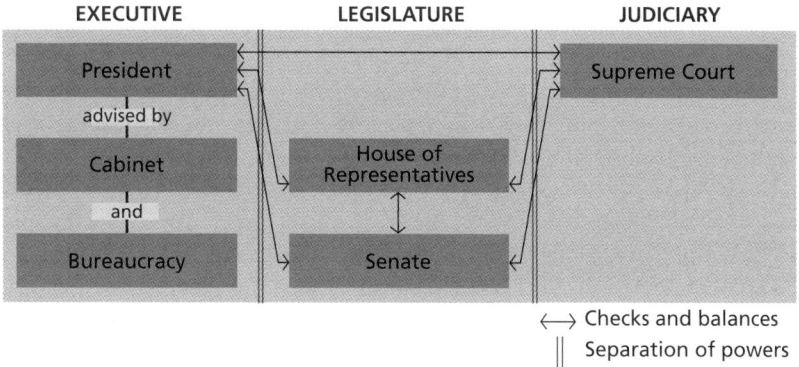

Members of the House of Representatives and the Senate have much more legislative power than their counterparts in the British parliamentary system both in terms of initiating bills and amending or vetoing those emanating from the executive. Party discipline is also much looser, so that even if a majority of the members of Congress belong to the same party as the president, there is no guarantee that the president's initiatives will be passed. The Supreme Court also has the power of judicial review and can overturn any legislation that it feels is in violation of the Constitution. Apart from the name of the upper chamber—the Senate—the Fathers of Canadian Confederation adopted virtually nothing from the U.S. system with respect to the internal operation of the federal and provincial governments. Figure 2.5 outlines the relationships among the American political institutions.

CANADIAN AND AMERICAN FEDERALISM

Canadian Confederation was the first attempt to fuse the principles of the British parliamentary system with those of federalism, although Australia would make a similar move shortly afterward. Since the United States was the leading federal state of the day, and the one closest to Canada, the federal aspects of the new **constitution** were directly related to those next door.

The Fathers of Confederation were dealing with a large piece of territory, one they hoped would soon become larger, someday equalling or exceeding that of the United States. They came from colonies that had separate identities and a previous semi-autonomous existence. In this respect, the model of American federalism could not help but influence the design of the new country. It would have to be a **federation** of some kind, with a division of powers between the central and provincial governments.

Confederation was, to a large extent, the work of John A. Macdonald, who went on to become the first prime minister of Canada. Macdonald preferred a unitary state or legislative union in which the new central government would have almost all the powers, and the provinces would be little more than municipalities. But Quebec and the Maritimes were not prepared to join such a system. Quebec in particular demanded an autonomous provincial government so that its linguistic and cultural concerns, such as education and civil law, would be placed in the hands of a French-speaking majority. The Maritimes, too, insisted on provincial governments because they did not want to lose their previously established identities, because they had little in the way of municipal government to handle local problems, and because they were far removed from the new capital in Ottawa. Hence, the logical compromise was a system that contained a central government to deal with common purposes, and provincial governments to look after local concerns. Although this principle was essentially that of American federalism, it was also consistent with the existing British colonial tradition of having two levels of government (Britain and local), so the Fathers of Confederation were accustomed to such divided jurisdiction.

Macdonald accepted a federal form of government, then, to allow the former colonies to retain some of their political and economic independence, but he intended the new country to be a highly centralized federation. He felt that its economic and defensive objectives required a strong central government, a conviction shared by most of the other participants because they believed that the American Civil War (which had just ended as they began their deliberations) had been the result of too much power at the state level. Some historians have added that most of the Fathers of Confederation had links to banks, railways, and manufacturing companies, all of which looked on the Confederation project primarily as a source of profit. By controlling the development of the country at the centre, these politicians would be free to exploit the hinterland.[4]

Federalism can be defined as a division of powers between central and regional governments such that neither is subordinate to the other. The Confederation settlement was not entirely consistent with this modern definition of federalism, however, because in certain respects the provinces were made subordinate to the central government. Some observers thus prefer to label the arrangement at its creation as "quasi-federal."[5] Ironically, the Fathers used the word "confederation," which in political science indicates a loose, decentralized federation, the opposite of what Macdonald intended. In the U.S. federal system, for example, the central government was given only certain delegated powers, while the residual powers remained at the level of the states. Macdonald was determined to reverse this pattern; he essentially gave the provinces 16 enumerated powers and left the residual powers at the centre. He was also careful to give Ottawa unlimited powers of taxation, broad powers to regulate trade and commerce, and power over such other important fields as defence and the criminal law.

Besides dividing powers between the two levels of government, constitutional architects in both Canada and the United States had to decide how the provinces or states would be represented at the national level. In both cases, the degree of democracy of the day required that the lower house of the legislature be based on the principle of representation by population, so that the most populous provinces or states would have the largest number of members in that chamber. To counterbalance this, and to protect the interests of the smaller states, the U.S. decided that each state, regardless of population, would have two senators at the national level. Some Fathers of Confederation preferred this idea, but others wanted representation by population in both houses of Parliament. The Canadian compromise was to base the Senate on the principle of equal *regional* representation rather than equal *provincial* representation.

Since Canadian politicians were already familiar with divided authority, it might seem that a fusion of the British parliamentary system and American federalism was not such a constitutional innovation. The colonial division of powers was of a somewhat different kind, however, and, more importantly, the whole ethos underlying the Canadian and U.S. systems was different. In the British parliamentary system, everything is designed to *facilitate* government action by concentrating power in the hands of the executive, whether in terms of its relationship with other institutions of government, such as Parliament and the courts, or with territorial units, such as local governments. In the American system, everything is designed to *inhibit* government action by preventing the concentration of power in the hands of any authority. Institutions of the national government—president, House of Representatives, Senate, and Supreme Court—should be able to veto each other, and they should collectively be kept in line by a division of powers that gives most authority to the states. It is largely because the British system is designed to facilitate government action and because the American system is designed to inhibit it that the fusion of the two systems in Canadian Confederation was such a distinctive phenomenon. John A. Macdonald saw the contradiction and tried to establish a federal system that was much more centralized than that next door.

One of the great ironies of Canadian constitutional development is that the country is now one of the most decentralized federations in the world. The evolution of Canadian federalism from a highly centralized to a highly decentralized state is discussed in Chapter 18. The reasons for this development include the enormous size of the country, strong regional sentiments, Quebec's endless quest for greater autonomy, and judicial decisions related to the division of powers that went against John A. Macdonald's intentions.

The only major change since the central institutional structure was established in Canada in 1867 was the adoption of the **Charter of Rights and Freedoms** in 1982. It added to the scope of judicial review with respect to the federal–provincial division of powers by importing American-style judicial authority in the area of protecting individual rights and freedoms. Henceforth, the courts could disallow federal or provincial legislation and other government actions that violated the Constitution either in terms of the division of powers or of the Charter of Rights.

· ·

PRINCIPLES OF THE CANADIAN CONSTITUTION

The preceding discussion has identified three basic principles of the Canadian Constitution: responsible government, which is the essence of the British parliamentary system; federalism; and judicial review, especially since 1982. At least three other fundamental principles are also embedded in the Canadian Constitution: constitutional monarchy, the rule of law, and democracy.[6]

· ·

PRINCIPLES OF THE CANADIAN CONSTITUTION

- Responsible government
- Federalism
- Judicial review
- Constitutional monarchy
- Rule of law
- Democracy

In terms of its head of state, Canada is a **constitutional monarchy**. This is not a principle that attracts much attention, largely because the monarch herself lives in another country and because her actual power, as well as that of her Canadian representative, the governor general, is not extensive. Nevertheless, as outlined in Chapter 21, the monarchical system underlies a great deal of the operation of government in Canada, largely in the form of the Crown.[7] The Crown can be defined as the sum total of residual or discretionary powers still left in the hands of the monarch. The term "constitutional monarchy" basically means that the monarch reigns according to the Constitution, and one that has put most of the powers of government into someone else's hands. Almost all of the powers once exercised by the monarch have been whittled away either by legislation or by constitutional convention.

The **rule of law** is another constitutional principle inherited from Great Britain that rests largely on convention and judicial precedent. In essence, it means that all government action must be based on law and that governments and government officials must obey the law. In other words, the law is supreme, and no one, including the lawmakers, is above it.[8] Courts in Canada as well as Britain have had occasion to overturn government decisions and actions that were not based on law.[9]

Finally, Canada is a **democracy**. This term, which is related to responsible government, constitutional monarchy, and the rule of law, will be analyzed more fully in Chapter 11. In Canadian terms, democracy has four components: popular sovereignty, meaning that the people ultimately rule, primarily through periodic elections; political equality, meaning that everyone has one vote on election day; political freedom, meaning that during and between elections people are free to organize and advocate for political purposes; and majority rule, meaning that except in defined situations designed to protect minority rights, the will of the majority prevails. Canada was hardly a democracy in 1867, however, and political equality in terms of universal suffrage was only achieved long afterward.

THE ROAD TO CANADIAN SOVEREIGNTY

Having outlined the development of the basic institutions and the fundamental constitutional principles of the Canadian political system, let us trace the evolution of Canada from British colony to sovereign state. Contrary to popular belief, the British North America (BNA) Act of 1867 (that is, the Constitution Act, 1867) did not directly advance the cause of Canadian independence. That act simply divided the powers that were already being exercised in Canada between a new central government and the provincial governments. British control still existed in many forms:

- British appointment of the governor general
- The power of the governor general to reserve Canadian legislation for the approval of the British Cabinet
- The power of the British government to disallow Canadian legislation
- The power of the British Parliament to amend the BNA Act
- The arbitrary extension to Canada of imperial legislation
- The paramountcy of any British legislation in conflict with Canadian statutes
- Canadian incapacity to pass legislation with extraterritorial effect
- The authority of the British Judicial Committee of the Privy Council as Canada's final court of appeal
- British control of Canadian foreign and trade policy

The act of Confederation made Canada a more respectable and viable entity and ultimately strengthened its case for greater autonomy, but it did not fundamentally alter the British–Canadian relationship.

Canada had succeeded in claiming the right to control its own tariffs even before Confederation, and between 1867 and 1914 it became increasingly autonomous in making commercial treaties with other countries. The same was true in terms of political treaties, although progress in this area came more slowly. One modest advance was the inclusion of Prime Minister Macdonald as a member of the British team that negotiated the 1871 Treaty of Washington. Relations with Britain were handled through the governor general, the Colonial Office, the Canadian High Commissioner in London after 1879, and in periodic Imperial Conferences after 1887.

By the end of the 19th century Canadian autonomy had progressed to the point that when Prime Minister Wilfrid Laurier sent an official contingent to the South African (Boer) War, it was done more in response to Canadian public opinion than to British pressure. In the Alaska Boundary dispute of 1903, however, the British representative on the Anglo-Canadian half of the judicial tribunal voted with the three American representatives to award the United States a long strip of the northern British Columbia coastline. In defending Canadian interests, Britain was apparently not prepared to jeopardize its relations with the United States.

The ultimate independence of Canada and of several other British colonies is usually attributed to developments connected to the First World War. Although Canada was automatically at war in 1914 as a result of British action, the Canadian government determined the extent of its own commitments, and Canada made a major contribution to the war effort. A series of conferences of Dominion prime ministers called the Imperial War Cabinet began in 1917, as Canada and the other dominions—Australia, New Zealand, and South Africa—demanded a policymaking role in return for their wartime efforts. Prime Minister Robert Borden and his counterparts took part in the Paris Peace Conference and signed the peace treaties, and the dominions became individual members of the League of Nations. Thus, by 1919, Canada had gained new international status as a result of both accomplishments on the battlefield and subsequent demands for recognition at the conference table.

The Vimy Ridge Monument commemorates the great battle in 1917. Some 3600 Canadian soldiers were killed and another 5000 injured, but it contributed to Canada's independence.

THE CANADIAN PRESS/Jonathan Howard

Postwar attempts to forge a unified Empire foreign policy broke down as various domin-ions sought to flex their fledgling muscles, and Prime Minister Mackenzie King insisted that Britain not co-sign the 1923 Halibut Treaty between Canada and the United States. Based on the Balfour Report, the Imperial Conference of 1926 ended with a proclamation of the com-plete equality in status of the United Kingdom and the dominions in internal, international, and imperial affairs. They were described in the proclamation as "autonomous Communities within the British Empire, equal in status, in no way subordinate one to another in any aspect of their domestic or external affairs, though united by a common allegiance to the Crown, and freely associated as members of the British Commonwealth of Nations."

Besides giving Canada complete autonomy in all policy fields, the 1926 declaration had implications for the position of the governor general. This official would no longer be an agent of the British government, but rather only a personal representative of the Crown. Disallowance of Canadian legislation by the British Cabinet and reservation of Canadian legislation by the governor general would now be obsolete. These arrangements were refined at another conference in 1930 and then constitutionalized in the **Statute of Westminster** of 1931. That statute provided that the Colonial Laws Validity Act (under which Dominion statutes were void if they conflicted with statutes of the Imperial Parliament) would no longer apply to the dominions, that in the future no Dominion statute was to be declared void because it was repugnant to the law of the United Kingdom, and that no act of the Imperial Parliament was to extend to a Dominion unless the latter had requested and consented to its enactment. The Statute also declared that a Dominion Parliament had the power to enact laws having extraterritorial operation.[10] The accompanying time line illustrates constitu-tional developments between 1867 and 1982.

. . . .

TIME LINE

Constitutional Developments, 1867–1982

1919	Member of the League of Nations
1926	Balfour Declaration—Imperial Conference confers autonomy on Dominions
1931	Statute of Westminster confirms independence from Britain
1949	Supreme Court of Canada becomes final court of appeal
1982	Made-in-Canada constitutional amending formula

The drive to loosen links with Britain was thus largely engineered by prime ministers Laurier, Borden, and King, without much apparent public pressure. Reducing British control would automatically increase the power of the Canadian state that these politicians con-trolled. O.D. Skelton, the trusted adviser of Liberal prime ministers in the early years of the 20th century, has also been identified as a leading advocate of breaking the British bonds in behind-the-scenes discussions with Laurier and King.

After 1931, therefore, Canada was completely independent of Britain, but a number of anomalies somewhat disguised this fact. First, Canada continued to share a head of state with Britain, although from the Canadian perspective, that person was King or Queen of Canada. Even though the Canadian government now had the power to select the governor general, prime ministers continued to appoint British aristocrats, diplomats, and war heroes until 1952. Of more importance, since Canada had not been able to decide how to amend the BNA Act within Canada, such amendments still had to be passed by the British Parliament, albeit only at Canadian request. In 1949 a procedure was developed to enact constitutional amendments in Canada if they affected only the federal level of government, but it was not until 1982 that a comprehensive domestic formula for making constitutional amendments was agreed to and enshrined in the **Constitution Act, 1982**. Also of great significance, the **Judicial Committee of the Privy Council (JCPC)** remained Canada's final court of appeal in criminal cases until 1933 and in all other cases, notably constitutional, until 1949. Other British legacies included the fact that, until 1965, the Union Jack and the Red Ensign, combining a smaller Union Jack in the corner with a Canadian crest, continued to serve as Canadian flags. In 1967 the government recognized "O Canada" rather than "God Save the Queen" as the Canadian national anthem, but it was not until 1980 that the former was designated officially.

Once Canada made an autonomous decision to take part, the Second World War saw the Canadian armed forces integrated with the Allied powers. Afterward, however, British–Canadian ties declined as Canada's population became more diversified in its ethnic origins, as Britain occupied a diminished role in world affairs, and as both Britain and Canada drew closer to the United States.[11] Although the definitive break occurred between 1914 and 1940, perhaps the final realization did not dawn until the Suez Crisis of 1956. The British and French bombardment of Egypt in defence of the Suez Canal in that year represented the first major international incident in which Canada found itself at odds with Britain.[12]

In the 21st century, Canada continues to share the Queen with Britain and several other countries and is part of the Commonwealth; nationals of both Canada and Britain have invested in each other's economies; the Canadian parliamentary and legal systems are based on those of Britain; a majority of Canadians speak a variant of the English language; and many are still linked to Britain by family ties. Otherwise, however, both Canada and Britain see each other as just another friendly, foreign country, with minimal influence and no control.

· ·

THE CHANGING ROLE OF THE STATE

Before concluding this chapter, we should mention the changing role of the state.[13] In brief, the state performed limited functions until the beginning of the 20th century, so that we often refer to the period before 1900 as that of the "negative state," and the period after 1900 as that of the "positive state." Before the 20th century, people expected the government to provide for their security, internal and external, of course, but it was basically an era of individual and family self-reliance and self-sufficiency. Canada had a relatively larger state role than most other countries at the time, such as in the construction of canals and railways and in Aboriginal, immigration, and tariff policies, but the wide array of public services to which we are accustomed today, such as education, health, and social services, were essentially left to the private sector or to charitable organizations.

As European and North American societies became increasingly democratic, the newly enfranchised women and working classes demanded that the government intervene to a larger extent to improve their lot. Mothers' allowances, minimum wage laws, old age pensions, and public protection of children were some of the marks of the early positive state. Other aspects of government intervention were prompted by the forces of population expansion, industrialization, and urbanization, as the excess of agricultural workers migrated to cities or found other types of employment. At the provincial level, the invention of the automobile had many implications for governments, especially the demand for the construction of roads. Wars were another common catalyst for increased government activity, and the First World War (1914–18) had precisely that effect. Canada increased the size of its armed forces, and afterward governments helped soldiers to get re-established in civilian life with pensions, housing, land, training, and other benefits. Since Canadians had never developed an animosity to the state that is characteristic of American society, it was natural to turn to the government to solve other problems with which people could not cope on their own.

Then came the Great Depression of the 1930s, and once again people sought help from the government. It was at that point that even the United States saw the need for dramatic public intervention, primarily in the form of the "New Deal." This initiative, like its diluted versions in Canada, brought the government into agricultural and other natural product marketing, more labour legislation, social security, housing, relief measures, and provision of employment by means of public works projects. In many parts of the world, the Depression was barely over before the outbreak of the Second World War (1939–45), which had the usual effect of greatly expanding the role of government.

In the late 1930s John Maynard Keynes, a British economist, made a powerful case for a much more interventionist government. Partly in response to the Depression, he argued that when private-sector economic activity declined and less money was being spent, the government should intervene with increased spending in order to balance out the extremes of the business cycle. The government, he argued, should even borrow money in such periods and spend it on transfers to individuals or on public works that would keep the economy moving. In contrast, when the private economy got overheated and was engaged in too much spending, the government should spend less and tax more, partly to take money out of the system and partly to repay the money it had borrowed during the previous downturn.

The articulation of **Keynesian economics** coincided with the arguments made by many other social scientists that there was a moral reason for the government to get more involved. These social scientists contended that ordinary people had a right to education, health care, housing, labour standards, and social services—ideas promoted by growing ranks of unionized workers and increasingly popular left-wing political parties. The state should step in to promote human welfare against the ravages of unemployment, poverty, illness, disability, and old age. A complementary case could be made in Canada that the government should provide transportation and communications links across the country that could probably not be operated at a profit by the private sector. Even business was in favour of government intervening to stabilize the economy.

As a result of such pressures, by 1950 or so Canada (and most Western European countries) had developed into a **welfare state** and was practising at least some degree of Keynesian economics. A wide range of social programs and government transfers to individuals had been created: unemployment insurance, family allowances, old age pensions, housing programs, and the beginnings of public health care. But the government also was heavily involved in the private-sector economy, with the Bank of Canada regulating interest rates, and the government basing its own expenditure and taxation policies on countercyclical budgeting.

Virtually all political parties were committed to this core public agenda, although governments started to diverge from the principle of balancing their budgets over the business cycle, seduced into running deficits in order to satisfy all the demands that came their way, whether through spending too much or not taxing enough.

The role of government in Canada and in most Western industrialized democracies continued to grow until the mid-1980s. At this point a profound reaction set in around the world against further government intervention, partly because public debts were getting troublesome. A growing consensus evolved that governments were spending, taxing, regulating, employing, owning, and owing too much, and that Keynesian economics was not working as prescribed. People wanted to keep more of their hard-earned incomes, they expected others to become more self-reliant, and "deregulation" and "privatization" became the new popular prescriptions for government.

Even political parties that believed in the virtues of government intervention were required to dilute their enthusiasm. The parties in power in Ottawa, including both the Mulroney and the Chrétien regimes, made massive cuts in government operations. Thus, Canada and other Western states entered the 21st century with a new philosophy of the role of government and with considerably pared-down government operations. This central shift in state policy, which coincided with increasing **globalization**, involved privatizing many Crown corporations and other public programs; removing many regulations, especially in areas of corporate behaviour; signing a series of free trade agreements that prohibited governments from acting in certain previously common ways; reducing government debts; cutting taxes; and providing social services of greatly reduced quality.

When referring to this new philosophy of government, the terms **neoliberalism** or **neoconservatism** are often used. These two words actually mean much the same thing in terms of a retreat from the welfare state: the government withdraws from the economy and allows it to operate on the pre-1900 capitalist principles of laissez-faire. Sometimes, however, the two terms are distinguished by the preference of neoconservatives to have government withdraw from *economic* policy but not from a role of promoting certain *social* values, such as the traditional role of men, women, and the family, and orthodox sexuality. Such neo- or social conservatives oppose employment equity, affirmative action, multiculturalism, and same-sex rights, and support activist state measures to regulate behaviour in such areas as education, abortion, marriage, and freedom of expression.

By the early years of the new century, however, governments could no longer ignore demands for more adequate public services, including an improved health care system. Thus, federal and provincial governments started to move beyond the neoconservative consensus of the previous 20 years: they began to take in more revenues and spend more money to compensate for earlier cutbacks.

Suddenly, at the end of 2008, the world economy nearly collapsed and most countries faced an economic crisis unlike anything since the Depression of the 1930s. Companies went bankrupt or laid off a large proportion of their employees, the banks in most states required massive bailouts in order to allow them to continue to extend credit, pension plans were threatened because their funds were invested in stocks of greatly depreciated value, and government revenues dried up. In these desperate circumstances, all governments—of whatever ideological stripe—began to borrow and spend money as they never had before. Thus, in the 2009–10 period, the Canadian federal and provincial governments ran up huge deficits and were prepared to continue such efforts if necessary for many years beyond.

. . . .
CONCLUSION

This chapter has shown how Canada developed from a British colony to a sovereign state. It also traced the evolution of government institutions along the way, focusing primarily on the foundations established in 1867. Those foundations consisted of the grafting of the British parliamentary and American federal systems, although certain aspects of the latter were deliberately avoided. The discussion has also revealed the fact that the question of French–English relations has been integral to Canadian constitutional development from the very beginning. The chapter concluded by illustrating the changing role of the state.

(SC) Canadian constitutional evolution usually resulted from the decisions of a small political elite. Whether this elite was British (1763–64), colonial (1864–67), Canadian (1980–82), or some combination thereof (1926–31), the state-centred approach is the most appropriate to apply to this development. Canada became more democratic within its own government structures and more autonomous from Britain in a gradual progression of statist decisions without a great deal of input from society as a whole.

[P] In some cases, however, such as in the establishment of colonial assemblies and then in the recognition of responsible government, such authorities were forced to respond to public pressure. It was only in the 1837 rebellions in both Upper and Lower Canada that such pressure took on violent proportions, and only for a short time. Thus, the pluralist approach would emphasize that if and when the public articulated its demands for constitutional change, whether peacefully or violently, the authorities eventually responded.

© It could also be said that constitutional developments reflected more than a mere desire for democracy or autonomy from Britain. Class analysts, for example, can identify the economic elites that had a hand in guiding constitutional developments, especially the decision to embark on Confederation in 1867. It served the profit-making purposes of the corporate elite to construct railways to outlying colonies if they would join the Confederation scheme. Many businessmen besides railway promoters felt that Confederation, with a strong central government, would be conducive to maximizing their profits. The changing role of the state between 1985 and 2000 was also generally the result of corporate interests that benefited in the process.

(G) Canada has always been subject to external forces, and this chapter confirms that globalization is not necessarily a new phenomenon. In fact, in a constitutional sense, Canada is more autonomous today than it has ever been. But at the same time, as the discussion of the post-1985 role of government shows, much of the pressure to reduce the role of the state came from ideas that were global in scope. Moreover, in a development elaborated upon in Chapter 10, the Canadian government voluntarily imposed restraints on itself by signing such international agreements as NAFTA and by joining such international organizations as the WTO, parts of the new "external constitution."

· ·

DISCUSSION QUESTIONS

1. After the Conquest, how would you characterize the British treatment of French Canadians?

2. How did the United Empire Loyalists change the face of Canada?

3. What aspects of the French–English political relationship were established before or at Confederation?

4. What is meant by the "Westminster model," and how does it differ from the U.S. system of government?

5. What aspects of American federalism did Canada adopt, and what aspects did it reject?

6. Is there an inherent contradiction between the British parliamentary system and the American federal system? Explain.

7. Has neoliberalism gone too far? Has the pendulum swung back?

8. How do you explain the massive government spending that began in federal and provincial government budgets in 2009?

· ·

NOTES

1. Some of the key sources on Canada's constitutional evolution are W.P.M. Kennedy, ed., *Documents of the Canadian Constitution, 1759–1915* (Toronto: Oxford University Press, 1918); R. MacGregor Dawson, *The Government of Canada*, 5th ed., revised by Norman Ward (Toronto: University of Toronto Press, 1970); and Bayard Reesor, *The Canadian Constitution in Historical Perspective* (Scarborough: Prentice Hall Canada, 1992). The following website is also useful: http://www.canadiana.org/citm/primary/primary_e.html.

2. Lord Durham, *Report of the Affairs of British North America*, Gerald M. Craig, ed. (Toronto: McClelland and Stewart, 1963).

3. P.B. Waite, *The Confederation Debates in the Province of Canada/1865* (Toronto: McClelland and Stewart, 1963); P.B. Waite, *The Life and Times of Confederation, 1864–1867*, 2nd ed. (Toronto: University of Toronto Press, 1962); and Donald Creighton, *The Road to Confederation* (Toronto: Macmillan, 1964).

4. Stanley B. Ryerson, *Unequal Union: Confederation and the Roots of Conflict in the Canadas, 1815–1873*, 2nd ed. (Toronto: Progress Books, 1973).

5. K.C. Wheare, *Federal Government*, 4th ed. (London: Oxford University Press, 1963).

6. Reesor, *The Canadian Constitution in Historical Perspective*, ch. 4.

7. David E. Smith, *The Invisible Crown* (Toronto: University of Toronto Press, 1996).

8. Reesor, *The Canadian Constitution in Historical Perspective*, pp. 66–71.

9. The most famous case is probably *Roncarelli v. Duplessis*, in which the courts found the premier of Quebec personally guilty of cancelling Frank Roncarelli's restaurant liquor licence merely because the latter had provided bail for Jehovah's Witnesses.

10. Dawson, *The Government of Canada*, p. 54.

11. Many observers and historians saw the King and St. Laurent governments as the villains in the Americanization of Canada after the Second World War, although J.L. Granatstein argues that British weakness was of greater significance in this regard than any deliberate Canadian government objective. See Donald Creighton, *Canada's First Century* (Toronto: Macmillan, 1970); George Grant, *Lament for a Nation: The Defeat of Canadian Nationalism* (Toronto: McClelland and Stewart, 1965);

and J.L. Granatstein, *How Britain's Weakness Forced Canada into the Arms of the United States* (Toronto: University of Toronto Press, 1989).

12. John Hilliker, *Canada's Department of External Affairs: The Early Years, 1909–1926* (Montreal: McGill-Queen's University Press, 1990).

13. For an alternative account, see Alasdair Roberts, "A Fragile State: Federal Public Administration in the Twentieth Century," in Christopher Dunn, ed., *The Handbook of Canadian Public Administration* (Toronto: Oxford University Press, 2002), ch. 2.

. . . .
FURTHER READINGS

Ajzenstat, Janet, Paul Romney, Ian Gentles, and William D. Gairdner, eds. *Canada's Founding Debates.* Toronto: University of Toronto Press, 2003.

Creighton, Donald. *The Road to Confederation.* Toronto: Macmillan, 1964.

———. *Canada's First Century.* Toronto: Macmillan, 1970.

Granatstein, J.L. *How Britain's Weakness Forced Canada into the Arms of the United States.* Toronto: University of Toronto Press, 1989.

Hilliker, John. *Canada's Department of External Affairs: The Early Years, 1909–1926.* Montreal: McGill-Queen's University Press, 1990.

Reesor, Bayard. *The Canadian Constitution in Historical Perspective.* Scarborough: Prentice Hall Canada, 1992.

Ryerson, Stanley B. *Unequal Union: Confederation and the Roots of Conflict in the Canadas, 1815–1873,* 2nd ed. Toronto: Progress Books, 1973.

Waite. P.B. *The Life and Times of Confederation, 1864–1867,* 2nd ed. Toronto: University of Toronto Press, 1962.

PART 2

The Societal Context: Cleavages and Identities

The next eight chapters deal with the main elements of the societal or socioeconomic context of the Canadian political system: principally regionalism, ethnicity, class, and gender. Political scientists generally believe that these aspects of Canadian society are the most relevant to politics because they represent deep, persistent divisions in society called cleavages. Each chapter examines the concrete statistical and historical base of the relevant societal characteristic, the demands each generates, and the current issues involved.

Another way to look at these characteristics of Canadian society is in terms of identities. Indeed, issues relating to ethnicity, gender, and sexual orientation are commonly referred to today as the "politics of identity" or the "politics of recognition," and some observers argue that such identities have become more important than traditional cleavages. It is at least a fact that if people are not conscious of a particular characteristic—if it is not part of their identity—they are unlikely to act on it politically. Regardless, many of the demands with which the authorities have to contend, and many of the interests that the authorities themselves represent, originate from such cleavages and identities.

Conflicting regional economic claims and distinctive regional identities have been constants of Canadian politics since the beginning and continue to be animating agents. The French–English question and the role of Quebec traditionally overshadowed other ethnic, linguistic, and cultural identities and cleavages, but recent political developments justify a discussion of Aboriginal peoples and other minority ethnocultural groups. The claims of the Aboriginal, French, English, and newer Canadian communities have been legitimated in policy, law, and the Constitution, such as in the recognition of Aboriginal rights, official bilingualism, and multiculturalism, but the achievement of such recognition did not end ethnic conflict. That is partly because of strong ethnic identities and of the contrasting perceptions that each group has of its own history and current status. Class cleavages have not been as obvious to many observers as some of the other divisions in society and class identities in Canada are generally weaker than the other identities mentioned. Chapter 8 will show, however, that class is an important factor in Canadian politics even if it is often overlooked. It is now also common to point to the increasing importance of gender identities and demands in the political system, especially with respect to women and sexual orientation.

Three other cleavages and identities are considered together in Chapter 9: religion, age, and urban/rural location. These three cleavages do not always achieve the same political salience as the others identified above, but they are of increasing importance. Religion and the urban/rural split are not new to the political agenda, but they seem to have gained a new lease on life in recent years.

For the sake of clarity, these identities and cleavages are discussed in separate chapters, but in real life they interact and overlap. Sometimes these factors reinforce each other (poor immigrant women; rich Anglo businessmen), but at other times they cut across each other. In any case, the different socioeconomic groups all compete for the attention of governments. For example, in his book *The Pursuit of Division*, Martin Loney argues that feminists and multicultural advocates have dominated the attention of governments over the past few decades at the expense of the poor. He asserts that even if women and recent immigrants constitute a large proportion of those living in poverty, it is their gender and ethnic identities that have predominated in public discourse.

If the factors mentioned constitute the principal components of the internal environment of the Canadian political system, they must be accompanied by a discussion of the external or global environment. The world has become a "global village," and international, multinational, transnational, and supranational factors are important elements of any national political system. This is especially true of canada which has always been open to such external influences.

Chapter 3

REGIONALISM

Alberta was enraged at the 1980 National Energy Program, and "western alienation" affected the whole western region of Canada. The Atlantic groundfish industry collapsed in the 1990s, and the softwood lumber dispute with the United States almost crippled the forestry industry, especially in British Columbia. Newfoundland and Labrador, Nova Scotia, and Saskatchewan fought to remove petroleum revenues from the calculation of equalization payments, Ontario argued that its residents paid $23 billion more in federal taxes every year than they got back from Ottawa, and a widespread sentiment exists in other regions that the federal government favours Quebec because of the threat of separation. Regionalism obviously animates a great deal of Canadian political activity.

The chapter will begin by outlining some theoretical considerations regarding the concept of regionalism. While regionalism has many dimensions, and is not entirely a question of geography and economy, an examination of these two aspects of Canada seems to be an appropriate place to start. That discussion includes key demands that regional cleavages and identities have generated, and some of the policies that have been made in response. The chapter then proceeds to deal with regional identities and related issues that are less connected to geography and economy.

THEORETICAL CONSIDERATIONS

Although there is no doubt that the Canadian political system is characterized by regionalism, no consensus exists on exactly what those regions are or on how that concept should be defined. One way of treating regionalism in Canada would be to equate regions with provinces and territories. Of course, the political-legal-constitutional basis of provinces and territories is not synonymous with the natural, physiographic (or even socio-psychological) basis of regions, and the fit between regionalism and provinces/territories is not perfect. Nevertheless, the connection is a compelling one, and in discussing the question of regionalism, the 1979 Task Force on Canadian Unity had this to say:

> Regional communities require an institutional framework if they are to become viable units which can express themselves and organize their collective life in an effective manner. For that reason, it seems to us that the provinces and the northern territories are the basic building blocks of Canadian society and the logical units on which to focus

a discussion of Canadian regionalism, even though they may not be the most "natural" regions from an economic point of view.[1]

To define regionalism in terms of such formal political-institutional boundaries would link it very closely to the question of federalism. The creation of provinces and territories had two primary effects as far as regional demands are concerned. On the one hand, if a region was identified with a political unit, that unit could become a persuasive transmitter of regional demands to Ottawa. Regional demands articulated by a provincial or territorial premier are harder to ignore than those that come from less authoritative sources. In fact, to politicize such regional demands in this way may well serve to magnify them, since premiers and bureaucrats can use such distinctiveness to justify an increase in their power. On the other hand, provinces and territories may be able to facilitate the decision-making process by handling local problems that are not controversial at the provincial/territorial level but that would cause great difficulty in Ottawa. The basic quest in the establishment of a federal system of government is to find the most appropriate division of powers and responsibilities between the national and provincial levels. This issue, the degree of centralization and decentralization in Canada, has never been settled to everyone's satisfaction. Canadians still raise demands about the design of the federal system as well as about policies within it. The peculiarities of the special case of Quebec are discussed more thoroughly in Chapter 5.

A second manner of defining regionalism would be to take an "environmental" or geographic approach. Regions would be defined in terms of their similarity of physical features and separated from other regions by prominent topographical barriers. Such a physical approach almost inevitably also includes a discussion of regional *economic* differences. To conceive of regions in this way is a fairly straightforward and useful enterprise, but it suffers from a rather static, rigid conceptualization that does not allow for change over time and that underplays the human element. It also implies, rather questionably, that a common environment leads to common political, social, and cultural characteristics.[2]

Some analysts prefer a third conception of regionalism which is somewhat more abstract. Regions are not fixed in political or geographic terms, but instead are fluid social creations that may change over time. They are "imagined communities" in which people feel that they have much in common with others. According to Richard Simeon, "regions are simply containers. . . . And how we draw the boundaries around them depends entirely on what our purposes are. . . ."[3] In this sense, regions are primarily a state of mind.

A fourth approach to regionalism comes from "dependency theory." It emphasizes the relations between different spatial entities, some dependent on others. In the Canadian case, this primarily relates to the dominance of central Canada over the outlying regions, and is often referred to in terms of the core and the hinterland or periphery, or the "metropolitan–hinterland" thesis. This approach focuses on the relations between the political and economic power of the centre and the underdeveloped periphery.[4]

This book will take advantage of all four concepts of regionalism, and usually employ the commonly accepted version of the following principal regions: Ontario, Quebec, the Prairies, the Atlantic region, British Columbia, and the North. The provinces were granted considerable power by the Constitution, but even in institutional terms, not every province is thought of as a region. Ontario and Quebec qualify as separate regions because of their size and provincial status. The Prairie provinces and the Atlantic provinces are sufficiently similar in character to be grouped together for many purposes as two regional units.

British Columbia's claim to regional status has gained increasing recognition because of its size and its geographic separation and economic distinctiveness from the Prairie provinces; Alberta, one should note, is increasingly being treated as a region separate from the Prairies. Newfoundland and Labrador often makes a claim for similar status at the eastern end of the country, but primarily because of its much smaller size, it is usually lumped with the three Maritime provinces to form the Atlantic region. The North, divided into three territories, is now also regarded as a separate region worthy of mention. To those on the periphery, on the other hand, Ontario and Quebec seem to constitute a single central dominant core.

. . . .

GEOGRAPHY
Physiographic Regions

In terms of size, Canada's is the second-largest country in the world. Prime Minister Mackenzie King once remarked that if some countries had too much history, Canada had too much geography.[5] In fact, St. John's, Newfoundland, is closer to London, England, than to Victoria, BC, and many Canadians live and feel closer to adjacent U.S. states than to other Canadian regions. Such tremendous distances have always had a crucial influence on the Canadian political system, especially in generating feelings of regionalism, alienation, and regional economic demands. Most importantly, such distances had much to do with the creation of the provinces and territories in the first place.

The distance problem is immensely complicated by divisions caused by physical barriers. Canada is usually divided into seven physiographic regions, five with significant population, as shown in Figure 3.1. In other words, the vast territory is divided into five main regions by natural barriers running in a north–south direction. It is often simpler to travel southward to the United States than to cross the barriers into another part of Canada. The main aspect of Canadian geography that counterbalances these north–south forces is the river and lake system. In this respect, the central historical role of the St. Lawrence River and the Great Lakes has often been noted.[6] After this natural east–west flow was enhanced by the construction of the St. Lawrence Seaway, ships were able to go halfway across the country, a fact that improves Canada's capacity to engage in international trade.

Transportation and Communications Systems

Apart from the Great Lakes–St. Lawrence water route, transportation and communications systems in Canada had to be constructed across the natural barriers. The establishment of each of these great transportation and communications projects dominated successive eras in Canadian politics.

Railways were the stuff of Canadian politics throughout the 19th and early 20th centuries. In particular, they formed a crucial part of the Confederation Settlement of the 1860s and 1870s. The Maritimes agreed to enter Confederation only if they were linked to central Canada by the Intercolonial Railway, and British Columbia was persuaded to join in 1871 with the promise of a transcontinental rail link within ten years.[7] John A. Macdonald brought the Canadian Pacific Railway (CPR) project to completion in 1885, only four years behind schedule, and it became one of his lasting monuments. Although it was a private company,

. . . .

Figure 3.1 Canada's Physiographic Regions

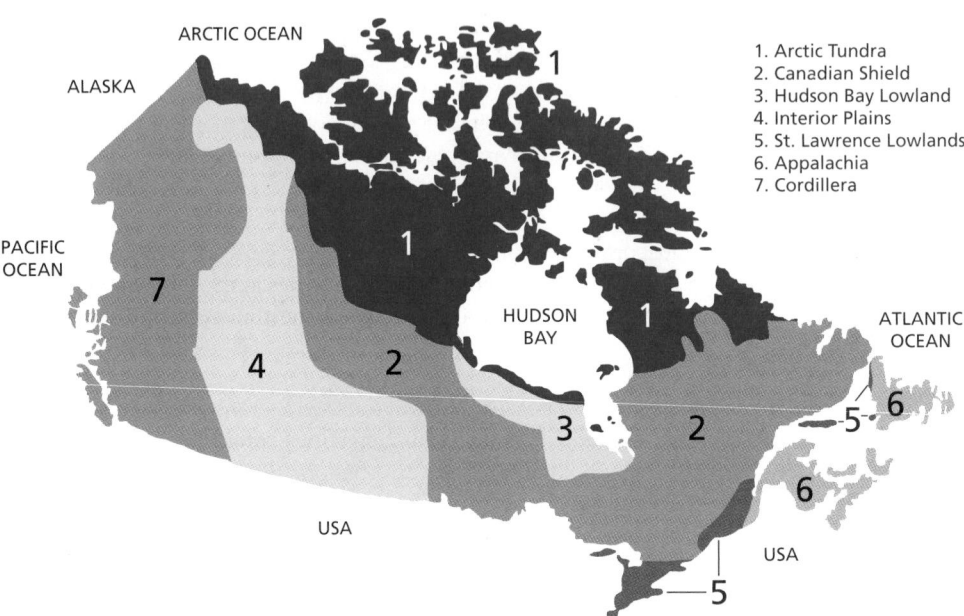

1. Arctic Tundra
2. Canadian Shield
3. Hudson Bay Lowland
4. Interior Plains
5. St. Lawrence Lowlands
6. Appalachia
7. Cordillera

the CPR received enormous government assistance in the form of cash and land grants that later became prime real estate in the centre of many Canadian cities. Although the building of the CPR was one of the great heroic events in Canadian history, it was also a classic example of the use of the state for the advantage of private capital.[8]

Because of a lack of competition (the "monopoly clause"), the CPR was allowed to charge high rates, and freight rates have been a constant complaint of Western Canadians since the day the CPR was completed. Other railways were eventually built, but even with government assistance many went into receivership, and in the 1919–23 period they were bailed out by the federal government in the creation of the Canadian National (CN) system. Thus, the establishment of CN as a Crown corporation could be seen not only as a service to isolated parts of the country but also as a benefit to bankrupt capitalist interests.

When both CP and CN wanted out of the passenger side of the business, a separate Crown corporation, VIA Rail, was created in 1977–78. When the Mulroney government discontinued half its routes in 1990, train enthusiasts howled in protest and argued that the extent of government subsidization of highway, marine, and air transport should be taken into consideration when railway deficits were discussed. The Chrétien government then privatized Canadian National by selling shares to the public.

The early 20th century was almost as obsessed with automobiles as the previous era was with railways. Since roads are primarily a provincial responsibility, however, their political significance was and continues to be greatest at that level. The federal government was mainly called on to ensure that a highway extended across the whole country for commercial, recreational, and symbolic purposes. Thus, in 1949, the federal government signed the

Trans-Canada Highway agreement with the provinces, under which Ottawa paid half the cost of bringing a transcontinental highway up to a national standard, and was eventually completed in 1962. In 1997, Prince Edward Island gained a "fixed link" to the mainland with the construction of the Confederation Bridge to replace the ferry service.

Given the distances involved, it is not surprising that demands also arose for a coordinated nationwide airline service carrying both passengers and cargo. The transport minister of the day, C.D. Howe, created Trans-Canada Airlines (now Air Canada) in 1937 as a Crown corporation. Air Canada was later one of the Mulroney government's first candidates for privatization. Official thinking in the late 1980s was that the country was now well served by a variety of private carriers and that the government airline no longer served a **public policy purpose**. The Canadian Transportation Agency retained some regulatory powers, but with the transfer of major airport ownership to local nonprofit authorities in the 1990s, and general deregulation, the federal government substantially evacuated the transportation industry, a field in which it was historically very active.

. . . .

MAJOR TRANSPORTATION AND COMMUNICATIONS LINKS AND AGENCIES

- Canadian Pacific
- Canadian National
- VIA Rail
- Trans-Canada Highway
- Trans-Canada Airlines/Air Canada
- Trans-Canada Pipeline
- Canadian Radio-television and Telecommunications Commission (CRTC)
- Canadian Broadcasting Corporation (CBC)
- Telesat
- Teleglobe

Oil and natural gas pipelines, a newer means of transportation, have figured prominently in Canadian politics over the past 50 years. Although they are privately owned, the building of pipelines requires government approval. The construction of the main natural gas line to Eastern Canada, the Trans-Canada Pipeline, was probably the most controversial issue on the Canadian political agenda in the mid-1950s. The haste of C.D. Howe in ramming related legislation through Parliament had a major role to play in the defeat of the St. Laurent government in 1957.

Transportation presents special challenges in the North. Roads and railways were virtually nonexistent there until the Diefenbaker government sponsored its "Roads to Resources" program, and the Yellowknife region of the Northwest Territories became linked to Edmonton. The Alaska Highway, which passes through Yukon on its way from British Columbia, has been a crucial part of that territory's development. Various pipeline proposals have also been significant to the North, especially the proposed Mackenzie Valley Gas Pipeline of the 1970s. That no such pipelines have yet been constructed in the North is more a matter of economics than of concern about Aboriginal peoples or the environment, but the issue is high on the political agenda again.

As far as communications are concerned, telegraph, telephone, radio, and television usually developed first in the private sector. But because some of these systems were natural monopolies or because of the limited number of frequencies available, they soon led to government regulation, now primarily the responsibility of the **Canadian Radio-television and Telecommunications Commission (CRTC)**. In most of these sectors demands also arose for public ownership, such as in the Prairie provinces' telephone systems. The **Canadian Broadcasting Corporation (CBC)** was created in 1932 in response to pressure for more Canadian content and more enlightened radio programming than was usually provided on local private stations, many of which carried U.S. programs. The CBC became operational in English and French with its own stations, as well as affiliated private stations, in 1936 and CBC television began in 1952. To supplement the country's terrestrial microwave system, the government took the initiative in 1969 to launch Telesat, a joint public–private supplier of domestic communications satellite services. Intercontinental communications via submarine cables and satellites are handled by Teleglobe Canada, which was a Crown corporation until the Mulroney government privatized it in 1987.

Thus, in the field of transportation and communications, demands to overcome distances and divisions have been dominant features of Canadian politics. Governments have primarily responded with assistance to private corporations, the establishment of Crown corporations, and the creation of regulatory agencies. To create and hold together a nation, Canadians built east–west institutions that ran counter to the natural north–south geographic features of the continent and the perpetual pull of the United States. In the neoliberal 1980s and cash-starved 1990s, however, both the Mulroney and the Chrétien governments privatized a number of government operations in this field, reduced support for others, and generally deregulated the transportation industry. Besides starting to dismantle these east–west links, governments began to sign north–south trade deals, leading many observers to question the continued existence of Canada as an independent nation-state. Symbolically, both CP Rail and the newly privatized CN Rail sold off track in Canada and laid off hundreds of employees while simultaneously becoming major players in the United States; CN now calls itself "North America's Railroad."

Population Distribution

Physical barriers are only one complication of the distances that characterize Canada; the distribution of population is another, for the people are not spread uniformly throughout this gigantic territory. It is commonly emphasized that the overall density of the Canadian population is one of the lowest in the world, some 3.0 people per km^2. But it is really more significant that no permanent settlements exist in nearly 90 percent of the country and that over 70 percent of the population is huddled within 150 km of the U.S. border.[9] Provincial and territorial population disparities affect the allocation of seats in the House of Commons—indeed the whole power structure in Ottawa—and the calculation of federal transfer payments. The population of the provinces and territories in 2009 can be seen in Table 3.1.

Geographers frequently speak of the "core," "heartland," or "metropolis" on the one hand, and the "periphery" or "hinterland" on the other, and **core–periphery analysis** can be usefully applied to political science. The Toronto–Ottawa–Montreal triangle obviously constitutes the core of Canada, and Ontario and Quebec combined contain 62 percent of its people.

TABLE 3.1   Population of Provinces and Territories, January 2009

Ontario	12 986 857	38.8%
Quebec	7 782 561	23.2%
British Columbia	4 419 974	13.2%
Alberta	3 632 483	10.8%
Manitoba	1 213 815	3.6%
Saskatchewan	1 023 810	3.1%
Nova Scotia	939 531	2.8%
New Brunswick	748 319	2.2%
Newfoundland/		
Labrador	508 990	1.5%
Prince Edward Island	140 402	0.4%
Northwest Territories	42 940	0.1%
Yukon	33 442	0.1%
Nunavut	31 556	0.1%
Canada	33 504 680	

Source: Statistics Canada. *Quarterly Demographic Estimates. Oct-Dec, 2008. Catalogue No. 91-002-X. Table 1-1.* Found at: http://www.statcan.gc.ca/pub/91-002-x/2008004/t002-eng.htm (Accessed May 25, 2009).

While central Canada constitutes the political core of the country, it is also the economic heartland, containing the largest concentration of corporate head offices, especially in the Toronto area. Moreover, it is the communications and cultural core, containing the headquarters of French and English CBC, CTV, Global, and private French television, many other Canadian cultural institutions, and most of the Canadian computer industry. The rest of the country—the hinterland or periphery, with its smaller population base—regularly complains that it is overlooked by both public and private decision makers. It is not surprising that many Westerners advocate a reformed Senate based on equal representation for each province that would give them more clout in Ottawa, while Quebec is extremely sensitive to its declining proportion of the total Canadian population, which by 1995 had fallen below a symbolic 25 percent.

In the 1990s, Quebec came closer than ever before to separating from the rest of Canada. If it were to leave with its existing borders intact (a somewhat debatable issue), Quebec would take with it almost one-quarter of the Canadian population, about 16 percent of the territory, and 21 percent of the Canadian gross domestic product. From a strictly geographic point of view, the separation of Quebec would raise the question of continuing transportation links between Atlantic Canada and Ontario, border-crossing impediments, and jurisdiction over the St. Lawrence Seaway.[10]

. . . .

ECONOMY

Having explored regionalism in geographic terms, we may now proceed to examine the Canadian economy. Such a discussion reveals striking regional economic differences that serve to reinforce geographic distinctions and create another pattern of demands on the Canadian political system.

Regional economic differences begin with primary industries—that is, the natural resource and energy base of the various provinces and territories. The importance of natural resources to the national economy has been a central tenet of Canadian political economy for generations; it is usually termed the **staples theory** and is identified with the famous economic historian Harold Innis.[11] It postulates that Canadian economic development has relied on a succession of resource exports (staples)—furs, fish, timber, wheat, minerals, and energy—rather than on manufacturing; Canadians are mere "hewers of wood and drawers of water." The staples theory also includes the notions of dependence, such as of interregional exploitation, especially in the relationship between inner and outer Canada. It involves an economy that remains underdeveloped and subject to the rise and fall of international markets, a second kind of dependence. In international trade, Canada continues to this day to rely primarily on exports of natural resources.

To economists, secondary industry consists of manufacturing, construction, and utilities, including electricity. Manufacturing includes the initial processing and refining of primary products as well as the making of finished goods, and generally produces more revenue and more jobs than primary industry, is less seasonal, and commands higher wages. Many observers have criticized the economic policy of almost all Canadian governments for having fostered the exploitation and exportation of raw natural resources rather than having developed an industrial policy that would give priority to manufacturing. Furthermore, the fact that both governments and corporations in Canada spend so little money on research and development (R&D) does not augur well for the future, when "high tech" and high productivity will be so important.

Economists then put transportation and communications, trade, finance, insurance and real estate, private services, and public administration into the tertiary or services category. Although the Canadian economy was never strong on manufacturing, much political attention in this "post-industrial" era is focused on the services sector. In outlining the trends in the Canadian labour force among the three divisions of the economy, Figure 3.2 demonstrates the contemporary importance of the tertiary sector.

The Atlantic Region

The Atlantic region has a distinctive and heavy reliance on fishing, which has rarely been a very prosperous industry. In the 1990s, however, the Atlantic fishery fell into deeper trouble than ever before, primarily because of a dramatic reduction in groundfish stocks, especially cod, and an oversupply of fishers, plant workers, and trawlers. The three Maritime provinces have a substantial agricultural base, which has provided prosperity for a few large firms but generally poor returns for most farmers. New Brunswick, Newfoundland and Labrador, and Nova Scotia also engage in forestry and mining, while Newfoundland and Labrador possesses great quantities of hydroelectric power. None of these resources has led to much general prosperity in

· ·

Figure 3.2 Employment in Canada by Sector

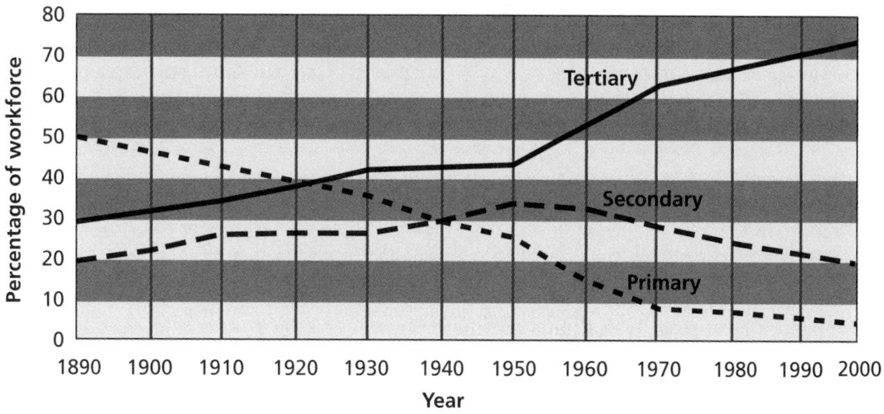

Source: Stephen Brooks and Andrew Stritch, Business and Government in Canada (Scarborough: Prentice-Hall Canada, 1991). Pg. 96; Statistics Canada. Distribution of Employed People, by Industry, by Province. Found at: http://www40.statcan.ca/l01/labor21a.htm (Accessed Sept. 25, 2006) (The figures for 2005 are Primary 4.0%, Secondary 20.7%, and Tertiary 75.2%).

the Atlantic region, however, and most of the larger projects have been developed by central Canadian or foreign firms. Some processing and refining of natural resources takes place in the region, but among other factors, the small local market and the distance from major population centres have left the region in a state of underdevelopment. Led by New Brunswick, a new emphasis on communications technology has revitalized Atlantic Canada's economy to some extent, because in the modern technological world physical distance is not the hindrance it was in the past. Newfoundland's offshore petroleum revenues have given the province a major boost, natural gas from the Sable Island Offshore Energy Project benefits Nova Scotia, and New Brunswick hopes to become a major energy exporter, Thus far, however, with the temporary exception of Newfoundland and Labrador, the Atlantic region is considerably below the national average in terms of per capita income or fiscal capacity.

Quebec

The Quebec economy is more diversified than that of the Atlantic region and somewhat more prosperous. Quebec's primary industries include farming in the St. Lawrence Lowlands, along with mining and forestry in the Canadian Shield. The shield is also traversed by numerous powerful rivers, making hydroelectricity Quebec's most valuable resource. Huge dams have been built on many of its rivers, including the controversial James Bay hydroelectric project of the 1970s. Electricity is the basis of Quebec's aluminum industry, for example, as well as of much other secondary industry. Quebec also stands out in the production of pulp and paper, especially newsprint. In addition, Quebec is much stronger than the Atlantic region in the more sophisticated aspects of manufacturing. Thus, besides the processing of metals and the traditional production of textiles, clothing, food, and beverages, Quebec now manufactures chemicals, aeronautics, electronics, pharmaceuticals, and transportation equipment. It also houses a large financial sector. The fact that economic power in Quebec used to rest largely in English-Canadian and foreign hands fuelled the nationalist debate in that province. But since 1960 a major transformation has occurred, and both the public and the francophone private sectors in Quebec have repatriated a great deal of industrial ownership. One means of doing so was the Caisse de dépôt et placement du Québec, which invested Quebec Pension Plan premiums in domestic firms. Still, Quebec remains below the national average in per capita income.

Ontario

Ontario has had the most diversified economy of any region and until 2008 was always among the richest provinces. It has an abundance of natural resources, including a great expanse of prime agricultural land in the Great Lakes Lowlands, vast stretches of trees, and a variety of minerals in the Canadian Shield. The province also contains several powerful rivers for the production of hydroelectricity, although it is increasingly dependent on nuclear power in this regard. Ontario's early development of hydroelectricity and of a steel industry gave it a head start over other regions. A skilled labour force, a large domestic market, proximity to key parts of the United States, and the advantage of federal tariff and banking policies also helped to make it the manufacturing heartland of the country. It now produces over half of the Canadian total, including automobiles, electronic products, machinery, and publishing, in addition to steel, food and beverages, smelting and refining, metal fabrication, and pulp and paper. Moreover, Ontario leads the country in the tertiary sector, such as finance, trade, and services, and the seats of the two largest governments in the country, in Ottawa and Toronto, also provide considerable employment. Unfortunately, the forestry and manufacturing sectors have been ailing for some time, and the worldwide economic meltdown at the end of 2008 forced Ontario into unprecedented have-not status.

The Prairie Region

The Prairie region is historically associated with agriculture, especially wheat, other grain, and livestock, and while the industry ebbs and flows, it continues to be important. The high value of primary industry in the Prairies has been largely a result of Alberta's oil and natural gas production, and that province has become the richest part of the country by almost any measure. As conventional supplies of crude petroleum declined, Alberta witnessed an enormous expansion of the oil sands as a source of synthetic oil. Petroleum is also of increasing significance in Saskatchewan, in concert with that province's other mineral resources, potash and uranium. In addition, Alberta possesses large amounts of coal, and Manitoba has nickel, copper, and zinc. Forestry has been an important industry in Manitoba and Alberta, while Manitoba's supply of hydroelectricity complements the petroleum of the other two Prairie provinces. Thus, although the Prairies can be compared with the Atlantic region to some extent in their relatively heavy dependence on primary industry, a contrast is readily apparent: resource extraction on the Prairies is a more profitable venture. The Prairies are also engaged in a certain amount of manufacturing, including food and beverages, transportation equipment, machinery, metal fabrication, chemicals, petrochemicals, and fertilizer. With the new wealth of the Western provinces, especially since the 1960s, the finance, trade, and service industries have expanded rapidly, and the Prairies are less dependent on Ontario in this respect than they used to be. In fact, much corporate power has moved westward, especially to Calgary. However, not even the Prairie provinces were spared by the recent global economic crisis, as petroleum revenues declined precipitously.

British Columbia

Mountainous British Columbia is the leading forestry province and also specializes in mining, including natural gas, copper, and coal. Several fertile river and lake valleys provide for farming, and, being a coastal province, BC also possesses a significant fishing industry. The mountains are the source of several large rivers that have been dammed for the production of hydroelectricity, and, as in Quebec, the abundant electricity is used to produce aluminum and is exported. Manufacturing is primarily related to the for-

An aerial view of the Syncrude oil sands upgrader in Fort McMurray, Alberta.

estry, mining, and agricultural bases of the BC economy: assorted wood products, such as lumber and pulp and paper; food and beverages; and the processing and refining of metals, petroleum, chemicals, and coal. Asian immigration has expanded the services sector, especially finance, but BC's heavy dependence on resource exports entails periodic economic downturns, especially for the forest industry in recent years. Fortunately for BC, as well as Alberta and Saskatchewan, China is taking a keen interest in their resource exports.

The North

The North—now divided into the three territories of Yukon, Northwest Territories, and Nunavut—has very limited agriculture and forestry, given its frigid climate, short growing season, and lack of soil. Mining has inspired many southerners to venture north over the years, especially in the gold rushes of the 1890s in Dawson City and the 1930s in Yellowknife. Other isolated mineral deposits have been found, but most proceeded with artificially high levels of government support, and many have since been abandoned. The prospects of oil and natural gas are more promising, especially in the Mackenzie River delta and the Beaufort Sea. The unstable world price, the uncertain supply in southern Canada and the United States, the outstanding Aboriginal land claims, and the cost and difficulty of transporting the petroleum southward have all combined to limit such a flow. Recently, however, the United States has exhibited renewed interest in northern petroleum resources. Northern Aboriginals used to be self-sufficient in hunting, fishing, and trapping, activities that continue to occupy them to some extent, while tourism is on the increase. In general, however, the inhospitable climate, the isolation, the small and transient labour force, and the poor transportation facilities conspire to retard economic development of the region. But recent positive signs include settlement of many Aboriginal land claims, the discovery of diamonds, and the creation of the eastern territory of **Nunavut** in 1999. Increased autonomy from Ottawa should better allow the territories to respond to local needs. Still, all three territories depend heavily on the federal government for financial support.

Regional Economic Demands

Since most natural resources fall within provincial jurisdiction, demands arising from the primary sector are often first addressed to the respective provincial government. Still, every primary industry has also sought federal government support of one kind or another over the years, and most other regional economic demands are primarily directed to Ottawa. In response, Ottawa's policy outputs have often benefited a certain industry throughout the country. At other times, its support of one region has also been in the national interest, such as in the creation of the **Canadian Wheat Board** to help Prairie farmers export more grain. Because these farmers could then pay higher federal taxes and buy more goods produced in other provinces, such a policy generally made the whole country more prosperous. Similarly, if Ottawa protects or promotes the Atlantic fishing or offshore petroleum industries, the rest of the country will pay less in employment insurance and equalization payments to that region.

Thus, as a result of regional economic differences, the national government regularly faces demands to assist a single industry or the economy of a single province or region. Many such demands have elicited a positive response, especially when the case was desperate, popular, or articulated by the right interest. Such outputs do not necessarily involve conflict between one region and another, and they sometimes benefit them all.

. . . .

HISTORIC REGIONAL CONFLICTS

More often than not, however, demands from one region do conflict with those from another. The most pervasive historical expression of such regional economic conflict has undoubtedly been between the Prairie and Ontario regions. Since Ontario's regional interests have historically been persuasive with the federal government, the analysis is usually put in terms of the central core versus the periphery of the country, especially the West. The principal historic economic complaints have involved the ownership, taxation, and regulation of natural resources; tariffs; transportation; and banking.[12]

Ownership of Natural Resources

The problem of natural resource ownership began in 1870 with the creation of the province of Manitoba. Although the Eastern provinces and British Columbia always had jurisdiction over their own natural resources, Ottawa decided to retain such control in the case of Manitoba, and when Saskatchewan and Alberta were created in 1905, these provinces were placed in the same subordinate position. The logic of John A. Macdonald in 1870 and Wilfrid Laurier in 1905 was that the federal government (i.e., central Canada) should control such resources in the national interest, allowing Ottawa to guide the development of the West. The Prairie provinces fought vehemently against this discrimination and were finally successful in gaining control of their natural resources in 1930.

Tariffs

The West also complained for generations that Canadian **tariff** policy was designed in the interest of central Canada at the expense of the Prairies. This was because as early as the 1879 **National Policy**, Macdonald saw the tariff as a means of promoting and protecting the industrial heartland of Ontario. Adding a tariff (an import tax) to the price of imported manufactured goods would raise their price above that of goods manufactured in Canada, even if foreign production costs were lower, so that domestic goods would cost less than imports to buy. In practice, it was largely foreign firms that established themselves in central Canada behind this tariff wall, but the tariff at least had the beneficial effect of creating jobs in Canada rather than in Britain or the United States. Ontario thus gained employment in producing tractors for Western Canada, for example, but Western Canadians felt that this was contrary to their interests because, in the absence of such a tariff, they would have been able to buy cheaper tractors from the United States. The West demanded lower tariffs at every opportunity, especially in the 1920s, when it sent its own farmer representatives to the House of Commons to fight on this front. Tariffs among all countries have gradually come down since 1945, but the issue took on a new life in the 1980s with the Western demand for free trade between Canada and the United States. Thus, the controversial Free Trade Agreement between the two countries, which took effect in 1989, can be seen in part as a response to 110 years of Western discontent with the tariff aspect of the National Policy.[13]

Transportation

Another aspect of Macdonald's National Policy that displeased the West was transportation, especially railways. In choosing to live so far from the central core of the country, Westerners expected to pay additional transportation costs, although many demanded that railway freight rates be subsidized by Ottawa. Indeed, the Crow's Nest Pass Act (or **Crow rate**) of 1897 was an attempt to do just that, and it provided a low rate for transporting Prairie grain to eastern ports. After successfully fighting to retain the Crow rate in the 1920s, many Westerners were greatly upset by the Trudeau government's increase in these rates, as well as by the Chrétien government's decision in 1995 to abolish the Crow rate entirely. But a more legitimate complaint was about peculiar inequities within the freight rate structure, including higher rates for finished goods than for raw materials (which discouraged manufacturing in the West), discrimination against short hauls, and deviations from the principle of distance determining price.

Banking

The West also protested against national banking policy. In contrast to community-based unit banks as in the United States, Canada deliberately developed a centralized branch banking system. This policy was in part an attempt to construct a sound, stable banking community that would avoid frequent local collapses, but the lack of competition was also favoured by the established banking interests themselves and provided more evidence of corporate pressure on government policy. The result was a handful of large national banks, usually with headquarters in Montreal or Toronto and with local branches spread across the country. From a hinterland perspective, money deposited in the local branch of a national bank would not remain in the community to be lent out for local purposes, but instead was sent to headquarters in central Canada to be used in the economic development of Ontario or Quebec. Moreover, decisions to make large loans were centralized at the head office, so that Western entrepreneurs would have to travel east if they wanted to borrow substantial sums. The operation of the banking system was another reason for the farmers' revolt of the 1920s, and such displeasure had much to do with the rise of the Social Credit Party in Alberta in the 1930s. In the 1970s, when the West became stronger in spite of this policy, the federal government finally responded. On the one hand, Ottawa eased restrictions on chartering regional banks, and several new Western banks were established; on the other, the existing national banks saw the merit of decentralizing decision making within their own operations, so that larger decisions could be made on location. Unfortunately, several of these new Western financial institutions faltered in the 1980s, largely because of a downturn in the region's economy that Westerners blamed on Trudeau's National Energy Program.[14]

These four policy areas—resources, tariffs, transportation, and banking—represent the most serious regional economic conflicts in Canadian history, but they can be seen in a broader context. The metropolitan–hinterland thesis suggests that the West was created as a colony of central Canada and was intended to be held in a subordinate and dependent relationship.[15] Western feeling about its situation was captured in a famous cartoon in the Grain

Source: "The Milch Cow," by Arch Dale (1882-1962), from the Grain Growers Guide (December 15, 1915). Reproduced courtesy of the Glenbow Archives, Calgary, Alberta (NA-3055-24).

Growers' Guide in 1915, and although it is depicted in agricultural terms, the image is still appropriate some 95 years later.

The Atlantic Provinces

Many of the Western economic conflicts with central Canada have been echoed by the Atlantic provinces. This was especially true of post-Confederation tariff policy, which also appeared to do the Maritimes more harm than good. Nova Scotia and New Brunswick entered Confederation in 1867 as proud and prosperous colonies, and although changes in marine technology (from wooden sailing ships to steel steamships) were probably the principal factor responsible, their economies quickly declined. Whatever the reason, Maritimers preferred to blame federal economic policy for much of their difficulty. The Atlantic provinces shared the West's concerns about federal freight rates, although they received subsidization in this area, too.

· ·

RECENT REGIONAL CONFLICTS

Against the background of historic regional conflicts, let us proceed to discuss more recent issues. Some of these are extensions of historic conflicts, while others are genuinely new.

Taxation and Regulation of Natural Resources

In the 1970s the original conflict over natural resources re-emerged, especially with respect to petroleum pricing. National energy policy in the 1950s and 1960s gave preference to the West because Alberta was guaranteed a market for its oil and natural gas as far east as Ontario. But the West overlooked that fact after the OPEC (Organization of Petroleum Exporting Countries) cartel agreed on an artificial rise in the international price of oil in 1973. At this point, federal policy began to favour the consumer/manufacturing interest of central Canada at the expense of the producer interest of the West. The height of the regional economic conflict occurred in 1980 with the Trudeau government's **National Energy Program (NEP)**, which imposed new federal taxes, retained a larger share of petroleum revenues for Ottawa, kept the national price below the world level, encouraged frontier—largely offshore—development, and promoted Canadianization of the industry, all objectives opposed by most Westerners. Eventually a partial compromise between central and Western interests was reached in 1981, and the Mulroney government later scrapped the NEP entirely. Nevertheless, the NEP had a profound effect on the Western Canadian psyche, especially when combined with the West's simultaneous opposition to Ottawa's constitutional initiatives and official bilingualism policy. Atlantic provinces also opposed federal resource policy in the 1980s, prompting them to fight for provincial ownership of offshore petroleum.

Other Regional Economic Conflicts

Another common complaint of the Atlantic and Western regions is that the federal government does most of its purchasing or procuring in central Canada. Although the economic complaints of the two outlying regions have thus often coincided, they have occasionally been at odds. In general, the East differed from the West to some extent on the Canada–U.S. Free

Environmentalist runs out of gas while protesting 'dirty oil.'

Trade Agreement, fearing that it would eliminate many of their subsidy programs. More distinctively, the Atlantic provinces complained of an insufficiently aggressive federal government when it came to protecting Atlantic fish stocks from foreign overfishing, with Newfoundland and Labrador wanting more provincial control over the industry.

Another regional issue is the environment. The Kyoto Accord was favoured by Quebec, for example, but condemned by the Alberta government. Even though the Harper Conservatives effectively abandoned Kyoto, Alberta feels increasing pressure from both inside and outside the province to take action to reduce the environmental devastation caused by the oil sands—to land, water, and air, especially greenhouse gases. Thus, besides dividing the political parties in their proposed solutions, climate change and other aspects of environmental degradation have generated a regional cleavage primarily between the petroleum (and coal) producers of Alberta and Saskatchewan and the rest of the provinces. The others generally endorse a "cap and trade" system, while Alberta and Saskatchewan have put their faith in "carbon capture and storage." This issue has dimensions beyond regionalism and is revisited in Chapter 8.

Smaller-scale regional economic disputes have also been a routine, if not daily, occurrence in Canadian politics. Awarding the CF-18 maintenance contract to Canadair of Montreal infuriated supporters of Bristol Aerospace of Winnipeg, which had submitted a superior bid and further reinforced Western alienation;[16] extending drug patent protection for multinational pharmaceutical firms in Quebec offended Canadian generic drug producers primarily located in Ontario; and promoting frontier petroleum exploration (including federal assistance to Newfoundland and Labrador's Hibernia project) upset conventional oil and gas producers in the west. When a single case of mad cow disease was discovered, the United States and Japan cut off all imports of Canadian beef, a situation that disproportionately affected the well being of farmers located on the Prairies. Somewhat similarly, the U.S. restrictions on the importation of softwood lumber from Canada hit British Columbia harder than any other province. On neither of these issues was the federal response deemed satisfactory.

Besides these regional economic conflicts that may or may not have engaged the attention of Ottawa, interprovincial conflicts sometimes develop. The most serious of these was probably the fight between Quebec and Newfoundland over the Churchill Falls hydroelectric project in Labrador. Ontario insisted that its residents be allowed to work in the construction industry in Quebec, the subject of a prolonged interprovincial battle, and Yukon and the Northwest Territories are promoting separate natural gas pipeline proposals—the Alaska Highway and the Mackenzie River routes, respectively.

Another issue, this time *within* the prairie region, concerns whether or not the Canadian Wheat Board (CWB) should retain its monopoly power to market western wheat and barley. The Harper government sided with those farmers (mostly located in Alberta) who want the right to market their own grain, but the majority of grain farmers in Manitoba and Saskatchewan favour the retention of the CWB monopoly power. Two courts rejected the Harper government's attempt to open up the barley market without parliamentary approval.

REGIONAL ECONOMIC DISPARITIES

Conflicts between regions are exacerbated in Canada because of regional economic inequalities or disparities. As mentioned, some have-not regions blame federal economic policies for their fate. Even if this charge has some truth to it, no observer can overlook other factors: Canada's primary resources are not evenly distributed and the regions have different sizes of territory and population and are at variable distances from key export markets.

Among the available measures of regional economic disparity are per capita provincial gross domestic product (GDP) (the total value of all goods and services produced divided by the population of the province), per capita income, and provincial unemployment rates. These measures for 2008 are shown in Table 3.2 and reflect the period before the economic crisis that began at the end of that year.

TABLE 3.2   **Provincial Gross Domestic Product Per Capita, Per Capita Income, and Unemployment Rate, 2008**

	GDP Per Capita	Per Capita Income	Unemployment Rate (Percentage)
Newfoundland and Labrador	38 748	30 504	13.2
Prince Edward Island	29 950	28 963	10.8
Nova Scotia	31 312	31 938	7.7
New Brunswick	31 667	31 080	8.6
Quebec	34 657	33 406	7.2
Ontario	41 305	37 309	6.5
Manitoba	35 310	33 329	4.8
Saskatchewan	40 923	35 400	4.1
Alberta	52 168	48 110	3.6
British Columbia	37 466	36 457	4.0

Sources: Adapted by author from: Statistics Canada. Data found at: http://www40.statcan.ca/101/cst01/ econ15.htm; CANSIM "Personal Income per Person,"; Table 384-0013; http://www40.statcan.ca/101/ cst01/labor07a-eng.htm?sdi=unemployment.

Traditionally, Canada had three categories of provinces: three rich ones (Ontario, Alberta, and British Columbia); four poor ones (the Atlantic provinces); and three intermediate provinces (Quebec, Manitoba, and Saskatchewan), although some shifting has occurred in recent years. Quebec has a larger economy than any province other than Ontario, of course, but this figure is not so impressive when expressed on a per capita basis. Per capita income statistics show that the average Albertan received about $20 000 more than the average person in Prince Edward Island, with the other provinces arrayed in between. It is also true as a general rule that the provinces with the highest unemployment rates have the highest provincial taxes, while Alberta's petroleum revenue allows it to get by with low income taxes and without a provincial sales tax at all.

In addition to developing national social programs and assisting various industries in a uniform national policy, successive governments have focused on two principal means to deal with the specific question of regional economic disparities. One is to give federal funding to have-not provincial and territorial governments, and the other is to engage in regional economic development programs.

In 1957 Ottawa finally responded to repeated provincial demands to make **equalization payments**.[17] These annual cash grants to the have-not provinces are designed to allow them to raise their services to an acceptable national level but can be spent for any purpose. In other words, they are unconditional grants, with no strings attached. The formula according to which provincial eligibility is calculated is extremely complex and designed to equalize the per capita yield of such provincial revenues across the country, that is, the fiscal capacity of the various provinces. The equalization formula used to be renegotiated every five years at federal–provincial conferences, but Ottawa sometimes altered the formula unilaterally. Equalization payments were entrenched in the Constitution in 1982 so that although the federal government may change the formula, it cannot withdraw from its responsibility in this regard. Section 36 reads as follows:

> Parliament and the government of Canada are committed to the principle of making equalization payments to ensure that provincial governments have sufficient revenues to provide reasonably comparable levels of public services at reasonably comparable levels of taxation.

Many find it puzzling that Quebec should qualify as a have-not province and, indeed, when its revenue shortfall is multiplied by its large population, that it should receive almost as much in equalization payments as all the other have-not provinces combined. The explanation seems to rest with the following facts: Quebec has less natural resource wealth than is commonly assumed, its industry was historically small-scale, its business profits were often taken out of the province and sent to corporate headquarters elsewhere, its steel industry was slow to get started, and it did not enjoy Ontario's proximity to the U.S. automobile industry. Moreover, until 1960 its labour force was not well trained and the Roman Catholic Church in the province discouraged entrepreneurial activity among its deferential flock. Whatever the reasons, Quebec does well by these federal payments, to which people in all provinces contribute through their federal taxes.

Many attempts have been made to identify the overall "winners" and "losers" of Confederation—that is, which provinces or regions have a net gain or loss when all their federal taxes and benefits have been totalled. This debate has particularly centred on Quebec, but the results of federalist and sovereignist studies are often contradictory. Two University of Calgary economists concluded, for example, that between 1961 and 1992 Quebec received $168 billion more in federal spending than it contributed in tax and other revenues to Ottawa, and it is still commonly assumed that Quebec is a net beneficiary of billions of dollars annually. On a per capita basis, however, there is no question that the Atlantic provinces benefit most.[18] As mentioned, Ontario claims to lose $23 billion per year, but without taking into account how much of that sum is redistributed across the country and later spent by other Canadians on buying goods and services from the province.

The three northern territories are far from being economically self-sufficient, and they depend heavily on financial resources from the federal government. The principal federal transfer is the Territorial Formula Financing (TFF), an annual unconditional transfer exceeding $2 billion. Nunavut contends, however, that if it could retain its natural resource revenues, it would not need such large annual transfers from Ottawa.

Equalization payments have become a leading regional issue in recent years, primarily pitting petroleum-producing provinces against the federal government. Newfoundland and Labrador and Nova Scotia claimed that for every dollar they took in from offshore petroleum revenue, 70 cents was clawed back by Ottawa by reducing their equalization payments. After aggressive protest, especially by Newfoundland Premier Danny Williams, Prime Minister Paul Martin signed a deal with the two provinces in 2005 under which their equalization payments would not be reduced over the following eight years, but Saskatchewan also wanted the same treatment of its nonrenewable resources. The provinces were unsuccessful in seeking a consensus on general changes to the formula in 2006, and the Harper government imposed a new formula in the 2007 federal budget. It was a more generous formula for all provinces, especially Quebec. While it allowed Newfoundland and Labrador and Nova Scotia to opt for a continuation of their Atlantic Accord signed with Martin, the new formula would be more generous for those two provinces, too, at least in the short-run. But the new formula included one-half of a province's nonrenewable resources, which Harper had originally promised to exclude, and it also had a cap that would kick in if a have-not province developed a higher fiscal capacity than a province that did not receive such payments. This choice only inflamed Williams' opposition to the new formula and to the Harper government. As noted in Chapter 18, in 2008–09 Alberta, Ontario, Saskatchewan, and British Columbia did not qualify for equalization payments. Due to the global financial meltdown, however, especially as it affected the manufacturing industry in Ontario, that province began to qualify in 2009–10, and in the 2009 budget, the federal government adjusted the new equalization formula to reduce its commitments in this field.[19]

The second means of reducing regional economic disparities is to establish federal **regional economic development programs**.[20] These payments and programs started in 1935 and have undergone many changes of organization and emphasis since. The basic thrust of these programs was to designate those parts of the country that needed economic assistance (essentially the whole country except Ontario's Golden Horseshoe—that is, Toronto and westward around the head of Lake Ontario), and then to provide grants to firms that would locate or expand existing operations in such areas. Some grants also went to provinces or municipalities to provide the basic infrastructure that might attract industry, such as highways, water and sewage systems, and industrial parks.

In 1987, another reorganization created several separate regional economic development agencies, which now consist of the **Atlantic Canada Opportunities Agency (ACOA)**, Federal Economic Development Initiative in Northern Ontario (FedNor), Western Economic Diversification Canada (WD), and Canada Economic Development for Quebec Regions (CED). Some of these agencies are attached to the Industry Canada department. In the 2009 budget, a new agency was added for beleaguered southern Ontario (the Southern Ontario Development Agency) so that the whole country is now covered by federal regional development agencies. Many cases could be documented of corporations receiving money without being in need of it or taking the money and not living up to their commitments to create jobs. However, some positive results have also occurred. In any case, federal politicians face a never-ending stream of appeals from have-not communities, have-not provinces, and corporations to use the federal power of the purse to make their lives a little easier.

REGIONAL IDENTITIES

Regional identities usually have some concrete, territorial foundation. Sharing a defined geographic area, interacting within it, and often possessing other common characteristics, such as ethnicity or class, people develop a perception of their collective interests and distinctiveness from other regions. However, since regions are to some extent a state of mind—an identity—they do not necessarily coincide with political boundaries or environmental divisions. Feelings of regionalism and regional identities can exist within a province or territory, such as in the northern parts of many provinces; regional sentiment can cut across provinces and territories, as in the case of people in northwestern Ontario feeling psychologically closer to Manitoba than to southern Ontario; and provinces and territories can be lumped together into regions, such as the Maritimes, the Prairies, or the North.

Regional identities may also coincide with distinctive clusters of ideological viewpoints or political cultures; they can sometimes compete with feelings of national identity and they may well result in peculiar patterns of political behaviour. In Canada, moreover, regional identities often correspond with feelings of regional alienation. Leaving aside Quebec for the time being, it is most common to speak of Western alienation, but such alienation varies to some extent from province to province and can also be found in other peripheral areas, such as Atlantic Canada or the North.

In 1980, Roger Gibbins defined **Western alienation** as follows:

A regionally distinct political culture through and within which are expressed economic discontent, the rejection of a semi-colonial status within the Canadian state, antipathy towards Quebec and French-Canadian influence within the national government, the irritation of the West's partisan weakness within a succession of Liberal national governments, and the demand from provincial political elites for greater jurisdictional autonomy.[21]

Dissatisfaction with both the Liberal and the Conservative parties' focus on Quebec issues in the 1980s and early 1990s led to deep feelings of Western alienation, and was largely responsible for the formation of the Reform Party, whose initial slogan was "The West Wants In." In the 1993 federal election, the Reform Party won the majority of seats west of Ontario, and almost all the seats in British Columbia and Alberta, and then repeated this feat in 1997. It then changed its leader and its name (to the Canadian Alliance) in an effort to become more appealing to the rest of the country, without notable success. In 2003, the Canadian Alliance merged with the Progressive Conservative Party, although it retained its Alberta-based leader, Stephen Harper. While he never lost sight of the regional base of the party, Harper strove to expand it, and by 2006, he managed to win enough seats in the rest of the country to form a minority government. At last, the West was in, but as in the past, the Harper government was also concerned with strengthening its base in Quebec!

It must also be acknowledged that Western alienation has a conservative ideological hue, especially in its most extreme dimension in Alberta. The collectivist strain in the Canadian political culture is weakest in that province, which generally favours individualist, nongovernmental solutions to public problems. To some extent, this preference for individual self-reliance is based on the relative prosperity of the region. Thus, in addition to opposition to the government regulation reflected in the Kyoto Accord, there was hostility to the gun registry and to the requirement in the Canada Health Act that publicly funded health services be provided in the public sector. Many Albertans are also opposed to the liberal interpretations of the Charter of Rights and Freedoms on such issues as sexual orientation and same-sex marriage. As noted in Gibbins' definition, a related theme is antagonism to official bilingualism and to constitutional reforms designed to appease Quebec.

Westerners have always felt that they are regularly out-voted in the House of Commons by MPs from central Canada. It is not so much that the Western provinces are unfairly represented in the Commons, based as it is on the principle of representation by population; it is just that central Canadian MPs tend to vote together to defeat proposals favoured by the West. The population of British Columbia and Alberta combined now exceeds that of Quebec, but even today most observers contend that the two Western provinces have no comparable impact on federal policies.[22] One possible solution to this problem advocated by many Westerners is to strengthen the capacity of the Senate to protect regional interests against the voting power of central Canada in the House of Commons. Alberta in particular has long advocated an elected Senate with more effective powers and with equal representation for each province regardless of population, so that the Senate could veto a policy like the National Energy Program. This question is further addressed in Chapter 23.

Even when the Mulroney Conservatives were in power, with strong representation from the West, decisions were still often made in the interests of central Canada, such as the CF-18 maintenance contract being awarded to Quebec. Thus, if the West can never find satisfaction in federal policies, another potential solution is to decentralize federal powers to the provinces. Many Westerners share the view of Quebeckers on this matter, for example, including the argument that the provinces should have a role in international agreements that affect provincial jurisdiction.

Although Western alienation is most prominent, other outlying regions in Canada also often feel isolated and discriminated against. In fact, the Atlantic and Northern regions probably have even more legitimate complaints, given their minimal representation in federal institutions and relative lack of financial resources. Most of these concerns are of an economic nature. Although the alienation felt by Western Canada and that experienced by the Atlantic and Northern regions have some similarities, they also have several differences. One difference is that Atlantic and Northern regions have more often sought security in electing Liberal MPs to the government side of the Commons. A second is that these regions have been easier to buy off with federal largess, such as changes to the employment insurance program and, possibly for that reason, they do not demonstrate the same anti-government ideological sentiment. A third difference is that they generally do not desire additional powers because they cannot afford to utilize them. But issues like Senate reform do resonate in Atlantic Canada.

Table 3.3 measures peripheral regional alienation during the 1997 federal election campaign. It reveals variations in alienation among Western provinces (especially between Alberta and Manitoba), as well as high levels in Newfoundland and Labrador and Nova

TABLE 3.3   Peripheral Regional Alienation (PRA) Index by Province, 1997

Province/ Territory	Mean PRA	Percentage Very High PRA
Newfoundland/ Labrador	3.72	13.04
Prince Edward Island	1.23	2.63
Nova Scotia	3.75	11.67
New Brunswick	2.87	11.54
Ontario	1.81	7.21
Manitoba	2.75	8.43
Saskatchewan	3.97	11.96
Alberta	4.56	19.82
British Columbia	3.57	15.96
Yukon	1.87	9.76
Northwest Territories	2.34	11.43

From Regionalism and Party Politics in Canada, edited by Lisa Young and Keith Archer. Copyright © Oxford University Press Canada 2002. Reprinted by permission of the publisher.

Scotia. The latter, interestingly enough, are the two Atlantic provinces with the greatest offshore petroleum revenues.

As implied, another striking aspect of regionalism in Canada is the party system, as evidenced by the differential success of various parties in different regions of the country.[23] The Liberal party has been weak in Western Canada ever since John Diefenbaker's Conservatives swept the region in the 1950s. Meanwhile, Quebec traditionally voted overwhelmingly for the Liberals, although that province's peculiar regional election results began to favour the Bloc Québécois after 1993. The main parties' popular vote in different regions in the 2008 federal election can be seen in Table 3.4.

TABLE 3.4   Regional Support for Main Parties in 2008 Federal Election

	Atlantic	Quebec	Ontario	West	North
Conservative	29.6%	21.7%	39.2%	52.4%	35.1%
Liberal	35.0%	23.7%	33.8%	16.3%	29.7%
NDP	26.1%	12.1%	18.2%	21.5%	25.4%
BQ	—	38.1%	—	—	—

Source: Elections Canada. Calculations by Author.

. . . .

CONCLUSION

The Canadian physical environment is primarily characterized by regionalism, and many demands stemming from such regions can be identified. Some demands seek improved transportation and communications links to bind the country more closely together. Others desire increased provincial or territorial autonomy in order to deal locally with their distinctive problems. A third set of demands relates to the specific interests of one province, territory, region, or industry under the label of regional economic cleavages and disparities. Since not all regional demands are economic in nature, however, the discussion of regionalism must also include questions of regional identities and regional alienation.

Regionalism is such a pervasive force in Canadian society that it figures in almost every chapter that follows. Given the close connection between the concepts of regions and provinces, issues that concern provinces as such are mainly dealt with in Chapter 5 (Quebec as a region), Chapter 17 (the constitution), and Chapter 18 (federalism). Regional identities and attitudinal differences are revisited in Chapter 11 (political culture), Chapter 19 (the Charter of Rights), and Part V (political institutions). The environment issue is mentioned again in Chapter 8, dealing with class and corporate power, and regional voting patterns and the regionalized party system are addressed again in Chapter 13, 14, and 15 (elections, parties, and election campaigns).

P Of the approaches outlined in Chapter 1, pluralism immediately comes to mind in the consideration of regionalism. First, pluralists point to the obvious geographic and economic diversities in Canada, and they argue that national policies must allow for regional variations. They mention that it was this diversity that led to the initial creation of the provinces and territories and the federal system. Power has been dispersed to the provincial and territorial political units because many of the diversities can be better accommodated at that level. Second, pluralists cite the interplay of many such forces at the national level and claim that a plethora of examples can be found to demonstrate that government policies have stemmed from vociferously articulated regional economic demands. However much one region or another feels neglected from time to time, pluralists claim that government decisions are usually compromises among various competing regional interests.

PC The next three approaches generally take the opposite point of view—that is, that in the interplay of regional forces, Ontario has usually dominated. Public choice theory, for example, emphasizes the voting power of central Canada in the design of most government policies in this field. Moreover, during the Pearson and Trudeau eras, when Quebec could be counted on to vote Liberal and the West went predominantly Conservative, elections were essentially fought out in Ontario, the province with not only the largest electorate but also the greatest number of "marginal" voters. This partly explains the thrust of Trudeau's constitutional and energy policies—especially the National Energy Program—which were strongly supported in Ontario but caused great anguish in the West.

SC The state-centred approach comes to much the same conclusion but for different reasons. It concentrates on the predominance of people from central Canada in such authoritative positions as the prime minister, Cabinet, House of Commons, and bureaucracy, and the ability of these authorities to operate autonomously, without public pressure. If 60 percent of members of Parliament and Cabinet ministers come from Ontario and Quebec, it is only to be expected that many federal policies will benefit the central part of the country. If the bureaucratic elite has similar geographic origins, this tendency will only be reinforced. In some periods in Canadian history Western or Atlantic regional demands were more satisfactorily addressed, usually when powerful regional ministers or strong provincial premiers engaged in a process of elite accommodation. But in the case of the 1980 National Energy Program, a combination of an unrepresentative Cabinet and an autonomous bureaucracy produced a policy to which the West reacted with hostility.[24] Partly in response to the NEP, Senate reform became a key point in constitutional discussions because the outlying provinces saw equal and effective provincial representation in that body as their only counterweight at the federal level to the predominance of central Canada in the House of Commons and Cabinet.

Ⓒ Class analysts also see a centralist thrust to most federal policies, but one that primarily facilitates the accumulation of capital among central Canadian corporations. Early railway policy, national tariff and banking policies, the bailout of the predecessors of CN, legislative support of private pipelines, corporate grants under regional development programs, the reliance on natural resource exploitation, and the reluctance to develop a Canadian industrial policy were all designed to benefit capitalist interests, most of which were headquartered in central Canada. Another way of expressing class analysis of Canadian regionalism is that the role of differential regional resource endowments is of secondary importance; uneven development is largely the result of political decisions primarily influenced by the process of capitalist accumulation.[25] Some such analysts also argue that parties have encouraged voters to think of Canadian politics in terms of conflict that "revolves around the allocation of power and resources across geographic units rather than, for example, among social classes."[26] In this perception, regions are less significant than classes and have been used to distract Canadians from class cleavages.

Ⓖ The regional economic differences and conflicts identified in this chapter have often had international connections, such as the attraction of American manufacturing companies to Ontario or American petroleum companies to the West. The interests of multinational corporations were often mixed in with the regional demands articulated to the federal government. But it is primarily in the post-1985 era of intensified globalization that such external forces are apparent in this field. The Canada–U.S. Free Trade Agreement, followed by NAFTA, resulted from both domestic and international pressures, but, having signed these agreements, Canadian governments suddenly discovered that they had given up the power to make public policies in many areas. Among the casualties were policies that might favour Canadian over American firms and industries, sometimes in the name of regional development. New Brunswick finds, for example, that it cannot expect any preferential treatment over New England states in gaining access to Sable Island natural gas, and softwood lumber producers have fought American interpretations of the treaties ever since they were signed. As Janine Brodie argues, such agreements severely limit "the ability of future Canadian governments to alleviate regional disparities and to contain regional conflict."[27] But globalization does not always favour or disadvantage the same regions: Alberta, which benefits from exporting additional petroleum to the United States under the free trade agreements, is the same province that protests most vociferously when Canada signs a multinational environmental treaty, such as the Kyoto Accord.

. . . .

DISCUSSION QUESTIONS

1. Which of the traditional regional demands and complaints in Canadian federal politics do you think are unjustified?

2. To what extent do you feel a regional identity?

3. Do you think decentralization of the federal system is an answer to conflicting regional demands?

4. Are there better ways to reduce regional economic disparities than through equalization payments and regional development programs?

. . . .

NOTES

1. Task Force on Canadian Unity, *A Future Together* (Ottawa: Supply and Services, 1979), pp. 26–27. The "provincialism" of this report was rejected by its government sponsor (Prime Minister Trudeau), but it may have inspired his successors.
2. Janine Brodie, "The Concept of Region in Canadian Politics," in David Shugarman and Reg Whitaker, eds., *Federalism and Political Community* (Peterborough: Broadview Press, 1989).
3. Richard Simeon, "Regionalism and Canadian Political Institutions," J. Peter Meekison, ed., *Canadian Federalism: Myth or Reality*, 3rd ed. (Toronto: Methuen, 1977), p. 293; Benedict Anderson, *Imagined Communities: Reflections on the Origins and Spread of Nationalism*, rev. ed. (London and New York: Verso, 1991).
4. Brodie, "The Concept of Region in Canadian Politics."
5. House of Commons, *Debates*, June 19, 1936.
6. Donald Creighton, *The Empire of the St. Lawrence* (Toronto: Macmillan, 1956). Harold Innis emphasizes the significance of the beaver fur trade, which utilized such river systems.
7. The whole romantic story is told in Pierre Berton's books *The National Dream* and *The Last Spike* (Toronto: McClelland and Stewart, 1970 and 1971).
8. For an analysis along these lines, see Robert Chodos, *The CPR: A Century of Corporate Welfare* (Toronto: Lorimer, 1973).
9. Statistics Canada, *Canada's Population from Ocean to Ocean* (Catalogue No. 98-120, January 1989), p. 16.
10. For a specifically geographic point of view on this question, see Scott Reid, *Canada Remapped* (Vancouver: Pulp Press, 1992).
11. Wallace Clement and Daniel Drache, *A Practical Guide to Canadian Political Economy* (Toronto: Lorimer, 1978), pp. 9–14; Wallace Clement and Daniel Drache, *New Practical Guide to Canadian Political Economy* (Toronto: Lorimer, 1985); Michael Howlett and Keith Brownsey, *Canada's Resource Economy in Transition: The Past, Present, and Future of Canadian Staples Industries* (Toronto: Emond Montgomery, 2008).
12. David Kilgour, *Inside Outer Canada* (Edmonton: Lone Pine Publishers, 1990); and Don Braid and Sydney Sharpe, *Breakup: Why the West Feels Left Out of Canada* (Toronto: Key Porter Books, 1990).
13. By this time many large central Canadian corporations also saw advantages for themselves in such a policy.

14. James L. Darroch and Charles J. McMillan, "Entry barriers and evolution of banking systems: Lessons from the 1980s Canadian western bank failures," *Canadian Public Administration* (June 2007).
15. Donald Smiley, *The Federal Condition in Canada* (Toronto: McGraw-Hill Ryerson, 1987), p. 159.
16. Robert Campbell and Leslie Pal, *The Real Worlds of Canadian Politics* (Peterborough: Broadview Press, 1989).
17. Robin W. Boadway and Paul A.R. Hobson, *Equalization* (Montreal: McGill-Queen's University Press, 1998); and Harvey Lazar, ed., *Canadian Fiscal Arrangements: What Works, What Might Work Better* (Kingston: McGill-Queen's University Press, 2005).
18. Robert Mansell and Ronald Schlenker, "The Provincial Distribution of Federal Fiscal Balances," *Canadian Business Economics* (Winter 1995), pp. 3–22, which also showed that Alberta lost $139 billion while Ontario lost $45 billion. A fuller account of federal–provincial/territorial finance is contained in Chapter 18.
19. Department of Finance Canada website, "Equalization Program," at http://www.fin.gc.ca/fedprov/ eqp-eng.asp; Heather MacIvor, *Parameters of Power: Canada's Political Institutions*, 5th ed. (Toronto: Nelson Education, 2010), ch. 4.
20. Among the early versions of such policy were the Prairie Farm Rehabilitation Administration (PFRA) of 1935, the Maritime Farm Rehabilitation Act of 1948, and the Agricultural Rehabilitation and Development Act of 1961. See also Donald J. Savoie, *Visiting Grandchildren: Economic Development in the Maritimes* (Toronto: University of Toronto Press, 2006).
21. Roger Gibbins, *Prairie Politics and Society* (Toronto: Butterworths, 1980), p. 191; and Roger Gibbins and Sonia Arrison, *Western Visions: Perspectives on the West in Canada* (Peterborough: Broadview Press, 1995).
22. Glen Williams, "Regions within Region: Canada in the Continent," in Michael S. Whittington and Glen Williams, eds., *Canadian Politics in the 21st Century*, 6th ed. (Toronto: Nelson, 2004), p. 145.
23. Lisa Young and Keith Archer, eds., *Regionalism and Party Politics in Canada* (Toronto: Oxford University Press, 2002).
24. Peter Foster, *The Sorcerer's Apprentices: Canada's Super-Bureaucrats and the Energy Mess* (Don Mills: Collins, 1982).
25. Janine Brodie, *The Political Economy of Canadian Regionalism* (Toronto: Harcourt, Brace, Jovanovich, 1990), p. 4.
26. Janine Brodie, "The Concept of Region in Canadian Politics," p. 36.
27. Brodie, *The Political Economy of Canadian Regionalism*, p. 223.

. . . .

FURTHER READING

Brodie, Janine. *The Political Economy of Canadian Regionalism*. Toronto: Harcourt, Brace, Jovanovich, 1990.

Canada. Task Force on Canadian Unity. *A Future Together*. Ottawa: Supply and Services, 1979.

Dyck, Rand. *Provincial Politics in Canada*, 3rd ed. Scarborough: Prentice Hall Canada, 1996.

Gibbins, Roger, and Loleen Berdahl. *Western Visions, Western Futures*. Peterborough: Broadview Press, 2003.

Howlett, Michael and Keith Brownsey, *Canada's Resource Economy in Transition: The Past, Present, and Future of Canadian Staples Industries*. Toronto: Emond Montgomery, 2008.

Savoie, Donald J. *Visiting Grandchildren: Economic Development in the Maritimes*. Toronto: University of Toronto Press, 2006.

Tomblin, Stephen. *Ottawa and the Outer Provinces*. Halifax: Lorimer, 1995.

Tomblin, Stephen G., and Charles Colgan, eds. *Regionalism in a Global Society: Persistence and Change in Atlantic Canada and New England*. Peterborough: Broadview Press, 2004.

Western Economic Opportunities Conference. *Documents and Verbatim Record*. Calgary, July 1973.

Young, Lisa, and Keith Archer, eds. *Regionalism and Party Politics in Canada*. Toronto: Oxford University Press, 2002.

Chapter 4

ABORIGINAL
Peoples

Given that they were here first, should Aboriginal peoples be allowed to hunt and fish at will? How can their land claims be dealt with fairly? How can the lives of urban Aboriginals be improved? Should Canada proceed with constitutional reform on other issues before it resolves Aboriginal concerns? How have the actions of the state affected Aboriginal people's sense of identity? How have Aboriginals mobilized to affect government policies? Although the way in which they have been governed over the past 150 years is obviously a failure, is Aboriginal self-government a realistic alternative? What does it mean? Is it possible for those Aboriginals who want to do so to return to a traditional way of life? In short, how can the claims of Aboriginal peoples who reside in Canada be addressed after 33 million "immigrants" have taken possession of most of the inhabitable land and completely transformed the country? Aboriginal issues have attracted widespread interest in recent years, but opinion is deeply divided on how to deal with them.

This chapter will begin with an analysis of some theoretical considerations and then detail the demographic profile of Canada's Aboriginal peoples today. It will examine the historical evolution of these indigenous peoples and outline the principal political issues they have raised since 1970, especially with respect to land and governance. Current issues are so unprecedented in Canadian political experience that they are not easily understood, and although concrete action has been taking place at a rapid rate in recent years, there is still a long way to go.

. . . .

THEORETICAL CONSIDERATIONS
Colonialism, Identities, and Changing Terminology

Any discussion of Aboriginal peoples has to begin with the concept of colonialism. Colonialism can be defined as the exploitation, domination, and subjugation of a people by an imperial power, exactly what was practised in the European settlement of Canada. Some early and isolated good relations and good intentions no doubt existed, but the 1876 Indian Act was clearly aimed at assimilating Aboriginals into the new white majority, and it represented a colonialism as obnoxious as European countries perpetrated anywhere else in the world. Some critics even use the word "genocide."[1]

When Europeans took control of the continent, they applied their own terminology to the Aboriginal peoples they encountered. Their first mistake, of course, was to call them "Indians." Although this term survives in the form of "North American Indians" in the Constitution Act, 1982, and in the Census, Aboriginals naturally prefer to use their own, more accurate words. The term "First Nation" came into common usage in the 1970s to replace the word "Indian" and refers to both status and non-status "Indians," but does not include the Métis or Inuit. Somewhat similarly, "Eskimo" became "Inuit," and many geographic terms, such as names of towns, have been changed from English or French to Aboriginal. The changes in terms are an illustration of the politics of identity; they reflect Aboriginal people's conceptions of themselves. The older terms were imposed by governments, while the newer terminology reflects the hard fought battles of Aboriginal peoples in the politics of recognition. Many would prefer to be known as "Aboriginal peoples who reside in Canada," reflecting the fact that they increasingly ground their sense of citizenship in their identity as a First Nation rather than as a citizen of Canada, or are internal "dual citizens." On the other hand, some critics argue that the term "First Nation" was deliberately chosen to enhance their claim for self-government status.

The census distinguishes between Aboriginal ancestry and Aboriginal identity, with the former being a larger number. There are the three official categories—North American Indian, Métis, and Inuit; Indians are divided between status and non-status, and the former are subdivided between on- and off-reserve. In some contexts, it is also useful to speak separately of Aboriginal women and men.[2] In other words, Aboriginals in Canada are a highly diverse group with many different identities, expectations, and political demands, and have even formed several specialized advocacy groups.

Theoretical Models

In theory, there are probably three main governance options that could be chosen to improve the condition of Aboriginal life in Canada.[3] The first would be integration and assimilation into the non-Aboriginal society. This was the route historically favoured by the Government of Canada, and one chosen by many Aboriginal people themselves. Integration and assimilation would presumably involve repeal of the Indian Act and treaties, abandonment of reserves, and denial of any kind of Aboriginal status, more or less as the 1969 Trudeau-Chrétien White Paper proposed. The migration of increasing numbers of Aboriginal people into urban areas is a variation on this option, mostly involving people who have left reserves because of the inadequacies of such an environment, but also including Métis who never had a land base.

Given the fact that in the pre-contact period, Aboriginals governed themselves, the second option would be a return to Aboriginal self-government, focused on reserves. For some, this means making reserves more autonomous of the Indian Affairs Department, perhaps with powers akin to municipalities; indeed, First Nations communities increasingly operate without detailed departmental bureaucratic supervision. This option would also include the example of the Nisga'a Treaty, where the powers of the First Nation exceed those of a municipality, including jurisdiction over natural resources. One step further would be to incorporate the concept of Aboriginal self-government as a third order of government, akin to federal and provincial levels, as proposed in the Charlottetown Accord. In this model, federal and provincial laws would still apply to Aboriginals in certain areas of jurisdiction.

Aboriginal self-government is at least theoretically feasible with a territorial base such as a reserve, but it is a much more questionable concept in situations where Aboriginals are intermingled with others, especially in an urban setting.

Some advocates would go further and speak of Aboriginal sovereignty. This third option would involve being independent of the Canadian state. This is the ideal of those who feel that the second option would leave Aboriginals in a "post-colonial," but still internal colonial relationship with the dominant non-Aboriginal authorities.[4] They see all the trappings of self-government processes, land claims agreements, and Aboriginal rights court cases as basically determined by the white society's ways and needs. But while this third option may be the underlying dream of many Aboriginals, only a few militants see independence as a realistic proposition.

· ·

ABORIGINAL DEMOGRAPHIC PROFILE TODAY

The Canada census asks about Aboriginal origin and Aboriginal identity, self-identifying questions that are subjective and probably understate the real numbers involved. In the 2006 census, Statistics Canada reported 1.2 million Aboriginals based on identity, that is, those who *felt* themselves to be Aboriginal, and about 1.7 million Aboriginals based on ancestry or ethnic origin. These figures, respectively, represent 3.8 percent and 5.5 percent of the total population.[5] Many Aboriginals reported multiple ancestries, often in combination with non-Aboriginal origins. Canadian authorities divide these numbers into three official categories: North American Indians (now usually called First Nations), Métis, and Inuit. Table 4.1 shows the breakdowns for Aboriginal origins and identity.

Aboriginal Canadians are not spread uniformly across the country. The largest absolute numbers live in Ontario, but First Nations and Métis have higher proportional concentrations in the western part of the country. On the other hand, about half of the Inuit live in Nunavut, and another 30 percent in parts of adjacent provinces (Nunavik in northern Quebec, Nunatsiavut in

TABLE 4.1 Aboriginal Origins and Identity, 2006 Census

	Origins	*Identity*
North American Indian (First Nations)	1 253 615 (72.5%)	698 025 (59.5%)
Métis	409 915 (23.7%)	389 780 (33.2%)
Inuit	65 885 (3.8%)	50 480 (4.3%)
Other and Multiple		34 500 (2.9%)
Total	1 729 415	1 172 790

Source: Statistics Canada, Ethnocultural Portrait of Canada Highlight Tables, 2006 Census. Found at: http://www12.statcan.ca/english/census06/data/highlights/ethnic/pages/Page.cfm?Lang=E; Statistics Canada. Aboriginal Peoples Highlight Tables, 2006 Census. Found at: http://www12.statcan.ca/english/census06/data/highlights/aboriginal/index.cfm?Lang=E (accessed March 6, 2009)

northern Labrador), and the Northwest Territories. Those at the top of the ranking in terms of Aboriginal proportion of population are Nunavut, NWT, Yukon, Manitoba, and Saskatchewan. Table 4.2 illustrates this distribution in terms of Aboriginal identity in 2006.

Turning from identities and ancestry to official, legal numbers, Indian Affairs and Northern Development Canada reports some 780 000 status or registered Indians, of whom about half live on reserves.[6] There are about 2700 reserves, with an average size of about 1150 hectares, and some 614 bands or First Nations. On the other hand, Statistics Canada found that about 54 percent of all Aboriginals live in urban areas; Winnipeg, Saskatoon, Regina, and Edmonton have the highest concentrations of urban Aboriginals, although large numbers also reside in Vancouver, Toronto, and Calgary.

Regardless of the legal and identity distinctions mentioned, there are 11 major Aboriginal linguistic families, the largest being Cree, Inuktitut (the language of the Inuit), and Ojibway, but more than 50 Aboriginal languages exist. About one-fifth of the Aboriginal population have an Aboriginal language as mother tongue, largely confined to the Inuit and those who live on reserves, but only 15 percent actually speak an Aboriginal language at home. This leads to much concern about the disappearance of Aboriginal languages.

TABLE 4.2 Distribution of Aboriginal Canadians by Identity, 2006 Census

	North American Indian	Métis	Inuit	Total	Percentage of Provincial/ Territorial Population
Atlantic Provinces	36 615	18 805	5 255	67 010	3.0
Quebec	65 085	27 980	10,950	108 425	1.5
Ontario	158 395	73 605	2 035	242 495	2.0
Manitoba	100 640	71 805	565	175 395	15.5
Saskatchewan	91 400	48 120	215	141 890	14.9
Alberta	97 275	85 495	1 610	188 365	5.8
British Columbia	129 580	59 445	795	196 075	4.8
Yukon	6 280	800	255	7 580	25.1
Northwest Territories	12 640	3 580	4 160	20 635	50.3
Nunavut	100	130	24 635	24 915	85.0
Total	698 025	389 780	50 480	1 172 785	3.8

Note: The total figure includes multiple and other responses. Some calculations by author.

Source: Source: Statistics Canada. Aboriginal Peoples Highlight Tables, 2006 Census. Found at: http:// www12.statcan.ca/english/census06/data/highlights/aboriginal/index.cfm?Lang=E (accessed March 6, 2009). The total figure includes multiple and other responses. Some calculations by author.

All three categories—First Nations, Métis, and Inuit—are increasing in numbers because of high birth and fertility rates, because fewer are missed in the Census than in the past, and because more individuals are identifying themselves as Aboriginal. The latter is especially true of the Métis. Almost half of the Aboriginal population is aged 24 and under, and overall, it is growing twice as fast as its non-Aboriginal counterpart.

These basic statistics present only part of the picture. At least of equal significance are the distressing statistics on Aboriginal poverty.[7] Many reserve families have incomes far below the poverty line, and apart from a few Aboriginal urban professionals, the same is true for most of those who live off-reserve. Related to this level of poverty are alarming rates of Aboriginal alcoholism, violence, mortality, low educational attainment, and high unemployment. The suicide rate among Aboriginal youth is at least five times the national average, and Aboriginal Canadians are much more likely to be murdered or to die from accidents, poisoning, or violence. The incidence of tuberculosis among residents of reserves is seven times that of other Canadians, while cardiovascular disease, diabetes, pneumonia and other respiratory diseases, gastroenteritis, rheumatic fever, ear infections, meningitis, hepatitis, intestinal infections, skin diseases, and disorders of the nervous system are all common. In 2009, several first nations were badly hit by an outbreak of the H1N1 (swine flu) virus. The overall life expectancy of Aboriginal Canadians is about 6.6 years shorter than that of non-Aboriginals, mostly because of poor lifestyles and inadequate health services. Housing on reserves is often sadly deficient, being severely overcrowded and in need of repair, and contaminated drinking water is a common problem (see Box 4.1).

Although the Canadian government is anxious to point out that considerable improvement has been recorded in on-reserve living conditions since 1960, it acknowledges that about 50 percent of dwellings on First Nations reserves still require renovation or replacement. On-reserve Aboriginal communities would rank 68th among 174 nations on the UN Human Development Index, and the UN Human Rights Commission criticized Canada for the high rates of poverty, infant mortality, unemployment, suicide, and abuse among Aboriginal peoples.

The following scenario is regrettably typical for many Aboriginals in Canada: having been stripped of their land, original livelihood, and culture, and having been placed on unproductive

| BOX 4.1 | E. Coli in Kashechewan |

In October 2005, the 1900 people living in the Kashechewan First Nation located on the Ontario James Bay coast learned that their drinking and bathing water was contaminated with E. coli bacteria. The tainted water had contributed to chronic diarrhea problems and skin conditions, such as impetigo, scabies, and eczema. The federally maintained water treatment plant had an intake pipe located downstream from Kashechewan's sewage lagoon. It was the provincial government, rather than Ottawa, that decided to evacuate the residents until they were healthy and their water supply was repaired. At the same time, nearly 100 First Nations across the country had boil-water advisories, one lasting for nine years.

reserves, they find themselves with little to do. The resulting poverty, unemployment, idleness, and reliance on welfare often lead them to seek solace in alcohol and drugs. Some Aboriginals also resort to family and other violence, which in turn brings them into trouble with the law. Not being able to pay their fines, and being subject to discrimination at the hands of the police, the courts, and other aspects of the justice system, they then go to jail, where they become even more alienated, depressed, and abused.

THE CANADIAN PRESS/Troy Fleece

First Nations leaders struggling to break the cycle of joblessness and poverty complain that their efforts are hamstrung by crumbling facilities such as this school in Saskatchewan.

Aboriginal Canadians have suffered from untold discrimination and indignity at every turn. Reflecting a colonial mentality, the Indian Act treated them like children and required bureaucratic approval for almost any band decision. In the past, babies were frequently removed from the reserves to be adopted by non-Aboriginal parents, and until the 1970s many Indian children were forced to go to residential schools, where they were punished, sometimes to the point of assault, for speaking their mother tongue or engaging in their own cultural and spiritual traditions.[8] Aboriginals were forced to renounce their identities and traditional forms of government and medicine were outlawed. Those living on reserves did not even have the right to vote in federal elections until 1960, and between 1927 and 1951 the Indian Act made it an offence for a band to hire a lawyer to bring a claim against Canada without government consent. As in the case of French Canadians, this protracted attempt to assimilate Aboriginals was a dismal failure.

Despite the picture painted above, there are many Aboriginal success stories, but part of the reason for so little progress in improving the condition of Aboriginal life in Canada is the relatively small number of people involved and hence the invisibility of the problem. The dispersion of Aboriginal peoples has also made it difficult for them to be elected to federal or provincial governments and has recently generated demands for guaranteed Aboriginal seats in Canadian legislatures. Another reason is the negative Aboriginal stereotype and the mistaken belief that Aboriginals have brought all these difficulties upon themselves.[9]

. . . .

HISTORICAL EVOLUTION

Aboriginal peoples have inhabited Canada for perhaps as long as 40 000 years, with most experts linking their origins to Asia. They are an extremely varied group in both origin and identity. Those who settled in the southern part of what is now Canada, as well as those in Yukon and the Mackenzie Valley of the north, are officially termed "North American Indians," but, given the erroneous origin of the label, they prefer to be called **"First Nations"** peoples. Those located in the eastern Arctic and northern islands used to be called Eskimo and are now referred to as "Inuit."

Before Europeans came to the continent, most Aboriginals functioned as nomadic hunters, but some were more permanent fishers, carvers, or farmers. They were self-sufficient and self-governing. Practising their own forms of government for thousands of years, they generally made decisions on the basis of consensus rather than by voting, and, in many cases, women (sometimes called clan mothers) and elders of both genders played a significant role. In their close attachment to the land, most did not think in terms of private ownership; instead, they believed in the shared use of land and saw themselves as trustees of the land for future generations.[10] They did not always exist in a peaceful state with their neighbours, however, even before the Europeans arrived.

It was the fur trade more than anything that led to the invasion by Europeans and to wars between the British and the French in North America. The fur trade was devastating for the Aboriginal peoples, totally disrupting their way of life and introducing new diseases, such as smallpox, that severely reduced their population.

In the **Royal Proclamation of 1763**, which divided up the territory acquired by Britain, Aboriginal rights were clearly defined, however much they have since been ignored.[11] In a large area called Indian Territory, the purchase or settlement of land was forbidden without Crown approval—that is, without a treaty between the Crown and the Aboriginal people concerned. This is sometimes called the principle of "voluntary cession." Shortly afterward, the Crown concluded land-cession agreements with Indians in what is now southern Ontario in order to provide land for the United Empire Loyalists moving in from the United States. Indians originally received a lump-sum payment and, later, annuities.

From about 1830 onward the system changed, and the Crown set aside reserves in exchange for the cession of Indian land, in addition to providing benefits, such as the right to hunt and fish on unoccupied Crown land. The first major treaties of this kind were the Robinson Treaties of 1850 in northern Ontario and the Douglas Treaties on Vancouver Island.

The 1867 Constitution Act gave jurisdiction over Indians and lands reserved for the Indians to the federal government. Parliament soon passed the **Indian Act**, which was consolidated in 1876 and provided for federal government control of almost every aspect of Indian life. One of the provisions of the Indian Act allowed for "enfranchisement," which encouraged Indians to give up their Indian status. Thus began the distinction between **status Indians**, those registered with the federal government according to the terms of the Indian Act, and non-status Indians, those no longer registered.

Meanwhile, the treaty-making process continued apace, with treaties numbered 1 to 11 covering most of northern Ontario and the Prairie provinces, and parts of British Columbia, Yukon, and the Mackenzie Valley of the Northwest Territories. These treaties were primarily designed to clear Aboriginal title so that the transcontinental railway could be built and Western immigrant settlement could begin. Such treaties contained an extinguishment clause, under which pre-contact Aboriginal rights were given up in exchange for treaty rights. In return for surrendering title to the lands involved, Indians received tracts of land for reserves as well as other benefits, such as small annuities, gratuities, schools, hunting and fishing rights, agricultural implements, cattle, and ammunition. In retrospect, almost everyone agrees that the Aboriginals were taken advantage of in these negotiations and that the land given them for reserves was usually small, remote, and lacking in resources.[12] Nevertheless, Aboriginals guard their treaty rights religiously because they have little else, and those in much of British Columbia and the Arctic with whom no treaties were signed at all fared even worse. Figure 4.1 is a map of the historic Indian treaties.

· ·

Figure 4.1 Historic Indian Treaties

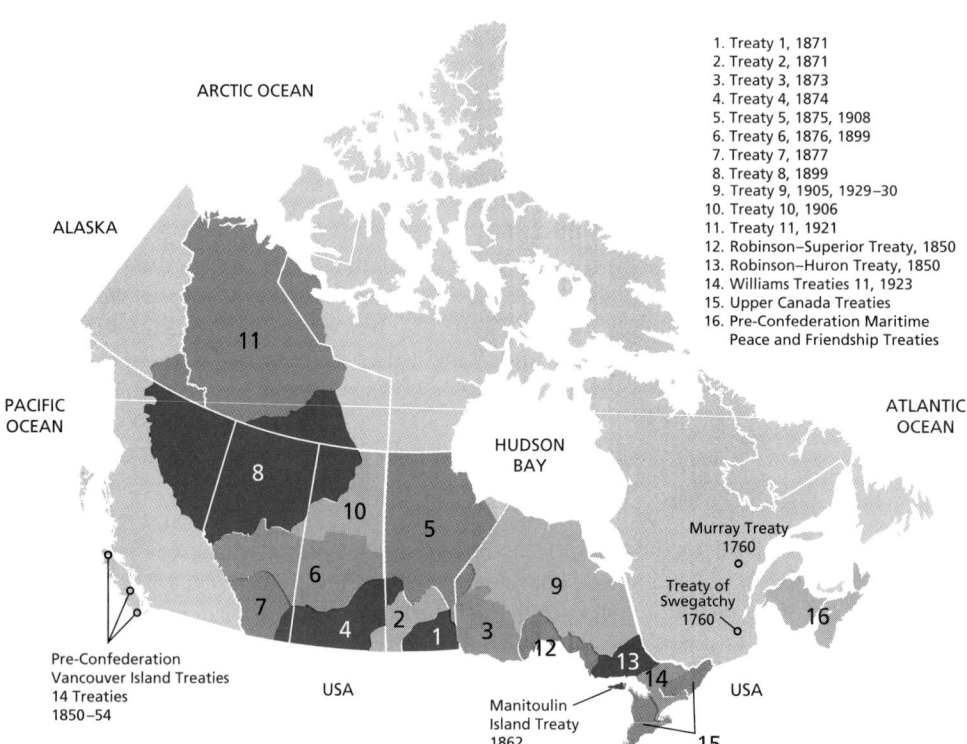

1. Treaty 1, 1871
2. Treaty 2, 1871
3. Treaty 3, 1873
4. Treaty 4, 1874
5. Treaty 5, 1875, 1908
6. Treaty 6, 1876, 1899
7. Treaty 7, 1877
8. Treaty 8, 1899
9. Treaty 9, 1905, 1929–30
10. Treaty 10, 1906
11. Treaty 11, 1921
12. Robinson–Superior Treaty, 1850
13. Robinson–Huron Treaty, 1850
14. Williams Treaties 11, 1923
15. Upper Canada Treaties
16. Pre-Confederation Maritime Peace and Friendship Treaties

Source: Historical Treaties of Canada. Indian and Northern Affairs Canada. Found at: http://www.ainc-inac.gc.ca/al/hts/tgu/mps/htoc-eng.pdf

By this time another identifiable group existed besides status, non-status, treaty, and non-treaty Indians. These were the Métis, essentially the descendants of French and Scottish fur traders and Indian women. Found largely on the Prairies, the Métis combined nomadic hunting with farming. They were not covered by the Indian Act or by treaties and were therefore left to the mercy of new white settlers and their provincial and territorial governments who displaced the Métis from their lands. It is not surprising, therefore, that Louis Riel took up their cause in 1885 in the second Riel Rebellion in Saskatchewan. After the rebellion was crushed, the Métis remained in an even weaker position to fend for themselves, and it is only in recent years that they have even been recognized in public policies.

The one group of Aboriginals left untouched by government, although not by fur traders, missionaries, and other whites, was the Eskimo or Inuit who inhabited the Northwest Territories, the coast of northern Labrador, and about 25 percent of northern Quebec. A 1939 Supreme Court ruling declared that the Eskimo came within the meaning of Indians in the 1867 Constitution Act (although not under the Indian Act), but it was not until the 1950s that the federal government began to deliver health and educational services to them and later to relocate them into about 50 permanent settlements, largely on the coast of the Arctic mainland, Hudson Bay, and northern Quebec.[13] This disruption of their traditional lifestyle based on hunting and trapping caused them to depend increasingly on social assistance and intermittent wages.

. . . .

ABORIGINAL POLITICAL ISSUES SINCE 1970

For a variety of reasons, Canada's Aboriginal peoples and their problems have become a major concern of Canadian politics since 1970. In part they were insulted by the terms of the 1963 Royal Commission on Bilingualism and Biculturalism, which spoke of the English and French as being Canada's two "founding races." They were also offended by the 1969 Trudeau–Chrétien **White Paper on Indians**, which called for their complete integration, if not assimilation, into the wider Canadian society. The paper reflected Trudeau's obsession with individual rights and his blindness to the concept of collective or group consciousness, similar to his attitude toward Quebec. More than any other single factor, the White Paper was the spark that ignited the Aboriginal movement in Canada. More positive influences were the sympathetic 1977 Berger Inquiry into the proposed Mackenzie Valley gas pipeline,[14] as well as the increased awareness of Aboriginal issues worldwide. Now that most European colonies around the world had been liberated, partly through the efforts of the United Nations, many observers came to see that indigenous peoples in the new world had also been victims of colonialism. In some places, such as South Africa, they could pursue self-determination through majority control of an independent country, but if that was unrealistic in Canada, the Aboriginals would at least insist on reclaiming their identities, ensuring their survival and development as distinct nations, and restructuring the Canadian political system so that they would have control over their own affairs.[15]

Aboriginal people organized and began to fight back, learning from the civil rights movement and the New Left of the 1960s and anti-colonial Third World liberation movements. The incidence of sit-ins, roadblocks and other blockades, rallies, court cases, hunger strikes, and international protests increased. Indeed, at the 1989 annual meeting of the **Assembly of First Nations**, a mutual defence pact based on the NATO agreement was signed to the effect that bands would support each other and send reinforcements when requested. Then, in 1990, two incidents helped place Aboriginal concerns prominently in the public consciousness: an Aboriginal MLA in Manitoba, Elijah Harper, was instrumental in defeating the Meech Lake Accord, and the Mohawks of Oka, Quebec, took the law into their own hands to protect what they considered to be their land from the expansion of a non-Aboriginal golf course.

Since 1970, then, the crowded Canadian political agenda has had to find room for a variety of Aboriginal issues, which are made all the more complex because of the diversity within the Aboriginal community. These issues include Aboriginal self-government, land claims, social conditions, economic development, Aboriginal languages, Aboriginal women, educational issues, and justice. For the purposes of this text, most of the issues can be discussed under the broad headings of land issues and governance issues. Although it is easier to visualize Aboriginal self-government when it is based on a specific piece of territory, the issues of land claims and governance have often proceeded somewhat independently of each other, although they are now often negotiated simultaneously in the form of modern treaties.

Land Issues

In much of the country, North American Indians signed treaties with the Crown under which they ceded the land to the government in return for protected reserves. But, especially in British Columbia and the North, few such treaties were signed, leaving North American Indians and Inuit in these regions without a recognized land base. The Métis never possessed any land, with the result that only about one-third of Aboriginal peoples have a land base on which to rely. This gives rise to the issue of **Aboriginal title**, that is, a claim to land on the basis of traditional occupancy and use rather than treaty.

Aboriginals have been making land claims since 1885, but governments never took them seriously. Indeed, as mentioned, between 1927 and 1951, the Indian Act made it an offence to raise funds or hire a lawyer to advance a land claim without the government's permission. The existence of such Aboriginal title was finally recognized in the *Calder* case in 1973 in connection with the Nisga'a band in British Columbia, but the Supreme Court of Canada was split on the question of whether such title had been subsequently extinguished. Nevertheless, the Trudeau government announced its intention to begin to negotiate Aboriginal title. Although this was a major step forward, the initial policy was not satisfactory because even where treaties had been signed, Indians were increasingly challenging their terms and implementation; some Métis also raised the land issue. A great variety of Aboriginal land claims have, therefore, been launched in the past 40 years. They fall into two categories: **comprehensive claims** based on Aboriginal title (that is, traditional use and occupancy of land) that have not been dealt with by treaty or other legal means, and **specific claims** arising from alleged non-fulfillment of Indian treaties and other lawful obligations.

NORTHERN LAND CLAIMS

North of the 60th parallel the federal government is in charge of both the land and the Aboriginals. As a result, many comprehensive claims have been settled in Yukon and the Northwest Territories. Besides providing land and money, such comprehensive claims clarify Native hunting, fishing, and trapping rights and clear obstacles to future economic development.[16] It should be noted, however, that as in other land claims settlements, the rights of current non-Aboriginal property owners have been protected. The creation of the northern territory of Nunavut is discussed under governance issues below.

SOUTHERN LAND CLAIMS

In the south, where Ottawa has responsibility for "Indians and lands reserved for the Indians" but where the provinces have jurisdiction over public ("Crown") lands, land claims have moved more slowly. Aboriginals have generally found provincial governments even less sympathetic to their issues than Ottawa, and conflict often develops between First Nations and natural resource companies as well as with other non-Aboriginals who now live on the land in question. Ottawa insists that provinces be party to such settlements and contribute to their costs, arguing that it is in the provinces' interest to establish certainty of title to lands and resources.

The first provincial comprehensive land claim settlement was the 1975 **James Bay and Northern Quebec Agreement** between the Cree and Inuit and the government of Quebec, supplemented by several subsequent agreements. In return for allowing Quebec to construct a giant hydro development project in the area, the James Bay Agreement gave the Aboriginals exclusive use of 13 700 km^2 of land and additional territory where they had exclusive hunting, fishing, and trapping rights, along with $225 million in cash. Although the deal was unprecedented and widely heralded in many quarters, one terrible side effect was the mercury poisoning of fish and of the people who ate them, resulting from an unanticipated chemical reaction between water and rock in the flooded land. This problem, the disruption of the caribou migration patterns, and the growing perception that the deal may have been less generous to the Aboriginal community than originally thought, led to the Crees' refusal to sign the second, "Great Whale," phase of the James Bay project.

Since 1975, several other comprehensive land claim successes can be reported below the 60th parallel, especially in Quebec, Labrador, and British Columbia. Many others are near completion and negotiation over others has begun. For current information on these fast-changing developments, readers are referred to the website of Indian Affairs and Northern Development Canada.

Since the province of British Columbia contains a large proportion of North American Indians and few treaties, the land claims issue has been particularly significant there. Unfortunately, the provincial government was reluctant to engage in such negotiations, and the BC Supreme Court was not much help. When the *Delgamuukw* case came to the Supreme Court of Canada in 1997, however, that court was more sympathetic. It ordered that in such cases, various kinds of oral history evidence be admissible and also provided its first comprehensive statement on Aboriginal title: a group must establish its exclusive occupation of the land in question before the time the Crown asserted sovereignty. Although the Supreme Court of Canada allowed for Crown infringement on Aboriginal title for valid legislative objectives, it specified that the groups with Aboriginal title need to be involved in the decision-making process around such a proposed infringement.[17]

As mentioned, the neighbouring Nisga'a tribe in northwest BC, which had been seeking recognition of their Aboriginal title for more than 100 years, took their claim to court in the 1973 *Calder* case. It was not until the 1990s, however, when governments of Canada and British Columbia signed a B.C. Treaty Commission Agreement with the First Nations of that province that serious negotiations began. The Nisga'a served as pioneers again when they finally signed the first modern-day treaty with Ottawa and the BC government in 1998. In this combined land and self-governance treaty, the Nisga'a gained 1930 km^2 of land, $190 million in cash, and self-government powers beyond those of municipal governments in return for giving up the right to future land claims and tax-exempt status. It was a complex document including sections on forestry, mining, wildlife and the environment, public access, the administration of justice, finance, taxation, and many more. Two years later, the treaty was ratified by the Nisga'a people in a referendum, as well as by the federal and BC legislatures. Although opposed by a minority of Nisga'a, some surrounding Aboriginals, and some in other provinces who felt that they had given up too much, the treaty's most vociferous opposition arose among non-Aboriginals in the BC legislature, where a demand for a provincial referendum was loudly voiced. Nevertheless, the Nisga'a treaty may well serve as a model for treaties with other Aboriginal groups,[18] and British Columbia is currently the site of a distinctive, busy, complex, and innovative land claims tribunal process.

Specific land claims result from alleged breaches of the government's legal obligations and dissatisfaction with treaties—especially the fact that bands did not receive the full amount of land that the treaties promised. It was not until 1973 that Ottawa agreed to hear them, but since then Canada has settled hundreds of specific claims, although not always to First Nations' satisfaction. There remained a serious backlog, however, such that a new system was adopted in 2008. The new Specific Claims Tribunal Act provided for an independent tribunal composed of superior court judges to make binding decisions on specific claims that the Minister rejected or did not approve within a three-year time period. Whether approved by the Minister or the Tribunal, a successful claim usually results in a cash settlement that can be used to purchase land to compensate for what was lost. In a related development, the Supreme Court of Canada ruled in 2002 that Aboriginals who can prove their forebears honestly believed that government authorities had created a reserve for them may have a case even if no specific order in council verified its creation.[19]

OTHER LAND ISSUES

Another dimension of land issues concerns what treaties allow Aboriginals to do on public lands. Aboriginal treaty rights, especially hunting and fishing rights, frequently conflict with provincial law. Some progress has been made on this front, especially in two Supreme Court of Canada decisions in 1990. In the *Sioui* case, the Court ruled that a 1760 Huron treaty was valid, and its provision that Indians be allowed "the free exercise of their Religion [and] their Customs" prevented Quebec from prosecuting Hurons for practising Native customs and fishing in provincial parks. The Court also gave Indians new hope in the *Sparrow* decision that stated that section 35(1) of the Constitution Act, 1982, affords Aboriginal people constitutional protection against provincial legislative power and that the clause should be given a generous, liberal interpretation. In this case the Court said that the Aboriginals' right to fish could override provincial regulations regarding the size of a net.[20]

In the 1999 *Donald Marshall* cases, the Supreme Court ruled that the treaty rights of the Mi'kmaq in Atlantic Canada allowed them to make a "moderate livelihood." Subject to government regulations with respect to conservation, they could catch lobster or eels during the period when the fishing season was closed to non-Aboriginals. In the 2005 *Bernard* case, however, the Court decided that not enough historic evidence existed to give Aboriginals in Nova Scotia and New Brunswick the same right to cut trees.[21] In Saskatchewan, Manitoba, and Ontario, landmark court decisions have held that even the provinces' Métis have hunting and fishing rights under the Constitution, no different from the rights of status Indians.

The Innu of Labrador protested in vain for several years against low-level NATO military training flights around Canadian Forces Base Goose Bay, which they claimed were a hazard to human health and the environment. Meanwhile, the government of Newfoundland and Labrador moved the Mushuau Innu community of Davis Inlet to an island off the Labrador coast, where they developed even worse social and health problems—including severe solvent abuse among children—and had even fewer economic opportunities than before. Later, Ottawa intervened to relocate them back to the Labrador mainland. Ottawa and Newfoundland and Labrador also signed a self-government framework agreement and land claims agreement with the Innu of Labrador, although the youth suicide rate remained alarming.[22]

Yet another aspect of the land question arose in the conflict at Oka, Quebec, in the summer of 1990, the most serious conflict between Aboriginals and authorities of modern times.[23] The municipal council's decision to expand a golf course on land claimed by resident Mohawks as sacred ground (a claim of traditional occupancy but not guaranteed by treaty) led to an armed standoff between Mohawk warriors and the Quebec provincial police in which one police officer was killed. The Mohawks were supported by the nearby Kahnawake reserve, which also set up barriers and blockaded the Mercier Bridge to Montreal. The Canadian Armed Forces were later brought in, and Aboriginal demonstrations took place across the country. Although some local non-Aboriginal residents stoned vehicles carrying Mohawk families, most Canadians hoped that the incident would speed up the process of settling hundreds of outstanding Aboriginal land claims before any worse violence occurred. Unfortunately, violence did erupt again—in a peaceful and legitimate land dispute in 1995 at Ipperwash, Ontario, in which a police officer killed an unarmed demonstrator, Dudley George. A third incendiary dispute began in 2006 in Caledonia, Ontario, over the development of a residential subdivision on what the Six Nations reserve near Hamilton claimed as their land. Roadblocks, barricades, angry confrontations, acts of violence, and unhelpful judicial rulings prompted the provincial government to try to solve the problem by buying the property from the developer.

THE CANADIAN PRESS/str-Shaney Komulainen

A Canadian solider and an Aboriginal protester come face-to-face in a tense standoff in Oka, Quebec, in September 1990.

Governance Issues

Aboriginal Canadians have long demanded improvements in government health, social, housing, and educational services, and some minor improvements have been made over the years. They began to feel, however, that they were too constrained by the Indian Act and that Aboriginal problems required Aboriginal solutions. They were tired of living at the mercy of non-Aboriginal politicians and bureaucrats, a fact highlighted by the Mulroney government's reduction in their postsecondary education support and cuts to their newspapers, broadcasting, organizations, and subsidized housing.[24] Yet most Aboriginals did not want to gut the Indian Act and existing government programs until they had something better to put in their place.

The first positive official response to Aboriginal discontent was the Hawthorn Report of 1966, *Survey of the Contemporary Indians of Canada*. It took the position that Aboriginal Canadians needed a greater degree of local autonomy and deserved a higher level of government services to compensate for everything that had happened in the past. Because non-Aboriginal Canadians had built a prosperous society on the lands and resources originally owned by Aboriginals, the latter should be considered "citizens plus." Nothing much came of this report at the time, and, indeed, the next initiative, the 1969 White Paper, took the opposite approach—that Aboriginal Canadians should be treated exactly the same as other Canadians and that reserves should be dismantled and treaties and the Indian Act should be repealed.

As mentioned, it was the angry Aboriginal response to the White Paper that finally sparked the beginning of changes in the issue of governance. Since they could hardly be expected to support the apparatus that created their current problems, Aboriginal Canadians began to argue that they should be able to choose their own decision-making processes, at least on reserves. Before the passage of the Indian Act, they had sophisticated and distinctive forms of government and many wanted to return to such traditional ways. Going well beyond changes in the decision-making machinery, however, they demanded **Aboriginal self-government**.[25] Aboriginals argued for more control their own affairs, but the specific structures of such proposed self-government were not clear-cut: they felt that an array of self-government arrangements and institutional models could be developed. In general, most of the desired responsibilities are within provincial—not federal—jurisdiction, which means that provinces need to be involved in the complex self-government negotiations. At the same time, it is widely acknowledged that most Aboriginal communities are not self-sufficient economically, and like have-not provinces and territories, they will require continued financial transfers from other levels of government.[26]

THE CONSTITUTION ACT, 1982, MEECH LAKE, AND THE CHARLOTTETOWN ACCORD

The first advance in the constitutional recognition of Aboriginal rights occurred after widespread protests in connection with the constitutional negotiations in 1981–82. The Constitution Act, 1982 ultimately contained two clauses of interest here. Section 25 guaranteed that the Charter would not be construed so as to abrogate or derogate from any Aboriginal, treaty, or other rights or freedoms pertaining to the Aboriginal peoples of Canada, including any rights recognized by the Royal Proclamation of 1763, and any rights or freedoms "that now exist by way of land claims agreements or may be so acquired." Section 35 recognized and affirmed the existing Aboriginal and treaty rights of the Aboriginal peoples of Canada, including the Indian, Inuit, and Métis peoples. Partly to conform with the equality rights clause in the Charter and partly to respond to a ruling of the United Nations Human Rights Committee in the Sandra Lovelace case, the Indian Act was amended to remove the clause that had previously taken Indian status away from Aboriginal women who married white men but granted such status to white women who married Indian men. Bill C-31 (1985) led to the reinstatement of nearly 100 000 Aboriginal women and their children, but since bands were allowed to control their own membership, a high proportion of those reinstated in status had difficulty in returning to the reserve. In 2005 Paul Martin named Sandra Lovelace Nicholas to the Senate.

Based in part on the recommendations of the 1983 Penner Report (Report of the Special Committee of the House of Commons on Indian Self-Government), a series of federal–provincial first ministers' conferences on Aboriginal rights was held between 1983 and 1987. In turn, prime ministers Trudeau and Mulroney tried unsuccessfully to get provincial premiers and Aboriginal leaders to agree to the terms of a constitutional amendment recognizing the principle of Aboriginal self-government. Several premiers insisted that the concept be clarified before they would agree even in principle, while Aboriginal leaders wanted the principle recognized as an *inherent* right. At the 1987 conference, Georges Erasmus, national Chief of the Assembly of First Nations, spoke as follows:

> Nothing short of Aboriginal self-government will achieve our aspirations for survival as distinct peoples. Attempts by governments at integration and assimilation over the years have failed and we have rejected them. We must be able to control our lives on our own lands and using our own resources.[27]

Manitoba MLA Elijah Harper withheld assent for the Meech Lake Accord because it did nothing for Canadian Aboriginals.

Although the constitutional talks broke down, two pieces of legislation were passed to provide for self-government in specific localities. The 1984 Cree-Naskapi (of Quebec) Act set in place self-government arrangements for the Indians of Quebec who were parties to the James Bay land claim agreement, and the 1986 Sechelt Indian Band Self-Government Act allowed the Sechelt band in British Columbia to assume control over their lands, resources, health and social services, education, and local taxation in what is usually called the "municipal model." Given the absence of constitutional advance, however, Aboriginals were understandably opposed to the Meech Lake Accord, which addressed Quebec's constitutional demands but completely overlooked their own. Even supporters of the Accord found it hard to blame Elijah Harper for withholding unanimous consent when it came before the Manitoba legislature for approval.

Elijah Harper's stand, together with the 1990 Oka affair, precipitated a dramatic breakthrough of constitutional concern with Aboriginal issues and full participation of Aboriginal leaders in post-Meech constitutional negotiations. For the first time, Aboriginal leaders were given the same status as premiers in the talks leading up to the 1992 Charlottetown Accord, and that document addressed Aboriginal concerns in a more extensive and satisfactory way than it did the demands of Quebec.

The Charlottetown Accord would have recognized the inherent right of Aboriginal peoples to self-government and acknowledged that such First Nations governments constituted a third order of government in Canada, analogous to the provinces. The document provided for self-government agreements to be negotiated among the three levels of government. Federal and provincial laws would remain in place until superseded by Aboriginal laws, but the latter would have to be consistent with the preservation of peace, order, and good government in Canada. In addition to provisions for Aboriginal self-government, Aboriginal peoples were to have a new role of one kind or another in the House of Commons, Senate, Supreme Court, first ministers' conferences, and the constitutional amending formula. Despite the enormous leap in official thinking that this section of the Accord represented, a majority of Aboriginal voters opposed it in the referendum. Some found the provisions lacking in detail, and many Aboriginal women worried that their individual (Charter) rights might be being sacrificed for new group rights.

Although few non-Aboriginals voted against the Charlottetown Accord because of its provisions regarding Aboriginal self-government, it should be noted that there was and is a cleavage between those who are sympathetic to Aboriginal demands and those who oppose them. Provincial premiers' reluctance to constitutionalize Aboriginal self-government and vehement opposition to the Nisga'a Treaty were previously mentioned. Some elements of the electorate contend that Aboriginals already receive preferential treatment. They cite, for example, the large annual budget of the Indian Affairs department with its high per capita federal spending on Aboriginal Canadians, certain tax exemptions, extensive subsidization of post-secondary education, and affirmative action programs, among others. In his "anti-Aboriginal phase," BC premier Gordon Campbell held a provincial referendum on eight questions negatively related to Aboriginals and received overwhelming support from those who voted, while many others boycotted the whole process.[28]

POST-1992 PROGRESS

After 1992, activity in the area of Aboriginal governance focused on legislative and administrative changes, such as experiments in delegating federal or provincial government powers to First Nations communities, and new self-government agreements.[29] In mid-1995, the Minister of Indian Affairs announced that Ottawa was launching new negotiations to give Aboriginals in all provinces much wider powers, and outlined how the government would implement the inherent right of Aboriginal self-government in practical, workable agreements. Not expecting to be able to achieve a formal constitutional amendment to this effect, the Chrétien government claimed that the principle was *already* contained in section 35 of the Constitution Act, 1982, and therefore *already* constitutionalized. According to the August 1995 ministerial statement, the principles of Aboriginal self-government are as follows:

- The inherent right is an existing Aboriginal right recognized and affirmed under the Canadian Constitution.
- Self-government will be exercised within the existing Canadian Constitution. It does not mean sovereignty in the international sense. Aboriginal peoples will continue to be citizens of Canada and the province or territory where they live.
- The Canadian Charter of Rights and Freedoms will apply fully to Aboriginal governments. The current provisions of the Charter that respect the unique Aboriginal and treaty rights of Aboriginal peoples will continue to apply.
- All federal funding for self-government will come from the reallocation of existing resources.
- Where all parties agree, rights in self-government agreements may be protected in new treaties under section 35 of the Constitution Act, 1982. They may also be protected through additions to existing treaties, or as part of comprehensive land claims agreements.
- Federal, provincial, territorial, and Aboriginal laws must work in harmony. Certain laws of overriding federal and provincial importance, such as the Criminal Code, will prevail.
- The interests of all Canadians will be taken in account as agreements are negotiated.

In its report a year later, the **Royal Commission on Aboriginal Peoples** identified four "touchstones" as a framework for its recommendations. These were (1) a new relationship between Aboriginal and non-Aboriginal people based on equality, respect, and reconciliation; (2) self-determination for Aboriginal peoples within Canada through self-government—that is, the right to control their collective futures; (3) economic self-sufficiency for Aboriginal peoples, including breaking the cycle of poverty and dependency on government transfers and creating meaningful employment opportunities; and (4) personal and collective healing for Aboriginal peoples and communities, to remedy the effects of decades of mistreatment and neglect. The commission endorsed Aboriginal self-government in its widest sense and the basic separation of Aboriginal and non-Aboriginal societies. Among other things, it proposed a division between "core" areas, where Aboriginal governments would be free to exercise authority and legislate on their own initiative, and "peripheral" areas, which would require self-government treaties or agreements with other governments. It also proposed an Aboriginal Parliament, dual Canadian–Aboriginal citizenship, an independent lands and treaties tribunal, an Aboriginal development bank, an action plan on health and social conditions, and an Aboriginal-controlled education system.[30]

The Chrétien government was reluctant to rush into the implementation of the royal commission's more exotic recommendations, preferring the course on which it had previously embarked. In 1997, the government issued a general response called *Gathering Strength—Canada's Aboriginal Action Plan*. It began with a Statement of Reconciliation, apologizing for past wrongs, especially the horrors of the residential school system. Next, in a Statement of Renewal, the document adapted the royal commission's four touchstones to the following basic principles: renewing the partnerships; strengthening Aboriginal governance; developing a new fiscal relationship; and supporting strong communities, people, and economies.

Whether or not the 1995 and 1997 federal declarations amounted to anything close to "inherent Aboriginal self-government," considerable progress continued to be made at the community level. Aboriginal people now control over 80 percent of Indian Affairs departmental program funding, and Aboriginal authorities increasingly deliver such services as education, language and culture, police services, health care and social services, housing, property rights, and adoption and child welfare. In this vein, Ottawa signed an agreement in 1997 with the Mi'kmaq chiefs in Nova Scotia, transferring education authority to First Nations' control. Many more First Nations were negotiating self-government agreements, whether dealing with a comprehensive range of jurisdictions, a single jurisdiction (for example, education), or combined self-government and land claims negotiations.

In the Northwest Territories, a 1992 plebiscite ratified a boundary division that led to the creation, in 1999, of a new territory called **Nunavut**, as seen in Figure 4.2. It is a public government, elected by Aboriginal and non-Aboriginal residents alike, with all the institutions associated with a province or territory. But Nunavut can be characterized as a form of Aboriginal self-government because the Inuit make up 85 percent of the population. In addition, several Yukon First Nations have signed final land claim and self-government agreements with the federal and territorial governments, which in many respects were a model for the Nisga'a Treaty. They require that each First Nation have a constitution and a citizenship code; they recognize the rights of non-Aboriginals; and they outline how First Nations powers relate to territorial and federal powers.[31]

In the 1999 *Corbiere* case, the Supreme Court gave band members living off-reserve the right to vote in First Nations' elections. Then, in 2002, Indian Affairs Minister Robert Nault introduced a new First Nations Governance Act (Bill C-61). His objective was to take quick action to ensure greater democracy and financial accountability on reserves, but most First Nations' leaders had other, longer-term priorities, notably more money, more power, and solutions to social problems. Because of such opposition, the bill was not passed by the time Paul Martin succeeded Jean Chrétien as prime minister, and the new government abandoned it.

. . . .

Figure 4.2   Nunavut Territory

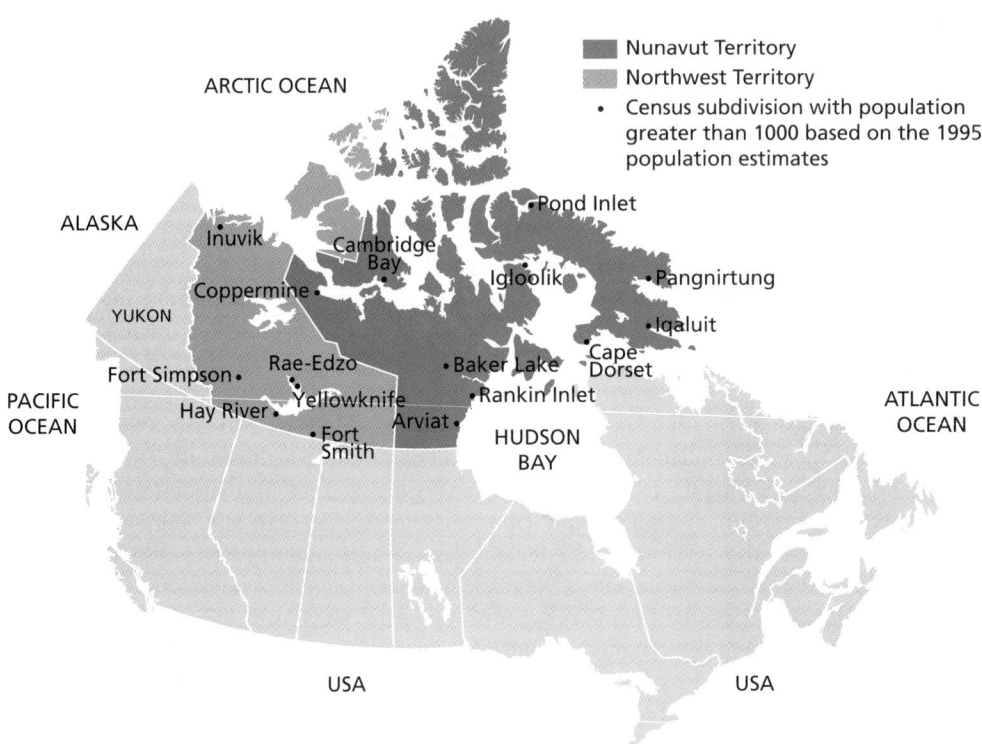

Source: Statistics Canada. Canadian Social Trends. Catalogue No. 11-008, Spring 1997, Number 44, p. 17. Found at: http://www.statcan.gc.ca/bsolc/olc-cel/olc-cel?catno=11-008-X&chropg=1&lang=eng

A specific aspect of Aboriginal governance relates to the high proportion of Aboriginals in Canadian jails. Indeed, some troubling criminal cases raised the question of whether they are treated fairly in the justice system: in the case of Donald Marshall, a Nova Scotia Mi'kmaq who was imprisoned for more than ten years for a crime he did not commit; in the rape and murder of Helen Betty Osborne, a First Nations girl in The Pas, by four white men; in the shooting of an Aboriginal leader, J.J. Harper, by a Winnipeg police officer; and in the Stonechild case, where an inebriated Aboriginal youth was left by the police to freeze to death outside the city limits of Saskatoon.[32] Inquiries into these tragedies have documented the discrimination against and brutalization of Aboriginals by every aspect of the criminal justice system. A 2006 report from the federal ombudsman for prisons admitted that Aboriginals are still subject to systemic discrimination once incarcerated.

It is sometimes proposed that an autonomous or parallel Aboriginal justice system be established in which Aboriginal cases would be diverted from the regular judicial process to allow convictions and sentences to be based on Aboriginal values and community traditions. So far, several provinces have allowed experimental judicial processes involving Aboriginal input; more Aboriginals have been hired as police officers; some reserves have their own Aboriginal police forces and justices of the peace; and a few even maintain their own correctional facilities. Increasingly, judges dealing with Aboriginal defendants follow Native traditions (or consult with elders) in imposing their sentences, such as restitution, restorative justice, and banishment. Perhaps with the high rate of Aboriginal incarceration in mind, the federal Parliament amended the Criminal Code in 1995 to read: "All available sanctions other than imprisonment that are reasonable in the circumstances should be considered for all offenders, with particular attention to the circumstances of Aboriginal offenders." The Supreme Court brought this clause to the attention of other judges in the 1999 *Gladue* case, and it was then applied by the BC Court of Appeal in the *Armbruster* decision.[33]

. . . .

RECENT ABORIGINAL ISSUES

Many developments have recently occurred on the Aboriginal front and many others remain on the Canadian political agenda. One is the question of apologies for the abuse that Aboriginal children endured in "residential schools." Most of the churches involved issued full and formal apologies for their part, and the Martin government began the process of providing financial compensation. Martin asked former Supreme Court judge Frank Iacobucci to work with the individuals and groups involved to come up with a general solution, which was announced in the early days of the Harper government. Then, in a moving ceremony in the House of Commons in June 2008, Stephen Harper issued a full official and historic apology for the residential school policy, and a Truth and Reconciliation Commission was established as part of the overall settlement of this problem.

A number of significant court decisions affecting Aboriginals have been made over the past few years. For example, the Supreme Court ruled in 2003 that the Métis people are a distinct Aboriginal group, with a constitutional right to hunt for food. The full implications of the ruling are not yet clear, but the decision certainly strengthens the bargaining position of this previously ambiguous group. [34] The Court also found that Aboriginals must be consulted on the development of logging, mining, or other resource projects on lands to which the title is still in dispute, although they have no veto over such projects. In a setback to Aboriginals, the Court ruled in 2005 that Mi'kmaq did not possess a right to cut logs on Crown land in Nova Scotia and New Brunswick without authorization, but in 2006 made a distinction between logging for commercial and domestic purposes. Chapter 19 includes discussion of such Charter cases.

On the revenue side, another Aboriginal political issue that arose in recent years is the extent to which First Nations have a right to operate gambling facilities on their reserves, now that casinos have become a leading source of revenue for governments in general. Another question relates to Aboriginal tax exemptions. In 1995, the federal government began to enforce its Indian Remission Order so that status Indians who earned employment income for duties performed off-reserve would have to pay income tax. Although several court cases emerged in this fuzzy area, tax exemptions are being negotiated away in such forums as the Nisga'a treaty. Meanwhile, Aboriginal leaders in the NWT signed a deal with a consortium to build the revived $5 billion Mackenzie Valley natural gas pipeline that could give them one-third ownership and a considerable share of the jobs involved. Aboriginals are also increasingly involved in employment, profit-sharing, and even sometimes partial owner-ship in Saskatchewan uranium mines, the Labrador nickel mine, and diamond mines in the Northwest Territories and northern Ontario. In addition, more funds are being made avail-able for Aboriginal economic development. Some of these are related to a private initiative of former Prime Minister Paul Martin, and others come from Asian investors who have their eye on natural resources on Aboriginal lands.

The fate of Aboriginals in a separate Quebec has also been discussed. In the event of a split between Quebec and the rest of Canada, it is widely anticipated that Aboriginal peoples in northern Quebec would prefer to remain with Canada. "Beyond claiming that they themselves constituted nations, Aboriginal leaders could invoke a constitutional fiduciary responsibility on the part of the federal government."[35] If so, this question could result in a nasty, even violent, confrontation. On the other hand, two more positive developments in Quebec are the creation of a new Regional Government of Nunavik involving the Inuit in the northern one-third of the province, and the Paix des Braves, which paved the way for the construction of more hydroelectric facilities with Aboriginal approval.

The auditor general has raised a variety of Aboriginal issues in recent reports. In 2003, she reported that the promises made in modern treaties were not being fully implemented. Aboriginal leaders cited a number of causes for this problem: the ignorance in key federal agencies about land-claims agreements, the "we don't take action until forced to do so" approach enforced by the federal Department of Justice, and the technical and minimalist interpretations of the agreements by those charged with their implementation. In 2005, the auditor general continued to report that the Indian affairs department had not been helpful in assisting First Nations to expand the size of reserves through transfers of Crown land or the purchase of land in urban areas.

Land claim settlements and Aboriginal self-government are not likely to affect the fate of the many Aboriginals who have left the reserve to live in urban centres. The rates of poverty, unemployment, violence, and substance abuse among urban Aboriginals are almost as high as those among Indians living on reserves. Aboriginal women in particular are con-cerned about issues of day-to-day survival in a harsh urban environment, such as housing, education, and the future of their children. Aboriginals are disproportionately represented among the inner-city poor all across the country, and this aspect of Aboriginal politics is likely to assume increasing importance in the future.[36] Another tragic issue is the number of Aboriginal women who have gone missing in certain large cities, some of them having been involved in the sex trade.

The Martin government convened a number of major meetings with Aboriginal leaders, culminating in the first ministers' and national Aboriginal leaders meeting in Kelowna in November 2005. Martin announced that Ottawa would contribute some $5 billion over five years toward a ten-year dedicated effort to closing the gap in the quality of life between Aboriginal peoples and other Canadians, with particular reference to health, education, housing, and economic development. The Harper government distanced itself from the Kelowna agreement, much to the annoyance of premiers and Aboriginals. The new adminis-tration also opposed a separate Aboriginal commercial fishery on the Fraser River, put more emphasis on accountability in reserve governance, and tried to promote individual rather than collective ownership of Aboriginal land. The House of Commons passed a private mem-ber's bill from the former PM to implement the Kelowna Accord, but the Harper government ignored it. A Supreme Court decision in June 2008 (*R. v. Kapp*) countered the Harper fishing policy and upheld an Aboriginal jump-start on salmon fishing in the Fraser River, based on the affirmative action provisions of the Charter of Rights.

One of the traditional weaknesses of the Aboriginal cause has been a general attitude of passivity and a lack of effective organization of Native groups. Recent years, however, have witnessed the emergence of strong and vocal advocacy groups, such as the Assembly of First Nations (status Indians), the Congress of Aboriginal Peoples (non-status Indians), the Métis National Council, the Inuit Tapiriit Kanatami, the Native Women's Association of Canada, and the Pauktuutit Inuit Women's Association, all of which were present at the 2005 meeting of first ministers and national Aboriginal leaders. While such organizations should strengthen the Aboriginal cause in the policymaking process, the fact that they represent different groups within the Aboriginal community means that their demands sometimes conflict with each other. Many other Aboriginal groups exist at the provincial or territorial level, such as the Council of Yukon First Nations.

Among other recent developments are the ratification and parliamentary approval of the Tsawwassen First Nation Final Agreement in British Columbia (the first modern urban treaty), and an amendment to the Canadian Human Rights Act, which extended the act to first nations, and met with their approval after being significantly changed. Although the process of signing comprehensive and specific land claims agreements seems to be exceedingly slow, many more can be anticipated over the next few years, as the Harper government resolved to speed up the resolution of treaty disputes. In response to the *Sharon McIvor* case before the BC Court of Appeal in 2009, the government agreed to amend the Indian Act to remove a continuing discrimination against Indian women who married non-Indian men. As for the general governments of the three northern territories, they are increasingly the recipients of a devolution of province-like powers, and each has a first minister who functions as, and now is called, a premier.

. . . .

CONCLUSION

Earlier in the chapter, three models of governance were proposed. Since most Aboriginals reject the assimilation model, and almost all Canadians reject the Aboriginal sovereignty model, the answer must lie somewhere in between. Aboriginals and non-Aboriginals must learn to live together. Primarily because many reserves are in a deplorable state, increasing numbers of First Nations people are leaving for a new urban existence, but reserves are likely to be with us for a long time to come. However, while eschewing assimilation, a certain amount of Aboriginal integration into the modern society may be advisable; this is what Alan C. Cairns calls "citizens plus." He and other thoughtful observers want to improve existing government programs; enlarge and strengthen reserves, attempting to make them more economically viable for those who choose to remain there; respect treaty rights; settle land claims; give Aboriginals more control over their daily lives; and treat them more fairly in the justice system. Although progress so far has been slight, a new generation of well-educated, articulate, and insistent Aboriginal leaders has arrived on the scene, and we witness almost daily announcements of tentative or final land claims agreements, self-government agreements, and judicial decisions relating to Aboriginal rights. Cairns reminds us that we are all in this together:

> Aboriginal nations, given their size and resources, cannot and will not opt for an independence that exceeds their governing capacity. Non-Aboriginal Canadians cannot

wipe out Aboriginal difference in pursuit of an idealized homogeneity that would make governance easier. So the choices we have to make for territorially based nations are the nature and extent of Aboriginal self-government and how we organize our common life in the areas beyond the reach of self-government.[37]

Armed with renewed identities and self-confidence, Aboriginals have placed their demands prominently on the political agenda in recent years. If the Nisga'a Treaty is used as a basis for other land claims/self-government agreements, it will establish certain government structures and practices that have never been seen in Canada before. Some non-Aboriginals hold Aboriginal peoples responsible for most of their own problems, resent the fact that in certain respects Aboriginals are treated more generously than other groups in society, and oppose such new solutions. Other non-Aboriginals support efforts to improve the conditions of Aboriginal life and welcome such solutions, arguing that government policies and corporate practices rather than the Aboriginals themselves are to blame for their plight in this country.

Aboriginal issues are revisited in several other points in this text. Aboriginal questions in Quebec are mentioned in the next chapter, and we also return to these issues in Chapters 7 (Gender) and 8 (Class). At the same time, the place of Aboriginals in the party and electoral systems is gaining increasing attention, and is included in Chapters 13 and 14. Aboriginal advocacy groups are mentioned in Chapter 16; the territories are mentioned again in Chapter 18 (Federalism); and Chapter 19 includes discussion of relevant Charter cases.

P The Aboriginal question confirms many of the tenets of the pluralist approach. Because their organizations were historically weak if not nonexistent, Aboriginals hardly ever even tried to exert any influence on the authorities and were flatly rejected if they did. But in recent years, they have converted this inertia into activism, and their organizations have functioned as effective advocacy groups. Indeed, in an almost corporatist manner, Aboriginal leaders have been integrated into the policymaking process since 1992, and the delegation of powers of self-government (and recognition of the inherent right to self-government) goes well beyond the pluralist–corporatist concept of delegating self-regulating powers to professional groups.[38] Even so, Aboriginal groups are generally less powerful than many other interests in society.

SC The state-centred approach is also particularly appropriate to this question. At first, almost every decision with respect to Canadian Aboriginals was made by the bureaucrats in the Indian Affairs department. In most cases, what the politicians and bureaucrats thought was in the interests of the Aboriginal peoples clearly was not. The relocation of the Inuit to the high Arctic was one of many such authoritative fiascoes. The repeated relocations of the Innu of Davis Inlet and Sheshatshiu are a more recent manifestation of the same paternalistic attitude. Even today, when many political and judicial decisions actually favour Aboriginal peoples, their progress is hampered by foot-dragging bureaucrats, as the auditor general has noted.

 Class analysts would fault large corporations as well as government elites for the sorry state of Aboriginal life in Canada. In the creation of Indian reserves and in later disputes, government policies generally allowed the corporate elite to preserve the most productive land for itself. Corporations have frequently challenged Aboriginal rights when valuable supplies of trees, minerals, petroleum, or fish were found on reserve land or on land or water that Indians had claimed as theirs by Aboriginal title. Confrontations between forestry companies and Aboriginals have occurred at Temagami in Ontario, Clayoquot Sound in British Columbia, and in New Brunswick, and vehement right-wing opposition broke out to the Nisga'a treaty in BC.

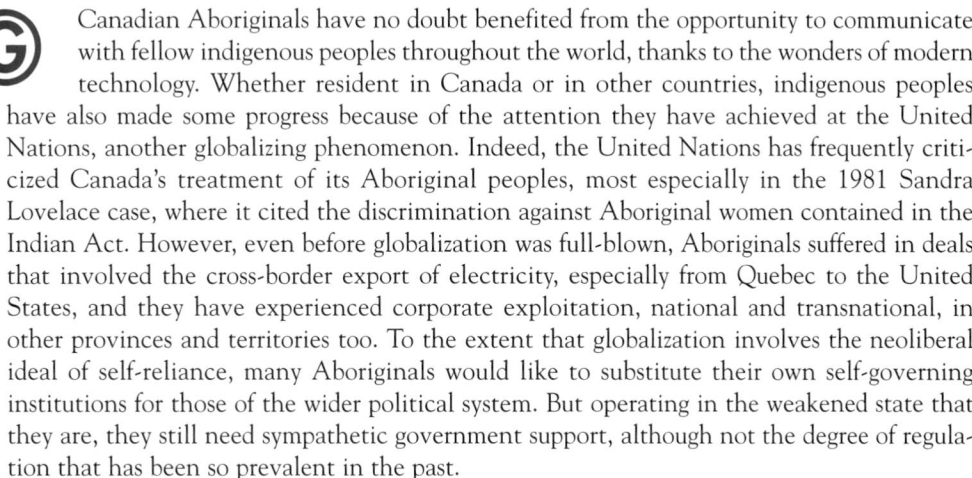 Canadian Aboriginals have no doubt benefited from the opportunity to communicate with fellow indigenous peoples throughout the world, thanks to the wonders of modern technology. Whether resident in Canada or in other countries, indigenous peoples have also made some progress because of the attention they have achieved at the United Nations, another globalizing phenomenon. Indeed, the United Nations has frequently criticized Canada's treatment of its Aboriginal peoples, most especially in the 1981 Sandra Lovelace case, where it cited the discrimination against Aboriginal women contained in the Indian Act. However, even before globalization was full-blown, Aboriginals suffered in deals that involved the cross-border export of electricity, especially from Quebec to the United States, and they have experienced corporate exploitation, national and transnational, in other provinces and territories too. To the extent that globalization involves the neoliberal ideal of self-reliance, many Aboriginals would like to substitute their own self-governing institutions for those of the wider political system. But operating in the weakened state that they are, they still need sympathetic government support, although not the degree of regulation that has been so prevalent in the past.

. . . .

DISCUSSION QUESTIONS

1. How have Aboriginal identities changed in recent years?

2. What are the causes of the generally poor condition of Aboriginal life in Canada?

3. What are the principal Aboriginal demands on the political agenda, and how far can or should the government go to address them?

4. What can be done to make First Nations reserves more economically viable?

5. What is meant by Aboriginal self-government? How far should it go?

6. How would an Aboriginal justice system interact with Canada's traditional justice system?

7. What can be done to improve the living conditions of urban Aboriginals?

. . . .

NOTES

1. For example, Taiaiake Alfred, *Peace, Power, Righteousness: An Indigenous Manifesto* (Toronto: Oxford University Press, 1999), xv.
2. On the subject of Aboriginal women, see the work of Joyce Green, including *Making Space for Indigenous Feminism* (Black Point, NS: Fernwood Books, 2007).

3. See the contrasting views on this subject in Alan C. Cairns, *Citizens Plus: Aboriginal Peoples and the Canadian State* (Vancouver: UBC Press, 2000); Cairns, *First Nations and the Canadian State: In Search of Coexistence* (Montreal: McGill-Queen's University Press, 2005); Thomas Flanagan, *First Nations? Second Thoughts* (Montreal: McGill-Queen's University Press, 2000); Tim Shouls, *Shifting Boundaries: Aboriginal Identity, Pluralist Theory, and the Politics of Self-Government* (Vancouver: UBC Press, 2003); Heidi Libesman, "In Search of a Postcolonial Theory of Normative Integration: Reflections on A.C. Cairns' Theory of *Citizens Plus*", *Canadian Journal of Political Science* (December 2005); and Mark Charlton and Paul Barker, eds., *Crosscurrents: Contemporary Political Issues*, 6th ed. (Toronto: Nelson Education, 2009), ch. 2.

4. Alfred, *Peace, Power, Righteousness*; Taiaiake Alfred, *Wasase: Indigenous Pathways of Action and Freedom* (Peterborough: Broadview Press, 2005); Kiera Ladner, "*Aysaka'paykinit*: Contesting the Rope Around the Nations' Neck," in Miriam Smith, ed., *Group Politics and Social Movements in Canada* (Peterborough: Broadview Press, 2008).

5. Statistics Canada, "Aboriginal Peoples in Canada in 2006: Inuit, Métis and First Nations, 2006 Census," Catalogue no. 97-558, available at http://www12.statcan.ca/English/census06/analysis/aboriginals. This report notes that Canada has the second-largest proportion of indigenous peoples of any country; New Zealand's proportion is 15 percent, while the United States has two percent.

6. Statistics from Indian Affairs Canada and Statistics Canada sometimes vary considerably. See Indian Affairs and Northern Development Canada, *Basic Departmental Data*, 2004 (December 2005), and the departmental website, Historical Trends—Registered Indian Population Canada 1982–2007, available at http://www.ainc-inac.gc.ca/ai/rs/pubs/sts/ht/ht-can-eng.pdf.

7. *Basic Departmental Data*; Peter R. Oberle, *The Incidence of Family Poverty on Canadian Indian Reserves* (Ottawa: Indian and Northern Affairs Canada, 1993); and Geoffrey York, *The Dispossessed: Life and Death in Native Canada* (Toronto: Lester & Orpen Dennys, 1989).

8. John Milloy, "*A National Crime*": *The Canadian Government and the Residential School System, 1879 to 1986* (Winnipeg: University of Manitoba Press, 1998).

9. National Chief of the Assembly of First Nations Phil Fontaine responded to charges about the corruption and nepotism practised by some chiefs by reminding us that most of the members of the former non-Aboriginal Grant Devine government in Saskatchewan were convicted of corruption.

10. In his book, *A Fair Country: Telling Truths about Canada* (Toronto: Viking Canada, 2008), John Ralston Saul contends that Canada's entire political culture is based on Aboriginal values.

11. The Royal Proclamation was a strong statement on Indian rights, and today's Aboriginal Canadians point to the significance of its inclusion in the 1982 Charter of Rights. It can be found, among other places, in Michael Asch, *Home and Native Land: Aboriginal Rights and the Canadian Constitution* (Toronto: Methuen, 1984) and at http://www.canadiana.org/citm/primary/primary_e.html. See Darlene Johnston, *The Taking of Indian Lands: Consent or Coercion?* (Saskatoon: University of Saskatchewan Native Law Centre, 1989).

12. Thomas R. Berger, *A Long and Terrible Shadow: White Values, Native Rights in the Americas* (Vancouver: Douglas & McIntyre, 1991).

13. A subsequent and controversial relocation occurred in 1953–55. See Royal Commission on Aboriginal Peoples, *The High Arctic Relocation* (Ottawa: Supply and Services Canada, 1994, Catalogue No. Z1-1991/1-41-3-1E).

14. Thomas Berger, *Northern Frontier, Northern Homeland: The Report of the Mackenzie Valley Inquiry* (Ottawa: Supply and Services Canada, 1977), republished by Douglas & McIntyre, Vancouver, 1988.

15. Asch, *Home and Native Land*, pp. 32–37, and Michael Asch, ed., *Aboriginal and Treaty Rights in Canada: Essays on Law, Equality and Respect for Difference* (Vancouver: UBC Press, 1997).

16. Indian and Northern Affairs Canada, *Comprehensive Claims Policy and Status of Claims*, March 2002; cited on February 11, 2003; available at http://www.ainc-inac.gc.ca/ps/clm/brieff_e.pdf; and Michael S. Whittington, "Aboriginal Self-Government," in Michael Whittington and Glen Williams, eds., *Canadian Politics in the 21st Century*, 6th ed. (Scarborough: Nelson, 2004).

17. *Delgamuukw v. British Columbia*, [1997] 3 S.C.R. 1010; *Calder v. Attorney General of B.C.*, [1973] S.C.R. 313; *Guerin v. The Queen*, [1984] 2 S.C.R. 335; and *Ontario (Attorney General) v. Bear Island Foundation*, [1991] S.C.R. 570; Mary C. Hurley, "Aboriginal Title: The Supreme Court of Canada Decision in *Delgamuukw v. British Columbia*," Library of Parliament Background Paper No. BP-459E

(February 2000); and Stan Persky, *Delgamuukw: The Supreme Court of Canada Decision on Aboriginal Title* (Vancouver: Douglas and McIntyre, 1998).

18. Mary C. Hurley, "The Nisga'a Final Agreement," Library of Parliament, PRB99-2E (September 2001); and Karen E. Lochead, "Whose Land is it Anyway? The Long Road to the Nisga'a Treaty," in Robert M. Campbell, Leslie A. Pal, and Michael Howlett, eds., *The Real Worlds of Canadian Politics*, 4th ed. (Peterborough: Broadview Press, 2004).

19. *Ross River Dena Council Band v. Canada*, [2002] 2 S.C.R. 816.

20. *R. v. Sioui*, [1990] 1 S.C.R. 1025; *R. v. Sparrow*, [1990] 1 S.C.R. 1075. See also Kiera Ladner, "Up the Creek: Fishing for a New Constitutional Order," *Canadian Journal of Political Science* (December 2005).

21. *R. v. Marshall*, [1999] 3 S.C.R. 456 and *R. v. Marshall*, [1999] 3 S.C.R. 533; Ken Coates, *The Marshall Decision and Native Rights* (Montreal: McGill-Queen's University Press, 2000); *R. v. Marshall*; *R. v. Bernard* [2005] 2 S.C.R. 220; and Kiera L. Ladner, "Up the Creek: Fishing for a New Constitutional Order."

22. Christopher Alcantara, "Explaining Aboriginal Treaty Negotiation Outcomes in Canada: The Cases of the Inuit and Innu in Labrador," *Canadian Journal of Political Science* (March 2007).

23. Geoffrey York and Loreen Pindera, *People of the Pines: The Warriors and the Legacy of Oka* (Toronto: Little Brown, 1991); Craig MacLaine and Michael Baxendale, *This Land Is Our Land* (Toronto: Optimum, 1990); and Robert Campbell and Leslie Pal, *The Real Worlds of Canadian Politics*, 2nd ed. (Peterborough: Broadview Press, 1991), ch. 4.

24. Murray Angus, *"And the Last Shall Be First": Native Policy in an Era of Cutbacks* (Toronto: NC Press, 1991).

25. Bruce Clark, *Native Liberty, Crown Sovereignty: The Existing Aboriginal Right to Self-Government in Canada* (Montreal: McGill-Queen's University Press, 1990), argues that this right already exists and that what Aboriginals need is money, land, and cooperation to be able to exercise this right.

26. Whittington, "Aboriginal Self-Government."

27. Georges Erasmus, "Opening Remarks," First Ministers' Conference on Aboriginal Constitutional Affairs, Ottawa, March 26, 1987. See also Frank Cassidy, ed., *Aboriginal Self-Government* (Halifax: Institute for Research on Public Policy, 1991).

28. In his subsequent "pro-Aboriginal phase," Premier Campbell became one of the strongest supporters of Aboriginal causes.

29. Whittington, "Aboriginal Self-Government"; and Audrey Doerr, "Building New Orders of Government—The Future of Aboriginal Self-Government," *Canadian Public Administration* (Summer 1997).

30. Royal Commission on Aboriginal Peoples, *Report of the Royal Commission on Aboriginal Peoples* (Ottawa: Supply and Services, 1996, Catalogue No. Z1-1991/1-1E).

31. Whittington, "Aboriginal Self-Government"; and Gurston Dacks, "Implementing First Nations Self-Government in Yukon: Lessons for Canada," *Canadian Journal of Political Science* (September 2004).

32. Suzanne Reber and Robert Renaud, *Starlight Tour: The Last, Lonely Night of Neil Stonechild* (Toronto: Random House Canada, 2005); Joyce Green, "From Stonechild to Social Cohesion: Anti-Racist Challenges for Saskatchewan, *Canadian Journal of Political Science* (September 2006).

33. *Corbiere v. Canada (Minister of Indian and Northern Affairs)*, [1999] 2 S.C.R. 203; and *R. v. Gladue*, [1999] 1 S.C.R. 688; *R. v. Armbruster*, [1999] BCCA 448.

34. *R. v. Powley*, [2003] 2 S.C.R. 207; *Haida Nation v. British Columbia (Minister of Forests)*, [2004] 3 S.C.R. 511; *Taku River Tlingit First Nation v. British Columbia (Project Assessment Director)*, [2004] 3 S.C.R. 550; *R. v. Marshall*; *R. v. Bernard*; *R. v. Sappier*; *R. v. Gray* (December 7, 2006).

35. Kenneth McRoberts, "Quebec: Province, Nation, or Distinct Society?" in Michael S. Whittington and Glen Williams, eds., *Canadian Politics in the 21st Century*, 6th ed. (Toronto: Nelson, 2004), p. 420.

36. Law Commission of Canada, *Urban Aboriginal Governance in Canada: Re-fashioning the Dialogue* (Ottawa, 1999, Catalogue No. JL 2-5-/1999E); and David Newhouse and Evelyn Peters, eds., *Not Strangers in These Parts: Urban Aboriginal Peoples* (Ottawa: Policy Research Initiative, 2003).

37. Cairns, *Citizen Plus*, p. 212; and Heidi Libesman, "In Search of a Postcolonial Theory of Normative Integration: Reflections on A.C. Cairns' Theory of Citizens Plus."

38. Tim Shouls, *Shifting Boundaries: Aboriginal Identity, Pluralist Theory, and the Politics of Self-Government.*

· ·

FURTHER READING

Alfred, Taiaiake. *Wasase: Indigenous Pathways of Action and Freedom*. Peterborough: Broadview Press, 2005.

Cairns, Alan C. *Citizens Plus: Aboriginal Peoples and the Canadian State*. Vancouver: UBC Press, 2000.

Cairns, Alan C. *First Nations and the Canadian State: In Search of Coexistence*. Montreal: McGill-Queen's University Press, 2005.

Campbell, Robert M., Leslie A. Pal, and Michael Howlett, eds. *The Real Worlds of Canadian Politics: Cases in Process and Policy*, 4th ed. Peterborough: Broadview Press, 2004.

Frideres, James S. and René Gadacz. *Aboriginal Peoples in Canada*, 8th ed. Toronto: Pearson Education Canada, 2008.

Green, Joyce, ed. *Making Space for Indigenous Feminism*. Black Point, NS: Fernwood Books, 2007.

Milloy, John. *"A National Crime": The Canadian Government and the Residential School System, 1879 to 1986*. Winnipeg: University of Manitoba Press, 1998.

Morrison, Andrea. *Justice for Natives: Searching for Common Ground*. Montreal: McGill-Queen's University Press, 1997.

Murphy, Michael, ed. *Canada: The State of the Federation 2003: Reconfiguring Aboriginal-State Relations*. Montreal: McGill-Queen's University Press, 2005.

Shouls, Tim. *Shifting Boundaries: Aboriginal Identity, Pluralist Theory, and the Politics of Self-Government*. Vancouver: UBC Press, 2003.

Warry, Wayne, *Ending Denial: Understanding Aboriginal Issues*. Toronto: University of Toronto Press, 2007.

Whittington, Michael S. "Aboriginal Self-Government." In Michael Whittington and Glen Williams, eds., *Canadian Politics in the 21st Century*, 6th ed. Toronto: Nelson, 2004.

Woolford, Andrew. *Between Justice and Certainty: Treaty Making in British Columbia*. Vancouver: UBC Press, 2005.

Chapter 5

French Canada
AND THE QUEBEC
Question

Canada experienced French–English conscription crises in both world wars. In the late 1960s, Parliament enacted the controversial Official Languages Act, making the federal government officially bilingual. In the 1970s and 1980s, Quebec introduced a French-only sign law and demanded constitutional recognition of the province as a distinct society. The increasing unilingualism of Quebec and the expansion of bilingualism in the rest of the country seemed unfair to many Canadians. The "rest of Canada" generally felt that Ottawa was giving preferential treatment to Quebec in government policy and spending to persuade it to stay within Confederation.

Whether considered in terms of ethnicity, language, or culture, the French minority is at least as problematic in Canadian politics as the regional conflicts discussed in Chapter 3, and the two reinforce each other in the question of Quebec's place in Confederation. Among all the ethnic/linguistic/cultural issues in Canada, the French question has always had the greatest significance, reflecting the fact that it is the largest such minority, that it has been here longer than any other group besides the Aboriginals, and that it has a territorial base in Quebec. The very size of Quebec and French Canada make them of crucial importance in federal politics, but this significance is complicated by the variety and strength of identities felt by different members of the French minority.

This chapter begins with a numerical profile of the French–English linguistic picture in Canada today,[1] and a brief survey of theoretical considerations, including questions of identity and Quebec nationalism. It then examines the history of French–English relations up to 1960, followed by a discussion of the Quiet Revolution in Quebec. After outlining contrasting visions held by different groups, the chapter traces developments in French–English relations at the federal level, in Quebec, and in the other provinces since 1970. It concludes with a review of contemporary issues.

THE FRENCH–ENGLISH DEMOGRAPHIC PROFILE IN CANADA TODAY

The distribution of French and English communities within and outside Quebec today is shown in Table 5.1. Although Statistics Canada gathers figures on ethnic origin, mother tongue, and language spoken at home, it is difficult to use statistics on ethnic origin because

TABLE 5.1		Mother Tongue in Quebec, the Other Provinces, Canada Outside Quebec, and Canada as a Whole (Percentages), 2006 Census					

	English	*French*	*Other*		*English*	*French*	*Other*
Quebec	8.2	79.6	12.3	British Columbia	71.2	1.4	27.4
New Brunswick	64.7	32.7	2.6	Newfoundland/ Labrador	97.6	0.4	2.0
Ontario	69.1	4.2	26.6	Yukon	85.4	3.9	10.8
Prince Edward Island	93.6	4.2	2.3	Northwest Territories	77.3	2.4	20.3
Manitoba	74.6	4.0	21.4	Nunavut	27.0	1.3	71.7
Nova Scotia	92.3	3.7	3.9	Canada Outside Quebec	73.3	4.1	22.6
Alberta	79.6	2.0	18.4	Canada	57.8	22.1	20.1
Saskatchewan	85.5	1.8	12.8				

Source: Statistics Canada. Population of non-official mother tongues, Canada, provinces, territories and Canada less Quebec, 1996 to 2006. Table A-1. Found at: http://www12.statcan.ca/english/census06/analysis/language/tables/ annexA1.htm; Table A-3. Found at: http://www12.statcan.ca/english/census06/analysis/language/tables/annexA3. htm; Table A-5. Found at: http://www12.statcan.ca/english/census06/analysis/language/tables/annexA5.htm

so many Canadians are now an ethnic mixture and because an increasing number prefer to call themselves "Canadians." It is more reliable to use figures for mother tongue, even though this is a measure of linguistics rather than ethnicity. Employing mother-tongue and home-language figures, then, we label the groups anglophone, francophone, and allophone, the last being those with a mother tongue other than English or French.

According to the 2006 census, the number of people in Canada as a whole having English as their mother tongue was 18.1 million, or 57.8 percent of the population, while those having French as their mother tongue numbered 6.9 million, or 22.1 percent. Both of these groups increased over the 1986–2006 period in absolute numbers, but their percentage of the total dropped, primarily because of the high immigration levels of those having other linguistic backgrounds. The number of Canadians with another mother tongue was 6.3 million, or 20.1 percent, but none of these allophone groups came close to the number of French; Chinese, the third-largest mother tongue, constituted only three percent.

The Quebec population is made up of 5.9 million francophones and 607 165 anglophones, or 79.6 and 8.2 percent, respectively. It also contains 911 895 or 12.3 percent allophones, those with a non-official language as their mother tongue. Although 85.8 percent of all Canadian francophones live in Quebec, almost one million francophones live outside Quebec, and about 1.5 million residents of Quebec have a mother tongue other than French. Thus, while Quebec is predominantly French, and Canada outside Quebec is predominantly English, an important distinction should be made between French Canada and Quebec (see Table 5.2). Outside Quebec, francophones are located primarily in Ontario and New Brunswick.

TABLE 5.2   Composition of French Canada Compared with Quebec

French Canada	Quebec
6 892 230 francophone Canadians, of whom	5 916 840 francophones
5 916 840 live in Quebec, and	607 165 anglophones
975 390 live outside Quebec	911 895 allophones

Source: Statistics Canada. Population of non-official mother tongues, Canada, provinces, territories and Canada less Quebec, 1996 to 2006. Table A-1. Found at: http://www12.statcan.ca/english/census06/analysis/language/tables/ annexA1.htm; Table A-3. Found at: http://www12.statcan.ca/english/census06/analysis/language/tables/annexA3. htm; Table A-5. Found at: http://www12.statcan.ca/english/census06/analysis/language/tables/annexA5.htm.

Statistics on official bilingualism reveal that 17.4 percent of the total population could carry on a conversation in both official languages, including 35.8 percent of francophones in Quebec and 83.6 percent of francophones outside Quebec. For Anglophones, the figures were about 70 percent in Quebec and 7.5 percent outside Quebec.[2] In other words, the highest rates of official bilingualism are among francophones outside Quebec and anglophones inside Quebec.

. . . .

THEORETICAL CONSIDERATIONS
Identities and Quebec Nationalism

Given this numerical distribution, there has never been a single French-Canadian or even Quebec identity, and such identities have changed considerably over the years. Most, but not all, francophones in Quebec have historically wanted protection or autonomy from the federal government. But content until 1960 with their identity as conservative, family-oriented Roman Catholics, they did not demand much else from the provincial government. This all changed in the 1960s with the Quiet Revolution in Quebec and a wholesale reversal of values. All of a sudden, francophone Quebeckers aggressively wanted control over all aspects of Quebec life, including the economy and language policy, and began to call themselves "Québécois." They increasingly saw themselves as a majority in Quebec rather than a minority within Canada, as they had in the past. The desire of most Quebec francophones for an activist provincial government led them to demand more autonomy from Ottawa than ever before: in many aspects of social and economic policy, they wanted to do things their own way. Francophones outside Quebec were similarly quite docile before 1960, accepting their minority status with resignation, and possessing a subdued identity. But energized by the Québécois, francophone minorities in the other provinces developed more positive identities over the past 50 years, sometimes associating themselves with their brethren in Quebec, but often linking themselves to each other. Their demands were mainly in the realm of language and culture, education, and the provision of provincial services in French. A small number of Quebec francophones identified with such a French Canada that extended across the country rather than with a more autonomous Quebec.

Related to such identities and central to the question of French–English relations and the position of Quebec in Canada is the phenomenon of Quebec nationalism. This feeling of primary loyalty to Quebec emanates from the widely held notion that it is home to a distinctive French-Canadian nation, centred on language, ethnicity, culture, history, and territory. Before 1960, these factors were reinforced by religion. Over the centuries, Quebec nationalism has taken many twists and turns, but it was always embraced by almost all francophone Quebeckers. It has been a driving force in both provincial and federal politics, and it has usually stood for a substantial degree of political autonomy or self-determination. Francophone Quebeckers valued autonomy because Quebec was different and because they felt that such autonomy had been guaranteed in 1867. Most considered that Confederation had been a pact between two ethnic groups, English and French, and many held to the "compact theory of Confederation" that no changes could be made to the constitution without the approval of both groups, or at least the consent of the province of Quebec.

Before 1960, Quebec nationalism was largely inward-looking and defensive, primarily concerned with ensuring that the federal government kept out of that province's affairs. It was a nationalism of "survival," and was closely tied to the Roman Catholic Church. The province's identity, as extolled by such historians as Lionel Groulx, promoted the superiority of a rural, religious, family-oriented, isolated, defensive, simple, and unsophisticated French way of life.

Dominated by the authoritarian Premier Maurice Duplessis from 1935 to 1960, the population was taught that only he could protect them from evil external influences, such as Ottawa. Duplessis governed with three main allies: the Church, which he empowered to oversee social policy; the farmers, who were overrepresented in the legislature; and American capital, which was encouraged to enter the province and create jobs for those who were no longer needed on the farm. Duplessis was unconcerned about working conditions in these new resource and manufacturing operations or about the fact that, because the companies were foreign owned, employees had to master English to be promoted.

The forces of modernization, urbanization, secularization, and democratization had become explosive by the time Duplessis died in 1959, and Quebec has possessed quite a different kind of nationalism since its "Quiet Revolution." After 1960, Quebec nationalism was characterized by a new collective self-confidence; it is urban, modern, secular, democratic, and bureaucratic. Rather than having an inward-looking obsession with survival, it became outward-looking and aggressive, and focused on expansion and growth. Post-1960 Quebec nationalism sought to protect and promote the French language and culture, to increase the powers of the provincial government, and to reverse the dominance of Anglo and external economic power in the province. As before, most francophone Quebeckers retained a primary loyalty to their province but not one that necessarily interfered with their allegiance to the wider country of Canada. A large proportion of the population turned their back on the Church, although most continued to be nominal Roman Catholics. As noted below, however, the ethnic and religious composition of the province soon began to change.

Different Conceptions of French Canada

The fact that most, but not all, francophones live in Quebec has given rise to two basic models with which to address the question of how to deal with the distinctiveness of French Canada. The first—the territorial principle—would recognize Quebec as the homeland of French Canada and give that province powers and resources to protect and promote its linguistic and cultural distinctiveness. Quebec would be granted some kind of special status, distinct from other provinces, and essentially be "French," while the rest of Canada would primarily be "English."[3] The second option—the personality principle—would treat Quebec as "une province comme les autres," recognize the existence of French Canada across the country, and promote bilingualism at the federal level and in the other provinces and territories.

English Canadians had difficulty accepting these demands, which seemed excessive and contradictory: making Quebec more French and more autonomous at the same time as promoting French in Ottawa and in the other provinces and territories. They did not understand that the two demands came largely from two different groups of francophones, with contrary conceptions of French Canada.

. . . .

HISTORICAL OVERVIEW OF FRENCH–ENGLISH RELATIONS
Pre-Confederation Developments

Almost every Canadian political decision since 1759 has reflected the French–English division to some extent, and the tensions that currently threaten the continued existence of the country can probably best be understood in historical context. As outlined in Chapter 2, the French first colonized what is now the province of Quebec, but when the British defeated them on the Plains of Abraham, many changes occurred in the colony. Except for the clergy and the seigneurs, the French elite retreated to France, leaving the British to take control of the economy. The British also formed the government, and the conquerors assumed that the population would soon become "English."

Certain things did not change, however. The people continued to speak French and attend the Roman Catholic Church, which became a highly influential and autonomous organization. It would probably have been impossible to transform Quebec into an Anglo-Protestant colony—at least without a great deal of coercion and immigration—and the British soon exhibited a policy of tolerance and accommodation. By the time of the **Quebec Act** of 1774, the British recognized the inevitable, and guaranteed the French their religious rights and their own system of civil law.

As "English" immigrants moved into what is now Ontario in the 1780s, especially the United Empire Loyalists from the new United States, it became logical to divide the colony into two: Lower Canada (Quebec) would be essentially French Catholic, and Upper Canada (Ontario) would be Anglo Protestant. This separation was recognized in the **Constitutional Act of 1791**.

Difficulties between the popular assembly and the appointed executive and legislative councils became increasingly serious after 1800, culminating in armed revolts in both colonies in 1837. The battle for more popular control in Lower Canada was complicated by the ethnic factor, as French Canadians were predominant in the assembly alone. Lord Durham felt that the ethnic problem could only be solved by another attempt to assimilate the French. Hence, he recommended that the two colonies be reunited into the colony of Canada, in which English would be the official language and the anglophone population of the rapidly expanding western portion (Ontario) would soon outnumber the French.

This final attempt at assimilation, incorporated in the **Act of Union**, was to no avail. In recognition of its failure, the French language was increasingly used along with English in the government, cabinets were usually alliances between English and French leaders, and the legislature operated on the informal principle of the double majority—legislation had to have the approval of a majority of representatives from both sections of the colony.

Given this historical evolution, the logic of Confederation and the cultural guarantees of section 133 of the **Constitution Act, 1867** are perfectly understandable. Both French and English could be used in all aspects of the new federal Parliament, and laws were passed in both languages. Both languages could also be used in whatever federal courts were later established. The francophone minorities in Ontario, Nova Scotia, and New Brunswick were inarticulate and ignored, even though the Acadian minority in New Brunswick constituted 16 percent of the provincial population. However, the anglophone minority in Quebec, at 20 percent and centred in Montreal, was well organized and in control of the economy of the province. This fact ensured that English could be used along with French in the legislature and courts of Quebec. None of these constitutional provisions was particularly controversial in 1867, and protection of the Protestant school system in Quebec and the Roman Catholic system in Ontario attracted greater interest. With religious rights seen in educational terms and language rights applying only to legislatures and courts, no constitutional rights were granted to minority-language schools.

· ·

OFFICIAL BILINGUALISM IN THE CONSTITUTION ACT, 1867

- Federal Parliament, proceedings, and laws
- Federal courts
- Quebec parliament, proceedings, and laws
- Quebec courts

Ethnic/Linguistic Conflicts, 1867–1960
THE RIEL REBELLIONS

Although the two language groups have been regularly accommodated in government circles since 1867, six serious linguistic conflicts erupted from the time of Confederation to 1960. The first Riel Rebellion precipitated the creation of the province of Manitoba in 1870, as the French-Catholic Métis Louis Riel led the fight for provincial status. During that uprising, and in a situation of uncertain government authority, an Ontario Orangeman was executed by a Métis court-martial. Riel maintained a fairly low profile afterward, but in 1885 he re-emerged in what is now Saskatchewan to lead the second Riel Rebellion on behalf of western Aboriginals who had been treated shamefully by the government. After quelling the rebellion, the federal government charged Riel with treason and he was found guilty in a famous trial in Regina. Ethnic and religious tensions across the country rose to a fever pitch, for while English Protestants regarded Riel as a murderer, traitor, and madman, French Catholics believed he was a patriot and a saint. To Prime Minister John A. Macdonald fell the unenviable decision of whether to let Riel hang or to use the executive power of mercy to spare him. Caught in the middle of this heated confrontation, Macdonald followed the will of the majority and had Riel hanged. This exacerbated the level of French-Catholic outrage across the country, especially in Quebec. As a result, Honoré Mercier and his Parti National were elected in that province in 1886, and the close attachment of the people of Quebec to Macdonald's Conservative Party was permanently damaged. Moreover, Mercier argued that the Riel affair had demonstrated the lack of French-Canadian influence in Ottawa, leading him to demand greater autonomy for the province of Quebec.

BILINGUALISM IN MANITOBA

The third linguistic conflict occurred in Manitoba in 1890. Since the small settlement was about equally divided between French and English, Riel had insisted that the 1870 Manitoba Act follow the Quebec precedent of giving the two languages official status in the new province's legislature and courts. (Because the province was equally divided between Protestants and Roman Catholics, the separate school system was also guaranteed.) After its creation, however, Manitoba attracted thousands of English-speaking immigrants and others who chose to identify with the anglophone community. Hence, in 1890, the anglophone majority passed the Official Language Act which removed the official status of French in the province's legislature and courts. To solidify its control of the province, the same group abolished the separate school system; both moves led to French-Catholic opposition within Manitoba and beyond.[4]

. . . .

TIME LINE

Major French–English Conflicts, 1867–1945

1870	First Riel Rebellion
1885	Second Riel Rebellion
1890	Manitoba's Official Language Act
1913	Ontario's Regulation 17
1917	First conscription crisis
1944	Second conscription crisis

FRENCH SCHOOLS IN ONTARIO: REGULATION 17

The fourth main linguistic conflict concerned minority French-language education rights in Ontario. Although minority-language schools had not been constitutionally guaranteed, the Protestant schools in Quebec, mostly in Montreal, naturally operated in English, and it was only logical that French-language schools be established in francophone parts of New Brunswick and Ontario. In 1913 the Whitney government issued Regulation 17, which virtually abolished the use of French in the Ontario school system; English was to become the sole language of instruction after the third year, and the study of French as a subject was limited to one hour a day. Whitney claimed that he was doing Franco-Ontarian citizens a favour by forcing them to learn English in an English-speaking province, but those affected denounced the regulation and challenged it in court. The 1917 *Mackell* case confirmed, however, that constitutional protection in educational matters applied only to religious minorities, not linguistic ones.[5]

THE FIRST CONSCRIPTION CRISIS

The Regulation 17 incident in Ontario had its greatest implications in Quebec during the **conscription crisis** of the First World War. As a British colony, Canada was automatically at war, but could determine its own degree of involvement. Despite small standing armed forces, the Conservative government of Robert Borden made major commitments. Appeals for volunteers had promising results initially, but as reinforcements were needed later in the war, few recruits came forward. The government therefore decided to resort to conscription—compulsory military service—in 1917. Borden knew that French Canada generally felt indifferent to the conflict and that conscription would divide the country along ethnic lines. Having few French Canadians in his Cabinet to start with, the prime minister appealed to Liberal leader Wilfrid Laurier to join him in a coalition government. Laurier refused the offer, although most of the anglophone Liberal MPs did join in a **Union Government** in 1917. The subsequent enforcement of conscription entailed considerable violence. A riot in Quebec City in the spring of 1918, which the federal government sought to quell by sending in the army, left four people dead and many others injured. This confrontation destroyed what little French-Canadian support remained for the Conservative Party after the execution of Louis Riel.

THE SECOND CONSCRIPTION CRISIS

Ontario repealed Regulation 17 in 1927 and French–English tensions returned to a normal, controllable level until they were inflamed by another conscription crisis during the Second World War. In 1939, the Liberal Prime Minister Mackenzie King was in power with a strong contingent of ministers and MPs from Quebec. Although still closely allied with Britain, Canada entered the war as an independent country, and its leader was extremely cautious in determining its degree of involvement. King knew that conscription would be resisted in French Canada, so he was even more reluctant than Borden to adopt it. After first promising not to impose conscription, he held a national plebiscite to let himself off the hook. Although 80 percent of voters outside Quebec agreed to release King from his promise, Quebeckers voted 73 percent against. On the basis of the slogan "conscription if necessary, but not necessarily conscription," King managed to postpone the adoption of compulsory military service until almost the end of the war. Given the sensitivity with which conscription was imposed on this occasion, King is credited by most observers with having skillfully kept the country together in the circumstances.

THE QUIET REVOLUTION: QUEBEC IN THE 1960S

As noted, the Quebec of the past 50 years is quite a different province and society from the one that existed before 1960. After that date, the province underwent a **Quiet Revolution**, consisting of a dramatic change of values, attitudes, and behaviour of French-Canadian Quebeckers, a new collective self-confidence, a new brand of nationalism, and an enormous expansion of the role of the provincial state. These features of the new Quebec had many implications for French–English relations in both the Quebec and the Canadian political systems.

The government of Jean Lesage (1960–66) took over many of the functions previously administered by the Church.[6] The most important of these was education, which was radically modernized. Health and welfare programs were also made public rather than charitable responsibilities. With the nationalization of private power companies, Hydro-Québec became a huge Crown corporation supplying all the electricity in the province. Lesage also reformed almost every piece of legislation on the books, especially labour and electoral laws; added reams of new ones; and created many government agencies.

. . . .

TIME LINE

French–English Relations, 1945–1970

1949–59	Opposition to Maurice Duplessis grows
1960–66	Quebec Quiet Revolution
1963–68	Royal Commission on Bilingualism and Biculturalism
1968	Pierre Trudeau becomes PM
1968–69	Official Languages Act
1970	FLQ crisis

All these new and expanded public responsibilities required substantial additional revenues, and Lesage put immense pressure on Ottawa to increase federal–provincial grants, to allow Quebec to opt out of the conditions attached to them, and to give the province a greater share of joint taxation. In areas of provincial jurisdiction, Quebec began to move toward distinctive programs, such as designing its own pension plan, which was then used as a model for the Canada Pension Plan. As time went on, the province demanded ever-larger powers, including international francophone links, leading to perpetual federal–provincial discord. In the Quebec private sector, francophones had lower incomes and lower-status jobs than anglophones, but the Lesage government did little of substance to rectify this situation, probably for fear of driving out Anglo-Canadian and foreign investment.

Much of the analysis of the Quiet Revolution centres on the concept of the **new middle class**—civil servants, teachers, professors, and other salaried professionals. Since upward mobility was still difficult in the English-dominated private sector, this new class used Quebec nationalism to further its own aspirations in the expansion of the Quebec state.[7] They sponsored an enormous increase in provincial government programs and agencies.

During the early 1960s, the federal government grappled somewhat haphazardly with Quebec's new demands. The Diefenbaker government (1957–63) introduced simultaneous English/French interpretation into Parliament, began printing all federal government cheques in a bilingual format, and appointed a French-Canadian governor general. Immediately after taking office, the Pearson government (1963–68) established the **Royal Commission on Bilingualism and Biculturalism** "to inquire into and report upon the existing state of bilingualism and biculturalism in Canada and to recommend what steps should be taken to develop the Canadian Confederation on the basis of an equal partnership between the two founding races." Even before the commission reported, however, Pearson felt obliged to act on Quebec's demands. He gave Quebec and the other provinces more federal funds and taxation power, removed conditions from many shared-cost programs, and permitted Quebec to make international arrangements with France.

At the same time, and partly due to the influence of his new Justice Minister, Pierre Elliott Trudeau, Pearson sought to strengthen the position of French Canadians at the federal level. One of their priorities was that French be used as a language equal to English in the corridors of power in Ottawa. Such federally-oriented Quebec francophones were also concerned about the fate of francophone minorities in the other provinces. The new self-confidence of the Québécois inspired these dwindling minorities to greater self-assertiveness.

Although the British North America Act of 1867 provided that either English or French could be used in the federal Parliament and courts, the extent of official bilingualism in Ottawa before 1960 was minimal in the executive branch, where English was the working language of the public service, at least at policymaking levels.[8] In response to the demands of francophones who did not focus on Quebec, Pearson and Trudeau introduced an Official Languages bill so that the Canadian public service would operate on a bilingual basis, much to the consternation of those unilingual public servants who were now pressured to learn French. Parliament passed the **Official Languages Act** in 1969, and since that time Canada has been officially and effectively bilingual in its federal institutions.[9] Ottawa also began to support French immersion educational programs as well as to assist francophone minorities in other provinces.

. . . .

PRINCIPAL PROVISIONS OF THE OFFICIAL LANGUAGES ACT, 1969

- Canada is a country with two official languages, English and French, and both languages have equal status, rights, and privileges in federal government institutions.
- Canadians have the right to full and equal access to Parliament and to the laws and courts and the right to be served by and communicate with the institutions of the federal government in either English or French in any office across the country or abroad where significant demand exists.
- Canadians employed by the federal government have the right to work in the official language of their choice wherever practicable, and both English- and French-speaking Canadians are ensured of equitable opportunities for employment and advancement in federal institutions so that the federal public service is representative of the two official language groups.
- The Canadian government is committed to supporting the vitality of English- and French-speaking minority communities, especially by encouraging and assisting the provinces and territories in providing minority-language and second-language education.

Trudeau succeeded Pearson as prime minister in 1968, and the question of French–English relations, or "national unity," was the principal political issue throughout the 16 years that he was in power. Trudeau fought against recognition of Quebec as the homeland of French Canada and opposed giving that province special recognition or power. He argued that any kind of special status would be the first step toward separation; he feared that a nationalistic French Quebec would go back to being inward-looking and intolerant; and he felt that francophone Quebeckers would have more opportunity if they followed his example, became bilingual, and participated in the life of a larger country. Part of Trudeau's popularity in English Canada stemmed from the perception that he was "anti-Quebec," but he was passionately "pro-French" in promoting bilingualism in Ottawa and across the country.

During the 1960s, advocates of a third option had also emerged: Quebec separatism. Those who advocated that Quebec become a separate, sovereign state took their nationalistic feelings to the extreme and argued that Quebec would be better off without its connection to Canada. Most such separatists or sovereignists were democratic by nature and proceeded to use persuasion to advance their cause, but a small wing of the movement, the **Front de libération du Québec (FLQ)**, resorted to violence. Periodic bombings killed several people and injured at least 27 others during the 1960s. Then, in October 1970, two small cells of the FLQ kidnapped a British diplomat and abducted and murdered Quebec cabinet minister Pierre Laporte. Trudeau invoked the coercive **War Measures Act**, giving the police and armed forces special

The invocation of the War Measures Act in 1970 in connection with the FLQ crisis included the visible presence of armed soldiers in Montreal and Ottawa.

THE CANADIAN PRESS

powers to quell the violence, and more than 400 innocent, peaceful separatist supporters were arrested in the process. By crushing the FLQ, by giving French Canadians more clout in Ottawa, and by constitutionalizing pan-Canadian bilingualism, Trudeau hoped to undercut any Quebec demand for special status or separation.

QUEBEC AND FRENCH CANADA SINCE 1970
The 1970s

Despite the fact that a centralist Trudeau government was in power, the first Robert Bourassa government in Quebec (1970–76) gained a degree of autonomy from Ottawa in the fields of family allowances and immigration. It also passed **Bill 22** to give primacy to the French language in many spheres in the province, such as in the operations and documents of public and para-public authorities. As far as education was concerned, immigrant children who did not already have a "sufficient knowledge" of English were obliged to go to French-language schools. This was an attempt to have such children join the majority French linguistic group in the province rather than become "English," as so many previous immigrants had done. Relying on immigration to bolster the francophone segment of the population became a vital issue when the French-Canadian birthrate plummeted after 1960. Bill 22 also aimed at the francization of the private sector by pressuring companies to use French as the language of internal corporate operations. The more Quebec moved in the direction of French unilingualism, of course, the more English Canada resisted Trudeau's policy of national bilingualism and the larger grew the number of anglophones who left Quebec.

The Parti Québécois (PQ) was elected to office in 1976 under René Lévesque with an even more nationalistic program.[10] Faced with a hostile Trudeau government in Ottawa, the PQ made few gains in provincial autonomy. But it did pass **Bill 101**, the Charter of the French Language, which extended Bill 22 by making French the predominant language in the province. Bill 101 generally turned the persuasive and optional aspects of Bill 22 into coercive and mandatory ones, raising strong opposition from English Quebeckers and English Canadians generally. It made French the only official language of the legislature (although laws continued to be translated unofficially into English); only individuals (not corporations) could use English in Quebec courts; the only children who could go to English schools in the province were those whose parents had done so; and all commercial signs had to be in French only.[11] All four of these clauses were subsequently ruled unconstitutional by the courts, but in other ways Bill 101 still stands: large companies must operate in French, and French continues to be the official language of the province.

The 1980s

In 1980 the PQ government held a **referendum** on the question of pursuing a more independent relationship with Canada called **sovereignty-association**. Sovereignty with continuing links to Canada could be considered as a fourth option for dealing with the French Canada situation, somewhere between "distinct status" and complete independence. Many federal politicians, including Trudeau, Justice Minister Jean Chrétien, and several provincial premiers

encouraged Quebeckers to defeat the PQ proposal, promising them "renewed federalism" if they did so.[12] When sovereignty association was turned down by a vote of 60 percent to 40 percent, new federal–provincial constitutional negotiations began, culminating in the **Constitution Act, 1982**. Ironically, even though the whole effort was supposed to appeal to the residents of that province, the Quebec government alone objected to the act. That was because it reflected the Trudeau vision of a centralized, symmetrical bilingual Canada rather than recognizing the distinctive French character of Quebec. Nevertheless, it became law in all parts of the country. As far as language was concerned, the act reinforced official bilingualism at the federal level and in New Brunswick, and guaranteed **minority-language education rights** in the provinces wherever numbers warranted. Many Quebeckers never forgave Trudeau and Chrétien for adopting such a significant constitutional document against the opposition of their provincial government.

When Brian Mulroney became prime minister in 1984 with a strategy of accommodating the views of the Quebec majority, even René Lévesque was willing to give Confederation another chance. Such a change of heart split the PQ, however, and the government collapsed. The second Bourassa government, elected in 1985, was first able to convince the Mulroney government to allow Quebec to play a fuller part in the **Francophonie**, the international French-speaking community. Then, in 1988, the Supreme Court of Canada declared the sign provision of Bill 101 to be unconstitutional as a violation of freedom of expression.[13] Bourassa responded by using the "notwithstanding clause" in the federal and Quebec charters of rights to pass **Bill 178**, which provided for French-only outdoor signs but allowed bilingual signs indoors. Violating what the Court had determined to be a constitutional right and giving preference to French collective rights over (English) individual rights produced a vehement reaction among English Quebeckers and an anti-Quebec, anti-French response in the rest of the country. It should be noted, however, that in 1983 some aspects of Bill 101 were voluntarily relaxed, and in 1986 Quebec ensured the provision of social and health services in English to its anglophone minority. Moreover, when the five-year limit on Bill 178 ran out in 1993, Bourassa replaced it with **Bill 86**, which allowed bilingual signs outside as well as inside stores, as long as the French lettering was predominant.

. . . .

TIME LINE

Quebec–Canada Relations, 1970–2000

1976	Election of Parti Québécois
1980	First Quebec Referendum
1982	Constitution Act, 1982
1987–90	Meech Lake Accord
1992	Charlottetown Accord and national referendum
1995	Second Quebec Referendum
1998	Supreme Court Reference on Quebec independence
2000	Clarity Act

The main item on the Bourassa–Mulroney agenda was the **Meech Lake Accord**. Designed to bring Quebec back into the Canadian constitutional fold, the accord provided for the recognition of Quebec as a **distinct society** within Canada, provincial nomination of senators and Supreme Court judges, a provincial veto on a wider range of constitutional amendments, constitutionalization of Quebec's rights in immigration, and provincial opting-out, with compensation, of federal programs set up within their jurisdiction. In many respects Meech Lake reflected the approach of the 1979 Task Force on Canadian Unity, which had been promptly shelved when its recommendations were contrary to Trudeau's vision of Canada. The Accord is discussed in more detail in Chapter 17.

The new model gained widespread acceptance until Trudeau himself came out of retirement to condemn it and until negative English-Canadian reaction emerged against Quebec's Bill 178. In the end, the Newfoundland and Manitoba legislatures failed to approve it before the 1990 deadline. Many Quebeckers felt betrayed again, Quebec began a much more aggressive campaign to wrest powers from Ottawa, and several Quebec members of Parliament quit their parties to sit as Quebec *indépendantistes* in the Bloc Québécois created by Lucien Bouchard.

The 1990s

After intense post-Meech Lake discussions, the Quebec legislature decided that a referendum on **sovereignty** would be held in the province in 1992. Those opposed to independence hoped that the rest of Canada would offer Quebec a model of a new federation before that time so that the voters would have an acceptable federalist option. Such a vision was embodied in the **Charlottetown Accord**. If ratified, Quebec would essentially have achieved fulfillment of its Meech Lake demands, including recognition as a distinct society within Canada based on its French-language majority, unique culture, and civil law tradition. All provinces would have received increased power over immigration, an enlarged veto over constitutional amendments, and compensation when opting out of national programs. Quebec and the other provinces would have secured some nine legislative powers in addition to immigration if they chose to use them. In the end, however, 56.7 percent of Quebeckers voted against the accord, presumably because it did not offer Quebec sufficient additional powers. Canadians outside Quebec did not like it much better.

After the disheartening, if not traumatic, experience of the Charlottetown Accord all federal parties decided to put constitutional issues on the back burner, especially the Chrétien Liberals, elected in 1993. However, the inadequacies and rejection of the Charlottetown Accord ignited a new surge of nationalism in Quebec, and in 1994 the Parti Québécois was re-elected under Jacques Parizeau. As in 1976, the PQ argued that it was "safe" to elect it to government, because sovereignty would be decided in a separate, subsequent referendum. The Parizeau government kept adjusting its concept of sovereignty and delaying the date of the vote until it thought it had a version that would be accepted by the Quebec public.

The referendum on Quebec sovereignty was held in October 1995. Although the PQ government ultimately proposed a kind of sovereignty that retained significant links to the rest of Canada (such as Canadian passports and citizenship and use of the Canadian dollar), its proposal was turned down by a vote of 50.6 percent to 49.4 percent. Such a close result was not particularly comforting to those who wanted to keep the country together, especially when the charismatic Bouchard succeeded Parizeau as Quebec premier immediately afterward. Nevertheless, Bouchard resigned in 2000 without having called another referendum, and as support for Quebec sovereignty continued to fall, his successor, Bernard Landry, was also forced to abandon any such plans. Meanwhile, as noted in Chapter 17,

Chrétien had asked the Supreme Court whether Quebec had a constitutional right to declare independence unilaterally, and he followed that up with the **Clarity Act**, which required any such referendum question to be approved by the federal House of Commons. Under that Act, even opposed by some moderate Quebec nationalists, the federal government would also decide if the size of the vote in favour of sovereignty was sufficient to trigger formal constitutional negotiations.

In any case, a federalist Quebec government was elected in 2003—the provincial Liberals under Jean Charest. He welcomed a Supreme Court decision upholding Quebec legislation that forced francophone parents to send their children to French-language schools. But noting the need for graduates to be increasingly bilingual, Charest did introduce English as a second language in

Prime Minister Stephen Harper developed a close relationship with Quebec Premier Jean Charest.

THE CANADIAN PRESS/Jacques Boissinot

French schools in grade 1 instead of grade 3. About this time it was revealed that the Chrétien government had given a number of large advertising contracts promoting national unity to Quebec communications firms that had, in turn, made financial contributions to the Liberal party. The effectiveness of such advertising was debatable, but even worse, this "sponsorship scandal" sometimes reached criminal proportions. Largely because of the scandal, the federal Liberals lost considerable support in Quebec in the 2004 election, while the Bloc Québécois picked up nearly 50 percent of the vote. In February 2004, Paul Martin decided to appoint Judge John Gomery to conduct a judicial inquiry into the whole operation. Partly because of opposition attacks based on revelations before the **Gomery inquiry**, the Martin government was defeated on a non-confidence motion in November 2005, setting the stage for the January 2006 election won by the Conservatives under Stephen Harper

Developments in Other Provinces and Territories

The Quebec government and most Quebeckers have been more concerned about internal matters than about what happens to French minorities in other provinces and territories. Nevertheless, the Quiet Revolution led francophones outside Quebec to regain their French identities and to seek to preserve their language and culture. Often under pressure from Prime Minister Trudeau, some provincial premiers hoped that by extending rights or services to their francophone minorities, they would help to forestall separatism in Quebec. Thus, considerable improvement was made in minority francophone rights in many provinces after 1965.[14] As mentioned, all provinces and territories were bound by the Constitution Act, 1982 to provide education in the minority official language where numbers warranted. In addition, the Supreme Court ruled that francophone parents must have some control over their children's French-language education.[15] Amendments to the Criminal Code in 1978 and 1988 forced all provinces and territories to provide for criminal trials in French, if demanded by the accused.[16]

Much has been written about the Trudeau government's creation of minority official-language education rights across the country. It has even been said that this was the real reason he pushed the concept of a Charter of Rights and Freedoms. Moreover, Ottawa helped to create the demand for French-language schools in the nine anglophone provinces by assisting the creation of advocacy organizations that would promote its own agenda.[17] The federal government then pressured such official-language minority groups to demand and establish French-language schools, as well as giving the provinces the money to finance them. All this was designed to undercut Quebec's claim that it was the homeland of French Canada, and it was a classic case of a government's not waiting for societal forces to demand what it wanted to do.

New Brunswick implemented its own Official Languages Act in 1969 to improve the Acadian educational system at all levels and to provide provincial government services in both languages. New Brunswick then became the only officially bilingual province in the Constitution Act, 1982.[18] The Richard Hatfield government embarked on a policy of cultural equality based on a "separate but equal" strategy rather than on individual or institutional bilingualism, with parallel unilingual school boards and other public bodies (Bill 88). Some years later, after an anti-bilingual party elected several members to the provincial legislature, New Brunswick constitutionalized Bill 88 in 1993 to further protect the right of English and French linguistic communities in the province to distinct cultural and educational institutions.[19] Finally, in 2002, Premier Bernard Lord strengthened the Official Languages Act, especially at the municipal level of government and in the health care field. Moncton declared itself the most bilingual city in Canada.

Ontario began to provide public French-language secondary schools in 1968 and later established the right of every Franco-Ontarian to go to a French-language school. Ontario then guaranteed French trials in the provincial courts and gradually extended French-language provincial services. Premier David Peterson passed Bill 8, which became effective in 1989 and provided for the translation of laws, simultaneous French-English interpretation in the legislature, and provincial government services in French in 22 designated regions of the province. The courts granted Franco-Ontarians the right to have French-language schools run by trustees elected by the francophone population. As in New Brunswick, the considerable voting power of the Franco-Ontarian community encouraged all parties to support such initiatives, but the combination of Quebec's Bill 178 and Ontario's Bill 8 was too much for many Ontarians to bear. In 1989–90, some 70 municipalities symbolically declared themselves officially unilingual, although such animosity subsided by the turn of the 21st century.

Manitoba moved very slowly on French-language initiatives but was pushed by a series of Supreme Court of Canada decisions beginning in 1979. The 1890 Official Language Act was declared unconstitutional (a violation of the 1870 Manitoba Act); all laws had to be passed in both languages; trials had to be available in French; and most government documents had to be published in a bilingual format.[20] Since then, governments have also expanded French-language services where required.

Given their small francophone minorities, Saskatchewan and Alberta took very little action on French-language issues. Indeed, even asking a question in French in the Alberta legislature originally created quite a controversy. In the 1988 *Mercure* case, however, the Supreme Court of Canada ruled that Saskatchewan (and, by implication, Alberta) was bound by an 1886 territorial statute to pass laws in both French and English.[21] The Court allowed the province to opt out of this requirement, however, by repealing the territorial law by means of a single, bilingual provincial statute! Both provinces proceeded to do so but did allow French to be spoken in their legislatures and courts. With federal arm-twisting and financial incentives, Saskatchewan also began to translate some of its English-only laws into French. Meanwhile, under federal government pressure, the northern territories granted French official status, but advances for francophone minorities in other provinces have been minimal.[22]

Linguistic minorities at the provincial and territorial level find it necessary to organize in order to pursue their objectives. Such groups include the Assemblée de la francophonie de l'Ontario (AFO), the Société franco-manitobaine, and the Société des acadiens et acadiennes du Nouveau-Brunswick. These French groups have also joined others in the Fédération des communautés francophones et acadienne du Canada. Meanwhile, the English minority in Quebec has also formed its own militant pressure group, Alliance Quebec.

. . . .

CONTEMPORARY ISSUES

Given that francophones constitute 22 percent of the Canadian electorate, given their historic constitutional rights, given their geographic concentration in Quebec and majority control of such a large province, and given their modern-day self-consciousness and self-confidence, the French fact in Canada cannot be ignored. If English Canada wants Quebec to remain part of the country, it cannot go back to the easy days of pre-1960 unilingualism and federal government centralization. Moreover, the Trudeau model is no longer an option: most Quebeckers expect the federal government to operate on a bilingual basis but are not overly concerned about francophone rights in the rest of the country. The goodwill or self-interest of Canadians outside Quebec in becoming bilingual is not enough to keep the country together; the only question really is: how autonomous should Quebec be?

Kenneth McRoberts reminds us of some of the characteristics that make Quebec distinct.[23] First, some 86 percent of Canadian francophones are located in Quebec, 80 percent of Quebeckers are francophone, and more than 90 percent of Canadians who use French at home live in that province. Second, Quebec's political institutions are distinctive in many ways: the civil law system, the downplaying of symbols of the Crown, and the plethora of state enterprises, many of them protecting or regulating language and cultural activities. Third, Quebec has pursued many policy differences from other provinces and territories, often with a social democratic flavour: laws that are more labour-friendly; distinctive child-care and pharmaceutical plans; multifunctional public clinics that combine health and social services; a more important role for the provincial government in immigration; and a distinctive form of collaboration among the state, capital, and labour. Fourth, Quebec is distinct in the separateness of its sources of news and entertainment and in many of the institutions of its civil society, such as advocacy groups and political parties. McRoberts concludes that "for most Quebec francophones, anything less than distinct society would not do justice to the reality of contemporary Quebec as they understand it."[24] They see Quebec as the heartland of French Canada, a province that needs special constitutional recognition and has the responsibility to protect itself in the North American English linguistic environment. Whether or not it is justified, many Quebeckers continue to have a "siege mentality" with respect to language and culture, and language has replaced the

Church as the focus of French-Canadian identity. The Quebec corporate elite is now a francophone group, and, along with the new middle class in the Quebec public sector, sees itself benefiting from increased provincial autonomy.

Recalling the fate of the Meech Lake and Charlottetown Accords, recognition of Quebec as a distinct society is not likely to be supported by enough other provinces (and their publics) to be constitutionally entrenched, although such recognition would be a bare minimum for most Quebeckers today. It may be enough in the short-term, however, to develop more asymmetrical arrangements with Quebec—treating it differently from other provinces in an informal way—and redressing what Quebec sees as a fiscal imbalance between the two levels of government. Paul Martin, Stephen Harper, and Jean Charest all seemed prepared to pick up on the work of Lester Pearson, Brian Mulroney, and Robert Bourassa in this respect. Many observers feel that the only hope of keeping the country intact in a recognizable form is to find a formula along these lines that would be supported by a majority of Canadians both inside and outside Quebec.[25]

Much greater autonomy would accrue to Quebec under a formula of sovereignty-association, that is, sovereignty with continuing links to Canada in some kind of political and economic partnership, and even more, of course, with outright independence. Support for Quebec sovereignty ebbs and flows, partly depending on the performance of federal and Quebec governments, but total independence has never attracted a majority of Quebeckers. The formula proposed in the 1995 referendum came close to a majority, but that involved an ambiguous question including considerable links to Canada.

As prime minister, Paul Martin and Stephen Harper both treated Quebec in a slightly different fashion from other provinces, usually referred to as "asymmetrical federalism." Harper appealed to Quebec with the promise of (decentralized) "open federalism," of fixing the "fiscal imbalance" between the two levels of government, and of giving Quebec a role in the Canadian delegation to UNESCO. He was also the author of a House of Commons resolution that recognized the Québécois as a nation within a united Canada.[26]

Within Quebec, new forms of nationalism can be identified. The nationalism of the 1960s and 1970s was closely related to the expansion of the provincial state, but as francophones repatriated the private sector in Quebec in the 1980s, especially in the era of globalization and neoliberalism, the concept of "market nationalism" emerged. The distinctiveness of Quebec was no longer threatened by market forces; indeed, controlled by francophones, they could be bulwarks in its defence.

About the same time, analysts began to distinguish between "civic" and "ethnic" nationalism in Quebec. As the proportion of allophones increased, a provincial policy of "interculturalism" appeared. New immigrants were told that they could retain their distinctive practices and cultures as long as they entered into the use of French as the common language of Quebec public life. Quebec nationalism would no longer be based on ethnicity and restricted to "pure laine" francophones. The new civic nationalism would welcome non-francophones who felt loyal to Quebec and recognized that the use of French was the essential condition for the cohesion of Quebec society. This distinction has left the concept of "Québécois" rather ambiguous—does it refer only to those of French ethnicity or to this wider, more varied group?

Related to that issue was the increasing concern among some residents about the number of immigrants in the province as well as about certain minority religious and ethnic group practices. Most observers felt that the future of the French language was secure, but others noted that the bulk of new immigrants settled in City of Montreal, where the proportion of residents with French mother tongue had fallen in the 2006 census to just over 50 percent. Then, in response to complaints about Islamic and other religious dress and symbols, Premier Charest appointed a two-person commission (Bouchard-Taylor) to hold public hearings and make recommendations with respect to the "reasonable accommodation" of such differences. Contrary to many of the briefs they heard, the commissioners believed that newcomers were not a threat to the Quebec way of life. They recommended that the government of Quebec should be totally secular, treating all religions alike but not denying them individual expression, and that people of all cultures and faiths should share in a common inclusive state defined by the French language.[27] Whether either allophones, especially of non-Christian faiths, or *pure laine* Quebeckers will actually embrace this official policy remains to be seen.

. . . .

CONCLUSION

The ethnic cleavages that are such a prominent feature of the Canadian political system are based in part on the number and variety of groups involved and on their contrasting identities—the perceptions that each group has of its own history and current status. The French are acutely conscious of their current minority position in the country as a whole, as opposed to constituting a majority within Quebec. They desperately want to preserve their language and culture against the pervasive forces of Anglo-American television and other media. Most Quebec francophones want to enlarge their capacity to govern themselves, and those outside Quebec want to maximize opportunities to use their own language. English-speaking Canadians, however, are still by far the largest single group in the land and resent the number of jobs, mostly in the public sector, that now require fluency in French. They also tend to support the idea of provincial equality and are skeptical about distinct status for Quebec. Yet, as McRoberts says, "the majority of Quebec francophones remain just as determined as ever that their distinctiveness be recognized and accommodated."[28]

The political significance of Quebec and French Canada ensures that they are featured in almost every chapter of this text. Readers have already encountered many of the issues relating to them in Chapter 2 (the institutional foundations of Canada), Chapter 3 (Quebec as a region), and Chapter 4 (Aboriginals issues in Quebec). The fact that northern Quebec is populated almost exclusively by Aboriginals, for example, has constituted a problem for sovereigntists; this is discussed more fully in Chapter 17 on constitutional reform. That chapter also reiterates how Pierre Trudeau designed the Constitution Act, 1982 in order to promote his vision of the relationship between Quebec and French Canada. Before that, Chapter 9 again notes the significant historic role of religion in Quebec, Chapter 11 picks up on this chapter to discuss a Quebec or French-Canadian subculture, and Chapters 13–15 emphasize the important part that that province plays in electoral and party politics in Canada. Throughout most of Canadian history, the party that won a majority electoral victory attracted considerable support in Quebec. In recent years, however, the Bloc Québécois has siphoned off a large number of Quebec seats in federal elections, making it difficult for any national party to win a majority. Nevertheless, all parties make special appeals to the voters of that province, choose leaders with some bilingual capacity, and in the case of the Liberals, normally alternate Anglophone and francophone leaders. Of course, Quebec is central to the discussion of Canadian federalism (Chapter 18), and several Charter cases have emerged from that province (Chapter 19). The four main institutions of government detailed in Part 5 also have to give considerable attention to the place of Quebec and language questions.

P Of the approaches outlined in Chapter 1, pluralism is probably most relevant to the discussion of the French–English cleavage. First, the French–English relationship in Canadian society is the very essence of pluralism: it is a basic fact of Canadian political life and animates much of the political activity in the country. The fundamental co-existence of two dominant ethnic groups establishes an underlying pluralism and also provides the foundation for most of the other pluralistic aspects of Canadian government and society. Second, the pluralist approach is clearly correct in anticipating regular bargaining between such groups in the policymaking process. Although such interaction does not necessarily assume equality of bargaining power or require the involvement of organized groups, it has been a fact of Canadian political life from the very start. French–English relations and the position of Quebec in the federation then became perhaps the most prominent issues after the Quiet Revolution of the 1960s.

SC The state-centred approach begins with the fact that the British and French "charter groups" have historically dominated positions of political power, although the British usually prevailed over the French.[29] Apart from two prime ministers and a few "Quebec lieutenants," French Canadians generally occupied minor positions in the federal Cabinet until 1968, when Pierre Trudeau drew his principal ministers from Quebec. A similar imbalance existed in the public service, but under the Official Languages Act, hiring and promotion preferences have given the French language and francophone public servants a more equitable, if not superior, position. The state-centred approach takes the perspective that many policies in this field reflect the interests or prejudices of the political elite rather than the demands articulated by the wider society. In particular, Trudeau's imposition of official bilingualism was carried out despite the opposition of a majority of the anglophone population and the indifference of a majority of francophones in Quebec. Moreover, his *dirigiste* approach is evident in his creation and financing of official-language minority advocacy groups throughout the country, his determination to guarantee their rights in the Charter, his funding of whatever official bilingualism he could persuade provincial and territorial governments to offer, and his determined opposition to the idea of treating Quebec differently from other provinces.

PC In terms of the public choice approach, French Canadians constitute nearly 25 percent of the electorate, which should be sufficient to demand much attention. However, Quebec voted Liberal so often that it did not figure prominently in any party's electoral calculations between 1896 and 1960. The neglect of bilingualism at the federal level was one result, although the delayed implementation of conscription in the Second World War is an indication that French Canada could not be completely taken for granted. After the Quiet Revolution, when their demands increased and were backed by the threat of separation, and especially after 1984, when their voting preferences became more volatile, Quebec francophones became the most courted group in the country. In terms of "rational choice," Matthew Mendelsohn has studied which aspects of their condition were uppermost in their mind as they decided for whom to vote.[30]

(C) Class analysts are interested in socioeconomic rather than ethnic cleavages but find certain linkages between the two.[31] They are particularly interested in the relationship between class and ethnicity in Quebec. In the pre-1960 period, the titans of big business in Quebec reflected the dominance of British, Anglo-Canadian, and Anglo-American backgrounds. They took little interest in promoting francophone concerns and made English the language of business. Premier Maurice Duplessis welcomed "English" capital into Quebec and did not object to the exploitation of French-speaking workers. Then, during the Quiet Revolution, a new middle class of francophone Quebeckers made itself felt in the province's public sector and passed laws to improve the lot of francophones in the private sector as well. These developments fostered the emergence of a new entrepreneurial class in the province, and the economic elite in Quebec today is francophone in character. Class analysts also argue that ethnic politics are a reflection of underlying economic, class-based forces. Some suggest that the capitalist-controlled political elite has chosen to emphasize the ethnic factor in Canadian politics in order to distract the population from any consciousness of class divisions. Capitalist forces did not want English and French working people across the country to realize how much they had in common. Finally, class analysts cite the use of the War Measures Act in 1970 as an unnecessary resort to coercion by the state.

(G) The forces of globalization also affect the Quebec question. The significance of post-1960 Quebec nationalism is related to the legacy of Anglo-American transnational corporations controlling much of the Quebec economy; to the global dominance, especially evident in North America, of the English language; and to the small proportion of French-speaking immigrants that choose to come to Canada, including Quebec. In this context, policies giving preference to the French language in the province are quite understandable, as is Quebec's desire to play a major role in the Francophonie and in other aspects of international affairs. However, partly as a result of such policies, the now francophone-dominant Quebec private sector thinks globally itself; some Quebeckers endorse the view that links to the United States and other markets reduce Quebec's reliance on the rest of Canada; and Quebec has developed some highly successful transnational companies of its own. On the other hand, given its nature as a "French island in a North American anglophone sea," there remains considerable concern about the difficulty of maintaining measures to protect its culture.

. . . .

DISCUSSION QUESTIONS

1. How would you characterize the interaction between the English majority and the French minority in Canadian history?

2. What are their respective visions of their place in Confederation?

3. Should the French minorities outside Quebec have the same rights and services as the English minority in Quebec?

4. Is the territorial or the personality principle a more realistic basis for language policy in Canada?

5. Why do most Quebeckers insist on constitutional recognition that Quebec is a distinct society within Canada? What additional powers do they seek?

6. What is likely to happen to official bilingualism if Quebec ever separates?

. . . .

NOTES

1. Although the label "English" is sometimes used in this chapter to refer to language, as opposed to ethnic origin, special mention should be made of the Scots in Canada, who historically controlled the fur trade, the banks and other financial institutions, the major universities, and much of the government. Many prime ministers, for example, were of Scottish background. See Pierre Berton, *Why We Act Like Canadians* (Toronto: McClelland and Stewart, 1982), pp. 77–78.

2. Jean-Pierre Corbeil and Christine Blaser, "The Evolving Linguistic Portrait, 2006 Census: Findings," http://www12.statcan.gc.ca/english/census06/analysis/language/index.cfm.

3. Kenneth McRoberts, "Making Canada Bilingual: Illusions and Delusions of Federal Language Policy," in David Shugarman and Reg Whitaker, eds., *Federalism and Political Community* (Peterborough: Broadview Press, 1989); and McRoberts, *Misconceiving Canada: The Struggle for National Unity* (Toronto: Oxford University Press, 1997). See also Guy Laforest, *Trudeau and the End of a Canadian Dream* (Montreal: McGill-Queen's University Press, 1995).

4. *A.G. Manitoba v. Forest*, [1979] 2 S.C.R. 1032. Canada's involvement in the British Boer War also complicated French–English relations to a limited extent.

5. *Ontario Roman Catholic Separate School Trustees v. Mackell*, [1917] A.C. 62.

6. Dale Thomson, *Jean Lesage and the Quiet Revolution* (Toronto: Macmillan, 1984).

7. Kenneth McRoberts, *Quebec: Social Change and Political Crisis*, 3rd ed. (Toronto: McClelland and Stewart, 1993); and Kenneth McRoberts, "Quebec: Province, Nation, or Distinct Society?" in Michael S. Whittington and Glen Williams, eds., *Canadian Politics in the 21st Century*, 7th ed. (Toronto: Thomson Nelson, 2008).

8. It was not until 1927 that postage stamps became bilingual; in 1934 bilingual bank notes were introduced; and in 1945 bilingual federal family allowance cheques were provided in Quebec. See Office of the Commissioner of Official Languages, *Our Two Official Languages Over Time*, rev. and updated ed. (Ottawa, 1996); and Graham Fraser, *Sorry, I Don't Speak French: Confronting the Canadian Crisis That Won't Go Away* (Toronto: McClelland and Stewart, 2006).

9. C. Michael MacMillan, "Active Conscience or Administrative Vanguard?: The Commissioner of Official Languages as an Agent of Change," *Canadian Public Administration* (June 2006).

10. Graham Fraser, *René Lévesque and the Parti Québécois in Power* (Toronto: Macmillan, 1984). For France's role in the whole saga, see J.F. Bosher, *The Gaullist Attack on Canada, 1967–1997* (Montreal: McGill-Queen's University Press, 1998).

11. William Coleman, "From Bill 22 to Bill 101: The Politics of Language under the Parti Québécois," *Canadian Journal of Political Science* (September 1981).

12. Gertrude J. Robinson *Constructing the Quebec Referendum: French and English Media Voices* (Toronto: University of Toronto Press, 1998).

13. *Ford v. Quebec (Attorney General)*, [1988] 2 S.C.R. 712.

14. C. Michael MacMillan, *The Practice of Language Rights in Canada* (Toronto: University of Toronto Press, 1998).

15. *Mahe v. Alberta*, [1990] 1 S.C.R. 342; Troy Q. Riddell, "Official Minority-Language Policy outside Quebec: The Impact of Section 23 of the Charter and Judicial Decisions," *Canadian Public Administration* (Spring 2003); and Michael D. Behiels, *Canada's Francophone Minority Communities: Constitutional Renewal and the Winning of School Governance* (Montreal: McGill-Queen's University Press, 2004).

16. See *R. v. Beaulac*, [1999] 1 S.C.R. 768, a case in which the Supreme Court reaffirmed the right of an accused person to be tried in his or her mother tongue.

17. Leslie Pal, *Interests of State: The Politics of Language, Multiculturalism, and Feminism in Canada* (Montreal: McGill-Queen's University Press, 1993).

18. New Brunswick court cases include *Jones v. A.G. New Brunswick*, [1975] 2 S.C.R. 182; *Société des Acadiens v. Association of Parents*, [1986] 1 S.C.R. 549; and *Société des Acadiens et acadiennes du Nouveau-Brunswick Inc. v. Canada*, [2008] 1 S.C.R. 383.

19. James Ross Hurley, *Amending Canada's Constitution: History, Processes, Problems and Prospects* (Ottawa: Supply and Services, 1996).

20. Manitoba cases include *A.G. Manitoba v. Forest*, [1979] 2 S.C.R. 1032; *Reference re Manitoba Language Rights*, [1985] 1 S.C.R. 721; *Order re Manitoba Language Rights*, [1985] 2 S.C.R. 347; *Bilodeau v. Attorney General Manitoba*, [1986] 1 S.C.R. 449; and *Reference re Manitoba Language Rights*, [1992] 1 S.C.R. 212. Parallel Quebec cases include *Attorney General of Quebec v. Blaikie*, [1979] 2 S.C.R. 1016; and *MacDonald v. City of Montreal*, [1986] 1 S.C.R. 460.

21. *Mercure v. Attorney General Saskatchewan*, [1988] 1 S.C.R. 234.

22. French minority educational rights were strengthened by a decision of the Supreme Court in the PEI case *Arsenault-Cameron v. Prince Edward Island*, [2000] 1 S.C.R. 3.

23. McRoberts, "Quebec: Province, Nation, or Distinct Society?"

24. Ibid., p. 399.

25. Kenneth McRoberts, *Misconceiving Canada*; and R.A. Young, *The Struggle for Quebec* (Montreal: McGill-Queen's University Press, 1999); see articles in *Policy Options*, December 2004/January 2005, April 2007, and July/August 2008.

26. Chantal Hébert, *French Kiss: Stephen Harper's Blind Date with Quebec* (Toronto: Knopf Canada, 2007).

27. The Bouchard-Taylor Report can be found at http://www.accommodements.qc.ca/documentation/rapports/rapport-final-integral-en.pdf. See also articles in *Policy Options*, September 2007.

28. McRoberts, "Quebec: Province, Nation, or Distinct Society?" (6th ed.), p. 424.

29. John Porter, *The Vertical Mosaic* (Toronto: University of Toronto Press, 1965); and Rick Helmes-Hayes and James Curtis, eds., *The Vertical Mosaic Revisited* (Toronto: University of Toronto Press, 1998).

30. Matthew Mendelsohn, "Rational Choice and Socio-Psychological Explanation for Opinion on Quebec Sovereignty," *Canadian Journal of Political Science* (July/August 2003).

31. Janine Brodie and Jane Jenson, *Challenge, Crisis and Change: Politics and Class in Canada Revisited*, 2nd ed. (Ottawa: Carleton University Press, 1990).

· ·

FURTHER READING

Behiels, Michael D. *Canada's Francophone Minority Communities: Constitutional Renewal and the Winning of School Governance*. Montreal: McGill-Queen's University Press, 2004.

Bothwell, Robert. *Canada and Quebec: One Country, Two Histories*, rev. ed. Vancouver: University of British Columbia Press, 1998.

Coleman, William. "From Bill 22 to Bill 101: The Politics of Language under the Parti Québécois." *Canadian Journal of Political Science* (September 1981), pp. 459–85.

Cook, Ramsay. *Canada, Quebec and the Uses of Nationalism*. Toronto: McClelland and Stewart, 1995.

Fraser, Graham. *Sorry, I Don't Speak French: Confronting the Canadian Crisis That Won't Go Away*. Toronto: McClelland and Stewart, 2006.

Gagnon, Alain-G., ed. *Quebec State and Society*, 3rd ed. Peterborough: Broadview Press, 2003.

Gagnon, Alain-G., and Raffaele Iacovino. *Federalism, Citizenship and Quebec: Debating Multinationalism*. Toronto: University of Toronto Press, 2006.

Hébert, Chantal. *French Kiss: Stephen Harper's Blind Date with Quebec*. Toronto: Knopf Canada, 2007.

Laforest, Guy. *Trudeau and the End of a Canadian Dream*. Montreal: McGill-Queen's University Press, 1995.

Maclure, Jocelyn. *Quebec Identity: The Challenge of Pluralism*. Montreal: McGill-Queen's University Press, 2003.

MacMillan, C. Michael. *The Practice of Language Rights in Canada*. Toronto: University of Toronto Press, 1998.

McRoberts, Kenneth. "Making Canada Bilingual: Illusions and Delusions of Federal Language Policy." In David Shugarman and Reg Whitaker, eds., *Federalism and Political Community*. Peterborough: Broadview Press, 1989.

———. *Misconceiving Canada: The Struggle for National Unity*. Toronto: Oxford University Press, 1997.

———. "Quebec: Province, Nation, or Distinct Society?" In Michael S. Whittington and Glen Williams, eds., *Canadian Politics in the 20th Century*, 7th ed. Toronto: Thomson Nelson, 2008.

Pal, Leslie. *Interests of State: The Politics of Language, Multiculturalism, and Feminism in Canada*. Montreal: McGill-Queen's University Press, 1993.

Salée, Daniel, and Michael Murphy. *Canada: the State of the Federation: 2005: Quebec*. Montreal: McGill-Queen's University Press, 2005.

Young, Robert A. *The Struggle for Quebec*. Montreal: McGill-Queen's University Press, 1999.

Chapter 6

ETHNOCULTURAL
Minorities

With high immigration rates from the developing world, the number of Canadians who belong to visible minorities increases daily. Many established Canadians welcome this development and cherish this diversity, but this multicoloured tapestry is not to everyone's taste. For example, employment equity and affirmative action programs designed to assist members of visible minorities and occasional involvement in "homeland politics" have generated much controversy. The Liberal Party was sometimes accused of entrenching multiculturalism in the Constitution to undercut Quebec nationalism or to attract immigrant votes, and many observers oppose public funding of multiculturalism and argue that newcomers should put more effort into absorbing traditional Canadian values. Whatever level of immigration Canadians prefer, there is general concern about how immigrants are treated once they arrive and about the country taking advantage of all immigrant skills.

Although Canadians of Aboriginal, English, Scottish, Irish, and French origin constitute minorities, this chapter focuses on other, usually more recent, ethnocultural and mostly visible minorities. These groups increasingly vie with Aboriginal and French–English issues on the political agenda. The three principal topics that arise in this area are immigration policy, preserving and promoting the identity of minority ethnic groups, and ensuring that individuals belonging to such groups are treated equitably and included in law and society. This chapter begins with a profile of ethnocultural minorities in Canada today and puts that portrait into historical context. It then raises some theoretical considerations regarding racism and ethnic identities, before discussing the historic pattern of discrimination that new Canadians experienced and their demands for equality and inclusion. The next part deals with responses to such demands in the period after 1970, especially their success in achieving the policy of multiculturalism and improving the equity situation. The chapter ends with an account of current issues with respect to large-scale immigration, multiculturalism, and employment equity.

A PROFILE OF ETHNOCULTURAL MINORITIES IN CANADA TODAY

The 2006 Census reported over 200 ethnic origins in Canada; however, these statistics are increasingly difficult to interpret because so many Canadians now have multiple ethnic origins and because a large proportion of them simply tell Statistics Canada that they are "Canadian." Recent immigrants are more likely to be of single ethnic origins, as well as to be visible minorities, although many non-Caucasian or non-white Canadians have lived here for generations. Table 6.1 provides statistics on the largest groups, and continues to emphasize the Caucasian character of the overall population.

On the other hand, Table 6.2, showing a typical recent year of immigration statistics, reveals the changing nature of ethnocultural minorities in Canada.

These immigration patterns give rise to the concept of **visible minorities**, defined in the Employment Equity Act as "persons, other than Aboriginal peoples, who are non-Caucasian in race or non-white in colour." The 2006 census reported that visible minorities now number over five million Canadians, or 16.2 percent of the population. The largest visible minority groups were South Asians, Chinese, Blacks, Filipinos, Latin Americans, Arabs, Southeast Asians, West Asians, Koreans, and Japanese. Except for Japanese and Blacks, most of these are first- or second-generation Canadians.

Almost all visible minorities live in a large urban centre. In fact, visible minorities make up the following percentages of the six largest cities: Toronto (43%), Vancouver (42%), Calgary (22%), Montreal and Edmonton (17%), and Ottawa (16%). Some suburbs of Toronto and Vancouver house even larger proportions of visible minorities; Halifax has a large Black population; and Winnipeg, a sizable Filipino community.[1]

Ethnicity in Canada can also be measured in linguistic terms. As noted in Chapter 5, the 2006 census indicated that the 6.3 million allophones (those with a mother tongue other than English or French) constituted 20 percent of the population. The third most common mother tongue was Chinese (at 3.3 percent of the population or just over one million Canadians).

TABLE 6.1	Largest Ethnic Groups in Canada, 2006 Census (Single and Multiple Responses)		
Canadian	10 066 290	Chinese	1 346 510
English	6 570 015	North American Indian	1 253 615
French	4 941 210	Ukrainian	1 209 085
Scottish	4 719 210	Dutch	1 035 965
Irish	4 354 155	Polish	984 565
German	3 179 425	East Indian	962 665
Italian	1 445 335	Russian	500 600

Source: Statistics Canada, 2006 Census of Population. Catalogue no. 97-562-XCB2006006. Ethnic Origins, 2006 counts, for Canada, provinces and territories – 20% sample data. Found at: http://www12.statcan.ca/english/census06/data/highlights/ethnic/pages/Page.cfm?Lang=E (retrieved March 10, 2009).

TABLE 6.2   Top Ten Source Countries 2007

Rank	Source Country	Number of Immigrants
1	China	27 014
2	India	26 054
3	Philippines	19 064
4	United States	10 450
5	Pakistan	9 547
6	United Kingdom	8 128
7	Iran	6 663
8	Republic of Korea	5 864
9	France	5 526
10	Columbia	4 833

Source: Citizenship and Immigration Canada. Facts and Figures 2007. Canada- Permanent Residents by Top Source Countries. Pg. 30. Found at: http://www.cic.gc.ca/englishpdf/pub/facts2007.pdf. (Accessed April 26, 2009). Reproduced with the permission of the Minister of Public Works and Government Services Canada, 2009.

The other leading language groups are Spanish, German, Italian, Punjabi, and Arabic. In total, more than 200 languages were mentioned in the 2006 census.[2]

THEORETICAL CONSIDERATIONS

Canada is not alone in containing a variety of ethnocultural groups; most modern states are characterized by cultural pluralism. Such ethnic collectivities normally share ancestry, language, religious beliefs, and cultural traditions, leading to a sense of identity, although to some extent these are socially constructed, as suggested in Chapter 1.[3] At one point in time, such heterogeneity gave rise to discussions of race and racism. Social and natural scientists today generally take the position that, despite appearances, there are no significant biological differences between such groups, and avoid the word "race" in this connection. Nevertheless, people may behave as if such differences are profound; they may demonstrate attitudes of "racism" despite what scientists say; and governments may resort to "racial profiling" such as in collecting statistics on crime. Such attitudes and policies could refer to the people of any group, but are more likely to relate to "visible minorities." This term, which has official status in the Canadian lexicon, has sometimes been criticized for being racist in itself. Nevertheless, it can be argued that some such term is necessary, not to tolerate racism, but rather to confront it. If we want to eradicate discrimination against non-Caucasians or non-white Canadians, for example, we need a term to describe the groups with which we are concerned.

Although there are no inherent biological differences among varied ethnicities, people often have feelings of identification with their own ethnic group. A change in immigrant identities occurred in the 1960s when the country was consumed with debates about upgrading the official status of the francophone component, and other ethnocultural groups began to ask about their place in Canadian society. Suddenly they were demanding some kind of official status, too, along with policies and public financial support to help them retain their languages, traditions, and cultures. The "politics of identity" particularly applies to members of such groups who began to feel strong ethnocultural identities in the 1970s and who began to demand "recognition."

This development raised the theoretical question, also noted in the previous chapters, about how the political system should treat ethnocultural differences. Prior to 1970, in the absence of an official policy, the general approach was to encourage assimilation into the dominant anglo-conformity of English Canada, and unequal treatment of non-British or non-French newcomers was not of much concern. Still, the U.S. ideal of the "melting pot"—of melting away ethnic differences and treating everyone alike—was never entrenched in Canada, and the alternative approach adopted by the Trudeau government in 1971 did not come out of thin air. Just as the proportion of "visible" immigrants began to exceed 50 percent of the annual intake, the government adopted an official policy of "multiculturalism." This policy will be discussed at length below, but it is obviously an alternative to assimilation into the dominant domestic ethnocultural group, and undoubtedly includes a greater commitment to the principle of equality and perhaps veers toward a kind of collectivism as opposed to individualism.[4]

HISTORY OF CANADIAN IMMIGRATION

Let us put the ethnocultural portrait into historical context. Aboriginal peoples settled in what is now Canada too long ago to be considered immigrants. The British and French might be labelled as immigrants, but they were almost the only other ethnocultural groups in Canada before 1867. Those three groups are sometimes considered the "founding peoples" of the country, although, ironically, Aboriginals had to fight to be included in the definition. Following the Aboriginals, the French, and the British, people from many other lands began to immigrate to Canada. By 1867, a sizable German contingent had already arrived, and, shortly afterward, the wide-open spaces of northern Ontario, the Prairies, and British Columbia attracted large numbers of immigrants from continental Europe as well as from Britain and the United States. Railway construction and Western settlement were two key objectives of the Macdonald government's 1879 **National Policy**, and the first dramatic surge of immigrants arrived during the 1880s, many of them homesteaders in the prairies. These included Danes, Dutch, Icelanders, Poles, Ukrainians, Finns, Norwegians, and Swedes. Between 1881 and 1884, nearly 16 000 Chinese were brought into British Columbia as contract labourers to work on the CPR. A substantial number of Blacks came to Canada to escape from slavery in the United States.[5]

Between 1910 and 1913, the largest number of immigrants in the country's history arrived in Canada—1.4 million over four years. The prosperous 1920s were another active decade, but immigration declined significantly during the Depression and the Second World War.

After the war, another huge wave of immigrants came to Canada, largely from southern Europe. They were supplemented by postwar refugees from around the world, one of the largest groups being from Hungary after its 1956 revolution. Figure 6.1 indicates the fluctuations in the number of immigrants arriving in Canada since 1860. The 1990s were the biggest decade in Canadian immigration history, with more than two million immigrants, but even more arrived in the first decade of the 21st century.[6]

Overall, Britain was the leading source of immigrants between 1900 and 1965. During that time, immigration policy favoured British, American, and European newcomers, since they were considered to be well educated and skilled and better able to assimilate. The blatant discrimination in Canadian immigration policies will be addressed below. Most people of British/Celtic background saw Canada as a "British" or "English" or Caucasian country, and immigrants in the post-Confederation period generally tried to fit into that mould. Nevertheless, even without official sanction, many retained their original languages and cultures, and developed hyphenated identities, such as an Italian-Canadian identity or a German-Canadian one. Their ethnocultural identity was essentially a low-profile private matter, however, and they rarely made political demands on this basis.

The **Immigration Act** was significantly amended in 1967, and Canadian immigration patterns changed radically over the following 50 years, as Figure 6.2 demonstrates. In 1957, more than 90 percent of the immigrants were from Britain or continental Europe, a figure that has fallen to about 16 percent. In contrast, Asian immigrants accounted for less than two percent of total immigrants in 1957 but now constitute about 50 percent annually.

. . . .

Figure 6.1   Immigration: A Historical Perspective, 1860–2001

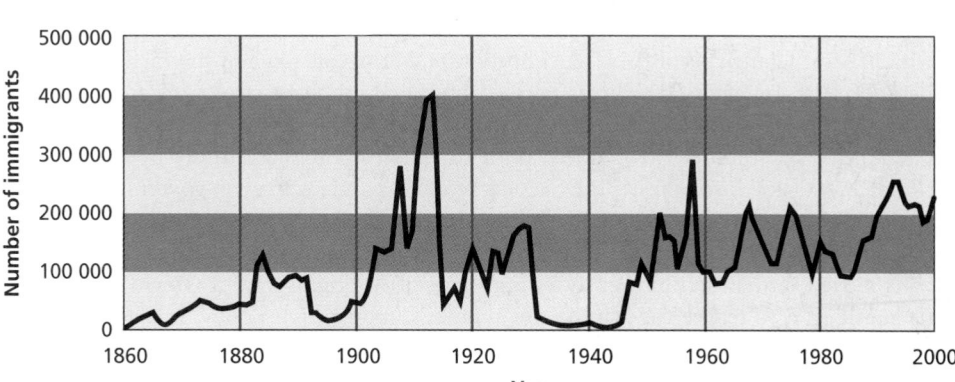

Source: Citizenship and Immigration Canada. Facts and Figures 2001: Immigration Overview. Found at http://www.cic .gc.ca/english/pub/facts2001/1imm-01html (Accessed Oct. 5, 2002) Reproduced with the permission of the Minister of Public Works and Government Services Canada, 2009.

· ·

Figure 6.2 Principal Sources of Immigrants to Canada, Selected Years (Percentages)

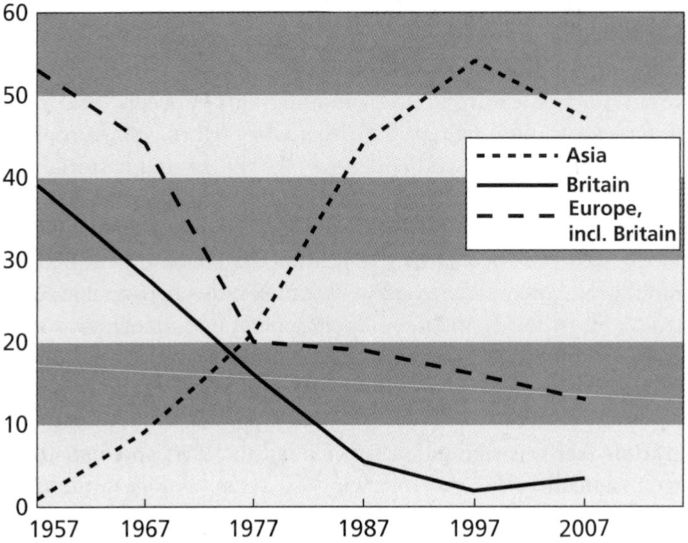

Source: Citizenship and Immigration Canada. Facts and Figures, 2007. Found at: http://www.cic.gc.ca/english/pdf/pub/ facts/2007.pdf (Accessed Mar. 10, 2009) Calculations by author.

· ·

RACIAL DISCRIMINATION

Racial or ethnic discrimination can be defined as unfavourable treatment based on prejudice regarding ancestry. A first encounter with such discrimination arises from the Immigration Act itself. Most Canadians of the 21st century would cringe at some of the racist comments made and racist immigration policies pursued by prime ministers stretching from John A. Macdonald to Mackenzie King.[7] For example, Chinese immigrants from 1885 onward had to pay a head tax to enter the country, prior to being prohibited entirely by the Chinese Exclusion Act of 1923, and during the Second World War, the Canadian government refused to accept Jewish refugees trying to escape from Hitler's Europe. As noted above, for 100 years Canadian immigration policy gave preference to Caucasians. As time went on, however, Canada moved further and further away from its British origins, and a growing number of Canadians began to realize the bias in the country's immigration policy. International and domestic pressure thus forced the Pearson government to revise the Immigration Act in 1967 to remove its preference for Anglo-Europeans.

Those immigrants who managed to meet the official criteria often settled in minority ethnic communities and started their own social and cultural organizations, such as clubs, choirs, folk dance troupes, and newspapers. Many families spoke the "old country" language at home, but the children generally became proficient in English at school, and the second generation often assimilated into the Anglo-Canadian way of life, as intended. Whatever their hyphenated identities, members of such ethnic minorities maintained a low public profile and made few demands. Once arrived, they were largely ignored by federal and provincial governments, although the occasional privilege was granted, such as promises to Mennonites and Hutterites of exemption from military service. In Manitoba between 1896 and 1916 it was legal to establish bilingual English and other-language schools in areas of concentrated ethnic minority settlement.

It was not always the case, however, that immigrants were ignored: once landed they were sometimes discriminated against on the basis of their ethnic origin and were subject to blatant racism. This discrimination was often written into laws beyond the Immigration Act, such as detention, electoral, and employment legislation. During the First and Second World Wars, some who had come from countries with which Canada was at war were treated harshly. In the first contest, Canada interned immigrants from the Ukraine, and because the federal franchise was sometimes based on provincial franchises, the bias against Asians in British Columbia carried over to federal elections. At the federal level itself, Canadian citizens who came from countries with which Canada was at war (principally Germany and Austria) had their vote taken away in the 1917 election.

Untold cases of discrimination against both visible and invisible ethnic minorities in the area of employment have occurred throughout Canadian history. In the early part of the last century, for example, British Columbia labour laws prohibited the hiring of Asians in order to preserve jobs for whites, and in Saskatchewan, Chinese Canadians were not allowed to employ white women. Such discrimination extended to government employment and was sometimes even authorized by law. Blacks faced racial segregation in Ontario and Quebec, including schools.

The worst case of federal government mistreatment of visible minorities (other than Aboriginals) was that of Japanese Canadians in the Second World War. When Japan entered the war, Canadian citizens of Japanese origin were automatically suspected of being loyal to Japan, a suspicion without any foundation. Canadian citizens of Japanese background were uprooted from the west coast, interned in "relocation centres," and had their property confiscated. At the end of the war, about 4000 were deported.[8] Moreover, until after the Second World War, Canadians of Chinese, Japanese, and East Indian descent had no vote unless they had served in the armed forces. Conversely, until 1975, British subjects resident in Canada could vote in federal elections even without becoming Canadian citizens.

Immigrants have also faced a number of extra-legal barriers that made it difficult for them to play an active part in mainstream politics and government and society in general. One such barrier was discrimination within political parties. People of minority ethnocultural origins were generally not welcomed into mainstream parties, and

Menial jobs waiting for immigrants in Canada's "Land of Opportunity."

when they did find entry, they were usually given only subordinate roles. They had a hard time winning party nominations, unless it was in a hopeless or clear-cut "ethnic" constituency. It was not until the Diefenbaker era, around 1960, that Canadians of Ukrainian background started to make inroads into the Conservative Party; only two MPs before 1964 were from visible minorities.[9]

Most people who belong to visible minorities (as well as Aboriginals) faced racial animosity, at least including abusive comments, on a regular basis.[10] Even when laws were passed to prohibit discrimination in the employment market, visible minority immigrants often found it difficult to secure employment because their education and experience were frequently discounted and their skills underutilized. Even if they were successful in getting hired, they were often victims of pay inequities or promotion blockages.[11]

OVERCOMING DISCRIMINATION: MULTICULTURALISM, EQUITY, AND INCLUSIVENESS

It has already been noted that changes to the Immigration Act in 1967 began to alter the ethnic composition of the Canadian population and with it, Canadians' traditional perceptions of themselves. This increase in the numbers of people of different ethnocultural origins gave them more leverage to demand improvements in their status as citizens. Changes in the 1970s and 1980s were largely positive for such groups and started with the adoption of the policy of multiculturalism.

The original mandate of the 1963 Royal Commission on Bilingualism and Biculturalism was to concentrate on the English and French languages and cultures and to make recommendations in the wake of the Quiet Revolution in Quebec. By that time, however, the number of people in the country belonging to other ethnocultural groups was sufficient to force a change in the commission's terms of reference. Largely because of pressure from Ukrainian Canadians, the Royal Commission was also asked to examine "the contribution made by other ethnic groups to the cultural enrichment of Canada and the measures which should be taken to safeguard that contribution." The term "multiculturalism" came into use at about this time, and the commission recommended that increased government attention be given to other ethnic groups, including public funding in certain areas. With this encouragement, such groups began to demand public financial assistance as well as verbal and moral support.

In 1971, partly because of the Royal Commission recommendations, group pressure, and politicians hoping to win votes, the Trudeau government announced a new official policy of multiculturalism within a bilingual framework.[12] **Multiculturalism** is the official recognition of the diverse cultures in a plural society; it involves encouraging immigrants to retain their linguistic heritages and ethnic cultures instead of abandoning them and assimilating with the dominant group. The government felt that it was "overdue for the people of Canada to become more aware of the rich tradition of the many cultures"[13] in the country. It argued that the Canadian identity would not be undermined by multiculturalism; indeed, cultural pluralism was the very essence of the Canadian identity. Such diversity makes Canada a more interesting place to live in terms of foods, restaurants, languages, entertainment, sports, and cultures. In providing links to virtually every other country in the world, this array of ethnic groups also enhances Canada's international image and influence.[14] At the same time, members of ethnocultural minorities were encouraged to integrate linguistically by becoming fluent in English or French.

. . . .

BASIC OBJECTIVES OF MULTICULTURALISM POLICY

- To assist cultural groups in retaining and fostering their identity
- To assist cultural groups in overcoming barriers to their full participation in Canadian society
- To promote creative exchanges among all Canadian cultural groups
- To assist immigrants in acquiring at least one official language

Ottawa established a number of new programs to implement the multicultural policy and a government department to administer them. To some people of such ethnic origins, however, the policy did not provide for complete equality because the policy of official bilingualism preserved the historic dominance of the British and French groups. Others saw multiculturalism as more of a symbolic than substantive policy, one that was primarily aimed at preserving ethnic folklore. Some Quebeckers viewed multiculturalism as an attempt to diminish their claim of being a distinct society within Canada, as "French" culture was treated as just one of many others in the country.

One of the fascinating aspects of the multiculturalism policy was the role of the Citizenship Branch of the Secretary of State Department in funding multicultural advocacy groups in order to demand services, legislation, recognition, and rights from the government. This was done at the direction of the Trudeau Liberal government and served to help the party implement its campaign commitments and advance its own vision of the country.[15] Besides its financial support of individual minority ethnic groups and their diverse projects, the government established the Canadian Consultative Council on Multiculturalism in 1973, which was later renamed the Canadian Ethnocultural Council.

Once in place, the policy of multiculturalism legitimized demands for many other changes, in terms of both promoting ethnocultural identities and removing barriers to equity and inclusiveness. The next stage was the government's creation of the Canadian Human Rights Commission in 1978. Most provinces already had such bodies to deal with complaints of discrimination in the private sector and to promote anti-discrimination educational programs, but the new commission closed certain loopholes within the federal government's jurisdiction.

Another advance was the **Charter of Rights and Freedoms** in 1982, which provided constitutional protection against discrimination by federal and provincial governments in the equality rights clause, section 15. Moreover, the Charter endorsed affirmative action programs to overcome past discrimination. After intense pressure from various ethnocultural minorities, section 27 was added to the Charter to the effect that it would be interpreted "in a manner consistent with the preservation and enhancement of the multicultural heritage of Canadians."

The multiculturalism ministry that began to take form in the 1970s gradually increased in status, and 1988 saw the passage of a new Canadian Multiculturalism Act. The act gave multiculturalism a stronger legal base by consolidating existing policies and practices into legislation, provided a more detailed policy statement on multiculturalism, and created the Canadian Multicultural Advisory Committee. In 1991 the Mulroney government created a

THE CANADIAN PRESS/Frank Gunn

Kindergarten children in Toronto represent the changing face of urban Canadian schools.

new Department of Multiculturalism and Citizenship. Citizenship was later combined with Immigration, while multiculturalism became part of the Canadian Heritage Department, which reduced it in status.

In 1986 the federal **Employment Equity** Act designated visible minorities, women, people with disabilities, and Aboriginals as groups that could benefit from employment equity programs with respect to hiring in the public service and in large companies dealing with the government. Although those not included complained about reverse discrimination, some minority ethnic leaders criticized the lack of specific goals and timetables in the legislation.[16] It was strengthened in 1995.

The treatment of Japanese Canadians during the Second World War nagged at the Canadian conscience for nearly 45 years until the Mulroney government announced a settlement package in the 1988 **Japanese Redress Agreement**, which provided, among other things, $21 000 for each of the surviving internees. This led to demands from other ethnic minorities that they be similarly compensated for wartime discrimination in Canada.

Some provinces also demonstrated support for the concept of multiculturalism. Ontario, for example, instituted a heritage language policy in its school system. Then, in 1993, it passed the strongest employment equity legislation in the country, although the law did not survive the new provincial PC government elected in 1995. In Quebec, however, while French-speaking immigrants were welcomed in order to bolster the francophone population, other immigrants were required to attend the French-language school system and were otherwise encouraged to assimilate into the majority French culture. Some, such as the Haitian community, managed to hang on to their own culture at the same time.

On the partisan front, the Liberal Party, in particular, began to welcome ethnic minorities into its ranks. Such groups were naturally inclined toward the Liberal Party anyway, seeing that it had usually been in power when they arrived in the country and that it was the party that initiated the policy of multiculturalism. A common practice in many large cities was to pack Liberal Party nomination and leadership delegate selection meetings with "instant Liberals" from various ethnocultural groups—primarily Sikh, Italian, Greek, Portuguese, Croatian, Korean, Macedonian, and Chinese. This effort had the advantage of integrating these immigrants into the Canadian political process and of giving these minority ethnic groups the political influence they had previously lacked. On the other hand, they were not necessarily encouraged to remain active party members, and the practice sometimes provoked animosity between two or more such groups as well as alienating those who had worked hard for the party for many years.

Taking their cue from Aboriginal, francophone, and anglophone minority groups, nearly every other ethnic group established a national organization to promote its culture and to function as an advocacy group from time to time. Examples include the National Congress of Italian Canadians, the German Canadian Congress, and the National Association of Japanese Canadians. As noted above, the government itself actively encouraged many such groups to organize, and they were to find common ground in the Canadian Ethnocultural Council, which also received considerable government funding. The council now consists of a coalition of nearly 40 national ethnic organizations.

. . . .

BACKTRACKING IN THE 1990S

If the responses to demands from the multicultural community were largely positive in the 1970s and 1980s, such was not entirely the case in the 1990s. Opposition surfaced toward immigration in general and visible minority immigration in particular, as well as toward multiculturalism, employment equity, and other related policies and practices.[17]

This opposition was partly a response to the recession of the early 1990s and the continuing high unemployment rate afterward. Most economists agree that immigration has little effect on the unemployment rate and that it causes as many jobs to be created as immigrants actually fill. Moreover, they add, with a low birthrate and an aging population, Canada needs a relatively high annual intake of immigrants for economic reasons alone. Such views, however, were rejected by many voters in the 1990s, who saw recent immigrants taking jobs away from long-time residents. As for the source of immigrants, while the level of Canadian acceptance and tolerance of nontraditional immigrants is high, it is not unlimited. The Reform Party was the first to break ranks with an all-party consensus on these issues, calling for a severe cut in annual immigration levels and a greater emphasis on skills. Other parties resisted to some extent, but the Chrétien government reduced the target from 250 000 to about 200 000 in 1994, imposed a $975 right-of-landing fee, and announced that it would withdraw from the direct delivery of immigrant integration services. This withdrawal would shift the cost of immigrant integration to provincial/territorial and local governments, families, and community groups. Opposition was probably also related to a small number of high-profile crimes committed by immigrants who had been ordered deported but who had remained in the country, as well as to the numerous illegal immigrants and bogus refugee claimants who continued to make a new home in Canada.[18]

The policy of official multiculturalism was also under increasing attack. In an era of neoliberalism and government fiscal restraint, more and more Canadians were reluctant to provide public funding for multicultural purposes, a sentiment first given official voice by the Spicer Commission in 1991.[19] Some members of the multicultural community even spoke out against the policy, especially writer Neil Bissoondath. They maintained that official multiculturalism was divisive, that it ghettoized visible minorities, fostered racial animosity, and detracted from national unity.[20] Such critics argued that multiculturalism emphasized our differences rather than our similarities as Canadians, and that with the concern about balancing the government's books, it was hardly appropriate to foster the maintenance of foreign traditions while starving national cultural institutions. The money would be better spent teaching immigrants about basic Canadian values.

Others attacked multiculturalism from a different angle. For example, in refuting the claim of systemic prejudice and discrimination against visible minorities, Martin Loney argued that the people at a real disadvantage in Canadian society are the poor—of every ethnic origin. The money provided for public subsidization of multiculturalism, Loney stated, would be better spent on those who truly need it.[21]

Even the positive treatment of multiculturalism in the 1992 Charlottetown Accord was greeted with mixed feelings. The framers of the Accord wrote that "Canadians are committed to racial and ethnic equality in a society that includes citizens from many lands who have contributed, and continue to contribute, to the building of a strong Canada that reflects its cultural and racial diversity." Some multicultural leaders complained, however, that this clause was only a statement of equality, building on section 15 of the Charter, and not an enhancement of the principle of multiculturalism, as contained in section 27. In other words, for some multicultural advocates, guaranteeing *equity* was not enough; they also wanted government to go further to protect and promote *identity*.[22]

Similarly, the 1990 decision of the RCMP to allow Sikh Mounties to wear turbans as a religious symbol produced considerable opposition. So did the wearing of turbans in the halls of the Royal Canadian Legion. On the other hand, the House of Commons lost no time in waiving a similar rule when the first turbaned Sikh MP was elected in 1993. Since most newcomers to Canada settle in Toronto, Montreal, and Vancouver, an increase in racial tensions in these three cities became apparent in the 1990s.

THE CANADIAN PRESS/Adrian Wyld

Ujjal Dosanjh became the first Indo-Canadian premier and later the federal Minister of Health.

Relations between the Black community and the Montreal and Toronto police forces were strained, and because some police forces believed that people of certain ethnic groups were disproportionately involved in crime, they engaged in the practice of racial profiling.

. . . .

CURRENT ETHNOCULTURAL ISSUES

Generally speaking, racial and ethnic discrimination has probably declined in Canada since the turn of the new century, but the number of areas in which equality and identity issues emerge has certainly increased. And, to some extent, new issues have replaced older ones that have been resolved.[23]

Canadians of nontraditional ethnic origins are sensitive to the way in which the media portrays them. In many cases, the complaint is that they are not portrayed at all, and that the media presents a picture of a homogeneous, white Canadian society. Immigrant and visible minorities continue to claim that the media do not devote much attention to stories of interest to them and, if they are mentioned, they are portrayed as criminals or as people who defraud the welfare system.[24] To some extent this is changing, however, as television stations now hire a number of anchors and reporters who are members of visible minority groups.

The Immigration Act and Refugee Protection Act was amended and renamed by the Chrétien government in 2002, and tweaked again by both the Martin and Harper governments. Even if the act is essentially colour-blind, it contains potential for discrimination and controversy. First, how many immigrants should Canada take per year? In recent years, the number has been quite consistently about 250 000 and while advocates of both larger and smaller numbers can be heard, the Harper government reduced the landing fee by one-half. Second, which categories of immigrants should be emphasized—family reunification, skilled immigrants, or entrepreneurs—and how many points should be allotted for different abilities and traits? What weight should be given to higher education, English- or French-language fluency, work experience, prearranged employment, and family ties? Should foreign students be allowed to work while attending school in Canada and to obtain work visas after graduating? In mid-2008, the Harper government gave the Minister of Citizenship and Immigration more power to control the number and type of people allowed in as permanent residents, a policy change defended on the grounds that it would fast-track skilled workers to meet the needs of the Canadian economy. This action provoked criticism, however, because it left considerable discretion to the minister, and because it could result in a reduction of immigrants admitted in the family reunification category.

Ministerial discretion is also often involved in individual immigration cases. This is largely because of the wide scope for minister-issued permits to remain in Canada when an immigrant is turned down by regular bureaucratic processes. Paul Martin's first immigration minister, Judy Sgro, resigned over this issue (allegedly involving strippers and pizza companies), while her accuser was deported back to India. But the problem of individuals, their lawyers, and their MPs appealing to the minister for special consideration is unfortunately very common, and ministerial decisions are often arbitrary and controversial.

The role of the provinces in the immigration process is definitely increasing. Although immigration is a concurrent constitutional responsibility of both levels of government, Quebec was the only province to take much interest in it until fairly recently. Over the years, Ottawa has gradually widened Quebec's authority to choose its own immigrants, as it preferred those who spoke French, but many of the other provinces have now sought similar involvement because they wanted larger numbers or were looking for particular skills. Because this devolution has been agreeable to both sides, it has not been particularly controversial, but some observers would question how much uniformity of standards has remained.

As for refugees, the Chrétien government tried to streamline the system and deal more effectively with bogus refugees and other undesirables. It also signed an agreement with the United States to turn back at the border refugee claimants who had come through that country on their way to Canada on the basis that asylum-seekers should be processed where they first land. Critics pointed out that this would disallow certain categories of refugees because the U.S. has a more restrictive refugee policy; moreover, if claimants somehow managed to get into Canada illegally, they would have the right to a formal hearing. Sure enough, the reciprocal refugee-processing agreement between Canada and the United States was criticized in a Federal Court decision for precisely the reasons listed.

Indeed, immigration cases constitute a large part of the workload of the Federal Court, as seen in Chapter 24. Sometimes ethnocultural cases also get to the Supreme Court of Canada. In a number of communities, for example, the issue of Sikh children wearing their kirpan (ceremonial dagger) to school was been raised, and a Supreme Court decision in 2006 which permitted such a practice has certainly not silenced those who feel that it constitutes a danger in the schoolyard.[25]

Canada has witnessed an increasing incidence of gang crime in recent years, and some such gangs are based on ethnicity. Inter-ethnic gang wars seem to be more common, especially in Vancouver and Toronto, and the latter experienced an explosion of gun-related murders in 2005, many of which police attributed to such gang warfare. Some observers contend, however, that gang warfare, either of ethnic or non-ethnic dimensions, is primarily related to poverty and the inadequacy of social support programs.

Speaking of poverty, studies of recent immigrants have concluded that they do not do as well financially as either earlier immigrants or Canadian-born counterparts, and in fact many live below the poverty line. One factor in this scenario is that recent immigrants have trouble entering the work force because their professional credentials are often not recognized by provincial or territorial accreditation bodies, although this problem is often due to inadequate knowledge of English or French. Immigrant women especially find it difficult to stay in one job long enough to qualify for employment insurance benefits, so that they often fall back on social assistance. The attributes of ethnicity, gender, and class often reinforce each other.

Many ethnocultural minorities continue to experience discrimination. Blacks, South Asians, and Chinese were the leading groups to report discrimination in a 2002 study, especially in the workplace and in retail settings.[26] After the events of September 11, 2001, it was often Canadian Muslims and Arabs who were victims of a backlash, especially being subjected to greater scrutiny by law enforcement and immigration officials and airport security personnel.[27] Besides being subjects of suspicion within Canada, many Muslims and Arabs found it difficult to enter the United States, and a few who did, such as Maher Arar, found themselves unjustly targeted as terrorists.

The integration of newcomers into Quebec society is a particular problem, especially for those whose sense of nationalism is based more on French ethnicity than being a resident of a civic, inclusive Quebec. When opposition to making concessions to immigrants flared up in the province, Premier Charest found it advisable to appoint a commission to make recommendations on "reasonable accommodation." That commission basically argued that immigrants were not a threat to the French character of Quebec, but that did not end the debate. Many Canadians outside Quebec would also like to demand a greater commitment to Canadian citizenship. A 2005 survey found that only 20 percent of respondents agreed with the statement that "the government should encourage immigrants to maintain their identity and culture," while 69 percent thought that immigrants "should integrate and become part of the Canadian culture."[28]

Members of ethnocultural minorities often complain that employment equity programs are insufficient in preventing discrimination, for even where they exist, visible-minority immigrants are underrepresented at senior levels of most organizations, including the Government of Canada. On the other side of this issue are those who claim that employment equity makes them victims of "reverse discrimination," a difference of perception that will probably never be resolved. The abolition of racially segregated schools was considered an advance, but ironically, Toronto recently established a black-centred school to try to counter the high drop-out rate among such students.

Once the Mulroney government enacted the Japanese Redress Agreement, other groups began to appeal for apologies or compensation for the way they had been treated in earlier eras of Canadian history. This included Ukrainian Canadians in the First World War and Italian Canadians in the Second, who had suffered somewhat similar treatment to Japanese Canadians. The Martin government signed a redress agreement related to the head-tax that was charged to Chinese immigrants between 1885 and 1923, which the Harper government completed with a compensatory grant of $20 000 to each survivor or his or her widowed spouse.[29]

Some observers also see the concept of dual citizenship as a problem. According to the 2001 census, about 700 000 Canadians are also citizens of another country. Arguments can be made on either side of this question, but on her appointment as governor general, Michaëlle Jean felt it appropriate to renounce the French part of her dual citizenship. Related to this is the charge that some immigrants are too engaged in homeland politics and that they bring internal ethnic conflicts to their new land. Some undoubtedly see themselves as "diaspora"— displaced from the homeland for various reasons, but hoping to return. The Sikh and Sri Lanka communities are sometimes singled out in this connection, but they are not alone. It is also said that involvement in politics abroad tends to deflect energies away from political participation in Canada. Stasiulis and Abu-Laban admit that homeland politics is a common occurrence among many ethnic minorities, but answer the criticism in these terms: "There is little evidence that an ethnic community highly politicized on homeland issues cannot simultaneously participate in Canadian politics."[30]

Although members of ethnic minorities are involved in all aspects of public policies, one particular area of interest to many of them is Canadian foreign policy. The Harper government, for example, was often criticized by Arab-Canadian groups for its staunch support of Israel in outbreaks of violence in the Middle East. This criticism was reinforced by what many regarded as a government hard line on questionable terrorist suspects, such as Omar Khadr, and the general Arab-Muslim focus of anti-terrorism policies.

For political scientists, the most interesting question about ethnocultural minorities is their role in political parties, elections, and the resulting political representation. Although political parties obviously discriminated against members of visible minorities as candidates in the past, for example, what is the current situation? The number of candidates and MPs from both visible and invisible ethnic minorities generally continues to increase, but still remains considerably below their proportion of the overall population.[31] Stasiulis and Abu-Laban explain this as follows:

> [T]he statistical underrepresentation of ethnic and visible minorities within the major parties can be explained in terms of a variety of structural, cultural, and organizational obstacles. For recent immigrants lacking official-language skills, linguistic barriers intersect with lack of familiarity with the Canadian political culture and system. Racial minorities confront discrimination practiced at the highest levels of party structures.... [F]or all marginalized groups, there is a legacy of exclusion that is reinforced by the hegemonic bicultural discourse of party politics, by patterns of recruitment through networks, and by party traditions such as the incumbency factor within the electoral process.[32]

Historically, as mentioned, the Liberal party had a virtual stranglehold on the minority ethnic vote, but somewhat surprisingly, the Conservative Party has recently found itself with the largest representation of visible minority MPs in its caucus. That party has found favour with more conservative-minded immigrant groups on such issues as low taxes, same-sex marriage, and feminism. After 2006, the Harper government vigorously wooed ethnocultural minorities through mailings and appearances at their celebrations, seeking to change their political persuasion from Liberal to Conservative, and made considerable headway in the 2008 election results.

. . . .

CONCLUSION

Various waves of immigration have challenged traditional conceptions of what it is to be Canadian. Given the current low birthrate, immigration is necessary for any expansion of the Canadian economy. Now coming primarily from developing countries, immigrants are increasingly demanding their share of political influence as well as more government support in their quest for equity and identity. Despite official multiculturalism and employment equity policies, many continue to experience considerable discrimination at an everyday level. Canada may well be a world leader in the way a variety of ethnocultural communities live together peacefully, but ethnic tensions are increasing, particularly in Canada's largest metropolitan centres. These tensions occasionally result in violence, including ethnic gang activity, which some observers relate to high levels of immigrant poverty and the reduction of social support programs in the 1990s. Although most Canadians value the policy of multiculturalism, they would also prefer to see immigrants integrate themselves more fully into the wider Canadian society.

Issues related to ethnocultural minorities are readdressed in Chapters 7 (gender) and 8 (class). They are mentioned again in Chapters 13, 14, and 15 in connection with parties and elections. Ethnocultural issues are revisited in Chapter 19 (Charter of Rights and Freedoms), and immigration cases constitute a large part of the workload of the Federal Court, as seen in Chapter 24.

| P | Ethnic diversity is the essence of the pluralist approach. Combined with the diversity of the Aboriginal, British, and French elements of the population, the influx of other ethnocultural groups makes Canada one of the most heterogeneous societies in the world. Even before the official policy of multiculturalism was enunciated, many Canadians of all origins celebrated this diversity as a key component of the Canadian national identity: a cultural mosaic in

contrast to the American melting pot. The pluralist approach therefore relates to the interaction of many ethnic advocacy groups as they seek to promote increased immigration (especially from their home country), good relations between Canada and the country of origin, multiculturalism, employment equity, constitutional status, and changes in traditional Canadian ways. Organized ethnic groups eventually took advantage of the slack in the system as their members grew in numbers and self-confidence, gained pride in their identities, worked with relevant government officials and agencies in a specialized and tightly knit policy community, and became active within political party organizations. Even so, it would be difficult to argue that such groups have obtained a position of equality with more established interests.

PC The public choice approach is also relevant to developments in multiculturalism in the past 40 years. When ethnic groups began to represent significant numbers of voters, the Liberal Party adopted policies fostering higher levels of immigration as well as multiculturalism. It promised even more in return for votes and participation, especially at its nomination meetings. The Mulroney Conservatives followed suit in the 1984–93 period. In the 1990s, however, parties had to be more circumspect. The Liberals tried to retain the support of the ethnocultural minorities with high immigration levels but, for a variety of reasons outlined above, faced the opposition of certain other voters, diluting the government's enthusiasm for both immigration and state-supported multiculturalism. Especially after 2004, the Conservative party made concerted efforts to woo the ethnocultural vote and had considerable success in breaking the Liberal–ethnocultural link.

SC The state-centred approach is most applicable to the pre-1970 period, in which politicians and bureaucrats formulated policies in this field isolated from societal pressures. Until recently, the state elite contained very few people of non-British or non-French origin, and most were not only insensitive to other ethnocultural concerns but were actually determined to keep the country as white as possible.[33] John Porter found such a *vertical mosaic* in the political elite as well as in all the other societal elites that he studied.[34] Cabinets and bureaucracies in Ottawa and certain provinces and territories have reflected more varied hues in recent years, but policy changes may be related more to voting power and public opinion than to actual changes within the state elite.

In another sense, the state-centred approach was particularly relevant to the Trudeau era. Around the time that the policy of official multiculturalism was adopted, the government sought to create multicultural advocacy organizations that would promote its own agenda. The politicians and bureaucrats justified their actions by arguing that such interests were inherently difficult to organize on their own. Fledgling minority ethnic groups (which just happened to represent large numbers of new voters) therefore required government support.[35]

© Class analysts emphasize the class nature of ethnicity in Canada; for them, ethnic inequalities are merely an aspect of economic and class inequalities in society and result from the capitalist pursuit of profit. Domestic and multinational companies often exploited immigrant labour—for example, indentured Chinese immigrants who built the CPR, workers in the garment trade in Toronto or Montreal, or seasonal agricultural workers. Individual affluent Canadian families may also have taken advantage of foreign domestics and caregivers. Supported by such corporations and other wealthy interests, traditional political parties tried to co-opt ethnic minority leaders and disguise the real interests of such groups by promising recognition of their cultural identities rather than genuine economic equality. However, many ethnic minority leaders preferred this kind of recognition.[36] Class analysts also point out that Canada continues to prefer business immigrants, while ordinary immigrants are increasingly falling below the poverty line.

(G) Canada has always been deeply involved in the migration of people from one state to another, both as a means of populating the country and as a humanitarian home to refugees. But the increasing number and diversity of such immigrants, especially since 1990 or so, is a mark of intensified globalization. The extent to which immigrants and refugees are seen as a tool to strengthen the competitiveness of the Canadian economy rather than in terms of valuing diversity and social justice is a particular influence of the contemporary neoliberal variety of globalization.[37]

. . . .
DISCUSSION QUESTIONS

1. What annual levels of immigration do you think are appropriate? What kinds of immigrants should Canada seek?

2. How has massive recent immigration affected the Canadian identity?

3. To what extent should immigrants be encouraged to retain their languages, cultures, and customs? Should such retention be supported by the public purse?

4. To what extent should established Canadian practices and customs be modified to accommodate recent immigrants?

. . . .
NOTES

1. Statistics Canada, *Canada's Ethnocultural Mosaic*, 2006 Census, Catalogue no. 97-562.
2. "2006 Census: Immigration, citizenship, language, mobility and migration," *The Daily*, December 4, 2007, available at http://www.statcan.gc.ca/daily-quotiden/071204/dq071204a-eng.htm.
3. Daiva Stasiulis and Yasmeen Abu-Laban, "Unequal Relations and the Struggle for Equality: Race and Ethnicity in Canadian Politics," in Michael Whittington and Glen Williams, eds., *Canadian Politics in the 21st Century*, 7th ed. (Toronto: Nelson Education, 2008), p. 288. Much of the following discussion relies on this source.
4. Ibid., p. 304.
5. Anne Milan and Kelly Tran, "Blacks in Canada: A Long History," *Canadian Social Trends* (Statistics Canada, Catalogue No. 11-008, Spring 2004).
6. Alain Bélanger and Eric Caron Malenfant, "Ethnocultural Diversity in Canada: Prospects for 2017," *Canadian Social Trends* (Statistics Canada, Catalogue No. 11-008, Winter 2005).
7. Stasiulis and Abu-Laban, "Unequal Relations," 7th ed., pp. 290–91, is one account of this bigotry.
8. Ann Gomer Sunahara, *The Politics of Racism: The Uprooting of Japanese Canadians during the Second World War* (Toronto: Lorimer, 1981).
9. Alain Pelletier, "Politics and Ethnicity: Representation of Ethnic and Visible Minority Groups in the House of Commons," in K. Megyery, ed., *Ethnocultural Groups and Visible Minorities in Canadian Politics: The Question of Access* (Toronto: Dundurn Press, 1991), p. 127.

10. For example, John Marlyn, *Under the Ribs of Death* (Toronto: McClelland and Stewart, 1957, 1964). Debra Thompson asks why racism has received so little academic examination in Canadian political science in "Is Race Political?" *Canadian Journal of Political Science* (September 2008).

11. Kelly Tran, "Visible Minorities in the Labour Force: 20 Years of Change," *Canadian Social Trends* (Statistics Canada, Catalogue No. 11-008, Summer 2004); and Boris Palameta, "Low Income among Immigrants and Visible Minorities," *Perspectives* (Statistics Canada, Catalogue No. 75-001-XPE, Summer 2004).

12. Many observers also feel that the policy of multiculturalism was a means of undercutting any recognition of Quebec's distinct culture or distinct status.

13. Prime Minister's Statement in the House of Commons, October 8, 1971; and Andrew Cardozo and Louis Musto, eds., *The Battle over Multiculturalism: Does It Help or Hinder Canadian Unity?* (Ottawa: PSI Publishing, 1997).

14. The most philosophical (but still very readable) discussion of multiculturalism in Canada can be found in the writings of Will Kymlicka, such as *Finding Our Way: Rethinking Ethnocultural Relations in Canada* (Don Mills: Oxford University Press, 1998).

15. Leslie Pal, *Interests of State: The Politics of Language, Multiculturalism, and Feminism in Canada* (Montreal: McGill-Queen's University Press, 1993).

16. Daiva Stasiulis, "Deep Diversity: Race and Ethnicity in Canadian Politics," in M.S. Whittington and G. Williams, eds., *Canadian Politics in the 1990s*, 4th ed. (Scarborough: Nelson Canada, 1995), p. 209.

17. Jean Leonard Elliott and Augie Fleras, *Multiculturalism in Canada: The Challenge of Diversity* (Scarborough: Nelson Canada, 1991), and *Unequal Relations: An Introduction to Race and Ethnic Dynamics in Canada* (Scarborough: Prentice Hall Canada, 1991); Audrey Kobayashi, "Ethnocultural Political Mobilization, Multiculturalism, and Human Rights in Canada," in Miriam Smith, ed., *Group Politics and Social Movements in Canada* (Peterborough: Broadview Press, 2008).

18. Stasiulis and Abu-Laban, "Unequal Relations and the Struggle for Equality," p. 389; and Donald E. Blake, "Environmental Determinants of Racial Attitudes among White Canadians," in *Canadian Journal of Political Science* (July/August 2003).

19. Citizens' Forum on Canada's Future, *Report to the People and Government of Canada* (Ottawa: Supply and Services, 1991).

20. Neil Bissoondath, *Selling Illusions: The Cult of Multiculturalism in Canada* (Toronto: Penguin, 1994).

21. Martin Loney, *The Pursuit of Division: Race, Gender, and Preferential Hiring in Canada* (Montreal: McGill-Queen's University Press, 1998).

22. Abu-Laban, "The Politics of Race and Ethnicity," p. 251.

23. See Institute for Research on Public Policy, *Policy Options*, June 2008.

24. Stasiulis and Abu-Laban, "Unequal Relations," 6th edition, p. 375.

25. *Multani v. Commission scolaire Marguerite-Bourgeoys*, [2006] 1 S.C.R. 256.

26. Mohammed Al-Waqfi and Harish C. Jain, "Racial inequality in employment in Canada: Empirical analysis and emerging trends," *Canadian Public Administration* (September 2008).

27. Stasiulis and Abu-Laban, "Unequal Relations," 6th ed., p. 371.

28. Globe and Mail/CTV poll conducted by The Strategic Counsel, *Globe and Mail*, August 12, 2005.

29. Matt James, "Recognition, Redistribution, and Redress: The Case of the 'Chinese Head Tax'" *Canadian Journal of Political Science* (December 2004); Stephen Winter, "The Stakes of Inclusion: Chinese Canadian Head Tax Redress," *Canadian Journal of Political Science* (March 2008).

30. Stasiulis and Abu-Laban, "Unequal Relations," 7th ed., p. 299.

31. Jerome H. Black and Lynda Erickson, "Ethno-Racial Origins of Candidates and Electoral Performance: Evidence from Canada," *Party Politics* 12, 4 (2006): 541–61.

32. Stasiulis and Abu-Laban, "Unequal Relations and the Struggle for Equality," 7th ed., p. 298.

33. Stasiulis, "Deep Diversity," pp. 196–98.

34. John Porter, *The Vertical Mosaic* (Toronto: University of Toronto Press, 1965); and Rick Helmes-Hayes and James Curtis, eds., *The Vertical Mosaic Revisited* (Toronto: University of Toronto Press, 1998).

35. Pal, *Interests of State*.

36. Karl Peter, "The Myth of Multiculturalism and Other Political Fables," in Jorgen Dahlie and Tissa Fernando, eds., *Ethnicity, Power and Politics in Canada* (Toronto: Methuen, 1981); Kogila Moodley,

"Canadian Multiculturalism as Ideology," *Ethnic and Racial Studies* (July 1983); and Loney, *The Pursuit of Division.*

37. Yasmeen Abu-Laban and Christina Gabriel, *Selling Diversity: Immigration, Multiculturalism, Employment Equity, and Globalization* (Peterborough: Broadview Press, 2002).

. . . .

FURTHER READING

Abu-Laban, Yasmeen, and Christina Gabriel. *Selling Diversity: Immigration, Multiculturalism, Employment Equity, and Globalization.* Peterborough: Broadview Press, 2002.

Bissoondath, Neil. *Selling Illusions: The Cult of Multiculturalism in Canada.* Toronto: Penguin, 1994.

Black, Jerome H., and Lynda Erickson. "Ethno-Racial Origins of Candidates and Electoral Performance: Evidence from Canada." *Party Politics* 12, 4 (2006): 541–61.

Cardozo, Andrew, and Louis Musto, eds. *The Battle over Multiculturalism: Does It Help or Hinder Canadian Unity?* Ottawa: PSI Publishing, 1997.

Day, Richard J.F. *Multiculturalism and the History of Canadian Diversity.* Toronto: University of Toronto Press, 2000.

James, Carl, ed. *Possibilities and Limitations: Multicultural Policies and Programs in Canada.* Black Point, NS: Fernwood Publishing, 2005.

Kelley, Ninette, and Michael Trebilcock. *The Making of the Mosaic: A History of Canadian Immigration Policy.* Toronto: University of Toronto Press, 1998.

Kernerman, Gerald. *Multicultural Nationalism: Civilizing Difference, Constituting Community.* Vancouver: UBC Press, 2005.

Kymlicka, Will. *Finding Our Way: Rethinking Ethnocultural Relations in Canada.* Don Mills: Oxford University Press, 1998.

Pal, Leslie. *Interests of State: The Politics of Language, Multiculturalism, and Feminism in Canada.* Montreal: McGill–Queen's University Press, 1993.

Pratt, Anna. *Securing Borders: Detention and Deportation in Canada.* Vancouver: UBC Press, 2005.

Stasiulis, Daiva. "Unequal Relations and the Struggle for Equality: Race and Ethnicity in Canadian Politics." In Michael Whittington and Glen Williams, eds., *Canadian Politics in the 21st Century,* 7th edn. Toronto: Nelson Education, 2008.

Stoffman, Daniel. *Who Gets In: What's Wrong with Canada's Immigration Program—and How to Fix It.* Toronto: Macfarlane Walter Ross, 2002.

Sunahara, Ann Gomer. *The Politics of Racism: The Uprooting of Japanese Canadians during the Second World War.* Toronto: Lorimer, 1981.

Troper, Harold, and Morton Weinfeld. *Ethnicity, Politics and Public Policy.* Toronto: University of Toronto Press, 1999.

Chapter 7

GENDER

Feminists seek gender equality—employment equity, pay equity, equity in law, equity in the various institutions of government, and equity in the family setting. Not all women agree on all these demands, however, and a large proportion of men support most of them. Although the proportion of women prominent in politics and government is generally increasing, it remains far below 50 percent. Sexual harassment and assault have become major societal concerns, as have abortion, divorce, child care, and many issues related to reproduction. Gender issues have created considerable political controversy and are of increasing significance as women take a more equal part in the economic and political systems. Child care, for example, was a prominent issue in the 2006 election campaign. Beyond the equality of women are other gender-related issues, specifically concerning the gay and lesbian communities, especially the question of same-sex marriage.

This chapter begins by looking at certain theoretical considerations regarding gender, before outlining the historical evolution of women's rights in Canada. It then examines issues relating to the women's movement today, which has brought a new set of demands onto the political agenda. After discussing the contemporary manifestations of such issues, the chapter concludes with an overview of gay and lesbian concerns.

THEORETICAL CONSIDERATIONS

Gender is more than meets the eye. Although the concepts of gender and sex are closely related, the distinction that is usually made between them is that sex refers to biological differences between men and women while gender refers to the behavioural, cultural, or psychological traits associated with one's sex; it is socially and politically constructed.[1] As explained in Chapter 1, structuralists emphasize the role of social structures—traditions, customs, practices, and institutions—in determining how individual members of society see themselves and behave. Such structures contribute to our identities, whether we realize it or not, and the concept of gender is closely related to that of identity.

Also referring back to the notion of hegemony in Chapter 1, the traditional way of looking at politics was through men's eyes because we just always thought in those terms. We operated within the context of the dominant values and expectations of society. Men were the main players in the political system, as well as the analysts and interpreters of that system; men made the decisions, and they defined what politics was all about.

Focusing again on identities, we all have multiple identities, and those most important to us can change over time. Because other cleavages and identities overshadowed gender for the first 100 years after Confederation, "farm women, working women, French-Canadian women, Protestant women, western women, [and] city women had quite different collective identities following from the ways in which class, religion, and place entwined in Canadian politics. There was no single identity, nor was there a single women's politics."[2] One of the main forces behind the whole discussion of identity politics in the past 40 years or so, however, has been the women's movement, as women increasingly put a priority on gender in determining their identity. As women became conscious of their fundamental difference from men in so many aspects of the political system, they began to emphasize gender politics and the politics of recognition. Of course, such women were not all agreed on what policies should be adopted in their interests—ideological differences among them remained—but they did share a new consciousness that it was their gender that was important. This movement also broadened the idea of what is "political." The feminist movement argued that the traditional male definition of politics was too narrow; for example, men had overlooked aspects of the political system in which women had been significant participants: community groups, charities, and other informal local networks.[3]

Given the feminist movement's basic objective of achieving gender equality, it has also alerted us to different conceptions of equality. Policies that provide for formal gender equality may seem to be desirable, but they may result in outcomes that do not achieve substantive equality. Feminists point out that in certain situations, women may have to be treated differently from men in order to achieve such genuine equality.

Strangely enough, in the 21st century, many women reverted to thinking of their identities in terms of their other demographic characteristics. Nevertheless, having put the gender stamp on the political system, women were soon followed by other interests that gave new emphasis to their gender identities, among them the gay, lesbian, bisexual, and transgendered communities.

. . . .

EVOLUTION OF WOMEN'S RIGHTS TO 1970

Men and male-oriented issues virtually monopolized Canadian politics before 1900. In those early years, when women were expected to marry and then became chattels of their husbands, they first had to fight for educational and occupational rights, such as admission to universities and to the medical and legal professions.[4] This battle was led by the first prominent feminist, Dr. Emily Stowe, who in 1880 was the first female to practise medicine in Canada. The first female lawyer was admitted to the bar in 1897. Women later demanded the right to make contracts and to own property, and they increasingly began to work in factories and offices, to become teachers and nurses, and to make major contributions on the farm. At the turn of the century, farm women in particular became active in reform organizations of many kinds, pressing for the prohibition of alcohol, the establishment of new public health facilities, better housing, and improved working conditions for women and children.

As influential as they were in promoting these causes, many women began to feel that their impact would always be limited until they could vote. Thus, in what is sometimes called the "first wave" of the women's movement, women demanded the franchise, an issue that did not necessarily pit all women against all men but still aroused great hostility. It was a conflict between those who saw women primarily as wives and mothers, whose influence could be best exercised within the home, and those who felt that women should be treated as equals of men in the wider society.

After the outbreak of the First World War, proponents of female suffrage had an additional argument—that women should be rewarded for their contribution to the war effort. Thus, after the vociferous efforts of some of the most articulate women of the day, Manitoba, Alberta, and Saskatchewan extended the right to vote in provincial elections to women in 1916; Ontario and British Columbia followed suit a year later; and all the jurisdictions except Quebec and the Northwest Territories shortly afterward. The first women legislators in the British Commonwealth, Louise McKinney and Roberta MacAdams, were elected in Alberta in 1917, and were replaced in 1921 by Nellie McClung and Irene Parlby. Mary Ellen Smith was elected to the BC legislature in 1918 and became the first Canadian female cabinet minister in 1921.

At the federal level, the Borden government deliberately manipulated the franchise for the 1917 election, in part by giving the vote to women in the armed services (mostly nurses) and to close relatives of soldiers fighting abroad—women who would likely support the war effort. With no adverse effects, the vote was extended a year later to all women, and they had their first chance to exercise this new right in the 1921 election.

Many reforms in social legislation took place immediately after the enfranchisement of women. These included mothers' allowances, child welfare acts, the prohibition of child labour, and an increase in the age for compulsory schooling and at which marriage could be

---

TABLE 7.1 Women's Franchise and First Woman Elected

	Franchise	*First Woman Elected*
Canada	1917–18	1921
Manitoba	1916	1920
Alberta	1916	1917
Saskatchewan	1916	1919
British Columbia	1917	1918
Ontario	1917	1943
Nova Scotia	1918	1960
New Brunswick	1919	1967
Yukon	1919	1967
Newfoundland	1925	1975
Quebec	1940	1961
Northwest Territories	1951	1970

Source: Penney Kome, Women of Influence: Canadian Women and Politics (Toronto: University of Toronto Press, 1985); Terence H. Qualter, The Electoral Process in Canada (Toronto: McGraw-Hill Ryerson, 1970).

THE CANADIAN PRESS/National Archives
of Canada PA-127295

Agnes Macphail, the first female
Member of Parliament in Canada.

solemnized within a province. At the federal level, the divorce law was amended to establish "equality of cause" between wife and husband, and the Old Age Pensions Act was passed.[5] These reforms and other advances were achieved only after constant pressure: organizing women's groups; writing leaflets, plays, and letters to the editor; engaging in demonstrations and debates; and lobbying politicians. Yet, although the right to vote entailed the right to hold office (except in New Brunswick until 1934), very few women were actually elected.

In 1921 Agnes Macphail was the first woman elected to the House of Commons and a second woman, Martha Black, was elected in 1935. Macphail stayed on until 1940 and then became one of the first two women elected to the Ontario legislature in 1943. A vigorous, articulate, and witty legislator, Macphail promoted radical and progressive causes of many kinds, but she could only do so much by herself to advance women's issues in such an entrenched male bastion.[6] The five most eastern provinces were slower to elect women, as Table 7.1 indicates. It was not until 1940 that Quebec women were enfranchised in provincial elections, largely as a result of the determined leadership of Thérèse Casgrain and after 13 previous bills to this effect were defeated. Even worse, the legal status of married women under the Quebec Civil Code was such that until 1955 a woman could not seek a separation on the grounds of her husband's adultery, and until 1964 had no right to carry on a trade without her husband's consent.[7]

The number of women who won seats in the House of Commons before 1970 was minuscule, as Table 7.2 demonstrates. Indeed, many of the pre-1970 female MPs were the widows or daughters of male members of Parliament. Female participation at the candidate level was inhibited by many factors. First, both sexes were traditionally socialized into the view that politics was a masculine pursuit and that women should remain in the home. Second, most women were constrained by the responsibilities of homemaking and child-rearing. Such roles had little prestige and prevented women from accumulating the money, contacts, and experience that political careers usually require. The long hours and unpredictable schedules of politicians conflicted with most women's family commitments, prevented them from being away from home for any length of time, and at least delayed a woman's entry into active politics. Third, political parties discouraged female candidacies, however much they needed women at the constituency level to raise money and stuff envelopes. Most parties set up a separate women's auxiliary organization rather than encourage their participation in the mainstream of the party. When consciousness of the lack of female candidates increased, women were nominated more frequently, but usually as sacrificial lambs against a strong male incumbent. This was especially evident in the two major parties, and led to the "law" that the closer a party is to power, the less likely it is to nominate women candidates.[8]

Until the late 1920s, no women had been appointed to the other house of Parliament, the Senate. When an enterprising group of Western women took this issue to court, the Supreme Court of Canada ruled in 1928 that women were not eligible for such appointment. In 1929 this decision was appealed to the Judicial Committee of the Privy Council, which in the **Persons case** overruled the Supreme Court and declared women to be "qualified

TABLE 7.2   Number of Women Elected in Federal Elections, 1921–1968

Election	Women	Election	Women
1921	1	1953	4
1925	1	1957	2
1926	1	1958	2
1930	1	1962	4
1935	2	1963	4
1940	1	1965	3
1945	1	1968	1
1949	0		

Source: Penney Kome, Women of Influence: Canadian Women and Politics (Toronto: University of Toronto Press, 1985); Terence H. Qualter, The Electoral Process in Canada (Toronto: McGraw-Hill Ryerson, 1970).

persons" within the meaning of section 24 of the 1867 Constitution Act and eligible to sit in the Senate. The women's movement continues to celebrate this decision in the form of the "Persons Day Breakfast." Prime Minister Mackenzie King immediately appointed Cairine Wilson to the Senate, but even here progress was slow. The second woman was not appointed until 1935, and 18 years would pass before three more received the call.

It was not until 1957 that the first woman, Ellen Fairclough, was appointed to the federal Cabinet, by John Diefenbaker; she was followed by Judy LaMarsh in 1963. The advance of women to the cabinet at the provincial level was also very slow. However, women were frequently elected to mayoralty posts and were often the backbone of quasi-political community organizations.

Nevertheless, gradual improvements continued to be made in federal and provincial programs and legislation. The federal Family Allowances Act of 1944, for example, provided a small monthly payment to each Canadian mother to help care for her children and often represented the only independent income the woman possessed. In 1952 Ontario passed the first equal pay legislation, to be followed by federal legislation two years later. The invention of the birth control pill in 1960 led to profound changes in many women's lives; amendments to the Criminal Code in 1969 allowed the advertisement of birth control devices in Canada; and a new Divorce Act in the same year made it easier for people to get out of an unfulfilling marriage.

This discussion of the advance of women in the formal political system has implied that women themselves did not play a very significant role, at least before 1970. Modern feminists challenge that view by arguing that the political participation and contribution of women should be seen in a broader light. They may have been scarce in the corridors of power, but they were active and important in "small-p" politics, often called "civil society" or organizations distinct from the family, state, and economy. This includes charities, nongovernmental organizations, community groups, women's groups, faith-based organizations, professional associations, unions, self-help groups, social movements, business associations, coalitions, and advocacy groups. As Jaquetta Newman argues, "we need to recognize these groups as *political*, not just social, actors. Their social networks and activism do not just "lead to" politics, but expand its definition.[9]

THE WOMEN'S MOVEMENT AFTER 1970

By 1970 attitudes toward women and their role in society had changed sufficiently that it was now possible to speak of the **women's movement**, and the word **feminist** became a common term. Such terms are used to describe those who seek to establish complete gender equality, to free men and women from restrictive gender roles, and to end the subordination of women. However, within the women's movement a variety of perspectives exist, including socialist feminists, Marxist feminists, radical feminists, and liberal feminists. As mentioned, there was even a call to "reinvent" the discipline of political science along feminist lines and to examine women's political participation in nontraditional forums. Moreover, it was shown that in such settings as the televised leaders' debate, the presence of a woman leader can make a difference.[10]

This "second wave" of the women's movement coincided with the **Royal Commission on the Status of Women**, appointed in 1967 and reporting in 1970. It "provided a solid statistical base and a framework for most of the feminist action that followed during the 1970s."[11] The Royal Commission made 167 recommendations, not all of which had been implemented some 40 years later. Since that time gender issues have become an important daily factor in Canadian politics, and most governments now designate a minister responsible for women's issues, a step that was pioneered at the federal level in 1971. In 1972 the federal government established the Office of Employment Opportunity, followed by the Canadian Advisory Council on the Status of Women in 1973; the first federal–provincial conference on women's issues convened in 1982, and in 1995 Ottawa issued the Federal Plan for Gender Equality. This plan committed the government to applying gender-based analysis in the development of all new legislation, policies, and programs. A major part of the government agency, Status of Women Canada, was the Women's Program, which supported the work of organizations promoting women's full participation in Canadian society.

Representation in Politics and Government

In the post-1970 era, women's participation in politics and government increased substantially. Table 7.3 shows the increase in the number and proportion of women in the House of Commons in this period. Many of the factors that inhibited women from becoming politicians before 1970 are still present, although in recent years some parties have created special funds to support female candidates. It is now an accepted truth of electoral politics that if a woman can manage to win a party nomination, she is at no disadvantage in the election to follow. However, the number and proportion of women elected appeared to plateau after 1997.

At the Cabinet level, Jeanne Sauvé was appointed in 1972, Monique Bégin and Iona Campagnolo in 1976, and Flora MacDonald in 1979, but by the 1980s one or two token female ministers were clearly insufficient. Brian Mulroney usually had six women in his cabinets after 1984, and the rest of the provinces and territories eventually appointed women ministers. Bob Rae came close to gender equality in his 1990 Ontario NDP cabinet: 11 women out of 26.

TABLE 7.3 Representation of Women in the House of Commons, 1972–2008

Election	Number Elected	Percentage of MPs
1972	4	2
1974	9	3
1979	11	4
1980	14	5
1984	27	10
1988	39	13
1993	53	18
1997	62	21
2000	62	21
2004	65	21
2006	64	21
2008	69	22

Source: Status of Women Canada, Towards Equality for Women—A Canadian Chronology, 1994. Reproduced with the permission of the Minister of Public Works and Government Services Canada, 2006; updated by author.

In the post-1970 period Canada finally saw women elected as political party leaders. Alexa McDonough (NDP) led the way in Nova Scotia in 1980, and the list of provincial parties led by women since then is too long to enumerate. After Rosemary Brown made a serious stab at the NDP national leadership in 1975 and Flora MacDonald for the PCs in 1976, it remained for Audrey McLaughlin to make history when she was elected leader of the federal New Democratic Party in 1989, the first woman to lead a major national party. Alexa McDonough succeeded her in 1995, and Elizabeth May became the national Green Party leader in 2006.

Two of these provincial leaders even served as premier. Rita Johnston inherited the BC premiership from her disgraced predecessor, Bill Vander Zalm, while Catherine Callbeck in Prince Edward Island was the first woman to be elected to premiership in 1993. Somewhat similarly to Johnston, Kim Campbell took over the federal PC leadership and prime minister-ship in 1993, only to lose the subsequent election to Jean Chrétien, at least partly because of the faults of her male predecessor.

Jeanne Sauvé pioneered women's political participation in several fields: she was the third federal woman Cabinet minister, the first woman Speaker of the House of Commons, and the first woman governor general (1984), followed by Adrienne Clarkson in 1999 and Michaëlle Jean in 2005. Meanwhile, Bertha Wilson became the first woman to sit on the Supreme Court of Canada in 1982. After 1989, the Supreme Court had either two or three women out of nine, until it increased to four as a result of Paul Martin's 2004 appointments. Women judges have also been appointed at an ever-increasing rate in other courts, and constitute about one-quarter of those appointed by the federal government.

Within the federal bureaucracy, the first women joined the RCMP in 1974, and the first woman deputy minister (Sylvia Ostry) was appointed in 1975; in the 1980s, women became eligible for full combat roles in the armed forces, and the first woman general was named in 1988. In 1993, Jocelyn Bourgon became the first woman to hold the top public service position in Ottawa, Clerk of the Privy Council and Secretary to the Cabinet. Women have also increased their participation in provincial and territorial government and politics beyond the positions mentioned above; many have become successful ministers of finance.[12] But despite these breakthroughs at the provincial, territorial, and federal levels in absolute numbers, many observers still raise the question of how much influence women have in the policy-making process.

To bring the discussion up to date, Table 7.4 reveals that the number and percent of women candidates and MPs elected in the 2008 federal election did not constitute a significant advance. The figures do show, however, that if a party or party leader is determined to increase the number of female candidates, it will have some effect, as Liberal leader Stéphane Dion was insistent that the party run more such candidates.

Beyond the question of candidates, political scientists are particularly interested in the behaviour of women voters.[13] As mentioned in Chapter 15, there is a tendency for women voters to prefer the Liberals and NDP to the Conservatives. Several observers have noted that the Harper Conservatives were unlikely to win a majority government without greater support from the female half of the electorate. Nevertheless, unlike its efforts to woo Quebeckers and ethnocultural minorities, that party did little to appeal to women voters after 2006. There were no women of significance in the 2006–08 Cabinet or wider administration, and several government decisions, such as the cancellation of the Court Challenges Program, were clearly contrary to women's interests, as noted in Chapter 19. More women were appointed to the post-2008 election Harper Cabinet, as seen in Chapter 21.

In terms of basic ideology, some parties and governments have moved back from the extremes of neoliberalism, but the Harper government remained relatively firm on "women's issues." For example, besides cancelling the Court Challenges Program and Martin's federal–provincial childcare agreements, it deliberately slipped a provision into the 2009 budget that

TABLE 7.4	Women Candidates and MPs in the 2008 Federal Election			
Party	Women Candidates	%	Women MPs	%
Liberal	113	36.8	19	24.7
NDP	104	33.8	12	32.4
Conservative	63	20.5	23	16.1
BQ	20	26.7	15	30.6
Green	90	29.7	0	0
Other	55	6.0	0	0
Total	445	27.8	69	22.4

Source: Parliament of Canada, Women Candidates in General Elections—1921 to Date, available at http://www.parl.gc.ca/Sites/LOP/HFER/hfer.asp?Language=E&Search=WomenElection.

took pay equity away from the jurisdiction of the Canadian Human Rights Commission and put it into the collective bargaining process. This occurred after the government was ordered to provide pay-equity compensation to a group of mostly female nurses in its employ.

Employment Issues

Since women constitute about 47 percent of the labour force, one major feminist concern is employment. Overall, some 58 percent of those over 15 years of age are part of the paid workforce, but this rate rises to 77 percent of women between the ages of 23 and 54.[14] Women have traditionally been paid less than men, underrepresented in managerial positions, and discouraged from undertaking nontraditional occupations. Demands for "equal pay for work of equal value" or **pay equity** have led to legislation at the federal level and in many provinces. By 1997 women's full-time earnings had risen to an average of about 70 percent of men's, where it plateaued, just like their political representation, and a federal task force report on pay equity in 2003 called for more vigorous legislation. The federal government got itself embroiled in a mammoth and protracted pay equity dispute with its own clerical staff, most of whom were female, which it finally settled in late 1999 for $3.6 billion. The federal Crown corporation Canada Post was ordered to pay $150 million in a similar case, and companies within federal jurisdiction, such as Bell Canada, refused to respond to pay equity demands of their employees until ordered to do so by the courts. However, the Supreme Court of Canada ruled that when the Province of Newfoundland was facing an "exceptional financial crisis" in 1991, it was justified in backtracking on a pay-equity commitment despite the equality rights provision in the Charter.[15]

Beyond pay equity is the broader subject of **employment equity**—that is, the elimination of discrimination in hiring and promotion, which is sometimes combined with **affirmative action** programs to give preference to women and other groups in order to make up for past systemic inequities. In 1980 the federal bureaucracy established a pilot project with respect to affirmative action in the hiring of women, and in 1983 affirmative action was made mandatory in all federal government departments. The 1984 *Report of the Royal Commission on Equality in Employment*, written by Rosalie Abella, became the foundation of the 1986 Employment Equity Act. This law extended employment equity requirements to all Crown corporations, all federally regulated companies with more than 100 employees, and other large companies in receipt of major government contracts. Ottawa strengthened the federal Employment Equity Act in 1995, and by 2007, women occupied 40 percent of executive jobs and constituted over 54 percent of the federal government work force.[16] Ontario passed an even more extensive Employment Equity Act in 1993, which was the subject of much controversy in the 1995 provincial election campaign and was quickly repealed by the Harris government.[17]

Because most businesses see employment equity as a drain on their bottom line, they generally oppose the idea. Indeed, the area in which women are most severely underrepresented is at the top of private sector corporations, a leading cause of overall pay differentials. In 2008, of Canada's Top 500 companies, only 30 were led by women with Heather Reisman at Chapters-Indigo and Elyse Allan at GE Canada being two of the most prominent. Women held only 15.2 percent of board director positions, 15.7 percent of corporate officer positions, and 6.2 percent of top earner positions.[18] The shortage of women in senior executive positions means that the pool of female candidates for board directorships is limited. As the example

Heather Reisman, CEO of Chapters-Indigo.

CP PHOTO/Frank Gunn

of Ontario shows, the predominant neoliberal ideology after 1985, along with its counterpart, globalization, often weakened government attempts to promote employment equity, but Crown corporations ranked much above the private sector in having women in senior officer roles.

In 2006, 67 percent of all employed women worked in teaching, nursing and related health occupations, clerical and other administrative positions, and sales and service occupations, and constituted a majority in each field. In many of these fields, pay is low and opportunities to advance are relatively few. However, it should not be overlooked that women have made gains in several professional occupations: in the same year, for example, women constituted 55 percent of all doctors and dentists in Canada, 52 percent of business and financial professionals, and 11 percent were self-employed.[19] Women make up about 70 percent of the part-time work force, sometimes by choice but often by necessity, and part-time workers generally have few benefits and little job security. In this era of global restructuring, companies are turning even more to part-time contract workers, and women usually suffer the most from such developments.

The value of work performed by women without pay is of increasing concern to many observers but has been difficult to estimate. Economists point out that although women who work for pay contribute to government revenues by paying income taxes, women who work in the home without remuneration generally carry out a variety of functions, such as caring for the young and seniors, which reduce the demand for public services. Unpaid work in the home makes a major contribution to the economy that does not show up in traditional statistics, but according to one 1992 estimate, its value was nearly $300 billion, or 41 percent of the gross domestic product.[20] The reduction in social programs after the advent of neoliberalism only increased the burden of unpaid caregiving roles performed primarily by women.

The 1992 study found that women performed two-thirds of unpaid work, such as household maintenance, caregiving, and volunteer work, which was worth some $16 580 per year on an individual basis. On average, women spent approximately 29 hours per week on housework, almost double that of men. By 2005, men were sharing this burden a bit more equitably, as shown in Figure 7.1: women averaged about 4.3 hours per day on unpaid housework, childcare, and shopping, compared to the male average of 2.5 hours. On the other hand, men averaged about two hours more per day on paid work.

Constitutional, Legal, and Aboriginal Women's Issues

A third category of post-1970 women's issues is related to constitutional and legal issues. The first of these was the question of equality rights in the 1982 Charter of Rights and Freedoms. This was especially important because the courts had made a mockery of the gender equality

· ·

Figure 7.1 Average Time Women and Men Spend per Day on Unpaid Domestic Work, 1986 and 2005

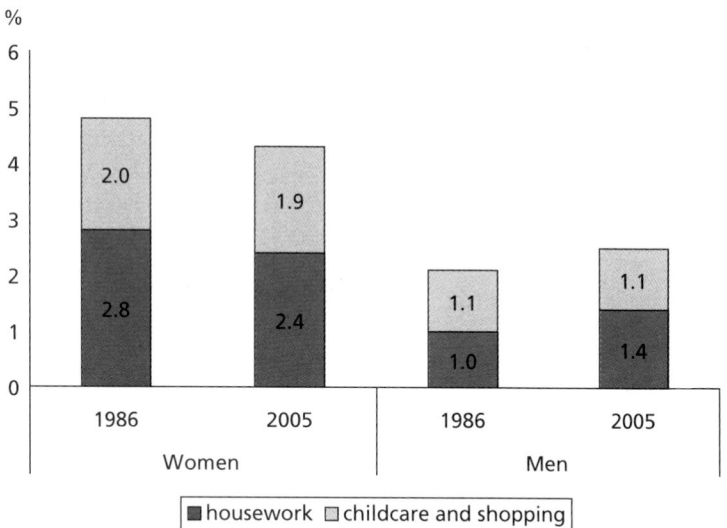

Source: Statistics Canada, The General Social Survey, Matter of Fact, No. 9, Catalogue no. 89-630-X, "Are women spending more time on unpaid domestic work than men in Canada?", available at http://www.statcan.gc.ca/pub/89-630-x/ 2008001/article/10705-eng.htm.

provision in the 1960 Bill of Rights. As the Charter emerged from federal–provincial nego-tiations, gender equality was to be lumped into section 15 with such other factors as race, religion, and age, which governments would be allowed to override with the notwithstanding clause. Such treatment at the hands of 11 male first ministers galvanized the women's move-ment as never before; as a result of pressure from women's groups, section 28 was added to the final document to give gender equality a place of its own and protection from the notwith-standing clause.[21]

Women thus became part of the coalition that included other Charter-based rights-bearers who used the Charter to advance their causes.[22] There followed a series of fem-inist challenges to laws that women felt discriminated against them. For example, women achieved the right to maternity leave under the Unemployment Insurance Act. Although they had mixed success in the so-called "rape-shield" cases (hoping to restrict questions about past sexual history put to defendants in a case of sexual assault), the courts agreed that "no means no" with respect to a woman's consent to sexual relations. Battered wives have been excused for murdering their offending husbands; gender discrimination in private employers' disability plans has been removed; and physical requirements that discriminate against women must be proven to be necessary for a job. The government itself encouraged such legal activity with the **Court Challenges Program** under which it subsidized the Legal Education and Action Fund (LEAF) in making such challenges. This was a continuation of Trudeau's attempt to strengthen the women's movement by funding advocacy groups.[23] When the Mulroney government cancelled the Court Challenges Program in 1992, women protested; it was reinstated by the Chrétien administration, only to be eliminated a second time by the Harper government.

The Supreme Court did *not* advance the cause of women in decisions dealing with such issues as the deduction of child-care expenses from a self-employed woman's income tax (the 1993 *Symes* case) and the taxation of women's support payments while men who made such payments deducted them from their income tax (the 1995 *Thibaudeau* case). But in both of these decisions the female justices on the court dissented.[24] The federal government then amended the Income Tax Act so that child support payments would no longer be deductible from the contributor's income tax and so that recipients of such payments would no longer need to declare them as taxable income. The Supreme Court also made some interesting decisions regarding the entitlements of women (and their children) upon divorce.

On the constitutional front, in the 1987–90 period the **National Action Committee on the Status of Women (NAC)** and certain subsidiary groups actively opposed the Meech Lake Accord. Having become part of the constitutional policy community in 1982, they demanded participation in any subsequent constitutional decisions and were concerned that the accord, drawn up by 11 men, had nothing to say about women's rights. NAC was also unhappy with the Charlottetown Accord because even though the equality of men and women was reiterated in the Canada clause, it was articulated in weaker language than that of other rights. Like Aboriginals, official francophone minorities, people with disabilities, and other groups that had achieved constitutional standing in 1982, women's groups were not satisfied with subsequent constitutional documents unless their status was further reinforced.[25]

Another long-standing legal issue was that of the equality of Aboriginal women relative to Aboriginal men. A provision in the Indian Act denied Indian status to Native women who married white men, but no such loss was involved when an Indian man married a white woman. After the *Lavell* case upheld this clause in the Indian Act, much pressure was brought to bear, including a critical decision by the Human Rights Committee of the United Nations involving Sandra Lovelace. In 1985 the provision was repealed, and the Indian Act was amended to restore Indian status and the right to be considered for band membership to Indian women (and their children) who had lost such status through intermarriage. Their fate continued to rest, however, with the band membership, but the *Sharon McIvor* case mentioned in Chapter 4 should finally resolve the problem. A year before, the Constitution itself was amended to recognize and affirm that Aboriginal and treaty rights were guaranteed equally to male and female persons.

Reproduction, Sexuality, Health, and Violence Issues

One of the main feminist rallying cries of the post-1970 period was that women must be able to control what happens to their own bodies. Many women's organizations supported Dr. Henry Morgentaler in his long fight (including several court cases, clinic raids, and jail terms) to reform the Criminal Code's provisions on abortion. Although amendments were made in 1968, feminists did not regard these as sufficient, and the Supreme Court of Canada threw out the abortion law in the famous 1988 *Morgentaler* case.[26] The prospect of having no law at all restricting abortion was appealing to most feminists, but a sizable proportion of public opinion disagreed; in 1990 the Mulroney government introduced a compromise abortion law, which was defeated in the Senate. The Mulroney government also appointed a Royal Commission on New Reproductive Technologies, whose 1993 report endorsed a cautious approach to this controversial subject and was not turned into legislation until a decade later.

Prostitution, pornography, sexual stereotyping, sexual harassment, and sexual assault are other major areas of concern to women's groups, although feminists are not totally united on the first two. While they universally oppose practices that exploit or demean women, some women defend the "freedom of expression" argument in discussions of pornography, and some, the "right to work" defence of prostitution. The courts have also become engaged in these issues and ruled in 1990, for example, that the existing law against soliciting was valid as a "reasonable limit" on freedom of speech.

Also of concern are the courts' treatment of sexual assault cases, sexual harassment in the workplace, and violence against women. In one study, 50 percent of all Canadian women reported that they had experienced at least one incident of violence by a male since the age of 16, and nearly 40 percent, one incident of sexual assault.[27] More often than not, women were the victims in cases of spousal assault, so the federal government embarked on an initiative to combat family violence after 1988 that, among other things, contributed to the creation of

shelters for battered women. By 2006, however, due to cuts by both Liberal and Conservative governments, federal funding for women's shelters had almost disappeared.[28]

Although on average Canadian women clearly live longer than men, women are concerned about their own particular health issues. Probably the main concern is breast cancer, which afflicts one woman in nine. Pressure has mounted on governments to take more initiative in this area, and some have responded, while occupational health problems are also of increasing concern.

The Feminization of Poverty and Child Care

Chapter 8 will reveal the large extent to which Canada has experienced the **feminization of poverty**. As pointed out there, in 2006 about 32 percent of sole-support mothers lived below the low-income cut-off, commonly accepted as the poverty line. This figure represented 40 percent of all the children living in poverty.[29] With or without a partner, large numbers of women with preschool children find it necessary to work outside the home to support themselves and their families. The Canada Child Tax Credit is designed to help poorer families with children, but provincial governments often reduce their own social assistance payments by the amount of the federal benefit so that the recipients are no further ahead. Pay equity, employment equity, higher minimum wages, increased unionization, and improved job training and literacy programs will also help decrease the incidence of women living in poverty.

One of the major unresolved "women's issues" today is that of daycare for children. Many women qualify for up to a year of maternity benefits under the Employment Insurance program, but then face the difficulty of finding, let alone financing, daycare for their children. The Mulroney government introduced legislation for a national daycare program in 1988, but when the bill failed to pass before the election, it fell victim to the budgetary restraints of 1989–92. A Liberal "Red Book" promise of 1993 also went unfulfilled until the Martin government negotiated individualized child-care agreements with each province and territory to provide significant funding in this field. Ottawa's flexibility on the issue detracted from any notion of a truly national daycare program, and only Quebec's $5-a-day child care (later raised to $7.00) approaches an adequate standard. In 2006, nearly 70 percent of mothers with children under the age of 3 were in the workforce, and over 75 percent with children between 3 and 5, yet only 811 000 licensed full-time daycare spaces were available across the country.[30] As seen in Figure 7.2, this was enough to cover 17.2 percent of children aged 0 to 12. Rather than work toward a national system of child-care spaces, the Harper Conservatives cancelled the Liberals' federal–provincial deals and began to pay families $1200 annually per child and let them find their own solutions.

Women's Centres and Women's Groups

Many women's centres were established across the country in the 1980s, financed by federal or provincial governments or both. Although such centres primarily served as support and referral agencies for battered wives and others seeking help, they also promoted a variety of other women's causes, such as abortion law reform. The Mulroney government cut the budget

. . . .

**Figure 7.2   Percent of Children Aged 0-12 for Whom a Regulated Child Care Space
was Available by Province and Territory, 2006**

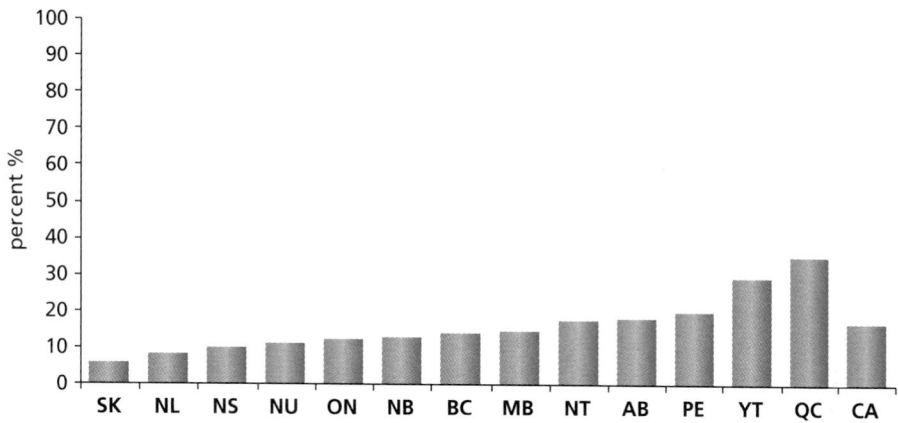

Source: *Childcare Resource and Research Unit, "Trends & Analysis 2007," p. 6, available at http://www.childcarecanada.
org/pubs/other/TandA/Trends_Analysis07.pdf.*

for such centres in 1989 and 1990, but then restored some of the funding after a vehement protest. With the demise of the Canada Assistance Plan under the Liberals in 1996, however, funding for women's centres and many other services for women were cancelled, while others were discontinued by the Harper government.

The National Council of Women of Canada (NCWC) was created in 1893 and still represents thousands of women in autonomous provincial, regional, and municipal councils. The Voice of Women (VOW) was formed in 1960 around peace issues, and the Canadian Advisory Council on the Status of Women (CACSW) was set up by the government in 1973 in response to the Royal Commission on the Status of Women.

The number of women's groups has increased remarkably in recent years. For many years, the foremost women's advocacy group was the National Action Committee on the Status of Women (NAC). It was established in 1972, largely in response to government inaction on the Status of Women report. It functioned as an umbrella lobbying group for more than 700 local and national member groups representing more than three million women. An indication of its importance and of politicians' consciousness of the female vote was the separate televised leaders' debate held on women's issues in 1984 and sponsored by NAC.[31]

Because it was less sympathetic to NAC and affiliated groups than the Trudeau regime and because it anticipated criticism of its cutbacks, the Mulroney government refused to attend NAC's annual meeting in 1989 and 1990 and even began to fund the rival organization, REAL Women. REAL (Realistic, Equal, Active for Life) Women was founded in 1984 and opposed all feminist demands. The Catholic Women's League and various anti-abortion ("pro-life") groups also played a major role on the abortion issue from the anti-feminist point of view. Thus, women themselves were divided on some or all of the issues raised.

When Ottawa changed the method of distributing grant money to women's groups to a project-by-project basis in 1998–99, NAC complained that the Chrétien government was treating it even more disrespectfully than the Conservatives had done. The organization has virtually collapsed because of the financial crisis as well as internal divisions—evidence that the female identity does not necessarily trump other identities. Status of Women Canada currently operates two modest programs, the Women's Community Fund and the Women's Partnership Fund.

. . . .

GAY, LESBIAN, BISEXUAL, AND TRANSGENDERED ISSUES AND IDENTITIES

Even more remarkable than the strengthening of women's identities after the second wave of the women's movement around 1970 was the sudden appearance of gay and lesbian identities and demands. Although most people with such identities were originally reluctant to reveal them, a variety of political issues related to homosexuality have arisen in recent years.[32] In most cases, however, politicians have preferred to avoid the demands coming from the gay and lesbian communities, forcing these groups to take their concerns directly to the courts.

One of the first demands in this area was for protection from individual discrimination in human rights codes, essentially to prevent discrimination in the private sector, such as in hiring or accommodation. Quebec was the first province to enact legislation prohibiting discrimination on the grounds of **sexual orientation**. The federal government was among the laggards in this area, not adding such a clause to the federal Human Rights Act until 1996. When the Charter of Rights was adopted in 1982, section 15 prohibited discrimination by government or in law on the basis of sex. Although sexual orientation was not explicitly included, the Supreme Court of Canada decided unanimously in the 1995 *Egan* case that the clause did indeed include sexual orientation. In 1998, the Supreme Court reaffirmed that the Charter included sexual orientation, ruling in the *Vriend* case that this ground be added to the Alberta Individual Rights Protection Act.[33] Thus, by the late 1990s, whether by legislation or court decision, sexual orientation had been added to all the human rights codes in Canada. Meanwhile, it was only with difficulty that Justice Minister Allan Rock was able to increase sentences for those convicted of committing hate crimes, including crimes against homosexuals, in 1995.

The next phase of the battle for equality in this area centred on gay and lesbian couples. In 1998, the Ontario Court of Appeal recognized same-sex survivor pension benefits in the *Rosenberg* case, and many employers in both the public and the private sectors extended employee benefits (health, dental, and retirement plans, and so on) to same-sex couples. In the *M. v. H* case in 1999, the Supreme Court outlawed the clause in the Ontario Family Law Act that restricted financial support to opposite-sex spouses after separation from their partner.[34] Henceforth a same-sex spouse could apply for such support just as in any common-law relationship. About the same time, the federal government passed pension legislation that granted survivor benefits to the gay and lesbian partners of its own employees and also withdrew objections to gay and lesbians receiving survivor benefits under the Canada Pension Plan.

In the wake of the *M. v. H.* decision and in response to pressure from gay and lesbian rights groups, the federal and most provincial governments introduced omnibus legislation in the 1999–2002 period to remove discrimination against same-sex unions. Thus, in a giant leap forward, same-sex couples are now treated equally with heterosexual couples in most aspects of the law. The 2001 census included a question on same-sex partners for the first time, and the 2002 changes to the Immigration Act included a gender-neutral clause.[35]

Perhaps the ultimate issue that arises in the gay and lesbian communities relates to marriage. Parliament passed a Reform Party motion in 1999 that upheld the traditional definition of marriage as a union between a man and a woman, but at the same time an Angus Reid poll indicated that more than 50 percent of Canadians were prepared to allow same-sex couples to marry. Meanwhile, Quebec passed pioneering legislation in 2002 to extend full parental rights to same-sex couples in the province. Under a "civil union," they would have the same status and obligations, including adoption rights, as heterosexual couples. Then, in 2003, in the case of *Halpern v. Canada (Attorney General)*, the Ontario Court of Appeal ruled that the ban on same-sex marriage was discriminatory and unconstitutional, and ordered the immediate recognition of such marriages. Between 2004 and 2005, virtually all provincial and territorial appeal courts made decisions similar to that of Ontario. When Prime Minister Chrétien referred the issue to the Supreme Court in the *Reference re Same-Sex Marriage*, the judges generally agreed with these lower court decisions and upheld the proposed legislation.[36] Despite the Supreme Court ruling, Parliamentary debate was bitterly divided. A slightly amended law (Bill C-38) was passed in July 2005, and a large majority in 2006 voted against reopening the issue.

. . . .

CONCLUSION

Although women's issues have been on the political agenda at least since the turn of the 20th century, today's politicians must pay much more attention to gender questions than ever before. Increased participation by women in the work force and in society in general has created dramatic changes in the political system. This chapter has shown that, although the record is mixed in the post-1970 period, women have made immense progress overall. By the start of the 21st century, the main obstacles to further progress included the fiscal restraint practised by all governments and a certain amount of backlash against employment equity programs. "Dismantling the state" was not generally good for the furthering of women's equality, which often depended on deliberate government intervention. The increasing number and proportion of women in influential positions, however, should guarantee that advances will be made in the future. At the same time, the gay and lesbian communities have recently experienced many victories in their struggle for equality. Most of their successes have so far been achieved in the courts.

Concerns about women's political involvement and representation reappear in Chapters 15 (election campaigns) and 23 (Parliament). The general feminization of poverty is discussed in Chapter 8 (class). The representation of women in the bureaucracy and judiciary are revisited in Chapters 22 (bureaucracy) and 24 (judiciary). There has been little improvement in other areas of concern to the feminist movement, and that movement continues to suffer from weakened advocacy groups as noted in Chapter 16. Legal issues relating to both women and the gay and lesbian communities primarily resurface in Chapter 19, which discusses the Charter of Rights and Freedoms.

P The pluralist approach emphasizes the vast increase in the number of women's groups in recent years and their increasing influence on public policymaking. Once again, organization and mobilization have effects on public policy, and to some extent this influence has been achieved within narrow status-of-women policy communities. Women's groups have also become part of the rough and tumble of constitutional politics and have played a significant part in some of the bargains adopted. This pluralism of Canadian society is enhanced by the increasing acceptance of the alternative lifestyles represented by the gay and lesbian communities but, as mentioned above, these latter groups have not had as much success in politics as within the legal system.

SC The state-centred approach explains the period of inaction on women's issues (1920–70) by the fact that women were largely excluded from the Cabinet and bureaucracy. When governments finally decided to act in this field, bureaucrats in status-of-women agencies had a large role in setting the government agenda. Leslie Pal emphasizes the close links between the bureaucratic agencies established in this field and the women's groups that the government was itself helping to support financially.[37]

Women are still seriously underrepresented in all organs of government, but the proportion of women elected to Parliament has regularly increased and their contingent on the Supreme Court is not likely to be reduced to less than one-third. Women can be *appointed* to some of these positions to increase their numbers, but greater female representation in the corridors of power will also require political parties and voters to *elect* more women to Parliament. Women are slowly rising to the top of some other institutions in society and are increasingly able to engage in processes of elite accommodation, but they remain almost invisible in the ranks of the influential corporate elite.

C Many radical, socialist, and neo-Marxist feminists take the view that women will never achieve full equality and emancipation in a capitalist system, which they claim depends on the exploitation of women. Some also point to the coercive aspect of the pre-1990 abortion laws, which were designed and passed primarily by men. Socialist feminists argue that "class and gender interact in the present system to produce women's inequality and that significant transformations in both are necessary for women's emancipation."[38] A quite different class-based analysis of feminism is offered by Martin Loney, who argues that the feminist movement has usurped the struggle for equality by concentrating only on women and left behind the traditional concerns of the working class: poverty, inequality of opportunity, and social marginalization of men, women, and children alike.[39]

PC Public choice theory focuses on the number of women voters, past voting restrictions, and the degree of gender consciousness among women voters. Women did not even have a vote for the first 50 years of Confederation, for example, and for a long time after that they seemed less concerned with gender than with other issues—ethnicity, region, religion, and class. Since 1970, more women are conscious of "women's issues," and governments are paying more attention to them. But although women make up one-half of the electorate, they are not united on such issues, and this provides a good excuse for governments not to take action, such as the Mulroney and Chrétien governments' abandonment of a promised national daycare program, and Harper's cancellation of Martin's initiative in this field.

(G) Globalization affects the women's movement in opposite ways. It is an advantage that women around the world can easily contact each other, learn from each other, and fight for their rights across state borders. One international body that has often been of benefit to women in Canada and elsewhere is the United Nations, which promotes gender equality in a variety of ways and has even seen fit to criticize the policies of the federal and provincial governments. On the other hand, women often feel they are among the main victims of globalization. For example, "employment equity has been subverted by the emergence of new neo-liberal norms," which emphasize "minimal state action in the economy and privilege the market."[40] As the state withdraws from employment equity and labour standards in deference to market forces, and as transnational corporations transfer work to part-time status or to foreign countries, women often bear the brunt—the loss or downgrading of jobs, the decreased compensation for work, and the necessity of picking up the slack in voluntary caregiving roles. Nevertheless, at least at the federal level, Canada has a legacy in this field that has "withstood some of the attacks upon it"; it is at the provincial level, such as in Mike Harris's Ontario, that employment equity suffered most at the hands of forces of neoliberalism and globalization.[41]

. . . .
DISCUSSION QUESTIONS

1. Are you personally affected by the gender cleavages and identities discussed in this chapter? If so, how?

2. How do you explain the lull in women's political activities after they obtained the vote?

3. How do you explain the increase in women's collective self-consciousness over the past 40 years?

4. Do female party leaders have a more difficult time getting their parties elected than male leaders?

5. To what extent should the private sector adopt employment equity programs?

6. How far should governments go in providing public daycare programs?

7. How far should legislation go in recognizing same-sex relationships?

. . . .
NOTES

1. Jacquetta Newman and Linda White, *Women, Politics, and Public Policy: The Political Struggles of Canadian Women* (Don Mills, ON: Oxford University Press, 2006), p. 12.
2. Jane Jenson, "Wearing Your Adjectives Proudly: Citizenship and Gender in Turn-of-the Century Canada," *Canadian Political Science Association* (May 1990), p. 12.
3. Jacquetta Newman, "Small-p Politics: Women Working Outside Formal Political Structures," in Mark Charlton and Paul Barker, *Crosscurrents: Contemporary Political Issues*, 6th ed. (Toronto: Nelson Education, 2009), pp. 266–69. On the related subject of social capital, see Elisabeth Gidengil and Brenda O'Neill, eds, *Gender and Social Capital* (New York: Routledge, 2006).

4. Early developments are outlined in a 1993 Status of Women Canada publication called *Toward Equality for Women—A Canadian Chronology*. Other books on the subject include Jean Cochrane, *Women in Canadian Politics* (Toronto: Fitzhenry & Whiteside, 1977); Penney Kome, *Women of Influence* (Toronto: University of Toronto Press, 1985); Janine Brodie, *Women and Politics in Canada* (Toronto: McGraw-Hill Ryerson, 1985); Linda Kealey and Joan Sangster, eds., *Beyond the Vote: Canadian Women and Politics* (Toronto: University of Toronto Press, 1989); and Sandra Burt, Lorraine Code, and Lindsay Dorney, eds., *Changing Patterns: Women in Canada* (Toronto: McClelland and Stewart, 1988).

5. Royal Commission on the Status of Women, *Report* (Ottawa: 1970), p. 338.

6. Doris Pennington, *Agnes Macphail, Reformer: Canada's First Female M.P.* (Toronto: Simon & Pierre, 1989); and Terry Crowley, *Agnes Macphail and the Politics of Equality* (Toronto: Lorimer, 1990).

7. Micheline D. Johnson, *History of the Status of Women in the Province of Quebec*, Background study for the Royal Commission on the Status of Women (Ottawa, 1968), p. 49.

8. Janine Brodie, *Women and Politics in Canada* (Toronto: McGraw-Hill Ryerson, 1985), and "Women and Political Leadership: A Case for Affirmative Action," in Maureen Mancuso, Richard Price, and Ronald Wagenberg, eds., *Leaders and Leadership in Canada* (Toronto: Oxford University Press, 1994); and Heather MacIvor, *Women and Politics in Canada* (Peterborough: Broadview Press, 1996).

9. Newman, "Small-p Politics: Women Working Outside Formal Political Structures," p. 269.

10. Jill Vickers, *Reinventing Political Science: A Feminist Approach* (Halifax: Fernwood Publishing, 1997); Sandra Burt, "Looking Backward and Thinking Ahead: Toward a Gendered Analysis of Canadian Politics," in Michael Whittington and Glen Williams, eds., *Canadian Politics in the 21st Century*, 5th ed. (Scarborough: Nelson, 2000); and Elisabeth Gidengil and Joanna Everitt, "Conventional Coverage/Unconventional Politicians: Gender and Media Coverage of Canadian Leaders' Debates, 1993, 1997, 2000," *Canadian Journal of Political Science* (July/August 2003).

11. Kome, *Women of Influence*, p. 86.

12. Jane Arscott and Linda Trimble, eds., *In the Presence of Women: Representation in Canadian Governments* (Toronto: Harcourt Brace, 1997).

13. Elisabeth Gidengil, "Beyond the Gender Gap," *Canadian Journal of Political Science* (December 2007); Marie Rekkas, Gender and Elections: An Examination of the 2006 Canadian Federal Election," *Canadian Journal of Political Science* (December 2008); and Sylvia Bashevkin, *Women, Power, Politics: The Hidden Story of Canada's Unfinished Democracy* (Toronto: Oxford University Press, 2009).

14. Statistics Canada, *Women in Canada: Work Chapter Updates*, available at http://www.statcan.gc.ca/bsolc/olc-cel/olc-cel?land=eng&catno=89F0133X; Statistics Canada, *Women in Canada: A Gender-Based Statistical Report* (Catalogue No. 89-503-XPE, March 2006), p. 14; Melissa Cooke-Reynolds and Nancy Zukewich, "The Feminization of Work," *Canadian Social Trends* (Statistics Canada, Catalogue No. 11-008, Spring 2004).

15. See *Newfoundland (Treasury Board) v. N.A.P.E.*, [2004] 3 S.C.R. 381.

16. Privy Council Office, *Fifteenth Annual Report to the Prime Minister on the Public Service of Canada* (2008), p. 35.

17. Yasmeen Abu-Laban and Christina Gabriel, *Selling Diversity: Immigration, Multiculturalism, Employment Equity, and Globalization* (Peterborough: Broadview Press, 2000).

18. Catalyst Canada, *2008 Catalyst Canada Census of Women Board Directors of the Fortune 500* and *2008 Catalyst Census of Corporate Officers and Top Earners of the Fortune 500*.

19. Statistics Canada, *Women in Canada: Work Chapter Updates*; Statistics Canada, *Women in Canada*, pp. 14, 113.

20. William Chandler, "The Value of Household Work in Canada, 1992," *National Income and Expenditure Accounts, Fourth Quarter 1993*, 41, no. 4 (Catalogue No. 13-001), based on the 1992 General Social Survey.

21. See Penney Kome, *The Taking of Twenty-Eight* (Toronto: Women's Educational Press, 1983), and *Women of Influence*, ch. 10.

22. Alan Cairns, *Disruptions: Constitutional Struggles, from the Charter to Meech Lake* (Toronto: McClelland and Stewart, 1991); and Rainer Knopff and F.L. Morton, *Charter Politics* (Toronto: Nelson Canada, 1992).

23. Leslie Pal, *Interests of State: The Politics of Language, Multiculturalism and Feminism in Canada* (Montreal: McGill-Queen's University Press, 1993); Christopher P. Manfredi, *Feminist Activism in the*

Supreme Court: Legal Mobilization and the Women's Legal Education and Action Fund (Vancouver: UBC Press, 2004); and *R. v. Lavallee*, [1990] 1 S.C.R. 852.

24. *Symes v. Canada*, [1993] 4 S.C.R. 695; *Canada v. Thibaudeau*, [1995] 2 S.C.R. 627.

25. Cairns, *Disruptions.*

26. Robert Campbell and Leslie Pal, *The Real Worlds of Canadian Politics*, 2nd ed. (Peterborough: Broadview Press, 1991); Janine Brodie, Shelley A.M. Gavigan, and Jane Jenson, *The Politics of Abortion* (Toronto: Oxford University Press, 1992); *R. v. Morgentaler*, [1988] 1 S.C.R. 30; *Borowski v. Canada (Attorney General)*, [1989] 1 S.C.R. 342; and *Tremblay v. Daigle*, [1989] 2 S.C.R. 530.

27. Holly Johnson, *Dangerous Domains: Violence Against Women in Canada* (Scarborough: Nelson Canada, 1996), based on Statistics Canada, *The Violence Against Women Survey, 1993.*

28. Sandra Burt, "Moving Forward or Stepping Back? Taking Stock of Current Policies on Women's Status in Canada," in Michael Whittington and Glen Williams, eds. *Canadian Politics in the 21st Century*, 7th ed. Toronto (Nelson Education, 2008), p. 273.

29. Statistics Canada, *Income in Canada—2006*, Catalogue no. 75-202-X, (May 2008), available at http:// www.statcan.gc.ca/pub/75-202-x200600-eng.htm, p. 21.

30. Childcare Resource and Research Unit, "Trends & Analysis 2007," p. 6, available at http://www .childcarecanada.org/pubs/other/TandA/Trends_Analysis07.pdf.

31. Jill Vickers, Pauline Rankin, and Christine Appelle, *Politics as If Women Mattered: A Political Analysis of the National Action Committee on the Status of Women* (Toronto: University of Toronto Press, 1993); Alexandra Dobrowolsky, "The Women's Movement in Flux: Feminism and Framing, Passion, and Politics," in Miriam Smith, ed., *Group Politics and Social Movements in Canada* (Peterborough: Broadview Press, 2008).

32. Didi Herman, *Rights of Passage: Struggles for Lesbian and Gay Legal Equality* (Toronto: University of Toronto Press, 1994); Miriam Smith, *Lesbian and Gay Rights in Canada: Social Movements and Equality-Seeking, 1971–1995* (Toronto: University of Toronto Press, 1999); David Rayside, *Queer Inclusions, Continental Divisions: Public Recognition of Sexual Diversity in Canada and the United States* (Toronto: University of Toronto Press, 2008); and Miriam Smith, "Identity and Opportunity: The Lesbian and Gay Rights Movement," in Smith, *Group Politics and Social Movements in Canada.*

33. *Egan v. Canada*, [1995] 2 S.C.R. 513; and *Vriend v. Alberta*, [1998] 1 S.C.R. 493.

34. *M. v. H.*, [1999] 2 S.C.R. 3.

35. Mary C. Hurley, "Sexual Orientation and Legal Rights," *Library of Parliament Current Issue Review* 92-1E (October 2001); website of EGALE (Equality for Gays and Lesbians) at http://www.egale.ca. For BC cases dealing with the educational system, see ch. 18.

36. J. Scott Matthews, "The Political Foundations of Support for Same-Sex Marriage in Canada," *Canadian Journal of Political Science* (December 2005).

37. Pal, *Interests of State.*

38. Burt, "Looking Backward and Thinking Ahead: Toward a Gendered Analysis of Canadian Politics," in Michael Whittington and Glen Williams, eds., *Canadian Politics in the 21st Century*, 5th ed. (Toronto: Thomson Nelson, 2000), p. 308.

39. Martin Loney, *The Pursuit of Division: Race, Gender, and Preferential Hiring in Canada* (Montreal: McGill-Queen's University Press, 1998).

40. Abu-Laban and Gabriel, *Selling Diversity*, p. 158

41. Ibid., p. 152.

. . . .

FURTHER READING

Abu-Laban, Yasmeen, and Christina Gabriel. *Selling Diversity: Immigration, Multiculturalism, Employment Equity, and Globalization.* Peterborough: Broadview Press, 2000.

Andrew, Caroline, and Sanda Rodgers, eds. *Women and the Canadian State.* Montreal: McGill-Queen's University Press, 1997.

Bashevkin, Sylvia. *Welfare Hot Buttons: Women, Work and Social Policy Reform.* Toronto: University of Toronto Press, 2002.

————. *Women, Power, Politics: The Hidden Story of Canada's Unfinished Democracy*. Toronto: Oxford University Press, 2009.

Brodie, Janine, Shelley A.M. Gavigan, and Jane Jenson. *The Politics of Abortion*. Toronto: Oxford University Press, 1992.

Burt, Sandra. "Moving Forward or Stepping Back? Taking Stock of Current Policies on Women's Status in Canada." In Michael Whittington and Glen Williams, eds., *Canadian Politics in the 21st Century*, 7th ed. Toronto: Thomson Nelson, 2008.

Dobrowolsky, Alexandra. *The Politics of Pragmatism: Women, Representation, and Constitutionalism in Canada*. Toronto: Oxford University Press, 1999.

Herman, Didi. *Rights of Passage: Struggles for Lesbian and Gay Legal Equality*. Toronto: University of Toronto Press, 1994.

Manfredi, Christopher P. *Feminist Activism in the Supreme Court: Legal Mobilization and the Women's Legal Education and Action Fund*. Vancouver: UBC Press, 2004.

Newman, Jacquetta. "Small-p Politics: Women Working Outside Formal Political Structures," in Mark Charlton and Paul Barker, eds., *Crosscurrents: Contemporary Political Issues*, 6th ed. Toronto: Nelson Education, 2009.

————, and Linda White. *Women, Politics, and Public Policy: The Political Struggles of Canadian Women*. Don Mills: Oxford University Press, 2006.

Pal, Leslie. *Interests of State: The Politics of Language, Multiculturalism and Feminism in Canada*. Montreal: McGill-Queen's University Press, 1993.

Rayside, David. *Queer Inclusions, Continental Divisions: Public Recognition of Sexual Diversity in Canada and the United States*. Toronto: University of Toronto Press, 2008.

Smith, Miriam. *Lesbian and Gay Rights in Canada: Social Movements and Equality-Seeking, 1971–1995*. Toronto: University of Toronto Press, 1999.

Tremblay, Manon, and Linda Trimbell, eds. *Women and Electoral Politics in Canada*. Don Mills: Oxford University Press, 2003.

Vickers, Jill. *Reinventing Political Science: A Feminist Approach*. Halifax: Fernwood Publishing, 1997.

Young, Lisa. *Feminists and Party Politics*. Vancouver: UBC Press, 2000.

Chapter 8

CLASS

A few Canadian families are among the richest people in the world, while a large number of others line up at soup kitchens and food banks because they cannot afford to buy food. Obsessed with their deficits and debts in the 1990s, governments usually blamed their fiscal woes on the costs of social programs, and they cut back sharply on social assistance. No adult can make ends meet on the minimum wage, but small businesses claim they will go bankrupt if the wage is raised. Many corporations pay minimal taxes, while Canadian history is replete with examples of workers being fired for trying to form unions and being clubbed by police when they went on strike.[1] Many university students emerge at graduation with staggering debts; other young people inherit huge fortunes. Hundreds of thousands of Canadians lost their jobs in the worldwide economic meltdown at the end of 2008 and many others lost a huge proportion of their pension plans and savings. All of these examples are related to class and class cleavages.

The concept of class is not as clear-cut as that of region, ethnicity, or gender, and Canadians are generally more conscious of regional and ethnic divisions. Nevertheless, class is an important generator of political activity in most countries, and Canada has its deep-seated class cleavages as well. A discussion of class in Canada must therefore not only clarify the concept but also explain why it is not a more significant factor in Canadian politics. This chapter will begin by discussing various theoretical considerations involving class, present a statistical profile of class in Canada, and then examine the political role of the upper, middle, and working classes, and of those below the poverty line. It concludes with a discussion of the social safety net—its rise and demise.

THEORETICAL CONSIDERATIONS

When dealing with the concept of class, it is customary to start with Karl Marx, who predicted that every capitalist economy would produce a class system consisting primarily of the **bourgeoisie**, the owners of the means of production, and the **proletariat**, the workers. The proletariat would sell their labour for a price; the bourgeoisie would pay them as little as possible (and less than they were worth), thereby accumulating profit or surplus value; and the state would respond to any resistance with **coercion**. Although religion and the prospect of a pleasant afterlife might keep them content for a while, the workers would eventually come to resent their low wages and exploitation, and finally engage in a violent revolt.

Capitalist societies have not evolved exactly as Marx predicted, and today's neo-Marxists, while adhering to the essence of their mentor, usually make certain alterations in his analysis. Marx did provide for a small **petite bourgeoisie** of farmers, small-business people, and self-employed professionals, but this class has become more significant than he expected. Furthermore, the **new middle class** of civil servants, teachers, nurses, and other salaried professionals was almost unforeseen in the mid-1800s, and it has become another large and important force. Thus, those who analyze politics in terms of class speak of the bourgeoisie (the economic elite), the petite bourgeoisie (the old or upper middle class), the new middle class, and the proletariat (the "working class"). As well, they often identify "fractions" within each class.[2]

Those social scientists interested in class but who are not neo-Marxists commonly divide individuals and families into the upper, middle, and working classes, based on such interrelated factors as income, wealth, occupation, and education. With these measures, the divisions between the classes are less clear-cut. Although such inequalities both produce and result from inequalities in other characteristics, such as education and occupation, income is the simplest measure to use in this discussion.

Regardless of approach, there is an obvious division in Canada between the rich and poor, or even between more nuanced income and occupational groups, but these cleavages are not usually as pronounced as others discussed in this section of the book. Neither are class cleavages as prominent in Canadian politics as in many other countries. Indeed, the contemporary emphasis in political science on the politics of identity is rarely focused on the characteristic of class. In some political systems, ethnicity or gender identities may be replacing class as a basis of political participation, but Canadian politics has rarely revolved around this fundamental characteristic of society. Since consciousness must precede identity, the principal explanation must be that the working and poor classes in Canada have a low level of **class-consciousness**. Why?

Wealthy concerned by widening gap between rich and poor.

Those who defend the lack of such consciousness argue that other social divisions take precedence in Canada, that the system permits social mobility, that most people feel they are middle class, that material benefits are widely shared, and that the political system has accommodated working-class interests along with those of other groups. Those who decry the lack of working-class class-consciousness argue that the upper classes, the petite bourgeoisie, and even the new middle class have defined what is politically relevant in society in regional, ethnic, and religious terms instead of in terms of class or ideology.[3] For example, the Liberal and Conservative parties were firmly entrenched when the franchise was extended to the working class and the new voters discovered that politics was about other social differences.

When politicians and political parties appeal to members of the working class as Albertans, francophones, or Protestants rather than as workers, the latter develop a perverted view of who is an enemy or a friend. Members of one union can be persuaded that they should be hostile to the demands of another, or that they should support coercive back-to-work legislation to end another union's strike. They can also be collectively hoodwinked into thinking that their wage demands fuel inflation and must be curtailed by programs of wage and price controls. In discussing the "myth of classlessness," Allahar and Côté pin the blame for this self-delusion on the predominant liberal ideology, reinforced by mass media ownership by the corporate elite, which explains social inequalities as stemming from varied individual effort and not from structured class relations.[4] In addition, of course, the poor, lacking in resources and often having given up, could hardly be expected to mount the kind of political organization that could challenge the defenders of the status quo. The concept of hegemony mentioned in Chapter 1, while incorporating societal elites in general, is usually applied to the dominance of the economic elite in particular.

Janine Brodie and Jane Jenson make the point that class-consciousness requires prior ideological and organizational activity by groups, such as unions, farmers, cooperatives, and other reformers. They demonstrate that classes as active and self-conscious social actors have to be created, and that class-based organizations must precede the expectation of class-based voting.[5] The attempts by farmers and unions to redefine Canadian politics in class terms were repelled by the traditional parties; their leaders were co-opted by the Liberal Party; and both organizations were internally divided. Moreover, many Canadian affiliates of American unions were encouraged to remain aloof from partisan politics. Despite such discouragement, a much stronger left-wing political presence developed in Canada than in the United States, especially in the form of the CCF/NDP, and the existence of a discourse of class and democratic socialism that those parties provided contributed to a stronger sense of class-consciousness in this country.

Another problem in analyzing social class is the distinction between "objective" and "subjective" class. Objective class refers to the class into which analysts place a person, according to criteria such as type of work or level of income, while subjective class means the class to which people think or feel they belong, even if it contradicts objective standards. Many people who consider themselves to be middle class would be categorized as working class by social scientists, and Marx himself foresaw the phenomenon of "false consciousness." Somewhat similarly, many people who do see themselves as working class adopt a deferential attitude toward their "betters."

A qualification that should also be added relates to the changing nature of class. Some analysts contend that those born after 1945 have distinctive "post-materialist" orientations that are less concerned with traditional class polarization than with "quality of life" and "lifestyle" questions, such as environmental, women's, identity, and minority group issues.[6] Others point out that class often overlaps with gender (women) and ethnicity (Aboriginal, ethnocultural minorities, and immigrants), putting many people at a double or triple disadvantage.

. . . .

A PROFILE OF CLASS DIVISIONS IN CANADA TODAY

Since those who prefer the neo-Marxist approach to measuring class divisions in Canada have rarely provided a concrete, numerical account of their understanding, Table 8.1 has been devised on the basis of that approach.[7]

A more common means of measuring income inequality is to divide the population into five groups of equal numbers, or quintiles, ranging from highest to lowest income, and to indicate the share of total income received by each group. Figure 8.1 presents such proportions for the year 2006 and shows that in terms of "market income" (before government transfers and taxes), the highest quintile held about 51 percent of the income and the lowest quintile had about two percent. Government transfers provide much of the income of the lowest quintile, and taxes take a little away from the rich to redistribute to the poor. Even after taxes and transfers, however, the highest-earning 20 percent of the population still received about 44 percent of the total income, while the lowest quintile received only five percent.

. . . .

THE UPPER CLASS
Identifying the Corporate Elite

It is not difficult to identify those who compose the upper class or **corporate elite**. Canada possesses many fabulously rich entrepreneurs and some of the wealthiest families in the world. Each December, *Canadian Business* magazine estimates the wealth of the 100 richest Canadians. The top ten for 2008 are shown in Table 8.2. Other analysts sometimes have slightly different

TABLE 8.1 Estimated Number and Percent of Voters by Class in Canada		
Class	*Voters*	*Percentage of Electorate*
Upper class	600 000	2.5
Middle class	3 600 000	15.0
Petite bourgeoisie	1 800 000	7.5
New middle class	1 800 000	7.5
Working class	16 200 000	67.5
Unionized	5 400 000	22.5
Not unionized	10 800 000	45.0
Poor	3 600 000	15.0
Working	1 800 000	7.5
Welfare	1 800 000	7.5

. . . .

Figure 8.1 **Income Shares of Quintiles: Market Income, Total Income (Income after Transfers and before Tax), and Income after Tax, 2006**

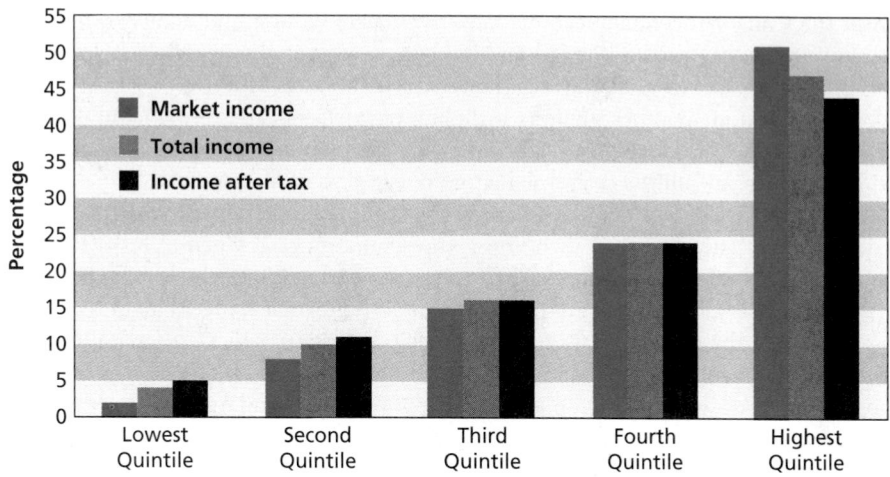

Source: Statistics Canada, *Income in Canada, 2006, Catalogue 75-202-X (November 2008), available at http://www .statcan.gc.ca/pub/75-202-x200600-eng.htm, pp. 76, 78, and 80.*

	TABLE 8.2 Ten Richest Canadians, 2008		
Rank	Name	Net Worth (billions)	Companies
1	Thomson Family	18.45	Thomson Reuters, Woodbridge Co. Ltd.
2	James (J.K.), Arthur, and John (Jack) Irving	7.11	Irving Oil Ltd., J.D. Irving Ltd.
3	Galen Weston	6.58	George Weston Ltd., Loblaw Cos. Ltd.
4	Edward (Ted) Rogers (*since deceased)	5.05	Rogers Communications Inc.
5	James (Jimmy) Pattison	4.93	Jim Pattison Group
6	Alex Shnaider	4.25	Midland Resources Holding Ltd.
7	David Azrieli	4.15	Canpro Investments Ltd.
8	Paul Desmarais Sr.	4.11	Power Corp. of Canada
9	Bernard (Barry) Sherman	3.77	Apotex Group of Cos.
10	Jeff Skoll	3.14	eBay Inc., Participant Media

Source: *Who Are the Richest Canadians? The 10th Annual 'Rich 100' for 2008. Canadian Business Online. Dec. 4, 2008. Found at: www.canadianbusiness.com. This list was compiled on November 3, 2008. (Accessed March 16, 2009).*

numbers or rankings, but these are the "usual suspects." The Thomson family used to be the main proprietor of Canadian newspapers, but by the time of his death in 2006, Ken Thomson concentrated on electronic information fields and had bought 40 percent of CTVglobemedia (CTV and *The Globe and Mail*). Ted Rogers died in 2008, but the family still owns a huge swath of the Canadian communications industry. Galen Weston and family own such food enterprises as George Weston Limited and Loblaws as well as the upper-class clothing store Holt Renfrew. The Desmarais family own Power Corporation in Montreal, a gigantic financial conglomerate, and many other interests including newspapers. The Irving family owns most of New Brunswick, including large tracts of woodlands, pulp mills, oil refineries, gas stations, trucking, bus lines, and all the English-language newspapers in the province.

Another category of wealthy Canadians is the corporate chief executive officers (CEOs) who do not necessarily own their own firms. The total average compensation of the top 100 CEOs in Canada for one year alone—2007—was over $10 million, which includes the exorbitant value of salary, bonus, incentives, shares, and other benefits. Over half of this compensation came from the net proceeds of cashing in stock options, which, as capital gains, were taxed at half the regular income tax rates.[8] This figure compared to $17 739 for the full year earnings of a person working at the average minimum wage, and $40 237 for the full year earnings at the average wage and salary in Canada.

Sometimes another distinction is made between the "indigenous elite" and the "comprador elite," the latter being made up of the executives of branches of foreign-owned firms.[9] The comprador elite take orders from the corporate headquarters abroad, a good example being Brian Mulroney when he was president of the Iron Ore Company of Canada, in which Hanna Mining of Cleveland had a controlling interest. However, many Canadian firms have now become transnationals themselves. Thomson, Weston, Desmarais, Irving, Bombardier, and the McCains are among those that have many assets abroad.

The individuals and families of great wealth or income identified above, and others of slightly inferior stature, own or control many of the large corporations operating in Canada. Some individuals and families own hundreds of firms, and the extent of intercorporate connections is high.[10] In recent years, many have been more concerned with taking over competitors (often reducing the labour force in the process) rather than creating any new wealth or jobs or investing in increased productivity in the country.

A final point here concerns the vital part that Canadian banks play in the operations of the corporate elite. They do so because much corporate activity is financed by large bank loans. Thus, many of the individuals named above sit on the boards of directors of major Canadian banks, where their presence assures their company or companies of preferential banking treatment.[11] Indeed, a whole theory has been advanced regarding the manner in which the banks have directed the development of the Canadian economy. They have contributed to the widespread foreign ownership in Canada because of their preference for financing foreign branch plants in Canada rather than domestic manufacturers; they have exacerbated regional disparities in their preference for central Canadian clients; and they have encouraged a resource-based economy by preferring export-oriented resource companies to manufacturing.[12]

Most members of the corporate elite inherited a good deal of their wealth; such a transfer is facilitated by the lack of a wealth or inheritance tax in Canada. As far as the other aspects of their social background are concerned, the near Anglo-Protestant monopoly of earlier years is beginning to change. Several of the largest corporate families are of Jewish background, and French Canadians are increasingly prominent in such circles, now including Paul Desmarais (originally from Sudbury) and his sons, the Bombardier family, Jean Coutu (drug stores), and Pierre-Karl Péladeau (Quebecor). Those of other ethnic backgrounds are also joining the corporate elite, with names such as Saputo, Azrieli, and Stronach. Although Toronto remains the financial capital of the country, the economic elite is also increasingly diverse in terms of geography, with a new Western flavour.

Demands of the Corporate Elite and Results

The social homogeneity of the members of the corporate elite may have started to change, but the upper class is no less unified in its basic values. The predominant value that still characterizes the members of this group is the desire to maximize their ownership and control of the private sector and to press the public sector to adopt such policies as will allow them to go about their business of "accumulation."

It is not difficult, therefore, to draw the general lines of the public policy demands of the economic elite. Essentially, they want to be left alone: they want to cut government spending on social programs, to balance the annual budget, and to reduce the accumulated national debt. If taxes are necessary, they advocate avoiding estate or wealth taxes as well as corporate and progressive individual taxes, while providing generous loopholes, write-offs, and tax shelters.[13] They also want to minimize government regulation, labour standards, and environmental protection, as well as anti-combines laws and other restrictions on corporate takeovers. As Peter Newman says, "what unites [the capitalist elite] is common resentment of the multiplying intrusions of politicians and bureaucrats into the once-sacrosanct ground of Canadian capitalism."[14]

Governments have normally responded positively to such demands. Under the Mulroney government, for example, the progressive nature of the personal income tax was reduced when ten tax brackets were reduced to three. The Chrétien Liberals allowed the Bronfman family to transfer $2 billion in Seagram shares to the United States, averting about $700 million in capital gains taxation in the process. The Paul Martin budgets managed to balance the budget by slashing transfers to the provinces, mostly for social programs. And when the executive branch of government was not forthcoming, the corporate elite sometimes found comfort in actions of the Senate or the courts; for example, the Supreme Court has extended to corporations aspects of the Charter of Rights and Freedoms that were intended to protect individuals.

In her book *Behind Closed Doors*, Linda McQuaig[15] shows how the rich use their political influence to obtain tax breaks that are paid for by those with lesser incomes. Canada's personal and corporate income tax systems are riddled with loopholes; large numbers of corporations pay suspiciously low, if any, federal and provincial taxes; and governments have greatly increased their reliance on personal income taxes over the post-1985 period while reducing taxes on corporations.

Figure 8.2 shows that as a result of such policies, "the rich are getting richer and the poor are getting poorer." Dealing with wealth rather than annual income, it divides the population into ten groups and reveals that between 1984 and 2005 the wealthiest ten percent of Canadian family units made extraordinary gains, while the wealth of the poorest 40 percent declined.[16]

In fact, the business community prides itself on having set the entire government agenda, especially after 1985 or so, in articulating and supporting the movement to neoliberalism

· ·

Figure 8.2 The Wealth of Canadian Families, 1984, 1999, 2005

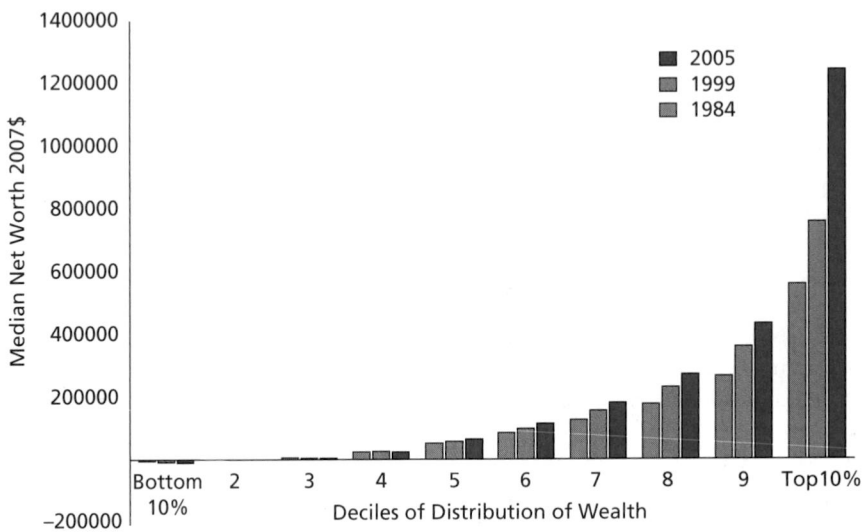

Source: Lars Osberg, A Quarter Century of Economic Inequality in Canada: 1981–2006. Fig. 9, The Wealth of Canadian Families 1984, 1999, 2005. Canadian Centre for Policy Alternatives, 2008. Found at: http://www.growinggap .ca/files/QuarterCenturyofInequality.pdf

in Canada. Big business was the principal advocate of free trade agreements, balancing the budget, reducing the debt, and then reducing taxes, and it emerged as a much "freer" and more powerful force in relation to the state. Nevertheless, the spate of corporate collapses, especially of companies involved in fraudulent accounting practices at the expense of shareholders and employees, has produced much anger. Conrad Black was charged with a variety of corporate crimes and the Canadian Democracy and Corporate Accountability Commission reiterated the call for internal corporate accountability.[17] Much of the worldwide financial crisis of 2008–09 can be attributed to the greed of certain corporate executives.

Three principal exceptions to big business's pressure to minimize the role of government must be noted. First, although the economic elite demands that governments minimize spending on others, it often expects sizable chunks of public funds for itself. The new "acquisitors," for example, have "exploited to [the] utmost the Canadian tradition of government subsidies in everything from offshore oil to horror films."[18] This tradition goes back as far as the end of the 19th century, when railway companies were given generous amounts of public funds and public lands; it has continued in a wide range of fields at the federal level ever since, especially in terms of regional economic development, and is carried on in giveaways to resource companies at the provincial and territorial level. The extent of actual government contributions to business was first made common knowledge by David Lewis in his 1972 book, *Louder Voices: Corporate Welfare Bums*.[19] Subsequent NDP leaders have reiterated that the "corporate welfare" involved often takes the form of capital cost allowances, deferred taxes, or "tax expenditures" (taxes forgone by the government). Bombardier was among the companies with such close ties to the Liberal government that it procured billions of dollars' worth of federal benefits, possibly to the extent of breaking international trading rules. Among many other favours, the Irving family extracted $35 million in loan guarantees from New Brunswick for a new diaper plant in Moncton."[20] Corporations often try to justify such requests as the means of creating jobs and generally promoting the trickling down of benefits from the top of the economic ladder to the bottom.

A second exception to the general pattern of corporate demands is the rare occasion on which the economic elite actually favoured new social programs. Motives here included increasing the purchasing power of the poor and working class, reducing the amounts that companies themselves had to pay in employee benefits, improving their corporate image, and ensuring the basic stability of society so that the upper classes did not have to worry about violent protests from the poor or unemployed. For example, companies operating in Canada gain a huge competitive advantage because they do not have to take much responsibility for the health insurance of their employees due to the universal public health program. Alvin Finkel writes of the reform measures adopted in the Depression of the 1930s: "The actions taken were those that businessmen-politicians and other pro-capitalist politicians believed would placate working-class and farmer demands while being assured at the same time that business power within the overall system would be preserved."[21]

In the third place, business leaders sometimes favour an expansion of government activity, usually in the provision of basic utilities or infrastructure, which will decrease their costs or increase their profits. For example, businessmen in Ontario shortly after 1900 encouraged the provincial government to create a Crown corporation to provide a cheap, reliable supply of electricity, and resource companies have often demanded that governments build roads and railways to save them the trouble.

As noted in Chapter 1, the Canadian state gives priority to big-business demands because it depends on the private sector, to a large extent, to create jobs. Many of the government handouts to corporations are predicated on job maintenance or job creation, although they do not always have this result. Beyond that, there are several reasons that politicians respond to the demands of the economic elite. First, corporate executives and politicians often come from the same ranks, including prime ministers and ministers of finance. Brian Mulroney, John Turner, and Paul Martin are good examples. Second, companies have many avenues of influence available: making a direct, personal pitch to governments; using professional lobby firms to help them make contact with public decision makers for a fee; and taking advantage of their membership in pressure groups. Among the hundreds of business pressure groups in existence, the **Canadian Council of Chief Executives** (formerly the BCNI) is probably the most powerful, representing as it does the chief executive officers of the 150 largest firms in the country.[22] Third, throughout their history both the Conservative and Liberal parties have largely been financed by large corporate contributions, and a link between corporate contributions and general public policy, if not to specific corporate favours, was not difficult to establish. In addition, in the 1988 election, Canadians witnessed an unprecedented parallel campaign in which the country's major corporations spent millions of dollars on top of their party donations to persuade Canadian voters of the merits of free trade. Fourth, the corporate elite also control the mass media to a large extent, with the potential to skew the nature of public discourse in the country. In short, an admirer of the corporate elite like Peter Newman could still write that "the combined power exercised by ... the new Canadian Establishment has seldom been exceeded in any nation that dares call itself a functioning democracy."[23]

Environmental protection has become one of the leading political issues in Canada and elsewhere, and to some extent can be framed as an issue pitting polluting corporations against ordinary citizens. Of course, the latter can also be forced or encouraged to change their behaviour in ways that would benefit the environment, but any serious reduction in greenhouse gases or other degradation of the environment will require curbs on the pollution emitted by large corporations. They were, in fact, the leading lobbyists against the Kyoto Accord or any effective post-Kyoto plan, whether it be a carbon tax, a "cap and trade" system, or simply a serious limit on emissions.[24] It is probably true that the Harper government's pro-business stance was never so obvious as in its lack of action in this field, although as noted in Chapter 3, this issue also possesses a strong regional dimension.

Occasionally corporations do not get everything they demand; for example, the large banks lobbied for authority to engage in mergers for some time without success.[25] The Harper government annoyed the corporate community (and many retirees) when it removed the tax advantages of corporate income trusts. And sometimes the most heinous corporate behaviour is punished, as when the federal and provincial governments demanded $10 billion from one of Canada's largest tobacco companies for having smuggled cigarettes into the country in the early 1990s. Eventually, two Canadian tobacco companies were indeed fined over $1 billion in 2008 after pleading guilty to orchestrating such a smuggling scheme. Although these were the largest fines ever levied in Canada, some observers noted that they were much smaller than originally proposed, that the companies had many years to pay them, and that the company executives who devised the scheme were not punished. Tobacco companies also got away with pressuring pharmaceutical companies to tone down promotion of smoking-cessation products, while they also fought against the government's attempt to ban the fraudulent words "light" and "mild" in cigarette labelling.

. . . .

THE MIDDLE CLASS

As outlined earlier, the traditional middle class, or "petite bourgeoisie," consists of affluent farmers, small-business people, and self-employed professionals, including doctors and lawyers. This group could also be called the old or upper-middle class. The "new middle class" consists of civil servants, teachers, and other salaried professionals, such as nurses, social workers, librarians, engineers, accountants, and the like. Neo-Marxists generally emphasize the importance of the ownership of the means of production, but as Leo Panitch says, the 20th century saw the development of a stratum of employees without such ownership or control but who "nevertheless dispose of labour in terms of managing, supervising, and controlling the labour of others."[26]

To some extent, these two fractions of the middle class have considerably different economic interests and therefore different identities and political demands. First, the members of the petite bourgeoisie are usually much wealthier than those of the new middle class and have many more tax breaks. Second, the petite bourgeoisie is made up of the self-employed and employers, while the new middle class is mostly composed of those who work for someone else. The new middle class largely works in the public sector, either directly for governments or in para-governmental institutions, such as schools, universities, and hospitals. Third, this public-sector branch of the new middle class is increasingly organized into unions, such as government employee unions, and nurses', teachers', and professors' associations. (While the new middle class now makes up a substantial portion of union membership in Canada, unions, as such, are discussed in the "working class" section below). The petite bourgeoisie, however, normally abhors unions almost as much as does the economic elite. Moreover, although it is common for members of the working class to think of themselves subjectively as middle class, the opposite may be true in the case of some nurses and teachers, who are in the process of being "proletarianized." Managerial changes to the way in which work is done and the severe funding cuts over the 1985–2000 period led rapidly growing numbers in these two professions to think of themselves and to act as members of the working class.[27]

Although the middle class is therefore far from being a unified force, its members are normally well educated and most are economically comfortable since they receive above-average levels of income. They own their homes and cars, and usually have assorted other material possessions. Some parts of the middle class have benefited in recent years from structural changes in the economy; indeed, the categories of management, administration, and health are among the few that have grown in both number of jobs and proportion of total income. However, some observers speak of the "hollowing out of the middle class" as it declines in numbers relative to those above and below it.

Unlike those in the upper class, members of the middle class may not be sufficiently affluent to finance their own educational and medical needs and those of their children, and usually demand and benefit from government programs in these fields. In addition, although not all members of the middle class can take advantage of the clauses written into the tax laws to benefit the wealthy,[28] they do enjoy such tax shelters as RRSPs and certain investment incentives (see Figure 8.3). The middle class is probably correct in feeling that it pays a disproportionate amount of the taxes to finance government programs of all kinds. Recent studies have shown, for example, that the deregulation of tuition fees in such professional schools as law and medicine has had a more serious impact on middle class students than on those above or below them because their parents cannot afford such increased fees and the students do not qualify for student assistance programs.

Many groups within the middle class are organized by profession, primarily at the provincial and territorial level. But there is no umbrella advocacy group that transmits the class's

· ·

Figure 8.3   Distribution of RRSP Tax Breaks by Income

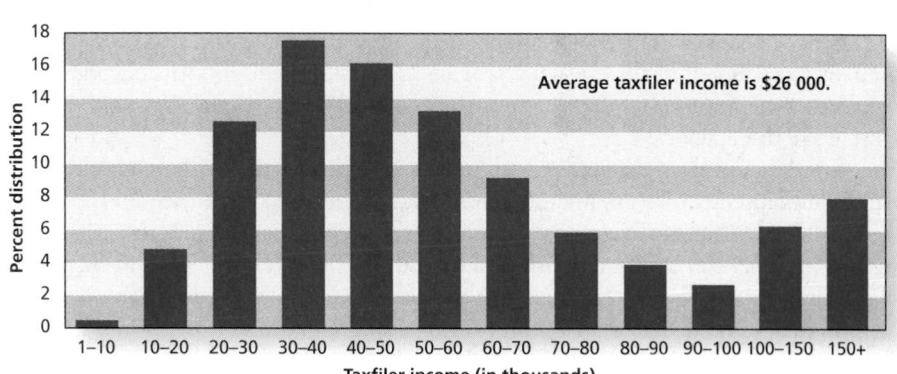

Source: Canadian Council on Social Development. Insight (April 1995). Reprinted by permission of Canadian Council on Social Development.

demands collectively to the authorities. Some—especially those who are unionized—have been attracted by NDP promises to shift the tax burden to the corporate sector and upper classes, but most continue to support the Liberal and Conservative parties because of their lack of sympathy with the NDP's links to industrial labour unions. To some extent, therefore, even the new middle class confirms Marx's contention that the petite bourgeoisie functioned primarily as an ally of the economic elite.

. . . .

THE WORKING CLASS

The working class is generally identified with manual or routine as opposed to intellectual work. Its members normally lack postsecondary education, but they are often qualified in a trade. They usually, but not always, receive less income than those in the middle class and are more frequently unionized. The typical member of the working class is engaged in resource exploitation, assembly line production, secretarial and clerical work, sales, and a variety of crafts and trades. (That portion of the working class living below the poverty line is discussed in the next section.) Although Marx categorized farmers as part of the petite bourgeoisie because of their ownership of land, most Canadian farmers have had to struggle for their existence. These less affluent farmers have sometimes cooperated with organized labour to support such organizations as the Co-operative Commonwealth Federation (CCF) and NDP.

The difference in economic status between unionized and nonunionized members of the working class is often profound, and the issue of unionization is a significant one for many of its members. Marx's predictions of a violent proletarian revolt were dealt a blow when the Macdonald government legalized trade unions in Canada in 1890 and when the franchise was extended to the working class. Since then, the courts have decided that labour legislation falls primarily within provincial jurisdiction, and the impediments to unionization vary across the country. Many provincial governments as well as many companies have been viciously hostile toward the formation of unions, and Canada has experienced a large number of violent strikes. Among the key labour struggles in Canadian history were the 1919 Winnipeg General Strike, the 1937 General Motors Strike in Oshawa, the 1945 Ford Strike in Windsor, the 1949 Asbestos Strike in Quebec, and the woodworkers strike in Newfoundland in 1959.[29] Labour legislation also deals with conciliation, mediation, arbitration, picketing, labour standards, occupational health and safety standards, and compensation for injury on the job. All of these usually provide minimal protection for the working class, as governments claim to be responding to labour demands but still seek to avoid offending their own corporate supporters.

Other things being equal, it is in the interests of members of the working class to belong to a union: unionized employees almost always have higher wages (sometimes higher than members of the middle class), adequate benefits, better working conditions, and more protection against arbitrary treatment and dismissal than those who do not engage in such collective bargaining. In other words, a union and the collective agreement bring the rule of law into the workplace. Table 8.3 compares unionized and nonunionized workers in a number of benefit categories.

In spite of these facts, the rate of unionization among those who work for wages (among employees who are not management and owners) is low and appears to be declining. Total union membership in 2008 was 4.6 million, or about 30 percent of the 15.1 million potential

TABLE 8.3	Unionized and Nonunionized Employees Covered by Employer-Sponsored Benefit Plans (Percentage)			
	Medical	*Dental*	*Life Insurance/Disability*	*Pension*
Unionized	83.7	76.3	78.2	79.9
Nonunionized	45.4	42.6	40.8	26.6

Source: Ernest B. Akyeampong, "Unionization and Fringe Benefits," Perspectives on Labour and Income. Adapted from the Statistics Canada publication, Catalogue 75-001-XPE (Autumn 2002), pp. 42–43.

members in the country.[30] The proportion of unionized workers in different sectors of the labour force is shown in Figure 8.4. In general, public sector workers now constitute close to 60 percent of the union movement, as the rate of unionization in that sector is about 75 percent, compared to 18 percent in the private sector. Public sector unions make up three of the seven largest unions in the country, as seen in Table 8.4 and, since 2004, more than 50 percent of union members have been women.

The 1980s and 1990s were not good years for the working class. Both decades began with a recession, and high unemployment diminished the bargaining power of Canadian workers, forcing them to concentrate on matters of job security rather than remuneration. Besides the recession in the 1990s, the ideology of neoliberalism resulted in government restraint

Figure 8.4   Labour Force Sectors with Highest Rates of Unionization, 2008

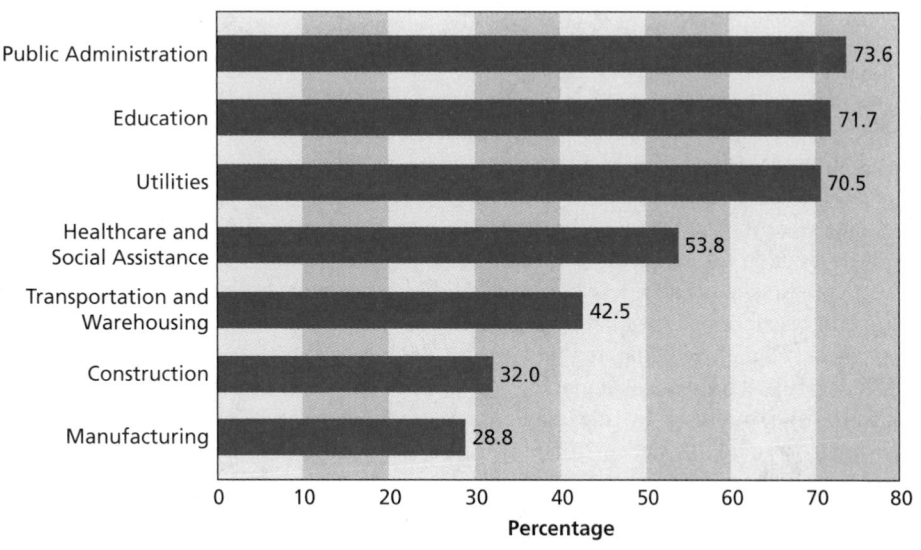

Source: Statistics Canada, Perspectives on Labour and Income. Unionization. Autumn 2008. Catalogue No. 75-001-XIE. Pg. 73.

TABLE 8.4   Largest Unions in Canada, 2008

Canadian Union of Public Employees (CUPE)	570 000
National Union of Public and General Employees (NUPGE)	340 000
United Steelworkers of America (USWA)	280 000
Canadian Auto Workers (CAW)	255 000
United Food and Commercial Workers (UFCW)	245 000
Public Service Alliance of Canada (PSAC)	174 000
Communications, Energy and Paperworkers (CEP)	146 000

Source: Union Membership in Canada-2008. Available from: http://www.hrsdc.gc.ca/eng/labour/labour_relations/info_analysis/union_membership/index.shtml. Human Resources and Skills Development Canada, 2009. Reproduced with the permission of the Minister of Public Works and Government Services Canada, 2009.

programs across the country. The forces of globalization and international trade agreements led multilateral corporations to close many large operations in Canada to take advantage of lower wages, unregulated working conditions, and an absence of environmental standards in other countries.

Although the official unemployment rate fell marginally around the turn of the 21st century, the unemployment insurance program is one of the most important concerns of the working class. This program was introduced in 1941 to help workers between jobs, but given the high national unemployment rates in the years since, especially in certain regions, it was used much more heavily than was originally anticipated. With such large numbers of workers drawing on the fund, it became both a vital source of individual and regional income and the subject of much political controversy. Made more generous in 1971 and renamed "Employment Insurance" (EI) in 1996, the program has been regularly restricted ever since, involving lower average payments, a shorter maximum duration of benefits, and a dramatic reduction in the percentage of the unemployed qualifying for benefits.[31] The decline hit women much harder than men. With thousands of unemployed workers eliminated from the EI program, it is no wonder that the fund accumulated an annual surplus of some $6 or $7 billion, which both the Chrétien and the Martin governments lumped into general revenues, helping them to balance the budget. Improvements have been made in recent years in the area of maternity, parental, and adoption leave, and political embarrassment and desperation for votes, especially in Atlantic Canada, led to a softening of restrictions immediately before the 2000 and 2004 elections. In 1989, 74 percent of those unemployed qualified for benefits, whereas since 1996, it has remained in the 40 percent range. This was particularly tragic after 2008, when the collapse of the economy produced a huge increase in the unemployment numbers and fewer than half received employment insurance benefits. In addition, the regional variations in the program were harshly criticized.

Organized labour has many other concerns, including provincial laws that make it difficult to form a union and inadequacies in child care, health care, education and training, pay equity, workers' rights, occupational health and safety, and pension and wage protection in the case of corporate bankruptcies. Labour works in conjunction with many allied groups in advancing these issues with the government. The trade union movement did not initially have much luck in taking its issues to the courts, but the Supreme Court made several recent decisions that were sympathetic to organized labour: it overturned an Ontario law that prohibited agricultural workers from forming unions; it upheld secondary picketing as a form of freedom of expression; and it ruled that the federal government had jurisdiction under its unemployment insurance power to provide maternity benefits. Most importantly, the Court overturned its own earlier ruling and decided that collective bargaining was indeed protected by the freedom of association clause in the Charter of Rights and Freedoms.[32]

The **Canadian Labour Congress (CLC)** is the lobbying body for more than three million workers. The CLC has the largest actual membership of any advocacy group in the country and therefore represents the greatest number of voters. Its influence is diminished, however, by its divergent values and its outsider status, as well as by the fact that not all unions belong to it. Whether it increased or decreased its influence by affiliating with the NDP in 1961 is still an open question. Many unions have not joined any central organization, and others have formed such rival groups as the Confédération des syndicats nationaux. The historic factionalism within the Canadian union movement has not helped the cause of the working class.[33] Thus, out of a potential 15 million paid (non-agricultural) workers, only two-thirds of the 4.6 million who have joined a union have affiliated with the largest central labour organization in the country.

. . . .

THE POOR

The poor can be defined as those living below the **poverty line**.[34] Among the many contested issues in this area is how to define poverty in the first place. Different organizations use varied definitions of poverty, which are sometimes highly ideological. Statistics Canada strenuously argues that its "Low-Income Cut-Off" (LICO) is a bureaucratic term, not a poverty line, but it is widely accepted as such. It is calculated as follows: any individual or family that spends more than 64 percent of their income on food, clothing, and shelter is considered to be living in poverty because that is 20 percent more than the average.[35] Some $10 billion annually would be required to bring all of these people up to the poverty line.[36]

Using this measure, it has to be acknowledged that the proportion of the population living in poverty declined from 25 percent in 1969 to 15.3 percent in 2005, with variations in between. In this connection, "before tax and transfer" figures present a much bleaker picture than "after tax and transfer" statistics, but the justification for using the former is that the poverty line is arbitrary and low, that a large group of near-poor exists just above it, and that many below it are *far* below it. Figure 8.5 shows the number of people, including children, below the poverty line in selected years. The actual number of people collecting social assistance was more than 1.7 million in 2005, down from more than three million in 1994–95, but this decrease was partly due to stricter eligibility rules rather than an improvement in these people's economic condition.

The aspect of poverty that is probably most heartbreaking is that nearly 25 percent of the poor people in Canada are children; in other words, about 11 percent of children live in poverty. The rate increases to 26 percent for children with disabilities, to 33 percent for Aboriginal and visible minorities, and to 47 percent for recent immigrants.[37] In 1986 the high-school dropout rate among children from poor families was 2.2 times the rate of others.

. . . .

**Figure 8.5   Number of Canadians (Including Children) Below the Poverty Line
(before Tax and Transfers) in Selected Years**

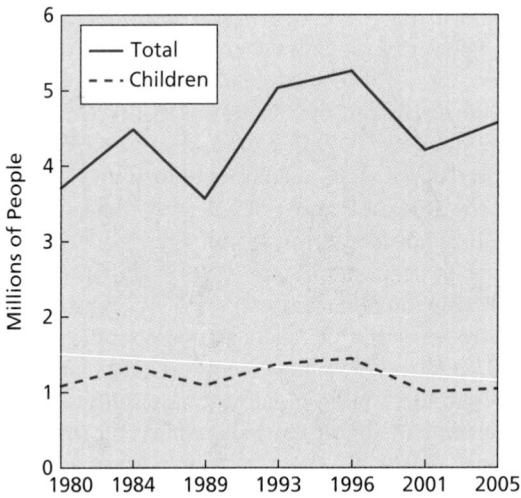

*Source: Poverty Profiles. National Council of Welfare, 1999 and 2001; Statistics Canada. Income of Canadians.
The Daily, March 30, 2006.*

This tie between low income and low education is self-perpetuating, and ways must be found
to encourage the children of poor families to pursue their education. The *Canadian Poverty
Fact Book* asserts that "the educational opportunities of children, whether at the primary,
secondary or postsecondary level, must not be limited by the economic circumstances of their
parents."[38] It also documents how children from low-income families stand out from their
better-off peers: "They are less healthy, have less access to skill-building activities, have more
destructive habits and behaviours, live more stressful lives, and are subject to more humilia-
tion. In short, they have less stable and less secure existences and as a result they are likely
to be less secure as adults."[39]

Although the House of Commons passed a resolution in 1989 to eliminate child poverty
in Canada by the year 2000, the number of children living in poverty actually increased by
50 percent during the 1990s. Because of the improved economy, fewer children lived in poverty by 2006, but even so, nearly 28 percent of families headed by a lone-parent mother were
below the poverty line.[40] In terms of depth of poverty, lone-parent mothers with children are
also further below the poverty line than other groups; hence the expression, the **feminization
of poverty**. Much could be said about each of the other categories of people living in poverty,
such as women, Aboriginals, people with disabilities, recent immigrants, and seniors.

A major dimension of poverty is the issue of housing, especially since all levels of government have virtually abandoned the field of social, public, or co-op housing. The high cost
of housing as a proportion of income is forcing the poor to reduce their spending on other
necessities, such as food, which puts an unbearable strain on a charitable food banks. Even
worse, an increasing number of poor people are now actually homeless.

Many poor people work full-time, and others part-time; as a result, the poor can be about equally divided between those who work and those who are unemployed or unemployable. The working poor try to scrape by on the minimum wage or have more than one low-paying job. Because the minimum wage is even lower than welfare benefits (both being below the poverty line), many working poor choose to go on welfare because they are often better off that way. Rather than raise the minimum wage, however, many provincial governments reduced welfare benefits in the 1990s. Even the combined incomes of two family members earning the minimum wage would not raise them above the poverty line. As with the working class above the poverty line, employment insurance is of vital importance to the working poor.[41] In the sweeping changes brought to the program by both the Mulroney and Chrétien governments discussed above, the lowest-income groups were the biggest losers.

When their EI runs out, the working poor become the welfare poor. Welfare benefits vary considerably across provinces and territories; they are not generous, contrary to the impression of many who have not had to rely on them. One must sell off most of one's possessions in order to qualify; studies repeatedly show that the incidence of welfare fraud is minimal; and earned income is usually deducted from welfare benefits, so it is often not worth the effort to find a job. Moreover, leaving the social assistance rolls usually means giving up free prescription drug and dental benefits and incurring new work-related expenses.[42]

Although the poor do try to fight back, they are generally unorganized and collectively inarticulate in the political system. They lack the skills to organize effectively as advocacy groups, primarily because they do not have the education, money, or time. However, a number of groups attempt to include the voice of the poor in the political process. One is the Canadian Council on Social Development (CCSD), which represents middle-class, bureaucratic, and even some corporate concern with the state of social policy in the country. It has often provided the blueprint for social reform and is an important source of data on social programs. Because the CCSD does not actually represent the poor, as such, the government sponsored the creation of the National Council of Welfare (NCW) in 1969 as an advisory group to speak on behalf of welfare clients themselves. Its members include welfare recipients, public housing tenants, and other low-income citizens as well as those involved in providing services to the poor. It also produces studies of the poverty problem and other social issues. Even though it is funded by the government, the NCW is usually more critical and radical than the CCSD. A third group, the National Anti-Poverty Organization (NAPO), was formed in 1971. It is an umbrella organization of some 700 local, provincial, and territorial anti-poverty groups and individuals across the country, representing Canadians living below the poverty line. Considering its lack of resources, it is surprisingly articulate. A number of other organizations also provide social policy analysis.

Couple living in car hope to use home renovation tax credit.

. . . .

THE RISE OF THE SOCIAL SAFETY NET

Reflecting the influence of the affluent economic elite, the North American predilection to abide by private market forces, and the assumption that jurisdiction over such matters rested primarily with the provinces, the federal government was slow to get involved in the provision of health and social service programs.[43] By the early 1980s, however, Canada had become a **welfare state** in which federal, provincial, and municipal governments were engaged in a wide range of programs that contributed to a **social safety net** that protected the weakest members of society, especially those unable or not expected to earn a living on their own. The principal federal measures can be divided into five basic fields—those relating to the young, seniors, people with disabilities, the unemployed, and health insurance. These programs, together with their dates of adoption, are listed as follows:

- Old Age Pensions (1927)
- Blind Persons' Allowances (1937)
- Unemployment Insurance (1941)
- Family Allowances (1944)
- Old Age Security (1951)
- Disabled Persons' Allowances (1954)
- Unemployment Assistance (1956)
- Hospital Insurance (1957)
- Canada Pension Plan (1965)
- Canada Assistance Plan (1966)
- Guaranteed Income Supplement (1966)
- Medical Insurance (1968)

- U.I. Amendments (1971)
- Spouse's Allowances (1975)
- Child Tax Credit (1978)
- Canada Child Tax Benefit (1993)
- National Child Benefit Supplement (1997)
- Universal Child Care Benefit (2006)

CP PHOTO/Boris Spremo

As CCF premier of Saskatchewan, Tommy Douglas pioneered public health insurance in Canada and was named "the greatest Canadian" in a CBC contest in 2005.

Almost all of these measures faced much upper-class and corporate opposition before being adopted. Virtually all were passed when a Liberal government was in office, although it should be added that the first unemployment insurance legislation was introduced by the Conservative R.B. Bennett but thrown out by the courts, and that the Diefenbaker government made incremental improvements to earlier Liberal measures.[44] In the case of hospital and medical insurance, the CCF pioneered the measures at the provincial level in Saskatchewan, and in several instances the Liberals introduced the federal programs when they were in a minority position in Parliament and depended on CCF or NDP support. The trade union movement, churches, and other progressive organizations like the CCSD were also responsible for popularizing such programs and pressing the government to implement them.

Other aspects of the social security net include special federal programs for war veterans and Aboriginals, and training schemes for the unemployed, while many provincial services supplement those outlined above. Primitive provincial welfare programs at the end of the 19th century gave way to mothers' allowances and family benefits after 1900, and child welfare programs, residential services, hospitals, workers' compensation, and student assistance can be found in every province and territory. Some provinces provide supplementary family allowances and assistance to seniors; some include dental, drug, optical, and paramedical services under medicare; and most offer a variety of other public health, crisis intervention, rehabilitation, and information and referral services. Some of these programs are partially funded through federal–provincial shared-cost programs. Thus, in spite of the resistance of the upper classes and the economic elite, the lot of the working class and poor in Canada could be and has been worse.

. . . .

THE DEMISE OF SOCIAL PROGRAMS

In fact, the plight of the poor became much worse after the middle of the 1980s. Both federal and provincial governments in the 1990s were obsessed with their accumulated debts and current budgetary deficits, which they, along with business interests and conservative think tanks, blamed on overspending on social programs. Although social programs loom large in federal, provincial, and territorial government budgets, Canada actually stands near the bottom of OECD countries in the proportion of gross domestic product spent on social programs, as seen in Table 8.5. In another measure, although the United Nations has repeatedly ranked Canada at or near the top in terms of its Human Development Index, we fell to 12th place in its Human Poverty Index. It is possible, therefore, that debts and deficits have been caused by under-taxation rather than by overspending; indeed, on a comparative basis, Canada derives less tax revenue from corporations than most of its major allies do. As noted earlier, Canada is also one of the few major Western industrialized countries without a tax on inheritance or wealth.[45]

Those in power from the mid-1980s onward agreed that social spending had to be chopped. Many observers saw Mulroney's package of economic policies—the Canada–U.S. Free Trade Agreement, privatization, deregulation, tax reform, reductions in transfers to the provinces and territories, and the many cutbacks in social programs—as an integrated strategy. Although the government claimed that these measures were introduced either to improve the economy or to cut the deficit (and the benefits might "trickle down" to the poor), they had the collective effect of reducing the standard of living of the poor and the working class. Several provinces, led by Alberta and Ontario, made their own massive cuts in social spending and would have done so regardless of reductions in federal transfers.[46]

Under the Chrétien Liberals, Paul Martin's 1995 budget cut transfers to the provinces and territories far beyond anything attempted by the Mulroney government, especially in health, postsecondary education, and welfare: a decrease of $7 billion over 1996–98.

TABLE 8.5	Total Social Expenditure as a Percentage of Gross Domestic Product, 2005, Aggregated Data (OECD Countries)		
Sweden	29.4	Greece	20.5
France	29.2	Switzerland	20.3
Austria	27.2	Czech Republic	19.5
Denmark	26.9	Japan	18.6
Germany	26.7	New Zealand	18.5
Belgium	26.4	Australia	17.1
Finland	26.1	Iceland	16.9
Italy	25.0	Ireland	16.7
Luxembourg	23.2	Slovak Republic	16.6
Hungary	22.5	CANADA	16.5
Norway	21.6	United States	15.9
Spain	21.2	Mexico	7.0
Poland	21.0	Korea	6.9
Netherlands	20.9		

Source: Data taken from OECD Social Expenditure-Aggregated data. Found at: http://stats/oecd.org/wbos/Index.aspx?datasetcode=SOCX_AGG

Besides lumping the three programs together under the label **Canada Health and Social Transfer (CHST)**, Ottawa repealed the Canada Assistance Plan and removed the conditions under which provinces received such funding. This meant that welfare would now have to fight it out with health and postsecondary education within provincial budgetary processes, and provincial governments could restrict social assistance eligibility and promote "workfare" schemes at will. In other words, although less was heard about it, the welfare sector bore the brunt of federal cutbacks even more than the health and education sectors.

The main cutbacks to social programs at both the federal and the provincial levels from 1985 to 2000 can be listed as follows:[47]

- Reduced social assistance levels in all provinces as well as cuts to supplementary benefits
- Cuts to services for people with disabilities—eligibility rules, home care, attendant care, and special transportation needs
- Social housing programs abandoned by the federal government and most provinces
- Severe federal cutbacks to employment insurance
- Repeal of the Canada Assistance Plan, reducing federal contributions to provincial welfare programs and removing federal standards
- Federal and provincial cuts to health care
- Introduction of provincial workfare schemes for those collecting social assistance

- Alarming increases in homelessness, especially in large cities
- Increased reliance on food banks, the number of which increased from 75 in 1984 to 625 in 1998
- Dramatic increases in university tuition fees in most provinces

All of these government cuts to social programs and the resulting deterioration in the way of life of millions of Canadians led to increasing protests around the turn of the 21st century. This was particularly true of the Ontario Coalition Against Poverty, whose leader, John Clarke, was arrested for a variety of offences and jailed for 25 days without trial. Many advocacy groups concerned with poverty have demanded that prohibitions on discrimination in federal and provincial human rights codes be extended to "social condition"—that is, level of income—to protect the poor.[48]

Even the United Nations scolded Canadian governments for what had transpired. Its Committee on Economic, Social and Cultural Rights criticized Canada in 1998 for its departure from the UN Covenant on these matters, especially given its obvious capacity to achieve a high level of respect for all UN Covenant rights. It slammed Ottawa and the provinces for having adopted the very policies listed above, "which exacerbated poverty and homelessness among vulnerable groups during a time of strong economic growth and increasing affluence."[49]

A few years into this decade, government revenues generally increased and ideological positions softened. Most provinces and territories began to make marginal improvements in their social programs, while Ottawa increased equalization payments and other transfers to the provinces and territories. About the time that a UNICEF study on child poverty ranked Canada 19th out of 26 OECD countries, the Martin government established the Early Learning and Child Care Initiative. This was a flexible distribution of $5 billion over five years to support provincial and territorial programs in these fields on a bilateral basis. Another move was to divide the Canada Health and Social Transfer into two constituent parts, health programs and social programs, so that the former would not absorb the entire fund. Then, having previously resurrected a federal role in the realm of housing, Martin made a budget deal with the NDP in the tense minority government situation in 2005 that put $4.5 billion into additional spending on the environment, social housing, foreign aid, and tuition reduction. A year earlier, Martin provided a major long-term boost to health care funding, with special emphasis on reducing waiting times.

A potentially serious problem, however, resulted from the Supreme Court decision in the *Chaoulli* case in 2005.[50] On the basis that waiting lists in the public system were too long, the Supreme Court ruled (5 to 4) that the Quebec law outlawing private medical insurance for core medical services was unconstitutional. Many observers feared that this decision would have a domino effect across the country and encourage two-tier medicare in Canada. Indeed, several provinces have moved in that direction.

As indicated earlier, improvement in the economy resulted in a decline in the proportion of people living below the poverty line. Unfortunately, this decline came to an abrupt end with the worldwide economic meltdown at the end of 2008. Among the ideas for how governments could improve the lot of the poor are the following:[51]

- Restore eligibility for Employment Insurance to earlier periods.
- Increase the federal minimum wage (partly as a model for the provinces and territories).

- Negotiate minimum standards for social assistance allowances based on the actual cost of a basket of essential goods.
- Increase the federal transfers to the provinces and territories under the Canada Social Transfer.
- End the provincial claw-back of the National Child Benefit Supplement.
- Increase federal allocations for child care and early learning.
- Increase federal allocations for affordable housing.
- Create specific programs to deal with poverty among immigrants, people with disabilities, and urban Aboriginals.

CONCLUSION

Whatever conception of class is employed, the existence of different classes in Canadian society cannot be denied. In this chapter, it was useful to divide the population into four classes: upper, middle, working, and poor. If such class cleavages do not usually result in much political activity at the lower levels, it must be that many Canadians are unaware of them, consider them acceptable, or feel powerless to change them.

Even though class in Canada is rarely given the attention that it receives in other political systems, the subject is connected to many other chapters of this book. Class has already been linked to preceding chapters in terms of the socioeconomic position of Aboriginal peoples, francophones, recent immigrants, ethnocultural minorities, and women, and class subcultures are mentioned in Chapter 11 (political culture). The role of multinational corporations is considered in Chapter 10 (the global environment), and of domestic corporations in Chapter 12 (media ownership) and Chapter 13 (financing political parties). Advocacy groups representing different classes are included in Chapter 16, and various class interests in the courts are raised in Chapter 19 (the Charter of Rights). Finally, the dominance of middle- and upper-class individuals and interests is emphasized in Part 5 on the institutions of government.

Ⓒ Of the approaches outlined in Chapter 1, class analysis is obviously the one most concerned with class cleavages. This approach maintains that the corporate elite is always the most powerful force in the political system and that in the post-1985 era of neo-liberalism such influence was only exacerbated. The corporate elite adopted a very effective strategy of placing on the national agenda, and making dominant, certain overarching themes: first, free trade, then, the deficit and debt, and, more recently, tax cuts. Each of these has as its inevitable product the reduction of the size and role of the state.

The class approach is also concerned with the lack of class-consciousness among the working class and the poor. Given such a weak sense of class-consciousness in the two lower classes, how do class analysts explain the social safety net? They argue that some such measures directly benefit the corporate sector, and the rest serve to legitimate the capitalist system and ensure social peace.[52] After the vote was extended to the working class, some minimal response had to be made to address its political demands, but not so much as to interrupt the accumulation activity of the bourgeoisie.

PC Public choice theory requires that voters be rational, self-interested, and conscious of their group position, something that many Canadian workers apparently are not. In spite of their numbers, such workers therefore rarely constitute a strategic group at election time. Politicians often promise programs of interest to the working class but do not fulfill them; sometimes they completely reverse their electoral commitments, as in the case of Pierre Trudeau's flip-flop on wage and price controls in 1974. Once the Chrétien Liberals were elected in 1993, they dragged their feet in implementing their Red Book commitments with respect to job creation and social programs. On rare occasions, however, politicians strike a bargain with the working class in which the former promise social programs in return for votes and then actually deliver.

SC State-centred theorists argue that because of the divisions within the working class and their low level of class-consciousness, politicians and bureaucrats can ignore their demands more easily than in the case of regional economic and ethnic demands. Moreover, since very few working-class politicians have ever been elected in Canada and most bureaucrats are of middle-class background, policies have been designed in the interests of those in power. Rodney Haddow has gone further to synthesize the class-based and state-centred approaches in his study of poverty reform in Canada. He shows that the bureaucrats in the influential finance department look at every issue through the eyes of big business, acting as an agent of capitalist class interests in the halls of power.[53] It should also be noted, however, that some bureaucrats take a wider view of the national interest. Those public servants in departments oriented toward lower classes, such as health, welfare, labour, and human resources development, along with their provincial counterparts, have been known to join organizations like the CCSD and do what they can to persuade the politicians to adopt their recommendations.[54]

P Pluralists emphasize the role of the one main working-class pressure group, the Canadian Labour Congress, and other groups speaking for the lower classes in the competition among societal interests. When faced with the resources available to business groups, however, this is a lopsided contest. Like the other segments of society, the labour movement has its own elite—the leaders of the largest unions in the country. But John Porter found that the composition of the labour elite was quite different from others. Lacking socioeconomic credentials, the labour elite has minimal links to the other elites, whether in terms of marriage, friendship, school ties, or politics.[55] What is even more striking is the absence of any group that could be said to represent the middle class. If policy is arrived at through advocacy group interaction, the middle class's unarticulated interests are ignored.

G The principal effect of globalization on class cleavages in Canada is the deepening of the divisions. The neoliberal ideology, of which globalization is a part, called for a withdrawal of government from society, allowing market forces to determine the distribution of income. Such a "state of nature" meant that stronger, wealthier interests prevailed. Globalization reinforces this ideological approach in the restrictions that states voluntarily impose upon themselves to regulate corporations by signing international agreements and by joining international organizations. Motivated by profit, transnational corporations are likely to make increasing inroads in the provision of social and medical services in Canada, which does not bode well for the working and poorer classes. However, the latter groups have found some comfort and camaraderie in other countries and in at least one global organization, the United Nations. In 2002, it was the policies of the Liberal government in British Columbia, a "massive assault on the social and economic rights of the poorest people," that were brought to the attention of the UN Committee on Economic, Social and Cultural Rights.[56]

DISCUSSION QUESTIONS

1. To what class do you and your family belong? Assess your family's class-consciousness.

2. What is the best way to define and distinguish among social classes?

3. Why do so many Canadians conceive of Canada as a middle-class nation?

4. Do you feel that the economic elite owe their wealth and power primarily to their own honest, individual efforts or to inheritance, exploitative forms of profit-making, and manipulation of the political system?

5. Given that unions are generally the best way of improving the lot of the working class, why are they not more popular among members of that class?

6. How do you explain the existence of the social safety net, given the lack of political power of the poor and working class?

7. What would you do to eliminate child poverty?

NOTES

1. Irving Abella, ed., *On Strike* (Toronto: James Lewis & Samuel, 1974).
2. Some readers will find this to be a great oversimplification of Karl Marx. Others will want to read modern variations, such as the Goldthorpe-Ericson class scheme which divides occupations into seven categories. See Gordon Marshall, et al., *Against the Odds? Social Class and Social Justice in Industrial Societies* (Oxford: Clarendon Press, 1997).
3. Janine Brodie and Jane Jenson, *Crisis, Challenge and Change: Party and Class in Canada Revisited* (Ottawa: Carleton University Press, 1988).
4. Anton L. Allahar and James E. Côté, *Richer and Poorer: The Structure of Inequality in Canada* (Toronto: Lorimer, 1998), pp. 24–26.
5. Brodie and Jenson, *Crisis, Challenge and Change*.
6. Neil Nevitte, Herman Bakvis, and Roger Gibbins, "The Ideological Contours of 'New Politics' in Canada: Policy, Mobilization and Partisan Support," *Canadian Journal of Political Science* (September 1989); and Neil Nevitte, *The Decline of Deference: Canadian Value Change in Cross-National Perspective* (Peterborough: Broadview Press, 1996).
7. Henry Veltmeyer's *Canadian Class Structure* (Toronto: Garamond Press, 1986) is the only attempt by a Canadian sociologist that I could find to estimate the actual number of people in each class, but see also Michael Ornstein and H. Michael Stevenson, *Politics and Ideology in Canada: Elite and Public Opinion in the Transformation of a Welfare State* (Montreal: McGill University Press, 1999).
8. Hugh Mackenzie, *Banner Year for CEOs* (Ottawa: Canadian Centre for Policy Alternatives, 2009). A similar list can be found in the *Globe and Mail Report on Business*, October 6, 2008.
9. Wallace Clement, *The Canadian Corporate Elite* (Toronto: McClelland and Stewart, 1975), and *Continental Corporate Power* (Toronto: McClelland and Stewart, 1977).

10. Tony Clarke, *Silent Coup: Confronting the Big Business Takeover of Canada* (Toronto: Lorimer, 1997); Anton L. Allahar and James E. Côté, *Richer and Poorer: The Structure of Inequality in Canada*; Jamie Brownlee, *Ruling Canada: Corporate Cohesion and Democracy* (Black Point, NS: Fernwood Publishing, 2005); and Diane Francis, *Who Owns Canada Now* (Toronto: HarperCollins, 2008).

11. Stephen Brooks and Andrew Stritch, *Business and Government in Canada* (Scarborough: Prentice Hall Canada, 1991), pp. 143–53.

12. R.T. Naylor, *The History of Canadian Business* (Toronto: Lorimer, 1975).

13. Linda McQuaig details "how the rich won control of Canada's tax system ... and ended up richer" in *Behind Closed Doors* (Toronto: Penguin, 1987). See also her *The Quick and the Dead* (Toronto: Penguin, 1991) and other writings.

14. Peter C. Newman, *The Canadian Establishment*, vol. 2: *The Acquisitors* (Toronto: McClelland and Stewart, 1990), p. 569.

15. McQuaig, *Behind Closed Doors*.

16. Lars Osberg, *A Quarter Century of Economic Inequality in Canada: 1981–2006* (Ottawa: Canadian Centre for Policy Alternatives, April 2008), cited on March 17, 2009, available at www.GrowingGap .ca. See also Rene Morissette and Xuelin Zhang, "Revisiting Wealth Inequality," *Perspectives on Labour and Income* (Statistics Canada, Spring 2007).

17. Havina S. Dashwood, "Canadian Mining Companies and Corporate Social Responsibility: Weighing the Impact of Global Norms," *Canadian Journal of Political Science* (March 2007) finds some evidence of corporate social responsibility.

18. Newman, *The Acquisitors*, p. 13.

19. David Lewis, *Louder Voices: Corporate Welfare Bums* (Toronto: James Lewis & Samuel, 1972). See also R. Chodos and R. Murphy, eds., *Let Us Prey* (Toronto: Lorimer, 1974); and Ontario Coalition for Social Justice, *Unfair $hares: Corporations and Taxation in Canada* (March 1998).

20. David Olive, *Toronto Star*, September 8, 2003.

21. Alvin Finkel, *Business and Social Reform in the Thirties* (Toronto: Lorimer, 1979), p. 176.

22. See Peter C. Newman, *Titans: How the New Canadian Establishment Seized Power* (Toronto: Penguin Books, 1998), in which Tom d'Aquino boasts of determining the government's entire agenda; Peter Clancy, "Business Interests and Civil Society in Canada," in Miriam Smith, ed., *Group Politics and Social Movements in Canada* (Peterborough: Broadview Press, 2008).

23. Newman, *The Acquisitors*, p. 578.

24. Douglas MacDonald, *Business and Environmental Politics in Canada* (Peterborough: Broadview Press, 2007).

25. Russell Alan Williams, "Mergers If Necessary, but Not Necessarily Mergers: Competition and Consolidation at Canada's 'Big Banks,'" in Robert M. Campbell, Leslie A. Pal, and Michael Howlett, eds., *The Real Worlds of Canadian Politics*, 4th ed. (Peterborough: Broadview Press, 2004).

26. Leo Panitch, "Elites, Classes, and Power," in Michael S. Whittington and Glen Williams, eds., *Canadian Politics in the 1990s*, 4th ed. (Scarborough: Nelson Canada, 1995), p. 168.

27. I owe this observation (as well as many other improvements to the book) to Prof. Jim Silver of the University of Winnipeg.

28. McQuaig, *Behind Closed Doors*.

29. Abella, *On Strike*; and Walter Stewart, *Strike!* (Toronto: McClelland and Stewart, 1977), ch. 4.

30. Human Resources and Skills Development Canada, available at www.hrsdc.gc.ca/en/labour/labour_ relations/info_analysis/union_membership/index.shtml. That is, as a percentage of non-agricultural paid workers. See also Statistics Canada, *Perspectives on Labour and Income*, "Unionization," (August 2008).

31. Z. Lin, "Employment Insurance in Canada: Recent Trends and Policy Changes," *Canadian Economic Observer* (July 1998).

32. *R.W.D.S.U., Local 558 v. Pepsi Cola Canada Beverages (West) Ltd.*, [2002] 1 S.C.R. 156; *Dunmore v. Ontario (Attorney General)*, [2001] 3 S.C.R. 1016; *Reference re Employment Insurance Act (Can.)*, ss. 22 and 23, [2005] S.C.R. 669; and *Health Services and Support—Facilities Subsector Bargaining Assn. v. B.C.*, [2007] 2 S.C.R. 391, which overturned the earlier 1987 Labour Trilogy case.

33. Gad Horowitz, *Canadian Labour in Politics* (Toronto: University of Toronto Press, 1968). See also David Camfield, "The Working-Class Movement in Canada: An Overview," and Charlotte Yates, "Organized Labour in Canadian Politics: Hugging the Middle or Pushing the Margins?" in Miriam Smith, ed., *Group Politics and Social Movements in Canada* (Peterborough: Broadview Press, 2008).

34. The field of social policy analysis is now blessed with a multitude of organizations that provide data relevant here. These include the Canadian Council on Social Development, the National Council of Welfare, the Caledon Institute of Social Policy, the National Anti-Poverty Organization, the Centre for Social Justice, the Ontario Coalition for Social Justice, the Canadian Labour Congress, and the Canadian Centre for Policy Alternatives.

35. National Council of Welfare, *Poverty Profile 2001* (Autumn 2004), *Welfare Incomes 2004* (Spring 2005), and *Welfare Incomes, 2006 and 2007* (Winter 2008). The "Market Basket Measure" is an alternative to the LICO way of measuring poverty.

36. National Council of Welfare, *Poverty Profiles* 1999, 2001, 2002, *and* 2003, and *Welfare Incomes, 2006 and 2007.*

37. The overall figure is national; the figures for specific groups are for Ontario. National Council of Welfare, *Poverty Profile, 2001* and *Welfare Incomes, 2004*; and Campaign 2000, *Putting Children First: 2005 Report Card on Child Poverty in Ontario.*

38. Canadian Council on Social Development, *The Canadian Poverty Fact Book—1989*, p. 93; and *The Progress of Canada's Children, 1997.*

39. *The Canadian Poverty Fact Book, 1994*, p. 2.

40. Statistics Canada, "Income of Canadians," *The Daily*, May 5, 2008; cited on March 18, 2009; available at http://www.statcan.ca/daily-quotidien/080505/dq080505a-eng.htm; Monica Townson, *Women's Poverty and the Recession* (Ottawa: Canadian Centre for Policy Alternatives, 2009); and Conference Board of Canada, How Canada Performs, at http://www.conferenceboard.ca/HCP/Details/society.aspx.

41. It was implemented shortly after the Depression, when unemployed men were placed in labour camps. When they began a trek from BC to Ottawa, they were blocked by police in the Regina Riot of July 1, 1935.

42. TD Economics, *From Welfare to Work in Ontario: Still the Road Less Travelled* (Toronto: TD Bank Financial Group, 2005).

43. Denis Guest, *The Emergence of Social Security in Canada*, 3rd ed. (Vancouver: UBC Press, 1998); Jacqueline S. Ismael, ed., *Canadian Social Welfare Policy: Federal and Provincial Dimensions* (Montreal: McGill-Queen's University Press, 1985).

44. P.E. Bryden, *Planners and Politicians: Liberal Politics and Social Policy 1957–1968* (Montreal: McGill-Queen's University Press, 1997).

45. Roger S. Smith, *Personal Wealth Taxation* (Toronto: Canadian Tax Foundation, 1993), p. iii; and Conference Board of Canada, "Canada's Record on Poverty Among the Worst of Developed Countries—And Slipping," September 17, 2009 at http://www.conferenceboard.ca/press/newsrelease/10-21.aspx.

46. Walter Stewart, *Dismantling the State* (Toronto: Stoddart, 1998); Don Waterfall, *Dismantling Leviathan: Cutting Government Down to Size* (Toronto: Dundurn Press, 1995); and Stephen McBride and John Shields, *Dismantling a Nation* (Halifax: Fernwood Publishing, 1993, 1997).

47. See, for example, publications of the National Council of Welfare, the Caledon Institute of Social Policy, NAPO, the Centre for Social Justice, and the Canadian Centre for Policy Alternatives.

48. The Supreme Court more or less rejected this argument in *Gosselin v. Quebec (Attorney General)*, [2002] 4 S.C.R. 429.

49. UN Committee on Economic, Social and Cultural Rights, "Concluding Observations on Canada's 3rd Periodic Report," (E/C. 12/1/Add. 31, 10 December 1998).

50. *Chaoulli v. Quebec (Attorney General)*, [2005] 1 S.C.R. 791.

51. National Council of Welfare, "Presentation to the Standing Committee on Finance," October 27, 2005; Campaign 2000, "Decision Time for Canada: Let's Make Poverty History: 2005 Report Card on Child Poverty in Canada"; and NAPO, "Election Issue Sheet on Poverty in Canada," 2005. See also Institute for Research on Public Policy, *Policy Options*, September 2008, and Canadian Centre for Policy Alternatives, *The Growing Gap*, at www.GrowingGap.ca.

52. Finkel, *Business and Social Reform in the Thirties.*

53. Rodney Haddow, *Poverty Reform in Canada 1958–1978: State and Class Influences on Policy Making* (Montreal: McGill-Queen's University Press, 1993); and Rianne Mahon, "Canadian Public Policy: The Unequal Structure of Representation," in Leo Panitch, ed., *The Canadian State: Political Economy and Political Power* (Toronto: University of Toronto Press, 1977).

54. Richard Splane, "Social Policy-Making in the Government of Canada: Reflections of a Reformist Bureaucrat," in S.A. Yelaja, ed., *Canadian Social Policy* (Waterloo: Wilfrid Laurier University Press, 1978); and Rand Dyck, "The Canada Assistance Plan: The Ultimate in Cooperative Federalism," *Canadian Public Administration* (Winter 1976). Carl Cuneo and Leslie Pal engaged in an interesting intellectual dialogue on the question of the significance of class in the bureaucracy in the March 1986 issue of the *Canadian Journal of Political Science*.

55. John Porter, *The Vertical Mosaic* (Toronto: University of Toronto Press, 1965), chs. XI and XVII; and Rick Helmes-Hayes and James Curtis, eds., *The Vertical Mosaic Revisited* (Toronto: University of Toronto Press, 1998).

56. See letter from the Poverty and Human Rights Project, dated February 11, 2002; cited on October 25, 2002; available at http://www.povnet.org/human_rights/ICESR_let.pdf.

. . . .

FURTHER READING

Allahar, Anton L., and James E. Côté. *Richer and Poorer: The Structure of Inequality in Canada*. Toronto: Lorimer, 1998.

Brodie, Janine, and Jane Jenson. *Crisis, Challenge and Change: Party and Class in Canada Revisited*. Ottawa: Carleton University Press, 1988.

Brownlee, Jamie. *Ruling Canada: Corporate Cohesion and Democracy*. Black Point, NS: Fernwood Publishing, 2005.

Canadian Centre for Policy Alternatives. *The CCPA Monitor*. Ottawa: monthly, and other assorted publications.

Clarke, Tony. *Silent Coup: Confronting the Big Business Takeover of Canada*. Toronto: Lorimer, 1997.

Guest, Denis. *The Emergence of Social Security in Canada*, 3rd ed. Vancouver: University of British Columbia Press, 1998.

Hale, Geoffrey. *The Uneasy Partnership: Politics of Business and Government in Canada*. Peterborough: Broadview Press, 2006.

MacDonald, Douglas. *Business and Environmental Politics in Canada*. Peterborough: Broadview Press, 2007.

McBride, Stephen, and John Shields. *Dismantling a Nation: The Transition to Corporate Rule in Canada*, 2nd ed. Halifax: Fernwood Publishing, 1997.

McQuaig, Linda. *Behind Closed Doors*. Toronto: Penguin, 1987.

National Council of Welfare. Various publications.

Ornstein, Michael, and H. Michael Stevenson, *Politics and Ideology in Canada: Elite and Public Opinion in the Transformation of a Welfare State*. Montreal: McGill University Press, 1999.

Osberg, Lars. *A Quarter Century of Economic Inequality in Canada: 1981–2006*. Ottawa: Canadian Centre for Policy Alternatives, April 2008, available at www.GrowingGap.ca.

Panitch, Leo, ed., *The Canadian State: Political Economy and Political Power*. Toronto: University of Toronto Press, 1977.

Stewart, Walter. *Dismantling the State*. Toronto: Stoddart, 1998.

Studies in Political Economy: A Socialist Review. Ottawa: Carleton University.

Chapter 9

Other Cleavages and Identities:
URBAN/RURAL LOCATION,
Religion, and Age

Is there a greater need to possess a rifle in rural than in urban communities? Is discourse in the House of Commons dominated by big-city issues? Is December 25 still Christmas or just a generic "holiday"? What are the implications of considerable Muslim immigration in recent years? Which group is in greater need of government support: seniors or children? Will the aging population soon bankrupt the public health care system?

Beyond the regional, ethnic, gender, and class cleavages and identities discussed earlier, the urban/rural split, religion, and age constitute three social factors that have considerable potential for political controversy in Canada.[1] Of the three, religion has been prominent in Canada's past, especially at the provincial level, while today's religious issues are of a somewhat different complexion. As the population grows older and as rural areas decline in numbers, at least relative to urban areas, the claims of seniors and of urban communities are increasing in political significance. At the same time, Canadians living in rural areas complain of neglect.

THEORETICAL CONSIDERATIONS

As with other social characteristics, rural, urban, religion, and age can be measured in numerical terms, and differences and divisions can be labelled as cleavages. But also in common with characteristics addressed in earlier chapters, numbers alone do not do full justice to their political implications. To be of political significance, such characteristics must have salience to the individuals involved, and that gives rise to the concept of identities. As mentioned in Chapter 1, such identities tend to be socially constructed. "You are only as old as you feel," it is said, and if people over 65 years of age do not feel "elderly," if they do not feel different, and if they do not seek recognition on the basis of their age, their political impact will be reduced. Nevertheless, the number and proportion of seniors in Canadian society is increasing rapidly, and they are likely to view their age as part of their identity. Numbers alone may not be significant with respect to those adhering to various religious denominations, for many of whom such adherence is only a formality. An index of religiosity therefore has to include frequency of public and private religious practice and the importance of religion to the person involved.

Indeed, 44 percent of Canadians place a high degree of importance on religion in their life.[2] While "rural" and "urban" might seem straightforward enough at first sight, the distinction between them is not necessarily clear-cut: some people have a foot in both camps or live in and identify with an ambiguous suburban, small town, or rural area adjacent to a big city. Moreover, some observers even regard "rural" and "urban" as social constructions based on "perceptions, identity, power, and symbols."[3] All of these identities are felt to be important by large proportions of the population.

URBAN/RURAL LOCATION

Statistics Canada categorized 80 percent of the population as urban and 20 percent as rural in the 2006 census, the basic definition of "urban" being centres of at least 1000 people. In these terms, the majority of Canadians have been designated as urban-dwellers since 1931, and the percentage has gradually increased in every decade since 1974, as seen in Figure 9.1. In 2006, the total urban population exceeded 25 million, while the rural population plateaued at about six million: between 2001 and 2006, remote rural areas lost population while those close to urban centres grew slightly. Some observers regard this definition of rural as too narrow, however, and would add in small towns with more than 1000 residents, which have many of the same concerns as rural populations.[4] Although there has always been some tension between urban and rural interests in Canadian politics, it has no doubt been exacerbated by such a pattern of steady urbanization. Many observers talk of a new cleavage in Canadian politics, although, ironically, both rural and urban interests feel that they are not getting the attention they deserve from Ottawa.

Figure 9.1 Proportion of the Canadian Population Living in Urban Regions Since 1901

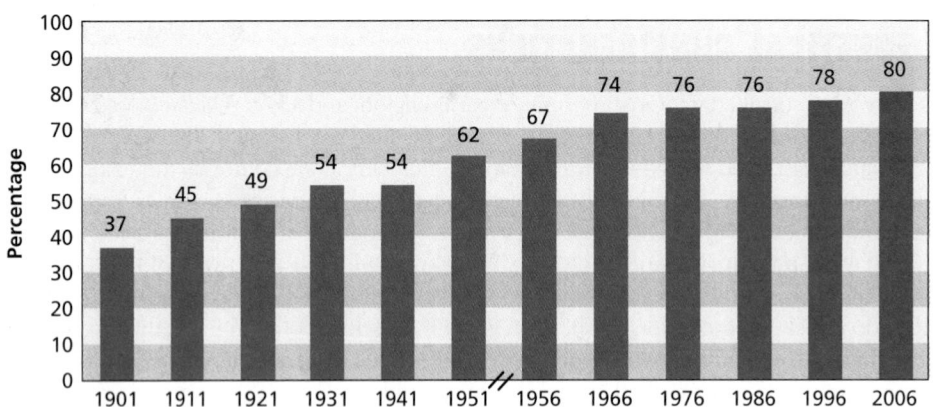

Source: Statistics Canada. Population of Canada, Provinces and Territories in the last 50 years. Fig. 5, Proportion of the Canadian population living in urban regions since 1901. Found at: http://www12.statcan.ca/census-recensement/2006/as-sa/97-550/figures/c5-eng.cfm

Chapter 3 observed that 62 percent of the population lives in Ontario and Quebec, and that the Toronto–Montreal–Ottawa triangle constituted the political and economic core of the country. But the distribution of the Canadian population is even more complicated. In addition to this national **core–periphery system**, a series of regional core–periphery systems exists across the country. Several metropolitan centres dominate their own regional hinterlands: Vancouver in British Columbia; Edmonton and Calgary in Alberta; Regina and Saskatoon in Saskatchewan; Winnipeg in Manitoba; Toronto in Ontario; Montreal in Quebec; and Halifax and St. John's in Atlantic Canada. The same could be said of Whitehorse in Yukon, Yellowknife in the Northwest Territories, and possibly Iqaluit in Nunavut. The interior of BC and northern Ontario are two examples of regions within a province that feel isolated from and exploited by their own economic cores, Vancouver and Toronto, respectively.

Such regional cores are heavily urbanized and are termed "census metropolitan areas" (CMAs) by Statistics Canada. As seen in Table 9.1, the 33 largest metropolitan centres in Canada, those with over 100 000 residents each, constituted 68 percent of the total population in 2006, and 45 percent of the population lived in the six largest cities alone. More than one politician has calculated that the support of only these highly urbanized areas would be enough to form a government.

An adequate discussion of Canadian urban and rural differences would be lengthy and complex. Just as they are hard to differentiate by definition, it is difficult to generalize about either sector—each is diverse, and each is in a state of change. Here, however, is a brief list of key aspects of rural Canada today:[5]

- Rural Canada is characterized by low-density as opposed to high-density living, with greater distances separating people and settlements, and a narrower range of services available to them.
- Rural communities provide transportation links between large urban centres and many of the recreation areas used by urban Canadians.
- Rural Canada is partly agricultural, but the number of people engaged in agriculture has been declining for decades.
- The rural agricultural population is no longer primarily defined in terms of family farms; the number of farms has decreased, the size has increased, and they are increasingly owned by corporations rather than by families.
- The remaining farm families usually have to supplement their incomes with off-farm and nonfarm work and now receive only 26.5 percent of their income from farming activities.
- Rural Canada is also the location of other primary industries: mining, forestry, petroleum, fishing, and hydroelectricity.
- Government concern with balancing budgets over 1995–2007 period, under the influence of neoliberalism, resulted in a substantial reduction in the number of schools, hospitals, post offices, and other government offices in rural areas and small towns.
- Rural Canada is characterized by an exodus of young people, often leaving for educational advancement and not returning.

Many of these factors have led to an angry sentiment of **rural alienation** in recent years, primarily reflecting a loss of power to the benefit of urban Canada. Until 30 years ago, the interests of rural Canada were more forcefully represented than their numbers deserved.

TABLE 9.1	Population of Census Metropolitan Areas, 2006 Census		
Toronto	5 113 149	Regina	194 971
Montreal	3 635 571	Sherbrooke	186 952
Vancouver	2 116 581	St. John's	181 113
Calgary	1 079 310	Barrie	177 061
Edmonton	1 034 945	Kelowna	162 276
Ottawa*	846 802	Abbotsford	159 020
Quebec	715 515	Sudbury	158 258
Winnipeg	694 668	Kingston	152 358
Hamilton	692 911	Saguenay	151 643
London	457 720	Trois-Rivières	141 529
Kitchener	451 235	Guelph	127 009
St. Catharines/Niagara	390 317	Moncton	126 424
Halifax	372 858	Brantford	124 607
Oshawa	330 594	Thunder Bay	122 907
Victoria	330 088	Saint John	122 389
Windsor	323 342	Peterborough	116 570
Gatineau*	283 959	TOTAL	21 500 000
Saskatoon	233 923		

*The author has separated Ottawa-Gatineau into two parts.

Source: Statistics Canada, Population and dwelling counts, for census metropolitan areas, 2006 and 2001 censuses, available at http://www.statcan.ca/census-recensement/2006/dp-pd/hlt/97-550.cm?TPL+P1.

Rural Canada is still somewhat overrepresented in the House of Commons, but the number of rural politicians has declined, leading to the realization that, politically speaking, rural Canada does not matter much in electoral terms. Moreover, governments, academics, and other "experts" view cities as the economic engines of the country and pay little attention to rural areas.

Rural Canada thus exhibits a growing belief that it is not in control of its own destiny, politically or economically, and that those in power do not understand its issues or take them seriously. Laws and regulations are made by "city-slickers" who know nothing about rural life; such rules generally reflect the needs of urban communities and do not always work when applied to the countryside. Tax assessments, land use regulation, and environmental issues are often cited as examples. The controversy over the annual Newfoundland and Labrador seal hunt might also be seen in urban–rural terms, while the Charter of Rights and Freedoms protects minority rights but not those of property owners. Somewhat similar to the phenomenon of Western alienation, rural Canada finds an institutional structure stacked against it, but does not have the comfort of provincial governments to defend its interests. Rural Canadians do have organized advocacy groups, including the Canadian Federation of Agriculture, the National Farmers Union, and the more militant Rural Revolution, but find it necessary to take to the streets in increasing numbers, protesting the level of farm incomes and sometimes blockading the food distribution system.

Almost all aspects of agriculture have sought federal government assistance at one time or another.[6] Persistent demands are made for agricultural credit and subsidies, often to match those given farmers in other countries, and to ensure that international trade agreements do not disadvantage Canadian farmers. Farmers remind us that they cannot continue to provide food for urban dwellers unless they derive an adequate financial return, and that they in turn purchase goods and services from those who depend on such food. Conflict often arises among producers of different commodities, and producers of the same commodity are sometimes divided among themselves, such as about the value of marketing boards, including the Canadian Wheat Board.[7] A more specialized case had to do with the discovery of mad cow disease in one Alberta cow in 2003, in response to which more than 30 countries restricted the import of Canadian beef and cattle. The U.S. and Japanese restrictions devastated the Canadian beef industry; farmers fought desperately for compensation and felt strongly that their concerns were not taken seriously.

Each of the other primary industries has its own demands, too numerous to mention here. But more general rural demands include guaranteed Internet access and more adequate health services, although these are really provincial issues.[8] Indeed, broadband Internet service can provide electronic delivery of health, education, and government services, such as telemedicine and telehealth innovations, in the absence of actual health care personnel and facilities. Rural residents fight for the restoration of postal and other government services, as well as private services, such as banks. The lack of public transportation is often a serious rural issue, while rural and urban communities have a shared concern with a safe environment. For example, the contamination of the public water system at Walkerton, Ontario, which killed seven people and made more than 2000 ill, was caused by E. coli bacteria contained in run-off from area farms that developed partly because of inadequate regulation. Another shared concern is the disappearance of prime agricultural land because of urban development and sprawl—subdivisions and shopping centres. Although everyone decries this situation from the point of view of having less land for the production of food, some farmers are happy to sell their land because it was not providing a good living for their families.

That is not to say that rural demands have been totally ignored. As mentioned, rural areas continue to be overrepresented in the House of Commons, although to make rural constituencies much larger in area would often take them beyond the capacity of a single MP to serve. Several agricultural commodities have federal marketing boards (and others have

Ontario farmer criticizes budget money to public transportation.

provincial boards); the Canadian Wheat Board has the mammoth mandate of marketing Canadian grain. Further, farmers do receive large annual subsidies for a variety of products, and the government ultimately provided hundreds of millions of dollars of compensation for the BSE (mad cow) crisis.[9]

Whether urban or rural, the country is divided into municipalities, and in the first instance, local issues are addressed at this level. Since municipalities constitute a subordinate level of government, however, local concerns often find their way onto the agenda of provincial and territorial governments as well. Generally speaking, there has been limited official contact between municipalities and the federal government, despite the fact that national policies often have significant implications at the local level.

The **Federation of Canadian Municipalities** is the collective national voice for all types of municipalities in the country. Although often dominated by large, urban forces, it also has a Rural Forum with representatives of communities of fewer than 10 000 people.[10] This forum articulates many of the rural demands mentioned above and proposes that federal programs cease to be based on a per capita formula that puts rural and northern communities at a disadvantage and be awarded on fiscal capacity instead.

As they grow larger and encounter more complex problems, major urban centres increasingly make demands on Ottawa to deal with such issues as poverty, housing, transportation, immigration, and crime. Periodically since about 1970, the federal government has established agencies concerned with urban problems, such as secretariats for urban issues. The Martin government revived such interest with an "Agenda for Cities," but when smaller communities wanted a piece of the action, it became the New Deal for Cities and Communities, and the Cities Secretariat in the Privy Council Office became the Ministry of State for Infrastructure and Communities. One of Martin's main promises in this regard was to help support urban public transportation systems by sharing the proceeds of the federal gas tax with municipalities. When smaller and rural municipalities immediately protested against this discrimination, the program was broadened to include all sizes of communities. The Harper government was less interested in a direct federal–municipal relationship.

Besides dealing with the municipal level of government on distinct local rural and urban issues, the federal government often faces different demands with respect to national policies from rural, urban, and suburban parts of the electorate, which reflect certain differences in values or needs. Perhaps the leading case was that of registering guns.[11] The "gun control" law of the 1990s was widely supported by urban voters and vehemently opposed by a majority of rural voters who claimed that hunting was part of their lifestyle, if not essential to their well-being. Of course, the law did not prohibit the ownership of hunting rifles, only requiring their registration, but many opponents argued that confiscation would follow. The Harper government announced a legal amnesty for long-gun owners who had not yet registered their guns; while it was unable to pass legislation to give full legal sanction to this decision, it continued to pursue the issue by means of a private member's bill.

Given that large urban centres have younger, more diversified populations in ethnic terms, more recent immigrants, higher average levels of education and incomes, and lower levels of religious attendance, other federal policies have had a differential appeal to urban and rural voters. One study based on early 1990s data emphasized two issues related to moral conservatism: homosexuality and feminism. People living in small places were more opposed to same-sex marriage than were those in larger centres, and were more likely to object to women working outside the home. Indeed, rural Canada rarely elects any female members of Parliament. There were also small differences on questions related to Quebec, such as the designation of that province as a distinct society.[12] It is usually thought that rural and urban areas also differ on such issues as immigration, multiculturalism, and abortion. In other words, urban Canadians are more open to diversity, change, new technology, and globalization; rural Canadians are more wary of social change, they value family bonds, and they may be more community-minded.[13]

Not surprisingly, Canada has experienced a certain rural–urban split in terms of party preference. The Liberal Party has essentially been an urban party for generations, as has the NDP, while the Conservative Party has not made many inroads into metropolitan centres except for Calgary. In this respect, considerable attention has been focused on suburban areas, such as the "905 belt" around Toronto, which tended to demonstrate conservative views in both federal and provincial elections. In the 2006 federal election, the Harper Conservatives were shut out of central Toronto, Montreal, and Vancouver, the three largest cities in Canada. Claiming that the lack of representation of these three centres around the Cabinet table would be dysfunctional for the government and the country, Prime Minister Harper appointed a senator to represent Montreal and lured David Emerson across the floor from the Liberals to speak for Vancouver. That Harper was prepared to face great controversy over these two moves indicates how important he felt such large-city representation to be, and the party did slightly better in urban areas in 2008.

. . . .

RELIGION

Historically, religious cleavages and identities coincided to a considerable extent with those of language and ethnicity, so that the interests of French Catholics were often at odds with those of Anglo-Protestants. Frequently, especially in the earlier years, the religious conflict even overshadowed the ethnic one, and it was most often a problem between Protestants and Roman Catholics within the Christian church. As this issue diminished to some extent in recent years, other religious issues have gained more prominence.

Separate Schools

The first main religious demand in Canada came from Roman Catholic and Protestant minorities who wanted their own separate school systems. The Protestant minority in Quebec and the Roman Catholic minority in Ontario were successful in having this right established in law at the elementary level before Confederation. Thus, in the **Constitution Act, 1867**, these two minority school systems were given constitutional protection in section 93:

> Nothing in any [provincial] Law shall prejudicially affect any Right or Privilege with respect to Denominational Schools which any Class of Persons have by Law in the Province at the Union. . . .

The section goes on to say that if the majority in either provincial legislature ever tried to abolish such separate school systems, the aggrieved minority could appeal to the federal Cabinet, which was empowered to introduce remedial legislation to restore them. Manitoba was created on the same basis, and the issue first came to a head in that province in 1890 when the Anglo-Protestant majority passed legislation abolishing the Roman Catholic separate school system. On appeal to the courts, the Judicial Committee of the Privy Council ruled that the legislation was valid: Catholics were not prohibited from establishing their own school system—they would merely have to help pay for the public system as well! They then appealed to the federal Cabinet under the terms of section 93. The Bowell government introduced remedial legislation, but it did not pass before the 1896 election, and the new prime minister, Wilfrid Laurier, proceeded to negotiate a compromise on the issue with the province rather than use the remedial power. When Laurier created Alberta and Saskatchewan in 1905, they were required to provide full-fledged parallel public and Catholic systems.

In Ontario, section 93 was considered to guarantee public funding of the existing separate school system up to grade 8. When an increasing number of students went further in school, Roman Catholic pressure resulted in partial funding being extended to grades 9 and 10. Then, in 1984, after having previously opposed any change in the situation, Progressive Conservative Premier Bill Davis suddenly announced an extension of full public funding to the end of high school. This was no doubt related to the fact that the Catholic proportion of the provincial population had reached a strategic 35.6 percent. Table 9.2 indicates the proportion of Canadians belonging to major religious denominations in 2001.

A Roman Catholic demand for greater public funding usually provokes a backlash among supporters of the public system. In the case of Ontario, the extension of funding in 1984 was challenged in the courts, but the Supreme Court upheld the new law. Although it was an apparent breach of the new Charter (adopted in 1982), this discrimination in favour of the Roman Catholic faith had been given constitutional protection in 1867.

TABLE 9.2 **Religion in Canada, 2001 Census**

Denomination	Number	Percentage
Roman Catholic	12 936 905	43.6
Protestant	8 654 850	29.2
No Religion	4 900 090	16.5
"Christian"	780 450	2.6
Muslim	579 640	2.0
Christian Orthodox	479 620	1.6
Jewish	329 995	1.1
Buddhist	300 345	1.0
Hindu	297 200	1.0
Sikh	278 410	0.9
Other religions	101 525	0.3
Total	29 639 030	

Source: Adapted from: Statistics Canada. Religion in Canada, 2001 Census. Found at: http://www12 .statcan/ca/english/census01/products/analystic/companion/rel/canada.cfm

In the case of Quebec, however, the outcome was different. After the Quiet Revolution, language superseded religion as the key to the identity of the great majority of Quebeckers. A consensus developed among all religious and linguistic groups that the provincial school system should be transformed into one based on language rather than religion. The constitutional amendment required to override section 93 passed the Quebec legislature easily, but it barely got through the House of Commons because many Catholic MPs worried that it might have a domino effect on separate school systems in other provinces.

In a sense, it did. When Newfoundland and Labrador entered Confederation in 1949, several different religious groups were guaranteed their own separate school systems. A shortage of finances and a spirit of ecumenicalism saw the three main Protestant groups voluntarily amalgamate their schools in 1968, however, while the Roman Catholics and Pentecostals were determined to maintain their own. By the 1990s, especially at a time of serious recession, the provincial government of Clyde Wells decided to establish one public school system in the province. A referendum on the issue held in 1995 approved the government plan, which would have left the churches with a limited role in the system. When the Roman Catholics and Pentecostals refused to cooperate, new Premier Brian Tobin called for a second referendum in 1997 that cut out the churches entirely, and his bill passed by a larger margin, eventually also being approved by the federal Parliament.

Other Religious Issues

As mentioned in Chapter 5, the Roman Catholic Church was a formidable force in Quebec politics (federal and provincial) until the Quiet Revolution of the 1960s. In that earlier era, religious cleavages regularly surfaced in terms of the proper proportion of people appointed as federal and provincial cabinet ministers and other public officeholders. Other federal issues with a Protestant–Catholic religious overtone included relations with the Vatican, immigration, birth control, divorce, and abortion. Whatever the official position of the Church, it was only after many Roman Catholics were quite obviously taking the birth control pill that the sale of contraceptive devices was legalized in 1968. By then, too, thousands of Roman Catholics were seeking divorces or annulments, so the Divorce Act was amended to permit divorce on grounds other than adultery, and to force Quebec and Newfoundland to handle divorces in their own courts, as in other provinces. Justice Minister Pierre Trudeau also amended the abortion laws, but it fell to Dr. Henry Morgentaler to challenge the still rigid provision in the Criminal Code, which the Supreme Court removed in 1988. Even after it was legalized, abortion continued to be opposed by many religious groups, including the Roman Catholic Church and evangelical Christians. Morgentaler's abortion clinic in Toronto was bombed in 1992, and his installation in the Order of Canada in 2008 ignited considerable protest.

Canadians of the Jewish race and faith have faced both governmental and private sector discrimination until recent times. Canada did not permit Jewish immigration from Europe in the 1930s, for example; the Christian elitism of Canadian politics of the time would not allow Mackenzie King to name David Croll to the federal Cabinet (later settling for an appointment to the Senate); and anti-Semitism pervaded society, especially in Quebec. Nowadays, however, it is conventional to find a place in the federal Cabinet for at least one person of Jewish background; Canadian foreign policy traditionally favoured Israel over Arab states in the Middle East; and in an appeal for Jewish votes, Conservative leader Joe Clark made an unfulfilled election promise in 1979 to move the Canadian embassy in Israel from Tel Aviv to Jerusalem. It was largely because of Jewish pressure that the government began to prosecute Canadians accused of killing Jews in Nazi concentration camps in Europe in the Second World War. Cases have also gone to court involving anti-Semitic denials of the Holocaust.

As early as the 1980s, court decisions outlawed the recital of the Lord's Prayer in Ontario public schools unless it was accompanied by readings from other religious groups. About the same time, the courts struck down the Lord's Day Act, which restricted commercial activity on Sunday for religious reasons. The Supreme Court did allow similar legislation to be passed if its limitations on Sunday activity were based on the desirability of a common day of rest, for which purpose Sunday just happened to be chosen, but most provinces have since removed any such restrictions.

One issue that was prominent in the 1990s was the question of Sikh members of the RCMP and other police forces being allowed to wear their turbans as part of religious tradition. As mentioned in Chapter 6, this issue also arose in the case of who was allowed to enter Royal Canadian Legion premises. Related to this was the issue of Sikh children wearing their kirpan daggers while attending public schools.

In some provinces, minority religions have persuaded the authorities to provide partial funding for religious schools other than Roman Catholic, but this has been quite controversial in Ontario. The Harris government rejected such calls from Jews, Muslims, and evangelical Christians, even after they sought and won support from the United Nations, but Harris's successor, Ernie Eves brought in a tax credit scheme in 2001 for parents whose children attended any kind of private school. The McGuinty government cancelled this initiative on obtaining

A Sikh RCMP officer is authorized to wear a turban.

THE CANADIAN PRESS/Toronto Sun/Paul Henry

office. When Ontario PC leader John Tory proposed to provide public funding for all religious schools in 2007, however, a backlash developed which guaranteed his loss in the election.

Meanwhile, earlier governments in Ontario had allowed the practice of settling certain family disputes in a Jewish court (a beit din) instead of using the regular courts, as long as all parties to the dispute were agreed. But when Muslims demanded the same right to employ Sharia law in the arbitration of their internal family conflicts in 2005, the McGuinty government cancelled the practice for all religious groups. At the federal level, faith-based groups have won CRTC approval for their own individual or ecumenical radio and television stations. One demand so far untouched by the politicians is the legalization of polygamy.

Current Religious Issues

In general, the traditional religious cleavage in Canadian society between Protestants and Roman Catholics is not one that is likely to engender much political conflict, especially at the federal level, in the 21st century. Figure 9.2 indicates that the proportion of the Canadian-born with no religious affiliation increased significantly over the 1985–2004 period, as did the group that had a religious affiliation but did not attend religious services. In 2004, their combined figures were close to 50 percent. On the other hand, those who immigrated to Canada over the past 20 years were more stable in these two respects, and did not exceed 35 percent.

As religious identity becomes less salient to many Canadians of longstanding residence, other religions denominations have grown in size and have developed a heightened sense

. . . .

Figure 9.2 Canadian-born Losing Faith More Than Immigrants

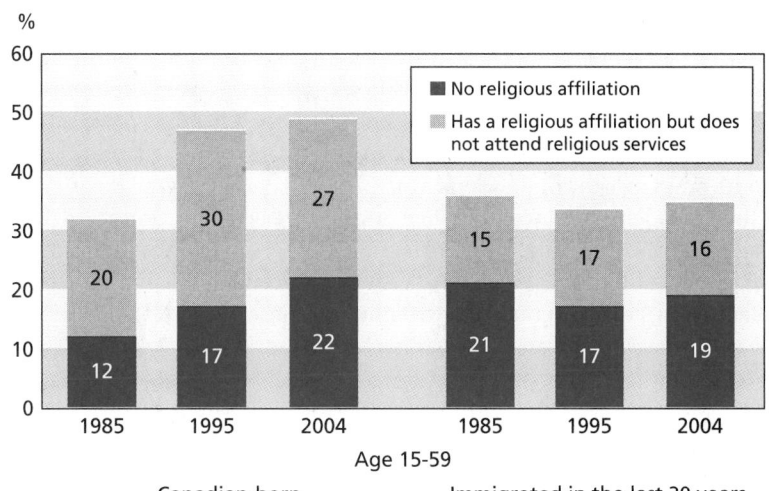

Source: Statistics Canada. Warren Clark and Grant Schellenberg. Who's Religious? Canadian Social Trends. *Summer 2008. Pg. 4. Graph: Canadian-born are losing faith, but immigrants stay the same. Catalogue No.11-008. Found at: http://www.statcan.gc.ca/pub/11-008-x/11-008-x2006001-eng.pdf*

that their identities should be reflected in public policies. These groups include Muslims and evangelical Christians, and the conflict is often between Christians collectively and non-Christians, or between the nonreligious and strong adherents in a variety of religions. The Harper government proposed changes to the Income Tax Act that would allow the Heritage Minister to deny tax credits to film or television projects that it deemed offensive or not in the public interest. Prominent evangelical activist Charles McVety, president of the Canada Family Action Coalition, took some credit for pushing the government in this direction. Under fire for its cultural policies in general, however, Harper later abandoned this proposal.

The main new religious issues in recent years involve Muslims, as their proportion of the population increases and as their issues become more prominent around the world. For example, forcing veiled Muslim women to show their faces if they wanted to vote became an issue, at least temporarily, in both federal and Quebec elections. The issue was clarified when protesters realized that anyone could vote by mail without showing election officials any part of their body. As mentioned in Chapter 6, after the terrorist attacks of 9/11, Canadian Muslims and Arabs were often victims of a backlash.[14] While a handful of home-grown Islamic terrorists have been charged and a few convicted, others remain in custody as mere suspects. Some who have been suspects, either of Canada or the United States, such as Maher Arar, have been cleared of any such connections.

The integration of newcomers into Quebec society, perhaps especially visible Muslim immigrants, is a particular problem for those whose sense of nationalism is based on French ethnicity rather than a more inclusive Quebec. When opposition to certain distinctive new practices flared up in the province, Premier Charest appointed a commission to make recommendations on "reasonable accommodation." As mentioned in Chapter 6, that commission basically argued that immigrants were not a threat to the French character of Quebec, but this conclusion did not end the debate.

Political scientists are especially interested in how people of various religions vote. One of the constants in the study of Canadian voting behaviour, at least until very recently, was that most Roman Catholics voted Liberal, and this was a major reason for the Liberal party being in government so much of the time. Despite this strong correlation, political science could not really explain it,[15] but this link has been weakening in recent elections. Despite its appeal to those with no religious affiliation, the CCF/NDP had a connection to the Social Gospel movement in its early years and even later attracted many United Church ministers to its ranks. Meanwhile, evangelical Christians took an active part in the Reform Party and the Canadian Alliance and were strong supporters of Stockwell Day when he won the leadership of the Alliance. After the new Conservative Party of Canada was established, people belonging to this creed were sometimes accused of capturing control of local party associations in order to choose a like-minded Conservative candidate. Nevertheless, Jonathan Malloy argues that **evangelicalism** is a much less significant force in Canadian than in American politics.[16]

The voting patterns of more recent immigrants with other religions—Muslim, Buddhist, and Hindu—have not been so firmly established. Opposition to the same-sex marriage issue and disgust with the Liberals' role in the sponsorship scandal may have lured many of them to support Stephen Harper's Conservative Party in 2006 and 2008. The Harper government certainly tried to woo Muslim and other such voters with some of its more conservative domestic policies, but its strong support for Israel in foreign policy and its rigid approach to "anti-terrorism," such as in its refusal to bring Omar Khadr home from Guantanamo Bay, were not conducive to this purpose. The Canadian Islamic Congress repeatedly felt snubbed by that government.

. . . .

AGE

Since society generally feels that neither the young nor seniors should be expected to work for a living, few people of any kind actually oppose in principle demands from these two sectors of the population. Indeed, as seniors make up an increasing proportion of the electorate, their concerns have greater impact on the political system than ever before. Policies relating to children and young adults are mostly provincial and territorial in nature and were mentioned earlier in the chapters on class and gender, while the issue of the lack of political engagement on the part of young people is addressed in Chapter 11 (which includes a graph on estimated voter turnout rate by age). This section will therefore concentrate on seniors.

Earlier Struggles

Seniors were one of the first groups in society identified for public support by the federal government. This occurred in 1926 with the passage of the Old Age Pensions Act, which provided a tiny monthly payment, based on a means test, to those aged 70 and over, jointly financed by

THE CANADIAN PRESS/*Toronto Star*/Rene Johnston

Mississauga Mayor Hazel McCallion, one of Canada's longest-serving mayors.

Ottawa and the provinces. In 1951, such pensions were transformed into a universal, federal Old Age Security (OAS) program; since then the monthly payment has increased regularly, and the age of eligibility has dropped to 65. Ottawa brought in the contributory Canada Pension Plan (CPP) in 1964, and in 1966 the Guaranteed Income Supplement (GIS) was added for those who had little or no other income. Finally, the Spouses' Allowance, introduced in 1975, provides a monthly payment to those between 60 and 65 who are spouses, widows, or widowers of a pensioner with little or no income. Several provinces and territories also provide supplementary old age benefits of one kind or another, and many of those in the labour force have workplace pensions to which both they and their employers contribute. But given the limitations of all these programs, it is no wonder that so many Canadians set aside money before they retire in Registered Retirement Savings Plans (RRSPs) and deduct the amount from their income tax.

The Mulroney government was the first to try to reduce its support of seniors by partially de-indexing the OAS from cost-of-living increases in 1985. This led to a spontaneous national protest of "grey power" that forced the government to change its mind. The seniors demonstrated an enviable vitality in mobilizing the National Pensioners and Senior Citizens Federation and other groups on this issue, which provided a rare example of applying sufficient pressure to change a provision in a national budget. However, seniors have not been as well organized since and have lost some ground. In the 1989 budget, the government reduced its commitment by clawing back OAS payments from those whose incomes were more than $50 000. A somewhat similar conflict occurred when Paul Martin engaged in massive cutbacks as finance minister in the 1995 budget. In this case, Martin and Prime Minister Chrétien came to an unprecedented brink of conflict, with the PM carrying the day before the budget was delivered.[17] In other words, even in the absence of an adversarial interest (except those who wanted to balance the budget), seniors have had to fight to maintain existing programs.

More positive responses were the creation of a National Advisory Council on Aging in 1980 and the designation by a number of governments of a cabinet minister to be in charge of seniors' affairs. Thus, like women, Aboriginals, immigrants, and ethnocultural minorities, seniors usually have a minister and a bureaucratic agency to speak for them within the political elite.

Population Projections

How is the population divided by age, and what does the future portend in this respect? The 2006 Census showed 5 579 835 people under age 15 (17.7 percent); 21 697 805 people between the ages of 15 and 64 (68.6 percent); and 4 335 255 people over 65 years of age (13.7 percent). The average age of the population has been increasing and will increase more as time goes on, as shown in Figure 9.3. In projecting future population figures, it is necessary to make assumptions about fertility rates, life expectancy, immigration, and emigration.[18]

The current Canadian fertility rate is about 1.5; that is, there is an average of 1.5 births per woman. Although a fertility rate of 2.1 is required to replace the existing population, the current rate should continue to increase the population until about 2025 because of the high proportion of women of childbearing age. After that, deaths will exceed births, so that any increase in population will depend entirely on immigration.

· ·

Figure 9.3   Proportion of Persons Aged 65 Years and Over in Canada, 1956 to 2006

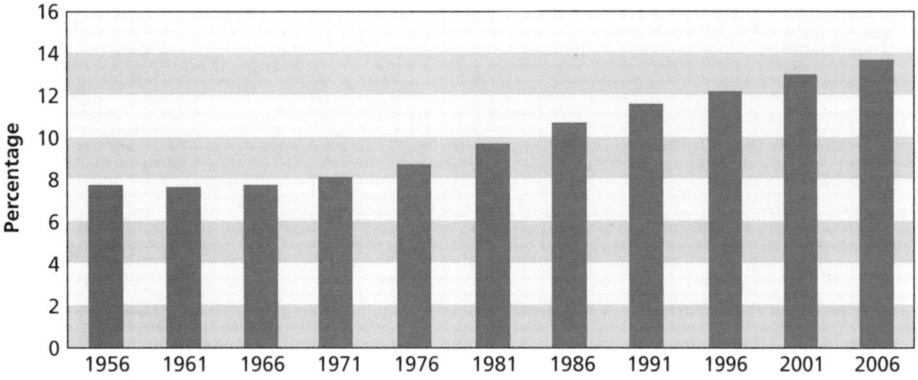

Source: Statistics Canada. 2006 Census. Fig. 2 Proportion of persons aged 65 years and over in the Canadian population, 1956 to 2006. Found at: http://www12.statcan.ca/census-recensement/2006/as-sa/97-551/figures/c2-eng.cfm

The future age structure in Canada shows that the number of seniors will increase from about 4.3 million in 2006 to 4.9 million in 2011. After that, as the postwar "baby boom" generation (those born between 1946 and 1966) reaches retirement age, the number of people aged 65 and over will rise dramatically to 9.1 million by 2031, including 400 000 over the age of 90! In short, the proportion of seniors will increase from 13.2 percent to 23.4 percent over the 2006–31 period. While the group over 65 is increasing, the proportion under 15 will decrease from 17.7 percent in 2006 to 14.6 percent in 2031. Taking the two groups together, they remain in the 30 percent range until 2011 and increase to 39 percent by 2031. According to Statistics Canada's 2006 "medium growth" projections, the number of seniors will begin to exceed the number of children about 2015, as indicated in Figure 9.4.

Statistics Canada refers to those between the ages of 15 and 64 as the "working-age population." Assuming they are in the labour force and financially self-sufficient, and assuming those under 15 and over 65 are not, sociologists talk of the **dependency ratio**—the proportion of the population that is financially dependent on others for the financing of pensions, social security, education, medical services, and other government programs. The dependency ratio is expressed as the number of people of dependent ages per 100 persons of working age. The dependency ratio was 44 in 2006 (i.e., for every 100 people between 15 and 65, there were 44 in the dependent age ranges). This should remain relatively constant to 2011 and then increase to 61 by the year 2031. Statistics Canada estimates that there will be 69 dependent people per 100 of working age in 2056. Within the dependent group, the number of seniors will exceed the number of children by 2015, as mentioned, and by 2031 there will only be 62 children per 100 seniors.

Two main public policy implications flow from the increasing dependency ratio and transformation of the dependent group from young to old. First, the financial burden of children is usually borne by the immediate family, but seniors make a larger claim on public resources—according

. . . .

Figure 9.4 **Number of Persons Aged 65 Years and Over and Number of Children Aged Less Than 15, 1956 to 2016**

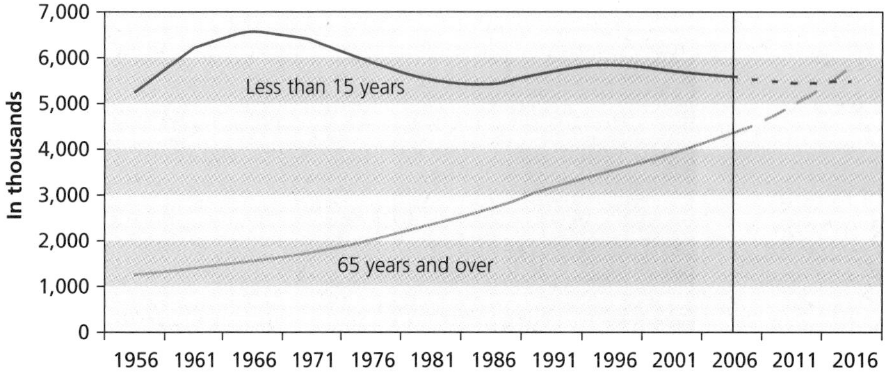

Source: Statistics Canada. 2006 Census. Fig. 1, Number of persons aged 65 years and over and number of children aged less than 15 years in the Canadian population, 1956 to 2016. Found at: http://www12.statcan.ca/census-recensement/2006/as-sa/97-551/figures/c1-eng.cfm

to some estimates, 2.5 times as much. Second, the senior group itself will also grow older, with those over 80 being more dependent than those between 65 and 79, and therefore even more expensive in support programs.

Current and Future Issues

This changing age structure, especially the increase in the proportion of seniors, is likely to have profound effects on the pattern of demands in the political system. Let us examine some of these concerns.[19]

As noted, seniors have had to fight to maintain existing public pension plans and will no doubt have to do so again; indeed, many would still like to remove the clawback in the Old Age Security system for those earning more than $50 000. Given the declining fertility rate, most observers see the need for large-scale immigration to bolster the number of contributors to public pension plans. Since public pensions provide barely enough for many people to live on, it is regrettable that fewer than half of seniors have registered pension and savings plans with which to supplement public programs. Many employer pension plans leave much to be desired, and most lost a substantial amount of their value in the worldwide economic meltdown of 2008–09. Even employers that remained standing had trouble meeting their pension obligations, and this continues to be a crucial issue for both provincial and federal governments to address.

The question of mandatory retirement has arisen in recent years, although this issue does not necessarily divide people on the basis of age. Some older people want to work beyond age 65, either for financial or psychological reasons, but many retire early. However, mandatory retirement is usually supported by the trade union movement as a means applying pressure for better pensions. The Supreme Court ruled that mandatory retirement policies or laws are discriminatory on the basis of age but justifiable as a "reasonable limit." Nevertheless, one jurisdiction after another has abolished mandatory retirement, either on the basis that it is discriminatory or because it is increasingly felt that the economy needs more people to work beyond 65 years of age.

Of utmost importance in the future will be the increased demand for health services. Ottawa provides huge annual grants to the provinces and territories for health insurance, but it is at the provincial and territorial level that demands for improved health care are generally articulated. Many seniors worry that in any future rationing of health care services, they will be considered expendable. Not only do they battle against any retraction of the health care system, but they also advocate an expansion—to include a national pharmacare program, for example.

The public purse will only be able to afford adequate medical care for seniors if a change is made from the emphasis on hospitalization to caring for them as much as possible in their own homes, partly by means of home support programs. This in turn raises the question of housing. The federal government reduced the role of Canada Mortgage and Housing Corporation in social and cooperative housing that was of interest to seniors, although some funding for home renovations has been added, and some provinces or municipalities provide seniors with a shelter allowance to reduce their burden of property taxes. Many localities are experiencing a crisis in long-term care: those in need of nursing home care often have to do without, needlessly occupy acute-care beds in hospitals, or end up in facilities far from where they and family members live. Many seniors want home care and long-term care to be included in the Canada Health Act. A related problem concerns the "sandwich generation," family members caught between the demands of caring simultaneously for both their children and related seniors. This stressful situation sometimes calls out for tax breaks, compensation, or at least information on long-term illnesses and disabilities.[20]

Seniors also protest against government cutbacks to its own agencies dealing with programs for seniors, including the New Horizons Program, and to the budget of outside advocacy groups. In fact, seniors have not been particularly well organized over the years, but since they have no real adversaries, several programs of benefit to them have been adopted after pressure from other quarters. The success of the National Pensioners and Senior Citizens Federation, which suddenly sprang into action in connection with the 1985 budget de-indexation affair, convinced Canadian seniors that they would have to fight their own battles. That organization continues to function, as does Canadian Pensioners Concerned and the Canadian Association of Retired Persons, but the strength of their voice does not reflect their growing numbers.

. . . .

CONCLUSION

This chapter has demonstrated the increasing chasm between rural and urban Canada, in which both interests compete for government attention. It also showed certain value differences between rural and urban Canadians. As for religion, although church attendance continues to fall, traditional issues, such as funding for separate schools, still surface periodically. A variety of new religious concerns have emerged in recent years, largely traceable to the arrival of diverse religious groups in Canada. In terms of age, the extent to which the Canadian population is growing older is quite dramatic, and the political system will have to devote more resources to the needs of this cohort of society.

Some issues raised in this chapter have links to previous ones, such as the connection between religion and ethnicity, whether French or ethnocultural minorities (Chapters 5 and 6). Urban and rural locations are linked to geography (Chapter 3), and age may be connected to class (Chapter 8). More importantly, the three concerns of this chapter reappear in terms of political parties and voting behaviour (Chapters 14 and 15) as well as of advocacy groups (Chapter 16). Geographic location is related to the electoral system and representation in Parliament (Chapters 13 and 23), and religion is revisited in Chapter 19 (the Charter of Rights and Freedoms).

P Pluralism is relevant to these three issues in the sense that each involves a number of organized interest groups: religions, seniors, and urban and rural interests. Indeed, an increasing number of new religious groups is making claims in the political system, to some extent supplanting the previous dominance of Protestants and Roman Catholics. But few groups in any of these areas are well organized and powerful players; although there is room in the system for them to have an impact, there is no equality of influence, for example, between rural and urban interests.

C Class analysis could help explain why many of the interests in these three areas are not very influential. For example, a large proportion of seniors are not well off, and the same could be said for most farmers and others living in rural areas. Indeed, class analysis would decry the poverty of so many seniors and rural residents, although it would also note the extent of poverty in urban areas as well.

PC Public choice analysis would look at the number of voters represented by various groups discussed in this chapter. The decline in the rural population, the increase in the urban population, the increase in the number of seniors, and the increase in the number and assertiveness of minority religious groups all have implications for the promises made by politicians seeking office.

SC The historic dominance of policymakers belonging to Christian faiths was referred to above, especially in the context of state discrimination against Jews. The religious background of politicians, bureaucrats, and judges is now more diverse, although to some extent it is also less significant than when such people were generally more serious about their religious beliefs. In terms of urban and rural location, the proportion of farmers in authoritative roles has declined, such that rural and agricultural concerns are not taken as seriously as they once were.

G Globalization has had an impact on the increasing diversity of religions in Canada, as recent immigration has fostered the existence of many minority religious communities. Such groups, in turn, have often tried to influence aspects of Canadian foreign policy, such as in the Middle East. Although Canada was always a major exporter of agricultural commodities, globalization has affected this industry, especially as trade agreements have required changes in Canadian agricultural policies.

. . . .

DISCUSSION QUESTIONS

1. To what extent are the concerns of urban and rural Canadians at odds with each other?
2. Does a declining share of the population mean rural concerns are destined to be increasingly ignored?
3. What historic demands of a religious nature continue to have political relevance today?
4. What are the more recent religious issues on the Canadian political agenda?
5. How much will the Canadian political agenda change as a result of the aging of the population?

. . . .

NOTES

1. I am indebted to my colleague Samuel Bottomley for the suggestion to include this chapter as well as for his advice on its contents.
2. Warren Clark and Grant Schellenberg, "Who's religious?" Statistics Canada, *Canadian Social Trends* (Summer 2006).
3. V. du Plessis, R. Beshiri, R. Bollman, and H. Clemenson, "Definition of Rural," Rural and Small Town Analysis Bulletin 3, no. 3, pp. 1–17, as quoted in Reimer, p. 73; Federation of Canadian Municipalities website.
4. Bill Reimer, "Rural and Urban: Differences and Common Ground," in Harry H. Hiller, ed., *Urban Canada: Sociological Perspectives* (Oxford University Press, 2005), p. 71.
5. Reimer, "Rural and Urban: Differences and Common Ground."
6. A good source of such demands is the Canadian Federation of Agriculture.
7. Grace Skogstad, "The Dynamics of Institutional Transformation: The Case of the Canadian Wheat Board," *Canadian Journal of Political Science* (September 2005).
8. For a practical look at nonagricultural rural issues, see Roger Fitzgerald, "Challenges Facing Rural Communities: A Newfoundland and Labrador Perspective," *Canadian Parliamentary Review* (Autumn 2005).
9. http://www.cbc.ca/news/background/madcow.
10. Federation of Canadian Municipalities, Policy Statement, "2005 Policy Statement on Rural Issues"; cited on January 15, 2006; available at http://www.fcm.ca/english/policy/rural.html.
11. Samuel A. Bottomley, "Locked and Loaded: Gun Control Policy in Canada," in Robert M. Campbell, Leslie A. Pal, and Michael Howlett, eds., *The Real Worlds of Canadian Politics: Cases in Process and Policy*, 4th ed. (Peterborough: Broadview Press, 2004).
12. Fred Cutler and Richard W. Jenkins, "Where One Lives and What One Thinks: Implications of Rural–Urban Opinion Cleavages for Canadian Federalism," in Hamish Telford and Harvey Lazar, eds., *Canada: The State of the Federation 2001* (Kingston: Institute of Intergovernmental Relations, 2002).
13. Michael Adams, "The Seeds of Electoral Realignment: The Urban–Rural Divide is Overtaking Region as a Predictor of How Canadians Will Vote," *Globe and Mail*, March 26, 2008.
14. Daiva Stasiulis and Yasmeen Abu-Laban, "Unequal Relations and the Struggle for Equality: Race and Ethnicity in Canadian Politics," in Michael Whittington and Glen Williams, eds., *Canadian Politics in the 21st Century*, 7th ed. (Toronto: Nelson Education, 2008).
15. André Blais, "Accounting for the Electoral Success of the Liberal Party in Canada," *Canadian Journal of Political Science*, 38 (2005): 821–40; André Blais, Elisabeth Gidengil, Richard Nadeau, and Neil

Nevitte, *Anatomy of a Liberal Victory: Making Sense of the Vote in the 2000 Canadian Election* (Peterborough: Broadview Press, 2002).

16. Jonathan Malloy, "The Politics of Canadian and American Evangelical Christians: Comparing Big Apples and Small Oranges?" in *American Review of Canadian Studies* (Fall 2009); "Christian Activists Capturing Tory Races," *The Globe and Mail*, May 27, 2005; Trevor W. Harrison, "Populist and Conservative Christian Evangelical Movements: A Comparison of Canada and the United States," in Miriam Smith, ed., *Group Politics and Social Movements in Canada* (Peterborough: Broadview Press, 2008).

17. Edward Greenspon and Anthony Wilson-Smith, *Double Vision: The Inside Story of the Liberals in Power* (Toronto: Doubleday Canada, 1996), ch. 16; Lawrence Martin, *Iron Man: The Defiant Reign of Jean Chrétien* (Toronto: Viking Canada, 2003), pp. 101–05.

18. In the projection shown, Statistics Canada assumes a continuing fertility rate of about 1.5, that life expectancy will rise by about four years by 2031, and that immigration will continue at between 250 000 and 300 000 newcomers per year.

19. See Canadian Pensioners Concerned, Submission to the Prime Minister's Caucus Task Force on Seniors, November 7, 2003; cited on January 17, 2006; available at http://www.canpension.ca/pages/briefs/brief14.html; their website, http://www.canpension.ca/pages/concerns.html; their monthly newsletter, CPC Viewpoint, at http://www.canpension.ca/pages/newsletter.html; the website of the National Pensioners & Senior Citizens Federation, http://www.npscf.ca/site/aboutus/aboutus.htm; and of the National Advisory Council on Aging, http://www.naca-ccnta.ca/naca_main_e.htm.

20. Cara Williams, "The Sandwich Generation," *Canadian Social Trends* (Statistics Canada, Catalogue No. 11-008, Summer 2005).

· ·

FURTHER READING

Blais, André, Elisabeth Gidengil, Richard Nadeau, and Neil Nevitte. *Anatomy of a Liberal Victory: Making Sense of the Vote in the 2000 Canadian Election.* Peterborough: Broadview Press, 2002.

Bottomley, Samuel A. "Locked and Loaded: Gun Control Policy in Canada." In Robert M. Campbell, Leslie A. Pal, and Michael Howlett, eds., *The Real Worlds of Canadian Politics: Cases in Process and Policy*, 4th ed. Peterborough: Broadview Press, 2000.

Hiller, Harry H., ed. *Urban Canada: Sociological Perspectives.* Oxford University Press, 2005.

Skogstad, Grace. "The Dynamics of Institutional Transformation: The Case of the Canadian Wheat Board." *Canadian Journal of Political Science* (September 2005).

Chapter 10

Canada's External Environment:
THE UNITED STATES
and the World

The Canadian armed forces participated in the first Gulf War, in Afghanistan, and in many United Nations and NATO peacekeeping operations, but in 2003 Canada opted to stay out of the war against Saddam Hussein in Iraq. The United States is a major market for Quebec's electricity and Alberta's petroleum, but is increasingly concerned about the environment. European and U.S. agricultural subsidies (and the Canadian weather) have seriously damaged the Canadian grain industry. Anglophone Canadians watch far more American TV shows than Canadian ones, and the United States does not understand why Canada wants to protect its own magazines. Many companies operating in Canada closed their doors as a result of the combined forces of global restructuring and free trade agreements. The World Trade Organization routinely overturns Canadian government policies, and the whole world, especially the United States, is obsessed with international terrorism. Along with the U.S. government, Ottawa stepped in to salvage General Motors in the 2009 global economic meltdown and now owns a share of the company.

Canada obviously does not exist in a vacuum; instead, it is linked to the rest of the world by all sorts of political, economic, defensive, cultural, demographic, and individual ties. These links constitute the global environment of the Canadian political system. They have an ever-increasing impact on it, causing Canadian governments more and more difficulty in pursuing their own policy preferences.

The country started as a combination of French and British colonies, with all basic decisions being made abroad. As Canada emerged into a sovereign state, however, the world was becoming increasingly interdependent so that even though we gained the legal powers to make decisions for ourselves, we faced a multitude of external influences. Given its location, Canada is particularly susceptible to influence from the United States, the world's only "hyperpower."[1]

This chapter details Canada's slow but steady absorption into the U.S. sphere of influence. It discusses the demands that the United States makes on the Canadian political system, the effects of the U.S. presence on Canadian values and opinions, and the policies that have been adopted to both foster and resist such absorption. But at the same time, the Canadian political system is increasingly subject to a wider variety of international, multinational, and supranational pressures, many of which can be subsumed under the heading of **globalization**. Thus, Canada has to contend with many external influences beyond those of the United States.

The chapter begins with a discussion of this wider context. In particular, it includes the foreign governments, international organizations, international agreements, and transnational corporations that constitute our principal external links, and introduces into this setting the new concern with international terrorism. Within that context, the rest of the chapter emphasizes the continuing importance of the United States, which affects Canada both in bilateral and multilateral dimensions.

. . . .

THE GLOBAL SETTING

Foreign Governments

Foreign governments make decisions every day in both foreign and domestic policy that can have some effect on Canada. Sometimes this impact is deliberate, but often it is unintentional. Of course, it is the responsibility of our foreign affairs officials (and, in really crucial situations, the minister of foreign affairs, the minister of finance, or even the prime minister) to put pressure on such governments so that their decisions are not harmful to Canada. Policies of the United States are far more likely than those of other foreign governments to have an impact on Canada, and these will be detailed later in the chapter in five sections: defence policy, foreign policy, border policy, economics, and culture.

An unending list of other countries' policies could also be provided, but a few examples will have to suffice. Looking at the European Union, disputes concerned the EU ban on the import of Canadian seal pelts and of furs from animals caught by using leg-hold traps. Another was the EU rejection of our lumber exports because of its concern about Canadian forestry practices, as well as the EU requirement that all softwood lumber imports from Canada be treated to kill the pinewood nematode beetle. There were also disagreements over the labelling of champagne and scallops exported from Canada. However, Canada long complained that a number of European countries overfished within Canadian territorial waters and had a major role in the destruction of the groundfish industry. European agricultural subsidies are also a source of great distress to Canadian policymakers. China is an increasingly important player on the international scene, but it took the Harper government several years to give it much attention.

CP PHOTO/Jake Wright

International Organizations

Canada has joined a multitude of international organizations with the aim of taking advantage of opportunities to influence other countries' policies, to expand external trade, and to promote joint objectives with other states. Nevertheless, such membership often entails obligations and responsibilities that influence Canadian domestic or foreign policies. A list of the principal international organizations to which Canada belongs is provided below, but a few examples of how such organizations have an impact on Canadian policies should be mentioned.

President Barack Obama visits Ottawa in February, 2009: sometimes Canadians appreciate U.S. influence.

Belonging to the United Nations gives a middle-ranking country a platform to promote its altruistic and its self-interested objectives. The UN has always been central to Canadian foreign policy: Canada has preferred to base its actions on **multilateralism** in this and other international organizations. But the UN also makes claims on Canada, such as to pay our regular share of its budget and to answer the call (and pay the bill) whenever it decides to set up a peacekeeping force in far-flung trouble spots around the world. The United Nations has also criticized several domestic Canadian policies, including Quebec's language legislation and federal and provincial laws on labour, Aboriginals, and women. As mentioned in Chapter 8, the UN Economic, Social and Cultural Affairs Committee raked Canada over the coals in 1998 for the deterioration of its social programs. Although the United Nations has few coercive resources to apply to governments that break their commitments to its covenants, the organization wields considerable prestige, and its moral suasion is sometimes enough to make governments change their domestic policies.

· ·

LEADING INTERNATIONAL ORGANIZATIONS TO WHICH CANADA BELONGS

- The United Nations (UN)
- The World Trade Organization (WTO)
- North Atlantic Treaty Association (NATO)
- North American Aerospace Defense Command (NORAD)
- The International Monetary Fund (IMF) and the World Bank
- The Organisation for Economic Co-operation and Development (OECD)
- The Commonwealth
- La Francophonie
- The Organization of American States
- The G8
- Asia-Pacific Economic Cooperation Council (APEC)

The **World Trade Organization (WTO)** can actually require its members to change their trading practices. For example, in response to American complaints regarding split-run magazines, the WTO ordered Canada to discontinue a federal excise tax and postal subsidies to protect domestic magazines. It has also ruled on such issues as the EU ban on Canadian beef, Canadian and Brazilian subsidies to their aerospace industries, what it deemed to be export subsidies to Canadian dairy products, drug patent policy, Australia's ban on imports of Canadian salmon, and the Canada–U.S. Auto Pact.[2] The WTO has thus become a huge impediment to the pursuit of Canadian government policies—that is, Canadian **sovereignty**, in a wide range of sensitive fields.

The WTO is not alone. The International Monetary Fund (IMF) puts pressure on member countries with respect to the size of national deficits, advising the Canadian government in 1991 not to raise public servants' salaries and, in 1999, to cut income taxes and the debt. When the leaders of the Asia-Pacific Economic Cooperation (APEC) summit met in Vancouver in 1997, the mistreatment of those who were protesting the ruthless dictators attending the meeting became a leading domestic political issue in Canada. International organizations to which Canada does not belong can also make decisions that have a major influence on domestic policies. The Organization of Petroleum Exporting Countries (OPEC) raised the international price of oil in the early 1970s with dramatic implications for Canadian petroleum policies as well as federal–provincial relations.

International Agreements

Beyond the obligations and covenants of such international organizations as mentioned above, Canada often signs international agreements with one or more foreign governments. Once again, such agreements usually present both opportunities and obligations and provide a certain amount of constraint on subsequent domestic policymaking. Of all such agreements signed by Canada over the years, the Canada–U.S. Free Trade Agreement and the North American Free Trade Agreement stand out.

THE CANADA—U.S. FREE TRADE AGREEMENT

The 1989 **Canada–U.S. Free Trade Agreement (FTA)** was probably the most significant agreement that this country ever signed. It is a wide-ranging pact that covers almost every aspect of the bilateral relationship.[3] The agreement essentially removed almost all barriers to the cross-border flow of goods and services between the two countries. Each could henceforth send its products to the other without tariffs, quotas, or other impediments, but each continued to apply its own tariffs to imports from other countries. For any subsequent conflicts in trade between the two countries, a complex **dispute-settlement mechanism** involving binational panels and binding arbitration was set up. If either country refused to abide by the final decision of the arbitrators, however, the other could retaliate ("countervail"), as before.

When it is said that "either country could send its goods and services across the border without impediment," what is meant is that in general neither government could regulate, restrict, or tax such goods and services as they crossed the border. This is because for most purposes the two countries were to be seen as a single market in which corporations based in either were to be treated equally. Both countries committed to give "national treatment" to each other's companies—to treat them the same way as their own. In other words, free trade deals are primarily about reducing the role of government and turning more powers over to corporations in the marketplace. It is a tremendous concession to corporations for governments to voluntarily abandon their powers in this way.

NORTH AMERICAN FREE TRADE AGREEMENT

The ink was hardly dry on the Canada–U.S. Free Trade Agreement when the Mulroney government began talks with the United States and Mexico about a **North American Free Trade Agreement (NAFTA)**. This 1994 agreement essentially extended the FTA to Mexico, and most provisions in the two agreements were identical. (Thus, the expression "NAFTA" is now commonly used to include both agreements.) Canada entered the agreement mainly to prevent the other partners from endangering its position, although some corporations pressured it to do so, seeing it as a means of enhancing the efficiency of their operations.[4]

Opponents feared that companies would move from Canada to Mexico because of the low wages and less stringent environmental standards in that country; they also complained that Mexico was able to negotiate stronger clauses on energy and culture than had Canada under the FTA. Although the Canadian government claimed that certain domestic services and industries were either protected or not affected by NAFTA (culture, water, environmental, health, safety and labour standards, and social programs), critics noted that the protective wording in these fields was weak. After about a decade of experience with NAFTA, many observers agreed that it had failed all three signatories: it had not ended Canada–U.S. trade disputes, it had not brought prosperity to Mexico, and it had not stopped the flow of illegal immigrants from Mexico into the United States. While some Canadians try to persuade themselves that a new North American identity has emerged, Stephen Clarkson basically answers "no" to the question: does North America exist?[5]

Transnational Corporations and Globalization

The pressures exerted by a foreign government are often made on behalf of corporations with head offices in that country, and, as mentioned, international agreements are often about removing government controls on corporate behaviour. This sometimes makes it difficult to distinguish between pressures exerted by foreign governments and those by **transnational corporations**, but here we will try to focus on corporations themselves. Transnational corporations have always made demands on domestic political systems wherever they established themselves, but traditionally these did not differ in kind from demands of companies headquartered in that country. Globalization is changing the nature of corporate behaviour, however, in both the economic and the political spheres. It is commonly characterized by the lowering of tariffs, the creation of larger free trading areas, and the increasing mobility of capital and worldwide corporate competition. Such "economic forces have pushed the issue of market liberalization to the forefront" and capital's perception "that there is too much government hindering the globalization process … had led to an assault on the powers of the nation-state."[6] The world is increasingly one integrated global economic unit in which national boundaries are much less significant than in the past.

The globalization characterizing corporate behaviour in recent years has meant that more companies are outgrowing their domestic state, that they are introducing new forms of technology at an incredible rate, that they are merging and taking over one another, and that they are opening or closing operations strictly on the basis of economic efficiency and without regard to traditional location. Corporate money, banking, finance, and investment flow between countries almost at will. Such globalization has had many implications for the Canadian economy, mostly the closing of transnational corporations' manufacturing plants in this country. As noted in Chapter 8, however, Canada has a number of transnational corporations of its own. The main political implication of globalization is that it is increasingly difficult for national, provincial, and territorial governments to maintain distinctive labour, tax, or environmental laws because such companies regularly threaten to move to other jurisdictions that they find more congenial.

. . . .

PRINCIPAL CHARACTERISTICS OF GLOBALIZATION

- Comprehensive free trade agreements
- Removal of state controls on corporate behaviour
- Cross-border capital flows
- Worldwide corporate competition
- Mega-mergers of the largest transnational corporations
- Massive diffusion of technological change, including the Internet
- Closure of transnational plants in developed countries and migration to the developing world
- Widespread movement of people through immigration, permeability of borders, and transnationalism

International Terrorism

Although the term is difficult to define, let us say that **terrorism** is any act intended to cause death or serious bodily harm to civilians…with the purpose of intimidating a population or compelling a government or an international organization to do or abstain from doing any act.[7] This activity can be committed by domestic or external groups, but after the bombing of the World Trade Center in New York City and the Pentagon in Washington, DC, on September 11, 2001 (often called "9/11" for short), the concern with international terrorism greatly increased. These suicide missions by al-Qaeda terrorists caused some 3000 casualties and represented a significant addition to the global context within which individual states operate. The attacks led to dramatic changes in American policies at home and abroad; most other states, including Canada, also took many actions in response, some of their own volition and some at the insistence of the U.S. Canada passed a comprehensive piece of anti-terrorism legislation that gave sweeping powers to the government, threatening individual freedoms, and it was also persuaded to become part of the military operations in Afghanistan.

Along with an increased integration of the two countries' armed forces, the American government has been adamant about beefing up security measures along the Canada–U.S. border. Considering that the United States has made the fight against terrorism its primary global mission and that the threat does appear to be more serious than ever before, international terrorism has become a new constant in the Canadian policymaking process. Former Prime Minister Martin created the Department of Public Security and Emergency Preparedness (now Public Safety Canada), and adopted a first-ever National Security Policy. Although the latter was also concerned with public health and other potential emergencies, its main focus was on anti-terrorism. Federal agencies in the security field mushroomed, but a number of controversial cases of individuals being treated as terrorists revealed a deplorable lack of coordination among them.[8] The U.S. tried to justify its invasion of Iraq as a pre-emptive, anti-terrorist move, but it may actually have encouraged additional terrorist attacks on American allies, such as in Madrid in 2004 and London in 2005. Some aspects of Canada's anti-terrorism legislation have been struck down by the courts; a few suspected terrorists have been convicted, and others continue to sit in Canadian prisons or live under strict bail conditions. Chapter 19 on the Charter of Rights and Freedoms follows up on this issue.

GLOBAL INFLUENCES IN DEFENCE, FOREIGN, AND BORDER POLICIES

Defence Policy

Shortly after Confederation, Britain withdrew its garrisons from Canada and left the colony to fend for itself militarily. Neither that nor Canada's colonial status stopped Britain from expecting Canadian assistance in the Boer War around the turn of the 20th century and much greater military support in the First World War, however irrelevant these wars were to Canada.

Canada's first military engagement after achieving full autonomy in 1931 was the Second World War, which began in 1939. A year later, Canada and the United States signed the Ogdensburg Agreement, which set up the Canada–United States Permanent Joint Board on Defence to study the common defence problems of the two countries. In 1941, the year the United States entered the war, the Hyde Park Declaration extended the planning of continental defence to cover the production of war materials.

After the war, the United States became increasingly obsessed with containing Soviet communism and persuaded Canada and most Western European countries to form a new military alliance, the North Atlantic Treaty Organization (NATO), in 1949. Commitments to NATO required a great increase in the size of the Canadian permanent armed forces. U.S. attention was then drawn to the confrontation between North and South Korea. The UN military intervention in the Korean War was effectively a U.S. effort, to which Canada made a significant military contribution and lost 1550 lives.

The next phase of the North Americanization of Canadian defence was a series of radar lines built across northern Canada in the 1950s to intercept anticipated Soviet bombers. These arrangements logically led to the North American Aerospace Defense Command (NORAD) of 1958. This agreement provided for a joint Canada–U.S. air defence system with headquarters in Colorado and with an American as commander-in-chief and a Canadian as second-in-command. A Defence Production Sharing Program was established in 1959, the same year in which the Diefenbaker government cancelled the legendary Canadian airplane, the Avro Arrow. The advisability of this cancellation continues to be debated, and it meant the continued reliance on foreign-produced aircraft for Canadian air defence.[9]

John Diefenbaker also encountered two serious missile crises in the 1957–63 period. When U.S. President John Kennedy announced a naval blockade of Cuba because of the establishment of Soviet missile bases in that country, the Canadian Cabinet waited three days before putting its armed forces in a state of highest alert. The Cuban missile crisis thus soured relations between the two leaders, a state of affairs compounded by American annoyance at Canada's stand with respect to BOMARC missiles. These had been established by the U.S. at two bases in Canada as part of the NORAD Agreement and were intended to be armed with nuclear warheads. Some Cabinet ministers wanted to take possession of the warheads as planned, but others argued that to place the warheads on Canadian soil would appear to foster the nuclear arms race. The Canadian–American defence relationship became a prominent issue in the 1962 and 1963 election campaigns. The Diefenbaker government eventually fell apart over the issue in 1963: it was defeated on a nonconfidence motion, and the Liberals won the resulting election under Lester Pearson. The new prime minister had the warheads installed as part of Canada's international commitments, but they were ultimately removed in 1971.

Pearson's successor, Pierre Trudeau, cut defence spending and, in a new emphasis on protecting domestic sovereignty, halved Canada's NATO contingent in 1969. The most prominent new issue had to do with the U.S. request to test the Cruise missile over Canadian territory because of the resemblance of our terrain to that of the Soviet Union. In spite of considerable popular protest, the Trudeau government allowed the tests to take place, as did succeeding governments.[10]

The Mulroney government promised to make defence a much higher priority than it was during the Trudeau years and published a hawkish White Paper on the subject in 1987. Partly because of public opposition, and partly because of budgetary considerations, the Paper was not implemented, a decision that was vindicated when the Cold War effectively ended a year or so later. However, when Iraq invaded Kuwait in 1990, Canada readily agreed to participate in the U.S.-led Gulf War coalition, which was, like the Korean affair, theoretically a United Nations operation. Canada then participated in the various phases of the Balkan war in the former Yugoslavia. Even though the Cold War was over, the Chrétien government renewed the NORAD agreement in 1996.

The election of George W. Bush as U.S. president added considerable pressure on other countries, especially Canada, to endorse the Ballistic Missile Defence (BMD) system. With much expert advice that the system was unproven and unnecessary, and supported by a majority of public opinion, Prime Minister Martin declined to take part. In any case, after the sharing of military operations in Kosovo and Afghanistan (i.e., the deployment of Canadian troops under U.S. command), there was increasing "interoperability" between the armed forces of the two countries, and they signed an accord to jointly deploy military forces and emergency services in the event of a terrorist attack or other disaster. When Bush attacked the Saddam Hussein regime in Iraq, he therefore expected Canadian participation. But Prime Minister Chrétien decided that the situation neither represented an imminent security threat nor had sufficient authority from the United Nations, and he declined to join the U.S.–UK coalition. At the same time, Canada more or less withdrew from its traditional peacekeeping contributions to the United Nations but became increasingly engaged in a fighting role in Afghanistan.

Independent of, but consistent with, U.S. pressure, both the Martin and Harper governments strengthened the Canadian military, which had been largely neglected during the Chrétien regime. At the same time, Canada has been increasingly concerned about defending its sovereignty in the Arctic, and both governments announced that Canadian forces would be more active and visible in the North. As global warming increases the possibility of using the Northwest Passage as a regular shipping route, including that of Alaska petroleum with associated threats to the environment, a major confrontation between the U.S. and Canada over sovereignty could occur. Do other countries need Canadian permission to use the passage and can Canada enforce its jurisdiction? Some suggest that the U.S. would be willing to recognize Canadian sovereignty if it were convinced that Canada was capable of intercepting terrorist threats in the area. The U.S. proceeded to establish a unified command within its armed forces (Northcom) to supplement NORAD with responsibility for coordinating activities of U.S. forces throughout North America, and in 2006 the two countries renewed the NORAD agreement.[11]

Troops of the Royal Canadian Regiment battle group hold an orders meeting in April 2007 in the bleak desert of Kandahar province of Afghanistan.

The Canadian military mission in Afghanistan, now under the auspices of NATO, soon became the most significant aspect of Canadian defence policy.[12] The mission was first extended to February 2009 and then to December 2011, even as Canadian casualties continued to mount. The Liberals supported the second extension initiated by the Harper government in return for some input into the wording of the motion, and it was widely anticipated that Canadian forces would remain beyond 2011 in a non-combat role. One of the many controversial aspects of that mission was what Canadian troops do with the enemy Afghan fighters they captured, called detainees. These prisoners were turned over to Afghan authorities but with concerns that they might be or have been tortured, which is contrary to the Geneva Convention on the conduct of war.

Foreign Policy

To the extent that foreign policy can be distinguished from defence policy, the degree of U.S. influence in this field has also been controversial.[13] Canada sees itself as a "middle power" that emphasizes multilateral approaches in global affairs. It prefers to work with many other states simultaneously to achieve its foreign policy objectives, whether through ad hoc arrangements or international organizations. Its most famous hour probably occurred when foreign minister Lester Pearson was responsible for the creation of the first UN peacekeeping force in 1956. At the same time, Canada is always under pressure to agree with the United States. Although we did not become directly involved in the Vietnam War, many Canadians would have preferred a foreign policy more critical of many U.S. military or diplomatic initiatives around the world. Nevertheless, the Canadian government was quick to respond to U.S. demands to contribute to its military efforts in the Gulf War and its peacekeeping mission to intervene in the fighting among warlords in Somalia, both ostensibly in the name of the United Nations. In response to broader international pressure, Canada made a major contribution in the Bosnian civil war, as well as in trying to end the tribal warfare in Rwanda. Canada has an impressive record as an international peacekeeper, having participated in 63 such exercises.

In the 1990s, Canada undertook a number of new foreign policy initiatives that had wide support around the world but often not as much from next door. Canada was a leader in the campaign to ban anti-personnel landmines, which culminated in an anti-landmines treaty signed in Ottawa in 1997. This country was also at the forefront of the effort to establish an International Criminal Court, building on its active participation in prosecuting former Yugoslavian war criminals before the UN International Criminal Tribunal. Former Foreign Affairs Minister Lloyd Axworthy put these and other initiatives (cross-border problems with illicit drugs, weapons, terrorism, refugees, and the environment) in the context of a move from concentrating on "state security" to "human security" and from peacekeeping to peacebuilding. During his last two years in office, Jean Chrétien made aiding Africa one of Canada's top foreign policy priorities.[14] Nevertheless, despite expressed concerns about the third world, Canada remains far below the international standard of contributing 0.7 percent of GNP to foreign aid. The Harper government's foreign policy was undistinguished, more oriented toward the Americas, and a 2007 Strategic Counsel public opinion poll indicated that Canadians generally felt it was too heavily influenced by the U.S.

Border Policy

Although Canadian and American authorities had always worked cooperatively along the "greatest undefended border in the world," the events of September 11, 2001, led to increased concern and collaboration.[15] In December 2001, the two countries signed the Smart Border Declaration and launched a joint 30-point action plan. The "secure flow of people and goods" involves collaboration in identifying security risks and high-risk goods, preferably before they arrive in North America, while expediting the flow of low-risk goods and low-risk travellers, by using biometric identifiers, such as fingerprints, facial recognition, and iris scanning. The two countries also pledged to relieve congestion at key crossing points by investing in border infrastructure and to identify and minimize threats to airports, ports, bridges, tunnels, pipelines, and the power lines that link them.

The two countries also promised to share information and intelligence and coordinate the work of enforcement agencies in addressing common threats. There could be some benefit to Canada in this initiative, but it was undertaken primarily at the behest of the United States and has not been entirely without problems. For example, the United States tends to engage in racial profiling at the border, hassling Canadian citizens or landed immigrants who are Muslim or of Arab origin, and both countries are in the process of arming their border guards. In 2003, Canada consolidated its border personnel into the Canada Border Services Agency, and in 2005, the United States announced that Americans and Canadians would need a passport or some new national identification card to enter the U.S., rather than a more widely held document like a driver's licence. Federal and provincial governments opposed this proposal on the grounds that it would be a major impediment to cross-border movement, especially trade, but were not capable of changing it. It also seems that nothing much came of the "Smart Border" declaration and that movement across the "thickening" Canada–U.S. border is only becoming more difficult. In general, American authorities seem unable to distinguish between the problems they have at the Canadian and Mexican borders.

GLOBAL ECONOMIC INFLUENCES ON CANADA

Among the global economic influences on Canada, that of the United States is even more pervasive than is its impact on defence, foreign, and border policy. This influence is felt in almost every aspect of Canadian life, including investment, trade, environment, energy, and labour unions. Much of this pressure predated the Canada–U.S. Free Trade and the North American Free Trade agreements, whose effects go far beyond trade, but was only exacerbated by those two treaties. In many ways, Canada constitutes a zone within the American economy rather than a distinctive national economy,[16] although in other ways Canada is increasingly under a broader range of external economic influences.

Foreign Investment

In the "British period" of Canadian history, a great deal of investment in Canada came from Britain. Some of this foreign capital was in the form of British companies operating in Canada, such as the Hudson's Bay Co., but to a large extent it took the form of Canadian borrowing in the London bond market in what is called "portfolio investment" or "debt securities." Interest had to be paid on such loans, but ownership remained largely in Canadian hands.

When Canada entered the "American period" of its history, the source of foreign investment largely shifted from Britain to the United States and the form of investment switched from loans to "direct" or "equity" investment—that is, control through the ownership of shares. Thus, to a large extent the Canadian economy has come to consist of branch plants of U.S. parent corporations. These companies typically operate in many other countries, too, and therefore gain the label of multinational or transnational corporations. Figure 10.1 indicates the shift from British to U.S. investment in Canada between 1900 and 1967.

This pattern of economic development was fostered in the first instance by the **National Policy** of 1879, which put a tariff on imported manufactured goods. Rather than export to Canada from the United States and pay the tariff, American companies set up branch plants within Canada behind the tariff wall. This was advantageous for the creation of employment in Canada and contributed to the general prosperity of the country, especially Ontario. A second factor favouring this pattern of development was the preference of Canadian banks to lend to established foreign companies.

Canadian banks also preferred to lend to foreign companies that sought to exploit Canadian natural resources. "A large proportion of the investment in resource exploitation reflected the needs of the United States investors for raw materials for their processing and manufacturing plants in the United States." This integration often had the practical impact "of reducing the likelihood of further processing activity of Canadian natural resources in Canada."[17] Thus,

· ·

**Figure 10.1   Percentage of British, U.S., and Other Foreign Investments in Canada,
1900–1967**

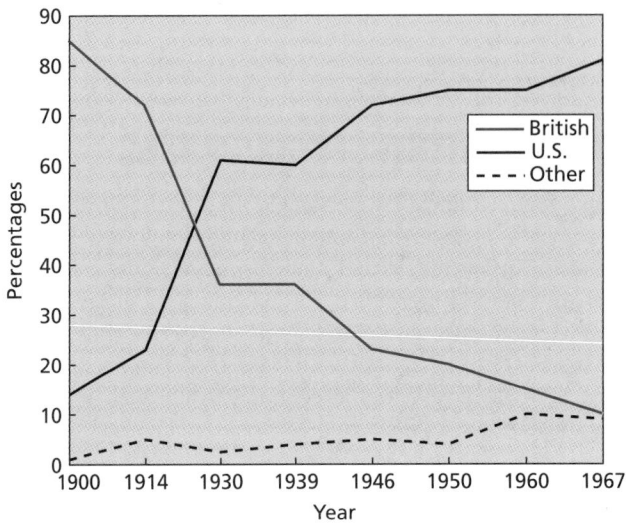

Source: *Foreign Direct Investments in Canada 1972, Page 15. Reproduced with the permission of the Minister of Public
Works and Government Services, 2009, and Courtesy of the Privy Council Office.*

along with many aspects of manufacturing, the mining, forestry, and petroleum industries
came to be characterized by a high degree of foreign, mostly U.S. ownership. In fact, the
Gray Report of 1972 (Foreign Direct Investment in Canada) began with these words: "The
degree of foreign ownership and control of economic activity is already substantially higher
in Canada than in any other industrialized country and is continuing to increase."[18] Some of
the largest multinationals operating in Canada are identified in Table 10.1

"Free market" economists are enthusiastic boosters of unlimited foreign investment. They
claim that maximum efficiency results from capital being able to flow to wherever it will yield
the greatest returns. In this case, they argue that Canada needs foreign capital and that such
investment creates jobs, which in turn raise the Canadian standard of living. They also say
that Canadians are too timid to take advantage of risky investment opportunities in their
own country and that efficiency is enhanced when multinationals transfer "state-of-the-art"
technology and well-trained managers and management techniques to their branch plants.

Others take the view that these advantages are short-term or short-sighted.[19] First, more
capital may eventually flow out of the country in interest and dividends than was originally
brought in. Second, multinationals are likely to purchase supplies and component parts from
the parent company or parent country rather than buying them and creating employment in
Canada. Third, such plants usually remain small and inefficient ("truncated") because they
are designed to serve only the Canadian market rather than being encouraged to compete
in export markets with the parent plant or branches set up in other countries. Finally, critics
also claim that a branch plant economy suffers because most of its research and development
(R&D) is done in the parent plant. This limits the number of interesting and challenging jobs

TABLE 10.1   Large Foreign-Owned Companies in Canada

Alcan (UK)	IBM Canada (U.S.)
Canada Safeway (U.S.)	Imperial Oil (U.S.)
Cargill (U.S.)	ING Canada (Netherlands)
ConocoPhillips Canada Resources (U.S.)	Novelis (India)
Costco Wholesale Canada (U.S.)	Pratt & Whitney Canada (U.S.)
Dow Chemical Canada (U.S.)	Sears Canada (U.S.)
Ford Motor Co. of Canada (U.S.)	Shell Canada (Netherlands)
General Motors of Canada (U.S.)	Sysco Food Services (U.S.)
Hewlitt-Packard (Canada) (U.S.)	Toyota Canada (Japan)
Home Depot Canada (U.S.)	Ultramar (U.S.)
Honda Canada (Japan)	Wal-Mart Canada (U.S.)
HSBC Bank Canada (UK)	Westcoast Energy (U.S.)
Husky Energy (Barbados)	

Source: Financial Post Business, FP 500 *(June 2008). Material reprinted with the express permission of:* "The National Post Company", *a Canwest Partnership.*

in science, engineering, and technology located in Canada. As convenient as it is to import such technology, this process hinders Canadian innovative efforts to develop distinctive export products and to increase productivity.

Critics of the situation also worry that if layoffs or shutdowns are necessary, these are usually slated for branch plants first, and such a high degree of U.S. ownership perpetuates the resource-export orientation of the Canadian economy. The ultimate symbolic disadvantage of foreign-owned companies is that they may occasionally choose or be required to conform to the laws of the country in which their parent is located rather than those of Canada. The extension of U.S. laws to branch plants located in Canada, typically under the Trading with the Enemy Act, is called **extraterritoriality**. On several occasions, when such branch plants in Canada tried to do business with countries on the U.S. "enemy list," they were told that they had to follow U.S. law, thus reducing production and job opportunities in Canada.

Statistics for 2006 on the state of foreign investment in various Canadian industries are shown in Figure 10.2. In general, the proportion of foreign control declined between 1971 and 1984 but increased since—to 21 percent of the total economy. Not surprisingly, the United States is the parental home to over half of the foreign-ownership in Canada (owning about 11.5 percent of the Canadian economy). The Canadian manufacturing industry is characterized by greater foreign ownership than any other sector of the economy.

The policies that Canadian governments have adopted to counter this threat of U.S. or other foreign ownership and control of the Canadian economy can be divided into four main categories. First, Crown corporations have been established, partly to ensure that the company involved remains in Canadian hands. Atomic Energy of Canada Ltd. and Petro-Canada were federal creations developed in response to demands that a Canadian presence in strategic industries be retained.

. . . .

Figure 10.2   Assets Under Foreign Control by Industry, 2006 (Percentages)

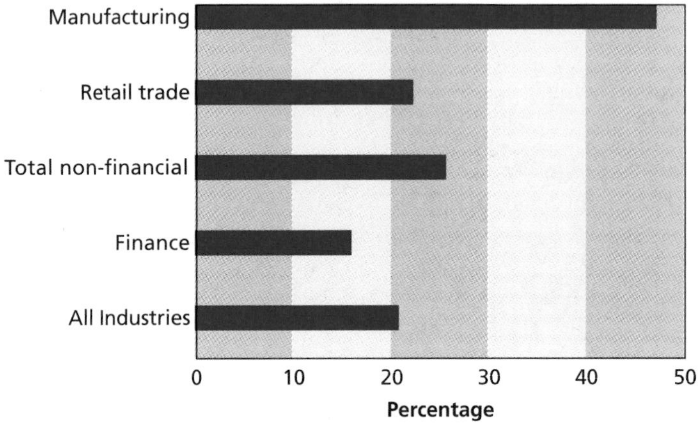

Source: Statistics Canada, "Corporations Returns Act," Catalogue 61-220-x (March 2009), available at http://www
.statisticscanada.gc.ca/pub/61-220-x/2006000/t-73-eng.pdf, retrieved on March 22, 2009.

Second, while leaving other corporations to function privately, the federal government often established regulatory agencies. The principal government response to the Gray Report was the creation of the **Foreign Investment Review Agency (FIRA)**. FIRA "screened" foreign takeovers of large Canadian companies and new ventures by foreign firms in Canada, approving the deal if it involved "significant benefit to Canada." Although the Cabinet rarely disallowed any such initiatives and imposed minimal conditions, the proportion of foreign ownership of Canadian industry declined while it was in place, and FIRA became a major irritant to the United States. The first act of the less nationalistic Mulroney government in 1984 was to replace FIRA with Investment Canada. In its recast form, the agency had the opposite objective of attracting increased foreign investment to Canada. Then, in the Canada–U.S. Free Trade Agreement, Investment Canada was restricted to screening acquisitions of firms with a value more than $150 million and could not impose any performance requirements. The National Energy Board, the Canadian Nuclear Safety Commission, and the Canadian Transportation Agency are other regulatory agencies designed to protect the Canadian national interest in important respects.

Third, ownership restrictions and tax incentives were introduced. Maximum foreign ownership limits exist in certain fields, such as broadcasting, financial institutions, newspapers, and publishing. Incentives to Canadian ownership were exemplified by the National Energy Program of 1980. Its incentive (largely tax write-offs) was sufficient to persuade the Reichmann brothers to buy Gulf Canada from its American owners. Finally, the government established funding agencies, such as the Business Development Bank of Canada, whose mandate is to encourage Canadian entrepreneurship when the commercial banks are not interested.

Many of these policies were half-hearted and others were later diluted under U.S. pressure. Many were weakened or withdrawn by the Mulroney government, both to increase foreign investment and to remove irritants in the Canada–U.S. relationship. Although the degree of foreign investment increased considerably after the mid-1980s, this was widely seen as a natural ingredient of globalization and the source of badly needed jobs. But the foreign take-overs of the Hudson's Bay Company, Molson, Labatt, Domtar, Inco, Falconbridge, Dofasco, and Fairmont Hotels in 2005–06 raised increased concern among economic nationalists. Other recent foreign takeovers include Alcan, Four Seasons' Hotels, Algoma Steel, Ipsco, LionOre Mining, North American Oil Sands, Stelco, and AbitibiBowater. As part of China's sudden emergence on the world economic scene, that country indicated an interest in investing heavily in Canadian resource industries, resurrecting the issue of whether foreign investment in Canada is always desirable. In 2008, the Harper government blocked the first foreign takeover since 1985. Industry Minister Jim Prentice told Alliant Techsystems Inc. that he was not satisfied that its proposed takeover of MacDonald-Dettwiler, a Canadian aerospace firm, would be of net benefit to Canada. Another concern is the tendency of Canadian companies to move some of their head-office functions to the United States, as in the case of Seagram, Nortel Networks, and Nova Chemicals; this is sometimes referred to as the "hollowing out" of corporate Canada.

Trade

External trade constitutes about 35 percent of Canada's GDP and provides about 25 percent of all jobs. At the same time as they tried to maximize their exports, countries used to seek to protect their domestic industry from foreign competition through the imposition of tariffs, quotas, customs duties, and the like. In 1947, however, Canada was among the signatories of the General Agreement on Tariffs and Trade (GATT), under which countries pledged to remove such trade restrictions on a multinational basis. GATT has since been transformed into the much more powerful World Trade Organization (WTO) which allows its members to go even further with bilateral agreements, as Canada and the United States did in defence production arrangements.

Canadian exports to the United States exceeded those to the United Kingdom after 1921 and edged up to nearly 85 percent by 2001, a year in which imports from the United States rose to 73 percent. Both figures have dropped slightly since then, as indicated in Table 10.2. Because of geographic proximity, it is only logical that Canada and the United States be closely linked by trade. It is even more likely because of their complementary resources and industries—the abundance of primary resources in Canada and the amount of manufacturing in the United States. Indeed, provinces trade more with neighbouring states than with one another, although much of this trade is of an intrafirm character rather than truly international. By 2004, China was the fourth-largest buyer of Canadian exports (after the U.S., the United Kingdom, and Japan), and the second-largest supplier of Canadian imports.

Given the degree to which Canadian prosperity depends on export trade, it is advantageous to have ready access to the U.S. market; it is also convenient to have such a close supply of goods that are not produced in Canada. However, to have put so many eggs in one basket means that in times of U.S. recession, demand for Canadian goods falls off and the Canadian economy takes a nosedive too, as was particularly evident after 2008. Furthermore, protectionist pressure in the United States for new or increased tariffs or quotas against Canadian exports can have a devastating effect on certain industries, such as softwood lumber.

Canadian policymakers had been concerned for some time that the country was dangerously dependent on the U.S. economy while being left out of the various regional trading

TABLE 10.2   Leading Buyers of Canadian Merchandise Exports and
Suppliers of Canadian Merchandise Imports, 2008 (Customs
Basis, Percentage)

	Exports	Imports
United States	77.7	52.4
United Kingdom	2.7	2.9
Japan	2.3	3.5
China	2.1	9.8
Mexico	1.2	4.1
Germany	0.9	2.9

*Source: Foreign Affairs and International Trade Canada. Canada's Merchandise Exports. Found at: http://
www.dfait-maeci.gc.ca/economist-economiste/assets/pdfs/PFACT_Annual_Merchandise_Trade_by_
Country-Eng.pdf (Accessed March 22, 2009)*

blocks being formed, especially the European Union. The Diefenbaker and Trudeau governments tried unsuccessfully to diversify the Canadian export market to Britain and Europe,
respectively, while the Pearson government signed the sectoral **Auto Pact** with the United
States to guarantee a balanced exchange of automobiles and parts. A protectionist mood
descended on the U.S. Congress in the early 1980s, and new barriers to many Canadian
exports were imposed.

Modern pressure for a free trade agreement with the United States came largely from
the corporate sector, led by the Business Council on National Issues and western Canadian
resource producers. Brian Mulroney was apparently converted to the idea when U.S. protectionist measures began to be felt in Canada and when the Macdonald Royal Commission on
the Economic Union and Development Prospects for Canada recommended that the country
take such a "leap of faith." Mulroney found an advocate of free trade in the White House, and
the Canada–U.S. Free Trade Agreement took effect on January 1, 1989.[20]

Those Canadians who favoured the agreement argued that in the absence of the deal the
United States would have continued to apply a series of protectionist measures, threatening
more jobs. Canadian firms would now have access to the huge unprotected U.S. market,
allowing them to expand and create employment. Supporters of the FTA admitted that many
Canadian firms would go under and thousands of Canadian jobs would be lost because of
the competition from larger American companies, but they claimed that such competition
would force Canadian corporations to become stronger, more specialized and efficient, and
more capable of functioning in the global economy. Defenders also hailed the likelihood of
increased U.S. investment in Canada, as well as higher levels of investment from other countries wanting to take advantage of Canadian access to the U.S. market. Many asked whether
any practical alternative existed.

Opponents of free trade argued that the deal would lead to a loss of jobs rather than
an increase, because the Canadian market would be inundated by U.S. exports and small
Canadian firms would not be able to compete. Massive layoffs and shutdowns were predicted,
especially in industries where the labour force was largely female. Jobs would also be lost

because U.S. branch plants would close, supplying the Canadian market instead from the parent plant south of the border, and some Canadian firms would move to the United States to take advantage of backward labour and environmental laws in certain states. It was clearly designed, they said, to enshrine neoliberal values and corporate rights and prevent the recurrence of such economic nationalistic measures as FIRA and the National Energy Program.[21] Opponents felt that for reasons outlined throughout this chapter, the existing degree of integration of the two countries' economies was already detrimental to Canadian interests.

Many opponents worried that the deal would endanger agricultural marketing boards, regional development programs, and the Canadian social safety net, and they expected pressure for policy harmonization in every field: taxation, pollution control, product standards, and social programs. They also saw threats to basic Canadian values, in which there would be pressure for less government, less caring and equality, and more social Darwinism ("survival of the fittest"). Finally, they felt that the Free Trade Agreement would reduce Canadian flexibility of action on the world stage and limit its ability to pursue an independent Canadian foreign policy.

As mentioned, a new agreement called NAFTA took effect in 1994. In most respects similar to FTA, NAFTA includes **Chapter 11**, under which a foreign company can sue a country on the grounds that a government policy reduced its profits. Canada lost at least two multimillion dollar lawsuits in this connection, the most infamous involving the gasoline additive MMT. Ethyl Corporation of Virginia used NAFTA rules to force Canada to roll back its ban on this ingredient, which is widely regarded as a hazard to health.[22]

After 20 years or so, the results of the trade agreements have been mixed. On the one hand, trade between Canada and the United States has boomed in both directions; on the other, thousands of Canadian manufacturing jobs have disappeared. Some of the broader fears may have been overblown, and where they have been realized, it is sometimes impossible to separate the effects of the free trade agreements from those of technological change, globalization, the value of the Canadian dollar, worldwide neoliberal forces, and the early 1990s recession. The number of conflicts has been large, however, and some of the same issues that precipitated the Free Trade Agreement have continued to be problematic, especially Canadian exports of softwood lumber; the agricultural sector, including the BSE or 'mad cow disease' problem; and cultural industries. In fact, when the softwood lumber dispute was resolved in 2006, it was outside the parameters of NAFTA, whose tribunals had usually ruled in Canada's favour. Other specific areas of dispute have included uranium, beer, magnesium, steel, swine, wheat, sugar, peanut butter, tobacco, milk, meat, paper, salmon and herring, poultry products, magazine publishing, wheat, patents, dairy products, and country-music television.[23]

Given the repeated refusal of the American administration to recognize NAFTA rulings that U.S. restrictions on softwood lumber violated the agreement, many Canadian observers advocated withdrawing from the agreement. They argued that the U.S. was taking the same bullying approach to trade arrangements with Canada as it was in its foreign policy around the world. Another issue—the "Buy American" program—surfaced during the Great Recession of 2009: it was only when individual states and municipalities in the U.S. cancelled contracts with Canadian suppliers that most people realized the free trade agreements applied exclusively to the two federal governments. On the other hand, some Canadians would prefer to cut Mexico out of NAFTA, since its relationship with the U.S. is so different from our own.

Such critics were more willing to trust the WTO than NAFTA, since the former seemed to make fairer decisions and had teeth to enforce them, and they pointed out that Canada could take advantage of increased markets in other parts of the world, such as China, India, and Brazil. It is true that Canada–China trade is increasing rapidly, and Canada has subsequently signed free trade agreements with Costa Rica, Israel, the European Free Trade Association (Norway, Switzerland, Iceland, and Liechtenstein), Peru, Jordan, Chile, and Colombia. Negotiations continue with several other countries, including South Korea and the European Union.

The Environment

Canadians have seriously damaged their own environment over the years, but the situation has been aggravated by proximity to the United States and some of its even less restrictive anti-pollution laws. The largest transboundary environmental issue is that of air pollution and acid rain. Canadian research generally shows that about 50 percent of the acid rain falling north of the Canada–U.S. border is caused by U.S. sources. These emissions flow northward and fall into Canadian lakes and rivers, killing plant and animal life and damaging trees, cars, and buildings. Canada welcomed the improvements in this area, but cross-border flows of polluted air remain problematic.

The pollution of the Great Lakes is the other serious bilateral environmental problem. Here again, most of the responsibility rests with the chemicals discharged from the larger proportion of factories and waste dumps situated on the U.S. shores of the lakes. Phosphorus levels were reduced in the 1970s, but the Great Lakes are still in a critical state because of toxic pollution. Another issue primarily relating to the Great Lakes—and that is of much concern to the Council of Canadians—is the threat that the United States will press Canada for bulk water exports. A recent study commissioned by the Munk Centre for International Studies reported that Canada remains vulnerable to water diversions to the United States because of the weak wording in the free trade agreements. Already the Great Lakes Annex Agreement allows the export of water in containers of 20 litres or less for human consumption, evidence of the enormous influence of the bottled water industry. In 2005, a dispute erupted over the potential contamination of Manitoba's rivers and lakes with the draining of Devils Lake in North Dakota, which flowed into the Red River system. Most observers did not regard the screening device that was eventually put in place as sufficient protection.

Fishing on Canada's east and west coasts has been another environmental problem. Because of the peculiarities of the boundary between British Columbia and Alaska, Canada and the United States have had continuing differences over west coast salmon. A boundary dispute was settled in 1984, but then a conflict erupted over conservation. Canadian salmon fishers voluntarily reduced their catch because of dwindling stocks, but neither U.S. fishers nor the U.S. government was prepared to follow suit. On the east coast, fishing constituted a long-standing environmental issue with European countries. A number of them historically hauled huge quantities of fish from the Grand Banks just outside Canadian territorial waters. They even defied multinational agreements to abide by annual quotas until, at least in the case of cod, too few fish were left for either Europeans or Canadians to catch.

Another external influence on environmental policy is the Kyoto Protocol, which Canada signed in 1997. It was a multilateral agreement in which countries committed to reducing greenhouse gases, which are almost universally believed to cause global warming and climate change. Many Canadians do not resent this particular external pressure, although there are differences of opinion within the country, as noted in Chapter 3. A principal problem, however, was that U.S. President George W. Bush refused to ratify the treaty. Among other implications, this would probably force Canadian corporations into a position of comparative disadvantage when they had to adhere to new restrictions that were not equally contingent on U.S. competitors. The Harper government abandoned Kyoto and appeared to be taking a position on greenhouse gases closer to that of George W. Bush. Once Barack Obama was elected as U.S. President, however, Canadian policies seemed to be closer to his. This was a rare case where U.S. policies were more progressive than Canadian ones.

Energy

In the energy sector, the voracious U.S. industrial complex usually wants to import Canadian electric power and petroleum. Governments in Quebec, New Brunswick, Manitoba, and BC have been eager to export electricity, and those of Alberta, Saskatchewan, BC, and Nova Scotia to supply oil or natural gas. The federal government has normally approved these sales with little hesitation, although the **National Energy Board** is charged with ensuring that long-term Canadian needs will not be compromised in the process. Aboriginal and environmental groups in some provinces have not been so favourably disposed to the hydro or nuclear plants necessary to produce the electricity, however, and Canadian nationalists worry about the future supply of petroleum for domestic purposes. Environmentalists on both sides of the border are concerned about the greenhouse gases, water pollution, and the

Graham Harrop/artizans.com

desecration of land involved in the massive operation of the Alberta oil sands, the source of much of the oil exports to the U.S.[24] Petroleum producers and the Alberta government are worried that the U.S. may turn its back on such oil imports for environmental reasons—an unusual case where the United States may actually be protecting rather than damaging the Canadian environment.

The degree of U.S. ownership of the Canadian petroleum industry also caused considerable conflict between the two countries. The **National Energy Program (NEP)** of 1980 set a target of 50 percent Canadian ownership of the oil and gas industry by 1990 and gave certain preferences to Petro-Canada and private Canadian firms. U.S. petroleum companies in Canada protested, and their government pressured Canada to remove these incentives to Canadianization. The Trudeau government made minor concessions, and the Mulroney Cabinet dismantled the NEP entirely and began to privatize Petro-Canada. The Canada–U.S. Free Trade Agreement created a North American energy pool in which prices could not be discriminatory (that is, Canada had to sell oil, gas, or electricity to the United States at the Canadian domestic price), and if cutbacks were ever necessary, domestic sales had to be reduced by the same proportion as exports. One implication was that New Brunswick could not claim preferential treatment over New England states when it came to the distribution of Sable Island natural gas via the Maritimes and Northeast Pipeline.

Trade Unions

Historically, Canadian trade unions were closely allied with those in the United States. Many unions in Canada, such as the United Steelworkers of America and the United Auto Workers, were part of "international unions" that had their headquarters in the United States. The Canadian union movement justified the relationship by arguing that as long as it had to bargain with multinational corporations, it needed the support of international unions, especially their larger strike funds. Membership in international unions peaked in 1965 at 67 percent of all union members in Canada. Since then, a nationalist trend has been apparent in the Canadian labour movement: several unions have cut their ties with the international headquarters, demanded greater autonomy, or defected to a different union. Thus, in 2007, only 28 percent of Canadian union members belonged to international unions.[25] The largest remaining international unions in Canada are the United Food and Commercial Workers, the Steelworkers, and the Teamsters, but at least the international Steelworkers is led by a Canadian.

The Canadian Economy in an Age of Globalization

The most influential recent book on the subject of the effects of globalization on Canada was Stephen Clarkson's *Uncle Sam and Us*. Clarkson advanced the interesting notion that the two North American trade agreements plus the WTO constitute an external or "supraconstitution" for Canada, which is as constraining on the operation of government as the "internal" Constitution. In fact, these three constraints, which involve the United States as well as wider global forces, not only severely limit what policies the federal, provincial, and territorial governments may pursue in the economic field but also have a similar influence on social policies, culture, and foreign policy. Clarkson added that it is hard to know whether the government decisions and non-decisions Canadians have witnessed since 1990 were the result of globalization as such or of its companion ideology, neoliberalism (or neoconservatism). To some degree, he argued, the constraints have been self-imposed.

. . . .

GLOBAL INFLUENCES ON CANADIAN CULTURE

Although Canadians have always wanted access to the cultural offerings of other countries, they have also sought to develop a vibrant culture of their own. The factors that have made it difficult to establish such a distinctive Canadian culture include our small, geographically dispersed, and diverse domestic population and the dominant external cultural industries next door. That there is any domestic content in Canadian cultural industries is largely the result of the efforts of committed nationalists in public institutions and in a small number of Canadian-owned private firms, for it is almost always easier to maximize profits by inundating the Canadian market with external content. As early as 1977, the president of the CBC talked of the "relentless American cultural penetration" of Canadian life, and David Bell adds: "ownership and control of the means of distribution of culture (including popular culture) are important determinants of what ideas get transmitted to the general public. Canada, unlike virtually any other country in the world, has a cultural-transmission system that is very largely in the hands of foreigners."[26] In light of ever-increasing global economic integration, "nations need strong domestic cultures and cultural expression to maintain their sovereignty and sense of identity." At the same time that the forces of globalization are making the task more difficult, they are also making it more imperative.[27] This section primarily examines global influences in the fields of broadcasting, magazine and book publishing, film, and sound recording. As in the case of defending the Canadian economy, the measures adopted to protect and promote Canadian culture include Crown corporations, regulatory agencies, ownership restrictions and tax measures, and funding agencies.

Television

Increasingly rivalled by the Internet, television probably remains the most significant cultural institution in the world, whether it is used for entertainment, information, or advertising. Broken down by language group, anglophones in Canada spend 72 percent of their television-viewing time watching foreign programs while francophones spend only 29 percent.[28] Canadians can access much U.S. programming on most domestic channels; in addition, about 85 percent of Canadian households have purchased cable television or satellite services, which offer all the U.S. networks as well as additional channels.

Anglophone Canadians watch their own news and public affairs programs quite conscientiously, but prefer U.S. programs in other categories. Indeed, U.S. public television stations near the border depend on Canadians to contribute funds to their operations. Canadian television has a higher reputation abroad than it does at home, and the few Canadian series that are produced are readily sold to foreign networks. There are two main reasons that Canadian television networks broadcast so much U.S. programming. First, it is much cheaper to buy a U.S. show or series than to produce a Canadian one, which cost about $100 000 and $1 million per hour, respectively. Second, U.S. programs generally attract a larger audience, so that they command higher advertising rates than do Canadian ones. If profit is the name of the game, then the best way to play is to provide U.S. fare.

By way of protecting and promoting Canadian culture in the broadcasting field, the **Canadian Broadcasting Corporation (CBC)**, a Crown corporation, in its radio and television networks, and Radio-Canada, its French-language equivalent, is a crucial agent of Canadian cultural expression. Unfortunately virtually all federal governments since 1984 have made serious cuts to the CBC's budget. Such reductions forced the CBC to rely more and more on advertising revenue, reducing the income potential of private television broadcasters and causing it to deviate from the high-quality cultural programming that Canadians rightfully expect from their public broadcaster.[29] Conservative governments, including that of Stephen Harper, have shown particular hostility to the CBC.

A second main pillar of the broadcasting industry is the regulatory agency, the **Canadian Radio-television and Telecommunications Commission (CRTC)**.[30] This agency issues broadcasting licences and Canadian-content regulations, which are more stringent for the CBC than for private stations and networks. The CRTC currently requires all television stations to provide at least 60 percent Canadian content over the year, although in prime time, private broadcasters can go as low as 50 percent; the Canadian-content rule for most specialty and pay-TV channels is only 30 percent.

Under strong industry and popular pressure to allow more U.S. outlets in Canada, the CRTC approved cable and pay television, which diluted the audiences of Canadian channels. Canadians had to buy cable TV to obtain the parliamentary channel and the CBC all-news channel, Newsworld (now CBC news network). In 1995, the CRTC authorized direct-to-home (DTH) satellite services. While it imposes minimal Canadian-content rules in this area, too, many nationalists accuse the CRTC of selling out to cable and satellite companies in their saturation of the Canadian television audience with U.S. fare. They fear for the future of Canadian content when the largely American 500-channel universe is beamed directly into Canadian homes. The government attempts to offset this problem to a small extent with the Canadian Television Fund which distributes funds to all conventional and specialty channels to promote Canadian production.

Magazines

Magazines are perhaps the second most important vehicle of popular culture, and this Canadian industry is also permeated by U.S. content. Although Canadian magazines surpass foreign magazines in terms of subscriptions in Canada, foreign magazines account for the great bulk of English-language newsstand sales. Overall, Canadian magazines have increased to about 50 percent of the total circulation, but as with television, the picture is much more positive on the French side than the English.

The main device used to protect Canadian magazines has involved the deduction of advertising expenses. After 1965, Canadian firms could deduct magazine advertising expenses from their income tax only if those advertisements were placed in magazines published in Canada. A major controversy occurred when these measures were introduced, especially because the Pearson government tried to deny the privilege to the "Canadian" or **split-run** editions of *Time* and *Reader's Digest*. Such editions added a minute amount of Canadian content to the American edition so as to masquerade as Canadian magazines, and then sold advertising to Canadian firms. The U.S. government threatened to withhold its assent to the Auto Pact, forcing Canada to treat these two magazines as Canadian. In the 1990s, *Sports Illustrated* started to produce a so-called Canadian split-run edition that challenged the law because such editions could now be physically printed in Canada via satellite.

As mentioned above, the WTO ordered Canada to abandon a federal excise tax and most postal subsidies that had been introduced to protect its domestic magazines, although the Canada Magazine Fund does provide limited financial support. When, on behalf of the publisher Time-Warner, the United States threatened to launch an all-out trade war over the issue of banning split-run magazines in 1999, Canada retreated. In the end, it allowed foreign magazines sold in Canada to carry up to 18 percent of Canadian ads without any Canadian content, and corporations could deduct advertising expenses from their income tax whether the magazine was foreign or domestic.

Film and Video

The Canadian film industry is even weaker than television or magazines, and the average Canadian moviegoer rarely sees a Canadian feature film. Canadian films have achieved a respectable reputation abroad but do not achieve box office success comparable to those of other countries in their domestic market. Less than five percent of the screen time in Canadian movie theatres is devoted to Canadian films (and most of that is in the sophisticated Toronto and Montreal markets), a figure that remains depressingly static. U.S. movie producers make many feature films in Canada every year, taking advantage of its scenic locations, its technical expertise, and the low Canadian dollar, but these are always disguised as U.S. movies by the time they hit the screen.

The problem has many causes, including the fact that the companies that dominate the large urban cinema markets are American-owned and that the film distribution system is U.S.-controlled. Other factors are the undeniable Canadian fascination with Hollywood, the small Canadian market, and a shortage of funds. Canadian feature films are dramatically underfunded in both production and marketing. The average Hollywood film has a production budget of more than $50 million and a marketing budget of more than $25 million, whereas the average Canadian feature film has a budget of less than $5 million, of which only about $250 000 is earmarked for marketing.

A number of instruments have been adopted to promote the Canadian film industry. First, another Crown corporation, the National Film Board (NFB), has an illustrious history, making impressive Canadian films and winning many international awards. It suffers from two serious disadvantages, however: insufficient funding to make feature films, with the result that it has concentrated on documentaries, shorts, and cartoons; and no effective mechanism for making its films available to the general public. To promote the production of more feature films, the government established a funding agency, Telefilm Canada. In addition to administering the Canadian Television Fund, it provides millions of dollars annually for the development, production, distribution, and marketing of Canadian feature films, and few if any would be made without it.[31] An assortment of tax credits is also available, while heritage ministers have repeatedly tried to reform the film distribution system so that theatres would screen more Canadian feature films.

Publishing

The Canadian publishing industry consists of Canadian companies and branches of foreign firms. Both kinds of companies also sell foreign titles in Canada, and estimates of imported books as a proportion of total book sales range from 45 percent to 70 percent. Canadian firms, such as Nelson Education, the publisher of this book, and McClelland and Stewart produce a much larger number of new titles in Canada than branch-plant firms that put greater efforts into distributing their U.S. titles. Books are like television shows: they are cheaper to import than to make domestically. The problem is aggravated by the lack of effort to sell Canadian books at Canadian bookstores. Paperback books at newsstands, drug stores, and supermarkets come almost entirely from the United States because the publishers and distributors who control the supply are U.S.-owned companies.

The Canadian government supports the production, distribution, and promotion of Canadian books in a variety of ways, including financial assistance.[32] As for foreign investment in the industry, when the parent publisher of a Canadian subsidiary is taken over by another foreign firm, the Canadian branch is supposed to be sold to a Canadian buyer, although this has not always happened. For example, a British firm, Pearson Education, was allowed to buy Prentice Hall Canada, an American company.

Newspapers, Radio, and Sound Recordings

The Canadian newspaper and radio industries are much more autonomous than the industries discussed above. Firms in these industries are required by law to remain in Canadian hands, and several aggressive Canadian chains are alive and well in both industries. Today, the publicly owned CBC radio is commercial-free, has virtually 100 percent Canadian content, and can be heard in almost every part of the country. Programs like *The Current, As It Happens*, and *Cross-Country Checkup* are widely regarded as crucial links in keeping the country together.

Nevertheless, the influence of the United States can be detected in these industries, too: the ready availability in some centres of such U.S. papers as *USA Today* and of U.S. radio stations; the reliance on U.S. newsgathering agencies abroad, such as American Press reports; the dependence on U.S. sources for comics, crossword puzzles, commentators, and personal-advice programs and columns; and the tendency to include a large proportion of news coverage of U.S. events.

The CRTC requires that AM and FM radio stations play 35 percent Canadian music, and this regulation has generally been seen as the catalyst for the explosion of the Canadian music industry over the past 30 years. In addition, the Canada Music Fund is designed to strengthen the Canadian sound recording industry by offering financial assistance for the production, distribution, and marketing of Canadian music products.[33] In 2005, the CRTC authorized satellite radio, which many observers did not feel included sufficient Canadian-content restrictions.

Other Cultural Industries

Other cultural fields could be mentioned, but the basic situation there is much the same: most aspects of Canadian culture are heavily influenced by U.S. institutions and values, and most Canadians accept this state of affairs without complaint. To a large extent the Canadian presence in such industries is the result of demands made by the nationalist minority for protection from U.S. domination and for promotion of Canadian content, a concern first given official expression in the **Massey Royal Commission** Report on National Development in the Arts, Letters, and Sciences in 1951.

That commission recommended that public financial assistance be provided to the arts, and, in response, the Canada Council (now the **Canada Council for the Arts**) was set up in 1957. It gives life-maintaining grants to hundreds of individual writers, artists, musicians, and playwrights as well as to almost every orchestra, theatre centre, art gallery, and ballet and opera company in the country. The Social Sciences and Humanities Research Council of Canada (SSHRCC) somewhat similarly subsidizes academic research and writing. Other than the measures mentioned above, Canada has imposed ownership restrictions in several areas of the cultural field, and Canadian immigration regulations require that before hiring a non-Canadian, employers must demonstrate that no qualified Canadian is available.

Canadian Cultural Industries in an Age of Globalization

Some observers believe that the technological changes and convergence characteristic of globalization have made it almost impossible to regulate the inflow and transmission of electronic content. Moreover, in another aspect of globalization, some of the measures that Canada has chosen in the past to promote and protect Canadian culture have fallen afoul of the rules of international trade organizations and agreements. One means that has been selected in the past to avoid the latter restrictions is to negotiate a broad exemption for cultural industries, but as examples cited above indicate, this has not always been successful. An alternative is to develop a new international instrument on cultural policies and trade that would allow Canada and other like-minded countries to maintain policies that promote their cultural industries. Such an instrument would have to state explicitly when domestic protectionist cultural measures would be permitted and would not be subject to trade retaliation. Many other countries share Canada's concerns about cultural sovereignty, but it would not be easy to counter the forces of globalization in order to treat trade in cultural goods and services differently from trade in other areas.

· ·

GLOBAL INFLUENCES ON OTHER ASPECTS OF CANADIAN POLITICAL LIFE

Defence, foreign, and border policies, economics, and culture may stand out, but even before the free trade agreements, American influence was also established in practically every other aspect of Canadian life. Many of these influences have been or will be noted in other chapters of this book, but a brief catalogue can be included here. In areas sometimes far removed from politics are the links of many religious organizations and fraternal groups, like the Kiwanis and Masons, which also have their headquarters in the United States. No one can deny the integration of Canadian and American professional sport, including the loss of some of the Canadian orientation of the National Hockey League.[34] A major area of scientific activity in Canada has been the development and refinement of the "Canadarm," this country's contribution to the U.S. space program. How predictable that the division of Spar Aerospace that produced this symbol of Canadian expertise was sold to U.S. interests in 1999!

In the semi-political realm, many social and political protest movements, including farmer and women's movements and anti-poverty and Aboriginal groups, have spilled over the border to some extent, although in some cases the external influences go well beyond the United States. In the political system, American influences (as well as those from other countries) can be seen in the changing nature of Canadian political values (less deference, demands for more popular participation) and in party ideologies (the shift to the right). Party leadership conventions have long been considered to be an adaptation of those in the United States, and many would regard the whole Reform Party/Canadian Alliance phenomenon as a U.S. transplant. Certainly its proposed Triple-E Senate was based precisely on the equivalent American chamber. The Canadian lobbying industry increasingly resembles that across the border, and the adoption of the Charter of Rights and Freedoms has had the tendency to legalize, and therefore Americanize, the operation of the whole political system.[35]

. . . .

CONCLUSION

Canada follows U.S. examples because of tradition, adoration, convenience, or economics; because the U.S. presence makes it necessary; and because of explicit U.S. government or corporate pressure. Most observers expected that, directly or indirectly, the free trade agreements would increase such U.S. influence on almost all aspects of Canadian policy. Thus, during the 20th century, Canada went from being a British colony to a colony of the United States, or from colony to nation to colony.[36] Furthermore, as political, economic, and environmental developments become common global problems, Canada must increasingly respond to transnational and supranational demands. As insistent as demands may be from forces in the domestic Canadian society, Canadian politicians must also pay greater attention to their global surroundings. Indeed, the government may already have signed away many of the powers that would be useful in attending to domestic problems.

Just as globalization in general and the influence of the United States in particular affect almost every aspect of Canadian life, they also come into virtually every chapter of this book. But they are especially central to the following two chapters, which deal with the Canadian political culture and the mass media. They are also an important part of the context of Part 4, the section on the constitution, federalism, and the Charter of Rights and Freedoms.

Ⓖ This whole chapter is about globalization, and nothing really needs to be added. It has been demonstrated that external forces increasingly affect Canadian policymaking, especially in the areas of defence, foreign, border, economic, and cultural policies. Although the U.S., as a state, remains the principal source of such external influences, that country and many others also have an impact on the Canadian political system through international agreements and organizations, transnational corporations, and international terrorism. As mentioned, Stephen Clarkson argues that although the three trade agreements Canada has signed have presented severe restraints on government policies in all areas, the self-imposed ideology of neoliberalism or neoconservatism may actually have had an even greater effect.

(SC) It is often contended in political science that a country's foreign policy is more state-centred than its domestic policy—that politicians and bureaucrats operate with greater autonomy in international affairs.[37] In Canada's case, the continentalism of postwar economic policies was largely the work of the American-born minister of trade and commerce, C.D. Howe, and others in the political and bureaucratic elites who shared his assumptions.[38] A more nationalistic elite briefly held sway in the late 1960s and 1970s, including Walter Gordon and Herb Gray. The concept of free trade emerged after Mulroney's election in 1984 even though it had not been mentioned during that election campaign and had not been preceded by widespread public demands. Moreover, governments usually sign international agreements in a highly secretive process, deliberately excluding those members of the public who are concerned. One of the principal criticisms of globalization is that international organizations make decisions without any kind of democratic accountability.[39]

(C) The class-based approach also has much to say about the external environment.[40] Indeed, a large part of the capitalist domination of Canadian government and society consists of multinational firms. Class analysts are foremost among those who criticize the extent to which the Canadian government has supported, and Canadian companies have been part of, the U.S. military–industrial complex. Multinational corporate links shape Canadian economic policy in many ways, including the reliance on resource exports, the weakness in manufacturing, and the virtual absence of research and development. Class-based analysis cites Brian Mulroney as an excellent example of the comprador elite, claiming that his upbringing in a U.S. company town in Quebec and his later stint as president of a U.S. subsidiary in that province left him with a markedly deferential approach to Canada–U.S. relations. Class analysts further decry the influx of foreign investment, the limited effort to diversify trade patterns, the international environmental devastation, and the limited control over national energy resources. As far as "free" trade is concerned, it was primarily the corporate sector that pressed for such deals because they would make the corporations freer of government encroachment. Many U.S. subsidiaries supported the Canadian Alliance for Trade and Job Opportunities, the ad hoc corporate group that pushed for free trade before and during the 1988 election campaign. Representatives of Canadian industry—both foreign and domestic—were part of the FTA negotiating process through Sectoral Advisory Groups on International Trade, but the Canadian Labour Congress was not involved. In addition, class analysts abhor the exploitation of Mexican labour, now that we are joined together under NAFTA, and are profoundly concerned about U.S. corporate influence on Canadian culture.

. . . .

DISCUSSION QUESTIONS

1. Is globalization just another name for giving multinational corporations free rein to maximize their profits?

2. How much scope does globalization leave to nation-states to make distinctive domestic policies?

3. How much scope does Canada have to develop an independent foreign policy?

4. What are the advantages and disadvantages of foreign investment in Canada? What are the advantages and disadvantages of the other economic relationships between the two countries?

5. What are the advantages and disadvantages of NAFTA? What alternatives were available in the increasing regionalization of world trading patterns?

6. What are the advantages and disadvantages of the close cultural relationship between Canada and the United States?

7. Does North America exist?

· ·

NOTES

1. Laura Macdonald, "In the Shadow of the Hyperpower: Beyond Canada's Middle-Power Image," in Michael Whittington and Glen Williams, eds., *Canadian Politics in the 21st Century*, 6th ed. (Toronto: Thomson Nelson, 2004).

2. Foreign Affairs and International Trade Canada, Trade Negotiations and Agreements, "Dispute Settlement"; cited March 23, 2009; available at http://www.international.gc.ca/trade-agreements-accords-commerciaux/disp-diff/index.aspx?lang=en.

3. Bruce Doern and Brian Tomlin, *Faith and Fear: The Free Trade Story* (Toronto: Stoddart, 1991); Robert Campbell and Leslie Pal, *The Real Worlds of Canadian Politics*, 2nd ed. (Peterborough: Broadview Press, 1991).

4. Government of Canada, *The North American Free Trade Agreement at a Glance* (1993, Catalogue No. E74-56/1-1993E); Jeffrey M. Ayres, *Defying Conventional Wisdom: Political Movements and Popular Contention against North American Free Trade* (Toronto: University of Toronto Press, 1998).

5. Stephen Clarkson, *Does North America Exist? Governing the Continent after NAFTA and 9/11* (Toronto: University of Toronto Press, 2008).

6. Stephen McBride and John Shields, *Dismantling a Nation: Canada and the New World Order* (Halifax: Fernwood Publishing, 1993), p. 20; Linda McQuaig, *The Cult of Impotence: Selling the Myth of Powerlessness in the Global Economy* (Toronto: Viking, 1998); and Stephen Clarkson, *Uncle Sam and Us: Globalization, Neoconservatism, and the Canadian State* (Toronto: University of Toronto Press, 2002).

7. Defined by a UN panel on March 17, 2005; see also Foreign Affairs and International Trade Canada, "International Crime and Terrorism," cited on March 22, 2009, available at http://www.international.gc.ca/crime/terrorism-terrorisme.aspx?lang=en; and David A. Charters, *The (Un)Peaceable Kingdom? Terrorism and Canada before 9/11* (Montreal: Institute for Research on Public Policy, October 2008).

8. Maher Arar, a joint Canadian and Syrian citizen, was detained by the United States on suspicion of terrorism and deported to Syria, where he was jailed for nearly a year and tortured. Arar was cleared of such accusations by a judicial inquiry, which was extremely critical of the RCMP. Besides the RCMP, which retains certain security functions, there is CSIS (Canadian Security Intelligence Service), CSE (Communications Security Establishment), Foreign Affairs Canada, Public Safety Canada, National Defence, FINTRAC (Financial Transactions and Reports Analysis Centre), CSBA (Canada Border Services Agency), CATSA (Canadian Air Transport Security Authority), and probably many more.

9. Knowlton Nash, *Kennedy and Diefenbaker* (Toronto: McClelland and Stewart, 1990); and H.B. Robinson, *Diefenbaker's World* (Toronto: University of Toronto Press, 1989).

10. J.L. Granatstein and Robert Bothwell, *Pirouette: Pierre Trudeau and Canadian Foreign Policy* (Toronto: University of Toronto Press, 1990).

11. Danford Middlemiss and Denis Stairs, *The Canadian Forces and the Doctrine of Interoperability: The Issues* (Montreal: Institute for Research on Public Policy, 2002); and J.L. Granatstein, *A Friendly Agreement in Advance: Canada–US Relations, Past, Present, and Future* (Toronto: C.D. Howe Institute, 2002); see also articles in *Policy Options* (May 2005).

12. For a fascinating account of how this came to be, see Janice Gross Stein and Eugene Lang, *The Unexpected War: Canada in Kandahar* (Toronto: Viking Canada, 2007); see also Institute for Research on Public Policy, *Policy Options*, December 2006/Janary 2007.

13. Government of Canada, *Foreign Direct Investment in Canada* (Ottawa: Supply and Services, 1972), ch. 19; K.R. Nossal, *The Politics of Canadian Foreign Policy*, 3rd ed. (Scarborough: Prentice-Hall Allyn Bacon Canada, 1997); Tom Keating, *Canada and World Order: The Multilateralist Tradition in Canadian Foreign Policy*, 2nd ed. (Oxford University Press, 2002); and the annual series *Canada among Nations* produced by the Norman Paterson School of International Affairs at Carleton University and published by McGill-Queen's University Press.

14. Lloyd Axworthy, *Navigating a New World: Canada's Global Future* (Toronto: Knopf Canada, 2004); and Jennifer Welsh, *At Home in the World: Canada's Global Vision for the 21st Century* (Toronto: HarperCollins, 2004); see also articles in *Policy Options* (February 2005).

15. See Foreign Affairs and International Trade Canada, Canada–U.S. Relations, "Border Cooperation," cited on January 26, 2006, available at http://www.dfait-maeci.gc.ca/Can-am/main/border/default-en .asp; Institute for Research on Public Policy, *Policy Options*, July/August 2006.

16. Glen Williams, "Regions within Region: Canada in the Continent," in Whittington and Williams.

17. *Foreign Direct Investment in Canada*, p. 14.

18. Ibid., p. 5.

19. Kari Levitt, *Silent Surrender: The Multinational Corporation in Canada* (Toronto: Macmillan, 1970).

20. Doern and Tomlin, *Faith and Fear*; Michael Hart, *Decision at Midnight: Inside the Canada–U.S. Free Trade Negotiations* (Vancouver: University of British Columbia Press, 1995); John Crispo, ed., *Free Trade: The Real Story* (Toronto: Gage, 1988); and Clarkson, *Uncle Sam and Us*.

21. John W. Warnock, *Free Trade and the New Right Agenda* (Vancouver: New Star Books, 1988), pp. 116–17.

22. For a list of Chapter 11 disputes, see Foreign Affairs and International Trade Canada, Dispute Settlement, "NAFTA—Chapter 11—Investment," at http://www.international.gc.ca/trade-agreements-accords-commerciaux/disp-diff/gov.asp. Canada actually won a Chapter 11 case with the rejection of the claim of United Parcel Service that Canada Post, as a Crown corporation, was competing unfairly against it.

23. For a list of other NAFTA disputes, including softwood lumber, see NAFTA Secretariat, Decisions and Reports, at http://www.nafta-sec-alena.org/en/DecisionsandReports.asp?x=312; for an assessment after 20 years, see Institute for Research on Public Policy, *Policy Options*, October 2007.

24. Andrew Nikiforuk, *Tar Sands: Dirty Oil and the Future of a Continent* (Vancouver: Greystone Books, 2008).

25. Human Resources and Skills Development Canada, *Union Membership in Canada—2007*, available at http://www.hrsdc.gc.ca/eng/lp/wid/union_membership.shtml, retrieved on March 23, 2009.

26. David V.J. Bell, "Political Culture in Canada," in Michael Whittington and Glen Williams, eds., *Canadian Politics in the 21st Century*, 7th ed. (Toronto: Thomson Nelson, 2008), p. 244.

27. Michael Dorland, ed., *The Cultural Industries in Canada* (Toronto: Lorimer, 1996); Foreign Affairs and International Trade Canada, "Canadian Culture in a Global World" (1999); cited on March 25, 2009; available at http://www.international.gc.ca/trade-agreements-accords-commerciaux/fo/cancul-ture.aspx?lang=en#tphp; and Clarkson, *Uncle Sam and Us*.

28. Statistics Canada, "Television Viewing," Catalogue no. 87F0006XIE, March 2006.

29. Department of Communications, *Report of the Task Force on the Economic Status of Canadian Television* (Ottawa, 1991), p. 9.

30. Herschel Hardin, *Closed Circuits* (Vancouver: Douglas & McIntyre, 1985); and Marc Raboy, *Missed Opportunities: The Story of Canada's Broadcasting Policy* (Montreal: McGill-Queen's University Press, 1990).

31. Canadian Heritage, Arts and Culture, "Film and Video"; cited on March 25, 2009; available at http://www.pch.gc.ca/pc-ch/sujet/arts-culture/index-eng.cfm.

32. Ibid.

33. Ibid.

34. Jim Silver, *Thin Ice: Politics and the Demise of an NHL Franchise* (Halifax: Fernwood Publishing, 1996).

35. S.M. Crean, "Reading between the Lies: Culture and the Free Trade Agreement," in Cameron, ed., *The Free Trade Deal*; and David Thomas, ed., *Canada and the United States: Differences That Count*, 3rd ed. (Peterborough: Broadview Press, 2008).

36. Donald Creighton, *Canada's First Century* (Toronto: Macmillan, 1970); and George Grant, *Lament for a Nation: The Defeat of Canadian Nationalism* (Toronto: McClelland and Stewart, 1965.) Northrop Frye notes that Canada passed from a pre-national to a post-national phase without ever having become a nation, in his Conclusion to Carl F. Klinck, ed., *The Literary History of Canada: Canadian Literature in English* (Toronto: University of Toronto Press, 1976).

37. Tom Keating, "The State, the Public and the Making of Canadian Foreign Policy," in Robert Jackson et al., eds., *Contemporary Canadian Politics: Readings and Notes* (Scarborough: Prentice Hall Canada, 1987); and Elizabeth Riddell-Dixon, "State Autonomy and Canadian Foreign Policy: The Case of Deep Seabed Mining," *Canadian Journal of Political Science* (June 1988), pp. 297–317.

38. Williams, "Regions within Region."

39. William D. Coleman, "The Politics of Globalization," in Rand Dyck, ed., *Studying Politics: An Introduction to Political Science*, 3rd ed. (Toronto: Nelson Education, 2009).

40. Wallace Clement, *Continental Corporate Power* (Toronto: McClelland and Stewart, 1977); Gordon Laxer, *Open for Business: The Roots of Foreign Ownership in Canada* (Don Mills: Oxford University Press, 1989); and Levitt, *Silent Surrender*.

. . . .

FURTHER READING

Axworthy, Lloyd. *Navigating a New World: Canada's Global Future*. Toronto: Knopf Canada, 2004.

Canada Among Nations. Annual. Montreal: McGill-Queen's University Press.

Clarkson, Stephen. *Does North America Exist? Governing the Continent after NAFTA and 9/11*. Toronto: University of Toronto Press, 2008.

Clarkson, Stephen. *Uncle Sam and Us: Globalization, Neoconservatism, and the Canadian State*. Toronto: University of Toronto Press, 2002.

Cohen, Andrew. *While Canada Slept: How We Lost Our Place in the World*. Toronto: McClelland and Stewart, 2003.

Dorland, Michael, ed. *The Cultural Industries in Canada*. Toronto: Lorimer, 1996.

Hart, Michael. *A Trading Nation: Canadian Trade Policy from Colonization to Globalization*. Vancouver: University of British Columbia Press, 2002.

Holloway, Steven. *Canadian Foreign Policy: Defining the Canadian National Interest*. Peterborough: Broadview Press, 2006.

McBride, Stephen. *Paradigm Shift: Globalization and the Canadian State*, 2nd ed. Black Point, NS: Fernwood Publishing, 2005.

McDougall, John. *Drifting Together: The Political Economy of Canada–US Integration*. Peterborough: Broadview Press, 2006.

McQuaig, Linda. *The Cult of Impotence: Selling the Myth of Powerlessness in the Global Economy*. Toronto: Viking, 1998.

Stein, Janice Gross, and Eugene Lang. *The Unexpected War: Canada in Kandahar*. Toronto: Viking Canada, 2007.

Thomas, David, and Barbara Boyle Torrey, eds. *Canada and the United States: Differences That Count*, 3rd ed. Peterborough: Broadview Press, 2008.

Urmetzer, Peter. *Globalization Unplugged: Sovereignty and the Canadian State in the Twenty-First Century*. Toronto: University of Toronto Press, 2005.

Welsh, Jennifer. *At Home in the World: Canada's Global Vision for the 21st Century*. Toronto: HarperCollins, 2004.

PART 3

Linking People to Government

Having examined the societal and external environments of the Canadian political system, we are ready to explore Canadian politics, as such. The three traditional elements of Canadian politics are the electoral system, political parties, and pressure groups, all of which, along with voting and the election campaign, are discussed in separate chapters in this part. But the context of values, attitudes, identities, opinions (and how they are acquired), and patterns of political participation in which these three familiar institutions operate must also be examined. Moreover, no one can deny the ubiquitous importance of the mass media and public opinion polls as links between people and government today. Thus, we begin with chapters on the Canadian political culture, and on political socialization, the mass media, and public opinion polls.

Chapter 11

THE CANADIAN
Political Culture

Most Canadians think they live in the best country on earth, but they do not get overly excited by national symbols like the flag or "O Canada." Others would prefer to live in an independent Quebec and some would not object to becoming part of the United States. Canadians have historically looked on the state as a benevolent force, although recent surveys indicate widespread disrespect for all institutions in society, including government. In the 2004 and 2006 election campaigns, Paul Martin claimed that the Liberal party reflected Canadian values better than Stephen Harper's Conservatives, but this assertion was of little help in the latter contest. The Meech Lake Accord was drawn up behind closed doors, and Canadians have since demanded more meaningful participation in the country's constitutional affairs. Conversely, the voter turnout rate in elections is not impressive.

All these phenomena and countless others are encompassed in the concept of political culture, which can be defined as the sum total of the politically relevant values, beliefs, attitudes, identities, and orientations in a society. Vague and elusive as these values and attitudes may be, they influence what is done within a political system and therefore demand investigation.

Political culture includes feelings people have toward the overall political community of Canada—reactions to national symbols (the flag, the national anthem, the Constitution) and feelings of patriotism, nationalism, and pride, including the question of how people feel toward their province or territory as opposed to the whole country. A second aspect of political culture involves beliefs regarding the role of the state—how large a part do Canadians want government to play in their lives and what kinds of policies should it adopt? Another variable consists of orientations to the decision-making apparatus. How do Canadians feel, in general, about the police, the bureaucracy, the courts, and the politicians? Do citizens trust them? Alternatively, do people feel that their participation in the political system can make any difference? And to what extent do they participate? Patterns of actual participation can also be considered part of political culture.

This chapter will focus on the Canadian commitment to democracy, distinguish between Canadian and U.S. political values, attempt to identify other aspects of the Canadian national identity, discuss the concept of subcultures or "limited identities," and examine patterns of Canadian political participation. Although political culture is usually considered to be fairly stable, it will also be necessary to sketch how, in the Canadian case, it seems to be changing.

. . . .

THEORETICAL CONSIDERATIONS

Given the abstract nature of the concept of political culture, let us first try to elaborate on its definition. David Bell provides this clarification: "Political culture consists of the ideas, assumptions, values, and beliefs that shape our understanding and behaviour as citizens in the world of politics. It affects the ways we use politics, the kinds of social problems we address, and the solutions we attempt."[1] Jane Jenson adds that political culture sets boundaries to political action and limits the range of actors that are accorded the status of legitimate participants, the range of issues considered to be included in the realm of meaningful political debate, and the policy alternatives feasible for implementation.[2]

If political culture sets the limits for what ideas and actions are appropriate for consideration in the political system, it is very close to the concept of hegemony that was mentioned in Chapter 1. In other words, political culture determines what is normal and acceptable and what is not; it indeed consists of the dominant values and expectations in the system. These values and expectations lead to the kinds of political decisions and behaviour that the various elites in society have deemed legitimate.

Bell points out that political scientists use two principal methods of identifying the ingredients of political culture.[3] One is to survey individual Canadians and ask them about their attitudes and values. If and when such values and attitudes are widely shared, they can be said to constitute the collective political culture. A second approach is to develop an understanding of the political culture from observing the operation of the political system and society more generally. This can be achieved, for example, from a reading of history and literature and from a study of government decisions and political institutions.

Emphasizing history, two influential contributions to the debate about the Canadian political culture are those of American academics Louis Hartz and Seymour Martin Lipset. Hartz enunciated the "fragment theory" according to which the dominant values established in different parts of North America were those held by the Europeans who first arrived on this continent and reflected the political culture of the country from which they came. Hartz argued that the dominant political value in France when Quebec was first settled was feudalism, with hierarchical and communitarian characteristics, and the political culture of Quebec and French Canadians has been distinctive ever since. On the other hand, the political culture that English-speaking settlers brought to North America favoured liberalism, individual freedom, and equality, the prevailing values of Britain at the time.[4] Canadian political scientist Gad Horowitz picks up the discussion to differentiate English Canada from the United States. He argues that those who objected to the dominant values in the United States, the United Empire Loyalists, came to Canada and, along with their liberal views, they brought other elements to the ideological mix, including a "Tory touch," which incorporated collectivism, paternalism, elitism, and a strong state. This legitimation of ideological diversity in Canada had the effect of allowing socialism to become part of the political culture as well, reinforced by waves of a later fragment—British working class immigrants. Thus, according to Horowitz, the Canadian political culture is dominated by liberalism, but it is accompanied by significant touches of conservatism and socialism.[5]

In Lipset's analysis, sometimes called the "formative events" theory, the dominant values of any society have their foundation in great historical events. That would be the American revolution, as far as the U.S. political culture goes, and the "counter-revolution," the reaction against that revolution that was a formative event in Canadian history.[6] Although Hartz and Lipset begin from completely different premises, they end up complementing each other's approach, and both give considerable emphasis to the United Empire Loyalists as the principal founders of the Canadian political culture. Interestingly enough, John Ralston Saul has recently challenged these theories with the argument that it is the Aboriginal values with which the Loyalists and other European settlers came into contact that were actually more important.[7] He calls Canada a Métis civilization, and is not the only commentator to disagree with Hartz and Lipset. They continue to have much influence in this discussion, however, raising the distinction between anglophone and francophone values in Canada as well as the difference between the dominant values of Canada as a whole and those of the United States. Of course, more recent waves of immigrants and more recent formative events have also had an impact on the Canadian political culture.

. . . .

THE TRADITIONAL CANADIAN POLITICAL CULTURE

Democracy

In the past, many features of the Canadian political system were undemocratic. At the time of Confederation, few even had that aspiration, but the "official thinking" soon purported to claim that Canada was a democracy. That example of hegemony—the commonly accepted view of things—was far from true, but Canada has become increasingly democratic over time. It could still be much improved in this respect, but the first conclusion that emerges from a quest for Canadian political values today is that almost all Canadians believe in democracy. The preamble to the 1982 Canadian Charter of Rights and Freedoms acknowledges democracy

Canadian students learn about democracy by viewing rowdy Question Period.

to be a foremost value in the country when it speaks of Canada as a "free and democratic society," but the Charter is not particularly enlightening about what this means. **Democracy** is defined in hundreds of ways, some of them quite contradictory, but in the modern Western world it usually includes the elements of popular sovereignty, political equality, political freedom, and majority rule.[8]

POPULAR SOVEREIGNTY

Popular sovereignty means that the people have the final say, which in large, modern political systems usually takes the form of elections at certain specified intervals. At the federal, provincial, and territorial levels in Canada, the Constitution requires that elections be held at least every five years, and tradition usually reduces this interval to four. For most Canadians, this is a sufficient opportunity for the exercise of popular sovereignty, although few would be content with anything less. Some states have a tradition of consulting the public more often or more specifically by means of plebiscites or referendums, but these devices are largely foreign to the Canadian mentality. Although their incidence is slightly higher at the provincial and municipal levels, only three national plebiscites or referendums have occurred since 1867: in 1898, on the prohibition of liquor sales; in 1942, on conscription; and in 1992, on the Charlottetown Accord. At least in the past, Canadians cherished "representative democracy," in which elected officials and appointed authorities made decisions on their behalf.

Popular sovereignty is thus normally exercised in periodic elections, which are, more than anything, mere opportunities to select those who will be responsible for making the big political decisions over the next four years or so on behalf of the whole population. As pointed out in Chapter 15, specific policy mandates in election campaigns are not as common as we might expect. Needless to say, it is an element of the law-abiding nature of most Canadians that everyone recognizes the legitimacy of the election results and accepts this expression of the popular will, whatever the defects in the electoral system. Although Canadians allow many public officials, such as judges, to be appointed, many observers think it is time to make the Senate an elected body.

POLITICAL EQUALITY

Given the significance of elections as the means of implementing the principle of popular sovereignty, a second aspect of democracy is that everyone is equal on election day. In essence, this means that every person has one vote and no more than one vote, as provided by the Canada Elections Act and the Charter of Rights and Freedoms. It is only in relatively recent times, however, that Canada has met this ideal, and at one time or another in the past several groups were excluded: women, those without property, Aboriginal Canadians, and various minority ethnocultural groups.

The principle of one person–one vote is a minimal expression of **political equality**. A major deviation from the ideal occurs if members of Parliament are not distributed among provinces and territories on the basis of "representation by population." Chapter 13 reveals significant deviations in this respect. Another discrepancy occurs if electoral districts are not of equal population size within a province, which is also a considerable problem because of Canada's huge uninhabited spaces. These are issues that concern political scientists more than the general public but are of increasing interest to the courts as well.

It should also be said that even if every vote carried exactly equal weight, considerable room for inequality remains in the electoral system. Political parties in Canada have, to a large extent, been privately financed and it may well be that those who contributed money to a party or candidate expected to get something in return. Thus, those who have the resources to help finance elections are likely to have more influence than those who merely vote. Beyond election day itself, tremendous inequalities in political influence begin to emerge, such as in advocacy group and lobbying activity. Such disparities may lie outside the scope of political equality as a bare ingredient of the definition of democracy, but they are of increasing concern to many observers.

POLITICAL FREEDOM

Just as the 1982 Charter of Rights and Freedoms enhanced protection of aspects of popular sovereignty and political equality, it also provided an explicit constitutional statement of **political freedom** in Canada, as discussed in detail in Chapter 19. According to section 2 of the Charter,

Everyone has the following fundamental freedoms:

(a) freedom of conscience and religion;
(b) freedom of thought, belief, opinion and expression, including freedom of the press and other media of communication;
(c) freedom of peaceful assembly; and
(d) freedom of association.

It is a mistake to think that the Charter created these political freedoms. While it may have clarified, strengthened, or expanded them, what the Charter basically provided was a new means of enforcing rights and freedoms—using the courts to invalidate legislation that infringed on them rather than having to persuade politicians to do so. It is therefore interesting to note the extent to which these freedoms were respected or violated before the adoption of the Charter.

Leaving aside government mistreatment of Aboriginals, which went way beyond denial of political freedom, government authorities as well as the general public generally supported political freedoms as a long-standing part of the Canadian political culture. As in the case of political equality, however, there were many breaches of this principle—and one might ask: political freedom for whom? Three of the most striking cases where political freedoms were seriously infringed upon occurred at the federal level.[9] The first interference with freedom of speech or assembly had to do with section 98 of the Criminal Code prohibiting "unlawful associations." It was introduced after the 1919 Winnipeg General Strike and not repealed until 1936. The language of section 98 was sufficiently wide "to encompass the extravagant rhetoric of a trade-union meeting," and was used by the police to spy on unions, socialist and social democratic organizations, and minority ethnic groups. The Communist Party was a particular target, and many party members were imprisoned or deported. The second major case involved the incarceration or deportation of Canadians of Japanese

THE CANADIAN PRESS/National Archives of Canada/Tak Toyota. C-046350

Japanese Canadians relocated to internment camps during the Second World War.

extraction during the Second World War, depriving this group of personal liberty, property, and livelihood, as well as freedom of expression. The third example, the invocation of the War Measures Act in 1970, outlawed support for the FLQ but was used to imprison more than 400 nonviolent Quebec separatists who had no connection to that organization. Some observers saw a fourth, post-Charter case of government infringement of political freedom in the anti-terrorism legislation after 2001.

The use of such measures on even three or four occasions raises the question of how committed the political authorities are to the principle of political freedom. Furthermore, the overwhelming popular support given to the implementation of such restrictive measures indicates a rather superficial commitment to political freedom on the part of the population at large.[10] This indifference relates to the strong Canadian feeling of deference to authority, which is discussed below. Although Canadians normally believe in political freedom, therefore, they seem prepared to let the authorities restrain such individual or group liberty at the least suggestion of violence.

Violations of political freedom have been more common at the provincial level, especially during the authoritarian regime of Maurice Duplessis in Quebec and with the peculiarities of the William Aberhart Social Credit government in Alberta. Some observers questioned the commitment to political freedom of more recent provincial authorities when in 1981–82 certain premiers insisted that the "notwithstanding" clause be inserted into the Charter of Rights and Freedoms. Federal and provincial governments are thereby both allowed to override the political freedoms guaranteed in the Charter merely by admitting that intention. In the first 25 years after adoption of the Charter, the Quebec sign law provided the most controversial exercise of the notwithstanding clause, which is an indication that the authorities are either committed to political freedoms or else believe their electorates would not tolerate infringements.

MAJORITY RULE AND MINORITY RIGHTS

The Canadian conception of democracy also incorporates the notion of **majority rule**—that is, in case of dispute, the larger number takes precedence over the smaller number. This principle is generally accepted in elections and in legislatures that result from elections. However, it is sometimes felt necessary to protect certain minorities from the actions of the majority, so that specific minority rights are given constitutional protection. The Constitution Act, 1867 recognized existing Roman Catholic and Protestant minority education rights in the provinces, as well as French and English minority language rights in the federal and Quebec legislatures and courts. Extension of these rights to Manitoba and their subsequent removal and resurrection were discussed in Chapter 5.

Over the past generation, Canada has extended minority rights in the Constitution to a considerable degree. The 1982 Charter of Rights guaranteed French and English language rights in the operation of the federal and New Brunswick governments, as well as French and English minority-language education rights in parts of all provinces and territories where numbers warrant. The Charter also guaranteed equality rights for women (who are not actually a minority, of course), and prohibited federal, provincial, and territorial discrimination against various types of minorities. The fact that the notwithstanding clause can be used to override minority rights other than those dealing with language or gender indicates that certain rights were considered more sacred than others, and that majority rule still applies in certain cases. But women and Charter-based minorities—official language, ethnocultural, and Aboriginal—have all used their new constitutional status to protect and promote their own interests.

Thus it is safe to say that almost every Canadian would claim democracy to be a fundamental political value of the country today and would support the four main ingredients identified. Despite many gaps, Canadian governments, both before and after 1982, have probably had as respectable records in refraining from the violation of democratic principles as any in the world. Nevertheless, given the fact that popular sovereignty is exercised only every four years or so, and given the limited scope of political equality, the apparent ease with which governments can violate fundamental freedoms, and the tension between majority rule and minority rights, the extent to which democracy is indeed a fundamental Canadian value should not be overstated.

Distinguishing between Canadian and American Values

Beyond the consensus on democracy, it is difficult to find widespread agreement on other values that constitute the Canadian political culture. One approach that bears promise, however, is to contrast widely held Canadian values with those of the United States. Of course, Canadian and American values are very much alike, but a focus on the differences can be quite revealing. A rich academic literature exists on this subject, the key proponent of this approach being the American sociologist Seymour Martin Lipset in his book *Continental Divide*. As mentioned above, Lipset's analysis ties in well with another prominent interpretation of Canadian values, often called the Hartz-Horowitz or fragment theory.[11]

Many observers have made the point that while the American Declaration of Independence lists the objectives of "life, liberty and the pursuit of happiness," Canada's 1867 Constitution Act talks about "peace, order and good government." Lipset goes on from this point to outline his basic distinction as follows: "Canada has been and is a more class-aware, elitist, law-abiding, statist, collectivity-oriented, and particularistic (group-oriented) society than the United States."[12] Among Canadian commentators on the subject, Pierre Berton noted that Canadians are law-abiding, peaceful, orderly, deferential toward authority, cautious, elitist, moralistic, tolerant, diffident, and unemotional.[13] Canada is often considered to be a "kinder, gentler" society than that next door. This approach leads us to identify five basic Canadian values that can be distinguished from those in the United States.

BALANCE BETWEEN INDIVIDUALISM AND COLLECTIVISM

If there is a value other than democracy to which most Canadians adhere, it is probably that of **individualism**, liberalism, or capitalism, often expressed as the sanctity of private enterprise or individual economic freedom. The general principle is widely shared that everyone should be free to go about their business as they choose and that those with the greatest talent or who work the hardest should reap the benefits of their abilities and labour. In Paul Sniderman's survey, for example, 65 percent of Canadians believed that people who have made a lot of money were "willing to work and take advantage of the opportunities all of us have,"[14] while 13 percent felt that they have usually done so at the expense of others. The extent of commitment to individualism can be best gauged, however, in comparison with the United States.

Although both countries have "mixed economies" today—that is, a combination of private enterprise and government involvement—the United States remains the world's last stronghold of liberalism or individualism with a relatively smaller public sector than other modern states. This is only to be expected, given its revolutionary origins—revolting against an oppressive foreign government—and its self-proclaimed role since 1945 as the leader of the "free world" and capitalist forces. Canada, however, has been less hostile toward public intervention and more inclined to rely on government. This is partly because of the geographic environment of the Canadian political system and the U.S. threat, as seen in Chapters 3 and 10, but it also stems from the basic Canadian value of collectivism or community, a value derived from the French feudal system and the arrival of the United Empire Loyalists. Both founding groups, to say nothing of a similar value shared by Aboriginal Canadians, saw society not as a mass of grasping, ambitious individuals, but as an organic community in which all people—high and low—had their place and did their respective part to contribute to the welfare of the whole. In Sniderman's survey, 58 percent of Canadians agreed with the statement that "I am glad that I have a government that looks after me in so many ways," while 32 percent disagreed; 50 percent of Canadians agreed that "the government should see to it that everyone has a job and a standard of living" compared to only 25 percent of Americans.[15]

The balance between capitalism and **collectivism** in Canada can be seen in Table 11.1, which shows, in terms of the total value of the economy, the percentage of all revenue taken by government, the percentage of all expenditure made by government, and the percentage of all tax receipts taken by government. In all three measures of the size of the public sector, Canada is in an intermediate position relative to other Western democracies, although slightly on the low side. This complements an observation made in Table 8.5 in Chapter 8 with respect to government social expenditures as a percentage of gross domestic product.

TABLE 11.1 Total Government Revenue, Expenditures, and Tax Receipts, as Percentage of GDP, OECD Countries, 2007

Government Revenue		*Government Expenditures*		*Tax Receipts*	
Norway	58.3	Sweden	52.6	Sweden	50.7
Sweden	56.0	France	52.4	Denmark	50.3
Denmark	55.6	Denmark	50.8	Belgium	45.4
Finland	52.6	Hungary	50.1	France	44.1
France	49.7	Belgium	48.8	Finland	44.0
Belgium	48.6	Austria	48.5	Norway	43.7
Iceland	48.3	Italy	48.5	Austria	42.1
Austria	47.9	Finland	47.3	Iceland	41.4
Italy	46.6	Netherlands	45.9	Italy	41.0
Netherlands	46.3	Portugal	45.8	Netherlands	39.1
Hungary	44.6	UK	44.6	Luxembourg	38.6
New Zealand	44.4	Germany	43.9	Czech Rep.	37.8
Germany	43.9	Czech Rep.	43.6	New Zealand	37.8
Portugal	43.1	Greece	43.3	Hungary	37.2
UK	41.8	Iceland	43.1	UK	36.5
Luxembourg	41.0	Poland	42.6	Spain	35.8
Spain	41.0	Norway	40.9	Portugal	34.8
Czech Rep.	41.0	New Zealand	39.9	Germany	34.8
Poland	40.5	**CANADA**	**39.3**	Poland	34.3
CANADA	**40.4**	Spain	38.7	**CANADA**	**33.4**
Greece	40.2	Luxembourg	38.0	Slovak Rep.	31.6
Ireland	37.2	Slovak Rep.	37.7	Australia	30.9
Australia	35.8	U.S.	36.6	Ireland	30.6
Switzerland	34.7	Japan	36.0	Switzerland	29.7
Japan	34.6	Switzerland	35.4	Japan	27.4
U.S.	34.2	Australia	34.9	U.S.	27.3
Slovak Rep.	34.0	Ireland	34.2	Greece	27.3
Korea	33.8	Korea	30.2	Korea	25.5
Mexico	21.7	Mexico	21.1	Mexico	19.9

Source: OECD in Figures, StatLink. Public finance, Government sector, 2007 Found at: http://dx.doi. org/10.1787/468155324423; OECD in Figures, StatLink. Public finance, Taxation, 2005. Found at: http://dx.doi.org/10.1787/468178478114

Thus, although Canadians might instinctively claim a commitment to capitalism and might still be less reliant on the state than many other countries, it would be more accurate to say that the accumulation of public demands has given Canada an economy almost equally divided between private and public sectors. Proof of this balance can be found in the surveys of the 2000 Canada Election Study, where Canadians were found to be divided evenly in their faith in free enterprise as opposed to the role of government.[16]

Canada is generally less collectivist than Western Europe, and although the difference between the two North American countries should not be overstated, much concrete evidence of a significant variation exists. The extent of federal and provincial Crown corporations, including broadcasting, transportation, and electricity and other resources, is unheard of south of the border; the Canadian public health insurance system stands out in great contrast to that of the United States; the Canadian social security system is considered more adequate; and taxes are generally higher in order to finance such collective activity. In just about every policy field, in fact, the extent of government intervention is greater in Canada than in the United States. Two other differences between the two countries are that individual property rights, so valued in the United States, are not guaranteed in the Canadian Constitution, and that while many private American individuals and corporations are generous philanthropists, Canadians prefer to have charitable causes funded by the government.[17]

PARTICULARISM, DIVERSITY, AND TOLERANCE

A second difference in the basic values of the two countries has to do with the distinction between "universalism" and "particularism," leading many to argue that pluralism is a more appropriate description of Canada than of the United States. This distinction is commonly expressed in terms of the melting pot and the mosaic: immigrants to the United States are urged to become "unhyphenated" Americans, whereas Canada encourages the retention of cultural particularisms; Canada is officially a "tossed salad" rather than a "blender." Sometimes this Canadian diversity or heterogeneity is simply called tolerance, and sometimes it is linked to the recognition of group rights as opposed to individual rights. The distinctiveness of the French-Canadian Roman Catholic community in Quebec was the original basis of this value, but it has now spread to policies of multiculturalism and recognition of other group rights, even in the Constitution.

As noted in Chapter 6, multiculturalism means encouraging the retention of minority ethnic cultures rather than trying to assimilate all newcomers into some kind of homogeneous Canadianism. This official policy is seen as a means of enriching and enlivening the country, encouraging new Canadians to feel at home, promoting tolerance and minimizing discrimination, and perhaps enhancing Canada's contribution to world harmony. In his writings, Will Kymlicka makes the point that Canada was a world leader in constitutionalizing multiculturalism, in accommodating national minorities through territorial autonomy (Quebec), and in constitutionalizing Aboriginal rights, treaties, self-government, and land claims. The federal government has recognized both National Multiculturalism Day (June 27) and National Aboriginal Day (June 21).[18] Figure 11.1 indicates that most Canadians believe that immigrants have a good influence on the country.

Even if an ethnic revival has occurred in many countries, including the United States, particularism in Canada can be extended to women in the sense that they, like minority groups, generally benefit from more advanced legislation than in the U.S. It could also relate to the greater secularism in Canada that permits a commitment to minority rights, such as same-sex marriage,[19] as well as being seen in terms of acknowledging the existence of social classes. Americans have even less class-consciousness than Canadians, being imbued with

. . . .

Figure 11.1 Immigrant Influence: "Overall, would you say immigrants are having a good or bad influence on the way things are going in [country]?"

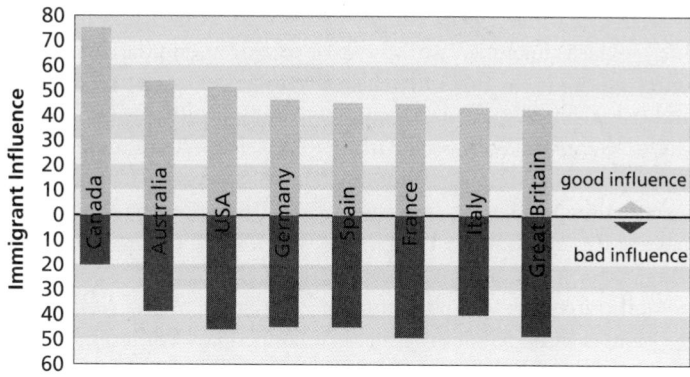

Source: Attitudes Towards Immigrants. International Social Trends Monitor, IPSOS MORI. May 2006. Found at: www.ipsos-mori.com/istu-may06.pdf

the belief that through hard work anyone can make it to the top, and more Americans than Canadians feel that they belong to the middle class. All of this affects the tolerance for trade unions, which is greater in Canada because middle-class America sees no need for them. Particularism has a territorial dimension, too—Canadian provinces are stronger than the American states. Decentralization in Canada is accompanied by stronger regional or provincial loyalties and identities, again because of the example set by Quebec. Finally, American universalism can also be seen in its foreign policy, which would brook no compromise with "evil empires" (Ronald Reagan) and the "axis of evil" (George W. Bush), whereas Canada has often played a useful negotiating role on the international scene because of the lessons of compromise and tolerance learned at home.[20]

DEFERENCE TO AUTHORITY

Another fundamental difference between Canadian and American values is the higher level of **deference to authority** in Canadian society.[21] Canadians demonstrate greater respect toward the law, judges, police, religious leaders, and many others with "legitimate power." Peace, order, and good government rather than individual liberty is the Canadian ideal, and many observers have noted that Canada is probably the only country where a police officer, the Mountie, is a national symbol—certainly a contrast to the U.S. hero Horatio Alger, the self-made man. Unlike Americans, Canadians are not instinctively suspicious of the state; indeed, Canadians have not seen the government in terms of an alien imposition, but as the authorized agent to respond to their individual and collective demands. Such respect for authority and trust in government goes so far as to permit much greater government secrecy in Canada than in the United States, to be less concerned about the admissibility of evidence obtained illegally by the Crown,[22] and even to allow the RCMP to engage in a wide range of illegal activities, such as opening mail.[23] Surveys seem to indicate that Canadians opt for security over civil liberty, having no concern with video cameras in public places, for example,[24] although the American obsession with terrorism since September 2001 might have changed many attitudes in that country on these issues.

Deference is related to other values already mentioned. Americans are the epitome of the "Protestant ethic"—that is, members of Protestant sects that emphasize hard work in this life as the key to entering the next. But in their frenzy to get ahead at all costs, individualistic, competitive, and achievement-oriented Americans may find it necessary to bend or break the law. Canadians, slightly less obsessed with material success, are more likely to obey a law even if they do not like it. Crime rates are considerably lower in Canada, gun control laws are stronger, and the drug problem is less severe.[25] Furthermore, the United States has many more lawyers per capita, and Americans are more litigious by nature, having a much greater propensity to take disputes to court.

Deference to authority comes in part from the monarchical and feudal traditions, which contain the idea of an organic community made up of people of different status. These values were reinforced by the two dominant churches in Canadian history, Roman Catholic and Anglican, which recognize priests, bishops, archbishops (as well as cardinals and popes, in the former case) in a great hierarchy between ordinary mortals and God. Americans, however, exalting the sovereignty of "We, the People," revolted against the monarchical system and, when it came to religion, turned to anti-elitist, Protestant sects in which power resided in the local congregation. Respect for authority and the law is also related to the settlement of the Western frontier. In the Canadian West and in the North the law and enforcement of the law by the RCMP preceded settlement, whereas in the violent American frontier, settlers arrived ahead of the law. This state of affairs not only provided Canada with a more peaceful settlement of its frontier (and, believe it or not, better treatment of its Aboriginals) but also reinforced the previously established respect for law and order.

EGALITARIANISM

One striking example of the claim that Canada is more egalitarian than the United States is in the constitutional equality of women. In the United States a proposed Equal Rights Amendment to the constitution failed to pass, whereas at about the same time, Canada adopted a strong guarantee of gender equality (including affirmative action) in the 1982 Charter of Rights and Freedoms. The Charter also aims to guarantee equality and prevent discrimination on many other grounds such as ethnicity, religion, age, and sexual orientation. Somewhat similarly, the health and welfare programs that flow from Canadian collectivism ensure a greater degree of equality for the poor and working classes.[26] A 2000 Statistics Canada study shows that the poorest 25 percent of Canadian families have more purchasing power than their U.S. counterparts, while the opposite is the case at the top of the income scale, and a 2005 study confirmed that Canada ranks higher on intergenerational social mobility.[27] Canada extends this redistributive egalitarianism to have-not regions as well as have-not individuals through equalization payments and regional economic development programs. The subtle differences in the public's commitment to equality in the two countries are revealed in that 47 percent of Americans agreed that "we have gone too far in pushing equal rights in this country," compared with only 31 percent of Canadians.[28]

Canadian **egalitarianism** is related to the comparative strength of class-consciousness, trade unions, and social democratic parties in the two countries. It can also be seen in a strong cooperative movement, stretching from Prairie grain elevators to Quebec's caisses populaires to the Antigonish movement in the Maritimes. Perhaps it also results from the feeling of noblesse oblige among those in the upper echelons of the hierarchy, the feudal concept that the lord was responsible for the well-being of his serfs. In any case, Lipset argues that Canadians are more committed to "redistributive egalitarianism, while Americans place more emphasis on meritocratic competition and equality of opportunity." He also admits that the United States has a greater hierarchy of educational institutions than is found in Canada. There is no need to rank Canadian universities, as *Maclean's* insists on doing: they are pretty much of equal quality.[29]

CAUTION, DIFFIDENCE, DEPENDENCE, IDEALISM, AND NONVIOLENCE

The fifth value difference to emerge from the Lipset analysis relates to Canadian caution and diffidence, sometimes called a national inferiority complex. It includes our historical dependence on other countries, the lack of will to be truly exceptional or to stand out from

Chantal Petitclerc leads Team Canada as she carries the Canadian flag at the opening ceremonies of the XVIII Commonwealth Games in Melbourne, Australia, in March 2006.

the crowd, and the absence of a spirit of innovation and risk taking.[30] Canadians delight in the security of savings and understatement, and the cautiousness of Canadian banking policy served the country well in the post-2008 worldwide economic crisis. Of course there have been many Canadian "winners" in all walks of life, in whose accomplishments Canadians vicariously share: Margaret Atwood, Glenn Gould, Wayne Gretzky, Karen Kain, Stephen Lewis, Donovan Bailey, Céline Dion, David Foster, David Suzuki, Louise Arbour, and Bryan Adams, for example, in addition to Nobel Prize winners Frederick Banting, Lester Pearson, and John Polanyi, and those who have been lost to other countries, such as Joni Mitchell and John Kenneth Galbraith. But Canadians sometimes take satisfaction in being "beautiful losers"; they are obsessed with "survival" rather than success; they are especially good at deprecating themselves and almost always think things American are superior. As Pierre Berton says, we are prudent and cautious, sober and solemn, and introverted, uncertain, and always questioning ourselves. Most Canadians take quiet satisfaction in their accomplishments—a 1995 survey showed that 89 percent of Canadians felt proud when they saw the Canadian flag or heard the national anthem—but they are reluctant to proclaim such feelings aloud.[31] Above all, as Constable Benton Fraser demonstrated on the TV series *Due South*, most Canadians are polite![32]

Although Canada made major contributions to two world wars, Canadians are not a warlike people. They abhor violence at home and abroad; they have no enemies, and their military establishment has been small. Instead, they have tried to be peacemakers and peacekeepers in international relations, putting special emphasis on the United Nations (another collective authority); trying to reduce the militancy of the foreign policy of the United States in quiet, backroom diplomacy; and helping to remove the causes of war through assistance to the developing world. Surveys show that a majority of Canadians are uncomfortable with the combative role that our forces began to play in Afghanistan after 2005.

Other Basic Values

At least in the past, four additional national characteristics based on geography, ethnicity, and political institutions have also been considered part of the basic Canadian political value structure. Some of these were identified as basic constitutional principles in Chapter 2.

First, Canadians are a northern people, attached to the land.[33] To a large extent we enjoy the wilderness, relish four distinct seasons, including the cold, and are immensely proud of the beauty and variety of our natural surroundings, whether it is the Rocky Mountains, the Prairie wheat fields, the rugged Canadian Shield, or picturesque Atlantic fishing villages.[34]

Second, Canada is an officially bilingual country. French and English are recognized as official languages, at least at the federal level, and since 1970 or so have become well established in national institutions. Governors general, prime ministers, ministers, Supreme Court judges, members of Parliament, and senior bureaucrats are increasingly expected to be able to function in both languages, and for those who arrive at such high office without the capability, second-language training is available at public expense. Federal publications, signs, services, and ceremonies all reflect this policy, and although it is not universally embraced, most see it as a key feature distinguishing Canada from the United States. The companion policy of official multiculturalism has already been discussed in terms of particularism and tolerance.

Third, Canada is a federation, with a division of powers between two levels of government such that neither is subordinate to the other. This characteristic of government was adapted from the United States, but Canadian federalism has developed its own unique features, as seen in Chapter 18, especially an extremely decentralized character. This has resulted from Quebec's promotion of provincial autonomy, with the governments of the other large provinces following suit.

Canada's adoption of the British parliamentary system is a fourth prominent national characteristic. Both federal and provincial governments operate with a strong executive, a relatively weak legislative branch, and, until 1982, a judiciary that had very limited powers of judicial review. The recent addition to the Constitution of a Charter of Rights and Freedoms granting authority to the courts to invalidate legislation conflicting with the Charter is a U.S. anomaly grafted onto the British institutional trunk. Other than the Charter and the French civil code used in Quebec, the Canadian legal system is based on that of Britain, including the British common law.

One potential place to look for a statement of basic Canadian political values would be in the Constitution. Unfortunately, in this respect, the Constitution Act, 1867 did not go much beyond "peace, order, good government," although the Charter of Rights and Freedoms, as mentioned, includes a catalogue of fundamental freedoms, as well as a variety of democratic, legal, and equality rights. The only serious attempt to construct a comprehensive list of national values was the **Canada Clause** in the 1992 Charlottetown Accord, which more or less confirms the values identified above. These fundamental characteristics include

- Democracy
- A parliamentary system of government
- A federal system of government
- Aboriginal peoples constituting one of three orders of government
- Quebec constituting a distinct society within Canada
- Official bilingualism (including official language minorities)
- Racial, ethnic, and cultural equality and diversity
- Individual and collective human rights and freedoms
- Equality of men and women
- Equality of the provinces, but recognition of diversity

When pollster Allan Gregg asked ordinary Canadians in 1995 what they thought was distinctive about Canada and Canadians, he received much the same results: nonviolence, tolerance of minorities, humane treatment of the poor and disadvantaged, official bilingualism, history, climate, and a reluctance to boast.[35]

. . . .

CANADA'S CHANGING POLITICAL CULTURE

Some observers claim that what has just been described is more myth than reality. Moreover, in the 1990s, many aspects of this traditional value structure seemed to be changing. Different concepts of democracy emerged, the distinction between Canadian and American values appeared to decline, and some of the other values identified above had diminishing support. Much of this transformation can be attributed to the presence of the United States, directly or indirectly; some of it is part of a worldwide change in political values; and some is not so easily explained.[36]

As far as democracy is concerned, the 1990s saw an upsurge in interest in the means of more direct popular participation. The most common prescription in this regard was the referendum, in which legislators are guided or bound by the frequent referral of policy questions to the electorate as a whole. Quebec has used this device twice on the question of sovereignty; certain other provinces now require it for approval of constitutional amendments; and some have prescribed its use for other issues, such as electoral reforms or significant tax increases. Many observers believe that since the Charlottetown Accord was put to a popular vote in 1992 any other major constitutional changes will require a national referendum as well, even though this is not mandated by the constitutional amending formula. Canada now possesses a Referendum Act that can be activated at any time.

Direct participation also includes the concept of the **initiative**, in which legislators respond to demands for policy changes expressed by voters in the form of a petition, and the **recall**, in which a member of Parliament could be forced to resign if a certain proportion of electors in a constituency sign a petition to this effect. The recall device was legislated only in BC, and in general, these three forms of direct democracy no longer appear to generate much enthusiasm. In their place, some observers advocate "e-democracy," in which citizens could participate more directly in public policy discussions via the Internet.

Another aspect of dissatisfaction with the traditional notion of democracy is the now commonly advanced idea that elected members of Parliament should vote on certain issues in accordance with the views of their constituents, rather than follow the party line. After 2003, Prime Minister Paul Martin was willing to give his backbench MPs more freedom in this respect, but, perhaps because of subsequent minority governments, Canada has reverted to rigid party discipline, with many incentives to toe the party line remaining in place.

Several of the Canadian values described above emanate from British, United Empire Loyalist, or French feudal origins and may lose their salience as these influences fade into the past or are diluted by immigration from other parts of the world. The distinctions between Canadian and American values are also threatened in at least three ways by the influence of the United States. First, given the extent of U.S. control over Canada and Canadian exposure to the U.S., values implicit in that country's popular culture, as transmitted by television, movies, books, magazines, and music, in business, and in the military, have likely had some impact on those north of the border. It is debatable whether distinctive Canadian values can withstand the homogenizing forces of modern technology and globalization, especially those originating from the south. Second, nationalists saw all these influences increasing under the Free Trade Agreement and NAFTA, and feared that the distinctiveness of Canadian values would suffer as a result. Third, some observers such as Lipset felt that the adoption of a U.S.-style Charter of Rights and Freedoms would have a profound effect on diminishing distinctive Canadian values. The Charter places the power of the state under judicial restraint and "makes Canada a more individualistic and litigious culture."[37] In a country that articulates its basic values so diffidently to start with, these powerful threats are not to be taken lightly.

There are several recent indications that feelings of deference in Canada are on the decline, one of which was the majority's refusal to endorse the Charlottetown Accord, a product of the political elite.[38] Neil Nevitte's book, *The Decline of Deference*, revealed that those Canadians expressing a high degree of confidence in government institutions fell from 36.9 percent in 1981 to 29.4 percent in 1990, and he argues that all advanced industrial

. . . .

Figure 11.2 Canadians' Trust in Public Action

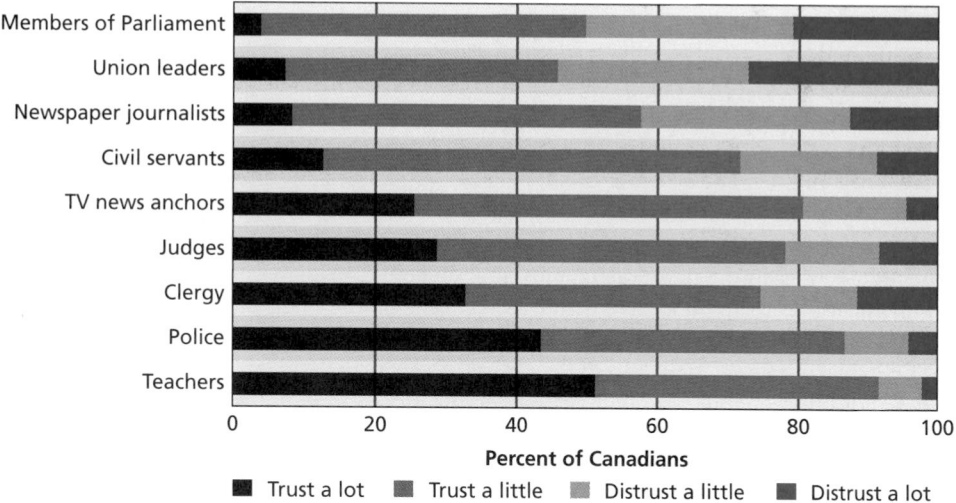

Source: POLLARA, *"Nurses, Doctors Still Top the POLLARA Public Trust Index," cited on February 5, 2003, available at http://www.pollara.ca/new/Library/surveys/intro~1.htm; http://www.pollara.ca/new/Library/surveys/1of3.htm; http:// www.pollara.ca/new/Library/surveys/3of3.htm. Reprinted by permission of POLLARA Inc.*

states experienced similar value transformations over that decade. Figure 11.2 shows that Canadians have developed an increasingly negative attitude toward politicians, no doubt in part because the Trudeau, Mulroney, and Chrétien governments destroyed much of Canadians' respect for and trust in government authority. The sponsorship scandal only exacerbated these feelings.

Although Canadians continue to be more supportive of government intervention than Americans are, the whole political spectrum shifted to the right after 1985 or so as a result of the worldwide influence of neoliberalism or neoconservatism. Governments reduced the scope of their operations, cut back social programs, were careful to balance their budgets, paid down their debts, lowered taxes, privatized Crown corporations, and engaged in deregulation. A study by the Canadian Policy Research Networks, for example, found a new emphasis on self-reliance and fiscal responsibility: "The strong sense of collective responsibility is now balanced by recognition that families and individuals must take more responsibility for themselves and their kind."[39] Somewhat similarly, Telford and Lazar argue that Canada has moved to the right on economic and fiscal issues, but that social attitudes have changed in a leftward, progressive, permissive direction.[40]

Another reason to expect that the traditional Canadian political culture has changed is related to the growth of postmaterialism. Nevitte divides the population into two main groups: those born before 1945, with their "materialist" orientations, and those born after 1945, the "postmaterialist" generation. He finds that this dividing line explains a great deal about differences in Canadian values.[41] If Canadians born after 1945 felt satisfied with their material well-being, not having been exposed to the Depression and the Second World War, they could turn their attention to other "quality of life" values and issues. These included the environment and individual rights. Although protecting the environment almost always necessitates increased government intervention, the protection of individual rights, such as with a constitutional charter, involves restricting the actions of government.

In his study of Canadian values, Michael Adams asserts that "the status associated with once-cherished institutions ... has gone into steep decline. Established authority has had its legitimacy questioned in every sphere." Canadians have rejected the power of traditional institutional authorities, and with that rejection comes a decline in civility and reluctance to break the rules.[42] On the other hand, Adams has produced evidence that Canadians and Americans are actually becoming increasingly different from each other at the most basic level of values. Some of these value differences are of recent origin, such as the American search for security in the traditional family and religion. Canadians are about half as religious as Americans, he writes, and divergent views of religion are one symptom of a growing disparity between the two cultures. But most differences reflect the five basic distinctions made earlier in this chapter, including collectivism, diversity, and idealism. Adams adds: "The values and cultures of our two countries remain distinct even in the face of powerful forces of globalization and continental free trade."[43]

Although the coming to power in 2006 of the Harper Conservatives could be taken as confirmation that support for collectivism has declined, it must be pointed out that in order to achieve election, that party had to move from the ideological right to the centre. Moreover, one survey showed that only 41 percent of those who voted Conservative in 2006 did so because they wanted a Conservative government; 54 percent just wanted change.[44] Indeed, it could be said that neoliberalism never really took hold in the Canadian political culture, and as the early 21st century evolved, at least some aspects of it seemed to have run their course. Moreover, the economic meltdown that began in 2008 required all governments to intervene massively in their economies. This conclusion would support the contention that the Canadian political culture has not really changed that much. It also resonates with a 2003 survey that showed 52 percent of Canadians would like to see Canada become less like the United States and only 12 percent to be more like the U.S. in the future. Table 11.2 shows the proportion of Canadians in a 2005 poll who felt that selected changes would alter the fundamental nature of Canada.

TABLE 11.2 Percentage of Canadians Feeling That Selected Changes Would Alter the Fundamental Nature of Canada

Eliminating public health care	85%
Abandoning two official languages	73%
Ceasing to engage in peacekeeping operations	69%
Establishing closer ties with the U.S.	66%
Eliminating the CBC	60%

Source: Centre for Research and Information on Canada (CRIC), *Portraits of Canada 2005* (January 2006), available at *www.cric.ca*, retrieved on January 20, 2006.

· ·

"LIMITED IDENTITIES": SUBCULTURES IN CANADA

Even before recent changes in basic Canadian political values, the latter were submerged to some extent by regional, provincial, and territorial political subcultures. For generations, political scientists and historians in Canada have debated whether a pan-Canadian political culture really existed, or whether it made more sense to emphasize **subcultures** or **limited identities**.[45] Subcultures are distinctive collections of values, beliefs, attitudes, identities, and orientations held by smaller groups within the society. Given the strong influences of region and ethnicity in Canadian society, it is not surprising that smaller clusters of values and attitudes based on these factors, and others, would constitute subcultures, supplementing whatever pan-Canadian values can be identified. In his recent study of this subject, for example, Nelson Wiseman primarily focuses on distinctive provincial political cultures.[46]

Regional and Provincial/Territorial Subcultures

Chapter 3 introduced the concept of regional and provincial or territorial identities, and Wiseman found that the same approaches used to analyze the national political culture can be adopted to study provincial political cultures, including different times and patterns of settlement ("fragments") and individualized "formative events." Strong local loyalties, variations in attachment to national political values, differences in such attitudes as political efficacy and trust in government, and distinctive party systems, patterns of political participation, and voting behaviour are all evidence of regional, provincial, and territorial political subcultures.[47] Many of these subjects will be examined in more detail in later chapters.

Canadians are frequently polled as to their respective federal and provincial loyalties. Surveys usually show that Ontarians have the least defined concept of a provincial identity, and see themselves as Canadians who happen to be situated in Ontario. Quebeckers have the strongest sense of being a "distinct society" and are the least attached to Canada. Even Westerners are quite centrally oriented, in spite of the fact that Alberta and British Columbia have increasingly strong self-images and that residents harbour feelings of **Western alienation**.[48]

Leaving aside Quebec for a moment, the Western political subculture has been most predominant in recent years. It is based on a sense of being underrepresented in national governments, of being subject to discriminatory federal economic policies, and of therefore wanting a decentralization of federal powers to the provinces. Westerners provide restrained support for the democratic principle of majority rule, which to them means that national policies are designed in the interests of central Canada. Many Westerners also reject the existing decision-making structure in which the Senate does not give them sufficient voting strength to overcome Ontario's influence in other branches of government. Generally speaking, the Western subculture is also more wedded to the principles of individualism and self-reliance than is the rest of the country, somewhat more conservative in social attitudes, such as on same-sex marriage, and perhaps more attached to the concept of populism. By the time of the 2006 election, however, less was heard of the earlier Western populist proposals such as frequent referendums, and in this respect, Prime Minister Stephen Harper seemed mostly concerned with establishing an elected Senate.

Wiseman advises us that each of the three Prairie provinces has a somewhat distinctive political culture, largely based on different patterns of settlement. Manitoba was historically dominated by ex-Ontario liberals and developed a "liberal" political culture; Saskatchewan became the home of a large contingent from the British working class, giving it a left-wing populist political culture; and Alberta attracted many ex-Americans—religious, radical, populist, individualistic, and often preoccupied with monetary theories—who provided the base for a right-wing, populist, plebiscitarian political culture.[49] Thus, the Western political subculture is more complicated than it appears at first sight—it varies from province to province and evolves over time.

Ethnic Subcultures

For francophone Quebeckers, distinctive provincial and ethnic subcultures coincide.[50] This best example of an ethnic subculture within Canada also illustrates the fact that values and attitudes can change over time. In the pre-1960 period, Quebec was extremely conservative in its attitudes and values, was heavily influenced by the Roman Catholic Church, had a low average level of education, and was less committed to the value of democracy than the rest of the country.[51] It was very inward looking and obsessed with survival and with being left alone.

To some extent, Quebec remains a distinct ethnic subculture today, but its values have changed. It is still concerned with the preservation of the French language and culture but no longer looks to the Church as a means of doing so. Instead, the Quebec provincial government has become the primary engine of French-Canadian "national" survival, and Quebeckers have become profoundly democratic. They now believe strongly in majority rule (at least within the province) and in political equality, for example, in regulating election contributions. French Canadians have become politically sophisticated; their culture has flourished; their attitudes have become more "progressive" than those of other Canadians on such issues as daycare, abortion, common-law marriages, and homosexuality; and they are becoming increasingly aggressive economically. A new francophone entrepreneurial elite is even confident of taking on the Americans under free trade. Although this Québécois subculture is inherently nationalistic, a July 1995 *Maclean's* survey revealed that 75 percent of Quebeckers felt pride when they saw the Canadian flag or heard the national anthem. Quebeckers' views on variations of sovereignty were discussed in Chapter 5, as was their reaction to their increasingly heterogeneous society.

New Aboriginal and minority ethnic subcultures are also increasingly evident in Canada. All these groups have been passive until recently, neither articulating their demands strongly nor even participating actively as political candidates or voters. At the beginning of the 1990s, however, they suddenly became more self-confident and aggressive, wanting to influence public policies and demanding their place as candidates or participants in constitutional negotiations. Aboriginals have a distinct conception of their place in Canadian society and most want to govern themselves, while the ethnocultural minorities want to be full participants in the overall political system.

Other Subcultures

Within the general Canadian political culture, different classes exhibit somewhat distinctive values, attitudes, and orientations, even where the individuals involved are lacking in class-consciousness. Attitudes of trust in government and feelings of political efficacy naturally decline from upper- to middle- to working-class groups and are lowest among the poor. It is also likely that the upper classes are less committed to communitarian and egalitarian values than the working classes and are more attached to elitism and hierarchy. In short, the upper classes have a political subculture distinguished by feelings of self-confidence, trust, and participation, and by demands for the retention of the status quo; the working classes have a political subculture characterized by alienation, lack of participation, and by demands for substantial economic reform. Most of the poor have dropped out of the political system entirely, evidence of a truly distinctive subculture.[52] As indicated in Chapters 7 and 9, other identities are increasingly important in Canadian politics. Thus, one could also speak of gender and religious subcultures, as well as those related to location and age.

. . . .

POLITICAL PARTICIPATION

Since many of the basic political values relate directly or indirectly to citizen participation in the political system, patterns of political participation can also be considered an aspect of political culture. Political participation consists of "those voluntary activities by citizens that are intended to influence the selection of government leaders or the decisions they make."[53] Numerous avenues of political participation exist, but actual participation takes effort, which not everyone is willing to exert, and which is partly related to the possession of **political efficacy**—a sense of political competence and a feeling that one can have some impact on the system. Participation also depends on the possession of such resources as time, money, and information. In the Canadian case, the opportunities for participation far exceed actual levels of involvement.

Electoral Participation

Voting on election day is a crucial aspect of democracy, as previously defined, and is the most common form of political participation in Canada. The voter turnout rate is also one of the few forms of participation that can be regularly and reliably measured. The overall average national turnout rate between 1900 and 1993 was about 73 percent, or nearly three-quarters of those eligible to vote. The turnout rate then fell to 67 percent in 1997,[54] to 64.1 percent in 2000, and to 60.9 percent in 2004. In 2006, the turnout rate increased to 64.9 percent, but then fell again in 2008—to 58.8 percent, as seen in Table 11.3.

Although the rate varies across provinces and territories, the 2004 and 2008 averages were historic modern-day lows. Some observers pointed out that even these figures were generous, since they are based on the percentage turnout of names on the voters' list, a list that probably contained no more than 85 percent of eligible voters. The explanation for this regularly decreasing turnout rate in Canadian federal elections is undoubtedly complex. Some voters may have abstained because they did not consider any of the alternatives very attractive (or

TABLE 11.3   Percentage Voter Turnout in Federal Elections, 1984–2008

1984	1988	1993	1997	2000	2004	2006	2008
75.3	75.3	69.6	67.0	64.1*	60.9	64.9	58.8

The figures for the 2000 election were revised by the Chief Electoral officer to the above numbers after the official report was published.

Source: Elections Canada. Found at: http://www.elections.ca/content.asp?section=pas&document=turnout& lang=e&textonly=false

very different), and others because they were perfectly content with things as they were. It would seem that some may also have felt that it was not worth the trouble to vote, given that the state performs fewer functions than it used to, and that many forces of globalization are beyond the power of the state. Some people probably feel that their vote would be wasted in the first-past-the-post system, as discussed in Chapter 13. In general, it was mostly poorly educated young people who abstained, those who were not interested in politics and not well informed.[55] The federal turnout rate in Canada is well above that of the United States but behind many other states, as statistics from the International Institute for Democracy and Electoral Assistance (IDEA) reveal at http://www.idea.int/vt/survey/voter_turnout2.cfm.

There has been much concern in Canada in recent years about the low turnout rate among people under the age of 30; it is estimated that only 25 percent of this cohort voted in the 2000 federal election. The three most common reasons for not voting given by those in this group were as follows: lack of interest (28 percent); lack of time (23 percent); and lack of appeal on the part of, or lack of faith in, parties, leaders, and candidates (20 percent). Most such young people lack a sense of civic duty and do not feel that voting is important for its own sake or that it is an essential obligation of living in a democracy. Most are neither cynical nor alienated; they are just not interested and do not see politics as relevant to their lives.[56] Elections Canada put much effort into a campaign to raise this youth voter turnout rate and calculates that it rose in 2004. Figure 11.3 shows its estimated turnout rate by age group in that election.

Within the group that does vote, we can distinguish among degrees of knowledge and involvement. As Chapter 15 indicates, the level of information of the typical voter should not be overestimated, and many who vote pay little or no attention to the campaign. Although 80 percent claim to expose themselves to television or newspaper coverage of the election campaign, only 20 percent follow politics closely on a daily basis between elections. The level of factual and conceptual knowledge increases with level of education and reading about politics in newspapers; significant regional variations are also evident, but viewing political programs on television was of negligible impact.[57]

A study of the 1984 election found that as a national average, voters could name 3.3 provincial premiers (out of ten) and 36 percent could define the concepts of left and right and place the NDP as the furthest left of the three main parties. A 2000 study revealed that only 26 percent could name the current prime minister, the minister of finance, and the Leader of the Opposition. In 2002, a poll showed that only 47 percent knew that the Canadian Alliance party was to the right of the New Democrats, while 18 percent said it was to the political left. And in various international studies of political knowledge, Canada

Figure 11.3 **Estimated Voter Turnout Rate by Age, 2004**

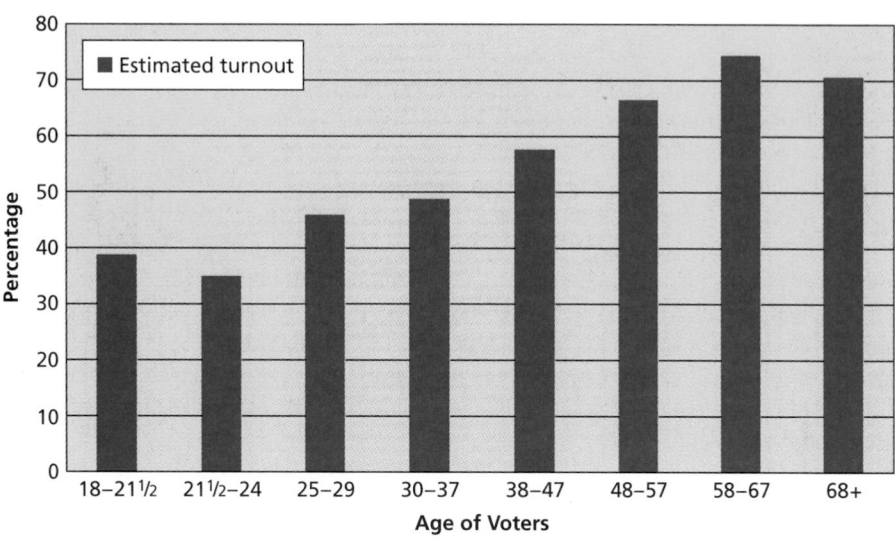

Source: Elections Canada. Estimation of Voter Turnout by Age Group at the 38th Federal General Election, June 28, 2004. Final Report, December 2005. Found at: http://www.elections.ca/loi/report-e.pdf

usually ranks in the middle or lower range.[58] Here is what the leading study of the subject recently concluded:

> The Canadian public contains deep pockets of political ignorance and political illiteracy. Over 40 percent of Canadians were unable to name the leaders of the federal political parties, even though they were being interviewed right after an election in which those leaders had figured prominently. As for the parties' issue positions, 30 percent of Canadians could not identify one single promise with the party making it. And most Canadians were unable to identify which party was on the left and which was on the right.[59]

Beyond those who cast an "informed vote," a smaller proportion of the electorate becomes actively involved in the election campaign. A small number attend all-candidates meetings; some work as deputy returning officers and poll clerks; some join a political party and vote at its local nomination meeting; some contribute money to political parties; some contribute time to a local candidate to do mailing, telephoning, or door-to-door canvassing; and a small number in each constituency become totally preoccupied with the local campaign. Members of this last group, including candidates themselves, are sometimes called "gladiators," as distinct from the great bulk of the population, who are primarily "spectators."[60]

Elections Canada tells us that about 75 000 Canadians made contributions of more than $100 to candidates in the 2000 federal election, and many more, about 200 000, also contributed to political parties. Even so, these figures represent only about one percent of the entire electorate, although an undetermined number donated smaller amounts.

Nonelectoral Participation

The political participation of most Canadians peaks at election time, but many avenues are open between elections in which to make demands, demonstrate support, or otherwise become involved in the political process. Most Canadian political parties do not maintain reliable lists of party members, but estimates of party membership never exceed three percent of the population.[61] It is known that many people sign up before or during the campaign and then let their membership lapse afterward.

Another means of political participation is to join a voluntary group, an action that at least 60 percent of Canadians claim to do.[62] As seen in Chapter 16, any group, whatever its primary orientation, can become an advocacy group so that membership in any group is potentially political. In the unlikely event that the group does take a political turn, however, passive members rarely do more than send the occasional preprinted postcard to their MP or the prime minister. However, active executive and staff members of such groups may become highly involved in political campaigns. Even more initiative is required to form such a group, usually to protest against some political decision or lack of action at the municipal, provincial, territorial, or federal level.

Such group participation usually involves communicating with the authorities in routine ways, but occasionally it takes the form of peaceful demonstrations (locally or on Parliament Hill), sit-ins and other types of civil disobedience, and the rare case of violent

. . . .

Figure 11.4　Percentage of Canadians Who Engaged in Selected Political Activities over the Previous Year, 2003

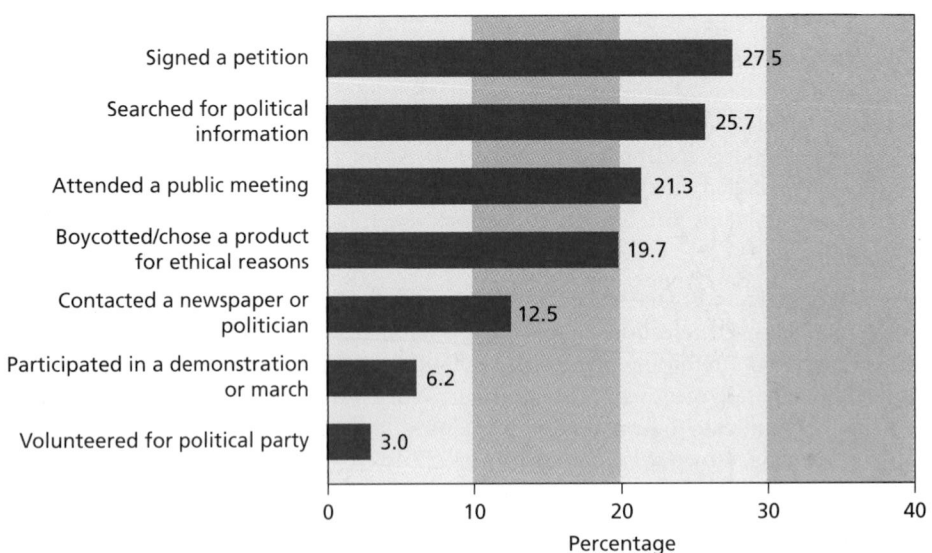

Source: "Percentage of Canadians Who Engaged in Selected Political Activities over the Previous Year, 2003," adapted from Statistics Canada publication 2003 General Social Survey on Social Engagement, Cycle 17: An Overview of Findings, Catalogue 89-598, released July 6, 2004.

protest. As noted above, Canadians are generally a peaceful lot, and instances of political violence are uncommon. The main historical incidents of violence were the two Riel Rebellions of 1870 and 1885, the conscription riots in Quebec City in 1918, the Winnipeg General Strike of 1919, the Regina Riot (of the unemployed) of 1935, various FLQ incidents of the 1960s culminating in the FLQ crisis of 1970, and the Mohawks' armed standoff at Oka in 1990.[63]

Canadians can also participate politically between elections as individuals—writing, faxing, or e-mailing letters to MPs or the prime minister; writing letters to the editors of newspapers; calling radio or television phone-in shows; signing petitions; or telephoning or meeting an MP. As with so many other aspects of political participation, however, it is difficult to obtain solid data on the degree of this category of individual involvement. Figure 11.4 reveals the percentage of Canadians who engaged in selected political activities in 2003.[64]

. . . .

CONCLUSION

Although the values and attitudes that constitute the political culture of any society are difficult to establish, certain Canadian political values can be identified, the foremost being a rudimentary belief in democracy. In many cases, it helps to see Canadian values in contrast to those of the United States. Canada has a more even balance between individualism and collectivism; it gives greater weight to particularism, tolerance, and deference to authority; it is also more egalitarian, cautious, diffident, and dependent. To some extent, however, these differences between Canadian and American values may be in decline. Efforts to define pan-Canadian values, attitudes, and identities are also complicated by the existence of regional, ethnic, and other political subcultures and identities. As for political participation in Canada, it "bears little similarity to the classical democratic ideal of widespread citizen involvement in all aspects of the political process."[65]

Because the political culture provides the value context within which the Canadian political system operates, the contents of this chapter are relevant to virtually everything else in the text. Previous chapters have already had connections to the values, attitudes, identities, and subcultures mentioned here. The global and especially the U.S. influence on Canada's political culture was also addressed earlier. The next chapter on political socialization, mass media, and public opinion polls is closely linked to political culture, especially in terms of asking where basic values and attitudes came from and how they can be measured, while the following four chapters—elections, political parties, voting, and advocacy groups—examine how political values impact on political behaviour. Part 4, the Constitutional Context, revisits such questions as amending the constitution to better reflect the contemporary political culture, how that political culture affects federal–provincial relations, and how the Charter has strengthened certain basic values. Finally, Part 5 examines the operation of the institutions of government in the context of the limits imposed by the political culture.

 The limited nature of Canadian democracy, combined with Canadian deference to authority, means that political authorities have considerable autonomy in making their decisions, as the state-centred approach suggests. It would be too

much to claim that the state is completely autonomous from the rest of society and from demands flowing from the public, but it now becomes clear why state authorities have, to a large extent, been able to pursue their own conception of the national interest. Canadians are also respectful of those in positions of authority in other segments of society, and this chapter has identified the various regional, provincial, territorial, and ethnic subcultures whose leaders come together in a process of elite accommodation. They devise compromise arrangements with which to satisfy the mass members of these groups.

In terms of participation, the authorities are still able to choose the most convenient date for the election and the message to be conveyed. Content in the knowledge that few people know what is going on and even fewer can be bothered to do anything about it, those in power carry on with their own agenda. Politicians may encourage popular participation when it serves their own purposes, but bureaucrats have been notoriously suspicious of public involvement. Even if the public is now demanding more meaningful participation, they are not turning out in impressive numbers on election day.

P Pluralists centre on the "limited identities" that characterize Canadian society and the many subcultures that exist in the country, each one providing a shading to the national values identified. They also focus on the values of particularism and tolerance. Rather than emphasize the elite interaction that emanates from such subcultures, however, pluralists note that most of these interests are organized into advocacy groups and that public policies are the outcome of a broader interplay among such groups. Pluralism emphasizes that individuals are free to join or form any group, and although more than half of Canadian adults do so, the passivity of most members comes as no surprise. This leads to inequalities among such groups.

PC This chapter also demonstrates that relatively few citizens are either well informed or participate beyond voting, surely a smaller number than the public choice approach would have anticipated. Whether such behaviour is based on a rational understanding that greater effort would not be worthwhile or on simple apathy and laziness, it is clear that the "public choice" is often not a well-informed one. Still, political parties do design election platforms that they think will attract the support of voters once the latter are spurred to take some temporary interest.

© Class analysts are generally critical of the Canadian values and attitudes identified in this chapter. In particular, they emphasize the narrow conception of democracy held by most Canadians, deriding the notion of one person–one vote as a genuine measure of political equality, the view that political freedom is meaningful in the absence of economic and social freedom, and the claim that an election every four years is an effective implementation of popular sovereignty. They also contend that the capitalist ethic is still predominant among the political and economic elite and that much of the government intervention that has occurred has been welcomed rather than opposed by the bourgeoisie. They put little stock in such "tory" ideas as trusting a concerned and paternalistic political or economic elite to advance the position of the working class. Such analysts emphasize class subcultures and view regional and ethnic subcultures largely in class terms. They argue, too, that Canadians have not respected their heritage of natural resources, that federalism has impaired Ottawa's capacity to ensure greater economic equality in the country, and that the state has not been strong in improving the conditions of the working class.

As for participation, class analysts claim that the bourgeoisie encourages the masses to vote, but only to choose between parties equally committed to the capitalist system. If political violence occurs, such as in the Winnipeg General Strike or the Oka incident, the authorities move the police in quickly to quell it, frequently exacerbating the situation with such coercive measures.

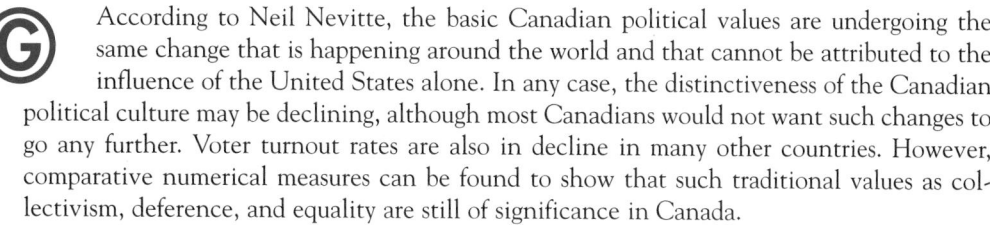

According to Neil Nevitte, the basic Canadian political values are undergoing the same change that is happening around the world and that cannot be attributed to the influence of the United States alone. In any case, the distinctiveness of the Canadian political culture may be declining, although most Canadians would not want such changes to go any further. Voter turnout rates are also in decline in many other countries. However, comparative numerical measures can be found to show that such traditional values as collectivism, deference, and equality are still of significance in Canada.

DISCUSSION QUESTIONS

1. Do you believe that periodic elections are a sufficient means of exercising the principle of popular sovereignty, and that the principle of one person–one vote is a sufficient mark of political equality?

2. How deep is the Canadian commitment to political freedom? What situations do you think justify government restriction of such freedom?

3. What kinds of minority rights should be protected in the Constitution, and in what circumstances should Canada follow the principle of majority rule?

4. To what extent has the traditional Canadian political culture been transformed in recent years?

5. How can the voter turnout rate, especially among young people, be increased?

6. What forms of political participation have you engaged in? Why haven't you or other Canadians participated more?

NOTES

1. See, for example, David V.J. Bell, "Political Culture in Canada," in Michael Whittington and Glen Williams, eds., *Canadian Politics in the 21st Century*, 7th ed. (Toronto: Thomson Nelson, 2008), p. 228.
2. Jane Jenson, "Changing Discourse, Changing Agenda," quoted in Bell, "Political Culture in Canada," p. 231.
3. Bell, "Political Culture in Canada," pp. 236–40.
4. Louis Hartz, *The Founding of New Societies* (New York: Harcourt, Brace and World, 1964).

5. Gad Horowitz, "Conservatism, Liberalism and Socialism in Canada: An Interpretation," *Canadian Journal of Economics and Political Science* (May 1966).

6. Seymour Martin Lipset, *Continental Divide* (New York: Routledge, 1990).

7. John Ralston Saul, *A Fair Country: Telling Truths about Canada* (Toronto: Viking Canada, 2008). Another recent treatment of the Canadian political culture is Andrew Cohen, *The Unfinished Canadian: The People We Are* (Toronto: McClelland and Stewart, 2007).

8. Henry B. Mayo, *An Introduction to Democratic Theory* (New York: Oxford University Press, 1960), ch. 4; Patrick Dunleavy and Brendan O'Leary, *Theories of the State: The Politics of Liberal Democracy* (London: Macmillan, 1987); and David Held, *Models of Democracy*, 2nd ed. (Stanford: Stanford University Press, 1996).

9. Thomas R. Berger, *Fragile Freedoms* (Toronto: Clarke, Irwin & Co., rev. and updated, 1982).

10. Paul M. Sniderman, Joseph F. Fletcher, Peter Russell, and Philip E. Tetlock, *The Clash of Rights: Liberty, Equality, and Legitimacy in Pluralist Democracy* (New Haven, CT: Yale University Press, 1996).

11. Lipset, *Continental Divide*, p. 8.

12. Ibid. John Ralston Saul, on the other hand, emphasizes that the phrase that was used in earlier versions of the BNA Act was "peace, *welfare* and government." See *A Fair Country*, Part II. He emphasizes "fairness" over "order."

13. Pierre Berton, *Why We Act Like Canadians* (Toronto: McClelland and Stewart, 1982).

14. Sniderman et al., *The Clash of Rights*, p. 91.

15. Ibid., pp. 99 and 123. Of course, the scope of government in the U.S. expanded enormously under President Barack Obama due to the Great Recession of 2009.

16. André Blais, Elisabeth Gidengil, Richard Nadeau, and Neil Nevitte, *Anatomy of a Liberal Victory: Making Sense of the Vote in the 2000 Canadian Election* (Peterborough: Broadview Press, 2002), p. 102.

17. Allan Gregg and Michael Posner, *The Big Picture: What Canadians Think About Almost Everything* (Toronto: Macfarlane Walter & Ross, 1990), pp. 11–13, 29. Such differences have probably narrowed due to the actions of President Obama.

18. Will Kymlicka, *Finding Our Way: Rethinking Ethnocultural Relations in Canada* (Don Mills: Oxford University Press, 1998), among many other works. In his book, *Utopia: The Surprising Triumph of Canadian Pluralism* (Toronto: Viking Canada, 2007), Michael Adams continues to argue that support for the Canadian mosaic is holding fast.

19. Michael Adams and others emphasize the secularism of Canada in contrast to the religiosity of the United States. One survey found 27 percent of Canadians opposed to same-sex marriages compared with 47 percent opposed in the U.S.

20. Given evidence of intolerance at home, this self-defined Canadian international image is a touch moralistic.

21. Edgar Friedenberg, *Deference to Authority* (White Plains, NY: M.E. Sharpe, 1980); and Judy M. Torrance, *Public Violence in Canada* (Montreal: McGill-Queen's University Press, 1986).

22. Section 24(2) of the Charter allows the admissibility of tainted evidence if it does not detract from the "repute" of the Court!

23. Sniderman, *The Clash of Rights*, p. 27.

24. Centre for Research and Information on Canada, *Portraits of Canada 2005* (January 2006), p. 10.

25. Statistics Canada, *Crime Comparisons between Canada and the United States* (Catalogue No. 85-002-XPE 2001, December 18, 2001); and Statistics Canada, "Homicides," *The Daily*, September 29, 2004. On a per capita basis, three times as many murders and twice as many aggravated assaults are committed in the United States as in Canada. Despite the law and order orientation of the Harper government, the crime rate has generally been in decline for some time.

26. For a recent perspective on the differences between Canadian and U.S. health care systems, see Statistics Canada, *Joint Canada/United States Survey of Health: Findings and Public-Use Microdata File*, available at http://www.statcan.ca/english/freepub/82M0022XIE/free.htm. Of course, President Obama may be successful in reducing such differences.

27. W. Wolfson and B. Murphy, "Income Inequality in North America: Does the 49th Parallel Still Matter?" *Canadian Economic Observer* (Catalogue No. 11-010-XPB, August 2000). See Miles Corak, "Equality of Opportunity and Inequality across the Generations: Challenges Ahead," *Policy Options* (March–April 2005), and Educational Policy Institute, Global Higher Education Rankings 2005 at http://www.educationalpolicy.org/pdf/Global2005.pdf.

28. Sniderman et al., *The Clash of Rights*, ch. 4.

29. Apart from all the methodological problems in *Maclean's* magazine's annual ranking of Canadian universities, the whole operation is essentially American-inspired and irrelevant to Canada. All Canadian universities are respectable, and the qualitative differences between them are minimal, unlike the situation in the United States.

30. Margaret Atwood, *Survival* (Toronto: Anansi, 1972); W.L. Morton, *The Canadian Identity* (Toronto: University of Toronto Press, 1961); and Dominique Clift, *The Secret Kingdom: Interpretations of the Canadian Character* (Toronto, McClelland and Stewart, 1989), p. 227.

31. Lipset, *Continental Divide*, ch. 4; *Maclean's*, July 1, 1995, p. 15; Michael Adams says that Canadians fear "committing an unforgivable act of hubris" if they praise their country, *Sex in the Snow: Canadian Social Values at the End of the Millennium* (Toronto: Penguin Books, 1998), p. xxi.

32. According to Walter Stefaniuk, *You Asked Us ... About Canada* (Toronto: Doubleday Canada, 1996), the Canadian habit of frequently adding "eh?" to a spoken sentence is a "politeness marker," designed to include the listener in the conversation, p. 1.

33. Morton, *The Canadian Identity*, articles by Carl Berger and Cole Harris in Peter Russell, ed., *Nationalism in Canada* (Toronto: McGraw-Hill, 1966), and Bell, "Political Culture in Canada," p. 239.

34. Not all foreigners were equally impressed: one unkind Englishman said that "Canada is Montreal and Vancouver with bugger all in between," and Voltaire referred to Canada disparagingly as "quelques arpents de neige."

35. *Maclean's*, July 1, 1995, p. 15.

36. Neil Nevitte, *The Decline of Deference: Canadian Value Change in Cross-National Perspective* (Peterborough: Broadview Press, 1996), argues that the change in Canadian values is consistent with changes in other advanced industrial states and is not the result of American influence.

37. Lipset, *Continental Divide*, p. 225.

38. Nevitte, *The Decline of Deference*; Gregg and Posner, *The Big Picture*, pp. 11–13, 54–56, 65–68, 204–5; Alan Frizzell, John H. Pammett, and Anthony Westell, *The Canadian General Election of 1988* (Ottawa: Carleton University Press, 1989), pp. 105, 112; and Peter C. Newman, *The Canadian Revolution 1985–1995: From Deference to Defiance* (Toronto: Viking, 1995).

39. Suzanne Peters, *Exploring Canadian Values: Foundations for Well-Being*, and *A Synthesis Report* (Canadian Policy Research Networks Inc., 1995), p. vi.

40. This is the theme of the book, Hamish Telford and Harvey Lazar, eds., *Canada: The State of the Federation 2001: Canadian Political Culture(s) in Transition* (Kingston: Institute of Intergovernmental Affairs, 2002).

41. Nevitte, *The Decline of Deference*.

42. Adams, *Sex in the Snow*, pp. xxv, 7, 16–17.

43. Michael Adams, *Fire and Ice: The United States, Canada and the Myth of Converging Values* (Toronto: Penguin Canada, 2003); and columns in *The Globe and Mail* on January 10, 2005; May 15, 2005; and December 28, 2005.

44. Environics Research Group, Environics/CBC 2006 Federal Election Survey, January 2006, at http://erg.environics.net/news/default.asp?aID=598.

45. J.M.S. Careless, "Limited Identities," *Canadian Historical Review* (March 1969), pp. 1–10.

46. Nelson Wiseman, *In Search of Canadian Political Culture* (Vancouver: UBC Press, 2007).

47. Telford and Lazar, *Canada: The State of the Federation 2001*. See also CRIC, Portrait of Canadians, 2005; and Ailsa Henderson, "Regional Political Cultures in Canada," *Canadian Journal of Political Science* (September 2004).

48. Statistics Canada, 2003 General Social Survey on Social Engagement, *The Perceptions of Canadians* (Sense of Belonging to Canada; Sense of belonging to province of residence); cited August 15, 2005; available at http://www.statcan.ca/english/freepub/89-598-XIE/2003001/perceptions.htm.

49. Nelson Wiseman, "The Pattern of Prairie Politics," *Queen's Quarterly* 88, no. 2 (Summer 1981); *In Search of Canadian Political Culture*; and "Provincial Political Cultures," in Christopher Dunn, ed., *Provinces: Canadian Provincial Politics*, 2nd ed. (Peterborough: Broadview Press, 2006).

50. Michael Ornstein, Michael Stevenson, and Paul Williams, "Region, Class and Political Culture in Canada: Is There an English-Canadian Subculture?" *Canadian Journal of Political Science* (June 1980). See also Philip Resnick, *Thinking English Canada* (Toronto: Stoddart, 1995), and Kenneth McRoberts, ed., *Beyond Quebec: Taking Stock of Canada* (Montreal: McGill-Queen's University Press, 1995).

51. Pierre Elliott Trudeau, "Some Obstacles to Democracy in Quebec," in *Federalism and the French Canadians* (Toronto: Macmillan, 1968).

52. Ornstein, Stevenson, and Williams, "Region, Class and Political Culture in Canada."

53. William Mishler and Harold D. Clarke, "Political Participation in Canada," in Michael S. Whittington and Glen Williams, eds., *Canadian Politics in the 1990s*, 4th ed. (Scarborough: Nelson, 1995), p. 130.

54. In 1993, a year-old voters' list—from the 1992 referendum—was used, such that the list of eligible voters was inflated because people who had moved or died were still on the list under their old address, while many were also added under their new address. The Chief Electoral Officer once estimated that the turnout rate was about 73 percent.

55. Blais et al., *Anatomy of a Liberal Victory*, ch. 3; André Blais, Agnieszka Dobrzynska, and Louis Massicotte, "Why Is Turnout Higher in Some Countries Than in Others?" Elections Canada, at http://www.elections.ca/content.asp?section=loi&document=index&dir=tur/tuh&lang=e&text only=false; and Jeffrey Simpson, *The Friendly Dictatorship* (Toronto: McClelland and Stewart, 2001).

56. Jon H. Pammett and Lawrence LeDuc, "Explaining the Turnout Decline in Canadian Federal Elections: A New Survey of Non-Voters" (March 2003), http://www.elections.ca/loi/tur/tud/TurnoutDecline.pdf; Anne Milan, "Willing to Participate: Political Engagement of Young Adults," *Canadian Social Trends* (Statistics Canada, Catalogue No. 11-008, Winter 2005); and Lawrence LeDuc and Jon H. Pammett, "Voter Turnout in 2006: More than Just the Weather," in Jon H. Pammett and Christopher Dornan, eds., *The Canadian General Election of 2006* (Toronto: Dundurn, 2006).

57. Ronald D. Lambert, James, E. Curtis, Steven D. Brown, and Barry J. Kay, "The Social Sources of Political Knowledge," *Canadian Journal of Political Science* 21, no. 2 (June 1988), pp. 359–74. See also Henry Milner, *Civic Literacy in Comparative Context* (Montreal: Institute for Research on Public Policy, 2001).

58. Paul Howe and David Northrup, "Strengthening Canadian Democracy: The Views of Canadians," *Policy Matters* (Montreal: Institute for Research on Public Policy) 1, no. 5 (July 2000), p. 40; Milner, *Civic Literacy in Comparative Context*, pp. 8–11; and Compas poll, April 29, 2002.

59. Elisabeth Gidengil, André Blais, Neil Nevitte, and Richard Nadeau, *Citizens* (Vancouver: UBC Press, 2004), p. 69.

60. Ibid., pp. 124–26.

61. R. Kenneth Carty, *Canadian Political Parties in the Constituencies*, Royal Commission on Electoral Reform and Party Financing Research Studies, vol. 23 (Catalogue No. 21-1989/2-41-23E); and R. Kenneth Carty, William Cross, and Lisa Young, *Rebuilding Canadian Party Politics* (Vancouver: UBC Press, 2000).

62. Statistics Canada, General Social Survey on Social Engagement, 2003.

63. Torrance, *Public Violence in Canada*.

64. See also Susan Crompton, "Vox Populi: Canadians Who Speak Up," *Canadian Social Trends* (Statistics Canada, Catalogue No. 11-008, Autumn 2002).

65. William Mishler, *Political Participation in Canada: Prospects for Democratic Citizenship* (Toronto: Macmillan, 1979), p. 36.

. . . .

FURTHER READING

Adams, Michael. *Fire and Ice: The United States, Canada and the Myth of Converging Values*. Toronto: Penguin Canada, 2003.

Ajzenstat, Janet, and Peter J. Smith, eds. *Canada's Origins: Liberal, Tory or Republican?* Montreal: McGill-Queen's University Press, 1995.

Bell, David. "Political Culture in Canada." In Michael Whittington and Glen Williams, eds., *Canadian Politics in the 21st Century*, 7th ed. Toronto: Thomson Nelson, 2008.

Cohen, Andrew. *The Unfinished Canadian: The People We Are*. Toronto: McClelland and Stewart, 2007.

Gidengil, Elisabeth, André Blais, Neil Nevitte, and Richard Nadeau. *Citizens*. Vancouver: UBC Press, 2004.

Gregg, Allan, and Michael Posner. *The Big Picture: What Canadians Think About Almost Everything*. Toronto: Macfarlane Walter & Ross, 1990.

Kymlicka, Will. *Finding Our Way: Rethinking Ethnocultural Relations in Canada*. Don Mills: Oxford University Press, 1998.

Laycock, David, ed. *Representation and Democratic Theory*. Vancouver: UBC Press, 2004.

Lipset, Seymour Martin. *Continental Divide*. New York: Routledge, 1990.

Milner, Henry. *Civic Literacy in Comparative Context*. Montreal: Institute for Research on Public Policy, 2001.

Nevitte, Neil. *The Decline of Deference: Canadian Value Change in Cross-National Perspective*. Peterborough: Broadview Press, 1996.

Telford, Hamish, and Harvey Lazar, eds. *Canada: The State of the Federation 2001: Canadian Political Culture(s) in Transition*. Kingston: Institute of Intergovernmental Affairs, 2002.

Thomas, David, ed. *Canada and the United States: Differences That Count*, 3rd ed. Peterborough: Broadview Press, 2008.

Wiseman, Nelson. *In Search of Canadian Political Culture*. Vancouver: UBC Press, 2007.

Chapter 12

Political Socialization,
THE MASS MEDIA,
and Public Opinion Polls

Many adults cannot identify their member of Parliament and more children can name American political officeholders than Canadian ones. The latter fact is often blamed on the inadequacies of the educational system or related to the high proportion of U.S. television to which Canadians are exposed. Given their reliance on the mass media as the source of their political information, another concern of many Canadians is the large number of media outlets owned by a few wealthy families. During election campaigns parties spend millions of dollars on media advertising and public opinion polls, and media coverage of elections is often focused on such polls.

It is now commonly observed that the mass media and public opinion polls are two of the most important elements in the political system. The mass media—principally television, newspapers, and radio—are the primary source of most Canadians' knowledge and opinion about topical political issues and current personalities. However important the traditional mass media in this respect, people are increasingly reliant on the Internet. Another important link between people and government is the public opinion poll, as parties, advocacy groups, governments, and the media themselves seek to discover Canadians' opinions on every conceivable matter.

This chapter begins by outlining the various agents of political socialization, a principal one being the mass media. It then surveys the state of the media in Canada, including the question of ownership. It examines the relationship between the media and the public and between the media and the politicians, and concludes with a discussion of the role of public opinion polls.

. . . .

THEORETICAL CONSIDERATIONS

Chapter 11 defined political culture as the collection of basic values, ideas, assumptions, and beliefs that shape our understanding and behaviour as citizens in the world of politics. That chapter emphasized that the dominant values and expectations of society are essentially what is meant by the concept of "hegemony." This chapter is largely about the acquisition or transmission of such values, attitudes, and orientations. Those who hold the dominant values and expectations would only be expected, consciously or unconsciously, to transmit them to the rest of society, including new immigrant arrivals and the younger generation. Sometimes these influential actors—these elites—will deliberately seek to own the mass media, one of the most important agents of political socialization; at other times, they will exert their influence through their control of other parts of the economy, the educational system, the bureaucracy, or religious or cultural organizations. Such a process of defining what is normal underlies much of the material in this chapter.

. . . .

POLITICAL SOCIALIZATION

Political socialization is the process by which individuals acquire their political values, attitudes, information, and opinions. Looked at in another way, it is the process by which society passes on its basic values or political culture from one generation to another. Political socialization is sometimes called political learning or education.

The process of political socialization consists in part of direct, individual observation of political phenomena, but is mostly performed by intermediaries or agents of socialization. It is relatively easy to identify the main agents of political socialization in Canada but much more difficult to evaluate their relative impact. We begin with the four traditional agents—family, school, peers, and the mass media—and then examine other such influences.

The Family

The portrait of a "family" is more varied today than in the past, but it remains the basic cell of Canadian society. Despite many modern pressures—the increasing incidence of mothers working outside the home, the high divorce rate, and competing influences, such as peers and the mass media—parents, stepparents, or sometimes grandparents are the first major influence on a child's attitudes and values. At the very least, families provide children with certain circumstances of birth, especially their regional and ethnic origins and their social class, all of which are bound to have some effect on children's political attitudes and behaviour.[1] Second, most children absorb attitudes and values, some of which are of political significance, in a kind of osmosis from their family's conversation and behaviour. Parents' casual comments about politics, politicians, parties, and police are good examples. Third, some parents deliberately try to indoctrinate their children with certain political values, such as supporting a particular political party or developing a sense of political efficacy. Since the degree of party identification in Canada is relatively weak, as seen in Chapter 15, the influence of parents in this respect should not be overestimated.[2] Nor should the more general political impact of the family in modern times, for political socialization is a process that continues throughout life.

The School

The school is the second main agent of political socialization. Although Canada has distinctive provincial and territorial educational systems, the decline of the family's influence and the greater use of child-care centres and kindergarten have probably increased the importance of the "school." Like the family, it is an early enough influence that it is likely to shape basic lifelong values. All school systems in Canada and elsewhere deliberately attempt to inculcate

Political socialization in the classroom setting.

certain basic values and attitudes, including some of a political nature, such as a feeling of affection or support for the country, the governmental apparatus, the head of state, the police, the flag, and the national anthem. Some, even in Canada, go beyond this to dwell on the virtues of capitalism, cooperation, or other ideological, moral, religious, or political values.

Given the diversity of Canadian society, many questions arise about the role of the school in the political socialization process. Since the provinces and territories have jurisdiction over education, do they deliberately contribute to distinctive regional political cultures and identities at the expense of the overall country? The radically different accounts of certain historical events found in French and English textbooks, such as whether Louis Riel was a traitor or a hero, are often cited as examples of the biased role of formal education in this process.[3] One point is clear: the forces of dualism, regionalism, and continentalism in Canadian society make it difficult for the school system to develop any pan-Canadian sense of national identity.[4]

Most observers feel that the current state of Canadian political education is deficient and that students are not exposed to enough direct teaching about politics. When it comes to current events, for example, high-school students usually demonstrate a deplorable lack of recognition of such figures as provincial premiers and federal Cabinet ministers and a lack of knowledge about which political parties form federal and provincial governments.[5] A recent study of 18–24-year-olds by the Dominion Institute found that only 46 percent could name Canada's first Prime Minister and only 26 percent knew the year of Confederation. Only

Ontario, Manitoba, Nova Scotia, and Quebec require high school students to take a dedicated Canadian history course to graduate.[6]

Peers

Peers are the third main agent of political socialization. Peers are simply friends, acquaintances, associates, cohorts, fellow students, coworkers, homemakers, and members of teams and clubs. The concept of "peer pressure" is probably most familiar at the adolescent level and is not usually concerned with political values, attitudes, and opinions; but we are all susceptible to peer influence at any stage of our lives. Wherever and whenever two or more people communicate, political issues of one kind or another may arise, and one person can influence the other. In any larger group setting, including peer-group discussions "around the water-cooler," one person often becomes dominant, because of that person's knowledge, position, or strength of character.

An excellent example of the use of peer-group leaders occurs during election campaigns when the Canadian Labour Congress tries to persuade its members to vote for the New Democratic Party. Given the leadership status of union stewards, it is expected that they will be successful in their effort to "talk up" the NDP at coffee or lunch breaks. Since all union members are probably affected by government in a similar way, this is a natural setting in which certain attitudes or opinions can be reinforced or changed.

The Mass Media

The mass media are the fourth main agent of socialization. They are more often instruments of entertainment than enlightenment, of course, and personal interaction with family members, teachers, or peers normally carries greater impact than passive, impersonal exposure to the media. Moreover, although the first three agents are likely to influence lifelong values and attitudes, the media primarily transmit opinions on topical issues and personalities. Such short-term stimuli are, however, very important in determining how people vote. The mass media, including the Internet, are examined in depth later in the chapter.

Other Agents of Political Socialization

The family, school, peers, and media are probably the main agents of political socialization in Canada but certainly not the only ones. Political parties, religions, groups of various kinds, corporations, think tanks, and the government itself are secondary influences on political attitudes, values, information, and opinions.

Political parties practise the art of persuasion and seek to influence opinions and party preferences on a daily basis. Those who already identify with a particular party find that the simplest means of forming an opinion on any issue is to take their cue from the party leader. The more a person identifies with a party or leader, the greater the propensity to defer to the partisan perspective expressed.

Like political parties, individual corporations are in the business of persuasion, trying to sell their own goods and services. Sometimes, however, companies will also try to influence political attitudes and opinions, an effort that is called **advocacy advertising**. Many such corporations were involved in the free trade debate, especially during the 1988 election campaign, expressing their support through "speeches, debates, letters, advertisements, information sessions with employees, and inserts in newspapers."[7] Others have used the media to try to influence Canadians' opinions on tax changes, the Kyoto Accord, drug patents, and nuclear energy. Sometimes employers also try to influence the opinions or voting preferences of their own employees with internal memos about how different parties or policies would affect the firm.

Although the power of religion in Canadian society is generally declining, churches have often influenced the political values, attitudes, and opinions of their members in the past. The classic case was the Roman Catholic Church in Quebec before 1960, when it had a close relationship with political authorities and did not hesitate to tell its members how to behave politically. That church continues to take a strong stand on many public issues, including abortion and same-sex marriage. Other religious denominations also articulate positions on political issues from time to time, such as the United Church and Jewish leaders. Two religious groups that appear to be taking an increased interest in politics in Canada are evangelical Christians and Muslims, and in such cases, religion may be becoming a more important factor in political socialization.[8] However, Canada is a more secular society than the United States, as pointed out in Chapter 11, and religion does not play as important a role in political socialization here as it does there.[9]

More than half of the Canadian population belongs to a group of some kind, and although the orientation of such groups is primarily non-political, all have the potential to influence their members' political views. Some, such as the Canadian Labour Congress, the Catholic Women's League, and the Canadian Medical Association, are quite determined to do so, as well as to extend their influence beyond their own members to the public at large. Others, such as the Boy Scouts or Girl Guides, try to instill in children an informed affection for the country. Some groups get involved in political indoctrination on rare occasions when the interests of the group are threatened by government action, such as the funeral directors' association fighting against the Goods and Services Tax. Recent immigrants closely attached to minority ethnocultural organizations may be strongly influenced by the groups' stand on Canadian policy toward their homeland or internal homeland politics.

Many interest groups are sources of useful information about public policy, and it is sometimes difficult to separate them from "think tanks," whose main purpose is to provide analyses of such policies. Canada now possesses a considerable number of the latter, and their studies often influence politicians, bureaucrats, and the public at large. Many are on the "right" side of the political spectrum—for example, the Fraser Institute, the C.D. Howe Institute, the Canada West Foundation, and the Donner Canadian Foundation. Those on the "left" that specialize in social policy include the Caledon Institute, the Centre for Social Justice, the Canadian Centre for Policy Alternatives, and the Council of Canadians.[10]

Finally, the government itself is often engaged in efforts to influence public views and behaviour. Sometimes this is done for what are widely recognized as legitimate purposes, such as encouraging physical fitness and discouraging smoking, impaired driving, racial discrimination, violence against women, and the use of drugs. Sometimes it is done for broadly acceptable political purposes, such as promoting tourism in Canada, the purchase of Canadian-made goods, or national unity. Governments are also expected to inform the public about new laws, regulations, and programs through pamphlets and the mass media, but it is a fine line between simple information and extolling the virtues of such initiatives for partisan purposes. The Mulroney government, for example, spent large sums of public funds flaunting the merits of the Free Trade Agreement and the Goods and Services Tax in advertising campaigns that most observers felt were excessive and self-serving. In the latter case, the Speaker declared such advertising to be an affront to the House of Commons, as it took place even before debate there had concluded. Governments often use public funds for "public education" purposes just before or during an election campaign, as they circumvent, at public expense, the spending ceilings of federal, provincial, and territorial electoral laws. The Harper government was roundly criticized for excessive advertising of its 2009 stimulus program.

After nearly losing the 1995 Quebec referendum, the government of Jean Chrétien spent hundreds of millions of dollars in a pro-Canada advertising campaign in that province. The money was spent to boost the federal government's profile by flying the Canadian flag as widely as possible in Quebec and by sponsoring sporting and cultural events. Quebeckers were generally insulted that they were considered so easily bought, but even worse, the auditor general revealed that the money was mismanaged. In fact, much of it went to advertising companies with close ties to the Liberal party, and in some cases the money made its way back in the form of political donations. Thus, the whole operation was not only counterproductive but also resulted in one of the worst scandals—the sponsorship scandal, subject of the **Gomery Report**—of modern Canadian history.

How Canadians individually and collectively acquire their political values, attitudes, and opinions is a complicated question. The whole process is so haphazard and complex and the stimuli in each person's own environment are so diverse that no deliberate effort is guaranteed to be successful. Instead, Canadians acquire many of their political values, attitudes, and opinions in an unconscious way. Moreover, many Canadians are only semi-socialized: they simply do not have many political values, attitudes, and opinions or much political information. The leading study of this subject concluded that not only is lack of information a serious problem, but even worse is the large degree of misinformation among the electorate. Many Canadians are misinformed about basic policy-relevant facts, such as underestimating the gap between rich and poor and the generally dismal condition of Canada's Aboriginal peoples, and overestimating the extent of crime.[11]

. . . .

THE MASS MEDIA

In surveying the state of the newspaper, radio, and television industries in Canada today, we should first note that the privately owned media exist primarily to make a profit, and that whatever political functions they serve are incidental.[12] There are significant costs involved in delivering comprehensive political information, and such costs are often cut in the interests of profit. Second, as in so many other aspects of Canadian life, the mass media are divided along linguistic lines, largely English and French, with an increasing number operating in other languages. Third, the mass media are the source of most Canadians' political information, while at the same time they have "considerable influence on the beliefs and perspectives presented to Canadians. These choices help to determine available role models, images of reality, definitions of what is political, concepts of community, and other elements of our political culture."[13]

Newspapers

Nearly five million copies of close to 100 Canadian newspapers are published daily and they are read by 14 million Canadians every week. Rather than being based on independently owned operations, the Canadian newspaper industry has been characterized by concentrated chain ownership for decades, although the names and faces have changed. By 2009, many of the traditional names had disappeared; in their place, the Asper family owned 13 daily newspapers (including the *National Post*) in addition to the CanWest Global television network, and the Péladeau family owned 37 dailies under the Quebecor/Sun Media label along with a French-language TV network. Transcontinental had ten; Glacier Ventures had nine; the Desmarais (Power Corp.) chain had seven; Torstar had four; and the Irving family owned the three English dailies in New Brunswick. CTVglobemedia owned the *Globe and Mail* as well as the CTV television network, and several small chains and independents completed the picture, as seen in Table 12.1. It is still true, however, that many of the wealthiest families in the country control much of the daily newspaper industry, and in some cases one owner has a monopoly in a single province (Irving in New Brunswick) or metropolitan area (CanWest in Vancouver).

Concentrated ownership of Canadian newspapers has always caused considerable concern in some quarters. Many fear that the owner of several papers will gain an unhealthy degree of influence over public opinion by establishing a common point of view for all papers in the chain. This anxiety deepened when there appeared to be collusion *between* the Southam and Thomson chains in 1980. These actions prompted an investigation under the Combines Act, and charges of collusion were laid. Nothing demonstrates the weakness of Canadian competition laws as much as the acquittal of Thomson and Southam chains of these charges,[14] although an earlier case against Irving's monopoly in New Brunswick met the same fate in the courts.

The incident led the Trudeau government to appoint the **Kent Royal Commission on Newspapers**, which called for some divestment of existing ownership as well as rigid control of future concentrations. Tom Kent expressed concern with the degree to which newspapers were involved in the ownership of radio and television stations, cable TV, and magazines, and recommended restrictions on multimedia holdings. He also sought to ensure that individual newspaper editors had complete autonomy so that they could not be told how to do their job by a common corporate owner. Under strong corporate pressure, however, the government took no action.[15]

When Conrad Black was a dominant force in the industry, he created considerable alarm because of his strong ideological perspective.[16] The Asper family turned out to be even more insistent than Black that their newspapers speak with one voice, namely their own. They prepared national editorials that had to be carried by every newspaper in the chain and with which local editorials could not disagree; they regularly spiked (that is, denied publication of) items, including editorial cartoons, to which they objected; they fired columnists, editors, or publishers who did not share their point of view; and they established a bureau at company headquarters to coordinate news coverage for all papers in the chain. At first, they were particularly insistent that their newspapers and television stations be supportive of Prime Minister Chrétien domestically and of Israel on the international front. But following the lead of the *National Post*, which they had bought from Conrad Black, they later turned to the right. In the 2006 election campaign owner Lawrence Asper publicly endorsed Stephen

TABLE 12.1 Chain Ownership of Canadian Daily Newspapers, 2009		
Owner	*Number*	*Examples*
Quebecor/Sun Media	37	*Toronto Sun, Sudbury Star, Le Journal de Montreal*
CanWest MediaWorks	13	*National Post, Ottawa Citizen, Calgary Herald, Vancouver Sun*
Transcontinental	10	*St. John's Telegram, Cape Breton Post, Moose Jaw Times-Herald*
Glacier Ventures	9	*Kimberley Daily Bulletin, Kamloops Daily News*
Power Corp.	7	*La Presse* (Montreal), *Le Soleil* (Quebec), *Le Droit* (Ottawa)
Torstar	4	*Toronto Star, Hamilton Spectator*
Brunswick News	3	*New Brunswick Telegraph Journal, Moncton Times & Transcript*
Continental	3	*Kelowna Daily Courier, Thunder Bay Chronicle Herald*
Alta Newspaper Group	3	*Lethbridge Herald, Medicine Hat News*
FP Canadian Newspapers	2	*Winnipeg Free Press, Brandon Sun*
CTVGlobemedia	1	*Globe and Mail*
Smaller chains & Independents	7	*Le Devoir* (Montreal), *Halifax Chronicle-Herald*

Source: Canadian Newspaper Association, About Newspapers—Ownership, cited on March 31, 2009, available at http://www.cna-acj.ca/en/aboutnewspapers/ownership.

Harper at a Conservative party rally. These initiatives confirmed the worst fears of what can happen when a large number of media outlets have a single owner who is determined to mould Canadians' thinking on public issues.

Many newspapers can now be read in whole or in part online. According to the Canadian Newspaper Association, 17 percent of Canadians read a daily newspaper on the Internet, although most of them also read the printed edition. Another new feature of the industry is free dailies. Five ownership groups now publish about 35 free daily newspapers in Canada, with an estimated daily circulation of 1.3 million copies. The largest are Torstar/Metro International (*Metro*) and Quebecor (*24 Hours*), both publishing free dailies in Toronto, Ottawa, Edmonton, Calgary, and Vancouver. Such developments do not bode well for the traditional newspaper industry.

Broadcasting

The radio and television industries are distinct from newspapers in two respects: the degree of government regulation involved—primarily through the **Canadian Radio-television and Telecommunications Commission**—and the public ownership of the English CBC and French Radio-Canada networks.

Canadians' radio listening has declined to about 18.3 hours per week on average.[17] The publicly owned **Canadian Broadcasting Corporation (CBC)** accounted for more than 12 percent of total listening in 2007, with the CBC being the favourite of university graduates, those in professional occupations, and seniors. Through hundreds of transmitter stations, coverage is almost nationwide. In addition, CBC operates northern services and Radio-Canada International. CBC radio has a sophisticated audience and plays a major role in transmitting information and opinion among Canadians in its extended newscasts and public affairs programs.

Apart from CBC/Radio-Canada, the Canadian radio industry consists of nearly 650 local, mostly private, stations, with FM now vastly exceeding AM in listeners. These stations put varying degrees of effort into newsgathering and public affairs programming. Stations used to be independently owned, but are increasingly characterized by chain ownership, just as in the newspaper industry. Ownership changes frequently, and over 60 percent of the radio market in Canada is controlled by the ten leading firms. Like newspapers, radio stations must be Canadian-owned, but the limited Canadian content on private radio stations became a problem. Since they mainly transmit music, the CRTC issued Canadian-content rules (35 percent of music played on a radio station between 6 a.m. and midnight must qualify as Canadian content according to CTRC conditions), as noted in Chapter 10. In 2005, the CRTC authorized satellite radio with what many observers felt were inadequate Canadian-content guarantees.

The average Canadian also watches about 22 hours of television per week and depends on that medium for most of his or her political information. The publicly owned CBC/Radio-Canada has stations across the country, with English production centred in Toronto and French production in Montreal. These are supplemented by agreements with several privately owned affiliated stations, which telecast a certain amount of CBC programming. This usually includes national news and public affairs, but not always drama or more sophisticated cultural programs.

The CBC also established its Newsworld channel in 1989 and its French equivalent, RDI, in 1995. These all-news channels cover many political events live and more extensively than the regular CBC, with which they work closely, and provide much regional coverage, documentaries, and in-depth interview programming. Newsworld is available only on cable or satellite, and although its audience is small, most members of the political elite tune in regularly. Keen observers of Canadian politics also watch the national parliamentary channel, now called the Cable Public Affairs Channel (CPAC), run by the cable companies. In some provinces another channel carries provincial legislative proceedings, and several provinces have educational television channels.

CBC television has a strong commitment to Canadian programming but suffers from a chronic shortage of funds. After severe bloodletting under the Mulroney government and the appointment of hostile members to its board of directors, the CBC had reason to expect better treatment under the Chrétien regime. Instead, that government slashed the CBC

Peter Mansbridge holds up his Gemini Award for Best News Anchor at the awards ceremony in 2003. Most Canadians get their political information from television.

budget even further, precipitating the resignation of the corporation's president. More major cuts occurred on the Harper watch in 2009.

On the private side of television, the CTV network consists of more than 24 stations centred in CFTO in Toronto; it also operates a 24-hours cable news channel and other specialty channels, and has ownership connections to *The Globe and Mail*. The Toronto-based CanWest Global system, owned by the Asper family of Winnipeg, now considers itself to be the third national English-language network, along with its own specialty channels. Several major cities also have one or more independent private English stations. On the French side, the TVA network, owned by Péladeau (Quebecor), is centred in Télé-Métropole in Montreal.

At least 85 percent of Canadian homes subscribe to cable or satellite television, more than in any other country. Cable stations receive television signals from large satellite dishes and transmit them by means of cables to individual subscribers. To some extent the CRTC regulates which channels they carry, but in general, cable television is designed to bring the major U.S. networks into almost every Canadian home. This gives most Canadians two chances to view popular U.S. shows— either on the originating network or on CTV or Global, which bid ferociously for such programs. The Canadian cable industry is dominated by the giants of Canadian television and radio: Rogers Communications, Shaw Cablesystems, Vidéotron, and Cogeco Inc. The variety of other channels on cable television, some of them of Canadian origin, is constantly increasing, but the more channels a subscriber desires, the higher the fee he or she must pay. As mentioned in Chapter 10, popular and industry pressure forced the CRTC to allow such a wide range of U.S. channels to be available on Canadian cable television, and in the 1990s, it authorized the first direct-to-home (DTH) satellite service.[18] The increase in the number of specialty, pay-per-view, and digital channels has served to dilute even further the audience of the conventional Canadian television stations.

Requiring Canadian television stations to be domestically owned or to telecast 50 percent or more Canadian content is virtually meaningless when almost all residents are within reach of a large assortment of U.S. television channels. On this point, Fred Fletcher talks of "American images crowding out Canadian ones,"[19] and Ed Black writes of the problem of trying to serve a small population in two language groups "who live in tempting, embarrassing, and almost smothering proximity to [ten times as many] Americans who speak the language of Canada's majority…. They also have the world's most penetrating and effective system for transmitting ideas en masse."[20] Peter Trueman adds:

I have felt for years that the greatest threat to Canada's integrity as a nation is not the crisis in Quebec ... but American television.... Think of the overwhelming preponderance of American programming, which in an unobtrusive way pumps us full of American values, American hopes, American history, even American patterns of speech.[21]

Although the CBC has recently gone to an almost all-Canadian format in prime-time hours, the private stations and networks realize that profits can generally be maximized by telecasting as much U.S. programming as the CRTC will allow. The production of Canadian programs on CTV and Global, apart from newscasts, is minimal. The most popular television shows among Canadian anglophones are all American, but we should not underestimate the attraction of Canadian national newscasts, *Hockey Night in Canada*, *This Hour Has 22 Minutes*, *Canada AM*, *The Morning News*, *the fifth estate*, *Marketplace*, *Téléjournal*, *Le Point*, and *W5*.

Figure 12.1 illustrates the percentage of time Canadians spend watching different types of television programs. Francophones watch more news and public affairs than anything else, while anglophones watch more drama. In terms of origin, francophones watch 65 percent Canadian content, compared with anglophones' 28 percent; in fact, in every category, francophones watch more Canadian content than anglophones. The latter watch more Canadian than foreign coverage in only one category—news and public affairs. What is probably most troubling is the low proportion of Canadian content in the drama category, especially on the anglophone side. In this sensitive situation, it is almost unbelievable that the CRTC would fail to enforce the Canadian-content commitments, especially in the drama category; that

. . . .

Figure 12.1 Percentage of Television Viewing Time Spent Watching Different Types of Programs, Canadian and Foreign, Anglophones and Francophones, 2004

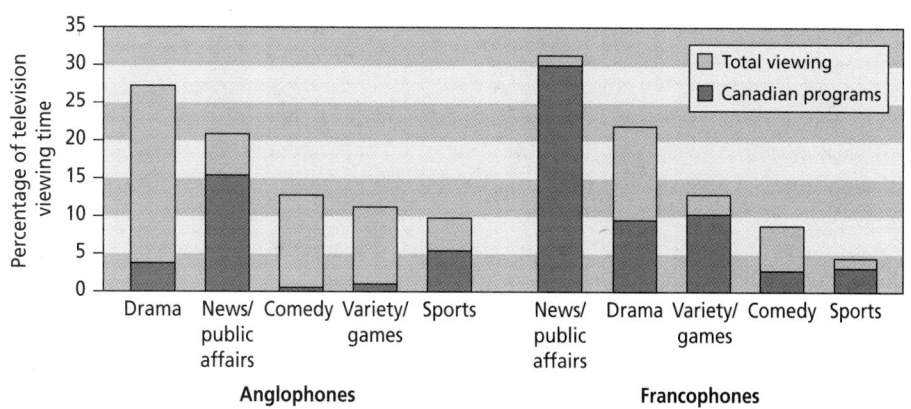

Source: Adapted from: Statistics Canada. Television Viewing: Data Tables. Sept. 21 to Dec. 21, 2003, released March 31, 2005. Catalogue 87F0006XIE.

it would continue to license numerous new American cable channels; and that successive federal governments would underfund the CBC.[22]

The Changing Media World

The basic political function of the mass media—to provide comprehensive and fair coverage of all aspects of the political system—is always open for debate, but few aspects of that system are under such drastic and interrelated change. David Taras has summarized the changes in the media world as a convergence of technologies, of news and entertainment, of cultures, and of corporations.[23] The first involves the merging of television, telephone, satellite, cable, and Internet technologies. Wireless carriers now offer television service on cellphones via the Internet and telephone companies are applying for licences to offer TV over their phone lines, all of which is creating a nightmare for the CRTC as it tries to protect Canadian content.[24] The convergence of news and entertainment relates primarily to making television news more entertaining while reducing its serious content, and the convergence of cultures refers to the expansion of American popular culture around the world.

The convergence of corporations is now rampant; in fact, it is almost impossible to keep up with the media conglomerations that have taken place in the United States. But the same tendency can be seen in Canada, and the four largest mass media conglomerates are listed in Table 12.2. The table reveals that the cross-media ownership often includes owning newspapers and television stations in the same cities. In a severely criticized ruling that was especially helpful to the Asper empire, the CRTC decided that a company that owned both newspapers and television stations would be allowed to have its reporters gather and exchange information freely with one another, although the management of such news operations was supposed to be kept separate. The CRTC has recently adopted new rules of media ownership that should preclude any further concentration of ownership.

Few if any of these changes are positive for the vital place of the media in the Canadian political system. Television, with its convergence of news and entertainment, provides a more superficial understanding of political developments than newspapers. Since reliance on television in English Canada usually means exposure to American television, this tendency detracts from public knowledge in a second way (the convergence of cultures). The increased concentration of ownership of newspapers, radio, and television (the convergence of corporations) is not a healthy development in any democracy that values the maximum diversity of opinions. Such ownership only enhances the predominance of the right-wing opinion already amply supplied by radio talk-show hosts, think tanks, columnists, and pundits. However, the opposite trend toward a fragmentation of audiences allows individuals to ignore broader public questions as they expose themselves to media coverage of only a few personal interests.

Many parts of the media industry have recently experienced economic trouble, and most have cut corners in order to stay in business, such that political news is often sacrificed in the process. Besides the general deterioration of political coverage, there has been a serious decline in local coverage—fewer local television and newspaper voices. The severe economic turndown of 2008–09 has only exacerbated such problems, including budgetary cuts at the CBC. Meanwhile, private networks use this excuse to sell unprofitable local stations and seek reductions in CRTC Canadian content regulations.

TABLE 12.2	The Four Largest Multimedia Conglomerates in Canada, 2009		
CanWest Global	**CTVglobemedia**	**Quebecor**	**Rogers**
conventional TV stations (including E! Channel)	CTV television network	daily newspapers	cable television and telephones
specialty channels	specialty channels	TVA television network	specialty channels
daily newspapers	*The Globe & Mail*	Internet services	Internet services
magazines	CHUM radio and television stations (A Channel)	publishing	magazines
Internet services		cable television	radio stations and telephones
Alliance/Atlantis Communications		magazines	video rentals
news service		video rentals	CITY-TV network

The Internet

Probably even more significant than changes in the existing media industry is the impact of the Internet. It is starting to rival newspapers, radio, and television as a medium of mass communications, in addition to its other functions.[25] Like them, it can be used as a source of information and entertainment; indeed, as one of its features, the Internet actually provides access to the other three forms of mass media and has had a negative effect on the newsprint and newspaper industries. Looked at another way, the three traditional media increasingly rely on the Internet to supplement their offerings, and regularly refer their audiences to their websites. Statistics Canada estimates that people in more than 60 percent of Canadian households own personal computers and that 68 percent of Canadians have access to the Internet at home, work, or school. Those who cannot afford to buy a computer or an Internet service can usually find free online access at university, college, or public libraries, and students who cannot afford to buy a good daily newspaper can now read it online!

In addition to providing an alternative source of coverage of topical political developments, the Internet is a vast reservoir of information, including websites of newspapers, television networks, Parliament, the courts, government departments and agencies, political parties, advocacy groups, and other actors in the political system. Among other things, the Internet is now an integrated part of parties' and many candidates' election campaigns. It often allows for direct and instantaneous feedback between the sender and receiver, brings together print and electronic communication methods into a single medium, and allows for the targeting of small segments of the population.

As quickly as society's dependence on the Internet grows, its potential has not yet been fully realized, and exciting new technological devices are being developed at a rapid pace. Although the Internet is a liberating force that permits people to gain information, connect with others who have similar concerns, and provide direct feedback to government, it does have a negative side. A "digital divide" still exists, largely based on age and class, between those who use it and those who don't, and it can also be used for antisocial purposes. As mentioned, it is also threatening the whole future of the newspaper industry, which has been such an important source of political information in the past.

Another feature of the Internet is the blog, that is, a web-based, self-published opinion piece. To some extent, the political blogging world is a small, interacting community made up primarily of party insiders and those who work in the media. Some of the party insiders are dissidents who use blogs to express unauthorized opinions, and some of the media types employ blogs to supplement their more orthodox output. Stephen Harper expelled Garth Turner from the Conservative party caucus in part because of the critical comments he made on his personal blog. The most prominent collection of bloggers in Canada is sponsored by *Maclean's* magazine—see www.macleans.ca/blogcentral. But anyone can become a blogger and many people participate in the discussion boards that media companies and other organizations establish on their websites. It is too early to evaluate the political significance of blogs in Canada, but it is apparent that members of the media use them as one of their sources, and some claim that blogging has already had some influence on the wider political world. The same might be said of YouTube and various social networking sites, such as Facebook and Twitter. These innovations are not primarily used for political purposes, but they occasionally can have an impact.[26]

The Media and the Public

PUBLIC PERCEPTIONS OF THE MEDIA

The influence of the mass media in the political system is profound and appears to be constantly increasing.[27] Most of the information Canadians receive about the political process comes from television, newspapers, radio, or the Internet, rather than from direct observation or other sources, such as books or magazines. Some recipients may be able to separate this information from whatever commentary or biases accompany it, but many are also swayed by the particular perspective that the media give to the data they present. When asked about their preferred medium for political information out of the three traditional sources, between 50 percent and 60 percent of people choose television, 25 percent to 30 percent prefer newspapers, and about 10 percent, radio.[28] Figure 12.2 shows the results of a 2003 survey of "frequent consumers" of news about their reliance on five different media. While television was in the lead, most such frequent consumers—quite likely peer-group opinion leaders—exposed themselves to more than one media source. Rather than having a direct impact on virtually every individual, in fact, it is likely that the media primarily influence such peer-group

Figure 12.2   Exposure to Different News Sources Among "Frequent Consumers" of News

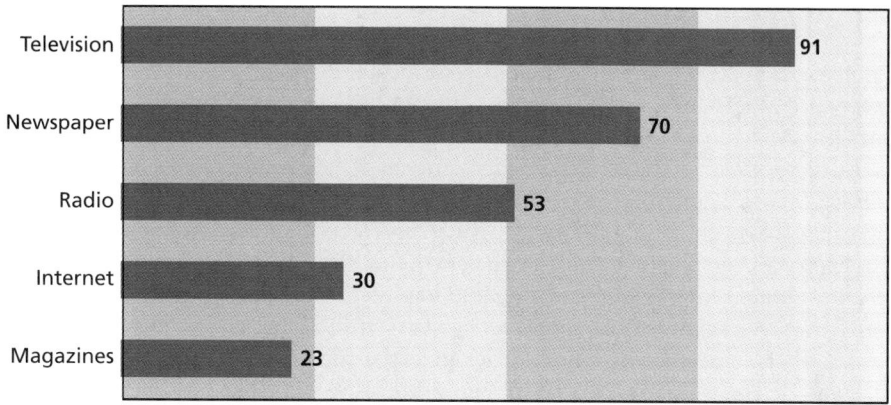

% of Frequent Consumers of News Aged 19 and Older

Source: Statistics Canada. Leslie-Anne Keown. Keeping Up with the Times: Canadians and Their News Media Diet. Canadian Social Trends, Statistics Canada, March 2007. Catalogue No. 11-008-XWE.

leaders—those people who pay close attention to political developments—who then, in turn, transmit this information and opinion to those around them.

It is usually said that the two most important effects of the media on the general public and opinion leaders alike are in the realm of setting the political agenda for the country and framing the issues.[29] In other words, the media tell people what to think about, what the important issues are, and which political personalities are significant. They help to define what is political. This is a function the media share with political parties and other institutions, and although the latter may be more important as initiators of issues, these will not likely remain on the agenda without media attention. Any given event can be "framed," that is, presented and explained, in a number of ways. A general election may be framed by journalists as a horserace among the party leaders, as a contest among ideologies and principles, or several other ways.[30]

The **parliamentary press gallery** is a key player in developing a consensus about what the issues are and how they should be framed.[31] In part, this reflects the influence of the daily Question Period in the House of Commons, which provides gallery reporters with snippets of controversial issues that are well suited to media, especially television, coverage. Reporters are also increasingly dependent on government hand-outs because they lack the time and expertise to indulge in much investigative journalism. In addition to their representatives in the press gallery, all media outlets receive wire or news services. The most important is Canadian Press, an agency collectively owned by member newspapers, which hires several CP reporters in Ottawa and wires their stories to all outlets. Stories originating in other cities by reporters of individual papers are sent to Canadian Press, rewritten, and wired to all other members. Canadian Press also has an electronic outlet, Broadcast News (BN). CP has been weakened in recent years by the withdrawal of CanWest and Quebecor, which have both set up their own news services. Many media outlets have closed their individual bureaus in Ottawa, and in relying on news services instead, do not provide the coverage of stories of local interest that they did in the past.

THE REALITY OF DIFFERENT MEDIA COVERAGE

Public perceptions of the merits of the different media, especially that television is superior to newspapers, are somewhat distressing to those who know the real advantages and disadvantages. Because of cost and time constraints, television is restricted in the number of items it can cover in any newscast and must present a shorter and more superficial account of political events than either radio or newspapers. It cannot present the whole story or very many stories, and such editing necessarily involves selection or bias on someone's part. In a 60- to 90-second "news clip" with a 10-second "sound bite" of the actual voice of political leaders, how something is said is usually more important than what is said. Recent research indicates that the length of the sound bite is even decreasing, and "Canadians are rarely exposed to their leaders for anything longer than the time it takes for them to blurt out 8 or 10 words."[32] The transcript of a 30-minute newscast would make up about one-third of a single newspaper page.[33]

Moreover, because it is a visual medium, television must aim to show colourful, dramatic, emotional, conflictual, or entertaining pictures. Riots, demonstrations, and political conventions usually make good television, but the daily routine of politics does not lend itself as well to compelling visual coverage. Witness the efforts taken by politicians and the media to find contrived and engaging settings in which to stage political happenings, make announcements, or tape interviews. From Question Period to election campaigns, political events are now designed to appeal to television's definition of the news. Television portrays images and impressions and is therefore much better at dealing with political leaders and personalities than with issues. When John Turner issued a 40-point policy manifesto just before the 1988 election, for example, "the electronic media ... could not cope with such a cornucopia of ideas that had not been predigested into a simple theme wrapped around a few easily grasped issues."[34]

These characteristics make television more open to distortion and exploitation, with the result that it may well be the least believable and most biased of the three media.[35] Television meets the needs of the average citizen with a short attention span who is looking for visual stimulation and who does not want to invest too much effort in understanding the political system.

This situation is exacerbated by the increasing tendency of political parties and politicians to gear their activities to the demands of television. Press conferences are now dominated by television lights and cameras; leaders' tours during election campaigns are "photo opportunities"; party conventions and leaders' debates are scheduled for maximum airtime; and governments convey public information via catchy, superficial television commercials rather than in detailed newspaper advertisements or pamphlets. In addition, in preparing for elections, parties put greater effort into designing television commercials and trying them out before focus groups than in devising solutions to the country's problems. The televised leaders' debate has become the single most important event in an election campaign, and elections may turn more on leaders' images than issues, policies, local candidates, or other leading figures in the party. The appearance, style, and general image of the party leader, including his or her ability to perform on television, have become of crucial importance.[36] This increasing emphasis on appearance, largely because of television, is often said to trivialize politics. Unfortunately,

Canada has one of the lowest rates of daily newspaper circulation and one of the highest rates of television-viewing among Western industrialized states; in other words, it suffers from a condition known as "television-dependency."[37] Distinct from newscasts, however, all-news channels like CBC Newsworld (now CBC news network), CPAC, and public affairs programs on other channels, have the time to delve into political issues in more depth, and students of Canadian politics are well advised to watch them.

Newspapers generally offer more comprehensive coverage of political events, presenting both greater factual information and a wider range of interpretation. Furthermore, the broadcast media and opposition parties tend to take their cues from newspapers. Although television is the most important channel for the distribution of news, daily newspapers remain the major news-gathering institutions in the media system.[38] In his account of newspaper coverage of the 2004 election campaign, Christopher Waddell was struck by the steady shift at newspapers from straight news reporting to providing context and analysis, which readers would not get from all-news channels and the Internet. Newspapers devoted more space to columns and less to news stories, and some journalists switched back and forth during the campaign between being reporters and commentator/columnists.[39]

Thus, although the "average" Canadian relies on television for political information, those with political influence—whether in government, parties, advocacy groups, or peer-group situations—depend on newspapers. Those who prefer newspapers over television have higher educations, higher incomes, and are better informed, and the degree of political participation increases sharply with a person's level of newspaper consumption. In other words, those who make the effort to increase their political information by reading a newspaper are not only better informed but are also most likely to go on to engage in some form of political participation.[40]

Among newspapers, *The Globe and Mail* is read by nearly three-quarters of Canada's top-level decision makers across the country and more than 90 percent of media executives; it thus tends to set the agenda for other news organizations, including the Canadian Press.[41] The independent but financially troubled *Le Devoir* occupies a somewhat similar position in French Canada. It is likely that few beyond the political elite read or are influenced by the editorials in such newspapers, however, and there is little evidence that editorial endorsement has much impact on the outcome of elections.[42]

The Media and the Politicians

Politicians need publicity and therefore have a great interest in how the media cover their behaviour. Even though they and their bureaucratic advisers have their own direct sources, these authorities also depend on the media to provide information they need about what is happening at home and abroad. The media, in turn, rely on the authorities for much of their information. A number of issues arise from this mutually dependent relationship.

POLITICIANS AND MEDIA OWNERS

In the newspaper era, when papers were individually owned by their editor, newspaper owners were generally on friendly terms with politicians, and regular confidential consultations took place. Several editors, including Joseph Howe and George Brown, were politicians themselves, and one politician, Henri Bourassa, founded a newspaper, *Le Devoir*. Most papers had a partisan perspective that was evident in both their news columns and editorials. However, such factors as chain ownership, the quest for a mass audience, and the public expectation that partisanship be restricted to the editorial page have changed the relationship between politicians and media owners. Indeed, to a large extent, the party press has been replaced by the critical press.[43] Some newspapers do retain partisan views (the *Toronto Star*—Liberal, the *National Post*—Conservative), and the Asper family seems to be a throwback to an earlier era.

POLITICIANS AND JOURNALISTS

A second issue is the relationship between working journalists and politicians. Both groups are essentially engaged in the same business, one needing publicity and the other, information. In principle, reporters should maintain enough distance from politicians to cover them objectively; however, it is often necessary to cultivate close relations to get the kind of information the media seek. Journalists also worry that a critical account of a politician on one occasion may jeopardize a good story the next time around.

Furthermore, since politicians often confidentially seek out the opinions of reporters, the latter sometimes have to agonize over whether to reveal information that was given to them "off the record"—that is, in the expectation that it will not be used. There is also the question of whether the media should transmit information that they are not supposed to have, such as when Global Television came into advance possession of a summary of the 1988 budget. Another problem the media have to face is how much privacy to leave politicians. When do a politician's personal habits or health problems begin to interfere with his or her public functions, and when should they be revealed?[44]

These issues also relate to the complex legal question of libel, often defined as "a false statement about a person that is to his or her discredit."[45] In general, the media in Canada are cautious in what they write or broadcast, and the politicians are fairly thick-skinned, so that court cases involving libel are relatively rare. Less serious instances of media bias or error are supposed to be handled by the CRTC, individual companies' "ombudsmen," or voluntary press councils.

NEWS MANAGEMENT

"News leaks" are yet another issue in the relations between media and politicians. When governments do not know what course to follow, they sometimes leak a proposal to the media as a "trial balloon," hoping for guidance from the kind of reaction received. Ed Black points out that this practice is necessary because today's politicians usually have little time to respond to problems and little chance to sit back and give them comprehensive consideration.[46]

Leaks are part of a broader problem of **news management** and manipulation, which appears to be increasingly common.[47] This relates especially to the timing and selective distribution of information, exaggerating the positive while keeping secret or past deadline time that which is negative, giving preference to friendly reporters over others, making prime ministerial requests for network television time for less than important announcements, or outright lying. News management also involves putting the best face on an unpopular government action or a politician's performance by having a partisan official tell the media how successful it actually was, in the hope that the media will transmit this evaluation to their audience. Those involved in such efforts are often called "media handlers" or **spin doctors**, because they try to put the best face, or "spin," on any event. As noted in Chapter 21, one of the most important parts of a Memorandum to Cabinet proposing new government action is the communications strategy. And, as Fletcher and Everett point out, the 200 members of the press gallery are greatly outnumbered by the government communications officers.[48] The Harper government started out being much less accessible to reporters than its predecessors, maintaining strict centralized control over the flow of information and insisting on choosing which reporters asked questions at news conferences.

An even more serious aspect of news management is censorship under the Official Secrets Act (now euphemistically renamed the Security of Information Act) or the War Measures Act (now replaced by the Emergencies Act). In 1970, for example, the media were prohibited from transmitting any stories that supported the FLQ. Short of actual censorship is the highly secretive tradition of Canadian governments. In 1982, however, the Access to Information Act made it somewhat easier for the media and other interested parties to obtain access to government information. The events of September 11, 2001, and the subsequent U.S. "war on terrorism" have provided an excuse for the government to function more secretively again, and contrary to expectations, the Harper government's Accountability Act did not provide for greater access to government information.

The ultimate problem in media–government relations is political interference with the "freedom of the press," or as the Charter of Rights puts it, "freedom of press and other media of communication." This is one of the sacred principles of democracy, as discussed in Chapter 11. The most blatant examples of such political interference have occurred at the provincial level. In Quebec, Maurice Duplessis kept the press under control by awarding advertising and printing contracts to newspaper owners and financial gifts to members of the press gallery.[49] In Alberta, the Social Credit government in the 1930s deliberately tried to force newspapers to retract any criticisms of the government. Occasional attempts have been made by the Prime Minister's Office over the years to have the CBC take a certain perspective on a vital national issue. Much has been written—both claiming and refuting bias—about the CBC's coverage of the Meech Lake Accord. Government pressure was also suspected in 1998 when the CBC suspended reporter Terry Milewski, who covered the APEC summit in Vancouver. On the French side, the Trudeau government accused the Radio-Canada network of being riddled with separatists who gave a biased interpretation of federal–provincial relations. Although there was probably some truth to the charge, it smacked of political interference.

. . . .

PUBLIC OPINION POLLS

Opinions are more specific, numerous, and changeable than the values and attitudes that were the subject of Chapter 11. Although very unstable, opinions about topical issues and current personalities often affect the political behaviour of individuals, especially in voting, and polls of the public's opinions frequently influence the actions of government.

Measuring Public Opinion

The phrase **public opinion** is sometimes used to imply that all members of the public hold a unanimous, informed view on a particular issue. In actuality, many opinions are held on any issue, and each issue interests only a certain segment of the population. Furthermore, most

ALRIGHT... OTHER THAN POLITICAL POLLSTERS, WHAT DO YOU CONSIDER THE GREATEST THREAT FACING OUR NATION?

Graham Harrop/artizans.com

Man considers political pollsters a threat to nation.

political opinions are not well informed. They are based on little information, they are simplifications of complex issues, and they are often internally contradictory. Indeed, it is frequently the case that people form their opinions first and then look for information to confirm them; at the very least, they "seek out information that conforms to their predispositions ... and avoid or reinterpret any contrary and non-supportive messages."[50]

Given this great conglomeration of viewpoints, public opinion is very difficult to gauge. Haphazard methods, such as reading editorials or letters to the editor or listening to open-line programs, are obviously unreliable, but so are many amateur public opinion surveys. However, professional polling agencies claim to be able to select a representative sample of people, ask carefully worded questions, and report with a high degree of accuracy the opinions of the whole population. Such polls have assumed an immense importance in contemporary Canadian politics: "no political party plans campaign strategy without them, no government is prepared to risk major policy initiatives without gauging public opinion, and for major news organizations they are an indispensable reporting tool, both between and during elections."[51]

Beyond the now common procedure for conducting a public opinion poll, two special techniques deserve mention. The first is "tracking," in which a polling firm telephones samples of hundreds of people nightly during an election campaign to see how day-to-day developments are affecting the various parties and to detect any shifting momentum. The results may well cause a party to change its approach. The second special technique is the "focus group," in which a party or candidate engages a firm to gather a number of people together with a professional moderator. The client, who watches the proceedings from behind a one-way mirror, will have previously worked out with the moderator what the respondents will be asked or shown, in the hope of capturing their "gut reaction." This can include their views on various leaders, issues, commercials, themes, or slogans, which can be presented in a variety of forms—text, pictures, graphics, jingles, and so on.

Who are these professional pollsters? Although the Canadian branch of the Gallup Poll has operated in Canada since 1941, political and governmental polling did not begin in earnest until about 1960. The Liberal and Conservative parties originally hired U.S. polling companies but then designated official party pollsters, Martin Goldfarb and Allan Gregg (Decima), respectively. Both of these pollsters also had corporate clients and did frequent, lucrative work for government departments when their respective parties were in power. Canada now possesses many successful public opinion polling companies that are regularly hired by media outlets, political parties, advocacy groups, governments, or government departments, and some of them are listed below. All of them also do much non-political polling, and many of them have become Canadian multinationals. A number of lobbying firms, especially Earnscliffe Strategy Group and Hill and Knowlton, also do polling as part of their comprehensive consulting work.

. . . .

LEADING PUBLIC OPINION POLLING FIRMS

- Nanos Research
- Angus Reid Strategies
- Compas Public Opinion and Customer Research
- Harris-Decima
- Ekos Research Associates
- Environics Research Group
- Ipsos Reid
- Leger Marketing
- Pollara Public Opinion and Market Research
- Strategic Counsel

These professional polling companies all have slightly different methodologies, but exactly how accurate are they? The only way a survey's accuracy can be tested is through a comparison of its results immediately before an election with the electoral outcome itself. The immediate pre-election findings of most professional agencies have usually been within the range of accuracy that the survey claimed, typically that the results were accurate within plus or minus four percent 19 times out of 20, but exceptional inaccurate predictions do occur.

When two or more firms are seeking the same information but produce different results, doubts naturally arise about their methodology. The way a question is worded, the optional responses available, the sequence of the questions, the degree to which respondents are telling the truth, and many other variables can influence the result and account for such differences. Timing is also an important consideration because results can sometimes be out of date by the time they are tabulated and reported. In the June 2004 election, almost all of the polls underestimated the Liberal vote. Pollsters explained this inaccuracy by claiming that a large shift in voter preference occurred in the last two days of the campaign. They rejected the frequently heard argument that telephone polling had become less accurate because so many people now possess cell (mobile) phones with numbers that are not listed in a directory. In January 2006, the pollsters were closer, with SES Research (now Nanos Research) the most accurate, as seen in Table 12.3.

The Importance of Polls in Elections

Public opinion polls are closely connected to elections. One main issue that arises in this connection is whether the pre-election predictions of such polls influence the actual election results. This question cannot be answered categorically, but it is unlikely that their direct effect is that great. First, most voters do not pay much attention to the poll results; second, not everyone believes them; and third, it is not important to everyone to vote for the winning side, even if this is clear in advance. Although some voters may want to jump on the victorious bandwagon—the **bandwagon effect**—at least a few are likely to switch to the predicted loser—"the underdog effect"—either out of sympathy or to try to prevent a majority victory for the prospective winner.[52]

However, polls may have a significant indirect effect on the election results. The media are as obsessed with the polls as the politicians are, and the survey results may well cause the

TABLE 12.3   SES Research Poll on Final Voting Preference versus Election Results (Percentage of Votes), 2006

	SES Research Prediction	*Election Results*
Conservatives	36.4	36.3
Liberals	30.1	30.2
NDP	17.4	17.5
BQ	10.6	10.5
Other	5.6	5.5

Source: SES Research poll released January 22, 2006 and Election Results January 23, 2006. Reproduced with permission of SES Research. www.sesresearch.com

media to concentrate on those parties and politicians who are in the lead, or ignore those who are trailing. Furthermore, polls have a considerable effect on party morale. A positive poll usually generates greater enthusiasm and effort, better candidates, and larger financial contributions, while a negative poll saps the spirit of leaders, candidates, and foot soldiers alike. Both of these results undoubtedly affect the subtle "momentum" of the campaign.

Another issue can be addressed more categorically: polls definitely detract from the discussion of real issues in the election campaign.[53] The media are fascinated by polls primarily because they are good for business, and, given the media's ability to influence the political agenda even during election campaigns, they emphasize the **horse-race effect** of the contest. The media tend to spend more time on trying to determine who is ahead than on comparative analysis of party platforms, asking leaders to comment on the latest poll results, for example, rather than on how the party would deal with a particular public problem. Now that the media actually hire polling firms, survey results are becoming major news items in themselves.[54] To avoid this criticism, the CBC has a policy of not conducting public opinion surveys during an election campaign; however, it is not above reporting on polls done by others. Polls sometimes also affect the voter turnout rate by generating feelings of complacency or hopelessness.

Many political losers have blamed their fate on the public opinion polls and some have called for the prohibition of polls during part or all of the campaign. Such bans do exist in many countries.[55] Whatever their faults, however, polls enliven the campaign and increase the information available, and many argue that to prohibit their publication in the media would not prevent parties, candidates, and others from conducting their own surveys. The main effect of a publication ban would be to give certain crucial information to those who could afford to conduct a survey and to deny it to the general public, a highly undemocratic suggestion.[56]

One of the amendments to the Canada Elections Act made in the wake of the Royal Commission on Electoral Reform was to prohibit, in the final three days of the campaign, the broadcast, publication, or dissemination of the results of new or scientifically conducted opinion surveys that would identify a political party or candidate. This restriction was soon challenged by the Thomson and Southam newspaper chains as a violation of freedom of the press, and their challenge was upheld by the Supreme Court of Canada.[57] A ban on the publication of polls on election day itself was subsequently enacted, and the law requires polling organizations to provide a full account of their methodology.

In his book *Margin of Error*, Claire Hoy reveals how important public opinion polls were in the 1988 election campaign. First, the Conservatives used many publicly funded polls to determine their election platform. Second, the Liberals surveyed public opinion in Quebec to see if a Senate veto of the Free Trade Agreement would detract from their support in that province. Third, the NDP avoided the free trade issue (and left the Liberals to capitalize on it) because party polling indicated that the NDP lacked public credibility on economic issues.[58] Indeed, the NDP used focus groups as early as 1984 to find that the phrase "ordinary Canadians" was preferable to "working Canadians" in its advertising.[59] When even the ideologically oriented NDP starts to base its strategy on focus groups and public opinion polls, it is hard to overstate their current significance.

Impact of Polls on the Authorities

Perhaps an even more significant question in the study of public opinion is the relationship between polls and the actions of the authorities.[60] For nearly 100 years after Confederation, governments had to act in the absence of a reliable survey, but governments nowadays spend huge sums of public funds on surveying public attitudes on various issues. A typical example was the polling done by the Liberal government before the 2000 pre-election budget. By using both traditional polls and focus groups, the Earnscliffe pollsters revealed that a majority of Canadians preferred a cut in the progressive income tax to a flat tax, as espoused by the Canadian Alliance, even if a flat tax would result in lower taxes for them personally. Such preferences were implemented in the budget, and Finance Minister Paul Martin's budget speech confidently ridiculed the flat tax approach. After criticizing the Liberal government for an excessive expenditure on public opinion polling, the Harper government was shown to have spent even more: it commissioned an average of two polls every working day in 2006–07 at a cost to taxpayers of $31 million.

Since opinion is likely to be considerably divided, however, polls do not always provide clear-cut policy guidance, and even when public opinion is clearly in favour of a certain course of government action, the authorities may decide otherwise. This may be the consequence of the politicians' own convictions, the recommendations of the public service, the pressure of advocacy groups and lobbyists, or the rigidity of party discipline. Indeed, some hold the view that even in a democracy, politicians are not obliged to follow public opinion; they may also lead it.[61] This is especially the case now that we realize how uninformed, superficial, and changeable most voters' opinions really are. Although politicians and bureaucrats may be accused of acting in their own self-interest if they do not follow a clear-cut preference among the public, they may actually be relying on a deeper understanding of the issue, the greater information at their disposal, a more sophisticated analysis of its implications, a concern for minority groups' rights, or a less prejudicial attitude. Capital punishment has been an issue on which public opinion was quite clear, for example, but one on which the authorities repeatedly went their own way. Should Parliament reinstate capital punishment in response to overwhelming popular opinion based on a mistaken impression about rising crime rates, a desire for retribution, and an assumption of deterrence?[62] Most political issues are even more complicated than capital punishment, and, on most, public opinion is much more divided; thus, the correlation between public opinion and public policy is not as strong as might be expected.

Christopher Page's study of this subject reinforces many of the observations made above.[63] In connection with the Trudeau initiative on constitutional reform in the early 1980s, Page observes that polls had little effect on the content of the Charter, but were useful in maintaining the government's resolve to go through with the reform as well as in designing the way to sell it to the public. Somewhat similarly, the Mulroney government had decided on the GST proposal before it did much polling; indeed, the policy was adopted in defiance of the polls. Nevertheless, government polling helped to decide the details of the policy (e.g., to exempt groceries) and how to reduce its unpopularity as it was communicated to the public. On gun control, the Chrétien government also made the decision to act before it polled the public on the subject. But Liberal polls which indicated a generally favourable public reaction were used to keep dissident MPs and provinces in line, and in the communications campaign with respect to implementation.

Thus, Page argues that on these three key issues, at least, the government policy was decided before it engaged in polling. Except perhaps on the GST, polling encouraged the government to pursue the policy upon which it had previously embarked, but it mostly affected government communications operations about a policy rather than the substance of the policy itself.[64] He also points out that in addition to their own polling, governments examine polls done by interest groups, the media, and other sources. Polls are used in every aspect of the policymaking process (outlined in Chapter 20), and are more often sponsored by the bureaucracy than ministers' offices or the Prime Minister's Office. Governments appreciate the security of a supportive poll, but they realize the superficiality of many peoples' opinions, and they actually lead public opinion as much as they follow it.[65]

It should be added that the incidence of and government reliance on public opinion polls severely undercuts the argument in favour of referendums. Public opinion polls already provide a quick, cheap, frequent, and accurate picture of the public's views, so there is little danger that the government will not know how the population feels about an issue.

. . . .

CONCLUSION

Students of political science and other readers of this book quite likely belong to the small proportion of the population for whom politics is a central concern and who are well informed about the subject. Such readers must be careful not to assume that the rest of the population is so well socialized into politics. In any case, this chapter has demonstrated the enormous significance of the media, especially television, daily newspapers, and increasingly the Internet, and documented the abundant use in all branches of politics of public opinion polls and polling firms. Individually and combined, the electronic media and public opinion polls have completely transformed Canadian politics in the past 50 years.

The media are central to many other aspects of the political system and are revisited in several other chapters. That particularly includes elections, political parties, and government—those in power and those in the House of Commons seeking to replace them. Indeed, the government and opposition are in a daily contest for favourable media coverage all aimed at improving their fortunes in the next elections. The media also constitute a vital link to Canada's external political environment, especially the United States. Public opinion polls are equally important for parties and in elections, but are also of daily significance in the policymaking process—by the party in power, the bureaucracy, and those whose responsibility it is to criticize their proposals. Political socialization is closely linked to the previous chapter on political culture.

© Of the approaches outlined in Chapter 1, class analysts have the greatest concerns about the subject matter of this chapter. They emphasize the deliberate attempt of the bourgeoisie to socialize the masses into an acceptance of the status quo. They argue that the public agents of socialization—the school and the media—transmit messages to serve the interests of the economic elite, the school through elite control of the political system, and the media through outright elite ownership. Traditional political parties and advocacy groups join in to help define politics in nonclass terms so that the lower classes are socialized into supporting a system that does not operate in their interests.[66] Socialization, in such observers' terms, is indoctrination into the virtues of capitalism.

Class analysts also have much to say about the political role of the media. First, nothing is as elitist in Canadian society as the ownership of newspapers and private radio and television stations, and such owners have been known to issue orders regarding coverage of political events. Second, the media elite also includes a small number of influential journalists and columnists from whom most of their colleagues take their lead. The media and political elites share socioeconomic characteristics and meet at social gatherings.[67] Third, even when owners do not deliberately interfere in the editorial operations of their companies, the media transmit role models and images of an elite version of reality. As Fletcher says, "the media tend to reinforce the dominant institutional and cultural patterns of authority. By setting the limits for public debate, the media generally exclude serious challenges to the status quo."[68] Some class analysts go further and argue that the media promote consumerism, the myth of "middle classness," and private ownership of property, and are "a powerful ideological weapon for holding the mass of people in voluntary submission to capitalism."[69]

The economic and political elites can use their control over the mass media to legitimate their power and reduce the extent to which they need to rely on coercion. Portraying protesters, radicals, and union leaders, among others, in an unfavourable light and trivializing political discourse will help enormously to maintain the status quo. Although the public is easily convinced of the dangers of public control of the media, it does not seem to be concerned about problems resulting from concentrated private ownership. It is even more difficult for the general public to see how state intervention—for example, regulating ownership—could protect the principle of freedom of the press.[70]

Wallace Clement and others point to the extent to which the richest and most powerful families in Canada either made their fortunes in the media business or else control media outlets alongside other interests.[71] They say, along with the Kent Report, that "freedom of the press is not a property right of owners."[72] The costs of establishing a new media outlet of any kind are prohibitive except to the wealthiest individuals in the land, and this pattern of ownership allows them to shield their economic operations from media scrutiny. Moreover, among the leading business pressure groups are the Canadian Association of Broadcasters (CAB), representing private radio and television companies, and the Canadian Newspaper Association. Through pressure on the CRTC and successive governments, the CAB has ensured its members a highly profitable position in the Canadian broadcasting system, while nothing so demonstrates the political dominance of the economic elite as the quick abandonment of the Kent Report because of pressure from the newspaper industry.

P In contrast, the pluralist approach emphasizes the multitude of media outlets in the country, including the increasing number of cable television channels and the creation of several morning tabloid newspapers, some of them free. People have many sources of information to choose from and considerable competition exists among them, although only a few large cities enjoy competitive daily newspapers. Pluralists also claim that the frequent revelations of the views of the public in the form of public opinion polls is a sign of the openness of government and society, while the Internet can be seen as a means for almost everyone to enhance their knowledge.

PC Public or rational choice theorists have identified a "media game" between the media and the politicians corresponding to the rational, self-seeking relationship between politicians and voters.[73] In this case, the two parties are engaged in an exchange in which each needs the other in order to maximize its self-interest, although the early Harper government had a somewhat hostile attitude toward the press. As for public opinion polls, the public choice approach is probably most relevant because polls are a principal means for the authorities to identify what the public wants from the government. In this view, the authorities detect what policies would get them the most votes and then promise such policies in the election campaign. As Taras writes, "polling tells the parties where the swing votes are—in which regions and among which income, ethnic, and age groups—and the messages that are most likely to move those votes."[74]

SC State-centred theorists begin by pointing out how the state can use the school system to encourage each new generation to feel satisfied with the status quo or helpless to change it. The authorities also engage in massive publicly financed advertising campaigns to persuade the electorate of the wisdom of their actions. The prime minister attempts to influence public opinion through press conferences and special televised statements, for example, and the bureaucrats use the media to foster favourable publicity about their program needs, especially when fighting for additional resources or against stringent cutbacks. Perhaps the main method of manipulation used by the bureaucracy, however, is not so much in what information is disseminated but in what is withheld. The state-centred approach also points out that the amount of money spent by governments and even bureaucrats to do their own polling is quite staggering.

G Globalization has a close connection to the mass media; indeed, the communications industry is the means by which much of the intensified contact among people, organizations, corporations, and governments occurs.[75] As mentioned, the term "convergence" is used in the media context to refer to such globalizing phenomena as the merging of technologies, companies, and cultures. Although Canadian newspapers remain fairly strong, U.S. mega-media companies in the communications industry are larger and more powerful than ever, and many wonder for how long the CRTC and CBC will be supported in protection and production of Canadian content. However, Canada is a leading exporter of television programs in its own right. Many Canadian public opinion polling firms also have partners or parents in other countries, and globalization even affects the agents of political socialization.

Modern students often develop an intimacy with the Internet that may rival their relationships with family, teachers, and peers, and these three socializing influences themselves increasingly represent a wider diversity of recent and visible immigrants.

· ·

DISCUSSION QUESTIONS

1. Think about the relative importance of the agents of political socialization in your own life. Can you decipher your own socialization process?

2. Does the fact that media companies have an impact on public opinion mean that concentrated ownership should be more restricted than in other industries?

3. What are the advantages and disadvantages of obtaining information from each of television, radio, newspapers, and the Internet?

4. What is the overall effect of the mass media coverage of politics?

5. Should the publication of public opinion polls be prohibited at some stage of an election campaign?

6. How seriously should the authorities take the results of public opinion polls? Is the government justified in taking so many public opinion polls at public expense? Explain.

· ·

NOTES

1. Ronald Landes, "Political Education and Political Socialization," in Jon Pammett and Jean-Luc Pépin, eds., *Political Education in Canada* (Halifax: Institute for Research on Public Policy, 1988), p. 17.
2. Jon Pammett, "The Development of Political Orientations in Canadian School Children," *Canadian Journal of Political Science* (March 1971).
3. Marcel Trudel and Genevieve Jain, *Canadian History Textbooks: A Comparative Study* (Ottawa: Royal Commission on Bilingualism and Biculturalism, 1970).
4. Landes, "Political Education and Political Socialization," p. 17.
5. John Ricker and Alan Skeoch, "The Contribution of Ontario's Schools to Political Education," in Pammett and Pépin, *Political Education in Canada*, p. 70.
6. See the Dominion Institute at http://www.dominion.ca.
7. Alan Frizzell, Jon H. Pammett, and Anthony Westell, *The Canadian General Election of 1988* (Ottawa: Carleton University Press, 1989), p. 69.
8. The Canadian Conference of Catholic Bishops has extended traditional Catholic concerns and made passionate appeals on poverty, unemployment, housing, and other class issues.
9. Michael Adams, *Fire and Ice: The United States, Canada and the Myth of Converging Values* (Toronto: Penguin Canada, 2003).
10. David Taras, *Power and Betrayal in the Canadian Media* (Peterborough: Broadview Press, 1999), ch. 8; and Stephen Brooks, "Policy Analysis in Canada," in Christopher Dunn, ed., *The Handbook of Canadian Public Administration* (Toronto: Oxford University Press, 2002), pp. 198–99.
11. Elisabeth Gidengil, André Blais, Richard Nadeau, and Neil Nevitte, *Citizens* (Vancouver: UBC Press, 2004).
12. Peter Trueman, *Smoke and Mirrors: The Inside Story of Television News in Canada* (Toronto: McClelland and Stewart, 1980); Paul Nesbitt-Larking, *Politics, Society, and the Media: Canadian Perspectives* (Peterborough: Broadview Press, 2001).

13. Frederick J. Fletcher and Robert Everett, "The Media and Canadian Politics in an Era of Globalization," in Michael Whittington and Glen Williams, eds., *Canadian Politics in the 21st Century*, 6th ed. (Toronto: Thomson Nelson, 2004), p. 428.

14. Stephen Brooks and Andrew Stritch, *Business and Government in Canada* (Scarborough: Prentice Hall Canada, 1991). The mutually advantageous simultaneous closings were deemed by the courts to be a coincidence and a normal part of doing business. Nesbitt-Larking has much to say about concentrated newspaper ownership in chs. 2 and 5 of *Politics, Society, and the Media*.

15. David Taras, *The Newsmakers* (Scarborough: Nelson Canada, 1990), pp. 8–17.

16. James Winter, *Democracy's Oxygen: How Corporations Control the News* (Montreal: Black Rose, 1997); Maude Barlow and James Winter, *The Big Black Book: The Essential Views of Conrad and Barbara Amiel Black* (Toronto: Stoddart, 1997); and John Miller, *Yesterday's News: Why Canada's Daily Newspapers Are Failing Us* (Halifax: Fernwood Publishing, 1998). See also Christopher Dornan and Heather Pyman, "Facts and Arguments: Newspaper Coverage of the Campaign," in Jon H. Pammett and Christopher Dornan, *The Canadian General Election of 2000* (Toronto: Dundurn, 2001), pp. 191–92.

17. Statistics Canada, "Radio Listening, 2007," *The Daily*, September 18, 2008.

18. The Supreme Court of Canada ruled in 2002 that satellite television service from U.S. companies was illegal in Canada and that the only two lawful Canadian distributors were Bell ExpressVu and Star Choice Communications (*Bell ExpressVu Limited Partnership v. Rex*, [2002] 2 S.C.R. 559).

19. Frederick J. Fletcher and Daphne Gottlieb Taras, "Images and Issues: The Mass Media and Politics in Canada," in Michael S. Whittington and Glen Williams, eds., *Canadian Politics in the 1990s*, 3rd ed. (Scarborough: Nelson Canada, 1990), p. 229. This is also one of the themes of Nesbitt-Larking's *Politics, Society, and the Media*.

20. Edwin R. Black, *Politics and the News: The Political Functions of the Mass Media* (Toronto: Butterworths, 1982), p. 80.

21. Trueman, *Smoke and Mirrors*, p. 161.

22. House of Commons Standing Committee on Canadian Heritage, *Our Cultural Sovereignty: The Second Century of Canadian Broadcasting* (June 2003).

23. Taras, *Power and Betrayal*; and Russell Mills, "Reflections on the State of Canadian Media," *Canadian Parliamentary Review* (Winter 2003–04).

24. Catherine McLean, "Television's Penetration May Force Policy Review," *The Globe and Mail*, January 18, 2006.

25. Tamara A. Small, "parties@canada: The Internet and the 2004 Cyber-Campaign," in Pammett and Dornan, *The Canadian General Election of 2004*; Darin Barney, *Communications Technology* (Vancouver: UBC Press, 2005); and Ann Dale and Ted Naylor, "Dialogue and Public Space: An Exploration of Radio and Information Communications Technologies," *Canadian Journal of Political Science* (March 2005).

26. Heather McIvor, *Parameters of Power*, 5th ed. (Toronto: Nelson Education, 2010), pp. 541–43.

27. The general thrust of David Taras in *The Newsmakers*. See Chapter 11 of his book for a discussion of how the media are performing functions previously the domain of political parties. See also Nesbitt-Larking, *Politics, Society, and the Media*.

28. Various surveys including André Blais, Elisabeth Gidengil, Richard Nadeau, and Neil Nevitte, *Anatomy of a Liberal Victory: Making Sense of the Vote in the 2000 Canadian Election* (Peterborough: Broadview Press, 2002), p. 35; Gidengil et al., *Citizens*, p. 26; Christopher Waddell and Christopher Dornan, "The Media and the Campaign," in Jon H. Pammett and Christopher Dornan, eds., *The Canadian General Election of 2006* (Toronto: Dundurn Press, 2006), p. 225.

29. Taras, *The Newsmakers*, pp. 30–31; Walter C. Soderlund, Ronald H. Wagenberg, Donald E. Briggs, and Ralph C. Nelson, "Regional and Linguistic Agenda-Setting in Canada: A Study of Newspaper Coverage of Issues Affecting Political Integration in 1976," *Canadian Journal of Political Science* (December 1980); Walter C. Soderlund, Walter I. Romanow, E. Donald Briggs, and Ronald H. Wagenberg, *Media and Elections in Canada* (Toronto: Holt, Rinehart and Winston, 1984); and Fletcher, *The Newspaper and Public Affairs*, p. 16.

30. McIvor, *Parameters of Power*, p. 522; Linda Trimble and Shannon Sampert, "Who's in the Game? The Framing of the Canadian Election 2000 by *The Globe and Mail* and the *National Post*," *Canadian Journal of Political Science* (March 2004).

31. Taras, *The Newsmakers*, ch. 3; and Allan Levine, *Scrum Wars: The Prime Ministers and the Media* (Toronto: Dundurn Press, 1993).

32. Taras, *Power and Betrayal*, p. 208.

33. Taras, *The Newsmakers*, p. 102.

34. Alan Frizzell et al., *The Canadian General Election of 1988*, p. 33; Waddell and Dornan, "The Media and the Campaign," ch. 9.

35. Taras, *The Newsmakers*, ch. 4.

36. Ibid., ch. 5; Howard K. Penniman, ed., *Canada at the Polls, 1984* (Durham, NC: Duke University Press, 1988), pp. 184 and 201; and Levine, *Scrum Wars*.

37. Henry Milner, "Civic Literacy in Comparative Context," *Policy Matters* (July 2001) (Montreal: Institute for Research on Public Policy), pp. 16–18.

38. Fletcher and Everett, "The Media and Canadian Politics in an Era of Globalization," p. 433.

39. Christopher Waddell, "The Newspaper Campaign," in Pammett and Dornan, *The Canadian General Election of 2004*.

40. William Misher, *Political Participation in Canada: Prospects for Democratic Citizenship* (Toronto: Macmillan, 1979), p. 73; and Gidengil et al., *Citizens*, pp. 25–35.

41. Fletcher, *The Newspaper and Public Affairs*, p. 30; and Taras, *The Newsmakers*, pp. 87–89.

42. Fletcher, *The Newspaper and Public Affairs*, p. 11.

43. Dornan and Pyman, "Facts and Arguments," pp. 192–94; and Nesbitt-Larking, *Politics, Society, and the Media*, chs. 2 and 5.

44. Allan Fotheringham, *Birds of a Feather: The Press and the Politicians* (Toronto: Key Porter Books, 1990), p. 249.

45. Siegel, *Politics and the Media in Canada*, p. 80.

46. Black, *Politics and the News*, p. 12; and Taras, *The Newsmakers*, p. 234.

47. See books by such press secretaries as Patrick Gossage, *Close to the Charisma: My Years between the Press and Pierre Elliott Trudeau* (Toronto: McClelland and Stewart, 1986), and Michel Gratton, *So, What Are the Boys Saying?* (Toronto: McGraw-Hill Ryerson, 1987) as well as Taras, *The Newsmakers*, pp. 125–30, 158, 172.

48. Fletcher and Everett, "The Media and Canadian Politics in an Era of Globalization," p. 432. See also Taras, *Power and Betrayal*, p. 52; and Craig Forcese and Aaron Freeman, *The Laws of Government: The Legal Foundations of Canadian Democracy* (Toronto: Irwin Law, 2005).

49. Pierre Laporte, *The True Face of Duplessis* (Montreal: Harvest House, 1960).

50. Black, *Politics and the News*, p. 168. In his definitive book, Christopher Page writes: "many people have opinions which are inconsistent, weakly held, and subject to change." *The Roles of Public Opinion Research in Canadian Government* (Toronto: University of Toronto Press, 2006), p. 168.

51. Frizzell et al., *The Canadian Federal Election of 1988*, p. 91. See also Nesbitt-Larking, *Politics, Society, and the Media*, ch. 12; and Michael Marzolini, "Public Opinion and the 2006 Election," in Pammett and Dornan, eds., *The Canadian General Election of 2006*, ch. 10.

52. John Turner's election in Vancouver Quadra in 1984 is often cited as an example of the underdog effect, given that all polls in the constituency indicated that he would lose.

53. Taras, *The Newsmakers*, pp. 187, 192–94; Peter Desbarats, *Guide to Canadian News Media* (Toronto: Harcourt Brace Jovanovich, 1990), p. 138; and Waddell and Dornan, "The Media and the Campaign," pp. 239–42.

54. Gidengil et al., *Citizens*, p. 65; and Trimble and Sampert, "Who's in the Game? The Framing of the Canadian Election 2000 by *The Globe and Mail* and the *National Post*."

55. Claire Hoy, *Margin of Error* (Toronto: Key Porter Books, 1989), pp. 219–20; and Taras, *The Newsmakers*, p. 193.

56. Hoy, *Margin of Error*, p. 228. Hoy discusses the government's first poll on the conscription issue in 1942, which it wanted to keep secret (p. 14).

57. *Thomson Newspaper Co. v. Canada (Attorney General)*, [1998] 1 S.C.R. 877.

58. Hoy, *Margin of Error*, pp. 1–5; and Penniman, ed., *Canada at the Polls, 1984*, p. 129.

59. Penniman, ed., *Canada at the Polls, 1984*, p. 131.

60. Richard Johnston, *Public Opinion and Public Policy in Canada* (Toronto: University of Toronto Press, 1986); and François Petry and Matthew Mendelsohn, "Public Opinion and Policy Making in Canada, 1994–2001," *Canadian Journal of Political Science* (September 2004).

61. Hoy writes that in one view "the essence of parliamentary democracy is that we elect politicians to lead, to take risks, to stand for something more than the latest popular sentiment or the collective public wisdom, which may be based more on short-term emotion or outright ignorance than on anything else," *Margin of Error*, p. 7.

62. In fact, support for capital punishment has fallen off dramatically to about 50 percent. This is no doubt due in part to the many miscarriages of justice that Canadians have witnessed in recent years.

63. Page, *The Role of Public Opinion Research in Canadian Government*.

64. Ibid., p. 184.

65. Ibid., Conclusion. For future issues that polls have revealed, see David Herle, "Poll-driven Politics—The Role of Public Opinion in Canada," Institute for Research on Public Policy, *Policy Options* (May 2007).

66. Janine Brodie and Jane Jenson, *Crisis, Challenge and Change: Party and Class in Canada Revisited* (Ottawa: Carleton University Press, 1988). Another theme of Nesbitt-Larking, *Politics, Society, and the Media*, is the exclusion of women, Aboriginals, the poor, and the working class from media coverage.

67. Fotheringham describes one such event, a Barbara Frum party, in *Birds of a Feather*, pp. 146–50.

68. Fletcher and Taras, "Images and Issues," pp. 233–34.

69. Ibid., p. 223; Black, *Politics and the News*, pp. 43–44; John Porter, *The Vertical Mosaic* (Toronto: University of Toronto Press, 1965), ch. XV; and Ted Magder, "Taking Culture Seriously: A Political Economy of Communications," in Wallace Clement and Glen Williams, eds., *The New Canadian Political Economy* (Montreal: McGill–Queen's University Press, 1989).

70. Desbarats, *Guide to Canadian News Media*, p. 69.

71. Wallace Clement, *The Canadian Corporate Elite* (Toronto: McClelland and Stewart, 1975), pp. 270–86.

72. Royal Commission on Newspapers, p. 1.

73. M.J. Trebilcock, D. Hartle, R. Prichard, and D. Dewees, *The Choice of Governing Instrument* (Ottawa: Supply and Services, 1982), and W.T. Stanbury, *Business–Government Relations in Canada* (Toronto: Methuen, 1986), pp. 147–48 and ch. 11.

74. Taras, *The Newsmakers*, p. 186.

75. Rowland Lorimer and Mike Gasher, *Mass Communications in Canada*, 4th ed. (Don Mills: Oxford University Press, 2001), ch. 11.

FURTHER READING

Barney, Darin. *Communications Technology*. Vancouver: UBC Press, 2005.

Butler, Peter M. *Polling and Public Opinion: A Canadian Perspective*. Toronto: University of Toronto Press, 2007.

Everitt, Joanna, and Brenda O'Neil, eds. *Citizen Politics: Research and Theory in Canadian Political Behaviour*. Toronto: Oxford University Press, 2002.

Fletcher, Frederick J., and Robert Everett. "The Media and Canadian Politics in an Era of Globalization." In Michael Whittington and Glen Williams, eds., *Canadian Politics in the 21st Century*, 6th ed. Toronto: Thomson: Nelson Canada, 2004; 7th edition, 2008.

Gidengil, Elisabeth, André Blais, Richard Nadeau, and Neil Nevitte. *Citizens*. Vancouver: UBC Press, 2004.

Miller, John. *Yesterday's News: How Canada's Daily Newspapers Are Failing Us*. Halifax: Fernwood Publishing, 1998.

Nash, Knowlton. *Trivia Pursuit: How Showbiz Values Are Corrupting the News*. Toronto: McClelland and Stewart, 1998.

Nesbitt-Larking, Paul. *Politics, Society, and the Media: Canadian Perspectives*. Peterborough: Broadview Press, 2001.

Page, Christopher. *The Roles of Public Opinion Research in Canadian Government*. Toronto: University of Toronto Press, 2006.

Pammett, Jon H., and Christopher Dornan, eds. *The Canadian General Election of 2000*. Toronto: Dundurn Press, 2001.

———. *The Canadian General Election of 2006*. Toronto: Dundurn Press, 2006.

Taras, David. *The Newsmakers*. Scarborough: Nelson Canada, 1990.

———. *Power and Betrayal in the Canadian Media*, updated ed. Peterborough: Broadview Press, 2001.

Winter, James. *Democracy's Oxygen: How Corporations Control the News*. Montreal: Black Rose, 1997.

Chapter 13

ELECTIONS AND
the Electoral System

If elections are a crucial component in the definition of a democracy, it is important that they be conducted in the most "free and fair" way possible. Anyone should be able to contest the election, everyone should be able to vote, every vote should be equal on election day, and every province and territory should be fairly represented in the House of Commons. In most technical respects, the Canadian electoral system meets such standards, but it does not fare so well in terms of proportionality. It does not award seats in proportion to a party's popular vote, and many critics advocate a more proportional system. Other observers are consoled by the fact that historically this electoral system usually produced a majority of seats for the winning party without having won a majority of the votes cast. But when such an "artificial majority" was created, Opposition parties were short-changed in the number of seats they obtained. Historically, too, much controversy surrounded the question of party and election finance, as contributions often came with strings attached, and some parties grossly outspent others.

This chapter examines the formal, legal, and official aspects of the electoral system, and has four parts: redistribution or redrawing the electoral map, the official organization of elections, an evaluation of the lack of proportionality in the electoral system and suggestions for reform, and party and election finance. The actual electoral contest between political parties and candidates and the questions of electoral behaviour and party support are discussed in Chapter 15.

. . . .

THEORETICAL CONSIDERATIONS

The primary function of elections is to allow the mass of citizens to choose their parliamentary representatives and, indirectly, their governmental leaders.[1] Besides recruiting political leaders, elections serve to inform the public, which is part of the political socialization function. Moreover, both political parties and advocacy groups take advantage of elections to articulate certain interests, and most parties try to aggregate interests in putting forward a comprehensive, attractive election platform. Elections also serve a legitimation function. That is, by exercising their franchise, voters legitimize the power of those elected by agreeing to be bound by their decisions. This activity presumably also generates popular support for the political system as a whole. Elections similarly help to integrate the country by putting everyone in it through a common national experience. To the extent that policy concerns are central to the campaign, elections may also provide policy guidelines for the authorities and a feeling of political efficacy for the voters. Even if such policy mandates are somewhat lacking, the electorate can at least remove a government whose policies or performance were judged to be inadequate.

The question of whether elections are free and fair arises in political systems that claim to be democratic.[2] Canadian elections are "free" in the sense that almost anyone or any party can enter the race, although there are built-in advantages for existing parties and disadvantages for smaller, newer entrants. These advantages and disadvantages relate primarily to media coverage and election finance. Another aspect of fairness is the question of proportionality, that is, the extent to which representation in the House of Commons reflects the wishes of the voters. A close relationship between the popular vote a party receives and its electoral representation is not a major objective of Canada's first-past-the-post system. In the recent past this electoral system was also incapable of producing a majority government, which used to be one of its leading claims; moreover, no majority appears to be in sight in the foreseeable future. Thus, Canada has seen much recent interest in electoral reform.[3]

. . . .

DRAWING THE ELECTORAL MAP

In a House of Commons where each MP represents a specific constituency, the electoral process begins by dividing the country into single-member electoral districts.[4] This process, called **redistribution**, involves two stages: first, deciding how many seats in the Commons to allot to each province and territory; and second, actually drawing constituency boundaries within the provinces.

Distribution of Seats among Provinces

The Constitution Act, 1867 requires that the readjustment process be repeated after each decennial census—for example, 1991, 2001, and 2011. Given the federal character of Canada, with its strong provincial and territorial loyalties, the search for a fair means of distributing seats in the House of Commons among the provinces and territories has been a long and unsatisfactory one. Different formulas have been used over the years, but none has ever commanded unanimous support. The formula used following the 2001 census and the one that resulted in the 308 seats in the House of Commons after the 2004, 2006, and 2008 elections was adopted by means of the Representation Act, 1985. Table 13.1 illustrates how such calculations were made, involving the following four steps:

1. Starting with 282 seats, one seat is allocated to each of the Northwest Territories, Nunavut, and Yukon, leaving 279 seats.

2. The total population of the ten provinces is divided by 279 to obtain the electoral quota or quotient.

3. This electoral quota is divided into the population of each province to obtain the number of seats each is entitled to.

TABLE 13.1   Representation Formula Using the 2001 Census Figures

	Minimum Number of Seats in Accordance with the Constitution Act, 1867[1]	Population 2001	National Quotient[2] 107 220	Rounded Result	Special Clauses[3]	Total	Electoral Quotient
Newfoundland and Labrador	7	512 930	107 220	5	2	7	73 276
Prince Edward Island	4	135 294	107 220	1	3	4	33 824
Nova Scotia	11	908 007	107 220	8	3	11	82 546
New Brunswick	10	729 498	107 220	7	3	10	72 950
Quebec	75	7 237 479	107 220	68	7	75	96 500
Ontario	95	11 410 046	107 220	106	0	106	107 642
Manitoba	14	1 119 583	107 220	10	4	14	79 970
Saskatchewan	14	978 933	107 220	9	5	14	69 924
Alberta	21	2 974 807	107 220	28	0	28	106 243
British Columbia	28	3 907 738	107 220	36	0	36	108 548
Nunavut	1	26 745	—	—	—	1	—
Northwest Territories	2	37 360	—	—	—	1	—
Yukon Territory	1	28 674	—	—	—	1	—
National total	282	30 007 094				308	

Notes:

[1] Assigns one seat each to Nunavut, the Northwest Territories, and the Yukon Territory (3 seats).

[2] Uses 279 seats and the population of provinces to establish national quotient (29 914/279 = 107 220).

[3] Add seats to provinces pursuant to "senatorial clause" guarantee in the Constitution and "grandfather clause" (based on 33rd Parliament).

Source: Elections Canada. Representation 2004. Representation Formula: Detailed Calculations for 2001 Census. Found at: http://www.elections.ca/scripts/fedrep/federal_e/repform_e.htm.

4. If these provincial seat allocations result in any province having fewer seats than it has senators, then (under the "senatorial clause") it obtains such additional seats as to equal its number of senators; if the allocations result in any province having fewer seats than it had in 1976, then (under the "grandfather clause") such additional seats are also added.

Drawing Constituency Boundaries

The second phase of the redistribution process, drawing constituency boundaries within each province, was historically the prerogative of the politicians. They regularly engaged in the process of **gerrymandering**—that is, manipulating constituency boundaries so as to ensure as far as possible the re-election of the members of the government party.[5] In the absence of any written rules, some constituencies had huge populations while others were extremely small. The Electoral Boundaries Readjustment Act of 1964 established a new system, however, so that beginning with the post-1961 redistribution, this task has been performed by independent commissions. An electoral boundaries commission is appointed for each province, chaired by a judge designated by the chief justice of the province. The other two members of each commission are appointed by the Speaker of the House of Commons and are often chosen from the political science community. All commissions depend extensively on the support and assistance of Elections Canada staff, and digital computerized technology now simplifies the task of drawing electoral maps.

The commissions swing into action as soon as the provincial population figures are available from the census. Theirs is a very delicate task of trying to arrive at a design that will provide constituencies of approximately equal population size throughout the province while also accounting for geographic characteristics, communities of interest, and other peculiarities. The most difficult problem is in dealing with sparsely populated rural or northern regions at the same time as concentrated urban centres. In recognition of this problem, the commissions in the 1960s and 1970s were allowed to deviate from the average population figure to a maximum tolerance of plus or minus 25 percent, but since then the law allowed them to exceed this limit "in circumstances viewed by the commission as being extraordinary" in order to arrive at a manageable geographic size for all districts. They must also consider the "community of interest or community of identity in or the historical pattern of an electoral district." Thus, rural and northern constituencies tend to be under the provincial quotient, and southern, urban ones tend to be slightly over it. The Royal Commission on Electoral Reform and Party Financing recommended a tolerance of 15 percent, but court decisions have been satisfied with plus or minus 25 percent.[6] In the 2003 operation, only two constituencies out of 308 exceeded the 25 percent limit (Labrador and Kenora), and only 19 exceeded plus or minus 15 percent of the provincial quotient.[7]

The publication of the map of proposed electoral boundaries is followed by a period of public hearings, which are normally held at several different locations in the province. During these hearings interested individuals, municipalities, groups, and MPs appear to express their views on the proposals. Then, within a year of the availability of the population data, the commissions must complete their reports. They are sent through the chief electoral officer to the Speaker of the House of Commons, who ensures that they are tabled and referred to the appropriate Commons committee. Written objections signed by at least ten MPs may be filed with this committee, which has 30 days while the House is sitting to discuss and raise objections to the report. The committee's proceedings are sent back to the electoral boundaries commissions, which have the authority to alter their report or leave it as is. Thus, it is the independent commissions and not the politicians who have the final say. Because of the time needed by the chief electoral officer, returning officers, and political parties to make adjustments in their operations, the new boundaries cannot be used at an election until at least one year after the date that the representation order encompassing the new boundaries is proclaimed. Because of such delays and the serious underrepresentation of Ontario, Alberta, and British Columbia, the Harper government considered a redistribution of Commons seats even before the 2011 census.

Since it takes fewer votes in smaller provinces and in rural parts of all provinces to elect a member of Parliament, such votes are worth more than those in large provinces or in urban areas. These deviations serve to undermine to some extent the basic democratic principle of political equality or "one person, one vote." John Courtney points out that within each province the degree of similarity in constituency size is increasing, but that between the different provinces there is a widening disparity in the size of constituencies.[8] In general, however, Canadians accept this deviation from the principle of representation by population or political equality out of ignorance or recognition of the fact that the Canadian population is peculiarly distributed. However, the democratic rights provision of the Charter of Rights and Freedoms opens up the possibility of a legal challenge on this subject. As mentioned in Chapter 19, several provincial redistribution schemes have been taken to court.

. . . .

THE OFFICIAL ELECTION MACHINERY

Setting the Date

Until 2007, the prime minister had the prerogative to set the date of the election within a five-year period from the previous electoral contest. Largely based on the government party's standings in the public opinion polls, the election was typically called about four years after the previous campaign. The average time between elections since 1867 has been about 41 months, reflecting the shorter tenure of minority governments. Going into the fifth year, especially to the five-year limit, was usually seen as a sign of political weakness, and most governments waiting that long have been defeated. The governor general had to approve the prime minister's request to **dissolve Parliament** in order to call an election, but this was normally automatic. Only once in Canadian history (1926), in rather peculiar circumstances, did a governor general refuse such a request, as discussed in Chapter 21. The defeat of a government in a nonconfidence vote in the House of Commons is the alternative way in which an election is precipitated, in which case the prime minister's leeway is limited to choosing the exact date. Such a defeat of the Paul Martin government led to the election of January 2006.

Public opinion polls can be wrong, of course, or public opinion can change between the calling of the election and the actual voting day, so that the apparent advantage for the party in power in choosing the election date is not absolute. John Turner was a victim of such a change in 1984 when an 11-point lead in June dissolved into a 22-point lag by September, and Chapter 15 discusses the highly volatile nature of Canadian party preferences. Nevertheless, because of the potential unfairness of the system and because the uncertainty of the date caused inconvenience to many of those involved, some observers advocated the establishment of fixed election dates. New Zealand demonstrated that this could be done within the British parliamentary system, and several provinces now have fixed election dates.

At the federal level, the Harper government passed legislation in 2007 which set fixed election dates, with the next supposed to be held on October 19, 2009. The law left a loophole for the Prime Minister to advise the governor general to call an election before that date, but this was intended to be used in the case of a non-confidence vote, as might have occurred in the minority government situation. Breaking the spirit of the new

Voter will vote for whoever promised trip to Mexico.

law, Harper employed the escape clause to call the October 14, 2008 election even without the government being defeated. The PM was thus still able to take advantage of calling an election when it suited his purposes.

Election Officials

The **chief electoral officer** is responsible for the overall administration of the election and must function with absolute impartiality.[9] This post is therefore filled by a resolution of the whole House of Commons, rather than by a regular public servant hired by the government. However, returning officers, who organize the election in each of the electoral districts (also called constituencies or ridings), have been chosen by the Cabinet, and were usually partisan appointees. Ironically, once appointed, returning officers were expected to function in a completely nonpartisan fashion. Before the election call, each returning officer will have divided the constituency into polling divisions (or polls) of about 350 voters each; a typical urban constituency will have about 225 polls. Because such preparations must be made beforehand, returning officers work part-time between elections and full-time during the campaign. They usually served until a different party came to power and replaced them with its own supporters. Many informed observers argued that this peculiar and paradoxical situation should be changed, and it finally was, in the Harper government's 2006 **Federal Accountability Act**.[10] Since then, the chief electoral officer chooses returning officers on a nonpartisan basis.

The Voters' List

In Canadian federal elections, the **voters' list** was historically compiled from scratch after the election writ was issued. This was done by means of a door-to-door enumeration in which the returning officer appointed two enumerators to collect the names of eligible voters in each polling division. It was largely because of this lengthy process that Canadian election campaigns used to last at least 47 days.

The 1993 reforms permitted the use of electoral lists prepared within the previous 12 months to substitute for a full-fledged enumeration. Because the 1992 referendum was held almost exactly a year before the 1993 election, there was no 1993 enumeration except in Quebec (which had held its own simultaneous referendum). This incident had implications for the voter turnout rate, as mentioned in Chapter 11.

Reforms introduced in 1996 provided for a National Register of Electors, the base of which was compiled in one last door-to-door enumeration in April 1997 (except in Alberta and

Prince Edward Island, which used the most recent provincial voters' list). Henceforth, that register is automatically revised from such sources as income tax, citizenship and immigration, driver's licence, and vital statistics files, although with such a modern mobile population, it is a struggle to keep it up-to-date. In any case, there is ample opportunity to correct the list during the campaign, and a ballot can even be issued on election day itself to a qualified person whose name is not on the list. A major advantage of a permanent voters' list is that the length of the election period could be reduced to 36 days. The main problem is to get new 18-year-olds onto the list in the first place. Elections Canada welcomes their approach at any time.

Nomination

About 95 percent of candidates are nominated at a meeting of a political party, but they must then submit formal **nomination** papers, endorsed by 100 people on the local voters' list, and a $1000 deposit. Candidates receive this deposit back if and when they file their financial statement. Official candidates of registered parties must obtain the party leader's endorsement to use the party name on the ballot. This requirement was mainly adopted to pre-empt the possibility of local conflicts over who was the legitimate standard-bearer of the party, but it effectively gives the leader a veto over nominations—with many implications.[11] In 1974, for example, Robert Stanfield denied the party label to Leonard Jones, who was nominated as the Conservative candidate in Moncton, because of Jones's outspoken opposition to official bilingualism. Similarly, Brian Mulroney refused to endorse discredited ex-Cabinet minister Sinclair Stevens in 1988. When a number of Liberal backbenchers voted against government bills in mid-1995, Jean Chrétien warned them that he might not sign their nomination papers in the next election, although only John Nunziata ultimately met this fate, and then ran successfully as an Independent.

Election Day

After nomination day, the returning officer arranges for the ballots to be printed and allows people to vote in advance polls or by special ballot. Recent reforms made voting much more convenient for those not at home on election day, including members of the armed forces, government officials posted abroad, and others temporarily out of the country. By this time, the returning officer is also busy hiring and training deputy returning officers and poll clerks to look after each polling station on election day and finding appropriate polling stations, typically in schools, church basements, or community centres.

Canadian federal elections are held on Mondays, and the polls used to be open from 9 a.m. to 8 p.m. local time. Because voters in the western part of the country complained that the winning party was often determined before their votes had even been counted, the Royal Commission on Electoral Reform and Party Financing proposed a system of staggered hours for different time zones. This recommendation was implemented for the 1997 and subsequent elections and meant that the polls closed at approximately the same real time all across the country. Thus, the ballots are counted and results announced more or less simultaneously. As before, however, the dissemination of results from one region

THE CANADIAN PRESS/Ryan Remiorz

Inmate at Montreal Detention Centre casts his ballot in the 2004 federal election after all inmates won the right to vote.

where the polls have closed to another where they are still open is not allowed. This issue then arose in the context of results being posted on the Internet in 2000 before all the polls had closed, and in a split decision, the Supreme Court upheld the law.[12] Voters are entitled to three consecutive hours off work in which to cast their ballot, and the sale of liquor is no longer prohibited during polling hours. Other recommendations of the Royal Commission that made the system more user-friendly include the provision for level access at polling stations, the establishment of mobile polls for seniors and those with disabilities, the appointment of interpreters, and the use of a template for those with vision impairments.

Voters mark their X in private on the ballot provided, and when the polls close the deputy returning officer and poll clerk count them, usually in the company of scrutineers from the various candidates who are allowed to challenge unorthodox markings on ballots and generally keep the whole process honest. Results are announced an hour or so after the polls close and the candidate with the most votes, the **first-past-the-post**, is declared elected. This means that the winner usually does not actually have a majority of the votes cast, only a plurality.

The Ballot

The secret ballot was introduced into federal elections in 1874. In the first two elections after Confederation, people voted orally and were subject to bribery or intimidation, including the threat of physical assault if they voted the wrong way! The candidates are listed in alphabetical order on the ballot, which contains their party affiliation, if any. The chief electoral officer keeps a registry of political parties, and a party need only have a single candidate to be registered and to use the party label on the ballot.[13] Such parties must also register their national and constituency official agents and auditors for the purposes of keeping track of the party's and candidates' finances. Twelve parties were registered for the 1988 election, 14 for 1993, 10 for 1997, 11 for 2000, 13 for 2004, 15 for 2006, and 19 for 2008.[14]

The Franchise

The extension of the **franchise** beyond males with substantial property was mentioned in passing in Chapters 4 to 8.[15] This evolution in Canada was complicated by the use of different provincial franchises in federal elections between 1867 and 1885 and between 1898 and 1917. The federal franchise between 1885 and 1898 required that males be property owners, but this qualification was gradually eliminated in most provinces about 1900. By this time, women had won the vote in certain municipal elections, and they gained the provincial franchise in Manitoba, Saskatchewan, and Alberta in 1916. In 1917 the federal franchise was manipulated so as to maximize support for the incumbent government. The vote was extended to women serving in the war, and female relatives of men serving overseas, but Canadian citizens who had come from "enemy alien" countries were denied the vote. In 1918 all women were granted the vote, and since 1920 a uniform federal franchise has existed that included all Canadian citizens with the exception of Aboriginals and those of Asian ancestry (especially those from Japan, China, and India). The latter were not allowed to vote in British Columbia provincial elections, and the federal law disqualified anyone who for reasons of race was denied the vote under provincial electoral statutes. Such restrictions were removed by 1948, and the vote was extended to the Inuit in 1953 and to Registered Indians in 1960. The voting age was reduced from 21 to 18 in 1970, and British subjects who were not Canadian citizens lost their vote in 1975.

. . . .

DATES OF EXTENSION OF THE RIGHT TO VOTE IN CANADIAN FEDERAL ELECTIONS

- 1918: Women
- 1948: Asian Canadians
- 1953: Inuit
- 1960: Registered Indians
- 1970: Persons 18 years of age
- 1988: Judges and people with mental disabilities
- 1999: Returning officers
- 2002: All prisoners

By 1975, the **Canada Elections Act** disqualified only the following individuals from voting: the chief and assistant chief electoral officers, returning officers (except in the case of a tie), federally appointed judges, prison inmates, those deprived of their liberty by reason of mental disabilities, and those convicted of corrupt or illegal electoral practices. During the 1988 campaign, however, three of these disqualifications were challenged in the courts in terms of the Charter of Rights and Freedoms, which guarantees the vote to every Canadian citizen. In the case of judges and those with mental disabilities, the provisions of the act were declared unconstitutional and the disqualifications removed. The courts made a number of contradictory decisions on whether prison inmates should be able to vote, and the 1993 amendments gave the vote in federal elections to inmates serving sentences of less than two years. In 1996, however, long-term prisoners were successful in persuading the courts to remove the two-year restriction, a decision confirmed by the Supreme Court of Canada in 2002.[16] In 1999, returning officers received the right to vote, and in the case of a tie in a constituency, a by-election will be held rather than have the returning officer cast a deciding vote.

Recent amendments to the Canada Elections Act include a provision that voters must prove their identity and address by providing a piece of government-issued photo ID before obtaining a ballot, or else be vouched for by another qualified voter. This requirement became especially controversial when it was applied to veiled Muslim women. Another amendment required superintendents of multiple-residence buildings (apartments, condos, etc.) to provide access to election campaigners.

. . . .

THE PROPORTIONALITY OF THE ELECTORAL SYSTEM

In each constituency, the candidate with the most votes wins, even if this is less than 50 percent. This type of electoral system is therefore called the "first-past-the-post" (FPTP) or single-member plurality system. Among the advantages of this electoral system are its simplicity for the voter, its quick calculation of results, and its provision of a clear-cut representative for each constituency. It may have other benefits, such as encouraging parties to make broad appeals across the country, rather than to seek a narrow base of support, and if it produces a single-party government, it probably helps the electorate hold the governing party accountable. FPTP has usually provided a majority government in Canada, which some observers also take as an advantage. When all the local results are cumulated nationally, however, the proportion of seats a party wins does not necessarily bear much relationship to its overall share of the **popular vote**, as seen in Table 13.2.

Take as an extreme, hypothetical example a two-person race in each constituency in which the Liberal candidate beat the Conservative candidate by one vote in every case: the Liberal Party would then win 100 percent of the seats from just more than 50 percent of the vote, and the Conservative Party would have zero percent of the seats from just less than 50 percent of the vote. In fact, this example is not so hypothetical: in the New Brunswick election of 1987,

TABLE 13.2   **Percentage of the Popular Vote and Percentage of Seats by Party for Federal Elections, 1993–2008**

		Liberal	PC	NDP	Reform / Alliance	BQ
1993	% Vote	41.3	16.0	6.9	18.7	13.5
	% Seats	60.0	0.7	3.1	17.6	18.3
1997	% Vote	38.5	18.8	11.0	19.4	10.7
	% Seats	51.5	6.6	7.0	19.9	14.6
2000	% Vote	40.8	12.2	8.5	25.5	10.7
	% Seats	57.1	4.0	4.3	21.9	12.6
		Liberal	Conservative	NDP		BQ
2004	% Vote	36.7	29.6	15.7		12.4
	% Seats	43.8	32.1	6.2		17.5
2006	% Vote	30.2	36.3	17.5		10.5
	% Seats	33.4	40.3	9.4		16.6
2008	% Vote	26.3	37.7	18.2		10.0
	% Seats	25.0	46.4	12.0		15.9

Source: Reports of the Chief Electoral Officer, adapted by the author.

the Liberals won 100 percent of the seats with about 60 percent of the popular vote. Many political scientists and other observers are therefore concerned that such overall disparities can occur between the percentage of seats that a party wins and the percentage of its popular vote. They look beyond the results in each electoral district and argue that there should be a more proportional representation of overall party support.

Discrepancies between Seats and Votes: National Level

The actual disparities can be analyzed for both the national and the provincial levels.[17] Overall, in 27 elections since 1921, the party with the largest popular vote almost always won more seats than it deserved, while the second party was usually somewhat underrepresented. When it comes to minor parties, those with concentrated regional support, like the Bloc Québécois, were often overrepresented, while those with broad national ("diffuse") support usually lost out. The CCF/NDP, for example, regularly received only about half as many seats as its popular vote merited.

As mentioned, some observers credit this electoral system with producing a majority government—the leading party obtaining more than 50 percent of the seats—even though a party rarely wins more than 50 percent of the popular vote. In only three federal elections after 1921 (1940, 1958, and 1984) did the winning party obtain at least 50 percent of the vote, and this automatically produced a majority government. On 11 other occasions, a minority government resulted. But on the remaining 13 occasions out of 27, this electoral system manufactured an artificial majority government in terms of seats, even though the leading party did not win a majority of the vote. Thus, this system does have a tendency to produce a majority government, although with four or five major parties, a minority government is likely even in a FPTP system. Moreover, on three occasions (1957, 1962, and 1979) the party with the second-largest popular vote ended up with more seats than the party that came first, and therefore went on to form the government, as often happens in the provinces as well.[18]

Historians and political scientists have even contributed to a misinterpretation of Canada's past by concentrating on seats rather than on votes, such as in exaggerating the Liberal sweep in Quebec in 1896 and the national Liberal victory in 1935, and in giving the NDP the image of a minor party because, as mentioned, it has usually elected only about half as many members as its popular vote actually justifies.

In the 1993 context, the Liberals and Bloc were overrepresented, but Reform, the NDP, and especially the PCs, deserved more seats in terms of their popular vote. Reform should have been the official opposition in the sense that it received more votes than the Bloc; the NDP deserved party status because seven percent of the vote would theoretically produce about 20 seats; and the Conservatives ran a close third to Reform in popular vote and more than doubled the vote of the NDP but suffered from ridicule of its two-member caucus. The 1997 election also gave the Liberals a majority of seats that their popular support did not justify, gave the regionally concentrated Bloc more seats than it merited, and continued to underrepresent the more nationally based PCs and NDP. The 2000 election awarded the Liberals with another undeserved majority, and was still unkind to the Conservatives and NDP. Then, in 2004, 2006, and 2008, no party won a majority of seats, but the NDP (and Greens) were seriously disadvantaged.

Discrepancies between Seats and Votes: By Province

Another set of disparities between popular vote and seat figures exists on a province-by-province basis. In this case, Alan Cairns was particularly struck by the disparity between the Conservative vote and seats in Quebec (1896–1984) and between the Liberal vote and seats in Western Canada (since 1957). Table 13.3 shows the distribution of seats won per province and territory and the breakdown of the seats–votes ratio for the 2008 election.

Cairns observed that such disparities affect parties in three principal ways: image, strategy, and policy. Each party's image is largely derived from the attention given to its number of elected members in the House of Commons rather than from its popular vote. Thus, when the Conservatives had virtually no members from Quebec before 1984, they gained a non-French or anti-French image, even though they usually obtained at least 13 percent of the popular vote in that province. Similarly, the Liberals acquired an image of an anti-Western party after 1957 because they rarely elected members west of Ontario, even though they normally received more than 20 percent of the Western vote. In 2000, the Canadian Alliance took

TABLE 13.3	Results of the 2008 Election: Seats, Percentage of Seats, and Percentage of Votes Won by Party by Province and Territory										
	Conservatives			Liberals			NDP			BQ		
	Seats	%S	%V	Seats	%S	%V	Seats	%S	%V	Seats	%S	%V
Newfoundland and Labrador	0	0	17	6	86	47	1	14	34	0	0	0
Prince Edward Island	1	25	36	3	75	48	0	0	10	0	0	0
Nova Scotia*	3	27	26	5	46	30	2	18	29	0	0	0
New Brunswick	6	60	39	3	30	32	1	10	22	0	0	0
Quebec*	10	13	22	14	19	24	1	1	12	49	65	38
Ontario	51	48	39	38	36	34	17	16	18	0	0	0
Manitoba	9	64	49	1	7	19	4	29	24	0	0	0
Saskatchewan	13	93	54	1	7	15	0	0	26	0	0	0
Alberta	27	96	65	0	0	11	1	4	13	0	0	0
BC	22	61	44	5	14	19	9	25	26	0	0	0
NWT	0	0	38	0	0	14	1	100	42	0	0	0
Nunavut	1	100	35	0	0	29	0	0	28	0	0	0
Yukon	0	0	33	1	100	45	0	0	9	0	0	0
Total	143	46	38	77	25	26	37	12	18	49	16	10

* One Independent in each of Nova Scotia and Quebec

Source: Elections Canada. Election 2008: Official Voting Results. Table 7, Distribution of seats, by political affiliation and sex. Found at: http://www.elections.ca/gen/rep/37g/table7_e.html. (Accessed April 3, 2009) Calculations by author.

nearly 24 percent of the vote in Ontario, but in winning only two seats in the province, it was thought to have been confined to the West.

As far as strategy is concerned, when Conservatives despaired of electing members from Quebec and felt they could form a government without much representation from that province, they ignored it, especially in 1957.[19] The Liberals often felt that campaigning in the West was a waste of time and money and therefore concentrated their effort elsewhere. Even in 2000, Liberal leader Jean Chrétien did not bother to stop in Calgary during the campaign. These strategies are not good for keeping the country together, one of the functions that political parties and elections are supposed to perform.

Finally, since the elected members of the party have a major role to play in the development of party policy, Conservative policy did not reflect the concerns of French Canada when the party lacked francophone and Quebec MPs, just as Liberal policy tended to ignore Western concerns because so few Liberals were elected from Western Canada. This is especially serious for the party that forms the government, when it has few or no MPs from a province or region to put into the Cabinet. Between 1962 and 1984, either Quebec or the West was effectively left out of national decision making at the Cabinet level. Residents of such provinces or regions understandably feel that national policy does not reflect their interests and turn to provincial governments to defend these interests or start to think in separatist terms.

Beyond the problems identified by Cairns, first-past-the-post is criticized in other ways. It is said to promote the over-representation of white males because each party can only nominate a single candidate in each constituency and may be tempted to choose the "lowest common denominator." It may discourage voter turnout because those who support candidates that are not likely to win will not bother to vote when their effort will be "wasted." And it may encourage voters to opt for their second choice candidate ("strategic voting") because their first choice has no chance of winning.

Remedies

Given these problems, especially when FPTP is no longer producing majority governments, reform of the electoral system is increasingly urged. The most extreme remedy would be a system of "proportional representation" in which constituencies would be eliminated and each party would receive as many seats in each province as its popular vote dictated. Although such a system has its advocates, most observers feel that Canadians do not want to part with local constituency representation. William Irvine first proposed a system somewhat akin to that in Germany—usually called "mixed member proportional"—in which about half of the MPs would be elected from constituencies, as they are now. The others, called "provincial MPs," would be designated on the basis of popular vote by party in each province to bring each party's proportion of popular vote and percentage of seats into line, both in individual provinces and in the country as a whole. Irvine hoped to overcome the lack of representation of important segments of opinion in party caucuses and the Cabinet, as well as to avoid the sense of regional–ethnic alienation that stems from the current situation.[20] It would probably be the prerogative of individual parties to draw up a list of candidates from which these "provincial MPs" would be selected. The positive side of such a process is that women and minority ethnocultural candidates could be placed at the top of the list and obtain increased representation as a result. It would also mean that fewer votes would be "wasted," because even if a person's vote did not help elect a constituency MP, it would likely contribute to the election of those MPs based on popular vote.

Sensing that such a reform might be too radical for Canadian taste, several authorities have suggested a more modest "top-up" system in which the first-past-the-post system would be supplemented by a smaller number of proportional MPs, say 50 or 60, who would overcome the worst problems of the existing system but still theoretically make majority government possible. This system would start with the regularly elected constituency MPs who are necessary to ensure the representation of all parts of Canada. But some 50 supplementary MPs would be added, to be distributed on the basis of popular vote by party by province. They would correct the greatest discrepancies between the proportion of seats and votes.

For the party in power, such supplementary MPs could provide provincial representation in the Cabinet; for opposition parties, they would speak up for their provinces in the caucus and in Parliament, improving the party's image and policies. Representing an entire province, it is not likely that such provincial MPs would be underemployed, and they would probably soon shed the status of "second-class" representatives. Alternatively, they could concentrate on committee and other legislative work in the Commons. To avoid the negative connotations of being chosen by party officials in "smoke-filled back rooms," they could be drawn from the party's candidates in each province who were most narrowly defeated in the general election and would seek re-election in a specific constituency the next time around.

Reform along more proportional lines was first officially endorsed by the Pépin–Roberts Task Force on Canadian Unity in 1979, and the idea appealed to both Pierre Trudeau and Ed Broadbent as party leaders at the time. It would favour all federalist parties in some ways, and perhaps the unity of the nation as a whole. On the other hand, some parties and politicians are concerned that it would benefit others more than themselves, while many are worried about the prevalence of minority or coalition governments. Some feel it would give party organizers too much power in choosing and ranking candidates, and others argue that parties should have to fight for victory solely in individual constituencies.

There has been much interest in electoral reform in recent years at the provincial level. In British Columbia, a Citizens' Assembly recommended that the province adopt a single transferable vote (STV) system consisting of multimember constituencies in which voters ranked candidates on their ballot. More proportional representation would be achieved with the election of a wider array of candidates at the local areas. In a referendum in 2005, the proposal received 57 percent support, but the government had previously set the threshold for change at 60 percent, so the proposal was abandoned until the election of 2009. In Prince Edward Island, a recommendation for a "top-up" system (17 constituency seats and 10 proportional members) was more decisively defeated in a referendum in the same year.

Ontario held a referendum on October 10, 2007 on whether to adopt a mixed-member proportional electoral system in which the legislature would have 90 electoral districts and an additional 39 MPPs based on popular vote from party lists. Voters would have two ballots, one for their local representative and one for their party preference. The proposal was soundly defeated: 37 percent voted for MMP and 63 percent voted to retain first-post-the-post.

When BC staged its second referendum on electoral reform in 2009, the results were almost opposite to those of 2005: only 39 percent supported the STV system. Still, there are serious advocates of electoral reform, like Fair Vote Canada, with considerable support from the political science community, who are not likely to let the problem die.[21]

. . . .

FINANCING ELECTIONS
Pre-1974

Before 1974, Canada had no effective laws with respect to party and election finance, and numerous irregularities and outright scandals occurred. The Liberal and Conservative parties relied almost completely on contributions from big business at the national level, which usually produced a surplus to be distributed to candidates' campaigns as well, and candidates were otherwise dependent on donations from small local firms. Both parties had fundraisers (sometimes called "bagmen")—often senators who could exploit their corporate connections and make use of their abundant spare time—assisted by corporate volunteers. Business also made contributions in kind, such as various skilled human resources. Corporate contributions were supplemented by fundraising dinners, but party leaders themselves occasionally had to come to the party's rescue. This was especially the case in the Depression elections of 1930 and 1935, when the Conservatives were led by a multimillionaire, R.B. Bennett. The CCF/ NDP depended primarily on individual membership fees, supplemented by union contributions, but in this case the flow of funds was reversed, and the local candidates had to help finance the central campaign. Overall, the Liberals and Conservatives raised and spent far more than the CCF/NDP, at both the national and the local levels.[22]

The secrecy surrounding party and election finance before 1974 makes it difficult to know how many irregularities and scandals actually took place. The first to come to light was the **Pacific scandal** of 1872, in which a group of businessmen eager to obtain the contract to build the CPR donated some $350 000 to John A. Macdonald's election campaign. When the scandal was revealed, Macdonald's government was defeated in the House of Commons, precipitating another election, which he lost. The second major scandal that came to public attention was the Beauharnois scandal of 1930, in which a similar group gave $600 000 to the Liberal Party in hopes of obtaining the contract to build the Beauharnois Dam on the St. Lawrence River. By the time the deal was publicly exposed, the Liberal Party was in Opposition, and its leader, Mackenzie King, rather incredulously denied any knowledge of such a large contribution.[23] In the 1960s, the Rivard scandal involved drug trafficker Lucien Rivard, who had been a regular contributor to the Liberal Party. He apparently felt that such donations, in addition to his attempted bribery of a government lawyer in a bail proceeding, should get him out of jail. These schemes did not work for him, but another—throwing a hose over the prison wall and escaping—turned out quite well!

The Rivard and other small-scale scandals in the 1960s, together with increasing public expectations of political morality, caused the Pearson government to appoint a commission on the subject of party and election finance in 1964. But when its recommendations were published two years later, no action was taken. It required the heightened sense of public outrage at political immorality in the United States (the Watergate scandal), along with

Opposition pressure in the minority government period of 1972–74, to produce legislation more or less as recommended in 1966. Amendments to the Canada Elections Act were passed in 1974 but did not take effect until the election of 1979.

Federal Election Finance Law and Its Results, 1974–2003

The Federal Election Finance Law had four basic provisions.[24] First, although no limit was placed on the size of contributions, a ceiling was imposed on both national party spending and on candidate expenditures. Second, the disclosure provision required that the names of those contributing more than $100 (later raised to $200) be filed with the chief electoral officer and that such records be open to public inspection. Third, a tax credit provision was added so that contributors with taxable incomes would receive a 75 percent income tax credit for contributions up to $100 (later raised to $200) and declining afterward, to a maximum tax credit of $500. Finally, candidates who received at least 15 percent of the vote would have a portion of their expenses subsidized by the public purse, the original formula being replaced by a flat 50 percent rate in amendments made in 1983. Parties that received a certain minimum percentage of the vote were also subsidized for a portion of their expenditures.

· ·

MAIN PROVISIONS OF FEDERAL ELECTION FINANCE LAW, 1974–2003

- Ceiling on national party spending and on local candidate spending
- Disclosure of contributions more than $200
- Tax credit of 75 percent for contributions up to $200
- Public subsidy to candidates receiving at least 15 percent of the vote and to parties receiving a certain minimum percentage of the vote

The objectives of the legislation were thus to increase the equity, transparency, and participatory nature of the electoral system. Equity would be enhanced in limiting candidate and national party spending, as well as by the public subsidy provision; the disclosure clause would make it difficult in the future for large, secret contributions to be made in return for some favourable government decision; and the tax credit would encourage individual contributions and reduce Liberal and Conservative dependence on corporations.

How did political parties obtain such funds? Liberal, PC, and later, Alliance parties tended to use well-connected corporate supporters to volunteer their time in soliciting funds from other members of the corporate elite. The largest corporations in the country often gave annual contributions of $100 000 or more to both Liberal and Conservative parties. All parties also used direct-mail techniques: after obtaining lists of people's names from magazines, professional organizations, or any other likely source, they mailed out hundreds or thousands of computer-generated letters soliciting contributions, highlighting the tax credit available. Sometimes parties conferred special benefits on those giving more than a certain sum, such as being invited to a reception with the leader. The Liberals and Conservatives especially also raised huge amounts of money at dinners ($100/plate, $500/plate, etc.) at which the party leader or other luminaries spoke. The NDP sometimes received a small number of large union donations.

Table 13.4 reveals the total contributions to parties throughout the 2000 election year, before the system was changed again for the 2004 election. It shows that the Liberals received

TABLE 13.4 Value of Individual, Corporate, and Union Contributions to Parties during 2000 (Dollars)

	Liberal	Alliance	PC	NDP	Bloc
Individual	6 966 801	11 954 957	2 778 118	5 752 150	1 663 967
Corporate	11 862 693	6 753 356	2 777 286	198 757	360 153
Union	77 331	0	0	3 022 480	36 008
Other	1 160 995	932 693	66 290	4 749	199 624
Total	20 067 820	19 641 006	5 621 694	8 978 136	2 259 752

Source: Elections Canada. Contributions to Political Parties. Table 1, Summary of contributions and expenses, by registered political party. Found at: http://www.elections.ca/ecFiscals/2000/table01_e.html. (Accessed December 15, 2002); Elections Canada. Contributions to Political Parties. Table 3, Contributions to registered political parties, by donor category. Found at: http://www.elections.ca/ecFiscals/2000/table03_e.html (Accessed December 15, 2002).

far more from corporations than from individuals; the PCs received about equal amounts from individuals and corporations; the Alliance still had more individual than corporate contributions; and the NDP received twice as much in individual contributions as from unions. The Bloc relied almost exclusively on individual contributions, reflecting its Quebec orientation where, at the provincial level, contributions were restricted to individuals.

Federal Election Finance Law after 2003

In the light of such disparities, compounded by the constant scent of scandal surrounding corporate contributions, it became increasingly common to propose the prohibition of corporate (and trade union) contributions, allowing only individual citizens to contribute to political parties. Quebec pioneered this system 30 years ago in its provincial elections, and Manitoba followed suit. The Chrétien government ran into an abundance of ethical problems in its third term, and as part of a package to clean up the way political parties and government operated, a new regime for election finance came into effect in January 2004.[25] The **Gomery Inquiry** into the sponsorship scandal even revealed that corporations did not always abide by the previous law. For example, in order to exceed the limits, company presidents would sometimes funnel corporate contributions through employees as individual contributions.

The most significant part of the reform was to virtually eliminate corporate and trade union contributions and to limit individual donations to $5000 per year. To compensate for such losses, parties were entitled to an annual public reimbursement of $1.75 for each vote they received in the preceding election. They were also entitled to a reimbursement of 50 percent of their election expenses. All the major political parties seemed satisfied that the loss of corporate (or union) contributions was more than made up for by the new taxpayer-funded allowance, and even the seat-less Green party now receives about $1 million a year based on its popular vote.

The Harper government made additional reforms of party and election finance in its Federal Accountability Act, such that corporations and trade unions can no longer contribute at all to elections, nominations, or leadership candidates. The following are the other main features of post-2006 party and election finance restrictions:

. . . .

ELECTIONS

- Individuals are limited to an annual contribution of $1000 to a party, a constituency association, and a candidate (adjusted for inflation to $1,100 in 2008).
- Individual contributions are eligible for a 75 percent tax credit for contributions up to $400, with the percentage declining thereafter.
- The identity of contributors of more than $200 must be disclosed.
- Candidates have a spending limit in the $90 000 range and must report their expenditures.
- A candidate who received at least 10 percent of the votes is eligible to be reimbursed for 60 percent of his or her election expenses.
- National parties have a spending limit based on 70 cents per person in all the constituencies they contest (in the range of $20 million if they contest all constituencies); they must report their expenditures.
- National parties that received at least two percent of the national vote (or at least five percent in the constituencies they contest) are eligible for an annual public subsidy of $1.75 per vote received in the previous election (adjusted for inflation to $1.95 in 2008).
- National parties are also eligible to receive a public rebate of 50 percent of their election expenses.

. . . .

LEADERSHIP CONTESTS

- Individual contributions are limited to $1000 (adjusted for inflation to $1100 in 2008).
- No spending limit is set, but contributions and expenditures must be disclosed.

. . . .

NOMINATION MEETINGS

- Individual contributions are allowed up to $1000 (adjusted for inflation).
- Contributions and expenditures must be disclosed if either exceeds $1000.
- Expenditures are limited.
- Those seeking the nomination can deduct daycare expenses.

It was anticipated that all parties would put great effort into raising contributions from individuals, but the Conservatives and NDP had more success in this regard than the Liberals. Table 13.5 reveals how much each main party spent in the 2008 election at the national level, including the fact that the NDP outspent the Liberals in that campaign. Table 13.6 shows each party's annual public subsidies for 2008, based on the 2006 election results. While such reforms have had a major impact on the electoral system, at least three controversial aspects remain. First, there is no restriction on party spending outside the election period. Thus, a party with a large war chest and which knows when the election will be held can gain a significant advantage over its adversaries by advertising in the unrestricted pre-election period. Second, the Conservatives, not really needing the public subsidies, tried to deny them to other parties. It was primarily this issue that came close to defeating the Harper minority government in

TABLE 13.5   National Party Expenditures, 2008 Election

Conservatives	$19 418 580
NDP	$16 813 891
Liberals	$14 531 853
BQ	$4 879 604
Green	$2 795 800

*Allowances are adjusted for inflation ($1.95 per vote in 2008).

Source: Elections Canada. Financial Reports: Registered Party Financial Transactions Return. Found at: http://www.elections.ca/scripts/webpep/fin2/summmary_report.aspx (Accessed May 2, 2009).

late 2008 and that was the main impetus to the proposed coalition of Liberals, NDP, and Bloc Québécois. Third, the Conservatives were accused of transferring funds between federal and constituency levels in the 2006 election in order to evade the legal spending limits.

Third-Party Advertising and the Royal Commission on Electoral Reform and Party Financing

Another major problem in the realm of election finance is **third-party advertising**—that is, spending by groups other than candidates and political parties. The 1974 act prohibited advocacy group spending during an election campaign that favoured or opposed a party or candidate. It was argued that the only way party and candidate spending ceilings could be effective was if any spending on their behalf by advocacy groups was included in the parties' budgets. But in the 1980s more and more groups began to advertise for or against various parties or candidates without having these expenses included in the parties' budgets. Although such advertising was clearly a violation of the spirit of the act as well as its specific terms,

TABLE 13.6   Public Allowances for 2008

Party	2006 Votes	Allowance ($)*
Conservatives	5 374 071	10 439 132
Liberals	4 479 415	8 701 263
NDP	2 589 597	5 030 290
BQ	1 553 201	3 017 092
Green	664 068	1 289 951

*Allowances are adjusted for inflation ($1.95 per vote in 2008)

Source: Elections Canada. Quarterly Allowances to Registered Political Parties, 2008. Found at: http://www.elections.ca/content.asp?section=pol&document=qua2008&dir=pol/qua&lang=e&textonly=false (Accessed April 4, 2009) Calculations by author.

the **National Citizens' Coalition (NCC)** challenged the act in the Alberta Court of Queen's Bench in 1984. That court ruled the clauses unconstitutional as a violation of the freedom-of-expression provisions of the Charter of Rights and Freedoms.

Third-party advertising increased enormously in the 1988 election campaign, especially in the case of the pro-free trade group, the Canadian Alliance for Trade and Job Opportunities. Receiving huge corporate contributions from such companies as Canadian Pacific, Alcan Aluminum, Shell, Noranda, Imperial Oil, the Royal Bank, Sun Life, Manufacturers' Life, Northern Telecom, IBM, Inco, Olympia & York, and Texaco, the group collected and spent more than $5 million.[26] With only one political party in favour of free trade, namely the Conservatives, any advertising that promoted the Free Trade Agreement also promoted the Conservative Party. Thus the Conservatives benefited from some $5 million in advertising by advocacy groups on top of their own national budget of nearly $8 million, with the same large corporations contributing to both causes. Such third-party advertising made a mockery of party spending ceilings and is widely thought to have helped the Conservatives achieve re-election by turning the momentum of the campaign back in their favour during the last two weeks, especially in Ontario.

In response to widespread public criticism of this problem and the retiring chief electoral officer's repeated recommendations for change in this and other aspects of the Canada Elections Act, the Mulroney government appointed a **Royal Commission on Electoral Reform and Party Financing** shortly after the 1988 election. Headed by Pierre Lortie, that commission identified several other concerns, held public hearings across the country, and commissioned extensive academic research. The royal commission recommended that spending during the election period by individuals or organizations other than candidates and political parties be restricted to $1000. The commission argued that to limit paid advertising by such advocacy groups during the 30- to 40-day period every four years was a "reasonable limit" on freedom of expression and would stand up to judicial scrutiny. This limit was legislated before the 1997 election, in a diluted form, but it was immediately challenged by the NCC, and Alberta courts once again found that it violated the Charter.

The new Canada Elections Act passed before the November 2000 election imposed an overall ceiling on third-party advertising during the campaign of $150 000, of which no more than $3000 could be spent in each electoral district on advertising for or against candidates. Of course, the NCC challenged these new spending limits, but they were finally upheld by the Supreme Court of Canada in 2004.[27] In the 2008 campaign, these ceilings were adjusted for inflation to a total of $183 300 and $3666 per electoral district. Some 62 third parties registered in that election. The National Citizens Coalition continued its tradition in this regard, but many of the other third parties were on the left of the spectrum, such as the Council of Canadians, Make Poverty History, Friends of Canadian Broadcasting, and many unions.

. . . .

CONCLUSION

Because elections are crucial to the operation of Canadian democracy, it is unfortunate that the electoral system is still somewhat flawed. Although the actual operation of the system on election day is now basically satisfactory, and most problems of party and election finance have been eliminated, the principle of representation by population is widely breached, and parties are not awarded seats in proportion to their popular support. The minority governments that currently result from the first-past-the-post system weaken the argument that, whatever its other faults, FPTP usually produces a majority government.

This chapter is closely related to the following two on political parties and the election campaign. It also has links to some of the demographic chapters earlier in the book as well as the Charter of Rights, especially in terms of the extension of the right to vote. Moreover, elections constitute the basis of the House of Commons, and therefore, as well, the Executive branch of government in Part 5 of the book.

© Of the approaches outlined in Chapter 1, class analysts make many points, especially with respect to the historic system of party and electoral finance. They had little difficulty in finding a quid pro quo for corporate contributions: governments gave corporations tax concessions of all kinds, loans, grants, and contracts; preferential legislation and regulations; and free trade. It was only the revelation of funding scandals that persuaded the Chrétien and Harper governments to eliminate such corporate contributions. Increasing the proportionality of the electoral system would probably also benefit left-wing parties such as the NDP. Class analysts would therefore point out that when provincial governments required a 60 percent majority in referendums on electoral reform, they were favouring the forces that sustain capitalist rule.

PC The public choice model is interested in the mechanics of the electoral system insofar as they determine which groups within the electorate must be accommodated by political parties in order to achieve victory. An electoral system that overrepresents some interests and underrepresents others will affect the promises political parties make. Moreover, if the relationship between seats and votes is skewed, public choice theorists note that certain interests can be ignored. The way in which the mechanics of the electoral system traditionally gave the Liberals more seats than they deserved in Quebec and fewer in Western Canada (with the reverse being true for the Conservatives) meant that both parties put greatest effort into Ontario, which is where such effort would pay them dividends. In any case, no party that wants to form the government can ignore the fact that Ontario contains more than one-third of the constituencies. Public choice also has things to say about how parties, once in office, can get around those planks of their election platforms that they never intended to implement. On another issue, rational choice scholars argue that politicians seek to shape the rules in their own interest. This would certainly apply to the historic pattern of party finance laws, as well as to resistance to adopt a more proportional electoral system in recent years.

P Pluralists note that the elimination of restrictions to the franchise is likely to increase the diversity of viewpoints expressed and members elected, although a more proportional electoral system is sometimes advocated on the grounds that it would likely increase the Parliamentary representation of women and ethnocultural minorities. Pluralists also argue that in the redistribution process it is often more important for a constituency to reflect a distinct "community of interest" than to have a number of voters exactly equal to that in other ridings.

State-centred theorists and neo-institutionalists emphasize how the mechanics of the electoral system can affect the results and how most of these mechanics are beyond the interest or comprehension of the general electorate. Such concerns include the way in which the redistribution process is handled, the discrepancies between votes and seats, and the rules with respect to party and election finance. One of the most blatant is how established parties rigged the rules to favour themselves in the distribution of broadcast time and in the subsidies for party advertising, as mentioned in Chapter 15.

DISCUSSION QUESTIONS

1. Given the peculiar distribution of the Canadian population, to what extent should we adhere to the principle of "representation by population"?

2. Should the party leader have a veto on local nominations? Why or why not?

3. Should the electoral system be reformed in a more proportional direction? If so, how?

4. Should further changes be made to the law governing party and election finance?

5. What are the arguments on each side of the debate over third-party advertising?

NOTES

1. Jon H. Pammett, "Elections," in Michael Whittington and Glen Williams, eds. *Canadian Politics in the 21st Century*, 7th ed. (Toronto: Thomson Nelson, 2008).
2. See, for example, Richard Rose, ed., *The International Encyclopedia of Elections* (Washington: CQ Press, 2000); and David Butler, Howard Penniman, and Austin Ranney, eds., Democracy at the Polls: A Comparative Study of Competitive National Elections (Washington: American Enterprise Institute, 1981).
3. See, for example, Ontario Citizens' Assembly Secretariat, *From Votes to Seats: Four Families of Electoral Systems;* and Denis Pilon, *The Politics of Voting: Reforming Canada's Electoral System* (Toronto: Emond Montgomery, 2007).
4. John Courtney, *Elections* (Vancouver: UBC Press, 2004), ch. 3.
5. For Sir John A. Macdonald's efforts, see R.M. Dawson, "The Gerrymander of 1881," *Canadian Journal of Economics and Political Science* (May 1935).
6. See Chapter 19; John C. Courtney, Peter MacKinnon, and David E. Smith, eds., *Drawing Boundaries: Legislatures, Courts and Electoral Values* (Saskatoon: Fifth House Publishers, 1992); and John Courtney, Commissioned Ridings (Montreal: McGill-Queen's University Press, 2001).
7. Elections Canada, "Federal Electoral Districts—Representation Order of 2003." For 1995, see Louis Massicotte, "Electoral Reform in the Charter Era," in Alan Frizzell and Jon H. Pammett, eds., *The Canadian General Election of 1997* (Toronto: Dundurn Press, 1997), p. 178.
8. John C. Courtney, "Parliament and Representation: The Unfinished Agenda of Electoral Redistributions," *Canadian Journal of Political Science* (December 1988); and Andrew Sancton, "Eroding Representation-by-Population in the Canadian House of Commons: The Representation Act, 1985," *Canadian Journal of Political Science* (September 1990).
9. Courtney, *Elections;* Louis Massicotte, "The Chief Electoral Officer of Canada," *Canadian Parliamentary Review* (Autumn 2003).
10. *Report of the Chief Electoral Officer of Canada*, p. 46; Democracy Watch, news release, January 27, 2006.
11. William Cross, *Political Parties* (Vancouver: UBC Press, 2004), ch. 4.

12. *R. v. Bryan*, [2007] 1 S.C.R. 527.

13. MacIvor, *Canadian Politics and Government in the Charter Era*, ch. 9. An amendment was made to the Canada Elections Act in 2001 that allowed a party with a minimum of 12 candidates—rather than the previous requirement of 50 candidates—to place the party label on the ballot, but in 2003 the Supreme Court overruled this decision as discriminatory: one candidate was enough. This case, centred on the Communist Party of Canada, also allowed smaller parties to issue tax receipts to donors and to retain unspent election contributions. See *Figueroa v. Canada (Attorney General)*, [2003] 1 S.C.R. 912.

14. In 2008: Conservative, Liberal, NDP, Bloc Québécois, Canadian Action, Green, Marxist-Leninist, Communist, Marijuana, Christian Heritage, Progressive Canadian Party, Libertarian, First Peoples National Party, Western Block Party, Animal Alliance Environment Voters Party, neorhino.ca, People's Political Power Party, Work Less Party, and Newfoundland and Labrador First Party.

15. Elections Canada, *A History of the Vote in Canada* (Ottawa: Public Works and Government Services, 1997); and Courtney, *Elections*, ch. 2.

16. Chief Electoral Officer, *Towards the 35th General Election* (Ottawa: 1994, Catalogue. No. SE 1-5/1993); Massicotte, "Electoral Reform in the Charter Era"; *Sauvé v. Canada (A.G.)*, [1993] 2 S.C.R. 438; *Sauvé v. Canada (Chief Electoral Officer)*, [1996] 1 F.C. 857; and *Sauvé v. Canada (Chief Electoral Officer)*, [2002] 3 S.C.R. 519.

17. Alan C. Cairns, "The Electoral System and the Party System in Canada," *Canadian Journal of Political Science* (March 1968).

18. The most prominent provincial examples are Quebec, 1944, 1966, and 1998; Saskatchewan, 1986 and 1999; BC, 1941 and 1996; and New Brunswick, 2006.

19. John Meisel, *The Canadian General Election of 1957* (Toronto: University of Toronto Press, 1962).

20. William Irvine, *Does Canada Need a New Electoral System?* (Kingston: Institute of Intergovernmental Relations, Queen's University, 1979).

21. Henry Milner, ed., *Making Every Vote Count: Reassessing Canada's Electoral System* (Peterborough: Broadview Press, 1999); Milner, ed., *Steps Toward Making Every Vote Count: Electoral System Reform in Canada and Its Provinces* (Peterborough: Broadview Press, 2004); Law Commission of Canada, *Voting Counts: Electoral Reform for Canada* (Ottawa, 2004); Fair Vote Canada at http://www.fairvotecanada.org/fvc.php; and Pilon, *The Politics of Voting: Reforming Canada's Electoral System*.

22. K.Z. Paltiel, *Political Party Financing in Canada* (Toronto: McGraw-Hill Ryerson, 1970).

23. T.D. Regehr, *The Beauharnois Scandal* (Toronto: University of Toronto Press, 1990).

24. W.T. Stanbury, "Regulating Federal Party and Candidate Finances in a Dynamic Environment," in H.G. Thorburn and Alan Whitehorn, eds., *Party Politics in Canada*, 8th ed. (Toronto: Prentice Hall, 2001); Cross, *Political Parties*, ch. 7.

25. Elections Canada, 2003 Electoral Reform—Political Financing, at http://www.elections.ca/content.asp?section=loi&document=major&dir=re3&lang=e&textonly=false; Cross, *Political Parties*, ch. 7; Craig Forcese and Aaron Freeman, *The Laws of Government: The Legal Foundations of Canadian Democracy* (Toronto: Irwin Law, 2005), pp. 100–132; Louis Massicotte, "Electoral Legislation Since 1997: Parliament Regains the Initiative," in Jon H. Pammett and Christopher Dornan, eds., *The Canadian Federal Election of 2006* (Toronto: Dundurn, 2006); and W. Scott Thurlow, "Financing Canadian Elections," *Canadian Parliamentary Review* (Winter 2008–09).

26. *Toronto Star*, December 9, 1989, p. C1.

27. Massicotte, "Election Reform in the Charter Era"; *National Citizens' Coalition Inc. v. A.G. Canada*, [1984] 11 D.L.R. (4th) 481; *Somerville v. Canada (A.G.)*, [1996] 136 D.L.R. (4th) 205 (Alta C.A.); *Libman v. Quebec (Attorney General)*, [1997] 3 S.C.R. 569; and *Harper v. Canada (Attorney General)*, [2004] 1 S.C.R. 827.

. . . .

FURTHER READING

Cairns, Alan C. "The Electoral System and the Party System in Canada." *Canadian Journal of Political Science* (March 1968).

Courtney, John. *Elections*. Vancouver: UBC Press, 2004.

Courtney, John C., Peter MacKinnon, and David E. Smith, eds. *Drawing Boundaries: Legislatures, Courts and Electoral Values*. Saskatoon: Fifth House Publishers, 1992.

Cross, William. *Political Parties*. Vancouver: UBC Press, 2004.

Forcese, Craig, and Aaron Freeman. *The Laws of Government: The Legal Foundations of Canadian Democracy*. Toronto: Irwin Law, 2005.

Gagnon, Alain-G. and A. Brian Tanguay, eds., *Canadian Parties in Transition*, 3rd ed. Peterborough: Broadview Press, 2007.

Law Commission of Canada. *Voting Counts: Electoral Reform for Canada*. Ottawa, 2004.

MacIvor, Heather, ed. *Election*. Toronto: Emond Montgomery, 2009.

Milner, Henry, ed. *Making Every Vote Count: Reassessing Canada's Electoral System*. Peterborough: Broadview Press, 1999.

———, ed. *Steps Toward Making Every Vote Count: Electoral System Reform in Canada and Its Provinces*. Peterborough: Broadview Press, 2004.

Pammett, Jon H. "Elections." In Michael Whittington and Glen Williams, eds., *Canadian Politics in the 21st Century*, 7th ed. Toronto: Thomson Nelson, 2008.

———, and Christopher Dornan, eds. *The Canadian Federal Election of 2006*. Toronto: Dundurn Press, 2006.

———, and ———, eds. *The Canadian Federal Election of 2008*. Toronto: Dundurn Press, 2009.

Pilon, Denis. *The Politics of Voting: Reforming Canada's Electoral System*. Toronto: Emond Montgomery, 2007.

Chapter 14

POLITICAL PARTIES AND
the Party System

Political parties are integral to the operation of almost every aspect of a modern political system, but Canadians are generally more attuned to their faults than their virtues. They are widely criticized for their partisan appointments, for their vicious attacks on each other and each other's leaders, and for their loud and often obnoxious behaviour during Question Period in the House of Commons. It is often difficult to appreciate the value of political parties, but they should not be known by their defects alone.

For most of the post-1867 period, the Liberal and (Progressive) Conservative parties dominated the Canadian political scene. The New Democratic Party became a stable contender after 1961, while various smaller parties—the Progressives, CCF, Social Credit, Créditistes, and Union Nationale—have come and gone, some of them forming governments at the provincial level. When the Conservatives self-destructed in 1993 and two new parties joined the fray, the Reform Party (later, the Canadian Alliance) and the Bloc Québécois, the Liberals gained a new lease on life. But they began to decline after 2000 and the two "right-wing" parties united in 2003. This led to a Liberal minority government after the 2004 election, and the new Conservative Party of Canada formed minority governments after the 2006 and 2008 elections.

This chapter is divided into four main sections: the historical evolution of Canadian political parties, interpretations of the Canadian party system, party ideology, and party organization. Party and electoral finance were examined in Chapter 13, and the role of parties in the electoral campaign, including electoral behaviour and party support, is discussed in Chapter 15.

. . . .

THEORETICAL CONSIDERATIONS

A **political party** can be defined as an organized group that nominates candidates and contests elections in order to influence the personnel and policy of government. Although some parties operate for long periods in the political wilderness and may be able to exert a certain amount of influence without being in power, almost every party ultimately hopes to form the government and make policy and personnel decisions on its own. Beyond this unique function, parties are distinct from other groups in society in two main ways. Whereas most other groups possess a fairly narrow focus and articulate a single interest, political parties are usually broader in scope and seek to aggregate, combine, consolidate, or appeal to many different interests or demands. In the process, parties reduce these demands to a manageable quantity called "issues." In addition, while other groups provide "functional" representation—economic, occupational, cultural, religious—political parties are closely tied to the formal institutions of government, including the electoral system and Parliament, all of which are based on territorial representation.

Another function of political parties is to recruit decision makers, primarily by means of the electoral system. They usually choose as candidates people who have been party members for some time and who have been "groomed" or trained. The government party also appoints certain political officeholders, often from the ranks of its own supporters, a practice referred to as **political patronage**. In addition to recruitment, parties engage in political socialization and citizen education as they point out their own strengths and their opponents' weaknesses in the daily partisan battle in Parliament as well as on the election trail.

Parties are also integrally involved in the legislative and executive operations of government. The formal and informal procedures of the House of Commons and Senate are completely imbued with partisan considerations, especially in the party discipline they display, while the Canadian Cabinet tradition is that all ministers are drawn from a single party, even in a minority government situation, so that they will be able to come to agreement more easily on government policy.

Beyond this list of functions, parties may be engaged in formulating public policy. In theory, at least, each party develops a distinctive election platform; the successful party then proceeds to implement it, while the opposition parties continue to provide clear-cut policy alternatives. In reality, the policymaking role of political parties is often minimal: parties do not always provide policy alternatives to the electorate; governments frequently ignore their election platforms in office; and they often obtain policy ideas from other sources.[1]

Theoretical considerations about political parties also centre around different kinds of parties. One way to categorize them is in terms of appeal. "Broker" parties generally try to appeal to a wide range of interests in society in order to form a majority government based on a coalition of groups, but in the process relinquish any claim to a focused ideological approach. Among the interests that are usually deemed of importance in Canada are region and ethnicity. Ideological or "missionary" parties, on the other hand, try to cut through such divisions by emphasizing a central message, usually based on class or a right- or left-wing ideology. Of course, parties could also be based on a single regional or ethnic interest.

Parties can also be categorized in terms of organization. Run by a small group of notables, "cadre" parties are not particularly democratic in structure or operation. "Mass" parties, on the other hand, tend to promote a large membership with significant influence in the functioning of the party. It is often the case that broker and cadre categories overlap, as do the missionary and mass designations. Heather McIvor deems that most of this terminology is obsolete, at least in the Canadian case, and that our four main parties can all be called "electoralist," and are basically focused on winning elections. Even so, she distinguishes between "catch-all" parties (Liberals and Conservatives) who mainly want to maximize their votes, and "programmatic" parties (NDP and Bloc Québécois) which retain a somewhat ideological agenda.[2] Such issues of ideology and organization will be examined later in the chapter.

A final theoretical point relates to the concept of hegemony. Most political parties want to gain power, so they will promote the dominant values and expectations of society. If such values change, however, mainline parties will probably respond in order to retain their control. Some parties stand for alternate values, of course, but they have a hard time becoming accepted as legitimate players in the electoral game. This is not only because they are rowing against the orthodox current, but also because the mainline parties have designed the rules of the game in their own interests.

. . . .

HISTORICAL EVOLUTION OF CANADIAN PARTIES

At this point, a brief discussion of the historical evolution of the Canadian political party system may be useful. Ken Carty suggests dividing this evolution into four parts, or four party systems; these can be distinguished by the number of parties in contention and their different approaches to seeking election, and can be structured around a list of prime ministers, their parties, and their dates of office.[3]

The First Party System, 1867–1921

Until 1921, the Conservative and Liberal parties virtually monopolized Canadian politics. David Smith points out that successful party leaders, such as John A. Macdonald and Wilfrid Laurier, sponsored great national projects on the one hand while being masters of detailed constituency and patronage politics on the other.[4]

. . . .

PRIME MINISTERS, 1867–1921

John A. Macdonald	Conservative	1867–73
Alexander Mackenzie	Liberal	1873–78
John A. Macdonald	Conservative	1878–91
John Abbott	Conservative	1891–92
John Thompson	Conservative	1892–94
Mackenzie Bowell	Conservative	1894–96
Charles Tupper	Conservative	1896
Wilfrid Laurier	Liberal	1896–1911
Robert Borden	Conservative	1911–20
Arthur Meighen	Conservative	1920–21

The Conservative Party is usually said to have had its beginnings in 1854 when John A. Macdonald formed a coalition of four pre-Confederation groupings: Tories and Moderates from Upper Canada (Ontario), along with English businessmen and French Conservatives from Lower Canada (Quebec). Party lines for individual politicians were quite flexible in those days, and many MPs were called "ministerialists" because of their promise to support

John A. Macdonald, the founder of the Conservative Party, served as prime minister for 19 years.

the ministry of the day in return for government favours. Alliances among groups were also unstable, but Macdonald's coalition gradually melded into an organized political party. The two main groups left out of this coalition—the French radicals in Quebec and the Clear Grits from Upper Canada—later became the nucleus around which an organized Liberal party took form.

After Macdonald was disgraced by the Pacific scandal, the Liberals took office between 1873 and 1878 under Alexander Mackenzie, but his government reflected this early lack of cohesion. Macdonald returned to power in 1878 and the Conservatives demonstrated increasing party unity as time went on. After the execution of Louis Riel, however, French-Canadian support started to fall away from the Conservative Party, helped by the fact that an attractive francophone, Wilfrid Laurier, soon became leader of the Liberal Party. Macdonald died in 1891, and his party experienced a period of great instability as it went through four leaders in the subsequent five years. Thus, with the government party in decline and the Liberals finally showing the marks of a well-organized national party, it is not surprising that Laurier won the watershed election of 1896.[5] At that time Canada moved from a situation of Conservative **one-party dominance** to a classic **two-party system** in which Liberals and Conservatives competed on equal terms. Thus, the "first party system" can be subdivided into two parts, before and after 1896.

Laurier governed quite successfully until he was beaten in 1911, when the two main issues were reciprocity (free trade with the United States) and the naval question (whether Canada should establish its own navy or contribute to that of Britain). Robert Borden's Conservatives took over and were soon confronted with the monumental task of managing Canada's war effort. In 1917, after three years of war, Borden concluded that conscription would have to be adopted, but, conscious of French-Canadian opposition, he proposed a coalition government with Laurier, who still led the Opposition Liberals. Most English-speaking Liberal MPs agreed to join the Conservatives in a **Union Government** in 1917, but Laurier and the French-Canadian Liberals remained in opposition, leaving that party badly split. With conscription, the Conservatives almost totally alienated French Canada, at the same time as the policies of both Conservative and Liberal parties upset the farming community in English Canada, notably the West. Thus, while Mackenzie King succeeded Laurier as Liberal leader in 1919 and skilfully pursued party reconciliation, Arthur Meighen inherited an unpopular Conservative Party in 1920 when he took over from Borden.

The Second Party System, 1921–1957

The 1921 election marked the end of the two-party system in Canada; from that point onward, there were always other parties in contention, leading to the label **two-plus** or **two-and-a-half party system**, at least until 1980. Moreover, in this period dominated by Mackenzie King and Louis St. Laurent, the Liberal government was characterized by decentralized ministerial accommodation in which strong regional Cabinet ministers exercised a great deal of individual power and then spoke for their regions in the development of a national consensus.

· ·

PRIME MINISTERS, 1921–1957

Mackenzie King	Liberal	1921–26
Arthur Meighen	Conservative	1926
Mackenzie King	Liberal	1926–30
R.B. Bennett	Conservative	1930–35
Mackenzie King	Liberal	1935–48
Louis St. Laurent	Liberal	1948–57

Wilfrid Laurier, Canada's first French-Canadian prime minister.

William James Topley/Library and Archives Canada/C-001971

In 1921, farmers entered the contest with their own Progressive candidates and elected more members than the Conservatives,[6] while two Labour members were also successful. Farmers were particularly unhappy with conscription, tariff, agricultural, and transportation policies, as well as prevailing political practices, such as party patronage and rigid party discipline in the House of Commons. Nevertheless, Mackenzie King led his Liberals to victory in 1921, in 1925, and again in 1926 (after a brief Conservative interruption caused by the King–Byng dispute discussed in Chapter 21), and by the late 1920s most of the Progressive MPs either had become Liberals or had been defeated. A few of the more radical farmers joined with the Labour members to form the Ginger Group in Parliament, while the Liberals were defeated in 1930, primarily because of the onset of the Great Depression.

By this time the Conservatives were led by R.B. Bennett. Although he exercised vigorous leadership and even departed from orthodox Conservative policy to some extent, Bennett could not cope with the unemployment, poverty, and general devastation wrought by the Depression. Along with almost every other government in office during this period, Bennett's Conservatives were defeated in 1935, and Mackenzie King's Liberals returned to power.

Besides contributing to this change of government, the Depression was the catalyst for the creation of several new political parties, and marks the division between two parts of the "second party system." The Co-operative Commonwealth Federation (CCF) was formed in Calgary in 1932, an amalgam of the parliamentary Ginger Group, the intellectual League for Social Reconstruction (largely centred in Toronto and Montreal), and various farmer and labour groups and scattered socialist and farmer–labour parties, primarily from the West. In 1933 the party adopted its radical platform, the Regina Manifesto, at its meeting in that city, and chose Labour member of Parliament J.S. Woodsworth as its leader. The party elected several MPs in 1935 and took office in Saskatchewan in 1944 under T.C. (Tommy) Douglas.[7]

The Social Credit Party was born in Alberta in 1935 around the charismatic evangelist William Aberhart. The party was originally concerned with the reform of the banking system as a means of dealing with the Depression but abandoned this platform when it proved to be both unworkable and unconstitutional. After Alberta became prosperous with the discovery of oil in the 1940s, Social Credit transformed itself into an orthodox conservative party under E.C. Manning. The party remained in power in Alberta for 36 years, came to power in British Columbia in 1952, and elected several Western MPs.[8]

In Quebec, a group of disgruntled progressive Liberals defected from their provincial party in 1935 to join forces with the chronically unsuccessful provincial Conservative Party in the formation of the new Union Nationale. The leader, Maurice Duplessis, quickly discarded the comprehensive reform program on which the party was elected a year later and became ultraconservative. Despite this shift in emphasis, the Union Nationale remained in power in Quebec until 1960 with only a four-year interruption between 1940 and 1944.[9]

None of these developments impeded the Liberal Party at the federal level; it continued to elect majority governments from 1935 to 1948 under Mackenzie King and then, until 1957, under his successor, Louis St. Laurent. King's conciliatory skills were severely tested during the Second World War (1939–45), but his government avoided a serious second **conscription crisis**. He also presided over the initiation of the Canadian welfare state. The St. Laurent period was one of great prosperity, largely financed by a tremendous inflow of American investment.[10]

The Conservative Party floundered for 20 years after 1935, having previously alienated French Canada and having been blamed, however unfairly, for the Depression. It changed leaders repeatedly, changed party policy to some extent, and changed the party name to Progressive Conservative in 1942, all to no avail.

The Third Party System, 1957–1993

The Liberal dominance was at least temporarily halted in the 1957 election. The next 35 years was a period of alternating minority and majority governments, Progressive Conservative and Liberal. David Smith contends that the Diefenbaker and Trudeau eras were marked by a more pan-Canadian approach, as each leader had a vision of the national interest that he sought to impose. In this period as well, television linked individual voters to these leaders without the need for regional intermediaries. Some of these characteristics might also be applied to the Mulroney era. From 1957 to 1980, the system was marked by two major parties and two minor parties.

• •

PRIME MINISTERS, 1957–1993

John Diefenbaker	Progressive Conservative	1957–63
Lester B. Pearson	Liberal	1963–68
Pierre Elliott Trudeau	Liberal	1968–79
Joe Clark	Progressive Conservative	1979–80
Pierre Elliott Trudeau	Liberal	1980–84
John Turner	Liberal	1984
Brian Mulroney	Progressive Conservative	1984–93
Kim Campbell	Progressive Conservative	1993

John Diefenbaker became Conservative Party leader in 1956 and led the party to a surprising minority government victory a year later and then to a record majority in 1958. This was partly due to the public's increasing resentment of Liberal complacency and arrogance, as demonstrated in the infamous **pipeline debate**. Diefenbaker's decline was almost as rapid as his ascent, however, as his government fell apart over defence policy. The party was reduced to a minority government position again in 1962, and defeated a year later, after which it engaged in a long period of bitter in-fighting over the leadership question.[11]

During the Diefenbaker period, significant developments in two minor parties took place. The CCF, which had seen its fortunes decline throughout the 1950s, decided to combine its efforts with those of the new national labour organization, the Canadian Labour Congress. The result was the creation of the New Democratic Party (NDP) in 1961. T.C. Douglas was persuaded to leave the premiership of Saskatchewan to become the first national NDP leader.[12] Then, out of the blue, a group of Social Credit or Créditiste MPs was elected from Quebec in 1962, just when the western wing of the party was starting to decline.[13]

Lester Pearson's Liberals were elected in 1963 and re-elected in 1965, but were never able to win a majority government. Nonetheless, in spite of his minority status, Pearson tackled many controversial issues, particularly the new nationalism in Quebec, the Canada Pension Plan, medicare, and a new flag. One opposition party or another supported each of Pearson's measures so that he was able to continue in office until he retired.[14]

In 1968, the Liberals gained a majority government under their new leader, Pierre Elliott Trudeau, but just narrowly defeated Robert Stanfield's Conservatives in 1972. In the resulting minority government, the Liberals worked closely with the NDP, but this support was withdrawn two years later. With Trudeau ridiculing Stanfield's proposal for **wage and price controls**, the Liberals were returned with a majority in 1974, only to turn around and implement such a policy themselves. By 1979, the Liberals had apparently accumulated other faults as well, for they were defeated by the Conservatives, now led by Joe Clark. Nine months later, the Clark government fell with parliamentary rejection of its budget, and Trudeau led his party back to power in early 1980.[15]

The 1980s can be considered the second part of the third party system and even labelled a **three-party system** because, at least between elections, the NDP became entrenched as a national party. At the same time, the separatist Parti Québécois formed the government of Quebec between 1976 and 1985 under René Lévesque. After persuading Quebeckers to give Canada one last chance in their 1980 referendum, Trudeau patriated the Constitution, together with a Charter of Rights and Freedoms, and enacted the controversial National Energy Program.[16] He resigned in 1984, turning the reins over to John Turner, who was pitted against the new Conservative leader, Brian Mulroney. In the 1984 election, the Conservatives won a landslide victory, including a startling majority of the seats in Mulroney's home province of Quebec.[17] After the negotiation of the Canada–U.S. Free Trade Agreement and the Meech Lake Accord, Mulroney led his party to a second successive majority government in 1988, only to see Meech Lake fail to acquire the unanimous approval of new provincial governments in 1990. A second attempt at comprehensive constitutional reform, the Charlottetown Accord, failed in a national referendum in 1992.

The Fourth Party System, 1993–

The Liberal Party's obsession with Quebec was the main reason that the West preferred the Conservatives after 1957. When Westerners perceived that the Mulroney Conservatives were likewise concerned primarily with holding on to their unprecedented Quebec support after 1984, however, many residents turned to support the new Reform Party headed by Preston Manning, son of the former Social Credit premier of Alberta. Then, with the collapse of the Meech Lake Accord, sovereignist sentiment increased in Quebec, and several Conservative and Liberal MPs defected to form a new federal separatist party, the Bloc Québécois. Thus, five parties of considerable strength contested the 1993 federal election, and produced a highly unusual result: the Liberals did well across the country, the Bloc Québécois displaced the Conservatives in Quebec, and the Reform Party routed the Conservatives in the West. The PCs held on to 16 percent of the popular vote but retained only two seats, and the NDP did badly everywhere. Given that a minimum of 12 seats is required for official party standing in the House of Commons, only three parties came back as recognized parties, two of them new, and it seemed that a real and regionalized **multi-party system** had developed.[18] The 1997 election returned five official but highly regionalized parties, at least in terms of seats won.

· ·

PRIME MINISTERS, 1993–

Jean Chrétien	Liberal	1993–2003
Paul Martin	Liberal	2003–06
Stephen Harper	Conservative	2006–

Given the fact that the Reform Party did not substantially increase its support in Ontario or the five easternmost provinces in the 1997 federal election, Manning began to promote the idea of a "United Alternative." He primarily hoped to attract the remaining supporters of the PC Party to join in a new right-wing party. In January 2000, the Reform Party transformed itself into the Canadian Reform Conservative Alliance, known as the Canadian Alliance, but most Progressive Conservatives steadfastly refused to join. Former Alberta provincial treasurer Stockwell Day then beat Manning for the leadership of the new party in July 2000.[19] The 2000 election also returned five official parties, all with regionalized support; the Liberals won another majority government and the Canadian Alliance formed the official Opposition. After the 2000 election, there was much internal criticism of Alliance leader Stockwell Day. Twelve Alliance MPs with no confidence in his leadership left or were kicked out of the party caucus. Calling themselves the Democratic Representative Caucus, they formed a kind of opposition coalition group with the Progressive Conservatives, led for a second time by Joe Clark, but when Day was replaced by Stephen Harper as Alliance leader in March 2002, most of them returned to the Alliance fold.

Peter MacKay replaced Clark as leader of the PCs in May 2003, while Paul Martin became Liberal leader in November of that year. A month later, breaking a promise never to negotiate with the Canadian Alliance, MacKay agreed to a merger of the two parties to "unite the right" in the new Conservative Party of Canada. The MacKay–Harper pact was promptly supported by a majority of the members of each party in hastily arranged votes, although many PC members, including Clark, refused to join, and the new combined party chose Harper as its leader in March 2004.

Since 1993, the Bloc Québécois has held more than 40 percent of the voter support in Quebec, significantly reducing the traditional Liberal dominance of the province. Indeed, if some 50 Quebec seats are automatically siphoned off by the Bloc, it is difficult for any party to

BOX 14.1	Evolution of Canadian Party System by Era		
Era	Major Parties	Minor Parties	Label
1867–96	Conservative	Liberal	One-party dominance
1896–1921	Liberal, Conservative		Two-party system
1921–35	Liberal, Conservative	Progressives	Two-plus party system
1935–57	Liberal	Conservative, CCF, Social Credit	One-party dominance
1957–80	Liberal, Conservative	CCF/NDP, Social Credit	Two-plus-two party system
1980–93	Liberal, Conservative, NDP		Three-party system
1993–2003	Liberal	Reform (Canadian Alliance), NDP, Conservative, Bloc Québécois	Multi-party system
2003–	Liberal, Conservative	Bloc Québécois, NDP	Two-plus-two party system

win a majority in the rest of Canada. Thus Canada has witnessed only minority governments since 2004. The Liberals and Conservatives were clearly the major parties, while the Bloc and NDP were significant minor players. It was Harper's Conservatives, however, that formed a minority government after the 2006 election.[20] The 2008 election gave the Conservatives 143 seats, still short of a majority, while the Liberals dipped to 77 seats; the NDP gained marginally, while the BQ remained about the same as in 2006. The whole evolution of the Canadian party system, together with sub-eras, can be summarized as in Box 14.1.

. . . .

INTERPRETATIONS OF THE CANADIAN PARTY SYSTEM

Faced with the rather unusual party system—or succession of party systems—just outlined, several political scientists have proposed theories or interpretations in order to explain them. Some of these theoretical considerations were mentioned at the beginning of the chapter, especially the distinction between broker and ideological parties.

The Broker System

The most traditional explanation of Canadian political parties is the **broker or brokerage** theory.[21] The essence of this interpretation is that, given the multiple cleavages in Canadian society and the function of parties to aggregate interests, political parties in Canada should be conciliators, mediators, or brokers among the cleavages already identified—that is, regions, ethnic and linguistic groups, genders, classes, religions, ages, and urban and rural locations. The theory suggests that maximizing their appeal to all such groups is not only the best way for parties to gain power, but, in the fragmented Canadian society, is also necessary in order to keep the country together. Thus, in their search for power, parties should act as agents of national integration and attempt to reconcile as many divergent interests as possible.

The interests to which parties give most attention are presumably those of greatest concern to the voters, reflecting their personal identities. In the past, religion was often prominent, while gender and age are emerging as increasingly important in the future. Throughout most of Canadian history, however, the two overriding cleavages or identities that have concerned people as well as parties have been those of region and ethnicity. Although the class cleavage is the central focus of politics elsewhere, it has usually attracted little attention in Canada, and the broker theory emphasizes the middle-class consciousness of most Canadians. The broker theory can thus be

Mackenzie King, the longest-serving prime minister, thwarted class politics with his successful pursuit of brokerage politics.

Library and Archives Canada/C-027645

seen to argue that the Liberal and Conservative parties have no basic ideological orientation and merely promise to satisfy the most important concerns felt by the voters at any point in time. Alternatively, they can be said to disguise their real ideological interests—protecting the capitalist system—by emphasizing ethnic and regional identities instead of class interests. In any case, ideological differences between these two parties are not profound. Defenders of the broker system argue that parties should not foment artificial class conflicts and ideological differences in a country that is already seriously divided—they should bring people together rather than drive them apart.

However appealing the broker system may appear, its negative implications should not be overlooked. By concentrating on regional and ethnic cleavages, parties minimize the role of ideology in Canadian politics. Parties are opportunistic and pragmatic rather than offering the electorate a choice of principled, distinctive programs. Parties do not generate innovative policy approaches but are content instead to respond to public opinion polls and advocacy group demands. What parties offer to the electorate in the place of a choice of solutions to national problems are alternative slogans and leaders, the latter especially important in a television age.

Ideological or Class-Based Parties

A second perspective on the Canadian party system, and a reaction to the broker approach, is the concept of **ideological or class-based parties**.[22] Like the broker model, this theory is partly an explanation of the existing system, but when it comes to prescribing an ideal situation, it rejects the national status quo. Class-based analysts expect that in the pre-democratic period, two parties will develop, both of which defend the capitalist system. When the vote is extended to the working class, however, a new left-wing, working-class party will emerge that either joins the competition or displaces one of the existing parties, generally forcing politics to take on an ideological and class-based character. This evolution clearly occurred in Britain, for example, and can also be seen to some extent in the United States.

In late-19th-century Canada, the Liberal and Conservative Parties both defended capitalism, and differentiated themselves on ethnic and religious grounds as well as on minor policy differences such as the tariff. When the vote was extended to the working class at the turn of the 20th century, some isolated labour, socialist, and communist political activity occurred, and by 1920 new class-based, ideological farmer and labour parties existed. But the newly enfranchised working class did not manage to create a successful class-based party, as the Liberals and Conservatives did everything in their power to discourage such a development, by using both seductive and coercive techniques.

Mackenzie King introduced policy innovations to attract farmer and labour voters and co-opted leaders of both farmer and labour movements into the Liberal Cabinet, while the Conservatives used force to quell the 1919 Winnipeg General Strike and the 1935 On-to-Ottawa Trek of the unemployed.[23] Eventually, the farmers' intense interest in politics declined, and the working class continued to support the two old-line parties on ethnic/religious and regional grounds, rendered content by the occasional piece of social legislation.

The Depression represented the collapse of the capitalist system and, as might have been expected, gave rise to new ideological parties. Of these, the CCF became the most sustained working-class party, but most members of that class continued to support the two traditional parties. Although unionization expanded significantly in the 1940s, the CCF's success was impeded by the Liberal Party's exploitation of divisions within the working class,[24] and by extremist anti-CCF propaganda sponsored by the business community. The CCF achieved its highest popular standing in the 1943–45 period, after which Liberal welfare initiatives helped to draw off working-class support. As mentioned, this decline led to the creation of the NDP in 1961 as a marriage of the CCF and the CLC, but even with the NDP's organic link to the labour movement, most working-class Canadians continued to vote Liberal or Conservative.

Explanations for the lack of class-consciousness among the Canadian working class were noted in Chapter 8.[25] As mentioned there, the Liberals and Conservatives were well established when the vote was extended to the working class, and they continued to define politics in non-class terms, either appealing to ethnic/religious and regional groups or else developing pan-Canadian appeals that diverted attention from class-based issues. These parties persuaded most voters that they belonged to the middle class and gave them the impression of inclusion and social mobility. At the same time, the upper and middle classes were always conscious of their own class position and voted accordingly.

Advocates of a class-based party system claim that it would provide ideological alternatives in elections that would make them more meaningful. Moreover, the broker system, with its emphasis on multiple cleavages, is dangerously destabilizing. If the Liberals and Conservatives are unsuccessful as brokers, an ethnic–regional unit can threaten to separate. In such circumstances, class could be the integrating ingredient: "A nation like Canada, which is in danger of falling apart on ethnic-regional lines, may be held together by a politics which unites the people of various regions and ethnic groups around the two poles of left and right."[26] Canadians would ideally be united by their common class position into two or three national class-based parties. Finally, it is said that class-based politics and parties are already the norm in Western Canadian provincial politics, so that this theory is quite a realistic proposition after all.

Chapter 15 indicates that although class-consciousness in Canada is low and explains very little of electoral behaviour, ideology is an important factor in the voting decision. In other words, ideology and class do not always coincide in people's minds. This observation leads to an examination of the right side of the political spectrum in recent years. As the section on party ideology in this chapter establishes, the Reform Party and the Canadian Alliance were clearly right-wing parties, while the Progressive Conservative party was more of a broker party. But the question is whether the new Conservative Party of Canada fits best into the broker or ideological category. The new party held a policy conference in March 2005, which generally produced a moderate policy output, and in the 2006 and 2008 election campaigns, Stephen Harper took a more brokerage approach, especially in his appeal to Quebec. There was, however, a right-wing tinge to some of his promises and to many of the policies of his government.

Other Interpretations

Three other interpretations of the Canadian party system can be mentioned briefly. These are the one-party dominance approach, the concern with the decline of political parties, and explanations for the existence of so many minor parties.

ONE-PARTY DOMINANCE

The one-party-dominance thesis is hardly appropriate to an era of minority governments. But Canadian government was characterized by majority governments for most of Canadian history before the year 2000. H.G. Thorburn maintains that instead of looking at the party system as being historically made up of two major parties, it was really dominated by one—the Liberals—after 1900.[27] The Liberals were the "government party," power-oriented rather than issue-oriented, attracting "winners" and "successes" as supporters and candidates, and maintaining themselves in office with the help of public service expertise, public opinion polls, and the chance to choose election day.[28] The Conservatives were seen as the "opposition party," ordinarily having to settle for the role of critics (from within the range of ideological conformity) but being elected to office only on those rare occasions when the people got thoroughly fed up with the Liberals. With their divisiveness, "opposition mentality," and lack of preparedness to govern, however, the Conservatives did not remain in power very long. Finally, the NDP could be termed the "innovative party," never really having a chance to govern nationally but being responsible for introducing new ideas from beyond the range of current ideological conformity, both at the federal and the provincial levels. As mentioned above, a return to one-party dominance is thwarted by the popularity of the Bloc Québécois in Quebec.

PARTY DECLINE

Another interpretation emphasizes the decline of political parties.[29] John Meisel suggests a number of reasons that the traditional functions of parties have been taken over by other institutions. In the first place, people prefer to participate directly in specialized voluntary associations rather than take their concerns to an omnibus political party, with the result that the number and strength of advocacy groups has greatly increased. Such issue-oriented individuals anticipate more prompt and effective satisfaction of their demands by participating in group action, quite possibly by interacting with the bureaucracy, than by going through traditional political party channels.[30]

The quantity and complexity of information with which governments have to deal has come to mean that generalist politicians can no longer cope with it, which leaves them increasingly dependent on the bureaucracy. This culminates in a situation in which advocacy groups confer with the bureaucrats and work out policies that the politicians can neither understand nor alter, further reducing the role of political parties in the policy-making process. Intergovernmental conferences and committees of all kinds have become the forum in which many public policies are ironed out, and once certain political and bureaucratic compromises have been made, there is little that other politicians or parties can do about them.

Meisel also notes that parties now gear most of their activity to the demands of the media, and to the extent that elections are dominated by leader images and leader debates, the need for traditional party organizations diminishes. Similarly, public opinion polls provide better feedback to politicians than their traditional discussion with party activists. Investigative journalism has reduced the role of the Opposition in Parliament; direct-mail appeals have replaced traditional forms of party fundraising; and modern transnational corporations are beyond the control of any party or government. Other recent developments

Artizans/Bruce MacKinnon

Why the Green and Marijuana Parties remain minor parties.

that have contributed to the decline of parties are the increasing power of the prime minister, the influence of election strategists and other specialist advisers, and the new role of the courts and the Charter of Rights and Freedoms.

Meisel's regretful critique of Canadian political parties has inspired other commentary suggesting that rather than on the decline, they are in a state of transition. Such observers admit that certain traditional functions are being performed by interest groups, the media, public opinion polls, and the bureaucracy, but argue that others are simply being carried out by parties in different ways.[31]

MINOR PARTIES

Because Canada has had so many minor parties, political scientists have also developed several theories to account specifically for them. Essentially, the existence of all these parties can be explained by the fact that at one time or another, ethnic, regional, or class grievances have gone unsatisfied by the broker parties. Moreover, new minor parties are only to be expected when individual voter identification with existing parties is generally weak and when ideological stagnation and opportunism characterize the broker system. In particular, if the working class never managed to establish a major party in Canada, it is not surprising that several minor working-class parties would be created.

On a more theoretical note, it has also been argued that the rigid party discipline enforced in the Canadian Parliament has encouraged the development of minor protest parties.[32] When certain interests felt frustrated by the requirement of toeing the party line in Ottawa, they turned to form minor parties, usually at the provincial level, to vent their grievances. Some observers have gone so far as to suggest that the parliamentary system, with its rigid party discipline, is unsuitable for such a diverse country.

Another prominent theory relating to minor parties is that of C.B. Macpherson in his explanation of the series of one-party-dominant eras in Alberta provincial politics.[33] He applies a kind of Marxist theory to explain the situation by arguing that the province was characterized by a homogeneity of class interests—the predominance of small, independent producers—so that little internal class conflict could be detected. Instead, the whole Alberta society was held in a quasi-colonial relationship by Eastern Canada. The feeling of being exploited by the privileged classes in the East led Albertans to unite behind a dominant provincial party. Macpherson has been faulted for exaggerating the extent of one-party dominance in the province, but Albertans continued to act as if they were a homogeneous society exploited by the East for decades after he identified this phenomenon.

The rise of the CCF in Saskatchewan has also attracted specific explanations, including the collectivist streak in the Canadian political culture, which seems particularly strong in that province. Disagreeable weather, social isolation, and corporate and federal government exploitation also encouraged cooperative behaviour and cooperative organizations that eventually became transformed into a political party, the Co-operative Commonwealth Federation.[34]

. . . .

PARTY IDEOLOGY

Discussions of party ideology might be a relatively straightforward task in some political systems, but they are not so in Canada. Parties often downplay their ideological differences in the search for votes, their positions change over time, and they are all internally divided to some extent. Some observers have concluded that no basic ideological differences exist between the Liberals and Conservatives:[35] either they are both pure broker parties with no ideology, responding pragmatically and opportunistically to public opinion polls in the pursuit of power, or else they are equally committed to the capitalist system but prepared to remedy its worst faults to maintain popular support. A second interpretation is that although no fundamental ideological differences exist between them, they maintain certain consistent policy differences.[36] In fact, however, they have reversed some of these historic stands (such as advocating free trade with the United States or decentralization of the federal system), and voters must be forgiven for being suspicious about how deeply held such differences are.

A more comprehensive and theoretical perspective that includes the NDP in the analysis is that genuine ideological differences do exist in Canada and that such ideologies as **liberalism**, **conservatism**, and **social democracy** can be found to differentiate these three parties to some extent. The ideological continuum can be sketched in diagrammatic form, as in Figure 14.1. This perspective is based on the writing of Louis Hartz, Kenneth MacRae, Gad Horowitz, William Christian, and Colin Campbell, and it is sometimes called the fragment theory, as mentioned in Chapter 11.[37] This theory suggests that the basic ideology in Canada is liberalism, but that traces of socialism and conservatism also exist, and that each of the ideologies is more or less represented by a corresponding party. Such liberalism seeks to liberate the individual and maximize each individual's freedom and potential, something that almost all Canadians would support. Differences emerge, however, about who should be liberated, about what the inhibiting agent is, and about how to go about such liberation, primarily focusing on the role of the state.

Conservatism seeks to liberate the individual from the restrictions of the state. Reducing the role of the state to a minimum and allowing private market forces to determine the distribution of power and wealth is often labelled **individualism**. Minimizing the tax burden on individuals is a key priority, but conservatism also advocates little government regulation and ownership, and leaving people to fend for themselves instead of being supported by public social programs. Conservatives do not cherish inequality, but if such policies result in inequalities or elitism, they are generally unconcerned; that is how it should be, because inequalities are both natural and deserved—some people are better and some work harder

. . . .

Figure 14.1 The Ideological Continuum in Canada

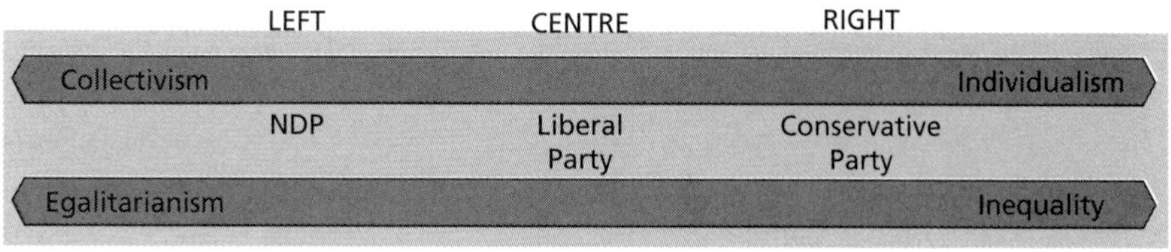

than others. These attitudes are labelled as being on the **right**. Historically, those who took this position were found primarily in the Conservative Party, and an even more extreme faction became the core of the Reform Party, and later the Canadian Alliance.

Social democracy, conversely, seeks to liberate the individual from the inequalities and exploitation of the capitalist system. It believes in equality, and it prescribes a large element of state action or **collectivism** in order to achieve such liberation and equality. These views are generally referred to as being on the **left**. In particular, this ideology emphasizes government planning, regulation, ownership of some of the major industries of the country, progressive taxation, and redistribution of income through social programs. Adherents are sometimes subdivided between "democratic socialists" and "social democrats," depending on the extent to which they want the state to intervene and the extent of equality they want to effect. The early CCF was certainly more socialistic than the current New Democratic Party, with the latter's majority being of the social democratic persuasion. The CCF/NDP take credit for introducing public health insurance when they formed the government of Saskatchewan, pressing for other social welfare programs, advocating a more progressive taxation system, creating a variety of Crown corporations in the provinces where they held power, and supporting the creation of several such government bodies in Ottawa.

Liberalism, almost by default, falls between the other two ideologies. In fact, it has a dual personality and can be subdivided into "welfare" and "business" variants. Business liberals believe that the state inhibits individual self-fulfillment and that its role should be minimized so that individualism can prevail. Welfare liberals, conversely, take the view that the state can be a positive agent in liberating individuals from the constraints of other forces including the private-enterprise economy. Welfare liberals therefore stand for a combination of individualism and collectivism and a combination of equality and inequality, which they usually label "equality of opportunity." Being composed of business and welfare liberals, the Liberal party is located in the centre of the Canadian ideological continuum. Although Liberals obviously hold private market forces in greater esteem than does the NDP, Liberal governments introduced old age pensions, family allowances, and many other social welfare programs over the years. Under bureaucratic influence, the Liberals brought **Keynesian economics** to Canada, and the CCF/NDP and Liberals both claim credit for the development of the Canadian **welfare state**. Historians generally point out that the Liberal Party made an ideological shift about 1919 from a business-liberal to a welfare-liberal orientation, although some observers saw a shift backward after 1993.

To complicate the picture to some extent, a second wing of the former Progressive Conservative Party was the "progressive" element, people who were sometimes called **red tories**. These conservatives combined beliefs in privilege and collectivism, seeing society as an organic whole, emphasizing community values as well as individualism, and standing for order, tradition, stability, and noblesse oblige. They believed in hierarchy, in which everyone should occupy his or her place, but they also had a paternalistic concern with the condition of all the people. This aspect of conservatism is not unique to Canada, being found quite commonly in Britain and the rest of Europe; it stands out only in contrast to a lack of such sentiment within American conservatism. Thus, the ideology of the Progressive Conservative Party was not clear-cut; it was somewhat divided, just as in the case of the other two parties. Pre-Mulroney Conservatives sometimes exhibited a strong red tory touch, such as in the creation of the RCMP, CBC, CNR, and the National Energy Board, in the Bennett New Deal, and in the Stanfield proposal for wage and price controls. It was sometimes difficult to distinguish among social democrats, welfare liberals, and red tories, and some New Democrats felt closer to red tories than to certain Liberals.[38]

If liberalism in the United States, that country's monolithic ideology, lacks the collectivist touch, how do we explain a collectivist presence in three Canadian party ideologies? One explanation focuses on the United Empire Loyalists, who removed most of the collectivist tendencies from the U.S. political culture when they migrated to Canada and left behind almost undiluted business liberalism. The United Empire Loyalists rendered ideological diversity legitimate in Canada and, because of their early predominance, made collectivism a respectable and important element in the Canadian political culture. In fact, they added to the collectivist approach already found in the feudal background of French Canada—that is, the ideas of hierarchy, order, stability, and community. Collectivism was reinforced by subsequent waves of British immigration, whose intellectual baggage included both red tory and socialist views, along with the influence of the Social Gospel movement.[39] Such collectivist tendencies were discussed in Chapter 11.

There is so much overlap in the ideological orientation of the Liberal and Conservative parties in particular that it is sometimes difficult to detect the distinctions made above, and political scientists often ask the question: "Does party matter?"[40] Indeed, from about 1945 to 1980 the Liberal and Conservative parties shared a basic ideological approach that emphasized economic growth based on foreign investment, expansion of the welfare state, and engagement in a certain amount of macroeconomic government regulation.[41] As time went on, however, this consensus broke down. Thus, especially after the Conservatives took office in 1984, policy and ideological differences between the two parties were more obvious, with the Mulroney government pursuing a business-liberal agenda in which renewed reliance was placed on market forces—privatization, deregulation, deficit reduction, and cutting social programs—and the extent of government intervention was actually reduced. In other words, conservatism up to this point had upheld the status quo and simply opposed further change, but the new brand of conservatism wanted to turn the clock back and "dismantle the state" to some degree.[42]

Indeed, after 1985, the whole ideological spectrum shifted to the right. For the first time in Canadian history, social programs were cut back rather than expanded; Crown corporations were privatized rather than created; taxes were cut rather than raised; regulations were repealed rather than promulgated; public debts and deficits were reduced rather than increased; and public servants were fired rather than hired. The phenomenon went beyond one or two parties; it happened around the world, and in Canada it affected governing parties of all ideological persuasions in the 1990s: the NDP, especially in Saskatchewan; the Parti Québécois; and Liberal governments in several provinces and in Ottawa.

The Reform Party was very much part of this shift to the right, and it exerted great influence at both federal and provincial levels even though it did not form the government. The other leaders of this right-wing crusade, Conservative premiers Ralph Klein in Alberta and Mike Harris in Ontario, followed the Reform program to a tee. Their actions were all consistent with a belief in individualism, which is unconcerned about whether it leads to socioeconomic inequalities. What distinguished Reform/Alliance from other Canadian parties was a complete absence of the collectivist value. In this respect, it was almost a clone of the U.S. Republican Party, with which it maintained contact.[43]

As mentioned in Chapter 2, this new philosophy of government is often called **neoliberalism** or **neoconservatism**. Although the two terms are often used to mean the same thing, a distinction can be made between them. Both advocate that government withdraw from economic policy, but sometimes neoconservatism is taken to mean a belief in a strong state that can promote certain traditional social values and regulate social behaviour. Neoconservatives were "social conservatives" who opposed abortion, public child care, gay rights, same-sex marriage, and employment equity. The Reform Party and the Canadian Alliance contained both neoliberals and neoconservatives, and were a particular magnet for social conservatives.[44]

It should be added that the Reform Party/Alliance had two other main concerns. First, it believed in populism—that is, it was against elitism and professed to value the wisdom of ordinary people. To some extent this is also an Americanism as opposed to the traditional Canadian belief in British parliamentary democracy. The second was a territorial focus—that the West was getting short-changed within Confederation.

To return to the shift to the right, the NDP began to occupy the previous position of the Liberal Party. The Chrétien government pursued the same kind of leaner government that it previously condemned under Mulroney, and Finance Minister Paul Martin dismembered parts of the welfare state which was largely the creation of his father, Paul Martin, Sr., a Liberal Cabinet minister from the 1940s to the 1960s. As a result, a crush occurred on the right-wing side of the spectrum. The Progressive Conservative Party found it difficult to identify its own ideological space between the Chrétien Liberals and the Reform Party or Canadian Alliance.

It seemed logical to Preston Manning to engineer some kind of merger of right-wing forces in the country, but many observers believed that there was more of an ideological divide between the two parties than met the eye. Tory leader Joe Clark declined the invitation, and PC conventions in 1999 and 2002 supported his position. It was left to two new leaders, Stephen Harper of the Alliance and Peter MacKay of the PCs to engineer a "reuniting of the right" in December 2003, to be called the Conservative Party of Canada. Although the new party chose Harper as its new leader, it would probably be inaccurate to refer to the merger as "an Alliance takeover." Over the next two years, party policies revealed an increasingly centrist approach, clearly influenced by the more moderate Progressive Conservative faction. This gradual transformation comprised three stages: the June 2004 election, for which party policy had to be instantaneously created; the 2005 policy convention; and the 2006 election campaign. In April 2005, for example, Harper repudiated a proposal from Preston Manning and Mike Harris that Ottawa should repeal the Canada Health Act. Conservative government policies after January 2006 generally brought the party back into the traditional range of the Canadian political culture. The party may no longer include many red tories, but it seemed to have abandoned its most extreme neoliberal and neoconservative views. Few observers believed that Harper had truly changed his values, but he and others at least realized that they had been out of touch with a majority of Canadians.

Indeed, as the 21st century dawned, the appeal of neoliberalism and neoconservatism decreased across the whole Canadian spectrum, as well as around the world. Policies had moved too far to the right, and too many people had suffered. Alexandra Dobrowolsky reminds us that British Labour Party Prime Minister Tony Blair sought out a "Third Way," between socialism and neoliberalism. Like neoliberalism before it, the third way has affected the ideological positions of parties everywhere, including Canada. Dobrowolsky emphasizes the policy convergence of Canadian parties in recent years, which reflects new centrist consensus.[45]

Harper's Conservative Party held a policy convention in November 2008, just after the election. Given the early signs of the economic slowdown, the leader urged the delegates to take a pragmatic, less ideological approach to the issues under discussion, although many right-wing resolutions were adopted. However, as the economic situation became a crisis, the government introduced a budget in January 2009 that provided for a deficit of some $64 billion over the next two years. Although virtually all countries were engaged in the same massive deficit-stimulus policy, many Canadian Conservatives were alarmed at this violent change in ideological direction, and *Maclean's* magazine proclaimed "the end of Canadian Conservatism." To some extent, the NDP once again began to influence the national agenda from the moderate left.

The Bloc Québécois stands alone with its one main objective: Quebec sovereignty. The question of nationalism generally overwhelms the left–right ideological approach in Quebec, but in some respects nationalism can be provided for within the format presented earlier. Nationalism is a kind of collectivism that usually involves a large role for the state, and at the pan-Canadian level—trying to make Canada more independent of Britain or the United States—it has been a consistent mark of left-wing parties, such as the NDP, as well as of red tories and left-wing Liberals. Although it is also possible for right-wingers to be nationalistic, the PQ has usually been placed on the left side of the continuum, somewhere between the Liberals and the NDP. The BQ, including people who were previously members of a variety of other parties, does not have a comprehensive program apart from Quebec sovereignty and therefore no clear-cut left–right ideological stance. Nevertheless, since its creation, it has usually adopted a slightly left-wing approach when required to take a stand on other issues.

Protecting the environment has now become one of the leading issues on the political agenda. While all parties have outlined approaches to dealing with this problem, the Green, NDP, and Liberal plans all involve greater government intervention, whether by taxing carbon, placing ceilings on emissions, or both, than the Conservative proposals. Thus, to a large extent, environmental protection falls on the left side of the ideological spectrum, but the Conservatives may be forced into taking government action by the stronger environmental laws adopted by the Obama administration in the United States.

. . . .

PARTY ORGANIZATION

A political party has been defined as an organized group, but the structure of such a group requires clarification. One main component of the party is the **parliamentary party** or **party caucus**—that is, the party's elected representatives in Parliament. Here we are more concerned with the **extra-parliamentary party** organization made up of party activists and executive members, the party headquarters or staff, and ordinary party members. The principal aspects of party organization that bear examination are party membership, party leadership selection and review, party policymaking, and general structures and operations. Party and election finance were discussed in Chapter 13.

Party Membership

All accounts of party membership in Canada find that it represents a tiny segment of the population. William Cross writes that there are two categories of party members: committed activists who maintain their membership year after year, and those attracted to a leadership or nomination contest who let their membership lapse afterward.[46] Looking at the various parties, the NDP is somewhat distinctive in this respect: it aspires to a large membership, and local activists often operate an annual, year-round membership and renewal drive. New members must take an oath that they support the party's principles, and only those who have been members for at least 30 days and who live in the constituency are allowed to vote at nomination meetings. Constituency association representation at party conventions is based on the size of the local membership, and the party is unique in having affiliated members—that is, members of trade unions that have voted to affiliate with the party. However, even in the NDP, membership grows with the prospect of voting at a nomination meeting or for a new party leader.

Although they may also conduct membership drives for a few weeks a year, the Liberals and Conservatives are normally more casual about the annual renewal of party memberships. They have a local core of activists, but for the most part their members join up in connection with the meeting to nominate a candidate for the next election, to choose delegates to a national convention, or to have a vote in a leadership contest. It is typical for aspiring candidates or delegates to sign up large numbers of new members to vote in their favour. Since party members do not usually need to be Canadian citizens, these temporary members are sometimes recruited from minority ethnocultural groups in urban centres and they often disappear from the party as soon as the meeting is over.

Political scientists and others who see the need for strong political parties in a democracy regret the weakness of party membership in Canada. Parties should be more than electoral machines, but even in that function, technology cannot do everything; a party can only be successful if it has a substantial membership base.

Party Leadership

Since the leader is such a dominant presence in any political party, it is important to examine how parties choose such leaders. The Liberals relied on the parliamentary party to select its leaders before 1919 and the Conservatives did so until 1927, but both then moved to choose their leaders at national delegate conventions.[47] The years and winners of party leadership contests are contained in Table 14.1.

The Liberals have alternated anglophone and francophone leaders, partly by accident and partly by design. The Conservatives did not have a francophone leader until Jean Charest in 1995, Brian Mulroney having been the first bilingual Quebecker to hold the post in that party. Most Liberal leaders have been Roman Catholics (King, Pearson, and Ignatieff excepted), while most PC leaders have been Protestants (with the exception of Clark, Mulroney, and Charest). All Liberal leaders have come from Ontario or Quebec, while the origin of most Conservative leaders was outside central Canada. Lawyers represent the most common occupational background (St. Laurent, Diefenbaker, Stanfield, Trudeau, Lewis, Turner, Mulroney, Charest, Chrétien, and Martin). Audrey McLaughlin was the first female national party leader in Canadian history, although Rosemary Brown (NDP), Flora MacDonald (PC), and Sheila Copps (Liberal) gave male contenders a run for their money in 1975, 1976, and 1990, respectively.

With the exception of Mulroney, Ignatieff, Preston Manning, and Jack Layton, all of the leaders have had some prior experience in the House of Commons or in provincial legislatures (Bracken, Drew, Stanfield, and McDonough), with Douglas having been both a premier and

TABLE 14.1 **Dates of Election of Major Party Leaders**

Liberal	Conservative	CCF/NDP
1919 Mackenzie King	1927 R.B. Bennett	1932 J.S. Woodsworth
1948 Louis St. Laurent	1938 Robert Manion	1942 M.J. Coldwell
1958 Lester B. Pearson	1942 John Bracken	1960 Hazen Argue
1968 Pierre E. Trudeau	1948 George Drew	1961 T.C. Douglas
1984 John Turner	1956 John Diefenbaker	1971 David Lewis
1990 Jean Chrétien	1967 Robert Stanfield	1975 Ed Broadbent
2003 Paul Martin	1976 Joe Clark	1989 Audrey McLaughlin
2006 Stéphane Dion	1983 Brian Mulroney	1995 Alexa McDonough
2008 Michael Ignatieff	1993 Kim Campbell	2003 Jack Layton
	1995 Jean Charest	
	1998 Joe Clark	
	2003 Peter MacKay	
	2004 Stephen Harper	

Reform/Canadian Alliance	Bloc Québécois
1991 Preston Manning	1990 Lucien Bouchard
2000 Stockwell Day	1997 Gilles Duceppe
2002 Stephen Harper	

an MP. What is quite striking in many cases, however, is the brevity of this parliamentary experience, and the Liberal tendency to co-opt an extra-parliamentary notable for their leader has often been noted, the most recent example being Michael Ignatieff. Especially in a television age, a fresh face may be just as important as legislative experience to obtain the job, although it might not be so useful afterward. Alternatively, in the case of Turner, Chrétien, and Harper, a period out of the Commons' spotlight was apparently considered advantageous by the delegates who chose them. Joe Clark is the only person to be elected leader on two widely separated occasions.

An even more democratic procedure than the leadership convention has been utilized in recent years—every card-carrying member of the party has been allowed to cast a vote for the leadership (one member-one vote [OMOV]). Such a procedure avoids much of the cost of holding a national convention, eliminates the unholy fight among various candidates for delegates at the constituency level, ensures that the decision is not left to the more affluent members of the party who can afford the travel costs, and removes the circus atmosphere of the convention. The Parti Québécois was the first party to move to such an OMOV leadership selection process, and many other provincial party leaders have now been elected on this basis. Party members can vote by phone, by mail, online, or by casting their ballot at the local level. Such procedures have potential problems of their own, however, including technological breakdowns, an unrepresentative electorate, and the involvement of voters who have no knowledge of the candidates or who actually support other parties. Many partisans also feel that the loss of the publicity value of a nationally televised convention is too high a cost and suggest that by imposing spending limits on candidates and subsidizing delegates' expenses some of the worst features of conventions can be avoided.

Despite the advantages of a full-fledged convention, all parties have been influenced by the pressure for more popular participation in the leadership selection process. The Liberal Party adopted a new system in 1992 which combined giving every party member a vote along with having a leadership convention. Every party member voted on the leadership candidates, as well as for delegates, and the latter were elected in proportion to the popular vote received by each leadership candidate at the local level. Once they got beyond the first ballot at the convention, however, such delegates could use their own judgment. In 2006, Stéphane Dion was in third place on the first ballot and then engineered alliances to win on the fourth.[48] After the "emergency" selection of Michael Ignatieff in late 2008, the Liberals adopted the OMOV system in May 2009 for the choice of leaders in the future.

The PC Party put its new leadership selection process into play in 1998. It gave each member of the party a vote but weighted these votes so that each constituency had equal power, regardless of the size of its membership. In 2003, the Progressive Conservatives used a hybrid system similar to that of the Liberals, combining OMOV and a delegate convention. In choosing Stephen Harper in 2004, the new Conservative Party reverted to a one member–one vote system, without a convention, except that each constituency had equal weight. In 2003, the NDP allowed all members to vote for leader and had a small convention to celebrate the occasion.

Most parties also have **leadership review** mechanisms in their constitutions, although these vary in detail. The NDP opens nominations for the position of leader at their national convention every two years so that, at least in theory, the leader can be immediately replaced. However, in the absence of a concrete challenger, no vote is needed.

As a result of the civil war within the party over John Diefenbaker's leadership between 1962 and 1967, the PC party added a leadership review provision to their constitution in 1974. It consisted of a vote at a convention on the question "Are you in favour of holding a leadership convention?" It was first invoked after the defeat of Joe Clark's government in 1981, but 66 percent of party delegates rejected the idea of a leadership convention. Two years later, an almost identical 67 percent opposed a leadership convention, but Clark decided this degree of support was insufficient, so he resigned. Although he ran to succeed himself in the subsequent leadership race, he was defeated by Brian Mulroney. At the same time, the leadership review mechanism that had caused so much turmoil in the party was changed: the question was put only at the first convention following an election that the party lost, a provision included in the constitution of the new Conservative Party.

The Liberals added a leadership review clause in 1966 to the effect that at the first convention after each election (win or lose), delegates vote on whether they want to have a leadership convention. Until 2002, the party always backed its leader, but it appeared that Jean Chrétien would lose the vote scheduled for February 2003 because a majority in the party wanted him to resign. By announcing his retirement, he was spared such a leadership review. Paul Martin won 88 percent backing after leading the Liberals to a minority victory in 2004, but announced his intention to step down immediately after the electoral defeat of January 2006. When Stéphane Dion led the Liberal party to its lowest ever results in 2008, he was forced to resign almost immediately—even before a leadership review. In fact, the Liberals were so desperate for a new leader and so concerned that in the minority government situation an election might be held before their scheduled convention in May 2009, that they used an emergency process to preclude a leadership convention. The party hierarchy pressured Dion to submit his resignation in December 2008 to take effect as soon as a new leader was chosen. The party executive opted to consult only the caucus, defeated candidates, and party officials. Previously declared leadership candidates Dominic LeBlanc and Bob Rae withdrew from the race, and the executive anointed Michael Ignatieff as the new leader. His leadership was merely confirmed by the party convention, and without opposition.

Party Policymaking

All political parties have difficulty designing their policymaking processes. On the one hand, some people join a party with the aim of contributing to party policy, but on the other, no party wants to be saddled with unrealistic policy commitments. Thus, they all struggle to combine these two forces in the most appropriate way, and membership input is usually the loser. Even more striking is that most parties put very little effort at all into policy research.

Liberal and Conservative national conventions or general meetings usually include a policy session and sometimes focus primarily on policy. But even if specific resolutions are debated and passed, which is not always the case, party leaders retain the right to determine official party policy. Although parliamentary leaders may be influenced by such discussions to some extent, they are in no way bound by the policy resolutions of the party organization.

The Liberal Party did not even hold a national convention between 1919 and 1948, and instead mainly relied on the public service for policy advice. When the Liberals found themselves in opposition after 1957, however, and cut off from the public service, Lester Pearson was forced to turn to the party organization to help develop new policy proposals. He convened a famous thinkers' conference in Kingston in 1960, followed by a party conference that debated the ideas brought forward. Once in power after 1963, the Pearson government quickly implemented most of the policies that the party had adopted. Under Pierre Trudeau, the party held several more party policy conferences, but did not pay much attention to the results.[49] Jean Chrétien tried to replicate the successful early 1960s experience with a policy conference in 1991, followed by a party convention a year later. The Red Book used as the party platform in the 1993 election drew substantially on these two party meetings. The Liberals did not have another serious discussion of policy within the party until after Paul Martin's defeat in 2006, but the ensuing leadership selection process eclipsed any serious discussion of party policy.

The Conservatives discussed policy to some extent at their many leadership conventions. But after the 1956 convention, Diefenbaker attempted to destroy all evidence of its policy proposals and governed for five years without any policy constraints from the party. When Robert Stanfield became leader, he was anxious to develop a stronger policy orientation and encouraged policy discussions within the party. Joe Clark was not guided by the party very much in his policies, and Brian Mulroney relied primarily on the public service, royal commissions, backroom advisers, and public opinion polls for policy guidance. The new Conservative Party held a policy convention in March 2005. After several heated debates, it adopted a 50-page Policy Declaration, which generally reflected a compromise position between the previous Canadian Alliance and Progressive Conservative positions. This document was helpful in designing the party's 2006 election platform. Indeed, it would appear that both Liberals and Conservatives have generally been more successful in election campaigns that were preceded by a serious effort at policy generation within the party.

The NDP has always claimed to be particularly distinctive in the realm of party policy-making. It has regular policy sessions every two years, which are indeed the predominant item on the convention agenda. Grassroots constituency associations are invited to submit resolutions in advance, and, resolutions passed by the convention are considered to be official and binding on the leader and the parliamentary party. The party's executive and council are allowed to submit resolutions of their own, however, and the council, which is subject to greater leadership manipulation than the convention, has the authority to "flesh out" the meaning of policies adopted. Instead of passing random policy resolutions at whim, riding associations since 1995 have primarily been expected to respond to papers prepared by groups within the party that are in possession of considerable policy resources and expertise. If the NDP policymaking process is now less distinctive from other parties, this party still gives greater priority to policy debate and takes more seriously the resolutions passed.

Given that the generation of policy is one of the weakest aspects of party operations in Canada, many recommendations have been made for reform. The Royal Commission on Electoral Reform and Party Financing, for example, strongly urged parties to establish foundations that would engage in serious policy research, whether or not their ideas were subject to approval of grassroots party members. Bill Cross comes to the same conclusion:

> Parliamentary parties in both government and opposition would benefit from serious study undertaken by their extraparliamentary parties toward providing policy alternatives and guidance to the parliamentary parties. Such activity would serve to encourage those Canadians with policy concerns to participate in party activity rather than looking to interest groups as a way to influence public policy. A beneficial side effect might also be a weakening of the growing concentration of government-party decision making within the prime minister's office.[50]

General Structures and Operations

CONVENTIONS

All parties have constitutions that outline their objectives, structures, and procedures. In theory, at least, the ultimate authority in each party is the party convention, which all parties now hold quite regularly at an average of about two-year intervals. The convention agenda normally includes the election of the party executive, constitutional amendments, policy discussions, and instruction in local election organization, but such conventions also serve important social and morale-building purposes. In the Liberal and Conservative parties, each constituency association is entitled to an equal number of delegates, while in the NDP, representation is based on the size of the local membership. All parties include certain ex-officio delegates, such as MPs, and, in some cases MPPs, MLAs, and nominated or recently defeated candidates. In the NDP, affiliated labour unions also send delegates. Both the Liberals and the NDP have tried to become more inclusive and representative with an array of women's, youth, campus, Aboriginal, ethnocultural, and other associated groups.

PARTY EXECUTIVE

Each party has a national executive, including a president, vice-presidents, treasurer, and so on, and each establishes a number of executive committees. These officials usually perform such duties on a part-time basis, although it is helpful for the president to be close to Ottawa and readily available for meetings, campaign organization, and other functions. Both the Liberals and the Conservatives have sometimes elected a senator as party president, since such a person has considerable free time and is on the public payroll, saving the party the cost of a presidential salary. The party president usually has the confidence of the leader, and the contest for the presidency is sometimes a surrogate vote on the leadership.

PARTY HEADQUARTERS

The three main national parties maintain a headquarters office in Ottawa, which is staffed by permanent party employees and headed by the national director. These chief executive officers maintain close relations with the leader and caucus, and, in the case of the party in power, the Prime Minister's Office (PMO). In each case, the size of the party staff varies considerably, depending on the state of party finances and the imminence of an election, and the PC and NDP offices were dramatically scaled down after the 1993 election. The role of party headquarters during election campaigns is outlined in Chapter 15. Between elections, headquarters perform a variety of functions, such as collecting money, ensuring local organizations are alive and well, arranging for speakers at local annual meetings, planning conventions, publishing newsletters, maintaining a website, conducting surveys, and researching policy.

THE IRON OF OLIGARCHY

To complete the analysis of party organization, the relationships among the party membership, the executive, the parliamentary caucus, and the party leadership should be examined. Political theorist Robert Michels claimed that a tendency toward elitism is inevitable within all political parties, giving rise to his famous **iron law of oligarchy**.[51] Even in parties that seek or profess to operate democratically, a small elite invariably develops such that rank-and-file party members have little real power.

THE CANADIAN PRESS/Nathan Denette

Liberal leader Michael Ignatieff speaks to the Empire Club in Toronto in January 2009.

One tendency is for party leaders, whether or not in government, to create a small coterie of advisers, who cut the leader off from party influence. This was particularly so in the Liberal Party during the tenure of Pierre Elliott Trudeau. As party leader, Trudeau virtually ignored the party organization, paying little attention to its policy-generation efforts, its increasing debt, and its cynical electoral strategies. In fact, he left almost all party and electoral matters in the hands of people who held no official position in the Liberal Party. Their style of operation and their ignoring of the party organization led to demands that party members take back control of the party policy, platform, appointments, and electoral strategy. The party's constitution was amended in 1992 to solidify these changes. Nevertheless, a great deal of control continues to reside with the leader and the surrounding personal advisers, professional consultants, pollsters, political strategists, and media and advertising experts.

A second common development is that the parliamentary wing of the party claims precedence over the extra-parliamentary party organization. In terms of policy, for example, when a party has official status in the House of Commons, it is entitled to hire a substantial number of researchers. Even in Opposition, the complement of publicly paid staff supporting the leader, caucus, and individual MPs clearly outnumbers the staff at party headquarters and may prescribe different policy approaches than come out of party policy discussions. Moreover, when a party forms the government, it has the entire public service to advise it, and may find that the world looks somewhat different from the position of public responsibility than from the Opposition benches. Caucus members are usually more concerned about getting re-elected than are policy-oriented party members, and may thus seek to tone down certain ideas emanating from the grassroots of the party.

In the third place, even though the party organization has periodic elections, a small group of executive members often seek re-election for many terms and effectively maintain control. They use their experience, their access to party information, their connections, their control of party funds, and their influence over party policy to do so. Member apathy is also a factor, for the great bulk of party members are inactive and quite happy to have a handful of activists take charge.

FEDERAL–PROVINCIAL PARTY LINKS

The federal nature of Canada and the existence of two levels of government at which political parties seek to influence policy and personnel raises the question of the relationship between national and provincial party organizations.[52] To oversimplify the situation, the Conservative Party could be said to have a "confederal" character—that is, the federal and provincial Conservative parties are essentially independent of each other and always have been. There is virtually no formal organizational or financial link between the two wings of the party, and the provincial wing is nonexistent in BC, Saskatchewan, and Quebec. Thus, federal and provincial party memberships are separate, and a complete set of federal riding associations and executives coexists with provincial party organizations at the grassroots level. Now, of course, the federal party has a different name (Conservative Party of Canada) from the Progressive Conservative parties at the provincial level.

By contrast, the NDP could be called an "integrated" party because, with the exception of Quebec, people join the NDP at the provincial level and automatically become members of the national party, almost as if it were an afterthought. Provincial offices of the party theoretically serve the needs of both wings of the party, and a provincial convention also deals with federal matters from its own perspective. To help overcome the inevitable provincial orientation of this combined operation and to combat the dormancy of the federal party at the provincial and constituency levels between federal elections, the party created a Council of Federal Ridings in each province, with mixed results. Federal organizers work out of provincial offices in the pre-election period and the provincial party headquarters devotes its full attention to the federal election campaign once it is called. The two levels of the party are also integrated financially. In Quebec, however, the federal party operates independently of any provincial party of the same name. The 1995 Renewal Convention sought to give the federal party a more stand-alone presence, such that revenue sharing is less important, and 75 percent of the federal council is elected at the federal convention of the party rather than at provincial conventions.

The Liberal Party is characterized by two different federal–provincial relationships. In Quebec, Ontario, and the four western provinces, the party is split into federal and provincial wings, each of which has separate finances, memberships, constituency associations, executives, conventions, and offices. The other provinces have a joint Liberal Party, although such an integrated relationship probably gives the party a provincial orientation. It is possible to join the federal party directly, but it is more common to join the provincial party and become an automatic member of the federal organization. The Liberals made constitutional changes in 2006 to strengthen the federal wing of the party, but the lack of a national membership list continued to hamper their fundraising efforts.

The Yukon legislature operates with political parties, and the territorial Liberals and NDP are each connected to their respective national parties. The Northwest Territories and Nunavut are characterized by nonpartisan, consensus government and do not have parties at the territorial level. Nevertheless, all three national parties have small organizations in each of the territories for federal political purposes.

FEDERAL–LOCAL PARTY LINKS: THE FRANCHISE MODEL

Besides the federal–provincial links within a political party, the relationship between the federal party and its local constituency associations should be mentioned, especially the "franchise model" pioneered by Ken Carty. It is based on the idea that Canadian parties are large national competitive organizations that have local branches or franchises that respond to the distinctiveness of their immediate environments, somewhat akin to Canadian Tire or McDonald's. As in the case of the private sector models, each organizational element of the party has its respective functions and not all local constituency associations operate exactly alike:

> Their central organizations are typically responsible for providing the basic product line—policy and leadership; for devising and directing the major communication line and appeal—the national campaign; and for establishing standard organizational management, training, and financing functions.... Local units ... provide the basic organizational home for most individual members, and are normally charged with delivering the product by creating organizations that can find and support candidates, as well as mounting campaigns to mobilize the vote on election day.[53]

This model has implications for all of the organizational questions considered above, including party membership, leadership, and policymaking, as well as for candidate selection and electoral effort as discussed in Chapter 15.

. . . .

CONCLUSION

However much Canadians tire of their endless bickering and lack of inspiration, political parties perform several crucial functions in the political system. In particular, they sort out the political issues and, in trying to bridge some of the many Canadian cleavages, make the political system more manageable. Many political observers are concerned about the danger of major political parties being outflanked by single-issue groups, whether as advocacy groups during and between election campaigns or as single-interest parties, in the representation of political interests and as the focus of political activity.[54] Such scholars argue that steps must be taken to strengthen mainline parties so that they can overcome their current lack of organizational depth and their weak membership base, and enhance their capacity to perform their representational and policymaking functions. Perhaps Canadians expect too much of their parties and place on them too much of the burden of keeping the country together. Perhaps parties do not perform their functions well and are also dysfunctional in some respects. Perhaps their functions and methods of operation are in a state of change. But they must not be allowed to deteriorate further.

While parties are mentioned with enormous frequency throughout the book, they figure most prominently in the preceding and following chapters on elections and election campaigns. They are also the essential determinant for the operation of the House of Commons. If the situation persists in which no party wins a majority, and if Canada ever opts for coalition governments as a result, inter-party relationships will also be central to the functioning of the Cabinet.[55]

PC Since parties are so central to the operation of the political system, all of the approaches outlined in Chapter 1 have something to say about them. Parties are one of the main objects of the public choice approach, for example, and the efforts of political parties to barter promises for votes can be seen in the attempt to develop attractive election platforms and in party policymaking processes. Politicians make such promises as will lead to their election, while rational, self-interested voters support the party whose policies are of greatest utility to them. At least in the Liberal and Conservative parties, such promises and policies are not seriously limited by ideological consistency. As noted in Chapter 15, however, the alleged quid pro quo takes place in an environment of vague proposals, slogans, and leader images as far as the parties are concerned, and prejudices, ignorance, and family traditions on the part of many voters.

P The pluralist model is particularly applicable to the broker system. In a country with many cleavages, it is not only desirable but also necessary that political parties seek to accommodate the demands of all major groups. Unlike class analysts, pluralists do not see class divisions as taking priority over ethnic, religious, regional, or other concerns. They also note the increased role of women and new ethnocultural groups in party operations.

© Class analysis can be seen in its critique of the broker system and in its prescription for a class-based, ideological party system. In such analysts' eyes, the Liberal and Conservative parties are apologists for the capitalist system but have deliberately defined Canadian politics in terms of region and ethnicity in order to disguise their true motives. Both parties are so intermeshed with the capitalist system that any apparent choice they provide to the electorate is purely illusory. Other elite theorists observe that party activists overrepresent "elite" characteristics in society in terms of ethnicity and gender, and emphasize the inevitable tendency toward oligarchy within all political parties, such that rank-and-file members have little real power.

(SC) The state-centred approach argues that it is largely irrelevant which party forms the government because the subsequent "government policy" is developed within the Cabinet and bureaucracy. Such policy is more related to social and economic conditions and to the authorities' priorities than to election promises or party platforms. When parties neglect to develop policy within their ranks and fail to provide distinctive election platforms, they serve to confirm this contention. Even if they do put effort into the generation of party policy and even if they do propose specific policy positions in the campaign, government policies are rarely enacted without some evidence of bureaucratic modification. On the other hand, when a party comes to power fully committed to a new approach, the results are obvious. A Pearsonian commitment to social welfare programs, a Trudeauesque obsession with linguistic rights, or a Mulroneyite determination for free trade, privatization, and deregulation (to say nothing of distinctive NDP or Conservative approaches at the provincial level) all demonstrate that the state apparatus is not immune from party and societal influences.

(G) Globalization affects political parties in two main ways. First, many parties have links with their counterparts in other countries. In some cases there are formal international organizations, such as the Socialist International and the Liberal International, which respectively incorporate all social democratic and liberal parties around the world; in other cases, there is just informal cooperation, such as between the Canadian Alliance and the U.S. Republican party. Second, globalization goes hand in hand with neoliberalism, which became a significant political ideology in Canada and elsewhere. In one respect, neoliberalism is an example of globalization—a new ideology spreading quickly around the whole world. In another, neoliberalism advocates the basic ingredients of globalization, such as a reliance on economic forces at the expense of government involvement in the economy. However, the new worldwide consensus on the "third way" is also an example of globalization, even if it is somewhat at odds with the policy objectives of that movement.

· ·

DISCUSSION QUESTIONS

1. Why are political parties so prominent at the federal and provincial levels of government in Canada and so insignificant at the municipal level in most cases?

2. What historical events, political personalities, or other factors have been determining influences in the evolution of the Canadian party system?

3. Given the negative implications of the broker system, do you feel it would be advantageous to move to a class-based, ideological system? Why or why not?

4. What is the best method of choosing party leaders and the best approach to leadership accountability?

5. Is it possible in this complex, technological, information-driven age for ordinary party members to make useful policy suggestions for national policies, or is it inevitable that the policymaking function be turned over to party leaders and their advisers, bureaucrats, and advocacy groups? Would party foundations help?

6. Is there a distinctive ideological base for the major parties in Canada? Is there at least a distinctive, consistent approach to policy questions? Is the new Conservative Party a broker or an ideological party?

. . . .

NOTES

1. William Cross, *Political Parties* (Vancouver: UBC Press, 2004).
2. Heather MacIvor, *Parameters of Power: Canada's Political Institutions*, 5th ed. (Toronto: Nelson Education, 2010), pp. 367–78.
3. R.K. Carty, "Three Party Systems: An Interpretation of the Development of National Politics," in Hugh G. Thorburn and Alan Whitehorn, eds., *Party Politics in Canada*, 8th ed. (Scarborough: Prentice Hall Canada, 2001).
4. David E. Smith, "Canadian Political Parties and National Integration," in Alain Gagnon and Brian Tanguay, eds., *Canadian Parties in Transition*, 2nd ed. (Scarborough: Nelson Canada, 1996). Carty and Smith divide the periods in the same way but use different criteria. See also Gagnon and Tanguay, *Canadian Parties in Transition*, 3rd ed. (Peterborough: Broadview Press, 2007).
5. J. Murray Beck, *Pendulum of Power* (Scarborough: Prentice Hall Canada, 1968); and John Duffy, *Fights of Our Lives: Elections, Leadership and the Making of Canada* (Toronto: HarperCollins, 2002).
6. W.L. Morton, *The Progressive Party in Canada* (Toronto: University of Toronto Press, 1950).
7. Walter Young, *Anatomy of a Party: The National CCF 1932–1961* (Toronto: University of Toronto Press, 1969); Walter Young, *Democracy and Discontent* (Toronto: Ryerson Press, 1969); and S.M. Lipset, *Agrarian Socialism: The Cooperative Commonwealth Federation in Saskatchewan* (Los Angeles: University of California Press, 1950).
8. Alvin Finkel, *The Social Credit Phenomenon in Alberta* (Toronto: University of Toronto Press, 1989).
9. H.F. Quinn, *The Union Nationale* (Toronto: University of Toronto Press, 1963).
10. Reginald Whitaker, *The Government Party: Organizing and Financing the Liberal Party of Canada 1930–58* (Toronto: University of Toronto Press, 1977).
11. J.L. Granatstein, *The Politics of Survival: The Conservative Party of Canada, 1939–1945* (Toronto: University of Toronto Press, 1967); and George Perlin, *The Tory Syndrome: Leadership Politics in the Progressive Conservative Party* (Montreal: McGill-Queen's University Press, 1980).
12. Lynn McDonald, *The Party That Changed Canada: The New Democratic Party, Then and Now* (Toronto: McClelland and Stewart, 1987); Desmond Morton, *The New Democrats 1961–1986: The Politics of Change* (Toronto: Copp Clark Pitman, 1986); and Alan Whitehorn, *Canadian Socialism: Essays on the CCF and the NDP* (Toronto: Oxford University Press, 1992).
13. Maurice Pinard, *The Rise of a Third Party: A Study in Crisis Politics* (Scarborough: Prentice Hall Canada, 1971); and Michael Stein, *The Dynamics of Right-Wing Protest: A Political Analysis of Social Credit in Quebec* (Toronto: University of Toronto Press, 1973).
14. Peter C. Newman, *The Distemper of Our Times* (Toronto: McClelland and Stewart, 1968); and Andrew Cohen, *Lester B. Pearson* (Toronto: Penguin Canada, 2008).
15. Jeffrey Simpson, *Discipline of Power: The Conservative Interlude and the Liberal Restoration* (Toronto: Personal Library, 1980).
16. Christina McCall-Newman, *Grits: An Intimate Portrait of the Liberal Party* (Toronto: Macmillan, 1982); and Stephen Clarkson and Christina McCall, *Trudeau and Our Times*, 2 vols. (Toronto: McClelland and Stewart, 1990 and 1994).
17. Alan Frizzell and Anthony Westell, eds. *The Canadian General Election of 1984* (Ottawa: Carleton University Press, 1985); and Graham Fraser, *Playing for Keeps* (Toronto: McClelland and Stewart, 1989).
18. R. Kenneth Carty, William Cross, and Lisa Young, "Building a Fourth Canadian Party System," in Thorburn and Whitehorn, eds., *Party Politics in Canada*; Alan Cairns, "An Election to Be Remembered: Canada 1993," *Canadian Public Policy* (September, 1994); Alan Frizzell, Jon H. Pammett, and

Anthony Westell, *The Canadian General Election of 1993* (Ottawa: Carleton University Press, 1994); and R. Kenneth Carty, William Cross, and Lisa Young, *Rebuilding Canadian Party Politics* (Vancouver: UBC Press, 2000).

19. Faron Ellis, "The More Things Change... The Alliance Campaign," in Jon H. Pammett and Christopher Dornan, eds., *The Canadian General Election of 2000* (Toronto: Dundurn, 2001).

20. Tom Flanagan, *Harper's Team: Behind the Scenes in the Conservative Rise to Power* (Montreal: McGill-Queen's University Press, 2007) provides a frank, insider's analysis of how all this happened.

21. H.G. Thorburn, "Interpretations of the Canadian Party System," in H.G. Thorburn, ed., *Party Politics in Canada*, 6th ed. (Scarborough: Prentice Hall Canada, 1991); Paul Fox, "Middle-of-the Road Parties Are the Canadian Tradition," in his *Politics: Canada*, 6th ed. (Toronto: McGraw-Hill Ryerson, 1987); Matthew Mendelsohn, "Four Dimensions of Political Culture in Canada Outside Quebec: The Changing Nature of Brokerage and the Definition of the Canadian Nation," in Hamish Telford and Harvey Lazar, eds., *Canada: The State of the Federation 2001* (Kingston: Institute of Intergovernmental Relations, 2002); and Anthony Sayers, "The End of Brokerage? The Canadian Party System in the 21st Century," in Michael Whittington and Glen Williams, eds., *Canadian Politics in the 21st Century*, 7th ed. (Toronto: Thomson Nelson, 2008).

22. Janine Brodie and Jane Jenson, *Crisis, Challenge and Change: Party and Class in Canada Revisited* (Ottawa: Carleton University Press, 1988); Charles Taylor, *The Pattern of Politics* (Toronto: McClelland and Stewart, 1970); and Gad Horowitz, "Toward the Democratic Class Struggle," in Trevor Lloyd and Jack McLeod, eds., *Agenda 1970* (Toronto: University of Toronto Press, 1968).

23. On seduction, see Whitaker, *The Government Party*, for example, the co-opting of Saskatchewan farm leader C.A. Dunning and Humphrey Mitchell from the labour movement; on coercion, see Judy Torrance, *Public Violence in Canada* (Montreal: McGill-Queen's University Press, 1986).

24. The Liberals actually welcomed communist support if such working-class divisions would weaken the CCF. Gad Horowitz, *Canadian Labour in Politics* (Toronto: University of Toronto Press, 1968).

25. Jon Pammett, "Class Voting and Class Consciousness in Canada," *Canadian Review of Sociology and Anthropology* 24, no. 2 (1987); Keith Archer, "The Failure of the New Democratic Party: Unions, Unionists, and Politics in Canada," *Canadian Journal of Political Science* (June 1985); Michael Ornstein, H. Michael Stevenson; A. Paul Williams, "Region, Class and Political Culture in Canada," *Canadian Journal of Political Science* (June 1980); and Elisabeth Gidengil, "Class and Region in Canadian Voting: A Dependency Interpretation," *Canadian Journal of Political Science* (September 1989).

26. Horowitz, "Toward the Democratic Class Struggle," p. 254.

27. Thorburn, "Interpretations of the Canadian Party System"; Whitaker, *The Government Party*; and Perlin, *The Tory Syndrome*.

28. Stephen Clarkson, *The Big Red Machine: How the Liberal Party Dominates Canadian Politics* (Vancouver: UBC Press, 2005); and André Blais, "Accounting for the Electoral Success of the Liberal Party in Canada," *Canadian Journal of Political Science* (December 2005).

29. John Meisel, "Decline of Party in Canada," in H.G. Thorburn, ed., *Party Politics in Canada*, 5th ed. (Scarborough: Prentice Hall Canada, 1985); John Meisel, "The Dysfunctions of Canadian Parties: An Exploratory Mapping," in Thorburn, ed., *Party Politics in Canada*, 6th ed; and Gagnon and Tanguay, eds., *Canadian Parties in Transition*, various editions.

30. Paul Howe and David Northrup, *Strengthening Canadian Democracy: The Views of Canadians* (Montreal: Institute for Research on Public Policy, July 2000).

31. Gagnon and Tanguay, *Canadian Parties in Transition*, 3rd ed.

32. S.M. Lipset, "Democracy in Alberta," *Canadian Forum* (November/December 1954); and Roger Gibbins, *Regionalism: Territorial Politics in Canada and the United States* (Toronto: Butterworths, 1982), ch. 5.

33. C.B. Macpherson, *Democracy in Alberta: Social Credit and the Party System* (Toronto: University of Toronto Press, 1953).

34. S.M. Lipset, *Agrarian Socialism, The Cooperative Commonwealth Federation*, rev. ed. Garden City, NY: Anchor Books, 1968); J.F. Conway, "Explaining the Roots of Canada's Third Parties," *Canadian Journal of Political Science* (1978).

35. Conrad Winn and John McMenemy, *Political Parties in Canada* (Toronto: McGraw-Hill Ryerson, 1976), pp. 4–5.

36. R.M. Dawson, *The Government of Canada*, 4th ed. (Toronto: University of Toronto Press, 1963), pp. 466–72; and J.R. Mallory, *The Structure of Canadian Government* (Toronto: Macmillan, 1971), p. 197.

37. Louis Hartz, *The Founding of New Societies* (New York: Harcourt, Brace and World, 1964); Gad Horowitz, "Conservatism, Liberalism and Socialism in Canada: An Interpretation," *Canadian Journal of Economics and Political Science* (May 1966); Gad Horowitz, "Notes on 'Conservatism, Liberalism and Socialism in Canada,'" *Canadian Journal of Political Science* (June 1978); William Christian and Colin Campbell, *Political Parties and Ideologies in Canada*, 3rd ed. (Toronto: McGraw-Hill Ryerson, 1990); and William Christian and Colin Campbell, *Parties, Leaders, and Ideologies in Canada* (Toronto: McGraw-Hill Ryerson, 1996).

38. Neil Nevitte, Herman Bakvis, and Roger Gibbins, "The Ideological Contours of 'New Politics' in Canada: Policy, Mobilization and Partisan Support," *Canadian Journal of Political Science* (September 1989).

39. Horowitz, "Conservatism, Liberalism and Socialism in Canada."

40. James McAllister, "Do Parties Make a Difference?" in Gagnon and Tanguay, eds., *Canadian Parties in Transition*; Winn and McMenemy, *Political Parties in Canada*.

41. Duncan Cameron, "Political Discourse in the Eighties," in Gagnon and Tanguay, eds., *Canadian Parties in Transition*; and Michael Ornstein and H. Michael Stevenson, *Politics and Ideology in Canada* (Montreal: McGill-Queen's University Press, 1999).

42. Walter Stewart, *Dismantling the State* (Toronto: Stoddart, 1998); and Stephen McBride and John Shields, *Dismantling a Nation: The Transition to Corporate Rule in Canada* (Halifax: Fernwood Publishing, 1997).

43. Brooke Jeffrey, *Hard Right Turn: The New Face of Neo-Conservatism in Canada* (Toronto: HarperCollins, 1999); and Trevor Harrison, *Of Passionate Intensity: Right-Wing Populism and the Reform Party of Canada* (Toronto: University of Toronto Press, 1995).

44. Trevor W. Harrison, "Populist and Conservative Christian Evangelical Movements: A Comparison of Canada and the United States," in Miriam Smith, ed., *Group Politics and Social Movements in Canada* (Peterborough: Broadview Press, 2008).

45. Alexandra Dobrowolsky, "Political Parties: Teletubby Politics, The Third Way, and Democratic Challenge(r)s," in Michael Whittington and Glen Williams, eds., *Canadian Politics in the 21st Century*, 6th ed. (Toronto: Thomson Nelson, 2004).

46. Cross, *Political Parties*, ch. 2; R. Kenneth Carty and Munroe Eagles, *Politics Is Local: National Politics at the Grassroots* (Toronto: Oxford University Press, 2005).

47. John C. Courtney, *The Selection of National Party Leaders* (Toronto: Macmillan, 1973); John C. Courtney, *Do Conventions Matter? Choosing National Party Leaders in Canada* (Montreal: McGill-Queen's University Press, 1995); Cross, *Political Parties*, ch. 5.

48. The 2006 Liberal convention is covered in articles in Institute for Research on Public Policy, *Policy Options*, February 2007.

49. Joseph Wearing, "Can an Old Dog Teach Itself New Tricks? The Liberal Party Attempts Reform," in Gagnon and Tanguay, eds., *Canadian Parties in Transition*.

50. Cross, *Political Parties*, p. 46; Irvin Studin, "Revisiting the Democratic Deficit: The Case of Political Party Think Tanks," Institute for Research on Public Policy, *Policy Options*, February 2008.

51. Robert Michels, *Political Parties* (New York: Free Press, 1966).

52. Donald Smiley, *Canada in Question: Federalism in the Eighties*, 3rd ed. (Toronto: McGraw-Hill Ryerson, 1980); and Rand Dyck, "Relations between Federal and Provincial Parties," in Gagnon and Tanguay, eds., *Canadian Parties in Transition*, 2nd ed.

53. Roland Kenneth Carty, "The Politics of Tecumseh Corners: Canadian Political Parties as Franchise Organizations," *Canadian Journal of Political Science* (December 2002).

54. Pierre Lortie, *The Challenge of Electoral Reform: Combining Innovation with Continuity*, Royal Commission on Electoral Reform and Party Financing, Winnipeg, November 26, 1990; Cross, *Political Parties*.

55. Peter H. Russell, *Two Cheers for Minority Government: The Evolution of Canadian Parliamentary Democracy* (Toronto: Emond Montgomery, 2008).

· ·

FURTHER READING

Campbell, Colin, and William Christian. *Parties, Leaders, and Ideologies in Canada.* Toronto: McGraw-Hill Ryerson, 1996.

Carty, R. Kenneth, William Cross, and Lisa Young. *Rebuilding Canadian Party Politics.* Vancouver: UBC Press, 2000.

Carty, R. Kenneth. *Canadian Political Party Systems.* Peterborough: Broadview Press, 1992.

Cross, William. *Political Parties.* Vancouver: UBC Press, 2004.

Flanagan, Tom. *Harper's Team: Behind the Scenes in the Conservative Rise to Power.* Montreal: McGill-Queen's University Press, 2007.

Gagnon, Alain-G. and A. Brian Tanguay, eds. *Canadian Parties in Transition*, 3rd ed. Peterborough: Broadview Press, 2007.

Horowitz, Gad. "Conservatism, Liberalism and Socialism in Canada: An Interpretation." *Canadian Journal of Political Science* (May 1966).

Jeffrey, Brooke. *Hard Right Turn: The New Face of Neo-Conservatism in Canada.* Toronto: HarperCollins, 1999.

MacIvor, Heather. *Parameters of Power: Canada's Political Institutions*, 5th ed. Toronto: Nelson Education, 2010.

Ornstein, Michael and H. Michael Stevenson. *Politics and Ideology in Canada.* Montreal: McGill-Queen's University Press, 1999.

Pammett, Jon H. and Christopher Dornan, eds., *The Canadian Federal Election of 2006.* Toronto: Dundurn Press, 2006.

———, and ———, eds. *The Canadian Federal Election of 2008.* Toronto: Dundurn Press, 2009.

Sayers, Anthony Sayers. "The End of Brokerage? The Canadian Party System in the 21st Century." In Michael Whittington and Glen Williams, eds., *Canadian Politics in the 21st Century*, 7th ed. Toronto: Thomson Nelson, 2008.

Thorburn, H.G., and Alan Whitehorn, eds. *Party Politics in Canada*, 8th ed. Toronto: Prentice Hall, 2001.

Chapter 15

PARTIES, VOTING,
and the Election Campaign

Following 12 years of Liberal government, why were Stephen Harper's Conservatives elected in 2006? After re-election in 2008, were they likely to fall to Michael Ignatieff's revived Liberal party? What are the components of a national election campaign? To what extent do the media coverage of the campaign and the leaders' debate influence the results? How are the campaigns of local candidates organized? What determines how people vote?

Elections are not only the most colourful and exciting element of the Canadian political system, but they are also in many ways the most important. Certain elections are great landmarks in a country's history and often change its course. Almost all the daily efforts of parties and politicians are ultimately geared toward maximizing their support in the next electoral contest. The election campaign constitutes the arena in which political parties, the mass media, public opinion polls, and political participation all come together to play their most extensive and interconnected role.

The official side of the electoral system having been examined in Chapter 13, this chapter explores the more lively side of the campaign—that dominated by political parties, party leaders, candidates, the media, and public opinion polls. The chapter has three main parts: the national party campaign, the local candidate campaign, and electoral behaviour and party support.[1]

THEORETICAL CONSIDERATIONS

Of the three main subjects contained in this chapter, the one that attracts the most theoretical consideration of political scientists is electoral behaviour and party support. Especially since the "behavioural revolution" in the discipline of political science, these questions have been of great interest. At some points, the discipline might have gone overboard with its obsession with numbers, primarily gained through the use of public opinion surveys, but studying the behaviour of voters remains a fascinating branch of Canadian political science, and what answers have been accumulated will be provided in the third part of the chapter.

. . . .

THE NATIONAL PARTY CAMPAIGN
Party Headquarters and Pre-Writ Preparations

The main motive for the choice of election date in 1997, 2000, and 2004 was that Liberal polling indicated the party was well ahead of its rivals in public opinion, although in selecting a date that was less than four years from the previous contest in the first two cases, Liberal strategists were somewhat concerned about possible charges of opportunism. Despite the fact that the governing party chose election day, however, in none of these contests were the Liberals particularly well prepared. The same could be said of the 2006 election, which was forced by the defeat of the Martin minority government on a nonconfidence motion. On the other hand, the opposition Conservatives were well prepared for it, having geared up for an election six months earlier when they expected the Martin government to fall. In 2008, the Conservatives ignored their own fixed election date law to call an election when they felt it to be advantageous, rather than wait to be defeated in the Commons.

At the national level, especially in an era of unstable minority governments, political parties begin thinking about the next election as soon as the last one has passed, and it is helpful to have at least a year in which to engage in planning the next campaign. This planning entails setting up a national campaign committee, which ponders such matters as strategy, policy, image, and budget. Most federal parties also have campaign committees in each province, with varying degrees of centralization or decentralization of authority. Parties usually hire extra organizers in the pre-election period and deploy them to reactivate local associations. Funds permitting, party headquarters also conducts public opinion polls throughout the inter-election period to see how the voters perceive the various leaders, parties, and issues. For the party in power, especially in a majority position, such polls used to be central to deciding when to call the election in the first place. Obvious election preparations on the part of the governing party encourage the other parties to get into the act, such that an unstoppable momentum usually develops. Nowadays, in a minority situation, the polls may be of even greater benefit to the Opposition parties in deciding when to defeat the government.

Another party activity that begins before the calling of the election is the search for good candidates. This is essentially a task of the local party organizations, and the party headquarters rarely imposes a candidate on an unwilling constituency association. However, the leader, regional lieutenants, and party organizers are always on the lookout for new blood, and head office may try to parachute a few "star" candidates into safe seats. The Liberals, Conservatives, and NDP all run a full slate of candidates, so where local organizations are weak, the national party sometimes has to take the initiative to find a candidate for them.

National fundraising is another activity that goes on between elections, although it intensifies immediately before and during the election period. This topic was discussed in Chapter 13, which noted that parties now get a substantial proportion of their revenues from the public purse, and are otherwise limited to small individual contributions.

Once the election is called, party headquarters continues to perform such activities as polling, fundraising, and candidate recruitment. Either before or immediately after the election call, headquarters also holds campaign colleges, schools, and seminars for candidates, campaign managers, and other local campaign officials. In addition, headquarters will design logos, other artwork, and one or more leaflets that candidates can order or adapt for their own local purposes. In some cases, nowadays, it even produces videos. Another headquarters activity is the preparation of draft "issue letters" and fact sheets for candidates to use, either in promoting their own party's platform or in attacking that of others. During the campaign, headquarters normally communicates with candidate campaigns on a daily basis, via fax or e-mail, in efforts to bolster morale, ensure uniformity of presentation, and alert candidates to a change in course.

Election Strategy

Election strategy involves deciding which groups within the electorate are to be targeted; whether to emphasize the leader or issues, and, if the latter, which issues; and whether to mount an offensive or defensive campaign. Strategists determine the itinerary of the leader's tour, the content and style of the party's advertising, and where extra organizational efforts will be concentrated. Once the election is called, the national campaign committee discusses such things as "modification to the leader's tour, daily tracking of polling results, and focus group findings, carries out ongoing testing of campaign slogans and phrasing, determines the final changes of the ads and when to replace one round of ads with subsequent ones, and makes preparations for the leaders' debates."[2] Nevertheless, accounts of all recent campaigns reveal how frequently the best-laid plans of electoral strategists go awry.

In a nutshell, the Liberals' strategy in 2004 and 2006 was to demonize Stephen Harper as Conservative leader, emphasizing extreme right-wing statements that he or others in the party had made in the past. They then crafted a campaign distinguishing between the basic values of the two parties. This was somewhat successful in 2004, but much less so in 2006 when Harper campaigned on a more moderate, centrist platform, laying out one promise a day. Unfortunately for the Conservatives in 2004, outspoken candidates often undermined the moderate approach that Harper was trying to take. The Liberals exploited these breaches unmercifully, claiming that they were indeed part of a hidden agenda. But in 2006, Conservative candidates were kept under strict control and did not cause Harper much embarrassment. By 2008, it was the Conservatives' turn to ridicule Liberal leader Stéphane Dion, both for his style and his main promise—the "Green Shift"—to raise taxes on those activities that damaged the environment and reduce other taxes proportionally.

Election Platform

One of the Liberals' great assets in the 1993 campaign was their "Red Book," *Creating Opportunity: The Liberal Plan for Canada.* To some extent the Red Book was based on a thinkers' conference in 1991 and policy debates at a party convention in 1992. Chrétien claimed that, if elected, he would adhere to every word, and the book provided a tremendous prop for a leader who was otherwise not policy-oriented in his public appearances.[3] The Liberals claimed by 1996 that they had implemented 78 percent of their promises, although conspicuously unfulfilled was their promise that was widely understood to mean that they would get rid of the GST. The Liberals put considerable effort into developing another comprehensive 102-page platform in 1997, but not so much in the elections of 2000, 2004, or 2006. By 2006, it was the Conservative platform that was most comprehensive and that attracted the most attention.[4] To some extent it was based on the new party's national policy conference in March 2005 in Montreal. Confirming the observation that opposition parties often offer a more comprehensive electoral manifesto than the government, Dion insisted that the Liberals focus on

THE CANADIAN PRESS/Jacques Boissinot

NDP leader Jack Layton sings in a radio interview in Quebec City in the 2008 election campaign.

the Green Shift idea in 2008, while the Conservatives had a modest platform that was only unveiled in its totality one week before election day.

The Leader's Tour

The leader's tour consists of each party leader crisscrossing the country many times over the campaign period. Similar to a royal tour, party officials go ahead of the leader to make sure that every detail is in place. The leader is then accompanied by a horde of strategists and support staff, as well as by reporters who pay to travel aboard the party-chartered plane or bus. All this effort is expended not only to attract attention in the areas visited but also to generate national media coverage. Since this kind of coverage is free, in contrast to paid advertising, and since televised news coverage is very important in reaching voters, parties spare no trouble or expense to obtain it. Stephen Harper ran an almost perfect leader's tour in 2006, following the advice of Frizzell and Westell, who wrote that parties

> should arrange events every day so that the TV crews, pressed by deadlines and demands from home stations for footage, will have little option but to picture the leader in a favourable setting ... [and] ensure that in every speech or statement there is a phrase that sums up the message in a couple of seconds.[5]

An innovation begun in 1997 was that instead of each network placing a complete crew of its own on each of the leader's tours, the five major television networks—CBC, CTV, Global, Radio-Canada, and TVA—pooled their resources and personnel on the party leaders' campaign planes and buses. Thanks to new communications technologies, from the 2000 election onwards, the team on each leader's tour was more closely connected to the party's "war-room" back in Ottawa than on previous occasions. This allowed each leader to react instantaneously to developments in the others' campaigns.

Media Coverage

Parties hope that the leader's tour will garner them one positive story every day on the national television news and in daily newspapers. Such was generally the case when there were only three national parties in the race, but with five party leaders to cover in 1993, 1997, and 2000, networks sometimes grouped different campaigns together so that each party did not get an individual item on the national news every night. Such numbers also reduced the length of leaders' sound bites.[6] Four parties (three outside Quebec) in 2004 and 2006 made it more manageable to provide individual attention, and the Green party gained considerable coverage in 2008.

Before 1997, television and newspapers gave virtually equal time or space to the various party leaders, although the kind of treatment was not always so equitable. But in 1997 and 2000, the different parties received a quite unequal quantity of treatment in both television and newspaper coverage. For example, a study of the four Toronto daily newspapers in 2000 showed that all concentrated on the Liberals and Canadian Alliance, and that the Progressive Conservatives and NDP received much less attention. Moreover, the coverage of all four parties in all four papers was generally negative in tone. Similar to newspapers in 2000, the Liberals and Alliance gained far more time than the other two parties on English-language television news, while on French-language television news, little was heard of any party beyond the Liberals and the Bloc.[7] In 2006, the *National Post* unashamedly cheered on the Conservatives, while owner David Asper even showed up at a Conservative party rally. A study of newspaper coverage in that campaign revealed that the *National Post*, *Calgary Herald*, and *Toronto Star* were all strongly biased in their editorials and among their columnists, but even they were relatively neutral in their news coverage.[8]

As noted in Chapter 12, large corporations control the ownership of most of the mass media. The lack of any major media support for the NDP, along with limited news coverage, reflects the hegemony argument made in Chapter 1 that the media do not provide equitable coverage to parties advocating policies that substantially challenge the status quo. *Globe and Mail* columnist Lawrence Martin regularly argues that the whole tone of the Canadian mass media is increasingly right wing.

National Media Advertising

Each party turns its national paid media advertising over to one or more advertising agencies, along with at least some indication of the party's campaign strategy. As noted in Chapter 12, the most important part of the media campaign is television, and most parties spend huge amounts of money on the production of television commercials alone. Each party's advertisements vary across languages and from region to region, so great differences exist in the messages voters receive. Nowadays, of course, parties increasingly also advertise on the Internet.

The purchase of broadcast time is regulated by the Elections Act. Representatives of registered parties meet with the Broadcasting Arbitrator before the election to try to agree on an allocation of commercial broadcasting time. If they cannot agree, the arbitrator makes the allocation within the guidelines of the act. It requires each broadcaster to make available, for purchase by registered political parties, six and one-half hours of prime time during the campaign. Such an allocation among parties is primarily based on the number of seats held in the House of Commons and on popular vote received in the previous election. No party can receive more than one-half of the total time, but candidates are allowed to purchase time for their own use outside what is allotted to parties. Having been awarded more than twice as much time as the Liberals and three times as much as the NDP in 1988, the Conservatives were allowed to saturate the airwaves in the last week of the campaign. In addition to purchasable time, parties are awarded free radio and television time in the same proportions.

Many observers, including supporters of minor parties, considered the earlier distribution of paid and free broadcasting time to be extremely unfair, and the Royal Commission on Electoral Reform recommended a more equitable system. In 1992, the Reform Party went to court and successfully challenged its original allotment for the forthcoming election. Since

TABLE 15.1   Allocation of Broadcasting Time, Major Parties, 2008 Election

	Paid Time (min:sec)	Free Time (min:sec)		
		CBC-TV	CBC Radio One	TVA/TQS
Conservatives	95:30	51:30	29:00	15:00
Liberals	82:30	44:30	25:00	13:00
NDP	45:00	24:30	13:30	7:00
Bloc Québécois	37:30	20:30	11:30	6:00
Greens	22:30	12:00	7:00	3:30

Source: Elections Canada. The Broadcasting Arbitrator. 2007 Allocation of Paid Time. Appendix A. Pg.6. Found at: http://www.elections.ca/content.asp?section=med&dir=all&document=index&lang=e&textonly=false

then, the Broadcasting Arbitrator uses discretion to increase the time of smaller parties. The results during the 2008 election for the larger parties are shown in Table 15.1. The other 14 registered parties received smaller amounts of both buyable and free time.

When the Reform Party case went to the Alberta Court of Appeal in 1995, that court struck down the clause that prevented a party from purchasing more than its allocated time on any station. Thus, from 1997 onward, parties were allowed to purchase more time than allocated to them under the act, providing stations were willing to sell them such time and subject to the overall limits on each party's election expenses. The official allocation therefore became most significant as the basis for the distribution of free time for each party. Another court case had effectively removed the blackout rules that prohibited *candidate* advertising on election day and the day before, although the decision left intact the prohibition on *party* advertising during the last 48 hours.[9]

One of the most memorable, if short-lived, negative commercials was that run by the Tories in 1993. It featured Jean Chrétien's face (the left side slightly paralyzed from a childhood disease) with such voice-over comments as "I personally would be very embarrassed if he were to become prime minister of Canada." After an instantaneous public uproar, Kim Campbell had the commercial removed.[10] Another striking advertisement in the 1997 campaign was sponsored by the Reform Party. It showed a red, slashed circle stamped over the faces of Jean Chrétien, Jean Charest, Gilles Duceppe, and Lucien Bouchard, which essentially said, "We've had enough political leaders from Quebec." Above all, this commercial was designed to undercut Jean Charest after his success in the leaders' debates. The Conservative commercials in 2006 attacked Liberal corruption, while Liberals were even more negative, attempting to scare voters with some of Stephen Harper's earlier assertions. Although both parties' "attack" ads probably had some effect, the Liberal commercials seemed wildly out of place with what Harper was now saying. Immediately after the Liberals elected Stéphane Dion as their leader, the Conservatives ran some viciously personal negative television ads. In fact, in one case the company involved in placing them refused to participate in the campaign. When Dion resigned as Liberal leader after the 2008 election, he attributed much of his lack of success to these ads, and new leader Michael Ignatieff told the Conservatives that they would be wise not to do the same to him.

The Leaders' Debates

The televised leaders' debates are another main aspect of the national campaign.[11] These have been held in every election since 1968 except 1972, 1974, and 1980. Debates tend to benefit the opposition party leaders who might otherwise have difficulty obtaining coverage, but it would be virtually impossible for the incumbent prime minister to refuse such a debate anymore. Originally a byproduct of the influence of American presidential politics, the debates have become a crucial aspect of the campaign because of the combined importance of leaders and television.

The leaders' debates are not mentioned in either the Canada Elections Act or the television broadcasting regulations, and the consortium of television stations that carry them essentially set the rules. The recommendation of the **Royal Commission on Electoral Reform and Party Financing** that the debates become obligatory and regulated has not been implemented. In 1993, with a large number of parties in the race, the consortium agreed that only five parties would take part: those that were represented in Parliament and that had had a consistent impact in public debates and public opinion. Mel Hurtig, leader of the new National Party of Canada, went to court to try to force his way into the debate, but did not succeed. The 1997 and 2000 debates also consisted of the leaders of the five largest parties, and those in 2004 and 2006 of only four, with some observers finding Gilles Duceppe of the Bloc Québécois rather out of place in the English debate. In 2008, Green Party leader Elizabeth May managed to get herself admitted to the leaders' debates at the last minute, even though the party had no seats in the House of Commons before the election (and none afterward, either).

Although they are carefully trained and briefed (speechwriters prepare opening and closing statements and one-liners), debates place the leaders in a much less controlled setting than they are used to. The debates are thus one of the few opportunities for the public to see them functioning on their own. The 1984 and 1988 debates each featured a dramatic one-on-one exchange between Brian Mulroney and John Turner that was also endlessly replayed afterward. Since then, the leaders' debates have been less dramatic, partly because there have been more leaders involved with less opportunity for one-on-one confrontations. Since 1984, there have been separate French and English debates on successive nights (and two in each language in 2006), making it virtually indispensable for a party leader to be bilingual.

As noted, each party immediately sends forth its **spin doctors** to persuade reporters that its leader won, but whether the public makes up its own mind on the winner or awaits the verdict of media commentators is not entirely certain. Each leader's performance is judged in relation to the others, as well as relative to the media's expectations. Studies show that approximately half of the voters watch the debates.[12] Those who do so tend to be well-informed, peer-group opinion leaders who may well influence others who failed to tune in. Partly because of the large size of the audience and partly because sound bites may be replayed afterward, the debates "dominate journalistic commentary for at least several days." However, the debates should not be overemphasized, especially if there is no clear-cut winner, because "they can also be rapidly overtaken by other campaign events."[13]

The televised leaders' debate, 2008 election.

The 2004, 2006, and 2008 Election Campaigns

With the popular Paul Martin as their new leader, the Liberals would probably have won a majority in the 2004 election had it not been for the sponsorship scandal, which angered people both inside and outside Quebec. Quebeckers were insulted that the federal government had tried to buy their loyalty by sponsoring events in that province, heavily laden with Canadian flags, especially when much of the money fell into dubious hands. Even though it happened on Jean Chrétien's watch, many voters thought Martin (as a key Minister from Quebec) knew or should have known about it and, in any case, he did not handle it well. Martin was also hobbled by the deep split within the Liberal party as a result of his long-standing challenge to the former leader.

On the other side, analysis of the campaign indicated that despite his efforts to be more moderate than his Alliance origins (even promising to extend public health insurance to include a national drug plan), Stephen Harper and his new Conservative party were still seen as too extreme for many voters. As mentioned, the Liberals' television commercials deliberately helped to reinforce this perception. The NDP also had a new leader in Jack Layton, and at one point in the campaign his party achieved levels of support twice as high as in 2000. But Layton was abandoned by many of these new supporters at the end of the campaign. Some of them were seduced by the Liberal call to vote strategically, that is, to vote Liberal instead of NDP to keep the Conservatives out. Given the poorly run Liberal campaign, the Conservatives began to take the lead. But a last-minute upsurge in Liberal support appears to have come from those who were undecided until the last 48 hours, as well as those who left both the Conservatives and the NDP as decision-time arrived; many were traditional Liberals who managed to overcome their anger at the sponsorship scandal.

In 2004, there were essentially two parallel campaigns. In Quebec, it was Liberals and the Bloc. Besides the federal sponsorship scandal, voters in that province were upset at certain provincial Liberal government policies, but nationalists and separatists were also impressed with the performance of Bloc leader, Gilles Duceppe. In the rest of Canada, it was a two- or three-party contest. None of the other three leaders stood out, so most voters were guided by values and issues, such as same-sex marriage, gun control, and social programs. The Liberals tried to differentiate themselves on health care, but in fact the Conservatives and NDP also stressed this issue.[14]

The 2006 campaign was in many ways a repeat of 2004 but spread over a longer period—November to January—and with a different result. By this time, the Gomery hearings into the sponsorship scandal had attracted a huge daily television audience, especially in Quebec, so the Liberals were even more on the defensive on that issue. At first it seemed that the Bloc would sweep Quebec, but as the Conservatives established themselves as the likely winner in English-Canada, Quebeckers suddenly paid more attention to Stephen Harper, who provided a federalist alternative to the discredited Liberals. As mentioned, Harper ran a well-orchestrated campaign, revealing one moderate policy a day, departing from some of his earlier views, and muzzling any extremist candidates. Saving some prime-time advertising until the end, Harper then hit the Liberals hard on the corruption issue. Meanwhile, although the economy was strong, the Liberals did not exploit that accomplishment. Except for televised attack commercials that were often the subject of ridicule, they ran a lackadaisical campaign that once again tried to distinguish between Liberal and Conservative values.

The 2006 campaign witnessed almost daily release of public opinion polls. One Strategic Counsel poll indicated that 66 percent of those surveyed said it was time for a change, for a new government, including 83 percent in Quebec. Another poll concluded that most people who voted Conservative did not do so because of the party's program; they were just angry with the Liberals and wanted them punished. The Canadian Election Survey found a remarkable stability in voter attitudes between 2004 and 2006, except for the salience of the corruption issue. For more complete analyses, see the Canadian Election Study at http://www .ces-eec.umontreal.ca.[15]

Breaking the spirit of the fixed-election date law, the initial 2008 election call was controversial, but that issue did not engage voters very long. For the first part of the campaign, the leading question was probably the Liberals' "Green Shift" proposal. With his limited English skills, however, Stéphane Dion had a difficult time defending it; the Conservatives distorted it, and the NDP and Greens argued that it was insufficient or the wrong approach to deal with the environment. Stephen Harper unveiled a very modest list of promises, Jack Layton and the NDP argued that huge planned corporate tax cuts should be rescinded, and Elizabeth May attracted more attention to the Green party than ever before. At the beginning of the campaign, it seemed that the Conservatives might make a breakthrough in Quebec sufficient to give them a majority, but the Prime Minister's musings on culture and crime (along with the realization that the Conservatives were offside with Quebeckers on other issues like Afghanistan and the environment) sent many voters back to the Bloc.

The second half of the campaign focused on the dismal economic news from around the world. At first the Conservatives declared that Canada had nothing to worry about, but while voters were increasingly concerned, they appeared to favour Stephen Harper to handle the problem, despite his denial that there was one. The fact that a minority government seemed to be in the works encouraged NDP and Green voters to stick with their party of choice rather than vote strategically in order to prevent a Conservative majority. On the other hand, many people decided not to vote at all, with a record low turnout rate of 59 percent. Liberal support was also at an all-time low, precipitating Stéphane Dion's resignation as leader, while the Conservatives made substantial gains in Ontario, finishing just short of a majority overall.[16]

. . . .

THE LOCAL CANDIDATE CAMPAIGN

Nomination

At the local level, each party's first priority is the **nomination** of its candidate. In the case of incumbents, ambitious newcomers, and those who anticipate the date of the next election, the nomination meeting is often held before the election is called. This allows many preparations, such as the production of lawn signs, to be made ahead of time so that the campaign can get off to a strong and early start.

Nominating candidates is one of the most important functions of political parties.[17] Unfortunately, it is another of their functions that leaves much to be desired. Although it is generally a wide-open opportunity for ordinary people to participate and influence the direction of the political system, the nomination process does not usually generate much interest. First, many party nominations are uncontested. Leaders often decree that incumbents should be re-nominated without competition, which is a serious constraint on democracy. But even without that edict, sitting MPs are rarely challenged for the nomination. Second, discussion of policy is usually discouraged in the nomination process, although an aspiring candidate will sometimes be the standard-bearer for a particular interest. Third, those seeking the party nomination often recruit hundreds of new members who turn out to vote for them, overwhelming more permanent party members. Although such a process allows for the integration of new Canadians into the political process, these "instant members" rarely stay around to become useful participants, especially if their favourite loses the nomination.

There are conflicting opinions about the intervention of the central party in the nomination process. Generally speaking, it is more democratic to allow the local constituency association to provide the candidate on its own. But central office guidance can sometimes produce a better candidate or lead to a more representative set of candidates across the country. Jean Chrétien acquired the right as Liberal leader to name local candidates without a nomination meeting, and used the power to recruit "star" candidates, women, and visible minorities, and occasionally to stop a candidate with objectionable views. The NDP once hoped to achieve gender parity in its candidates but was later content with having nearly 50 percent women or members of minority groups. This effort often entails difficult negotiation between headquarters and riding associations, but the NDP normally ends up with the most representative roster of candidates. Stéphane Dion promoted the nomination of women in 2008, and in advance of the election, the central Conservative party stripped the party nomination from several candidates chosen at the constituency level. In any case, under the Canada Elections Act, the party leader must approve each candidate's nomination, a significant centralizing power.

Given the explicit recruitment function of elections, it turns out that parties have nominated a set of candidates quite unrepresentative of the general population. Nominated candidates overrepresent all the "elite" variables in Canadian society—class (upper-middle), ethnicity (anglophone), religion (prestige Protestant and Roman Catholic), and gender (male). Historically, the largest single category of candidates has been lawyers, although other professionals and businesspeople of the same socioeconomic status are now common as well. Parties usually nominate francophones in French-Canadian constituencies, but other candidates who are members of ethnocultural minority groups appeared only recently.

Besides the working class, women have been the most underrepresented of any demographic group. The number of women candidates increased significantly in 1993 to 476, before falling to 408 in 1997 and to 373 in 2000. Starting in 2004, a candidate could deduct daycare expenses when seeking the party nomination, but still only 391 women were nominated in that campaign. In 2006, the total number of women candidates was 380 out of 1634, or 23.3 percent. In 2008, as mentioned in Chapter 7, women candidates increased to 27.8 percent (445 out of 1601)—still fewer than 15 years before. This time, due to the insistence of Dion, the Liberals had the most: 113, compared to 104 New Democrats, 90 Greens, 63 Conservatives, 20 Blocquistes, and 55 others.[18] However, as Bill Cross points out, "[t]here is no evidence that voters are less likely to support a female or minority candidate either in a nomination contest or in a general election. In fact, when women seek party nominations they succeed in numbers equal to men, and when women are nominated in competitive ridings, they are elected at rates similar to men."[19]

The Local Campaign

Once the nomination has taken place, a campaign committee headed by the campaign manager is established (see Figure 15.1). In most campaigns the other key official is the canvass organizer, who sets up the door-to-door "foot canvass" to distribute literature or the telephone canvass. Whether canvassers contact voters on the doorstep or on the phone, the object is only secondarily to spread the party's message, which is now sometimes contained on short videos or CDs rather than printed leaflets. Canvassers primarily hope to discover the party or candidate preferences of prospective voters and to seek out their own supporters. Armed with a voters' list, they will put a positive, negative, or other distinguishing mark beside the names of all voters contacted. To cover an entire constituency in this fashion, especially if it is done two or three times as is often attempted by the NDP, requires a veritable army of volunteers and an elaborate hierarchical organization.[20] Since the campaign will need volunteers for many other tasks as well, and since few people relish door-to-door canvassing, the canvass organizer will probably not have enough workers and therefore have to concentrate efforts in priority polls. If money is more plentiful than personnel, the local campaign may rely instead on media advertising, but as at the national level, the increasing fragmentation of the television audience raises doubts about whether this is a good investment.

Figure 15.1   Structure of a Typical Local Campaign Committee

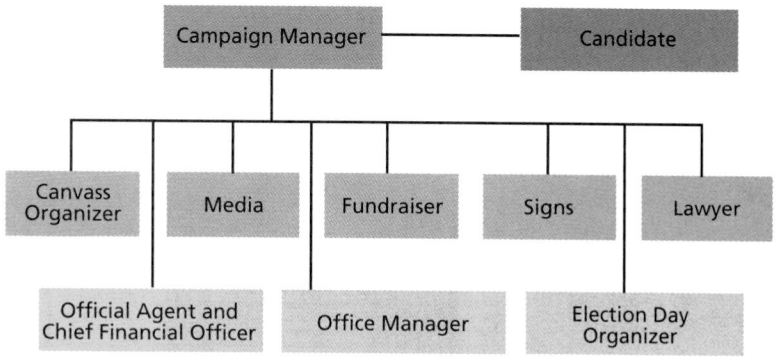

In recent elections, some constituency associations have done their own local polling, and since a permanent voters list makes it easier to find voters' phone numbers and addresses, parties are employing even more sophisticated techniques. Rather than just identifying supporters and opponents, for example, parties use massive phone banks to find out which issues concern individual voters, especially marginal ones, and to follow up with a customized letter or even candidate visit to address such issues. The Conservatives were the first party to become expert at computer-assisted mail and telephone campaigning directed at members of key groups in targeted constituencies.[21] Although such customized targeting such as by email is still in its infancy, most local campaigns now require the services of a webmaster to oversee the candidate's website and other Internet operations. In the past, much of this work was voluntary, but campaigns increasingly engage paid staff. The local campaign is thus a complex operation requiring more and more sophistication, staffing, and funding. Parties will no doubt continue to find further innovative ways to contact voters involving new technological devices.[22]

Since this book would like to encourage people to be more active in, as well as better informed about, the Canadian political system, it assures its readers that they would be welcomed with open arms if they went to the local headquarters of the candidate of their choice and volunteered their services. They might be asked to canvass or to put up signs, or their computer skills might be used in some way. In time, with more experience, they might be invited to be part of the campaign committee.

All this activity culminates on election day, when the organization tries to have party scrutineers placed in all the polls. Ideally, an inside scrutineer in each poll keeps track of which people on the list have cast their ballot, while an outside scrutineer periodically collects this information and then heads out to encourage all those previously identified as party supporters to get out to vote.

EXPLAINING CANADIAN VOTING BEHAVIOUR

Political scientists have studied the voting behaviour of Canadians in all recent elections, and have now accumulated considerable evidence to explain why people vote the way they do. Of course it is often a complex matter to determine why an individual decided how to vote, making it quite difficult to account for the actions of the entire electorate. Those who studied the 2000 election put forth a complicated multi-stage analytical framework focusing on the factors that seem to have had the greatest impact on the greatest number of voters, as shown in Figure 15.2. This comprehensive model considers almost every possible factor that could be involved.[23]

Sociodemographic Bases of Party Support

The first factor that influences the voters' choice is their socio-demographic characteristics, such as their geographic region, the type of setting they live in (rural or urban), their ethnic background, their religion, and their gender. These relate to the cleavages and identities discussed in Chapters 3 to 9 and were heavily emphasized in the early research on voting behaviour.[24]

· ·

Figure 15.2 Explaining the Voting Decision

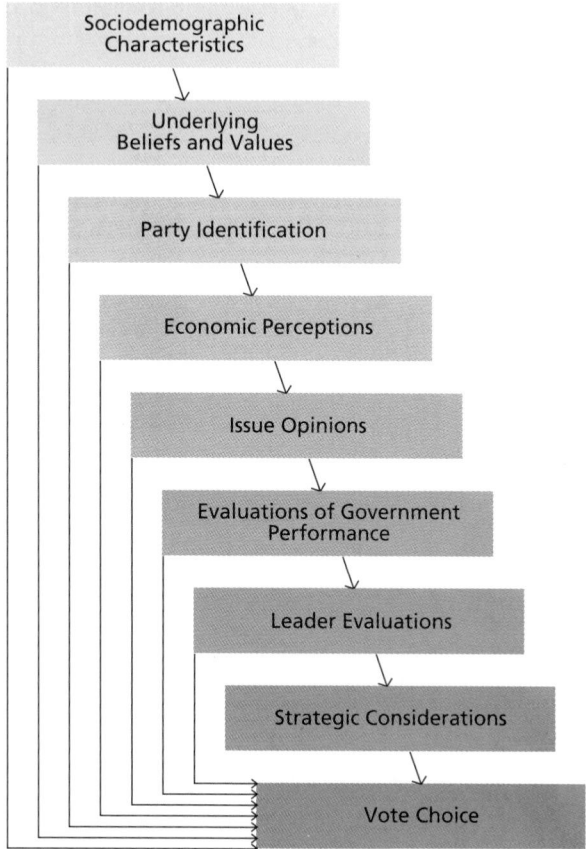

First, there are wide variations in regional support for different parties, some of which have been constant for generations and others that are of more recent origin. Between 1957 and 1993, the Conservatives were dominant in the West, and before 1984 the Liberals almost always had Quebec to themselves. In 1993, the Reform party challenged the Conservatives in the West, and since that date the Bloc Québécois has attracted the most support in Quebec. In 2004, there were only two parties in contention in Quebec, the Liberals and the Bloc Québécois; in the rest of Canada, the Liberals were the major player in Ontario, the newly unified Conservative party dominated the West, and the NDP had pockets of support across the country. In 2006, the Conservatives were more competitive in Ontario and Quebec than before, while retaining their Prairie strongholds, and the three parties battled it out in British Columbia. Table 3.4 showed a breakdown of party support by region in 2008, which was less distinctive than in previous campaigns.

A second locational factor is the rural–urban split. For example, the Liberals and NDP have always attracted more urban than rural votes, in contrast to their conservative opponents, whatever the party name. In 2008, the successful Conservatives still won no seats in the core of three largest cities—Toronto, Montreal, and Vancouver, although they had considerable support in the suburbs and smaller urban areas.

A third marked pattern in Canadian voting behaviour emerges on the basis of religion.[25] Roman Catholics have been strongly inclined to vote Liberal, whether they were French, English, or of other ethnic background and regardless of where they lived in the country. Political scientists have always found it difficult to explain this historic Liberal–Catholic connection,[26] although it has recently been in decline. There has been a similar historic tendency for those with no formal religion to vote NDP, with the Conservatives picking up a disproportionate amount of the Protestant vote. The Reform Party and Canadian Alliance seemed particularly attractive to evangelical Christians, who then cast their lot with the new Conservative party after 2004.

Turning to ethnicity, the Liberal Party has traditionally appealed to French-Canadian voters, both outside and inside Quebec. Within francophone Quebec, the Conservatives did well only in the Mulroney era; after 1993, the BQ always had a stronger appeal than the Liberals to Quebeckers of French origin; but the Liberals gained the support of almost all those of English, non-English, and non-French ethnicity. The Liberal Party was severely damaged among Quebec francophones by the "sponsorship scandal" in 2004 and 2006, however, leaving room for the Conservatives to capture significant federalist vote in that province in the latter campaign.

For decades, the Liberal party attracted the support of most post-Second World War immigrants, including new Canadians of non-European origin (increasingly members of visible minorities) who apparently reacted with gratitude to the fact that the Liberal Party was in office when they arrived. The 2006 election was the first to find many people in ethnocultural minority groups favouring the Conservatives, whether because of the Liberal party scandals, its stand on same-sex marriage, its failure to apologize for the Chinese head tax, or its rejection of a judicial inquiry into the Air-India bombing. The Conservatives' efforts at courting ethnocultural minorities after 2006 paid considerable dividends in the 2008 election and further reduced Liberal support.

It is mostly in Quebec that age is a significant factor, as younger voters in that province prefer the Bloc but, generally speaking, older voters across the country find the Conservatives most appealing. A certain amount of gender gap has recently been uncovered: men tend to be slightly more attracted to conservative parties, and women to the Liberals or NDP. Recent studies of the significance of gender have found this to be a complicated issue.[27]

A final demographic factor is social class, the expectation being that upper-class citizens would vote for right-wing parties, the middle class would support the Liberals, and the working and poorer classes would vote NDP. In most Western democracies such a pattern is quite significant, but it is not borne out well in Canada, which generally lacks strong **class-consciousness.** As indicated in Chapter 8, only a small proportion of the working class has ever voted for working-class parties, and what distinctive support the NDP once received from those who belonged to unions or those with lower incomes now seems to have disappeared.[28] Alan Whitehorn adds, "even NDP supporters do not see the class cleavage between the corporate-funded Liberal party vs. the labour-funded NDP, a tell-tale sign of brokerage politics blunting working class consciousness."[29] In 2006, one prominent labour leader, Buzz

Hargrove, urged working-class Canadians to vote strategically, either Liberal or NDP, to keep the Conservatives out. Hargrove was expelled from the NDP, and Stephen Harper aimed to corral a segment of the working class vote for himself.

Of all the socioeconomic factors, Roman Catholics and ethnocultural minorities were the bedrock of Liberal support for decades. But the support of both groups dwindled considerably over the past decade, and that in itself explains much of the fact that the Liberals dropped to a record low in the 2008 election.[30]

Core Values and Beliefs

The second major factor that influences how Canadians vote relates to their core values and beliefs; the 2000 election study shows that values and beliefs have a substantial impact on voter choice.[31] Within Quebec, the electorate was split down the middle on one question: Quebec sovereignty. Those in favour of this concept voted for the Bloc Québécois, and those against it voted Liberal. Outside Quebec, there was a more traditional ideological division between left and right connected to faith in the free market system as opposed to the desirability of government intervention. Those more inclined to government intervention tended to choose the Liberals or the NDP. In other words, although little or no class voting is now apparent, ideological voting is still significant, perhaps more than otherwise thought.[32] This is presumably why the Liberals tried to focus on the differences in "values" in both 2004 and 2006, claiming to be more collectivist and compassionate. The ideological differences in party preferences from 2001 revealed in Figure 15.3 are still compelling, even though there is no longer any budget surplus.

· ·

Figure 15.3 Spending the Surplus: Priorities by Party Preference

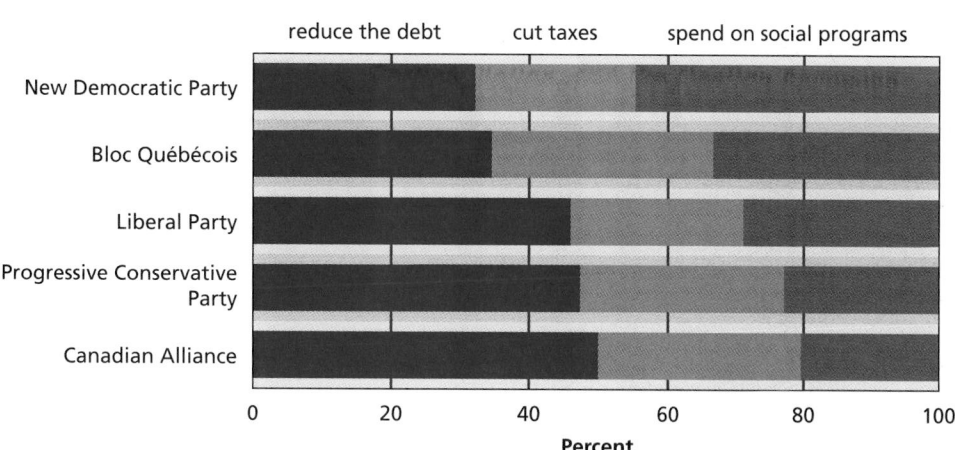

Source: COMPAS poll cited in the National Post's State of the Nation, June 16, 2001. Reprinted by permission of COMPAS and the National Post.

The role of core values is further complicated by the question of social values. Many Canadian Alliance supporters, for example, had a distinctive view of the role of the family and the role of religion, and to some extent Alliance and PC voters parted company on whether a strong state should intervene to enforce traditional social values, such as on questions of censorship, homosexuality, or abortion. The new Conservative Party continued to attract social conservatives but tried to avoid mention of most of their issues.

Party Identification

Ever since they began studying electoral behaviour, Canadian political scientists have been wrestling with the question of **party identification**—that is, whether voters have a feeling of closeness or psychological attachment to a particular political party.[33] It has generally been thought that the degree of party identification was considerably lower in Canada than in most other countries, resulting in the fact that we had few **safe seats.** But the 2000 election study found that Canadians had a stronger feeling of attachment to a party than previously thought. Between 50 percent and 60 percent of voters demonstrated a consistent party preference, and a full 25 percent of the electorate considered themselves to be Liberals. The other parties followed far behind.

At that time two significant implications seemed to follow from the Liberal Party having about one-quarter of the electorate on its side before the election was even called. First, since about half of the electorate had made up its mind before the campaign started, the campaign was primarily a struggle to win over the other half.[34] Second, the Liberals would lose the election only if all the short-term factors that influence the noncommitted voters—leadership, candidates, issues, and so on—were slanted in favour of some other party. By 2008, however, the Liberals had lost their head start of greater numbers of core supporters; in fact, by then, more voters identified with the Conservative party.[35]

In his take on this issue, Pammett writes that about one-third of the electorate is composed of flexible partisans who have a low degree of interest in politics, while just over one-quarter of the electorate constitutes flexible partisans with a high degree of political interest. He also emphasizes that differences in the results from one election to another can be the result of conversion or replacement, the latter being composed of new voters, or those who only turn out occasionally.[36]

The Economy, the Issues, and the Government's Performance

The next three factors that are expected to influence voters are the state of the economy, the issues raised in the campaign, and the voters' assessment of the incumbent government's performance. They are lumped together here because in recent years they have not been very significant influences on the overall results.[37]

It is often speculated that voters will re-elect an incumbent government in favourable economic circumstances and vote against the government party if the economy is faltering. Several election studies have reinforced casual observation of this point, especially in terms of the unemployment rate. It seems that in recent elections, however, the state of the economy was relatively strong, such that it was taken for granted and did not have much impact on the voting decision. In 2006, for example, the Liberals did not even promote the fact that the economy was booming. It may well be a more important factor as the economy recovers after the worldwide crisis that began in 2008, as it was in the Great Depression of the 1930s.[38]

Political scientists have given the question of issues a great deal of study. On the one hand, it would be logical if voters made their choice on the basis of party positions relating to current political issues, that being the general understanding of what elections are all about and that being what voters often claim to do. On the other hand, many voters prove to have only the most simplistic understanding of public issues and often have difficulty articulating their thoughts on the issues that supposedly influenced them. Of course, there are elections dominated by one particular issue, such as the "free trade" election of 1988, but the 2000, 2004, and 2006 elections were not in this category. Health care was usually mentioned by voters as the most salient issue, but it did not really influence which party they chose to support. In this case, the 2000 election study demonstrated that, as mentioned above, basic values and a general ideological orientation were more important than specific issues in influencing the voters' decision.[39] If a single issue predominated in the 2008 contest, it was probably the Liberal proposal for a "green" tax shift, but it attracted more opposition than support.

Somewhat related to the performance of the economy is the general performance of the incumbent government. In theory, a voter satisfied with the current government's performance would support it and one dissatisfied would vote for an opposition party. This factor did not count for much in the 2000 contest, but it became increasingly important in 2004 and 2006. It was not so much that voters disputed Liberal government policies, but rather, their behaviour—their "culture of entitlement." Liberal arrogance in general, and several actions of questionable integrity, primarily the sponsorship scandal, led many in the electorate to vote for a "change." On the other hand, in 2008 voters were not generally alienated by the first two years of Harper government.

How federal leaders propose to weather the economic storm.

Leadership

In most election surveys, respondents are asked whether their vote was based primarily on party leader, candidate, issues, or the party generally, a distinction not always easy for voters to make.[40] The role of the local candidate has rarely elicited much attention, and as mentioned above, issues did not count for much in most recent elections while general party preference did. But what about the party leader? For a time, political scientists thought that the importance of party leader in the voting decision was on the increase as a result of the enormous power of the prime minister's position, the growing importance of television as a source of electoral stimulation and information, the fact that television primarily focused on party leaders, and the belief that party identification was weak in Canada.[41] It is now more common to downplay the significance of the party leader, especially since the days of Pierre Elliott Trudeau and because party identification seems to be stronger than once thought. As Pammett puts it, "despite the fact that popular commentary is fond of debating the effects of the leaders' appearance, dress, hairstyles or speaking styles on the public, the bulk of the population does not rate these things highly when it comes to making up their minds."[42] On the other hand, as revealed in 2008, a leader who is deemed to be weak by the public will drag the party down.

Strategic Voting

Strategic voting is defined as voting for the second-favourite party when it is perceived to have a better chance than the first choice of defeating the party disliked most.[43] Such a practice reverses the decision that the voter had come to at the end of the long sequence of influences and is an attempt to make a vote count when it might otherwise be "wasted." Although strategic voting is increasingly common in the vocabulary of election analysis, it requires a sophisticated voter to appreciate it. The 2000 election study revealed that it was nonexistent in Quebec and practised by only three percent of voters outside that province— mostly by people who would otherwise have voted PC or NDP but wanted to ensure the defeat of a Liberal or Alliance candidate. There was much talk of strategic voting in 2006, especially by Buzz Hargrove and both of the party leaders he endorsed, but probably no more than a handful of NDP votes went to the Liberals as a result.

. . . .

THE ABSENT MANDATE

The preceding analysis casts doubt on the question of whether elections provide a policy mandate for the successful party—hence the concept of the **absent mandate.** First, Canadian parties do not always present a comprehensive election platform. Next, government parties do not seem to feel bound by the specific policies they proposed in the campaign, such as the Liberal opposition to wage and price controls in 1974 and to the GST in 1993. Third, the limited role that issues play in the campaign seriously detracts from the claim of any government that it has a mandate to pursue a particular policy. For example, free trade was never mentioned in the 1984 campaign and the GST was almost totally overlooked in 1988. Fourth, even on the rare occasion that a single issue figures prominently, the winning party almost never obtains a majority of the total votes cast and certainly not a majority in all regions of the country, "so a national mandate is absent."[44] The free trade issue in 1988 provided the closest thing to a policy mandate for any Canadian government in recent times, yet the Conservatives received only 43 percent of the overall popular vote and less than 40 percent in six provinces and territories.[45] The Liberals made much of their Red Book during and immediately after the 1993 campaign, but as time went on, they strayed farther and farther from it. The next comprehensive election platform was that of the Conservative party in 2006, *Stand Up for Canada*. From that document, Stephen Harper reiterated five basic promises throughout the campaign, and arguably implemented them over the next two years. But, as mentioned, many people voted for the party despite its promised policies. Finally, as emphasized in Chapter 11, there is a huge degree of ignorance and even misinformation on the part of the electorate, such that the extent of rational voting should never be overstated.[46]

· ·

CONCLUSION

Although public opinion polls are increasingly common, elections remain the definitive measure of the public will. As such, elections leave much to be desired, because they rarely produce a victorious party with a specific policy mandate. Parties may offer only vague slogans like "national unity"; elections frequently turn on leader or party images; successful parties often renege on their policy promises once in office; and a large proportion of voters pay little attention to the campaign. As defective as elections are, however, caution should be exercised before jumping on populist bandwagons, like holding frequent referendums on specific issues. In many cases, the electorate—having less incentive to be accommodating—takes policy positions that are more extreme and emotional and less well informed than those of political parties. Referendums are at odds with the virtues of representative democracy and may endanger the rights of certain ethnic, linguistic, religious, ideological, or other minorities.

This chapter is closely related to the preceding two on the formal electoral system and political parties. It also has links to the chapter on the mass media and public opinion polls, and in dealing with the kinds of candidates who get elected, it has connections to Chapter 23 on the House of Commons.

PC Of the approaches outlined in Chapter 1, the public choice model is, at least at first sight, the one most relevant to elections. Extensive public opinion polling by political parties confirms the claims of this approach that parties make calculated promises to get elected, concentrating on strategically located groups. Parties tend to ignore their committed supporters as well as those who are hostile, and then, within a certain ideological range, promise whatever the polls tell them will maximize their electoral success. Nevertheless, the preceding account of voting behaviour puts into question some of the other claims of the public choice approach, at least with respect to its assumption of rational and well-informed voters. The average person spends more time researching the purchase of a television set or perusing the weekly supermarket fliers than in comparing party platforms. The successful party also emerges with a less specific policy mandate than the public choice model suggests.

(C) Class analysts add that the bargains struck between parties and voters during the campaign may not be honoured afterward. Promises made to middle-income voters and the working class—for example, that social programs are a "sacred trust" or that wage controls will not be adopted—are often broken by the victorious party in record time. At least in the past, as discussed in Chapter 13, class analysts attributed this to the issue of party finance. That is, once in office, parties did what their financial supporters or such corporate-funded bodies as the Canadian Council of Chief Executives or the C.D. Howe Institute wanted them to do, which was often at odds with their promises. Class analysts add that parties nominate and voters support a set of candidates who bear little resemblance to the general population, overrepresenting all the "elite" variables in Canadian society.

(P) Pluralists emphasize the necessity of designing a party's election platform so that it appeals to many groups in society—all major ethnocultural categories, industries, regions, genders, and classes. Such platforms are usually classic brokerage documents. Election manifestoes are increasingly based on what public opinion polls indicate the public wants or is willing to accept. Pluralists also point to the socioeconomic group preferences that have been evident in elections and emphasize the extent to which each party appeals to a coalition of certain groups. In addition, they note the increasing involvement of advocacy groups in the election campaign.

(SC) Even this most "popular" aspect of the political system reveals the extent to which the state is relatively autonomous from the rest of society, as state-centred theorists contend. This is primarily because the focus of election campaigns is not usually on policy. If voters are uninformed about issues, if they make their decision on the basis of leader or party images, and if parties present only vague policy directions that few politicians or voters take seriously in any case, post-election policy innovation will stall or be dominated by the prime minister, Cabinet, and bureaucracy. If the authorities decide to adopt policies that were not mentioned in the campaign or to leave unfulfilled promises that were made, they merely resort to publicly paid advertising campaigns to demonstrate the necessity of the statist decision.

. . . .
DISCUSSION QUESTIONS

1. Can anything be done to give more emphasis to the substance of each party's campaign (platform) and less to its presentation (personality, image, and advertising)?

2. Is the distribution of media time during election campaigns fair? If not, how could it be improved?

3. Is it fair to exclude minor party leaders from the leaders' debates?

4. How rational and well informed is the average voter?

5. If you voted recently, explain how you came to your decision.

. . . .

NOTES

1. Alan Frizzell and Anthony Westell, eds., *The Canadian General Election of 1984* (Ottawa: Carleton University Press, 1985); Alan Frizzell, Jon H. Pammett, and Anthony Westell, eds., *The Canadian General Election of 1988* (hereafter referred to as *1988*) (Ottawa: Carleton University Press, 1989); Alan Frizzell, Jon H. Pammett, and Anthony Westell, eds., *The Canadian General Election of 1993* (hereafter referred to as *1993*) (Ottawa: Carleton University Press, 1994); Alan Frizzell and Jon H. Pammett, eds., *The Canadian General Election of 1997* (hereafter referred to as *1997*) (Toronto: Dundurn Press, 1997); Jon H. Pammett and Christopher Dornan, eds., *The Canadian General Election of 2000* (hereafter referred to as *2000*) (Toronto: Dundurn, 2001); Jon H. Pammett and Christopher Dornan, eds., *The Canadian General Election of 2004* (hereafter referred to as *2004*) (Toronto: Dundurn, 2004); and Jon H. Pammett and Christopher Dornan, eds., *The Canadian General Election of 2006* (hereafter referred to as *2006*) (Toronto: Dundurn, 2006).

2. Alan Whitehorn, "Alexa McDonough and the Atlantic Breakthrough for the New Democratic Party," in Frizzell and Pammett, eds., *1997*, p. 94.

3. Stephen Clarkson, "Yesterday's Man and His Blue Grits: Backward into the Future," in Frizzell et al., eds., *1993*, p. 33.

4. More comprehensive election manifestoes are a characteristic of the "Fourth Party System," according to R.K. Carty, William Cross, and Lisa Young, *Rebuilding Canadian Party Politics* (Vancouver: UBC Press, 2000). But Stephen Clarkson challenges the distinctiveness of that system in "The Liberal Threepeat" in Pammett and Dornan, eds., *2000*. See also Faron Ellis and Peter Woolstencroft. "A Change of Government, Not a Change of Country: The Conservatives in the 2006 Election," in Pammett and Dornan, eds., *2006*, ch. 3.

5. Frizzell and Westell, in Frizzell, Pammett, and Westell, eds., *1988*, p. 75; and David Taras, *The Newsmakers* (Scarborough: Nelson Canada, 1990), pp. 154–67.

6. Christopher Dornan, "The Television Coverage: A History of the Election in 65 Seconds," in Frizzell and Pammett, eds., *1997*, p. 165.

7. Clarkson, "The Liberal Threepeat"; Christopher Dornan and Heather Pyman, "Facts and Arguments: Newspaper Coverage of the Campaign," in Pammett and Dornan, eds., *2000*; and André Blais, Elisabeth Gidengil, Richard Nadeau, and Neil Nevitte, *Anatomy of a Liberal Victory: Making Sense of the Vote in the 2000 Canadian Election* (Peterborough: Broadview Press, 2002), p. 38.

8. Stuart Soroka and Antonia Maioni, "Little Sign of Bias in News Coverage," *Toronto Star*, February 1, 2006, p. A17; and Christopher Waddell and Christopher Dornan, "The Media and the Campaign," in Pammett and Dornan, eds., *2006*, ch. 9.

9. *Reform Party of Canada et al. v. Canada (Attorney General)*, Alberta Court of Appeal, March 10, 1995; and *Somerville v. Canada (Attorney General)*, Alberta Court of Appeal, June 5, 1996.

10. Peter Woolstencroft, "'Doing Politics Differently': The Conservative Party and the Campaign of 1993," in Frizzell et al., eds., *1993*, p. 20; Lionel Lumb, "The Television of Inclusion," in Frizzell et al., eds., *1993*, p. 122; and Walter I. Romanow, Michel de Repentigny, Stanley B. Cunningham, Walter C. Soderlund, and Kai Hildebrandt, *Television Advertising in Canadian Elections: The Attack Mode, 1993* (Waterloo: Wilfrid Laurier University Press, 1999).

11. Lawrence LeDuc, "The Leaders' Debates: (...And the Winner Is...)," in Frizzell and Pammett, eds., *1997*; Lawrence LeDuc and Richard Price, "Great Debates: The Televised Leadership Debates of 1979," *Canadian Journal of Political Science* (March 1985); David Lanoue, "Debates That Mattered: Voters' Reaction to the 1984 Canadian Leadership Debates," *Canadian Journal of Political Science* (March 1991); Taras, *The Newsmakers*, pp. 167–75; and Paul Attallah and Angela Burton, "Television, the Internet, and the Canadian Federal Election of 2000," in Pammett and Dornan, eds., *2000*.

12. LeDuc, "The Leaders' Debates," in Frizzell and Pammett, eds., *1997*, p. 212; and Attallah and Burton, "Television."

13. LeDuc, "The Leaders' Debates," pp. 207–8

14. Pammett and Dornan, eds., *2004*.

15. Pammett and Dornan, eds, *2006*; and The Canadian Election Study. See also Institute for Research on Public Policy, *Policy Options* (March 2006).

16. For articles on the 2008 election, see Institute for Research on Public Policy, *Policy Options*, November 2008.

17. William Cross, *Political Parties* (Vancouver: UBC Press, 2004), ch. 4; William Cross, "Grassroots Participation in Candidate Nominations," in Joanna Everitt and Brenda O'Neill, eds., *Citizen Politics: Research and Theory in Canadian Political Behaviour* (Toronto: Oxford University Press, 2002); R.K. Carty, "The Politics of Tecumseh Corners: Canadian Political Parties as Franchise Organizations," *Canadian Journal of Political Science* (December 2002); and William Cross, "Candidate Nomination in Canada's Political Parties," in Pammett and Dornan, eds., *2006*, ch. 7.

18. Parliament of Canada website, "Women Candidates in General Elections—1921 to Date," available at http://www2parl.gc.ca/Sites/LOP/HFER/hfer.asp?Language=E&Search=WomenElection.

19. Cross, *Political Parties*, p. 74. See also Jerome H. Black and Bruce M. Hicks, "Visible Minority Candidates in the 2004 Federal Election," *Canadian Parliamentary Review* (Summer 2006); and Jerome H. Black, "The 2006 Federal Election and Visible Minority Candidates: More of the Same?" *Canadian Parliamentary Review* (Autumn 2008).

20. Jerome H. Black, "Revisiting the Effects of Canvassing on Voting Behaviour," *Canadian Journal of Political Science* (June 1984); Tom Brook, *Getting Elected in Canada* (Stratford: Mercury Press, 1991); and Lynda Erickson and R.K. Carty, "Parties and Candidate Selection in the 1988 Canadian General Election," *Canadian Journal of Political Science* (June 1991).

21. George Perlin, "Opportunity Regained: The Tory Victory in 1984," in Howard R. Penniman, ed., *Canada at the Polls, 1984* (Durham, NC: Duke University Press, 1988), p. 85; and Attallah and Burton, "Television."

22. Munroe Eagles, "The Effectiveness of Local Campaign Spending in the 1993 and 1997 Federal Elections in Canada," in *Canadian Journal of Political Science* (March 2004).

23. Blais et al., *Anatomy of a Liberal Victory*, ch. 5.

24. Amanda Bittner, "The Effects of Information and Social Cleavages: Explaining Issue Attitudes and Vote Choice in Canada," *Canadian Journal of Political Science* (December 2007) is one researcher who gives more emphasis to other factors in more recent times.

25. Blais et al., *Anatomy of a Liberal Victory*, p. 93.

26. André Blais, "Accounting for the Electoral Success of the Liberal Party in Canada," *Canadian Journal of Political Science* (December 2005).

27. Blais et al., *Anatomy of a Liberal Victory*, ch. 6; Elisabeth Gidengil, "Beyond the Gender Gap," *Canadian Journal of Political Science* (December 2007); and Marie Rekkas, "Gender and Elections: An Examination of the 2006 Canadian Federal Election," *Canadian Journal of Political Science* (December 2008).

28. Blais et al., *Anatomy of a Liberal Victory*, p. 94.

29. Alan Whitehorn, "The 2000 NDP Campaign: Social Democracy at the Crossroads," in Pammett and Dornan, eds., *2000*, p. 119.

30. Elisabeth Gidengil, Joanna Everitt, Patrick Fournier, and Neil Nevitte, "Anatomy of a Liberal Defeat," paper presented at the 2009 Canadian Political Science Association.

31. Blais et al., *Anatomy of a Liberal Victory*, ch. 7.

32. Ibid., p. 112.

33. Ibid., p. 115.

34. Jon H. Pammett, "The People's Verdict," in Pammett and Dornan, eds., *2000*, p. 306.

35. Gidengil et al., "Anatomy of a Liberal Defeat."

36. Pammett, "Elections," in Michael Whittington and Glen Williams, eds., *Canadian Politics in the 21st Century*, 7th ed. (Toronto: Thomson Nelson Canada, 2008), pp. 158–60.

37. Blais et al., *Anatomy of a Liberal Victory*, chs. 9, 10, and 11.

38. As pointed out by Fred Cutler, many voters have a hard time distinguishing between the effects of federal and provincial government economic policies, "Whodunnit? Voters and Responsibility in Canadian Federalism," *Canadian Journal of Political Science* (September 2008).

39. Blais et al., *Anatomy of a Liberal Victory*, p. 153.

40. Pammett, "The People's Verdict," p. 298; and André Blais, Elisabeth Gidengil, Agnieszka Dobrzynska, Neil Nevitte, and Richard Nadeau, "Does the Local Candidate Matter? Candidate Effects in the Canadian Election of 2000," *Canadian Journal of Political Science* (July/August 2003).

41. Blais et al., *Anatomy of a Liberal Victory*, p. 165.

42. Pammett, "The Voters Decide," in Frizzell and Pammett, *1997*, p. 234; see also Pammett, "The People's Verdict," pp. 298–99.

43. Blais et al., *Anatomy of a Liberal Victory*, p. 181.

44. Harold D. Clarke, Jane Jenson, Lawrence LeDuc, and Jon H. Pammett, *Absent Mandate* (Toronto: Gage, 1984), p. 182.

45. Surveys indicated that only about one-half of the voters claimed to make up their mind primarily on the basis of the free trade issue, some on each side. Frizzell et al., eds., *1988*, p. 124; and Richard Johnston, André Blais, Henry E Brady, and Jean Crête, "Free Trade and the Dynamics of the 1988 Canadian Election," in Joseph Wearing, ed., *The Ballot and Its Message* (Toronto: Copp Clark Pitman, 1991).

46. Elisabeth Gidengil, André Blais, Richard Nadeau, and Neil Nevitte, *Citizens* (Vancouver: UBC Press, 2004); see also Pammett, "Elections," p. 164.

. . . .

FURTHER READING

Blais, André, Elisabeth Gidengil, Richard Nadeau, and Neil Nevitte. *Anatomy of a Liberal Victory: Making Sense of the Vote in the 2000 Canadian Election*. Peterborough: Broadview Press, 2002.

Brodie, Janine, and Jane Jenson. *Crisis, Challenge and Change: Party and Class in Canada Revisited*. Ottawa: Carleton University Press, 1988.

Cross, William. *Political Parties*. Vancouver: BC Press, 2004.

Cross, William, ed. *Political Parties, Representation, and Electoral Democracy in Canada*. Toronto: Oxford University Press, 2002.

Gidengil, Elisabeth, André Blais, Richard Nadeau, and Neil Nevitte. *Citizens*. Vancouver: UBC Press, 2004.

Nevitte, Neil, André Blais, Elisabeth Gidengil, and Richard Nadeau. *Unsteady State: The 1997 Canadian Federal Election*. Toronto: Oxford University Press, 2000.

Pammett, Jon. "Class Voting and Class Consciousness in Canada." *Canadian Review of Sociology and Anthropology* 24, no. 2 (1987).

———. "Elections." In Michael Whittington and Glen Williams, eds., *Canadian Politics in the 21st Century*, 7th ed. Toronto: Thomson Nelson Canada, 2008.

———, and Christopher Dornan, eds. *The Canadian General Election of 2006*. Toronto: Dundurn Press, 2006.

Thorburn, H.G., and Alan Whitehorn, eds. *Party Politics in Canada*, 8th ed. Toronto: Prentice Hall, 2000.

Wells, Paul. *Right Side Up: The Fall of Paul Martin and the Rise of Stephen Harper's New Conservatism*. Toronto: McClelland & Stewart, 2006.

Young, Lisa, and Keith Archer, eds. *Regionalism and Party Politics in Canada*. Toronto: Oxford University Press, 2002.

Advocacy Groups, SOCIAL MOVEMENTS, and Lobbying

Over the years, the **Canadian Federation of Students (CFS)**, representing half a million students, and the Canadian Association of University Teachers, speaking for 65 000 professors, librarians, and researchers, have both tried to persuade federal and provincial governments to restore public funding to postsecondary education and freeze tuition fees. The Canadian Council of Chief Executives, conversely, applauded the governments' balanced-budget doctrine, with its increased reliance on market forces. The petroleum companies took out newspaper ads to oppose the Kyoto Protocol, while environmentalist groups advocated its immediate implementation. Canada's Research-Based Pharmaceutical Companies, a national association of large multinational pharmaceutical firms, pressed the government to protect their patent monopoly on new drugs, while the Canadian Generic Pharmaceutical Association, representing the Canadian-based part of the industry, argued that such protection only increased the cost of drugs to the patient and the taxpayer.

Such groups as these develop in almost every political system when individuals or companies with common concerns band together to strengthen their cause. They are often called **interest groups** or **pressure groups** and can be defined as any group that seeks to influence government policy without contesting elections—that is, without putting forward its own candidates. Alternatively, they have been defined as "organizations whose members act together to influence public policy in order to promote their common interest."[1] Although the terms are basically interchangeable, it could be said that an interest group *becomes* a pressure group when it actively pursues an objective with government, while **advocacy group** is a more generic term.[2] Most such groups originally form for non-political purposes and retain non-political functions, but they almost inevitably get drawn into political activity from time to time because of the pervasiveness of government. This discussion must also include **social movements**, which generally possess a less formal structure and bring new values into the political system. The term "civil society" is often used to refer to institutions and organizations that exist between the individual and family on the one hand and the government or state on the other—churches, unions, charities, athletic organizations, recreational groups, social movements, and especially advocacy groups. It is often argued that a civil society characterized by widespread participation in such groups is a prerequisite to a strong democratic political system.

The term **lobbying** is used to refer to any organized attempt to influence the authorities, an activity that is most commonly undertaken by pressure groups but could of course be done by individuals, companies, or other political actors. Increasingly, however, pressure groups have been joined by professional lobbying firms in this activity.

Once having established their functions and discussed certain other theoretical considerations, this chapter proceeds to identify some of the leading Canadian advocacy groups and social movements, to outline their targets and methods of operation, to assess their resources, and then to examine the activity of professional lobbying firms.

. . . .

THEORETICAL CONSIDERATIONS

In the traditional discussion of functions performed in the political system, advocacy groups are assigned the primary task of "interest articulation." They normally have a narrow focus and are organized around a single, central interest which they try to impress on those in authority. National advocacy groups often experience internal regional, provincial/territorial, ethnic, or class tensions that must be bridged in constructing the message that they want to articulate, so that such groups also play a limited part in the aggregation of interests. Paul Pross prefers to speak of the "interest promotion" function of such groups. Sometimes groups are referred to as "special interests," a term that has become more common as a wider array of "identity groups," such as women or minority ethnocultural groups, make themselves heard. Such a disparaging label is usually applied to previously marginalized interests by those who have dominated the policymaking process in the past.[3]

The party and electoral systems were originally assumed to be the principal means of accommodating various interests within the Canadian political system. Individuals would take their concerns to parties; parties would respond to any interest that appeared to be important; and regional, ethnic, religious, economic, professional, and other interests could be encompassed within the territorial representation provided by the electoral system. As society became more complex, however, Canadians increasingly demonstrated a preference to form or join more specialized, functional groups rather than rely exclusively on the territorial representation of parties and elections. Thus, in the promotion of interests, advocacy groups provide a supplementary kind of functional representation, especially between elections.[4]

Besides interest articulation and aggregation, such groups engage in political communication. They transmit demands from the people to the authorities, as well as disseminate information in the other direction. In addition, groups may assist in the communication between different parts or different levels of government. They frequently communicate among themselves and build temporary alliances or coalitions around common problems.

Advocacy groups are also involved in the policymaking process. The enhanced complexity of society has meant that public issues now require reliance on information that is so technical and voluminous that politicians and parties, lacking both time and expertise, cannot handle it well. Consequently, advocacy groups regularly interact with the bureaucracy to work out technical arrangements to their mutual satisfaction and present these proposals to the politicians and parties as a fait accompli. Although this chapter will emphasize the role of advocacy groups in taking the initiative to interact with government, it is increasingly the case that the bureaucracy actually seeks out their expertise. This fundamental transformation of the policymaking process will be emphasized in Chapter 20. Advocacy groups are even involved in the application or administration of government programs and in regulatory functions.

Pross adds that such groups are also engaged in the function of legitimation. When groups participate peacefully and cooperatively, they demonstrate support for the political system and confer legitimacy on both it and those with whom they are interacting. Governments encourage groups to lend them such legitimacy and support by welcoming their advances, by "drawing them into a privileged advisory position," and sometimes by helping to create them. By keeping the authorities abreast of current demands and societal changes, advocacy groups promote "general political stability."[5] If they can successfully achieve accommodations across regional and ethnic cleavages, they also become important unifying agents in Canadian society.

Reverting to some of the observations made in Chapter 1, let us mention the concepts of structuralism and hegemony. The basic point is that the realm of advocacy groups, social movements, and lobbying is not a level playing field: some interests are stronger than others. As Miriam Smith writes,

> structural theories of the role of social forces in the political process stress that the power relations are not the result of individual choices but of socially patterned behaviour, collective action, and institutional and organizational configurations. Individual choices are overwhelmed by the structural forces that shape behaviour. The pattern of group formation is affected by factors such as economic and social inequality, which create systematic obstacles for marginalized groups in the political system.[6]

While advocacy groups are never entirely satisfied with their lot in the political system, most of them are an integral part of that system. In other words, they operate within and support the context of the dominant values and expectations of society, perhaps without even realizing it. But however difficult it is to think beyond the hegemonic status quo, one of the challenges to the traditional way of doing things comes from social movements, which engage in a struggle to expand the boundaries of the existing system. They begin at the margins of the political system and possess an alternative set of values and expectations. Although they rarely have much immediate impact, many have managed to change society's way of thinking over time. They bring new issues into the system, but are forced to try to alter social values before they can succeed in changing specific government policies. Social movements are thus an important part of the concerns of this chapter.

. . . .

THE ARRAY OF CANADIAN ADVOCACY GROUPS

The number of advocacy groups operating in Canada is in the thousands, so not all can be identified here. Instead, only some of the largest, most influential, or more interesting will be mentioned. Such a selective list can be seen in Table 16.1.

TABLE 16.1 Leading National Canadian Advocacy Groups

Business
Canadian Council of Chief Executives
Canadian Chamber of Commerce
Canadian Manufacturers & Exporters
Canadian Federation of Independent
   Business
Retail Council of Canada
Canadian Bankers Association
Canadian Association of Broadcasters
Canadian Construction Association
Canadian Association of Petroleum
   Producers
Canadian Life and Health Insurance
   Association
Mining Association of Canada
Canada's Research-Based Pharmaceutical
   Companies
Canadian Generic Pharmaceutical
   Association
Forest Products Association of Canada
Canadian Home Builders' Association

Agriculture
Canadian Federation of Agriculture
National Farmers Union

Labour
Canadian Labour Congress

Professions
Canadian Bar Association
Canadian Medical Association
Canadian Nurses Association
Canadian Association of University
   Teachers
Canadian Association of Chiefs of Police
Canadian Teachers' Federation
Canadian Federation of Students

Ethnic
Fédération des communautés francophones
   et acadienne du Canada
Assembly of First Nations
Canadian Ethnocultural Council
National Congress of Italian Canadians
National Association of Japanese Canadians

Religious
Canadian Council of Churches
Canadian Conference of Catholic Bishops
United Church of Canada
Canadian Jewish Congress

Public Interest Groups
Council of Canadians
John Howard Society
Canadian Civil Liberties Association
National Action Committee on the
   Status of Women
Canadian Council on Social Development
National Council of Welfare
Greenpeace Canada
Mothers Against Drunk Driving
   (MADD Canada)
Non-Smokers' Rights Association
National Anti-Poverty Organization
Sierra Club of Canada

Other
Canadian Taxpayers Federation
Royal Canadian Legion
Consumers' Association of Canada
Egale Canada
Federation of Canadian Municipalities

Business Groups

In the case of business, nothing prevents individual companies from lobbying on their own behalf for grants, subsidies, tariff changes, loan guarantees, tax write-offs, government contracts, or policy changes, and many firms do so on a regular basis. In addition, it is evident from Table 16.1 that despite their supposed or real competition, the private firms within almost every industry have organized a common pressure group to promote the interests of the industry as a whole.[7] Thus, to a large extent, the "system of business interest associations in Canada is highly fragmented, consisting of many small, narrowly focused organizations."[8] William Coleman counted about 600 business groups that were active in Canadian federal politics, about 40 percent of which were in the manufacturing sector. He summarizes the business pressure group scene as follows:

> A relatively small number of associations with members that are generally large firms, operating in large oligopolistic sectors. These associations spend in excess of $1 million annually, employ a minimum of 10 to 15 people, are institutionally bilingual, and have an officer, if not their head office, in Ottawa. Associations in this category are visible to the attentive public; their leaders are quoted frequently in the business press and move freely in government circles.... The several roles they play gives them a system of comprehensive political contacts, ranging from lower and middle technical levels of the bureaucracy to senior officials, MPs, and Cabinet ministers.[9]

Superimposed on these industrial groupings are such "peak" organizations as the **Canadian Council of Chief Executives (CCCE)**, the **Canadian Manufacturers and Exporters (CME)**, the Canadian Chamber of Commerce (CCC), and the Canadian Federation of Independent Business (CFIB). The Canadian Council of Chief Executives, formerly known as the Business Council on National Issues, represents the chief executive officers of the 150 largest firms in the country. The CCCE sees itself as Canada's "premier business association," and was particularly influential with the Mulroney Conservative government. It fought hard for the Canada–U.S. Free Trade Agreement, after which it then sought "to broaden public understanding of the need for more responsible fiscal policies." Those policies included balancing the budget and reducing taxes, all of which meant reducing the role of government. Like most other groups, it has recently developed a new focus on global issues. Although Canada thus lacks a single peak voice for the business community as a whole, that community may be even more influential for being represented by at least four national organizations.

THE CANADIAN PRESS/Fred Chartrand

Nancy Hughes Anthony, then president of the Canadian Chamber of Commerce, and Thomas d'Aquino, president of the Canadian Council of Chief Executives, propose an alternative to the Kyoto Protocol, September 2002. Ms. Hughes Anthony then became the head of the Canadian Bankers Association.

On the agricultural side of business, about 100 active associations vie for influence.[10] The broadest is the Canadian Federation of Agriculture (CFA), which represents 200 000 farm families as well as some 20 provincial farm and commodity organizations. The National Farmers Union (NFU) is a more radical group, and many other specific commodity groups exist independently, such as the Canadian Cattlemen's Association.

Nonbusiness Groups

The **Canadian Labour Congress (CLC)** functions as a common voice for organized labour, but only 75 percent of Canadian union members actually belong to unions affiliated with the CLC. It maintains a link to the New Democratic Party, as do many of its individual unions, and is unique among Canadian advocacy groups in demonstrating such an overt partisan preference.

Many of the minority ethnocultural groups in Canada have their own organizations, such as the National Congress of Italian Canadians, the German Canadian Congress, the National Association of Japanese Canadians, and the National Association of Canadians of Origins in India. Some 30 such groups have been brought together, with government support, in the peak organization the Canadian Ethnocultural Council, although it has weakened over time. The largest of several Aboriginal groups is the **Assembly of First Nations**. The English and French are organized only where they are minorities—the anglophone Alliance Quebec and the Fédération des communautés francophones et acadienne du Canada, which incorporates provincial units, such as the Assemblée de la francophonie de l'Ontario. Most of the religious denominations in Canada function as advocacy groups from time to time, with the Canadian Conference of Catholic Bishops, the United Church of Canada, the Canadian Council of Churches, and the Canadian Jewish Congress probably being most influential.

Most professions have organizations that speak for their members on relevant issues, the Canadian Medical Association and the Canadian Bar Association being two of the oldest and most important. In addition to serving the needs of its own members, the CMA advises the government on other health matters in the broader public interest. Besides representing the interests of lawyers, judges, notaries, law teachers, and law students, the CBA is uniquely involved in the legislative process, since it has expertise in every aspect of the law.

The Royal Canadian Legion is by far the largest veterans' organization, going back to 1926 and representing those who served in Canada's armed forces or who are associated with them. Besides working for better pensions and other benefits for its own members and a strong military establishment, the Legion is prominently involved in public service and charitable work.

Other Categorizations of Advocacy Groups

However much any of the above-mentioned groups claim to be pursuing the public interest, they can be generally categorized as "self-interested" groups because their principal concern is to improve their own position, usually economic. The true "public interest" group exists to promote causes that it sees as beneficial to society as a whole and that do not directly benefit its own members: the John Howard Society (improving prison conditions and the lot of ex-inmates), the Canadian Council on Social Development (promoting better social policy), the Canadian Civil Liberties Association (protecting civil liberties from government infringement), and a variety of environmental groups, among others.

Most of the groups named above and many others are called **institutionalized groups** because they are permanent, well-established, formal organizations. Almost all maintain a head office in Ottawa with a full-time staff, a sizable budget, and a reasonably stable membership. Most have developed continuous links with the authorities and represent their members' interests on a daily basis, year after year.

These characteristics are not possessed by all advocacy groups, however, and other labels have been attached to them. Some groups spring up spontaneously around a specific issue, and once the issue is resolved, they fade away. Such **issue-oriented groups** lack the institutionalized groups' permanence, office, staff, budget, membership, and access to the authorities. Instead, they more likely resort to attracting public attention to their cause through media coverage of actions like demonstrations. Since issue-oriented groups usually disappear when the issue has been resolved, they are not as familiar as institutionalized groups, but several famous examples can be cited. In the early 1970s the Stop Spadina group opposed extension of the Spadina Expressway in Toronto and the People or Planes group fought against building the proposed Pickering airport east of that city; later, "Bread Not Circuses" opposed Toronto's bids to host the Olympic Games. Somewhat similar was the group called Thin Ice, which was successful in the bitterly fought campaign to prevent the spending of vast amounts of public funds to keep the NHL's Winnipeg Jets in Winnipeg.[11] Other recent cases include Rural Dignity, a spontaneous national group that sprang up to fight against the deterioration of rural and small-town life in general, and of its mail service in particular, and the Foundation for Equal Families, which fought for same-sex amendments to federal statutes. Proposed reform of the Divorce Act, especially with respect to custody matters, spawned a variety of fathers' rights and even grandparents' rights groups. If their issue is not resolved, or if they anticipate further challenges, such groups may become a more permanent fixture, gradually evolving from an issue-oriented group to the institutionalized category.

Other categorizations are sometimes useful in discussing advocacy groups. Most groups are "autonomous" in the sense that they develop without government initiative, although they may later seek government financial support. However, politicians or bureaucrats may actually be involved in the creation of such groups, whether for personal gain or in the hope of promoting a certain public policy objective. In the late 1960s, for example, the federal government began to fund anti-poverty, women's, minority official language, Aboriginal, and other ethnic groups.[12] The Mulroney government cut back on grants to Aboriginal, women's, and anti-poverty groups, and to groups representing people with disabilities, however, both for fiscal and for ideological reasons, something the Trudeau government had also done on occasion when a particular group became too critical of the hand that fed it. Such grant reductions demonstrate a lack of political sincerity as well as the dangers involved in a group's becoming too critical and too dependent.[13]

A distinction can also be made between "active" groups, which have a formal organization and a name, and "categoric" groups, which are simply a number of unorganized individuals who share a common characteristic. Categoric groups are potential advocacy groups, since an issue could come along that would bring them to life, but if their numbers are sufficient, the authorities will pay attention to them even in their latent state.

Social Movements

Political scientists often find it useful to distinguish between pressure groups and social movements. Many of the issue-oriented groups referred to are, in fact, part of larger, unstructured social movements, of which the environmental, women's, peace, human rights, and consumers' movements have been most prominent. Other examples include the Aboriginal, gay liberation, and animal rights movements. A social movement has been defined as an informal network of organizations and individuals who, on the basis of a collective identity and shared values, engage in political or cultural struggle intended to expand the boundaries of the existing system and undertake collective action designed to affect both state and society.[14] They begin at the margins of the political system, possessing an alternative vision of "the good life," and have to invest much effort at changing social behaviour before they can even hope to alter public policies. They usually consist of coalitions of small, local groups that have not (yet) hardened into a cohesive national pressure group.[15]

The **National Action Committee on the Status of Women (NAC)** and the Canadian Environmental Network are loose coalitions of hundreds of women's and environmental groups, respectively.[16] Such movements run into much bureaucratic and political party resistance and often do not achieve immediate success. In the long run, however, they widen the scope of public discourse, and parties and other mainstream political institutions eventually respond. Take recent improvements in legislation with respect to women and the environment, for example, and changes in public attitudes toward war, Aboriginals, homosexuals, and the treatment of animals.

THE CANADIAN PRESS/Andrew Vaughan

In July 2006, Vanessa Rose unrolls a 26-metre petition containing the names of Canadians who want the federal–provincial childcare agreements to continue, expanding the public agenda.

As mentioned above, social movements are one of the most effective means, over time, of changing basic societal values.

The Council of Canadians is a citizens' movement of about 100 000 members that provides a critical voice on key national issues, such as safeguarding social programs, promoting economic justice, renewing democracy, asserting Canadian sovereignty, preserving the environment, and promoting alternatives to corporate-style free trade. It has been active on such issues as trade agreements, public pensions, bank mergers, media ownership, genetically modified foods, health care, and the sale of Canadian water. The Internet facilitates both national and international grassroots political campaigns, and such international social movements and networks are often seen as one of the few counterweights to corporate globalization in the modern world.[17] The Council of Canadians is indeed part of an international network called the Blue Planet Project, which seeks to protect the world's fresh water from the threats of trade and privatization.

The Solidarity Network was an even broader coalition of labour, women's, anti-poverty, health, peace, farming, cultural, environmental, Aboriginal, student, faith, youth, and seniors' groups working to foster greater solidarity in the struggle for democratic change and social justice. It no longer exists, but the Council of Canadians works closely with other groups, such as the CLC, the CFS, the Sierra Club, NAC, and the Canadian Centre for Policy Alternatives. The CCPA produces regular reports, including the annual *Alternative Federal Budget*, a detailed, sophisticated document that is meant to show that despite globalization and fiscal pressures, there *are* alternatives, contrary to what governments have said.

. . . .

ADVOCACY GROUP STRUCTURES

A word should be added about the structure of advocacy groups. Issue-oriented groups may burst forth anywhere an issue arises—at the federal, provincial, territorial, or municipal level. Institutionalized groups, conversely, tend to be organized wherever government decisions regularly affect them. The federal nature of the country means that authoritative decisions are made at two (or even three) levels of government, and most institutionalized groups parallel the federal structure of government. They find it advantageous to be organized at both levels because, as discussed in Chapter 18, the division of powers between the federal and the provincial governments is so blurred. The Canadian Medical Association comprises 12 autonomous provincial and territorial divisions (such as the Manitoba Medical Association), the Canadian Chamber of Commerce has strong provincial branches (such as the Ontario Chamber of Commerce), and so does the Canadian Labour Congress (such as the Nova Scotia Federation of Labour). The CCC and CLC in particular also maintain municipal organizations—local chambers of commerce or boards of trade in every sizable community and local labour councils across the country.

Many groups, including teachers, nurses, and professors, are actually more strongly organized at the provincial level than in Ottawa. This is because they are more affected by decisions of provincial governments than by federal ones. Some, such as the medical and legal professions, are even delegated powers by provincial and territorial governments to regulate themselves.

By increasing the number of decision-making centres in the political system, federalism generally makes it easier for groups to block government action but harder to initiate new programs. Sometimes the national organization requests assistance from the provincial wings in dealing with an issue in Ottawa, while at other times a provincial unit seeks support from the national organization. For example, the insurance industry and the medical profession first fought against medicare in Saskatchewan when it was introduced there, then transferred the fight to Ottawa to oppose a national program, and finally went back to individual provinces to try to persuade them to stay out of the national scheme.[18] At other times, certain groups use their closer relations with provincial governments to transform the provinces into allies in the group's attempt to pressure Ottawa, such as in the insurance industry's opposition to the Canada Pension Plan, the mining industry's fight against federal tax reform, the petroleum industry's campaign against the National Energy Program and the Kyoto Accord, or the Assembly of First Nations' efforts to gain the federal government's attention.[19]

Many national groups are beset by regional and linguistic problems, and the Quebec wing of many national organizations has a distinct status of one kind or another. Other groups seem to handle the cleavages fairly well, having a regular provincial branch in Quebec, attempting to operate on a bilingual basis at the national level, and striving to reconcile regional–ethnic differences within the organization.[20]

. . . .

TARGETS AND METHODS OF ADVOCACY GROUP ACTIVITY

Besides being affected by the federal system, Canadian interest groups are very much influenced in their operations by the fact that they exist in a parliamentary system. This, despite the name, places most of the decision-making power in the hands of the bureaucracy, the prime minister, the Cabinet, and individual ministers. Advocacy groups that understand this basic truth direct most of their attention to these parts of the executive branch of government.

Policy Communities and Policy Networks

In discussing advocacy groups, the concepts of **policy communities** and **policy networks** should be mentioned.[21] These concepts are based on the premise that each field of public policy is discrete and specialized, with its own constellation of participants. Each policy *community* consists of a set of government agencies, advocacy groups, corporations, institutions, media people, and individuals, including academics, who have an interest in that particular policy field and attempt to influence it. Paul Pross argues that every policy community is divided into two parts. The first, the "sub-government," includes a "lead government agency," other policymaking agencies, and a small group of interests with the right to be consulted on a daily basis; the second, the "attentive public," is composed of the other actors mentioned. In either case, these actors initially attempt to establish their legitimacy with the lead agency, and if they achieve such recognition and status, they may be appointed to advisory committees and be made part of the agency's information flow. Pross cites the examples of the Canadian Bankers Association and the Canadian Tax Foundation as groups that have achieved such legitimacy, as opposed to the National Farmers Union, which has not. Once such groups are given the privilege of consultation and access to strategic information, they normally behave quite cooperatively, and the whole policy community becomes cohesive and mutually supportive.

Policy *networks* constitute a narrower set of actors within the policy community with a higher level of interest in the policy field and who interact with each other in a formal, frequent, organized way.[22] The literature on policy networks emphasizes that government consultation with outside groups is far more important than ever before and is just as often initiated by public policymakers as by the external interests that want to influence them. A major contributing cause of this development was the downsizing of government departments in the 1990s, which cost them crucial analytical capacities. While becoming more dependent on outside sources, however, governments began to pay them millions of dollars to produce such knowledge. Thus, policy networks emphasize the role of information and expertise rather than only the articulation of interests.[23] Beyond the *need* for expertise, the new emphasis on policy networks is based on the widespread feeling that governments *should* seek the contribution and cooperation of the third, nonprofit, or **voluntary sector** of individuals, public interest groups, policy-oriented organizations, think tanks, and the like—in order to produce and execute better policy. Such outside groups contribute to the legitimation of government policies and often help in their implementation. There is an increasing sentiment among authorities that civic engagement can lessen widespread public cynicism about government.

More will be said about such policy communities and policy networks in Chapter 20, but for now it is sufficient to emphasize the specialized nature of different policy fields, the varied configurations of actors they contain, and the increasing reliance of governments on self-initiated collaboration with the "third" and private sectors.

The Bureaucracy

As will be discussed in Chapter 22, the bureaucracy advises the prime minister, the Cabinet, and the ministers on almost all of their decisions; it drafts legislation and regulations according to the Cabinet's general instructions; it proposes budgets and spends government money; and it implements policies and programs once they have been given Cabinet or legislative approval. All of these areas hold considerable scope for bureaucratic discretion.[24] It is for this reason that institutionalized groups in particular direct their messages at the bureaucratic target more than at any other institution of government. Many group demands involve technical matters that only the bureaucracy understands and that it may be able to satisfy without reference to the politicians. Such groups try to cultivate close relationships with senior public servants so that they feel comfortable in contacting these officials on an informal, direct, day-to-day basis. This contact can take the form of telephone calls, meetings, letters, e-mails, faxes, and business lunches. If a first-name relationship emerges, so much the better.[25] The Canadian Construction Association, for example, holds an annual meeting at Meech Lake with a number of deputy ministers and other senior government officials from about eight departments to discuss the issues of the day and ensure the continuation of an open and productive dialogue.

As mentioned, a close relationship often develops between an advocacy group and its most relevant government department. This relationship is increasingly a reciprocal one, as desirable for the public service as it is for the group. In return for the various ways in which the bureaucracy can respond to group demands, the group may possess information that the department needs or desires in order to understand certain situations with which it is trying to deal, and the executive directors of many such groups are accustomed to regular calls for advice. Moreover, as issues become too complex for politicians—ministers or MPs—to understand, and larger numbers of issues, constituents, and obligations eat up their time, legislation is drafted in skeletal form with the specifics delegated to the bureaucracy to be added later in the form of regulations or "delegated legislation." Bureaucrats regularly consult interested groups as they draft such legislation, design new programs, and draw up regulations. As president of the Canadian Tobacco Manufacturers' Association, for example, Bill Neville managed to dilute the original regulations dealing with the anti-smoking message that the Health Department imposed on packages of cigarettes.[26] A group may also be a valuable ally in persuading other bureaucratic agencies or Cabinet to do what the department wants and in various "output" functions described below.

Thus, what is called a **clientele relationship** sometimes develops between such groups as the Royal Canadian Legion and Veterans Affairs Canada, between the Canadian Federation of Agriculture and Agriculture and Agri-Food Canada, between the Canadian Medical Association and Health Canada, between the petroleum and mining associations and Natural Resources Canada, and between business organizations and Finance Canada and Industry Canada. The relations between such an agency or department and its allied advocacy groups may become so close that it is difficult to tell them apart. The agency or department almost becomes an extension of the group, making policy in the interest of the group and promoting within the higher councils of government the interests they both represent. The minister, deputy minister, and Department of Finance speak for the business community, while the minister, deputy minister, and Agriculture Canada speak for the farming community, and so on.

Although advocacy groups are usually seen in terms of their "input" function—making demands or "policy advocacy"—they may also perform various implementation or "output" functions. A group may be better equipped to inform its specialized membership or audience about new laws, regulations, or programs than a department that is restricted to the conventional media or other regular channels of communication. Minority ethnocultural groups, for example, can help Citizenship and Immigration Canada in the dissemination of information about policy changes to a specialized audience. In addition, the cooperation of the group might be indispensable to the successful execution of a program, such as the role of the medical profession in the administration of medicare. In some cases, as noted, certain groups are even delegated powers of self-regulation, especially the medical and legal professions at the provincial and territorial level. As governments coped with decreasing funds in the 1990s, they often sought private-sector partnerships as a way of offloading services, improving service delivery, and encouraging civic engagement.[27]

Besides such direct, personal, informal contact, interest groups interact with the bureaucracy through numerous permanent and ad hoc advisory committees. Most departments set up several advisory committees and offer representation on them to the advocacy groups most affected. The National Council of Welfare is a classic case of a group that was not only created by government to serve as an advisory committee directly representing poor people but was even given a home and staff within the building housing the Welfare Department (now Human Resources and Skills Development Canada).

In addition, public servants themselves may be members of interest groups. For example, bureaucrats in social services departments often belong to the Canadian Council on Social Development, a situation that naturally assists the group in maximizing its influence; medical bureaucrats may belong to the Canadian Medical Association; and legal bureaucrats, to the Canadian Bar Association. In fact, considerable movement of personnel takes place between interest groups and the higher levels of the public service: officials often move from advocacy group jobs to the bureaucracy or vice versa.

The Prime Minister, the Cabinet, and Ministers

The prime minister, the Cabinet, and ministers form the second branch of government that advocacy groups frequently try to influence. This is because they make the major governmental decisions in a parliamentary system, as discussed in Chapter 21. Since many decisions are made by single ministers or Cabinet committees, it is probably most productive to submit single-issue representations to individual ministers, who actually spend much of their time in meetings with such groups.[28] If a minister stays in one position long enough, an advocacy group may be able to construct a more personal, informal relationship, as did the Canadian

Federation of Agriculture with Jimmy Gardiner, who served as minister of agriculture from 1935 to 1957. Unfortunately for such groups, the practice of shuffling ministers from one department to another every couple of years decreases the likelihood of developing such intimacy. The social scene in Ottawa should also be mentioned because parties and receptions provide excellent opportunities for Cabinet ministers, deputy ministers, and established group representatives (especially corporate representatives) to meet and mingle. Occasionally, ministers are themselves members of the interest group, in which case this interlocking membership is probably an advantage to the group. Less institutionalized groups, however, may have to forgo such close relationships with Cabinet ministers in favour of letters, faxes, or other means of more formal or mass communication.

The concept of **elite accommodation** is particularly relevant to this process. It claims that most public decisions in Canada emerge from the interaction of three agents: the Cabinet, the senior public service, and pressure groups, especially in the business field. The individuals who occupy the top positions in these sectors are elites both in the sense of being small numbers of people with disproportionate amounts of power (compared with ordinary citizens) and in terms of their exclusive socioeconomic backgrounds, coming from families of higher social class, higher incomes, and higher educations. Robert Presthus thus postulates that the common backgrounds and values of political, bureaucratic, and corporate leaders help to facilitate agreement among them.[29] Commanding the heights of these sectors of society, they easily accommodate each other in the working out of public policies. Lobbyists from professional lobbying firms also fit perfectly into this arrangement.

Parliament

The third main branch of the government is the legislature or Parliament, but, as is discussed in Chapter 23, it largely legitimizes decisions previously taken by the executive. That being the case, the House of Commons is not as often the target of advocacy group activity, but it does remain the object of considerable attention. One of the main reasons that a bill is usually sent to a legislative committee during its passage is to allow interest groups to make representations on it, and such committee scrutiny of bills involving group submissions may carry on for weeks. Especially in a majority government situation, however, ministers have traditionally been reluctant to accept amendments proposed at the legislative stage, so that groups were better advised to make their case at the executive level before the bill was made public. It has even been said that the sight of a pressure group at the legislative level in Canada is a sign that the group already failed at the level of the bureaucracy and the Cabinet. Nevertheless, many group-inspired amendments to legislation have been accepted in recent years, perhaps most notably the changes made to the Charter of Rights before its final adoption in the early 1980s as a result of pressure from women's, Aboriginal, people with disabilities', and minority ethnocultural groups. The Standing Committee on Finance, with its pre-budget hearings, is integrated into the expenditure management system and listens to established groups on an annual basis. Groups also converge on MPs in their offices or inundate them with letters, e-mails, or postcards from group members. For example, while not diminishing its influence at the levels of Cabinet and bureaucracy, the Canadian Chamber of Commerce is particularly adept at applying pressure on MPs through its base in almost every constituency across the country. Groups also meet with chairs of Commons standing committees, individual party caucuses, or caucus committees. Certain MPs may already belong to the interest group or may be persuaded to join, in which case they can be expected to speak on behalf of the group on a committee or in the Commons, in another aspect of interlocking membership between groups and authorities. Many groups hold receptions on Parliament Hill to develop a positive image with its hungry, thirsty denizens.

The upper chamber of Parliament, the Senate, can also be lobbied by groups, but it may be involved in a somewhat different dimension. At least in the past, many senators had close corporate connections and functioned regularly as lobbyists for big business, such that the Senate was called a "lobby from within."[30] During passage in that chamber, much legislation was considered by the Senate Committee on Banking, Trade and Commerce, many of whose members held directorships in Canadian banks and other large corporations. Such holdings did not deter committee members from active consideration of questions relating to financial institutions in what appears to be a classic case of conflict of interest. Most of today's senators are not so closely tied to the corporate sector.

Other Targets

Advocacy groups have many targets beyond these three main branches of government. If they can find a legal or constitutional angle to their demand, for example, such groups may take cases to the courts. Corporations have sometimes challenged federal or provincial legislation in the courts as a violation of the division of powers. Francophone groups have used the courts to uphold constitutionally guaranteed minority group language rights when politicians were reluctant to do so, and Aboriginal groups are increasingly using the courts to recognize or broaden the meaning of treaty and Aboriginal rights. The Charter of Rights and Freedoms provides added potential for targeting the courts by actually inviting individuals and groups to challenge federal or provincial legislation they consider to be discriminatory. Women's groups have been involved in many such cases, and same-sex groups made major advances in the courts at the end of the 20th century.[31] Earlier in the post-1982 period, the government actually encouraged disadvantaged groups to use the courts as part of their struggle with financial support from the Court Challenges Program. As shown in Chapter 19, however, it was corporate interests that most often challenged laws against the Charter.

As mentioned, only the Canadian Labour Congress has seen fit to attach itself formally to a political party. This strategy may have reduced the group's impact on Liberal and Conservative governments as it awaited an NDP victory. Other groups remain scrupulously nonpartisan so that they can exert equal influence on whichever party is in power.

Another target of group activity is the **royal commission**. These elaborate investigations of public problems normally invite interest groups and experts to submit briefs

Artizans/Michael de Adder

Supreme Court butts-out Big Tobacco.

in public hearings to supplement whatever original research the commission itself undertakes, as well as to generate support for its recommendations. Sometimes an interest group is actually represented on the commission itself, as in the case of the Canadian Medical Association and the Hall Royal Commission on Medical Services in the 1960s.

Besides their direct representations to government, advocacy groups increasingly try to influence public opinion in the hope that the authorities will respond to a clear message from the public. In what is called **advocacy advertising**, corporations and groups also use paid media advertising in an attempt to sway public opinion to their point of view.[32] For example, both Canada's Research-Based Pharmaceutical Companies and the rival Canadian Generic Pharmaceutical Association have taken out media advertisements to make their case on the question of patent protection for new pharmaceuticals. In 2002, there was massive advertising on both sides of the Kyoto Protocol, and in 2005, by the Canadian Nuclear Association. The Internet has allowed groups to mobilize both domestically (through such social networks as Facebook) and internationally.

Many advocacy groups increase their public profile once an election has been called.[33] This phenomenon, discussed in Chapter 13, is usually called "third-party" advertising. They often seek the response of parties and candidates to questions of concern to the group, and then indicate their support or opposition, sometimes through media advertising. Groups on both sides of the abortion debate and the **National Citizens' Coalition** are regular examples, while the Canadian Alliance for Jobs and Trade Prospects and its anti-free-trade counterpart, the Pro-Canada Network, were particularly visible in 1988. National or local groups sometimes target particular politicians, especially ministers, for defeat.

Such coalitions are an increasingly prominent part of the political system. The Council of Canadians helped to found the Pro-Canada Network and the Action Canada Network. The Canadian Environmental Network, the Solidarity Network, and the Canadian Health Coalition are only a few other examples. The Canadian Federation of Students and the Canadian Association of University Teachers both joined the Public Education Network, among others.

If all else fails, the group may resort to demonstrations, protest marches, tractor parades, sit-ins, and road and bridge blockades.[34] Some of these are peaceful and legal, such as the orderly demonstrations that are an almost daily occurrence on Parliament Hill and that frequently greet prime ministers on their travels. The Canadian Federation of Students organized the pan-Canadian Days of Action in October 1998, featuring protest marches, rallies, sit-ins, and informational pickets, and opponents of gun control participated in a demonstration to burn their firearm registration forms. But the frustration of Aboriginal, environmentalist, and other radical or issue-oriented groups increasingly takes the form of civil disobedience. Opponents of clear-cut logging and related forestry practices have spiked trees and chained themselves to trees, and Greenpeace engages in other dramatic escapades that demand widespread media coverage. The armed Aboriginal standoff at Oka, Quebec, in 1990 was one of the rare occasions in which a group actually resorted to violence.

In light of the violence and arrests that occurred at the Quebec Summit of the Americas and other such "globalization" gatherings (in Seattle, Genoa, etc.), various protest groups and other social movements have been forced to rethink their tactics. Some are leaning toward training participants in how to behave when confronted by police, while others are more inclined to avoid situations that could lead to violence, especially since the public has yet to be convinced that such violent confrontations are justified.

Advocacy groups are not restricted to one target and method, of course, and groups may use a variety of methods directed at a number of different targets. The Canadian Labour Congress, for example, was so distraught over the wage and price control program in 1975 that beyond its direct daily contact with government officials, its annual brief to the Cabinet, and its affiliation with the NDP, it challenged the legislation in the Supreme Court and organized a national day of protest. Five years later, the CLC held one of the largest demonstrations in Canadian history on Parliament Hill. Despite a few tense moments, it ended peacefully, much to the relief of the anxious House of Commons security guards.

As political issues increasingly cross national borders, advocacy group action now often takes a transnational form. Miriam Smith demonstrates three ways in which this happens: appealing to international organizations to pressure the Canadian state, forming alliances with other groups outside Canada to pursue common objectives, and mobilizing to influence politics elsewhere in the world.[35] Aboriginal and women's groups in Canada are good examples of groups using the United Nations to further their domestic causes. Both have also developed links with similar groups in other countries, as have groups opposed to comprehensive trade agreements and those aiming to protect the environment. Groups in Canada are also active in protesting certain policies of other states.

. . . .

GROUP RESOURCES AND DETERMINANTS OF SUCCESS

The fact that an institutionalized group like the CLC could fight an issue on so many fronts and still lose leads to the question why are groups sometimes successful and sometimes not? A variety of factors are involved in accounting for such success and failure, including the following:

- sympathy of and access to the government
- information
- financial position of government
- members
- cohesion
- money
- leadership and prestige
- popularity of the cause
- absence of opposition

The sympathy of the government and access to policymakers are probably most important.[36] If a basic correspondence exists between the demands of the group and the government's stated objectives—if they share basic values—the advocacy group will have greater success than if there is a vast gap in ideological perspective. Contrast the CCCE, which was widely seen as actually *setting* the agenda of the business-oriented Mulroney government,[37] with the CLC, which was virtually ignored. Similarly, the minister responsible for the Status of Women in that Cabinet repeatedly refused to meet the National Action Committee on the Status of Women because of its intense criticism of Conservative policies. At the same time, the Mulroney government cut NAC's grant and gave the first federal grant to its rival, REAL Women (Realistic, Equal, Active for Life). Left-leaning groups would presumably have more influence with NDP (provincial) governments than with Liberal or Conservative ones.

The sympathy of the government should normally entail ready access, especially at the political level. But, as the discussion of policy communities and policy networks revealed, groups may well establish their standing with bureaucratic policymakers, regardless of the party in power. Another aspect of access, to be discussed below, is that provided by consultant lobbyists. Whether at the political or bureaucratic levels, such hired guns are often able to provide groups or corporations with the kind of contact they desire.

Information is a second crucial resource in advocacy group politics.[38] Especially at the bureaucratic level, where much of this politics takes place, any vital information that is lacking as the public service drafts technical laws and regulations will be eagerly accepted. Even at the political level, the group may be able to present data and alternative analyses of policy that will lead ministers to rethink their proposals. Closely associated with information is the professional expertise of the advocacy group's staff, and in this connection, the large business groups are able to produce mounds of well-researched and glossy documents. The Canadian Bar Association makes frequent representations to parliamentary committees, royal commissions, and government departments, and because of its expertise in both the substance of many issues and the drafting of legislation, is often asked for advice. The CBA and Canadian Chamber of Commerce are among many groups that constantly monitor federal political issues and the passage of legislation and keep their members informed via monthly newsletters.

Since many group demands relate to the spending of public money, the financial position of the government will often influence a group's success, as the Canadian Federation of Students could attest. In the prosperous and free-spending 1960s and 1970s, for example, requests for funds were more likely to be fulfilled than in the 1980s, the 1990s, and in the early years of the new century, which constituted an era of government restraint.

The size of the group is also important: since membership numbers represent votes, the authorities feel comfortable ignoring very small groups because the electoral consequences would be minimal. In this respect, the Canadian Labour Congress, with some three million members, should be regularly successful in having the authorities respond to its demands because it is the largest advocacy groups in Canada.

The fact that the CLC is not usually very influential points to the importance not just of a large membership but also of the cohesiveness of the organization.[39] First of all, as mentioned, only about one-third of paid workers belong to unions and only 75 percent of Canadian union members belong to the CLC, so that the labour movement as a whole is not very cohesive. Second, this membership is indirect; members first belong to a group or a union that is itself attached to the national body. But even among those who are members of the CLC, unity, commitment, and militancy are notoriously lacking. In addition to the weak sense of class-consciousness in Canada, there is a lack of union-consciousness, an unwillingness of one union to support another. The CLC's ultimate threat to Liberal or Conservative governments is that the more unhappy the group is, the more likely its members are to vote NDP. But even on those occasions when the CLC "declared war" on the government, the bulk of its members continued to vote for the old-line parties. Liberal and Conservative governments apparently feel that the CLC is so incapable of mobilizing its members behind the demands issued by its leadership that it can often be ignored. In 2006, after a spat during the election campaign, the Canadian Auto Workers even detached itself from the NDP. The Canadian Federation of Students is another organization that could also benefit from greater cohesion.

In contrast, other groups, such as the Royal Canadian Legion or the Canadian Chamber of Commerce, have such cohesion that they are able to mobilize their local branches and members to inundate the authorities with demands for concerted action. The CCC, for example, issues periodic action calls that tell its members to "use the facts and arguments outlined in this bulletin [to] deliver the message in your own words on your own letterhead to your Member of Parliament by letter, phone, fax or in person. Send a copy of your message directly to the Minister of Finance and the Prime Minister."[40]

As in other aspects of politics and life in general, money is an important resource. In the case of advocacy groups, money can buy staff, offices, organization, expertise, publicity, and other useful weapons with which to get the group's message across. The four peak business groups, especially the Canadian Council of Chief Executives, are very well endowed financially, which gives them the capacity both to generate the information to strengthen their case and to transmit it to relevant targets. In fact, except for those representing big business or highly paid professions, most groups struggle with their finances.[41] On rare occasions, however, the very poverty of the group or its members may actually be an asset in seeking government assistance: it sometimes strengthens the case for public support.

The quality of group leadership and the prestige of the group are other important factors. In recent years, for example, even the Canadian Labour Congress has quite deliberately sought to choose articulate, attractive leaders to make its case. When dealing with a Liberal or Conservative government, however, organized labour probably does not rival doctors, lawyers, or businesspeople as far as prestige is concerned. Another factor is the sharing of a professional orientation between group leaders and authorities, especially in the bureaucracy. Many examples could be given of the success of a group because its officials shared the professional norms of the relevant public servants in their reciprocal, clientele relationship. A government or societal guilty conscience can sometimes also be helpful, such as in the provision of grants to Aboriginal, Japanese-Canadian, Chinese-Canadian, or anti-poverty groups.

It will also help if the cause is supported by public opinion—if it is consistent with the prevailing values of society in general. For example, although Canadian banks are used to getting their way with government, it was largely because of the negativity of public opinion that various governments have rejected bank mergers since 1998–99.[42]

Finally, a group will be more influential if it has no organized opposition. One of the reasons for the success of the Canadian Medical Association over the years, for example, was that it had medical politics almost all to itself.[43] Contrast that situation with the evenly divided forces on both sides of the abortion or tobacco advertising debates. Somewhat similarly, the Canadian Federation of Students finds its message diluted and contradicted by minor rival groups. Alternatively, success can be influenced by whether another group expresses more or less the same point of view, such as in the competition between the Canadian Federation of Agriculture and the National Farmers Union.

Taking all these resources into account, who wins in the competition among advocacy groups? The answer has already been suggested in Chapter 8 and implied in other parts of the book: business usually gets its way. This conclusion not only follows from a catalogue of group resources but also results from wider forces in the political system.[44]

. . . .

LOBBYING IN CANADA

The tendency of the rich and powerful, including big business, to benefit from pressure group politics and elite accommodation can only be enhanced by recent developments in the practice of lobbying in Canada. If lobbying is the activity of trying to influence the authorities, it is, of course, a perfectly legitimate activity for anyone to undertake in a democracy. Traditionally, individuals, companies, unions, and advocacy groups of all kinds have done their own lobbying, but in recent years Canada has seen the mushrooming of professional lobbying—consultant lobbyists or government relations firms that lobby on behalf of an individual, company, advocacy group, or other organization in return for a fee.

Emergence of Modern Lobbying

Those engaged in the new lobbying industry justify their existence largely in terms of the increasing size and complexity of government. The federal government grew enormously in the 1960s and 1970s, and the policymaking process was restructured so that corporations and advocacy groups could no longer find their way around Ottawa.[45] That the hostile budgets of 1980 (National Energy Program) and 1981 (corporate tax reform) caught the business community by surprise also contributed to the development of new means through which the corporate sector could make its voice heard more effectively.

The early 1980s was thus a period in which new avenues of influence were being sought, and an expansion of lobbying firms appeared to take place about the time the Mulroney government was elected in 1984. Many of the leading figures in the initial establishment of professional lobby firms were cronies of the prime minister.[46] Certain leading legal firms also set up lobbying operations. Given that the bureaucracy can satisfy many of the corporations' needs, several bureaucrats left government employment to join or form lobbying firms in order to capitalize on their inside knowledge and connections. Conflict-of-interest guidelines were supposed to preclude senior government ex-employees from dealing with their former departments for a certain time after their departure from public employment, but these rules were sometimes broken.

Legalizing Lobbying: The Registration System

After the emergence of such professional lobbying firms, a consensus developed among politicians that legislation, registration, and regulation were necessary. The registration idea was part of the Mulroney Conservatives' ethics package unveiled after its early troubled record of Cabinet resignations due to conflicts of interest and numerous legal charges against Tory backbenchers.[47]

According to the 1989 Lobbyists Registration Act, a lobbyist is an individual who, for payment, on behalf of any person or organization ... undertakes to arrange a meeting with a public office holder or to communicate with a public office holder in an attempt to influence

(a) the development of a legislative proposal . . .

(b) the introduction, passage, defeat or amendment of any bill or resolution . . .

(c) the making or amending of any regulation . . .

(d) the development or amendment of any policy or program . . .

(e) the awarding of any monetary grant or contribution or other financial benefit . . . or

(f) the awarding of any contract.

The legislation acknowledged that lobbying public officeholders was a legitimate activity, but it required lobbyists to register because it was desirable that officials and the public knew who was attempting to influence government and because paid lobbyists should not impede free and open access to government. It excluded representations made to parliamentary committees or other cases where the representations were a matter of public record and submissions made in direct response to a written request for advice or comment from a public officeholder.

The law divided lobbyists into two categories: those who worked for a client for a fee were classified as "Tier I" lobbyists, while "Tier II" lobbyists included those who engaged in traditional pressure group or corporate lobbying—that is, "in-house" employees whose duties involved communicating with public officeholders on behalf of the organization that employed them. Both types of lobbyists had to register their activities in the Registry of Lobbyists.

Many critics felt that the legislation was very weak and contrasted it with the U.S. law on this subject, which was adopted in 1946.[48] Some lobbyists did not register, and even when they did, the disclosure provisions in the Canadian law were quite minimal. The law did not require revelation of the specific object of the representations and was almost totally lacking in an effective enforcement mechanism.

The whole procedure provided a lucrative living to those who could claim to be intimates of ministers or ministries and favoured those who could afford to hire such professional lobbyists. In what John Sawatsky calls "one of the most odious lobby campaigns in the history of Canada," the fight of the Pharmaceutical Manufacturers Association of Canada to extend drug patent protection, "Gerry Doucet handled the PMAC file in GCI's (Government Consultants International) office; his brother Fred handled the issue in the Prime Minister's Office."[49] In the Mulroney era, ministers were allowed to set up large offices full of personal or partisan assistants headed by a chief of staff with which to provide stronger direction to the bureaucracy. As a result, lobbyists' efforts were often focused on ministers' offices, and Tory partisan links were particularly important. Partly because of the newness of the phenomenon, much of the early lobbying was a fairly crude process of selling access to ministers and their staff. The parliamentary committee hearings and judicial inquiry into the Mulroney-Schreiber affair revealed many shocking stories about the lobbying industry in its infancy, including the prominent role of Mulroney-confidant, Frank Moores.

A parliamentary committee reviewed the Lobbyists Registration Act in 1993 and the Liberal Party promised in the Red Book to take the recommended action. Not surprisingly, the lobbyists lobbied ferociously against greater transparency in their operations, and the amendments adopted in 1995 were a pale imitation of what had been recommended by the committee and promised during the election campaign. Tier II lobbyists were divided between in-house Corporation lobbyists and in-house Organization lobbyists, and the information required for the registration of each lobbying effort included the following:

- if the client is a corporation, the name and business address of the parent corporation and those subsidiaries that directly benefit from the lobbying activity;
- if the client is a coalition, the name and business address of each corporation or organization that is a member of the coalition;
- subject matters, including the specific legislative proposal, bill, resolution, regulation, policy, program, grant, contribution, financial benefit, or contract sought;
- name of each department or other governmental institution lobbied;
- source and amount of any government funding provided to the client;

- whether payment is contingent on the success of the lobbying; and
- communication techniques used, including grassroots lobbying, that is, appeals to the public through the mass media or direct communications that seek to persuade members of the public to communicate directly with and apply pressure on the public office-holder.[50]

As can be seen, the new legislation was somewhat more rigorous in what had to be reported. Coalitions and grassroots lobbying efforts had to be registered for the first time, and if contingency fees were involved, this had to be disclosed. As for enforcement, the six-month limitation of proceedings on contraventions was extended to two years. The ethics counsellor previously appointed by the Liberal government to administer the Conflict of Interest Code for ministers was required to work with interested parties to develop a code of conduct for lobbyists, which took effect in March 1997.[51]

Lobbying under the Chrétien, Martin, and Harper Governments

In the Chrétien government, ministers were forced to get by with a small number of partisan assistants, and the bureaucracy was allowed to operate with greater independence. Hence, the focus of lobbyists' efforts switched to some extent from ministers' offices to the level of the senior bureaucracy. Having Liberal connections was still important for lobbyists, however, because a knowledge of Cabinet thinking helped them influence decisions actually taken by the bureaucracy. Another distinctive mark of the Chrétien government was its massive consultation program: it sought the views of the stakeholders involved in so many issues that it almost overwhelmed both traditional advocacy groups and lobbyists.

Lobbying became more sophisticated over time. Instead of (or in addition to) promising access to ministers, lobbyists now had to be able to tell their clients what the government was thinking and where it was going and to provide strategic advice on how and whom to lobby. In arranging for a client's visit, lobbyists typically communicate with ministers and their offices, telling them what to expect from the representation. The lobbyist thus acts as a mediator between the public official and the client, calling the official back after the meeting and perhaps arranging another. If the client's issue is not on the minister's agenda, the lobbyist will approach the relevant public servant lower down in the hierarchy.

Although the revised law was a slight improvement, it remained highly defective. "By leaving vague the definitions of lobbying, and by excluding any lobbying associated with a consultative exercise, the government ... left much room for those sincerely wishing to avoid disclosing their activities or their aims to do so."[52] The point at which lobbyists must register is when they communicate with a public official on behalf of a client. If they work under a general retainer, monitoring federal government activities or providing strategic advice on how or whom to lobby, they can charge for their services but do not have to register. Hence, much of the work of legal firms in this area is not registered.

Moreover, the enforcement of the Lobbyists Registration Act itself was defective. It was not until 1999 that the RCMP looked into its first potential violation of the act in connection with a Liberal activist, René Fugère, a man close to the prime minister, who did not register as a lobbyist but met civil servants on behalf of a Shawinigan hotel owner who received a $100 000 government cheque to expand his operations. After the RCMP investigation into the affair, the prosecutors decided not to file a criminal charge, even though Fugère clearly engaged in

artizans.com

Artizans/Bruce MacKinnon

Tories Clean Air Bill emits pollution from Parliament: corporate lobbying successfully resisted environmental regulation.

lobbying without registering. Two later cases were reviewed by the registrar of the Lobbyists Registration Branch but were not even referred to the RCMP for further investigation.

There were other serious problems with lobbying during the Chrétien regime. For example, a former top aide to Health Minister Allan Rock was hired as chief lobbyist for Monsanto, famous for its expertise in genetic modification, only weeks after he left the minister's employ. Some two years previous, he had been involved in a file dealing with approval of new Monsanto genetically modified (GM) potato seeds.[53] Another development was the increasing dependence of government departments themselves on lobbying firms. In particular, because such firms often include polling in their repertoire of services, departments started hiring them for advice that involved gauging the state of public opinion. Paul Martin employed the lobbying firm Earnscliffe to do pre-budget polling in 2000, and Ottawa observers noted that Earnscliffe was closely tied to virtually everything done by Martin and the Department of Finance while he was there. Many claim that there was a blatant conflict of interest when Earnscliffe both lobbied the Department on behalf of clients on the one hand and did communications and polling for the department on the other. Many at Earnscliffe were later at the heart of Martin's campaign to seek the Liberal leadership. Indeed, many lobbyists worked part-time for the Liberal Party or for individual Liberal leadership contenders.

The Chrétien government made further amendments to the Lobbyists Registration Act in 2003, but because of opposition from the industry, the law was not made effective until mid-2005. At the same time, however, new cases of wrongdoing were revealed during the Martin regime. First, high tech firms hired lobbyists to obtain millions of dollars in investment financing from the Technology Partnerships Canada (TPC) program. It became clear that many people had functioned as lobbyists in the matter without registering under the LRA and that many were paid a contingency or "success" fee. Second, former Liberal Minister David Dingwall was implicated in the scheme, both for not having registered and for having obtained nearly half a million dollars as a lobbying fee. When he raised controversy as well in his role as the patronage-appointed president of the Royal Canadian Mint, he left the position with a generous severance package, arguing that he was "entitled to his entitlements."

The **Gomery Report** on the Quebec sponsorship scandal supported further revisions to the lobbying registration scheme, incorporating some, but not all of the recommendations made by the organization Democracy Watch.[54] The **Federal Accountability Act** renamed the act the **Lobbying Act**; it banned contingency fees; it provided for the appointment of a commissioner of lobbying as an independent agent of Parliament with additional investigatory powers; it prohibited ministerial staffers, ministers, and senior public servants from registering as lobbyists for five years after leaving office; it required that lobbyists record telephone calls and in-person meetings (but not e-mails) with senior public officeholders; and it extended the period during which infractions could be investigated to ten years. Nevertheless, most of its provisions did not come into effect until July 2008 and others were watered down in the regulations issued under the Act; most lobbying firms in Ottawa were happy to take on new Conservative partners who would undoubtedly prove to be positive additions.

The ineffectiveness of enforcement was further weakened in a Federal Court of Canada judgment that the Registrar of Lobbyists had exceeded his jurisdiction by investigating alleged violations of the act rather than notifying police. Recent exposés of the industry can be found in *The Hill Times* (February 25, 2008), the *Ottawa Citizen* (January 22, 2008), and *the Globe and Mail* (May 30, 2008). One of the most controversial moves was the hiring of Ian Brodie, former chief of staff to Prime Minister Harper, by Hill and Knowlton. To function as a lobbyist would violate the Lobbying Act, so he was titled "Senior Counsellor" at the lobbying firm.

Official documents on this subject are available at from the Office of the Commissioner of Lobbying in Canada at http://ocl-cal.gc.ca/epic/site/lobbyist-lobbyiste1.nsf/en/h_nx00269e .html. In 2009, 870 consultant lobbyists had 2241 active registrations; these were supplemented by1436 in-house Corporation lobbyists and 2204 in-house Organization lobbyists.[55] Table 16.2 lists some of the largest such firms and their principal clients in 2009. According to *The Hill Times*, some of the leading consultant lobbyists are David Angus and Joe Jordan (Capital Hill Group), Michael Robinson and Harry Near (Earnscliffe), Michael Coates and Goldy Hyder (Hill & Knowlton), and Torrence Wylie and Randy Pettipas, (Global Public Affairs).[56]

Because of the fees involved, big corporations and business pressure groups make the greatest use of consultant lobbyists; many corporations are clients of more than one professional lobbying firm, and many employ their own in-house lobbyists as well. Traditional pressure groups sometimes engage professional lobbyists to supplement their supplications to government because consultant lobbyists tend to be better strategists and can be used to build coalitions and share expenses on matters in which such cooperation is advantageous. Only a small number of trade unions, First Nations, and other nonprofit organizations have employed

TABLE 16.2 Largest Consultant Lobbying Firms and Principal Clients, 2009	
Firm	*Clients*
Global Public Affairs	Shell Canada, Petro-Canada, Canadian Association of Petroleum Producers, Weyerhauser
Capital Hill Group	Molson Canada, Bombardier, Bell Canada
Hill & Knowlton	Bell Canada, Merck Frosst, Canada's Research-Based Pharmaceutical Companies
Earnscliffe Strategy Group	Microsoft, General Motors, Canadian Pacific, Monsanto, CIBC

Source: Created by author using data from Office of the Commissioner of Lobbying of Canada. Found at: http://ocl-cal.gc.ca/eic/site/lobbyist-lobbyiste1.nsf/eng/home (Accessed April 13, 2009)

lobbyists. That partisan ties continue to play a significant part in the lobbying process makes the system doubly objectionable. Moreover, companies can deduct lobbyist fees (or the fees of belonging to an advocacy group) from their corporate income tax. Young and Everitt would like to level the playing field a bit by allowing tax credits for contributions to genuine public interest groups.[57]

Statistics from the Commissioner of Lobbying in mid-April 2009 show that the four government institutions most actively lobbied were Industry Canada, Finance Canada, the Privy Council Office, and the Prime Minister's Office. The most common subject matter of active registrations at that time were industry, environment, taxation and finance, and international trade.[58] These two sets of figures reveal two unsurprising developments: most of the lobbying is done with respect to economic issues (that is to say, by business interests), and given the centralized operation of the Harper government, the PCO and PMO became two of the agencies most heavily subject to lobbying efforts. Since the official registration reports are still not particularly forthcoming, it is fortunate that a private company, Advocacy Research Centre (ARC), fills the gap with a biweekly edition of the *Lobby Monitor*. This publication details the major lobbying efforts currently in progress, the techniques being used, and the people involved. A more critical account comes from periodic revelations of Democracy Watch, which reminds us of the continuing secrecy over lobbyists' fees and the cost of a lobbying campaign, subjects that are transparent in the corresponding U.S. law.

. . . .

CONCLUSION

This discussion confirms the contention that advocacy groups and lobbying are becoming increasingly important in the Canadian political system. The number and activity of such groups have grown over time, and however much they are an unintended appendage to the system, modern government could simply not do without them. More and more, government is actually seeking their involvement in the policymaking process. Much has been said in academic circles in recent years about how advocacy groups are displacing political parties, and a comparison of the budgets and staff of the parties and leading pressure groups only confirms the disparities in their resources. As for lobbying, the Harper government's Federal Accountability Act made some improvements, although this murky underside of Canadian politics can still use additional regulation and transparency. One main issue is the continuing unlevel playing field among business and professional interests on the one hand and social movements and unorganized interests on the other. The lobbying industry in particular has given corporate interests a powerful means of influence at the very time that corporate contributions to political parties were prohibited on the ground that they contributed to the "democratic deficit."

This chapter is thus primarily linked to Chapter 8 (class) and the various branches of government, discussed in Chapters 20 to 24, especially the bureaucracy. But advocacy groups based on ethnicity, gender, religion, age, and location were also encountered in Chapters 4, 5, 6, 7, and 9, and Chapter 13 included "third-party" engagement in election campaigns.

P Of the approaches outlined in Chapter 1, pluralism is at first sight most relevant to the subject of advocacy groups. It argues that public policy emerges from the competition and accommodation among organized groups. Pluralists claim that all interests in society are free to organize and participate in the group competition, as the array of advocacy groups mentioned in this chapter at least partly confirms. They contend that the political system is not tightly controlled by any elite, business or otherwise; it contains much "slack," which any interest can fill by merely getting organized. Each policy field has its own specialized audience and participants, so that different groups are influential in different areas. Pluralists would endorse public financial assistance to those interests that are truly lacking in organizational resources and would advise issue-oriented groups to seek cheap media publicity if they do not have well-established links to the authorities or the capacity to impress them in the usual behind-the-scenes way. But Miriam Smith argues that the contentions of pluralism are seriously flawed and that it is impossible not to recognize the persistent social inequality that creates barriers to the formation of advocacy groups that represent the permanently marginalized interests in society.[59]

SC Given the frequency and intensity with which the authorities are approached by advocacy groups and other lobbyists, it would take a resolute government indeed to ignore such group reaction, as is argued by the state-centred approach. In discussing the autonomy of the state, therefore, the concept of policy communities and policy networks and the close relationship between a government department and a principal client group commend themselves. As Coleman and Skogstad write, "sectoral state actors appear more able to control the policy agenda ... when they enjoy the support of well organized client interests. Close state–societal relations may augment the state's ability to proceed with its state–societal agenda."[60] The concept of policy communities, therefore, combines the pluralist and state-centred approaches. It also bears a certain resemblance to elite accommodation.

© Class analysts refute the pluralist claim that with a little effort any interest can organize itself into a group; doing so is beyond the capacity of many interests. Such analysts are among those most alarmed at the disparity in resources and consequent influence between affluent business groups and hard-pressed labour, farmer, consumer, Aboriginal, women's, and anti-poverty groups. Many "have-not" groups depend heavily on government support for their very existence but then find it cut just when they are beginning to make themselves heard. Moreover, class analysts add, nearly half the population does not belong to any advocacy group, the poorest and weakest part at that. Furthermore, businesses can lobby as individual firms, in functional pressure groups, or in peak business groups, so that they have more approaches from which to choose. The recent advent of expensive professional lobby firms, which few beyond the corporate sector can afford, merely heightens the disparities between business and other groups.

Class analysts and others contend that the predominance of business groups is not only a matter of material resources but also flows naturally from the marriage of a capitalist economy with a democracy and reflects the dominant ideology of the two parties that have alternated in government. Leo Panitch writes that "it is not that political and bureaucratic officials decide to favour capitalist interests in case after case; it is rather that it rarely even occurs to them that they might do other than favour such interests."[61] In the same vein, Ralph Miliband says that "it is easier for ministers to ditch their stocks and shares when appointed to public office than it is to ditch their basic sympathies and predispositions toward the business world."[62] Moreover, the state is dependent on businesses and business groups for the performance of the economy, so that the government takes seriously any promise to create jobs or any threat to contract employment.[63] In his book *Titans*, Peter C. Newman argues that the Canadian Council of Chief Executives (then the BCNI) under President Tom d'Aquino set the agenda for all recent Canadian governments. First it was free trade, then deficit reduction, and, after that, tax cuts, each of them reducing the size and role of the state. "The regimes of Brian Mulroney and Jean Chrétien came to agree that what was good for the BCNI was good for Canada," and d'Aquino emerged as "the most powerful influence on public policy formation in Canadian history."[64] In 2009, d'Aquino was succeeded as president by former Liberal cabinet minister John Manley.

Ⓖ If globalization means the increasing insignificance of national boundaries, it is certainly evident in the actions of advocacy groups. More than ever before, such groups have established links with their counterparts in other countries and must confront problems that are global in scope. Some issues are common to a variety of nation-states, and some are truly transnational.[65] As mentioned above, the Internet has made it possible for grassroots organizations to mobilize across national boundaries as a counterweight to governments, transnational corporations, and free trade agreements. But they must take on individual transnational corporations and influential groups, like the Canadian Council of Chief Executives, that actively promote a globalizing, neoliberal agenda. Even lobbying firms are increasingly transnational in scope, either establishing their own branches in other countries or developing partnerships that will serve their clients with concerns beyond Canadian borders.

. . . .

DISCUSSION QUESTIONS

1. Are you a member of any groups that at least occasionally try to influence government policy? Are you familiar with any local issue-oriented groups or social movements?

2. Why do business groups have more influence than other kinds of groups? Do they have too much?

3. How could the unorganized be helped to organize and how could weak groups be strengthened in order to offset the influence of business?

4. In what sense do advocacy groups act as integrating agents in society? On balance, are they more divisive or integrative in nature?

5. What factors led to the growth in the professional lobbying industry in Canada in recent years?

6. Even after the Harper government's Federal Accountability Act, how could the Lobbying Act be strengthened?

NOTES

1. Paul Pross, *Group Politics and Public Policy* (Toronto: Oxford University Press, 1986).
2. Lisa Young and Joanna Everitt, *Advocacy Groups* (Vancouver: UBC Press, 2004).
3. Ibid., pp. 21–22; and Miriam Smith, "Interest Groups and Social Movements," in Michael Whittington and Glen Williams, eds., *Canadian Politics in the 21st Century*, 7th ed. (Toronto: Nelson Education, 2008).
4. Pross, *Group Politics and Public Policy*, esp. ch. 11. See also Miriam Smith, *A Civil Society? Collective Actors in Canadian Political Life* (Peterborough: Broadview Press, 2005); and Miriam Smith, ed., *Group Politics and Social Movements in Canada* (Peterborough: Broadview Press, 2008).
5. Pross, *Group Politics and Public Policy*, pp. 92–93.
6. Miriam Smith, "Interest Groups and Social Movements," 7th ed., p. 171; Miriam Smith, *Group Politics and Social Movements in Canada*, ch. 1.
7. William D. Coleman, *Business and Politics: A Study of Collective Action* (Montreal: McGill–Queen's University Press, 1988); Stephen Brooks and Andrew Stritch, *Business and Government in Canada* (Scarborough: Prentice Hall Canada, 1991), ch. 7; W.T. Stanbury, *Business–Government Relations in Canada* (Toronto: Methuen, 1986), esp. ch. 7; Geoffrey Hale, *The Uneasy Partnership: Politics of Business and Government in Canada* (Peterborough: Broadview Press, 2006); Peter Clancy, "Business Interests and Civil Society in Canada," in Smith, *Group Politics and Social Movements in Canada*; and group websites.
8. Coleman, *Business and Politics*, p. 6.
9. Ibid., p. 45. In 1994 he counted more than 600 in "One Step Ahead: Business in the Policy Process in Canada," in Mark Charlton and Paul Barker, eds., *Crosscurrents: Contemporary Political Issues*, 2nd ed. (Scarborough: Nelson Canada, 1994).
10. Grace Skogstad, *The Politics of Agricultural Policy-Making in Canada* (Toronto: University of Toronto Press, 1987).
11. Jim Silver, *Thin Ice: Money, Politics and the Demise of an NHL Franchise* (Halifax: Fernwood Publishing, 1996).
12. Leslie Pal, *Interests of State: The Politics of Language, Multiculturalism, and Feminism in Canada* (Montreal: McGill–Queen's University Press, 1993).
13. See William Coleman and Grace Skogstad, eds., *Policy Communities and Public Policy in Canada* (Mississauga: Copp Clark Pitman, 1990); and Young and Everitt, *Advocacy Groups*, pp. 76–82.
14. Susan D. Phillips, "New Social Movements in Canadian Politics: Past Their Apex?" in J.P. Bickerton and A.G. Gagnon, eds., *Canadian Politics*, 3rd ed. Peterborough: Broadview Press, 1999; William K. Carroll, ed., *Organizing Dissent: Contemporary Social Movements in Theory and Practice*, 2nd ed. (Toronto: Garamond Press, 1997); Smith, "Interest Groups and Social Movements"; Jill Vickers, *Reinventing Political Science: A Feminist Approach* (Halifax: Fernwood Publishing, 1997); and Matt James, *Misrecognized Materialists: Social Movements in Canadian Constitutional Politics* (Vancouver: UBC Press, 2006).

15. Claude Galipeau, "Political Parties, Interest Groups, and New Social Movements," in Alain Gagnon and Brian Tanguay, eds., *Canadian Parties in Transition* (Scarborough: Nelson Canada, 1989).

16. Alexandra Dobrowolsky, "The Women's Movement in Flux: Feminism and Framing, Passion, and Politics," and Judith I. McKenzie, "The Environmental Movement in Canada: Retreat or Resurgence?" in Smith, *Group Politics and Social Movements in Canada*.

17. Jeffrey M. Ayres, *Defying Conventional Wisdom: Political Movements and Popular Contention against North American Free Trade* (Toronto: University of Toronto Press, 1998); and R.S. Ratner, "Many Davids, One Goliath," in Carroll, ed., *Organizing Dissent*.

18. Malcolm Taylor, *Health Insurance and Canadian Public Policy* (Montreal: McGill-Queen's University Press, 1978).

19. M.W. Bucovetsky, "The Mining Industry and the Great Tax Reform Debate," in Paul Pross, ed., *Pressure Group Behaviour in Canadian Politics* (Toronto: McGraw-Hill Ryerson, 1975); Glyn Berry, "The Oil Lobby and the Energy Crisis," *Canadian Public Administration* (Winter 1974); and Glen Toner and Bruce Doern, "The Two Energy Crises and Canadian Oil and Gas Interest Groups," *Canadian Journal of Political Science* (September 1986).

20. William D. Coleman and Tim A. Mau, "French–English Relations in Business-Interest Associations: 1965–2002," *Canadian Public Administration* (Winter 2002).

21. Pross, *Group Politics and Public Policy*, ch. 6; Coleman, *Business and Politics*, ch. 4; Leslie A. Pal, *Beyond Policy Analysis: Public Issue Management in Turbulent Times*, 3rd ed. (Toronto: Thomson Nelson, 2006), ch. 6; and Smith, "Interest Groups," p. 223.

22. Pal, *Beyond Policy Analysis*, ch. 6; Young and Everitt, *Advocacy Groups*, p. 7; Donald J. Savoie, *Breaking The Bargain: Public Servants, Ministers, and Parliament* (Toronto: University of Toronto Press, 2003), ch. 6; Steve Patten, "Democratizing the Institutions of Policy-Making: Democratic Consultation and Participatory Administration," *Journal of Canadian Studies* (Winter 2001); and Eric Montpetit, "Public Consultations in Policy Network Environments: The Case of Assisted Reproductive Technology Policy in Canada," *Canadian Public Policy* (2003).

23. Pal, *Beyond Policy Analysis*, p. 261.

24. Paul Pross, "Parliamentary Influence and the Diffusion of Power," *Canadian Journal of Political Science* (June 1985).

25. Pross, *Group Politics and Public Policy*; Brooks and Stritch, *Business and Government in Canada*, ch. 7; Coleman, *Business and Politics*; and Stanbury, *Business–Government Relations in Canada*, ch. 7.

26. Brooks and Stritch, *Business and Government in Canada*, pp. 237–38.

27. Leslie Seidel, *Rethinking the Delivery of Public Services to Citizens* (Montreal: Institute for Research on Public Policy, 1995); and Coleman, *Business and Politics*, ch. 3.

28. Pross, "Parliamentary Influence and the Diffusion of Power."

29. Robert Presthus, *Elite Accommodation in Canada* (Toronto: Macmillan, 1973). On corporatism, see Stephen McBride, "Public Policy as a Determinant of Interest Group Behaviour: The Canadian Labour Congress' Corporatist Initiative, 1976–1978," *Canadian Journal of Political Science* (September 1983).

30. Colin Campbell, *The Canadian Senate: A Lobby from Within* (Toronto: Methuen, 1983), and John McMenemy, "The Senate as an Instrument of Business and Party," in Paul Fox and Graham White, eds., *Politics: Canada*, 7th ed. (Toronto: McGraw-Hill Ryerson, 1991). See also David McInnes, *Taking It to the Hill: The Complete Guide to Appearing before Parliamentary Committees*, 2nd ed. (Ottawa: University of Ottawa Press, 2006).

31. Miriam Smith, *Lesbian and Gay Rights in Canada: Social Movements and Equality-Seeking, 1971–1995* (Toronto: University of Toronto Press, 1999); Young and Everitt, *Advocacy Groups*, pp. 112–15; and Smith, "Interest Groups," p. 225.

32. Brooks and Stritch, *Business and Government in Canada*, pp. 260–64; Stanbury, *Business–Government Relations in Canada*, ch. 12; and Smith, "Interest Groups," p. 226.

33. Young and Everitt, *Advocacy Groups*, pp. 195–11; and Smith, "Interest Groups," p. 222.

34. Young and Everitt, *Advocacy Groups*, pp. 115–21; and Smith, "Interest Groups," p. 220.

35. Smith, "Interest Groups," pp. 226–28.

36. Young and Everitt, *Advocacy Groups*, pp. 131–32.

37. Peter C. Newman, *Titans: How the New Canadian Establishment Seized Power* (Toronto: Penguin, 1998), pp. 154–62.

38. Young and Everitt, *Advocacy Groups*, pp. 133–34.
39. David Camfield, "The Working-Class Movement in Canada: An Overview," and Charlotte Yates, "Organized Labour in Canadian Politics: Hugging the Middle or Pushing the Margins?" in Smith, *Group Politics and Social Movements in Canada*.
40. The Canadian Chamber of Commerce, "Action Call," 1990.
41. Young and Everitt, *Advocacy Groups*, pp. 47–51.
42. John A. Chenier and Scott R. Duncan, eds., *The Federal Lobbyists, 1999* (Ottawa: ARC Publications, 1999), pp. 225–29; and Russell Alan Williams, "Mergers If Necessary, but Not Necessarily Mergers: Competition and Consolidation at Canada's 'Big Banks,'" in Robert M. Campbell, Leslie A. Pal, and Michael Howlett, eds., *The Real Worlds of Canadian Politics*, 4th ed. (Peterborough: Broadview Press, 2004).
43. Malcolm Taylor, "The Role of the Medical Profession in the Formulation of Public Policy," *Canadian Journal of Economics and Political Science* (February, 1960).
44. Young and Everitt, *Advocacy Groups*, pp. 135–136; Hale, *The Uneasy Partnership: Politics of Business and Government in Canada*; and pretty well every other source cited in this chapter.
45. Peter Aucoin, "Organizational Change in the Machinery of Canadian Government: From Rational Management to Brokerage Politics," *Canadian Journal of Political Science* (March 1986).
46. Brooks and Stritch, *Business and Government in Canada*, ch. 4; and Craig Forcese and Aaron Freeman, *The Laws of Government: The Legal Foundations of Canadian Democracy* (Toronto: Irwin Law, 2005), ch. 8.
47. Ian Greene, "Conflict of Interest and the Canadian Constitution: An Analysis of Conflict of Interest Rules for Canadian Cabinet Ministers," *Canadian Journal of Political Science* (June 1990).
48. Brooks and Stritch, *Business and Government in Canada*, p. 240; and John Sawatsky, *The Insiders: Government, Business, and the Lobbyists* (Toronto: McClelland and Stewart, 1987), Epilogue.
49. Sawatsky, *The Insiders*, pp. 315–16.
50. Lobbyists Registration Branch website, "A Guide to Registration"; cited on September 23, 2006; available at http://www.strategis.ic.gc.ca/epic/internet/inlobbyist-lobbyiste.nsf/en/home.
51. Ibid.
52. John A. Chenier, ed., *The Federal Lobbyists, 1995* (Ottawa: ARC Publications, 1995), p. ii; and Forcese and Freeman, *The Laws of Government*, p. 465.
53. *The Globe and Mail*, March 12, 2001.
54. Democracy Watch, "The System is the Scandal," press release issued on April 14, 2005, as well as press releases of November 22, 2004 and August 18, 2005, which can be found on the Democracy Watch website at http://www.dwatch.ca; Forcese and Freeman, *The Laws of Government*, ch. 8.
55. Office of the Commissioner of Lobbying of Canada, http://ocl-cal.gc.ca/eic/site/lobbyist-lobbyiste1.nsf/eng/h_nx00274.html.
56. *The Hill Times*, "The Top 100 Lobbyists," February 16, 2009.
57. Young and Everitt, *Advocacy Groups*, pp. 82–86.
58. Office of the Commissioner of Lobbying of Canada, http://ocl-cal.gc.ca/eic/site/lobbyist-lobbyiste1.nsf/eng/home.
59. Smith, "Interest Groups and Social Movements," 7th edition, pp. 170–71.
60. Coleman and Skogstad, *Policy Communities and Public Policy in Canada*, p. 6.
61. Leo Panitch, ed., *The Canadian State: Political Economy and Political Power* (Toronto: University of Toronto Press, 1977), p. 14.
62. Ralph Miliband, *The State in Capitalist Society* (London: Quartet Books, 1973), p. 55.
63. Brooks and Stritch, *Business and Government in Canada*, ch. 1; and Coleman, *Business and Politics*, ch. 1.
64. Newman, *Titans*, pp. 154–62.
65. Smith, "Interest Groups and Social Movements," 7th ed., pp. 181–82.

· ·

FURTHER READING

Ayers, Jeffrey M. *Defying Conventional Wisdom: Political Movements and Popular Contention against North American Free Trade*. Toronto: University of Toronto Press, 1998.

Brock, Kathy, ed. *Delicate Dances: Government and the Nonprofit Sector in Canada*. Montreal: McGill-Queen's University Press, 2003.

Carroll, William K., ed. *Organizing Dissent: Contemporary Social Movements in Theory and Practice*, 2nd ed. Toronto: Garamond Press, 1997.

Coleman, William, and Grace Skogstad. *Policy Communities and Public Policy in Canada*. Mississauga: Copp Clark Pitman, 1990.

Democracy Watch. Periodic press releases.

Forcese, Craig, and Aaron Freeman. *The Laws of Government: The Legal Foundations of Canadian Democracy*. Toronto: Irwin Law, 2005.

Hale, Geoffrey. *The Uneasy Partnership: Politics of Business and Government in Canada*. Peterborough: Broadview Press, 2006.

Howlett, Michael, and M. Ramesh. *The Political Economy of Canada: An Introduction*. Toronto: McClelland and Stewart, 1992.

James, Matt. *Misrecognized Materialists: Social Movements in Canadian Constitutional Politics*. Vancouver: UBC Press, 2006.

The Lobby Monitor. Ottawa: ARC Publications, biweekly.

McInnes, David. *Taking It to the Hill: The Complete Guide to Appearing before Parliamentary Committees*, 2nd ed. Ottawa: University of Ottawa Press, 2006.

Newman, Peter C. *Titans: How the New Canadian Establishment Seized Power*. Toronto: Penguin, 1998.

Pal, Leslie A. *Interests of State: The Politics of Language, Multiculturalism, and Feminism in Canada*. Montreal: McGill-Queen's University Press, 1993.

———. *Beyond Policy Analysis: Public Issue Management in Turbulent Times*, 4th ed. Toronto: Nelson Education, 2010.

Phillips, Susan D. "Interest Groups, Social Movements, and the Voluntary Sector: En Route to Reducing the Democratic Deficit." In James Bickerton and Alain-G. Gagnon, eds., *Canadian Politics*, 4th ed. Peterborough: Broadview Press, 2004.

Sawatsky, John. *The Insiders: Power, Money and Secrets in Ottawa*. Toronto: McClelland and Stewart, 1987.

Smith, Miriam. *A Civil Society? Collective Actors in Canadian Political Life*. Peterborough: Broadview Press, 2005.

———. ed. *Group Politics and Social Movements in Canada*. Peterborough: Broadview Press, 2008.

———. "Interest Groups and Social Movements." In Michael Whittington and Glen Williams, eds., *Canadian Politics in the 21st Century*, 7th ed. Toronto: Nelson Education, 2008.

Young, Lisa, and Joanna Everitt. *Advocacy Groups*. Vancouver: UBC Press, 2004.

PART 4

The Constitutional Context

The constitutional context of Canadian government and politics forms the framework of the "government" part of the political system. In this analysis, Part 4 picks up from Chapter 2 but goes into much greater depth. Chapter 17 discusses the Canadian Constitution in general and the succession of attempts to make major changes to it. One of the most important parts of the Constitution is the relationship between the different levels of government, and Chapter 18 examines all aspects of Canadian federalism. The other central feature of the Constitution since 1982 is the Charter of Rights and Freedoms. Chapter 19 reveals how it has been interpreted and how it has affected the operation of the whole Canadian political system.

Chapter 17

The Canadian
CONSTITUTION AND
Constitutional Change

What is the Canadian Constitution? What are its principal parts? What process should be used to amend it? Should the division of powers between Ottawa and the provinces be altered? Should Quebec be granted constitutional recognition as a distinct society? Should the Constitution be given a new, inspiring preamble? These and related constitutional questions have obsessed Canadian policymakers and scholars for years, yet many remain unresolved. Canada has gone through several attempts at constitutional review since 1960, but most of the issues involved spilled over into this century.

The Canadian Constitution would be easier to comprehend if it consisted of a single piece of paper by that name. In the absence of such a document, we can define a **constitution** as the whole body of fundamental rules and principles according to which a state is governed. To be more specific, the Constitution provides for the basic institutions of government and the relations among them, the relations between national and provincial governments, and the relations between governments and citizens.[1] In other words, the constitution provides the basic framework for the operation of the whole political system. Such a comprehensive definition suggests that the final product will not be neat and tidy and that some of its ingredients may not be written down at all.

This chapter begins by examining the ingredients of the Canadian Constitution and then considers successive attempts at constitutional change. The latter include the search for a domestic amending formula, the quest for a constitutional Charter of Rights, and the pressures for constitutional change arising from the Quiet Revolution in Quebec, especially the Constitution Act, 1982, the 1987 Meech Lake Accord, the 1992 Charlottetown Accord, and post-Charlottetown developments, all attempting to resolve the "Quebec problem."

COMPONENTS OF THE CANADIAN CONSTITUTION

In the search for the components that fit the definition of a constitution provided above, it will be seen that the Canadian Constitution is a great hodgepodge. Unlike the United States and many other countries, Canada does not have a single document called "the Constitution."

Instead, some parts of it are written and other parts are unwritten. The principal components of the Canadian Constitution are as follows:

- the Constitution Act, 1867
- formal amendments to the Constitution Act, 1867
- British statutes and orders in council
- organic Canadian statutes
- the Constitution Act, 1982
- judicial decisions
- constitutional conventions

The Constitution Act, 1867

We turn first to the formal, legal documents, the most important of which is the **British North America (BNA) Act, 1867,** which in 1982 was officially renamed the **Constitution Act, 1867.**[2] This was the law passed by the British Parliament that joined Nova Scotia, New Brunswick, Ontario, and Quebec together as the new Dominion of Canada, as mentioned in Chapter 2. The act contained many components that would be expected in a constitution, providing for much of the basic machinery and institutions of government and establishing a federal system.

The act lacks an inspirational introduction, and its preamble is seriously out of date. It merely states that the four original provinces have expressed their desire "to be federally united with a constitution similar in principle to that of the United Kingdom." Many of the subsequent 147 clauses are also obsolete, and several have actually been repealed. Box 17.1 illustrates its main provisions.

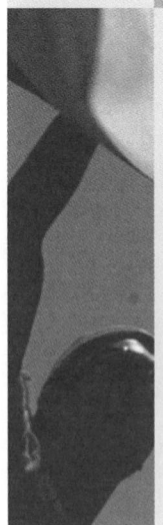

BOX 17.1	Main Provisions of the Constitution Act, 1867

Part III: Executive Power: Queen, Governor General, and Canadian Privy Council. Note that the Prime Minister and Cabinet are not explicitly mentioned.

Part IV: Legislative Power: Senate and House of Commons

Part V: Provincial Constitutions: Lieutenant Governor; Ontario and Quebec legislatures. This part is especially sketchy.

Part VI: Distribution of Legislative Powers: s. 91, federal powers; s. 92, provincial powers; s. 93, education; s. 95, concurrent powers.

Part VII: Judicature: s. 96, federal appointment of superior court judges; Parliament may set up a general court of appeal, but note that the Supreme Court of Canada is not explicitly established.

Part VIII: Revenues, debts, assets, and taxation, including provincial possession of their own public lands

Part IX: Miscellaneous: s. 132, treaty power; s. 133, official languages

Part X: Admission of other Colonies

The Constitution Act, 1867 was thus very brief on the executive and judicial branches of government, and it included virtually nothing about limiting the powers of government in relation to the people. The act also lacked any mention of the means to amend the act, but since it was a statute of the British Parliament, most formal changes have been made by the British Parliament at Canadian request.

Amendments to the Constitution Act, 1867

Formal amendments to the 1867 act are indeed the second ingredient of the Canadian Constitution. Schedule I to the Constitution Act, 1982, lists 17 amendments to the 1867 act made by the British Parliament and another eight made by the Canadian Parliament. The former were often termed "British North America Acts" of whatever year in which they were passed, but in 1982, they were mostly renamed "Constitution Act" of the appropriate year. The most important of the 17 British amendments to the 1867 Act are as follows:

- Constitution Act, 1907: established a new regime of federal–provincial grants
- Constitution Act, 1915: established a new distribution of Senate seats
- Constitution Act, 1930: transferred ownership of natural resources to Western provinces
- Constitution Act, 1940: added unemployment insurance to the list of federal powers
- Newfoundland Act, 1949: joined that province to Canada
- Constitution Act, 1951: allowed Ottawa to legislate with respect to old age pensions
- Constitution Act, 1960: made it mandatory for provincial superior court judges to retire at age 75
- Constitution Act, 1964: extended federal power in the concurrent field of old age pensions

British Statutes and Orders in Council

The third major component of the Canadian Constitution is a collection of British statutes and orders in council. Chief among these is the **Statute of Westminster**, 1931, which declared Canada to be totally independent of Britain. Then there were four main British orders in council—that is, decisions of the British Cabinet—that added the Northwest Territories, British Columbia, and Prince Edward Island to Canada. These, along with the 1949 amendment that incorporated Newfoundland and Labrador, completed the territorial dimensions of what we now know as Canada and are included in the Constitution for that reason. These are as follows:

- Rupert's Land and North-Western Territory Order, 1870: transferred Hudson's Bay Company lands to Canada
- British Columbia Terms of Union, 1871: joined that province to Canada
- Prince Edward Island Terms of Union, 1873: joined that province to Canada
- Adjacent Territories Order, 1880: added Arctic Islands to Canada

Organic Canadian Statutes

"Organic" Canadian statutes are laws passed by the Parliament of Canada that are of special or quasi-constitutional status. To start with, these would include the Canadian statutes that carved provinces out of the Northwest Territories: the Manitoba Act of 1870 and the Saskatchewan and Alberta Acts of 1905. Most observers would also include many other Canadian laws of constitutional significance, including the Supreme Court Act, an ordinary law that fleshes out the provisions of the 1867 act with respect to the judicial branch of government, along with the Federal Court Act, the Parliament of Canada Act, the Bill of Rights, the Canada Elections Act, the Indian Act, the Citizenship Act, the Emergencies Act, the Canadian Human Rights Act, the Yukon Act, the Nunavut Act, and the Constitutional Amendments Act. Where to stop in formulating such a list is not clear.

Constitution Act, 1982

The **Constitution Act, 1982** was, in a sense, the last amendment to the 1867 Constitution Act to be passed by the British Parliament, but it is worthy of separate mention. Although Canada was completely self-governing after 1931, many amendments to the 1867 act still had to be made by the British Parliament because no formula had been developed to do so in Canada. The Constitution Act, 1982 contained such a domestic constitution-amending formula. That Canadian statute was appendixed to the **Canada Act**, passed by the British Parliament, and finally terminated all British authority over Canada.[3] As noted in Chapter 21, however, the constitutional documents of 1982 did not alter the position of the monarchy in Canada. The same person continues to be recognized as Queen of Canada as is claimed by several other countries, including Britain.

THE CANADIAN PRESS/Ron Poling

Queen Elizabeth signs Canada's constitutional proclamation in Ottawa on April 17, 1982, as Prime Minister Pierre Trudeau looks on.

The second main aspect of the Constitution Act, 1982 was the **Charter of Rights and Freedoms**. The Charter guaranteed fundamental, democratic, legal, egalitarian, and linguistic rights and freedoms against government intrusion. In other words, the Charter of Rights and Freedoms imposed formal new limitations on the government in interaction with its citizens. In addition, it changed the manner in which such civil liberties were protected, now relying more on judicial interpretation than parliamentary restraint. The Charter is examined in depth in Chapter 19.

The 1982 act also contained statements on equalization payments to have-not provinces, multiculturalism, and Aboriginal rights. As far as the division of powers was concerned, a new section, 92A, was added that clarified and extended provincial powers over natural resources.

According to the Constitution Act, 1982, the Constitution of Canada consists of the British statutes and orders in council and some of the Canadian statutes mentioned above. These formal, legal documents make up the Constitution in the narrow sense of being subject to the constitutional amending formula adopted in 1982. Important as they are, these documents are silent on so many vital aspects of the fundamental rules and principles according to which Canada is governed that they cannot possibly constitute the entirety of the Canadian Constitution. Most authorities would therefore cast a much wider net in selecting the ingredients of the Constitution in its broader sense.

Judicial Decisions

The definition of the constitution must also include judicial decisions that have clarified or altered provisions of the 1867 act or other parts of the Constitution. The largest body of such decisions consists of the judgments of the British **Judicial Committee of the Privy Council (JCPC)**, Canada's final court of appeal until 1949, which significantly affected the division of powers between the federal and provincial governments. As mentioned in Chapter 18 on Canadian federalism, it was John A. Macdonald's intention to create a strong central government, but the Judicial Committee interpreted the 1867 act in such a way as to minimize federal powers and maximize those of the provinces. The court decisions that effected such a wholesale transformation of the federal nature of the country have to be considered part of the Constitution alongside the actual provisions of the original act.

A few early court decisions also imposed restrictions on government power vis-à-vis its citizens—that is, in the area of rights and freedoms—and many such decisions have been made since the Charter of Rights was adopted in 1982. These "rights and freedoms" decisions are part of the Constitution, along with the "division of powers" decisions mentioned.

Constitutional Conventions

Thus far, each of the ingredients listed can actually be found in written form, however difficult it would be to collect them all together. The final component of the Constitution, however, has never been confined to writing. It consists of **constitutional conventions**, defined as unwritten rules of constitutional behaviour that are considered to be binding by and on those who operate the Constitution but that are not enforceable by the courts.[4] Conventions develop from traditions and through constant recognition and observance become as established, rigid, and sacrosanct as if they were written down. Many of these informal rules have been inherited from Britain, some have been modified in the Canadian environment, and others are unique to Canada. Some conventions may be recognized by judges even if they cannot be enforced by the courts. But, as in Britain, conventions are no less real for remaining in an unwritten form, and many are among the most important parts of the Canadian constitution. As Peter Hogg writes, "[w]hat conventions do is prescribe the way in which legal powers shall be exercised. Some conventions have the effect of transferring effective power from the legal holder to another official or institution. Other conventions limit an apparently broad legal power, or even prescribe that a legal power shall not be exercised at all."[5] Many constitutional conventions, for example, relate to the executive branch of government, which is given slight attention in the 1867 act. These include the very position of prime minister and Cabinet, their dominant role even when the written words give formal powers to the governor general, and the principle of responsible government—that the Cabinet must resign or call an election if it loses the confidence of the House of Commons. Others will be discussed at relevant points in subject chapters.

It should be added that some actions that are *legal* according to the formal written words of the constitution may actually be *unconstitutional* if they violate a convention that has superseded a written power. An example would be the power of the governor general to withhold assent from a piece of legislation. But if the courts cannot enforce conventions, why are they consistently obeyed? Hogg replies that breach of a convention would result in "serious political repercussions"—dismissal, defeat, disgrace—and eventually to changes in the law so that it would not happen again.

The Constitution of Canada, therefore, is a rather complex phenomenon. It has two central documents—the Constitution Act, 1867 with its amendments, and the Constitution Act, 1982; it contains other written documents, including other British statutes and orders in council, Canadian statutes, and British and Canadian court decisions; and, in its unwritten part, it incorporates a whole series of constitutional conventions that fill in gaps or alter the way in which written provisions are implemented. For better or worse, the widest definition of a constitution requires the inclusion of all these components. Many observers would prefer a neater Constitution; some want it to be updated; and others would like it to be more inspirational so that it could function more satisfactorily as a symbol of unity. Thus far, however, attempts to recast the Canadian Constitution in any of these ways have foundered.

. . . .

THE QUEST FOR CONSTITUTIONAL CHANGE

Constitutional change has almost always been on the Canadian political agenda. In the early years of Confederation, one principal concern involved completing the territorial integrity of Canada with the eventual creation of ten provinces and now three territories. Another early constitutional issue was achieving autonomy from Britain by means of the Statute of Westminster, along with the abolition of court appeals to the Judicial Committee of the Privy Council. Two other persistent constitutional questions also arose before 1960: the search for a formula by which the 1867 act and the Constitution generally could be formally amended in Canada, and the proposal that rights and freedoms or civil liberties be given constitutional protection. These two issues then became enmeshed in constitutional demands inspired by the **Quiet Revolution** in Quebec. The simultaneous consideration of many large constitutional issues—amending formula, charter of rights, division of powers, institutional change, status of Quebec, and later Aboriginals—has acquired the label of "mega-constitutional change." The four key packages of constitutional changes were the 1970 Victoria Charter, the Constitution Act, 1982, the 1987 Meech Lake Accord, and the 1992 Charlottetown Accord. Of these four documents, only one was ultimately adopted, and many constitutional issues remain unresolved. Some of these developments were previously raised in Chapter 5 on French Canada and Quebec.

A Domestic Constitutional Amending Formula

As the final thrust toward full Canadian independence took place after the Balfour Declaration of 1926, it became clear that Canadians would have to find a way to amend the 1867 act in Canada. For the next 55 years, federal and provincial governments wrestled with the problem without being able to agree on an acceptable balance between rigidity and flexibility: a constitution should not be too easy to amend, but neither should it be impossible.

Attempts to find a domestic **constitutional amending formula** began in 1927, but since no success was achieved before 1931, the Statute of Westminster contained a clause allowing the British Parliament to amend the 1867 act at Canadian request. Further attempts were made in 1935–36, and in 1949 a partial domestic amending formula was adopted that became the BNA Act Amendment (#1) of 1949. That act added a clause to section 91 to the effect that in matters of concern to the national government alone, the federal Parliament could make constitutional amendments in Canada, without reference either to the provinces or to Britain. However, five exceptions remained, the most important being that any amendment affecting the provinces would still have to be made by the British Parliament. The basic question was whether such amendments should first require the unanimous approval of the provincial governments. This was the position taken by virtually every government of Quebec in order to protect its rights and powers and is referred to as the "compact theory" of Confederation. In this view, Confederation was a compact among the provincial signatories, such that no part of it could be changed without unanimous provincial consent. Many other provinces also came to support this theory, even though it was of dubious legal standing and was ultimately rejected by the Supreme Court of Canada.

In the absence of a resolution of this problem, a constitutional convention developed such that the federal government would not request an amendment to the federal–provincial division of powers without the unanimous consent of the provinces. Thus, in the case of the amendments in 1940, 1951, 1960, and 1964, Ottawa did not ask Britain to act until it had obtained the agreement of all the provinces.[6]

Further attempts to find a complete domestic formula were made around 1950 and 1960, and federal–provincial agreement was reached on the Fulton–Favreau formula in 1964. It provided that unanimous federal and provincial consent be required for changes to the division of powers (ss. 91, 92, and 93) and language provisions (s. 133), but on other matters affecting the whole country, the agreement of the federal government plus two-thirds of the provinces representing at least 50 percent of the population would be sufficient. After having agreed to this formula, the Jean Lesage government of Quebec rescinded its approval—ironically now fearing that the unanimity requirement would prevent making certain changes that Quebec wanted—and the formula died.

As discussed above, a domestic constitutional amending formula was finally adopted as part of the Constitution Act, 1982. Part V of the act actually provided for five such formulas, depending on the subject matter of the amendment:

1. unanimous consent of federal and provincial legislatures
2. consent of Parliament and seven provincial legislatures representing at least 50 percent of the population
3. consent of Parliament and one or more provinces affected
4. consent of Parliament alone
5. consent of a provincial legislature alone

The essence of these five formulas is presented in Box 17.2.

In general, the rigidity and opting-out provisions of the 1982 amending formula were considered a victory for the provinces and a trade-off for accepting the federal government's Charter of Rights.[7] The formula required that the federal Parliament and provincial *legislatures*

BOX 17.2	Canada's Constitutional Amending Formulas, 1982

1. Section 41 requires unanimous federal and provincial consent to amend any of the following items:

   (a) the office of the Queen, the Governor General and the Lieutenant Governor of a province;

   (b) the right of a province to a number of members in the House of Commons not less than [its] number of Senators ...;

   (c) the use of the English or the French language [at the federal level];

   (d) the composition of the Supreme Court of Canada; and

   (e) changes to this list of subjects requiring unanimous consent.

2. Section 38, dealing with other matters affecting both levels of government, requires the approval of the federal Parliament and the legislatures of two-thirds of the provinces representing at least 50 percent of the Canadian population. However, no amendment that reduces provincial powers, rights, or privileges can affect a province that does not agree to it. Section 39 provides that if such an amendment relates to education or culture, Canada must provide compensation to any province to which the amendment does not apply. Thus, if nine provinces and the federal government agreed to transfer education from provincial to federal jurisdiction, Ottawa must pay compensation to the province that continues to operate its own education system.

   For greater clarity, section 42 lists certain subjects to which the two-thirds and 50 percent formula applies, including:

   (a) the principle of proportionate representation of the provinces in the House of Commons;

(b) the powers of the Senate and the method of selecting Senators;

(c) the number of members by which a province is entitled to be represented in the Senate and the residence qualifications of Senators;

(d) the Supreme Court of Canada [other than its composition];

(e) the extension of existing provinces into the territories; and

(f) the establishment of new provinces.

3. Section 43 stipulates that constitutional matters applying to one or more but not all provinces, including boundary alterations and changes to the use of the English or French languages within a province, can be amended with the approval of the federal Parliament and the legislative assembly of each province to which the amendment applies.

4. Section 44 provides that constitutional provisions relating to the executive government of Canada or the Senate and House of Commons can be amended by the federal Parliament alone. This was previously the situation according to the partial amending formula adopted in 1949 and allowed that clause to be repealed.

5. Section 45 states that each province can amend its own constitution in matters not affecting any other jurisdiction (or the position of lieutenant governor), as had previously been the case.

approve such amendments, not just *cabinets*, as had often sufficed in the past. This innovation had later implications for the Meech Lake Accord, for although it was initially adopted by all ten provincial *premiers*, it ran into trouble when it came before certain provincial *legislatures*. The formula also allows constitutional amendments to be made without the consent of the Senate if they are adopted a second time by the House of Commons after 180 days. Thus, the 1982 amending formula was not a simple one and was not designed to approve amendments easily. It did, however, put an end to requests to the British Parliament to make Canadian constitutional amendments on our behalf.

A Constitutional Charter of Rights

Given the lack of a constitutional charter of rights in Britain and that country's generally respectable record of protecting civil liberties, based on parliamentary restraint, the common law, public opinion, and political culture, Canadians were not originally concerned about the absence of a bill of rights in their Constitution. It was only after witnessing federal mistreatment of Japanese Canadians in the Second World War; provincial discrimination against Asians (BC) and Jehovah's Witnesses and political dissidents (Quebec); and violations of freedom of the press (Alberta) that some Canadians began to advocate a constitutional bill of rights. One person who felt very strongly about this question was John Diefenbaker, and when he became prime minister he had Parliament pass a Bill of Rights in 1960. The bill had major structural weaknesses, however. Such deficiencies led many observers to recommend constitutionalizing the bill, which was part of the rationale for the adoption of the Charter of Rights and Freedoms, as part of the Constitution Act, 1982, which is discussed in detail in Chapter 19.

The Quiet Revolution in Quebec

The unresolved issues of a domestic amending formula and a constitutional charter of rights then became part of the third main thrust of change, which emanated from the Quiet Revolution in Quebec. This was primarily related to Quebec's place in the Canadian federation as well as to the general division of powers between the two levels of government. Such demands for mega-constitutional change dominated Canadian politics for more than 45 years,[8] and to some extent, they still threaten the continued existence of the country as we know it. The accompanying timeline lists the significant constitutional developments over the period 1960–2010.

. . . .

MEGA-CONSTITUTIONAL DEVELOPMENTS, 1960–2010

1. Quiet Revolution in Quebec, 1960–66
2. Confederation of Tomorrow Conference, 1967
3. Federal–provincial constitutional conferences, 1968–71
4. Victoria Charter, June 1971
5. Trudeau's proposal for patriation and amending formula, 1975–76
6. Election of Parti Québécois, 1976
7. Trudeau's Bill C-60, Phase I, 1978
8. Federal–provincial conferences, October 1978 and February 1979
9. Task Force on Canadian Unity, January 1979
10. René Lévesque's sovereignty-association proposal, November 1979
11. Quebec referendum, May 1980
12. Federal–provincial constitutional conferences, June and September 1980
13. Federal unilateral package, October 1980
14. Supreme Court decision on unilateral package, September 1981
15. Federal–provincial conference, November 1981
16. Proclamation of Constitution Act, 1982, April 17, 1982
17. Bourassa government's five demands, 1985
18. Meech Lake conferences, April and June 1987
19. Legislative ratification of Meech Lake Accord, 1987–90
20. Federal–Provincial Conference on Meech Lake Accord, May 1990
21. Death of Meech Lake Accord, June 1990
22. Allaire and Bélanger–Campeau Reports, 1991
23. Citizens' Forum, November 1990–June 1991

24. New federal constitutional reform package, September 1991

25. Dobbie–Beaudoin Committee, February 1992

26. Federal–provincial–territorial–Aboriginal negotiations, April–August 1992

27. Charlottetown Accord, August 1992

28. National referendum, October 26, 1992

29. Election of PQ government in Quebec, 1994

30. Quebec referendum on sovereignty, October 30, 1995

31. Calgary Declaration, September 1997

32. Supreme Court decision on unilateral declaration of independence, August 1998

33. Social Union Framework Agreement, 1999

34. Clarity Act, 2000

35. Quebec response, 2000

The Victoria Charter

As noted in Chapters 5 and 18, many of Quebec's demands could be and were addressed by bureaucratic, legislative, and judicial decisions at the federal level, in Quebec, or in other provinces, and did not require formal constitutional changes. By the end of the 1960s, however, the government of Quebec was demanding changes of a constitutional nature, demands often echoed by certain other provinces. Following the Confederation of Tomorrow Conference in 1967, a series of federal–provincial conferences over the 1968–71 period led to agreement on the Victoria Charter in June 1971.

The **Victoria Charter** contained a constitutional amending formula and a constitutionalized bill of rights, provided for provincial consultation on Supreme Court appointments, guaranteed equalization payments to redress regional disparities, and represented some progress on changes to language rights and to the federal–provincial division of powers. But after endorsing the document in Victoria, Quebec's Bourassa government changed its mind; in responding to nationalist public opinion in the province, it vetoed the package because Quebec had not received sufficient additional powers in the field of social policy.

The Constitution Act, 1982

The 1970s and early 1980s thus saw a constitutional tug-of-war between Ottawa and Quebec, with the other provinces arrayed in between, over the amending formula, the Charter of Rights, the Supreme Court, the Senate, language rights, and the division of powers. As noted in Chapter 5, the Trudeau strategy continued to be based on the constitutionalization of the Official Languages Act and the extension of French-language services from coast to coast to coast in order to undermine Quebec's claim to be linguistically distinctive and therefore to require additional powers.[9] Increasingly, Trudeau had to fight the other provinces, too, as most of them also demanded greater decentralization.

After the collapse of the Victoria Charter, Trudeau tried a number of devices to pre-empt the election of a separatist government in Quebec and, after its success in 1976, to convince

Quebeckers to follow his lead instead. The Pépin–Robarts Task Force on Canadian Unity might have been a fruitful basis on which to approach the problem, but because its recommendations differed from Trudeau's own principles of centralization, symmetrical federalism, and national bilingualism, he immediately dismissed them. In May 1980, four years after its election, the Parti Québécois government asked the people of Quebec for a mandate to negotiate **sovereignty-association** with the federal government—that is, Quebec would be a sovereign state but with continued economic links to the rest of Canada. Trudeau and other federal ministers entered the referendum campaign, promising that if Quebeckers turned down the PQ plan, Ottawa would initiate a process of constitutional renewal. When Quebec rejected Lévesque's proposal by a margin of 60 percent to 40 percent, Trudeau immediately embarked on a new round of federal–provincial constitutional discussions.

By October 1980, however, Trudeau abruptly gave up on trying to reach federal–provincial agreement and issued his own package of constitutional reform proposals, which he intended to have adopted by the British Parliament without provincial consent. This package was particularly provocative to the Quebec government and a large proportion of Quebeckers because it reflected Trudeau's vision rather than the kind of constitutional reform—a distinct status and increased powers for Quebec—that they assumed he had promised in the referendum debate. Many observers feel that Trudeau misled Quebeckers in the speeches he made in the 1980 referendum campaign.[10]

Upset at both the substantive and the procedural aspects of the Trudeau initiative, several other provinces also challenged it in the courts. In one of its most famous decisions, the

André-Philippe Côté (Le Soleil). Reproduced with permission.

Supreme Court of Canada ruled that nothing in *law* prevented the federal government from unilaterally requesting that such an amendment be made by Britain. However, it agreed with the dissenting provinces that unilateral federal action would violate the constitutional *convention* that provincial consent should be secured beforehand. In a rare example of judicial recognition of conventions, the Court went on to interpret the convention as requiring a "substantial degree of provincial consent" but not necessarily unanimity. A majority of the Court argued that the federal nature of Canada would be greatly changed if Ottawa could unilaterally alter the powers of the provincial governments in this way.[11]

Meanwhile, Trudeau's package had been subject to Parliamentary hearings in which a multitude of interest groups presented briefs to support and/or strengthen the document, as the Charter of Rights section became particularly popular. The governments of Ontario and New Brunswick had always supported it, and the addition of s. 92A giving the provinces enhanced jurisdiction over natural resources brought the federal NDP onside. Nevertheless, the Supreme Court decision prompted Trudeau to sit down with the premiers again and they engaged in three days and nights of tough negotiations in November 1981. The constitutional amending formula was a major stumbling block (with an alternative referendum proposal discussed), and Quebec insisted that it receive financial compensation if it opted out of any federal programs. Several provinces, principally Alberta, Saskatchewan, and Manitoba, disliked the Charter, especially in that it would give additional powers to the courts. This impasse was broken with the addition of the innovative notwithstanding clause, which allowed governments to pass a law in violation of certain Charter rights for a maximum five-year period, although disagreement continued over which parts of the Charter would be subject to it. Although other provinces had sided with Quebec's objections on various issues throughout the week, when René Lévesque went to sleep on November 4, the other nine provinces continued negotiations with the federal government during "the night of the long knives." Lévesque arose to find that the others had come up with compromises on all sides to reach a consensus, which, according to the Supreme Court, did not require unanimous consent. He was outraged, expressed his dissent, and stormed back home, the great irony being that Quebec had been the inspiration behind the whole exercise in the first place. The amended package was passed by Parliament, approved by the British Parliament as the Canada Act (1982), and signed by the Queen on April 17, 1982 on Parliament Hill.[12]

The act itself has already been extensively discussed. It contained a domestic constitutional amending formula and a Charter of Rights. It also included the constitutional entrenchment of equalization payments to have-not provinces and an amendment to the division of powers that enhanced provincial control over natural resources. The Charter essentially constitutionalized the federal and New Brunswick Official Languages Acts to guarantee the rights of official-language minorities to government services, trials, and so on. It also established the rights of official-language minorities to schools in their own language wherever numbers warranted. The clear objective of these provisions was to entrench official bilingualism across the country to the extent that Prime Minister Trudeau could persuade provincial premiers to do so. However, the Constitution Act, 1982, did not respond to any of the demands for constitutional change emanating from Quebec. It is not surprising that Quebec Premier René Lévesque refused to sign it, but it is doubtful that a federalist premier of that province would have reacted much differently.

The Quebec government sent a reference to the Supreme Court asking it to recognize that, by convention, Quebec had a veto on constitutional amendments, so that the Act was unconstitutional. The Court denied that Quebec ever had such a veto, even in conventional terms. Thus, the province was legally bound by the document in almost all respects. This imposition created much hostility within Quebec toward Trudeau, Justice Minister Jean Chrétien, the other provinces, and the Charter itself. Until the PQ government was defeated in 1985, it symbolically invoked the notwithstanding clause on every piece of legislation passed by the Quebec legislature.

The Meech Lake Accord

Although the 1982 act was operative in Quebec, when he became prime minister, Brian Mulroney was determined that Quebec should symbolically rejoin the Canadian constitutional family "with honour and enthusiasm." He therefore asked the new federalist Quebec premier, Robert Bourassa, to outline his conditions for such a reunion. The Quebec government proceeded to make five demands:

1. constitutional recognition of Quebec as a "distinct society" within Canada
2. a veto on constitutional amendments
3. increased jurisdiction over immigration
4. participation in Supreme Court appointments
5. financial compensation when Quebec opted out of national programs set up by Ottawa within provincial jurisdiction

After considerable preparation, Mulroney called the premiers together at Meech Lake in April 1987 and with surprising speed they agreed to a document that addressed Quebec's demands and became known as the **Meech Lake Accord**. The prime minister secured unanimous provincial consent by extending to the other provinces most of the same rights as were demanded by Quebec. The document also contained clauses that constitutionalized the Supreme Court of Canada, provided for provincial participation in Senate appointments, and guaranteed annual first ministers' conferences on the Constitution and on the economy.[13]

Despite the relative ease with which it was drafted, the Meech Lake Accord generated much controversy. On the negative side, many critics did not approve of the designation of Quebec as a distinct society within Canada and especially objected to the phrase that it was the role of the government and legislature of Quebec to "preserve and promote" that distinctiveness. No one was sure what implications the **distinct society** clause would have for the federal–provincial division of powers, leaving it for judicial clarification on an issue-by-issue basis. Some felt that in a federation all provinces had to have exactly equal status, and many argued that, armed with the distinct society clause, Quebec would immediately begin to challenge federal powers in a variety of fields. Others worried about the status of the anglophone and Aboriginal minorities within Quebec, as well as the francophone minorities in other provinces and territories, and some women's groups argued that the distinct society clause might be used to override the gender equality provisions of section 28 of the Charter of Rights and Freedoms.

A second objection to the accord was that it enlarged the list of subjects that required unanimous provincial consent in the constitutional amending formula, especially the list contained in section 42, such as changes to most aspects of the Senate and the creation of new provinces. Many critics felt that Senate reform and the transformation of the northern territories into provinces would be virtually impossible if such amendments required agreement of all ten provinces instead of only seven.

Objections to Quebec's expanded role in immigration and to provincial involvement in the nomination of judges to the Supreme Court of Canada were also raised by those opposed to increases in provincial power. But concerns expressed more vehemently related to the provision allowing provinces to opt out of national programs within provincial jurisdiction and be compensated by Ottawa. Fears were expressed that satisfactory new national social programs (such as a national daycare program) would never materialize because provinces would be compensated for programs that merely met national *objectives*, not national *standards*. Apart from criticizing what was in the accord, many opponents faulted it for what was left out. The North was not allowed to nominate senators or Supreme Court judges, Aboriginal rights were not strengthened, and multiculturalism was ignored.

Others condemned the process through which the accord had emerged—a behind-the-scenes gathering of (male) first ministers. In the post-Charter era, individual Canadians insisted on being part of the constitutional amendment process; moreover, the primacy of Quebec's concerns was rejected by those given constitutional standing by the Charter—women, Aboriginals, and members of multicultural and other minority groups.[14] The public now demanded more meaningful participation in the process of constitutional change.

The leading opponent of Meech Lake was former prime minister Pierre Trudeau, whose vision of a centralized, symmetrical, bilingual federation was at odds with the document. He was alarmed that it would give the provinces more power and recognize Quebec as a distinct society, acknowledging that French-speaking Canadians are centred in Quebec. On the other hand, many political scientists and other constitutional authorities to this day believe that the adoption of the Meech Lake Accord, to complement the Constitution Act, 1982, might have spared the country much of its constitutional anguish ever since.

According to the constitutional amending formula adopted in 1982, the accord then had to be approved by the federal and all provincial *legislatures* within three years—that is, before June 23, 1990.[15] In most cases such legislative approval came rather easily, but governments changed in New Brunswick and Manitoba before the accord could be ratified by the legislatures of those two provinces, and their new governments had reservations about the accord. In the case of Manitoba, the new Gary Filmon government was in a minority position, while the new Clyde Wells government in Newfoundland, seeing the issue in the same way as Trudeau, rescinded the approval that that province's legislature had previously given to the accord.

Thus, with three provinces left to ratify the accord, Prime Minister Mulroney convened a first ministers' conference in Ottawa in May 1990. After a week of protracted, behind-the-scenes negotiations, the participants emerged with a modest companion resolution, adapted to the satisfaction of Manitoba and New Brunswick. Still with his substantive and procedural reservations, Clyde Wells would only agree to put it before the Newfoundland legislature, not to endorse it. Amid a bitter public exchange between Wells and the federal government, the Newfoundland legislature did not vote on the accord a second time before the deadline. Meanwhile, the accord also ran into additional difficulty in the Manitoba legislature, where Aboriginal MLA Elijah Harper delayed passage beyond the deadline because of the absence of any advance for Aboriginal peoples.

THE CANADIAN PRESS/Chuck Mitchell

Prime Minister Brian Mulroney makes a pitch for the Meech Lake Accord in the House of Commons in June 1990.

The Charlottetown Accord

With the death of the Meech Lake Accord, most Quebeckers felt betrayed for a second time in ten years. Nationalist and separatist sentiment mushroomed over the next year or so as the Quebec Liberals and Parti Québécois issued new constitutional proposals. The Liberal position first appeared as the Allaire Report, which called for a highly decentralized federation in which Quebec and the other provinces would have almost all powers, including 22 new ones. According to the report, Quebec would insist on exercising its full sovereignty in the areas of jurisdiction already exclusive to it according to the present Constitution, notably social affairs, urban affairs, culture, education, housing, recreation, family policy, manpower policy, natural resources, health, and tourism. It would do the same in other fields that it somewhat dubiously claimed were currently either shared with Ottawa or not mentioned in the Constitution, such as agriculture, unemployment insurance, communications, regional development, energy, environment, language, research and development, and public security. Ottawa and Quebec would share jurisdiction over Aboriginal affairs, revenue and taxation, immigration, financial institutions, justice, fisheries, foreign policy, post office, telecommunications, and transportation, and the federal government would have exclusive power over only defence, customs and excise, and management of the national debt.

Representing both major parties as well as other interests in the province, Quebec's Bélanger–Campeau Committee report argued that unless a satisfactory proposal for a new constitutional arrangement was forthcoming from the rest of Canada, Quebec should separate. It therefore recommended that a referendum on Quebec sovereignty be held in 1992. Bélanger–Campeau anticipated that in the interim, the rest of Canada would offer Quebec some kind of new partnership, perhaps along the lines of the Allaire Report, so that Quebeckers would essentially have two alternatives before them when they cast their vote.

Responding to the criticism that the public had been shut out of the Meech Lake negotiations, the Mulroney government appointed the Citizens' Forum on Canada's Future in November 1990. Headed by Keith Spicer, it encouraged ordinary Canadians to discuss constitutional issues in a variety of settings and transmit their views to the committee. A large proportion of Canadians engaged in angry exchanges, the Constitution becoming a lightning rod for every conceivable grievance in the country. After listening to some 400 000 Canadians over an eight-month period, the forum's June 1991 report supported recognition of Quebec's distinctiveness, Aboriginal self-government, and settlement of Aboriginal land claims. However, the forum suggested that official bilingualism was a divisive issue and government funding for multiculturalism should be cut.

Meanwhile, in response to another problem central to the defeat of Meech Lake, the federal government set up a joint House of Commons–Senate Committee to study the constitutional amending formula. This Beaudoin–Edwards Committee also reported in June 1991 and endorsed a change in the formula that would restrict the requirement for unanimous provincial consent and replace it with regional vetoes, as well as allow national referendums on a new Constitution.

The prime minister appointed Joe Clark as the minister responsible for constitutional affairs and set up a special Cabinet committee on Canadian unity and constitutional negotiations. The committee agreed on a 28-point package of constitutional proposals in September 1991 called *Shaping Canada's Future Together*. Yet another joint Commons–Senate committee was set up to gather public reaction to the package and other reports on the subject. The government decided to supplement its hearings with a series of specialized public forums on specific constitutional issues, and the Dobbie–Beaudoin Committee on the Renewal of Canada issued its report in February 1992.

Meanwhile, Clark was persuaded to try to develop a collective federal–provincial– territorial–Aboriginal response to offer to Quebec before the looming referendum. After several rounds of negotiations, Clark, the nine premiers, the territorial first ministers, and the Aboriginal leaders all agreed on a comprehensive constitutional proposal in July. Quebec Premier Bourassa considered that it was promising enough to return to the bargaining table for the first time since the demise of the Meech Lake Accord, and a full-fledged constitutional conference took place in Ottawa in mid-August. After nearly a week of hard bargaining, the leaders unanimously signed a new constitutional accord on which they put the final touches in Charlottetown a week later.[16] **The Charlottetown Accord** had four main parts: the Canada clause, a Triple-E Senate, Aboriginal self-government, and changes to the division of powers, as indicated in Box 17.3.

BOX 17.3	Main Provisions of the Charlottetown Accord

Canada Clause: retained recognition of Quebec as a distinct society within Canada, as well as enumerating other fundamental values and characteristics of the country.

Triple-E Senate: each province would have six Senators (equal) and each territory, one. They would be elected, except in Quebec. Some Senate powers would be reduced, but others strengthened (effective). To compensate Ontario and Quebec for their loss of 18 senators each, these two provinces would be given 18 additional seats in the House of Commons, and Quebec was guaranteed a minimum of 25 percent of Commons seats in perpetuity.

Aboriginal Self-Government: the inherent right to Aboriginal self-government would be enshrined in the constitution, and Aboriginal governments would constitute a third order of government, analogous to the federal and provincial governments.

Division of Powers: retained the provisions of the Meech Lake Accord, but Ottawa offered to withdraw from many other fields.

Other: retained the provisions of the Meech Lake Accord with respect to the Supreme Court; changed the constitutional amending formula somewhat; and added a social charter to guarantee rights to health care, social services, and education; workers' rights; and protection for the environment.

The 1992 Referendum

Although supported by all those around the table, the accord would be of no effect until ratified by Parliament and the ten provincial legislatures. Before ratification, however, the federal government announced that a national **referendum** would be held on the new constitutional deal on October 26, 1992, the same date selected by Quebec for its constitutional referendum, now to be held on the Charlottetown Accord rather than on sovereignty. The decision to hold such a referendum was based on three main considerations: Alberta and BC laws required a referendum on constitutional amendments, so three provinces would be voting on the accord in any case; Meech Lake had been criticized for lack of public input; and public approval would lend legitimacy to the agreement and spur the 11 legislatures into speedy affirmative action.

On a national basis the referendum result was 55 percent no and 45 percent yes. As shown in Table 17.1, majorities voted no in Quebec, Nova Scotia, the four Western provinces, and Yukon. Even though the referendum was not legally binding, there was no point in bringing the constitutional package before legislatures for ratification: the Charlottetown Accord was dead.

Public opinion polls showed that rather than base their decision on the contents of the accord, as such, many people who voted "No" did so to vent their anger and frustration with

TABLE 17.1 Results of the National Referendum on the Charlottetown Accord (Percentages)		
	Yes	**No**
Newfoundland and Labrador	63.2	36.8
Prince Edward Island	73.9	26.1
Nova Scotia	48.8	51.2
New Brunswick	61.8	38.2
Quebec	43.3	56.7
Ontario	50.1	49.9
Manitoba	38.4	61.6
Saskatchewan	44.7	55.3
Alberta	39.8	60.2
British Columbia	31.7	68.3
Northwest Territories	61.3	38.7
Yukon	43.7	56.3
Total	45.0	55.0

Source: Elections Canada. Chief Electoral Officer of Canada, Referendum 92: Official Voting Results (Ottawa, 1992), Pg. 4.; Directeur general des elections du Quebec. Rapport des resultats officiels du scrutin - Referendum du 26 Octobre 1992 (Sainte-Foy, 1992), Pg. 49.

Prime Minister Mulroney, the premiers, politicians, and governments in general.[17] Such was the problem of holding the vote during a period of severe recession and at a time when respect for incumbent politicians was at an all-time low. Voters were not in a generous frame of mind, and rather than seeing the accord as a multi-sided compromise, they generally felt that it gave too much to others and not enough to themselves. Thus, the negative vote in Quebec was largely based on the view that the accord was a dilution of Meech Lake and did not give Quebec sufficient new powers, but many outside Quebec argued that that province got too much. Many Westerners did not see the proposed reforms to the Senate as sufficient protection of their interests in Ottawa, and many Aboriginal Canadians were dissatisfied with the provisions on self-government. Indeed, although the accord was primarily designed to address the constitutional insecurity of Quebec, Aboriginal Canadians, and Western and smaller provinces, a majority in all three groups believed that their elites had not bargained hard enough on their behalf. Pierre Trudeau and Reform Party leader Preston Manning were two of the leading opponents.

Post-Charlottetown Constitutional Developments

One year later, in 1993, the Chrétien Liberals were elected on the promise that they would concentrate on improving the economy and put constitutional issues aside. However, the Parti Québécois returned to power in Quebec in 1994 on the exact opposite platform—that it would move quickly to take Quebec out of Confederation. When the polls showed that Premier Jacques Parizeau could not persuade a majority of Quebec voters on the question of his choice—complete independence—he succumbed to the pressure of public opinion and from Bloc leader Lucien Bouchard and agreed to an extensive list of continuing links to Canada.[18] This seriously watered down proposal was ratified in an agreement between the PQ, the BQ, and Mario Dumont, leader of the small party Action Démocratique du Québec (ADQ). The legislature passed a bill setting the referendum date for October 30, 1995. The convoluted question put to the people of Quebec was as follows: "Do you agree that Quebec should become sovereign, after having made a formal offer to Canada for a new economic and political partnership, within the scope of the bill respecting the future of Quebec and of the agreement signed on June 12, 1995?"

The bill in question would allow a sovereign Quebec to use the Canadian dollar as its currency and its residents to retain concurrent citizenship and use Canadian passports. It anticipated the adoption of a new Quebec constitution and retention of Quebec's existing boundaries. The government of Quebec was then to propose a treaty of economic and political partnership with the rest of Canada. The treaty would set up a joint Council (executive), Secretariat (bureaucracy), Assembly (legislature), and Tribunal (court); establish rules for the division of assets and debt; and provide for the free movement of goods, individuals, services, and capital. If agreement with the rest of Canada on such a treaty was not achieved within a year, Quebec would unilaterally declare its sovereignty and expect recognition by other states, later claiming to have had secret support from France. It also anticipated continued membership in the North American Free Trade Agreement. Premier Parizeau virtually vacated the leadership of the "Yes" campaign when it became obvious that the cause had a chance only if the much more popular Bouchard became its effective leader.

The federal government stuck to its position that if Quebeckers could be persuaded that "Yes" meant actual separation, a majority would vote "No." Even when the question was toned down, Ottawa made no counteroffers until polls showed that its strategy was seriously flawed and could lead to defeat. In the final week of the campaign, Prime Minister Chrétien promised change—constitutional, if necessary, but not necessarily constitutional—if Quebeckers voted "No." The three principal changes he alluded to were some kind of recognition of Quebec as a distinct society, some kind of veto over constitutional amendments, and some kind of decentralization of powers from Ottawa. The other dramatic development of the last few days was a gigantic "No" rally in downtown Montreal, made up primarily of Canadians from coast to coast who "invaded" the city to tell Quebeckers how much the rest of Canada wanted them to stay.

The result of the 1995 referendum could not have been closer: 50.6 percent voted "No," while 49.4 percent voted "Yes." The turnout rate was a record 92 percent. Considerable controversy surrounded the high number of rejected ballots (most of them favouring the "No" side), but it was clear that nearly 60 percent of the francophones in the province had voted "Yes." Close but still defeated, Parizeau promptly resigned the premiership in favour of Bouchard.

After the suspenseful Quebec referendum results, Prime Minister Chrétien had Parliament pass a resolution recognizing Quebec as a distinct society within Canada. He also had Parliament pass a law to the effect that regardless of the official constitutional amending formula, no constitutional amendments would be passed without the approval of each region of the country (including Quebec). In addition, labour-market training would be transferred from federal to provincial jurisdiction wherever desired. Such measures were part of "Plan A" or the "carrot" approach of being nice to Quebec.[19] The government also pursued the "stick" approach or "Plan B," the principal part of which was to refer a hypothetical question to the Supreme Court of Canada, asking it to rule on the legality of a unilateral declaration of independence by Quebec.

As a result of these actions, the constitutional amending formula provided for in the Constitution Act, 1982 has been informally amended and now rests on the 1996 Constitutional Amendments Act instead. In the case of any proposed amendment that requires the approval of at least seven provinces representing at least 50 percent of the population, the federal government will henceforth not act until the change has acquired the approval of each of the following:

- Ontario
- Quebec
- British Columbia
- two or more of the Prairie provinces representing a majority of the Prairie provinces' population (which would have to include Alberta)
- two or more of the Atlantic provinces representing at least 50 percent of the region's population[20]

In September 1997, nine provincial premiers (excluding Lucien Bouchard) and two territorial first ministers gathered in Calgary to see if it would be productive to talk about the Constitution again before Quebec's next election. The premiers' declaration tried to reconcile the "unique character of Quebec society" with the equality of all the provinces. Although substituting "unique" for "distinct" and emphasizing provincial equality might attract some support in English Canada, it was less certain that the Calgary Declaration would appeal to most Quebeckers.

In August 1998, the Supreme Court delivered its decision on the legality of Quebec separation.[21] It answered the specific questions in the negative: "secession of a province 'under the Constitution' could not be achieved unilaterally"; furthermore, international law does not give Quebec the right to unilateral secession from Canada because "Quebec does not meet the threshold of a colonial people or an oppressed people, nor can it be suggested that Quebecers have been denied meaningful access to government to pursue their political, economic, cultural and social development."

Although that part of the judgment pleased federalists, the Court did not stop there. It went on to say that "the continued existence and operation of the Canadian constitutional order could not be indifferent to a clear expression of a clear majority of Quebecers that they no longer wish to remain in Canada." In other words, "a clear majority vote in Quebec on a clear question in favour of secession would confer democratic legitimacy on the secession initiative which all of the other participants in Confederation would have to recognize."

The Court added that "although there is no right, under the Constitution or at international law, to unilateral secession, the possibility of an unconstitutional declaration of secession leading to a *de facto* secession is not ruled out. The ultimate success of such a secession would be dependent on recognition by the international community."

Bouchard then called an election for November 30, 1998. Although he won the largest number of seats, Jean Charest's Liberals actually collected a greater number of votes. This lukewarm public endorsement forced Bouchard to postpone plans for yet another referendum on some variation of Quebec sovereignty. However, Ottawa and the provinces came to an agreement on the "social union framework," discussed in more detail in Chapter 18, but as in the case of the Constitution Act, 1982, Quebec did not agree. All of these developments left the constitutional crisis hanging.[22]

As mentioned in Chapter 5, Prime Minister Chrétien then introduced the **Clarity Act**, drafted by federal–provincial affairs minister Stéphane Dion. It essentially translated into law the Supreme Court decision denying Quebec's right to a unilateral declaration of independence. Although the bill stopped short of articulating what a "clear majority" would be in numerical terms, it did specify that the federal government would not recognize a Quebec referendum result that did not involve a clear expression of the will of the population that the province should cease to be part of Canada. The federal government would not tolerate a question that involved continuing economic or political arrangements with Canada, nor engage in negotiations that did not address the division of assets and liabilities; border changes; the rights, interests, and territorial claims of Aboriginal peoples; and the protection of minority rights.

Chrétien believed such legislation was required because the questions asked in the Quebec referendums of 1980 and 1995 were deliberately vague. The new act did not incite the inflammatory backlash in that province that some observers had expected, and the Liberals actually improved their position in Quebec in the November 2000 federal election. Nevertheless, one month later, Quebec passed an "Act respecting the exercise of the fundamental rights and prerogatives of the Quebec people and the Quebec state." It declared that Quebec would determine its own referendum question without intervention from Ottawa.

When Jean Charest won the 2003 Quebec provincial election, he indicated that constitutional reform would not be a priority—he would work to improve the operation of the federal system for Quebec in other ways, such as rectifying the "fiscal imbalance" between the federal and provincial governments. He had generally good relations with Prime Minister Martin until the end of 2005, and then with Stephen Harper, who reversed his earlier position on such matters as the need for provinces to have more revenue, the distinctiveness of the province of Quebec, and the acceptability of Quebec taking a formal role in UNESCO, as mentioned in the next chapter.

On another constitutional front, a number of constitutional amendments of a less comprehensive nature have been passed since 1982. They are listed in Box 17.4. The first was adopted under section 38 of the Constitution Act, 1982—that is, it required the approval of seven provinces representing at least 50 percent of the population (in fact, all but Quebec approved it), while the next six were adopted under section 43, the part of the amending formula involving the federal Parliament and the single province affected. The final two, adopted under section 44, affected the federal government alone.[23]

. . . .

FUTURE CONSTITUTIONAL CHANGE?

Reverting to the discussion of mega-constitutional change, it must be said that many demands for constitutional changes have not been satisfied. In particular, Quebec has not formally agreed to the Constitution Act, 1982, because the minimum changes that virtually all Quebeckers agree on (as embodied in the Meech Lake and Charlottetown Accords) have not been made. Similarly, Aboriginal Canadians have not had the principle of Aboriginal self-government, another aspect of the Charlottetown Accord, enshrined in the constitution. Beyond those two fundamental demands, many of the institutional changes raised by Western or smaller provinces continue to fester. With the threat of Quebec separation always in the air, it is often argued that another round of mega-constitutional negotiations is required.[24]

BOX 17.4	Single-Issue Constitutional Amendments Since 1982

1983: Constitution Amendment Proclamation, 1983: Added a new section 25(b), new sections 35(3) and (4), a new section 35.1, and a new section 37, all relating to Aboriginal peoples

1985: House of Commons: Changed the formula for representation therein

1987: Newfoundland: Added Pentecostals to the list of religious denominations that had a right to operate their own schools

1993: New Brunswick: Strengthened the principle of French–English dualism in the province's public institutions

1993: Prince Edward Island: Provided that the Confederation Bridge would replace the federal government's obligation of a steamship service to the province

1997–98: Newfoundland (two amendments): Reduced the role of the churches in the province's school system

1997: Quebec: Permitted a change in the structure of the school boards in the province from a religious to a linguistic basis

1999: Nunavut: Provided representation in the House of Commons and Senate separate from the Northwest Territories

2001: Newfoundland and Labrador: Changed the name of the province

Others contend that such large-scale negotiations are not likely to succeed because there are too many conflicting interests in question. Given the rigidity of the formal amending formula, to say nothing of the notion that a national referendum would be required to ratify the results, mega-constitutional failure is almost guaranteed. It might be better to live with the current dissatisfaction than the depression or disruption that inevitably result from the failure of intense efforts at constitutional change. Perhaps the system can carry on with further reforms of a nonconstitutional nature.[25] Box 17.5 lists some of the instruments that have been used since 1982 to address unsolvable constitutional issues by circumventing formal constitutional amendments as well as possible uses in the future. Many of these measures are addressed in the two chapters that follow, falling as they do within the realms of federalism and the Charter of Rights and Freedoms.

. . . .

CONCLUSION

Canada has one of the oldest constitutions in the world. Although it has been altered incrementally over its long existence by formal amendments, judicial interpretation, and conventions, its basic provisions remain intact. Ever since the Quiet Revolution, the issue

BOX 17.5	Instruments to Circumvent Formal Constitutional Changes

1. Parliamentary resolutions and declarations (recognizing Quebec as a distinct society within Canada; recognizing the Québécois as a nation within a united Canada; recognizing the principle of the inherent right to Aboriginal self-government)
2. Organic statutes (changing the constitutional amending formula; Senate reform?)
3. Federal–provincial agreements

    (a) delegation of powers, e.g., labour market training
    (b) on initiating new federal programs (e.g., Social Union Framework Agreement)
    (c) on inter-provincial trade (e.g., Agreement on Internal Trade)
    (d) international role for provinces (e.g., Quebec and UNESCO)

4. Federal-provincial finance (solving the "fiscal imbalance" with increased transfers; more health care funding; curtailing the federal "spending power"?)
5. Aboriginal treaties, land claims, self-government, and other agreements (e.g., Nunavut; Nisga'a Treaty; delegation of responsibility for programs)
6. Judicial decisions (e.g., place of private health care insurance; same-sex marriage; Aboriginal cases)
7. Constitutional conventions (inviting territorial leaders to first ministers' meetings; creation of the Council of the Federation; Parliamentary ratification of Supreme Court appointments?)

of mega-constitutional change has never been far from the top of the Canadian political agenda. The incomplete success of 1982 led to the dismal failures of 1990 and 1992. For the time being, therefore, we have resorted to less formal means of achieving some of the stated objectives.

This chapter is linked in particular to Chapter 5 on French Canada and Quebec and to the following chapters on federalism and the Charter of Rights and Freedoms.

(SC) Of the approaches outlined in Chapter 1, the state-centred theory is most relevant to the Constitution and constitutional change. For most of our history, these questions have primarily been the preserve of federal and provincial political and bureaucratic elites. Before 1982, constitutional accommodations could be made among first ministers and their advisers at federal–provincial conferences and only needed to be ratified by federal and provincial cabinets. After 1982, legislative approval was also required, but that did not necessarily involve the wider society. Elite theorists would add to the picture the involvement of only a small number of representatives from the intellectual elite—constitutional law professors, political scientists, historians, economists, and journalists.

[P] Although Matt James argues that social movements have been involved in Canadian constitutional politics for a long period of time,[26] pluralists generally point to the increasing public interest in such matters in recent years. They emphasize that several elite-designed proposals have foundered once exposed to public opinion: the Fulton–Favreau formula and the Victoria Charter in Quebec, and Meech Lake in other parts of the country. The public now demands more meaningful participation in the process of constitutional change. This participation was provided for in the public hearings of legislative committees on Meech Lake and the subsequent Citizens' Forum. When three provinces decided to hold a referendum on the Charlottetown Accord, a national referendum was held, and it is commonly thought that if the issue of mega-constitutional reform is ever revisited, a referendum will be required again, even though it is not necessary according to the constitutional amending formula.

(C) Class analysts see the Constitution as legitimizing arrangements for the capitalist elite to control the political system. They also consider constitutional issues as a device used by politicians to distract the public from the real issues of unemployment, the exploitation of workers, and the unfair distribution of wealth. They think of what might have happened if all the effort that went into constitutional discussions could have been directed toward pressing social issues. Many class analysts would also argue that the decentralized thrust of recent constitutional initiatives has the same result as the drive for free trade, the elimination of the deficit, and the campaign for tax cuts: they all are intended to weaken the central state. Moreover, they are pushed by many of the same people, especially the C.D. Howe Institute and the Canadian Council of Chief Executives. A specific and dramatic case of the latter's influence in even this field can be found by comparing a BCNI constitutional proposal to the nearly identical Calgary Declaration.[27]

As mentioned in Chapter 10, the Canadian government has actually reduced foreign ties in recent years with respect to being able to amend its own Constitution at home without requesting action from the British Parliament. However, the whole neoliberal-inspired globalization phenomenon has meant that Canada has sacrificed constitutional powers of both levels of government to international organizations.

· ·

DISCUSSION QUESTIONS

1. Is the 1982 constitutional amending formula too rigid? If so, how should it be changed? Did the informal change in 1996 help?

2. What is your assessment of the key provisions of the Meech Lake and Charlottetown Accords? Would we have been better off if one or the other had been adopted?

3. To what extent should politicians be guided by popular referendums on constitutional matters?

4. What are the advantages and disadvantages of "mega-constitutional change"—Canadians attempting to address all their constitutional problems simultaneously?

5. To what extent can Canadians resolve their "constitutional" problems in extra-constitutional ways?

· ·

NOTES

1. Alan C. Cairns has defined the Constitution in similar terms as follows: "[It] is the body of understandings defining the basic institutions of government and the relations between them, plus the relationships between governments in the federal system, and between the citizens and those governments," in *Constitution, Government, and Society in Canada* (Toronto: McClelland and Stewart, 1988), p. 31. See Craig Forcese and Aaron Freeman, *The Laws of Government: The Legal Foundations of Canadian Democracy* (Toronto: Irwin Law, 2005), ch. 2.

2. The act has not been included in this book but can be found at http://www.canlii.org/en/ca/const/const1867.html or http://www.solon.org/Constitutions/Canada/English/ca_1867.html. See Bernard Funston and Eugene Meehan, eds., *Canadian Constitutional Documents Consolidated* (Scarborough: Carswell, 1994); and Bernard Funston and Eugene Meehan, *Canada's Constitutional Law in a Nutshell*, 2nd ed. (Toronto: Carswell, 1998).

3. The Constitution Act, 1982 is a Canadian statute that is an appendix to the Canada Act, a British statute, and the Charter of Rights and Freedoms is part of the Constitution Act, 1982.

4. Many definitions of conventions exist and are discussed by Andrew Heard in *Canadian Constitutional Conventions* (Toronto: Oxford University Press, 1991). My definition is an amalgam of those he cites. See also Heard, "Constitutional Conventions and Parliament," *Canadian Parliamentary Review* (Summer 2005).

5. Peter Hogg, *Constitutional Law of Canada*, 2nd ed. (Toronto: Carswell, 1985), p. 12. Craig Forcese and Aaron Freeman also have a good discussion of constitutional conventions in their book, *The Laws of Government: The Legal Foundations of Canadian Democracy*. The question of judicial recognition of such conventions is addressed below.

6. On about ten other occasions constitutional amendments were made without prior consultation with the provinces because Ottawa considered that they were of exclusive federal concern. These included repeated redistributions of seats in the House of Commons and the entry of Newfoundland and Labrador into Confederation. See Guy Favreau, *The Amendment of the Constitution of Canada* (Ottawa:

Queen's Printer, 1965); and Paul Gérin-Lajoie, *Constitutional Amendment in Canada* (Toronto: University of Toronto Press, 1950).

7. Cairns, *Constitution, Government, and Society in Canada.*

8. Edward McWhinney, *Quebec and the Constitution 1960–1978* (University of Toronto Press, 1979); Edward McWhinney, *Canada and the Constitution 1979–1982* (University of Toronto Press, 1982); and Peter Russell, *Constitutional Odyssey*, 3rd ed. (Toronto: University of Toronto Press, 2004).

9. Kenneth McRoberts, *Misconceiving Canada: The Struggle for National Unity* (Toronto: Oxford University Press, 1997); Ian Greene, *The Charter of Rights* (Toronto: Lorimer, 1989), pp. 37–38; and Michael Mandel, *The Charter of Rights and the Legalization of Politics in Canada* (Toronto: Wall and Thompson, 1989; rev. ed. 1994), pp. 17, 20, 22, and 111.

10. See, for example, Gordon Robertson, *Memoirs of a Very Civil Servant: Mackenzie King to Pierre Trudeau* (Toronto: University of Toronto Press, 2000). Robertson is even more appalled at Trudeau's intervention in the debate over the Meech Lake and Charlottetown Accords.

11. *Reference re Amendment of the Constitution of Canada*, [1981] 125 D.L.R. (3rd) 1. See Heard, *Canadian Constitutional Conventions*, and Mandel, *The Charter of Rights*, pp. 22, 24–34, 111. In another political decision, the Court decided that Quebec had never had a veto on constitutional amendments: *Re: Objection to a Resolution to Amend the Constitution*, [1982] 2 S.C.R. 793. See Marc Gold, "The Mask of Objectivity: Politics and Rhetoric in the Supreme Court of Canada," *The Supreme Court Law Review* 7 (1985).

12. Keith Banting and Richard Simeon, eds., *And No One Cheered: Federalism, Democracy and the Constitution Act* (Toronto: Methuen, 1983); Roy Romanow, J. Whyte, and H. Leeson, *Canada … Notwithstanding: The Making of the Constitution 1976–1982* (Toronto: Methuen, 1984); and Ross Sheppard and M. Valpy, *The National Deal: The Fight for a Canadian Constitution* (Toronto: Macmillan, 1984).

13. Michael Behiels, ed., *The Meech Lake Primer: Conflicting Views of the 1987 Constitutional Accord* (Ottawa: University of Ottawa Press, 1989); *Canadian Public Policy* (September 1988); Roger Gibbins, ed., *Meech Lake and Canada: Perspectives from the West* (Edmonton: Academic Printing and Publishing, 1988); Peter Hogg, *Meech Lake Constitutional Accord Annotated* (Toronto: Carswell, 1988); and K.E. Swinton and C.J. Rogerson, *Competing Constitutional Visions: The Meech Lake Accord* (Toronto: Carswell, 1988).

14. Cairns, *Constitution, Government, and Society in Canada*; and Alan C. Cairns, *Disruptions: Constitutional Struggles, from the Charter to Meech Lake* (Toronto: McClelland and Stewart, 1991).

15. The former Cabinet secretary and clerk of the Privy Council, Gordon Robertson, argued strenuously that no such deadline existed but to no avail.

16. Alan C. Cairns, *Reconfigurations: Canadian Citizenship and Constitutional Change* (Toronto: McClelland and Stewart, 1995); Curtis Cook, ed., *Constitutional Predicament: Canada after the Referendum of 1992* (Montreal: McGill-Queen's University Press, 1994); Kenneth McRoberts and Patrick Monahan, eds., *The Charlottetown Accord, the Referendum and the Future of Canada* (Toronto: University of Toronto Press, 1993); Peter H. Russell, *Constitutional Odyssey*, 3rd ed.; Patrick C. Fafard and Douglas M. Brown, *Canada: The State of the Federation 1996* (Kingston: Institute of Intergovernmental Affairs, 1996); and F. Leslie Seidel, *Seeking a New Canadian Partnership: Asymmetrical and Confederal Options* (Montreal: Institute for Research on Public Policy, 1994).

17. Richard Johnston, André Blais, Elisabeth Gidengil, and Neil Nevitte, *The Challenge of Direct Democracy: The 1992 Canadian Referendum* (Montreal: McGill-Queen's University Press, 1996).

18. Réjean Pelletier, "From Jacques Parizeau to Lucien Bouchard: A New Vision? Yes, But ..." in Lazar, *Canada: The State of the Federation 1997.*

19. Robert Howse, "Searching for Plan A: National Unity and the Chrétien Government's New Federalism," in Lazar, *Canada: The State of the Federation 1997*; and Gordon Gibson, *Plan B: The Future of the Rest of Canada* (Vancouver: Fraser Institute, 1994).

20. Jennifer Smith, "Informal Constitutional Development: Change by Other Means," in Herman Bakvis and Grace Skogstad, eds., *Canadian Federalism: Performance, Effectiveness, and Legitimacy* (Toronto: Oxford University Press, 2002).

21. *Reference re Secession of Quebec*, [1998] 2 S.C.R. 217; David Schneiderman, ed., *The Quebec Decision: The Supreme Court Case and Commentary* (Toronto: Lorimer, 1999).

22. Robert A. Young, *The Struggle for Quebec: From Referendum to Referendum?* (Montreal: McGill-Queen's University Press, 1999).

23. J.R. Hurley, *Amending Canada's Constitution: History, Processes, Problems and Prospects* (Ottawa: Minister of Supply and Services Canada, 1996).

24. The advisability of making another attempt at "mega-constitutional change" is debated by Kathy Brock and Michael Lusztig in Mark Charlton and Paul Barker, eds., *Crosscurrents: Contemporary Political Issues*, 4th ed. (Scarborough: Nelson, 2002), ch. 6; Russell, *Constitutional Odyssey*.

25. Harvey Lazar, ed., *Canada: The State of the Federation 1997: Non-constitutional Renewal* (Kingston: Institute of Intergovernmental Relations, 1997); and Fafard and Brown, *Canada: The State of the Federation 1996*.

26. Matt James, *Misrecognized Materialists: Social Movements in Canadian Constitutional Politics* (Vancouver: UBC Press, 2006).

27. Paula Mallea, *Brief to the Manitoba Legislative Task Force on Canadian Unity*, Brandon, January 15, 1998 (Winnipeg: Canadian Centre for Policy Alternatives—Manitoba, 1998). I am indebted to Jim Silver for this information.

• •

FURTHER READING

Cairns, Alan C. *Constitution, Government and Society in Canada.* Toronto: McClelland and Stewart, 1988.

———. *Disruptions: Constitutional Struggles, from the Charter to Meech Lake.* Toronto: McClelland and Stewart, 1991.

———. *Reconfigurations: Canadian Citizenship and Constitutional Change.* Toronto: McClelland and Stewart, 1995.

Forcese, Craig, and Aaron Freeman. *The Laws of Government: The Legal Foundations of Canadian Democracy.* Toronto: Irwin Law, 2005.

Funston, Bernard, and Eugene Meehan, eds. *Canadian Constitutional Documents Consolidated.* Scarborough: Carswell, 1994.

Heard, Andrew. *Canadian Constitutional Conventions.* Toronto: Oxford University Press, 1991.

Hogg, Peter. *Canada Act Annotated.* Toronto: Carswell, 1982.

———. *Meech Lake Constitutional Accord Annotated.* Toronto: Carswell, 1988.

Hurley, J.R. *Amending Canada's Constitution: History, Processes, Problems and Prospects.* Ottawa: Minister of Supply and Services Canada, 1996.

James, Matt. *Misrecognized Materialists: Social Movements in Canadian Constitutional Politics.* Vancouver: UBC Press, 2006.

Lazar, Harvey, ed. *Canada: The State of the Federation 1997: Non-constitutional Renewal.* Kingston: Institute of Intergovernmental Relations, 1997.

McRoberts, Kenneth. *Misconceiving Canada: The Struggle for National Unity.* Toronto: Oxford University Press, 1997.

McRoberts, Kenneth, and Patrick Monahan, eds. *The Charlottetown Accord, the Referendum and the Future of Canada.* Toronto: University of Toronto Press, 1993.

McWhinney, Edward. *Quebec and the Constitution 1960–1978.* Toronto: University of Toronto Press, 1979.

———. *Canada and the Constitution 1979–82: Patriation and the Charter of Rights.* Toronto: University of Toronto Press, 1982.

Romanow, Roy, J. Whyte, and H. Leeson. *Canada ... Notwithstanding: The Making of the Constitution 1976–1982.* Toronto: Methuen, 1984.

Russell, Peter. *Constitutional Odyssey*, 3rd ed. Toronto: University of Toronto Press, 2004.

Schneiderman, David, ed. *The Quebec Decision: The Supreme Court Case and Commentary.* Toronto: Lorimer, 1999.

Seidel, F. Leslie. *Seeking a New Canadian Partnership: Asymmetrical and Confederal Options.* Montreal: Institute for Research on Public Policy, 1994.

Young, Robert A. *The Struggle for Quebec: From Referendum to Referendum?* Montreal: McGill-Queen's University Press, 1999.

Chapter 18

The Provinces
AND THE FEDERAL
System

Liberal Prime Minister Mackenzie King once said that he would not give "one red cent" to a Tory provincial government. Federal–provincial squabbles are a daily occurrence in Canadian political life, and provincial party leaders often centre entire election campaigns on complaints about Ottawa. In the 1930s, the courts threw out federal legislation aimed at alleviating the Depression, ruling that only the provinces could pass such laws. In the postwar period, though, Ottawa introduced a multitude of national programs within provincial jurisdiction and through financial inducements persuaded the provinces to join them. Throughout the 1990s, the federal government cut back on such transfers, to considerable provincial and public complaint. Early in the 21st century, health care, the environment, equalization payments, and the "fiscal imbalance" constituted fertile ground for further federal–provincial conflict, even though Ottawa was already transferring some $60 billion annually to the provinces and territories. The whole situation was complicated by the worldwide economic meltdown at the end of 2008.

The federal character of Canada is designated in the Canadian Constitution and its impact is seen in almost every aspect of governance and society. The federal system is closely related to regional economic cleavages and regional identities, is important for ethnic cleavages and identities, influences the Canadian political culture, and affects the operation of the electoral system, political parties, and advocacy groups. Federalism also has a major impact on the institutions of the national government.

In a formal sense, **federalism** can be defined as a division of powers between central and regional governments such that neither is subordinate to the other. This definition distinguishes the relationship between national and provincial governments from that between provincial and municipal governments; in the latter case the municipalities are clearly subordinate entities while in the former, provinces are "coordinate" or equal in status to the central government. This equality of status is provided for in the constitutional division of powers between the two levels of government, which is found primarily in sections 91 and 92 of the Constitution Act, 1867. Other aspects of federalism are also important, however, such as federal–provincial financial relations (taxing and spending) and joint policymaking mechanisms. Moreover, the institutions of federalism are embedded in a very diverse "federal society" that supports such a two-tier structure of government. As the Supreme Court said in the *Quebec Secession* case, "federalism is a legal response to the underlying political and

....

Figure 18.1 Map of the Provinces and Territories and Their Capitals

cultural realties that existed at Confederation and continue to exist today."[1] Figure 18.1 shows the division of Canada into provinces and territories, and their capitals.

This chapter begins by sketching the political systems of the provinces and outlining the federal system in Canada at its creation; it then traces the evolution of the federal system, especially through changes in the division of powers and federal–provincial financial relationships. In the following section this evolution is depicted in chronological phases, as the federal system veered between centralization and decentralization. The chapter concludes with a discussion of Canadian federalism today.

....

THE PROVINCIAL POLITICAL SYSTEMS

Canada comprises ten provinces and three territories. The provinces are autonomous within the powers given them by the Constitution, but the territories are constitutionally subordinate to the federal government. Although the territories increasingly function as provinces, exercising similar powers, these powers could theoretically be revoked.

Each province has considerable political and economic significance in its own right and can be considered a separate political system. Each one has a full complement of governmental institutions, which are subject to societal demands in much the same way as this book earlier outlined at the federal level. Each province also has a somewhat distinctive political culture,[2] party system, and array of advocacy groups. In presenting a quick picture of these provincial political systems, it will be seen that their operations bear a striking resemblance to those at the federal level.

Each province is theoretically headed by a lieutenant governor, who is appointed by the federal prime minister and who represents the Queen. The lieutenant governors function as the monarch and governor general do, primarily performing ceremonial and social functions. Apart from emergency situations, they no longer exercise personal discretion in the operation of government. The effective head of the provincial government is the premier, the equivalent of the prime minister, along with the cabinet, who are officially called the Executive Council. The provincial cabinet typically sets priorities, decides how much money to raise and spend, and how to do so, determines policies, gives direction for the preparation of legislation, oversees departmental administration, and makes order in council appointments. Premiers usually select their ministers from the elected members of the legislature and try to balance various interests; the size of the cabinet varies in proportion to the size of the province and averages about 18 ministers.

Provincial cabinets now operate with formal procedures and a cabinet committee system, usually dominated by committees concerned with social and economic development respectively. A cabinet secretariat has emerged to provide policy, procedural, and secretarial assistance to the premier, the cabinet, and cabinet committees. Although ministers are said to be individually responsible for their departments and collectively responsible for government policy, determined premiers can make their presence felt throughout the provincial government's operations in an even more effective way than is possible for the prime minister in Ottawa.[3]

The provincial legislatures are the elected representatives of the people, usually chosen at four-year intervals. These representatives are termed MLAs (members of the legislative assembly) in seven provinces, MPPs (members of the provincial parliament) in Ontario, MHAs (members of the house of assembly) in Newfoundland and Labrador, and MNAs (members of the national assembly) in Quebec. Each provincial legislature has only one chamber, which is divided between government and opposition members. With the expansion of provincial government activity over the past 50 years or so, legislative sessions became longer, committee work became more extensive, members of the legislature were deluged with constituents' problems with the provincial bureaucracy, and the position eventually became a full-time job. When in session, each provincial legislature has a daily oral question period that provides the focus for most of the mass media coverage. Provincial legislatures are busy and often exciting forums, and private members can now do a better job than in the past in the areas of criticizing, questioning, and informing the cabinet. Nevertheless, premiers and cabinets continue to make the crucial decisions, and legislators are not much closer to being involved directly in the decision-making process.[4]

Given the expansion of provincial government operations, at least until 1990 or so, provincial politicians are increasingly dependent on the bureaucracy or public service to advise them on their decisions and the implementation of their programs. In addition to providing services, enforcing rules, collecting taxes, and engaging in other administrative activities, the public service must draft regulations that contain the detailed substance of the law in question. This may involve consultation with relevant advocacy groups. Thus, the modern provincial bureaucracy is no mere neutral agent in providing advice; it is a power to be reckoned with in its own right.

The most important provincial responsibilities in Canada are health and education, meaning that these departments are usually the largest in terms of budgets and personnel. Finance departments are also significant at this level of government, as are such central agencies as cabinet secretariats and treasury or management boards. In addition, each province has an array of semi-independent agencies, boards, commissions, and Crown corporations operating outside the ordinary departmental structure. These typically include a public hydro-electricity commission, a public utilities commission, a human rights commission, a workers' compensation board, a labour relations board, and a liquor commission, although provinces engaged in widespread privatization programs from 1985 to 2000.[5]

Although provincial cabinets, legislatures, and bureaucracies may regularly interact with their federal counterparts, they do so on a basis of autonomy and equality. However, the federal and provincial judicial systems in Canada are officially integrated, as noted in Chapter 24. Each province establishes its own hierarchy of courts, at the base of which are "provincial courts," whose judges are appointed by the provincial cabinet. Above this level, the judges are appointed by the federal government. The element of integration can also be seen in the passage of criminal laws by Ottawa, by its dependence on the provinces for enforcement, and in appeals from provincial courts of appeal to the Supreme Court of Canada. The latter includes appeals of reference cases that provincial cabinets can refer to their own supreme court.

Every province also establishes a municipal level of government, typically including cities, towns, villages, townships, counties, and rural municipalities. The province determines the structures, responsibilities, and financial powers of these local governments. They are usually responsible for services to property, such as streets, sidewalks, water, sewers, garbage, police and fire protection, recreation, and libraries. As for the provision of services to people, such as health, welfare, and housing, these responsibilities may be largely delegated to municipalities, retained by the province, or shared. In most provinces, a second local authority, the school board, is elected separately from the municipal council; however, a recent trend has seen such school boards lose much of their power to the provincial department of education.

Many observers have noted that, especially since about 1970, Canada has seen a phenomenon of **province-building**, as provincial and territorial governments expanded their operations in both absolute terms and relative to Ottawa. Province-building is usually related to increases in provincial revenues and in the size of provincial bureaucracies, the creation of provincial Crown corporations and central planning agencies, and the willingness and capacity of provincial governments to intervene in the process of industrial development and diversification. Even if both levels slimmed down considerably after 1985, the operation of provincial/territorial and municipal governments is of tremendous significance. Table 18.1 compares employment and expenditure figures for these various levels for 2008.

Municipal governments are thus important parts of the overall government structure in Canada. Constitutionally, as mentioned, they are subordinate to provincial and territorial governments, and in that sense they are not part of the "federal" system. However, there are many reasons that Ottawa and municipal governments should be able to deal directly with each other, rather than through the provincial or territorial intermediary. Actions of the federal government—for example, in immigration and transportation—often have serious consequences for municipalities, especially large urban ones, and Ottawa might

TABLE 18.1 Federal, Provincial/Territorial, and Municipal Employment and Expenditure, 2008

	Employment	*Expenditure (Dollars)*
Federal	506 119	$237 021 000 000
Provincial/Territorial	1 684 729	$332 424 000 000
Municipal	1 128 670	$112 167 000 000 (2007)

Source: Adapted from Statistics Canada website. Found at: http://www40.statcan.gc.ca/101/cst01/ govt54a-eng.htm, http://www40.statcan.gc.ca/101/cst01/govt49b-eng.htm, http://www40.statcan.gc.ca/ 101/cst01/govt55a-eng.htm, http://www40.statcan.gc.ca/101/cst01/govt52a-eng.htm.

benefit from municipal input. The federal government might also want to help municipalities solve some of their problems. More and more observers are recommending that large cities be somehow brought into the ambit of Canadian federalism. As mentioned in Chapter 9, Paul Martin embarked on a New Deal for Cities and Communities with particular reference to sharing the proceeds of the federal gas tax to support urban public transportation systems.[6]

THE CONFEDERATION SETTLEMENT

The fundamentals of Canadian federalism, often called the **Confederation Settlement**,[7] were incorporated into the **British North America Act, 1867**, which in 1982 was renamed the **Constitution Act, 1867**. As noted in Chapter 2, the principal architect of Confederation was Sir John A. Macdonald, who intended the new country to be a highly centralized federation. In many ways, in fact, the Confederation Settlement was not consistent with the modern definition of federalism because in certain respects the provinces were made subordinate to the central government.[8]

The Confederation Settlement consisted of five principal components: (1) the division of powers between the central and provincial governments, (2) the division of financial resources, (3) federal controls imposed on the provinces, (4) provincial representation in the central institutions, and (5) certain cultural guarantees.

As far as the **division of powers** between the central and provincial governments was concerned, the Fathers of Confederation gave the provinces 16 specific **enumerated powers** in section 92 (e.g., hospitals and municipal institutions) and then left everything else—the **residual powers**—to Ottawa, in section 91. For greater certainty, however, section 91 also included a list of 29 federal powers, such as trade and commerce and national defence. Two **concurrent powers**—agriculture and immigration—were listed in section 95, and section 132 provided the federal government with the power to implement Empire treaties, regardless of their subject matter (see Box 18.1).

BOX 18.1	The Core of the Federal–Provincial Division of Powers		
	Federal Powers	*Provincial Powers*	*Concurrent Powers*
	Trade and commerce	Direct taxation within	Agriculture
	Any form of taxation	the province	Immigration
	National defence	Public lands	Old age pensions
	Banking	Hospitals and health care	
	Aboriginals	Municipal institutions	
	Criminal law	Education	
	Interprovincial	Property and civil rights	
	transportation and	Administration of Justice	
	communication		

In the division of financial resources, federal dominance was even more clear-cut. The Fathers gave Ottawa the power to levy any mode or system of taxation, which included both **direct** and **indirect taxes**. Since the only tax widely used at the time was the customs duty (an indirect tax), provincial power over direct taxation was not considered to be very significant. Instead, the provinces were expected to raise their revenues from the sale of shop, saloon, tavern, and auctioneer licences, as well as to rely on federal subsidies. The federal government was to pay each province an annual per capita grant of 80 cents plus a small subsidy to support its government and legislature. The federal government also assisted the provinces by assuming their pre-Confederation debts. It should be added that the provinces were authorized to raise revenues from their natural resources, but this source was not taken very seriously at the time because few such resources (except trees) had yet been discovered.

In a clear departure from what is now regarded as the federal principle, Ottawa was given several means of controlling the provinces. The federally appointed lieutenant governors had an alternative to giving royal assent to a provincial law—the power of **reservation**. They could reserve provincial legislation for the consideration of the federal Cabinet, which could then approve or reject it. Even if the lieutenant governor gave assent to a piece of provincial legislation, however, the federal Cabinet could subsequently disallow it—the power of **disallowance**. Then, under section 92(10)(c), the federal government could declare any local work or undertaking to be for the general advantage of Canada and thus place it within federal jurisdiction—the **declaratory power**.

Given the highly centralized nature of the division of powers, the limited financial resources of the provinces, and the federal controls, it is clear that the Confederation Settlement of 1867 placed the provinces in a subordinate position, somewhat akin to municipalities, rather than giving them the equal or coordinate status provided for in the modern definition of federalism.

In the light of the federal government's dominant position, it is not surprising that the provinces were concerned with their representation in the national policymaking system. The fourth aspect of the Confederation Settlement, therefore, was agreement on provincial representation in the House of Commons and the Senate, a question of much greater concern at the time than the division of powers. The great compromise that allowed Confederation to go forward was that the provinces would be represented according to population in the

Commons but that *regional* equality would prevail in the Senate. Thus, each of the three original regions—the Maritimes, Quebec, and Ontario—was to receive 24 senators, appeasing smaller provinces that could be easily out-voted in the lower chamber.

Such concern about provincial representation *within* the institutions of the national government has come to be called "intrastate federalism," as opposed to an emphasis on relations *between* federal and provincial governments, which is sometimes termed "interstate federalism."[9] Beyond the House of Commons and the Senate, interests of the various provinces can be represented within the Cabinet and, perhaps less explicitly, within the bureaucracy and Supreme Court, an issue that arises in the discussion of these institutions in the next part of the book. To some extent, federal–provincial (or interstate) tensions can be reduced if intrastate mechanisms are working effectively so that the people of all provinces feel adequately represented within the national policymaking process. But rigid party discipline, representation by population in the House of Commons, and unilateral federal appointment of senators and Supreme Court judges may diminish such confidence, and, as a result, provincial premiers often come to be the principal articulators of provincial interests.

Confederation was more than just a union of provinces: it was also a uniting of two cultural groups—English and French. (Nobody gave Aboriginals much thought at the time.) Thus, the fifth aspect of the Confederation Settlement might be called cultural guarantees. Considering the anxiety of French Canadians about the preservation of their language and culture, these guarantees were surprisingly minor. Section 133 of the 1867 act made French and English official languages in the federal Parliament and federal courts as well as in the Quebec legislature and Quebec courts—but nowhere else. At the time, religion was probably of greater concern than language, so existing separate school systems in the provinces (especially Ontario and Quebec) were guaranteed by allowing the federal government to step in to restore them, if necessary, according to section 93. French Canada was also protected by giving power over property and civil rights to the provinces so that Quebec could maintain certain cultural particularisms, including its civil law system.

Since the evolution of French-language rights is discussed in Chapter 5 and since the question of representation is addressed in Chapter 23, this chapter will proceed to track the development of the Confederation Settlement in its other three aspects—the division of powers, financial resources, and federal controls.

. . . .

EVOLUTION OF CANADIAN FEDERALISM

In discussing the evolution of Canadian federalism, a key concern will be to explain how the very centralized federation created in 1867 became the highly decentralized Canada of today. This trend can be documented in all three areas—the division of powers, financial resources, and federal controls.

Division of Powers

The evolution of the division of powers between federal and provincial governments can be examined in two respects: formal constitutional amendments that altered the division of powers, and judicial decisions that interpreted sections 91, 92, and 132 of the Constitution Act, 1867. It will be seen that the latter development was by far the more important.

CONSTITUTIONAL AMENDMENTS

Since 1867, only five formal constitutional amendments have been adopted that directly affected the division of powers. First, in 1940, unemployment insurance was added to the list of federal powers in section 91 after the courts had earlier declared it to belong to the provinces. Second, in 1951, old age pensions were made a concurrent power, allowing the federal government into this area as well. Third, in 1964, federal jurisdiction in the pensions field was enlarged to include widows' and survivors' benefits and disability pensions. Fourth, in 1949, the federal Parliament was allowed to amend the Constitution unilaterally in areas of purely federal concern, a power previously held by Britain. (This amendment was repealed in 1982 with the adoption of a more general amending formula.) Finally, in the **Constitution Act, 1982**, the new section 92A increased provincial jurisdiction over natural resources, while the Charter of Rights and Freedoms generally reduced the powers of both levels of government. Thus, in the first three cases, the net result was a slight increase in federal powers, but, as pointed out in Chapter 17, this increase was accomplished with the unanimous consent of the provinces. The 1982 natural resources amendment was the only formal constitutional amendment that in any way increased provincial powers at the expense of Ottawa.

JUDICIAL INTERPRETATION

Judicial interpretation of the federal and provincial powers in the 1867 act is a much more complicated subject. Before 1949, the **Judicial Committee of the Privy Council** (JCPC) in London was Canada's final court of appeal, and most constitutional decisions were rendered by that body. There is no doubt that its decisions had a major impact in transforming the nature of Canadian federalism from a centralized to a decentralized system, whether it acted out of ignorance or by deliberate design. The JCPC decisions can be examined primarily in terms of the Peace, Order, and Good Government clause, the Trade and Commerce power, and the Treaty power.

Section 91 of the 1867 act has two parts. First, the **Peace, Order, and Good Government clause** says that all powers not given to the provinces in section 92 are left with the federal government. This is also known as "POGG" or the residual clause, and reads as follows:

> It shall be lawful for the Queen, by and with the Advice and Consent of the Senate and House of Commons, to make laws for the Peace, Order, and good Government of Canada, in relation to all matters not coming within the Classes of Subjects by this Act assigned exclusively to the Legislatures of the Provinces; and for greater Certainty, but not so as to restrict the Generality of the foregoing Terms of this Section, it is hereby declared that (notwithstanding anything in this Act) the exclusive Legislative Authority of the Parliament of Canada extends to all Matters coming within the Classes of Subjects next hereinafter enumerated.

Then, for greater certainty, a list of 29 examples of federal powers is included, a clause that was logically unnecessary and eventually became counterproductive. In a nutshell, in the course of its judgments, the Judicial Committee drove a wedge between these two parts of section 91, decided that the list of 29 examples constituted the *real* federal powers, and ignored the Peace, Order, and Good Government clause except in time of national emergency. How it managed to transform the residual clause into an emergency clause, the so-called **emergency**

doctrine, is very difficult to fathom, and is the subject of much scholarly discussion and whole books and courses on Canadian constitutional law. However, the JCPC gave an extremely broad interpretation to section 92(13), property and civil rights in the province, finding that almost any matter that was the subject of a federal–provincial constitutional dispute could be incorporated within this provincial power. That is why so little was left over for the federal residual clause. A brief summary of the leading POGG cases is included in Box 18.2.

BOX 18.2   A Brief Summary of the Leading POGG Cases[10]

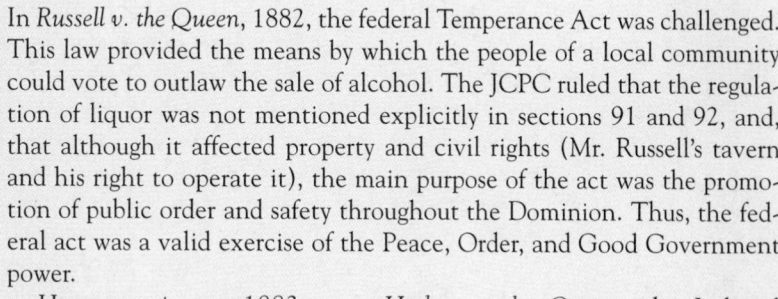

In *Russell v. the Queen*, 1882, the federal Temperance Act was challenged. This law provided the means by which the people of a local community could vote to outlaw the sale of alcohol. The JCPC ruled that the regulation of liquor was not mentioned explicitly in sections 91 and 92, and, that although it affected property and civil rights (Mr. Russell's tavern and his right to operate it), the main purpose of the act was the promotion of public order and safety throughout the Dominion. Thus, the federal act was a valid exercise of the Peace, Order, and Good Government power.

However, in an 1883 case, *Hodge v. the Queen*, the Judicial Committee ruled that there was a double aspect to the regulation of liquor—"subjects which in one aspect and for one purpose fall within s. 92, may in another aspect and for another purpose fall within s. 91." This decision opened the door for provincial action in the liquor field as well. In 1892, in the *Maritime Bank* case, provincial lieutenant governors were given equality of status to the Governor General, an equality which generally applied to the two levels of government as a whole. Then, in the Local Prohibition case of 1896, the JCPC said that the Peace, Order, and Good Government clause was merely supplementary to the powers listed in section 91, and that POGG would come into play only if a subject could not be found in the list of powers in either section 91 or 92, and if the subject had attained such dimensions as to affect the body politic of the country as a whole. From this point, at which the POGG clause was divorced from the rest of section 91 and the examples effectively became *the* federal powers, matters in dispute were increasingly found to fit into property and civil rights in the provinces.

POGG was then transformed into an emergency clause in a series of cases in the 1920s. In the 1922 *Board of Commerce* case, the Privy Council said that the regulation of prices and profiteering would normally fall within section 92(13), and only in special circumstances, such as war or famine, could such matters become of national importance. In the 1924 *Fort Frances* case, federal regulation of the price and supply of newsprint

BOX 18.2   A Brief Summary of the Leading POGG Cases (*continued*)

was upheld because it had been done in wartime, an emergency that justified federal action in a field that would ordinarily be provincial.

Finally, in the 1925 *Toronto Electric Commissioners v. Snider* case, federal legislation to deal with serious strikes was ruled unconstitutional since labour–management relations were normally matters of property and civil rights in the province and could only become the subject of federal action in an emergency. Faced with the disparity between this line of interpretation (that POGG was only an emergency clause) and that used in the *Russell* case (that POGG was a simple residual clause), the JCPC resorted to a reinterpretation of the earlier case: the evil of drunkenness at the time of the *Russell* case must have amounted to a national emergency!

A series of "New Deal" cases followed in the 1930s in which federal laws in the fields of unemployment insurance, labour standards, and the marketing of farm products were ruled invalid because they dealt with property and civil rights in the provinces and because the legislation was intended to be permanent rather than deal only with the temporary emergency of the Depression. In other words, federal actions based on the emergency doctrine had to be temporary measures. These highly controversial decisions rendered Ottawa impotent in dealing with the human devastation wrought by the Depression. Strangely enough, however, when the *Russell* case was duplicated in the 1946 Canada Temperance Federation case, the JCPC disavowed the emergency doctrine and reverted to the simple residual basis of POGG.

When appeals to the Privy Council were abolished in 1949, all eyes were on the Supreme Court to see which line of interpretation it would take with respect to POGG—emergency power or residual clause? The record has been unclear, but in general the federal level has won more cases than it did before 1949. Perhaps this reflects the Supreme Court's better understanding of the Canadian situation or its reaction to the excessive provincial orientation of the JCPC. Some of these federal victories have been based on POGG as a simple residual clause (with an issue having national but not emergency dimensions), such as the *Johannesson* case, which reaffirmed federal control over aviation and airports; the BC and Newfoundland and Labrador off-shore minerals cases, which gave Ottawa jurisdiction over the area beyond the BC and Newfoundland and Labrador coasts; and *Munro v. National Capital Commission*, which permitted federal regulation of property in the National Capital Region. But in the leading decision, the Anti-Inflation Act reference of 1976, the Court was badly split. The majority of judges who upheld it did so for different reasons: some adhered to the emergency doctrine, while others were prepared to accept a broader interpretation of POGG.

More recent cases, such as *Crown Zellerbach* in 1988 and *Oldman River* in 1992, strengthened federal jurisdiction over pollution control with extra-provincial implications. The Court seems to have concluded that POGG can be used in nonemergency cases to cover single, distinctive, indivisible subjects that have reached national dimensions and that a province would be unable to deal with properly on its own (the "provincial inability test"). Some such cases involved the federal criminal law power, which was also used by the Supreme Court to uphold the federal government's gun registration law in the *Firearms Act Reference*. Ottawa's control over telephones and telecommunications has also been enhanced; federal maternity benefits have been upheld as part of the Employment Insurance Act; and in a case involving LEGO, the federal power over trade marks prevailed.[11] Even if a recent pro-Ottawa stance can be detected, however, now often relying on the criminal law power, the net effect of judicial interpretation of the Peace, Order, and Good Government clause since 1867 was a great increase of provincial powers at federal expense.

A similar fate awaited the federal **Trade and Commerce clause**, section 91(2). The Fathers of Confederation deliberately expressed this clause in wide, general, unlimited terms, "the regulation of trade and commerce," but as early as the *Parsons* case in 1881 the JCPC basically restricted federal power to international and interprovincial trade. Besides drawing an unanticipated rigid line between interprovincial trade (federal) and intraprovincial trade (provincial), the courts created a no-man's land wherever the two kinds of trade were unavoidably combined. The general result of this interpretation was to enhance the provincial power over property and civil rights, and to downgrade the federal commerce power. Since 1949, the Supreme Court has rendered more realistic judgments in this area, recognizing the complexity of the situation and often favouring the federal side.

The **Treaty power**, section 132, effectively says that in cases of Empire treaties, the division of powers becomes inoperative and the federal government can implement them regardless of subject matter. Such was the decision of the *Aeronautics* case of 1932, and the *Radio* case of the same year applied this rule to non-Empire treaties as well. However, in the 1937 *Labour Conventions* case, the JCPC reversed itself and said that Ottawa could only implement treaties the subject matter of which was within federal jurisdiction. In this particular case, the subject matter fell instead into property and civil rights.

The combined effect of the judicial interpretation of the Peace, Order, and Good Government clause, the Trade and Commerce clause, and the Treaty power has been to reduce significantly the intended dominance of the federal government and to increase substantially the scope of provincial powers, especially with the broad interpretation given to property and civil rights. This influence has been controversial in political, judicial, and academic circles because it was clearly contrary to John A. Macdonald's conception of Canadian federalism and because it did not permit Ottawa to take many initiatives desired by centralist advocates.[12] The JCPC could deal only with the cases brought before it, of course, so that the decentralized results of its interpretation depended on a greater number of challenges to federal than to provincial laws. Several such cases were initiated by corporations that expected to be given a freer hand in their pursuit of profits if power remained at the provincial level. Other cases were started by provincial premiers with the support of their cabinets and advisers, which followed naturally from the legitimation in a federal constitution of subnational elites.

However, many observers contend that the Judicial Committee's line of interpretation was consistent with the increasing size and distances that characterized the country as time went on, as well as with societal forces and public orientations, at least outside Ontario.

They argue that Canada has a federal, decentralized, diversified *society*, and the provincial bias pervading so many of the JCPC's decisions was "in fundamental harmony with the regional pluralism" of that society. However desirable centralization may have seemed at the outset, it was inappropriate in the long run "for the regional diversities of a land of vast extent and a large, geographically concentrated, minority culture."[13] Most French-Canadian observers, for example, were quite happy with the work of the JCPC. Thus, Alan Cairns finds it impossible "to believe that a few elderly men in London deciding two or three constitutional cases a year precipitated, sustained, and caused the development of Canada in a federalist direction the country would otherwise not have taken."[14] Moreover, he observes,

> the discovery and amplification of an emergency power in Section 91 may have done an injustice to the intentions of Macdonald for the residual power, but it did allow Canada to conduct herself virtually as a unitary state in the two world wars in which centralized government authority was both required and supported.[15]

Federal–Provincial Finance

In the Confederation Settlement, the federal government was given the power to levy any kind of tax, while the provinces were restricted to direct taxation.[16] Ottawa assumed provincial debts (also paying debt allowances to those provinces with smaller debts) and paid unconditional grants to the provinces based on 80 cents per capita and in support of governments and legislatures. Although the intention was thus to create a highly centralized federation, the financial factor also ultimately contributed to the increased power of the provinces. This situation came about because the provinces successfully lobbied for larger federal grants, mostly unconditional in nature, than were set out in 1867; because the provinces levied direct taxes, such as income taxes, which they were not expected to use; and because some provincial revenues, such as those from natural resources, turned out to be more significant than anticipated.

Provincial revenues proved to be inadequate from the beginning, and special grants and arrangements had to be made immediately. A wholesale change in the grant system followed in 1907. By this time, too, the provinces had begun to levy their own direct personal and corporate income taxes, a situation complicated by the federal entry into the same fields during the First World War.[17] About the same time, the **conditional grant** made its appearance. This was a grant paid by the federal government to the provinces in an area of provincial jurisdiction but for which provincial revenues were deemed to be inadequate. The provinces usually had to match the federal share of 50 percent, as well as adhere to whatever conditions or standards Ottawa imposed. The most important conditional grant in the early years was the old age pension, which started in 1927.

With both levels of government taxing the same personal and corporate incomes, but in a totally uncoordinated fashion, and with the two levels starting to become intertwined in conditional grant programs, the federal–provincial financial situation became increasingly complicated. This muddied state of affairs worsened with the advent of the Depression, when even fewer funds were available to go around. The result was the appointment of the **Rowell–Sirois Commission**, officially the Royal Commission on Dominion–Provincial Relations, in 1937. One of the recommendations of its 1940 report—that the costly responsibility for unemployment insurance be transferred to the federal government—was quickly implemented by means of a constitutional amendment.

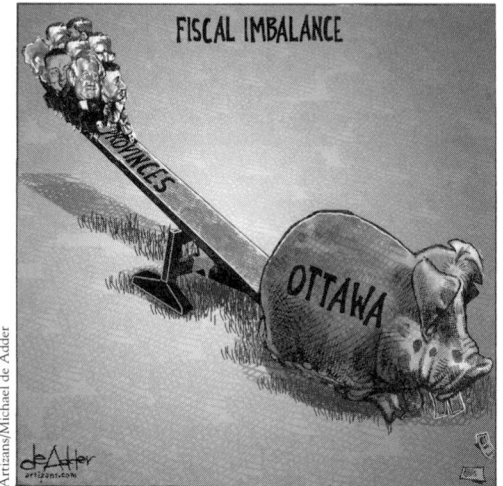

FISCAL IMBALANCE

Provinces' view of Fiscal Imbalance teeter-totter.

Before 1940, therefore, the two levels of government operated with relative independence on both the taxation and the expenditure sides of public finance. Since the Second World War, however, they have become intimately intertwined, and Ottawa has taken the lead (sometimes with provincial encouragement) in coordinating the various ingredients of the federal–provincial financial relationship. The complicated federal–provincial financial situation since 1940 might be simplified somewhat by taking three aspects separately: taxation agreements, conditional and block grants, and equalization payments.

FEDERAL-PROVINCIAL TAXATION AGREEMENTS

After 1942 the taxation side was characterized by a series of five-year federal–provincial agreements. The name and terms of the **taxation agreements** changed over the years—tax rental, tax sharing, tax collection, and so on—but the basic objective was the same: to effect a degree of coordination in the field of federal–provincial taxation. The main taxes in question were personal and corporate income taxes. Between 1962 and 2000, for example, the provincial portion of personal income tax was calculated as a percentage of the federal income tax ("tax on tax"), so that although the federal tax was standard across the country, except for Quebec, the provincial portion was allowed to vary. In recent years, several provinces have harmonized their retail sales taxes with the federal GST.

CONDITIONAL AND BLOCK GRANTS

The Rowell–Sirois Report frowned on shared-cost programs, preferring that each level of government operate independently. Nevertheless, joint programs expanded considerably after 1940, as pressure from the CCF, industrial unions, and other newly articulated interests on the left forced federal and provincial governments into the joint development of a **welfare state**. The most important shared-cost social programs were postsecondary education (1952), hospital insurance (1957), the Canada Assistance Plan (CAP) (1966), and medical insurance (1968). Hospital and medical insurance were later combined as health insurance.

Federal grants for postsecondary education have always been of a **block grant** variety—that is, a sum of money given to each province for the operating costs of postsecondary educational institutions, without any detailed conditions or strings attached. Between 1967 and 1977 these grants were based on a formula of providing 50 percent of such expenditures.

The other major **shared-cost programs** originally fell into the conditional grant category. The usual pattern here was that after it had laid down certain conditions, the federal government paid approximately 50 percent of the cost of each program. In the case of hospital insurance, for example, Ottawa would pay half the cost of provincial programs that provided their residents with basic hospital care without charge. The provinces could finance their half of the program costs from premiums or general tax revenues. Medical insurance was an extension of the prior program to cover basic doctors' services. Under the Canada Assistance Plan, Ottawa similarly provided half the funding for almost any provincial or municipal program that provided social assistance and welfare services based on need.

Most of these programs fell constitutionally within provincial jurisdiction, but Ottawa maintained that its **spending power** allowed it to make payments to individuals, institutions, and other governments in fields over which Parliament did not necessarily have the power to regulate. Moreover, the federal government was often responding to provincial demands. It even claimed that it could attach conditions to such spending and often did so. The constitutional status of this argument was addressed by the courts in several cases.[18]

Although a combination of provincial pressure and federal political and bureaucratic expansionism inspired most of these programs, the provinces often criticized the federal conditions attached as being out of place in areas of provincial jurisdiction. Quebec in particular took this point of view in the early 1960s. The Pearson government responded by allowing provinces to opt out of certain conditional grant programs and continue to receive federal funding as long as they maintained an equivalent program. Then, in the 1970s, Ottawa became upset at the rapidly escalating costs of many of these programs, along with its commitment to finance 50 percent of whatever the provinces spent on them.

In 1977 the federal government therefore transferred health insurance from the conditional to the block grant category, under the Established Programs Financing Act. Ottawa removed the detailed conditions attached to the health insurance programs, as many provinces wanted, but in return, the federal government no longer felt obliged to pay 50 percent of the provincial program costs. The federal grants now took the form of tax transfers as well as cash, and henceforth, Ottawa would increase its funding of such programs by only a certain annual percentage, which would no longer cover one-half of their overall costs. The tax transfers represent federal tax revenue forgone as a result of a coordinated reduction of federal taxes and an increase in provincial taxes, such that the position of the taxpayer is left unchanged.

Removing the conditions from health insurance grants, however, led to problems with hospital user fees, doctors' double-billing, and the provinces' use of health care funds for other purposes. Federal and public displeasure at these developments led Ottawa to pass the **Canada Health Act** in 1984, to much provincial chagrin. This law allows the federal government to penalize provinces that do not meet its five conditions in the provision of public health insurance:

1. *Comprehensive*: covering all necessary health services provided by hospitals and medical practitioners
2. *Universal*: covering the whole population
3. *Portable*: covering the costs of provincial residents while temporarily absent from the province
4. *Accessible*: not impeding or precluding reasonable access to services by extra charges
5. *Publicly administered*

The Canada Assistance Plan remained a conditional grant program, with Ottawa continuing its 50 percent contribution, until the Mulroney government put a ceiling on its CAP contributions to the three richest provinces.

The 1995 federal budget brought in by Finance Minister Paul Martin inaugurated a major transformation of federal–provincial transfer payments. Postsecondary education, health insurance, and the Canada Assistance Plan were combined into one block grant, beginning in 1996–97, called the **Canada Health and Social Transfer (CHST)**. It was a combination of cash payments and tax points, but represented a significant reduction in previous amounts, and Ottawa's expenditures were no longer driven by provincial costs. As a block grant, the CHST would not contain the previous conditions of CAP; the only condition on welfare transfers was that provinces not impose a minimum residency requirement. Ottawa felt that it could not retain previous conditions when it was reducing its contributions and was particularly loath to provoke the PQ government of Quebec immediately before the 1995 referendum.

All the federal off-loading, including the CHST and the shift to tax points, had serious consequences for many social programs, especially in have-not provinces. Because the latter do not have a strong tax base, they benefit more from the transfer of dollars than of tax points. These and other developments in fiscal federalism thus constituted some of the ways in which the "redistributive state" was eroded. Moreover, few social reformers trusted provincial governments to spend the smaller transfers on social programs. The federal Liberal government announced that it would continue to enforce the principles of the Canada Health Act, however, and fought with Alberta over the funding of private health clinics that charged "facility fees."

After the turn of the century, federal transfers began to increase. Table 18.2 shows how much each province and territory received in 2009–10 in major federal transfers, by which time the CHST had been replaced by the Canada Health Transfer (CHT) in support of health care and the Canada Social Transfer (CST) in support of other social programs including postsecondary education. Table 18.2 includes Equalization Payments, discussed below, but excludes nearly $7 billion in Infrastructure, Labour Market Training, and Wait Times Funding, as well as $1.5 billion in various trust funds, for a grand total of over $60 billion.

EQUALIZATION PAYMENTS

The third aspect of federal–provincial finance consists of **equalization payments**.[19] In 1957 the federal government began to pay unconditional grants to have-not provinces based on provincial need, so that all provinces could offer a relatively equal standard of services. At first only three provincial taxes were considered in the equalization formula, but the number later increased to 33—including almost every conceivable source of provincial revenue. Typically, Ontario, British Columbia, and Alberta were above the national average and did not receive equalization payments, but Alberta petroleum revenues raised the national average so high that Ontario began to qualify in 1980, and an adjustment to the formula had to be made. Any province whose total per capita revenue is below the average receives a payment based on the per capita shortfall multiplied by the province's population. Equalization payments were not touched by the federal reforms of 1995, but became very controversial after 2000, as will be discussed below.

TABLE 18.2 Major Federal Transfers to the Provinces and Territories, 2009–2010 ($ billions)

	Health Transfer	Social Transfer	Equalization Payments	Total
Newfoundland/Labrador	450	164	—	615*
Prince Edward Island	104	45	340	490
Nova Scotia	700	304	1 391	2 395*
New Brunswick	557	242	1 689	2 489
Quebec	5 799	2 518	8 355	16 671
Ontario	9 233	4 223	347	13 803
Manitoba	903	392	2 063	3 359
Saskatchewan	843	342	—	1 186
Alberta	1 962	1 170	—	3 132
British Columbia	3 354	1 431	—	4 785
Yukon	26	11	612**	649
Northwest Territories	27	14	864**	905
Nunavut	27	11	1 022**	1 060
Total	23 987	10 868	14 185	52 184

*Newfoundland/Labrador and Nova Scotia also received Offshore Accord funding of $465 million and $180 million respectively, which are included in the grand total.

**The Territories receive Territorial Formula Financing rather than Equalization Payments. They are not included in the Equalization Payments column total, but are included in the grand total.

Source: Department of Finance Canada. Federal Support to Provinces and Territories. Found at: http://www .fin.gc.ca/fedprov/mtp-eng.asp (Accessed April 17, 2009). Reproduced with the permission of the Minister of Public Works and Government Services, 2009.

Figure 18.2 shows the evolution in major federal transfers to the provinces over the 1991–2014 period. These figures do not include the money that the federal government spends in myriad specific jointly funded projects in the provinces and territories, including significant infrastructure transfers related to the post-2008 economic downturn.

OTHER PROVINCIAL AND TERRITORIAL REVENUES

The provinces and territories have discovered and levied more than 30 forms of direct taxation that were unanticipated in 1867.[20] The enormous natural resource revenues that some provinces receive on top of direct taxation and federal contributions are also significant. Over and above the revenue that is collected in the form of corporate income taxes, provinces obtain specific natural resource revenues from forests, including taxes on logging operations; leases and rentals of Crown lands; and royalties, rentals, and stumpage fees from timber

Figure 18.2 Major Federal Transfers Will Continue to Grow

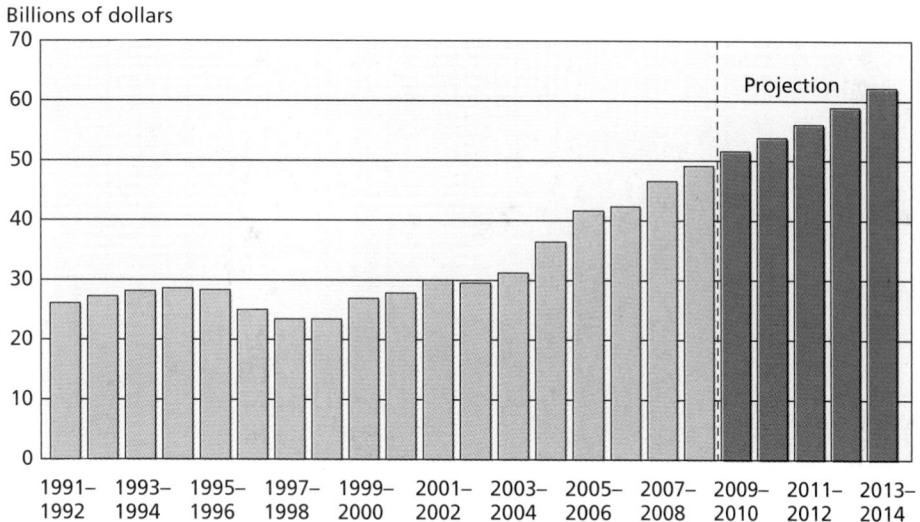

Source: Department of Finance Canada. The Budget Plan. Chart 3.5, Major Federal Transfers Will Continue to Grow. Pg. 189. Found at: http://www.budget.gc.ca/2009/plan/bptoc-eng.asp. Reproduced with the permission of the Minister of Public Works and Government Services, 2009.

and forest management. They also obtain revenues from mines, including taxes on mining operations, acreage taxes, licence and permit fees, rentals and lease payments, and royalties on mineral production. In addition, the petroleum-producing provinces collect revenue from oil and gas, including proceeds from the sale of Crown oil and gas leases, taxes on oil and gas production, royalties, freehold taxes, lease rentals, and fees and permits.[21] Given such petroleum revenues, Alberta in particular often takes in more revenue than it knows what to do with, and typically receives nearly one-third of its revenues from this source. The percentage of total provincial and territorial revenues from their own sources, including natural resources, can be seen in Figure 18.3.

Thus, the combination of unanticipated federal grants, direct taxes, and natural resource revenues has contributed significantly to the enhanced status of the provinces in the Canadian federal system. It should be added that pressure for decentralization and for turning taxation power over to the provinces comes from those provinces that have substantial personal and corporate incomes to tax. The Atlantic provinces and Manitoba sometimes fight against decentralization because they would not benefit if their taxation powers were expanded while Ottawa's were lessened. They want to keep the federal government strong so that it can redistribute revenues at least by means of equalization payments.[22] It should also be repeated that the two levels of government began by operating more or less independently of each other, taxing and spending in different areas, with federal grants being unconditional in nature. As time went on, the federal and provincial governments became closely intertwined by taxation agreements on the revenue side and by conditional and block grant programs in terms of expenditures.

. . . .

**Figure 18.3   Provincial and Territorial Own Source Revenue as Percentage of
Total Revenue, 2008**

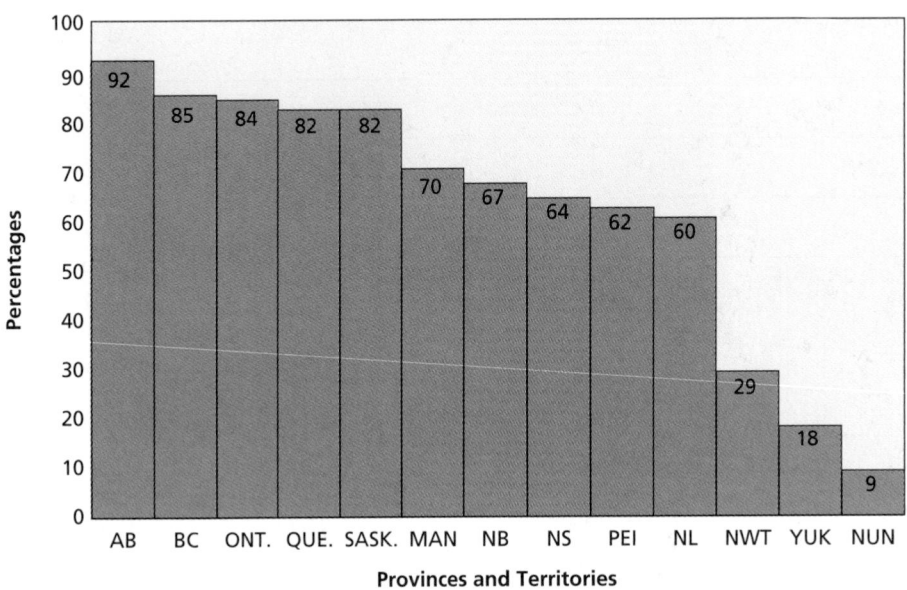

*Source: Adapted from: Statistics Canada. Consolidated provincial and territorial government revenue and expenditures,
by province and territory. Found at: http://www40.statcan.gc.ca/l01/cst01/govt56a-eng.htm*

Federal Controls

As mentioned, the 1867 Constitution Act contained three specific federal controls over
the provinces: reservation, disallowance, and the declaratory power. The decline in the use
of these powers has also enhanced the stature of the provinces. In the first 30 years after
Confederation all three controls were actively employed, and this had the effect of keeping
the provinces subordinate to Ottawa.[23] Their use gradually decreased after that, the two
major exceptions being the combating of anti-Asian legislation in BC around 1900 and the
outlawing of Social Credit legislation in Alberta in the 1930s. Overall, reservation was used
70 times, on 14 of which the federal government assented to the provincial legislation that
the lieutenant governor had reserved, and it was last exercised in 1961. The federal Cabinet
used its disallowance power 112 times, most recently in 1943. The declaratory power was
resorted to on 470 occasions, mostly to put local railroads into federal jurisdiction in the early
years, but not since 1961. It is now a convention of the Constitution, superseding the written
words of the 1867 act, that Ottawa not use these federal controls,[24] and the Charlottetown
Accord would have removed them. As these were the federal powers that originally precluded
Canada from being classified as a true federation, their disuse has meant that the provinces
have shrugged off their subordinate status. Canada is now a genuine federation and a highly
decentralized one at that.

Of the five parts of the Confederation Settlement, three have contributed to the decentralization of Canadian federalism: the division of powers, federal–provincial finance, and federal controls. But some of the societal forces underlying this decentralizing evolution should be identified explicitly. Among others, they include geography—the distances, divisions, and sometimes very large provinces; the development of strong, distinctive provincial and regional identities and political cultures; and Quebec nationalism, characterized by demands for more powers, which were often echoed by other provinces.[25] As Cairns reminds us, institutional developments were consistent with the basic evolution of the "federal" Canadian society.

. . . .

PHASES OF CANADIAN FEDERALISM

Canadian federalism can also be examined by dividing the years since 1867 into a number of eras.[26] These divisions demonstrate pendulum-like swings between centralization and decentralization and show that the evolution from a centralized to a decentralized federal system has not been a unilinear process.

Canadian Federalism, 1867–1945

The period 1867–96 can be classified as one of quasi-federalism, in which the provinces were subordinate to Ottawa. The courts gave the intended broad interpretation to federal powers, especially the Peace, Order, and Good Government clause; the federal level was still predominant in finance; and John A. Macdonald made widespread use of the federal controls of reservation, disallowance, and the declaratory power.

The period 1896–1914 can be termed one of classical federalism. During these years the two levels were equal in status and independent. By now, the courts generally favoured the provinces, the latter had more money to spend, and the federal government made little use of its controls, so that the provinces were no longer subordinate. This was also the period before taxation agreements and conditional grants—that is, federal and provincial governments functioned independently of each other.

Classical federalism was displaced by emergency federalism during the war years, 1914–20. In this era the courts permitted the federal government virtually unlimited powers under the emergency doctrine and the War Measures Act. The federal government also increased its financial resources in this period with the imposition of personal and corporate income taxes. Ironically, in this most centralized phase of Canadian federalism—more centralized even than in the first 30 years—the use of the federal controls was unnecessary because of the courts' emergency interpretation of the Peace, Order, and Good Government clause.

Between the wars, from 1920 to 1939, Canada reverted to another period of classical federalism. In these years, again, the two levels of government were equal in status (neither subordinate to the other) and operated more or less independently. Only a few conditional grants, for example, were developed during this time.

During the Second World War, from 1939 to 1945, Canada entered another period of emergency federalism. Once again, the courts allowed Ottawa to operate almost like a unitary government under the emergency interpretation of POGG and the War Measures Act.

Public finance was also highly centralized with the development of the Wartime Taxation Agreements, under which the federal government took complete control over personal and corporate income taxes and succession duties. As in the First World War, any additional use of the federal controls was unnecessary.

Executive Federalism, 1945–1984

The postwar world brought with it a completely new phase: cooperative federalism. The essence of this concept is that although neither level is subordinate to the other (the same as in classical federalism) they are closely intertwined, rather than operating independently. Here the crucial variable is financial relations. As noted in that connection earlier, the post-1945 period was marked by federal–provincial taxation agreements on the revenue side and a host of shared-cost programs in terms of expenditures.

Cooperative federalism results from several developments.[27] First, federal and provincial objectives often must be harmonized if public policy is to be effective, such as in the case of countercyclical fiscal policy. Second, public pressure forces the federal government to establish minimum standards throughout the country in the provision of certain public services within provincial jurisdiction, such as health care. Third, the two levels of government compete for tax revenues and end up needing to coordinate these efforts to some extent, at least for the convenience of taxpayers. Fourth, given a generally vague division of powers, federal and provincial ministers and bureaucrats all seek to maximize their jurisdiction and eventually overlap with the other level of government. Federal and provincial government operations are no longer confined to separate "watertight compartments."

Cooperative federalism is made operational by a great deal of federal–provincial interaction at all levels—first ministers, departmental ministers, deputy ministers, and even lesser officials, who engage in almost continuous consultation, coordination, and cooperation. Cooperative federalism can be conducted on a multilateral basis, involving the federal government and several or all provinces, or, alternatively, on a bilateral basis, in which Ottawa interacts with individual provinces. Since this interaction is not always cooperative, and since the ministers and bureaucrats involved are all part of the executive branch of government, cooperative federalism came to be labelled **executive federalism**. Two main implications of executive federalism are that legislatures, political parties, and the public at large are not given much role to play in decisions that emerge from the secrecy of meetings of executive officials, and that federal–provincial conflicts are worked out in conferences rather than referred to the courts.

Executive federalism can therefore be defined as "relations between elected and appointed officials of the executive branches of the two levels of government." At the highest level is the **first ministers' conference**, that is, a **federal–provincial conference** of premiers and the prime minister (to which territorial premiers were usually invited after 1992). This institution is not provided for in the written Constitution and rests on a conventional base.[28] Nevertheless, after 1945 many significant Canadian policy decisions were made in this forum, especially with respect to constitutional issues, shared-cost programs, and taxation and fiscal arrangements.[29] Some of these had to be ratified later by federal and provincial legislatures, but legislative approval was usually a formality. Such agreements could rarely be altered in any legislature because they would then have to be changed in all 11.

Executive federalism conducted at the level of departmental ministers and leading bureaucrats is sometimes labelled "functional" or "bureaucratic" federalism. This form of executive federalism is frequently more successful than first ministers' conferences, partly because the officials involved often share certain professional norms, and once they reach a consensus, these experts may be able to "sell" it to their departmental ministers. Functional federalism works best with cabinets in which individual federal and provincial ministers and deputy ministers have considerable autonomy so that they can interact productively with their counterparts at the other level of government. Such interaction was therefore hampered by the trend between the mid-1960s and 1993 of decision-making processes dominated by cabinet committees and under the guidance of powerful central agencies, such as finance departments, treasury boards, and Cabinet offices, as discussed in Chapter 21.[30]

Canadian federalism between 1945 and 1960 may have been "cooperative" in the sense that the two levels of government were closely intertwined, but it continued to be highly centralized in the immediate postwar period. The ministers and bureaucrats in Ottawa who had almost single-handedly run the country during the Second World War were reluctant to shed their enormous power. Moreover, they had discovered **Keynesian economics**, which prescribed a leading role for the central government in guiding the economy.[31]

The Diefenbaker government after 1957 was more sensitive to provincial demands, and the whole picture was increasingly complicated from about 1960 onward by the Quiet Revolution in Quebec, when cooperation was sometimes harder to come by. Moreover, for the first time since 1890 or so, language and culture became important again in a constitutional sense. An extension of official bilingualism and the concept of provincial opting-out were hallmarks of this phase of Canadian federalism, which saw a significant degree of decentralization take place, especially under Lester Pearson.

Then, between about 1970 and 1984, federal–provincial relations became quite confrontational. Quebec and the other provinces were more aggressive than ever, but the Trudeau government was not prepared for any further decentralization. Thus, block funding replaced conditional grants in important areas, leaving the two levels less intertwined than before. Moreover, first ministers' conferences frequently failed to come to any agreement, and Ottawa often chose to act unilaterally. Besides politicians displacing bureaucrats in this phase, federal–provincial conflicts were more frequently referred to the courts, resulting in a renewed emphasis on the division of powers.

THE CANADIAN PRESS/Peter Bregg

With his diplomatic skills, Lester Pearson personified the operation of cooperative federalism.

The Trudeau era was characterized by years of federal–provincial discord over resource and energy policies, especially the National Energy Program, federal–Newfoundland conflict over offshore oil, and federal–Saskatchewan conflict over the regulation and taxation of that province's oil and potash industries. When these disputes coincided with Trudeau's unilateral attempt to amend the Constitution and to entrench official bilingualism as a national policy, many Western Canadians began to re-examine their place in the federation. Some of the heat was reduced when Trudeau conceded the new section 92A, which recognized enhanced provincial jurisdiction over natural resources, in order to secure federal NDP support for the 1982 constitutional package and as a peace offering to the West.

Canadian Federalism, 1984–2000

When Brian Mulroney came to power in 1984, he was determined to improve federal–provincial relations and embark on another period of decentralized, Pearsonian cooperative federalism. During his first term many would say he succeeded, for much of the federal–provincial animosity of the Trudeau years seemed to dissipate. Western and Eastern concerns about energy resources were resolved to a large extent in the 1985 Western and Atlantic Accords. The highlight of the Mulroney approach, of course, was the 1987 Meech Lake Accord, which was designed to bring Quebec symbolically into the new constitutional framework and which would have generally increased provincial powers at Ottawa's expense.[32] Trudeau was the leading dissenter, feeling that Mulroney had given too much away.

During its second term, however, the Mulroney government increasingly aroused provincial anger, especially as it became obsessed with deficit reduction and cut back on grants to the provinces. The Mulroney government also enforced the Liberals' Canada Health Act, which imposed penalties on provinces that allowed doctors to extra-bill or permitted hospitals to charge user fees. Ontario, Alberta, and BC objected to the 1990 policy of reducing their grants under the Canada Assistance Plan, and several provinces were opposed to the Canada–U.S. and North American Free Trade Agreements. Mostly by designing the trade agreements to minimize their interference in provincial jurisdiction, Mulroney succeeded in getting them adopted.[33] But the major federal–provincial dispute of the Mulroney years concerned the Goods and Services Tax (GST), although to some extent it was just "good politics" for provincial premiers to jump on the anti-GST bandwagon because of widespread popular opposition. At first, only Quebec agreed to partial integration of its sales taxes with the new federal tax, even though many mutual advantages would have accrued to other provinces had they done so.

The Chrétien Liberals were initially popular with provincial governments in offering funds under the national infrastructure program and somewhat successful in negotiating a reduction in barriers that provinces imposed to the free movement of people, goods, services, and capital across the country. This was called the **Agreement on Internal Trade** and came into effect in July 1995.[34] The Chrétien government had no initial success in implementing their promise to replace the GST, however, only managing to persuade three Atlantic provinces to harmonize their retail sales taxes with the federal tax. Moreover, Ottawa made the provinces angry with reductions in their transfers from 1995 to 1999. The principal complaints included severe reductions in health, postsecondary education, and welfare transfers, as a result of Finance Minister Martin's Canada Health and Social Transfer, which combined the three programs into one block grant. At the same time, most provinces supported the principle of reducing government deficits, and seven were pleased that Ottawa did not cut equalization payments.[35]

In the wake of the defeat of the Charlottetown Accord and then the 1995 Quebec referendum, Ottawa decided to cede Quebec's foremost demand—provincial control over labour-market training. Rather than risk embarking on a form of asymmetrical federalism, however, the Chrétien government offered to transfer this responsibility to all provinces via bilateral and slightly different federal–provincial deals.[36] Then, the 1997 federal budget replaced the Child Tax Benefit with a new integrated National Child Benefit system developed through federal–provincial cooperation and supported by all ten provinces. Whether or not this new system had much effect on reducing the child poverty rate, it was a model of federal–provincial cooperation.[37]

Despite several significant federal–provincial agreements during the post-1995 period, many issues remained unresolved, and federal and provincial governments continued to crave some authoritative rules for their ongoing relationship. Among the concerns of the federal government were provinces not spending federal funds for the purposes intended (including violations of the Canada Health Act) and continuing barriers to social mobility across provinces and territories despite the Agreement on Internal Trade. Perhaps most of all, Ottawa demanded the right to use its spending power to make transfers to individuals, such as the Millennium Scholarships, which Quebec in particular opposed. The provinces, conversely, wanted to end unilateral federal changes in jointly funded programs (such as the Canada Health and Social Transfer cutbacks of 1995–99): they sought to ensure that any joint program offered to one province would be available to all, they insisted that Ottawa obtain provincial consent before establishing new joint social programs, and they expected at least to be consulted on programs in which Ottawa made direct transfers to individuals.

After many difficult negotiating sessions at the ministerial level, an agreement was finalized among the premiers and Prime Minister Chrétien (with Quebec dissenting) in February 1999 called the **Social Union Framework Agreement (SUFA)**. Such congeniality was encouraged by the simultaneous delivery of a multibillion-dollar increase in federal transfers to the provinces in the 1999 budget. The two most significant points were that the federal government agreed not to introduce new social programs involving transfers of money to the *provinces* without the support of a majority of provinces, and that Ottawa retained the right to use its spending power to make transfers directly to *people*.

· ·

CANADIAN FEDERALISM IN THE 21ST CENTURY

Canadian federalism in the 21st century demonstrates aspects of both continuity and change.[38] Despite the fact that the formal Constitution lists only three concurrent powers, despite the reduction in the role of all governments from about 1985 to 2000, and despite the attempt to disengage over the previous 15 years or so, federal and provincial governments continue to be intertwined in programs in almost every policy field. Thus, even though first ministers rarely meet collectively in formal conferences any more, there is probably as much federal–provincial interaction as ever at the ministerial and bureaucratic levels. Indeed, most of the action in the realm of Canadian federalism is taking place in political-bureaucratic circles rather than in the courts or in terms of constitutional reform. Meanwhile, at the initiative of Quebec Premier Jean Charest, the annual premiers' conference was transformed into the **Council of the Federation**. Its objective was to speak with a strong, united voice for the provinces and territories in their relations with the federal government, and considerable progress was made on institutionalizing the Council. Prime Minister Paul Martin promised the premiers a closer relationship than that of his predecessor, while Stephen Harper came to power with expectations of further decentralization. Indeed, the whole structure of Canadian federalism was somewhat transformed by new players and new relationships: how do Aboriginal self-government, direct contact between the federal government and cities, and relations between provincial governments and foreign states fit in?

Active Areas of Federal–Provincial Interaction

What are the main lines of federalism in the early years of the 21st century? Although some of the many active fields were the traditional ones, others gained new significance on the federal–provincial agenda. Health care, federal–provincial finances in general, equalization payments in particular, and the place of Quebec are almost always on the table, while the environment and Aboriginal affairs are among the newer issues in Canadian federalism.

TAXATION AGREEMENTS

Apart from Quebec, Alberta was the first province to withdraw from the 40-year-old integrated federal–provincial income tax system. This was because it wanted to adopt a "flat tax" that was incompatible with the base of the federal system. The other provinces soon disengaged as well because with federal tax cuts, a provincial "tax on tax" would have led to decreased revenues. All the provinces have now disengaged their provincial income tax rates from the federal income tax scheme and apply the provincial tax directly to residents' income. The new system is called "tax on income" instead of "tax on tax," and an enviable precedent of a nation-wide system with provincial variations has disappeared. All provinces except Quebec still allow the federal Canada Revenue Agency to collect their taxes for them, but the use of a different base complicates this task.[39] Ottawa reminds the provinces that they are free to raise their own taxes rather than always seeking larger federal transfers.

HEALTH CARE

Even before the publication of the Romanow report on the future of health care, which recommended larger federal health grants, the provinces persuaded Ottawa to increase its transfers in this field. This was primarily because the federal government had reduced its contributions when it brought in the Canada Health and Social Transfer and because it began running a budget surplus. In September 2000, for example, the federal government committed to invest $21.1 billion of additional cash through the CHST over five years. That did not satisfy the provinces, however, and they undertook a media campaign in 2002 to try to engage the public to demand even more federal financial support in this field. The 2003 First Ministers' Accord on Health Care Renewal promised the provinces an increase of

Prime Minister Paul Martin and his provincial and territorial counterparts at the first ministers' conference on Health in September 2004.

$35 billion over five years, and the 2003 budget foresaw the creation of two separate transfers as of 2004: a Canada Health Transfer and a Canada Social Transfer. When Paul Martin became prime minister, he called another first ministers' conference on health care in September 2004, which eventually agreed to an additional $18 billion in federal funding over the following six years. The "asymmetrical" dimension of the deal aroused some controversy, with Quebec being treated somewhat differently from the other provinces.[40] Although this money was intended to solve the health care problem for a generation, it did not take long for the provinces to ask for more.

A related issue was the apparent violation of the Canada Health Act in one way or another by almost all provinces.[41] Alberta was the worst culprit, allowing private (profit-oriented) clinics to perform surgical procedures, later including overnight stays, under the provincial health care system. Although Ottawa rarely penalized offending provinces, as it had a legal right to do, the provinces often complained that it should not be up to the federal government alone to police the Canada Health Act. Consequently, in 2002, Ottawa agreed to set up a three-person panel to resolve federal–provincial disputes over the Canada Health Act. But the federal government would continue to have the ultimate power to fine a province, regardless of the panel's recommendation. On the basis of the Romanow report, the Health Council of Canada was established as an independent body to advise Canadians on the performance of their health system, although Alberta and Quebec were reluctant to join.

The whole Canadian health care system then received a jolt when the Supreme Court of Canada ruled in the June 2005 *Chaoulli* case that Quebec's ban on private insurance in the provision of core health services was unconstitutional. The province was given a year in which to ensure that the public system provided timely treatment.[42] But in 2006, Quebec, British Columbia, and Alberta all announced plans to rely more heavily on private health care facilities in order to reduce wait times. These provinces argued that such an addition of profit-oriented services would not violate the Canada Health Act as long as those who were forced to use them had their costs covered by the public program.

A new aspect of federal–provincial relations in the health field has to do with public health threats, such as the SARS epidemic in Ontario in 2003, the possibility of health emergencies caused by terrorism, and H1N1 (swine flu) in 2009. Considerable discussion about the respective roles of the two levels of government has taken place in recent years on this issue.

EQUALIZATION PAYMENTS

As prime minister, Paul Martin agreed to revise the equalization formula in another first ministers' conference in 2005. Besides the demand for a general increase in the amount of such payments, Nova Scotia and Newfoundland and Labrador had a specific complaint with respect to their offshore petroleum industries. They claimed to be losing 70 cents in equalization payments for every new dollar of petroleum revenue they took in. At first, Ottawa rejected the claim, but Martin later negotiated side-deals with those two provinces that allowed them to retain offshore petroleum revenues with no reduction of equalization payments.[43] At this point, Ontario complained about an annual $23 billion gap between what it sent to Ottawa and what it received back. It ended up receiving several billion dollars over five years for immigration services, labour-market training, international border infrastructure, and meeting Kyoto requirements.

THE KYOTO PROTOCOL

Never before has an environmental issue caused so much federal–provincial discord as the Kyoto Protocol. As with other treaties, Ottawa has the constitutional power to sign and ratify the treaty, but not necessarily the complete jurisdiction to implement it. In 2002, Prime Minister Chrétien suddenly announced the ratification of Kyoto before any interprovincial agreement was in place. In Alberta's eyes, in particular, Kyoto appeared as a reincarnation of the NEP, although when it become clear that neither the Chrétien nor the Martin governments had any specific plan for implementation, the provinces stopped complaining.[44]

ABORIGINALS

Aboriginal issues remain near the top of Canada's political agenda and although Aboriginals are theoretically under federal jurisdiction, these issues increasingly assume a federal–provincial dimension. This is partly because land claims often involve Crown land owned by the province. Aboriginal peoples have usually fallen into a constitutional void, with the result that services to them, federal or provincial, are woefully inadequate. Moreover, there are different levels of government responsibility for different categories of Aboriginal people—status

Indians, non-status Indians, Métis, and so on. "The system is complex and involves many changing sites of initiative":[45] first ministers' conferences, the Supreme Court, comprehensive land claims, specific land claims, self-government agreements, program transfers and devolution, and relations between Aboriginal governments and urban-based Aboriginals on the one hand and provincial, territorial, and municipal governments on the other. As difficult as it is for Aboriginal peoples to achieve agreement from Ottawa, negotiation with most provincial governments is even more troublesome. On the positive side, federalism provides a model for Aboriginal self-governments to be raised, ultimately, to a third order of government in Canada, but much work needs to be done on a practical level to provide Aboriginals with the services they should be able to expect as Canadian citizens.

Aboriginal issues were a priority for the Paul Martin government. As mentioned in Chapter 4, he convened a first ministers and national Aboriginal leaders meeting in Kelowna in 2005. Martin announced that the federal government would commit $5 billion over five years toward a ten-year effort to close the gap in the quality of life between Aboriginal peoples and other Canadians. The premiers were enthusiastic participants and pledged to make significant contributions of their own.

CHILD CARE AND EARLY CHILDHOOD DEVELOPMENT

After repeated Conservative and Liberal promises of national child-care programs, or at least substantial federal support for such programs in the provinces, the federal government provided the provinces with $2.2 billion for early childhood development in 2000. In 2003, it increased federal assistance for child care as well as raising the National Child Benefit. But in 2005, under Social Development Minister Ken Dryden, the Martin government brought in "the first new national social program in a generation." As mentioned in Chapter 8, agreements were signed with each province, with few strings attached, in which they would share some $5 billion for this purpose over five years. Action in this field as well as in health can be seen as "targeted" federal funding (rather than conditional or block grants, as such): federal transfers that are specified for certain areas of policy but that may not require provinces to meet specific conditions. This new type of transfer still allows the federal government to direct the shape of provincial programs.[46]

BRINGING IN THE CITIES

For the most part, Canadian federalism has ignored municipal governments in the past. "This is primarily because of the way in which provinces have generally resisted ... any direct involvement by the federal government in helping local governments deal with persistent urban problems."[47] But large metropolitan centres were now demanding more powers, as well as the right to be directly involved in federal–provincial discussions dealing with their needs. They were asking for more taxation powers and more federal funding for such problems as mass urban transit, other infrastructure, housing, health, the environment, and public education for immigrant children. They would also like to see the re-creation of a federal department of urban affairs and to carve out a non-subordinate niche within the Constitution.

As noted in Chapter 9, Paul Martin promised a "new deal for cities." He provided considerable opportunity for cities to contribute to federal policy, eventually creating a Ministry of

State for Infrastructure and Communities, and exempted municipalities from paying the GST on their purchases. But his government's major contribution to cities (and other communities) was to share the revenues from the federal gasoline excise tax: Ottawa would transfer the equivalent of five cents per litre to a total of $5 billion over five years. Tailored bilateral agreements with the provinces would provide that these transfers be passed on to municipalities to help finance environmentally friendly infrastructure projects.

PROVINCES AND EXTERNAL RELATIONS

Besides being complicated by direct communication between the federal government and the cities, Canadian federalism is being challenged by provincial demands to play a role in external relations.[48] A certain amount of interaction between provinces and foreign states has taken place for many years, highlighted by Quebec's role in the Francophonie and Ottawa's consultation with forestry-producing provinces in connection with the softwood lumber dispute. Quebec now wants to play an even more prominent role on the world stage, while other provinces, especially Alberta, demand a say in Canadian foreign and trade policies that affect them. With its enormous daily cross-border trade with the United States, Ontario is concerned with maintaining an open border in the post–9/11 era.

Stephen Harper's Conservatives

Stephen Harper came to power in 2004 with a policy of **open federalism**, meaning the adoption of an even more decentralist approach.[49] Several of his priorities affected the provinces, and many involved reversing Martin's initiatives. The promise to lower the Goods and Services Tax had minor implications for those provinces that had harmonized their retail sales tax with the GST. Harper did not honour the full Kelowna commitment with respect to additional funding for Aboriginal problems, and did not object to the privatizing initiatives of some of the provinces in the health care field, even though these appeared to contradict both his election platform and the Canada Health Act. This may have been because a reduction in wait times was one of its first five election priorities. The promise to scrap the new early childhood and child care agreements that the Martin government had just finished signing with all ten provinces raised considerable provincial, municipal, and other objections. Instead, Harper had campaigned on the proposal to make an annual payment of $1200 for each child under six and allow families to use it in whichever way they chose to care for their children. Harper persuaded the provinces to accept a new softwood lumber deal with the United States and the new government hoped to make some progress on the issue of a national system of regulating the securities industry, a longstanding problem.

With the environment so prominent on the political agenda these days, the question arises whether its protection is a federal or provincial responsibility. In short, "environmental protection" is such a vast subject that aspects of it fall into both federal and provincial jurisdiction. If a taxation approach is pursued (e.g., carbon tax), Ottawa has unlimited taxation powers, but the provinces might design a legitimate tax as well. If a regulatory approach is used (e.g., emissions caps), the subject is even more complicated. Former Alberta premier Peter Lougheed has predicted a major constitutional confrontation between the federal and Alberta governments over capping emissions from the oil sands, but the Harper government rejected the Kyoto Protocol in favour of a less stringent approach to environmental protection. It was only when the new Obama administration in the United States threatened to cut off imports of Canadian petroleum not meeting new environmental standards that Harper began to take greenhouse gas emissions seriously. Even so, Alberta and Saskatchewan resisted.

Harper also promised to redress the so-called **fiscal imbalance** between the two levels of government, a constant refrain from Quebec in particular.[50] The 2007 federal budget did indeed seek to "fix" it with a boost in long-term funding support for training, post-secondary education, and infrastructure projects. As for equalization, as mentioned in Chapter 3, a new formula considerably increased the total amount of the transfer, especially for Quebec. Inspired by the O'Brien Report, it was based on only five taxes: personal income tax, business income tax, consumption tax, property tax, and one-half of a province's non-renewable resource revenues. It used a 10-province average, but imposed a cap on the payments a province would receive if it exceeded the fiscal capacity of a non-recipient province. Newfoundland and Labrador and Nova Scotia were permitted to stay with the Atlantic Accord if they wished, but the new formula would be more generous in the short-term, at least. Newfoundland premier Danny Williams was alarmed at Harper's change of heart with respect to not exempting resource revenues as well as the imposition of the cap and campaigned against him in the 2008 federal election. Nova Scotia later signed a side-deal, as well as receiving over $700 million as a result of a settlement of the 1985 agreement.[51]

Harper was particularly solicitous of Quebec. Besides the federal–provincial financial generosity mentioned above, he fulfilled that province's demand to have a seat in the Canadian delegation to UNESCO. Harper sponsored a resolution in the House of Commons that recognized the Québécois as a nation within a united Canada, and allowed Quebec to sign a labour-mobility agreement with France. Such actions continued Martin's approach of **asymmetrical federalism**.

The Federation of Canadian Municipalities argued that $123 billion was required by cities to bring bridges, roads, and water systems up to a minimum state of repair. The Harper government had only promised them $33 billion over seven years for infrastructure investments, coming from a full refund of all GST monies paid by municipalities and the transfer of a portion of the federal gasoline tax.[52] But after the 2008 economic meltdown, such infrastructure projects became a much higher priority of the government. In fact, by means of the Building Canada Fund, Ottawa was not only helping provincial and municipal governments, but also ensuring that their infrastructure spending was aligned with federal thinking.

It is clear that the federal structure of the country complicates the solution of many public problems, including those listed immediately above.[53] These issues and others demonstrate that despite the formal constitutional division of powers, Canada is characterized by a large amount of *de facto* concurrent jurisdiction.[54] Given the enormous degree of federal–provincial interaction that will be required in the future and an extremely rigid constitutional amending formula, the two or three levels of government have no choice but to work together in non-constitutional channels.

CONCLUSION

Federalism in Canada is both based on and intensifies regional, economic, and ethnic cleavages. In the beginning, the Canadian federal system was highly centralized, but this original design was soon found to be inappropriate for the society in which it operated. When the cleavages became difficult to overcome, and as "province-builders" competed with "nation-builders," Canada gradually became a very decentralized federation. Both in the courts and in negotiations with Ottawa, the provinces successfully fought for more powers and more financial resources. Although federalism often seems to be an unending source of intergovernmental discord, as well as a convenient excuse at both levels of government for not responding to demands, the importance of the continuing maze of cooperative federal–provincial interaction cannot be overestimated. In this respect, the original division of powers between the two levels of government has almost become irrelevant.

This chapter is closely linked to the preceding one on the Constitution. Chapter 3 on regionalism is also connected to federalism, but almost every chapter of the book reveals the effects of this central principle of the Canadian political system.

(SC) As in the case of the Constitution, the state-centred approach is most relevant to the Canadian federal system. It maintains that federal and provincial governments act in their own interests or in accordance with their own conception of the public interest, without much regard for the wishes of the general public. Ministers and bureaucrats usually want to maximize their own power and responsibility, so that both levels of government have expanded operations to the point of considerable overlap. Federal authorities argue for greater jurisdiction, revenue, conditions, standards, and controls, while provincial authorities fight for maximum provincial revenue, flexibility, and freedom.

Some state-centred theorists contend that much of the federal–provincial discord is an artificial competition among federal and provincial politicians and bureaucrats, rather than a real fight reflecting public opinion. Provincial governments demand powers, money, and constitutional vetoes in the name of their residents, but the residents themselves may be indifferent as to whether they are taxed, regulated, or provided for by federal or provincial governments. The cooperative mechanisms of executive federalism and the central role of the public service in bureaucratic federalism can also be seen as evidence of the state-centred approach. The public can do little but accept whatever arrangements are worked out among and federal and provincial bureaucrats and then sold to their ministers.[55]

The centralist and decentralist swings identified above are sometimes analyzed in terms of the concepts of nation-building as opposed to province-building. The overarching concern of the national political elite—prime ministers, federal cabinets, and leading bureaucrats—has been to construct a strong central government. But the creation of provinces produced counterbalancing provincial political elites—premiers, provincial cabinets, and bureaucrats—who were more interested in building strong provinces. In short, province-building means that the provincial state plays a significant role within the confines of the provincial society. Strong provincial governments want more powers, autonomy, and money, a demand that explains much of the pressure for decentralization in the Canadian federal system since 1960 or so.

P Nation-building and province-building are not confined to government elites. In each case, they have been supported by certain societal forces. At the national level, these include elements of the business community (banking, transportation, communications, manufacturing) and by most of the anglophone intellectual elite. Provincial political elites had support within their societies, primarily including natural resource companies, professionals, and others concerned with property. Pluralists also note that provincial political and bureaucratic elites genuinely represent diversified provincial societies and that it was in response to the scattered and diverse population with its different interests and regional loyalties that a federation was originally established. Pluralist theorists are among those who contend that the Judicial Committee of the Privy Council was farsighted in interpreting the division of powers in a decentralist direction; contrary to the intentions of John A. Macdonald, its decisions were entirely consistent with the "federal society" into which Canada evolved. Federalism allows provincial governments to take action in the interests of their own cultural majorities or distinctive industries that would generate much controversy at the national level. It permits experimentation in social policies, such that those that prove successful at the provincial level (e.g., medicare) can later be adopted in other provinces and at the national level.[56] Federalism also maximizes the number of organized groups that can make their voices heard, some at the national level and others in the provinces.

Ⓒ Most class analysts decry decentralization of the federal system for its stifling of creative, national programs.[57] They would prefer new and stronger national social programs and labour and environmental standards, which are not possible because of broad provincial jurisdiction. Generally speaking, class analysts assume that the federal government is more likely than the provinces to produce "progressive" policies. They want a strong and redistributive central state with high uniform national standards, and they are suspicious of what provincial governments would do with federal health grants without conditions attached. While arguing for greater centralization, class analysts point out how frequently private corporate interests have taken the opposite position. The corporate elite has often used its influence with friendly provincial governments to frustrate national initiatives and has challenged the federal government in court in order to enhance provincial jurisdiction in places where it has been more influential at that level.[58] More generally, business wants a relatively weak, non-redistributive federal government, and to some extent class analysts argue that constitutional debates and seemingly obscure skirmishes over the details of fiscal federalism have been a veil behind which a struggle has been waged over the size and character of the central state. Corporate preference for decentralization is not absolute, however; it depends on what actions provincial governments try to take. In Saskatchewan in the 1970s, mining and petroleum companies challenged the constitutionality of provincial NDP legislation they opposed, and in Alberta in the 1930s and 1940s, the banks took oppressive Social Credit banking legislation to the courts.

PC Public choice theorists see Ottawa's relations with the provinces in electoral terms. If Ontario and Quebec have the largest number of marginal seats at stake, for example, federal authorities will be most responsive to the demands articulated by their governments. This can be seen in the case of the National Energy Program (supported by Ontario) or in awarding Quebec instead of Manitoba the CF-18 maintenance contract. From 2004 onward, Stephen Harper's Conservatives were anxious to win more seats in both Quebec and Ontario and therefore tried to tailor their policies to voters in those two provinces; unfortunately for them, ideology often interfered with this objective.

Between 1985 and 2000, or so, Canada practised "disengaging federalism," which was undertaken under the influence of neoliberalism, the ideological lynchpin of globalization that reduced the role of both levels of the state. An example is the 1995 Agreement on Internal Trade, a counterpart to international trade agreements, in which federal and provincial governments agreed to create an internal "free market" by reducing interprovincial barriers to trade. The whole thrust of the Chrétien–Martin obsession with balancing the budget in the 1990s, to a large extent by reducing transfers to the provinces for health, social assistance, and postsecondary education, could also be seen as evidence of the globalization mentality affecting Canadian federalism. Now that neoliberalism has passed its peak, globalization affects Canadian federalism primarily in the concerns provinces have to influence federal trade and foreign policy, as well as to interact directly with other jurisdictions around the world.

DISCUSSION QUESTIONS

1. Are you a centralist or a decentralist? Why? What are the advantages and disadvantages of centralization and decentralization in Canadian federalism?

2. Do the residents of most provinces want a decentralized federal system or is it just the politicians and bureaucrats in such provinces who do?

3. Is it possible to have a clear-cut division of powers between federal and provincial governments in a modern era of such extensive government activity?

4. Should the federal government be able to spend money for any purpose, even within provincial jurisdiction? Should it be able to set conditions on provincial medicare programs?

5. Should federal grants to the provinces take the form of conditional, block, or unconditional grants? Why?

6. What are the advantages and disadvantages of executive federalism?

7. How have the weaknesses of intrastate federalism contributed to the importance of interstate federalism?

NOTES

1. *Reference re The Secession of Quebec*, [1998] 2 S.C.R., p. 244.
2. Nelson Wiseman, *In Search of Canadian Political Culture* (Vancouver: UBC Press, 2007).
3. Christopher Dunn, "Premiers and Cabinets," in Christopher Dunn, ed., *Provinces*, 2nd ed. (Peterborough: Broadview Press, 2006).
4. Graham White, "Evaluating Provincial and Territorial Legislatures," in Dunn, *Provinces*.
5. Rand Dyck, "Provincial Politics in the Modern Era," in Dunn, *Provinces*.
6. C. Richard Tindal and Susan Nobes Tindal, *Local Government in Canada*, 7th ed. (Toronto: Nelson Education, 2009).
7. Donald Smiley, *The Canadian Political Nationality* (Toronto: Methuen, 1967).
8. K.C. Wheare, *Federal Government*, 4th ed. (London: Oxford University Press, 1963).
9. D.V. Smiley and R.L. Watts, *Intrastate Federalism in Canada* (Toronto: University of Toronto Press, 1985).

10. Peter Russell, Rainer Knopff, and Ted Morton, *Federalism and the Charter* (Ottawa: Carleton University Press, 1989); Peter Russell, et al., *The Court and the Constitution: Leading Cases* (Toronto: Emond Montgomery, 2008); Peter Hogg, *Constitutional Law of Canada* (Toronto: Carswell, Student Edition, 2006); Patrick J. Monahan, *Constitutional Law* (Toronto: Irwin Law, 1998); and Bernard Funston and Eugene Meehan, *Canada's Constitutional Law in a Nutshell*, 2nd ed. (Toronto: Carswell, 1998).

11. *R. v. Crown Zellerbach Canada Ltd.*, [1988] 1 S.C.R. 401; *Alberta Government Telephones v. Canada (Canadian Radio-television and Telecommunications Commission)*, [1989] 2 S.C.R. 225; *Friends of the Oldman River Society v. Canada (Minister of Transport)*, [1992] 1 S.C.R. 3; *Ontario Hydro v. Ontario (Labour Relations Board)*, [1993] 3 S.C.R. 327; *Téléphone Guèvremont Inc. v. Quebec (Régis des télécommunications)*, [1994] 1 S.C.R. 878; *R. v. Hydro-Quebec*, [1997] 3 S.C.R. 213; *Reference Re: Firearms Act (Can.)*, [2000] 1 S.C.R. 783; *Reference re Employment Insurance Act*, [2005] 2 S.C.R. 669; and *Kirkbi AG v. Ritvik Holdings Inc.*, [2005] 3 S.C.R. 302. See also *Reference Re: Canada Assistance Plan (B.C.)*, [1991] 2 S.C.R. 525; and Gerald Baier, "Judicial Review and Canadian Federalism," in Herman Bakvis and Grace Skogstad, eds., *Canadian Federalism: Performance, Effectiveness, and Legitimacy* (Toronto: Oxford University Press, 2002).

12. V.C. MacDonald, "Judicial Interpretation of the Canadian Constitution," *University of Toronto Law Journal* 1 (1935–36); and the O'Connor Report, Senate of Canada, 1939. It is ironic that judicial interpretation contributed to decentralizing a centralized Canadian federation but centralized a decentralized federation in the United States. See Roger Gibbins, *Regionalism* (Toronto: Butterworths, 1982), ch. 4.

13. Alan C. Cairns, "The Governments and Societies of Canadian Federalism," *Canadian Journal of Political Science* (December 1977).

14. Alan C. Cairns, "The Judicial Committee and Its Critics," *Canadian Journal of Political Science* (September 1971), and reprinted in Cairns, *Constitution, Government and Society in Canada* (Toronto: McClelland and Stewart, 1988). See also John T. Saywell, *The Lawmakers: Judicial Power and the Shaping of Canadian Federalism* (Toronto: University of Toronto Press, 2003).

15. Cairns, *Constitution, Government, and Society in Canada*, p. 63.

16. Canadian Tax Foundation, *Finances of the Nation* (Toronto: Annual); David B. Perry, *Financing the Canadian Federation, 1867–1995: Setting the Stage for Change* (Toronto: Canadian Tax Foundation, 1997); and Robin W. Boadway and Paul A.R. Hobson, *Intergovernmental Fiscal Relations in Canada* (Toronto: Canadian Tax Foundation, 1993).

17. Direct taxes are derived from the very people who are intended to pay them, while indirect taxes are extracted from one person or company in the expectation that they will be passed on to someone else.

18. Not only does Ottawa have the power to spend; it can also abruptly stop spending! *Reference re Canada Assistance Plan (B.C.)*, [1991] 2 S.C.R. 525; *Finlay v. Canada (Minister of Finance)*, [1993] 1 S.C.R. 1080; Keith Banting, *The Welfare State and Canadian Federalism* (Kingston: McGill-Queen's University Press, 1982), pp. 52–54; D.V. Smiley and R.M. Burns, "Canadian Federalism and the Spending Power: Is Constitutional Restriction Necessary?" *Canadian Tax Journal* 17 (1969), pp. 468–82; Andrew Petter, "Federalism and the Myth of the Federal Spending Power," *Canadian Bar Review* (September 1989); and Christopher Dunn, "The Federal Spending Power," in Dunn, ed., *The Handbook of Canadian Public Administration* (Toronto: Oxford University Press, 2002), ch. 13.

19. T.J. Courchene, *Equalization Payments: Past, Present and Future* (Toronto: Ontario Economic Council, 1984); and Robin W. Boadway and Paul A.R. Hobson, *Equalization* (Kingston: McGill-Queen's University Press, 1998).

20. G.V. La Forest, *The Allocation of Taxing Powers under the Canadian Constitution*, 2nd ed. (Toronto: Canadian Tax Foundation, 1981).

21. Canadian Tax Foundation, *Provincial and Municipal Finances, 1989*, p. 12:1.

22. Jim Silver, "Constitutional Change, Ideological Conflict and the Redistributive State," in James McCrorie and Martha MacDonald, eds., *The Constitutional Future of the Prairie and Atlantic Regions of Canada* (Regina: Canadian Plains Research Center, 1992).

23. G.V. La Forest, *Disallowance and Reservation of Provincial Legislation* (Ottawa: Queen's Printer, 1965).

24. Andrew Heard, *Canadian Constitutional Conventions* (Toronto: Oxford University Press, 1991).

25. Garth Stevenson, "Federalism and Intergovernmental Relations," in Michael Whittington and Glen Williams, eds., *Canadian Politics in the 21st Century*, 7th ed. (Toronto: Thomson Nelson, 2008).

26. This discussion is loosely based on J.R. Mallory, "The Five Faces of Canadian Federalism," in P.-A. Crépeau and C.B. Macpherson, eds., *The Future of Canadian Federalism* (Toronto: University of Toronto Press, 1965).

27. Donald Smiley, *Canada in Question: Federalism in the Seventies* (Toronto: McGraw-Hill Ryerson, 1972), p. 56.

28. Heard, *Canadian Constitutional Conventions*, pp. 110–16.

29. Richard Simeon, *Federal–Provincial Diplomacy* (Toronto: University of Toronto Press, 1972).

30. J. Stefan Dupré, "Reflections on the Workability of Executive Federalism," in Richard Simeon, ed., *Intergovernmental Relations* (Toronto: University of Toronto Press, 1985); D.V. Smiley, *The Federal Condition in Canada* (Toronto: McGraw-Hill Ryerson, 1987), pp. 87–89; and Carolyn M. Johns, et al., "Formal and Informal Dimensions of Intergovernmental Administrative Relations in Canada," *Canadian Public Administration* (March 2007).

31. J.L. Granatstein, *The Ottawa Men: The Civil Service Mandarins 1935–1957* (Toronto: Oxford University Press, 1982).

32. The Meech Lake Accord is discussed in Chapter 16.

33. Grace Skogstad, "International Trade Policy and Canadian Federalism: A Constructive Tension," in Bakvis and Skogstad, *Canadian Federalism*, ch. 9.

34. Robert H. Knox, "Economic Integration in Canada through the Agreement on Internal Trade," in Harvey Lazar, ed., *Canada: The State of the Federation 1997: Non-Constitutional Renewal* (Kingston: Institute of Intergovernmental Relations, Queen's University, 1997); and Mark R. MacDonald, "The Agreement on Internal Trade: Trade-Offs for Economic Union and Federalism," in Bakvis and Skogstad, *Canadian Federalism*, ch. 11.

35. Among the best sources on this subject are the reviews published annually since 1980 by the Queen's University Institute of Intergovernmental Relations.

36. Herman Bakvis, "Checkerboard Federalism? Labour Market Development Policy in Canada," in Bakvis and Skogstad, *Canadian Federalism*, ch. 11.

37. Ken Battle, "The 1997 Budget and the Child Benefits Package," in Thomas J. Courchene and Thomas A. Wilson, *The 1997 Federal Budget: Retrospect and Prospect* (Kingston: John Deutsch Institute for the Study of Economic Policy, 1997); and Linda A. White, "The Child Care Agenda and the Social Union," in Bakvis and Skogstad, *Canadian Federalism*, ch. 6.

38. Bakvis and Skogstad, *Canadian Federalism*.

39. Douglas M. Brown, "Fiscal Federalism: The New Equilibrium between Equity and Efficiency," in Bakvis and Skogstad, *Canadian Federalism*, p. 73; Stevenson, "Federalism and Intergovernmental Relations," (2008), p. 90.

40. Tom McIntosh, "Intergovernmental Relations, Social Policy and Federal Transfers after Romanow," *Canadian Public Administration* (Spring 2004).

41. See *The Globe and Mail*, December 13, 2002, for a list of such violations up to that time.

42. *Chaoulli v. Quebec (Attorney General)*, [2005] 1 S.C.R. 791.

43. *Achieving A National Purpose: Putting Equalization Back on Track* (Ottawa: Department of Finance Canada, May 2006); Stevenson, "Federalism and Intergovernmental Relations," (2008), p. 91.

44. Mark S. Winfield, "Environmental Policy and Federalism," in Bakvis and Skogstad, *Canadian Federalism*, ch. 7.

45. Frances Abele and Michael J. Prince, "Alternative Futures: Aboriginal Peoples and Canadian Federalism," in Bakvis and Skogstad, *Canadian Federalism*, ch. 12.

46. Gérard Boismenu and Peter Graefe, "The New Federal Toolbelt: Attempts to Rebuild Social Policy Leadership," *Canadian Public Policy* 30:1 (2004).

47. Andrew Sancton, "Municipalities, Cities, and Globalization: Implications for Canadian Federalism," in Bakvis and Skogstad, *Canadian Federalism*, ch. 14; Robert Young and Christian Leuprecht, *Canada and the State of the Federation 2004: Municipal–Federal–Provincial Relations* (Kingston: Institute of Intergovernmental Relations, 2005); and Tindal and Tindal, *Local Government in Canada*.

48. Christopher J. Kukucha, "From Kyoto to the WTO: Evaluating the Constitutional Legitimacy of the Provinces in Canadian Foreign Trade and Environmental Policy," *Canadian Journal of Political Science* (March 2005); Heather MacIvor, *Parameters of Power*, 5th ed. (Toronto: Nelson Education, 2010), pp. 112–16.

49. Adam Harmes, "The Political Economy of Open Federalism," *Canadian Journal of Political Science* (June 2007), emphasizes the neoliberal component of the policy.

50. Sujit Choudhury, et al., *Dilemmas of Solidarity: Rethinking Redistribution in the Canadian Federation* (Toronto: University of Toronto Press, 2006); Institute for Research on Public Policy, *Policy Options*, September 2006 and March and April 2007 issues.

51. MacIvor, *Parameters of Power*, pp. 101–05.

52. Enid Slack and Richard M. Bird, "Cities in Canadian Federalism," *Institute for Research on Public Policy, Policy Options* (December 2007/January 2008).

53. Stevenson, "Federalism and Intergovernmental Relations," (2008), pp. 79, 86, and 100; Irvin Studin, "Process Before Product: A New Federal–Provincial Logic for a New Century," Institute for Research on Public Policy, *Policy Options* (September 2008).

54. Bakvis and Skogstad, "Canadian Federalism: Performance, Effectiveness, and Legitimacy," in *Canadian Federalism*, p. 11.

55. Richard Simeon and David Cameron, "Intergovernmental Relations and Democracy: An Oxymoron If There Ever Was One?" in Bakvis and Skogstad, *Canadian Federalism*, ch. 15, write that any notion that democracy and federalism coincide is an oxymoron!

56. Ironically, it was the later foe of decentralization, Pierre Trudeau, who told the socialist academic community in 1961 that they should not be so obsessed with centralization, that progressive social policies could sometimes be pioneered more successfully at the provincial level. "The Practice and Theory of Federalism," in Michael Oliver, ed., *Social Purpose for Canada* (Toronto: University of Toronto Press, 1961).

57. See, for example, John Porter, *The Vertical Mosaic* (Toronto: University of Toronto Press, 1965).

58. J.R. Mallory, *Social Credit and the Federal Power in Canada* (Toronto: University of Toronto Press, 1954); and Silver, "Constitutional Change, Ideological Conflict and the Redistributive State."

· ·

FURTHER READING

Bakvis, Herman, and Grace Skogstad, eds. *Canadian Federalism: Performance, Effectiveness, and Legitimacy.* Toronto: Oxford University Press, 2002.

Cairns, Alan C. *Constitution, Government, and Society in Canada.* Toronto: McClelland and Stewart, 1988.

Canadian Tax Foundation. *Finances of the Nation.* Toronto, annual (under various authors).

Harrison, Kathryn, ed. *Racing to the Bottom? Provincial Interdependence in the Canadian Federation.* Vancouver: UBC Press, 2005.

Hogg, Peter. *Constitutional Law of Canada*, student ed. Toronto: Carswell, 2006.

Institute of Intergovernmental Relations, Queen's University. *Canada: The State of the Federation*, annual (under the name of various editors).

LaSelva, Samuel. *The Moral Foundations of Canadian Federalism: Paradoxes, Achievements, and Tragedies of Nationhood.* Montreal: McGill-Queen's University Press, 1997.

Monahan, Patrick. *Constitutional Law*, 2nd ed. Toronto: Irwin Law, 2002.

Rocher, François, and Miriam Smith, eds. *New Trends in Canadian Federalism*, 2nd ed. Peterborough: Broadview Press, 2003.

Russell, Peter, et al. *The Court and the Constitution: Leading Cases.* Toronto Emond Montgomery, 2008.

Saywell, John T. *The Lawmakers: Judicial Power and the Shaping of Canadian Federalism.* Toronto: University of Toronto Press, 2003.

Stevenson, Garth. "Federalism and Intergovernmental Relations," in Michael Whittington and Glen Williams, eds., *Canadian Politics in the 21st Century*, 7th ed. Toronto: Thomson Nelson, 2008.

Tindal, C. Richard, and Susan Nobes Tindal. *Local Government in Canada*, 7th ed. Toronto: Nelson Education, 2009.

Chapter 19

THE CHARTER OF
Rights and Freedoms

Does the right to freedom of expression permit unrestricted access to pornography? Is regulation of Sunday shopping a violation of the freedom of religion of non-Christian groups? Does a person have the right to call a lawyer when stopped by a police officer and asked to take a breath test? Does freedom of association guarantee the right to strike? Does a person who has a terminal illness have a right to assisted suicide? Should tobacco companies be allowed to advertise cigarettes? Should police officers be able to enter dwellings without a search warrant? Does the state have a right to outlaw private health insurance? In the case of sexual relations, does no mean no? And in any of these cases, who should have the last say—legislatures or judges?

Civil liberties consist of rights and freedoms that individuals enjoy beyond the reach of the government or the state. Such rights and freedoms are an integral part of a democratic political system and represent territory into which the government is not allowed to enter as it makes and enforces public policy for a society. Chapter 16 pointed out that a constitution typically provides for the relationship between government and citizens, but that the Constitution Act, 1867, did not have much to say in this regard. Although many such civil liberties have always existed in Canada, they were constitutionalized and enlarged upon in 1982 in the form of the Charter of Rights and Freedoms, and it is increasingly the task of the judiciary to determine if and when governments have encroached on those rights. The Charter has had a profound influence on the Canadian political system in protecting such rights and freedoms, but it has also affected the operation of many other aspects of the system. On the other hand, its impact should not be exaggerated.

This chapter begins by defining such rights and freedoms and discussing the means of protecting them in Canada before 1982. The central part of the chapter examines the provisions of the Charter of Rights and Freedoms and some of the principal court cases that interpreted each clause in its first 25–30 years of existence. It concludes by discussing the implications of the Charter for the overall political system.

. . . .

DEFINING AND PROTECTING RIGHTS AND FREEDOMS

Rights and freedoms are commonly classified into four categories.[1] The first relates to political liberties, including the fundamental freedoms of speech, press, assembly, and religion. The second, legal rights, includes the procedural rights of a person suspected or accused of committing a crime, a liberty encompassing that person's right to legal counsel, a presumption of innocence, bail, and a fair trial. The third aspect of such rights and freedoms involves equality rights—that is, freedom from discrimination on such bases as gender, race, religion, or age. Canadians almost universally support these three categories of rights and freedoms, and they are therefore embedded in the Charter. The fourth category, economic rights, is more controversial. Although the right to own property, for example, is recognized in law as well as in the Canadian Bill of Rights, it was not enshrined in the Charter.[2]

Political systems that value such rights and freedoms have adopted two principal methods to protect them. The British approach is to make Parliament supreme but on the presumption that neither the legislature nor the executive would infringe civil liberties, because both are held in check by public opinion, tradition, the political culture, and self-restraint. Such rights and freedoms are so deeply ingrained in the values of the people and politicians alike that the latter would never think of infringing them, even though, in theory, Parliament could do so. Although the courts cannot overturn legislation in Britain—that is, they do not have the power of **judicial review**—they have wide **judicial discretion** in the interpretation of laws, and many civil libertarian values have been introduced into the law as canons of interpretation.[3] Thus, even in the British system, judicial precedents accumulated into the common law offer protection against arbitrary government action. So does the basic constitutional principle, the **rule of law**, which requires that every official act be based on law. In typical British manner, then, the fact that they were not written down did not mean that civil liberties did not exist.

The American approach, derived in reaction to an imperial government that *did* encroach on colonial liberties, is to provide for a written statement of civil liberties (usually called "civil rights") in a constitutional Bill of Rights. Then, if legislation is passed or the executive takes action that is felt to violate a person's rights, such acts can be challenged in the courts. It is up to the courts to determine whether the government has infringed civil rights as defined in the Constitution. The courts thus have the power of judicial review and can overturn offensive legislation or executive acts.

Neither the British nor the American system remotely approaches perfection, and both are designed only to restrict the actions of *governments*. In most cases, that is, bills and charters of rights do not extend to *private*, interpersonal relationships. Prohibitions against private discrimination, such as in employment and accommodation, are instead generally covered by human rights codes. Each province and territory in Canada has such a code, as does the federal government, and they are enforced by human rights commissions through investigation, conciliation, and, if necessary, adjudication of disputes.

. . . .

EN ROUTE TO THE CHARTER

A discussion of protecting rights and freedoms in Canada can be divided into three eras.[4] In the first, Canada inherited the British system based on parliamentary restraint within **parliamentary supremacy**. For the most part, therefore, Canadians' civil liberties depended on politicians' voluntarily respecting them or protecting them in legislation. Although many abuses can be enumerated, the Canadian record reflected the tenor of the times, and was probably as good as that of any other contemporary state—certainly no worse than the U.S. system where such rights were embedded in the constitution.

Unlike the UK, however, the Canadian situation was complicated by the adoption of federalism. Hence, Canada possessed two supreme legislatures, one in Ottawa and another in the provinces, each operating within its own constitutional jurisdiction. Federalism allowed the courts to engage in judicial review in the sense of invalidating federal or provincial legislation that violated the division of powers. In so doing, federalism also opened the door to judicial review in the protection of rights and freedoms. That is, if the courts could show that either level of government infringed civil liberties in the process of exceeding its jurisdiction in terms of the division of powers, then the courts could strike down the law.

Thus, even before the adoption of a constitutional bill or charter of rights, the Canadian courts were able to intervene to a limited extent to overturn legislation that violated such rights. The simultaneous violation of the division of powers and civil liberties most often took place at the provincial level, where the courts found provincial legislation infringing federal power in the realm of criminal law.

The courts sometimes supplemented this ground for their decisions by citing the preamble to the 1867 Constitution Act. It speaks of Canada's desire to have "a constitution similar in principle to that of Great Britain." Since civil liberties were generally recognized in Britain (albeit without judicial review), they should be applicable to Canadians, too. This interpretation, sometimes called an **implied bill of rights**, would have allowed the courts to go beyond the division of powers in striking down legislation that violated rights and freedoms, but it was rarely and inconsistently applied.[5]

Many abuses of rights and freedoms were never taken to court, and of those that were, most were dismissed. But three principal cases of judicial protection of such rights and freedoms in the period before 1960 can be cited. First, freedom of the press was at issue in the 1938 *Alberta Press Bill* case. The Alberta legislation allowed the government to order newspapers to reveal the sources of unfavourable comment and gave it the right to respond to criticism. The courts found this legislation invalid because it was an infringement of the federal criminal law power.[6] In the 1950s the freedom of religion of Jehovah's Witnesses in Quebec was at stake, such as in requiring them to obtain permission from the chief of police before they could distribute their literature on the sidewalk. Once again the federal criminal law power and the preamble proved to be useful in overturning a provincial law.[7] In 1957 the Supreme Court disposed of Premier Maurice Duplessis's **Padlock Law** on the same grounds. This law had given the premier and attorney general the power to padlock any building that Duplessis considered was being used for the propagation of communism and bolshevism, but having left these terms undefined, it was used against opposition groups of any kind.[8]

Another means of protecting rights and freedoms even in the pre-1960 period was to find executive actions to be contrary to the rule of law. This ground was used successfully on three occasions with respect to police and government treatment of Jehovah's Witnesses in the Duplessis period in Quebec. In the most famous case, the court found the premier himself had acted contrary to the rule of law: that is, he took action based not on law but on his dislike of Jehovah's Witnesses when he personally cancelled a tavern owner's liquor licence.[9]

John Diefenbaker, the architect of the Canadian Bill of Rights, 1960.

Violations of civil liberties that did not also offend the division of powers or rule of law gave the courts little discretion. For example, in a 1903 case that concerned denial of the vote to Asians in British Columbia provincial elections, the courts ruled that such electoral matters were entirely within the jurisdiction of provincial politicians.[10] Neither did Canadian Blacks find any satisfaction in the courts when they challenged discriminatory practices.[11] Although the federal government was generally more sensitive to rights and freedoms than the provinces were, its record left much to be desired, especially in the case of Aboriginals, women, radical speech, and minorities of various kinds, including its treatment of citizens of certain ethnocultural origins during the two world wars. Ottawa's internment of Canadian citizens of Japanese extraction during the Second World War proved both that the federal government was not above reproach and that the courts could do nothing about it.[12]

Thus, before 1960, both federal and provincial politicians were guilty of violating civil liberties. This fact and the realization that the courts could rarely be counted on to invalidate such actions persuaded John Diefenbaker to enact the **Canadian Bill of Rights** in 1960.[13] He was also influenced, as were many other states about the same time, by the United Nations' adoption of the Universal Declaration on Human Rights; indeed, the province of Saskatchewan had pioneered such a bill on Canadian soil. The Bill of Rights therefore inaugurated the second era in the protection of rights and freedoms in Canada.

The document's apparent aim was to allow the courts to invalidate legislation that they found to conflict with the Bill of Rights, but if so, this aim was not clearly articulated. The courts were never completely certain if they had been given this power or not. Other serious gaps in the bill were that it applied only to the federal government, not to the provinces; that it allowed legislation to be passed that overrode the bill, as long as this was acknowledged (a notwithstanding clause); that as an ordinary piece of legislation, the bill could be amended in the routine way; and that it was superseded by the War Measures Act, at the very time when it might be needed most.

Not surprisingly, the courts made limited use of the Bill of Rights. Only once, in the *Drybones* case of 1970, did they decide that a clause of an act violated the Bill of Rights and was therefore inoperative.[14] The Bill was more useful in clarifying legal rights and was referred to in several cases to fill in gaps in such definitions as what was meant by the "right to counsel," the "right to an interpreter," and the "right to a fair hearing." Several other cases arose regarding violations of rights and freedoms within federal jurisdiction, but in each case the Court found a way around applying the Bill of Rights. Provinces occasionally violated civil liberties in the post-1960 period, too, but the Bill of Rights was of even less assistance in these cases.[15]

. . . .

THE CHARTER OF RIGHTS AND FREEDOMS

Recognizing the limitations and ambiguities of the Canadian Bill of Rights, and wanting to incorporate new kinds of rights into the Constitution, several politicians, most notably Pierre Trudeau, attempted to improve it. Ironically, in the midst of this quest, Trudeau invoked the War Measures Act in 1970 and used it not only to fight the terrorist FLQ but also to encroach on the freedom of speech of innocent, nonviolent Quebec separatists. Finally, in 1982, with the adoption of the **Charter of Rights and Freedoms**, part of the **Constitution Act, 1982**, he accomplished his objective. The Charter essentially replaced the Bill of Rights, using much of its language in the sections on fundamental freedoms and legal rights, but going beyond it to include democratic, linguistic, mobility, egalitarian, and limited Aboriginal rights.

Trudeau wanted to remedy the deficiencies in the Bill of Rights. But he was also determined to entrench official bilingualism, as well as official minority-language education rights across the country, in an effort to undercut Quebec's claim that it represented French Canada. Moreover, Trudeau hoped to counter centrifugal forces throughout the land and pressures for general decentralization to the provinces by creating an instrument that the courts could use to cut down self-serving provincial laws. As a new national symbol, the Charter would also serve to increase the allegiance of all citizens to the national government.[16]

The Charter is generally a much stronger document than its predecessor. Besides being broader in scope, the Charter applies equally to both federal and provincial governments, and, being entrenched into the Constitution, it is difficult to amend. It states very clearly that the courts are to invalidate any government actions or legislation that they feel are in conflict with the provisions of the Charter.

However, the rights articulated in the Charter are not absolute. In the first place, section 1 indicates that such rights are subject to "such reasonable limits, defined by law, as can be demonstrably justified in a free and democratic society." The courts are thus allowed to find that although a piece of legislation does violate certain rights, it is still acceptable according to their definition of reasonable limits. Second, in the areas of fundamental freedoms, legal rights, and equality rights, either level of government is allowed to pass legislation contrary to the Charter by means of the notwithstanding clause, section 33. Governments were not expected to acknowledge in advance that legislation was contrary to the Charter, so the notwithstanding clause would normally come into play when legislation was introduced to override a judicial decision regarding a Charter right. Such a bill can be exempted from the provisions of the Charter only for a five-year period, after which it becomes inoperative if not re-passed for another five years.

The Charter of Rights and Freedoms has profoundly affected the operation of the Canadian political system. Let us now examine the provisions of the Charter and see how they have been interpreted by the courts, especially the Supreme Court of Canada. The following discussion only sketches the broad lines of Charter interpretation during its first 25–30 years of operation and is not intended to be a definitive statement of the law.[17]

The Reasonable Limits Clause

Section 1 is often called the **reasonable limits clause** and reads as follows:

> The Canadian Charter of Rights and Freedoms guarantees the rights and freedoms set out in it subject only to such reasonable limits prescribed by law as can be demonstrably justified in a free and democratic society.

The Supreme Court has made extensive use of section 1, upholding many laws that it considered to be in violation of Charter rights but that were saved by being reasonable limits on them. In interpreting the limits that can be "demonstrably justified in a free and democratic society," the Court developed guidelines in the *Oakes* case, which have come to be called the **Oakes test**. First, the objective of the government in limiting a right must be pressing and substantial; second, the means must be proportional to that objective. Three criteria are attached to this second point: the limit must be rationally connected to the government objective; it should impair the right as little as is necessary in order to achieve the objective; and the costs of the impairment to the right must be proportional to their benefits. The Oakes test has been applied in subsequent interpretations of the reasonable limits clause in a large proportion of Charter cases.[18]

The 2001 *Sharpe* case on child pornography presents a useful example of how the Court applies the reasonable limits clause. Although the judges ruled that the law prohibiting the possession of child pornography infringed Sharpe's freedom of expression, it was upheld as a reasonable limit on that Charter right because

- the *objective* of the law criminalizing the possession of child pornography (eradicating the sexual exploitation of children) was "pressing and substantial"
- the *means* chosen by Parliament (prohibiting the possession of child pornography) were "rationally connected" to the objective
- the law represented a "minimal impairment" of the Charter right by allowing minor and reasonable exceptions (e.g., innocent photographs of a baby in the bath)
- the "benefits" of prohibiting such materials outweighed any "costs" or deleterious effects to the right to freedom of expression since the law does not interfere significantly with speech possessing social value[19]

Fundamental Freedoms

Section 2 lists the following **fundamental freedoms**:

(a) freedom of conscience and religion;

(b) freedom of thought, belief, opinion and expression, including freedom of the press and other media of communication;

(c) freedom of peaceful assembly; and

(d) freedom of association.

FREEDOM OF RELIGION

With respect to freedom of religion, the Supreme Court invalidated the Lord's Day Act as an infringement of freedom of religion because its restrictions on Sunday activities were clearly related to the Christian Sabbath and discriminated against other religions. The Court did, however, uphold the Ontario Retail Business Holidays Act, designed to preserve Sunday as a day of rest on a secular rather than a religious foundation. But given public enthusiasm for Sunday shopping, provincial and municipal governments have essentially ignored this ruling. A number of cases have taken the view that a child welfare authority may approve of a blood transfusion for a child despite the parents' religious beliefs to the contrary. Public schools may no longer hold an exclusively Christian school prayer or religious studies classes, but Ontario's publicly funded Roman Catholic separate school system was upheld as a pre-Charter constitutional right even though it discriminated against other religions. In 1985, Aboriginal religious rights were not taken seriously, but in 2006, the Supreme Court ruled that Sikh students could carry their ceremonial daggers (called kirpans) to school, based on freedom of religion backed up by Canadian commitment to multiculturalism.[20]

FREEDOM OF EXPRESSION

With respect to freedom of expression, a wide range of issues has been brought before the courts. Perhaps most controversial was the Supreme Court's rejection of the French-only sign provision of Quebec's **Bill 101**, which was held to be a violation of Quebec's own Charter of Rights as well. The Court decided that freedom of expression included not only the freedom to express ideas but also the freedom to choose the language in which to express them. Moreover, the concept of freedom of expression incorporated "commercial expression." In this case, the Court hinted that it would be a reasonable limit if the law provided for the *predominant* rather than the *exclusive* use of French on commercial signs. Freedom of commercial expression was also involved in Quebec's successful effort to restrict advertising aimed at children. But the Supreme Court disallowed the federal prohibition of cigarette advertising: the Court ruled that a *partial* ban would be more acceptable, and the government amended the legislation accordingly. As weak as Parliament's response was, the tobacco industry immediately began a freedom of expression challenge against the new Tobacco Act, but the Supreme Court upheld it in 2007.[21]

In cases involving anti-Semitic denials of the Holocaust, a majority of the Court concluded that the section of the Criminal Code prohibiting the dissemination of hate literature was a reasonable limit on freedom of expression.[22]

Several freedom of expression cases have involved the labour movement. The Court ruled that freedom of expression includes the freedom of trade unions to engage in picketing, even secondary picketing, and that the right to distribute leaflets regarding a labour dispute is even more extensive. However, it is a reasonable limit on that right to prohibit the picketing of courthouses by court employees, even during a legal strike.[23]

Other cases have arisen in connection with election campaigns. Attaching posters on public property, including utility poles, was protected by freedom of expression, and paying a portion of the campaign expenses of candidates and parties from the public purse does not infringe a taxpayer's right to freedom of expression. After limits on third-party advertising during election campaigns were invalidated several times in the Alberta courts, the Supreme Court of Canada finally upheld them. However, the provision in the Canada Elections Act prohibiting the publication of public opinion polls during the final three days of a federal election campaign was overturned and later limited by law to election day itself. Federal legislation prohibiting public servants from engaging in electoral work for a political party or candidate was found to be invalid, but the more balanced Ontario legislation on the subject was upheld.[24]

Freedom of expression encompasses freedom of the press and the media, and several cases have dealt with this issue. The Court has usually sided with the media, such as in allowing the CBC to show the movie *The Boys of St. Vincent* even if it might have prejudiced upcoming sexual abuse trials. The Court upheld the right of the media to expose police tactics used to entice confessions from murder suspects and said that police search warrants should be open to media scrutiny unless their exposure would cause genuine harm. But the judges found it a reasonable limit that the Criminal Code prohibits the publication of the name of the victim of sexual assault if the victim so requests, and to clear the court in the case where public knowledge would further victimize the victim of sexual assault. They also agreed it was reasonable to restrict media coverage of the Paul Bernardo case before his trial. The Nova Scotia legislature was even allowed to limit media access to its proceedings.[25]

Obscenity also falls into this category, where one main case stands out, *R. v. Butler*.[26] The Court divided pornography into different categories, saying that portrayals of sex with violence and sex that is degrading or dehumanizing can be restricted by the authorities, but that a portrayal of explicit sex that is neither violent nor degrading is generally acceptable unless it depicts children. Parliament strengthened the provisions dealing with child pornography, which were upheld in the *Sharpe* case, as mentioned. When judges later ruled that Sharpe's fictional pornographic writings and an artist's depiction of children in various sexual activities both had artistic merit, Parliament debated whether this loophole should be closed.

As for prostitution, the Supreme Court upheld the prohibition on communicating for the purposes of sidewalk solicitation, Chief Justice Brian Dickson feeling that this was a reasonable limit on freedom of expression. Interestingly, the two women on the Court dissented, finding that the Code infringed both freedom of expression and freedom of association and was not just a reasonable limit on them.

FREEDOM OF PEACEFUL ASSEMBLY AND ASSOCIATION

Freedom of association has often been involved in labour union cases. In 2001, for example, the Supreme Court invalidated an Ontario law that prohibited the unionization of agricultural workers and upheld a Quebec law that forced construction workers to join one of five unions in the industry. In other words, freedom of association carries with it the right, or in some cases the obligation, to join a union. However, in an earlier set of less labour-friendly decisions, the Court ruled that freedom of association does not guarantee the right of trade unions to strike. Thus, freedom of association did not prevent federal or provincial legislatures from passing back-to-work legislation or otherwise interfering in the collective bargaining process. Justices Dickson and Wilson dissented on this decision, arguing that the freedom to belong to a union is of little value if the union cannot threaten or engage in a strike as a last resort. Labour was happier with the ultimate disposition of the *Lavigne* case, in which the Court rejected his objection to part of his union dues going to support causes with which he did not agree. Then, in 2007, the Supreme Court reversed itself on the question of whether collective bargaining was protected by the Charter right of freedom of association. In siding with the BC Hospital Employees' Union, the Court struck down a provincial law that had ripped up their contracts and privatized thousands of health-care jobs.[27]

Democratic Rights

Under **democratic rights** in sections 3 to 5, the Charter guarantees that every citizen of Canada has the right to vote in federal and provincial elections; that no Parliament can continue for more than five years from the previous election, except in time of real or apprehended war, invasion, or insurrection; and that each Parliament must sit at least once every year. A number of cases regarding elections were already mentioned in terms of freedom of expression, while section 3 has been cited in several cases dealing with federal and provincial electoral laws that deny the vote to certain categories of people. At the national level, it was used in the 1988 election to invalidate provisions in the Canada Elections Act that withheld the vote from federally appointed judges and people with mental disabilities. Many similar cases have arisen in connection with provincial electoral laws, especially relating to prisoners, persons on parole, and those remanded but not yet charged. In 1993 the Supreme Court agreed with the Federal Court of Canada that denying prisoners the right to vote violated section 3, but in the meantime, the law had been amended to allow those serving less than two years to vote. When the amended law was challenged in turn, all prisoners were awarded the vote in federal elections.[28]

Another interesting application of section 3 arose in cases involving the drawing of provincial electoral maps, especially in BC and Saskatchewan. Indeed, the courts surprised many observers by ruling that such a matter came within the scope of section 3 at all. In the 1989 *Dixon* case in British Columbia, the map was disallowed because electoral boundaries did not approach "equality of voting power" and such disparities could not be justified on any other grounds. In Saskatchewan, the Court of Appeal invalidated that province's electoral map in 1991 primarily because of disparities between the size of urban and rural ridings, but a quick appeal to a divided Supreme Court of Canada re-established it. Even though the electoral map systematically overrepresented rural voters, a majority of the Court decided that they would not insist on greater equality in the size of constituencies because "effective representation" had been achieved.[29]

The democratic rights section was also used to invalidate sections of the Canada Elections Act that required a political party to run 50 candidates before it could be registered. These provisions meant that an unregistered party could not use its label under the candidate's name on the ballot, issue tax receipts for contributions, or retain unspent election contributions. The Supreme Court argued that smaller parties serve a purpose in the electoral process, even if they are unlikely to win, and the law was eventually amended to allow the registration of a party with only a single candidate.[30]

Mobility Rights

Under section 6, **mobility rights**, every citizen of Canada has the right to enter, remain in, and leave Canada, and every citizen or permanent resident has the right to take up residence and pursue the gaining of a livelihood in any province. However, laws providing for reasonable residency requirements for receiving public services are acceptable, as are laws that give preference to local residents if the unemployment rate in that province is higher than the national rate. Mobility rights were included in the Charter because of Pierre Trudeau's concern that some provinces were restricting the entry of residents of other provinces, as in the case of cross-border employment. Mobility rights have not featured frequently in judicial interpretation but have arisen in unanticipated ways. It is often professionals—usually lawyers—denied permission to practise in a particular province who have tried to use mobility rights to their advantage. They have generally been unsuccessful because the Court has said that section 6 does not guarantee the "right to work," and it has upheld the right of each province to establish its own professional qualifications. The Court also ruled that PEI legislation that taxed non-residents at a higher level than residents did not violate section 6.[31]

Legal Rights

Legal rights are contained in sections 7 to 14. In section 7, everyone has the right to life, liberty, and security of the person and the right not to be deprived thereof except in accordance with the principles of fundamental justice. "Security of the person" was used as the main basis for throwing out the abortion provision of the Criminal Code in the famous *Morgentaler* case in 1988. A majority of the Court ruled that that law, with all its arbitrary and bureaucratic procedures, violated the security of the person of the woman concerned and constituted a "profound interference with a woman's body." Having invalidated the abortion law in the *Morgentaler* case, the Court declined to rule in the absence of any legislation in the *Borowski* case on whether the "right to life" included fetal rights. But in the *Daigle* case, the Court found no fetal right to life in the Quebec Charter of Rights, the Canadian Criminal Code, or the common law, and ruled that the "father" had no right to prevent an abortion. In the 1999 *Dobson* case, the Court ruled that a woman could not be sued for having harmed her fetus during pregnancy.[32]

Canada has had two high-profile euthanasia or mercy-killing cases. In the first, Sue Rodriguez tried to persuade the Court that since she was dying of Lou Gehrig's disease, security of the person should provide her with the right to an assisted suicide. The judges were divided, but the majority ruled against her. Then, when Robert Latimer took the life of his daughter, who had severe disabilities, because he could not bear to see her in such pain, the Supreme Court unanimously upheld the provisions of the Criminal Code with respect to murder and refused to recognize this as a special case.[33]

Security of the person was also involved in the *Operation Dismantle* case dealing with the attempt to halt the testing of the American Cruise missile in Canada. The Supreme Court ruled that the causal link between missile testing and the threat to the security of the person because of the potential escalation of the international arms race was uncertain, speculative, and hypothetical.[34]

Perhaps the most controversial decision with respect to section 7 concerned the public health care system in the 2005 *Chaoulli* case.[35] The question was whether the waiting times characteristic of the public system jeopardized the life, health, and psychological well-being of Canadians. The Court was evenly divided on whether the provincial law that banned the purchase of private health insurance for core medical services was unconstitutional according "life, liberty, and security of the person," but Madam Justice Deschamps tipped the balance against the law by referring only to the Quebec Charter. Thus, although the decision was limited in the first instance to Quebec, a number of provinces used the case to justify allowing an expansion of private health care facilities to which people capable of paying the fee could go to shorten their wait times for treatment. The thrust of the decision itself deeply concerned many observers who felt that it could lead to the end of the public medical care system in the whole country and who were alarmed at the degree of judicial intervention in political controversy as well as by the arrogance of the four-judge majority in overturning a sacred public policy.

"Security of the person" and "fundamental justice" combined in the *Singh* case to require the Immigration Department to provide an oral hearing for refugee claimants when their life could be in danger if deported. Fundamental justice necessitated giving such claimants an opportunity to state their case and to know the case against them. This decision was the cause of much of the subsequent backlog in the immigration department. In 2003, the Court upheld the Criminal Code provision with respect to the possession of marijuana (which it spells marihuana) against the view that the law violated the principles of fundamental justice.[36]

Fundamental justice is often linked to the presumption of innocence in section 11(d). For example, in the *Daviault* case, the Supreme Court allowed an extreme state of drunkenness to be used as a rare defence in a rape case; otherwise, it ruled, the accused's right to fundamental justice and presumption of innocence would have been violated. The government quickly amended the law to prevent a recurrence of this interpretation. In the *Stinchcombe* case, the Court said that section 7 strengthened the obligation of police and prosecutors to hand over relevant evidence to the accused well before trial. In 2004, in connection with two people implicated in the Air India explosion, the Court upheld provisions of the Anti-Terrorism Act that allowed for investigative hearings in which judges could compel witnesses to speak.

In a major blow to the women's movement, the *Seaboyer* decision invalidated the rape-shield law that had prohibited the use of evidence of the complainant's previous sexual activity. But Parliament responded by amending the Criminal Code, primarily by tightening up the concept of consent (no means no). Then, in another case that attracted much public attention, the Supreme Court overturned the acquittal of an Alberta man who had sexually assaulted a young woman during a job interview in a trailer. Although the woman said "no" three times to his sexual advances, the Alberta courts considered his actions "less criminal than hormonal," and were roundly criticized by the Supreme Court for dealing in "inappropriate myths and stereotypes." Parliament also amended the Criminal Code to overcome Supreme Court rulings with respect to being not criminally responsible on account of mental disorder and the production of medical records in sexual assault proceedings, while the Court partially reversed the *Seaboyer* decision with respect to the admission of a complainant's confidential counselling records.[37]

Section 8 establishes the right to be secure against unreasonable search and seizure. In dismissing the charge of collusion between the Southam and Thomson newspaper chains, the Court extended this right to corporations and decided that a reasonable search by the police or other government authorities had to be authorized by statute and issued by an impartial arbiter, almost exclusively a judge. This decision did nothing to remedy the feebleness of the Competition Act. Many cases in this realm have arisen with respect to drug seizures, with the general rule being that a search will not be wrongful if authorized by law, if the law itself is reasonable, and if the search is conducted in a reasonable manner. However, routine use of strip searches by police, even when they suspect the presence of narcotics, has been outlawed. A police officer's demand to see a person's driver's licence and insurance card during a spot check is not an unreasonable search, and male prisoners can be frisked by female guards. But taking blood samples without legal authorization and strip searches at Canadian border points without the opportunity to contact counsel were declared to be Charter violations.[38]

In at least two cases with respect to section 8, Parliament passed legislation to counter the effect of Supreme Court decisions. To offset the *Feeney* decision, an amendment to the Criminal Code made it easier for police to enter a dwelling house in order to make an arrest of a fleeing suspect. Another amendment facilitated the obtaining of bodily substances, such as hair samples, for forensic DNA analysis after the decision in the *Stillman* case that such was not provided for. Then, in the 1999 *Godoy* case, the Supreme Court ruled that police officers responding to a 911 call had the right to enter a dwelling house in order to ascertain the health and safety of the caller.[39]

In 2003, the Court upheld the power of the state to obtain a warrant to seize bodily samples from an accused to analyze their DNA, while rejecting the right of the police to frisk or search the pockets of a person they have detained on the street unless there is a threat to the officer's safety or the safety of others. However, the police are allowed to use infrared heat-detection equipment to search for indoor marijuana growing operations.[40]

Section 9 grants the right not to be arbitrarily detained or imprisoned, and section 10 reads that, on arrest or detention, everyone has the right to be informed promptly of the reasons and the right to contact a lawyer without delay and to be informed of that right. A huge number of Charter cases have arisen in this connection: for example, the Court has ruled that random police spot checks are a reasonable limit on the right not to be arbitrarily detained and that roadside breath tests do not include the right to retain counsel. However, if a person fails that test and is asked to accompany the officer to a police station, the individual has a right to retain counsel before taking the police station breathalyzer test. In the *Clarkson* case, an intoxicated woman who voluntarily waived her right to counsel and then proceeded to confess to the murder of her husband was acquitted because she was not aware of the consequences of not having counsel present. The double-murder confessions of a man with an IQ of less than 80 were not admitted as evidence because he did not understand his rights. The Court has ruled that a person has the right to be told of his or her right to a lawyer as well as to legal aid and must have a reasonable opportunity to exercise these rights. In a 1995 case, for example, a man convicted of rape and murder was granted a new trial because he had been subjected to an "intensive and manipulative interrogation by police" during which his repeated requests to consult a lawyer were ignored.[41]

Section 11 includes a variety of rights available to a person charged with an offence. "To be tried within a reasonable time" has been extremely controversial after the *Askov* decision, which found that a delay of almost two years between a preliminary hearing and a trial had been excessive.[42] The lower courts took this to mean that everyone had a right to a trial within six to eight months of being charged, and some 34 500 cases were stayed, dismissed, or withdrawn in Ontario alone. The Supreme Court then took the unprecedented initiative to point out in a speech by one of its members that this was not what the *Askov* decision intended.

Persons charged cannot be compelled to testify against themselves, cannot be denied reasonable bail without just cause, and are presumed innocent until proven guilty according to law in a fair and public hearing by an independent and impartial tribunal. Self-incrimination was addressed in the *Hebert* and *Broyles* cases, while "impartial tribunal" was dealt with in the *Valente* case, and is cited again in Chapter 24. The *Oakes* case dealt with the presumption of innocence: under the "reverse onus" clause of the Narcotics Control Act, a person found to be in possession of a narcotic was also presumed to be guilty of trafficking, and it was up to the person charged with possession to prove his or her innocence on the trafficking charge.

Although many observers find this to be a perfectly acceptable requirement when large quantities of drugs are involved, the *Oakes* case invalidated this clause as an unreasonable limit on the presumption of innocence. However, a person occupying the driver's seat of a vehicle, even if it is not moving, is presumed to have "care and control." The Court has also ruled that indiscreet remarks by politicians about a case before the courts, however regrettable, cannot be used as a defence to throw the case out. Persons charged are guaranteed trial by jury where the maximum punishment for the offence is imprisonment for five years or more and, whether finally acquitted of the offence or found guilty and punished, cannot be tried for it again.[43]

Everyone has the right not to be subjected to any cruel and unusual treatment or punishment. In this connection, the Court ruled that a minimum sentence of seven years for illegally importing any quantity of narcotic into Canada was excessive. Indeterminate sentences for dangerous offenders have, however, been upheld. Robert Latimer's case, mentioned above, also hinged on the question of "cruel and unusual punishment." The Court rejected this argument: the minimum mandatory sentence of ten years in jail was not grossly disproportionate, given the gravity of the offence. In the *Burns* case, the Supreme Court refused to extradite two men to the United States without assurances that they would not face the death penalty. In 2004, the Court upheld the Criminal Code provision that allowed parents and teachers to use reasonable force in spanking a child or pupil for correctional purposes.[44]

Section 14 provides that a party or witness in any proceedings who does not understand or speak the language in which the proceedings are conducted or who is deaf has the right to the assistance of an interpreter. In the *Tran* case, the Supreme Court ruled that an accused must receive a continuous, precise, impartial, competent, and contemporaneous interpretation of what is said, reinforcing section 14 with section 27 on the multicultural heritage of Canada.[45]

TERRORISM AND THE CHARTER

Increasing concern about **terrorism** since 9/11 has raised serious questions about the balance between national security and many legal rights, including life, liberty, and security of the person, and right to counsel, as well as several fundamental freedoms. Sometimes these issues are related to the Anti-Terrorism Act and sometimes to the Immigration and Refugee Act. In a 2002 deportation case dealing with a Tamil Tiger deemed to be a terrorist, the Supreme Court ruled that a new deportation hearing was in order because the person in question could be subject to torture once back in Sri Lanka. In other cases, security certificates permit the government to detain suspected terrorists for several years without trial and without revealing the evidence against them, after which they can be deported, still ignorant of their alleged crime.

As terrorist charges worked their way up the judicial hierarchy, the *Charkaoui* case challenged the provisions of the Immigration and Refugee Protection Act that allowed the government to imprison security suspects for an indefinite period without even knowing the case against them. In a 2007 decision, the Supreme Court ruled that the use of secret testimony to imprison and deport foreigners as possible terrorist suspects violates the Charter's guarantee of fundamental justice and a fair hearing. The Court suspended its ruling for a year, allowing parliament to draft a new law compatible with the Charter. The revised law, Bill C-3, was at least initially upheld in a Federal Court challenge. This left somewhat unclear the status of several men held under security certificates who could not be deported because they faced the prospect of torture in their home states.

Then, in June 2008, Charkaoui won a second Supreme Court decision when it ordered CSIS to stop systematically destroying interview notes and other evidence gathered during national security probes. In the fall of 2009, most of the surveillance restrictions on Charkaoui and some of the others involved in stalled security-certificate cases were eased when the Crown said it would rather drop the case than reveal how CSIS had obtained its information against them. Meanwhile, in May 2008, the Supreme Court ruled that Omar Khadr, detained by the U.S. at Guantanamo Bay, was entitled to see the documents relevant to the charges against him, including the records of CSIS interviews in the possession of the Canadian Crown. In another case, the Federal Court ruled in April 2009 that the government must demand that U.S. authorities return Khadr to Canada on the basis of fundamental justice. Somewhat similarly, the Federal Court told the Harper government to bring Abousfian Abdelrazik home from Sudan, since all charges against him had been dropped. Earlier in 2009, however, Momin Khawaja was convicted on seven terrorist charges and acquitted of two others, while several of the suspects in the "Toronto 18" terrorism case were found guilty.[46]

Equality Rights

Equality rights are contained in section 15, which reads as follows:

(1) Every individual is equal before and under the law and has the right to the equal protection and equal benefit of the law without discrimination and, in particular, without discrimination based on race, national or ethnic origin, colour, religion, sex, age or mental or physical disability.

(2) Subsection (1) does not preclude any law, program or activity that has as its object the amelioration of conditions of disadvantaged individuals or groups including those that are disadvantaged because of race, national or ethnic origin, colour, religion, sex, age or mental or physical disability.

In the *Andrews* case the Supreme Court laid down a two-step process for interpreting equality rights. The Court first determines if the case in question involves an inequality in law or treatment in terms of the personal characteristics listed in section 15 (or of others analogous to them), and then whether there has been a discrimination—that is, a harmful or prejudicial effect. In other words, inequalities and distinctions are permitted if no negative discrimination or disadvantage—social, political, or legal—is involved. According to Ian Greene, the Court made it clear that "it intends to interpret section 15 to help clearly disadvantaged groups in society."[47] Still, the Court has had some difficulty in pursuing a consistent line of interpretation, although it tried to do so in the 1999 *Law* case, in which it denied Canada Pension Plan survivor benefits to a widow under 35 years old.

To cite only some examples, the Supreme Court overturned the 1978 Bill of Rights decision that allowed the Unemployment Insurance Commission to discriminate against pregnant women. In addition, it agreed that provincial human rights codes must not prevent girls from playing on boys' athletic teams. In the *Corbiere* case, it ruled that band members living off-reserve have the right to vote in First Nations elections, and in the *Eldridge* case, that the equality rights of deaf people are violated if the people are not provided with sign language interpreters in a hospital. But in the case of mandatory retirement, the Court said that, however discriminatory, it was reasonable for laws to require retirement at age 65. Somewhat similarly, the government of Newfoundland and Labrador was allowed to back away from pay equity because of the severe fiscal situation of the time; Quebec was allowed to pay lower welfare allowances to people under 30 years of age, and the BC health system was not required to fund specialized programs for autistic children.[48]

Canadian Supreme Court agrees to gay marriage.

Many section 15 cases have dealt with sexual orientation. In the 1995 *Egan* case, the Supreme Court ruled unanimously that the Charter prohibited discrimination on the basis of sexual orientation, even though this ground was not explicitly listed in section 15. (The Court has recognized citizenship and marital status as other analogous grounds to the rights enumerated in section 15 but has so far rejected social condition or poverty.) Then, in the *Vriend* case, it reaffirmed this decision and ordered Alberta to add that ground to its Individual Rights Protection Act. Same-sex benefits received a major boost in the 1999 *M. v. H.* case, in which the Ontario Family Law Act was found to be a violation of section 15 when it provided support only for an opposite-sex spouse. And, as mentioned in Chapter 7, the Ontario Court of Appeal ruled in 2002 that the definition of marriage between a male and a female discriminated against same-sex couples. After similar decisions in most other provinces, the Chrétien government sent a reference case to the Supreme Court of Canada, which generally agreed with lower appeal court decisions, and Parliament passed a law confirming the change.[49]

In another case, the Surrey (BC) school board's ban of kindergarten stories of same-sex parents was rejected by the Supreme Court. But while the Court has thus been quite liberal in its interpretation of equality rights with respect to various gay and lesbian issues, it upheld the policy of the teacher education program of Trinity Western University in Vancouver to condemn "sexual sins including … homosexual behaviour." The Court purported to make a distinction between holding such a belief and acting on it. It also ruled that unlike legally married couples, common-law partners (of any gender) cannot claim an equal division of matrimonial property if their relationship breaks down.[50]

Subsection (2) of section 15 permits **affirmative action** programs that give preference to those who have been discriminated against in the past. This clause has rarely been involved in Charter decisions, although one significant case allowed Aboriginals to get a one-day jump-start on fishing for salmon in the Fraser River.[51]

Box 19.1 lists what the author believes to be the 15 most important Charter decisions, at least from a political science point of view. This list does not include significant Supreme Court decisions based on non-Charter grounds.

BOX 19.1	The 15 Most Important Charter Decisions

1. *Hunter* [1984]: Extends search and seizure protection to corporations
2. *Singh* [1985]: Gives refugee claimants the right to a full oral hearing on the basis of security of the person and fundamental justice
3. *Big M Drug Mart* [1985]: Strikes down Lord's Day Act restriction on Sunday shopping as a violation of freedom of religion
4. *Oakes* [1986]: Establishes guidelines for interpreting section 1, the reasonable limits clause
5. *Ford* [1988]: Strikes down the Quebec sign law as an infringement of freedom of expression
6. *Morgentaler* [1988]: Outlaws Criminal Code restrictions on abortion, primarily on the basis of security of the person
7. *Keegstra* [1990]: Decides that freedom of expression does not extend to disseminating hate literature
8. *Askov* [1990]: Sets a limit for the right to be tried within a reasonable time
9. *Butler* [1992]: Limits freedom of expression in relation to pornography
10. *Rodriguez* [1993]: Decides that security of the person does not include the right to assisted suicide
11. *Egan* [1995]: Decides that equality rights include sexual orientation
12. *Delgamuukw* [1997]: Defines Aboriginal title to land and rules that oral evidence is valid in making such a claim
13. *M v. H* [1999]: Extends sexual-orientation protection to same-sex couples
14. *Chaoulli* [2005]: Overturns the monopoly of public health care insurance for core medical services
15. *BC Health Services and Support* [2007]: Overturns earlier decision (Labour Trilogy) that freedom of association did not guarantee the right to collective bargaining.

Source: Adapted from Andrew Heard, "The Judiciary: The Power behind the Throne," in Rand Dyck, ed., *Studying Politics: An Introduction to Political Science*, 3rd ed. (Toronto: Nelson, 2009), p.261.

Official Languages of Canada

Sections 16 to 22 of the Charter constitutionalize the federal and New Brunswick official languages acts and reaffirm the limited official bilingualism of Quebec and Manitoba. These sections guarantee that certain federal and New Brunswick government agencies will operate on a bilingual basis, as discussed in Chapter 5. Although judicial interpretation of linguistic rights has been extensive, it related mostly to the original provisions of the 1867 Constitution Act as well as the 1870 Manitoba Act, rather than to the 1982 Charter. The extension of official bilingualism in the federal and New Brunswick official languages acts was ruled valid; several aspects of Quebec's Bill 101 were invalidated because they conflicted with section 133 of the 1867 act; the 1890 Official Language Act of Manitoba, which removed French as an official language in the province, was considered a violation of the Manitoba Act; and the Supreme Court then required Manitoba to translate all its laws into French. As noted above, the unilingual sign provisions of Bill 101 were challenged in terms of freedom of expression rather than on the basis of sections 16 to 23. A new section, 16.1, was added to the Charter in 1993 to reinforce the equality of the two official languages in New Brunswick. That being the case, the Supreme Court ruled in 2008 that RCMP officers working as a provincial police force in New Brunswick had to be bilingual.[52]

Pierre Trudeau promoted minority-language education rights as the central element of the Charter of Rights and Freedoms.

Minority-Language Education Rights

Section 23 deals with **minority-language education rights,** and some would argue that they were the part of the Charter with which Pierre Trudeau was most concerned.[53] Section 23 requires provinces to provide anglophone and francophone minorities with education in their own language, where numbers warrant. Thus, the Supreme Court struck down the provision in Bill 101 that allowed only the children of parents who were themselves products of the English school system in Quebec to go to that system, essentially those who were already there (the "Quebec clause"). Indeed, section 23 (the "Canada clause") was deliberately drafted so that it would conflict with this clause, ensuring that Canadian citizens who moved to Quebec could also send their children to the English schools. In other provinces, the Supreme Court has decided not only what number of francophone students warrant a French-language school but also that it must have a "distinct physical setting" and that French-language parents must have a say in the "management and control" of it.[54]

Enforcement

Section 24 makes clear, where the Bill of Rights did not, that the courts have the power to interpret the Charter and to invalidate laws or government actions that conflict with it. It also moves in the American direction with regard to the admissibility of evidence. The Charter does not actually bar illegally obtained evidence, as in the United States;

the admission of such evidence is acceptable as long as it does not bring the administration of justice into disrepute. The Supreme Court laid the basis for interpreting this section in the *Collins* case.[55] First, evidence should be excluded if it would prejudice the fairness of the trial, and second, the more seriously the obtaining of the evidence violates the Charter, the more compelling is the need to exclude it. Third, however, if to exclude the evidence would bring the judicial system into disrepute, the evidence should not be excluded. Such questionable evidence usually related to a violation of the right to counsel or to an unreasonable search or seizure.

General Provisions

Sections 25 through 30 relate to specific groups in society and were discussed in relevant chapters earlier in the book. Section 25 says that the rights and freedoms in the Charter should not be construed so as to abrogate or derogate from any Aboriginal, treaty, or other rights or freedoms that pertain to the Aboriginal peoples of Canada, including any rights or freedoms that have been recognized by the Royal Proclamation of October 7, 1763, and any rights or freedoms that may be acquired by the Aboriginal peoples of Canada by way of land claims settlement. A more positive Aboriginal clause in the Constitution Act, 1982, is section 35, which is not actually part of the Charter itself. The potential of the 1982 document to advance Aboriginal rights has never been clear, but encouraging signs emerged from the *Sparrow*, *Sioui*, and the first of the *Marshall* cases. In acquitting an Aboriginal from the offence of using a bigger fishing net than authorized by law, the Supreme Court asserted that governments must bear the burden of proving that laws are necessary if they have a negative effect on any Aboriginal right. In another early case on the subject of treaty rights, the Court ruled that an ancient treaty-based fishing right took precedence over a Quebec law that prohibited fishing in provincial parks. Then, as mentioned in Chapter 4, the *Delgamuukw* case provided a comprehensive statement on Aboriginal title and opened the door to accepting oral history evidence for purposes of such land claims.[56]

In 2003, the Supreme Court ruled that the Métis people are a distinct Aboriginal group, with a constitutional right to hunt for food. The Court also decided that Aboriginals must be consulted on the development of logging, mining, or other resource projects on lands the title to which is still in dispute, but that they have no veto over such projects. The Court found in 2005 that the Mi'kmaq did not possess a right to cut logs on Crown land in Nova Scotia and New Brunswick without authorization, although a year later logging for domestic use was allowed.[57]

Section 27, which has been cited sparingly, asserts that the Charter shall be interpreted in a manner consistent with the preservation and enhancement of the multicultural heritage of Canadians, and section 28 reads that notwithstanding anything in the Charter, the rights and freedoms referred to in it are guaranteed equally to male and female persons. The women's movement considered the addition of section 28 essential so that governments would not be able to use the notwithstanding clause (section 33) to override the gender equality provision of section 15. Section 29 protects section 93 of the 1867 Constitution Act, which guaranteed existing Protestant and Roman Catholic separate schools. Although section 93 clearly discriminates against other religions, the drafters of the Charter did not want to take responsibility for altering rights established in the original Constitution.[58]

Application of the Charter

Section 32 clarifies that the Charter applies to the Parliament and government of Canada, including Yukon and the Northwest Territories (and now Nunavut), and to the legislature and government of each province. By implication, it also applies to the municipal level of government. Thus, all legislation in Canada must be consistent with the Charter, as must all actions of government executives—ministers, public servants, police officers, and so on. The Charter is not intended to apply to the private sector, but certain institutions occupy an ambiguous position. Although the courts interpret the Charter, for example, it is not certain whether their own actions are governed by it. The Charter has been applied to law societies, because they have been delegated governmental powers, and to community colleges, but more autonomous semi-public institutions, such as hospitals and universities, are exempt in their internal operations. As mentioned earlier, federal and provincial human rights codes rather than the Charter regulate certain aspects of the private sector. But since such codes take the form of laws, they must also remain consistent with the Charter.[59]

The Notwithstanding Clause

Section 33 is the famous **notwithstanding clause**. Parliament or legislatures may exempt laws from three parts of the Charter—fundamental freedoms (section 2), legal rights (sections 7–14), and equality rights (section 15)—but not from democratic rights, mobility rights, or linguistic rights. This provision was a compromise between the provincial premiers, who wanted the clause to apply to the whole Charter, and Prime Minister Trudeau, who was adamant that it could not be used to circumvent the sections about which he cared most. For the sections it covers, a federal or provincial legislature merely has to expressly declare in a statute that the act or a provision thereof shall operate notwithstanding a specific provision of the Charter. If such action is taken, however, it is only valid for five years, after which it lapses or must be re-enacted.

Despite the number of times the Supreme Court has invalidated federal or provincial legislation since 1982, governments have rarely re-enacted such provisions under section 33. Over the first 20 years, it was used in only three high-profile situations.[60] The government of Grant Devine used section 33 to pass back-to-work legislation to settle a 1986 public service strike in Saskatchewan. During the first Parti Québécois period in Quebec, up to 1985, the notwithstanding clause was routinely applied, as a matter of principle, to all new legislation passed in that province. The Liberal government of Robert Bourassa discontinued that practice but used the notwithstanding clause to get around the Supreme Court decision with respect to bilingual signs in the province. As mentioned, when the Supreme Court ruled that French-only store signs violated their owners' freedom of expression, Bourassa invoked section 33 (and the equivalent clause in the Quebec Charter of Rights) and then passed what he considered to be a compromise law that allowed certain bilingual signs inside the store.

This incident, together with a general public adoration of the Charter and a distrust of politicians who sought to find ways around it, gave the notwithstanding clause a negative reception in most of English Canada. Since 1988, politicians have rarely even contemplated its use. As noted, Quebec has its own reasons to dislike the Charter, but Alberta otherwise provides the main locus of anti-Charter sentiment, and a number of incidents arose in that province that tempted the government to use section 33. One was to prevent the victims of a sterilization program (from an earlier period in the province's history) from appealing for compensation. Another was when the Supreme Court of Canada ruled that sexual orientation had to be added to the Alberta Individual Rights Protection Act, and a third occurred when the Supreme Court legalized same-sex marriages. The Alberta-based Reform Party also asked the federal government to use the notwithstanding clause to override a lower BC court decision justifying the possession of child pornography as an element of freedom of expression, but this decision was eventually overturned by the Supreme Court of Canada.[61]

Nevertheless, section 33 is often defended as a general principle: it allows democratically elected legislators to have the final say. It also takes pressure off judges to solve political crises because they know that politicians can, if necessary, override their strictly legal decisions.[62] Reflecting the fact that it was born of political compromise, the notwithstanding clause in the Charter leaves Canadians with a strange system under which the courts can overrule the legislatures and the legislatures can overrule the courts. Rank Canadian political compromise that it is, this system of protecting civil liberties may turn out to be superior to either total legislative supremacy or exclusive judicial review. Some observers advocate the abolition of the notwithstanding clause, but others, not wanting to entrust their fate entirely either to legislatures or to courts, prefer the checks and balances that they provide to each other.

. . . .

IMPLICATIONS OF CONSTITUTIONALIZING THE CHARTER OF RIGHTS

After more than 25 years of experience, the Charter of Rights and Freedoms continues to attract both lively support and opposition. Supporters and opponents alike agree, however, that the Charter has significantly changed the operation of the Canadian political system. The courts have become involved in most of the difficult political issues that have arisen over the past quarter century: Aboriginal rights, abortion, assisted suicide, Cruise missile testing, French-only signs, gender equality, health care, impaired driving, mandatory retirement, minority-language schools, official bilingualism, political rights of public servants, pornography, prostitution, redistribution of constituency boundaries, the right to strike, same-sex marriage, separate schools, sexual assault, sexual orientation, Sunday shopping, terrorism, and tobacco advertising. Such cases have enmeshed the courts in considerable political controversy and, as Russell says, the Charter has "judicialized politics and politicized the judiciary."[63]

The first major implication of constitutionalizing the Charter, therefore, was to increase the role of the courts in the political process at the expense of the elected politicians. Adopted at a time when politicians were generally regarded with considerable cynicism and disrespect, the Charter was embraced by the Canadian public as a welcome addition to the Constitution. In fact, it became a hallowed national symbol in just the way Trudeau hoped it would. Many Canadians, especially young people, were oblivious to the fact that most of these rights existed before 1982, but in any case, the vast majority had more faith in judges than in parliamentarians and believed that their rights would be better protected that way, as indicated in Table 19.1.

TABLE 19.1 Courts versus Legislatures: Who Should Have the Final Say?	
	Percentage of Respondents
Courts	59.6
Legislature/government	26.5
Don't know/refused	13.9

Source: Paul Howe and David Northrup, "Strengthening Canadian Democracy: The Views of Canadians," Policy Matters, (Montreal: Institute for Research on Public Policy) vol. 1, no. 5 (July 2000), p. 100. Reproduced by permission of Institute for Research on Public Policy (IRPP, Montreal).

Some observers take the opposite view, the most scathing attack on the "legalization of politics" in Canada having been made by law professor Michael Mandel. He and his supporters mount five main arguments from the left. First, an enormous leeway exists within which the courts make highly political decisions, but judges disguise their work through legal interpretations and abstract principles that are unintelligible to the general public. Mandel challenges the generally accepted view that while politicians make popular, political, self-serving decisions, judges' decisions are impartial, objective, technical, rational, and in the public interest. Marc Gold supports Mandel in this view by writing that "judicial rhetoric functions both to obscure the true basis for the decision reached and to sensitize the audience into accepting the result as both legitimate and appropriate."[64] Especially given the reasonable limits clause, almost every Charter case could have been decided differently, and the content of Canadians' rights has "depended to a large extent upon which judges happened to sit on the panels that heard the cases."[65] Canadian scholars are thus beginning to examine the records of individual Supreme Court judges and to categorize them ideologically, and the Court itself has made some very political moves.[66]

Mandel's second argument is that although the Charter has been sold as enhancing democracy and the power of the people, it has really reduced the degree of popular control over government by transferring power from representative, accountable legislatures and politicians to unrepresentative, unaccountable, and unrestrained judges, courts, and an elitist legal profession. He adds: "It is both simpler and cheaper to get to see your MP than to get to see a judge."[67]

In the third place, legalized politics enhances individual and corporate rights against the collective welfare of the community, as in the tobacco advertising and health care decisions. The adoption of individualistic American values in the Charter, as opposed to traditional Canadian collectivism, is strengthened by the tendency of the courts to cite American precedents when making their decisions.[68] Radha Jhappan reminds us that the Charter deals primarily with individual rights, and that the few collective rights included relate to francophone minority groups and Aboriginals.[69]

Mandel's fourth point is that legalized politics is conservative, class-based politics that defends existing social arrangements and undermines popular movements. For a variety of reasons, including the cost of litigation, the background and attitudes of judges, and the biases in the law and the Charter, the socially disadvantaged and labour unions were better off without the document. He says: "The Charter is capable of opposing every kind of discrimination but class discrimination." Joel Bakan adds that the Charter is "Just Words" and that its principles have failed to promote social justice because it is interpreted by such a conservative institution and because it cannot force government into taking action—it can only strike down initiatives already undertaken.[70] Jhappan adds that most of the rights and freedoms are of a negative variety, with the guarantee of minority-language education rights being the best example of positive rights.[71] She adds that many of the interests that are actually mentioned in the Charter and that needed it most, such as women and Aboriginals, have been bitterly disappointed.

Finally, Mandel argues that Canadians have come to attribute such significance to Charter rights that we are in danger of forgetting the much more important social rights about which it is silent. Is the right to have children educated in a certain language more important than to educate children at public expense? Is the right of a doctor to work in a hospital after 65 years of age more important than a basic right to public health services? In making these points, Mandel at least offers a reminder to question the face value of court decisions; to refrain from glorifying the Charter, judges, lawyers, and courts; and to remember traditional ways of making public decisions.

A second main implication of the Charter is that public consciousness of the policymaking role of the courts has created greater interest in the quality of judicial appointments. In some ways this is advantageous, for that quality was not overly impressive in the past. However, to begin selecting judges on the basis of their ideological orientations would be another regrettable element in the Americanization of the Canadian system.

A third implication of the adoption of the Charter, as Peter Russell, Mandel, and others have pointed out, is that minority groups increasingly bypass the usual political processes—legislatures, cabinets, and bureaucracies—and take their demands directly to the courts instead.[72] To some extent this has happened when such groups were unable to accomplish their goals through traditional political activity, in which case this alternative avenue is advantageous. After all, it can be argued, democracy is more than majority rule; it is also about individual rights, which in some cases might be better protected by courts than by legislatures.[73] However, groups may simply believe that it is less trouble to go to court than to engage in the struggle of mobilizing popular support for their cause. But few observers, even in the legal profession, would welcome a general transformation of all political activity into legal activity with the attendant loss of political and organizational skills that traditionally characterize a democracy. Seymour Martin Lipset fears that the Charter will remove one of the last traits that distinguish Canadians from Americans by increasing the litigious character of citizen–state relations and bring about a "rights-centred" political culture.[74]

In the fourth place, the Charter has had an effect on the federal–provincial relationship. In its first ten years of operation, the Supreme Court invalidated more substantive provincial statutes than federal ones, many involving minority-language rights, and often in Quebec. In this and other policy fields, Morton and Knopff argued that the Charter has "transferred authority ... out of provincial legislatures and into the federal courts." Indeed, they coined the term "court party" to describe the link between "Charter groups," such as official-language minority groups, feminists, civil libertarians, Aboriginals, visible minority groups, people with disabilities, and gays and lesbians, and the ascendancy of judicial power in Canadian politics. They argued that "Ottawa has been able to forge a strategic alliance with select, non-territorial-based interest groups and with sympathetic federally-appointed judges" at the expense of the provinces.[75] If this is true, the Charter was working even more to his liking than Trudeau anticipated!

WINNERS, LOSERS, AND DIALOGUE

Morton and Knopff are actually more concerned about which interests have gained from the Charter than whether it has weakened provincial powers. This leads to a debate between right and left over the effects of the Charter. Coming from the right, they are upset that Charter decisions have benefited women and various minority groups against what they believe to be the majoritarian views of elected legislatures and the general public. They construct a kind of conspiracy theory that it has all happened, contrary to the public interest, because the judges who sought more power for themselves have been aided and abetted by the very groups in society that are mentioned in the Charter and that stood to benefit from judicial rather than political decisions.[76]

Although both left and right critics accuse the judiciary of deliberately expanding its powers, and although both are unhappy that the fate of so many Canadian public policies now rests in the hands of judges rather than politicians, they part company over which interests in society have taken most advantage of the opportunities provided by the Charter or reaped the greatest benefits from this transformation. Concentrating on "users" rather than "winners," Gregory Hein shows that corporations, not women or minority groups, are the single biggest interest in taking Charter cases to the courts, as seen in Figure 19.1.

Regardless of frequency of use, can we generalize about winners and losers in Charter interpretation? Undoubtedly, official-language minorities, criminals, and the gay and lesbian communities are among the biggest winners, but Mandel is not the only one to hold that business has also been a major beneficiary. The editors of *Charting the Consequences: The Impact of Charter Rights on Canadian Law and Politics* remind us that many Charter rights have been extended to corporations and that businesses have used the Charter "to challenge all variety

· ·

Figure 19.1 Organized Interests in Court, 1988–1998

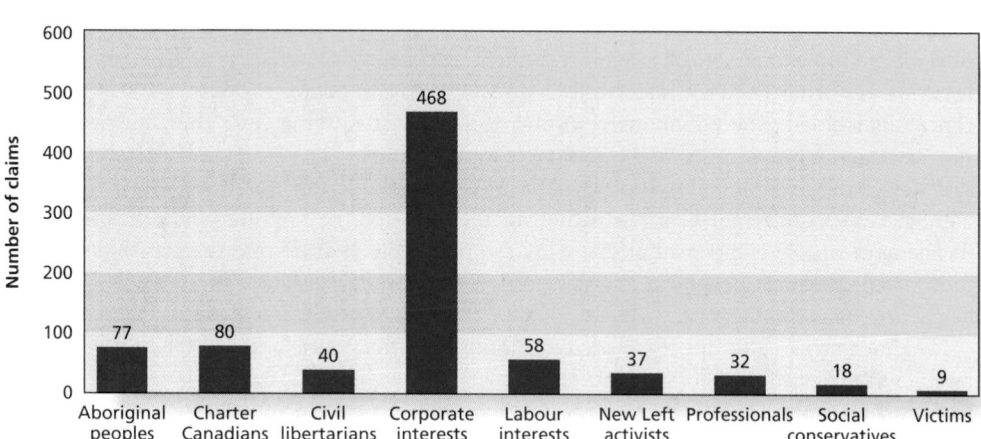

Source: Greg Hein, "Interest Group Litigation and Canadian Democracy," Choices (Montreal: Institute for Research on Public Policy) vol. 6, no. 2 (March 2000), p. 9. Reproduced by permission of Institute for Research on Public Policy (IRPP, Montreal).

of legislative measures."[77] As for such social movements as women, people with disabilities, and Aboriginals, the record is not as clear as Morton and Knopff imply. Liberal governments brought in the Court Challenges Program to level the playing field for disadvantaged interests, and Conservative governments abolished it, and all such groups have experienced wins and losses. Moreover, the Charter has often caused internal divisions within such groups over whether to pursue a legal or political strategy, and these groups' agendas "have had to conform to a more liberal, individualistic path than they might otherwise have chosen to follow."[78]

Although there is a grain of truth in the arguments of both left and right, the consequences of adding the Charter to the Canadian constitution are probably not as drastic as either contends. It should also be said that the courts have become increasingly deferential to existing laws. For example, in the second decade of the Charter's existence, the Supreme Court nullified fewer provincial statutes than in the first and appeared to have become more deferential to legislatures in general.[79] Despite all the criticism of its decisions, the Court found that most of the challenged laws were *not* violations of the Charter; in a high proportion of other cases, it invoked the reasonable limits clause to allow laws to stand even though they violated one Charter right or another. When governments chose to defend existing laws, they were usually successful, and they have been able to "Charter-proof" new ones without too much effort.[80] Moreover, the new political role of the courts has sometimes been exploited by the politicians. The latter are "often quite relieved to have controversial and unpredictable issues transformed into 'nonpartisan' questions about rights and about the correct interpretation of the Constitution to be taken off their hands and resolved in the courts."[81]

Scholars now talk about a "dialogue" between legislatures and courts. Such a dialogue is likely to result in incremental changes in legislation rather than judicial rejection of entire laws. Janet Hiebert and Kent Roach have provided the most comprehensive and balanced analyses of the interplay between the Supreme Court and Parliament. They both conclude that the definition of rights and freedoms should not be the prerogative of the courts alone. Parliament also has a role to play—it "shares responsibility with the judiciary for determining how the Charter should direct social conflicts."[82] Parliament and the courts look at many Charter issues from understandably different perspectives, neither of which is right or wrong. Hiebert finds that Parliament has sometimes been too deferential to the judicial definition of rights and freedoms (for example, in the case of tobacco advertising) and too inclined to revise laws so that they will meet the Court's legalistic standards rather than what legislators really feel is in the public interest. She declares that in some cases the Court has been negligent in not providing a stricter timetable for legislatures to revise their laws (for example, same-sex laws in certain provinces), while in others, the Court has not given Parliament enough time to reformulate a law, which might well involve holding public hearings and engaging in widespread consultations. She also points out that despite the greatly increased judicial role in the policymaking process, only a fraction of legislative decisions will ever be subject to judicial review.

The increasing calm in the debate over the role of the courts and the Charter was shattered by the *Chaoulli* decision in 2005 regarding the public health care system. As mentioned, the court was split 3–3 on whether the waiting times for core health services in the public system were a threat to life, liberty, and security of the person. The judgment even contained a heated debate among the judges themselves regarding the issue of deferring to legislators on such an obviously political rather than legal issue. It is the clearest case yet of individual rights usurping collective values. Even those observers who favoured a two-tier health care system argued that it should be the outcome of political debate, not judicial fiat. The decision also clearly established that judicial activism does not always come from the left.

. . . .

CONCLUSION

The protection of civil liberties in Canada historically occupied an intermediate position between the parliamentary sovereignty of Britain and the judicial review of the United States. The adoption of the Charter of Rights and Freedoms in 1982 had a profound effect on the operation of the whole Canadian political system in transferring power from politicians and legislatures to judges and courts. However, the reasonable limits and notwithstanding clauses in the Charter are unique Canadian responses and reassert the involvement of politicians in the process of defining rights and freedoms.

The significance of the Charter is such that it is linked to almost every other chapter of this book. Primarily related to Chapter 17 on the Constitution and Charter 24 on the Judiciary, it also has an impact on the institutions of government—the executive, bureaucracy, and Parliament—which are subject to Charter constraints. But Charter decisions have also affected many socio-economic issues discussed in Part 2, such as Aboriginals, official languages, gender, ethnocultural and religious minorities, corporations, unions, and age—even relations with the United States. Similarly, the mass media, elections, political parties, and advocacy groups have also been subjects of Supreme Court decisions based on the Charter.

P Of the approaches outlined in Chapter 1, pluralism is most relevant to the addition of the Charter of Rights in the protection of civil liberties in Canada. In emphasizing individualist values and lauding the Charter in protecting them, pluralists draw their inspiration from the ideology of liberalism as articulated by such philosophers as John Locke and John Stuart Mill. Liberalism emphasizes the basic rationality of all people and advocates equality and liberty as embodied in the fundamental freedoms—of speech, press, religion, and association—and in the rule of law. Pluralists thus point out how often ordinary people have gained from Charter restraints on police and from such decisions as the right to be informed of the right to legal aid. Pluralists expect that equality rights together with affirmative action programs will help remove various kinds of discrimination. They also observe that judicial decisions have been ideologically balanced, citing cases that have favoured both business and labour. Rather than be concerned that the legalization of politics has discouraged groups and popular movements from engaging in traditional political organization, pluralists welcome an additional means by which such demands can be advanced, and they point to special programs to fund certain kinds of Charter challenges.

C Class analysts have a less positive view of the Charter, following the general line of argument made by Mandel. Charter rights have often been extended to benefit corporations rather than individuals, such as in Sunday shopping, tobacco advertising, and search and seizure cases. The stringent search requirements laid down in the *Southam* case constituted another blow to the already weak laws restricting corporate collusion in Canada.[83] Mandel cites the *Singh* and *Morgentaler* cases as two of the few where the socially disadvantaged appeared to have benefited from a Charter decision, but he reminds us to look at subsequent attempts by governments to dilute these victories through legislation and regulation. Moreover, the costs of taking cases to the courts are generally prohibitive except to wealthy individuals and corporations, and in 1992 the Mulroney government cancelled the Court Challenges Program that had funded many Charter cases. After the Liberals resurrected the Program, the Harper government cancelled it for a second time. Mandel also stresses the Charter's preference for individualism over collectivism, adding that it "unites people against the state but the result is to leave them at the mercy of private power."[84]

Class analysts also emphasize the elitist background of judges and question whether they can make fair decisions for the ordinary mortals who appear in court. For example, Andrew Petter writes,

> there is nothing about the Canadian judiciary to suggest that they possess the experience, the training or the disposition to comprehend the social impact of claims made to them under the Charter, let alone to resolve those claims in ways that promote, or even protect, the interests of lower income Canadians.[85]

(SC) In one sense, a Charter of Rights or other means of restraining government action is contrary to the view of state-centred theorists. The *Singh* decision, for example, necessitated a complete overhaul of the refugee admission system, and the *Askov* decision created chaos in the Ontario court system. However, state-centred theorists emphasize the frequency with which the Supreme Court has used the "reasonable limits" clause to justify state infringement of Charter rights. In addition, they point out that the Charter has been used far more often to restrict individual police actions than to overturn major government policies, such as in Operation Dismantle.

(G) Globalization is relevant to the Charter of Rights and Freedoms in a number of ways. First, the Charter is about limiting government action, which fits perfectly into the neoliberal ideological basis of globalization. Although it may be pure coincidence, the Charter was adopted just as neoliberalism was becoming a dominant philosophy throughout the Western world. Second, in the same vein, the Supreme Court decided to apply the Charter to the rights and freedoms of corporations, providing the latter with another means—beyond trade agreements—to strike down government restrictions on their market-driven operations. Third, since most other Western democracies also possess a similar document, and with even Britain moving in the same direction to some extent, there is a natural tendency for Canadian judges to look at how the issues before them have been addressed by other courts around the world. Although the claim is sometimes made that they always look first at the American courts, it would be more accurate to emphasize the wide range of foreign precedents they examine.

. . . .

DISCUSSION QUESTIONS

1. What are the advantages and disadvantages of the "reasonable limits" clause in the Charter?

2. What are the advantages and disadvantages of the "notwithstanding" clause in the Charter?

3. Are Canadian fundamental freedoms and other democratic values better protected since 1982? Why or why not?

4. Does legalized Charter politics inherently favour business interests and discriminate against those with social disadvantages?

5. Does the Charter discourage traditional political activity?

6. Should Parliament play a larger role in the definition of rights and freedoms in Canada?

. . . .

NOTES

1. For example, Peter Hogg, *Constitutional Law of Canada*, student ed. (Toronto: Carswell, 2006).
2. Alexander Alvaro, "Why Property Rights Were Excluded from the Canadian Charter of Rights and Freedoms," *Canadian Journal of Political Science* (June 1991).
3. Although the British courts do not have such power, the European Court of Justice, part of the European Union, can make nonbinding decisions on whether British acts violate civil liberties. Moreover, the European Convention has now been incorporated into the British Human Rights Bill. Although the British courts do not have the explicit right to strike down public law that they deem to be in conflict with the European Convention, the Human Rights bill virtually obliges the government to rewrite statutes in response to criticism by the courts.
4. Good discussions of this early period are found in Radha Jhappan, "Charter Politics and the Judiciary," in Michael Whittington and Glen Williams, eds., *Canadian Politics in the 21st Century*, 7th ed. (Toronto: Thomson Nelson, 2008) and Heather MacIvor, *Canadian Politics and Government in the Charter Era* (Toronto: Thomson Nelson, 2006). See also Constance Backhouse, *Colour-Coded: A Legal History of Racism in Canada, 1900–1950* (Toronto: University of Toronto Press, 1999).
5. It was first articulated in the *Alberta Press Bill* case and used as a supplementary argument to criminal law in several cases but never on its own.
6. *Reference re Alberta Statutes*, [1938] S.C.R. 100.
7. *Saumur v. City of Quebec*, [1953] S.C.R. 299.
8. *Switzman v. Elbling and Attorney-General of Quebec*, [1957] S.C.R. 285.
9. *Roncarelli v. Duplessis*, [1959] S.C.R. 121. In *Chaput v. Romain*, [1955] S.C.R. 834, police had broken up a private meeting of Jehovah's Witnesses, and in *Lamb v. Benoit*, [1959] S.C.R. 321, the police arrested Jehovah's Witnesses for distributing their literature. In all three cases, action of the authorities was ruled contrary to the rule of law.
10. *Cunningham v. Tomey Homma*, [1903] A.C. 151. However, the federal power over naturalization and aliens had allowed the Court to overturn an earlier anti-Asian law in BC in *Union Colliery Co. of B.C. Ltd. v. Bryden*, [1899] A.C. 580.
11. Ian Greene, *The Charter of Rights* (Toronto: Lorimer, 1989), p. 18; Backhouse, *Colour-Coded: A Legal History of Racism in Canada, 1900–1950.*
12. Thomas Berger, *Fragile Freedoms*, rev. ed. (Toronto: Clarke Irwin, 1982). Greene also refers to the secret trials held in connection with the Gouzenko spy affair in 1945, in *The Charter of Rights*, p. 21.
13. Walter Tarnopolsky, *The Canadian Bill of Rights*, 2nd rev. ed. (Toronto: McClelland and Stewart, 1975); Christopher MacLennan, *Toward the Charter: Canadians and the Demand for a National Bill of Rights, 1929–1960* (Montreal: McGill-Queen's University Press, 2003). Saskatchewan had an earlier provincial Bill of Rights, while Alberta and Quebec each passed one later. These provincial bills of rights could not be constitutionally entrenched any more than the federal one was.
14. *R. v. Drybones*, [1970] S.C.R. 282. The Indian Act created a liquor offence that had harsher penalties for Indians than the equivalent offence for non-Indians.
15. *Brownridge v. The Queen*, [1972] S.C.R. 926; *A.-G. Ont. v. Reale*, [1975] 2 S.C.R. 624; and *Lowry and Lepper v. The Queen*, [1974] 26 D.L.R. (3rd) 224; *Robertson and Rosetanni v. The Queen*, [1963] S.C.R. 651 (upholding the regulation of operating hours of a bowling alley based on the Lord's Day Act); *A.G. Can. v. Lavell and Isaac v. Bédard*, [1974] S.C.R. 1349 (upholding a distinction in the Indian

Act between men and women marrying whites); *Hogan v. The Queen*, [1975] 2 S.C.R. 574 (denying the right to counsel before taking a breathalyzer test, after the *Brownridge* case had upheld such a right); *Oil, Chemical and Atomic Workers International Union v. Imperial Oil Ltd. and A.-G. B.C.*, [1963] S.C.R. 584 (denying unions the right to contribute to the NDP via a checkoff procedure); *Walter v. A.-G. Alta.*, [1969] S.C.R. 383 (upholding Alberta legislation restricting the settlement of Hutterites); *Morgan v. A.-G. P.E.I.*, [1976] 2 S.C.R. 349 (upholding PEI legislation restricting the ownership of land in the province to PEI residents); *A.-G. Can. and Dupond v. Montreal*, [1978] 2 S.C.R. 770 (upholding a Montreal bylaw prohibiting parades and public gatherings); and *Nova Scotia Board of Censors v. McNeil*, [1978] 2 S.C.R. 662 (upholding provincial film censorship boards).

16. Peter Russell, "The Political Purposes of the Canadian Charter of Rights and Freedoms," *Canadian Bar Review* (March 1983).

17. For a more comprehensive account, see Heather MacIvor, *Canadian Politics and Government in the Charter Era*; Sharpe, Robert J., and Kent Roach. *The Charter of Rights and Freedoms*, 3rd ed. (Toronto: Irwin Law, 2005); and Thomas Bateman, et al., *The Court and the Charter: Leading Cases* (Toronto: Emond Montgomery, 2008).

18. *R. v. Oakes*, [1986] 1 S.C.R. 103; Janet Hiebert, *Limiting Rights: The Dilemma of Judicial Review* (Montreal: McGill-Queen's University Press, 1996); and MacIvor, *Canadian Politics and Government in the Charter Era*, pp. 25–31.

19. *R. v. Sharpe*, [2001] 1 S.C.R. 45.

20. *R. v. Big M Drug Mart Ltd.*, [1985] 1 S.C.R. 295. Of course, Big M itself had no religion, but "worshipped only the Almighty Dollar." Michael Mandel, *The Charter of Rights and the Legalization of Politics in Canada*, rev. ed. (Toronto: Wall & Thompson, 1994), p. 316; *R. v. Edwards Books and Art Ltd.*, [1986] 2 S.C.R. 713 (Chief Justice Dickson's famous passage about a restful, recreational Sunday is located on p. 770); *Zylberberg et al. v. The Director of Education of the Sudbury Board of Education* (1988), 65 O.R. 641 (Ont. C.A.); *Alder v. Ontario*, [1996] 3 S.C.R. 609; *Re Davis* (1982), Can. Charter of Rights Ann. 9.1-1 (Alta. Prov. Ct.—Fam. Div.); *B. (R.) v. Children's Aid Society of Metropolitan Toronto*, [1995] 1 S.C.R. 315; *Jack and Charlie v. R.*, [1985] 2 S.C.R. 332; *Multani v. Commission scolaire Marguerite-Bourgeoys*, [2006] 1 S.C.R. 256; and MacIvor, ch. 8.

21. *Ford v. Quebec (Attorney General)*, [1988] 2 S.C.R. 712; *Devine v. Quebec (Attorney General)*, [1988] 2 S.C.R. 790; *Irwin Toy Ltd. v. Quebec (Attorney General)*, [1989] 1 S.C.R. 927; *RJR-MacDonald Inc. v. Canada (Attorney General)*, [1995] 3 S.C.R. 199; and *Canada (Attorney General) v. JTI-Macdonald Corp.*, [2007] 2 S.C.R. 610. See also *Rocket v. Royal College of Dental Surgeons of Ontario*, [1990] 2 S.C.R. 232, and Janet Hiebert, *Charter Conflicts: What Is Parliament's Role?* (Montreal: McGill-Queen's University, Press, 2002), ch. 4.

22. *R. v. Keegstra*, [1990] 3 S.C.R. 697; *R. v. Zundel*, [1992] S.C.R. 731; Mandel, *The Charter of Rights*, rev. ed., pp. 369–76; MacIvor, *Canadian Politics and Government in the Charter Era*, p. 395; and Kent Roach, *September 11: Consequences for Canada* (Montreal: McGill-Queen's University Press, 2003).

23. *RWDSU v. Dolphin Delivery Ltd.*, [1986] 2 S.C.R. 573; *B.C.G.E.U. v. British Columbia (Attorney General)*, [1988] 2 S.C.R. 214; Mandel, *The Charter of Rights*, rev. ed., ch. 5; and *R.W.D.S.U., Local 558 v. Pepsi-Cola Canada Beverages (West) Ltd.*, [2002] 1 S.C.R. 156.

24. *Ramsden v. Peterborough (City)*, [1993] 2 S.C.R. 1084; *MacKay v. Manitoba*, [1989] 2 S.C.R. 357; *Osborne v. Canada (Treasury Board)*, [1991] 2 S.C.R. 69; *Thomson Newspapers Co. v. Canada (Attorney General)*, [1998] 1 S.C.R. 877; *Libman v. Quebec (Attorney General)*, [1997] 3 S.C.R. 569; and *Harper v. Canada (Attorney General)*, [2004] 1 S.C.R. 827.

25. *Canadian Newspapers Co. v. Canada (Attorney General)*, [1988] 2 S.C.R. 122; *Canadian Broadcasting Corp. v. New Brunswick (Attorney General)*, [1996] 3 S.C.R. 480; *Dagenais v. Canadian Broadcasting Corp.*, [1994] 3 S.C.R. 835; and *New Brunswick Broadcasting Co. v. Nova Scotia (Speaker of the House of Assembly)*, [1993] 1 S.C.R. 319; *R. v. Mentuck*, [2001] 3 S.C.R. 442; and *Toronto Star Newspapers Ltd. v. Ontario*, [2005] 2 S.C.R. 188.

26. *R. v. Butler*, [1992] 1 S.C.R. 452; and *R. v. Skinner*, [1990] 1 S.C.R. 1235.

27. *Reference re Public Service Employee Relations Act, Labour Relations Act, and Police Officers Collective Bargaining Act of Alberta*, [1987] 1 S.C.R. 313. Two other simultaneous cases completed the "labour trilogy": *Public Service Alliance of Canada v. The Queen*, [1987] 1 S.C.R. 424; and *Saskatchewan v. Retail, Wholesale and Department Store Union*, [1987] 1 S.C.R. 460. See also *Lavigne v. Ontario Public*

Service Employees Union, [1991] 81 D.L.R. (4th) 545 (S.C.C.); Joel Bakan, *Just Words: Constitutional Rights and Social Wrong* (Toronto: University of Toronto Press, 1997); *Dunmore v. Ontario (Attorney General)*, [2001] 3 S.C.R. 1016; and *R. v. Advance Cutting and Coring Ltd.*, [2001] 3 S.C.R. 209. The reversal case was *Health Services and Support—Facilities Subsector Bargaining Assn. v. British Columbia*, [2007] 2 S.C.R. 391.

28. *Canadian Disability Rights Council v. Canada*, [1988] 3 F.C. 622; *Sauvé v. Canada (Attorney General)*, [1993] 2 S.C.R. 438; *Sauvé v. Canada (Chief Electoral Officer)*, [2002] 3 S.C.R. 519; and MacIvor, *Canadian Politics and Government in the Charter Era*, ch. 9.

29. *Dixon v. British Columbia (Attorney General)*, [1989] 59 D.L.R. (4th) 247 (B.C.S.C.); and *Reference re Provincial Electoral Boundaries (Sask.)*, [1991] 2 S.C.R. 158. Other cases have not gone as far as the Supreme Court of Canada, but the PEI electoral map was disallowed by the courts of that province, while the Alberta map was upheld.

30. *Figueroa v. Canada (Attorney General)*, [2003] 1 S.C.R. 912.

31. *Law Society of Upper Canada v. Skapinker*, [1984] 1 S.C.R. 357; *Black v. Law Society of Alberta*, [1989] 1 S.C.R. 591; and *Basile v. Attorney-General of Nova Scotia*, [1984] 11 D.L.R. (4th) 219 (N.S.C.A.).

32. *R. v. Morgentaler*, [1988] 1 S.C.R. 30; *Borowski v. Canada (Attorney General)*, [1989] 1 S.C.R. 342; Mandel, *The Charter of Rights*, rev. ed., pp. 405–33; *Dobson (Litigation Guardian of) v. Dobson*, [1999] 2 S.C.R. 753; MacIvor, *Canadian Politics and Government in the Charter Era* contrasts Morgentaler's fate before and after the adoption of the Charter, pp. 77–79.

33. *Rodriguez v. British Columbia (Attorney General)*, [1993] 3 S.C.R. 519; and *R. v. Latimer* [2001] 1 S.C.R. 3.

34. *Operation Dismantle Inc. v. The Queen*, [1985] 1 S.C.R. 441; and Mandel, *The Charter of Rights*, rev. ed., pp. 74–81.

35. *Chaoulli v. Quebec (Attorney General)*, [2005] 1 S.C.R. 791.

36. *Singh v. Minister of Employment and Immigration*, [1985] 1 S.C.R. 177; *Re B.C. Motor Vehicle Act*, [1985] 2 S.C.R. 486; *R. v. Beare; R. v. Higgins*, [1988] 2 S.C.R. 387; and *R. v. Malmo-Levine; R. v. Caine*, [2003] 3 S.C.R. 571. See also *R. v. D.B.* [2008] 2 S.C.R. 3 regarding sentences under the Youth Criminal Justice Act.

37. *R. v. Daviault*, [1994] 3 S.C.R. 63; *R. v. Stinchcombe*, [1991] 3 S.C.R. 326; *R. v. Seaboyer*, [1991] 2 S.C.R. 577; *R. v. Ewanchuk*, [1999] 1 S.C.R. 330; and *Application under s. 83.28 of the Criminal Code (Re)*, [2004] 2 S.C.R. 248. Janet Hiebert discusses the sexual assault cases and the interplay between the courts and Parliament in *Charter Conflicts*, ch. 5.

38. *Hunter v. Southam Inc.*, [1984] 2 S.C.R. 145; *R. v. Dyment*, [1988] 2 S.C.R. 417; *R. v. Beare; R. v. Simmons*, [1988] 2 S.C.R. 495; *R. v. Hufsky*, [1988] 1 S.C.R. 621; *R. v. Thomson*, [1988] 1 S.C.R. 640; *R. v. Ladouceur*, [1990] 1 S.C.R. 957; *Weatherall v. Canada (Attorney General)*, [1993] 2 S.C.R. 872; and *R. v. Golden*, [2001] 3 S.C.R. 679. See also *R. v. Kang-Brown* [2008] 1 S.C.R. 456 regarding the police use of sniffer dogs.

39. *R. v. Feeney*, [1997] 2 S.C.R. 13; *R. v. Stillman*, [1997] 1 S.C.R. 607; and *R. v. Godoy*, [1999] 1 S.C.R 311. Hiebert discusses the interplay between the courts and Parliament in the cases of *Feeney* and *Stillman* in *Charter Conflicts*, chs. 6 and 7.

40. *R. v. S.A.B.*, [2003] 2 S.C.R. 678; *R. v. Mann*, [2004] 3 S.C.R. 59; and *R. v. Tessling*, [2004] 3 S.C.R. 432.

41. *R. v. Therens*, [1985] 1 S.C.R. 613; *R. v. Thomsen*, [1988] 1 S.C.R. 640; *Clarkson v. The Queen*, [1986] 1 S.C.R. 383; *R. v. Manninen*, [1987] 1 S.C.R. 1233; *R. v. Brydges*, [1990] 1 S.C.R. 190; *R. v. Burlingham*, [1995] 2 S.C.R. 206; *R. v. Evans*, [1991] 1 S.C.R. 869; and *R. v. Woods*, [2005] 2 S.C.R. 205. See also *R. v. Singh*, [2007] 3 S.C.R. 405 regarding the section 7 right to silence.

42. *R. v. Askov*, [1990] 2 S.C.R. 1199; and *R. v. Rahey*, [1987] 1 S.C.R. 588.

43. *R. v. Hebert*, [1990] 2 S.C.R. 151; *R. v. Broyles*, [1991] 3 S.C.R. 595; *Valente v. the Queen*, [1985] 2 S.C.R. 673; *R. v. Oakes*, [1986] 1 S.C.R. 103; *R. v. Whyte*, [1988] 2 S.C.R. 3; *R. v. Holmes*, [1988] 1 S.C.R. 914; and *R. v. Vermette*, [1988] 1 S.C.R. 985.

44. *R. v. Smith (Edward Dewey)*, [1987] 1 S.C.R. 1045; *R. v. Lyons*, [1987] 2 S.C.R. 309; *R. v. Milne*, [1987] 2 S.C.R. 512; *Kindler v. Canada (Minister of Justice)*, [1991] 2 S.C.R. 779; *R. v. Latimer*, [2001] 1 S.C.R. 3; *United States v. Burns*, [2001] 1 S.C.R. 283; and *Canadian Foundation for Children, Youth and the Law v. Canada (Attorney General)*, [2004] 1 S.C.R. 76.

45. *R. v. Tran*, [1994] 2 S.C.R. 951.

46. *Suresh v. Canada (Minister of Citizenship and Immigration)*, [2002] 1 S.C.R. 3; *Charkaoui v. Canada (Citizenship and Immigration)*, [2007] 1 S.C.R. 350; Ronald J. Daniels, Patrick Macklem, and Kent Roach, eds. *The Security of Freedom: Essays on Canada's Anti-Terrorism Bill* (Toronto: University of Toronto Press, 2002); Kent Roach, *September 11: Consequences for Canada* (Montreal: McGill-Queen's University Press, 2003); Irwin Cotler, "From Professor to Justice Minister: Charter Rights and Anti-Terrorism," Institute for Research on Public Policy, *Policy Options* (November 2007).

47. Greene, *The Charter of Rights*, p. 172; *Andrews v. Law Society of British Columbia*, [1989] 1 S.C.R. 143; *R. v. Turpin*, [1989] 1 S.C.R. 1296; Mandel, *The Charter of Rights*, rev. ed., pp. 337–53; David Schneiderman and Kate Sutherland, eds., *Charting the Consequences: The Impact of Charter Rights on Canadian Law and Politics* (Toronto: University of Toronto Press, 1997), chs. 6, 7, 8, and 9; Bakan, *Just Words*; Mary C. Hurley, *Charter Equality Rights: Interpretation of Section 15 in Supreme Court of Canada Decisions* (Ottawa: Parliamentary Research Branch, Background Paper BP-402E, 2005); and MacIvor, *Canadian Politics and Government in the Charter Era*, ch. 11.

48. The Bill of Rights case was *Bliss v. A.-G. Can.*, [1979] S.C.R. 183; the Charter case that overturned it was *Brooks v. Canada Safeway Ltd.*, [1989] 1 S.C.R. 1219; the Supreme Court refused to review the Ontario Court of Appeal ruling in the *Blainey* case, which found that this was not a case of reasonable limits; and *McKinney v. University of Guelph*, [1990] 3 S.C.R. 229, where the Court said it would defer to legislatures in the area of mandatory retirement. See also *Eldridge v. British Columbia (Attorney General)*, [1997] 3 S.C.R. 624; *Corbiere v. Canada (Minister of Indian and Northern Affairs)*, [1999] 2 S.C.R. 203; *Law v. Canada (Minister of Employment and Immigration)*, [1999] 1 S.C.R. 497; *Newfoundland (Treasury Board) v. N.A.P.E.*, [2004] 3 S.C.R. 381; *Gosselin v. Quebec (Attorney General)*, [2002] 4 S.C.R. 429; *Auton (Guardian ad litem of) v. British Columbia (Attorney General)*, [2004] 3 S.C.R. 657; and *New Brunswick (Human Rights Commission) v. Potash Corporation of Saskatchewan Inc.* [2008] 2 S.C.R. 604.

49. *Egan v. Canada*, [1995] 2 S.C.R. 513; *Vriend v. Alberta*, [1998] 1 S.C.R. 493; *M. v. H.*, [1999] 2 S.C.R. 3; *Reference re Same-Sex Marriage*, [2004] 3 S.C.R. 698; and Mary C. Hurley, *Sexual Orientation and Legal Rights* (Ottawa: Parliamentary Research Branch, Background Paper 92-1E, 2005). Hiebert discusses these cases and the interplay between courts and legislatures in *Charter Conflicts*, ch. 8.

50. *Trinity Western University v. British Columbia College of Teachers*, [2001] 1 S.C.R. 772; *Chamberlain v. Surrey School District No. 36*, [2002] 4 S.C.R. 710; and *Nova Scotia (Attorney General) v. Walsh*, [2002] 4 S.C.R. 325.

51. *R. v. Kapp*, [2008] 2 S.C.R. 483.

52. *Jones v. A.G. New Brunswick*, [1975] 2 S.C.R. 182; *Attorney General of Quebec v. Blaikie*, [1979] 2 S.C.R. 1016; *A.G. Manitoba v. Forest*, [1979] 2 S.C.R. 1032; *Reference re Manitoba Language Rights*, [1985] 1 S.C.R. 721; *Order re Manitoba Language Rights*, [1985] 2 S.C.R. 347; *Bilodeau v. Attorney General Manitoba*, [1986] 1 S.C.R. 449; *Reference re Manitoba Language Rights*, [1992] 1 S.C.R. 272; *Société des Acadiens et Acadiennes du Nouveau-Brunswick Inc. v. Canada* [2008] 1 S.C.R. 383; and Mandel, *The Charter of Rights*, rev. ed., ch. 3.

53. Kenneth McRoberts, *Misconceiving Canada: The Struggle for National Unity* (Toronto: Oxford University Press, 1997).

54. *Attorney General of Quebec v. Quebec Association of Protestant School Boards*, [1984] 2 S.C.R. 66; *Mahe v. Alberta*, [1990] 1 S.C.R. 342; and *Arsenault-Cameron v. Prince Edward Island*, [2000] 1 S.C.R. 3. In *Doucet-Boudreau v. Nova Scotia (Minister of Education)*, [2003] 3 S.C.R. 3, the Supreme Court made an interesting decision with respect to the implementation of its decisions in ruling that a Nova Scotia judge was right to order the province to speed up the construction of French-language schools. In other words, judges may actively supervise how governments are carrying out their orders.

55. *R. v. Collins*, [1987] 1 S.C.R. 265.

56. *R. v. Sparrow*, [1990] 1 S.C.R. 1075; *R. v. Sioui*, [1990] 1 S.C.R. 1025; *Delgamuukw v. British Columbia*, [1997] 3 S.C.R. 1010; *Ontario (Attorney General) v. Bear Island Foundation*, [1991] 2 S.C.R. 570; *R. v. Marshall*, [1999] 2 S.C.R. 456 and 533; Mandel, *The Charter of Rights*, rev. ed., pp. 353–69; and Schneiderman and Sutherland, *Charting the Consequences*, ch. 5.

57. *R. v. Powley*, [2003] 2 S.C.R. 207; *Haida Nation v. British Columbia (Minister of Forests)*, [2004] 3 S.C.R. 511; *Taku River Tlingit First Nation v. British Columbia (Project Assessment Director)*, [2004] 3 S.C.R. 550; *R. v. Marshall; R. v. Bernard*, [2005] 2 S.C.R. 220, *R. v. Sappier; R.v. Gray*, [2006] 2 S.C.R. 686; *R. v. Kapp* (June 27, 2008).

58. *Reference re Bill 30, An Act to Amend the Education Act (Ont.)*, [1987] 1 S.C.R. 1148.
59. *RWDSU v. Dolphin Delivery Ltd.*, [1986] 2 S.C.R. 573; Mandel, *The Charter of Rights*, rev. ed., p. 283; and *McKinney v. University of Guelph*; *Lavigne v. Ontario Public Service Employees Union*, [1991] 2 S.C.R. 211; see also MacIvor, ch. 1. The *Blainey* case found that a clause in the Ontario Human Rights Code allowed discrimination against women in sports organizations, and since this was inconsistent with the Charter, it was held to be of no force or effect and was later repealed. This case demonstrates how the Charter can indirectly affect the private sector, as does the *Vriend* case.
60. It has been used on about 14 other occasions of no public significance. See Tsvi Kahana, "The Notwithstanding Mechanism and Public Discussion: Lessons from the Ignored Practice of s. 33 of the Charter," *Canadian Public Administration* 44, no.3 (2001); and MacIvor, *Canadian Politics and Government in the Charter Era*, p. 379.
61. The distinctive Quebec and Alberta approaches to the Charter are discussed in Schneiderman and Sutherland, *Charting the Consequences*, chs. 1 and 2; see also Rainer Knopff and F.L. Morton, *Charter Politics* (Scarborough: Nelson Canada, 1992). Alberta actually used the notwithstanding clause regarding same-sex marriage, but the subsequent Supreme Court ruling that it was within federal jurisdiction made that moot.
62. Greene, *The Charter of Rights*, p. 107; and Mandel, *The Charter of Rights*, pp. 87–96.
63. Peter Russell, "The Political Purposes of the Canadian Charter of Rights and Freedoms." There were many retrospectives on the Charter on its 20th anniversary, for example, Institute for Research on Public Policy, *Policy Options* (February 2007).
64. Marc Gold, "The Mask of Objectivity: Politics and Rhetoric in the Supreme Court of Canada," *The Supreme Court Law Review* 7 (1985), p. 458.
65. Andrew Heard, "The Charter in the Supreme Court of Canada: The Importance of Which Judges Hear an Appeal," *Canadian Journal of Political Science* (June 1991).
66. The Court repeatedly linked Quebec and Manitoba language cases, for example, to balance pro-French with pro-English cases, and backtracked on language rights after the Parti Québécois was safely out of power. Even more political were the Court decisions that paved the way for the adoption of the Charter in the *Patriation Reference* of 1981 and the *Quebec Veto Reference* of 1982. Marc Gold writes, for example, that "however much a judicial opinion may reflect how the court actually reached its decision, it is clear that the opinion should be viewed primarily as a portrayal of how the court wanted itself to be viewed in reaching that decision," in "The Mask of Objectivity," p. 457.
67. Mandel, *The Charter of Rights*, rev. ed., p. 69.
68. Christopher Manfredi, "The Use of United States Decisions by the Supreme Court of Canada under the Charter of Rights and Freedoms," *Canadian Journal of Political Science* (September 1990).
69. Jhappan, "Charter Politics and the Judiciary," p. 193.
70. Mandel, *The Charter of Rights*, rev. ed., p. 440; and Bakan, *Just Words*.
71. Jhappan, "Charter Politics and the Judiciary," pp. 193–95.
72. Russell, "The Political Purposes of the Canadian Charter of Rights and Freedoms"; Schneiderman and Sutherland, *Charting the Consequences*, chs. 6–9; and Miriam Smith, *Lesbian and Gay Rights in Canada: Social Movements and Equality-Seeking, 1971–1995* (Toronto: University of Toronto Press, 1999).
73. Robert Martin and Philip L. Bryden debate whether the Charter is undemocratic in Charlton and Barker, eds., *Crosscurrents*, 3rd ed.
74. Seymour Martin Lipset, *Continental Divide* (New York: Routlege, 1990).
75. F.L. Morton and Rainer Knopff, "The Charter Revolution and the Court Party," *Osgoode Hall Law Journal* (Fall 1992); Knopff and Morton, *Charter Politics*; MacIvor, *Canadian Politics and Government in the Charter Era*, ch. 7; and Jeremy A. Clarke, "Beyond the Democratic Dialogue, and Towards a Federalist One: Provincial Arguments and Supreme Court Responses in Charter Litigation," *Canadian Journal of Political Science* (June 2006).
76. F.L. Morton and Rainer Knopff, *The Charter Revolution and the Court Party* (Peterborough: Broadview Press, 2000).
77. Schneiderman and Sutherland, *Charting the Consequences*, p. 346, and chs. 3 and 4. The BC Health case may soften this assessment, but see Jhappan, "Charter Politics and the Judiciary," pp. 199–200.
78. Schneiderman and Sutherland, *Charting the Consequences*, p. 344.
79. York University Centre for Public Law and Public Policy, 1999, posted on the Canada Watch website (http://www.yorku.ca/robarts/projects/canada-watch/); and Patrick Monahan and Michael J. Bryant,

"The Supreme Court of Canada's 1996 Constitutional Cases: The End of Charter Activism?" *Canada Watch*, April 1997.

80. Schneiderman and Sutherland, *Charting the Consequences*, pp. 344–45; James B. Kelly, *Governing with the Charter: Legislative and Judicial Activism and Framers' Intent* (Vancouver: UBC Press, 2005) emphasizes the "Cabinet-centred" approach to constitutional review, rather than judicial activism.

81. Heard, "The Charter in the Supreme Court of Canada."

82. Hiebert, *Charter Conflicts*, p. xii. See also Kent Roach, *The Supreme Court on Trial: Judicial Activism or Democratic Dialogue* (Toronto: Irwin Law, 2001); MacIvor, *Canadian Politics and Government in the Charter Era*, ch. 4; Matthew A. Hennigar, "Expanding the "Dialogue" Debate: Canadian Federal Government Responses to Lower Court Charter Decisions," in *Canadian Journal of Political Science* (March 2004); and Gary O'Brien, "Legislative Scrutiny and the Charter of Rights: A Review of Senate Practices and Procedures," *Canadian Parliamentary Review* (Spring 2005).

83. Ontario Attorney General Roy McMurtry, one of the authors of the Charter, actually foresaw this possibility and referred to it in an address to a group of corporate lawyers in which he emphasized the value of the Charter for big business. See Mandel, *The Charter of Rights*, rev. ed., pp. 168–69.

84. Ibid., p. 301.

85. Quoted in Ibid., p. 43.

. . . .

FURTHER READING

Bakan, Joel. *Just Words: Constitutional Rights and Social Wrongs*. Toronto: University of Toronto Press, 1997.

Bateman, Thomas, et al. *The Court and the Charter: Leading Cases*. Toronto: Emond Montgomery, 2008.

Borovoy, Alan. *When Freedoms Collide: The Case for Our Civil Liberties*. Toronto: Lester & Orpen Dennys, 1988.

Daniels, Ronald J., Patrick Macklem, and Kent Roach, eds. *The Security of Freedom: Essays on Canada's Anti-Terrorism Bill*. Toronto: University of Toronto Press, 2002.

Greene, Ian. *The Charter of Rights*. Toronto: Lorimer, 1989.

Hiebert, Janet. *Charter Conflicts: What Is Parliament's Role?* Montreal: McGill-Queen's University Press, 2002.

———. *Limiting Rights: The Dilemma of Judicial Review*. Montreal: McGill-Queen's University Press, 1996.

Hogg, Peter W. *Constitutional Law of Canada*, student ed. Toronto: Carswell, 2006.

Jhappan, Radha. "Charter Politics and the Judiciary." In Michael Whittington and Glen Williams, eds., *Canadian Politics in the 21st Century*, 7th ed. Toronto: Thomson Nelson, 2008.

Kelly, James B. *Governing with the Charter: Legislative and Judicial Activism and Framers' Intent*. Vancouver: UBC Press, 2005.

Knopff, Rainer, and F.L. Morton. *Charter Politics*. Scarborough: Nelson Canada, 1992.

MacIvor, Heather. *Canadian Politics and Government in the Charter Era*. Toronto: Thomson Nelson, 2006.

MacLennan, Christopher. *Toward the Charter: Canadians and the Demand for a National Bill of Rights, 1929–1960*. Montreal: McGill-Queen's University Press, 2003.

Mandel, Michael. *The Charter of Rights and the Legalization of Politics in Canada*, rev. ed. Toronto: Wall and Thompson, 1994.

Morton, F.L., and Rainer Knopff. *The Charter Revolution and the Court Party*. Peterborough: Broadview Press, 2000.

Roach, Kent. *The Supreme Court on Trial: Judicial Activism or Democratic Dialogue*. Toronto: Irwin Law, 2001.

Sharpe, Robert J., and Kent Roach. *The Charter of Rights and Freedoms*, 3rd ed. Toronto: Irwin Law, 2005.

PART 5

Governing

Having examined the societal and constitutional contexts of the political system and the means of linking people to government, we now begin to focus on the authorities themselves or what might be termed "governing." This section, therefore, examines the individual institutions of government in detail. These institutions are the executive, including the Crown, the prime minister, and the Cabinet; the bureaucracy or public service; Parliament, including the House of Commons and the Senate; and the judiciary. The functions and operations of each branch of government are outlined, as are the kinds of outputs or authoritative decisions that each can make. Initially, however, Chapter 20 briefly discusses government in the early years of the 21st century and puts these institutions into the context of the policymaking process. It thus provides an overview of how these institutions interact with one another to produce public policies. It also outlines the array of policy instruments from which the authorities choose.

Chapter 20

The Policymaking
PROCESS AND POLICY
Instruments

To many citizens, "Ottawa" is one big blur; it is "the government." Some people with a little more sophistication disparage "the politicians," "the bureaucrats," or "the judges" but without much knowledge of who is really responsible for the decisions about which they are complaining. Although the institutions of government interact in many and mysterious ways, it is the job of political science to distinguish one from the other and to analyze how they operate both individually and collectively.

The discussion of the individual institutions of government that follows in subsequent chapters will be more meaningful if it is first put into the context of government in the new century and of the policymaking process. This chapter provides an overview of that process, indicating in a general way how the various institutions interact with one another in the making of public policy. This is followed by an elaboration of the concept of policy communities and networks, which was first broached in Chapter 16. The chapter ends with an overview of policy instruments—that is, the various devices among which the authorities choose to give effect to their decisions.

GOVERNMENT IN THE 21ST CENTURY

Government was defined in Chapter 1 as the set of institutions that make and execute collective public decisions for a society. That chapter explained how most Canadians initially try to satisfy their needs and wants without government intervention—that is, in the private or voluntary sectors—but may eventually call for some kind of collective, public sector action.

Until about 100 years ago, the role of government in society was very limited.[1] But over the first 85 or so years of the 20th century, government operations expanded enormously. Most Canadians saw the government as an extension of themselves, and as long as it did not unduly interfere with their own efforts to get ahead, they welcomed its expansion.

After 1985 or so, however, politicians, bureaucrats, the media, commentators, think tanks, and many citizens in all Western industrialized countries said that we had too much government: too much government expenditure, too much taxation, too much regulation, and too much government debt. Governments of all ideological persuasions were consumed with balancing their budgets and downsizing and restructuring their operations in what constituted a new relationship among governments, markets, and civil society. The general consensus was that "government over the past forty years has grown too big, absorbs too many resources, and is a drag on both economic performance and civic independence."[2]

In principle, it was probably a valuable exercise for politicians and bureaucrats to re-examine everything that government was doing to see if it was really necessary or whether it could be done better in other ways. Unfortunately, the reality was that the poorest segment of society bore the greatest burden of this downsizing of government, which had many painful and devastating effects. Moreover, as mentioned in Chapter 8, one school of thought argued that there was never a spending problem at all—the imbalance was caused by an unwillingness to tax and an abundance of tax loopholes. These observers assert that the concern with the deficit was just an excuse to embark on a neoliberal ideological tangent to reduce the role of government and make the world safe for market forces. Figure 20.1 illustrates the decline in federal departmental spending between 1994–95 and 1998–99, the period in which the largest cuts were made.

At the start of the 21st century, the federal government's debt stood at $580 billion, while other governments' debts in Canada brought total public indebtedness to at least $750 billion. Some provinces passed laws to prohibit adding to their debts, most governments budgeted surpluses with which they reduced their debts, and it seemed unlikely that any governments would spend excessively in the future. Ottawa itself was spending about $220 billion per year, but more than one-quarter of that was paying interest on the previously accumulated debt. Although only 2.8 million people or roughly 20 percent of the labour force work in the public sector (including all levels of government), total government taxes and expenditures are equivalent to about 40 percent of the gross domestic product (GDP), the total value of all production in the economy.[3] Thus, even the downsized public sector was a force to be reckoned with. Now that governments were balancing their books on an annual basis, however, they operated more even-handedly than in the preceding 15 years, reacting prudently but positively to public needs that could not be met without their intervention.

Suddenly at the end of 2008, there was a global economic crisis and everything changed. Federal and provincial governments in Canada all reacted in the same way. The consensus was that the fastest and most effective way to cope with the deep recession was for governments to pick up the slack; they should spend enormous amounts of money and run annual budgetary deficits for years to come, adding substantially to their respective public debts. As the private sector contracted, governments should provide fiscal stimulus to promote economic growth. The 2009 federal budget forecast a deficit of some $64 billion over the following two years, which soon proved to be optimistic, with a balanced budget unlikely until 2014, as seen in Table 20.1. Most of the provinces made similar calculations. The fiscal stability of Canadian governments over the 2000–08 period was shattered as a Conservative government that believed in lower taxes, balanced budgets, and debt reduction had to dramatically shift gears.

Figure 20.1   **Departmental Spending, 1998–1999 Relative to 1994–1995**

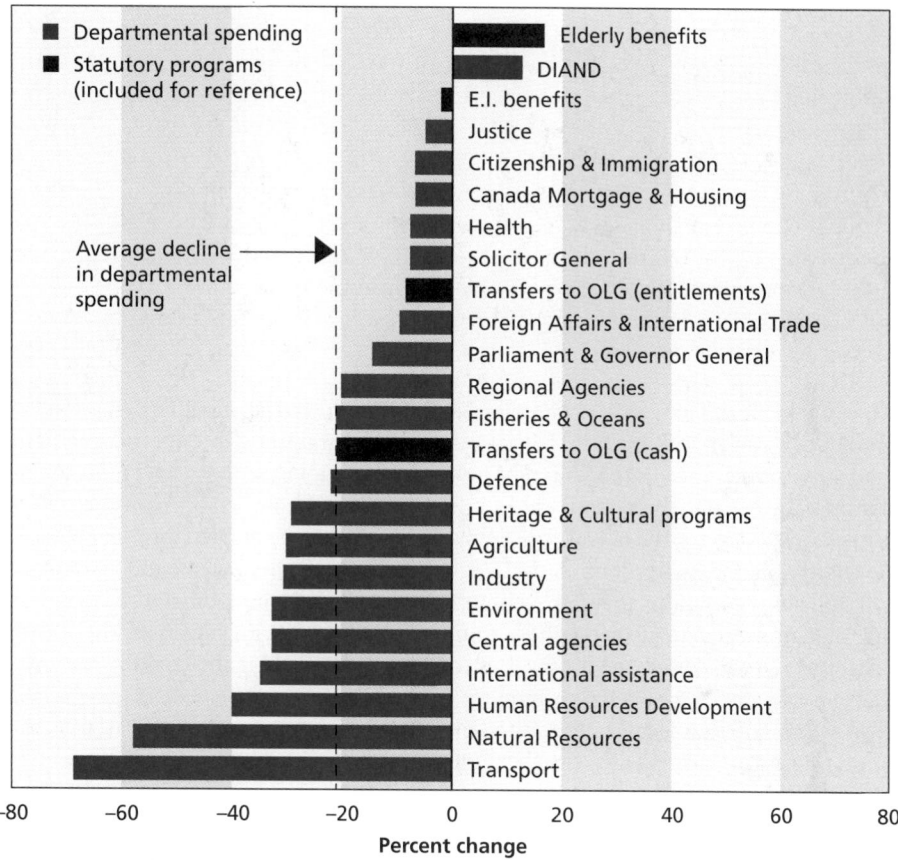

Source: Department of Finance. Budget Plan 1996. Chart 3.1 Departmental Spending. Pg. 38. Found at: http://www.fin.gc.ca/budget96/bp/bp96e.pdf

THE POLICYMAKING PROCESS

Public policy can be defined as "a course of action or inaction chosen by public authorities to address a given problem or interrelated set of problems."[4] Leslie Pal adds that every policy has three key elements: the definition of the problem, the goals to be achieved, and the instruments or means chosen to address the problem and to achieve the goals. In Chapter 1, a model of the whole political system was presented; it included such components as demands, support, outputs, feedback, the authorities, and the environment. Now imagine focusing in more detail on the authorities part of that model. The result would be an enlargement of that part of the system directly involved in the policymaking process and would look something like the model

TABLE 20.1   Federal Budgetary Projections, 2008–2009 to 2013–2014
(in billions of dollars)

	2008–2009	2009–2010	2010–2011	2011–2012	2012–2013	2013–2014
Revenues	236.4	224.9	239.9	259.4	276.4	294.3
Expenses	237.4	258.6	269.7	272.3	283.7	293.7
Balance	-1.1	33.7	29.8	13.0	7.3	0.7
Federal Debt	458.7	492.4	522.2	535.2	542.4	541.8

Source: Department of Finance Canada. 2009 Federal Budget. Table 1.1 Summary Statement of Transactions. Pg. 29. Found at: http://www.budget.gc.ca/2009/pdf/budget-planbugetaire-eng.pdf (Accessed April 20, 2009). Reproduced with the permission of the Minister of Public Works and Government Services, 2009.

shown in Figure 20.2. Here, as in the model shown in Chapter 1, it should be emphasized that the process is circular and ongoing, without a definable beginning or end, in which policies adopted at an earlier stage or in a different policy field or problems that develop in the implementation stage become the reasons behind the initiation of new demands on the state.

As the model suggests, the actual policymaking process can be divided into six phases: initiation, priority-setting, policy formulation, legitimation, implementation, and interpretation. Not all policies or decisions involve such an elaborate process including all the institutions of government; indeed, many can be made unilaterally by the prime minister, the Cabinet, a minister, the bureaucracy, or the courts. But the model shows the policymaking process in its broadest form—that is, a policy that requires the passage of a new law or an amendment to an existing law and that is later interpreted by the courts. Such a model does not necessarily imply that decision makers within each phase will function with complete rationality: they may equally well act out of expediency or habit.

Initiation

The authorities are bombarded daily with hundreds of demands. These demands emanate from many different sources: the provinces and territories, opposition parties, the media, advocacy groups, lobbyists, corporations, royal commissions, election promises, personal concerns of ministers or the prime minister, the government caucus, the bureaucracy, foreign countries (usually the United States), or other forces within the internal or external environments of the political system. The policymaking process is set in motion when the prime minister and Cabinet, frequently termed "the **government**" have been impressed with the articulation of a demand and decide to look into the matter further. On a smaller scale, a single minister may also make such a decision. Donald J. Savoie reminds us, however, not to underestimate the extent to which ministers pursue initiatives recommended to them in "mandate letters" from the prime minister.[5] It is at this point that a "demand" is sometimes said to become an "issue." An issue, therefore, is a demand that has made it onto the public agenda and that is under serious consideration by the authorities. In such a case, the Cabinet ordinarily sends a directive to the bureaucracy that it wants more information on the matter.

Figure 20.2 **The Canadian Policymaking Process**

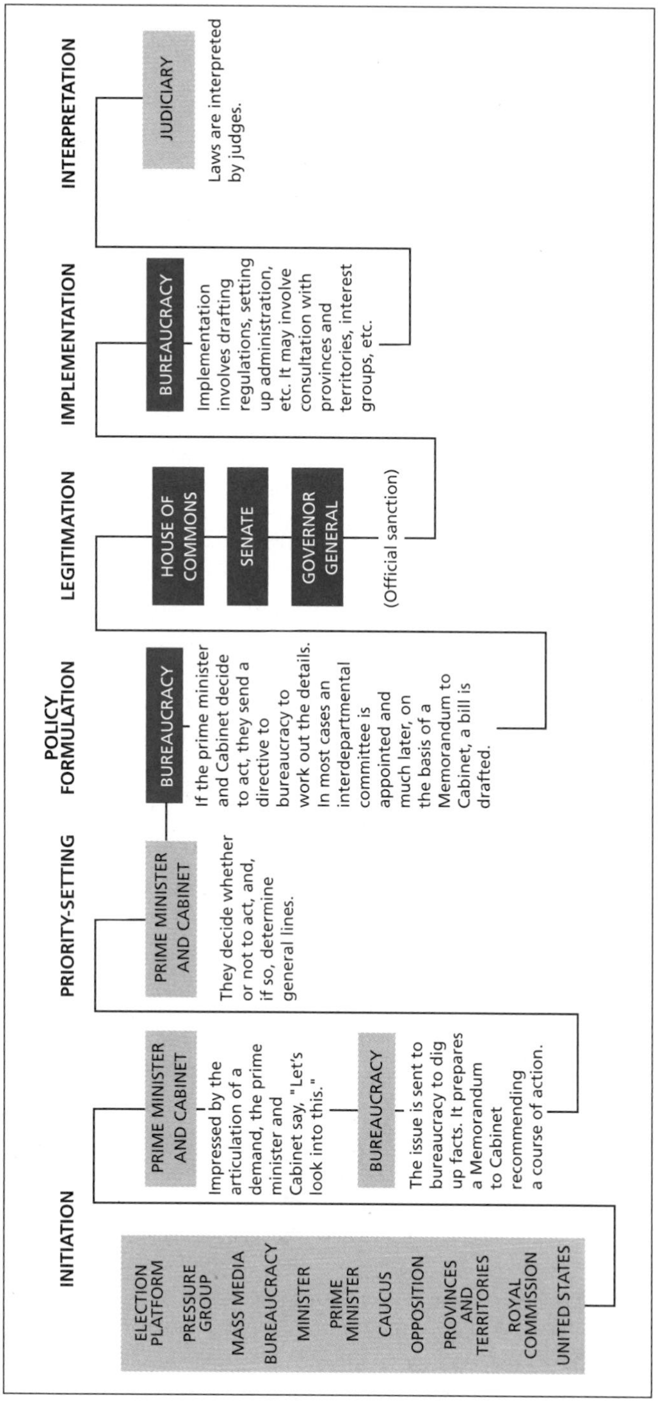

Priority Setting

The second phase of the policymaking process involves the prime minister and Cabinet again, this time in their priority-setting capacity. Responding to a course of action recommended by the public service, they decide which of the proposals they have selected for consideration are worthy of adoption. In other words, the prime minister and Cabinet (or, on lesser issues, an individual minister) must decide whether or not to take action on the issue, and, if they decide to act, they must determine the general lines of the new initiative. At this point the Cabinet may also choose which policy instrument will be most appropriate to achieve their objective. Here a major constraint is the cost of the proposal, since almost all such proposals face fierce competition for the scarce financial resources available. If the Cabinet and PM are not sure about what course to follow, they may publish policy alternatives in "coloured papers" and make them available to the public. A "Green Paper," for example, consists of an early consideration of an issue, with little indication of the direction of government policy.[6]

Policy Formulation

Once it has approved a proposal in principle, the Cabinet usually sends another directive to the bureaucracy to work out the details in what is called the policy formulation phase. This is often a very time-consuming process that requires coordination among many federal government departments (now called "horizontal management"[7]) and may also involve consultation with provincial governments, interest groups, and others. Policy communities and policy networks play an increasingly important role at this stage, and questions may be referred back to the Cabinet for further direction. On major, complex policy initiatives, the Cabinet sometimes issues a "White Paper," which provides a clear indication of its intentions but still leaves room for public input with respect to details. If the proposal requires legislative action, the policy formulation stage culminates in a bill being drafted on the basis of the Memorandum to Cabinet. During this process, the minister will probably discuss the principles of the proposal with interested members of the government caucus. Once a bill has been drafted and approved by the responsible minister, it is sent to the leader of the government in the House of Commons. After reviewing its consistency with relevant Cabinet decisions, this minister reports to Cabinet and seeks authority for the introduction of the bill into the House of Commons.

Legitimation

The proposal then enters the legislative arena, that is, Parliament—the House of Commons and the Senate. The relevant minister may accept technical alterations to the bill as it proceeds through the House of Commons and the Senate, but opposition amendments often challenge the basic integrity of the original draft and are therefore not encouraged. Certainly the main intent or principle of the bill cannot be changed without going back for the Cabinet's approval. The legislative stage is referred to as legitimation because the bill is put under the scrutiny of all the democratically elected representatives of the people and made legitimate by their approval. The Cabinet and members of Parliament contribute political expertise to the process, but given the shortage of time and limited technical expertise that are characteristic of the legislative branch, most such bills are passed in "skeletal" form—that is, a statute usually contains only the general principles or objectives that the authorities want to achieve, and the act delegates authority to the relevant minister, on the advice of the bureaucracy, to issue regulations to flesh it out later in the process. The legitimation stage ends with the token approval of the governor general, which is the sign that the policy has been officially sanctioned.

Implementation

Royal assent is by no means the end of the policymaking process. Few laws attain any significance just by sitting on the statute books; they must be implemented in order to be made effective. Implementation normally requires the setting up of new administrative machinery—new staff, new agencies, new field offices, and new operational manuals, among other things. It is therefore not surprising that most legislation does not automatically take effect on royal assent; it is not "proclaimed" or made operational until the government is ready to implement it.

Implementation almost always involves the drafting of detailed **regulations** by the bureaucracy, to add meat to the skeleton of the statute. These officially go by the name "statutory instruments," but they are also called subordinate or delegated legislation and are necessary because MPs lack the time and expertise to put such technical details into the law itself. Because the regulations are not in the law, they can also be changed fairly easily and are often developed in close consultation with the outside interests affected. Even though they have the same legal standing as if they were part of the enabling statute, the regulations that a law authorizes the executive to make are given only slight scrutiny by Cabinet, ministers, or Parliament, and thus are almost the exclusive preserve of the bureaucracy. Regulations are published in the *Canada Gazette* but are not likely to be noticed except by the interests to whom they apply. Nevertheless, they are so significant that the Privy Council Office issues detailed instructions on this subject.[8] Afterward, the regulations are scrutinized by the Standing Joint Committee of the Senate and House of Commons on Statutory Instruments. It has a staff of lawyers who devour the regulations to ensure that they do not contain any objectionable provisions. If they do, these are reported to the MPs and senators on the committee, who suggest changes to the bureaucratic drafters, and if the recommendations are rejected, the committee can propose a disallowance resolution to their respective chambers as a whole.

Interpretation

The policymaking process may well end, at least for the time being, with the implementation phase. But if new legislation is involved, it is often subject to judicial interpretation. Its constitutionality may even be challenged in the courts. Thus, especially since 1982, it is appropriate to add a sixth phase to the policymaking process, that of judicial interpretation. Judges always had an impact on a law by means of how they interpreted it, but if a statute is actually challenged in the courts, the judiciary must decide whether its provisions are contrary to the Charter of Rights and Freedoms or to the division of powers between federal and provincial governments.

. . . .

POLICY COMMUNITIES AND POLICY NETWORKS REVISITED

Although this section of the book focuses on the operation of the authoritative "governmental" policymaking institutions, they operate within a never-ending "political" environment. Indeed, if various interests know that the government has a problem under active consideration, they usually step up their attempts to influence the course of that discussion. Moreover, policymakers are finding it increasingly advantageous if not necessary to consult and even to develop partnerships with relevant organized external interests. It is in this context that the concept of **policy communities** and **policy networks** should be mentioned again.[9]

Although Figure 20.2 provides a framework in which to understand the policymaking process and the interaction of various government institutions in general, it must be emphasized that distinctive policy communities, participants, and processes are involved in different policy fields. Power is dispersed in many directions, and different politicians, bureaucrats, advocacy groups, and individuals participate in different sectors of public policy. The prime minister, Cabinet, and central policy structures are at the core of the whole process regardless of subject matter, but each policy community has its own "lead government agency," normally a department or section of a department of government: health for health policy, fisheries and oceans for fisheries policy, and so on.

Each lead agency is surrounded by associated Crown corporations and regulatory agencies, such as the CBC and CRTC, which operate at arm's length from the Canadian Heritage department or the Canadian Transportation Agency and VIA Rail, which are linked to Transport Canada. Still within the "subgovernment" circle, which might also be called the *policy network*, are the major advocacy groups, lobbyists, think tanks, corporations, provincial governments, and parliamentary committees interested in their respective policy fields. The wider "attentive public," which might be labelled the *policy community*, consists of other interest groups, other provincial governments, and other parliamentarians, corporations, and individuals interested in a particular policy field but who are not part of the inner circle. Paul Pross's 1986 model of the policy community, as seen in Figure 20.3, remains instructive to this day.

Interaction between government departments and advocacy groups has always been a two-way street, and bureaucrats have found it helpful to consult with affected interests as they went about making policy. For a variety of reasons, however, the reliance of policymakers on outside interests has become much heavier in recent years, a development that Donald Savoie phrases as "looking elsewhere for policy advice."[10] Governments now regularly integrate citizens, groups, clients, experts, academics, and other stakeholders as part of the policy development process.

The most significant factor in this development was the loss of expertise within the government itself. To balance federal and provincial budgets in the mid-1990s, and then to be able to reduce taxes, as neoliberalism prescribed, drastic cuts were made in public employment. Although most citizens noticed the effects at the level of the reduction or disappearance of government services, there was also a serious deterioration in the internal policy analysis capacity of governments.

Apart from this loss, the related theory of new public management advocated closer connections between the **public** and **private sectors**, as discussed in Chapter 22. But the role of the third or **voluntary sector** was also enhanced in this process. Almost all advocacy groups possess information that governments would find useful, and many perform quite sophisticated

· ·

Figure 20.3   The Policy Community

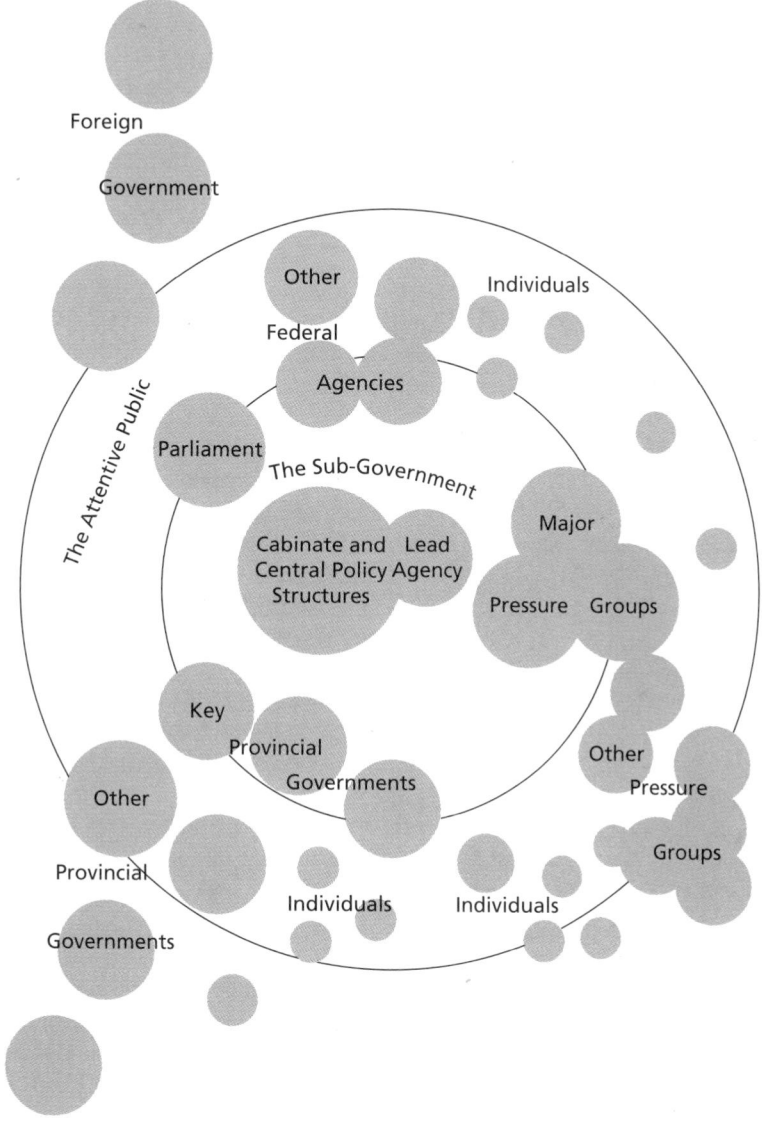

Source: A. Paul Pross, "Pressure Groups: Talking Chameleons," in Michael S. Whittington and Glen Williams, eds., **Canadian Politics in the 1980s,** *2nd ed. (Toronto: Methuen, 1984), p. 304.*

policy analyses on their own. In fact, it is sometimes difficult to distinguish between think tanks and the advocacy groups that engage in serious research and analysis. The evidence that extensive interaction with the third sector was considered something valuable in itself is that the same governments that had reduced their internal analytical capacities began to hand over huge sums of money to think tanks and related organizations to encourage external policy analysis. The Privy Council Office established a Voluntary Sector Initiative to this effect, and as policy analysts moved back and forth, the line between employment in the bureaucracy and in think tanks began to blur. The new buzzwords of public administration were "consultation" "engagement," "partnering," and "collaboration."

A third factor in encouraging greater government reliance on external actors was simply the increasing number of such groups in society: more social movements, more public interest groups, more community groups, more identity groups, more advocacy coalitions, more think tanks, and so on. Chapter 16 noted the preference of most Canadians to join such groups rather than to participate in political parties as a vehicle to promote their individual public policy concerns.

Thus, in the initiation stage of the policymaking process, demands primarily arise from the responsible minister, lead agency officials, associated government agencies, advocacy groups, lobbyists, corporations, and interested parliamentarians within each distinctive policy community. When a minister or the Cabinet seeks advice on whether or not to take action on a particular problem, they refer the problem to the lead agency in each field.

In the priority-setting phase, it may take only a single minister to make the decision to go forward. But on controversial issues or policies involving major expenditures, decisions are taken out of the specialized policy community and made subject to the critical review and veto of Cabinet committees or the Cabinet as a whole, acting on the advice of such central agencies as the Department of Finance Canada, the Treasury Board Secretariat, or the Privy Council Office.

Once a policy initiative has survived the priority-setting barrier, however, the minister or Cabinet refers the matter back to the lead agency to coordinate the efforts involved in policy formulation. An interdepartmental committee representing every government agency with an interest in the policy is usually appointed at this stage, and, as mentioned, if groups, lobbyists, and interested corporations are aware that a new policy is under consideration, they will do their best to get involved. Advocacy groups, provincial governments, or other interested actors may be formally consulted in this phase of the process, but in any case, the officials in the lead agency are sure to be conscious of the views of their "attentive public" and take its past representations and anticipated reaction into account. Moreover, before the minister or Cabinet gives final approval to a new policy or bill, these officials will likely have been subject to further pressure from within the policy community.

When legislation is required to implement the policy, the legitimation phase is dominated by those parliamentarians with a particular interest in the subject. This phase also attracts the attention of the major pressure groups, the key provincial governments, and the individuals within the general public who are part of the specialized policy community. If a bill goes to a parliamentary committee, for example, the committee is made up of interested MPs, before whom specialized bureaucrats, advocacy groups, and other experts make representations.

Again at the next phase, the lead agency is primarily responsible for implementing the policy. But it often does so in close consultation with the advocacy groups and provincial governments most intimately involved. They may be asked, for example, to comment on the first draft of the regulations. It is especially at this level that new partnerships are being formed between the lead agency and the most relevant voluntary- or private-sector actors. Reductions in government funding, for example, may leave departments little choice other than to bring such groups into the implementation process.

Finally, if the legislation is challenged in court, the challenger is usually a corporation, pressure group, provincial government, or individual member of the "attentive public" whose views are not consistent with the final version of the policy. The government defends its legislation on the advice of the lead agency and the Department of Justice Canada.

This discussion thus indicates that although a fairly uniform process exists for the making of Canadian public policy, regardless of subject matter, the specific individuals, corporations, groups, and lead agencies involved vary to a large extent from one policy field to another. Such key players in each distinctive policy network or policy community are often referred to as **stakeholders**.

. . . .

POLICY INSTRUMENTS

Once the authorities decide to take action on a problem, they must choose the means of addressing the issue. The specific techniques, tools, or devices chosen are often called **policy instruments**. Such instruments constitute government intervention in society and are commonly categorized according to the degree of intervention, intrusiveness, or coerciveness they represent. Some theorists have suggested that governments will instinctively choose the least intrusive instrument, because that is what they and the public prefer. Such is not always the case. Sometimes politicians and bureaucrats *want* to change aspects of society, and sometimes the electorate expects them to. Thus, the instruments could also be ranked according to how much change they represent or how much they improve the lives of those left behind by the forces of the private marketplace. Politicians and bureaucrats do not always choose policy instruments on an ideological basis, however; legal, technical, and administrative factors are often involved. Nicolas Baxter-Moore includes nine stages of intervention in his discussion of policy instruments.[11]

Privatization

The full range of policy instruments theoretically encompasses the decision to take no action at all. It is very common for the government to decide to leave the problem to be handled entirely by the forces of the private sector. Baxter-Moore refers to such public inaction as the privatization of conflict and points out that it can assume two forms: the government can either completely ignore the problem or explicitly decide to refer the question to some private-sector authority. An example of the latter would be the self-regulation of professional bodies, such as medical and legal associations.[12] Because of the changed philosophy of government after 1985, governments made increasing use of this policy instrument. They decided to ignore a greater proportion of demands than previously and even vacated many areas of former public activity in favour of leaving issues to be dealt with by private market forces.

Symbolic Response

The second policy instrument is the symbolic response. This can take the form of issuing a statement of government concern, consulting with those raising the problem, passively disseminating information, appointing a task force or a royal commission, or setting up a new government department. All of these, at least in the short run, are substitutes for any substantive government action. It is commonly held, for example, that a royal commission is appointed to take the heat off the government in connection with some problematic situation in the hope that by the time the commission reports, the problem will have evaporated. Since this instrument is also consistent with the philosophy of downsizing government, it has been popular in recent years.

Exhortation

The third degree of intervention is often called exhortation. This instrument goes one step further than the symbolic response because in this case the government urges the public to change its behaviour in some way. Exhortation uses persuasion in an attempt to secure voluntary compliance with government objectives without recourse to threats or rewards. Commercials to encourage physical fitness are one example, while others are pleas to restrain wage demands, to conserve the use of water or electricity (without any accompanying rate increases or regulations), or to promote the use of "blue box" programs or condoms. Because of its need to change public attitudes in order to accept major policy shifts, especially the Free Trade Agreements and GST in the 1980s, and to highlight equity and lifestyle policy concerns, the federal government became the country's largest advertiser. But in the new governance environment since then, information-based instruments have become even more important.[13]

Tax Expenditures

Tax expenditures are the fourth category of policy instrument. These consist of tax credits and tax deductions that individuals or companies can claim by spending money in certain ways: putting money into retirement plans, contributing to political parties, making certain kinds of investments, donating to charities, and so on. Some of these tax expenditures are included in Table 20.2.[14] Tax expenditures do not actually involve taxing or spending by government; rather, they are tax-based incentives to use individual or corporate income in particular ways. Tax expenditures are widely used because they are basically invisible and do not attract much

TABLE 20.2	Revenues Forgone through Selected Tax Exemptions or Credits, Projections 2010
Registered Pension Plans	$16 790 000 000
Registered Retirement Savings Plans	$12 125 000 000
Partial inclusion of Capital Gains	$4 335 000 000
Charitable donations	$2 955 000 000

Source: Department of Finance Canada. Tax Expenditures and Evaluations 2008. Found at http://www.fin.gc.ca/ taxexp-depfisc/2008/taxexp08_2-eng.asp (Accessed April 21, 2009). Reproduced with the permission of the Minister of Public Works and Government Services, 2009.

criticism; they neither *seem* to cost any money nor involve any sort of coercion. Although tax expenditures are a popular policy instrument, as corporations and individuals vigorously seek them out in order to reduce their taxes, it should be added that they do come at a cost. They result in reducing the amount of revenue that the government would otherwise receive by billions of dollars a year, funds that it could use for redistributive purposes. Those who are unaware of or do not qualify for such tax credits, especially lower-income individuals, end up paying higher taxes to make up the difference.

Public Expenditures

The fifth policy instrument, one that is much more obvious, is public expenditures. Unlike tax expenditures, public spending involves the actual disbursement of funds acquired and controlled by the state. The size of modern government budgets is an indication of how frequently the authorities have tried to solve problems by spending public money. The instrument of public expenditure has many subcategories. Governments provide transfer payments to individuals, such as in employment insurance, old age security, and social assistance programs; the federal government advances money to the provinces for health care, postsecondary education, and many other purposes; governments subsidize farmers, fishers, painters, and orchestras, and give contracts, grants, loans, and loan guarantees to corporations. The "spending power" of the federal government—that is, its right to spend money for any purpose it chooses—was discussed in Chapter 18. The government also engages in public expenditure in the provision of public services—helping the unemployed find jobs, defending the country, or engaging in research. In an age of retrenchment, of course, governments tried to avoid this policy instrument and reduced their expenditures and services quite dramatically, as demonstrated in Figure 20.1. But public spending became a very popular means of combating the Great Recession of 2008–09.

Regulation

Government becomes more intrusive still when it chooses the sixth policy instrument: regulation.[15] Almost every aspect of our lives is now regulated by government, although we may not always be aware of it. Examples include minimum wage laws; highway speed limits; restaurant and elevator inspections; the grading of eggs; building codes; consumer product safety; rent controls; pollution emissions; hunting, fishing, driver, and liquor licences; store hours; seat belt laws; Canadian content on radio and television; telephone rates; and bilingual labelling.

Government regulation interferes with individual or corporate freedom more than any instrument listed previously and is therefore more frequently criticized. But such regulations were obviously considered necessary by one government or another in order to promote some greater public purpose, such as public health, safety, or order; Canadianization; bilingualism; or protection from corporate exploitation. Many of these regulatory functions have been delegated to semi-independent regulatory agencies, such as the CRTC, marketing boards, provincial rent control tribunals, or liquor licensing boards, rather than to regular government departments. Such agencies are discussed in more detail in Chapter 22. Ordinarily, the less money the government has available to spend the more heavily it will rely on the instrument of regulation. But in the era of neoliberalism, the corporate sector, in particular, pressed for a pulling back of government in this area, too, resulting in a large amount of **deregulation**. International trade agreements have also constrained the use of regulatory instruments.

Taxation

Taxation, the seventh type of policy instrument, is generally considered even more intrusive than regulation because although it also has the effect of constraining behaviour, it actually takes something away from the individuals or corporations on whom it is imposed.[16] Previous chapters have provided some indication of the number and kinds of taxes levied by both federal and provincial governments. Personal and corporate income and general sales taxes are used by both levels of government, to say nothing of excise taxes; special taxes on alcohol, tobacco, amusement, and gasoline; natural resource levies; health insurance premiums; payroll taxes; and the property taxes used by municipal governments. Just as in the case of regulation, however, many people are not conscious of all the taxes they pay. Thus, the relative extent of the intrusiveness of taxation is somewhat subjective, depending on the awareness of and degree of constraint imposed by various taxes, as well as on the level of consciousness of and support for the public programs they are used to finance. The public became aroused over the very visible GST, for example, even though it largely replaced the invisible manufacturers' sales tax.

In the post-1985 environment, governments primarily balanced their budgets by reducing expenditures rather than by increasing their taxes. Indeed, as soon as a balanced budget was in sight, there were demands for tax cuts. However, various charges and fees for special benefits and services grew in use.[17] Besides user fees imposed on many social services in recent years, bridge and highways tolls are becoming more common.

Public Ownership

The eighth policy instrument is **public ownership**, typically taking the form of a Crown corporation. Governments routinely regulate and tax private companies, of course, but to "nationalize" them—to take them into public ownership or to create Crown corporations—obviously represents a greater degree of government intervention. At both federal and provincial levels, the "collectivist" streak in the Canadian political culture has given rise to the existence of a large number of important state enterprises, including the Canadian Broadcasting Corporation, the Canada Mortgage and Housing Corporation, the Bank of Canada, Farm Credit Canada, Atomic Energy of Canada Ltd., Canada Post, and electric power corporations in most provinces. Governments usually resort to public enterprise only as a last resort, however, when taxation and regulation fail to meet their objectives.[18] In the wave of neoliberalism that swept the country in the late 1980s and 1990s, the Mulroney and Chrétien governments privatized several Crown corporations, including Air Canada and Canadian National, putting such organizations (back) into the private sector **(privatization)**. Several provincial governments also privatized some of their Crown corporations.

State of Emergency: Harper and Flaherty row boat in sea of red ink, 2009.

State of Emergency

Baxter-Moore completes his catalogue of nine policy instruments with the **state of emergency**.[19] In a situation of natural disasters, domestic insurrection, or external military threat, governments can usually invoke emergency powers. These powers give special coercive functions to the police and military to assist the government in achieving its policy objectives. The use of the **War Measures Act** in the First and Second World Wars is the best Canadian example. Prime Minister Trudeau invoked the War Measures Act again in 1970 to deal with the FLQ crisis. Armed forces personnel suddenly appeared on the streets of Ottawa and Montreal, the police were given extraordinary powers, and certain civil liberties were suspended. Acknowledgment that the War Measures Act was inappropriate in these circumstances led to the creation of a less coercive Emergencies Act in 1988. Happily, the state of emergency is used less frequently than any other policy instrument in Canada, although the armed forces have been called on to help out in natural disasters, such as severe flooding in Manitoba, the ice storm in central Canada and New Brunswick, and a heavy snowfall in Toronto.

. . . .

THE ENVIRONMENT AS A CASE STUDY

The issue of the environment provides a good example (oversimplified here) of how a newly recognized public problem can be addressed by using different policy instruments. Historically, of course, the pollution problem was ignored, and was later given token, symbolic recognition without any substantial government action. The third stage was exhortation, which has now been common for some time. Individuals have been urged by government to "reduce, reuse, and recycle," such as in blue box campaigns, and corporations have been drawn into signing voluntary agreements to reduce their emissions of various kinds. There have also been tax expenditure programs designed to cope with environmental pollution—tax credits for investing in abatement equipment, for example, and governments have been spending increasing amounts of their budgets on environmental measures, such as air and water testing and cleaning up certain sources of toxic soil contamination.

Nowadays, climate change has led governments to get more serious about protecting the environment, with the Alberta oil sands and coal-fired electricity plants as particular targets because of their greenhouse gas emissions. Federal and provincial governments are contemplating various regulatory and taxation schemes. One idea is a carbon tax, pioneered in different forms in Quebec and British Columbia, and the focus of the Liberal party's Green Shift concept in the 2008 federal election. A carbon tax could be imposed on heavily polluting companies or on consumers who buy carbon-based products such as coal, oil, natural gas, and gasoline. An alternative policy instrument would be the imposition of concrete caps on such polluters (regulation), or a cap and trade system in which companies that are capped could buy credits from others that operated below their regulated limit. While there remains much dispute about which of these approaches is more realistic and effective, some environmentalists advocate using both taxation and regulation simultaneously. There is probably no appetite to nationalize companies in order to force them to reduce their pollution of the environment, but some environmentalists are almost at the point of advocating the declaration of a state of emergency!

Interestingly enough, the global economic meltdown of 2008 led the Canadian government to exempt some emergency infrastructure projects from environmental assessments. And because the new concern with global warming in the United States might lead that country to adopt measures that would restrict imports of petroleum from the Alberta oil sands, Canada may simply decide to adopt President Obama's environmental standards.

. . . .

CONCLUSION

This discussion of the policymaking process and policy instruments provides a framework on which to hang the remaining chapters of the book, which deal in greater detail with the individual institutions of government. It also introduces the range of devices available to a government in order to achieve its objectives.

This chapter is closely linked to the four which follow, dealing with each of the main institutions of government in turn. It is also related to Chapter 16, which discussed the role of advocacy groups and policy communities in the policymaking process.

PC In terms of the approaches outlined in Chapter 1, public or rational choice theory argues that in the initiation and priority-setting phases the Cabinet will choose to look into and then act on those issues that provide benefits to marginal voters. In choosing policy instruments, the authorities will similarly be guided by the anticipated reaction of these same marginal groups. Public choice theorists argue, in fact, that such groups are not just *a* factor but are *the* foremost factor in the selection of which policy instrument to use.[20] There is a close link between public choice theory and that concerning policy instruments, partly because economists are prominent in both schools of thought.

(SC) The state-centred approach contends that the policymaking process functions without significant input from society as a whole. The initiation phase is dominated by demands from politicians and bureaucrats themselves, and the authorities define as "issues" only those demands that are of interest to them. Most of the other phases of the policymaking process are carried out behind closed doors by bureaucrats and politicians, and when their actions are unveiled to the public in the legitimation phase, members of Parliament must toe the party line and are not allowed to respond to the demands of their constituencies. State-centred theorists also emphasize that the bureaucracy is present in more phases of the policymaking process than any other institution of government. It must be said, however, that the increasing reliance of government on outside sources of policy advice somewhat diminishes the claims of the state-centred approach.

(C) The class analysis model assumes that whatever the formal phases of the policymaking process, the political system ultimately responds to the demands of the bourgeoisie or corporate elite. This school of analysis emphasizes the connections between the state and corporate elites and, although discovering much evidence of such linkage, adds that "the economically powerful have not had to seek political office directly [for] their interests are usually served by those who are already there."[21] Class analysis finds that the political, bureaucratic, and corporate elites share many characteristics and values.[22] At least until recently, the Cabinet, higher public service, and pressure group leadership was made up of men who had family, corporate, educational, geographic, and social ties.[23]

Class analysts also have the most to say about the choice of policy instruments. They divide policy outputs between those that facilitate the accumulation of capital for the bourgeoisie, those that encourage the legitimation of the capitalist system by promoting social harmony, and those that provide for coercion if accumulation is seriously threatened by proletarian elements. Such analysts also distinguish among the transparency, intrusiveness, and coerciveness of various policy instruments in terms of the classes to whom they are applied.[24] The state will often disguise its activities on behalf of capital accumulation by using less visible instruments, while it will employ more obvious instruments when it seeks to legitimize its rule. The state will use less intrusive instruments (e.g., tax expenditures) against dominant-class interests and more intrusive policies (e.g., taxation) against subordinate classes or groups. However, it will respond to corporate demands for government assistance with public expenditures, while it will offer only symbolic responses to working-class demands. Finally, if the state must take action against dominant-class interests, it will not attach significant coercive penalties to such instruments, but it tends "to enforce all instruments more coercively when they are targeted at labour and other subordinate groups."[25] In this instance, the small fines handed out to corporate polluters can be contrasted with the "heavier financial penalties for unions involved in unofficial strikes ... and heavy police presence at sites of labour unrest."[26] Class analysts would take exception to the widespread consensus in recent years that "if possible, [government] policy should depend on market mechanisms and individual choice, and minimize spending and regulation."[27]

(G) Globalization has a profound effect on both the policymaking process and the policy instruments. First, external forces, including transnational corporations, foreign governments, and international organizations, increasingly place demands on the Canadian government to take actions or desist from taking actions contrary to the government's own choosing. Second, in the neoliberal context in which globalizing forces operate, they often urge the government to choose the least intrusive policy instrument possible, preferably to take no action at all. Transnational corporations, backed up by foreign governments and international organizations, usually want Canada to give them free rein to do as they will—not to be pressured, regulated, taxed, or bought. Not all neoliberal influences are external, however, and, after 1985 or so, many internal pressures also urged governments to reduce their degree of intervention in society and the economy.

. . . .

DISCUSSION QUESTIONS

1. How did the environment of governance change between 1985 and 2000? Why? How did it change after 2008?

2. Do all demands have an equal chance of coming to the attention of the prime minister and Cabinet?

3. To what extent do the social background characteristics of the prime minister and Cabinet ministers skew their choice of issues? To what extent are electoral considerations dominant in their choice?

4. Do you agree with the sequence of policy instruments outlined in the continuum of degree of government intrusiveness?

5. Do you agree with the class analysis view that the degree of intrusiveness and coerciveness of policy instruments varies according to the class that is subject to the intervention?

. . . .

NOTES

1. John C. Strick, *The Public Sector in Canada: Programs, Finance and Policy* (Toronto: Thompson Books, 1999).
2. Leslie A. Pal, *Beyond Policy Analysis: Public Issue Management in Turbulent Times*, 4th ed. (Toronto: Nelson Education, 2010), ch. 2.
3. See Table 11.1 in this book.
4. Pal, *Beyond Policy Analysis*, p. 2.
5. Donald J. Savoie, *Governing from the Centre: The Concentration of Power in Canadian Politics* (Toronto: University of Toronto Press, 1999), pp. 137–38, 324, 343.
6. Kenneth Kernaghan and David Siegel, *Public Administration in Canada: A Text*, 2nd ed. (Scarborough: Nelson Canada, 1991; 3rd ed., 1995), pp. 128–30.
7. Herman Bakvis and Luc Juillet, *The Horizontal Challenge: Line Departments, Central Agencies and Leadership* (Ottawa: Canada School of Public Service, 2004).
8. Privy Council Office, *Guide to Making Federal Acts and Regulations, Part 3*, available at http://www .pco-bcp.gc.ca/docs/information/Publications/legislation/pdf-eng.pdf.
9. Pal, *Beyond Policy Analysis*, ch. 6; Paul Pross, *Group Politics and Public Policy* (Toronto: Oxford University Press, 1986), especially ch. 6; William Coleman and Grace Skogstad, *Policy Communities and Public Policy in Canada* (Mississauga: Copp Clark Pitman, 1990); and previously discussed in this book in Chapter 16.
10. Donald Savoie, *Breaking the Bargain: Public Servants, Ministers, and Parliament* (Toronto: University of Toronto Press, 2003), ch. 6; Pal, *Beyond Policy Analysis*; Donald E. Abelson, *Do Think Tanks Matter? Assessing the Impact of Public Policy Institutes* (Montreal: McGill-Queen's University Press,

2002); and Kathy Brock, ed., *Delicate Dances: Government and the Nonprofit Sector in Canada* (Montreal: McGill-Queen's University Press, 2002).

11. Nicolas Baxter-Moore, "Policy Implementation and the Role of the State," in Robert Jackson, Doreen Jackson, and Nicolas Baxter-Moore, eds., *Contemporary Canadian Politics: Readings and Notes* (Scarborough: Prentice Hall Canada, 1987). Other sources on the subject include Michael Howlett and M. Ramesh, *Studying Public Policy: Policy Cycles and Policy Subsystems* (Toronto: Oxford University Press, 1995), ch. 8; Pal, *Beyond Policy Analysis*, ch. 4; and Privy Council Office, *Guide to Making Federal Acts and Regulations*.

12. Baxter-Moore, "Policy Implementation and the Role of the State," p. 340.

13. Pal refers to exhortation as information-based instruments.

14. Department of Finance Canada, *Tax Expenditures and Evaluations 2008*, available at http://www.fin .gc.ca/taxexp-depfisc/2008/taxexp08_2-eng.asp, retrieved on April 21, 2009.

15. John C. Strick, *The Economics of Government Regulation: Theory and Canadian Practice*, 2nd ed. (Toronto: Thompson Books, 1993).

16. There is some disagreement about these points in the literature: sometimes regulation is considered more intrusive than taxation, and at other times taxation is treated as a type of regulation.

17. Pal, *Beyond Policy Analysis*, p. 178.

18. Allan Tupper and Bruce Doern, *Public Corporations and Public Policy in Canada* (Montreal: Institute for Research on Public Policy, 1981).

19. See also Craig Forcese and Aaron Freeman, *The Laws of Government: The Legal Foundations of Canadian Democracy* (Toronto: Irwin Law, 2005), ch. 10.

20. M.J. Trebilcock, D. Hartle, R. Prichard, and D. Dewees, *The Choice of Governing Instrument* (Ottawa: Economic Council of Canada, 1982); M.J. Trebilcock, D. Hartle, R. Prichard, and D. Dewees, *The Choice of Governing Instrument: Some Applications, Technical Report 12* (Ottawa: Economic Council of Canada, 1981); and M.J. Trebilcock, *The Prospects for Reinventing Government* (Toronto: C.D. Howe Institute, 1994).

21. Dennis Olsen, *The State Elite* (Toronto: McClelland and Stewart, 1980), p. 21; and Wallace Clement, *The Canadian Corporate Elite: An Analysis of Economic Power* (Toronto: McClelland and Stewart, Carleton Library, 1975).

22. Clement, *The Canadian Corporate Elite*, p. 258; Robert Presthus, *Elite Accommodation in Canada* (Toronto: Macmillan, 1973); and Rodney Haddow, *Poverty Reform in Canada 1958–1978: State and Class Influence on Policy Making* (Montreal: McGill-Queen's University Press, 1993).

23. See, for example, John Porter, *The Vertical Mosaic* (Toronto: University of Toronto Press, 1965); and Rick Helmes-Hayes and James Curtis, eds., *The Vertical Mosaic Revisited* (Toronto: University of Toronto Press, 1998).

24. Baxter-Moore, "Policy Implementation and the Role of the State," pp. 346–48.

25. Ibid.

26. Ibid.

27. Pal, *Beyond Policy Analysis*, 3rd ed., p. 178. This prescription is not included in the fourth edition published in 2010.

. . . .

FURTHER READING

Bakvis, Herman, and Luc Juillet. *The Horizontal Challenge: Line Departments, Central Agencies and Leadership.* Ottawa: Canada School of Public Service, 2004.

Baxter-Moore, Nicolas. "Policy Implementation and the Role of the State: A Revised Approach to the Study of Policy Instruments." In Robert Jackson, Doreen Jackson, and Nicolas Baxter-Moore, eds., *Contemporary Canadian Politics: Readings and Notes.* Scarborough: Prentice Hall Canada, 1987.

Courchene, Thomas J., and Donald Savoie, eds. *The Art of the State: Governance in a World Without Frontiers.* Montreal: Institute for Research on Public Policy, 2003.

Forcese, Craig, and Aaron Freeman. *The Laws of Government: The Legal Foundations of Canadian Democracy.* Toronto: Irwin Law, 2005.

Haddow, Rodney. *Poverty Reform in Canada 1958–1978: State and Class Influence on Policy Making.* Montreal: McGill-Queen's University Press, 1993.

Inwood, Gregory J. *Understanding Canadian Public Administration: An Introduction to Theory and Practice,* 3rd ed. Toronto: Pearson Education Canada, 2009.

Lecours, André, ed. *New Institutionalism: Theory and Analysis.* Toronto: University of Toronto Press, 2005.

Pal, Leslie A. *Beyond Policy Analysis: Public Issue Management in Turbulent Times,* 4th ed. Toronto: Nelson Education, 2010.

Pross, Paul. *Group Politics and Public Policy.* Toronto: Oxford University Press, 1986.

Savoie, Donald J. *Breaking the Bargain: Public Servants, Ministers, and Parliament.* Toronto: University of Toronto Press, 2003.

———. *Governing from the Centre: The Concentration of Power in Canadian Politics.* Toronto: University of Toronto Press, 1999.

Strick, John C. *The Public Sector in Canada: Programs, Finance and Policy.* Toronto: Thompson Books, 1999.

Chapter 21

The Executive: Crown,
PRIME MINISTER,
and Cabinet

During a royal visit, Queen Elizabeth is often mistakenly referred to as Queen of England rather than Queen of Canada. Some Canadians are very attached to the monarchy, but others cannot understand what all the fuss is about. On the political front, few events in Ottawa match the suspense and speculation of the naming of a new Cabinet or a major Cabinet shuffle. Almost every member of Parliament aspires to become a Cabinet minister someday, and many ministers hope to become prime minister. These positions offer many perks and much prestige, the possibility of influencing the shape of public policy, and the opportunity to do favours for the minister's constituency, province, and friends.

As seen in Chapter 20, the prime minister and Cabinet are active in many phases of the Canadian policymaking process. Their decisions will sometimes be overturned by the courts, and occasionally even by Parliament, and are usually based to a considerable extent on advice from the bureaucracy. But in the end, the prime minister and Cabinet do make and are responsible for making the biggest political decisions in the country. This chapter begins with a discussion of the Crown, including the monarch and governor general, and then examines the political executive: the prime minister and Cabinet.

THE CROWN

To classify Canada as a **constitutional monarchy** means that it is a democracy headed by a king or queen. In other words, the Queen is the Canadian head of state, but she reigns according to the Constitution. Canada is also said to have "dual executive"—the formal and largely symbolic executive powers are given to the Queen, but the effective executive is made up of the prime minister and Cabinet.

The concept of the **Crown** revolves around the head of state and can be defined as the collectivity of executive powers exercised by or in the name of the monarch. Many executive decisions are made as "advice" to the Queen or governor general, even if the latter has no real control over them and must take the advice, whether welcomed or not. But the Crown is not only the collectivity of executive powers; it also represents the entire state and embodies what belongs to the people collectively—it is a metaphor for the country. This can be seen in Crown corporations (state-owned corporations) or Crown lands (state-owned lands). The Crown is also central to the legal system: Crown attorneys, those who prosecute crimes on behalf of society; court cases initiated in the name of the Queen referred to as *R.* (for *Regina*) *v. John Doe* or court cases against the government (*Smith v. The Queen*); branches of the judiciary called the Court of Queen's Bench; and lawyers awarded the title of Queen's Counsel (QC). The term "royal" is also widely used in Canada to refer to institutions that function for the advantage of all in the name of the Queen: the Royal Canadian Mint; royal commissions, which investigate problems for the general good; and the Royal Canadian Mounted Police, whose job is to capture violators of society's laws. Three important aspects of Parliament also reflect the existence of the monarchical system: royal assent, the speech from the throne, and Her Majesty's Loyal Opposition. "Loyal Opposition" demonstrates that criticism of the government has been legitimized and institutionalized in the name of the Queen. In this sense, the Crown performs useful functions in the Canadian political system that are of a symbolic and ceremonial nature.

The concept of the Crown is not widely understood by Canadians, and, as David Smith writes, it is largely "invisible" to them.[1] For example, since the Queen represents the whole state and its people, oaths of allegiance to the Queen are really pledges of support for the Canadian political system, and "God Save the Queen" really means "God help us to govern ourselves."[2] To put the Queen's picture on stamps or coins, in classrooms or courtrooms, is not to glorify her personally, but to recognize her as a unifying symbol of the state. Nearly

Queen Elizabeth II poses with Canadian veterans on Juno Beach, France, on the 60th anniversary of the D-Day landings.

every state finds it useful to have such a decorative, ceremonial figure. Similarly, in speaking of the powers of the Crown, it is best to see them as being in the possession of the Queen but exercised by the prime minister and Cabinet. The monarch "holds the powers on behalf of the people," as a custodian or trustee. She does not use them, but her presence keeps those who do wield them from becoming too powerful or irresponsible. As mentioned, it is an elegant fiction that the government of the day advises the Crown on the use of such powers. It is probably beneficial to divert favourable popular feelings to the harmless head of state because politicians might abuse such popularity. Another misconception is that the adoption of the Constitution Act, 1982 affected Canada's relationship with the Queen. That act allowed Canada to amend its own Constitution, but it left the Queen in place as the Canadian head of state: it is a personal relationship that no longer has anything to do with the country called the United Kingdom.

The Governor General

The Queen of Canada, Elizabeth II, is also Queen of other countries, and normally resides in Britain. That means that she needs a local representative in Canada—the governor general. The Queen remains the Canadian head of state, but in her absence the governor general may perform any of her functions and exercise any of her powers. Until 1926 the governor was a double agent: besides being the representative of the Queen, he was an agent of the British government, and as long as Canada was a British colony, the governor general exercised authority over Canada on behalf of the British Cabinet. Today, the governor general is only the personal representative of the Queen and has no connection whatsoever to the British government. The Canadian prime minister actually chooses the governor general, who serves a term of approximately five years. Surprisingly, even though the Canadian government has made the selection since 1926, it continued to appoint British governors general until 1952, when Vincent Massey became the first Canadian-born person to hold the post. Since then, as indicated in Table 21.1, Canada has alternated anglophone and francophone appointments.

Powers of the Crown

The Queen of Canada and governor general derive their powers, all of which are exercised according to firmly established constitutional conventions, from three main sources: the Constitution Act, 1867, the Letters Patent, and the royal prerogative. Section 9 of the 1867 act declared that the "Executive Government and Authority of and over Canada is ... vested in the Queen," and section 15 made her commander-in-chief of Canada's military forces. Among the powers explicitly given to the Queen was the one to appoint extra senators, as was done by Brian Mulroney in 1990, although this must be done on the recommendation of the governor general. The 1867 act gave the governor general the power to appoint regular senators and judges, to appoint the Speaker of the Senate, to give royal assent to legislation, and to recommend money bills to the House of Commons. In addition, it referred to the governor general's power to summon and dissolve Parliament. The governor in council, meaning the Cabinet operating in the name of the Crown, was given the power to appoint lieutenant governors and other officers. In fact, the act was somewhat sloppy in not carefully distinguishing

TABLE 21.1 Governors General Since 1952

Vincent Massey	1952–1959
Georges Vanier	1959–1967
Roland Michener	1967–1974
Jules Léger	1974–1979
Edward Schreyer	1979–1984
Jeanne Sauvé	1984–1990
Ramon Hnatyshyn	1990–1995
Romeo Leblanc	1995–1999
Adrienne Clarkson	1999–2005
Michäelle Jean	2005–

between the governor general and the governor in council, which suggests that even as early as 1867 the governor was normally expected to act on the advice of the Cabinet.

The Letters Patent is an obscure document that creates the office of governor general and accords it additional authority. The Letters Patent confer on the governor general all powers of the monarchy with respect to Canada, including the title of commander-in-chief, the power to appoint and remove ministers and judges; the power to summon, prorogue, and dissolve Parliament; and the power of pardon.

The royal prerogative or **prerogative powers** involve the residual authority of the Crown that remains from the days when the monarch was almost absolute. These are unwritten powers, based on custom and convention, although some of them, such as the right to summon and dissolve Parliament, are mentioned in the constitutional documents. Being unwritten, the prerogative powers are vulnerable to parliamentary restriction. Many such powers have been taken away and given to the prime minister and Cabinet—such as the power to nego-tiate treaties, to declare war and peace, and to appoint ambassadors—and those that remain could be removed if Parliament chose to do so.

Despite the impressive theoretical list of powers possessed by the Queen and governor general, there is no doubt that in a democratic age almost all of them must be exercised on the advice of the government—the prime minister and Cabinet—of the day. It would be totally unconsti-tutional, for example, for the governor to refuse to give assent to any piece of legislation. The Queen retains a minimal right to decide on certain honours herself, primarily within Britain, but the governor general was stripped of this power in the early years of this century. Canada created its own set of honours in 1967, the Order of Canada, and although such honours are presented by the governor general, they are decided on by a nonpartisan committee consisting of the chief justice of Canada, the clerk of the Privy Council, the deputy minister of Canadian Heritage, the chair of the Canada Council, the president of the Royal Society of Canada, and the chair of the board of the Association of Universities and Colleges of Canada.

The most important prerogative power of the governor general is the appointment of the prime minister, but this must be performed on the basis of constitutional convention.[3]

In ensuring that the office of prime minister is never vacant, the governor general normally relies on the operation of political parties and elections, and does not have far to look. On two occasions in the 1890s, however, the governor had to help find a person to be prime minister. This action was necessitated by the sudden death of John A. Macdonald in 1891 and then of John Thompson in 1894; in both cases the Conservative Party did not possess an obvious successor. Political parties are better organized today and prefer to choose their own leader. Thus, if the position should suddenly become vacant, such as through the death of the prime minister, the Cabinet or government caucus would name an acting leader pending a leadership convention.

The two most controversial acts of Canadian governors general took place in 1896 and 1926, when the governors in question acted on their own initiative in refusing the advice of the prime minister and Cabinet. The first concerned the question of making government appointments. Many appointments are officially authorized by the governor general, even though they are actually decided on by the prime minister or Cabinet. But the Charles Tupper government chose to retain office after it lost the 1896 election (awaiting defeat in the House of Commons), and during that interim period presented a list of several recommended appointments to the governor general, which he refused to make. Lord Aberdeen felt that the newly elected Wilfrid Laurier, rather than the recently defeated Tupper, had the authority to make such appointments. Aberdeen thought that he was actually upholding the Constitution by interceding.

The second famous case of refusing government advice, the **King–Byng dispute**, had to do with the **dissolution of Parliament**. The governor general normally summons and dissolves Parliament on the advice of the prime minister, but in 1926 Lord Byng refused Mackenzie King's request to dissolve Parliament and call an election. In this case, the governor general was primarily influenced by the fact that a motion of censure against the government regarding a scandal in the Customs Department was under debate in the House of Commons. The request for a dissolution appeared to be an attempt to curtail debate and avoid defeat in the Commons. In addition, the opposition Conservatives actually had more seats than the governing Liberals (who had been kept in power with the support of the Progressives), and an election had been held only eight months before. Thus, it seemed logical to Lord Byng to try to avoid an election when an alternative government might be available. As in 1896, the governor general felt that he was upholding the Constitution against unscrupulous behaviour by the government rather than subverting the democratic will.

Most authorities agree that King's advice was inappropriate and that Byng was right in not automatically acceding to the advice.[4] However, many feel that Byng should not have refused until he had assured himself that another viable government could be found. When the Meighen government fell three days later and was granted a dissolution, it appeared that the governor had acted in a partisan way. Byng's position was further weakened when the electorate returned King to office in the subsequent election. Although it should not be thought that the voters understood the subtleties of the situation or cast their ballots primarily on this issue, the impression that the election results repudiated the governor general's intervention has probably made subsequent governors wary of using their prerogative powers.

Another potential prerogative power of the governor general is to dismiss a government. Constitutional convention allows a governor to do so if the government refuses to resign after an election defeat or refuses to resign or call an election after a clear vote of nonconfidence. This has never happened at the federal level in Canada, and is never likely to, but the power was exercised as recently as 1975, amid great controversy, in Australia. Indeed, in the 1981–82 period in Canada, Governor General Edward Schreyer contemplated forcing an election (tantamount to dismissing a government) if the Trudeau government had not backed down from its threat to impose unilateral amendment of the Constitution and agreed to further negotiations with the provinces.

The great Canadian constitutional scholar Eugene Forsey staunchly defended Lord Byng's refusal in 1926, arguing that such intervention was valid as long as the governor general could find another government to take responsibility for his action. Indeed, Forsey noted many other hypothetical situations in which he would approve of similar intervention. Others find it impossible to specify the exact circumstances in which a governor general might refuse the advice of a prime minister. A third view is that in a democratic age, the governor general should leave even outrageous government behaviour to the will of the electorate. Everyone is agreed, however, that in normal circumstances governors general must act on the advice of the prime minister and Cabinet. Before they invoke such emergency powers, "they must be sure they have reached the danger point, and that their actions will stand up to the subsequent judgment of other institutions and the people."[5]

The governor general has been called an insurance policy against the unforeseeable, or a "constitutional fire extinguisher" whose emergency powers can be used only "when normal controls cannot operate and a crisis gets out of hand."[6] Andrew Heard adds that "governors should intrude into the democratic process only to the minimum extent absolutely required for the basic functioning of Parliamentary government."[7] Since the governor general is to be seen as an impartial symbol of unity, any act that could remotely be interpreted as partisan must be avoided.

Two incidents occurred toward the end of 2008 that raised the question of the governor general's discretionary powers. The Harper government had passed legislation for fixed election dates, with the next to be held in October 2009. However, rather than wait for the parliamentary defeat of his minority government, the PM asked the governor general for an election for October 2008. Most observers felt that the loophole in the law that allowed for an earlier election was designed to come into play only upon the defeat of the government on a nonconfidence vote. Given that the previous election had been a full two years before, however, no one really expected the governor general to object, even if Harper was breaking the spirit of his own law.

That election returned the Harper government, but it was still short of a majority. In December, when the minister of Finance introduced an almost universally ridiculed economic update amidst a worldwide economic meltdown, the three opposition parties signed a coalition agreement, in which they declared their readiness to form an alternative Liberal–NDP government with Bloc support to avoid an election. In order to cling to power, Harper delayed a scheduled nonconfidence vote, and then pre-empted it with a request to Governor General Michäelle Jean to prorogue Parliament to avoid the vote altogether. Harper argued that he would recall Parliament at the end of January 2009 with a full-fledged budget which would reflect the real economic situation and involve ample public consultation in the interim. The Conservatives also engaged in a powerful propaganda campaign to discredit the coalition, protesting that it would have made Stéphane Dion the Prime Minister when he had been soundly defeated in the recent election campaign, and that the coalition was supported by the separatist Bloc Québécois, although that party would not actually have been included in the cabinet. Expert opinion was divided as to whether the governor general should accept the PM's advice to prorogue because if this request was not a violation of the unwritten rules of the constitution (constitutional convention), it came very close.[8] But in the end, she took his advice, perhaps believing that a cooling-off period was in order and also in part because the government had survived a confidence vote on the Throne Speech shortly before the economic update.

Other Functions of the Crown

Leaving aside these very rare occasions, the governor general primarily plays a ceremonial and symbolic role. The governor general presides over the opening of Parliament, reads the government's speech from the throne, lays a wreath at the national war memorial on Remembrance Day, and leads Canada Day celebrations. The governor general is busy entertaining at Rideau Hall: visiting dignitaries must be wined and dined, honours and awards must be presented, and receptions of every kind must be held. Foreign diplomats present their credentials to, and take their leave of, the governor general acting as the Canadian head of state. Although extremely busy in Ottawa, the governor general is also expected to maintain a hectic travel schedule, promoting national unity, demonstrating moral leadership, encouraging good works as patron of many service organizations, and performing other ceremonial functions across the country. Adrienne Clarkson and Michaëlle Jean both excelled at such functions.[9] The Stanley and Grey Cups were both donated by governors general, and the Lady Byng trophy by Lord Byng's wife.

Between the drastic intervention of the emergency powers and the glamorous ceremonial activities lies the traditional advisory role of the monarch: the right to be consulted, the right to encourage, and the right to warn the prime minister in their regular confidential meetings.[10] Prime ministers often find it helpful to confide certain problems to the governor general that cannot be discussed with anyone else, and on which the governor general might be able to offer sage advice. Because of the limited term of office, the usefulness of the governor general to a Canadian prime minister cannot compare with the Queen's experience in advising a British prime minister in this respect, but many prime ministers have spoken warmly of these relationships.[11]

Advantages and Disadvantages of the Monarchy

The fact that the Queen's role as Canadian head of state is left over from the time Canada was a British colony has given rise to considerable dissatisfaction with the position.[12] Some Canadians feel that it is inconsistent with their country's independent status and find that her British background and residence seriously detract from her ability to perform one of her main functions—to serve as a symbol of Canadian national unity. On the other hand, supporters of the monarchy point out that the Crown played a part in allowing French-speaking Canadians to retain rights and privileges after the Conquest,[13] and that the monarchy helps to legitimize the pluralism of society by attracting attention to groups and demands that might otherwise be overlooked. The Aboriginal question is one of many worthy causes that can benefit considerably from the impartial prestige and media power of the monarchy. It is also argued that Canada gains from the worldwide celebrity status of the Queen and her capacity for pomp and ceremony. Moreover, apart from paying the costs of a royal visit, Canada gets all

Governor General Michäelle Jean marks Daffodil Month with cancer victim Dana El Sherif.

the prestige of the monarchy free of charge. The monarchy also helps to distinguish Canada from the United States, and as head of the Commonwealth, the Queen provides a link between Canada and many other countries.

Supporters of the monarchy also point out that the great advantage of dividing the head of state and head of government functions is to make the best use of the prime minister's time. The latter can concentrate on the serious business of governance, while the governor general tends to the ceremonial functions. It is difficult for a partisan prime minister to serve as a symbol of unity, but, being above the partisan fray, it is theoretically possible for a governor general or Queen to do so. Even if a consensus developed over an alternative head of state for the country, however, Canada has made it almost impossible to amend the constitution in this respect.

THE PRIME MINISTER AND CABINET

The prime minister and Cabinet are usually referred to as the "government" of the day, as in "the Harper government." Although the ministers are also members of Parliament, it is in their capacity as the **government** that they perform the leadership function in the political system. This section of the chapter is largely concerned with how they carry out this function.[14] It begins by examining the powers of the political executive in Canada and then discusses the pre-eminent position of the prime minister. The composition and operation of the Cabinet, including Cabinet committees, are addressed in the following sections, after which an outline of Cabinet support agencies is provided.

Powers of the Prime Minister and Cabinet

Given the importance of the prime minister and Cabinet, it is ironic that they are not provided for in the written parts of the Constitution; instead, their functions and powers rest on custom and convention. What *is* provided for in the 1867 Constitution Act is a Privy Council to advise the governor general in the exercise of the powers of that office. As mentioned above, at other points the 1867 act refers to the governor in council, which essentially means the Cabinet functioning as the Privy Council. In fact, the Cabinet acts as a committee of the Privy Council, but rather than merely advising the governor general, it actually makes the decisions in question. With the rare exception of governors general intervening on their own discretion, the prime minister and Cabinet exercise whatever powers are given to the Queen or the governor general in the Constitution. It is from this source that many decisions made by the Cabinet take the form of **orders in council**.

Thus, after an election, the governor general calls on the leader of the party with the most members elected to the House of Commons to become prime minister and to form a government. If there is any doubt about who won the election, an incumbent prime minister has the right to remain in office until defeated in the House of Commons, but the transfer of power usually takes place within a few weeks of the election and before Parliament meets. The prime minister assumes the title "Right Honourable"[15] and selects the Cabinet ministers, all of whom are sworn into the Privy Council. This allows them to use the title "Honourable" as well as the initials "PC" (Privy Councillor) behind their name. Since these are lifelong appointments and titles, members of former Cabinets remain in the Privy Council, such that it contains about 400 members. But only those in the Cabinet of the day are invited to Cabinet meetings, hence the concept of the Cabinet as a committee of the Privy Council. Periodically other prominent people are appointed to the Privy Council as an honour, but they are not invited to Cabinet meetings either, and the Privy Council as a whole hardly ever meets. The title "president of the Privy Council" can be assumed by the prime minister, but it is often bestowed on another Cabinet minister, such as the minister of intergovernmental affairs.

In normal circumstances, then, the prime minister and Cabinet exercise the powers of the Crown.[16] These powers include the summoning, proroguing, and dissolving of Parliament and the appointment of senators, judges, and other officials. The prime minister and Cabinet, rather than the governor general, really recommend money bills to Parliament, and all international acts and the general conduct of foreign relations are the prerogative of the Cabinet, including declaring war and peace, sending troops abroad, signing treaties, appointing ambassadors, and recognizing foreign governments. The Cabinet may feel it politically advantageous to have Parliament debate these issues and may need to submit legislation to Parliament to make treaties effective, but unlike in the U.S. system, such international acts are essentially within the purview of the executive, not the legislature. In the case of the Kyoto Protocol in 2002, the Chrétien Cabinet could have ratified the treaty within the executive branch but thought it advisable to get parliamentary approval first, and the Harper government allowed a "take-note" (non-voting) debate on Canadian military action in Afghanistan.

Exercising the powers of the Crown is only a small part of the reason that the prime minister and Cabinet are the centre of gravity in the Canadian political system, however. More important is their responsibility for providing overall political leadership and determining priorities for the country. That is, the prime minister and Cabinet decide which problems to deal with, establish the general thrust and direction of new policies, and determine the spending priorities of the government. As noted in Chapter 20, the Cabinet is bombarded by demands but chooses to look into only a few of them in the initiation phase of the policymaking process, and then gives the green light to even fewer in the priority-setting phase. In the British and Canadian systems, the responsibility for initiating legislation rests primarily with the prime minister and Cabinet. As will be seen in Chapter 23, opportunities do exist for other members of Parliament to introduce bills, but most of the time of the House of Commons is set aside for government business.

The **speech from the throne** provides the prime minister and Cabinet with an opportunity to outline their legislative program at the beginning of the session, while the Constitution requires that any bill to raise or spend money must also originate with the Cabinet. The Cabinet's virtual monopoly over the passage of legislation should ensure coordination among government policies, while its total monopoly over financial legislation is designed to guarantee a close relationship between policies adopted and the funds to make them effective. Such strong executive leadership, based on tradition, necessity, and the Constitution Act, has evolved over many centuries and has generally proven itself to be an effective way to run a country. As noted below, such leadership is based on the twin concepts of collective and individual ministerial responsibility.

Beyond the powers of the Crown and this general leadership function, Cabinet power is also derived from specific acts of Parliament. Almost every law delegates to a minister or the governor in council the power to make decisions of one kind or another. These include the quasi-legislative power to issue **regulations** under a law, sometimes called delegated or subordinate legislation. That is, on the advice of their bureaucrats, ministers are given the power to flesh out the bare bones of the statute with detailed stipulations that Parliament did not have the time or expertise to discuss. The Cabinet is similarly given many quasi-judicial powers, such as hearing appeals from regulatory tribunals like the Canadian Radio-television and Telecommunications Commission (CRTC).

It is also on the basis of such acts of Parliament that individual ministers are charged with supervising the administration of their departments. They provide direction and leadership, establish priorities, and transmit the prime minister's or their personal or party perspectives, all in an effort to ensure that public servants remain accountable to democratically elected leaders and public opinion. In addition, ministers are involved in Parliament, answering questions about the department's operations, defending departmental spending proposals, and piloting bills emanating from the department. Nowadays, it is common to refer to a minister's "portfolio" as including the department along with any service agencies, administrative tribunals, and Crown corporations that are linked to the minister but operate at arm's length.

The principle of individual **ministerial responsibility**—each minister being held responsible to Parliament for everything that goes on in his or her department—was once thought to entail a minister's resignation over errors of public servants, even those that the minister knew nothing about.[17] In an age of big government, however, the principle has lost most of its meaning. Ministers can still be criticized for departmental failures and are expected to correct them, but they rarely resign except in cases of serious personal mistakes and conflicts of interest.[18] The sanction for error rests more with the prime minister (demotion or forced resignation) than with Parliament.

The Prime Minister

The system of government that Canada inherited from Britain has traditionally been called **Cabinet government**, because the Cabinet was a collective decision-making body. But such a label does not do justice to the modern pre-eminence of the prime minister. Most observers agree that Cabinet government has been transformed into a system of **prime ministerial government**,[19] and no one doubts that the prime minister has enormous power and should be singled out for special attention.

Prime ministers have always lent their name and style to the government, such as the "Trudeau Cabinet" or the "Mulroney government," and "the ebb and flow of the fortunes of the government are directly linked to their performance."[20] Donald J. Savoie demonstrates how this pre-eminence begins before the prime minister is even sworn into office. An elaborate transition-planning process led by the Privy Council Office and involving the entire deputy minister community is designed to give the incoming PM all he or she needs to know about forming and operating a government, and many significant decisions are made in this transition period. This process requires such a focus because at that point in time, the PM is the only known member of the incoming Cabinet.[21] Party leaders who realistically expect to defeat the incumbent government now establish an advisory partisan transition team well before the election results show whether it will be needed. The Privy Council document *Accountable Government: A Guide for Ministers* talks of the prime minister leading the process of setting the general direction of government policy, choosing the principal holders of public office, deciding on the organization and procedures of the Cabinet, determining the broad organization and structure of the government, establishing standards of conduct for ministers, and having special responsibilities for national security, federal–provincial–territorial relations, and the conduct of international affairs.[22]

The pre-eminence of the prime minister over Cabinet colleagues can consequently be seen in ten of the PM's principal powers, rights, or responsibilities, and can be enumerated as follows:

1. Cabinet-maker
2. Chair of Cabinet meetings
3. Party leader
4. Chief policymaker
5. Leading player in the House of Commons
6. Chief personnel manager
7. Controller of government organization
8. Adviser to governor general
9. Chief diplomat
10. Public persuader

First, the prime minister is the Cabinet-maker.[23] Prime ministers select their own ministers and, subject to certain conventions discussed below, decide what portfolios to assign them. Ministers are also issued with "mandate letters" that inform them of the PM's policy expectations in their portfolio.[24] Ministers thus owe allegiance to the prime minister, who can promote and demote them, ask for their resignation, and, if necessary, dismiss them. All of these possibilities tend to keep ministers submissive if and when there is any difference in their policy priorities. Prime ministers are usually reluctant to drop or demote ministers who have outlived their usefulness, although appointment to the Senate has sometimes provided a valuable safety valve in this connection.

The prime minister's chairing of Cabinet meetings is a second main source of power. To start with, the prime minister

CP PHOTO/Tom Hanson

Stephen Harper gave new meaning to the concept of prime ministerial government.

determines the agenda of such meetings. A former Cabinet secretary wrote, for example, that for any reason the prime minister deems sufficient, the order of business may be altered, and an agenda already settled may be set aside in favour of other subjects of greater importance and urgency. The PM may suspend meetings, summon additional meetings, dispense with or extend the normal record kept by the secretary, or modify or set aside the normal rules of procedure.[25] In addition to the usual advantages of a chair, the prime minister receives advice from the Privy Council Office on various ministers' views on each agenda item and on how to achieve the PM's own objectives in the meeting. The prime minister is also advantaged by the peculiar way in which Cabinet decisions are arrived at. Rather than by motions and votes, the decision is reached when the PM summarizes the discussion and "calls the consensus." If and when this bears little resemblance to the actual tenor of the meeting,[26] ministers who do not agree with this interpretation either keep quiet or resign. Even though many decisions are now made by Cabinet committees, the prime minister decides which committees will be struck, who will chair them, who will sit on them, and which matters will be sent to them, so that this delegation of power from the full Cabinet does not necessarily reduce the PM's control.[27]

Third, the prime minister is the leader of the party. The PM's pre-eminence has probably increased over the years as political parties have become more cohesive and as election campaigns have come to focus on party leaders.[28] In fact, many ministers may have been elected on the leader's coattails. Some prime ministers, like Pierre Trudeau, may ignore and neglect the party between elections, but others, like Brian Mulroney, seemed to be more clearly in personal control of the party machine. As leader, the prime minister can control party organization, personnel, strategy, and policy.[29] Moreover, unlike other ministers, some of whom may have specialized constituencies of support within the party, the PM has been chosen by the party as a whole and can usually count on a broad base of support. As a party leader, the prime minister's power is further enhanced by his or her authority to approve of candidate nominations.

Fourth, the prime minister could be called chief policymaker. It has already been shown how the PM has the first word on government policy, such as in deciding how seriously to take the party's election platform and in issuing mandate letters to new ministers. But he or she also has the last word, whether in personal interaction with individual ministers, within the Cabinet chamber, in Parliament, or in other forums, such as the media. Modern government, of course, is too complex for a political leader to have an active role in formulating all policies, but the prime minister can pursue a number of personal priorities, as well as play a critical role in defining other problems.[30] In extreme examples, R.B. Bennett delivered a startling series of radio broadcasts in 1935 that committed his Conservative Party to a wide-ranging, radical "new deal"; Pierre Trudeau returned from a meeting with West German Chancellor Helmut Schmidt in 1975 to announce a major restraint program without even consulting his minister of finance; and Jean Chrétien bulldozed ahead with his Clarity Act despite widespread opposition from Cabinet colleagues and the Liberal caucus. Two of Stephen Harper's key decisions that did not even receive Cabinet discussion included the motion to recognize the Québécois as a nation and the ill-fated economic update in late 2008 that came close to causing a constitutional crisis. In any case of real or apparent policy conflict between the party organization and the government, between two ministers, or between a minister and the prime minister, the PM rules. However, he or she may retreat in order to preclude the resignation of an important minister, such as sometimes occurred in the strange relationship between Jean Chrétien and his finance minister, Paul Martin.[31]

Fifth, the prime minister is the central player in the House of Commons.[32] Even though prime ministers now delegate direction of the business of the House to a government House leader, they are still expected to be there every day for the oral Question Period (in contrast to Britain, where the prime minister appears only once a week), in which they set the tone for the government as a whole.[33] However, on a day that they expect a particularly rough reception from the Opposition, prime ministers can find an excuse to absent themselves from the House and leave their ministers to answer for some problem. As the leading parliamentarian, the PM decides how his or her MPs will vote on almost every matter and what kind of behaviour requires expulsion from the government caucus.

A sixth source of prime ministerial pre-eminence is an enormous power of appointment. Besides ministers, this includes the appointment of senators, Supreme Court judges, deputy ministers, heads of a wide range of government agencies, certain diplomats, lieutenant governors, and judges. In many cases, these order in council appointments are made on a patronage basis.[34] The appointment power can serve to keep those hopeful for appointment docile and supportive, as well as to impose the PM's ideological position on much of the government.

Given the extent and power of the bureaucracy today, the prime minister's control over government organization—the seventh power—is also significant. Subject to usually routine parliamentary approval, and on the advice of the Machinery of Government section of the Privy Council Office, the PM can decide to create new departments and set out their mandates. Prime ministers can also reorganize government departments, such as Trudeau's amalgamation of Trade and Commerce and External Affairs to give the latter a more commercial orientation. Under Mulroney and Chrétien, it became more common to abolish departments or agencies that predecessors had established and privatize Crown corporations. Stephen Harper re-amalgamated several departments and agencies that Paul Martin had severed from each other.

Eighth, the prime minister personally advises the governor general on such matters as when to call the next election.[35] This power is sometimes thought to be important in permitting prime ministers to get their own way in conflicts with ministers, government backbenchers, or the parliamentary Opposition because these members do not want to risk their seats and the many benefits of public office. The fixed election date law was supposed to eliminate this power, but a loophole allowed the prerogative to continue.

Furthermore, in an era of globalization and summit diplomacy, the prime minister increasingly overshadows the minister of foreign affairs on the world stage.[36] The prime minister doubled as secretary of state for external affairs until 1946 and still functions as Canada's chief diplomat in annual bilateral meetings with the U.S. president, annual meetings of the Group of Eight leading industrial countries, Commonwealth conferences, meetings of the Francophonie and APEC, and occasional appearances at the United Nations.

Finally, the prime minister is also the chief "public relations officer" of the government, or "public persuader."[37] Television has become the main instrument for transmitting the prime minister's message to his or her party, the government, and the public, and survival in the "battleground" of media relations "threatens to become the key determinant of prime ministerial success."[38] Pearson, Trudeau, Mulroney, Chrétien, and Martin all made televised appeals to seek support on various issues, for example, but the PM does not need to search out publicity or national media attention—it is always there.[39] A crucial position in the Prime Minister's Office is the press secretary, who organizes the prime minister's media appearances and often speaks on the PM's behalf.[40] Stephen Harper was unusual in his rather antagonistic attitude toward the media.

To perform these ten varied and significant functions, the prime minister must be adequately advised. It is not surprising, therefore, that both Trudeau and Mulroney substantially enlarged their two principal sources of advice, the Prime Minister's Office (PMO) and the Privy Council Office (PCO), and Chrétien, Martin, and Harper relied heavily on both. These two agencies will be examined in detail below.

Given all these powers, especially in a situation of being supported by a deferential majority in the House of Commons, the PM can usually succeed in controlling the policy and personnel of government. Richard Crossman and others trace the historical evolution of the centre of power in the British parliamentary system from monarch to Parliament, from Parliament to Cabinet, from Cabinet to public service, and from public service to prime minister.[41] In many respects, in fact, the Canadian prime minister with a **majority government** in the House of Commons is more powerful than the American president, except of course in terms of international clout. To get his agenda adopted, the latter must bargain with Congress, in which party discipline is not strong. Indeed, the expansion of the PCO and PMO, the holding of prime ministerial news conferences, the making of televised addresses to the nation, luxurious travel arrangements, and other conspicuous trappings of power have led many observers to criticize the presidentialization of the office of prime minister.[42] Although he may overstate the situation slightly, in *Governing from the Centre*, Donald Savoie writes that within the operation of the government itself, in a majority situation, the PM has few constraints other than lack of time.[43]

Many observers were surprised at how quickly British Prime Minister Margaret Thatcher (the "Iron Lady") was dumped when her party decided to remove her. In Canada, however, even unpopular PMs have stayed on well beyond their "shelf life." The main exception was in 1896 when Mackenzie Bowell's Cabinet rebelled and forced him from office, whereas, in 1963, John Diefenbaker survived a Cabinet revolt by appealing over the heads of the Cabinet to his supporters in the government caucus.[44]

Others emphasize the restraints on the power of the prime minister: he or she may be forced to compromise, especially in a minority situation, even within the internal operation of government, and is certainly subject to external constraints, such as limited finances, a hostile media, opposition from the provinces and strong advocacy groups, international influences, and the limits to which government policy of any kind can effect societal change. The prime minister is often at the mercy of events, and they may cause the PM to lose public support and in turn much of his or her overall influence. Graham White concludes that the prime minister has "formidable raw power" but falls short of being an autocrat.[45]

A LAME-DUCK AND MINORITY GOVERNMENT PRIME MINISTER

After his third election victory, Jean Chrétien was increasingly stubborn and unpopular and ignored the majority feeling—both within his party and among the general public—that he should retire. Moreover, his immensely popular rival, Finance Minister Paul Martin, had taken control of the party organization and was widely regarded as the heir-apparent.[46]

Given his own age, however, the longer Martin was made to wait, the slimmer his chances of succeeding became. Although he was a powerful Cabinet minister, he quite openly organized a leadership bid and probably planned a challenge at the Liberal leadership review scheduled for February 2003. Chrétien fired Martin as minister of finance, essentially for refusing to tone down his leadership campaign, but that campaign just kept getting stronger. Thus, instead of facing a leadership vote that he would probably lose, Chrétien announced in August 2002 that he would retire in February 2004. This would make him a "lame-duck" leader for an incredible 18 months, but it would also make Martin that much older and leave time for someone else to organize against him.

The powers of a lame-duck prime minister are still an open question. Beyond the fact that he was forced to retire before he had planned to do so, Chrétien lost several other battles: he was obliged to announce package after package of reforms to improve the ethical performance of the government; his caucus supported an opposition motion to elect Commons committee chairs rather than have them appointed by the PM; and the Liberal Party scheduled the leadership convention for November 15, 2003, more than two months before he planned to leave. However, freed from the constraints of seeking re-election, Chrétien actually adopted a more activist agenda in 2003 than in the preceding nine years, including refusal to participate in the Iraq war.

When Paul Martin finally assumed the prime ministership, he was soon reduced to a **minority government** position in the 2004 election, and when he lost power two years later, Stephen Harper also led minority governments from 2006–08 and again after 2008. Since this situation could well be repeated in the future, it is worth addressing the question of how much power a prime minister has when not backed up by a majority in the Commons. In the first place, executive decisions that do not require Parliamentary approval can be made in the same confident way, whether the government has a majority or not. These include government appointments, treaties, the summoning of Parliament, and so on. For example, the Martin government ignored the House of Commons' rejection of more than one of its executive appointments.

But a minority government has to be more careful with respect to any decisions that need to be passed by Parliament, such as legislation or spending proposals. (That said, the Opposition in Parliament could always base a nonconfidence motion on some action that was entirely within the scope of executive powers.) In a typical minority situation, the prime minister must negotiate delicate compromises with one or more opposition parties, making policy concessions in return for support. The Martin government was nearly defeated in the spring of 2005, only managing to hold on by amending its budget so that it gained the approval of the NDP. But the Martin Liberals lost a motion of nonconfidence in November of that year when even the NDP voted against them because they would not compromise on health care policy.

The government's own backbenchers in a minority position are usually more solid than in a lame-duck situation because they all support the leader and want to avoid an election; thus, survival primarily depends on gaining the support of a sufficient number of Opposition members. The main question, then, is whether or not opposition parties are ready for an election. Do they have enough funds, are they organizationally prepared, and would the public approve if they precipitated an early vote? The PM of a minority government can function in a bullying manner if the opposition parties are afraid of causing an election; in this case, they can always find excuses and means to keep a government in office. Even though Harper came to power in 2006 with five main priorities that had scant support among any opposition parties, he managed to see at least four of them adopted with some concessions.

PRIME MINISTERIAL TENURE AND STYLE

Out of 21 prime ministers between 1867 and 2006, nine held the position for two years or less, while 12 served at least a four-year term of office, as shown in Table 21.2. Of the 12 longest-serving PMs, nine were lawyers, seven were anglophone Protestants, four were francophone Catholics, and Brian Mulroney was a bilingual anglophone Catholic. Robert Borden came from the Atlantic region, five hailed from Quebec, four from Ontario, and R.B. Bennett and John Diefenbaker spent their adult lives in the West. At least two (Bennett and Trudeau) were extremely wealthy, and several others (Chrétien, St. Laurent, Mulroney, and King) had abundant corporate connections. Lester Pearson and Mackenzie King came from elitist academic–public-service backgrounds.

Michael Whittington provides a thumbnail sketch of the styles of recent prime ministers.[47] Mackenzie King was a broker and coalition-builder, avoiding action as much as possible; John Diefenbaker had a charismatic appeal to the public, and Lester Pearson had a collegial style of leadership with cabinet colleagues, opposition leaders, and provincial premiers. Pierre Trudeau began with a "cool" image in public but emphasized stern rationality in making decisions; Brian Mulroney was suave and businesslike but craved popularity; and Jean Chrétien promoted the image of a backwoods "hick" behind which he used his considerable political acumen to manage affairs as he intended. After his stellar performance as finance minister, Paul Martin disappointed most observers as PM, consulting too widely on too many priorities and not being able to make decisions until a crisis loomed. Stephen Harper was a shrewd, self-disciplined planner and organizer with clear priorities and the will to keep his colleagues in line.

TABLE 21.2 Prime Ministers of Canada, Ranked by Tenure in Office

Mackenzie King	21 yr., 5 mo.	Alexander Mackenzie	4 yr., 11 mo.
John A. Macdonald	19 yr.	Paul Martin	2 yr., 2 mo.
Pierre Elliott Trudeau	15 yr., 5 mo.	John Thompson	2 yr.
Wilfrid Laurier	15 yr., 3 mo.	Arthur Meighen	1 yr., 8 mo.
Jean Chrétien	10 yr., 1 mo.	John Abbott	1 yr., 5 mo.
Brian Mulroney	8 yr., 9 mo., 1 wk.	Mackenzie Bowell	1 yr., 4 mo.
Robert L. Borden	8 yr., 9 mo.	Joe Clark	9 mo.
Louis St. Laurent	8 yr., 7 mo.	Kim Campbell	133 days
John Diefenbaker	5 yr., 10 mo.	John Turner	80 days
R.B. Bennett	5 yr., 3 mo.	Charles Tupper	69 days
Lester Pearson	5 yr.		

Composition of the Cabinet

In theory, all Cabinet ministers are equal, although in practice this is far from the case. Pierre Trudeau periodically designated one minister as deputy prime minister, and Stephen Harper was the first prime minister afterward not to appoint such a deputy. A forerunner to the deputy prime minister was the francophone "lieutenant" of various anglophone first ministers. Ernest Lapointe (1923–41) and Louis St. Laurent (1941–48), the Quebec lieutenants of Mackenzie King, were each given wide discretion to deal with issues from that province. Macdonald used George-Étienne Cartier in a similar role for a few years, and to some extent C.D. Howe was an anglophone lieutenant to Louis St. Laurent.[48]

Below the deputy PM, if there is one, are the regular departmental ministers, each normally in charge of a single department. An informal ranking of these departments may result in variations in influence among this group of ministers, with finance, foreign affairs, justice, trade, health, treasury board, industry, human resources, and transport usually being among the key portfolios. Next, a handful of ministers may not have full-fledged departments to administer but be attached to larger departments, and the list is completed with the government leaders in the House of Commons and the Senate.

PMs sometimes also appoint junior ministers, variably called ministers without portfolio, ministers of state, or secretaries of state. Unlike in Britain, the Canadian tradition was that all ministers, even these junior ones, were included in the Cabinet. However, Jean Chrétien's nine or ten secretaries of state were in the ministry but not in the Cabinet. They came to Cabinet meetings at the invitation of the PM, and attended Cabinet committee meetings when specific items of interest to them were on the agenda. They each had a small staff and operating budget and received 75 percent of a Cabinet minister's pay. Paul Martin had many junior ministers, but they were theoretically equal in status to departmental ministers, while Stephen Harper originally established a much smaller Cabinet in which almost every minister had a department to run. In 2007, he added five junior ministers called *secretaries of state*, who were not in the Cabinet. In his post-2008 election Cabinet, however, Harper included 11 *ministers of state* who were not in charge of a department, but were full-fledged ministers with Cabinet committee assignments and invited to rare meetings of the full Cabinet.

Since the Cabinet occupies such a central position in the Canadian policymaking process, every interest in the country would like to be represented around the Cabinet table.[49] This desire alone creates pressure to expand its size. In general, the Cabinet contained about 13 or 14 ministers before 1911, then rose to around 20 until about 1960, increased to 30 under Trudeau, and to around 40 in the Mulroney period. Chrétien reduced the size of his Cabinet to 23 in 1993, but it rose to 28 in his second and third terms. Martin had close to 40, and while Harper started out with only 27, he later had a Cabinet of 38.

Although the prime minister decides who will sit in the Cabinet, several conventions have come to constrain the PM's prerogatives in the selection of ministers.[50] In the first place, reflecting the fact that Canada is a democracy and that ministers represent the people, all Cabinet ministers must have a seat in Parliament. As in Britain, and unlike the United States, ministers sit in the legislative branch of government at the same time as they form the executive.

A seat in Parliament would theoretically include a seat in the Senate. A number of senators sat in the early post-Confederation cabinets—indeed, senators Abbott and Bowell served briefly as prime minister in the 1890s—but the modern tradition is to include only one senator in the Cabinet. This senator serves as government leader in that chamber and usually has no departmental responsibilities. The Diefenbaker Cabinet functioned between 1958 and 1962 without a single senator, however, while Brian Mulroney gave Senator Lowell Murray important responsibilities as minister of federal–provincial relations in the Meech Lake period.

Almost all ministers therefore have a seat in the House of Commons. It is possible for the prime minister to name someone to the Cabinet who has not won election to the Commons, but convention dictates that such a person run in a by-election as soon as possible to obtain a seat. This sometimes happens when a PM chooses to appoint someone of unusual qualifications from outside parliamentary life, rather than a sitting backbencher, a practice that does not reflect well on the party's parliamentary caucus. In at least two cases such appointees lost the by-election in which they sought entry to the House and ultimately resigned from the Cabinet, confirming the view that it is impossible to sit in the Cabinet very long without a seat in Parliament.[51] Having been selected as Liberal leader in 1984 after an absence from politics, John Turner even served briefly as prime minister without a seat, but this was only temporarily legitimate.

A prime minister will usually feel compelled to appoint veteran MPs to the Cabinet, including those who served in previous Cabinets or those who ran for the party leadership. It is often thought safer to put leadership rivals into the Cabinet, subject to all its constraints, than to leave them to continue their campaigns outside. As a result, able newcomers are often overlooked. The prime minister may also be concerned with the ideological slant of the Cabinet, seeking either to balance various ideological factions within the party or else to ensure that a particular stream predominates.

The next constraint on the prime minister is the convention that each province be represented in the Cabinet. This flows from the fact that Canada is a federation and that the Senate has never performed its intended role of representing provincial interests in Ottawa. Thus, with the occasional exception of Prince Edward Island, every province that has elected a member to the government side of the chamber has always been awarded a Cabinet position. In both the Trudeau and Clark governments, the prime minister chose to appoint more than a single senator to the Cabinet in order to represent provinces that had not elected any or enough government members (the three Western provinces in the former case and Quebec in the latter). Harper's first cabinet had two senators, one the government leader, and the other to compensate for his lack of an MP from Montreal. Nunavut and PEI were both represented in Harper's second cabinet, but Newfoundland and Labrador failed to elect a single Conservative, so Nova Scotia's Peter MacKay was designated to represent both provinces in the cabinet, just as he doubled for PEI after the 2006 election. The convention of provincial representation usually results in some ministers being appointed only because their province needs a Cabinet representative rather than because of their merits, leaving worthy MPs from other locations excluded because their region is already adequately served.

It is not only that residents of a province feel more secure if one of their number is in the Cabinet; it is also useful for the Cabinet itself to have such provincial representation.[52] In fact, ministers essentially wear two hats: they speak for their department as well as for their province. This arrangement is functional for patronage as well as policy purposes: those government appointments and contracts awarded on a partisan basis will be the responsibility of the relevant provincial minister, often called the "political minister" for that province.

Larger provinces are not content with a single minister, of course, and in a Cabinet of 30 or more, Ontario and Quebec have sometimes exceeded ten. In such cases the ministers can be distributed so that each region within the province gains its own representative. Before 1984 Quebec was usually underrepresented in the Cabinet when the Conservatives were in power, largely because not many PC members were elected from that province, while the West was inadequately represented in the Pearson and Trudeau cabinets. Table 21.3 indicates the regional distribution of federal Cabinet ministers (including the prime minister) when each new government took office.

The next convention of Canadian Cabinet-making is the need for a balance of ethnic representation. A proper balance of anglophone and francophone ministers may result almost automatically from the carefully constructed provincial representation. French Canadians

TABLE 21.3   Regional Distribution of Federal Cabinet Ministers at the Beginning of Each Ministry

	Atlantic	Quebec	Ontario	West	Total
Macdonald (1867)	4	4	5	—	13
Mackenzie (1873)	5	3	6	—	14
Macdonald (1878)	5	4	4	1	14
Laurier (1896)	4	5	4	1	14
Borden (1911)	4	5	7	2	18
Borden (1917)	6	4	9	3	22
Meighen (1920)	5	3	6	3	17
King (1921)	4	6	6	3	19
Bennett (1930)	4	5	7	3	19
King (1935)	5	5	4	2	16
St. Laurent (1948)	4	6	7	3	20
Diefenbaker (1957)	8	3	6	4	21
Pearson (1963)	4	7	11	4	26
Trudeau (1968)	6	10	10	3	29
Clark (1979)	5	5	11	9	30
Trudeau (1980)	5	12	12	4	33
Turner (1984)	5	10	12	2	29
Mulroney (1984)	5	11	11	13	40
Chrétien (1993)	3	5	10	5	23
Martin (2003)	5	9	17	8	39
Harper (2006)	3	5	9	10	27

Source: W.A. Matheson, The Prime Minister and the Cabinet (Toronto: Methuen, 1976), updated by author.

were underrepresented even in Liberal governments before 1963, however, and often grossly underrepresented in Conservative cabinets. It was only in the Pearson, Trudeau, and Mulroney cabinets that francophone ministers achieved or exceeded fair numerical representation. Those of other minority ethnocultural origins were not proportionately represented in Canadian Cabinets until the Clark and Mulroney periods, but every Cabinet now has a more diversified ethnic hue, including a few members from visible minority groups.

As for other social divisions, the religion factor was much more important in the pre-1900 period than it is today. A balance between Protestants and Catholics and even of different Protestant sectors was originally a concern, but ministers increasingly decline to declare a religious affiliation. To some extent, prime ministers now aim to go beyond the Christian group; the Jewish community has usually claimed one or two spots since the initial appointment of Herb Gray in 1969, and other faiths have recently been represented. Nowadays, prime ministers are more concerned with appointing women to the Cabinet. The number gradually increased from one in 1957 to 11 of 38 in 2008.

Matheson writes of a representative Cabinet as follows:

> Adherence to the representation principle first introduced by Sir John A. Macdonald in 1867 has brought together the elites from the various subcultures and provided them with a means whereby they can work together to stabilize the Canadian political system. Thus in the Canadian context the Cabinet has filled a dual role, for in addition to exercising the usual functions of executive leadership, the Cabinet has provided an arena in which the elites may counter the dysfunctional and unstabilizing effects of cultural, regional, and religious fragmentation.[53]

Once the PM has chosen the people who will form the Cabinet, they must be assigned portfolios—that is, departmental responsibilities. Certain traditions surround this task, too, such as that finance usually goes to an anglophone in whom the business community has confidence; fisheries and oceans is normally given to someone from Atlantic Canada (or BC); and agriculture has traditionally (but not always) gone to a Westerner. Justice was historically awarded to a Quebecker, primarily because of the dual system of law in that province, and public works was also often claimed by a minister from Quebec. It was sometimes argued that francophone ministers preferred Cabinet posts that dispensed a great deal of patronage, while only anglophones were trusted with the big economic portfolios.[54] Whatever truth there might once have been in this portrait, it changed dramatically under Trudeau, as he appointed the first francophone ministers of trade and commerce and finance.

It is not normally expected that ministers will be experts in the field to which they are appointed, partly because the electorate is not likely to furnish the prime minister with members of Parliament with such credentials. Indeed, an argument can be made that a semi-expert is more dangerous than a total amateur since the latter will have enough sense to listen to the real experts within the department, while the former might try to substitute his or her limited knowledge for theirs. Thus, apart from the minister of justice's being a lawyer, there is no necessary relationship between ministers' training or pre-political occupation and their departmental assignment.

Parliamentary secretaries are not Cabinet ministers, although they are sometimes seen as "ministers-in-waiting." They have been a permanent fixture on the political scene since 1943 and have been provided for in legislation since 1959. They are MPs of the government party who "assist the minister in such manner as the minister directs," which most often takes the form of making speeches on behalf of the minister, receiving deputations, sitting in for the minister in House debates (whether of government or private members' bills or on adjournment), defending the department's Estimates, and maintaining liaison with other MPs. Paul Martin gave his parliamentary secretaries added status by swearing them into the Privy Council; they then became "honourable" for life and played a larger part in substituting for the minister. Harper discontinued this practice but did mandate parliamentary secretaries to play an active role in the government, primarily by sitting on the relevant Commons standing committee.[55]

Operation of the Cabinet
COLLECTIVE RESPONSIBILITY, CABINET SOLIDARITY, AND SECRECY

The Cabinet was traditionally seen as a collective decision-making body. Significant exceptions to this notion now include the prime minister's making some decisions single-handedly, decisions made by Cabinet committees, and decisions made by individual ministers. Regardless of which or how many ministers are involved in making such decisions, however, the Cabinet operates on the principle of collective ministerial responsibility. In other words, all members of the Cabinet are collectively responsible for carrying out the government's policies. Because of the fact that individual ministerial responsibilities often overlap or have implications for other ministers, members of the Cabinet engage in extensive formal and informal consultation with each other, part of a process called horizontal management.[56]

Collective responsibility is closely related to the principle of **Cabinet solidarity**, which means that all ministers must publicly defend all Cabinet policies or else resign. The most extreme manifestation of Cabinet solidarity can be seen in terms of the annual **budget**, the most important government policy statement of the year. Only the finance minister and PM usually know much about it until the budget is delivered in Parliament. Matheson writes:

> This procedure is unfortunate, in that it prevents the experience of the Cabinet from being utilized in the preparation of the budget and makes a mockery of the idea of Cabinet responsibility, since ministers must assume responsibility for something they have had little or no voice in preparing. It also illustrates the great influence of the civil servants who advise the Minister of Finance on this matter.[57]

Ministerial resignations because of policy differences are very rare in Canada, perhaps only 30 since 1867,[58] which suggests that the thought of giving up the perks of office engenders considerable flexibility in ministers' principles. In 2007, Michael Chong resigned from the Harper government on a matter of principle: not being able to support the motion that the "Québécois represent a nation within a united Canada." Cabinet solidarity has been suspended only in the case of parliamentary debates and votes on capital punishment and abortion.

Cabinet solidarity and collective responsibility are also linked to a third principle, that of **Cabinet secrecy**, confidentiality, or "cabinet confidences." Cabinet operations are shrouded in secrecy and ministers are not supposed to disclose information about its deliberations. Such confidentiality protects state secrets, protects the Cabinet against opposition and media exploitation of ministerial discord, and protects senior civil servants from identification and public criticism. Cabinet secrecy is also justified as the only way in which ministers can engage in no-holds-barred discussion of crucial issues and in which public servants can render impartial advice. Cabinet documents are not normally made public for 20 years, and, as a result, we do not know as much about how the Cabinet operates as about decision-making bodies that meet in public.[59] However, clever ministers are conscious that information represents power and that a well-timed leak can sometimes benefit them when involved in a battle within Cabinet. A Privy Council document reveals how these three principles are related:

> Ministers are bound by their oath as Privy Councillors. This oath reflects parliamentary government's core convention of Cabinet solidarity, by which Ministers share collective responsibility for the actions of government and speak to Parliament and Canadians with a single voice. This requires frank discussion in Cabinet and confidentiality in Cabinet decision making.[60]

DEPARTMENTAL, INSTITUTIONALIZED, AND PRIME MINISTER-CENTRED CABINETS

As mentioned, Cabinet-level decisions can be made by the prime minister alone, by the Cabinet collectively, by a Cabinet committee, or by a single minister. In this connection, a distinction is sometimes made between a **departmental Cabinet** and an **institutionalized Cabinet**. The former was characteristic of the Canadian Cabinet before 1960 or so, perhaps especially in the Mackenzie King and St. Laurent eras, in which ministers and departments were largely autonomous. Each developed its own policies and programs with little regard for central coordination and with only minimal prime ministerial interference. Strong ministers could make many decisions and policies without consulting their colleagues, and such ministers tended to remain in charge of a single department for long periods, rather than being shuffled on a regular basis. Such autonomous departmental ministers often doubled as strong regional ministers, who were also allowed to handle regional responsibilities on their own.[61] In addition, senior appointed officials usually served their careers within a single department and became "carriers of the interests, traditions, skills and memories of these particularized bureaucratic organizations."[62] At the same time, however, prime ministers could make certain decisions unilaterally, and some interfered in the operations of various departments more than others. R.B. Bennett and John Diefenbaker gained reputations for excessive interference, for example, while Louis St. Laurent was said to give too much authority to individual ministers.[63]

Despite the assumption of collective Cabinet decision making, the institutionalized or collegial Cabinet is really a product of the period after 1960 and the enormous expansion of government activity in the next 25 or so years. As society and its problems became more complex, individual ministers and departments could no longer make decisions and policies in isolation. The policies of one department almost inevitably affected those of another. More consultation and coordination were called for, with the result that ministerial collegiality replaced departmental autonomy. To some extent the need for policy coordination coincided with the view that Cabinet ministers should have greater control over the bureaucracy, while another stimulus was the development of techniques for more rational government decision making. The Pearson era was transitional in this respect, and the institutionalized Cabinet became fully developed in the Trudeau period, coinciding with his approach of increasing the rationality of government policymaking.[64]

In the new approach, the Priorities and Planning Committee of Cabinet established the overall priorities of the government so that policymaking was no longer so ad hoc and incremental. Then, the Prime Minister's Office and the Privy Council Office were expanded and strengthened so as to provide independent policy analysis to the prime minister and Cabinet. The Department of Finance and the Treasury Board Secretariat also became more effective central agencies, advising the Cabinet on its financial decisions. This change gave the prime minister and Cabinet the resources to challenge bureaucratic initiatives that were often rubber-stamped before.

Next, to avoid Cabinet overload and to enhance specialization within it, most of the Cabinet's work was done in committees. Cabinet procedures were also rigidly adhered to, including agendas, advance notice of issues, and advance circulation of background documents. In addition, new techniques of policy analysis, especially at the bureaucratic levels, provided ministers with a more rational basis for their decisions. Moreover, the attempt to go beyond traditional departmental thinking on problems led to the setting up of new ministries of state and task forces, and public discussion of policy options was encouraged by means of publishing Green Papers and White Papers on a subject before the Cabinet had made up its mind.

All of these measures tended to render Cabinet decisions more coordinated, organized, disciplined, political, and rational, hence the term "institutionalized Cabinet." Whatever the benefits of this approach, however, it also had negative implications. First, ministers did not have the time or capacity to study all the background documents that were prepared for them. Second, departmental bureaucrats often became subordinate not to their ministers but to the new central agencies, the PCO, PMO, Treasury Board Secretariat, and Department of Finance. Third, policies were often coordinated and analyzed to the point of paralysis.[65] Fourth, as was usually the case in previous governments, a small, informal group of trusted ministers and intimate advisers emerged as a "supergroup" who made key decisions regardless of the authorized channels.[66] Finally, since this decision-making model was generally replicated at the provincial level, it had particularly negative effects on federal–provincial relations.

John Turner and Brian Mulroney dismantled much of the "rational" policymaking machinery, both of them feeling that it was too elaborate, complex, and slow. They also argued that the responsibility of individual ministers should be restored, and, being distrustful of the bureaucracy, Mulroney relied excessively on the PMO and ministers' offices, and underutilized the PCO.[67] Jean Chrétien announced his intention to revert to the St. Laurent model of a departmental Cabinet in which individual ministers and departments were allowed to look after their own affairs and the maze of Cabinet committees was reduced. Even in an era of government downsizing, however, the complexity of issues required more coordination and consultation than the 40-year-old model could provide. The finance department began to fill the gap, partly because the budget and the deficit were the driving forces of the day, but also because some kind of coordinating device was needed. Insiders reported that the influence of other central agencies, especially the PCO, was also stronger than ever in the Chrétien government. If such a Cabinet is neither

THE CANADIAN PRESS/Winnipeg Free Press/Jeff De Booy

Joe Clark, a short-term Prime Minister in 1979, who pioneered the two-tier cabinet.

departmental nor institutionalized, Christopher Dunn suggests that we call it a "prime minister-centred Cabinet." This is consistent with the argument that we now have prime ministerial government rather than Cabinet government and is also in keeping with Donald Savoie's theme that power is increasingly concentrated around the PM.[68] This would be a good label for the Harper Cabinet, too.

CABINET AND CABINET COMMITTEES

Historically, the Cabinet as a whole met for about three hours once a week. When such a meeting is scheduled, the Privy Council Office proposes an agenda for the prime minister, including supporting documents, which is circulated in advance. Ministers sit around the Cabinet table in order of precedence, while the clerk of the Privy Council, two deputy secretaries, and one or two note-takers sit along the wall. These officials are rarely asked to speak, but they may pass notes to the prime minister. The PCO will have prepared a scenario note suggesting issues that the PM may want to raise and including guidance in getting through the meeting successfully. The chief of staff of the PMO is also usually present.

Since the mid-1960s, more and more Cabinet work has been done by Cabinet committees rather than by the full Cabinet.[69] In the Pearson, Trudeau, and Mulroney regimes, the Priorities and Planning Committee was clearly the most important Cabinet committee. Its special functions included setting priorities, allocating budgets, reviewing other committee decisions, making many important decisions itself, and supervising federal–provincial relations. Being chaired by the prime minister and containing the most important ministers also added to its significance. However, Joe Clark pioneered the two-tier Cabinet in Canada by explicitly naming an inner Cabinet instead of a Priorities and Planning Committee. In fact, that brief period saw another major departure from the usual collective decision-making process because the full Cabinet rarely met. Chrétien did not have a P&P Committee, while Martin's was short-lived, but the latter's Operations Committee served similar purposes. Under Chrétien and Martin, committee decisions were normally annexed to the agenda of the full Cabinet meeting and did not require further discussion, while under both leaders the frequency of meetings of the full Cabinet declined.

Under Stephen Harper the full cabinet only met about once a month.[70] Instead, he had two active executive committees of Cabinet, the Priorities and Planning Committee, with its traditional functions including expenditure management, and the Operations Committee. Operations, which met on Mondays (and additionally as required), was seen as a firefighter, dealing with unforeseen events, issue management, legislation, parliamentary management, and communications, including oversight of government advertising. The Operations Committee was particularly important because of the minority government situation, which required management of government business on a day-to-day, blow-by-blow basis, including relations with the opposition parties in Parliament. The Priorities and Planning Committee, chaired by the PM, met on Tuesdays, and ratified most other committee decisions. Harper's other Cabinet committees—called policy committees—were treasury board, social affairs, economic growth and long-term prosperity, and foreign affairs and national security. He later added Environment and Energy Security and a committee on Afghanistan.[71]

Each Cabinet committee normally meets once a week or as required, and ministers are likely to be members of two or more Cabinet committees. Unlike Cabinet meetings, ministers may bring advisers—usually their deputy ministers—to Cabinet committee meetings when they are sponsoring an item that is subject to consideration or may be called to speak to an issue. Furthermore, it has become common practice to invite officials from the Treasury Board Secretariat and the Department of Finance, if financial considerations may be raised, or the Department of Justice, to answer questions regarding legal issues.

The Memorandum to Cabinet (MC), prepared by the sponsoring department and signed by its minister, is the main decision-making instrument on which to make a committee recommendation (CR) to Cabinet (see Box 21.1). Less formal instruments are used where no decision is required. Under Harper's "command and control" management style, policy committees were left little room for unscripted policy deliberation. The scheduling of items on the committee agenda is the prerogative of the PCO in consultation with the PM. Before an item gets to committee, much interdepartmental discussion and negotiation will have taken place, including sounding out the views of stakeholders, parliamentarians, and provinces. The sponsoring minister is expected to have performed a political check by having consulted

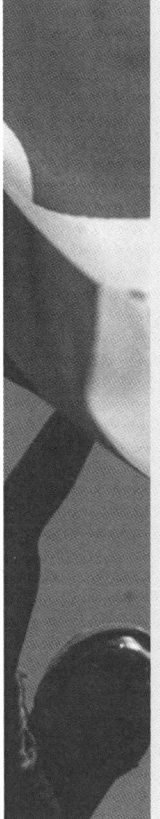

| BOX 21.1 | The Memorandum to Cabinet |

A **Memorandum to Cabinet (MC)** is "the key instrument of written policy advice to Cabinet and, as the tool an individual Minister uses to obtain the support of Cabinet colleagues for a proposed course of action, it plays a pivotal role in the Cabinet decision-making process."[72]

The MC starts in an individual department, which develops a policy or legislative proposal. MCs are usually drafted in response to priorities laid out in the minister's mandate letter, the speech from the throne, or the budget, but pressures may come from other sources, including international obligations. The department and minister may also have their own priority policy or legislative proposals that are not part of the announced government priorities which they want to pursue through the Cabinet committee system. When such a proposal involves many departments, a lead minister is designated, with other ministers being considered as co-sponsors of the proposal. Normally, agreement between sponsoring ministers and the PCO is required before the proposal can proceed for consideration. A draft is prepared by the lead department in consultation with sponsoring departments, and once it is sufficiently well developed, it is presented at an interdepartmental meeting of officials to which are invited all relevant departments and agencies, including central agencies. Resolution of any differences with central agencies as well as with other departments greatly enhances the chances that the proposal will succeed. Once the MC is signed by the sponsoring minister, it is sent to the PCO which must give authorization to print and distribute the document, and it is the prime minister's prerogative to determine to which Cabinet committee each MC is referred.

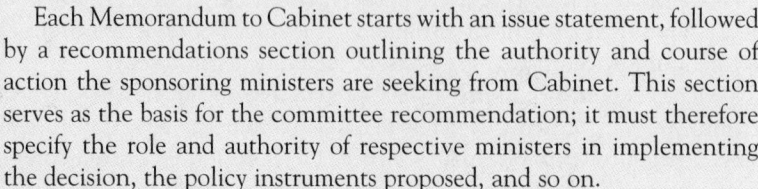

BOX 21.1   The Memorandum to Cabinet (*continued*)

Each Memorandum to Cabinet starts with an issue statement, followed by a recommendations section outlining the authority and course of action the sponsoring ministers are seeking from Cabinet. This section serves as the basis for the committee recommendation; it must therefore specify the role and authority of respective ministers in implementing the decision, the policy instruments proposed, and so on.

The next section is the rationale, which outlines why the action is required, what options were considered, and what arguments support the course selected. The section on "considerations" includes possible consequences of proceeding and not proceeding; horizontal policy impacts; key groups or interests consulted; and the privacy, official languages, regional, gender, environmental, and international implications. The risks and strategies section outlines adverse consequences and criticisms and articulates strategies for managing these risks. In some instances, these strategies will have been developed from consultations held with stakeholders. The section on financial, asset, and human resources implications must be signed off by the departmental comptroller, and the MC ends with a short summary of communications considerations.

Each MC must contain annexes consisting of a parliamentary plan and a strategic communications plan. The former, particularly important in a minority government situation, details the position of other political parties, the government caucus, the minister's strategy, proposed timing, engagement of Commons and Senate committees, and so on. The latter requires an assessment of public opinion, target audiences, expected media reaction, the key messages involved, and links to the government's overall messages.

Most MCs also include a background analysis section to detail the factual information and analytical context of the issue. An MC can also include a discussion paper, such as when the government wants to undertake extensive consultations either with stakeholders or with a standing committee of Parliament. Other annexes can be included where appropriate, such as drafting instructions for the Department of Justice if the proposal has a legislative component, or a detailed cost breakdown of options detailed in the MC.

As mentioned earlier, the PCO prepares briefing notes for the committee chair that outline the issue and the positions of the Treasury Board Secretariat and Department of Finance, and provide supporting background information and the PCO recommendation. The scenario note also scripts the best way to get successfully through the meeting, with potential decision points.

with caucus. Each committee is supported by a secretariat within the PCO that works with the sponsoring department.

The sponsoring minister presents the item to the committee and answers questions from other ministers. The departmental deputy minister and Treasury Board Secretariat (TBS), finance, or justice officials may also be asked to clarify technical issues. Other officials who are likely to be in attendance include the deputy secretary to the Cabinet, the assistant secretary to the Cabinet responsible for the committee, and other officials from the PCO, including a note taker, while the PMO normally has one or two officials in the room as well. As in the case of Cabinet as a whole, officials may pass notes to ministers or to the chair.

The Chair summarizes the discussion and where a consensus has been achieved, the item is given approval in principle. Following the meeting, the PCO issues a committee recommendation for ratification at an upcoming meeting of the P&P Committee or Cabinet as a whole. Where consensus cannot be reached in the committee, the Chair can recommend that the sponsoring minister report back with a modified proposal in order to respond to the concerns raised.

The **Treasury Board** operates somewhat differently from other Cabinet committees. It has its own support agency, the TBS, and the Cabinet committee sits in judgment as TBS officials across the table present cases for the proposed expenditure of funds. Paul Martin expanded the Treasury Board's mandate to include the previous functions of the Special Committee of Cabinet (ratifying most orders in council and regulations), while Harper added responsibility for accountability and ethics. In other words, Treasury Board now has a policy orientation function, being responsible for the Federal Accountability Act.

When Donald Savoie asserts that "Cabinet is no longer where the important decisions are made,"[73] he is in part stating a matter of fact that the full Cabinet does not really make decisions because they have already been made in Cabinet committees. But his theme is that ministers and Cabinet as a whole are increasingly subordinate to the prime minister, who can influence decisions of Cabinet committees as well as individual ministers in a variety of ways. The flow of government business is often from the centre to the departments, instead of from departments to the centre, and ministers have moved from being sources of power to being mere advisers to the PM. With a few exceptions, they are not the most influential advisers either. In short,

> power in the federal government has shifted away from line ministers and their departments towards the centre, and also, within the centre itself, power has shifted to the prime minister and his senior advisers at both the political and public service levels and away from Cabinet and Cabinet committees.[74]

Central Agencies

In addition to the regular departments that advise individual ministers and which are the subject of Chapter 22, four main agencies exist to support the prime minister and the Cabinet as a whole. These **central agencies**, already mentioned in passing, are the Privy Council Office, the Department of Finance, the Treasury Board Secretariat, and the Prime Minister's Office, although the PMO, being partisan, is not officially recognized as a central agency by the bureaucracy.

Sue Dewar/artizans.com

THE PRIME MINISTER'S OFFICE

The **Prime Minister's Office (PMO)**, made up of temporary, partisan loyalists, was considerably expanded by both Trudeau and Mulroney. It deals with such matters as the prime minister's relations with ministers, caucus, and party; partisan appointments; correspondence; media relations; public appearances; travel; constituency matters; and speeches; and it briefs the PM on legislative proceedings.[75] It also organizes the PM's hectic schedule of appointments and meetings, monitors political developments, offers policy advice from a partisan point of view, and helps the PM handle crises.[76]

When Brian Mulroney first came to office, he put all his closest advisers into the PMO and expanded its influence even beyond the level it enjoyed under Trudeau. However, after a series of political mistakes, most of these original advisers were let go and a new chief of staff brought order to the operation. Ironically, Mulroney seconded a career public servant, Derek Burney, to transform this partisan office. Under each of Jean Chrétien, Paul Martin, and Stephen Harper, the PMO had a reputation for imposing the prime minister's will on almost everything. Chretien's PMO was allegedly implicated in the sponsorship scandal; Martin brought most of his coterie of longtime advisers ("the Board") into the PMO, with limited success, and however feared, Stephen Harper's PMO also made mistakes. Harper's first Chief of Staff, Ian Brodie, was replaced after the 2008 election with Guy Giorno, who had served Ontario Premier Mike Harris in the same capacity. Recent PMOs have been primarily involved in communications and media relations work, being the ultimate "spin doctors" in the government.[77]

THE PRIVY COUNCIL OFFICE

To cope with the increased demands on the system because of the pressure of war, the **Privy Council Office** was recognized as the Cabinet Secretariat in 1940.[78] Ever since, the PCO has been responsible for organizing and supporting the decision-making system of Cabinet and its corresponding committees. Although it is not directly responsible for broad policy development, its role is to challenge and coordinate departmental policy proposals. It engages in medium- and long-term policy research through the Priorities and Planning Secretariat and the Policy Research Initiative, and provides secretariat services to Cabinet and Cabinet committees. These functions serve to ensure that government policy and programs are horizontally coordinated and that the institutions of government are well structured to respond to the needs of Canadians.

The PCO is comprised of senior public servants, unlike the partisans of the PMO. Indeed, the head of the PCO, the **clerk of the Privy Council and secretary to the Cabinet**, is the highest-ranking public servant in the government, and the responsibilities of the office radiate from the clerk's three primary functions: the prime minister's deputy minister, secretary to the Cabinet, and head of the public service.[79] As the deputy minister to the PM, the clerk provides advice on and support of the PM's role as head of government. "This includes advice on appointing senior office holders in the public service and organizing the government, on the Cabinet decision-making system, overall policy directions, intergovernmental relations, and the management of specific issues." As secretary to the Cabinet, the clerk "assists the Prime Minister in maintaining the cohesion of the Ministry and giving direction to it. In this role, the Clerk...provides support and advice to the Ministry as a whole to ensure that the Cabinet decision-making system operates according to the Prime Minister's design." As head of the public service, the clerk "serves as the principal link between the Prime Minister and the Public Service of Canada, and is responsible for the quality of expert, professional and non-partisan advice and service provided."[80]

Thus, the PCO provides logistical support for the Cabinet, ensures its smooth operation, and protects Cabinet confidences. This involves preparing agendas and approving relevant Cabinet documents, organizing meetings, writing and distributing background material, taking minutes, and communicating Cabinet decisions on a "need-to-know" basis. It performs the same services for Cabinet committees; in fact, a branch of the PCO headed by a committee secretary serves as a secretariat for each Cabinet committee. This official, as indicated above, is responsible for managing all aspects of the operation of a committee's meetings and provides advice to the chair of the committee on agenda items.

All of this is much more than a mechanical, secretarial function: the PCO "plays a key role in the elaboration of government policy, supporting the Prime Minister in providing leadership and direction to the Government." In its policy coordination role, the PCO works closely with line departments, as well as with the other principal central agencies "to ensure that new proposals are consistent with the Government's overall objectives and policies, and that all affected interests have been consulted."[81] Trudeau's original intention in expanding the Privy Council Office was to establish a source of policy advice for himself as prime minister, independent of regular departments, with which he could counter regular bureaucratic recommendations. As with his predecessors, Harper relied heavily on the PCO for policy advice, but he also cut the size of it by about 150 positions, sending these officials back to individual departments.

Next, the PCO provides advice on such matters as "the broad organization of government, the appointment of individuals to key positions, and the mandates of these senior office holders."[82] Because he or she is responsible for the quality of expert, professional advice and service provided by the bureaucracy to the political executive, the clerk advises on the machinery of government and the appointment, mandates, and promotion of deputy ministers.

Last, the PCO supports several other ministers in their functions. These include the leaders of the government in the House of Commons and in the Senate. The Legislation and House Planning Secretariat assists the House leaders in the pre-parliamentary and parliamentary stages of legislation and in maintaining communications with the opposition parties. The PCO also provides leadership and coordination in all aspects of federal–provincial relations, and a whole section of the office serves the minister of intergovernmental affairs.

Besides the clerk, the senior management group within the PCO includes the associate secretary to the Cabinet and the national security advisor to the PM, and deputy secretaries of operations, plans and consultation, machinery of government, senior personnel, and intergovernmental affairs. The clerk chairs a meeting of senior PCO officials every morning to identify issues to raise with the PM. The clerk and the chief of staff of the PMO meet daily (sometimes jointly) with the prime minister to review problems and, respectively render nonpartisan and partisan advice. Even though these two key officials provide advice from different angles, they usually (but not always) have little problem in their relationship.[83] The prime minister will be supported throughout the day with detailed strategy notes with regard to attending meetings, talking to important people in the office, or making critical telephone calls, all of which helps the PCO obtain the kind of results it considers best.

Thus, it could be said that the clerk of the Privy Council is the lynchpin of the government of Canada. This chapter has already established that the prime minister vastly outranks individual Cabinet ministers, and the clerk, the closest adviser to the PM, has his or her "safe pair of hands" on almost everything that really counts.[84] This includes preparing transition books for a new government, drafting the speech from the throne, working with the finance department and the Treasury Board Secretariat on the budget, organizing the machinery of government, writing mandate letters for ministers and deputy ministers, appointing and evaluating deputy ministers, chairing the coordinating committee of deputy ministers, keeping an eye on Memorandums to Cabinet, helping to strategize Cabinet and Cabinet committee meetings, and keeping track of federal–provincial relations. The prime minister may be the most important player in the actual making of government decisions, but the clerk will be advising on almost every one. To quote the Gomery report, "the Prime Minister sits at the apex of the political hierarchy, while the Clerk sits at the apex of the bureaucratic hierarchy. Together, they wield a great deal of power and influence."[85]

THE DEPARTMENT OF FINANCE

The **Department of Finance** and the Treasury Board Secretariat primarily supply financial advice to the Cabinet and have historically exercised a cautioning, restraining influence on new program proposals.[86] The finance department is responsible for the government's overall revenue and expenditure situation (macroeconomic policy), including its accumulated debt and annual deficit (if any), and advises on allocations among departments. Under the powerful deputy minister, the department is also the chief adviser on taxation policy and on transfer payments to the provinces and territories. Although reporting directly to the minister of finance and in that sense an ordinary department of government, Finance has a special responsibility of advising the Cabinet collectively on such matters, being incorporated into the process of developing Memorandums to Cabinet as well as preparing the annual budget.

The finance department has always enjoyed considerable pre-eminence, but in an age of government restraint and retrenchment, its influence necessarily increased; especially in the first term of the Chrétien regime, the finance department really determined the government's agenda.[87] When finance said that there was no more money available, for example, Red Book promises were ignored. To some extent it was the minister of finance talking, but in large measure he was repeating what his senior officials told him to say.

THE TREASURY BOARD SECRETARIAT

The Treasury Board is a committee of Cabinet chaired by the minister called the president of the Treasury Board, who is in turn in charge of a full-fledged government department, the **Treasury Board Secretariat**.[88] This secretariat, under the secretary of the Treasury Board, has the overall responsibility for controlling regular departmental spending, being involved in the detailed development of departmental budgets, the Estimates, and overseeing the actual expenditure of funds. The TBS is also in charge of labour relations in the public service and issues policies on personnel, administration, and finance. Although its perspective is more detailed than that of finance, the two agencies usually see things in a similar light, and the Treasury Board Secretariat's influence also increases when a government is obsessed with its deficit. Under Stephen Harper, the mandate of the department was broadened to include supervision of the Federal Accountability Act and other ethics issues.

. . . .

CONCLUSION

Although it is anomalous for Canada to share its head of state with other countries, there are advantages in having a head of state separate from the head of government. On a daily basis, of course, the political executive is the most significant part of the policymaking process. MPs want to be appointed to the Cabinet, and societal interests want to feel represented there. Given its importance, the composition of the Cabinet and the manner in which the political executive makes decisions are of great interest to political science. This chapter has shown how the executive decision-making process has changed over time and how power has come to be concentrated in the hands of the prime minister and central government agencies.

This chapter is primarily linked to the two that follow. As the political executive, the prime minister and Cabinet depend very heavily on the bureaucracy, the permanent executive, in both the formulation and implementation of their policies. The PM and Cabinet also need Parliament to authorize many of their decisions, but this is a more conflictual relationship that is open to public view. Being the most powerful part of the government, where almost everything in the system comes together, the prime minister and Cabinet are also related to every other chapter of the book.

(SC) In terms of the approaches outlined in Chapter 1, the state-centred theory has much to say about the political executive, given the obvious power of the prime minister and Cabinet. Most prime ministers had some personal conception of the public interest that they sought to pursue, but some were more courageous than others in imposing their own agenda in the absence of public support. In any case, the prime minister and Cabinet must rely on advice from the bureaucracy. In fact, they often do little more than prioritize problems and then charge the public service with finding solutions to them. Trudeau's objective of rendering the whole decision-making process more rational reflected a *dirigiste* mentality—government directing society rather than responding to it. However, in emphasizing privatization, deregulation, and deficit reduction, Mulroney determined that government should not direct society to the same extent, ironically attempting to lead society to be less reliant on the state. Chrétien also wanted to reduce the deficit, but later, in search of a legacy, sponsored a more activist agenda. Stephen Harper came to power with a well-developed set of priorities that he was determined to enact, but was otherwise forced by economic circumstances to take many actions that he had never previously contemplated.

Ⓒ Class analysts claim that the prime minister and Cabinet either come from or respond to the whims of the bourgeoisie. Historically, most Cabinet ministers were lawyers or businesspeople drawn largely from the petite bourgeoisie or upper-middle class rather than the corporate elite. Nevertheless, the big-business connections of Cabinet ministers are quite striking.[89] At the time of Confederation, for example, many ministers were simultaneously directors of railway companies. During the Borden period, ministers were required to divorce themselves from their former business connections, although there was some backtracking later. It is only since about 1960 that ministers have been required to resign directorships and sever active business connections under various versions of conflict-of-interest guidelines. Most have done so, although occasional abuses continued. In the midst of Prime Minister Chrétien's multifaceted ethical problems, it was revealed that Finance Minister Paul Martin received regular briefings on the activities of his company, Canada Steamship Lines.

Class analysts maintain that even if ministers are required to resign corporate positions and put their investments into some kind of trust, their previous corporate connections will never be far from their mind. Moreover, ministers will be contemplating their post-political existence. Significant numbers of ex-ministers, including Brian Mulroney, have been appointed to corporate boards; many others assumed active executive positions in the business or lobbying communities; and John Turner and Jean Chrétien both worked among big businesspeople during their brief respites from politics. Such evidence of the close connection between Cabinet members and the business community bolsters the class analysis critique, especially when only two labour leaders have ever been named to the Cabinet. Class analysts, such as John Porter, found considerable intermarriage and other family connections among the political, bureaucratic, corporate, and intellectual elites.[90]

Ⓟ Pluralists can hardly argue against the elitist nature of the Cabinet, but they do emphasize the conventions of provincial and regional representation therein, and point out that the Cabinet is becoming more diverse in social background over time. Even one of his critics acknowledged that of all political leaders of his generation, Mackenzie King alone really understood that "the essential task of Canadian statesmanship is to discover the terms on which as many as possible of the significant interest groups of our country can be induced to work together in a common policy."[91]

PC Mackenzie King was also perhaps the ultimate practitioner of "public choice" politics. He carefully calculated the electoral consequences of every decision, took whatever decisions were necessary to retain power, and felt that political security usually lay in inaction rather than action.[92] Much evidence of bending to the public choice can also be found in the records of other prime ministers and cabinets, even those of Trudeau and Mulroney, who claimed to be unconcerned with the electoral consequences of their policies. Similarly, Stephen Harper adopted many policies that were anathema to him in his earlier career. Consistent with the public choice approach, every Cabinet document contains a "communications strategy which spells out in considerable detail how policies should be sold."[93]

(G) The forces of globalization may be taking power away from individual states, and the associated forces of neoliberalism may have taken power away from governments, but globalization has also extended the scope of prime ministerial activity in Canada, and in some ways probably increased the powers of the office. Many international powers were always within the jurisdiction of the executive branch, such as signing and ratifying treaties, and some of these treaties, such as Kyoto, actually allowed governments to clamp down on corporate behaviour. But the globalization of many issues and the constant communication between heads of government have increasingly led the prime minister to make commitments to other states, which individual ministers, the Cabinet in general, and Parliament are then forced to approve. The coordinated response of the G20 to the Great Recession of 2008–09 is perhaps the best example. Prime Ministers are out of the country a great deal of the time, travelling from one international meeting to another, and even when at home spend much of their day in contact with other heads of government or otherwise dealing with global issues.

· ·

DISCUSSION QUESTIONS

1. Was Lord Byng justified in 1926 in refusing to grant Prime Minister Mackenzie King a dissolution of Parliament?

2. What are the advantages and disadvantages of recognizing the Queen as our head of state?

3. Do the prime minister and Cabinet, backed up by a majority in the House of Commons, have too much power in the Canadian system of government?

4. Do you think "Cabinet government" or "prime ministerial government" is a more accurate label for the Canadian system of government? In the absence of the American system of checks and balances between president and Congress, what constraints must the prime minister live with?

5. What were the advantages and disadvantages of the Trudeau effort to make Cabinet decision making more rational? Describe the operation of the Chrétien, Martin, and Harper prime ministerships.

6. Do you agree with the Gomery Report that the powers of the Clerk of the Privy Council should be reduced?

· ·

NOTES

1. Indeed, David E. Smith, *The Invisible Crown* (Toronto: University of Toronto Press, 1995), writes that "the Crown is the organizing force behind the executive, legislature, administration, and judiciary in both the federal and province spheres of government ... [and] reaches into every area of government activity," p. x.

2. Frank McKinnon, *The Crown in Canada* (Calgary: McClelland and Stewart West, 1976), p. 13.

3. Edward McWhinney, *The Governor General and the Prime Ministers: The Making and Unmaking of Governments* (Vancouver: Ronsdale Press, 2005). McWhinney offers ten rules for a governor general to follow. See also Craig Forcese and Allan Freeman, *The Laws of Government: The Legal Foundations of Canadian Democracy* (Toronto: Irwin Law, 2005), pp. 28–31.

4. See, for example, MacKinnon, *The Crown in Canada*, pp. 127–132; J.R. Mallory, *The Structure of Canadian Government*, rev. ed. (Toronto: Gage, 1984), pp. 51–57; and Eugene A. Forsey, *The Royal Power of Dissolution of Parliament in the British Commonwealth* (Toronto: Oxford University Press, 1943; reprinted 1968).

5. MacKinnon, *The Crown in Canada*, p. 124.

6. Heard, *Canadian Constitutional Conventions*, p. 123.

7. Ibid., p. 47.

8. Peter H. Russell and Lorne Sossin, eds. *Parliamentary Democracy in Crisis* (Toronto: University of Toronto Press, 2009).

9. Even so, Opposition parties in the Commons cut the Estimates of the GG's budget by $400 000 as a reprimand for Clarkson overspending on her circumpolar trip. Adrienne Clarkson, *Heart Matters* (Toronto: Viking Canada, 2006).

10. Walter Bagehot, *The English Constitution* (London: Collins, 1963), first published in 1867; and McWhinney, *The Governor General and the Prime Ministers*, p. 166.

11. See, for example, MacKinnon, *The Crown in Canada*, pp. 56, 101, 103; and Vincent Massey, *What's Past Is Prologue* (Toronto: Macmillan, 1963).

12. David E. Smith, *The Republican Option in Canada, Past and Present* (Toronto: University of Toronto Press, 1999), does not find a republican spirit in either Canada's past or present.

13. W.L. Morton, *The Canadian Identity* (Toronto: University of Toronto Press, 1961); Smith, *The Invisible Crown*; and Colin M. Coates, ed., *Majesty in Canada: Essays on the Role of Royalty* (Toronto: Dundurn, 2006).

14. Michael S. Whittington, "The Prime Minister, Cabinet, and Executive Power in Canada," in Michael Whittington and Glen Williams, eds., *Canadian Politics in the 21st Century*, 7th ed. (Toronto: Thomson Nelson, 2008); Graham White, *Cabinets and First Ministers* (Vancouver: UBC Press, 2005); and Andrew Heard, *Canadian Constitutional Conventions* (Toronto: Oxford University Press, 1991), ch. 3.

15. This title was originally based on appointment to the British Privy Council, but Lester Pearson created "Right Honourable" as a Canadian title, which is bestowed on the prime minister, governor general, and chief justice of the Supreme Court.

16. Forcese and Freeman, *The Laws of Government*, pp. 31–37, 337–49. In 2004, in an exercise of the royal prerogative, Foreign Affairs Minister Bill Graham refused to issue a passport on grounds of national security.

17. Kenneth Kernaghan and David Siegel, *Public Administration in Canada: A Text*, 4th ed. (Scarborough: Nelson Canada, 1999), p. 541; Privy Council Office, *Accountable Government: A Guide for Ministers and Ministers of State* (Ottawa: Government of Canada, 2008); cited on April 22, 2009; available at http://www.pco-bcp.gc.ca/docs/information/Publications/ag-gr/2008/docs/ag-gr-eng.pdf; and Forcese and Freeman, *The Laws of Government*, ch. 6, pp. 384–92.

18. Ministers who resigned or were fired or dropped recently for such reasons include Art Eggleton, Andy Scott, Lawrence MacAulay, and Maxime Bernier.

19. The concept was first popularized by Richard Crossman in Britain in his "Introduction" to Walter Bagehot's *The English Constitution* (London: Collins, 1963) and elaborated in *The Myths of Cabinet Government* (Cambridge, MA: Harvard University Press, 1972). See also Patrick Weller, *First among Equals: Prime Ministers in Westminster Systems* (London: Allen & Unwin, 1985); Donald J. Savoie, *Governing from the Centre: The Concentration of Power in Canadian Politics* (Toronto: University of

Toronto Press, 1999); and Jeffrey Simpson, *The Friendly Dictatorship* (Toronto: McClelland and Stewart, 2001), p. 4.

20. Savoie, *Governing from the Centre*, p. 71.

21. Ibid., pp. 81–82.

22. Privy Council Office, *Accountable Government: A Guide for Ministers, 2006*, pp. 20–21; Leslie Pal and David Taras, eds., *Prime Ministers and Premiers: Political Leadership and Public Policy in Canada* (Scarborough: Prentice Hall Canada, 1988); and Peter Aucoin, "Prime Ministerial Leadership: Position, Power, and Politics," in Maureen Mancuso, Richard G. Price, and Ronald Wagenberg, eds., *Leaders and Leadership in Canada* (Toronto: Oxford University Press, 1994).

23. W.A. Matheson, *The Prime Minister and the Cabinet* (Toronto: Methuen, 1976), ch. III; and R.M. Punnett, *The Prime Minister in Canadian Government and Politics* (Toronto: Macmillan, 1977), ch. 4.

24. Savoie, *Governing from the Centre*, pp. 137–39, 343.

25. A.D.P. Heeney, "Cabinet Government in Canada: Developments in the Machinery of the Central Executive," *Canadian Journal of Economics and Political Science* (August 1946); and Savoie, *Governing from the Centre*, p. 125.

26. Savoie, *Governing from the Centre*, p. 328.

27. A book by a long-time secretary to the Cabinet Gordon Robertson, *Memoirs of a Very Civil Servant: Mackenzie King to Pierre Trudeau* (Toronto: University of Toronto Press, 2000), contains much interesting material on the working style of prime ministers King, St. Laurent, Pearson, and Trudeau.

28. Leslie Pal, "Prime Ministers and Their Parties: The Cauldron of Leadership," in Pal and Taras, *Prime Ministers and Premiers*.

29. Matheson, *The Prime Minister and the Cabinet*, pp. 127–28.

30. Leslie Pal, "Hands at the Helm? Leadership and Public Policy," in Pal and Taras, *Prime Ministers and Premiers*, p. 25; and Savoie, *Governing from the Centre*, p. 316.

31. Lawrence Martin, *Iron Man: The Defiant Reign of Jean Chrétien* (Toronto: Viking Canada, 2003), pp. 100–03; Edward Greenspon and Anthony Wilson-Smith, *Double Vision: The Inside Story of the Liberals in Power* (Toronto: Doubleday, 1996), pp. 256–66; and Eddie Goldenberg, *The Way It Works: Inside Ottawa* (Toronto: McClelland & Stewart, 2006).

32. Punnett, *The Prime Minister in Canadian Government and Politics*, ch. 6; and Matheson, *The Prime Minister and the Cabinet*, ch. IX.

33. Savoie, *Governing from the Centre*, p. 94.

34. Privy Council Office, *A Guide Book for Heads of Agencies: Operations, Structures and Responsibilities in the Federal Government* (August 1999) lists 3500 governor in council appointments: judges, diplomats, agencies, boards, commissions, Crown corporations, and government departments; see also Simpson, *The Friendly Dictatorship*, pp. 14–18; Jeffrey Simpson, *Spoils of Power* (Toronto: Collins, 1998); and Forcese and Freeman, *The Laws of Government*, pp. 238–46.

35. Simpson, *The Friendly Dictatorship*, p. 39.

36. Kim Richard Nossal, "Political Leadership and Foreign Policy: Trudeau and Mulroney," in Pal and Taras, *Prime Ministers and Premiers*; and Savoie, *Governing from the Centre*, pp. 134–37.

37. Frederick Fletcher, "The Prime Minister as Public Persuader," in Hockin, *Apex of Power*. See also Punnett, *The Prime Minister in Canadian Government and Politics*, p. 22.

38. David Taras, "Prime Ministers and the Media," in Pal and Taras, *Prime Ministers and Premiers*, p. 36.

39. Savoie, *Governing from the Centre*, p. 72. In fact, an obsession with media attacks on minor points often distracts PMs from more important aspects of their work.

40. Gossage, *Close to the Charisma*; Michel Gratton, *So, What Are the Boys Saying?* (Toronto: McGraw-Hill Ryerson, 1987); and Bill Fox, *Spinwars: Politics and New Media* (Toronto: Key Porter Books, 1999).

41. Fred Schindeler, "The Prime Minister and the Cabinet: History and Development," in Hockin, *Apex of Power*, p. 22.

42. Denis Smith, "President and Parliament: The Transformation of Parliamentary Government in Canada," in Hockin, *Apex of Power*, p. 315.

43. Savoie, *Governing from the Centre*, pp. 87–97, 108.

44. Peter C. Newman, *Renegade in Power* (Toronto: McClelland and Stewart, 1963).

45. White, *Cabinets and First Ministers*. On page 83, White outlines what an autocrat would be like and concludes that this is not a good description of the prime minister. But he does not challenge the

basic argument put forward by Savoie and others that Canadian first ministers wield remarkable power (p. 99). For other accounts of constraints, see Paul Barker, "The Limits on the Power of the Prime Minister," in Mark Charlton and Paul Barker, eds., *Crosscurrents: Contemporary Political Issues*, 5th ed. (Toronto: Thomson Nelson, 2006).

46. Simpson, *The Friendly Dictatorship*, pp. 9–14; Michael M. Atkinson and David C. Docherty, "Parliament and Political Success in Canada," in Michael Whittington and Glen Williams, *Canadian Politics in the 21st Century*, 6th ed. (Toronto: Thomson Nelson, 2004), pp. 11 and 22.

47. Whittington, "The Prime Minister, Cabinet, and Executive Power in Canada." See also Patrice Dutil, "Prime ministers and public administration," *Canadian Public Administration* (June 2008); and Michael Bliss, *Right Honourable Men: The Descent of Canadian Politics from Macdonald to Chrétien* (Toronto: HarperCollins, 2004). A panel of academics rated Lester Pearson as the best PM in the last 50 years. See *Policy Options*, June/July, 2003. For an early look at Stephen Harper, see *Policy Options* (March 2006).

48. F.W. Gibson, *Cabinet Formation and Bicultural Relations* (Ottawa: Queen's Printer, 1970), ch. VIII; John English, "The 'French Lieutenant' in Ottawa," in R.K. Carty and W.P. Ward, eds., *National Politics and Community in Canada* (Vancouver: University of British Columbia Press, 1986); and Matheson, *The Prime Minister and the Cabinet*, pp. 34–38.

49. Matheson, *The Prime Minister and the Cabinet*, chs. II and V.

50. Heard, *Canadian Constitutional Conventions*.

51. General A.G.L. McNaughton served for more than nine months as minister of defence in 1944–45, suffering a by-election loss and a general election loss before finally resigning from the Cabinet. Pierre Juneau resigned as secretary of state when he failed to win a by-election in 1975. Chrétien appointed three ministers from outside the House: Stéphane Dion, Pierre Pettigrew, and Brian Tobin. Then, despite his emphasis on doing things more democratically than his predecessors, Stephen Harper convinced one newly elected Liberal to cross the floor to continue to serve in the Cabinet and appointed an unelected Conservative to the Senate to represent Montreal in the Cabinet.

52. Herman Bakvis, *Regional Ministers* (Toronto: University of Toronto Press, 1991). Bakvis has other interesting things to say about ministerial quality in "Cabinet Ministers: Leaders or Followers" in Mancuso et al., eds., *Leaders and Leadership in Canada*.

53. Matheson, *The Prime Minister and the Cabinet*, pp. ix, 22–23.

54. See the case studies in the study of the Royal Commission on Bilingualism and Biculturalism edited by Frederick W. Gibson, *Cabinet Formation and Bicultural Relations*. Gibson argues that francophones had no monopoly on the desire for patronage, p. 172.

55. Privy Council Office, *Accountable Government: A Guide for Ministers and Ministers of State*, 2008, pp. 9–10.

56. Ibid.; Forcese and Freeman, *The Laws of Government*, p. 370–84.

57. Matheson, *The Prime Minister and the Cabinet*, pp. 90–91.

58. S.L. Sutherland, "Responsible Government and Ministerial Responsibility: Every Reform Is Its Own Problem," *Canadian Journal of Political Science* (March 1991), p. 101. In Paul Martin's government, a junior minister resigned from Cabinet over same-sex marriage.

59. In a July 2002 decision, the Supreme Court of Canada upheld the principle of Cabinet confidentiality but ruled that it is not absolute. The case involved the Canada Evidence Act, which allows the Cabinet to refuse to disclose confidential information, but the Court ruled that courts can require the Cabinet to supply basic information about a requested memorandum, such as the date, title, author, and recipient. *Babcock v. Canada (Attorney General)*, [2002] 3 S.C.R. 3; and Forcese and Freeman, *The Laws of Government*, ch. 9.

60. Privy Council Office, *Accountable Government: A Guide for Ministers and Ministers of State*, 2008; Nicholas d'Ombrain, "Cabinet Secrecy," *Canadian Public Administration* (Fall 2004).

61. Bakvis, *Regional Ministers*.

62. Donald Smiley, *The Federal Condition in Canada* (Toronto: McGraw-Hill Ryerson, 1987), p. 88.

63. Matheson, *The Prime Minister and the Cabinet*, p. 178.

64. G. Bruce Doern and Peter Aucoin, eds., *The Structures of Policy-Making in Canada* (Toronto: Macmillan, 1971); *Public Policy in Canada* (Toronto: Macmillan, 1979); Colin Campbell and George Szablowski, *The Superbureaucrats* (Toronto: Macmillan, 1979); and Peter Aucoin, "Organizational

Change in the Machinery of Canadian Government: From Rational Management to Brokerage Politics," *Canadian Journal of Political Science* (March 1986).

65. Peter Aucoin, "Organizational Change in the Machinery of Canadian Government."

66. Punnett, *The Prime Minister*, p. 110; Walter Stewart, *Shrug: Trudeau in Power* (Toronto: New Press, 1971), ch. 11.

67. Aucoin, "Organizational Change in the Machinery of Canadian Government."

68. Savoie, *Governing from the Centre*, p. 325; Jocelyne Bourgon, *Third Annual Report to the Prime Minister on the Public Service of Canada* (Ottawa: Privy Council Office, 1995), p. 16; and Christopher Dunn, "The Central Executive in Canadian Government: Searching for the Holy Grail," in Christopher Dunn, ed., *The Handbook of Canadian Public Administration* (Toronto: Oxford University Press, 2002).

69. Earlier Cabinet committees were primarily used in the First and Second World Wars. See descriptions in Punnett, *The Prime Minister in Canadian Government and Politics*, pp. 72–74, and Matheson, *The Prime Minister and the Cabinet*, pp. 83–87.

70. This account is based on PCO documents as well as interviews with key PCO officials, especially Tomo Yokoyama, for which I am extremely grateful.

71. Prime Minister's Office, Cabinet Committees, available at http://www.pm.gc.ca/eng/feature .asp?pageId=53, retrieved April 22, 2009.

72. Privy Council Office's document, *Memoranda to Cabinet*, supplemented interviews with PCO officials.

73. Savoie, *Governing from the Centre*, p. 260.

74. Ibid., pp. 7–8, 338.

75. Marc Lalonde, "The Changing Role of the Prime Minister's Office," *Canadian Public Administration* (Winter 1971); Privy Council Office, *Decision-Making Processes and Central Agencies in Canada: Federal, Provincial and Territorial Practices* (Ottawa, 1998), pp. 2–3; and Simpson, *The Friendly Dictatorship*, p. 34.

76. Savoie, *Governing from the Centre*, p. 99; and Thomas Axworthy, "Of Secretaries to Princes," *Canadian Public Administration* (Summer 1988).

77. Whittington, "The Prime Minister, Cabinet, and the Executive Power in Canada."

78. A.D.P. Heeney, *The Things That Are Caesar's* (Toronto: University of Toronto Press, 1972), ch. 6; and Gordon Robertson, "The Changing Role of the Privy Council Office," *Canadian Public Administration* (Winter 1971).

79. Privy Council Office, *The Role and Structure of the Privy Council Office* (Ottawa, 2008), p. 1. Patrice Dutil, ed., *Searching for Leadership: Secretaries to Cabinet in Canada* (Toronto: University of Toronto Press, 2008).

80. Privy Council Office, "About the Clerk"; available at http://www.pco-bcp.gc.ca, retrieved on April 22, 2009.

81. Privy Council Office, *Decision-Making Processes and Central Agencies in Canada*, p. 3.

82. Ibid.

83. Much of the early success of the Harper government was attributed to the advice of Privy Council Clerk Kevin Lynch, who apparently had a good relationship with Harper's Chief of Staff Ian Brodie; but Lynch found the new Chief of Staff, Guy Giorno, more difficult to work with and decided to retire in favour of new Clerk, Wayne Wouters.

84. Donald Savoie's description, *Governing from the Centre*, ch. 5.

85. Commission of Inquiry into the Sponsorship Program and Advertising Activities, *Restoring Accountability* (Ottawa: Minister of Public Works and Government Services, 2006), p. 147.

86. Donald J. Savoie, *The Politics of Public Spending in Canada* (Toronto: University of Toronto Press, 1990), ch. 4.

87. Edward Greenspon and Anthony Wilson-Smith, *Double Vision: The Inside Story of the Liberals in Power* (Toronto: Doubleday Canada, 1996).

88. Savoie, *The Politics of Public Spending in Canada*, ch. 5.

89. Matheson, *The Prime Minister and the Cabinet*, pp. 121–25.

90. John Porter, *The Vertical Mosaic* (Toronto: University of Toronto Press, 1965), ch. XVII.

91. F.H. Underhill, *In Search of Canadian Liberalism*, quoted in Hockin, *Apex of Power*, p. 290.

92. "Mackenzie King genuinely believed and frequently said that the real secret of political leadership was more in what was prevented than in what was accomplished." Pickersgill, *The Mackenzie King Record*, vol. 1, p. 10.
93. David Taras, "Prime Ministers and the Media," in Pal and Taras, *Prime Ministers and Premiers*, p. 38.

. . . .

FURTHER READING

Bliss, Michael. *Right Honourable Men: The Descent of Canadian Politics from Macdonald to Chrétien.* Toronto: HarperCollins, 2004.

Dunn, Christopher, ed. *The Handbook of Canadian Public Administration.* Toronto: Oxford University Press, 2002.

Forcese, Craig, and Allan Freeman. *The Laws of Government: The Legal Foundations of Canadian Democracy.* Toronto: Irwin Law, 2005.

Goldenberg, Eddie. *The Way It Works: Inside Ottawa.* Toronto: McClelland & Stewart, 2006.

Greenspon, Edward, and Anthony Wilson-Smith. *Double Vision: The Inside Story of the Liberals in Power.* Toronto: Doubleday Canada, 1996.

Heard, Andrew. *Canadian Constitutional Conventions.* Toronto: Oxford University Press, 1991.

Matheson, W.A. *The Prime Minister and the Cabinet.* Toronto: Methuen, 1976.

McWhinney, Edward. *The Governor General and the Prime Ministers: The Making and Unmaking of Governments.* Vancouver: Ronsdale Press, 2005.

Pal, Leslie A. *Beyond Policy Analysis: Public Issue Management in Turbulent Times*, 3rd ed. Toronto: Thomson Nelson, 2006.

Privy Council Office. *Accountable Government: A Guide for Ministers and Ministers of State.* Ottawa, Government of Canada, 2008.

Savoie, Donald J. *Governing from the Centre: The Concentration of Power in Canadian Politics.* Toronto: University of Toronto Press, 1999.

Simpson, Jeffrey. *The Friendly Dictatorship.* Toronto: McClelland and Stewart, 2001.

Smith, David E. *The Invisible Crown.* Toronto: University of Toronto Press, 1995.

———. *The Republican Option in Canada, Past and Present.* Toronto: University of Toronto Press, 1999.

White, Graham. *Cabinets and First Ministers.* Vancouver: UBC Press, 2004.

Whittington, Michael S. "The Prime Minister, Cabinet, and Executive Power." In Michael Whittington and Glen Williams, eds., *Canadian Politics in the 21st Century*, 7th ed. Toronto: Thomson Nelson, 2008.

Chapter 22

THE BUREAUCRACY

Federal public servants deliver the mail, issue old age security cheques and passports, process income tax and GST forms, admit immigrants, approve new drugs and search for illicit ones, guard penitentiaries, negotiate treaties with domestic Aboriginals as well as with foreign countries, and provide myriad other services that are often taken for granted by the general public. For the most part, the federal bureaucracy performs these functions in a more than satisfactory manner, but if any hitch occurs, Canadians are quick to condemn the "red tape" and "slow-moving bureaucrats" in Ottawa. Whether such faults are more characteristic of government than of large, private-sector corporations and whether the downsizing of the bureaucracy in the 1990s changed its methods of operation for better or worse remain open questions.

Even though the bureaucracy, or public service, is generally not as visible as the other three branches of government, it is no less important. Most citizens encounter public servants in the provision of services, but the bureaucracy is probably even more significant in its advisory role. Modern government is so pervasive and complex that the prime minister and ministers hardly ever make a move without the advice of their permanent, expert staff. Most public servants work in various government departments, but these are supplemented by a vast array of Crown corporations and administrative agencies of many kinds. In fact, the bureaucracy has become so large and indispensable that many observers wonder whether it can be kept under political control.

This chapter begins by examining the functions and powers of the bureaucracy. It then deals in turn with the three main kinds of bureaucratic organization: the government department, the Crown corporation, and administrative agencies. The chapter concludes with a discussion of controlling the bureaucracy and recent attempts to reform it.

FUNCTIONS AND POWERS OF THE BUREAUCRACY

The traditional function of the bureaucracy is that of policy implementation—that is, administering policies established by the prime minister, Cabinet, and Parliament. Although this is still an important part of its work, the bureaucracy is equally involved in the function of policy-making. Besides advising the politicians in their capacity as rule makers, the bureaucracy is delegated wide "quasi-legislative" powers to make subordinate rules on its own. And although the courts are the foremost adjudicators of disputes in society, the bureaucracy has also encroached on their territory in the adjudication function, such that many disputes are now resolved by "quasi-judicial" regulatory tribunals. Less formally, the bureaucracy engages in interest articulation, in the sense of various departments speaking up for their own concerns or helping to advance the demands of their principal clientele, and it also has an important communications role in seeking out the views of the public and transmitting the government's response.

If the significance of the bureaucracy can be seen in its performance of all of these functions, this can also be demonstrated by examining its presence in the model of the policy-making process presented in Chapter 20. First, it plays a crucial part in the initiation phase. The bureaucracy may be a source of demands, whether these are self-interested or on behalf of its clientele, since administrators of a program may be among the first to recognize its inadequacies. Even if a demand reaches the prime minister and Cabinet from other sources, once the politicians decide to look into an issue further, the public service will usually be asked to provide them with additional information and advice.

If the prime minister and Cabinet decide to take action at the priority-setting stage, the bureaucracy is then centrally involved in the policy formulation phase. With its concentration of technical information and experience, the public service spends a great deal of its time in formulating policies, since the details of such policies are usually beyond the grasp of the politicians. This phase may also involve extensive contact with useful sources of expertise beyond the walls of government.

Once the policy, program, or law has received political authorization in the legitimization phase, implementation is almost exclusively a bureaucratic responsibility. Because of the time and informational constraints on Parliament, most bills are passed in rather general or skeletal form, and the real meat or substance of the law is expressed in the **regulations** issued under it. These are published under the authority of the minister or Cabinet in the *Canada Gazette*. The implementation of a law may thus see the bureaucracy making decisions that constitute quasi-legislative outputs that involve time-consuming negotiations with the provinces or with relevant interest groups.

Once the date set for the start of a new program arrives, it is the bureaucracy that actually provides the service, does the regulating, or performs whatever other activities are necessary to apply the law. Implementation also requires disseminating information to the public about new policies or programs. Governments now spend great quantities of public funds advertising their programs on the grounds that this is essential if they are to be fully effective. A final aspect of implementation is program evaluation—that is, an assessment of the adequacies of a policy after a period of operation. Program evaluation is becoming a more sophisticated addition to the field of policy analysis.

Given its role in almost all phases of the policymaking process, reference to "bureaucratic power" in political science or contentions that the bureaucracy is more powerful than the legislature or even the prime minister and Cabinet should not be surprising. It is more conventional to say that the prime minister and Cabinet make the most important decisions in the political system and that they theoretically control the bureaucracy. The bureaucrats *advise* on almost every decision, but the prime minister and ministers actually *make* the political decisions. Donald Savoie argues that career officials "respond whenever *clear* and *consistent* political direction is given,"[1] but this is not to deny the extent of bureaucratic power in the modern state.

It is difficult to pin down exactly how many people work for the Government of Canada, partly because they are divided into many and sometimes ambiguous categories. In regular departments, the number is probably about 200 000, but when all the assorted agencies are added, it grows to about 400 000 people, which includes 65 000 armed forces personnel and 20 000 in the RCMP. Then about 100 000 people work in federal business enterprises, making a grand total of about half a million people, which includes both part-time and full-time employees.[2]

. . . .

GOVERNMENT DEPARTMENTS
Number, Structure, and Size

Government **departments** are created and reorganized by Acts of Parliament, which also set out the responsibilities of each. But the prime minister and Cabinet can determine the internal structure of the department and even have the power to transfer responsibilities from one department to another.

A major consolidation of departments took place under Prime Minister Kim Campbell in 1993, reducing the overall number from 25 to 20. The most significant changes were the creation of Human Resources Development Canada, which incorporated employment, welfare, and labour; and Canadian Heritage, made up of secretary of state, multiculturalism, and communications. Table 22.1 lists the size of government departments as of 2008.

TABLE 22.1 Size of Work Force of Government Departments, 2008	
Agriculture and Agri-Food	6396
Canadian Heritage	2075
Citizenship and Immigration	3731
Environment	5964
Finance	1039
Fisheries and Oceans	9692
Foreign Affairs and International Trade	4272
Health	8935
Human Resources and Skills Development	22 259
Indian Affairs and Northern Development	4026
Industry	5220
Justice	5013
National Defence	24 064
Natural Resources	4264
Privy Council Office	743
Public Safety	837
Public Works and Government Services	12 197
Transport	4897
Treasury Board Secretariat	1042
Veterans Affairs	3816
Western Economic Diversification	377

Source: Employment Equity in the Public Service of Canada 2006–2007 and 2007–2008. Found at: http://www.tbs-sct.gc.ca/rp/0608ee06-eng.asp. Treasury Board of Canada Secretariat, 2008. Reproduced with the permission of the Minister of Public Works and Government Services Canada, 2009.

The government department assumes a pyramidal shape, with the minister at its apex. Since ministers in this system (unlike in the United States) are chosen from among the politicians elected to Parliament, it is too much to hope that they will be experts in the work of the department or able managers. All that is expected is that they are individuals with intelligence, ideas, common sense, and an ability to relay government priorities and public opinion to departmental experts as well as to relate expert advice from the department to Parliament and the public. Ministers will naturally develop some expertise if they stay in one Cabinet position for any length of time, but nowadays they are often shuffled to another department just as they are getting the hang of it.

Responsibility and Accountability at the Top of the Department

Ministers are responsible for their department in the sense that they are expected to provide overall direction and accept criticism for its faults. In other words, ministers take most of the credit or blame for what the department does, whether or not they know what is going on within it. As pointed out in Chapter 21, the principle of individual **ministerial responsibility** was once thought to mean that ministers had to resign over serious mistakes made by their public servants, even if unaware of the errors. Whether this theory was ever practised in Canada is questionable—there are no cases of such resignations since 1867—but certainly in this age of big government it is not a realistic proposition. What does ministerial responsibility mean today? First, ministers occasionally resign over their personal mistakes, but not as routinely as in Britain. Second, they must take political responsibility and answer to Parliament for all the actions of their officials. The minister must explain and defend the actions of the department in Parliament, especially during Question Period, and when a bureaucratic error is made, the minister must apologize and promise to correct the mistake. Third, although ministers may discreetly discipline the offender, they should not violate the traditions of public-service anonymity.[3]

Several serious bureaucratic errors occurred during the Chrétien regime that prompted much questioning of the notion of responsibility and accountability. One was in Human Resources Development Canada (HRDC) in the 1990s in connection with its job-creation programs. Since no one accepted responsibility for the fiasco, the auditor general had this to say in his final report: "Canada has never modernized its doctrine to distinguish between the minister's area of public responsibility and that of his senior public servants. To me, there is a certain lack of realism in holding ministers ultimately accountable for everything."[4] The second major bureaucratic blunder concerned the massive overspending of the national gun registry, and the third was the infamous sponsorship scandal. The apparent lack of accountability in these cases will be further addressed toward the end of the chapter.

The more permanent head of the department is the **deputy minister**. Appointed by the prime minister (on the advice of the secretary to the Cabinet), "deputies" or "DMs" are usually career public servants. In other words, they are rarely patronage appointments. Deputy ministers have two principal roles: they act as chief policy adviser to the minister and function as manager of the department; they, not the minister, run the department.[5] This again raises the question of whether DMs should therefore be responsible for departmental mistakes. Such officials used to spend a lifetime working their way to the top of a single department and became great experts in its subject matter. Since the 1962 Glassco Report, which recommended the adoption of private-sector managerial techniques in the public sector, emphasis in the appointment of deputy ministers has switched from expertise in the subject matter of the department to managerial skills that can be applied in any administrative setting. In recent years they, too, have been frequently shuffled from one department to another. Even so, the deputy minister is usually in the department longer than the minister and is thus likely to develop greater knowledge of its work. Deputy ministers also interact regularly with DMs in other federal departments, provincial DMs in corresponding departments, and the heads of advocacy groups particularly interested in the department's work.[6]

The relationship between the minister and the deputy minister is of great interest and concern to political science and public administration.[7] In theory, the minister sets the priorities for the department, based to some extent on the party platform, the prime minister's objectives, and the minister's own projects. Whether in determining priorities or in implementing them, the DM ideally provides a number of options among which the minister can choose. The deputy should give the minister advice that is not only based on administrative, technical, and financial considerations but is also sensitive to the political context. Evidence exists that the reality of the relationship sometimes approaches this theoretical ideal. However, weak ministers may be mere puppets of their bureaucratic advisers, and even strong ministers may encounter bureaucratic resistance to new initiatives, such as in being denied relevant information, having it delayed, or in having new policies implemented without enthusiasm.[8] In any case, ministers are busy doing other things and do not spend much time in their departmental offices. In most cases (Finance being an exception), the minister and deputy minister only see each other during a weekly briefing session.[9]

Besides their loyalty to their department, deputy ministers nowadays have strong links to the centre of government, especially the Privy Council Office. The clerk of the Privy Council chairs weekly deputy minister committee meetings, monthly luncheons, and semi-annual retreats. Deputy ministers have been appointed by the centre, their promotion prospects depend on "the centre," and they spend a great deal of their time "managing sensitive files for the centre."[10] Through the clerk, deputy ministers have a connection to the prime minister that increasingly approaches the importance of the relationship with their own minister. The problem of deputy ministers' reconciling their loyalty to their minister and to the clerk and the PCO was singled out for considerable attention in the Gomery Report.[11]

Exempt Staff

It is not easy for a single, solitary, temporary, amateur minister to impose his or her will on the deputy minister and the hundreds or thousands of other expert, permanent public servants who have established departmental attitudes, values, policies, and procedures. In this situation, the small personal staff that ministers are allowed to appoint may be of some assistance. The "political" or **exempt staff** provides ministers with advisers and assistants who share their political commitment and who can complement the professional, expert, and nonpartisan advice and support of the public service. The exempt staff is primarily engaged in promoting the image and reputation of the minister and doing favours for supporters and friends. Although they may provide partisan policy advice, any effort to interfere in the administration of the department will be strongly resented by the deputy minister.[12] In the Mulroney regime, ministers set up large offices headed by a powerful chief of staff whose authority rivalled that of the deputy minister and who was, among other things, the target of most lobbying efforts. As in other ways, Chrétien reverted to an earlier era by reducing the size and significance of ministerial offices, and one sign of the lesser importance of such offices was that lobbyists transferred their attention to the bureaucracy.

Exempt staff became another issue at the **Gomery Inquiry** for two reasons. First, it was a common practice to leave the minister's office to become lobbyists, and second, those who had worked for a minister for at least three years were allowed to slip into public service positions at the same level as they previously occupied.[13] Stephen Harper agreed: his **Federal Accountability Act** prohibited ministers, staffers, and senior public servants from becoming lobbyists for five years after leaving office, and required ministerial staffers to compete for internal job postings.

Although the policy differences among Canadian parties are usually rather small, Opposition parties often accuse the public service of becoming too sympathetic to a longstanding government party (e.g., in the 1935–57 and 1963–84 Liberal periods). But the Diefenbaker, Clark, and Mulroney Cabinets felt a need for bureaucratic expertise and did not rid themselves of more than one or two senior officials. The Harper government undertook a major internal shuffle of senior officials, but stopped short of dismissals. At the provincial level, however, this issue has on occasion been a problem for NDP governments or those that followed them.

The Rest of the Department

Below the deputy minister, the department is typically divided into several branches, each headed by an assistant deputy minister (ADM); these in turn are subdivided again and again. Figure 22.1 illustrates the hierarchical structure of a hypothetical government department. Those divisions of a department that actually carry out services and interact with the public are said to be performing "line" functions. Except for the top managerial posts, most of the line positions in any department will be located in the "field"—in local offices in communities across the country. But every department will also have "staff" divisions that serve such internal needs as policy development and research, personnel, financial, information, and

· · · · · · · · · · · · · · · · · · · ·

Figure 22.1 Organizational Chart of a Hypothetical Government Department

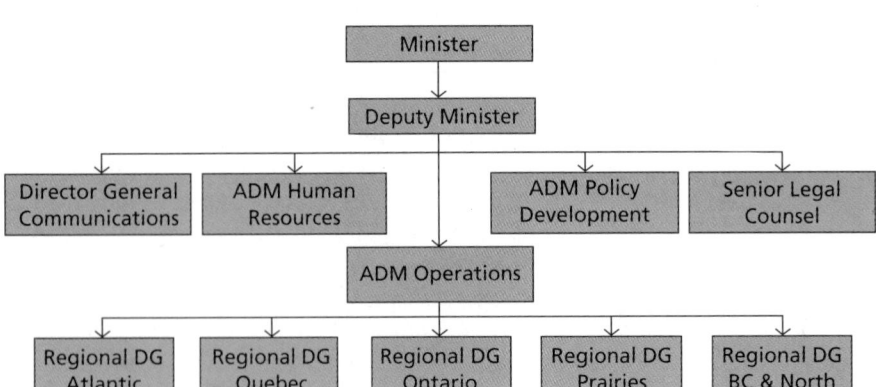

legal services. These positions are normally located in Ottawa along with the heads of the line divisions.

The hundreds or thousands of public servants in the department are ranged in descending levels of authority under the deputy minister and share four basic characteristics: they are expert, permanent, impartial, and anonymous. First, they are chosen on their merits—ability, knowledge, training, or experience—for the duties their positions entail. Second, they are career public servants, who normally remain within the public service until retirement. Third, they are nonpartisan and expected to serve whichever party comes to power with equal loyalty and enthusiasm. Fourth, bureaucrats are not normally identified in public; instead, the minister speaks for the department and takes the public and parliamentary responsibility for its performance. Even when public servants brief the media about new policies, for example, they are only referred to as "officials of the department."

The federal public service is divided into six occupational categories, within which are a large number of more specific occupational groups:

1. Executive group (e.g., senior management)
2. Scientific and professional (e.g., nursing, auditing)
3. Administrative and foreign service (e.g., personnel administration, program administration)
4. Technical (e.g., drafting)
5. Administrative support (e.g., clerical and regulatory, secretarial and stenographic)
6. Operational (e.g., correctional, firefighter)

Relations with Other Departments and Central Agencies

The operation of a government department is complicated by the necessity of interacting with other departments as well as by the authority of various central agencies to intervene in its affairs. Since almost any law, policy, or program affects a variety of departments, many interdepartmental committees exist. Beyond these, whenever a new policy is under active consideration, an ad hoc interdepartmental committee is appointed to look into it. Not only must the problem be examined from a number of departmental perspectives, but it is also subject to considerable bureaucratic "politics" and territorial claims. Ministers as well as deputy ministers constantly have to reconcile their departmental interests with the need to coordinate their activities with other departments, and they generally cannot act unilaterally if such action would have any impact on other departments' programs or policies. The increasing necessity of collaboration among a number of departments and agencies in the development of a new law, policy, or program is labelled **horizontal management**.[14]

The central agencies that complicate the life of a department include the Public Service Commission (PSC), the Treasury Board Secretariat (TBS), the Privy Council Office (PCO), the Department of Finance, and the Prime Minister's Office (PMO), most of which were mentioned in Chapter 21. The **Public Service Commission** is a three-member board that safeguards the principles of competence, nonpartisanship, and representation, and that is theoretically in charge of all hiring, promotions, and dismissals. In practice, however, the PSC delegates much of its authority to deputy ministers in individual departments.

It is primarily concerned with policing the merit system—that is, preventing appointments and promotions from being made on partisan or discriminatory grounds.

The **Treasury Board Secretariat** was discussed in Chapter 21, but its role merits re-emphasis, especially in human resources, financial, and expenditure management. The TBS essentially determines the terms and conditions of employment for the public service. It is in charge of the classification or reclassification of positions and represents the employer in the collective bargaining process. On the financial management side, the TBS is responsible for the preparation of the Estimates, which normally involves cutting back on departmental spending proposals. The TBS also establishes the policy framework in such areas as information technology, contracting, and accounting; oversees the actual expenditure of public funds; and tries to improve departmental management through such devices as program evaluation.[15] Along with the TBS, the **Department of Finance** is usually an opponent of new department spending programs and an advocate of retrenchment.

Under the 2003 Public Service Modernization Act, even more flexibility was delegated from the PSC and the TBS to departmental deputy ministers in the hiring process. In fact, the definition of "merit" was changed to eliminate the necessity of competitions as long as the candidate met the "essential qualifications for the work to be performed." Rather than do their own hiring, however, departments increasingly rely on private employment agencies to furnish them with candidates. In 2009, the human resources functions of the Canada Public Service Agency were reintegrated with the TBS under the new Office of the Chief Human Resources Officer.

The Privy Council Office's relations with regular government departments have also been referred to above. They primarily arise in connection with policy development and coordination, the reallocation of programs among departments, the reorganization of departments, and senior management appointments. Although the deputy minister will probably have had a hand in the mandate letter given to the new minister of the department, these letters are ultimately drafted by the PCO with the approval of the PM. The PCO will also take a great interest in any new policy proposal emanating from the department, typically in a Memorandum to Cabinet. The Prime Minister's Office, however, does not interact frequently with departments except with respect to new policy initiatives or political problems (i.e., crises) engaging the prime minister.

The Merit Principle and a Representative Bureaucracy

For about 40 years after Confederation, the Canadian public service operated on the **spoils system**, under which the party that won an election could replace those holding civil service positions with its own friends and supporters. One of the main motives for entering the political arena in that era was to reward family and friends with **political patronage**—government jobs and contracts.[16] Such partisan, amateur personnel proved to be increasingly inadequate as government operations grew more complex after the turn of the century, hence the passage of the Civil Service Amendment Act in 1908, which created the Civil Service Commission (predecessor to the Public Service Commission). It meant that public servants in Ottawa were hired on the **merit system**, and, after the adoption of the 1918 Civil Service Act, field positions were also to be based on merit. Politicians, however, were reluctant to give up their traditional right to reward their supporters with government jobs, and it is difficult to say exactly when the merit system was finally entrenched. The foundations of the modern merit system in Ottawa were laid in the 1930s at External Affairs, Finance, and the Bank of Canada.[17]

Almost as soon as the merit system was fully effective, the call began to be made that the bureaucracy should be more representative of the society it served. Given the power of the public service and the assumption that its recommendations and decisions would reflect the origins, identities, and pre-public-service values of its members, many critics argued that the public service could be responsive to all parts of society only if it included a proportional representation of various groups in the population. The senior levels of the public service had always overrepresented males, anglophones, the middle and upper classes, the well educated, and Ontarians.[18] Thus, it was claimed that policy recommendations and implementation reflected an insensitivity to women, francophones, and other minority ethnocultural groups, to the peculiarities of hinterland regions and provinces, and to the working class and the poor.

The first main concerns in the establishment of a **representative bureaucracy** were the small number of francophones in the higher reaches of the bureaucracy and the virtual absence of the use of the French language at the policymaking levels. The passage of the **Official Languages Act** of 1969 essentially made the executive branch of government bilingual. It gave both English- and French-speaking citizens the right to deal with head offices of government departments in either official language, as well as with local offices where numbers warranted. It also expanded language-training programs started by the Pearson government in 1964, made recruitment and promotion of francophones a higher priority, and designated certain positions as bilingual. The Treasury Board Secretariat was given authority to oversee the whole language-policy program, and the position of commissioner of official languages was created to be responsible for assessing the implementation of the policy, dealing with complaints, and reporting back to Parliament. It was fortunate that the Quebec educational system had improved by this time so that the new policy involved little or no loss of quality in government appointments and promotions. It did, however, ignite a backlash against the preference given to French Canadians and to bilingualism.

As of 2004, 39 percent of public service positions (64 938) had been designated as bilingual, 50 percent (83 354) as English-essential, five percent (8010) as French-essential, and another six percent (9009) as requiring either official language. It has thus become increasingly indispensable for public service executives to be bilingual. In 1998, for example, new second-language proficiency requirements were imposed for those at or aspiring to the assistant deputy minister level, and in 2003–04, the official bilingualism policy across the whole public service was further strengthened. By 2009, 70 percent of public servants declared English to be their first official language and 30 percent declared French.[19] Given that French mother tongue constitutes less than 25 percent of the population in general, francophones are now overrepresented at every level, which is probably because they are mostly bilingual.

Women also began to be targeted for increased representation in the higher levels of the public service in the 1960s and 1970s.[20] In addition, the pay equity program of the 1980s and 1990s was primarily designed to ensure that women received equal pay for doing work that had the same value as that done by men. It is not easy to compare the value of dissimilar jobs, but many occupational groups made up largely of women have had their salaries increased as a result. The government and the Public Service Alliance of Canada (PSAC) fought for years over a union demand for back-pay for some 200 000 current and former secretaries and clerks, largely women. The union won at both the Canadian Human Rights Commission and the Federal Court of Canada, leading to a $3.6 billion negotiated settlement. In 2009, the Harper government removed pay equity issues from the CHRC and made them subject to the collective bargaining process.

The next stage of making the public service more representative of society came in 1983, when an explicit affirmative action program was adopted for women, Aboriginals, and people with disabilities; two years later the list was expanded to include members of visible minorities. Once again, this did not necessarily result in a decline in the quality of appointments and promotions, but it sparked opposition from those who did not fall into the designated categories. A new Employment Equity Act in 1995 required identification and elimination of employment barriers against persons in the four designated groups and the adoption of positive policies and practices that would ensure that such people achieved a degree of representation in each occupational group proportional to their numbers in the Canadian work force. Table 22.2 indicates the number and percentage of people in the four designated groups in each of the six main occupational categories. In terms of workplace availability, women, Aboriginals, and people with disabilities are slightly overrepresented in the federal public service, while members of visible minorities are somewhat underrepresented. Women make up over 40 percent of the Executive group and over 80 percent of the Administrative Support category. The employment equity program extends to corporations with federal government contracts worth $200 000 or more, but it has probably had little impact on such companies.

The Estimates System

As noted at several earlier points in the book, the authorities spend a great deal of their time discussing the expenditure of public funds. Members of Parliament want money for their constituencies, premiers and federal ministers press to get funds for their provinces, and bureaucrats seek funding for their programs and departments. In addition, much of the pressure on the authorities from interest groups, lobbyists, and corporations consists of demands for federal funds. In earlier eras such spending was the prerogative of individual politicians or governing parties and was carried out on a patronage basis.[21] Nowadays, the spending process has been highly bureaucratized, and it is the function of the **Estimates** system to decide how such funds will be allocated in any fiscal year. The Estimates documents provide more than just the amount of money that each department and agency plans to spend in the next fiscal year: they are a valuable source of information on departmental plans and priorities and also contain departmental performance reports.

Under the current expenditure management system, the Cabinet decides on the advice of the Finance department, the Treasury Board Secretariat, and the Privy Council Office what the government's financial priorities and overall level of government revenue and expenditure will be. New policy proposals and new spending initiatives must also be specifically approved at this level. The whole budgetary process has been portrayed as a contest between "spenders" and "guardians."[22] The spenders are most of the ministers and departments in whose interest it is to increase their budgets. Spenders try to introduce new programs and expand existing ones in order to raise their prestige and enhance the support of their clientele. The guardians are essentially the minister of finance and the president of the Treasury Board, along with their respective departments, which are ordinarily seen as villains by almost everyone else involved.

Many government programs are automatically funded by the statutes that create them. The expenditures for these programs, called "statutory appropriations," cannot be changed without amending the relevant statutes; they are therefore more or less fixed and uncontrollable.

TABLE 22.2 Public Service by Employment Equity Groups, 2007–2008

	Women		Aboriginals		People with Disabilities		Members of a Visible Minority Group		Total
	Number	%	Number	%	Number	%	Number	%	Number
Executive	2042	41.7	165	3.4	278	5.7	326	6.7	4898
Scientific & Professional	12 385	45.3	697	2.5	1094	4.0	3662	13.4	27 350
Administrative & Foreign Service	55 832	61.8	4121	4.6	5554	6.2	8533	9.5	90 284
Technical	5663	32.5	612	3.5	896	5.1	1106	6.3	17 422
Administrative Support	21 719	80.9	1395	5.2	2093	7.8	2730	10.2	26 849
Operational	3948	19.8	1200	6.0	1086	5.4	850	4.3	19 951
Total	101 589	54.4	8190	4.4	11 001	5.9	17 207	9.2	186 754

Source: Employment Equity in the Public Service of Canada 2006–2007 and 2007–2008. Found at: http://www.tbs-sct.gc.ca/rp/0608ee06-eng.asp. Treasury Board of Canada Secretariat, 2008. Reproduced with the permission of the Minister of Public Works and Government Services Canada, 2009.

Since these appropriations constitute about three-quarters of the total budget, they seriously limit the Cabinet's discretion in altering the level or pattern of government expenditure.

The preparation of the Estimates involves projections of the cost of new and existing programs at the departmental level within the limits and guidelines laid down by higher authorities. A great deal of interaction between the managerial personnel of each department and the Treasury Board Secretariat takes place, as deputy ministers and ministers try to maximize their departmental allocations while TBS personnel engage in cutting them back. At the end of the process, the Estimates are consolidated for Cabinet approval and introduced into Parliament by the president of the Treasury Board before the beginning of the next fiscal year. They now consist of a separate volume for each department and agency. Since the Estimates are prepared so far in advance of actual spending, several sets of Supplementary Estimates are usually necessary to provide for unforeseen contingencies throughout the fiscal year.

Departmental Interaction with Provinces and the Public

Ministers and leading departmental officials do not interact only with other ministers and other officials within the federal government. Two other common forms of interaction are with the provinces and with external policy advisers and advocates and the public.

As noted in Chapter 18, much of the interaction between federal and provincial governments takes place at the bureaucratic level. Because the division of powers between federal and provincial governments is often vague and because both levels usually try to maximize their jurisdiction, the two levels end up operating programs in the same fields. Limitations on provincial finances have also prompted the provinces to request federal financial assistance, to which Ottawa has usually attached conditions, making itself even more intertwined with provincial governments. At the height of cooperative federalism, federal and provincial program administrators would interact harmoniously in the design and operation of such integrated programs.[23] It is still the case that in almost every federal department, officials interact regularly with their provincial counterparts, often by letter, fax, e-mail, or telephone, and sometimes more formally in federal–provincial conferences at the bureaucratic level.

In addition to such vertical department-to-department interaction, each level of government has set up bureaucratic agencies to supervise federal–provincial relations. Although these central agencies are necessary to keep track of the maze of such interaction and although they may facilitate federal–provincial bureaucratic cooperation in some instances, they often complicate the friendly relations that individual federal departments have established with their provincial counterparts.

The close relationship between advocacy groups and the bureaucracy was already discussed in Chapter 16. Groups that want to influence either the formulation or the implementation of policies and programs are active in taking their message to the relevant government department. Sometimes public servants resist the approach of self-seeking groups, but at other times the department may actually welcome it, especially if the group has vital, reliable information that will lead to the development of a more effective program, if the group can help muster support for the departmental initiative among other key players in the policymaking process, or if it can serve as a channel of communication to that part of the public that is interested in the particular proposal.

These mutually advantageous contacts between a group and a department may become so close and congenial that a symbiotic **clientele relationship** develops. The department gives official recognition to the group, regularly consults it on policy development and implementation, and gives it representation on advisory committees. It is in this connection that Chapters 16 and 20 spoke of policy communities and policy networks. Where such a congenial, supportive group does not already exist, it may even be necessary for the department to create it.[24]

As has been mentioned earlier, it is partly because the government lost much of its policy analysis capacity in the severe downsizing of the 1990s that bureaucrats depend more heavily on outside advice today. It may also be that that era had the effect of enhancing the value of public consultation (and polling). For example, 2001 produced an Accord between the Government of Canada and the voluntary sector, which committed both sides to extensive interaction. Another factor is probably that more outside information is available than ever before, whether in universities, advocacy groups, research institutes, or think tanks. Some of the latter include the Canadian Centre for Policy Alternatives, the Institute for Research on Public Policy, the Canadian Tax Foundation, the C.D. Howe Institute, and the Canada West Foundation. In any case, it is almost as normal nowadays for bureaucrats to seek out information and support from outside actors as it is for advocacy groups to impose pressure on their own initiative.[25]

. . . .
CROWN CORPORATIONS

The second most important form of bureaucratic organization is the **Crown corporation**. These are government-owned operations that assume a structure similar to a private corporation. Crown corporations may be private firms that have been nationalized by the government by buying their shares (CN and Petro-Canada), they may be transformed from regular departments (Canada Post), or, most typically in Canada, they may be created from scratch (Canada Mortgage and Housing Corporation). Canada has about 45 parent Crown corporations at the federal level, which have a total of about 60 subsidiaries. Table 22.3 lists some

TABLE 22.3 Major Federal Crown Corporations and Number of Employees, 2008	
Canada Post Corporation	61 557
Canadian Broadcasting Corporation	7784
Atomic Energy of Canada Ltd.	4728
VIA Rail Canada Inc.	3017
Canada Mortgage and Housing Corporation	1888
Business Development Bank of Canada	1732
Bank of Canada	1183
Export Development Canada	1068
Farm Credit Canada	1457

Source: Annual Report to Parliament - Crown Corporations and Other Corporate Interests of Canada 2008. Found at: http://www.tbs-sct.gc.ca/reports-rapports/cc-se/2008/cc-sepr-eng.asp?format=print (Accessed April 23, 2009). Treasury Board of Canada Secretariat, 2008. Reproduced with the permission of the Minister of Public Works and Government Services Canada, 2009.

major federal Crown corporations and the number of people they employ. In total, Crown corporations have over 90 000 employees.

The corporate structure referred to includes a board of directors, president, vice-presidents, and general manager. The Cabinet appoints the president or CEO and the board of directors, which theoretically set the general policy of the corporation. Many patronage appointments to the CEO position were made in the past, some of the most controversial by the Chrétien government, and it fell to Paul Martin to fire the partisan heads of Canada Post, VIA Rail, and the Royal Canadian Mint. The Cabinet also appoints the directors, who often have even less credibility, normally being part-time, patronage appointees. The auditor general pointed out that Crown corporation boards were packed with partisans lacking the basic skills needed to oversee such large businesses, and the Gomery Report called for an end to political involvement of CEOs and directors of Crown corporations.[26] The Harper government planned to establish a Public Appointments Commission for this purpose, but abandoned the idea when its choice of chair was rejected by opposition parties.

A second distinguishing feature of the Crown corporation is that it is not subject to day-to-day political direction. The statute that creates the corporation sets out its objectives to some extent and the Cabinet may issue certain general policy guidelines, but the corporation otherwise operates more or less independently. The Cabinet minister to whom the Crown corporation is attached largely acts as a channel of communication between it and Parliament, passing on answers to parliamentary inquiries but not being held responsible for the corporation in the same way as for a regular department. However, because the government created the Crown corporation, appoints its leading personnel, and usually provides some of its funds, the minister and Cabinet cannot totally avoid responsibility for its actions. Crown corporations must now submit a corporate plan to the minister as well as an annual year-end report to Parliament. In some cases the Cabinet can issue a directive to the corporation if informal persuasion to change its ways has not been effective, and a government can make deep cuts in a Crown corporation's budget, as the CBC repeatedly discovered.

Third, because many of them compete with private-sector firms, Crown corporations are expected to function without undue interference from bureaucratic administrative policies. They are not usually subject to the same personnel supervision of the Public Service Commission, for example, or quite the same financial control of the Treasury Board Secretariat. The Financial Administration Act contains different categories of Crown corporations, ranged in order of increasing independence from government control; as a general rule, the greater the financial self-sufficiency of the corporation, the greater its autonomy.

The Crown corporation is a logical structure for a governmental operation of a commercial or industrial nature; it may also be used in politically sensitive areas, such as broadcasting; and the case for a Crown corporation rather than a department is always stronger if the operation has private-sector competition. Canada once had a unique blend of public and private corporations in such areas as air and rail transportation, broadcasting, and petroleum that led one observer to refer to Canada's "public enterprise" political culture.[27]

Like other government operations, then, Crown corporations have a **public policy purpose**. They are created where, for one reason or another, the private sector has not met public needs, often because no profit would be feasible in serving the widely dispersed Canadian population. The basic objective of Crown corporations is to provide a public service, not to make a profit, but because most Crown corporations need annual public subsidies, they are often criticized for being inefficient. In fact, however, they are usually just as efficient as private companies; the subsidies are necessary to finance operations that are simply unprofitable by any standard.

The 1980s witnessed a worldwide trend toward the **privatization** of public enterprises, led by Margaret Thatcher in Britain, and the Mulroney government happily jumped on the privatization bandwagon. Such privatizations were largely made for ideological reasons: Conservative governments in particular had an instinctive preference for the private sector, and the proceeds from the sale of Crown corporation shares often helped to reduce the national deficit. Sometimes privatizations were undertaken to create an "entrepreneurial climate"—that is, to send a signal to corporations that a jurisdiction was "open for business" and was a place where profits could be made. Privatizers also argued that such Crown corporations no longer served a public policy purpose and that they would operate more efficiently as private companies. Moreover, the leading officials of Air Canada and Petro-Canada themselves recommended privatization in order to allow them to compete more freely with other private companies. When shares are purchased by a broad cross-section of Canadians, or when a nonprofit corporation is established (e.g., St. Lawrence Seaway), the privatization has not been as controversial as when the corporation is sold to a single company or to a foreign firm. Table 22.4 lists some of the main privatizations at the federal level.

By 1993 the new Liberal government claimed, somewhat contentiously, that privatization was no longer an ideological issue. Finance Minister Paul Martin (a "business liberal") argued that privatization freed up scarce resources for deficit reduction or new initiatives, that government was rethinking its role in society, that privatization reduced the scope of government to essentials, and that it improved service delivery, exposed government organizations to competitive business pressures, and broadened ownership of the Canadian economy. Against this background, the government announced that it would privatize the second-largest Crown corporation, the historic Canadian National Railway Company.

Other changes in the operation of Crown corporations are also afoot. In recent years, several—especially local port corporations—have become shared-governance structures. The Canadian Wheat Board also became a shared-governance corporation, with farmers electing 10 out of 15 members of the board of directors. Newly created Crown corporations include the Canada Pension Plan Investment Board, the Canada Employment Insurance Financing

---

TABLE 22.4 Major Federal Privatizations, 1984–2003

Air Canada	Eldorado Nuclear (Cameco)
Canada Development Corporation	Fishery Products International
Canadair	Northern Canada Power Commission
Canadian Arsenals Ltd.	Northern Transportation Company
Canadian Communications Group	Petro-Canada
Canadian National Railway	St. Lawrence Seaway Authority
Co-Enerco Resources	Teleglobe Canada
de Havilland Aircraft	Telesat

Board, and PPP Canada, Inc., a federal public–private partnership designed to promote shared investment in infrastructure projects.

. . . .

ADMINISTRATIVE AGENCIES

Administrative agencies, sometimes called administrative or regulatory tribunals, constitute a third form of bureaucratic organization. Some of the most important are listed in Table 22.5. In structure, most such agencies and tribunals bear considerable resemblance to Crown corporations. They are usually made up of a chair and board, which are appointed by the Cabinet, and advised by a permanent, expert staff. They typically receive policy guidelines from the Cabinet, but ministers are kept at arm's length from their day-to-day operations. Like Crown corporations, they are at least somewhat exempt from the Public Service Employment Act and Treasury Board Secretariat human resource policies. The incidence of partisanship in appointments to the chair and board has unfortunately been quite large: indeed, such agencies remained one of the last refuges of patronage in the political system. Of 36 new members appointed by the Harper government to the National Parole Board, for example, 23 were retired police officers who would be expected to have a "get-tough" approach. Harper also fired the President of the Canadian Nuclear Safety Commission and the President of the Canadian Wheat Board, and quarrelled with or contributed to the resignation of a number of other agency heads.

One specific type of agency, **regulatory tribunals**, may make **quasi-legislative** rules and regulations, such as in the case of the Canadian-content regulations of the **Canadian Radio-television and Telecommunications Commission**. A typical regulatory tribunal also makes **quasi-judicial** decisions based on the Cabinet's policy guidelines and its own regulations.

TABLE 22.5 Leading Agencies, Boards, Commissions, and Tribunals	
Atlantic Canada Opportunities Agency	Canadian Transportation Agency
Canada Border Services Agency	Correctional Service of Canada
Canada Revenue Agency	Immigration and Refugee Board
Canadian Dairy Commission	Library and Archives Canada
Canadian Food Inspection Agency	National Energy Board
Canadian Environmental Assessment Agency	National Film Board
Canadian Human Rights Commission	National Parole Board
Canadian International Development Agency	National Research Council
Canadian Nuclear Safety Commission	Parks Canada Agency
Canadian Radio-television and Telecommunications Commission	Public Health Agency of Canada
	Royal Canadian Mounted Police
Canadian Space Agency	Statistics Canada

They issue radio and television licences, approve long-distance telephone rates (CRTC), decide contentious immigration cases (Immigration and Refugee Board), review transportation rates (Canadian Transportation Agency), approve exports of natural gas and electricity (National Energy Board), and allow prisoners out of jail (National Parole Board).

These functions could presumably be performed by regular government departments, but they are given to semi-independent regulatory tribunals in order to divorce them from political and especially partisan considerations. Such functions are usually of an adjudicative nature and could also be performed by the courts. But these kinds of decisions demand a technical expertise not expected in judges, and it is hoped that the decisions of regulatory agencies will be made more quickly and more cheaply than those of the courts.

At the same time, however, regulatory tribunals are expected to provide an impartial, court-like hearing, and in many cases lawyers are present in the same capacity as in court. Decisions of such agencies are normally appealable to the courts on procedural grounds but not on the substance of the case. Some are appealable to the Cabinet on the merits of the case (e.g., CRTC decisions on long-distance telephone rates), but the Cabinet usually declines to overturn the agency's decision.

Two main criticisms of regulatory tribunals have been made in recent years. On the one hand, it was argued that there are too many regulatory agencies with too much power. Hence, **deregulation** was a companion ingredient to privatization in the neoliberalism of the 1980s and 1990s. The Mulroney government issued a regulatory reform strategy in 1986 and proceeded to deregulate the transportation industry. On the other hand, it is said that regulatory agencies become captives of the very industries they are supposed to be regulating. The agency and the industry operate as their own little policy community, divorced from other influences. In this connection the consumer interest is often overlooked as the regulatory tribunal falls victim to corporate pressure. This problem is sometimes lessened by allowing consumer groups to intervene in the hearings of regulatory tribunals or in government funding of intervener groups.

There is a wide variety of other administrative agencies. Such "structural heretics"[28] include royal commissions, advisory councils like the National Council of Welfare, funding bodies, agents of Parliament, and other one-of-a-kind agencies. The largest such agencies are the Canada Revenue Agency, Canada Border Services Agency, the Canadian Food Inspection Agency, Statistics Canada, and Correction Services of Canada. Some of the most popular are funding agencies, such as the National Research Council and the Social Sciences and Humanities Research Council. These agencies exhibit varying degrees of independence from the minister but generally operate at some distance.

The relationship between the government and independent agencies like the RCMP or the Canadian Security Intelligence Service (CSIS) is always somewhat problematic. The excessive manner in which the RCMP handled protests during the 1997 APEC summit in Vancouver, for example, was partly blamed on directions from the Prime Minister's Office. In an era of anti-terrorism, the secretive activities of such security-related agencies as the RCMP and CSIS, the rivalry between them, and their relations with U.S. agencies have caused considerable concern, such as in the case of the Arar Inquiry.

Agents of Parliament are most independent because they are agencies attached to Parliament rather than to the executive branch of government. They are divorced from the government of the day, either because they are meant to be critical or because they are supposed to serve all members impartially. The principal such agents are listed in Table 22.6.

TABLE 22.6   Agents of Parliament
Auditor General
Chief Electoral Officer
Commissioner of Lobbying
Commissioner of Official Languages
Conflict of Interest and Ethics Commissioner
Information Commissioner
Privacy Commissioner
Public Sector Integrity Commissioner

Royal commissions are a traditional instrument of policy advice, with about 450 having been appointed since 1867. Generally speaking, royal commissions are very formal, in-depth inquiries set up by the Cabinet to investigate some difficult problem for which the resources of the regular public service are considered inadequate. Royal commissions may be made up of from one to ten commissioners, usually people of stature and expertise, and normally involve extensive public hearings and an elaborate research program. They are often regarded somewhat cynically because of the length of time it takes them to produce a report, and because they cost a great deal of money. The cynics also point out that governments have not had a good record of implementing royal commission recommendations and that such commissions are often appointed to take the heat off a particular issue.

Sometimes royal commissions are also seen as devices with which to educate the public to the government's way of thinking or of generating support for a policy the government already had in mind. Nevertheless, many royal commissions have served a useful purpose, and many public policies, such as equalization payments, medicare, official bilingualism, and free trade, owe their existence, at least in part, to royal commission reports. The Royal Commission on Aboriginal Peoples (RCAP) and the Commission on the Future of Health Care are the most significant in recent times. Royal commissions are often referred to by the name of their chair, such as Rowell–Sirois (Federal–Provincial Relations, 1940), Hall (Health Services, 1964–65), Macdonald (Economic Prospects, 1985), and Romanow (Future of Health Care, 2002). Rather than royal commissions, the Harper government appointed a number of small, short-term advisory panels or task forces, such as John Manley's review of Canada's role in Afghanistan and Bernard Lord's study official languages.

CONTROLLING THE BUREAUCRACY

Given the enormous influence and considerable power of the bureaucracy in the modern state, democracies are understandably concerned about keeping the public service under control. A number of means of doing so can be identified.

Prime Minister, Ministers, and Cabinet

In the first place, the prime minister, individual ministers, and the Cabinet as a whole are supposed to provide political control of the bureaucracy. The minister both gives direction to the public service and has the power to veto any of its proposals, at least in theory. Real ministers have provided varied accounts of what actually happens in practice: some argue that ministers can control their departments, while others feel that they were often manipulated by their public servants. Even where the minister in charge is weak or manipulated, however, the prime minister or Cabinet as a whole may step in from time to time to reject bureaucratic advice and opt for an alternative proposal whose political implications are more to their liking.

Bureaucrats Controlling Bureaucrats

In the second place, the power of some bureaucrats is controlled by other bureaucrats, such as the financial control of the Treasury Board Secretariat and the Finance department, the personnel control of the Public Service Commission, and the policy control of the Privy Council Office. To some extent the central agencies operate on the orders of the prime minister, Cabinet, or Cabinet committees, so that these agencies supplement the political control mentioned above. The Martin government, for example, provided the TBS with a clearer focus to scrutinize departmental plans, performance, and spending. The comptroller general was upgraded to a distinct office within the TBS, reporting to the minister, and with close ties to comptrollers in departments and agencies. In addition, the Martin government's "whistle-blowing" legislation, strengthened by Harper's Accountability Act, was designed to allow bureaucrats to be safe from punishment for revealing improper activities of their colleagues or superiors.

House of Commons

The third line of defence against bureaucratic power is the House of Commons.[29] Although its operations will be examined in more detail in Chapter 23, one principle of parliamentary government is that the executive (Cabinet or bureaucracy) is not allowed to either raise or spend money without parliamentary approval. In practice, proposals for tax changes as well as spending proposals all originate with the executive, they are rarely altered in the legislative process, and the taxing and spending usually begin before Parliament has given its consent. But ultimately Parliament must pass all such financial measures. The process of examining the Estimates gives the House of Commons an opportunity to question and criticize ministers and deputy ministers about all aspects of their departmental spending, programs, and policies. Furthermore, the **auditor general** keeps an eye on the spending process and informs Parliament of instances where funds were spent unlawfully or unwisely. The **Public Accounts Committee** of the House (chaired by an opposition member) goes through the auditor general's report and calls onto the carpet those ministers or deputy ministers who have committed the worst financial faults.

Three other principal means are used by the House of Commons to control the bureaucracy. The first is the daily oral Question Period. In this case, the Commons must act through the intermediary minister who is theoretically responsible for everything the department does. Although the minister is expected to take the blame for bureaucratic errors, public servants seek to avoid bringing such embarrassment or disrepute upon their minister and department. Second, members of Parliament receive requests on a daily basis from their constituents to intervene on their behalf to speed up or correct bureaucratic decisions. MPs and their staff normally handle such problems with a telephone call or a letter to the public servant or minister concerned. A third kind of parliamentary control of the bureaucracy is exercised by the Standing Joint Committee on the Scrutiny of Regulations, which attempts to review the reams of regulations that the bureaucracy produces annually.

The Judiciary

A fourth kind of control of the bureaucracy is provided by the judiciary. The power of the courts to overturn decisions of bureaucrats in regular government departments is essentially restricted to breaches of the law or actions taken beyond the public servant's jurisdiction. Such cases are rare, but the Charter of Rights and Freedoms provides more scope for this kind of judicial review of bureaucratic action than in the past. In the *Singh* case, for example, the Supreme Court ruled that the immigration department had to provide an oral hearing for refugee claimants. In the *Little Sisters* case, the Supreme Court of Canada told customs officers that they must not discriminate against gay or lesbian material and that all sexually oriented material must be judged by the same criteria. The Charter's effect on the bureaucracy primarily relates to police officers, a special kind of public servant, and most often employed at the provincial or municipal level. Regulatory agencies are usually expected to operate in a court-like manner, and their decisions can be overturned by the courts for procedural abuses as well as for exceeding their jurisdiction. The Federal Court of Canada, to be discussed in Chapter 24, specializes in hearing appeals from such regulatory agencies.

Watchdog Agencies

Every Canadian province except Prince Edward Island has supplemented these four means of controlling the bureaucracy with the appointment of an ombudsman, an official of the legislature to whom people can complain about bureaucratic decisions, mistakes, abuse, discrimination, delays, or indecision. Ombudsmen try to correct such errors by persuasion, but, if that fails, they can resort to the power of legislative and media publicity. Canada has no overall ombudsman at the federal level, but several watchdog officials exist to deal with specialized complaints, usually as independent officers of Parliament. The correctional investigator looks into complaints from inmates against prison authorities; the commissioner of official languages investigates public or bureaucratic claims regarding infringement of the Official Languages Act; and the privacy commissioner investigates complaints from citizens who believe that their privacy rights have been invaded. For example, after being criticized by the privacy commissioner, customs officials changed their practice of routinely opening certain heavy private mail and sending it to immigration officials when they suspected it might contain information on illegal immigration and fraudulent documents.

THE INFORMATION COMMISSIONER

One of the most important of these watchdog agencies is the **Information Commissioner**. Canadian governments traditionally functioned under a thick cloak of secrecy at both the Cabinet and the bureaucratic levels. This tradition prevented the opposition and the public from knowing what alternative policies were considered in the executive branch, what kind of public opinion polling was carried out, and what advice was actually offered by the bureaucracy to the Cabinet. The **Access to Information Act** was passed in 1983 and considerably improved the situation, although the many exemptions in the act meant that it was not entirely effective. When citizens, journalists, companies, or interest groups apply to a department for a piece of government information, they are supposed to receive it within 30 days. If they are denied such government information, they can appeal to the information commissioner, who can overrule the department in the matter, with a final to appeal to the Federal Court.

Auditor General Sheila Fraser releases her annual report on May 1, 2007.

Former Information Commissioner John Grace repeatedly reprimanded the bureaucrats for the culture of secrecy that continued to flourish long after the passage of the act. His successor, John Reid, also had a rocky relationship with the Chrétien government. Along with citing the usual litany of cases of uncooperative government departments and agencies, the commissioner himself went to court to try to ensure that documents within the PMO or ministers' offices were covered by the Access to Information Act.[30] He also proposed an "Open Government Act," with recommendations to strengthen the Access to Information Act. Reid's proposals were endorsed by the Gomery Report, especially the idea of a mandatory requirement for public servants to keep written records. Bureaucrats should have to document their decisions and recommendations, and failure to do so or destruction of such documentation would be an offence.[31] Much was expected of the Harper Federal Accountability Act in this respect, but that government turned out to be even more secretive than its predecessors.

THE AUDITOR GENERAL

Although the auditor general was mentioned before as one means of parliamentary control over the bureaucracy, the office deserves specific attention.[32] The auditor general's staff function something like secret agents within the public service, recording any decisions or practices that are illegal, immoral, wasteful, or otherwise ill advised. These agents are not narrow financial auditors—they have no hesitation in making broad policy recommendations to the government in the periodic auditor general's reports to Parliament. Being an officer of Parliament gives the auditor almost complete independence from the government of the day.

The auditor's exposure of deficiencies in the financial management of job-creation programs of Human Resources Development Canada were mentioned earlier in the chapter. The firearms registry was supposed to be almost financially self-sufficient, but the Department of

Justice estimated in 2000 that the program would cost at least $1 billion by 2005. What troubled the auditor general even more than the cost overruns, however, was that the department and government generally did not reveal this information to Parliament but rather tried to hide the dramatic increase. It was also Sheila Fraser who first discovered the abuses in the sponsorship scandal, as bureaucrats directed government advertising contracts to corporate friends of the Liberal Party. Rather than recommending a strengthening of the role of the auditor general, however, Gomery Inquiry focused on giving the Public Accounts Committee substantially more money to hire its own administrative, research, and legal staff.[33] Harper's Accountability Act, however, singled out the auditor general for special attention, granting the office more powers and resources.

· ·

DYSFUNCTIONS AND REFORM OF THE BUREAUCRACY

Dysfunctions of the Bureaucracy

Apart from the problems of pure bungling and of keeping the bureaucracy under some kind of democratic accountability or control, three other problems or dysfunctions are often identified. First, from the public's perspective, there is the constant accusation of "red tape." This generally includes a collection of sins that characterize the behaviour of all large organizations, including delays, a multitude of forms, excessive rules and regulations, difficulty of communicating with the official who could solve the problem, and lack of helpful, personal attention. If these dysfunctions are more characteristic of government than of large private firms, it is partly because governments are required to function according to the law and the rules and regulations issued under the law. Government must also treat everyone in exactly the same way, so, unlike private firms, which may be able to modify their rules, services, and prices, it cannot show favouritism or make individual deals. Delays may be the result of public servants wanting to be certain that any decision is absolutely right, because mistakes may be criticized in Parliament or in the media. There is no excuse for public servants not to be prompt and courteous, but the public environment in which they work requires an equality of treatment that many people are not accustomed to in the private sector.

A second general criticism of bureaucracy is that it is inefficient because it lacks the profit motive of the private sector. Officials in private firms are said to move more quickly because they are in greater danger of losing their jobs and because minimizing costs is a higher priority. To some extent this is true. The essential difference between the public and private sectors, however, is that the bureaucracy is charged with providing a public service, and it should be judged primarily on the adequacy of that service. Nevertheless, there was a widespread belief among the business community, politicians, and the public at large that a great deal of "fat" could be squeezed out of the bureaucracy, at least until the dramatic layoffs in the Mulroney and Chrétien regimes.

From a management point of view, the main dysfunction of the public service is that deputy ministers and other managerial personnel are too hemmed in by rules and regulations and their authority is too limited by central agencies. Changes to alleviate this problem started to be made in 1986, and they continue: many TBS rules and regulations have been rescinded and deputy ministers have been given enhanced responsibility for human resources management in their departments.

Reform of the Bureaucracy

The issues mentioned above were involved in a major transformation of the Canadian federal public service over the 1985–2000 period that had parallels around the world and were part of the **New Public Management (NPM)**.[34] General factors leading to such public-service reform included debts and deficits, changing public- and private-sector expectations, an altered international trading environment (globalization), new technologies, growing doubts about the capacity of state institutions to fulfill their mandates, and citizen demands for direct political participation. In other words, NPM was not just about bureaucratic reform; it was part of the ideology of neoliberalism and the dismantling of the state. It should be said, therefore, that not everyone thinks the reality of NPM matches the rhetoric of its promoters, and, as will be noted, many observers do not believe it to be a good idea at all.

Prime Minister Kim Campbell restructured the executive branch of government.

Apart from giving managers more autonomy, privatizing Crown corporations, and reducing the powers of regulatory agencies, the first major reform began with a dramatic restructuring of government departments in 1993. This idea had long been in the works, and the installation of the Kim Campbell government seemed to be a good time to implement it. The personnel implications were felt most heavily at the assistant deputy minister level, over 50 of whom were laid off.

The second major reform, inaugurated by the 1994 and 1995 budgets, was generally labelled Program Review and involved rethinking what government did and how it did it—in essence, redefining the role of government.[35] The Program Review process asked the following six questions of virtually every government activity:

- Is the program still in the public interest?
- Is its delivery a legitimate and necessary role for government?
- Is the current federal role appropriate or should the program be realigned with the provinces?
- Should it be delivered in partnership with the private or voluntary sector?
- How can it be redesigned for efficiency?
- Is it affordable, given fiscal constraints?

Through this process, the federal government determined which activities it could continue to deliver or support within a much reduced budget. It also identified the activities it had to cease providing, scale back, devolve, or deliver or finance differently. It involved reducing subsidy programs, increasing user fees, and putting many government activities on a commercial basis.[36] In the 1995 budget the minister of finance ensured that real Program Review would happen when he declared his intention to eliminate over 50 000 public-service jobs by 1998 to help the government reduce its deficit. Some public servants were eligible for buyouts and early retirement packages, and some were able to swap jobs with those who wanted to leave, but the announcement still aroused great opposition from public-sector unions.

The third major reform was called **Alternative Service Delivery (ASD)**.[37] ASD is a generic term covering a variety of innovative means of providing government services that arise from a congruence of circumstances and objectives: reducing the size and expense of government, making government more citizen-oriented, involving users in service delivery, providing more flexibility in service delivery, enhancing employee motivation, and incorporating new developments in information technology. ASD consists primarily of special operating agencies, service agencies, partnerships, and the commercialization of certain government services.

Special operating agencies (SOAs) are units that function with relative autonomy within government departments. In most cases they have the potential to become self-financing, and the basic objective is to deliver a service along private-sector lines—that is, in a manner that is more sensitive to client requirements while promoting a more creative, entrepreneurial working environment and bringing savings to government. These units have a minimal role in policy advice, and their autonomy is based on a framework agreement with the department and a departmentally approved business plan. The head of the unit reports to the deputy minister, and the departmental minister retains political responsibility. Passport Canada and the Translation Bureau are examples of the 17 SOAs established. Even so, the Canadian effort pales in comparison with that in Britain, where 67 percent of the civil service were transferred to executive agencies by 1996 and where the head of the agency reports to the minister, not to the equivalent of the deputy minister.[38]

Service agencies are somewhat akin to SOAs, being defined as a mission-driven, client-oriented organizations established under constituent legislation to manage the delivery of federal services. They remain within the federal government and under the direction of a minister, but the intention is to provide more responsive and streamlined operations and to partner with the provinces to provide services to citizens in an efficient manner. Two of the first main initiatives in this category were the Canadian Food Inspection Agency (CFIA) and the Canada Revenue Agency (CRA). The CFIA combines the food inspection services previously provided by three separate federal departments and opens the way for provincial government involvement. The CRA is a transformation of the Canada Customs and Revenue Agency into an agency responsible for collecting most federal taxes; with provincial representation on its board of directions, it provides better coordination with provincial tax-collection efforts. The CRA is by far the largest agency-type initiative in Canada, including approximately one-quarter of the federal public service. The chief commissioner reports directly to the minister and is not encumbered by the central-management controls of the Treasury Board Secretariat and Public Service Commission.[39]

Partnerships have already been mentioned in passing, and they embrace a wide array of new administrative arrangements based on the principle that government does not need to "do it all" for the public interest to be well served.[40] The federal government could enter partnerships with private firms, other governments, or nonprofit, noncommercial, or volunteer organizations. The government–private company relationship behind the construction and operation of the Confederation Bridge between Prince Edward Island and New Brunswick and the creation of local authorities to operate Canadian airports are prominent examples. Another form of collaborative partnership is the Labour Market Development Agreements that Ottawa signed with the provinces between 1996 and 1998.[41]

Commercialization could involve turning a government function over to a nonprofit corporation, such as in the creation of NAV Canada to replace the government's air traffic control system. The NAV Canada board of directors includes representatives of the airlines, government, and employee unions, and sets its rates so that it breaks even. Commercialization also includes contracting out government services or encouraging employees to deliver services from the private sector that they previously provided as public servants, as has been done with some Parks Canada functions.

Once the budget was balanced in the late 1990s, bureaucratic reform centred less on reducing its size and more on making the public service a better place to work and on strengthening its policy capacity. La Relève was an initiative undertaken in 1997 to address "the quiet crisis of downsizing, pay freezes, criticism, insufficient recruitment, and premature departure of experienced public servants."[42] La Relève basically evolved into the Leadership Network in 1998, a separate agency reporting to the Cabinet secretary to ensure the effective management of ADMs as a valued corporate resource. Modernizing the framework for human resources management was the rationale for the 2003 Public Service Modernization Act. Meanwhile, in 1996, the government established a Policy Review Committee that was mandated to anticipate the policy issues of greatest importance to Canada in the future. Later called the Policy Review Initiative (PRI), it sought to strengthen the federal government's policy research capacity.

One of the most recent innovations in government operations is "e-government"—that is, making government "electronic" and putting it "online." Ottawa hoped that Canadians would be able to access all government information and services on the Internet by 2004.[43] Not all Canadians use the Internet, of course, and the Martin government created an agency, Service Canada, which aimed to provide easy-access, one-stop delivery of federal government services in many forms. Besides online access, it provides toll-free telephone service and operates hundreds of Service Centres across the country. It hopes to increase the range of its offerings, integrating as many departmental services as possible.

THE VERDICT ON THE NEW PUBLIC MANAGEMENT

Because it was basically inspired by neoliberal ideology, many observers are critical of the New Public Management. They correctly associate it with the dramatic reduction in the size of the public service, the abandonment of programs, and privatization, deregulation, and contracting out, rather than simple bureaucratic reform. Although it was one strategy to balance the budget, alternative strategies could have been followed. NPM obviously had severe consequences, especially for the lower echelons of society who disproportionately depended on such services. With many services provided by semi-independent partnerships for which Cabinet ministers could no longer be held responsible, NPM also reduced the degree of democratic accountability in the system. Indeed, the auditor general was forced to issue an enhanced definition of accountability to cover such means of alternative service delivery.

However, Peter Aucoin reminds us that it could have been much worse.[44] The federal government never wholeheartedly embraced the New Public Management, with its rigid separation of policymaking and service delivery (with the latter predominantly contracted out) and its glorification of private-sector management practices. This was because, at the national level at least, neoliberalism itself never fully took hold. NPM was more pragmatically adopted in Canada than in Britain, New Zealand, and Australia, and resort to agency-type structures, such as SOAs and service agencies, was limited and implemented in a diluted form. Indeed, even with the cutbacks and changes, Canada never abandoned the ideal of the political executive working closely with the central agencies within the bureaucracy nor the objective of maintaining the policy capacity of the public service. If that capacity was marginally reduced, it brought with it the advantage of engaging the external research community in policy development. Aucoin also makes the point that NPM in Canada continued to treat the public as citizens rather than as customers of public services.

Improving the operation of the massive federal public service is an on-going challenge. Much needs to be done to build on the successes and repair the damage of NPM. As head of the public service, Kevin Lynch, the clerk of the Privy Council and secretary to the Cabinet between 2006 and 2009, embarked on a wide-ranging process called "public service renewal." It centred on attracting new recruits to replace people retiring (good news for students using this book!), developing and renewing the capacities of those continuing their careers, and looking for new skills and new ways of doing things to meet the future challenges.[45]

. . . .

SPONSORSHIP, GOMERY, RESPONSIBILITY, AND ACCOUNTABILITY REVISITED

In the wake of its near-defeat in the 1995 referendum on Quebec sovereignty, the Chrétien government got into serious ethical problems on the issue of government-financed advertising and sponsorship programs to promote Canada at sporting and cultural events in Quebec. More than $23 million went to Groupaction Marketing, the federal government's agent in awarding such contracts, a firm that had close ties to the Liberal Party and had contributed to it financially. While it was orchestrated in the PMO, the auditor general reported that senior bureaucrats broke nearly every rule in the book in awarding questionable contracts, while the RCMP investigated several cases. These various incidents forced Chrétien to introduce a series of measures to upgrade the government's behaviour on this score. When Paul Martin became prime minister, he appointed an independent ethics commissioner, who would review the actions of all MPs, including the prime minister and ministers, and report to the House of Commons. Martin also revised various codes of conduct within the bureaucracy, and appointed the Gomery Inquiry to get to the bottom of the "sponsorship scandal."

In his first report, Gomery documented widespread abuse. In short, he established that there had been partisan political involvement in the administration of the Sponsorship Program; insufficient oversight by senior public servants; deliberate actions taken to avoid compliance with federal legislation and policies; a culture of entitlement among political officials and public servants involved with Sponsorship initiatives; and the refusal of Ministers, senior officials in the Prime Minister's Office, and public servants to acknowledge any responsibility for the mismanagement that had occurred.[46]

In his second report, Gomery called for a rebalancing of the relationship between Parliament and government and an assignment of clearer accountability to both politicians and public servants. One recommendation was to reduce the powers of the prime minister and the clerk of the Privy Council. A number of academic background studies argued that the clerk had too much power, partly because deputy ministers in departments had difficulty reconciling their loyalty to their minister when they depended on the clerk for promotion. This recommendation was ignored, and the Clerk is as powerful as ever.

A second key concern of the Gomery Report had to do with the principle of individual ministerial responsibility as opposed to the role of deputy ministers in running their departments.

This issue had been questioned for some time, especially with respect to the problems in HRDC and the firearms registry, where serious errors were committed but the public found it hard to nail anyone with accountability. Indeed, in the earlier Al-Mashat affair in 1991, when the former Iraq ambassador to the U.S. was illegally admitted to Canada as a landed immigrant, ministers took the unusual step of blaming public servants for the errors.[47]

As noted, the minister is not really expected to know everything that is going on in his or her department and yet is theoretically responsible. Meanwhile, the deputy minister, who really runs the department, is not held responsible. The official view has been that ministers are accountable to Parliament even for the statutory obligations of their deputies; deputy ministers are "answerable" on behalf of their ministers before Parliamentary committees but not "accountable." Gomery recommended significant reforms. First, to become more familiar with their departments, deputy ministers should remain in their posts for a longer period of time, at least three years and preferably five. Second, deputy ministers and senior public servants should be held accountable for their legal responsibilities before the Public Accounts Committee.[48] The first recommendation was widely supported, but the second met with mixed reaction.

New prime minister Stephen Harper shared Gomery's concern about accountability, and his wide-ranging Federal Accountability Act is mentioned in several other chapters. It was a mammoth document that affected almost every aspect of government operations. Harper actually went beyond the Gomery Report (except with respect to the information commissioner) in creating or strengthening mechanisms that would ensure that the politicians and bureaucrats operated at a higher ethical level than in the past. That included beefing up the "whistleblower" legislation that the Martin government had introduced, after the public servant who first complained about the sponsorship scandal lost his job.

On the question of making deputy ministers somewhat more accountable for the operation of their departments, Harper did not go as far as Gomery recommended. DMs were designated as "accounting officers" and *answerable* for their departments before the Public Accounts Committee; they remained *accountable* to their ministers, however, who in turn continued to be responsible or accountable to parliament.[49]

. . . .

CONCLUSION

This chapter illuminates the usually invisible world of the Canadian bureaucracy, an exceedingly complex operation that is charged to undertake an incredible number of tasks. It is a challenge to organize and coordinate the nearly half a million people performing such specialized functions, and, as in any large organization, informal relationships based on individual personalities may deviate from formal lines of authority. A central question that arises in any discussion of the bureaucracy is whether it is out of control. This issue primarily relates to the delicate relationship between the public service and the politicians. Several means of control were discussed above, but the question remains. Another main issue that this subject raises is ensuring that the public service is well positioned to offer the best possible advice to the government and that it provides services to the public in the most satisfactory way. The Canadian bureaucracy continues to strive to improve its performance in both respects, and its only half-hearted embrace of the New Public Management may well have been a blessing.

This chapter is primarily linked to the preceding one on the political executive; indeed, the operations of the two parts of the executive are very closely connected. It is also tied to the policymaking discussions in Chapters 16 (advocacy groups) and 20, and less directly, to most other chapters.

(SC) Bureaucratic power is central to the state-centred approach, which generally contends that the bureaucracy is a world unto itself. Ministers are so busy with Cabinet and Cabinet committee meetings, parliamentary responsibilities, public-speaking engagements, meetings to listen to advocacy group and lobbyist demands, and the job of looking after their constituencies that they have little or no time left to spend in their departments. They have only the most superficial idea of what their departments are doing; for the most part, these are self-governing operations, subject only to the authority of other bureaucratic central agencies. Even the prime minister and Cabinet as a whole can do little but take the advice of the secretary to the Cabinet, the deputy minister of finance, the secretary of the Treasury Board, the governor of the Bank of Canada, and a handful of other key officials, as outlined in this chapter as well as in Chapter 21.

State-centred theorists do not necessarily argue that such officials act only in their own narrow self-interest, however; they may pursue the public interest as they see it. The period between 1935 and 1957, for example, is sometimes seen as the era of the powerful **mandarins**, who brought **Keynesian economics** to Canada and developed the government's whole postwar social and economic program.[50] Although such a small group of mandarins may not have exercised the same kind of innovative influence during the past 50 years or so, the politicians have become even more dependent on the bureaucracy as a whole. In an example from the 1960s, federal welfare officials pushed the politicians for reforms that in their opinion would help the poor and working classes.[51] State-centred advocates must acknowledge, though, the increasing extent to which the bureaucracy relies on outside actors to furnish them with information and advice.

[P] Pluralists are not alarmed at the extent of bureaucratic power because they see it limited by the power of the Cabinet, the House of Commons, the courts, and other agencies. Furthermore, pluralists emphasize the rivalry and competition within the bureaucracy, which make it difficult for any single bureaucrat, department, or agency to become authoritarian. They also see the widespread interest group interaction with departments as a way of influencing the outputs of government. The concept of government as a plethora of specialized policy communities or policy networks, each with its own minister, department, associated agencies, advocacy groups, and interested individuals, is particularly appealing to pluralists and brings this approach together with that of state-centred theorists.

[PC] The "bureaucratic game" is another aspect of bargaining that is central to public or rational choice theory. In their rational, mutually self-seeking relationship with ministers, bureaucrats seek to increase their jurisdiction, their staff, their status, their budget, and their salary, and pursue or recommend policy options that are most convenient and congenial to themselves. Politicians are agreeable to these bureaucratic objectives as long as public servants help them stay in power by keeping them out of trouble and by pacifying electorally strategic interest groups. Donald Savoie contends, however, that the traditional bargain between the public service and the politicians has been broken.[52]

Ⓒ Class analysts argue that the bureaucracy primarily serves the interests of the corporate elite.[53] This is historically related to the commonalities in socioeconomic characteristics of the senior public service and the business community, and the elite accommodation that goes on among the bureaucracy, Cabinet, and pressure groups.[54] In the modern "globalized" world, the bureaucracy joins all other agencies of government in being even more sensitive to the mobility of capital and the need to defer to the value of capital accumulation. Class analysts reject the argument that privatization and the various tenets of the New Public Management are non-ideological issues, and make the basic point that it is groups that speak for the corporate elite, such as the Canadian Council of Chief Executives and the C.D. Howe Institute, that have set the overall context for the reduction in the size and range of activities of the state.

It has also been noted that in its never-ending search for profitable investment outlets, capital is seeking to gain access to the public sector. In *The Unconscious Civilization*, John Ralston Saul observes that privatization involves corporations trying to get their hands on easy profits—profits from administering that which already exists—rather than seeking to make profits by being innovative in the development of new products and services.[55] Despite the conditions of the Canada Health Act, for example, public health care provides a major target for such privatization efforts. Delisting of services at the provincial level has created room for private health insurers, the closing of hospitals has meant big opportunities for private profit-oriented home care companies, and this is probably only the beginning.[56] Class analysts also note that a similar process is under way in public education and in public–private partnerships (P3s) at the municipal level.[57] Some public servants apply a class analysis to their own employment situation. Years of pay freezes and cuts to public-service jobs caused them to feel exploited themselves. Many feel that public-sector restraint programs were simply designed "to advance business interests behind a facade of protecting the public." They point to "the frequent use of back-to-work legislation, the jailing of union leaders, and reducing the right to strike by designating an increasing number of public sector workers as essential."[58]

Ⓖ There are several ways in which globalization is affecting the operation of the Canadian bureaucracy. First, virtually all public servants must be increasingly aware of developments abroad that are relevant to their work. Second, more public servants than ever before are actually involved in work that spans Canadian borders, and in many cases these individuals and the departments and agencies in which they are situated are taking precedence over those that deal with the declining number of purely domestic questions. Third, public servants employed by the Canadian Border Services Agency are now armed and have received instruction on how to use a gun. Fourth, at least until recently, Canadian bureaucrats were working in a new neoliberal environment that prescribed the dismantling of the state, largely to the benefit of transnational corporations. Although Canada did not embrace this ideology, nor its handmaiden, the New Public Management, as enthusiastically as many other countries have done, neoliberalism had a major impact on the size and operation of the Canadian public service.

. . . .

DISCUSSION QUESTIONS

1. What is the ideal relationship between the minister and the deputy minister and between the deputy minister and Parliament?

2. Do central agencies interfere excessively with the deputy minister's responsibility to manage the department?

3. To what extent should Canada establish a "representative bureaucracy"?

4. What limits, if any, should be put on the political activity of public servants? On their right to bargain collectively and to strike?

5. Given the necessity of the bureaucracy in the modern state, are the democratic controls on its power sufficient?

6. How do you feel about downsizing the public service, privatizing Crown corporations, deregulation, and other aspects of the New Public Management?

. . . .

NOTES

1. Donald J. Savoie, *Governing from the Centre: The Concentration of Power in Canadian Politics* (Toronto: University of Toronto, 1999), pp. 7–8.

2. Statistics Canada, the Treasury Board Secretariat, and the Public Service Commission unfortunately provide widely different numbers! I am using Statistics Canada, *Public sector employment, wages and salaries (employees)*, available at http://www40.statcan.gc.ca/101/cst01/govt54a-eng.htm, retrieved on April 24, 2009. The Clerk of the Privy Council put the number at 263 000 in 2009 including regular departments and agencies and CRA, Parks Canada, CFIA, and NRC.

3. S.L. Sutherland, "Responsible Government and Ministerial Responsibility: Every Reform Is Its Own Problem," *Canadian Journal of Political Science* (March 1991); Kernaghan and Siegel, *Public Administration in Canada*, pp. 425–32; S.L. Sutherland, "The Al-Mashat Affair: Administrative Responsibility in Parliamentary Institutions," *Canadian Public Administration* (Winter 1991); Nicholas d'Ombrain, "Ministerial responsibility and the machinery of government," *Canadian Public Administration* (June 2007); and Privy Council Office, *Accountable Government: A Guide for Ministers and Ministers of State*, 2008, cited on April 25, 2009, available at http://www.pco-bcp.gc.ca/docs/information/Publications/ag-gr/2008/docs/ag-gr-eng.pdf.

4. Auditor General's Report, *Reflections on a Decade of Serving Parliament* (February 2001), p. 57. See Donald J. Savoie, *Breaking the Bargain: Public Servants, Ministers, and Parliament* (Toronto: University of Toronto Press, 2003).

5. Savoie, *Governing from the Centre*, p. 248.

6. Privy Council Office, *Accountable Government: A Guide for Ministers*, 2006, pp. 10–13.

7. Gordon Osbaldeston, *Keeping Deputy Ministers Accountable* (Toronto: McGraw-Hill Ryerson, 1990); Jacques Bourgault, "The Role of Deputy Ministers in Canadian Government," in Christopher Dunn, ed., *The Handbook of Canadian Public Administration* (Toronto: Oxford University Press, 2002), ch. 23; and Maurice Henrie, *The Mandarin Syndrome: The Secret Life of Senior Bureaucrats* (Ottawa: University of Ottawa Press, 2006).

8. See the exchange between Flora MacDonald and Mitchell Sharp in Paul Fox and Graham White, eds., *Politics: Canada*, 7th ed. (Toronto: McGraw-Hill Ryerson, 1991); and between Flora MacDonald

and Don Page in Mark Charlton and Paul Barker, eds., *Crosscurrents: Contemporary Political Issues*, 2nd ed. (Scarborough: Nelson Canada, 1994).

9. Savoie, *Governing from the Centre*, pp. 241–42.

10. Ibid., p. 10.

11. John H. Gomery, *Restoring Accountability: Phase 2 Report* (the Gomery Report), (Ottawa: Commission of Inquiry into the Sponsorship Program and Advertising Activities, 2004), ch. 8.

12. Privy Council Office, *Accountable Government*, p. 37; Blair Williams, "The Para-Political Bureaucracy in Ottawa," in Harold D. Clarke, Colin Campbell, F.Q. Quo, and Arthur Goddard, eds., *Parliament, Policy and Representation* (Toronto: Methuen, 1980); and Kenneth Kernaghan and David Siegel, *Public Administration in Canada: A Text*, 4th ed. (Scarborough: Nelson Canada, 1999), pp. 417–19.

13. Gomery Report, ch. 7, pp. 135–37.

14. Herman Bakvis and Luc Juillet, *The Horizontal Challenge: Line Departments, Central Agencies and Leadership* (Ottawa: Canada School of Public Administration, 2004); Leslie A. Pal, *Beyond Policy Analysis: Public Issue Management in Turbulent Times*, 4th ed. (Toronto: Nelson Education, 2010), ch. 7; and Savoie, *Governing from the Centre*, pp. 13, 56–57, and 62.

15. Pal, *Beyond Policy Analysis: Public Issue Management in Turbulent Times*, ch. 7; and Savoie, *Governing from the Centre*, pp. 295–96.

16. On the question of patronage, see Jeffrey Simpson, *Spoils of Power* (Toronto: Collins, 1988); and S.J.R. Noel, "Leadership and Clientelism," in David Bellamy, Jon Pammett, and Donald Rowat, eds., *The Provincial Political Systems* (Toronto: Methuen, 1976).

17. J.L. Granatstein, *The Ottawa Men: The Civil Service Mandarins 1935–1957* (Toronto: Oxford University Press, 1982).

18. John Porter, *The Vertical Mosaic* (Toronto: University of Toronto Press, 1965); Dennis Olsen, *The State Elite* (Toronto: McClelland and Stewart, 1980); Kernaghan and Siegel, *Public Administration in Canada*, ch. 24; and Bryan Evans, et al., "Profiling the Public-Service Elite: A Demographic and Career Trajectory Survey of Deputy and Assistant Deputy Ministers in Canada," *Canadian Public Administration* (Winter 2007).

19. Privy Council Office, *Sixteenth Annual Report to the Prime Minister on the Public Service of Canada* (March 2009), available at http://www.pco-bcp.gc.ca/index.asp?lang=eng&Page=information&Sub= publications&Doc=ar-ra/16-2009/table-eng.htm, retrieved on April 25, 2009.

20. Kathleen Archibald, *Sex and the Public Service* (Ottawa: Queen's Printer, 1970); Task Force on Barriers to Women in the Public Service, *Beneath the Veneer, vol. 1* (Ottawa: Supply and Services, 1990); and Caroline Andrew, "Women and the Public Sector," in Dunn, *The Handbook of Canadian Public Administration*.

21. Noel, "Leadership and Clientelism."

22. Donald J. Savoie, *The Politics of Public Spending in Canada* (Toronto: University of Toronto Press, 1990); David A. Good, *The Politics of Public Money: Spenders, Guardians, Priority Setters and Financial Watchdogs inside the Canadian Government* (Toronto: University of Toronto Press, 2007).

23. Rand Dyck, "The Canada Assistance Plan: The Ultimate in Cooperative Federalism," *Canadian Public Administration* (Winter 1976).

24. Paul Pross, *Group Politics and Public Policy* (Toronto: Oxford University Press, 1986); and William D. Coleman and Grace Skogstad, eds., *Policy Communities and Public Policy in Canada* (Mississauga: Copp Clark Pitman, 1990).

25. Pal, *Beyond Policy Analysis: Public Issue Management in Turbulent Times*, ch. 6; and Savoie, *Breaking the Bargain: Public Servants, Ministers, and Parliament*, ch. 6.

26. Auditor General's Report, *Reflections on a Decade of Serving Parliament*, p. 18; Auditor General, *Status Report*, February 15, 2005, ch. 7; and Gomery Report, *Restoring Accountability*, ch. 10, pp. 188–90.

27. Herschel Hardin, *A Nation Unaware: The Canadian Economic Culture* (Vancouver: J.S. Douglas, 1974); Herschel Hardin, *The Privatization Putsch* (Halifax: Institute for Research on Public Policy, 1989).

28. J.E. Hodgetts, *The Canadian Public Service: A Physiology of Government, 1867–1970* (Toronto: University of Toronto Press, 1973); and Jeffrey Graham Bell, "Agents of Parliament: A New Branch of Government?" *Canadian Parliamentary Review* (Spring 2006).

29. Paul Thomas, "Parliament and the Public Service," in Dunn, *The Handbook of Canadian Public Administration*; and David A. Good, "Parliament and Public Money: Players and Police," *Canadian Parliamentary Review* (Spring 2005).

30. See *Canada (Attorney General) et al. v. Canada (Information Commissioner)*, Federal Court, March 24, 2004. See documents from Democracy Watch and the Open Government Canada coalition, especially Access to Information Review Task Force, *From Secrecy to Openness: How to Strengthen Canada's Access to Information System* (Ottawa: Government of Canada, 2001); cited on October 2, 2006; available at http://www.atirtf-geai.gc.ca/submissions/ogc2001-07-05-e.html; as well as from the Office of the Information Commissioner of Canada website, at http://www.infocom.gc.ca; and Craig Forcese and Aaron Freeman, *The Laws of Government: The Legal Foundations of Canadian Democracy* (Toronto: Irwin Law, 2005), ch. 9.

31. Gomery Report, *Restoring Accountability*, ch. 10, pp. 180–85; Alasdair Roberts, "Administrative Discretion and the Access to Information Act: An 'Internal Law' on Open Government?" *Canadian Public Administration* (Summer 2002).

32. S.L. Sutherland, "On the Audit Trail of the Auditor General: Parliament's Servant, 1973–80," *Canadian Public Administration* (Winter 1980); and S.L. Sutherland, "The Politics of Audit: The Federal Office of the Auditor General in Comparative Perspective," *Canadian Public Administration* (Spring 1986); and see Auditor General's reports.

33. Gomery Report, *Restoring Accountability*, ch. 4, pp. 75–80.

34. Pal, *Beyond Policy Analysis*; O.P. Dwivedi and James Iain Gow, *From Bureaucracy to Public Management: The Administrative Culture of the Government of Canada* (Peterborough: Broadview Press, 1999); B. Guy Peters and Donald J. Savoie, *Taking Stock* (Montreal: McGill-Queen's University Press, 1998); David Johnson, *Thinking Government: Public Sector Management in Canada*, 2nd ed. (Peterborough: Broadview Press, 2006); Gregory J. Inwood, *Understanding Canadian Public Administration: An Introduction to Theory and Practice*, 3rd ed. (Toronto: Prentice Hall Canada, 2009); F. Leslie Seidel, *Rethinking the Delivery of Public Services to Citizens* (Montreal: Institute for Research on Public Policy, 1995), ch. 4; and Savoie, *Governing from the Centre*, pp. 142–46.

35. Jocelyn Bourgon, *Third Annual Report to the Prime Minister of Canada*, 1995, pp. 19–21; Savoie, *Governing from the Centre*, pp. 172–81; and Treasury Board, *Getting Government Right: Governing for Canadians*, February 1997, p. 5.

36. Bourgon, *Third Annual Report to the Prime Minister of Canada*, 1995, p. 20.

37. David Zussman, "Alternative Service Delivery," in Dunn, *The Handbook of Canadian Public Administration*.

38. Canadian Centre for Management Development, *Key Characteristics of Departments and Executive Agencies in the Westminster Democracies* (Ottawa, 1996); Seidel, *Rethinking the Delivery of Public Services to Citizens*, ch. 2; and Savoie, *Governing from the Centre*, p. 216.

39. Kernaghan and Siegel, *Public Administration in Canada*, 4th ed., p. 302; Peter Aucoin, "Beyond the 'New' in Public Management Reform in Canada: Catching the Next Wave?" in Dunn, *The Handbook of Canadian Public Administration*.

40. Bourgon, *Fourth Annual Report to the Prime Minister of Canada*, 1997, pp. 11–12.

41. Jim Armstrong and Donald G. Lenihan, *From Controlling to Collaborating: When Governments Want to Be Partners* (Toronto: Institute of Public Administration of Canada, 1999); and Aidan R. Vining and Anthony E. Boardman, "Public–private partnerships in Canada: Theory and evidence," *Canadian Public Administration* (March 2008).

42. Bourgon, *Fifth Annual Report to the Prime Minister*, 1998, p. 18; *Fourth Annual Report*, ch. 6; Savoie, *Governing from the Centre*, pp. 227–31; and Leslie A. Pal, ed., *How Ottawa Spends 1999–2000: Shape Shifting: Canadian Governance Toward the 21st Century* (Toronto: Oxford University Press, 1999).

43. Jeffrey Roy, *E-Government in Canada: Transformation for the Digital Age* (Ottawa: University of Ottawa Press, 2006).

44. Aucoin, "Beyond the 'New' in Public Management Reform in Canada."

45. Privy Council Office, *Sixteenth Annual Report to the Prime Minister on the Public Service of Canada*.

46. Gomery, *Restoring Accountability*, p. 197; see also articles in *Policy Options*, June 2005 and June 2006; Ian Greene and David Shugarman, "Commission of Inquiry into the Sponsorship Program and Advertising Activities, Phase I Report and Phase II Report," *Canadian Public Administration* (Summer 2006); and Savoie, *Breaking the Bargain: Public Servants, Ministers, and Parliament*.

47. S.L. Sutherland, "The Al-Mashat Affair: Administrative Responsibility in Parliamentary Institutions."

48. Gomery Report, *Restoring Accountability*, ch. 5.

49. Reg Whitaker, "Politics versus Administration: Politicians and Bureaucrats," in Michael Whittington and Glen Williams, eds., *Canadian Politics in the 21st Century*, 7th ed. (Toronto: Thomson Nelson, 2008); Jonathan Malloy and Scott Millar, "Why Ministerial Responsibility Can Still Work," in G. Bruce Doern, ed., *How Ottawa Spends, 2007–2008: The Harper Conservatives—Climate of Change* (Montreal: McGill-Queen's University Press, 2007); Heather MacIvor, *Parameters of Power: Canada's Political Institutions*, 5th ed. (Toronto: Nelson Education, 2010).

50. Granatstein, The Ottawa Men.

51. Richard Splane, "Social Policy-Making in the Government of Canada: Reflections of a Reformist Bureaucrat," in S.A. Yelaja, ed., *Canadian Social Policy* (Waterloo: Wilfrid Laurier University Press, 1978).

52. Savoie, *Breaking the Bargain: Public Servants, Ministers, and Parliament.*

53. Ralph Miliband, *The State in Capitalist Society* (London: Weidenfeld and Nicolson, 1969).

54. Robert Presthus, *Elite Accommodation in Canadian Politics* (Toronto: Macmillan, 1973).

55. John Ralston Saul, *The Unconscious Civilization* (Concord, ON: House of Anansi Press, 1995).

56. Colleen Fuller, *Caring for Profit: How Corporations Are Taking Over Canada's Health Care System* (Vancouver: New Star Books, 1999).

57. Canadian Centre for Policy Alternatives, *The Education Monitor and Education* and *Limited* (both quarterly publications).

58. Kernaghan and Siegel, *Public Administration in Canada*, p. 558; and Leo Panitch and Donald Swartz, *The Assault on Trade Union Freedoms: From Wage Controls to Social Contract*, rev. ed. (Toronto: Garamond Press, 1993).

- -

FURTHER READING

Bakvis, Herman, and Luc Juillet. *The Horizontal Challenge: Line Departments, Central Agencies and Leadership.* Ottawa: Canada School of Public Service, 2004.

Bell, Jeffrey Graham. "Agents of Parliament: A New Branch of Government?" *Canadian Parliamentary Review* (Spring 2006).

Dunn, Christopher, ed. *The Handbook of Canadian Public Administration.* Toronto: Oxford University Press, 2002.

Forcese, Craig, and Aaron Freeman. *The Laws of Government: The Legal Foundations of Canadian Democracy.* Toronto: Irwin Law, 2005.

Inwood, Gregory J. *Understanding Canadian Public Administration: An Introduction to Theory and Practice*, 3rd ed. Toronto: Prentice Hall Canada, 2009.

Johnson, David. *Thinking Government: Public Sector Management in Canada*, 2nd ed. Peterborough: Broadview Press, 2006.

Pal, Leslie A. *Beyond Policy Analysis: Public Issue Management in Turbulent Times*, 4th ed. Toronto: Nelson Education, 2010.

Privy Council Office. *Accountable Government: A Guide for Ministers and Ministers of State, 2008.* Ottawa: Government of Canada, 2008.

Savoie, Donald J. *Breaking the Bargain: Public Servants, Ministers, and Parliament.* Toronto: University of Toronto Press, 2003.

———. *Governing from the Centre: The Concentration of Power in Canadian Politics.* Toronto: University of Toronto Press, 1999.

PARLIAMENT

Almost every day the elected representatives of the Canadian people meet in open, verbal combat in Question Period in the House of Commons. Members of Parliament on the opposition side of the House attack the prime minister and other ministers for acts of omission and commission, while the government responds with laudatory statements and statistics on its own performance. In these exchanges and other debates, politicians' reputations are often made and broken. The House of Commons is the central link between the public and the government in Canadian democracy, and, as such, is the furnace of national politics. Most interests in society are represented there in one way or another, and they clash on a regular basis. The Commons is the primary battleground for the hearts and minds of Canadian voters, and House debate is a "lead-up" to the subsequent election campaign. The Senate, on the other hand, is normally a much more peaceful place and is viewed by many Canadians as a group of unelected, elderly party hacks who collect generous remuneration for doing little work. This impression is not entirely correct, however, and when the Senate's majority belongs to a different party from that in the Commons, its work becomes much more interesting.

Every four or five years (or more often with minority governments), voters in each local constituency elect their representative to the House of Commons. Because they have a direct part in electing its members, because it operates publicly, and because they often see it in action on television, Canadians are generally more familiar with the House of Commons than with any other political institution. This familiarity has sometimes led such voters and viewers to think that the Commons has more power in the policymaking process than it actually does. Although it is largely to enhance that power that the procedures of the House are regularly reformed, the institution has other functions that are probably not widely understood.

As well as the House of Commons, the **Parliament of Canada** includes the Queen and the Senate, and a law must be approved by all three parts. Indeed, every federal statute begins with the words, "Her Majesty, by and with the Advice and Consent of the Senate and House of Commons of Canada, enacts as follows...." In this respect Canada is sometimes said to employ the **Westminster model** of government because it is based on the British system. As noted in Chapter 2, this model begins with a bicameral legislature: an elected lower house with primary legislative powers answerable to the polity through elections, and an upper house with limited legislative powers, in law or in fact. The executive is part of the lower house and through the Cabinet drives or "energizes" the legislative process. The government or Cabinet is in charge of and responsible for the conduct of parliamentary business, while an institutionalized opposition has the right to criticize the government and the ability to make that criticism felt. The Westminster model, therefore, promises potent government and political stability through the prime minister and Cabinet, along with political accountability through open debate.

In popular parlance, however, the word "Parliament" is often used synonymously with the Commons, which is by far its most important part. Hence members of the House of Commons are called members of Parliament or MPs. MPs can be largely divided into three main groups: those who also serve as Cabinet ministers (the government), those who support the Cabinet (government **backbenchers**), and those who oppose the government (the **opposition**).

This chapter examines the House of Commons from a number of perspectives. These include its functions and powers, its composition, the parliamentary timetable, party discipline and the party caucus, stages and kinds of legislation, the organization and officers of the House, the committee system, members' services, the roles of MPs, the government–opposition balance, minority government, and reform of the institution. The chapter later explores the role of the Senate.

. . . .

FUNCTIONS AND POWERS OF THE HOUSE OF COMMONS

Historically, a basic principle of Canadian government was the sovereignty or **supremacy of Parliament**—that is, apart from interfering in provincial jurisdiction and with other minor exceptions, Parliament could pass laws of any kind that were virtually beyond review by any other organ of government, including the courts. This principle was considerably transformed in 1982, however, with the adoption of the Canadian Charter of Rights and Freedoms. The courts have now been given the power to review both federal and provincial legislation in terms of the Charter and to invalidate such legislation to the extent of any contradiction. However, the courts have often suggested that the legislation be redrafted to fit within the boundaries of the Charter, and the "notwithstanding" clause allows for the reassertion of parliamentary sovereignty on many points. As noted in Chapter 19, the courts and Parliament are engaged in a dialogue of sorts on these issues.

The principal function of the House of Commons (and Senate) is to pass laws, although, as the previous two chapters have shown, these are usually formulated in the executive branch. MPs (and senators) articulate local and other interests, and party caucuses try to come up with compromises in which diverse interests are aggregated. The Commons also engages in political recruitment and political communication, such that its non-legislative functions may actually be more important than its legislative role. Another way to address the functions of the House of Commons is in its relationship to the prime minister and Cabinet. The House of Commons does not make policy or govern, but, in the first instance, through motions of confidence and nonconfidence, it decides who will form the government; second, it provides that government, on behalf of the people, with the authority, funds, and other resources necessary for governing the country; third, by acting as a constant critic and watchdog, it makes the government behave; and fourth, it provides an alternative government by enabling the opposition to present its case to the public and become a credible choice for replacing the party in power.[1]

In discussing the functions of the House of Commons it is also instructive to examine its role in the chart of the policymaking process outlined in Chapter 20. In the first place, Parliament may be involved in the initiation phase by raising issues in the daily Question

Period and in general debates, in criticizing existing spending programs, or by means of private members' bills. It is then virtually nonexistent in the priority-setting and policy formulation phases. Where the Commons dominates the picture is in the legitimation stage. Whether or not bills are refined in the course of their passage through the House of Commons, they are at least legitimated. This means that Cabinet proposals embodied in bills are made legitimate by their passage through the formal, authorized, democratic channels of the Commons. It may not make many significant changes, but the House does subject bills to extended debate and publicizes their advantages and disadvantages before converting them into laws or statutes. C.E.S. Franks calls this process the "mobilization of consent."[2] The legislative stage serves to inform the public of the content of new policies, and out of this "prolonged warfare," consent or acceptance is eventually obtained. This debate essentially prepares the electorate for its decision on how to vote in the next election. The House then has little say in the fifth and sixth phases, the implementation and interpretation of laws, including scant supervision of regulations issued by the executive.

The various ways of looking at the functions of the House of Commons noted above emphasize the role of the institution as a whole. Individual members also have interest-articulation, representational, and ombudsman functions, as they speak out for their constituencies and generally take care of their constituents.

. . . .

COMPOSITION OF THE HOUSE OF COMMONS

The basic principle in establishing the House of Commons is that each province is represented in proportion to its population. Chapter 13 outlined how the 308 seats in the Commons are distributed among the provinces and territories, with the following results: Ontario, 106; Quebec, 75; BC, 36; Alberta, 28; Manitoba, 14; Saskatchewan, 14; Nova Scotia, 11; New Brunswick, 10; Newfoundland and Labrador, 7; PEI, 4; Northwest Territories, 1; Nunavut, 1; and Yukon, 1.

Even if members of Parliament other than Cabinet ministers have only a limited role in the policymaking process, they are important enough to justify an inquiry into their social-background characteristics. Since they are elected to represent territorial units and usually live in or near their constituencies, MPs almost automatically become representative of the population in a geographic sense. Although it is not quite so inevitable that they will be representative in terms of ethnic background, this also turns out to be true, at least in the case of English and French origins. The Constitution Act, 1867, required from the beginning that all House documents be printed in English and French, but the absence of simultaneous interpretation until 1958 and the unilingualism of most MPs served to limit the interaction between the two linguistic groups within the institution. Nowadays, they are increasingly bilingual.

However, members of Parliament do not reflect the population as well in terms of other ethnocultural groups, although the number of visible-minority MPs continues to increase. Then, although not as exclusive as Cabinet ministers, MPs have higher educational levels and higher-status occupations than the general population. Historically the legal profession furnished the largest single group in the Commons, but the number of MPs with a business background has exceeded the number of lawyers since the 1984 Conservative victory. A rough indication of the leading occupations of members of Parliament elected in 2008 is provided in

Table 23.1, which shows that educators, administrators, and "consultants" are now as numerous as lawyers, but that the working class continues to be severely underrepresented.

Members are also unrepresentative of the population with respect to gender. Relatively few women have been elected to the House of Commons, although the number is on the increase, reaching 39 out of 295 in 1988, 54 in 1993, 62 of 301 in both 1997 and 2000, 65 of 308 in 2004, 64 in 2006, and 69 in 2008. The high proportion of MPs without any previous service in elected office at the provincial level should also be mentioned. With less than ten percent of MPs elected in 2006 or 2008 having previously served in a provincial legislature, it is evident that federal and provincial political careers in Canada are quite distinct, although 20 to 25 percent of MPs come with municipal government experience.

What is probably most striking about Canadian members of Parliament, especially compared with other legislatures around the world, is their rapid turnover in office. With such a small number of **safe seats**, the proportion of new members after each election is about 40 percent, and the average length of time in office is less than ten years.[3] This means that Canadian MPs are transient amateurs who engage in "avocational politics."[4] Few members remain in Parliament long enough to develop an understanding of the institution, to master their extra-parliamentary responsibilities, or to stand up to a long-serving prime minister. The 1993 turnover was more than 75 percent, because of the decimation of the Conservatives and NDP, but even the relatively calm 1997 and 2000 elections produced a turnover of 30 percent and 15 percent, respectively. It jumped to 35 percent in 2004 and fell to about 20 percent in each of 2006 and 2008.

. . . .

THE PARLIAMENTARY TIMETABLE

Perhaps the best way to get an overview of the work of the House of Commons is by examining the parliamentary timetable—the agenda of a typical session and a typical week. The

TABLE 23.1 Occupational Distribution of MPs, 2008	
Field	*Number of MPs*
Business	71
Administration and management	57
Law	51
Education	51
Consultant	47
Agriculture	22
Political assistant	18
Director	18

Note: Many MPs listed more than one occupation.
Source: *Parliament of Canada. Top 10 Occupations in the House of Commons. Found at: http://www2.parl.gc.ca/ Parlinfo/Lists/Top10Occupations.aspx?Menu=PARL-HOC (Accessed April 26, 2009).*

Constitution requires that Parliament meet at least once a year, but it now sits for about 25 weeks, or 135 days, per year, from mid-September to mid-December, and from early February to mid-June, incorporating a weekly break per month. A session of Parliament is normally completed every 12 months, but it has often spilled over to two or even three years.

The Typical Session

A session begins with the **speech from the throne**, prepared by the prime minister (and advisers) and read by the governor general. Its function is to outline the government's legislative plans for the session, although the speech is often worded so vaguely that it is not a reliable guide. That speech introduces the throne speech debate, a six-day debate in which MPs can talk about anything under the sun. Party leaders and Cabinet ministers may use the occasion to articulate their priorities, while backbenchers often expound on the wonders or troubles of their constituency.

The second major event of the session is the **budget** and the budget debate. The budget itself is the annual financial statement of the government delivered by the minister of finance, chiefly concerned with tax changes and the broad outlines of expenditures for the forthcoming fiscal year. Among other things, the budget usually fleshes out the vague promises of the speech from the throne. So that no one can take advantage of tax changes beforehand, the budget is shrouded in secrecy until its delivery, and real or apparent "budget leaks" always generate great controversy. The budget sets the stage for a four-day freewheeling debate and provides the opposition with a second opportunity to try to defeat the government. Majority governments need not worry, but the Trudeau and Clark minority governments were defeated on their budgets in 1974 and 1979, respectively, and the Martin and Harper minority governments were forced to amend their respective 2005 and 2009 budgets. Legislation incorporating the specific tax changes mentioned in the budget comes along later, although the changes usually take effect as of budget night.

The details of the government's spending proposals for the next fiscal year are contained in the **Estimates**. Their presentation is the third major item of business in the session. Once tabled, however, the Estimates are transmitted to standing committees of the House for scrutiny, so that they actually occupy little time of the Commons as a whole. The Estimates are part of the "supply" process, that is, granting the government a supply of funds with which to finance its activities.

A fourth element of the session consists of the 22 days when the opposition parties choose the subject of debate and the government in turn responds. These are related to granting the government supply, and therefore variously called "supply," "allotted," or **opposition days**. These are divided proportionately among the opposition parties and distributed throughout the session, at the rate of approximately one per week.

Other than these four components, the time of the House of Commons is essentially taken up with the discussion of bills, and most of that time with bills introduced by the government. Indeed, it is partly because of the volume of government legislation that some sessions of Parliament exceed a year in length, but the cycle of events just outlined is ideally repeated on an annual basis. This annual parliamentary cycle has an internal logic that is difficult to refute.

When the government wants to take a break within a session, it "adjourns" the House; when it wants to bring a session to an end, it "prorogues" the Commons; and an election call results in the **dissolution of Parliament**. It is partly because government bills not passed by prorogation die and must start again from scratch in the next session that governments are tempted to allow sessions to continue beyond one year until all current legislation is disposed of. On the other hand, the Harper government prorogued the House in December 2008, less than a month after it began, to avoid a nonconfidence motion.

The Typical Week

The weekly House of Commons schedule can be seen in Figure 23.1. The 1982 reforms eliminated the traditional evening sittings in favour of meeting in the morning, now starting at 11:00 a.m. on Monday, 10:00 a.m. on Tuesday, Thursday, and Friday, and 2:00 p.m. on

. . . .

Figure 23.1   Weekly Order of Business

Hours	Monday	Tuesday	Wednesday	Thursday	Friday
10:00 – 11:00		Routine Proceedings		Routine Proceedings	Government Orders
11:00 – 11:15	Private Members' Business				Statements by Members
11:15 – 12:00					Oral Questions
12:00 – 1:00	Government Orders	Government Orders		Government Orders	Routine Proceedings
1:00 – 1:30					Government Orders
1:30 – 2:00					
2:00 – 2:15	Statements by Members	Statements by Members	Statements by Members	Statements by Members	Private Members' Business
2:15 – 2:30	Oral Questions	Oral Questions	Oral Questions	Oral Questions	
2:30 – 3:00					
3:00 – 5:30	Routine Proceedings Government Orders	Government Orders	Routine Proceedings Notices of Motions for the Production of Papers Government Orders	Government Orders	
5:30 – 6:30		Private Members' Business	Private Members' Business	Private Members' Business	
6:30 – 7:00	Adjournment Proceedings	Adjournment Proceedings	Adjournment Proceedings	Adjournment Proceedings	

Source: House of Commons, Journals Branch. Reproduced with permission.

Wednesday, and finishing at 7:00 p.m. from Monday to Thursday and at 2:30 on Friday. Wednesday mornings are reserved for party caucus meetings. The items on the daily agenda are statements by members, Question Period, government orders (usually government bills), private members' business (usually private members' bills), and the adjournment proceedings. "Routine proceedings" include the tabling of documents, statements by ministers, presentation of petitions and committee reports, and introduction and first reading of bills.

The highlight of the day is the 45-minute **Question Period**.[5] This period offers the opposition its best opportunity to criticize and embarrass the government as it grills the prime minister and Cabinet ministers about their deficiencies and faults. Ministers are not given notice of such questions, but before going into the chamber they are briefed by aides who try to anticipate what questions might be asked. Even greater daily effort goes into the preparation and rehearsal of questions by opposition party leaders and their staff. The **Leader of the Opposition** and the leader of any other recognized party begin the attack, and the Speaker of the House distributes questions to various opposition parties in a rough proportion to their numbers. Government backbenchers are also allowed to participate, but they usually ask "planted" questions to which ministers give prepared and self-serving replies. Since ministers often respond in a deliberately vague manner, supplementary questions to those initially posed are allowed, but the objective of the opposition is not so much to elicit information as to portray the government in a negative light. Such exchanges, along with corridor interviews and hallway "scrums"—a melee of reporters, microphones, and cameras—based on Question Period, find their way onto the television news and form the backbone of all media reporting on the House. Exciting as it is, many observers regret that Question Period gets so much attention and other aspects of Commons activity receive so little. Provision is also made for written questions from MPs who are genuinely concerned with seeking detailed information.

The 15 minutes preceding Question Period each day are set aside for members' statements, during which MPs can get something off their chests in 60 seconds, such as reminding the House that this is "cancer month" or that a constituent has won some kind of award. After Question Period, the regular business is the discussion of government orders, usually government bills, debates that are the basic routine of Commons life. At this point in the day most of the **parliamentary press gallery** and MPs leave the chamber in search of more pressing or more interesting activity, and the deputy speaker replaces the Speaker, completely changing the atmosphere of the House. The speeches in these debates, even with their 20-minute time limit, are often dull, although the "question and comment" period after each speech sometimes adds a modicum of life to the proceedings. But the public and media can hardly be blamed for paying so little attention to them when MPs themselves rarely listen to one another. The few members assigned to make up quorum on any day are more likely to be answering their mail, reading the newspaper, or working on their laptops!

Only five hours a week are reserved for **private members' bills** and motions. These bills and motions, introduced either by government supporters not in the Cabinet or by opposition members, are usually even more uninteresting than government bills and very few become law. As mentioned below, however, they have attracted a little more attention in recent years.

Finally, the adjournment proceeding, or "late show," is a half-hour opportunity at the end of the daily sitting (6:30 to 7:00 p.m.) four times a week to pursue issues that MPs feel were inadequately answered in the Question Period. Three members have five minutes each to restate their question, and a parliamentary secretary representing the minister has five minutes to respond.

Given the sharply adversarial nature of Question Period and the relative dullness of the rest of the parliamentary day, television coverage of the House of Commons does little to enhance the public's support of the government or politicians in general. However, "the all-consuming ritual of adversarial combat completely dominated by political parties" has its defenders. It serves the functions of keeping government conduct under constant surveillance and of providing an alternative regime,[6] and it presents a clear-cut picture to the electorate of which party is responsible for everything that has been done.[7]

PARTY DISCIPLINE

Probably the most significant aspect of the operation of the House of Commons is that everything is organized along party lines and that **party discipline** is so rigid. Almost all members belong to one party or another, and, with rare exceptions, the MPs of each party vote together. The most obvious reason that members of Parliament so consistently toe the party line, at least on the government side of the House, is the system of **responsible government**. It is generally believed, both inside and outside Parliament, that if the Cabinet is defeated on a major measure, it must resign or call an election; therefore, its backbenchers always have to put party loyalty ahead of the consideration of their own views or those of their constituents to ensure that Cabinet proposals are passed.[8] That perception is not entirely valid, however, and the principle of responsible government could be interpreted more flexibly to apply only to the speech from the throne, the budget, the Estimates, and explicit nonconfidence motions, as discussed later in the chapter. The Martin government moved in that direction, but the Harper administration often bullied MPs into submission by considering every vote to be one of confidence.

Apart from the fact that some degree of party discipline is a corollary of the principle of responsible government, several reasons can be cited to explain why MPs of any party stick together in parliamentary votes. One is the tendency of people who belong to a political party to see things in a similar light—a natural cohesiveness common to most organized groups. Related to this cohesiveness is an equally natural deference to the leadership of the party and a desire to present an image of party unity to the public. In addition, MPs are encouraged to support the party line because of the prospects of promotion. Government backbenchers who are well behaved can become committee chairs, parliamentary secretaries, or Cabinet ministers, while even in opposition parties MPs can be moved up to more important responsibilities.[9] Members also want to participate in the distribution of perks available in parliamentary life: the best offices, the best committees, opportunities to travel at public expense, and the chance to participate in Question Period, all of which are generally in the control of the party whips. Those who demonstrate greatest party loyalty can be rewarded with such favours. Another inducement is to receive full support of the party organization in the next election, including campaign funds and a visit by the party leader. Moreover, many MPs depend on the government to provide them with employment if they suffer defeat and are not unmindful of this future dependence while serving in the House. The ultimate sanctions for disloyal behaviour are expulsion from the party caucus, involving relegation to the unpleasant status of an independent, and denial of the party label in the next election. For all these reasons, parties usually vote as blocs, and a government with a majority of seats in the Commons has always felt confident that it could get parliamentary approval for almost anything it wanted. Party discipline is probably even more rigid in a minority government situation.

A system of rigid party discipline has major advantages, and opponents sometimes fail to appreciate the merits of an executive-centred system. Forcing MPs to toe the party line has allowed the executive to pursue a collectivist public interest beyond the narrow interests of constituencies, regions, and provinces, and has permitted Canadian governments to be more activist and welfare-oriented than legislature-centred systems, such as in the United States.[10] The inability of the Clinton administration to persuade Congress to enact a public health care system is often cited as a typical contrast. Party discipline protects MPs individually and collectively from the threats of single-interest pressure groups and lobbyists, whose presence is increasing, and frees the prime minister from time-consuming negotiations with individual MPs. Because it makes clear that the government party is responsible for everything that is done, party discipline also promotes the accountability of that party to the electorate. This argument is related to the fact that most people vote for the party, including the leader and the platform, rather than for the local candidate. That is to say, MPs have been elected on the basis of their party label rather than their ability to represent their constituents, and must at least balance these two loyalties.

The British House of Commons is the model for the Canadian House in many ways, but party discipline is looser in that chamber and even in a majority situation, legislation is frequently defeated without entailing the resignation of the government.[11] C.E.S. Franks attributes this significant difference in the operation of the two chambers to several factors: the larger number of members in Britain means that discipline is harder to enforce; incumbent British MPs can be sure of renomination, regardless of their degree of party loyalty; and the large proportion of safe seats results in fewer members being dependent on party patronage for their post-parliamentary livelihood. Moreover, long-serving British MPs usually coexist with short-term prime ministers and are not so obsessed with promotion to the Cabinet. They are more content than their Canadian counterparts to remain on the backbenches or to act as committee chairs, combining outside interests with their parliamentary responsibilities.[12]

It has become increasingly fashionable in Canada to advocate more **free votes** and greater opportunity for MPs to represent the interests of their constituencies rather than slavishly follow the dictates of the party. The Mulroney government allowed "free votes" on capital punishment and abortion that featured a dramatic split among Tory MPs, and a "compromise" abortion bill was defeated in a free vote in the Senate. At the same time, three Conservative MPs were expelled from the party caucus and two were denied the party's candidacy.[13]

Jean Chrétien took a hard line on party discipline.

CP PHOTO/Adrian Wyld

Jean Chrétien took a hard line on party discipline. In 1995, for example, when many Liberal backbenchers absented themselves from the vote on the government's gun registration bill and three voted against it, the PM quickly retaliated by removing the latter from their committee assignments. When Warren Allmand voted against the 1995 budget, the prime minister's attempt to remove him as a committee chair was delayed by Reform MPs, who disagreed with what he said but defended his right to dissent from the Liberal line. Chrétien even threatened not to sign the nomination papers of Liberal candidates in the next election if they voted against government measures. Such a fate befell John Nunziata, who was expelled from the Liberal caucus for his attack on the government for not removing the GST. Nevertheless, he ran successfully in 1997 as an Independent, but was defeated in the 2000 election.

Soon afterward, about half of the Chrétien caucus began to feel that it was time for him to resign, most of them favouring Paul Martin as his successor. They and others in the party organization forced Chrétien to set a retirement date. As he thus declined into lame-duck status in 2002, the caucus rejected one of his ethics package provisions related to them—revelation of their spouses' assets. Then, in an unprecedented revolt, on an opposition motion based on Martin's proposal to allow standing committees to elect their own chairs rather than have them imposed by the PMO, 55 Liberal backbenchers broke with the government to ensure its passage.

Paul Martin came to power with a promise of reducing the rigidity of party discipline. He instituted a scheme involving three categories of votes: first, where Liberal MPs had to support the government; second, where the government told MPs how it wanted them to vote, but where private members were allowed to dissent; and third, a free vote even for ministers. In his regime, most bills fell into the second category, with only votes of confidence and a limited number of matters of fundamental importance to the government falling into the first. The Liberal caucus split on free votes on same-sex marriage in both the Chrétien and the Martin regimes and, during Martin's watch, on Canadian participation in the U.S. Ballistic Missile Defence system. In Martin's minority, two government bills were defeated—both connected to the division of foreign affairs and international trade into separate departments—but since the government did not consider these to be confidence votes, it ignored their defeat. Thus, it was only on a straightforward nonconfidence motion that the Martin government was defeated in November 2005. Stephen Harper dismissed Garth Turner from the Conservative caucus in 2006 for his individualistic behaviour (primarily involving blogging), and took the same strict approach to party discipline that Chrétien had done. After sitting as an Independent, Turner joined the Liberal caucus, but he was defeated as a Liberal candidate in the 2008 election.

Meanwhile, Liberal leader Stéphane Dion removed Joe Comuzzi from that party's caucus for supporting the 2007 Conservative budget, and he later joined the Conservatives. Conversely, Bill Casey was dismissed from the Conservative caucus for voting against the 2007 Budget and was re-elected in 2008 as an Independent. Harper gave the House of Commons an opportunity to revisit the issue of same-sex marriage in a free vote in December 2006, but the majority voted against reopening the issue.

. . . .

CAUCUS MEETINGS

The other side of this public display of party discipline is that MPs are allowed to speak their mind in the secrecy of the **party caucus**.[14] The caucus consists of all the elected members of each party (and senators who choose to attend) and meets behind closed doors on Wednesday mornings. As in the case of Cabinet secrecy, however, members occasionally "leak" caucus information for their own benefit. Provincial and regional caucus meetings of each party are held before the general caucus meeting, and caucus committees are often appointed. MPs of like mind can also form informal task forces.

Unlike the practice in Britain, the prime minister and Cabinet ministers attend the government party caucus meeting. Most prime ministers use caucus primarily to inform their backbenchers of government plans; others are reasonably receptive to backbench arguments and suggested alternatives; and some do both. Ministers may discuss the principles of a new policy with interested backbenchers in the course of its development, but it would breach the tradition of the House to show the caucus an actual bill before it is introduced in the Commons. Although no votes are taken, sufficient backbench dissatisfaction may occasionally carry the day. Many examples could be cited, even in the Chrétien era, where the caucus had a significant influence on Cabinet policy, and the aforementioned Mulroney compromise abortion bill was probably unique in actually being written by a committee of four ministers and eight backbenchers.[15] Martin ordered his ministers to discuss every new proposal with the relevant caucus committee. Whether backbench MPs argue strenuously in caucus and whether they persuade the Cabinet to change position, the whole process is shrouded in secrecy, so voters are not aware of it; all that is evident in public is MPs voting as their leader tells them.

. . . .

STAGES AND KINDS OF LEGISLATION

The great bulk of legislation introduced takes the form of **public bills**. These are general bills that relate to matters of public policy and affect all Canadians, such as the Income Tax Act or the Canada Health Act. Most public bills (and virtually all that involve the raising or spending of money) are sponsored by the government and introduced by a Cabinet minister, thereby being titled **government bills**. They are numbered from C-1 to C-200 in each session. As noted earlier, most of the weekly and yearly agenda is taken up with such government business.

A certain amount of time, however, now normally five hours per week, is set aside for members who are not in the Cabinet to introduce legislation and motions of their own. Since these MPs (on whichever side of the House) are private members, their proposals are called private members' bills and are numbered from C-201 upward in each session.[16] These bills are also of a general public policy nature, but until 1995 they could not involve the expenditure of public funds. Since then, private members' bills that entail spending can be introduced, but they require a "royal recommendation" before third reading and they still cannot impose or increase taxes. Private members' bills almost never reach the statute books unless they are embraced by the government. Historically, the most that private members could hope for was that the Cabinet might incorporate their ideas into a government bill, and this still sometimes happens.

Since 1986, however, there has been provision for a more in-depth examination of a larger number of private members' bills and motions. The names of 30 private members are randomly drawn at the beginning of a Parliament. If any of these MPs have bills or motions to offer, they are heard first, and the list is later replenished. Such bills and motions are now allowed two hours of debate, and almost all are votable. In many cases, private members' bills are not "whipped"—that is, are not subject to party discipline—so MPs can exercise their own discretion. If a private member's bill passes, it goes on to committee for further review. Examples of private members' bills that made it to the statute books include those upholding nonsmokers' rights, changing the name of Trans-Canada Airlines to Air Canada and the name of electoral districts, recognizing the beaver as a symbol of Canadian sovereignty, hockey as Canada's national winter sport and lacrosse as our national summer sport, eliminating the excise tax on jewellery, and extending hate propaganda to sexual orientation.[17] Private members' bills that passed in recent minority government periods include John Godfrey's Federal Sustainable Development Act and former Prime Minister Paul Martin's bill to implement the Kelowna Accord, but they were ignored by the Harper government.

Private bills, on the other hand, refer to a specific person or private corporation. They originate in a petition, and require the payment of a fee. Certain divorces used to be effected by Acts of Parliament and took the form of private bills, while today this category mostly consists of bills incorporating companies and religious denominations. Other recent examples included a bill for the City of Windsor to acquire the Canadian portion of the Windsor–Detroit Tunnel, and those that allowed certain couples to marry even though they were related to each other within prohibited degrees of consanguinity. Private bills now originate in the Senate and occupy very little of the Commons' time.

Turning to the stages of the legislative process, Figure 23.2 shows the labyrinth that a bill must go through in order to become a law—essentially three readings in each chamber. Most government bills originate in the Commons, although, with the exception of money bills, they may be first introduced in the Senate. First reading simply means that a bill has been introduced—it is tabled, printed, and made public—and may be briefly explained. Some days later, the bill comes up for second reading. This stage involves a debate on the principle of the bill and may last several days or even weeks if it is controversial. The individual clauses of the bill are not discussed or amendable at this stage, and a favourable vote at the end of the second-reading debate therefore means that the bill has been approved in principle, although not necessarily in detail.

Even if the opposition has little hope of defeating a bill, it may expect that prolonged exposure of the flaws in the legislation will persuade the government to amend it. Failing that, public opinion can be aroused through television or other media coverage to the extent that the electorate will remember the incident when the next election occurs. Excessive opposition debate is called a **filibuster**, but government and opposition rarely agree on what is excessive. In 1913, during protracted opposition to the government's Naval Bill, the Borden government introduced **closure**, a rule allowing a majority government to cut off debate. This device was used with discretion until the **pipeline debate** of 1956, and it is widely believed that the abusive resort to closure helped to defeat the government a year later.[18] The closure rule is still on the books and has been used more routinely in majority government situations in recent years. However, it is both more common and more civilized to negotiate with the opposition parties over the time to be allocated to debating various issues. Standing Order 78 provides for three kinds of time-allocation motions depending on how much opposition consent can be acquired, and is considered less draconian than closure. Minority government encourages the government to come to agreement with opposition parties on scheduling various debates rather than cutting them off.

Figure 23.2 Legislative Process in the Canadian Parliament

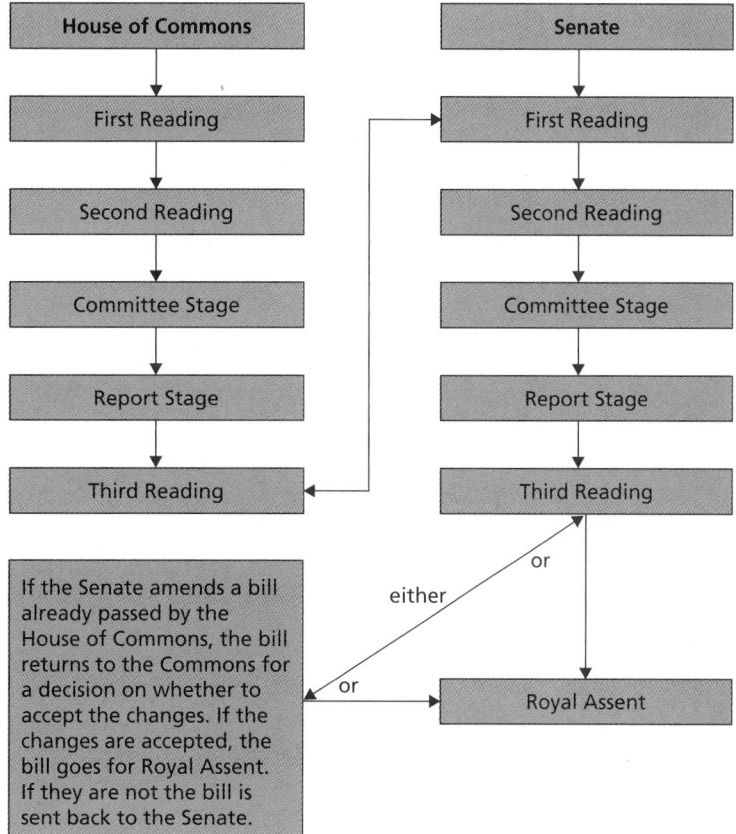

It is partly to avoid long debates that government legislation deliberately leaves wide discretion to the executive to issue regulations so that acts will not have to come back to the House for frequent amendments. Similarly, the government often introduces omnibus bills that deal with several different issues simultaneously because a number of individual bills would take longer to pass. The Harper government's Federal Accountability Act was such a bill.

Following second reading, a bill goes to committee, where it is examined in detail. In the small, informal confines of a Commons committee, ministers, public servants, advocacy groups, and other experts offer explanations or criticisms, after which the committee members scrutinize the bill clause by clause, voting on each, and occasionally amending them.

After being approved, sometimes with amendments, the bill is reported back to the House in what is called the Report stage. This phase gives all members of the House, especially those not on the committee, an opportunity to move other amendments. In 1999, the opposition discovered a new delaying tactic by moving hundreds of amendments at the report stage. The Canadian Alliance used this device to delay the Nisga'a Treaty, and the Bloc Québécois to prolong debate on the Clarity Act. After the 2000 election, however, the House gave the Speaker greater authority to limit such amendments. Once the bill is concurred in at the Report stage, it goes to third reading for a final, overall appraisal.

Assuming that the bill started in the Commons, it must then go through the same procedure in the Senate, but there it is usually disposed of in much faster order. In the rare case that the Senate amends a bill already approved by the Commons, the bill will have to go back to that house to see if it is acceptable in its amended form. If the Senate and House of Commons continue to disagree, the bill is usually abandoned, although a rarely used provision exists for a conference between representatives of the two houses.

Once a bill is passed in identical form by both houses, it is given royal assent in a special ceremony held in the Senate. The governor general or, more likely, a Supreme Court judge acting as "deputy governor general" nods in approval, and the bill becomes a law or statute, although it may not be immediately proclaimed. An alternative new procedure allows royal assent to be conferred by a simple written declaration by the governor general at Rideau Hall or by the deputy governor general in the Supreme Court building.[19]

Although this may seem like an overly complicated process, each stage has a distinctive purpose and most bills must be debated for some time before the media and public begin to pay attention to them and absorb their merits and faults. Reasonably lengthy consideration of the bill helps the electorate to make up its mind about whether to re-elect the government that introduced such legislation or to opt for an opposition party that criticized it effectively.

In 1994, the House adopted rule changes that allowed a bill to go to committee after first reading, before it had been approved in principle. Such a procedure considerably widens the scope of committee influence, but it applies only to government legislation and can be used only with the minister's consent. According to another new procedure, a committee can be directed to study an issue and prepare a bill. This was done in the case of the post-1991 redistribution process. These changes illustrate a slight loosening up of the Cabinet's dominance of the legislative process, but such devices are not often used.

. . . .

ORGANIZATION AND OFFICERS OF THE COMMONS

The Speaker

The layout of the Commons chamber is illustrated in Figure 23.3. The leading official of the House of Commons is the presiding officer, the **Speaker**, for whom one deputy and two acting speakers can substitute in the chair. In addition to ceremonial and administrative functions, the Speaker interprets and enforces the written rules of the Commons, which are called the **Standing Orders**,[20] as well as unwritten traditions, practices, conventions, and usages. Given the powers of the Speakership—recognizing which member can speak and ruling on whether motions are in order, whether debate is relevant, whether questions are urgent, and whether an unruly MP should be expelled—it is important for the person selected to be competent as well as totally impartial. Speakers were historically chosen by prime ministers from among their party's MPs and thus carried the suspicion of being biased in favour of the government. In seeking eventual reward beyond the Speakership, such as promotion to the Cabinet, some also feared displeasing the prime minister, the dispenser of such rewards.

A major change adopted in 1986 allowed MPs to choose their own Speaker by secret ballot, rather than merely ratifying the nomination of the prime minister. In 1988, the Speaker was given new authority to "name" (i.e., suspend) a member for the rest of the day and for a period of five days for a second breach of the rules. Peter Milliken was elected Speaker of the Commons after the November 2000 election, and was re-elected in 2004 and again in both 2006 and 2008, even though he then sat in Opposition. In 2008, he issued a rare "Speaker's warrant" to force Karlheinz Schreiber to appear before MPs to ensure that he answered questions before being extradited to Germany.

. . . .

Figure 23.3 Layout of the House of Commons Chamber

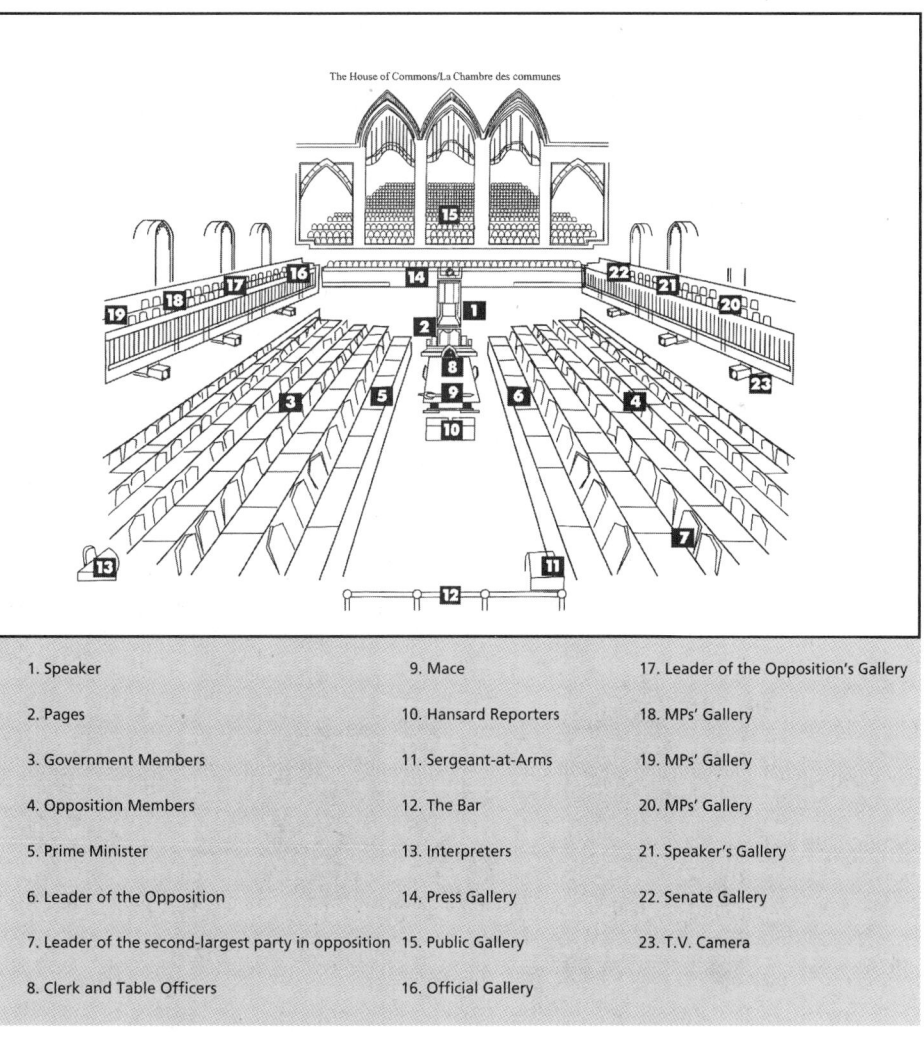

The House of Commons/La Chambre des communes

1. Speaker	9. Mace	17. Leader of the Opposition's Gallery
2. Pages	10. Hansard Reporters	18. MPs' Gallery
3. Government Members	11. Sergeant-at-Arms	19. MPs' Gallery
4. Opposition Members	12. The Bar	20. MPs' Gallery
5. Prime Minister	13. Interpreters	21. Speaker's Gallery
6. Leader of the Opposition	14. Press Gallery	22. Senate Gallery
7. Leader of the second-largest party in opposition	15. Public Gallery	23. T.V. Camera
8. Clerk and Table Officers	16. Official Gallery	

Source: Library of Parliament

Anyone who has observed Question Period is likely to be upset at the rowdy behaviour of members of Parliament, and it is true that the British chamber is more sedate. However, the rules demand a certain amount of civility, such as a prohibition on name-calling or accusations of lying, and require MPs to speak to each other through the Chair and to refer to each other by the name of their constituency, as the "Honourable Member for...."

The Speaker can vote only in the case of a tie, and Milliken was twice forced to break a tie in the Martin minority period in May 2005. The vote on a supplementary budget bill was the first time a Speaker was ever required to break a tie on a nonconfidence vote, and he followed precedent by voting with the bill so that debate on it could continue. Speakers cannot articulate the needs of their constituency or constituents in the Commons, as such, but in compensation, ministers and bureaucrats are especially sensitive to the concerns that the Speaker discusses with them outside the chamber.

House Leaders, Party Whips, and Clerk

From within their ranks, each party selects a House leader and a party whip. The government **House leader** is a Cabinet minister who manages the government's business in the Commons. This minister seeks to work out an agenda for House business with the opposition House leaders, who function as procedural strategists for their parties and often speak for their parties if their leaders are absent. Especially in a minority government situation, it is essential for the various party house leaders to work well together. **Party whips** are responsible for ensuring that their members are present for important votes and that they vote the right way.[21] Whips must therefore know the whereabouts of their MPs at all times. They also distribute members' offices, assign members to parliamentary committees, and line up the order of party speakers in Question Period and debates. It is largely through the whips, therefore, that party leaders impose discipline on their members. Members' opportunities to speak, to serve on the committee of their choice, and to travel as part of parliamentary delegations are largely influenced by their degree of party loyalty. In return, whips seek out backbench opinion on various matters and transmit it to the party leadership. Given the power of the party whips and party House leaders to organize its business, independent MPs and those MPs who belong to a party with fewer than 12 members find little opportunity to participate.

The chief permanent official of the Commons is the clerk of the House. This position is analogous to a deputy minister in a government department. As chief procedural adviser to the Speaker and manager of the support staff attached to the Commons, the clerk is also required to act in a totally nonpartisan manner. The clerk is assisted at the table by the deputy clerk and several principal clerks. Since the sergeant-at-arms rarely has to wield the mace to escort unruly MPs out of the chamber, that position also has administrative responsibilities attached.

Voting

Turning to the voting procedure in the Commons, decisions are in the first instance made orally when the Speaker invites members to say "aye" or "nay." In declaring which side won, the Speaker is guided by the numbers rather than the volume on each side, and on a routine matter in a majority situation, this will probably suffice. When either side wants a formal recorded vote it will request a **division**. In this case the division bells ring until the government and official Opposition party whips agree that all their available members have arrived, at which time a standing vote is conducted. It used to be that if either whip refused to give the go-ahead, the bells could ring indefinitely, but after the two-week "bell-ringing incident" of 1982, a 30-minute limit was adopted in 1986. A new procedure in 1994 allowed for deferred divisions with all-party consent, so that most votes are now held between late Monday and late Wednesday, when most members are there. To save time, if several votes are to take place in sequence, the result of one vote can be "applied" to subsequent votes with unanimous consent.

MPs sometimes engage in the practice of "pairing," in which two members on opposite sides make arrangements so that if one is legitimately absent for a vote, the other does not vote either. Party whips are involved in putting members' names in the registry of pairs, and paired members are listed at the end of the division list printed in *Hansard*. In general, pairing is advantageous only for the government, so that it will not be defeated on a crucial vote, and opposition parties are therefore not enthusiastic about the practice. Indeed, in slim majority and minority government situations, ministers sometimes have to cancel trips in order to be present for a vote or, to reduce the numbers on the other side, face the unappetizing alternative of taking an opposition member along with them!

Speeches

The length of speeches that MPs are allowed to make has been severely curtailed over the past 25 or so years. The 1982 reforms generally shortened them from 40 minutes to 20, but this depends on who is speaking, in what debate, and at what stage of the debate. In many cases, especially as a debate drags on, the maximum length is reduced to 10 minutes. Since each party's first speech in a debate has no limit, however, the Canadian Alliance MP who began the debate on the Kyoto Protocol in 2002 spoke for several days—a modern marathon.

What is said in such speeches is also of interest here. Of all the **parliamentary privileges** and rights of MPs, individual and collective, the most important is the protection from libel action for anything said in the chamber. Occasionally MPs take advantage of their privileged position in this respect by declining to repeat outside the House certain remarks they have made within.[22] Another form of Parliamentary privilege is to find someone in contempt of Parliament. This fate recently befell the Deputy Commissioner of the RCMP, who was accused of misleading MPs.

. . . .

THE COMMITTEE SYSTEM

Much of the important legislative work of the House takes place outside the Commons chamber in a variety of committees. These include standing and special committees of the Commons itself, as well as joint standing and special committees of the Commons and Senate combined. Committees allow a small number of people to develop expertise in a particular field and to examine proposals in depth; moreover, if several committees operate simultaneously, a greater volume of business can be accomplished. In an ideal situation, committees could allow private members to make constructive contributions to the governing of the country and to do so in a consensual rather than an adversarial atmosphere. In Britain, committees have always had an autonomous position, including the choice of their own chair, and many members have found career satisfaction at this level rather than yearning for appointment to the Cabinet.

Committees were not used in a systematic way for most of Canadian history, and membership was so unstable that they failed to develop expertise. Repeated reforms of the Commons committee system since 1968 have made it more significant; in fact, most observers focus on committee work as the most promising way of making legislatures more meaningful. David Docherty reminds us that committees are usually more relaxed and less partisan than the House as a whole, committee members are more directly engaged in policy discussions, committees encourage specialization, they have significant powers of investigation, and they are staffed by nonpartisan employees of the legislature.[23]

Standing committees are set up more or less permanently in most of the substantive areas of government policy, such as fisheries and oceans or natural resources. They have two principal functions: to examine the Estimates—that is, the government's spending proposals—and to examine legislation at the committee stage.[24] The Estimates of Health Canada, for example, are scrutinized by the Standing Committee on Health. In examining bills after second reading, committees question ministers, public servants, advocacy groups, and other expert witnesses, who either try to convince committee members to approve the bill as introduced or else to effect changes. Sometimes a minister will ask a standing committee to study a problem in the absence of legislation. The Standing Committee on Finance is perhaps most important and now engages in wide-ranging pre-budget consultations. The newest is the Standing Committee on Government Operations and Estimates which is designed to examine all public spending and federal operations not formally examined by any other parliamentary committee. It is intended to complement the work of the Standing Committee on Public Accounts.

As a result of the 1986 changes, standing committees have additional functions and resources. Since they largely parallel government departments, they are authorized to investigate any aspect of the departments with which they are associated, including a review of non-judicial government appointments. However, even a negative vote will not necessarily prevent the government from making such appointments. Committee clerks are employees of the House of Commons and provide administrative and procedural support, but committees also have a budget to hire supporting staff and researchers, and thus to develop independent expertise. They normally request the services of the staff of the Library of Parliament (Research Branch), but they can also apply for funding to hire outside personnel.

Smaller, more stable, and more expert membership has served to increase the effectiveness of standing committees. Representation on all committees is proportional to party standings in the House, so that in the Martin and Harper minority periods, most of the 24 twelve-member committees had five or six government members and the rest from opposition parties. Standing committees frequently set up smaller subcommittees to expedite discussion of a variety of concerns. The Standing Committees in 2010 are listed below.

· ·

HOUSE OF COMMONS STANDING COMMITTEES, 2010

Aboriginal Affairs and Northern
   Development
Agriculture and Agri-Food
Canadian Heritage
Citizenship and Immigration
Environment and Sustainable
   Development
Finance
Fisheries and Oceans
Foreign Affairs and International
   Development
Government Operations and Estimates
Health
Human Resources, Skills and Social
   Development and the Status of Persons
   with Disabilities

Industry, Science and Technology
International Trade
Liaison
National Defence
Natural Resources
Official Languages
Procedure and House Affairs
Public Accounts
Public Safety and National Security
Status of Women
Transport, Infrastructure and
   Communities
Veterans Affairs

Committee chairs are elected by committee members but until 2002 were usually pre-selected by the Prime Minister's Office. At that point, however, a large group of Liberal backbenchers joined with the opposition parties to force a change in this procedure so that chairs were henceforth elected by secret ballot. The Harper PMO reverted to the earlier practice of indicating the MP it wanted as the committee chair. In the recent minority periods, most chairs were from the government side except for committees on access to information, privacy and ethics, government operations and estimates, and public accounts. Each committee also had two vice-chairs, one from the official Opposition and the other from another opposition party. Cabinet ministers do not sit on committees, but the presence of the relevant parliamentary secretary provides a link, positive or negative, to the government and the corresponding minister and department.

The **Standing Committee on Public Accounts** has been chaired by an opposition MP since 1958. It has the important function of examining the reports of the **auditor general**, the official of Parliament who audits the government's accounts. The Gomery Report on the sponsorship scandal put great emphasis on strengthening this committee, recommending that it be given substantially more money to hire its own research personnel, legal, and administrative staff, and that membership on the committee be more stable.[25]

The Auditor General is the most famous independent agent of Parliament, but as mentioned in Chapter 22, several other officials fall into this category including the Information Commissioner, the Privacy Commissioner, the Commissioner of Official Languages, the Conflict of Interest and Ethics Commissioner, the Lobbying Commissioner, and the

Chief Electoral Officer. A new such officer created in 2008 was the Parliamentary Budget Officer (PBO), who is available to MPs to review the expenditures of any part of government and the general financial picture of the country. A dispute arose, however, over how independent the PBO, Kevin Page, really was, while he had to fight for adequate resources.[26]

Special committees are occasionally established for some specific, temporary purpose, especially if the government party has an excess of backbenchers and some issue arises that is beyond the normal jurisdiction of standing committees. Special committees usually have an investigatory function—to examine an issue before the government has made up its mind on how to deal with it. Such committees may therefore be an important part of the initiation phase of the legislative process. The House occasionally appoints a "legislative committee" to examine a specific piece of legislation.

In addition to the standing and special committees of the House of Commons alone, the Commons and Senate sometimes work together in **joint committees**. Joint committees obviously avoid duplication and also give senators a chance to get involved at an earlier stage of the process than is usually the case. The most important is the **Standing Joint Committee on Scrutiny of Regulations**, which has the vital but unenviable responsibility of scrutinizing the mounds of **regulations** and other subordinate legislation issued by the executive branch each year. If the legal staff of the committee find something objectionable about a set of regulations, and the committee members agree, it usually is able to persuade the relevant department informally to make changes. If not, it has the power to recommend rescission of offensive delegated legislation. Special joint committees can also be established, such as the one that was involved in the development of the Constitution Act, 1982.

Finally, there is the committee of the whole. This is simply the entire Commons membership sitting in the chamber as a committee. In such a case, the Speaker is replaced in the chair by the deputy speaker, and the rules are somewhat relaxed. This committee is only used to debate appropriation bills (once the Estimates have been approved), urgent bills (such as back-to-work legislation), and certain noncontroversial bills. Otherwise, the House prefers to use smaller committees that can meet simultaneously in committee rooms outside the Commons chamber.

It is primarily the transformation of the committee system in recent years that has enhanced the position of ordinary MPs in the legislative process. As committees became smaller, more stable in their membership, and more expert in their field, and as their members developed greater collegiality, they sometimes shed some of their partisanship. Between 1986 and 1993, for example, many of these committees developed a consensus on the issues before them that cut across party lines. Such committees became newly independent sources of power in the legislative system, and this led to the acceptance of an unprecedented number of committee amendments to government bills. Since 1993, and especially in the five-party Parliaments after 1997, committees found it more difficult to achieve such a cross-party consensus. Some of the standing committees functioned well between 2006 and 2008, while others almost came to a standstill due to extreme animosity between Conservative and Opposition members. The Harper regime developed a manual for committee chairs explaining how to manipulate witness lists, circumvent Opposition motions, and limit criticism of the government.[27]

One advantage of all committees that meet outside the Commons chamber is that they can listen to representations from advocacy groups, bureaucrats, and other experts.[28] It was traditionally said that pressure groups and lobbyists did not make much use of the legislative branch of government because the crucial decisions had previously been made in the executive. There is always a possibility that the committee recommendations can change the government's mind, however; for example, substantial changes were made to the proposed Constitution Act, 1982 as a result of group representations to the parliamentary committee which studied it.

. . . .

MEMBERS' SERVICES AND ETHICS

Deciding how much to pay members of Parliament is an intractable problem. Paying MPs considerably more than the average industrial wage is to ensure public criticism, but as a general rule, the higher the level of remuneration, the better the quality of person that will be attracted to parliamentary life. The peculiar insecurity of political office in Canada must also be taken into account. In 2001, parliamentarians voted themselves a raise and incorporated their previous tax-free expense allowance into their overall salary. The basic pay for MPs in 2009 was just under $160 000, while senators received about $130 000. On top of this basic income, large numbers of MPs receive additional payments for supplementary responsibilities. These supplementary payments, as of 2009, are indicated in Table 23.2.

In addition to this basic pay, backbench MPs receive many other benefits and services at public expense or on a subsidized basis. MPs are given an annual budget of about $300 000 which is mostly used to hire staff. They are provided with an office on Parliament Hill and in the constituency, and virtually unlimited office expenses, telephone, mailing, printing, and travel privileges. Parliamentary parties receive funds for research purposes, and additional funds are provided for the operation of the offices of opposition leaders, whips, House leaders, and caucus chairs. Such funding is provided only to recognized parties in the House—that

TABLE 23.2 Selected Supplementary Allowances for Additional Responsibilities, 2009, on Top of $157 700	
Prime Minister	$157 700
Speaker, Cabinet minister, Leader of the Opposition	75 500
Minister of State	56 700
Leaders of other parties	53 700
Deputy Speaker, Opposition House leader	39 000
Chief government and Opposition whip	28 400
Parliamentary Secretaries, House leaders of other parties	15 800
Whips of other parties, Committee chairs	11 100

Source: Parliament of Canada. Indemnities, Salaries and Allowances, Members of the House of Commons. Found at: http://www2.parl.gc.ca/Parlinfo/Lists/Salaries.aspx?Menu=HOC-Politic&Section=03d93c58-f843-49b3-9653-84275c23f3fb&Year=2009 (Accessed April 26, 2009).

is, groups of at least 12 members—a major blow to the Conservatives and the NDP after the 1993 election. More controversial is the MPs' pension plan. In 1995, the Liberals removed some of the extremely generous provisions for newly elected MPs: they would have to wait to age 55 to collect; they could not "double-dip," collecting their pensions and other government salaries at the same time; and they could opt out entirely. Some Reform MPs who opted out later re-entered the plan.

The lot of backbench members of Parliament is obviously much improved from earlier eras, and their every need is now provided for. Although their remuneration and services might seem excessive, the expenses of serving some 100 000 constituents and the insecurity of parliamentary life should not be underestimated. If their expenses were not completely covered, only wealthy individuals could seek federal political office.

Although Canada has had a Conflict of Interest Code for cabinet ministers for some time, such a code for ordinary MPs was only adopted in 2004 as part of the ethics package that Prime Minister Chrétien introduced when his government was facing assorted charges of unethical behaviour, including the sponsorship scandal.[29] Among other things, it required disclosure of assets held and gifts and hospitality received, and possible breaches of the Code were examined by the ethics commissioner. The system did not function well, but Harper's **Federal Accountability Act** strengthened and renamed the office: the conflict of interest and ethics commissioner.

· ·

ROLES OF MEMBERS OF PARLIAMENT

The roles that members of Parliament perform can be seen in two different lights. First, in terms of how they vote, MPs can be classified as trustees, constituency delegates, or party delegates. "Trustees" would be MPs who feel obliged to vote according to their own conscience, their own understanding of the issue in question, or their own conception of the national interest. Alternatively, "constituency delegates" would be MPs who vote the way they think a majority of their constituents would want them to vote or in their conception of the best interests of their constituency. In other words, in situations where the two did not coincide, trustees would place their own views above those of their constituents, while constituency delegates would do the reverse. However much MPs may claim to fall into either of these categories, in practice they rarely deviate from the party line. In fact, then, they could usually be labelled "party delegates." If the party caucus determines a position that conflicts with either their own views or those of their constituents, MPs almost always put the party position first. The reasons for such rigid party discipline were discussed earlier in the chapter.

The other way to examine the roles of MPs is in terms of how they spend their time or what their priorities are.[30] The first role in this respect is the lawmaker, devoting attention to the legislative process and committee work, such as introducing, amending, and debating legislation. MPs are supported in these tasks by the Research Branch of the Library of Parliament, but since this role is almost completely irrelevant to their constituents, this is not a priority for many members. Another role is being a propagandist for one or more causes. This involves using every opportunity available—Question Period, general debates, and even public speeches outside of Parliament—to press for certain reforms they believe in. Determined crusaders for proportional representation or freedom of information reform would be good examples.

Then there is the goal of promoting their constituency and bringing back public favours, a role that could be called representational. This requires lobbying ministers and public servants for new public buildings, roads, wharves, and other facilities so that they will have something "concrete" to show for themselves by the time of the next election. Finally, all MPs perform the daily function of ombudsmen or social workers for their individual constituents, intervening with ministers or public servants to hasten administrative decisions, to correct bureaucratic errors, and to repair governmental injustices. There will always be constituents with passport, immigration, employment insurance, pension, and many other kinds of problems, and some MPs specialize in trying to resolve them. This "caseload" of MPs is now so heavy that they are provided with considerable administrative assistance in both their Ottawa and their constituency offices so that they will have some time left over for their other duties.[31] Figure 23.4 presents, in graphic form, a picture of how MPs spend their time.

The life of an MP is extremely busy; MPs are constantly engaged in meetings and talking with individual and groups of constituents, interest groups, the media, bureaucrats, party officials, staff, and other parliamentarians. Besides assuming heavy responsibilities in Ottawa, they are expected to be seen frequently in the constituency, both in their offices and at myriad social events, usually on weekends or when Parliament is recessed. All this activity interferes with a normal family life, whether those with spouses and children move their families to Ottawa or leave them at home to be visited when time permits.

· ·

Figure 23.4   How an MP Spends the Day: Percentage of Working Time Devoted to Different Tasks

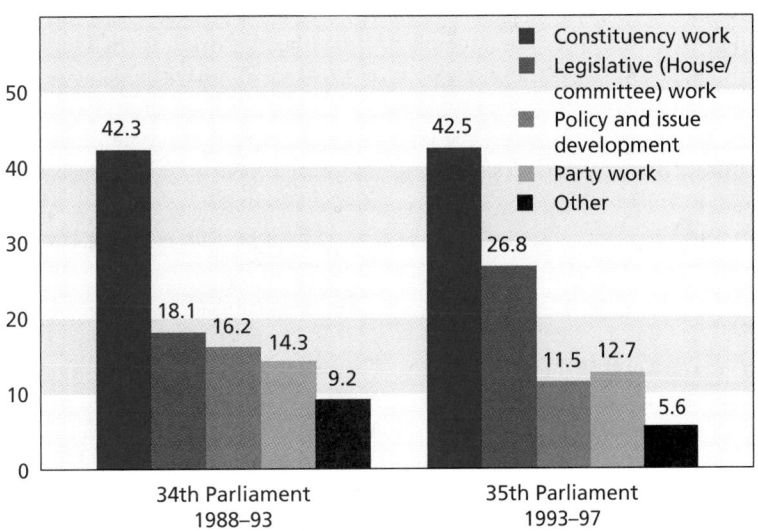

Source: David C. Docherty, Mr. Smith Goes to Ottawa: Life in the House of Commons (Vancouver: UBC Press, 1997), p. 129. Reproduced with permission.

. . . .

THE GOVERNMENT–OPPOSITION BALANCE

An objective look at Parliament reveals a basic dilemma: the government wants to get legislation passed expeditiously, but the opposition must have time to articulate constituency needs as well as a chance to criticize government proposals in order to make the public aware of their defects. One manner of addressing this conflict is to summarize the ways in which the Cabinet controls the Commons, especially in a **majority government** position, and then the ways in which the Commons controls the Cabinet.

The prime minister and Cabinet, through the governor general, summon, prorogue, and dissolve Parliament, and then basically determine the agenda of parliamentary business. The Cabinet has a monopoly on the introduction of financial legislation and a virtual monopoly on the legislation that actually is passed. The prime minister and Cabinet control almost all parliamentary committee work and also have the power to introduce closure to cut off debate or time-allocation motions to curtail it. Backing up all these specific devices of Cabinet dominance are two other general powers. Through the whip, the prime minister and Cabinet enforce party discipline on their MPs in order to achieve their ends, and they have at their disposal the vast informational resources of the public service. Thus, it is sometimes said that the prime minister and Cabinet operate as a virtual dictatorship until they have to face the electorate again some four or five years down the road.

Parliamentary control over the Cabinet, on the other hand, refers mainly to opportunities to criticize and to delay, rather than any real power to alter the Cabinet's proposals or to throw the government out. MPs, especially on the opposition side, have the daily option to ask oral questions of ministers, in addition to the 15 minutes set aside for members' statements, and 30 minutes for adjournment proceedings four times per week. They can also submit written questions seeking detailed information. MPs have the throne speech and budget debates in which to criticize the government generally or raise their own alternatives, as well as 22 opposition days per session to select the topic of debate. Marginal reforms were made in 2001 to strengthen the role of backbenchers: more money was allocated to registered parties for research and other caucus services; members' office budgets were increased; the housing allowance was raised; and the research capacity of the Library of Parliament was increased. MPs can introduce legislation in the form of private members' bills, criticize specific Cabinet measures at the second-reading stage, introduce amendments at the committee and report stages, and scrutinize the government's spending proposals. Opposition MPs may at least delay the adoption of government measures by prolonging debates and by raising procedural points. But when all is said and done, the prime minister and Cabinet usually get their way.

. . . .

MINORITY GOVERNMENT

The foregoing account assumes that the government is in a majority position in the Commons. Increasingly, Canada is characterized by a **minority government** situation—in which the government is outnumbered by opposition members—and the government is less dominant. The government may have to negotiate with opposition parties to some extent, such as to amend its proposals, abandon them, or even accept opposition initiatives. Many observers who deplore the normal arrogance of a majority government and who regret that so much opposition talent and so many opposition ideas ordinarily go to waste actually prefer to have a minority government in office.

Eugene Forsey reminds us that minority government is not exceptional, is not necessarily weak and indecisive, and does not have to be short-lived.[32] Between 1867 and 2010 there were 12 minority governments in Canada: 1921–25 (King), 1925–26 (King), 1926 (Meighen), 1957–58 (Diefenbaker), 1962–63 (Diefenbaker), 1963–65 (Pearson), 1965–68 (Pearson), 1972–74 (Trudeau), 1979–80 (Clark), 2004–06 (Martin), and 2006–08 and 2008– (Harper). Few of these governments could have been called weak and indecisive because of their minority position; many, such as the 1957–58 Diefenbaker government, were more active and courageous than the majority governments that preceded or followed them. Some were exceptionally bold and decisive, especially the Pearson governments and the Trudeau minority which were particularly sensitive to opposition demands. Although minority governments did not last as long as majority governments, not all of them ended by being defeated. The first Diefenbaker, Pearson, and Harper governments, for example, ended when the prime minister himself decided to call an election.[33]

In a minority government situation, much is made of one or more opposition parties holding the balance of power. On occasion, for example, this position has allowed the CCF or NDP to force a Liberal minority to adopt some of its policies. But holding the balance of power is not normally an enviable position, especially if the opposition cannot amend or defeat a government measure without throwing out the whole government. If any such defeat were taken as a vote of nonconfidence in the government, it would probably precipitate another election. Such an opposition party may not have the finances to engage in a quick succession of election campaigns, and is sometimes thought to suffer at the hands of an electorate that blames it for the inconvenience and expense of another vote.

This leads to a discussion of the principle of responsible government—that the Cabinet must have the confidence of the Commons or else call an election or resign. It is not always clear whether the Cabinet is required to take such drastic action. In a majority situation the problem is most unlikely to arise, but does a government in a minority position have to resign or call an election over any and every defeat? Atkinson and Docherty refer to the "erroneous notion that the defeat of any government-sponsored bill requires the government's resignation. No such requirement exists, except perhaps in the minds of MPs."[34] In 1968, the Pearson government was defeated on a piece of financial legislation, but the PM argued that the defeat was a fluke and that his government should be allowed to carry on. Since there is no question about the defeat of the government on a **nonconfidence motion**, including the speech from the throne and the budget, the matter was decided when the Cabinet subsequently survived an explicit nonconfidence motion. Some of the excitement over the defeat of the minority Martin government in 2005 is captured in Box 23.1. As mentioned, two of the Martin's bills were defeated, but he carried on regardless.[35] Such an understanding of what constitutes nonconfidence—explicit motions rather than defeat of ordinary bills—could be extended to majority situations as well.

More excitement followed the election of the Harper minority government in 2006. The polls showed that none of the parties was likely to win a majority in the foreseeable future, so they collectively found ways to ensure that the government would not be defeated on a nonconfidence vote or a vote that could be seen as one of nonconfidence. Both sides made

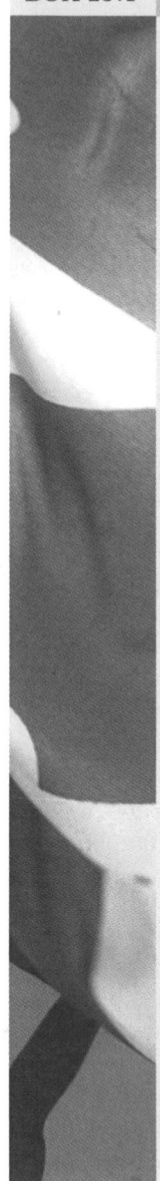

| BOX 23.1 | The Fall of the Martin Minority Government |

The 2004 federal election resulted in a minority government: 135 Liberals, 99 Conservatives, 54 Bloc Québécois, 19 NDP, and one Independent (Chuck Cadman). The Liberal total later declined to 133 with the ousting from the caucus of Carolyn Parrish and the voluntary withdrawal of David Kilgour, both choosing to sit as Independents. The Martin minority survived the vote on the speech from the throne by the almost unprecedented action of accepting opposition amendments to the speech. Two government bills were defeated, but since these were not considered confidence votes, the government ignored their defeat. That left the passage of the 2005 budget as the government's biggest obstacle. On the key second-reading vote, the Bloc and NDP opposed the budget, while the Conservatives took the unusual stance of abstaining. Meanwhile, the atmosphere in the House was extremely fractious, mostly because of revelations before the Gomery Inquiry, such that the Conservatives and Bloc nearly brought parliamentary business to a standstill. At this point, Martin went on national television to plead for a resumption of civility until such time as the allegations were dealt with in Gomery's final report. Martin promised to call an election within 30 days of the publication of that report. But not being certain that the budget would get through its final stages, Martin made a deal with the NDP for a supplementary budget. It would delay the corporate tax cuts and increase spending over two years by some $4.5 billion in the fields of housing, foreign aid, postsecondary tuition fees, and gas tax assistance for cities. The next problem was to get this bill, which was also a confidence vote, through the Commons. At this point, Conservative MP Belinda Stronach crossed the floor and was immediately elevated to the Martin cabinet. Nevertheless, the vote was a cliffhanger: 131 Liberals joined with 19 New Democrats, along with Independents Parrish and Cadman, for a total of 152. On the other side were 97 Conservatives, 54 Bloquistes, and Independent David Kilgour, for a total of 152. Speaker Peter Milliken broke the tie, and the government survived. The Liberals then lost Pat O'Brien to the Independent ranks on the same-sex marriage bill, while in July, Chuck Cadman died. The House adjourned for the summer, but in November, Conservative leader Stephen Harper introduced a general non-confidence motion supported by all the opposition parties, and the Martin government was defeated.

concessions from time to time, but the most common way to avoid a government defeat was for the Liberals to abstain. Harper called an election in October 2008 before being defeated, but then came close to defeat shortly afterwards, as discussed in Chapter 21. When the government introduced a superficial and partisan economic update, the three opposition parties signed a coalition agreement, in which they declared their readiness to form an alternative Liberal–NDP government with BQ support. In order to cling to power, Harper delayed a

Gilles Duceppe threatens to pull plug on Stephen Harper's minority government.

scheduled nonconfidence vote, and then pre-empted it with a successful but controversial request to the governor general to prorogue Parliament to avoid the vote altogether. In early February 2009 the Liberals supported the Conservative budget (with minor amendments), and the Harper minority government carried on.[36] Later in the session, the Liberals withdrew their support of the government and it began to depend on the NDP.

The difficulty of forming a majority government in Canada nowadays has resulted in a search for solutions to parliamentary instability. The events of late 2008 introduced the notion of a coalition government in the minds of Canadians who may no longer see it as a foreign concept. Even though this particular coalition had certain defects, did not take office, and was vilified by the Conservatives, the experience emboldened the opposition in its mandate to act as a check against the government. If the opposition parties were unanimously and thoroughly fed up with the government especially shortly after an election, they now realized that the passage of a nonconfidence motion would not necessarily precipitate an election.[37]

REFORM OF THE HOUSE OF COMMONS

The imbalance between government and opposition is so great, at least in a majority situation, and the legislative role of ordinary MPs has been so ineffective that parliamentary reform is never far from the minds of political scientists and politicians alike. Reform proposals have primarily been designed to remedy excessive partisanship, Cabinet domination, and the lack of influence of the private member.

At the end of the 1960s, changes in the committee system, the provision for timetabling the business of the House, and the funding of parliamentary parties for research purposes "inaugurated the modern era of parliamentary government."[38] Then, in the 1970s, MPs saw considerable improvement in their services, especially in parliamentary and constituency offices and staff. In addition, the proceedings of the Commons began to be televised in 1977, with later provision being made to televise some committee proceedings. One of the ways in which television changed members' behaviour was that they began to applaud instead of pound on their desks to indicate approval, something that was also appreciated by the simultaneous interpreters![39] In 1982, a severe altercation occurred between the Trudeau government and the Conservative opposition over the form and substance of the National Energy Program, such that the opposition left the division bells ringing for 15 days. The incident led all concerned to strive to improve Commons procedures. This momentum for reform survived the 1984 election, and as a result of the McGrath Committee, further reforms were made in 1986.[40]

In 1991, the Mulroney government introduced further changes. They were aimed at accomplishing as much parliamentary work in less time, giving MPs more time in their constituencies, and making the committee system more effective. Several modest changes were made after 1993, primarily related to the committee system, including reviewing government appointments and electing their own chair,[41] and to private members' bills. The temporary loosening of party discipline under Paul Martin and the creation of an independent ethics commissioner reporting to Parliament are probably the most significant reforms in modern times. Such changes enhanced the legislative role of backbenchers, but Franks argues that this is at the expense of the advantages of an executive-centred system. He feels that reform should be advocated with caution and that "Parliament is more in need of understanding than change."[42] Moreover, any future changes will probably need to be related to the now common occurrence of minority government.

PURPOSES AND POWERS OF THE SENATE

The ideal of democracy was still not enthusiastically accepted in the 1860s and the Fathers of Confederation felt it advisable to provide for an appointed body that would exercise "sober second thought" with respect to measures emanating from the popularly elected House of Commons. Thus, the Senate was to be the equivalent of the British House of Lords, an older, conservative influence, with a minimum age of 30, appointment for life, and a relatively high property qualification ($4000 of equity in land in the province or territory of residence and a net worth of $4000 over and above all debts). Sir John A. Macdonald argued that the Senate should protect minorities and the rich were always fewer in number than the poor![43]

Second, the smaller provinces would agree to join Confederation and accept representation by population in the House of Commons only if they were overrepresented in the Senate. The Fathers settled on a Senate that would be based on equal *regional* representation, a compromise between equal provincial representation (as in the United States) and the principle of representation by population. Such a system gave the Maritimes and Quebec a limited amount of protection against the voting power of Ontario in the Commons. It followed that senators were supposed to represent their regions and provinces within the national policy-making system.

A third function of the Senate, not explicitly provided for in 1867 but that can also be seen as part of the concept of sober second thought, is to improve legislation from a technical point of view. This function—to act as a non-ideological, routine revising chamber that picks up on flaws in legislation that have not been noticed during its passage through the busy Commons—has become one of the Senate's most important roles over the years.

As far as powers were concerned, the Senate was given a veto over all legislation, a power that was not restricted as in the case of the British House of Lords. The only point of Senate inferiority to the Commons was that "money bills," that is, legislation involving the raising or spending of money, had to be introduced in the lower chamber. Nothing in law prevented the Senate from delaying, amending, or vetoing any bills, whether or not they involved money, although in the latter case, amendments could not *increase* taxes or expenditures. It was only the Standing Orders of the House of Commons that claimed the Senate could not amend money bills, an assertion never accepted by the Senate.

It was not until 1982 that the Senate's power was in any way reduced, and that had to do only with constitutional amendments, not ordinary legislation. According to the Constitution

Act, 1982, the Senate can delay a constitutional amendment only for 180 days. If the Senate has not approved such an amendment by then, it can be re-passed by the Commons and bypasses the Senate in the process of ratification.

· ·

COMPOSITION OF THE SENATE

As mentioned, the basic structural principle of the Senate agreed to at the time of Confederation was equal regional representation. Thus Ontario, Quebec, and the Maritimes received 24 senators each. In the case of Quebec, the province was divided into 24 senatorial regions so that an appropriate balance of anglophone and francophone representatives would be chosen. Otherwise, senators do not officially represent a specific region of their province, although prime ministers usually give some attention to geographic balance, and on an individual, unofficial basis, senators themselves may choose to concentrate on one part of the province. When Prince Edward Island joined Confederation, it received four of the 24 Maritime senators, reducing Nova Scotia's and New Brunswick's share to ten each. In a general reform in 1915 the West was designated as a senatorial region with 24 senators, preserving the principle of equal regional representation, with six allocated to each Western province. In 1949, Newfoundland was awarded six senators in addition to the 96 already allotted, so as to leave the Maritime contingent intact. Finally, in 1975, Yukon and the Northwest Territories were given one senator each, as was Nunavut in 1999, so that the total became 105 (4 x 24 + 6 + 3), allowing for only slight deviations from the principle of equal regional representation.

Section 24 of the 1867 Constitution Act gives the governor general the power to appoint senators, but by convention this is done on the "advice" of the prime minister. Prime ministers have usually chosen partisan supporters, such as MPs seeking a safe haven, defeated MPs or candidates, those who have served the party organization well, retired premiers or other former provincial politicians, and federal Cabinet ministers who have outlived their usefulness. Rewarding party services, regenerating the Cabinet, and maintaining party unity were the main considerations in the prime minister's mind. Hence, almost all of those appointed could be called "party hacks," and the image of the Senate was set: a home for the aged, a pension scheme for retired party warriors, and a reward for businessmen's contributions to the party war chest. More positively, however, most senators could be seen as possessing valuable political experience.

In addition to rewarding faithful service to the party in the past, many appointments were made on the assumption that the new senator would continue to promote the party in the future. Such senators carried on as party fundraisers, party presidents, party organizers, election campaign strategists or managers, or in other partisan capacities. Most prime ministers have made the occasional nonpartisan or cross-party appointment, perhaps as a "cover" for yet more partisan nominees, and because the Senate was already overwhelmingly stacked with Liberals, Pierre Trudeau deliberately replaced a Tory with a Tory on six occasions.[44]

In the past, senators were traditionally English or French male lawyers or businessmen, many of whom maintained active business connections after their appointment. Most saw nothing wrong with carrying on as directors of various corporations or even being appointed to new ones at the same time as they held public office. They always had spare time, they welcomed the supplementary income, and they could be useful links between the corporate and political worlds. Because of ideological opposition to the whole concept of an appointed

IF DRAFTED — I WILL NOT RUN... IF ELECTED — i WILL NOT serve... IF APPOINTED TO THE SENATE — WELL, THAT'S A WHOLE DIFFERENT BALL OF WAX!

harrop ©

artizans.com

Graham Harrop/artizans.com

chamber, left-wing groups have refused the occasional offer of appointment, leaving labour and working-class representation in the Senate virtually nonexistent.

The Constitution Act, 1867 speaks of "qualified persons" being eligible for appointment to the Senate, and this was originally understood to include only men. In one of the most famous court cases in Canadian history, however, an enterprising group of women challenged this interpretation, and in the 1929 **Persons case**, the Judicial Committee of the Privy Council decided that "persons" did indeed include women.[45] Henceforth women were eligible to sit in the Senate, and their number reached 35 at the end of the Martin era. Such a large contingent of women has actually altered the Senate's operation to some extent, as noted below. In addition, ethnic and religious considerations have often played a part in Senate appointments. From the Diefenbaker period onward, prime ministers sought to diversify Senate membership in ethnocultural terms, and senators have been appointed as representatives of the Aboriginal, Ukrainian, Italian, Greek, Icelandic, and Black communities, among others.

Senators originally served for life, and many lived to the ripe old age of 80, 90, or 100. Lester Pearson had a constitutional amendment passed in 1965 to the effect that incumbent senators could stay until death or retire at 75 with a pension, but all subsequent appointees would have to retire at 75. In normal circumstances only one senator sits in the Cabinet (the government leader in the Senate). But both Joe Clark (1979–80) and Pierre Trudeau (1980–84) had three or four senators in their Cabinets to fill in gaps in their provincial representation, and Stephen Harper started out with two, one to represent Montreal. Because Harper believed in an elected Senate, he initially left many vacancies unfilled—18 as of December 1, 2008. However, because these vacancies actually disadvantaged the Conservative party in the Senate, Harper suddenly filled them with partisan supporters before the end of the year. He appointed a second batch of supporters with strong party ties in mid-2009, and hoped that he would soon have a Conservative majority in the chamber.

OPERATION OF THE SENATE

In the light of its intended functions, what can be said about the actual operations of the Senate? First, as for acting as a conservative influence on legislation and representing the interests of property, two examples stand out, the first being the Senate's defeat of the first

Old Age Pensions bill in 1925. But after an election in which Mackenzie King was deemed to receive a mandate for the legislation, the Senate passed the bill a year later. The other was the Senate's repeated refusal until 1936 to repeal the notorious section 98 of the Criminal Code that had been passed at the height of the Winnipeg General Strike in 1919 and clearly infringed freedom of speech.

The Senate has also been accused of being a lobby for the business community. At the time that Colin Campbell wrote his book *The Canadian Senate: A Lobby from Within*, many senators had corporate connections, especially those who sat on the Senate Committee on Banking, Trade and Commerce. He wrote of the Senate's adopted function of "business review," as its members "bargain and negotiate on business's behalf for amendments which are essential for a favourable financial and commercial climate." Campbell revealed the "one-sided review which takes place in a legislature created by a political system which bends over backwards to ensure that business has preferential access to the policy process."[46] The "new breed" of senators appointed since Campbell wrote are much less likely to come from the business community, however; they are more likely to be women and generally have a wider perspective.

Second, it must be concluded that the Senate has never effectively represented provincial and regional interests in the national policymaking process. This is not particularly surprising when senators owe their appointment to the federal prime minister and not to any provincial or regional constituency. Moreover, many senators settle down in the comfortable environs of Ottawa and rarely go near the region they ostensibly represent. As a result, the regional representation function was soon undertaken by the Judicial Committee of the Privy Council, regional ministers in the federal Cabinet, and provincial premiers in federal–provincial conferences.

Of the Senate's original purposes, then, the first has been rendered archaic and the second has been assumed by other agencies. Today's senators therefore justify their existence primarily in terms of the third function mentioned—routine, technical revision of bills. R.A. MacKay argues that the nonpartisan, noncontroversial revising function of the Senate is virtually indispensable, and F.A. Kunz calls it one of great usefulness.[47] In addition to routine revision of government bills, the Senate sometimes undertakes detailed examination of complex legislation, such as the Bankruptcy Act or the Criminal Code. Similarly, the rules allow a bill to be introduced simultaneously in both chambers so that the Senate can engage in an unhurried "pre-study" of the bill rather than wait until it has passed three readings in the Commons. This provision is rarely used, but the Anti-Terrorism Act was a recent example.

Senators also seek to emphasize other important aspects of their work.[48] One is the Senate's consideration of private bills. These concern individuals, companies, and other institutions, and are a nuisance to the busy House of Commons, which is often backlogged with public bills. Since 1934, almost all private bills have been introduced in the Senate, where the background work can be done so that the Commons can approve them routinely at a later date. For a period the Senate functioned as a divorce court for Quebec and Newfoundland, when religious opposition to divorce in those two provinces pre-empted turning this responsibility over to their courts. Divorces were a special kind of private bill, and between 1964 and 1968 (when they finally became a judicial matter in those two provinces) divorces were disposed of by the Senate without reference to the Commons.

Another kind of work not originally provided for is the study of various public problems by Senate committees in what Colin Campbell calls "social investigations." Senators often have the experience, expertise, independence of mind, and time to conduct inquiries that relieve the pressure on the House of Commons and are cheaper than royal commissions. Among the memorable reports of the Senate over the years were those on poverty, aging, unemployment, the mass media, science policy, land use, national defence, fisheries, Canadian–American relations, and the Canadian Security Intelligence Service. Senate committees now churn out reports at a dizzying pace on a wide range of subjects. Two of its most famous recent reports were on the legalization of marijuana and the Kirby Report on health care. Although the former did not achieve its objective, and marijuana has not been legalized, the Kirby Report had a major impact on health care discussions, especially regarding guaranteed maximum wait times and catastrophic drug coverage.[49] The government also implemented the recommendation of the Carstairs Report on end-of-life care that income security and job protection be extended to family members who care for the dying. Senate committees usually have more success when the government requests them to study an issue than when they undertake their own initiatives.

Finally, the Senate reviews regulations issued by various government departments. The Standing Joint Committee on the Scrutiny of Regulations has the responsibility of reviewing the great quantity of subordinate legislation issued every year. Although this is a joint Commons–Senate committee, the senators who sit on it have more time to devote to its tedious work and perhaps more independence of mind in approaching it.[50]

The question still arises: worthy as all of these new-found functions are, do they collectively justify the expense of the Senate? Many mediocre appointments have been made over the years, but the chamber has always had a number of impressive occupants. Although some senators have done virtually no work for their paycheques, others have made useful contributions. Many have outside interests, so that only a handful are totally focused on their senatorial responsibilities. Senator Colin Kenny, for example, led a crusade against the tobacco industry and persuaded the government to take a number of anti-smoking initiatives that led to the dissolution of the Canadian Tobacco Manufacturers' Council. He then became a leading spokesperson on defence issues. Given its lack of a popular base, however, any good work that the Senate does will always be somewhat suspect and not given the respect it deserves.

The Senate timetable is rather lax. Attendance is taken, and most senators show up three days a week for no more than 27 weeks a year. There being no shortage of time, the rules are quite relaxed; the Speaker is chosen by the prime minister and has a vote on all matters. There is a question period, but it is a challenge for the one senator who normally sits in the Cabinet to answer for the whole range of government activity. Prime ministers and Cabinets have often been disrespectful of the institution, leaving many vacancies for long periods of time and expecting it to pass large quantities of legislation quickly at the end of a session.

The Senate's exercise of its power to amend or veto legislation must be put into the context that an appointed legislative chamber lost much of its legitimacy with the spread of democratic sentiment shortly after Confederation. Thus, the Senate did not usually feel justified in defying the will of the popularly elected House of Commons.[51] Moreover, given the partisan nature of Senate appointments, the majority in that chamber usually corresponds to the partisan complexion of the Commons. Both had a Conservative majority for about the first 30 years and both usually had a Liberal majority after 1900.

As for amendments, Kunz and MacKay calculated that before 1960 the Senate made amendments to about 15 or 20 percent of the bills coming from the Commons.[52] This figure fell to between five percent and ten percent over the past 50 years. It must be said that in many cases such amendments were introduced in the Senate by the Cabinet itself, reflecting its second thoughts on the matter after a bill had been approved by the Commons, and most of the others were of a technical nature. To reinforce this point, it made little difference to the number of amendments whether or not the majority in both chambers belonged to the same party. Most of the technical amendments to government bills that are moved in the Senate are accepted by the Commons, but this is partly because they have been cleared in informal discussions beforehand.[53]

On the other hand, partisanship is most striking when we consider the Senate's vetoing of Commons legislation. In almost all such cases, a Liberal majority in the Senate has obstructed a Conservative majority in the Commons, or vice versa. According to MacKay, of approximately 4200 public bills passed by the Commons between 1867 and 1960, about 100 failed to pass the Senate, although many of these were withdrawn voluntarily by the government. Kunz found 18 vetoes out of 1918 bills between 1926 and 1963. Rather than concentrate on total numbers, Table 23.3 lists the 15 most controversial Senate vetoes. In addition, in 1961 the Senate held up the government bill firing James Coyne as Governor of the Bank of Canada until he had had a chance to defend himself before it. MacKay argues that in these and other cases the Senate has never defeated the real will of the people when clearly expressed;[54] if it

---

TABLE 23.3 The 15 Most Controversial Senate Vetoes

1.	1875: Rejection of a bill for the construction of the Esquimalt–Nanaimo railway
2.	1899–1900: Rejection of a bill to readjust representation in the House of Commons for Ontario
3.	1912: Amendment of Highways bill that government rejected
4.	1912: Amendment of Tariff Commission bill that government rejected
5.	1913: Rejection of Borden's Naval bill
6.	1914: Rejection of amendment of the BNA Act regarding provincial representation in the Senate
7.	1914: Rejection of Farmers Bank Depositors' Relief bill
8.	1923: Rejection of bill for construction of CNR branch lines
9.	1926: Rejection of Old Age Pensions bill
10.	1926, 1927, 1928, 1929: Rejection of repeal of s. 98 of Criminal Code
11.	1936: Rejection of amendment of the BNA Act regarding allowing provinces to levy sales taxes
12.	1937: Rejection of bill expanding jurisdiction of Board of Transport Commissioners
13.	1961: Rejection of amendment to the Customs Act
14.	1991: Rejection of Mulroney abortion bill
15.	1996: Rejection of Liberal bill reversing the privatization of Pearson airport

objects to a provision in a bill, the Senate will often accept it with "observations," pointing out its concerns to which the Commons may or may not respond.

Brian Mulroney had considerable difficulty with the Senate, when, between 1984 and 1991, a Liberal majority in that chamber coincided with a Conservative majority in the Commons. The Senate delayed many government bills, and it repeatedly passed amendments to them, only retreating at the last minute.[55] The Senate also tried to alter the Meech Lake Accord, and its amendments had to be overridden by the Commons after the expiry of the 180-day limit on constitutional amendments. Then, in mid-1988, at John Turner's direction, the Liberal majority in the Senate held up the Canada–U.S. Free Trade Agreement until the electorate had a chance to express its will on such an important measure. After the 1988 election, the Senate bowed to the popular will and passed the agreement, but later dug in its heels on other bills, especially the Goods and Services Tax (GST).

It is unlikely that the GST would have passed if Mulroney had not invoked an obscure clause in the 1867 Constitution Act, section 26, which allowed him to appoint eight additional senators (two for each of the four senatorial regions) to tip the balance in favour of the Conservatives.[56] After the GST was approved in an atmosphere of great bitterness, the Senate went ahead and defeated the government's compromise abortion bill (on a tie vote). This became the first measure in 30 years that the Senate actually defeated, but it was a peculiar case in that the government allowed a "free vote," and some Cabinet ministers were probably secretly relieved that the Senate had exercised such a rare veto.

Besides the intense partisan confrontation between the two chambers, the Mulroney period was exceptional for two reasons: first, the government had embarked on a new, neoliberal ideological agenda; and second, the Liberal ex-ministers in the Senate had a difficult time accepting the fact that they were no longer in power. In most of these cases, ironically, the House of Commons was acting in a more conservative manner than the Senate, which suddenly saw itself as protecting the little people.

By the time the Liberals came to power in 1993, the Conservatives had established a clear majority in the Senate, so positions were reversed, and the Liberals began to pay for their intransigence of a few years earlier. On a rather nonpartisan note, though, the Senate responded to demands from the academic community to veto a bill that would have merged the Social Sciences and Humanities Research Council with the Canada Council. The Conservative majority in the Senate was particularly incensed about the Liberal bill related to the privatization of the Toronto Pearson Airport, and the bill was defeated on a tie vote. The PC-controlled Senate then stalled the Liberals' redistribution bill to the point of abandonment, which was also the fate of pro-labour amendments to the Canada Labour Code. The Senate defeated the Newfoundland and Labrador constitutional amendment with respect to removing denominational schools, until it was overridden after 180 days.

Even after the Liberals regained a majority in the Senate, the second chamber remained a more active place than normal, as it amended the government's own Canada Wheat Board bill. But it then did the government a favour by defeating a private members' bill (dealing with profiteering from crime) that had slipped unnoticed through the Commons.[57]

The Senate declined to pass a number of bills that Jean Chrétien wanted adopted before he left office, including a bill creating an independent ethics commissioner, arguing that it wanted a separate ethics officer for senators. It also failed to pass the bill that would have sped up the redistribution process so that Paul Martin could have called an election early in 2004. Another long-standing bill that the Senate refused to pass was that on increasing penalties for animal cruelty. Once Martin was in office, however, the first two of these bills went through, and the Senate got a separate ethics officer.

Stephen Harper formed a government in 2006 in the unusual situation of holding a minority of seats in both the Commons and the Senate. Although the Conservatives were vastly outnumbered, especially until the end of 2008, the upper chamber generally functioned quite cooperatively with the government, such as with reasonable amendments to the Federal Accountability Act. On the other hand, the Senate insisted on keeping an ethics officer of its own, and it did not cooperate with Harper's efforts to reform the upper house.

Andrew Heard argues that a modern convention has developed such that the Senate can make purely technical amendments or others that it knows will be acceptable to the Commons and to the government. Although it should not act to frustrate the general thrust of Commons legislation put before it, the Senate can on rare occasions make substantive amendments "when the government has no clear support from the majority of Canadians to implement a policy that adversely affects some individuals or groups." If legislation is re-passed by the Commons, however, the Senate should give way.[58]

· ·

SENATE REFORM

Given the limited value of the Senate as it traditionally operated, its reform has always been high on the political agenda. One option is abolition, the official policy of the CCF/NDP because of the undemocratic nature of the Senate and its traditional links to the business community. Colin Campbell also recommended abolition because of the Senate's illegitimate defence of corporate interests and the impossibility of making the institution more effective and more democratic without interfering with the will of the House of Commons.

Many reformers have advocated reactivating the Senate's role of representing regional and provincial interests at the federal level because the existing mechanisms of "intrastate federalism" have been flawed. The Trudeau government first attempted to make the Senate a House of the Federation in 1978, with half its members selected by the provinces. However, the Supreme Court held that such changes to the structure of the Senate required provincial approval.[59] Of course, even if the prime minister retained the formal appointment power, he or she could name people nominated by the provinces. In the 1987 Meech Lake Accord, Prime Minister Mulroney promised to appoint senators from lists provided by the provinces, but by the time the Accord died three years later, and this interim measure with it, Mulroney had appointed only a handful of senators from provincial lists.

Meanwhile, Alberta began pushing its **Triple-E Senate** proposal: senators would be *elected*, the Senate would have additional powers to make it *effective*, and each province would have an *equal* number of representatives in the chamber.[60] Triple-E advocates were not entirely clear on what powers they saw as necessary to make the Senate "effective," but since they generally felt that laws currently emanating from the House of Commons were designed in the interests of central Canada, such proponents were not overly concerned about deadlock between their revamped Senate and the lower house. A constitutional amendment to effect such changes, however, would not be easily achieved.

The government of Alberta felt so strongly about an elected Senate that it held a "senatorial election" in 1989 when a vacancy occurred during the period in which Mulroney asked for a list of provincial nominees. The Reform Party candidate won the province-wide contest (coinciding with municipal elections); Premier Don Getty forwarded his name to the prime minister, and Mulroney reluctantly gave in. Senate reform was then a prominent part of the 1992 Charlottetown Accord, with changes approximating Triple-E, but when the accord went down to popular defeat, the Senate remained unreformed. Little on the subject was heard for about 15 years afterward, except for Alberta's holding of another senatorial election in 1998. Chrétien slyly filled a vacancy from that province a month before the election, appointing a former Tory, who sat as an Independent, so the two Reform candidates "elected" became "senators in waiting." Alberta held a third senatorial election in 2004, and one of the few early Senate appointments Stephen Harper made was that of Bert Brown, "elected" in both 1998 and 2004. Apart from the election issue, there is considerable debate about altering the regional or provincial representation in the chamber.[61]

To some extent, the Senate is changing through informal means. For example, Paul Martin appointed younger and often female senators from a wider diversity of professional backgrounds who were usually prepared to put in more effort than the male corporate lawyers who were previously dominant. In recent years, senators have taken more of their own initiatives and made many useful and objective responses to those of the government. The Senate aims to become the "think tank of the Canadian government." Although the lack of democratic accountability will always cloud the senators' work, their considerable accumulated political experience can be a considerable asset.

Because so much of its committee work is both impressive and ignored, the Senate has begun to televise some of its committee hearings, although not the proceedings of the Chamber as a whole. Other reforms recently recommended include setting up a regional affairs committee, assuming a specialized role of scrutinizing government appointments and treaties, making an even stronger investigation of regulations, working longer hours, and improving its attendance record.[62]

As mentioned, the benefit of appointed senators, at their best, is that a premium can be put on expertise, experience, and continuity, as well as gender and minority representation. But since the appointment process will always dog its accomplishments, one proposal is to set up an independent appointments committee (akin to that involved in recommending the appointment of judges) that would take the partisanship and favouritism out of the PM's hands. Stephen Harper, however, came to office determined to have senators elected. Because of the rigidity of the constitutional amending formula, he did not expect to achieve his objective in that direction. So he tried to obtain Triple-E through ordinary legislation. Harper's first bill proposed an eight-year term for new appointees, but the Liberal majority in the Senate decided not to proceed with it until the bill had been referred to the Supreme Court regarding its constitutionality. The second bill provided for popular consultation before senators were formally appointed by the PM; such informal senatorial elections could coincide with either federal or provincial elections. The constitutionality of this bill was also in question, and has not been debated beyond first reading in the Commons.

. . . .

CONCLUSION

This chapter demonstrates that apart from MPs who double as Cabinet ministers, the role of the House of Commons in the policymaking process is not impressive and that of the Senate even less so. However, both chambers have significant functions: in debating public issues, in keeping the government honest, and in educating the electorate. The prime minister and Cabinet can win almost every "battle" with Parliament, but may still lose the next electoral "war" if the opposition has alerted the public to their faults via the media. Concentrating the responsibility for public policy in the hands of the prime minister and Cabinet has advantages, but these could still be achieved if better use were made of the talent in the House of Commons and that increasingly evident in the Senate. Individual MPs also have important constituency responsibilities.

This chapter is primarily connected to Chapter 21 on the Executive, especially considering that the prime minister and Cabinet ministers are members of Parliament and need to retain the confidence of the House of Commons. It is also linked to chapters on parties and elections, since MPs owe their office to election, devote much of their efforts to being re-elected, and perform in a very partisan manner. Although partisanship overwhelms most of its operations, the socio-economic representation of parliamentarians is of considerable importance, and links this chapter to Part 2 of the book.

P In terms of the approaches outlined in Chapter 1, pluralists note the diversity in the social background of MPs, such as the rising numbers of women and ethnocultural minorities, and emphasize the opportunities available to MPs to articulate a variety of interests. Pluralists also point to the participation of parliamentary committees and individual MPs in various policy communities, and see advocacy groups interacting more regularly with MPs than in the past. However, pluralists question whether the rigid party discipline in the Canadian House of Commons is appropriate for such a pluralistic society. Such rigidity has forced various regional, ethnic, and class interests to form their own political parties when they felt unable to make themselves heard within traditional national parties. It has also led many people to look to provincial governments and premiers to articulate regional concerns. As for the Senate, pluralists emphasize its increasingly diversified membership and the wide range of its social investigations. Although it was once the preserve of French and English males, the Senate now contains more than one-third women and representation from a variety of ethnocultural groups.

PC Public choice theory sees the House of Commons as the focal point of party conflict between elections in order to influence the electorate in its next trip to the polls. Much of the activity in the Commons is designed to manipulate public opinion, as all parties try to present themselves in the best possible light and have nothing but condemnation for their opponents. This chapter has shown the many opportunities available in the Commons to pursue this intensely adversarial activity. Since media coverage of the Commons is usually dominated by opposition criticism, however, the Cabinet does its best to ignore the House and to interact (and bargain) directly with the public.

C Class analysts find that the "Commons" is still an elitist institution. Very few of its members come from manual occupations, for example, and a high proportion have postsecondary education. Even more telling are the results of a survey that indicated MPs overestimate the economic well-being of the other members of society.[63] At the very least, class analysts advocate more working-class representation in Parliament. But that in itself would be of limited value since MPs are largely impotent as representatives of the general public, and in class analysts' eyes, the prime minister and Cabinet generally act at the command of the corporate elite.

Class analysts charge that the Senate performs one principal role: the systematic review of legislation from the standpoint of the interests of business.[64] As mentioned, at least in the past, many senators simultaneously sat on various corporate boards and lobbied fellow senators, MPs, bureaucrats, and Cabinet ministers on behalf of individual corporations or the general capitalist cause. Campbell quotes one senator as follows: "without us the Cabinet and the bureaucracy would never get the type of cooperation out of the private sector which is needed to make the system run."[65] Class analysts argue that "technical review" is in reality "business review" and, at least until the Mulroney period, senatorial vetoes were usually in the corporate interest. At the same time as one Senate committee recommended the legalization of marijuana in 2002, another supported the big banks in their desire to merge.

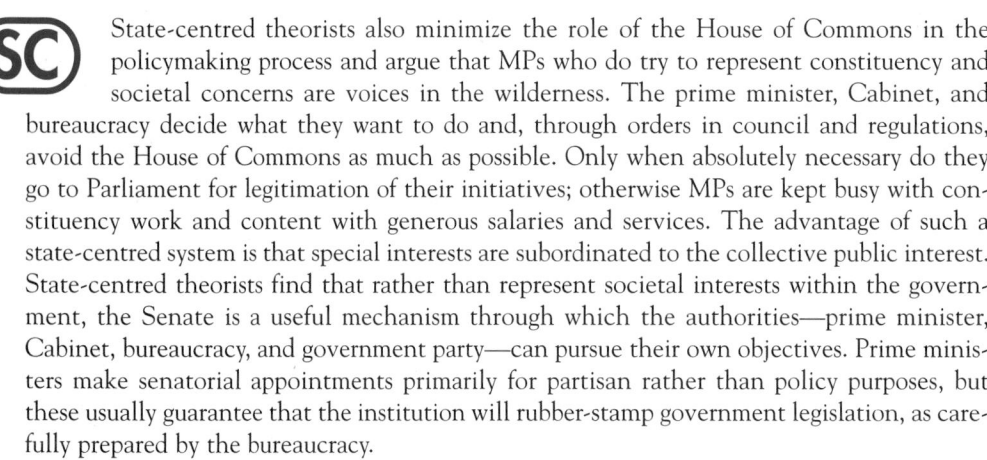 State-centred theorists also minimize the role of the House of Commons in the policymaking process and argue that MPs who do try to represent constituency and societal concerns are voices in the wilderness. The prime minister, Cabinet, and bureaucracy decide what they want to do and, through orders in council and regulations, avoid the House of Commons as much as possible. Only when absolutely necessary do they go to Parliament for legitimation of their initiatives; otherwise MPs are kept busy with constituency work and content with generous salaries and services. The advantage of such a state-centred system is that special interests are subordinated to the collective public interest. State-centred theorists find that rather than represent societal interests within the government, the Senate is a useful mechanism through which the authorities—prime minister, Cabinet, bureaucracy, and government party—can pursue their own objectives. Prime ministers make senatorial appointments primarily for partisan rather than policy purposes, but these usually guarantee that the institution will rubber-stamp government legislation, as carefully prepared by the bureaucracy.

. . . .

DISCUSSION QUESTIONS

1. If Parliament does not play a significant part in the policymaking process, what are its basic functions?

2. What are the advantages and disadvantages of rigid party discipline in the House of Commons?

3. Should the concept of "confidence" be limited to nonconfidence votes, the speech from the throne, and the budget, or applied more broadly?

4. What other aspects of the House of Commons, if any, should be reformed?

5. How does minority government affect the significance of the House of Commons in the policymaking process?

6. Does the Senate do enough to justify its existence, or should it be abolished?

7. What are the pros and cons of the Triple-E Senate? How else could the Senate be reformed?

8. If elected, to what extent should the Senate be able to interfere with the will of the Cabinet and the House of Commons?

. . . .

NOTES

1. C.E.S. Franks, *The Parliament of Canada* (Toronto: University of Toronto Press, 1987), p. 5. John Stewart, *The Canadian House of Commons: Procedure and Reform* (Montreal: McGill-Queen's University Press, 1977) lists essentially the same functions: "first, to support a government; second, to prevent clandestine governing; third, to test the government's administrative policies and legislative proposals; fourth, to constrain the ministers; and fifth, to educate the electorate," p. 30.
2. Franks, *The Parliament of Canada*, p. 216.
3. Franks, *The Parliament of Canada*, p. 73; David C. Docherty, *Mr. Smith Goes to Ottawa: Life in the House of Commons* (Vancouver: UBC Press, 1997), ch. 2.
4. John Porter, *The Vertical Mosaic* (Toronto: University of Toronto Press, 1965), p. 402.
5. Jeffrey Simpson, *The Friendly Dictatorship* (Toronto: McClelland and Stewart, 2001), pp. 36–45; and David C. Docherty, *Legislatures* (Vancouver UBC Press, 2005).
6. Franks, *The Parliament of Canada*, p. 142.
7. Stewart, *The Canadian House of Commons*, pp. 29–30.
8. Eugene Forsey and Graham Eglington, "Twenty-Five Fairy Tales about Parliamentary Government," in Paul Fox and Graham White, eds., *Politics: Canada*, 7th ed. (Toronto: McGraw-Hill Ryerson, 1991), argue that this is a mistaken belief; Docherty, *Mr. Smith Goes to Ottawa*, ch. 6; and Simpson, *The Friendly Dictatorship*, pp. 45–53.
9. Sometimes the concept of a "shadow cabinet" is used by opposition leaders, but if the party becomes the government, there is no guarantee that "shadow critics" will be given the corresponding Cabinet post.
10. Franks, *The Parliament of Canada*, pp. 6, 29, 96, 268; Michael M. Atkinson and David C. Docherty, "Parliament and Political Success in Canada," in Michael Whittington and Glen Williams, *Canadian Politics in the 21st Century*, 7th ed. (Toronto: Thomson Nelson, 2008).
11. Andrew Heard, *Canadian Constitutional Conventions* (Toronto: Oxford University Press, 1991), p. 80.
12. Franks, *The Parliament of Canada*, pp. 110–14. Donald Savoie confirms my contention that in Canada, almost every MP wants to be a minister, in *Governing from the Centre: The Concentration of Political Power in Canada* (Toronto: University of Toronto Press, 1999), p. 83.
13. Heard, *Canadian Constitutional Conventions*, p. 83.
14. Paul Thomas, "Parliamentary Reform through Political Parties," in John Courtney, ed., *The Canadian House of Commons: Essays in Honour of Norman Ward* (Calgary: University of Calgary Press, 1985); and Paul Thomas, "The Role of National Party Caucuses," in Peter Aucoin, ed., *Party Government and Regional Representation in Canada* (Toronto: University of Toronto Press, 1985). Savoie, *Governing from the Centre*, pp. 91–93, quotes MPs as referring to caucus as "bitching sessions."
15. Thomas, "The Role of the National Party Caucuses"; and Atkinson and Docherty, "Parliament and Political Success in Canada," p. 20.
16. Bills introduced in the Senate have an S designation.
17. The Speaker allowed a private member's bill that would make contributions to Registered Educational Savings Plans tax deductible and it was passed with the combined strength of the opposition parties, even though it was considered a money bill. The government later found a procedural way to have it quashed. See documents on House of Commons website: *Private Members' Business: Practical Guide*, 9th ed. (Ottawa: Parliament of Canada, 2008), retrieved on April 27, 2009, available at http://www.parl.gc.ca/information/about/process/house/PMB_PracticalGuide/PractGuide_4PMB-e.htm.
18. The government's resort to closure on every stage of the bill was seen as the work of Trade and Commerce Minister C.D. Howe, who was obsessed with getting the construction of the pipeline started.

19. Jessica J. Richardson, "Modernization of Royal Assent in Canada," in *Canadian Parliamentary Review* (Summer 2004).

20. For a compilation of the rules, see the most recent edition of *Standing Orders of the House of Commons*, available at http:www.parl.gc.ca/information/about/process/house/standingorders/toc-e.htm. For a discussion of the Speaker, see "The Impartiality of the Speakership: A Round Table," *Canadian Parliamentary Review* (Summer 2004).

21. Martin Westmacott, "Whips and Party Cohesion," *Canadian Parliamentary Review* (Autumn 1988).

22. Terry Moore and James Robertson, "An Introduction to Parliamentary Privilege," in *Canadian Parliamentary Review* (Autumn 2001).

23. Docherty, *Legislatures*, pp. 165–66; Atkinson and Docherty, "Parliament and Political Success in Canada," p. 21; Jonathan Malloy, "Reconciling Expectations and Reality in House of Commons Committees: The Case of the 1989 GST Inquiry," *Canadian Public Administration* (November 1996); House of Commons Canada, *Committees: Practical Guide*, 9th ed. (Ottawa: Parliament of Canada, 2008), cited on April 27, 2008, available at http://www.parl.gc.ca/information/about/process/house/CommitteesPracticalGuide/CmtesPG2008__cover-e.htm.

24. Jack Stilborn, "Parliamentary Review of Estimates: Initiatives and Prospects," *Canadian Parliamentary Review* (Winter 2006-07).

25. Gomery Report, *Restoring Accountability*, ch. 4, pp. 75–80, and ch. 6, pp. 117–19; Jonathan Malloy, "The Standing Committee on Public Accounts," in *Restoring Accountability: Research Studies*, Volume 1.

26. Gary Levy, "A Parliamentary Budget Officer for Canada," *Canadian Parliamentary Review* (Summer 2008); Jeffrey Graham Bell, "Agents of Parliament: A New Branch of Government?" *Canadian Parliamentary Review* (Spring 2006).

27. Heather MacIvor, *Parameters of Power: Canada's Political Institutions*, 5th ed. (Toronto: Nelson Education, 2010), p. 224.

28. Grace Skogstad, "Interest Groups, Representation and Conflict Management in the Standing Committees of the House of Commons," *Canadian Journal of Political Science* (December 1985); and David M. McInnes, *Taking It to the Hill: The Complete Guide to Appearing Before (and Surviving) Parliamentary Committees* (Ottawa: University of Ottawa Press, 1999).

29. C.E.S. Franks, "Parliamentarians and the New Code of Ethics," *Canadian Parliamentary Review* (Spring 2005).

30. Docherty, *Mr. Smith Goes to Ottawa*, ch. 5.

31. Docherty estimates that constituency work takes up 35 percent of the average MP's time and recommends that more resources at the local level would free up MPs for policy and legislative research, *Legislatures*, pp. 89–90.

32. Eugene Forsey, "The Problem of 'Minority Government' in Canada," *Canadian Journal of Economics and Political Science* (February 1964); Peter Dobell, "What Could Canadians Expect from a Minority Government?" (Montreal: Institute for Research on Public Policy, 2000); and Paul E.J. Thomas, "Measuring the Effectiveness of a Minority Parliament," *Canadian Parliamentary Review* (Spring 2007).

33. Peter H. Russell, *Two Cheers for Minority Government: The Evolution of Canadian Parliamentary Democracy* (Toronto: Emond Montgomery, 2008).

34. Atkinson and Docherty, "Parliament and Political Success in Canada," pp. 8–9.

35. According to Franks, the Trudeau minority was actually defeated on 18 of 81 votes between 1972 and 1974 but chose to resign on the defeat of the 1974 budget; the Pearson government had suffered two other defeats without much fanfare. Franks, *The Parliament of Canada*, p. 139. Andrew Heard discusses another controversial vote in May 2005 in "Just What is a Vote of Confidence? The Curious Case of May 20, 2005," *Canadian Journal of Political Science* (June 2007).

36. Peter H. Russell and Lorne Sossin, eds., *Parliamentary Democracy in Crisis* (Toronto: University of Toronto Press, 2009).

37. Russell, *Two Cheers for Minority Government*.

38. Franks, *The Parliament of Canada*, p. 132; and John Stewart, "Commons Procedure in the Trudeau Era," in John Courtney, ed., *The Canadian House of Commons: Essays in Honour of Norman Ward* (Calgary: University of Calgary Press, 1985).

39. One of the more controversial aspects of television was the rule that the camera could focus only on the person recognized by the Speaker, rather than show what was going on elsewhere in the chamber.

40. *Report of the Special Committee on Reform of the House of Commons* (Ottawa: House of Commons, 1985).

41. Atkinson and Docherty, "Parliament and Political Success in Canada," p. 37.

42. Franks, *The Parliament of Canada*, pp. 9, 261. See also Thomas S. Axworthy, "Parliamentary Reform—Everything Old is New Again," Institute for Research on Public Policy, *Policy Options*, June 2008; Centre for the Study of Democracy, http://www.queensu.ca/csd/.

43. Quoted in R.A. MacKay, *The Unreformed Senate of Canada*, rev. ed. (Toronto: McClelland and Stewart, 1967), pp. 47–48.

44. MacKay, *The Unreformed Senate*, pp. 91–95; and F.A. Kunz, *The Modern Senate of Canada 1925–1963: A Re-appraisal* (Toronto: University of Toronto Press, 1965), pp. 337–47. Andrew Heard argues that a constitutional convention is emerging that the Senate may not insist on altering the financial provisions of money bills. *Canadian Constitutional Conventions*, p. 94.

43. MacKay, *The Unreformed Senate*, ch. 9; and Kunz, *The Modern Senate of Canada*, ch. 2, both discuss socioeconomic backgrounds up to 1960 and 1963, respectively.

44. When Paul Martin appointed Dr. Lillian Dyck (no relation to this author) to the Senate, she sat as a New Democrat, but the NDP were reluctant to acknowledge her and she joined the Liberals instead!

45. Kunz, *The Modern Senate of Canada*, discusses this issue on pp. 53–56. The case was officially referred to as *Edwards v. Att. Gen. of Can.*, [1930] AC 124.

46. Campbell, *The Canadian Senate: A Lobby from Within* (Toronto: Macmillan, 1978), pp. 10–11; and John McMenemy, "The Senate as an Instrument of Business and Party," in Paul Fox and Graham White, eds., *Politics: Canada*, 7th ed. (Toronto: McGraw-Hill Ryerson, 1991), p. 455.

47. MacKay, *The Unreformed Senate*, p. 110; and Kunz, *The Modern Senate of Canada*, p. 186.

48. The Senate has started to publish a quarterly newsletter called *The Senate Report*, available on the Senate website, as well as *The Senate Today* and *The Senate This Week*.

49. Campbell, *The Canadian Senate: A Lobby from Within*; and Jeffrey J. MacLeod and Howard Chodos, "The Senate Committee Study on Canada's Health Care System," *Canadian Parliamentary Review* (Spring 2003).

50. Paul Salembier and Peter Bernhardt, "Understanding the Regulation Making Process," *Canadian Parliamentary Review* (Spring 2002).

51. MacKay, *The Unreformed Senate*, writes that it is an "institutional survival of a pre-democratic age" (p. 10) and that "in a democratic age an appointed upper house labours under the handicap that it has no political foundation" (p. 62).

52. MacKay, *The Unreformed Senate*, p. 87; and Kunz, *The Modern Senate of Canada*, pp. 116–17.

53. See Parliament of Canada, *Bills Introduced in the House of Commons and Amended by the Senate, 1960 to Date*"; available at http://www.parl.gc.ca/Parlinfo/Compilations/HouseOfCommons/Legislation/HOCBillsAmendedbySenate-aspx.

54. MacKay, *The Unreformed Senate*, pp. 96–112.

55. See the justification offered by Senator Lorna Marsden in "Doing Its Thing—Providing 'Sober Second Thought': The Canadian Senate, 1984–1990," in Fox and White, *Politics: Canada*.

56. In 1873 Alexander Mackenzie had asked the British government to summon additional senators but was refused on the ground that it was not necessary at the time.

57. The Senate also made a small amendment to the Liberals' Youth Criminal Justice Act in 2002.

58. Heard, *Canadian Constitutional Conventions*, p. 95.

59. *Reference Re Legislative Authority of Parliament to Alter or Replace the Senate*, [1980] 1 S.C.R. 54.

60. See, for example, Peter McCormick, "Canada Needs a Triple-E Senate," in Fox and White, eds., *Politics: Canada*; H. McConnell, "The Case for a 'Triple-E' Senate," *Queen's Quarterly* (Autumn 1988); and Simpson, *The Friendly Dictatorship*, pp. 18–29.

61. Special Senate Committee on Senate Reform, "Report on the Motion to Amend the Constitution of Canada (western regional representation in the Senate)" (Ottawa, October 2006).

62. For a fine account of the Senate in recent times, see Serge Joyal, ed., *Protecting Canadian Democracy: The Senate You Never Knew* (Montreal: McGill-Queen's University Press, 2003). Many contributors to the book, from both inside and outside the Senate, come to a consensus on many of these points.

63. Franks, *The Parliament of Canada*, p. 69.

64. Campbell, *The Canadian Senate*, p. 9.

65. Ibid., p. 71.

. . . .

FURTHER READING

HOUSE OF COMMONS

Atkinson, Michael M., and David C. Docherty. "Parliament and Political Success in Canada." In Michael Whittington and Glen Williams. *Canadian Politics in the 21st Century*, 7th ed. Toronto: Thomson Nelson, 2008.

Bejermi, John. *Canadian Parliamentary Handbook*. Ottawa: Borealis Press, annual.

Docherty, David C. *Legislatures*. Vancouver: UBC Press, 2005.

———. *Mr. Smith Goes to Ottawa: Life in the House of Commons*. Vancouver: UBC Press, 1997.

Franks, C.E.S. *The Parliament of Canada*. Toronto: University of Toronto Press, 1987.

Heard, Andrew. *Canadian Constitutional Conventions*. Toronto: Oxford University Press, 1991.

Russell, Peter H. *Two Cheers for Minority Government: The Evolution of Canadian Parliamentary Democracy*. Toronto: Emond Montgomery, 2008.

Smith, David E. *The People's House of Commons: Theories of Democracy in Contention*. Toronto: University of Toronto Press, 2006.

SENATE

Campbell, Colin. *The Canadian Senate: A Lobby from Within*. Toronto: Macmillan, 1978.

Joyal, Serge, ed., *Protecting Canadian Democracy: The Senate You Never Knew*. Montreal: McGill-Queen's University Press, 2003.

Kunz, F.A. *The Modern Senate of Canada 1925–1963: A Re-appraisal*. Toronto: University of Toronto Press, 1965.

Mackay, R.A. *The Unreformed Senate of Canada*, rev. ed. Toronto: McClelland and Stewart, 1967.

Smith, David E. *The Canadian Senate in Bicameral Perspective*. Toronto: University of Toronto Press, 2004.

Chapter 24

THE JUDICIARY

In 2006, Marshall Rothstein was interviewed by a House of Commons committee—the first time such a procedure preceded appointment to the Supreme Court of Canada. The BC courts ruled that it is possible for child pornography to have artistic value, and the Supreme Court of Canada opened the door to two-tier medical care in Canada. The Supreme Court also decided that jurors can be challenged for racial bias when an accused person is a member of a group subject to widespread prejudice, has told lower court judges to find alternatives to putting offenders in prison, and has denied Quebec the right to make a unilateral declaration of independence. The Federal Court of Canada quashes decisions of the Immigration and Refugee Board, overruled the government on many so-called security cases, and upheld a major public servants' pay equity claim. Women's and minority ethnocultural groups criticize the general dominance of white male judges across the country, and Aboriginals demand a parallel Aboriginal justice system. The public is appalled at residual patronage appointments to the bench and troubled by cutbacks to legal aid plans. The Harper government took a hard line on crime that included changing the procedure for appointing judges.

Canadian political science was traditionally interested in the judiciary or court system primarily in terms of its interpretation of the federal–provincial division of powers. Now that the **Charter of Rights and Freedoms** has catapulted the courts into the middle of many heated political issues, however, political scientists are giving this fourth branch of government much more attention. Chapter 19 considered the role of the courts in interpreting the Charter of Rights and Freedoms and included a wider discussion of the role of judges in the policymaking process. This chapter examines the judiciary as an institution of government, discussing the function of adjudication, categories of laws, the structure of the courts, the Supreme Court of Canada, and the appointment, retirement, removal, and independence of judges.

THE FUNCTION OF ADJUDICATION

The judiciary has always been associated with the rule adjudication function in the political system, although other institutions may perform part of this function, too. Adjudication can be defined as interpreting the law in cases of dispute, of settling disputes by applying the law to them, or of making a judgment based on the law. Peter Russell defines the term as follows: "providing authoritative settlements in disputes about the law."[1]

Judges engage in the authoritative resolution of legal disputes, but many legal disputes are resolved without going to court or before going through the entire judicial process. Such an "out-of-court" settlement, especially one between individuals or between governments, is likely to be some sort of personal or political compromise. It is only when an accommodation satisfactory to both sides cannot be reached that the formal adjudicatory process is pursued to the bitter end.

The function of the judiciary therefore is to render formal, impartial, authoritative judgments in the case of legal disputes between two parties that cannot be settled otherwise. It is a process that generally relies on the adversarial system, with lawyers representing each side. The judge, clothed with the coercive powers of the state, acts as an independent referee and decides which of the disputants is legally right. As a result, the process usually culminates in the designation of a winner and a loser, rather than in the achievement of some middle ground acceptable to both sides.

Other governmental structures also engage in rule adjudication, especially a great variety of administrative tribunals, as discussed in Chapter 22, and the distinction between them and real courts is often subtle. Moreover, the judiciary also has certain non-adjudicative functions. Because of their prestige and impartiality, for example, judges have frequently been appointed to head royal commissions or other commissions of inquiry. The nature of many such commissions has unfortunately been more political than judicial, and observers often feel that this is an inappropriate use of judicial personnel, especially given backlogs in their regular adjudicative work.

Apart from the civil law system in Quebec, Canadian federal, provincial, and territorial legal systems operate in the tradition of the English **common law**. The basis of that system is the accumulation over the centuries of judicial precedents, both in England and more recently in Canada. Thus, in a typical court case, the two sides seek to find precedents—previous court decisions—favouring their respective points of view. The judge (and sometimes the jury) has to decide which precedents most closely resemble the case currently before the court. The principle that precedents are binding on successive decisions is called **stare decisis**.

If the law were always comprehensive and crystal clear, and if the situations to which it applied were always simple and straightforward, rule adjudication would be fairly routine and the judiciary would not have much discretion in performing this function. The real world is more complex, however, and the law may not be clear on all points or provide for every conceivable situation. Moreover, judges can usually avoid a precedent they dislike by "distinguishing" it—that is, deciding that the facts in the case before them are sufficiently different from the facts of the precedent case that to follow the latter would be inappropriate.[2] Russell refers to the "inescapable generality of the law" such that, although judges theoretically settle disputes according to pre-existing law, they actually shape and develop the law in the very process of settling disputes about it. They "put flesh on the bare skeleton of the law and shape its substance."[3]

The judiciary and the function of judicial interpretation were included in the chart of the policymaking process in Chapter 20. Rather than occurring subsequent to policymaking, where it once was placed, rule adjudication can now be considered as part of the policymaking process. Unlike Americans, Canadian observers did not give much recognition to the concept of judicial involvement in this process until recently. But Russell argues that this Canadian approach "wrongly assumes that all important public policies are expressed in statutes passed by legislatures ... and overlooks the extent to which [such] policies...are shaped through the process of being applied in particular cases by judges and administrators."[4] He cites such examples as the large element of discretion left to judges in the sentencing process, the decision of the Canadian courts to give little weight to the Canadian Bill of Rights,

CPImages/Adrian Wyld

The nine justices of the Supreme Court in ceremonial robes on February 19, 2009.

and the increasing judicial supervision of the operation of administrative agencies. In addition, judicial interpretation of anti-monopoly laws "decisively shaped industrial policy by making it nearly impossible to convict corporations for monopolistic practices."[5] In the course of adjudicating disputes, therefore, the courts are inherently involved in policymaking.

One step beyond **judicial discretion** is the explicit power of **judicial review**. Rather than merely interpreting laws with discretion, judicial review is the power of the courts to declare them invalid, refuting the principle of the **supremacy of parliament**. The original Constitution Act of 1867 did not contain any such provision, although the courts soon appropriated this power in one respect. Chapter 18 detailed the extent to which the courts invalidated federal and provincial legislation as violations of the division of powers between the two levels of government. In rendering federal or provincial legislation void if either encroached on the jurisdiction of the other level of government, the decisions of the courts had a significant effect on the shape of Canadian federalism. The court's power of judicial review was greatly enhanced with the adoption of the Canadian Charter of Rights and Freedoms in 1982, and the effects of the first 25–30 years of that review were discussed in Chapter 19. Peter McCormick writes in this connection: "we should recognize that judges have always had power, have always affected our society by the decisions they make.... The Charter has simply made a longstanding reality more immediately visible and directed us belatedly to an assessment of the implications of judicial power."[6]

Access to and Costs of Justice

Many people, even in the middle class, cannot afford to hire a lawyer to defend them in court, yet the objective of the judicial process must be the search for truth and the obtaining of justice, goals that have traditionally rested on the adversarial system. To give those without the financial resources a fairer chance to achieve justice, legal aid programs financed jointly by the federal and provincial governments have been established. These vary from one province to another, cover only certain kinds of legal work, and have been subject to severe funding cutbacks in recent years so that they are less adequate than ever. Community legal clinics serve a similar function, and other proposals have been suggested to improve the prospects of less affluent persons in obtaining a fair hearing.[7] Very few ordinary people can afford to take a case all the way to the Supreme Court of Canada and the Court Challenges Program designed to help finance Charter challenges has twice been eliminated by Conservative governments. Increasingly, people are trying to defend themselves without legal counsel, a generally regrettable development.

A related means of reducing the costs of the administration of justice as a whole are the practices of plea-bargaining and pre-trial conferences. Plea bargaining involves discussions between defence and Crown attorneys with the aim of achieving agreement on charges to be pursued, typically by having the accused plead guilty to one charge and the Crown agree to drop other charges. This practice is routine at the provincial or territorial court level and avoids a lengthy, costly trial. In the higher trial courts it is common for the judge to hold a pre-trial conference with the lawyers for each side. Such conferences can result in a negotiated settlement or at least a time-saving clarification of the issues involved. They have also proved to be useful at the level of family and small-claims courts. Although plea-bargaining and pre-trial conferences must not be allowed to subvert justice, they are valuable devices to cut costs for everyone involved (including the public) and to reduce the workload of the often congested court system.

CATEGORIES OF LAWS

The law can be defined as "society's system of binding rules."[8] Laws are commonly divided into different categories, primarily "civil" and "criminal." A **civil law** regulates relationships between two private parties, such as individuals or corporations, and if private agreement cannot be reached in the case of dispute, one party may take the other to court. Most aspects of civil law in Canada are within provincial jurisdiction, largely because of the provincial power over property and civil rights. Civil cases often involve disputes over commercial contracts or property, and such cases are normally resolved by the court's ordering one party to pay damages to the other. Civil cases are decided on the basis of the "balance of probabilities" of the merits of each side.

Criminal law, on the other hand, is primarily a federal responsibility; it is thus more or less uniform throughout the country and has been consolidated in the **Criminal Code**. In this case, the commission of a crime, such as murder, sexual assault, or theft, is considered to be a wrong against society as a whole, and the state takes the initiative to bring the suspect to justice by means of the police and Crown attorneys. In criminal cases, judges may impose fines or prison sentences if the accused is found guilty, such guilt having been proven "beyond a reasonable doubt."

One of the peculiarities of Canadian federalism is that although criminal law is within federal jurisdiction, it is usually the provincial attorneys general and their agents, the Crown attorneys, who are responsible for initiating proceedings against the person who is charged. This situation has come about because the provinces have jurisdiction over the administration of justice. Sometimes a case contains both civil and criminal elements, such as a drunken driver who does damage to another person's car. The state pursues the violation of the Criminal Code, but the victim's insurance company would have to take the initiative to sue for property damage.

Instead of this basic division between civil and criminal law, a distinction is sometimes made between public and private law. Private law is essentially the same as civil law described above—that is, law that centres on private interests. Beyond the contracts and property mentioned, however, private law includes torts, wills, company law, and family law. Public law, primarily involving the public interest or the government, goes beyond criminal law to include constitutional law, administrative law, and taxation law. Constitutional law has traditionally involved questions about federal or provincial jurisdiction, and governments themselves have often been the parties to a constitutional case. With the adoption of the Charter of Rights and

Freedoms, a whole new aspect of constitutional law in Canada has emerged. Administrative law concerns the operation of government departments and agencies, and as government activity expanded over the years, this branch of law also increased in significance.

By giving the provinces jurisdiction over property and civil rights, the Fathers of Confederation allowed Quebec to retain its distinctive private or civil law system based on the French Napoleonic Code. A new edition of the **Code Civil du Québec** came into force in 1994. The private law system in the other provinces and territories is based on the English common law tradition. The theoretical distinction between the two systems in terms of form is that while the common law consists of a hodgepodge of judicial precedents, the Code Civil is a single, comprehensive document. As Gall puts it, "in a common law system, the courts extract existing principles of law from decisions of previous cases, while in the civil law system, the courts look to the civil code to determine a given principle, and they then apply the facts of an instant case to that principle."[9] The state has far greater ability to assert its authority and power through the written code than in the common law tradition, where the law is written in more general terms and is susceptible to interpretation and application by judges and juries. There are also certain differences in substance, but although much attention is given to this distinction in Canadian legal and political life, the actual difference between the two systems is probably not as great as is often assumed. Lawyers and judges in the civil law system cannot help but pay some attention to precedents within that system and cannot avoid being influenced by the common law system surrounding them.[10]

. . . .

STRUCTURE OF THE COURTS

Because the provinces that formed Confederation in 1867 already possessed a court system, and because the Judicial Committee of the Privy Council continued to function as a court of appeal for the whole British Empire, it was not necessary to devote much attention to the judiciary in the Constitution Act, 1867. The new federal government was allowed to establish a general court of appeal and any additional courts, but the provinces were otherwise given responsibility for the administration of justice, which included the establishment of a provincial court system. McCormick describes the logic of the Canadian court structure as follows:

- First: Identify the more routine cases and those that involve less serious possible outcomes and assign them to an accessible high-volume, low-delay court, preferably one that sits in many different centres (provincial courts).
- Second: Assign the less routine and more serious cases to a lower-volume court that can devote more time and more focused attention to each individual case (superior trial courts).
- Third: Establish a court of appeal to correct simple errors and to promote uniformity in the application of the law within each province (provincial courts of appeal).
- Fourth: Establish a "general court of appeal" to promote uniformity in the application of the law within the country as a whole and to provide judicial leadership (Supreme Court of Canada).
- Fifth: Create a system of federal courts for cases directly involving the federal government as a party or raising issues concerning the administrative law applied by federal departments (Federal Court of Canada).[11]

As shown in Figure 24.1, the court systems within each province developed into a reasonably uniform three-level hierarchy. At the top are two "superior" courts—the superior trial court and the court of appeal, although they go by different names from province to province. At the bottom are provincial courts. Most provinces originally set up district or county courts between these two levels, but over the 1975–95 period they abolished this intermediate tier and integrated it with their superior courts.[12] Each of the territories has a similar court structure.

Because of the assumption that provinces could not be trusted to make worthy appointments to superior, district, and county courts, the Fathers of Confederation provided that the judges of these courts would be appointed by the governor general, conventionally meaning the federal Cabinet or minister of justice. Such judges were also paid by the federal government. Thus, in another peculiarity of Canadian federalism, each province determines how many superior court judges it needs, but they are appointed and paid by Ottawa.[13] Since these courts were provided for in section 96 of the 1867 document, they are often called "section 96 courts," and their judges, "section 96 judges." Below the level of section 96 courts, each province established various "provincial courts" to which provincial Cabinets appoint the judges. A brief discussion of each level of the judicial hierarchy follows.

Provincial Courts

Whatever their structure or name, provincial courts generally have the functions listed in Box 24.1. Provincial courts have a monopoly on summary (less serious) offences except in some provinces where even lower tribunals, such as justices of the peace, have been given this responsibility. There is increasing concern that few JPs have the kind of legal training that would prepare them to deal with the complex legalities they must often confront. More serious crimes, called indictable offences, can be subdivided into three categories. Some, like

· ·

Figure 24.1   The Court Structure in Canada

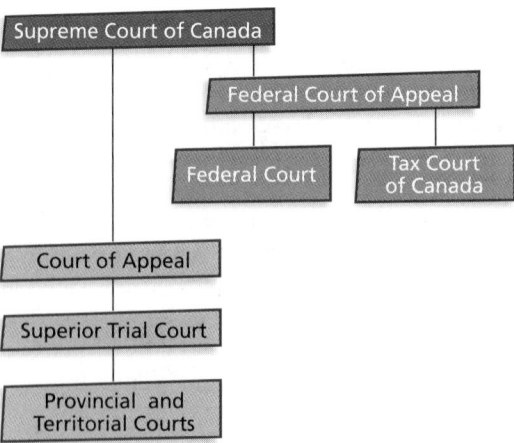

BOX 24.1	Functions of Provincial and Territorial Courts

- Summary offences including less serious crimes, provincial and municipal offences
- Most aspects of indictable offences, some mandatory and others optional
- Preliminary hearings for most serious crimes
- Bail hearings
- Youth Criminal Justice Act offences
- Family law, except divorce and proceedings flowing from divorce
- Small civil cases

murder, are reserved for superior courts; some, like theft, are assigned to provincial courts; and those in an intermediate category can be tried in either section 96 or provincial courts. The federal Youth Criminal Justice Act covers offences committed by those aged 12 to 18. This is a complex area of federal–provincial interaction, but as far as courts are concerned, the offences are tried in provincial courts or special youth courts established in some provinces. Family law is another area of great federal–provincial complexity. Several provinces have tried to overcome the problem by experimenting with a "unified family court" presided over by a section 96 judge, but most authorities would prefer to unify family law jurisdiction at the provincial court level.[14]

Provincial and territorial courts, sometimes in a civil division, also have jurisdiction over disputes involving small amounts of money, although some provinces have established small claims courts for this purpose. Each province and territory determines the monetary limit for cases that can be considered at that level, with disputes involving larger sums being initiated at the section 96 court level. Some provinces have also tried to remove the adversarial nature of small claims disputes and other civil lawsuits by instituting mediation services, such as Alternative Dispute Resolution (ADR), by professional mediators. These promise a cheaper, quicker, and possibly fairer resolution, and help to free up the backlog of cases before the courts.

The Superior Trial Court

The functions of the superior trial court in the provinces and territories, whatever its name, are listed in Box 24.2. In this court, the accused often has the option of trial by judge alone or trial by judge and jury. Although to be judged by a jury of peers is a sacred legal principle, the use of juries continues to decline. Besides the legislation that has reduced the availability of juries, prosecutors and judges are pressured for financial reasons to resolve cases quickly through plea-bargaining rather than through a protracted trial by jury. In addition, there is a growing concern that jurors cannot appreciate the complexity of the law and are more likely than a judge to be swayed by a charismatic lawyer in the courtroom.

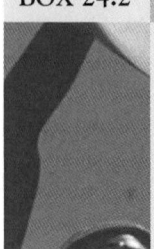

BOX 24.2	Functions of Superior Trial Courts

- Some mandatory and other elective indictable offences
- Civil matters over a given monetary amount
- Divorces and proceedings flowing therefrom
- Appeals from lower courts regarding summary convictions, juvenile, and family cases
- Administrative law cases

Provincial and Territorial Courts of Appeal

Provincial and territorial courts of appeal hear criminal, civil, and other appeals, some of which have already been appealed from a lower court to a section 96 trial court. Although some of its judgments are appealed to the Supreme Court of Canada, in most cases the decision of the provincial or territorial court of appeal is final, which adds to the significance of this level of court.[15] The basic function of an appeal court is to correct errors or injustices that one side claims were made in a lower court, but an appeal court is primarily interested in legal rather than factual issues. The second function of the appeal court is to render an opinion in a reference case—that is, on a constitutional issue referred to it by the provincial Cabinet. Russell thus speaks of the "law-making" role of appeal courts because their legal interpretations have a "creative legislative dimension."[16] Decisions of the court of appeal are binding on all courts below it and are "strongly persuasive" for trial courts in other provinces and territories. Courts of appeal normally sit in banks of three judges, but the size of these panels can be increased to five for very important cases. Each side of a case submits a brief or "factum" in advance that summarizes its arguments, and lawyers then engage in oral argument.

The Federal Court of Canada

The **Federal Court of Canada** was established in 1971 to replace the Exchequer Court created in 1875. It was intended to relieve the Supreme Court of hearing routine appeals from certain federal administrative agencies and **regulatory tribunals** and to develop a more unified and cohesive body of federal administrative law.[17] Although it is not well known to the public, the Federal Court has significant powers over the operation of the federal government. The Federal Court of Appeal consists of a chief justice and 12 other judges who sit in panels of at least three members. The Federal Court, formerly known as the trial division, contains the chief justice and 32 other full-time and assorted part-time judges. Between its two divisions, the Federal Court has the functions listed in Box 24.3.

The work of the Federal Court is dominated by cases involving the Immigration and Refugee Protection Act and the Immigration and Refugee Board. The Federal Court also handles many admiralty and patent cases, and cases involving Employment Insurance, penitentiaries, the Parole Board, the Public Service Commission, and the Public Service Labour Relations Board. In recent years the Federal Court upheld the decisions of the Canadian Human Rights Commission with respect to pay equity in the federal public service, at Canada Post and at Bell Canada. It has seen a growth in Aboriginal cases dealing with monetary and constitutional issues, land entitlements, and natural resources. Of great interest to political

---

BOX 24.3 **Functions of the Federal Court of Canada**

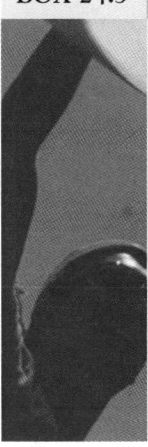

- Cases involving admiralty law, and copyright, trademark, and patent disputes
- Citizenship and immigration appeals
- Appeals from other federal administrative tribunals
- Civil cases involving the federal government
- Cases involving bills of exchange, promissory notes, aeronautics, and interprovincial works and undertakings
- Appeals from boards of referees under the Employment Insurance Act
- Prerogative writs (e.g., injunctions) applying to agencies of the federal government
- Appeals regarding the Access to Information and Privacy Acts
- Issuance of Canadian Security Intelligence Service warrants

---

science, the Federal Court also hears appeals regarding the Access to Information and Privacy Acts and decides on requests for warrants from the Canadian Security Intelligence Service to plant bugs, open mail, and engage in other surreptitious activities. Several Canadians accused of terrorism have recently (and often successfully) taken their cases to the Federal Court.

The Tax Court of Canada is a judicialized version of its predecessor, the Tax Review Board. It provides an easily accessible and independent tribunal for the disposition of tax disputes between citizens and the federal government. It deals primarily with matters arising under the Income Tax Act, the Employment Insurance Act, and the Excise Tax Act. Headed by a chief judge, it consists of 26 other full-time and assorted part-time judges, who hear cases across the country. Some of its decisions are appealable to the Federal Court of Appeal.

THE SUPREME COURT OF CANADA

The Supreme Court of Canada sits at the apex of the Canadian court system. About 85 percent of its work consists of hearing appeals from the provincial and territorial courts of appeal in civil and criminal cases,[18] but it also receives cases from the Federal Court of Appeal in administrative law matters. Besides hearing actual appeal cases from lower courts, the Supreme Court can be asked by the federal Cabinet to consider an important question of law, in what are called **reference cases**. Such cases are usually of a constitutional nature and have always been taken seriously, even though occasional doubt has been expressed as to whether they carry the same weight as an actual case. Table 24.1 lists selected reference cases.

That part of the Supreme Court's work of most interest to political science involves constitutional law, whether in terms of the division of powers between federal and provincial governments or interpretations of the Charter of Rights and Freedoms. Although the Supreme Court hears fewer cases than any lower court—it issues about 75 judgments per year—it is interested almost exclusively in questions of law.[19] Thus, of all courts, it is the most heavily engaged in a "law-making" role, and its decisions are binding on all lower courts across the country.

TABLE 24.1 **Selected Leading Reference Cases**

- *Anti-Inflation Act Reference, 1976*: A Trudeau government reference regarding the constitutionality of its own program of wage and price controls
- *Patriation Reference, 1981*: A case that combined three provincial reference cases concerning Prime Minister Trudeau's intention to ask the British Parliament to enact the Constitution Act, 1982 without provincial consent
- *Quebec Veto Reference, 1982*: A Quebec reference case clarifying whether that province had a right to veto constitutional amendments
- *Milgaard Reference, 1992*: A federal request to reopen the David Milgaard case because of suspicions of a miscarriage of justice
- *Goods and Services Tax Reference, 1992*: An Alberta reference of the federal law imposing the Goods and Services Tax
- *Quebec Education Act Reference, 1993*: A Quebec reference regarding the constitutionality of changing the basis of the province's education system from religious to linguistic
- *Quebec Secession Reference, 1998*: A federal reference regarding the constitutionality of a unilateral Quebec declaration of independence
- *Firearms Act Reference, 2000*: An Alberta reference challenging the constitutionality of the federal firearms registration scheme
- *Same-Sex Marriage Reference, 2004*: A federal reference seeking approval of a proposed federal law on this question

Until 1949, the Supreme Court was a seriously deficient institution. First, its decisions could be appealed to Canada's pre-1949 final court of appeal, the **Judicial Committee of the Privy Council (JCPC)** located in London, and it was bound by JCPC precedents. But even more humiliating, appeals could also go directly to that Empire court from provincial appeal courts, completely bypassing the Supreme Court of Canada. Before 1949, 253 cases went to the JCPC from the Supreme Court of Canada and 414 went there straight from provincial appeal courts.[20] This weakness in authority was enhanced by the relatively poor quality of judges appointed to the Supreme Court in that earlier period, apart from such individuals as Lyman Duff and Ivan Rand.[21]

Canada could have cut off appeals to the Judicial Committee after obtaining complete independence in 1931, and pressure mounted to do so after the unpopular "New Deal" decisions of 1935 that were mentioned in Chapter 18. But the Second World War intervened, and it was unclear whether the provinces would have to be involved in this decision because their appeals could already go directly to the JCPC. If so, there was some question of whether the provinces would agree to it, since they had been so well served by the Judicial Committee over the years. In 1947 it was determined that Ottawa could unilaterally curtail all such appeals, and it promptly did so. The Supreme Court of Canada has not been formally bound by Judicial Committee decisions since 1949 and has explicitly overruled them on occasion.

Until 1974, the Supreme Court had little discretion in deciding which cases it heard, but since then it has basically been in control of its own agenda. Today, only two categories of cases have an automatic right of appeal to the Supreme Court: provincial reference cases, and murder cases in which the provincial or territorial court of appeal was split on a question of law. Applications for leave (that is, permission) to appeal discretionary cases are normally handled in writing by a panel of three judges, but sometimes the panel hears the applications live, giving lawyers 15 minutes to make their case, via two-way satellite television if they choose. These panels annually hear about 550 applications for leave to appeal, accepting just over ten percent: those that involve a question of public importance or an important issue of law. Although the panels give no reasons for agreeing or refusing to hear an appeal, it can be assumed that they agree with the lower court decision if they refuse the appeal. Such discretion considerably enhances the stature of the institution. Figure 24.2 outlines the Supreme Court appeal process.

Although an increasingly important institution of government, the Supreme Court rests primarily on the **Supreme Court Act** rather than being embedded in any constitution act as such.[22] The Supreme Court Act now provides for a nine-member court (six from 1875 to 1927 and seven from 1927 to 1949). Three of the nine must come from Quebec, with its distinctive civil law system, while convention dictates that the other six be selected from a variety of locations, normally three from Ontario, two from the West, and one from Atlantic Canada. The act requires that at least five judges constitute a quorum, with the result that civil law cases from Quebec can be heard by a five-member panel, including a majority (three) from the civil law system. The position of Chief Justice normally alternates between francophone and anglophone members, simultaneous interpretation is available, and Supreme Court judges are now expected to be at least functionally bilingual. Among other provisions of the Supreme Court Act are those that lay out the grounds for appeal and reference cases and those that stipulate that judges hold office during good behaviour until the age of 75. One of the merits of the Meech Lake and Charlottetown accords would have been to "constitutionalize" the Supreme Court in order to give it a firmer foundation and to clarify how it could be changed.

. . . .

Figure 24.2 Supreme Court Appeal Process

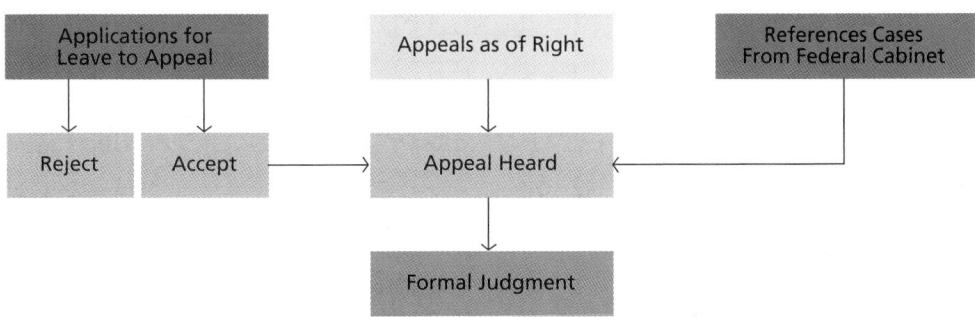

The Court holds three sessions of about two months each per year and adjourns in between to write up its decisions. Justices usually wear black silk robes at sittings of the Court, but have ceremonial robes of bright scarlet trimmed with Canadian white mink for special occasions. As much as possible, the Court tries to hear cases with a full complement of nine. Judges study the lower court proceedings and judgments in advance, along with the written arguments of the lawyers for each side. In preparing for the case, as well as in writing the first draft of decisions, each Supreme Court judge is assisted by three outstanding new law school graduates called law clerks. They help the busy judges search for and sift through precedents and other relevant material, including academic articles on the issues involved. The Court usually hears two cases per day, and oral arguments for each case normally last only two hours, during which time the judges often ask trenchant questions. In some instances the Court also grants "intervener status" to provincial governments and interest groups that are concerned about a case but not directly a party to it. Figure 24.3 shows the areas of law involved in the appeals heard in 2008. Public law cases, especially criminal and constitutional, now clearly predominate over private law disputes on the Supreme Court docket.

Once the arguments are completed, the judges usually "reserve judgment" and meet in private conference to discuss the case. Starting with the most recent appointee, each gives his or her tentative decision, and, if there is a consensus, the Chief Justice asks one member to draft the judgment. The Court tries to come to a unanimous decision, which it achieves in about 75 percent of cases,[23] but even so, not all the judges may come to the common decision by the same route. If it is a split decision, two or more judges are asked to prepare statements of their point of view. These drafts are then circulated among all the judges on the case and evoke comments before being revised. Judges sometimes compete to write certain judgments, as well as lobby one another for support.[24]

So much effort is put into the process of preparing their opinions that a decision is typically not issued until about six months after the Court hears the case, and it has occasionally

. . . .

Figure 24.3 Appeals Heard 2008: Type

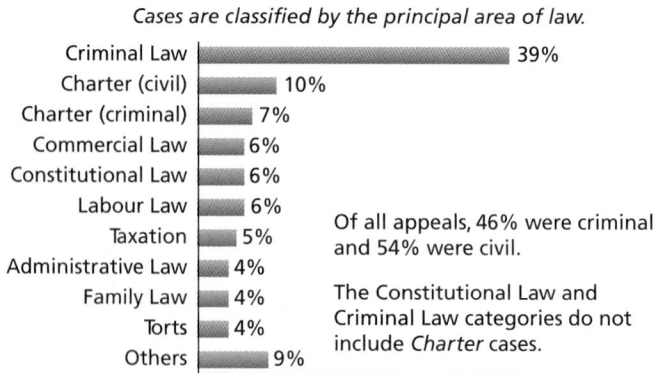

Cases are classified by the principal area of law.

Criminal Law — 39%
Charter (civil) — 10%
Charter (criminal) — 7%
Commercial Law — 6%
Constitutional Law — 6%
Labour Law — 6%
Taxation — 5%
Administrative Law — 4%
Family Law — 4%
Torts — 4%
Others — 9%

Of all appeals, 46% were criminal and 54% were civil.

The Constitutional Law and Criminal Law categories do not include *Charter* cases.

Source: Supreme Court of Canada. Statistics 1998–2008 Bulletin of Proceedings: Special Edition. Pg. 6. Reproduced with the permission of the Supreme Court of Canada, 2009.

taken over a year for all members of the Court to make up their minds, write their opinion, or concur with a colleague. When it comes to citing other cases as a basis for their decisions, the Supreme Court of Canada most frequently mentions its own decisions, followed by those of the Ontario Court of Appeal; in the 1984–94 period, about 15 percent of its citations were to English courts and seven percent to U.S. courts.[25] Decisions are usually released in written form by depositing them with the Registrar, but the Court can pronounce formal judgments in the courtroom. Recent membership in the Supreme Court can be seen in Table 24.2.

This discussion of the structure of Canadian courts reveals an essentially integrated, vertical court system rather than two parallel systems of federal and provincial/ territorial courts. With the exception of some federal matters that must be initiated in the Federal Court of Canada, both the provincial/territorial court systems and the Supreme Court of Canada hear cases dealing with federal, provincial, and territorial laws. The judicial system is further integrated with provincial and territorial governments prosecuting federal crimes and with the federal Cabinet appointing judges to section 96 courts within the provinces and territories. Some aspects of the federal–provincial/territorial judicial integration could be improved, such as in the areas of Young Offenders and family law. Federal–provincial conflict has occasionally arisen over provincial attempts to enhance the powers of their provincial courts and administrative tribunals at the expense of section 96 courts. However, most authorities argue strenuously in favour of maintaining such an integrated system.[26]

TABLE 24.2 Recent Membership in the Supreme Court of Canada

Appointment	Name	Retirement (Death)
1989 (Mulroney)	Beverley McLachlin CJ* 2000	
1990 (Mulroney)	William Stevenson	(1992)
1991 (Mulroney)	Frank Iacobucci	2004
1992 (Mulroney)	John C. Major	2005
1997 (Chrétien)	Michel Bastarache	2008
1998 (Chrétien)	Ian Binnie	
1999 (Chrétien)	Louise Arbour	2004
2000 (Chrétien)	Louis LeBel	
2002 (Chrétien)	Marie Deschamps	
2003 (Chrétien)	Morris Fish	
2004 (Martin)	Rosalie Abella	
2004 (Martin)	Louise Charron	
2006 (Harper)	Marshall Rothstein	
2008 (Harper)	Thomas Cromwell	

*Note: *CJ = Chief Justice*

THE APPOINTMENT OF JUDGES

As has already been established, Supreme and Federal Court of Canada judges, as well as judges of provincial and territorial superior courts are appointed by the federal Cabinet, while provincial court judges are appointed by provincial cabinets. There are approximately 1000 judges in each category. All of the first group must be qualified lawyers of at least ten years' standing, as must provincial court judges in Ontario and Quebec. Elsewhere, provincial court judges have to be members of the bar for a minimum of five years.

In a high proportion of cases over the years Canadian cabinets at both federal and provincial levels have used judicial appointments to reward faithful party supporters, often defeated candidates.[27] Legal expertise was also taken into account in some cases, but it was rarely the primary criterion. The prospect of a judgeship accounts in part for the active involvement of lawyers in many party organizations, while the promise of government legal business explains another part. **Political patronage** raises three main problems in this area: unsuitable individuals are appointed because of their partisan connections; well-qualified candidates are overlooked because of their lack of service to the party in power; and partisan judges may favour their former political colleagues.[28] This patronage system of appointing judges is still alive, although it is not as blatant as it once was.

At the federal level, Pierre Trudeau as minister of justice in 1967 instituted an informal practice of submitting names of potential judicial appointments to the National Committee on the Judiciary of the Canadian Bar Association. To his credit, the next justice minister, John Turner, appointed several prominent judges of non-Liberal backgrounds. Trudeau sullied his own government's record in this field with the appointment of six high-profile Liberal partisans in 1984, including the minister of justice himself and another minister who was not even assessed by the CBA committee. After an even more partisan record of judicial appointments during its first term,[29] the Mulroney government established a somewhat more satisfactory appointment system in 1988 for all "federal" judges except those on the Supreme Court of Canada, and modified it slightly in 1991.

An independent **Commissioner for Federal Judicial Affairs** maintains a record of those interested in federal judicial appointments. When a vacancy occurs, this official submits such names to a committee set up in each province or territory, which includes a section 96 judge; one nominee of each provincial or territorial law society, the provincial or territorial branch of the CBA, and the provincial or territorial attorney general, and three nominees of the federal minister of justice. This committee used to rank each candidate as "highly recommended," "recommended," or "not able to recommend," and the minister made the final decision, not being restricted to the highly recommended names. Given its law-and-order-orientation, the Harper government changed the procedures by adding a representative from the police community to the judicial advisory committees and abandoned the distinction between highly recommended and recommended. These changes were severely criticized, even by the Chief Justice of Canada. Many observers feared that besides entrenching greater partisanship into judicial appointments, the move would add an ideological ingredient—right-wing judges who would be hard on crime—which might compromise the principle of judicial independence.[30]

The minister may also consult senior members of the judiciary and the bar and the provincial and territorial attorney general, but it is possible to skip over the names high on the list to find ones lower down with partisan connections. Greene and colleagues found that even in the late 1990s a high proportion of appeal court judges had been candidates, party activists, or at least party members.[31] Similarly, Forcese and Freeman calculate that between 40 percent and 50 percent of federal judicial appointees in 2003 had made donations to the Liberal party, which is "broadly suggestive of a deeper political involvement."[32] Moreover, most appellate court judges are recruited from the ranks of trial judges, but once appointed at the trial level, there is no subsequent evaluation system when it comes to promoting them.

Appointments to the Federal Court are usually given minimal attention, but the Chrétien government's appointment of Michael Kelen in 2001 raised considerable controversy. Anti-tobacco advocates were upset because he had been the general counsel for the Canadian Tobacco Manufacturers' Council, where he fought against federal tobacco-control measures. Although reputed to be a good lawyer, he was also a generous donor to the Liberal Party. Despite increasing pressure to remove political patronage from this whole system, the early actions of the Harper government were not encouraging.

The prime minister chooses the chief justice in each province, almost always from the existing bench, as well as new members of the Supreme Court of Canada. Patronage has not been a problem on the Supreme Court since the appointment of Finance Minister Douglas Abbott in 1954.[33] Prime ministers consulted widely before making such appointments, managed to overcome their penchant for partisanship in this one area, and were pleased to be evaluated on the quality of their choices. Chief Justices Bora Laskin and Brian Dickson, and the first female appointee, Bertha Wilson, are outstanding examples. The Supreme Court of Canada is usually composed of seven judges with experience on provincial appeal courts, one from the Federal Court, and one without judicial experience, representing the "practising bar."[34]

At the provincial court level, the province's attorney general usually consults with the local judicial council or equivalent in making such appointments. For example, a central nonpartisan nominating commission, half of them non-lawyers, was established in Ontario in 1988, originally headed by political scientist Peter Russell. It advertises widely, encourages women and minority candidates to apply, and screens judicial applicants on their merits. Through the Liberal and NDP regimes, the attorney general almost always appointed those so recommended, but one commission member resigned in 1997 because the new Tory attorney general sometimes bypassed the commission. However, party service or legislative experience should not automatically disqualify a worthy candidate from a judicial appointment.[35]

Another controversial aspect of judicial appointments concerns the Supreme Court of Canada alone. Because this Court must adjudicate federal–provincial disputes,

Beverley McLachlin, the first female Chief Justice of Canada.

CP PHOTO/Jonathan Hayward

concern has been expressed in some quarters that all of its members are federally appointed. In theory, once appointed, judges act with total impartiality, and their independence is protected in various ways. Nevertheless, it may not appear as if justice has been done. As early as 1971, federal–provincial agreement was achieved on provincial consultation in the appointment of Supreme Court judges, but such agreement was never implemented. Later, the Meech Lake and Charlottetown accords provided for Ottawa to make Supreme Court of Canada appointments from lists provided by the provinces, but this too was ultimately abandoned. The 1992 document also proposed federal and provincial consultation with Aboriginal peoples in the appointment process.[36] While some mechanism for federal–provincial consultation in this area may eventually be adopted, to begin to regard Supreme Court judges as provincial representatives would do great disservice to the principle of judicial independence.

If a proper geographic balance is characteristic of Canadian judges, what can be said of their other socioeconomic characteristics? Partly as a consequence of geography, judicial appointments have also balanced francophone and anglophone origins at both federal and provincial court levels, especially in recent years as provinces have made more French-language court services available. Those of other origins have generally been excluded, but such names as Laskin (Jewish), Sopinka (Ukrainian), and Iacobucci (Italian) have appeared on the Supreme Court of Canada and increasingly on lower courts as well. Thus, the most serious aspects of judicial underrepresentation relate to women and the working class. In this connection, Paul Weiler writes:

> It is very natural that well-to-do families of the founding races and religions in Canada, especially those with a background of professional and/or public involvement, will produce the sons who will get the right kind of education, and thus the entrée into the kind of practice or position which produces a likely candidate for the Court.[37]

Just as in the case of ethnocultural minorities, however, more female and working-class law school graduates are becoming available for judicial appointments, and governments have at least begun to recognize the necessity of appointing greater numbers of female judges. The Supreme Court finally saw its first woman member in 1982, and after 2004, it had a total of four women out of nine. Such female judges have sometimes used their position to point out the male bias in legislatures, judiciaries, and laws.[38] Ian Greene calculates that women now make up about one-quarter of all judges in Canada.[39]

As noted in Chapter 4, Aboriginal Canadians have serious misgivings about the Canadian judicial system, feeling that it discriminates against them at every turn. While an increase in the number of Aboriginal judges might improve this situation, they often advocate instead the establishment of a parallel justice system (at least where it would do no harm to non-Aboriginals) that would reflect their own distinctive concepts of guilt and punishment. Although it seems unlikely that a separate Aboriginal justice system will be created in the near future, the regular courts increasingly recognize traditional Aboriginal concepts in relevant cases: sentencing circles (including a judge, police, elders, peers, family, and victims), elder sentencing panels, and community mediation processes.[40]

Given the significant law-making potential of higher-level judges, another dimension of the appointment process is a consideration of candidates' views on other issues. Chapter 19 noted that the decisions rendered by the Supreme Court of Canada depended to some extent on the makeup of the panel considering the case. That being so, those who appoint judges are able to take into account the predilections of candidates with respect to being hawks or doves on criminal matters or Charter enthusiasts as opposed to legislative deferentialists.[41] This issue prompts some authorities to recommend public hearings in a House of Commons committee to fathom the views of judicial nominees or at least to add an element of transparency to the process.[42] Ironically, in the eyes of many observers, appointments to the Supreme Court that are made without a formal consultation procedure have been superior to those to other federal courts in which an elaborate consultation process is in place.

Jacob Ziegel proposed the establishment of a Supreme Court nominating commission whenever a vacancy arises. This nine-member body, representing a variety of constituencies, would present the prime minister with a shortlist of candidates from which the federal government would have to pick one.[43] In 2005, Irwin Cotler, justice minister to Paul Martin, proposed a formalized procedure for choosing Supreme Court judges, which was then used toward the end of the year to replace retiring Justice John Major.[44] The minister of justice conducted widespread consultations from which an initial list of six candidates was developed. An advisory committee of nine people was established, consisting of a representative from each recognized party in the House of Commons, a retired judged named by the Canadian Judicial Council,

Marshall Rothstein "waxes poetic" during Supreme Court interview.

a representative of the provincial attorneys general and of the law societies of the region involved, and two eminent laypeople nominated by the minister of justice. This committee provided an unranked shortlist of three, from which the minister of justice was to make a recommendation to the prime minister, but at this point the process was suspended because of the 2006 federal election campaign. The new Harper government allowed the process to continue, selected one of the three, and then insisted that the nominee be subject to a televised interview by an informal Commons committee before being officially appointed by the prime minister. Members of the committee were instructed to use characteristic Canadian reserve in questioning the appointee, and Marshall Rothstein convinced the committee that he would do a good job.

The procedure to replace Mr. Justice Bastarache in 2008 was supposed to be similar to the one used to choose Rothstein, except that rather than a committee of nine, a panel of five MPs was about to assess a list of qualified candidates and present the government with an unranked shortlist of three. Ostensibly because of the need to make a timely appointment and because of the 2008 election call, even this revised process was abandoned. The government appointed Mr. Justice Thomas Cromwell without any parliamentary involvement, although no one objected to his appointment.

. . . .

RETIREMENT, REMOVAL, AND INDEPENDENCE OF JUDGES

Whatever the process involved in making judicial appointments, and whatever biases exist in the composition of the courts, judges are expected to abide by the principle of **judicial independence** or impartiality once they are on the bench. They are supposed to adjudicate without fear or favour with respect to private or political interests, and especially without any incentive to give preference to the government side where it is involved.

The independence of judges is primarily based on security of tenure, and it is difficult for the government to remove them before their scheduled date of retirement. Judges on the Supreme and Federal Courts of Canada and provincial superior courts have a mandatory retirement age of 75 years, and provincial court judges of 65 or 70. The general rule for all federally appointed judges and most provincial court judges is that they serve on "good behaviour"—that is, they do not serve at the pleasure of the government and cannot be removed unless they have been guilty of misbehaviour. Although the meaning of these terms has never been definitively established, judges are certainly removable for serious criminal acts and possibly for reasons of infirmity or incapacity, failure to execute their duties, or bringing the judicial system into disrepute. However, they cannot be removed merely because the government regards their decisions as erroneous or contrary to government policy, nor because they ruled against the Crown.

The process of removing a judge varies with the level of the position, and the degree of difficulty increases with the judge's rank in the hierarchy. Except in Ontario, where legislation is required, provincial court judges can be removed by an order in council of the provincial cabinet but only after an inquiry has been conducted by one of the judge's peers or by the provincial judicial council. It is even more difficult to remove judges of the provincial superior courts and the federal courts. In that situation, the Canadian Judicial Council conducts an inquiry and reports to the minister of justice, after which the passage of a joint address of both houses of Parliament is required.

The **Canadian Judicial Council**, created in 1971, consists of all the chief justices and associate chief justices of courts staffed by federally appointed judges, and it is chaired by the Chief Justice of the Supreme Court of Canada. Like the provincial judicial councils, its primary purpose is to deal with complaints raised against individual judges, but it also has a role in the continuing education of judges, provides a forum for developing consensus among its members, and makes representations to government with respect to judicial salaries and benefits.

Although a number of judges have been reprimanded by judicial councils, the issue of judicial removal has rarely arisen. Several provincial court judges have been removed over the years, a practice that is increasingly common as the public becomes less tolerant of their faults. In 2001, the Supreme Court upheld the removal of Judge Richard Therrien from the Court of Quebec on the grounds that when he was appointed a judge he failed to disclose to the authorities that he had been sentenced to imprisonment for one year for unlawfully giving assistance to the FLQ. But only four judges at the old intermediate county and district level met this fate since 1867, and not a single superior court judge has been removed from office. Such proceedings were initiated in several cases, but judges either died or resigned during the removal process. For example, Jean Bienvenue of the Quebec Superior Court eventually resigned in 1997 after the Canadian Judicial Council asked the federal Parliament to remove him for having said on the bench that women can be more cruel than men and that even Nazis exterminated Jews painlessly.[45] Two years later, Robert Flahiff of the same court lost his position when he was sentenced to three years in jail after being found guilty of laundering $1.7 million in drug money when he was a practising lawyer. Two recent cases involved judges on the Ontario Superior Court. A majority of the Council voted not to remove Mr. Justice Matlow, but when the Council recommended removal of Mr. Justice Cosgrove, he resigned.[46]

Besides security of tenure, judicial independence involves financial, administrative, and political independence, and judges are increasingly in control of the administration of the court system.[47] Salaries and pensions are fixed in such a way that judges cannot be individually or collectively intimidated by government threats to reduce them, although some judges went to court to challenge freezes or reductions in their salaries as part of provincial government restraint programs. The Supreme Court ruled that each province should create a salary commission to determine judges' remuneration.[48] Provinces proceeded to set up compensation commissions that based their decisions on the grounds that the high incomes of leading lawyers in private practice necessitated substantial judicial salaries. In a 2005 case, however, the Supreme Court clarified the 1997 decision and dismissed pay complaints by judges in several provinces.[49] Nevertheless, judges at all levels never cease asking for increases in pay.

Judges must also be able to function without political pressure—from Cabinet ministers, legislators, bureaucrats, or other judges—whether in public or in private. At both federal and provincial levels, cases have occurred of Cabinet ministers contacting judges, but however innocent their questions might seem, this must not be done.[50] Greene and colleagues report that judges increasingly feel their independence is threatened by certain interest groups, political correctness, media criticism, political criticism, and even demonstrations. However, individual judges have occasionally made outrageous sexist, racist, or other inappropriate comments from the bench.

It is sometimes thought that the prospect of promotion from one court to another might bias a judge's decisions, but no evidence has been found to justify this fear. Judges are rarely promoted from "provincial" to "federal" courts, but, as mentioned, 70 percent of appeal court judges have previous judicial experience.[51] In 1988 it was also felt (by fellow judges) that to deny judges a vote in federal elections was not necessary to guarantee their independence. On the other hand, judges are not supposed to make public speeches that could compromise their impartiality. For example, when Tom Berger of the BC Supreme Court publicly criticized the 1982 Constitution Act for its omission of Quebec and virtual neglect of Aboriginals, his actions were investigated by the Canadian Judicial Council. Although its recommendation was not to dismiss him, he resigned to protest the process employed.[52] Supreme Court judges are giving more public speeches and interviews than previously, but these attempts to engage in a dialogue with the public sometimes get them into hot water. Mr. Justice Bastarache made public comments that were investigated by the Judicial Council of Canada, for example, and was warned that "it is clearly preferable for judges to exercise restraint when speaking publicly."

. . . .

CONCLUSION

Rule adjudication remains the basic function of the judiciary, one that is becoming increasingly important in the political system. Judges also engage in pre-trial mediation of one kind or another and are occasionally called on to head commissions of inquiry. Other branches of government, especially administrative tribunals, also exercise the rule adjudication function to some extent, but this function can be generally equated with the courts. This chapter has shown, however, that many aspects of the legal system are highly political. The Supreme Court of Canada and the Federal Court of Canada are involved on almost a daily basis in deciding controversial political cases.

This chapter is primarily linked to those on federalism and the Charter of Rights and Freedoms. But the judiciary is also connected to all of the other institutions of government discussed in this part of the book.

© In terms of the approaches outlined in Chapter 1, class analysts looking at the judiciary begin with the argument that entry into law school has traditionally been restricted to the middle and upper classes (and may be again with deregulated law school tuition fees in some provinces), and then note the powers of the legal profession to govern itself. Moreover, those authorities who make judicial appointments are usually lawyers themselves, and consultation with the Canadian Bar Association or judicial councils on new appointments gives the legal profession yet another avenue of influence in the selection of judges. Indeed, a disproportionate number of judges have previously served on the CBA executive.[53] "Appointing judges is part of the process of recruiting a society's governing elite," and with cabinets looking "for someone very much like themselves," the result is a judiciary that bears little resemblance to the general population in socioeconomic background.[54] The elitist nature of the judiciary in terms of gender and ethnicity was noted above, while of the first 50 judges of the Supreme Court, only two came from working-class origins, as did only one among senior judges between 1961 and 1973.[55] Even Russell admits that "as long as judges are recruited entirely from the ranks of successful lawyers ... the bourgeois orientation of the Canadian judiciary is unavoidable. This may very well mean that when class issues are clearly at stake in adjudication, the Canadian judiciary is not impartial."[56] The elitist origins of judges, combined with the expense involved in going to court, leads class analysts to talk about a class system of justice. Michael Mandel notes that in a typical trial, "in terms of social class, the crown attorney, defence counsel, and judge have far more in common with each other than they have with either the victim or the criminal and vice versa."[57]

Class analysts dismiss notions of judicial impartiality and independence "as rhetorical facades behind which judges are free to exercise raw political power on behalf of themselves or their 'political masters,' or against their political or economic opponents."[58] Class analysts remember how often the courts responded to corporate claims in invalidating federal legislation that might have benefited the working class and point to the judicial emasculation of laws prohibiting corporate monopolies. Olsen mentions the high proportion of cases before the courts dealing with the protection of property, the high rate of incarceration of those accused who do not own property, the inadequacies of legal aid schemes, and the limited provision for "class action" suits in Canada, in which small consumers can collectively take on giant corporations. He concludes that the judiciary provides legitimacy for the established social order, arguing that the chief function of the higher judiciary is to rationalize formal arrangements for the elites and the privileged classes. By articulating these as principles and precedents, such judges impose norms and values downward on the lower courts and hence on the behaviour of the lower classes. In this task they are heartily joined by the various political elites who passed the controlling legislation in the first place.[59]

McCormick adds that "to make the courts more representative of women, of Canadians other than French and English, of visible minorities, and so on perhaps simply disguises, and may well reinforce, the extent to which they continue to be unrepresentative on a class basis."[60]

(SC) State-centred theorists argue that the judiciary is part of the state apparatus and is not as independent of other institutions of government as is commonly assumed. Judges are appointed, promoted, and occasionally dismissed by politicians; judges are called on to assist politicians in conducting inquiries; and judges are of the same elitist origins as politicians and bureaucrats and move in many of the same social and professional circles. Many provincial authorities have felt, rightly or wrongly, that the Supreme Court of Canada was an agent of the federal government, rather than a totally impartial referee of federal–provincial disputes, and others could argue that the Canadian Judicial Council is too eager to reprimand a judge who has criticized government policy.[61] Then, although some judicial decisions can be modified or overturned by subsequent legislation, state-centred theorists point out that the judiciary is the branch of government most insulated from public opinion. However objective its decisions, it has sometimes aided and abetted government policy that was at odds with public sentiment, such as in the Supreme Court's series of decisions with respect to official bilingualism and its endorsement of two-tier health care.

[P] Pluralists, however, argue that the judiciary adds a relatively independent point of authoritative decision making to the political system and counterbalances the other institutions of government. In Russell's words, "to liberals who are distrustful of an excessive concentration of power in the hands of any group or bureaucrats, the political pluralism fostered by a judiciary enjoying a high degree of independence is fundamental to maintaining political liberty."[62] Public opinion polls have repeatedly indicated greater confidence in judges than in politicians and a preference for courts rather than legislatures to have the final say in the interpretation of the Charter of Rights.[63] Pluralists also note the division of appointing power between federal and provincial governments, the different procedures involved, and the increasing proportion of female and minority ethnocultural appointments. They are encouraged by the number of suits launched by interest groups and by the practice of allowing such groups to become interveners in constitutional cases. McCormick concludes that despite all the undemocratic aspects of the judiciary, "the law and the courts are nothing more than the continuation of politics by other means,"[64] and are likely to be an even more prominent part in the future.

DISCUSSION QUESTIONS

1. Should the Supreme Court of Canada be constitutionalized?

2. Should all vestiges of patronage be removed from the appointment of judges, or have existing reforms in this area gone far enough?

3. Should the provinces be involved in the appointment of provincial superior court judges? Of judges of the Supreme Court of Canada? If so, how?

4. Are you satisfied with the consultation process involved in the appointment of judges to the Supreme Court of Canada?

5. What should be the criteria for reprimanding or removing a judge? Should Mr. Justice Tom Berger have been able to engage in public criticism of the 1982 Constitution Act?

6. How can justice be ensured for women involved in the courts?

7. How can justice be ensured for the working class?

8. Should Canada establish a parallel Aboriginal justice system?

NOTES

1. Peter Russell, *The Judiciary in Canada: The Third Branch of Government* (Toronto: McGraw-Hill Ryerson, 1987), p. 5.
2. Ian Greene, Carl Baar, Peter McCormick, George Szablowski, and Martin Thomas, *Final Appeal: Decision-Making in Canadian Courts of Appeal* (Toronto: James Lorimer & Co., 1998), p. 201.
3. Russell, *The Judiciary in Canada*, p. 5.
4. Peter Russell, "The Effect of a Charter of Rights on the Policy-Making Role of the Canadian Courts," *Canadian Public Administration* (Spring 1982), p. 2.
5. Ibid., p. 12.
6. Peter McCormick, *Canada's Courts* (Toronto: James Lorimer & Company Ltd., Publishers, 1994), p. 3.
7. Ian Greene, *The Courts* (Vancouver: UBC Press, 2006), p. 72. Chief Justice McLachlin has weighed in on this problem in public speeches.
8. Russell, *The Judiciary in Canada*, p. 6.
9. Gerald L. Gall, *The Canadian Legal System*, 4th ed. (Toronto: Carswell, 1995), p. 30.
10. Greene et al., *Final Appeal*, pp. 32 and 85.
11. McCormick, *Canada's Courts*, p. 23. Reproduced with permission.
12. Gall outlines this integration on pp. 157–59 of the third edition of *The Canadian Legal System*. See also Peter Russell, ed., *Canada's Trial Courts: Two Tiers or One?* Toronto: University of Toronto Press, 2007.

13. Occasional federal–provincial disputes have occurred over this point. See Russell, *The Judiciary in Canada*, pp. 122–23.

14. Ibid, pp. 229–35; Peter Hogg, *Constitutional Law of Canada*, 2nd ed. (Toronto: Carswell, 1985), pp. 546–49.

15. Greene et al., *Final Appeal*, p. x; and McCormick, *Canada's Courts*, p. 56.

16. Russell, *The Judiciary in Canada*, p. 290.

17. Russell, *The Judiciary in Canada*, p. 313.

18. Greene et al., *Final Appeal*, p. 149.

19. Statistics Canada, *Statistics 1998–2008 Bulletin of Proceedings: Special Edition*, available at http://www.scc-csc.gc.ca/stat/pdf/doc-eng.pdf. In 2007, the number of judgments issued was only 58.

20. Greene et al., *Final Appeal*, p. 141.

21. James G. Snell and Frederick Vaughan, *The Supreme Court of Canada: History of the Institution* (Toronto: Osgoode Society, 1985); and Russell, *The Judiciary in Canada*, p. 337.

22. Peter Russell, "Constitutional Reform of the Judicial Branch: Symbolic vs. Operational Considerations," *Canadian Journal of Political Science* (June 1984). See also Emmett Macfarlane, "Administration at the Supreme Court of Canada: Challenges and change in the Charter era," *Canadian Public Administration* (March 2009).

23. Supreme Court of Canada, *Statistics 1998–2008 Bulletin of Proceedings: Special Edition*. In 2007, the rate of unanimity dropped to 62 percent.

24. Ellen Anderson, *Judging Bertha Wilson: Law As Large As Life* (Toronto: University of Toronto Press, 2002); see also Matthew E. Wetstein and C.L. Ostberg, "Strategic Leadership and Political Chance on the Canadian Supreme Court: Analyzing the Transition to Chief Justice," *Canadian Journal of Political Science* (September 2005).

25. Greene et al., *Final Appeal*, pp. 151–56.

26. In 1981, the Supreme Court ruled that Ontario legislation had given Residential Tenancy Commissions powers that could reside only in the courts. Russell, *The Judiciary in Canada*, pp. 49–54, 327–29; and Hogg, *Constitutional Law in Canada*, ch. 7.

27. Carl Baar quotes an oft-repeated maxim that "to become a judge in the United States, you must be elected; to become a judge in Canada, you must be defeated," in "The Structure and Personnel of the Canadian Judiciary," in Paul Fox and Graham White, eds., *Politics: Canada*, 7th ed. (Toronto: McGraw-Hill Ryerson, 1991), p. 513. See also Craig Forcese and Aaron Freeman, *The Laws of Government: The Legal Foundations of Canadian Democracy* (Toronto: Irwin Law, 2005), ch. 4.

28. Andrew Heard, *Canadian Constitutional Conventions* (Toronto: Oxford University Press, 1991), p. 135.

29. A study of the first-term record of the Mulroney government revealed that 48 percent of all judges appointed were known Conservative supporters, compared with seven percent who supported opposition parties. Peter Russell and Jacob Ziegel, "Federal Judicial Appointments: An Appraisal of the First Mulroney Government's Appointments and the New Judiciary Advisory Committees," *University of Toronto Law Journal* 41 (1991).

30. Heather MacIvor, *Parameters of Power: Canada's Political Institutions* (Toronto: Nelson Education, 2010), p. 333–34.

31. Greene et al., *Final Appeal*, p. 36.

32. Forcese and Freeman, *The Laws of Government: The Legal Foundations of Canadian Democracy*, pp. 265–69.

33. Two or three subsequent appointments had marginal partisan pasts, including Julien Chouinard and Michel Bastarache. See MacIvor, *Parameters of Power: Canada's Political Institutions*, p. 354.

34. Greene et al., *Final Appeal*, p. 101.

35. McCormick, *Canada's Courts*, p. 112.

36. On the question of Aboriginal cases, see Larry Chartrand, et al., "Reconciliation and Transformation in Practice: Aboriginal Judicial Appointments to the Supreme Court," *Canadian Public Administration* (March 2008).

37. Dennis Olsen, *The State Elite* (Toronto: McClelland and Stewart, 1980), p. 47. See also Russell, *The Judiciary in Canada*, pp. 164–65; and Greene et al., *Final Appeal*, p. 42.

38. Bertha Wilson said that men didn't understand abortion in the Morgentaler case, but Peter McCormick, *Canada's Courts*, p. 115, discounts the distinctiveness of the judgments of women or visible minorities.

39. Greene, *The Courts*, p. 60.

40. R.G. Green, *Justice in Aboriginal Communities: Sentencing Alternatives* (Saskatoon: Purich Publishing, 1998).

41. McCormick, *Canada's Courts*, p. 165. C.L. Ostberg and Matthew E. Wetstein, *Attitudinal Decision Making in The Supreme Court of Canada* (Vancouver: UBC Press, 2007); Donald R. Songer and Susan W. Johnson, "Judicial Decision Making In the Supreme Court of Canada: Updating the Personal Attribute Model," *Canadian Journal of Political Science* (December 2007); and Donald R. Songer and Julia Siripurapu, "The Unanimous Decisions of the Supreme Court of Canada as a Test of the Attitudinal Model," *Canadian Journal of Political Science* (March 2009).

42. F.L. Morton and H. Patrick Glenn debate this subject in Mark Charlton and Paul Barker, eds., *Crosscurrents: Contemporary Political Issues*, 3rd ed. (Scarborough: ITP Nelson, 1998), ch. 15. See also note 43.

43. Joseph S. Ziegel, *Merit Selection and Democratization of Appointments to the Supreme Court of Canada* (Montreal: Institute for Research on Public Policy, 1999). An aborted attempt at parliamentary review occurred in 2004, see MacIvor, *Parameters of Power*, pp. 339–40.

44. Department of Justice Canada, *Speaking Notes for the Minister of Justice and Attorney General of Canada, Vic Towes, Q.C., Ad Hoc Committee to Review a Nominee for the Supreme Court of Canada* (February 27, 2006); available at http://www.justice.gc.ca/eng/news-nouv/spe-disc/2006/doc_31772.html, retrieved on April 28, 2009.

45. Another famous case concerned Leo Landreville of the Supreme Court of Ontario. See Gall, *The Canadian Legal System*, pp. 231, 238–39; Russell, *The Judiciary in Canada*, pp. 176–79; and Greene, *The Courts*, pp. 94–103.

46. Canadian Judicial Council website; MacIvor, *Parameters of Power*, p. 358.

47. The classic statement on this question was made by Mr. Justice LeDain in *Valente v. the Queen*, [1985] 2 S.C.R. 673; see also Perry S. Millar and Carl Baar, *Judicial Administration in Canada* (Montreal: McGill-Queen's University Press, 1981); Peter McCormick, "New Questions about an Old Concept: The Supreme Court of Canada's Judicial Independence Decisions," *Canadian Journal of Political Science* (December 2004); and Greene, *The Courts*, pp. 88–93.

48. *Manitoba Provincial Judges Association v. Manitoba (Minister of Justice)*, [1997] 3 S.C.R. 3; *Reference re Remuneration of Judges of the Provincial Court of PEI*; and *Reference re the Independence and Impartiality of Judges of the Provincial Court of PEI*, [1998] 1 S.C.R. 3.

49. *Provincial Court Judges' Assn. of New Brunswick v. New Brunswick (Minister of Justice)*, [2005] 2 S.C.R. 286. See also MacIvor, *Parameters of Power*, pp. 347–49.

50. See Heard, *Canadian Constitutional Conventions*, p. 128; Russell, *The Judiciary in Canada*, pp. 78–81, especially regarding the "Judges Affair"; and Greene, *The Courts*, p. 77.

51. According to Russell and Ziegel, "Federal Judicial Appointments," former party ties count in promotions.

52. Heard, *Canadian Constitutional Conventions*, p. 131; Russell, *The Canadian Judiciary*, pp. 85–89; Gall, *The Canadian Legal System*, pp. 236–38; McCormick, *Canada's Courts*, pp. 130–31; and Greene, *The Courts*, pp. 95–96.

53. Russell, *The Judiciary in Canada*, p. 163; Olsen, *The State Elite*, p. 48; and Russell and Ziegel, "Federal Judicial Appointments"; for Ian Greene's criticisms of the courts, see *The Courts*, p. 163.

54. Russell, *The Judiciary in Canada*, p. 107; and Olsen, *The State Elite*, p. 46.

55. Russell, *The Judiciary in Canada*, p. 164; and Olsen, *The State Elite*, p. 51.

56. Russell, *The Judiciary in Canada*, p. 165; Greene et al., *Final Appeal*, p. 42, also admit that judges are elitist but are not overly concerned either.

57. Michael Mandel, *The Charter of Rights and the Legalization of Politics in Canada* (Toronto: Wall and Thompson, 1989), p. 135.

58. Russell, *The Judiciary in Canada*, p. 4.

59. Olsen, *The State Elite*, p. 58.

60. McCormick, *Canada's Courts*, p. 115.

61. Despite all of his excellent work on the Supreme Court, there was some suggestion that Chief Justice Bora Laskin was too close to Prime Minister Trudeau in some of his judgments and in his eagerness to reprimand Tom Berger. Michael Mandel, *The Charter of Rights and the Legalization of Politics in Canada*, pp. 17, 20, 22, 111; and Greene, *The Courts*, pp. 58–65.

62. Russell, *The Judiciary in Canada*, p. 24.
63. Russell, *The Judiciary in Canada*, p. 35; Heard, *Canadian Constitutional Conventions*, p. 138; Maureen Mancuso, Richard G. Price, and Ronald Wagenberg, eds., *A Question of Ethics: Canadians Speak Out* (Toronto: Oxford University Press, 1998), pp. 41–43. In *The Courts*, p. 149, Ian Greene writes: "It is disturbing in a democratic polity that so many citizens would prefer to have issues ... decided by courts rather than by elected legislatures.... There would be many benefits to having these kinds of issues debated and resolved more frequently through the political process, and public debate that surrounds it, than through the courts. Public debate can have an educative effect, allowing misinformation created by such factors as stereotyping to be challenged."
64. McCormick, *Canada's Courts*, ch. 12.

. . . .

FURTHER READING

Gall, Gerald. *The Canadian Legal System*, 4th ed. Toronto: Carswell, 1995.

Green, R.G. *Justice in Aboriginal Communities: Sentencing Alternatives*. Saskatoon: Purich Publishing, 1998.

Greene, Ian. *The Courts*. Vancouver: UBC Press, 2006.

Greene, Ian, Carl Baar, Peter McCormick, George Szablowski, and Martin Thomas. *Final Appeal: Decision-Making in Canadian Courts of Appeal*. Toronto: James Lorimer & Co., 1998.

Heard, Andrew. *Canadian Constitutional Conventions*. Toronto: Oxford University Press, 1991.

MacIvor, Heather. *Parameters of Power: Canada's Political Institutions*. Toronto: Nelson Education, 2010.

McCormick, Peter. *Canada's Courts*. Toronto: Lorimer, 1994.

Russell, Peter. *The Judiciary in Canada: The Third Branch of Government*. Toronto: McGraw- Hill Ryerson, 1987.

Glossary[1]

(Numbers in parentheses refer to the chapter(s) containing the main discussion of the term.)

Aboriginal self-government. A demand by Aboriginal groups that they be able to govern themselves. Aboriginals also want recognition that the right is inherent (in their having been here first), and not a gift of the current occupants of their land. (4, 17)

Aboriginal title. The Aboriginal claim to land on the basis of traditional occupancy and use rather than treaty, as recognized in the 1973 *Calder* case and defined in the 1997 *Delgamuukw* case. (4)

Absent mandate. The notion that governments come to power without a clear-cut policy mandate. (15)

Access to Information Act. The 1983 act that gave citizens, journalists, and others the right to gain access to government documents, with certain exceptions, and established the office of Information Commissioner. (22)

Act of Union. The 1840 act that united the colonies of Upper and Lower Canada into the colony of Canada, partly designed to assimilate the French. (2, 5)

Administrative agencies. Government agencies established to administer a politically sensitive area of public policy and that operate at arm's length from the Cabinet. (22)

Advocacy advertising. Advertising that advocates a political point of view rather than trying to sell a good or service. (12, 16)

Advocacy, interest, or pressure group. Any group seeking to influence government policy without contesting elections; organizations whose members act together to influence public policy in order to promote their common interest. (16)

Affirmative action. A law or program that gives preference to individuals with certain characteristics in the hiring or promotion process. (7, 19)

Agreement on Internal Trade. A federal–provincial agreement signed in 1995 in which provinces promised to remove preferences for local individuals and companies and other barriers to the free movement of goods, services, and people across provincial borders. (18)

Alternative Service Delivery (ASD). Part of the New Public Management movement, ASD embodies a variety of innovative means of providing government services distinct from the traditional departmental model. (22)

Assembly of First Nations. The largest advocacy group representing status Indians, who now prefer to be called First Nations peoples. (4, 16)

---

[1] A fuller description of many of these terms can be found in John McMenemy, *The Language of Canadian Politics: A Guide to Important Terms and Concepts*, 4th ed. (Waterloo: University of Waterloo Press, 2006).

Asymmetrical Federalism. An approach to federal–provincial relations in which Ottawa is open to treating provinces differently from each other. (5, 18)

Atlantic Canada Opportunities Agency (ACOA). The federal agency that seeks to reduce regional economic disparities in the Atlantic region primarily through grants and loans to private firms. (3)

Auditor General. The official of Parliament whose staff audits the expenditures of government departments and who provides periodic reports on instances of funds being unlawfully or unwisely spent. (22, 23)

Auto Pact. The 1965 bilateral Canada–U.S. agreement under which automobiles and auto parts flowed across the border duty-free as long as the value of purchases equalled that of production in each country. (10)

Backbenchers. Members of Parliament on the government side who sit on the backbenches and are not in the Cabinet, or those similarly distant from important posts in opposition parties. (23)

Bandwagon effect. The notion that, if and when they know which party or candidate is going to win the election, voters will move en masse in that direction. (12)

Bill 22. The 1974 language law passed by Quebec that sought to enhance the status of the French language in that province and, among other things, required that immigrant children go to French-language schools unless they could already speak English. (5)

Bill 86. The 1993 language law, passed by Quebec when Bill 178 expired, that permitted bilingual signs outside as well as inside commercial establishments if French lettering was larger than English. (5)

Bill 101. The 1977 Quebec language law that sought to make French the official language of Quebec and put restrictions on the use of English in the courts, schools, and private sector. For example, all commercial signs had to be in French only. (5, 19)

Bill 178. The 1988 language law, passed by Quebec under the notwithstanding clause, that continued to require unilingual French signs on the outside of commercial establishments but permitted bilingual signs inside if French lettering was larger than English. (5)

Block grant. A federal–provincial grant that is given for a specific purpose, such as postsecondary education, but does not contain rigid conditions or standards. (18)

Bourgeoisie. A Marxist term referring to those who own the means of production, otherwise known as the corporate elite. (8)

British North America (BNA) Act, 1867. The act of the British Parliament that created Canada by combining Ontario, Quebec, Nova Scotia, and New Brunswick and that also provided some of the essential elements of the new country's Constitution. Renamed the Constitution Act, 1867, in 1982. (2, 17, 18)

Broker or brokerage. A kind of party system in which political parties try to appeal to many different interests and "broker" compromises among them, rather than having any distinct ideology. (14)

Budget. The annual financial statement of the government usually issued in the early spring by the minister of finance that introduces tax changes and gives an overview of government spending for the next fiscal year. (21, 23)

Cabinet government. A system of government in which the major political decisions are made by the Cabinet as a whole, as opposed to one in which the prime minister acts with considerable autonomy. (21)

Cabinet secrecy. A convention that Cabinet and Cabinet committee meetings are held behind closed doors and that all documents and discussions relating thereto are strictly confidential. (21)

Cabinet solidarity. A convention that all Cabinet ministers publicly support whatever decisions the Cabinet has taken, whatever their personal views. (21)

Canada Act. The 1982 act passed by Britain that terminated all British authority over Canada and under which Canada passed the Constitution Act, 1982, with a domestic constitutional amending formula. (17)

Canada Clause. The clause in the 1992 Charlottetown Accord that attempted to define the fundamental characteristics of Canada. (11, 17)

Canada Council for the Arts. The government agency established in 1957 as the Canada Council to provide financial support to all aspects of the artistic community. (10)

Canada Elections Act. The act that governs all aspects of federal elections. (13)

Canada Health Act. The 1984 act that re-imposed conditions on federal block grants to the provinces for health programs, especially to prevent extra-billing or other moves toward a profit-oriented, two-tier health system. (18)

Canada Health and Social Transfer (CHST). The annual federal block grant to the provinces that replaced the Canada Assistance Plan and Established Program Funding (health insurance and postsecondary education) after 1996–97, later split into two parts. (8, 18)

Canada–U.S. Free Trade Agreement. The agreement signed by Canada and the United States that came into effect in 1989 and that gradually eliminated tariffs between the two countries and otherwise prohibited governments from interfering in the private marketplace. (10)

Canadian Bill of Rights. An act of the Canadian Parliament passed in 1960 that outlined the basic civil liberties of Canadians but whose defects caused judicial confusion and limited the bill's effectiveness. (19)

Canadian Broadcasting Corporation (CBC). The large, national Crown corporation (including its French equivalent, Radio-Canada) with radio and television arms whose mandate is to promote meaningful communication among all parts of the country. (3, 10, 12)

Canadian Council of Chief Executives (CCCE). The most powerful peak business pressure group in Canada, representing the 150 largest firms in the country, formerly known as the Business Council on National Issues (BCNI). (8, 16)

Canadian Federation of Students. The largest advocacy group for post-secondary students in Canada. (1,16)

Canadian Judicial Council. An agency composed of the federal and provincial chief justices that disciplines federally appointed judges and otherwise provides leadership and coordination among federal and provincial judicial systems. (24)

Canadian Labour Congress (CLC). The largest labour advocacy group in Canada; the political voice of about three million union members. (8, 16)

Canadian Manufacturers and Exporters (CME). A large and powerful business advocacy group representing a wide range of Canadian manufacturers and exporters; a merger of the Canadian Manufacturers' Association and the Canadian Exporters' Association. (16)

Canadian Radio-television and Telecommunications Commission (CRTC). The regulatory agency established to police the communications industry, including radio, television, telephones, and telecommunications. (3, 10, 12, 22)

Canadian Wheat Board. A federal Crown corporation established to help grain farmers market their product in an aggressive way and to provide equitable returns to producers. (3)

Central agencies. Government agencies, such as the PMO, the PCO, the Treasury Board Secretariat, and the Department of Finance, that have certain coordinating functions across the whole federal public service and that prevent individual departments from acting with too much autonomy. (21)

Chapter 11 (NAFTA). A clause in the North American Free Trade Agreement that allows a foreign company to sue a government if a decision or policy reduces the firm's profits. (10)

Charlottetown Accord. The constitutional agreement of 1992 that responded to Quebec's demands for distinct society status, Aboriginal demands for self-government, and the West's demand for a Triple-E Senate that was approved by federal, provincial, territorial, and Aboriginal leaders, but then turned down in a national referendum. (5, 17)

Charter of Rights and Freedoms. That part of the Constitution Act, 1982, that guaranteed fundamental freedoms and rights (legal, democratic, linguistic, mobility, egalitarian, and limited Aboriginal) to individual Canadian citizens. (2, 6, 17, 19, 24)

Chief electoral officer. The independent and impartial official who is in charge of the operation of the whole electoral system. (13)

Civil law. A branch of the law dealing with relations between private parties, such as individuals and corporations, that do not involve government. (24)

Civil liberties. Liberties or freedoms, including the fundamental freedoms of speech, press, religion, and assembly, that citizens enjoy and that cannot be infringed or encroached upon by government. (19)

Clarity Act. The Act sponsored by Prime Minister Chrétien in 2000 that fleshed out the Supreme Court decision on Quebec separation and requires federal government approval for the question asked. (5, 17)

Class-based (ideological) parties. Political parties that appeal to a single socioeconomic class or ideology; when all parties do so, they constitute a class-based party system. (14)

Class-consciousness. An awareness of the social class to which one belongs, which is notoriously lacking in the case of most working-class Canadians. (8, 15)

Clerk of the Privy Council and Secretary to the Cabinet. The head of the Privy Council Office and head of the federal public service; the chief nonpartisan adviser to the prime minister and Cabinet. (21)

Clientele relationship. The intimate and mutually advantageous relationship that sometimes develops between a government department or agency and the advocacy group with which it most frequently interacts. (16, 22)

Closure. A rule in the House of Commons in which a Cabinet minister introduces a motion to cut off debate. (23)

Code Civil du Québec. The unique system of civil law used in Quebec and based on the Napoleonic Code. (24)

Coercion. Power based on authorized physical force (including police, armed forces, jails, etc.) on which government has a near monopoly. Also used by class analysts as a term for what government does (at the behest of the corporate elite) when the state cannot otherwise get the public to accept its decisions. (1, 8)

Collective responsibility. A convention holding that all Cabinet ministers are collectively responsible for government policy. (21)

Collectivism. An ideology holding that the public interest is enhanced by substantial collective action, normally via government, as opposed to individualism, which minimizes the role of government. (11, 14)

Commissioner for Federal Judicial Affairs. The official in charge of coordinating the process for the appointment of those judges who fall under the federal minister of Justice. (24)

Common law. The basis of the British and Canadian legal systems, apart from the civil law system in Quebec, that consists of the accumulation of judicial precedents and seeks out the previous decisions in cases most closely resembling the one at hand. (24)

Comprehensive claims. Aboriginal land claims based on Aboriginal title—that is, traditional use and occupancy—rather than on treaties or other legal documents. (4)

Concurrent powers. Powers officially shared by the federal and provincial governments, which in the Constitution Act, 1867, were agriculture, immigration, and, later, old age pensions. (18)

Conditional grant. A federal grant to the provinces, usually in support of a subject within provincial jurisdiction, to which Ottawa attaches conditions or standards before the province receives the money. (18)

Confederation Settlement. The deal made among the Fathers of Confederation that entailed setting up a new federal system of government with a division of powers, a division of financial powers, federal controls over the provinces, provincial representation in federal institutions, and certain cultural guarantees. (18)

Conscription crises. Two political crises in Canada, one in each world war, in which the population and government were divided, largely on French–English lines, over the necessity of compulsory military service. (5, 14)

Conservatism. A political ideology generally characterized by a belief in individualism and a minimum of government intervention in the economy and society, as well as by tradition, elitism, and opposition to change. (14)

Constitution. The whole body of rules and principles according to which the state is governed that, in the Canadian case, consists of a conglomeration of documents and conventions. (2, 17)

Constitution Act, 1867. The new name (changed in 1982) for the British North America Act, 1867. (2, 5, 9, 17, 18)

Constitution Act, 1982. A major amendment to the Canadian Constitution that added a Charter of Rights and Freedoms, an amending formula, clauses on equalization and Aboriginal rights, and a change to the division of powers with respect to natural resources. (2, 5, 17, 19).

Constitutional Act of 1791. The British law that divided Canada into two separate colonies, Upper and Lower Canada, each with a governor, executive and legislative councils, and an assembly. (2, 5)

Constitutional amending formula. The process for amending the Constitution, consisting of five different parts. (17)

Constitutional conventions. Unwritten rules of constitutional behaviour that are considered to be binding by and upon those who operate the Constitution, but that are not enforceable by the courts. (17)

Constitutional monarchy. The official designation of the Canadian form of government, characterized by a monarch who is head of state but who rules according to the Constitution, which confides almost all governmental power into other hands. (2, 21)

Cooperative federalism. A variant of Canadian federalism, in place in the post-1945 period, in which neither level of government is subordinate to the other and in which there is an extensive degree of interaction between them. (18)

Core–periphery system. A geographical term referring to population distribution in which the bulk of the people live in the core, heartland, or metropolis of the country (or province), which has political and economic domination over those living in the distant, sparsely settled periphery or hinterland. (3, 9)

Corporate elite. A synonym for "big business" or the bourgeoisie—that is, the collection of individuals who own or manage the largest corporations in the country. (8)

Council of the Federation. An organization created by Quebec premier Jean Charest—an institutionalizing of the annual premiers' conference—that encourages the provinces to work together in interprovincial and especially federal-provincial relations. (18)

Court Challenges Program. A program established after the adoption of the Charter of Rights and Freedoms in which the federal government helped finance those (especially francophone minorities and women) who challenged laws on the basis of the Charter, on the assumption that the costs involved would otherwise be prohibitive. (7)

Criminal Code. A federal document that codifies most of the criminal law in the country. (24)

Criminal law. That branch of the law dealing with wrongs committed against others that are considered to be offensive to society as a whole, for which the state takes the initiative to investigate, and for which perpetrators can be fined or jailed. (24)

Crow rate. A subsidized rail freight rate for Western goods, named after the Crow's Nest Pass, that was established in 1897, reduced in the 1970s, and eliminated in 1995. (3)

Crown. The collectivity of executive powers exercised by or in the name of the monarch. (21)

Crown corporation. A corporation owned by the government that assumes a structure similar to that of a private company and that operates semi-independently of the Cabinet. (22)

Declaratory power. The power in section 92(10)(c) of the Constitution Act, 1867, under which Ottawa can declare any local work or undertaking to be for the general advantage of Canada and thereby place it under federal jurisdiction. (18)

Deference to authority. A value considered to be part of the Canadian political culture in which citizens are respectful of government authority and accept its word and orders with little question. (11)

Democracy. A political system characterized by popular sovereignty, political equality, political freedom, and majority rule. (2, 11)

Democratic rights. A section of the Charter of Rights and Freedoms that, among other things, guarantees the vote to every Canadian citizen. (19)

Department. A kind of government organization headed by a minister who is politically accountable for its operations and a deputy minister who is in charge of its hierarchical administrative apparatus. (22)

Department of Finance. The government department that has overall responsibility for the government's finances and its role in the economy and that has a powerful influence on all government policy. (21, 22)

Departmental Cabinet. A Cabinet characterized by ministers and departments that operate with substantial autonomy from the prime minister, other ministers, departments, and central agencies. (21)

Dependency ratio. The proportion of the population dependent on others for financing government programs, usually referring to those under the age of 15 and over the age of 65, and expressed as a percentage of those of working age. (9)

Deputy minister. The public servant who heads each government department, manages the department, and advises the minister. (22)

Deregulation. A government policy that removes previous regulations, especially those affecting the corporate sector. (20, 22)

Direct taxes. A category of taxation that can be used by either level of government to extract money from the very person or corporation that is intended to pay it. (18)

Disallowance. A power given to the federal government in the Constitution Act, 1867, but now long obsolete, under which the prime minister and Cabinet can disallow any provincial law. (18)

Dispute-settlement mechanism. A clause in the Canada–U.S. Free Trade Agreement designed to settle such trade disputes as might arise under the treaty by means of binational panels. (10)

Dissolution of Parliament. The ending of a Parliament, usually after four to five years, by calling an election, an act normally in the hands of the prime minister but that formally requires the approval of the governor general. (13, 21, 23)

Distinct society. A controversial description of Quebec, found in the Meech Lake Accord and slightly modified in the Charlottetown Accord, claiming that Quebec constituted, within Canada, a distinct society. (5, 17)

Division. A formal standing, roll-call vote in the House of Commons in which members' names are recorded in Hansard. (23)

Division of powers. The distribution of legislative powers between the federal and provincial governments, largely contained in sections 91 and 92 of the Constitution Act, 1867. (17, 18)

Durham Report. The 1839 report by Lord Durham that recommended the union of Upper and Lower Canada and the granting of responsible government to the colony of Canada. (2)

Egalitarianism. As opposed to elitism, the philosophy or practice of providing everyone with an equal amount of power and/or of treating everyone more or less equally. (11)

Elite accommodation. The notion that public policies emerge from the interaction of various elites (small groups of people with a disproportionate amount of power) in society, who, sharing many socioeconomic characteristics and values, find it relatively easy to come to agreement. (1, 16)

Embedded state. The notion that the operations of the state are so extensive that they are connected to virtually every aspect of society, and that government therefore cannot act independently of societal forces. (1)

Emergency doctrine. A constitutional doctrine invented by the Judicial Committee of the Privy Council that in times of national emergency the Peace, Order and Good Government clause of the 1867 Constitution Act became an emergency clause, allowing the federal government to exercise extensive temporary powers. (18)

Employment equity. A policy that seeks to guarantee fairness in hiring, promotion, or remuneration, regardless of gender, ethnicity, and so on, and that may incorporate affirmative action, preferences to compensate for past systemic discrimination. (6, 7)

Enumerated powers. The powers of the provincial governments explicitly listed in section 92 of the Constitution Act, 1867. (18)

Equality rights. A section of the Charter of Rights and Freedoms that prohibits governments from discriminating against certain categories of people. (19)

Equalization payments. A large annual cash payment made by the federal government to have-not provinces to help them provide a satisfactory level of public services. (3, 18)

Estimates. The annual spending plans of government departments and agencies for the following fiscal year. (22, 23)

Evangelicalism. A term referring to the active political participation of fundamentalist Christian (usually Protestant) groups who espouse socially conservative views on such issues as abortion and homosexuality. (9)

Executive federalism. A variant of cooperative federalism characterized by extensive federal–provincial interaction at the level of first ministers, departmental ministers, and deputy ministers, such as the process that produced the Meech Lake Accord. (18)

Exempt staff. Partisan staff hired by the prime minister and Cabinet ministers who are not subject to the rules and regulations of the regular public service appointment process. (22)

Extra-parliamentary party. That part of a political party beyond its members of Parliament—that is, party members, local and national executives, and party headquarters. (14)

Extraterritoriality. The ability of a state to pass laws having authority beyond its borders, especially related to the United States telling Canadian branches of U.S.-based transnational corporations with whom they can trade. (10)

Federal Accountability Act. The wide-ranging Act sponsored by Stephen Harper in 2006 that dealt with party finance, lobbying, government appointments, ethics, the Auditor General, and other subjects, all designed to make the entire operation of government more accountable. (13, 16, 22, 23)

Federal Court of Canada. A court established by the federal government dealing with cases involving that level of government and other specialized subjects within federal jurisdiction. (24)

Federalism (federation). A system of government characterized by two levels of authority (federal and provincial) and a division of powers between them, such that neither is subordinate to the other. (2, 18)

Federal–provincial conferences. Periodic meetings of federal and provincial officials, especially first ministers or departmental ministers, characteristic of executive federalism, often making decisions that legislatures are not allowed to change. (18)

Federation of Canadian Municipalities. The organization to which all Canadian municipalities belong that functions as an advocacy group for that level of government; although not always taken seriously by federal and provincial governments, it is sometimes granted official status in the policy process. (9)

Feminist. A person who believes in removing barriers to the full equality of men and women. (7)

Feminization of poverty. The notion that a high proportion of people living below the poverty line are women, usually sole-parent women with children. (7, 8)

Filibuster. An organized attempt by the opposition in the House of Commons to prolong debate and delay adoption of government measures. (23)

First ministers' conference. A federal–provincial conference consisting of the prime minister and provincial premiers (and sometimes territorial and Aboriginal leaders). (18)

First Nations. The new term that can refer to the Indian peoples of Canada, both status and non-status, or that can replace the word "band." (4)

First-past-the-post. The kind of electoral system used in Canada in which the candidate with the most votes wins, regardless if it is over 50 percent; synonymous with single-member plurality system. (13)

Fiscal imbalance. A claim made by some provincial governments, especially Quebec, that the federal government has greater revenues than the provinces and that the provinces have insufficient revenues to finance their responsibilities. (18)

Foreign Investment Review Agency (FIRA). The agency established in the early 1970s to screen foreign investment in Canada and approve of foreign takeovers of Canadian firms; discontinued by the Mulroney government. (10)

Franchise. The right to vote. (13)

Francophonie. The international organization of French-speaking countries. (5)

Free vote. A vote in the House of Commons (or Senate) in which members are not required to abide by the party line. (23)

Front de Libération du Québec (FLQ). The terrorist wing of the Quebec separatist movement in the 1960s and 1970s. (5)

Fundamental freedoms. Political freedoms—of speech, religion, press, assembly, association, and so on—that governments are not supposed to encroach on and that are guaranteed by the Charter of Rights and Freedoms. (19)

Gerrymandering. An attempt to design constituency boundaries in the interests of the government party of the day in order to maximize the number of that party's seats and minimize the seats won by the opposition. (13)

Globalization. The modern phenomenon characterized by nation states declining in stature and power as they give way to the demands of transnational corporations via comprehensive free trade agreements, by massive diffusion of technological change, and by worldwide corporate competition or megamergers. (1, 2, 10)

Gomery Inquiry and Report. The Report written by Judge John Gomery in 2005–06 who was appointed by Paul Martin to investigate the sponsorship scandal in Quebec under Jean Chrétien. (5, 12, 13, 16, 22)

Government. (1) The set of institutions that make and enforce collective, public decisions for a society, and (2) the group of people—the prime minister and Cabinet—and their supporters in Parliament who are currently charged to make such decisions. (1, 20, 21)

Government bill. A bill introduced by a Cabinet minister on behalf of the government (prime minister and Cabinet), the kind of bill dominating discussion in the House of Commons. (23)

Gray Report. The government report authored by Herb Gray in 1972 expressing concern about the extent of foreign investment in Canada and recommending a screening agency. (10)

Horizontal management. The increasing involvement of a wide range of bureaucratic interests in the development of government policy. (22)

Horse-race effect. The notion that election campaigns have degenerated into a "horse race" where everyone, especially the media, is concerned with which party is ahead, not with how parties would tackle serious public issues. (12)

House leader. The person appointed by each party in the House of Commons to deal with counterparts in other parties with respect to scheduling Commons business. (23)

Ideological or class-based parties. Political parties that appeal to a single socioeconomic class or ideology; when all parties do so, they constitute a class-based party system. (14)

Immigration Act (now the Immigration and Refugee Protection Act). The law that regulates the immigration process and determines the qualifications, categories, and, to some extent, the origins of immigrants. (6)

Implied bill of rights. The notion that even before the enactment of the Canadian Bill of Rights or the Charter of Rights and Freedoms, the Constitution, especially in its preamble, contained an implied bill that protected civil liberties to some extent. (19)

Indian Act. The act that has governed almost all aspects of Indian life in Canada since the 1870s, giving extensive authority to government bureaucrats and minimal discretion to Indians themselves. (4)

Indirect taxes. A category of taxation, especially a tariff or customs duty, restricted to the federal government, in which the party that pays the tax is assumed to pass it along to some other customer. (18)

Individualism. An ideology that individuals should have maximum freedom or liberty to do as they please, especially in economic terms, and that governments should not get involved in taxation, regulation, redistribution, or ownership. (11, 14)

Information Commissioner. The official of Parliament who encourages government to operate on a more open and transparent basis and makes judgments in cases where departments withhold information under the Access to Information Act. (22)

Institutionalized Cabinet. A Cabinet characterized by collective ministerial decision-making and strong central agencies that support collective Cabinet operations. (21)

Institutionalized group. A kind of advocacy group characterized by permanence, resources, government acceptance, and well-developed links with the authorities. (16)

Interest group. *See* Advocacy, interest, or pressure group. (16)

Iron law of oligarchy. A theory about political parties that they almost always come to be controlled by a small group of permanent professional politicians and officials who are in charge of policy, finance, and strategy. (14)

Issue-oriented group. A kind of advocacy group that springs up around an issue and disappears once that issue has been resolved. (16)

James Bay and Northern Quebec Agreement. The deal signed in 1975 by the government of Quebec and its northern Aboriginal residents that gave the latter land, cash, and hunting rights in return for surrendering land for the James Bay hydroelectric project. (4)

Japanese Redress Agreement. The deal signed by the Mulroney government in 1988 to compensate Japanese Canadians for their internment and the confiscation of their property during the Second World War. (6)

Joint committee. A parliamentary committee containing members from both the House of Commons and the Senate. (23)

Judicial Committee of the Privy Council (JCPC). A committee of the British Parliament that functioned as Canada's final court of appeal until 1949. (2, 17, 18, 24)

Judicial discretion. The leeway inevitably bestowed on the courts when they interpret laws, even when they do not, or have no power to, overturn them. (19, 24)

Judicial independence. The constitutional principle that the courts should function independently of the rest of the government apparatus—that is, the politicians and bureaucrats—with implications for security of tenure and remuneration. (2, 24)

Judicial review. The power of the courts to overturn legislation or an action of the executive branch of government. (2, 19, 24)

Kent Royal Commission on Newspapers. The Royal Commission established in 1980 to investigate the newspaper industry after a rash of takeovers and closures in the 1970s. (12)

Keynesian economics. An economic theory first enunciated by John Maynard Keynes that to promote general economic stability, government should counterbalance the private sector, spending (running deficit budgets) in periods of unemployment when the private sector doesn't spend, and taxing (running a budget surplus) in periods of inflation when the private sector is spending too much. (2, 14, 18, 22)

King–Byng dispute. The dispute in 1926 between Prime Minister Mackenzie King and Governor General Lord Byng over King's request for a dissolution of Parliament, which Byng denied. (21)

Leader of the Opposition. The leader of the main opposition party in the House of Commons, normally the party with the second-largest number of seats. (23)

Leadership review. A clause in the constitutions of some political parties that allows party members to review the leader's performance and to vote on whether they want a leadership convention. (14)

Left. That part of the ideological spectrum that believes in equality in society and the intervention of government via such collectivist measures as taxation, regulation, redistribution, and public ownership to effect such equality. (14)

Legal rights. The rights of a person suspected or accused of committing a crime, now listed in the Charter of Rights and Freedoms. (19)

Liberalism. An ideology based on a belief in the rationality of the individual and on maximizing individual freedom, liberty, and self-fulfillment. Before 1900 this was assumed to entail a minimal role for government, but post-1900 liberalism usually advocated a larger role for the state and therefore was placed on the centre-left of the spectrum. (14)

Limited identities or subcultures. The notion that while the overall Canadian national identity is elusive, Canadian society is made up of all sorts of more limited identities or subcultures—regional, ethnic, linguistic, and so on. (11)

Lobbying. Any organized attempt to influence the authorities, now often performed by professional lobbying firms. (16)

Lobbying Act. The law, originally passed in 1989 as the Lobbyists' Registration Act, that sought to have lobbyists register with a government agency and submit certain information about what they were doing to influence government. (16)

Majority government. A situation in which the party in power has over 50 percent of the seats in the House of Commons. (2, 21, 23)

Majority rule. An element in the definition of democracy that in any decision-making setting involving a difference of opinion, the larger number should carry the day. (11)

Massey Royal Commission. A 1951 Royal Commission that expressed concern about the future prospects of Canadian culture and recommended ways to promote and protect it. (10)

Meech Lake Accord. The 1987 package of constitutional amendments intended to bring Quebec back into the constitutional fold. (5, 17)

Memorandum to Cabinet (MC). The formal written document that a minister submits to Cabinet seeking to initiate or change a government policy. (21)

Merit system. A system of hiring or promoting public servants on the basis of their merits (education, training, experience, etc.) rather than on party preference or other considerations. (22)

Ministerial responsibility. The principle that Cabinet ministers are individually responsible to the House of Commons for everything that happens in their department. (21, 22)

Minority government. A situation in which the government party has less than 50 percent of the seats in the House of Commons. (2, 21, 23)

Minority-language education rights. Rights established by the 1982 Charter of Rights and Freedoms whereby French-speaking Canadians have the right to send their children to French-language schools, wherever their numbers warrant, applying to English-speaking Canadians as well. (5, 19)

Mobility rights. A category of rights in the Charter of Rights and Freedoms guaranteeing the freedom to move from one province to another and seek employment there. (19)

Multiculturalism. A policy of encouraging minority ethnocultural groups to maintain their customs and traditions, often with public financial assistance. (6)

Multilateralism. The historic cornerstone of Canadian foreign policy, based on acting with other similarly minded governments and through international organizations rather than unilaterally. (10)

Multi-party system. Typically European in nature, a party system characterized by many parties, without any one having a majority in the legislature. (14)

National Action Committee on the Status of Women (NAC). Before its recent decline, the largest and most vocal women's advocacy group. (7, 16)

National Citizens' Coalition. A right-wing advocacy group once headed by Stephen Harper that challenged limitations on third-party advertising during election campaigns. (13, 16)

National Energy Board. A regulatory agency that makes decisions relating to exports of electricity and petroleum. (10)

National Energy Program (NEP). A 1980 initiative associated with Pierre Trudeau and designed to skim off more petroleum tax revenue for Ottawa, keep the price of petroleum below world levels, encourage conservation, and Canadianize the industry, which met with great opposition in Western Canada. (3, 10)

National Policy. A broad nation-building policy of John A. Macdonald unveiled in 1879 that included tariff protection for central Canadian manufacturing, massive immigration, and the construction of a national transportation system. (3, 6, 10)

Neoconservatism. An ideological term characterizing parties or politicians in the 1980s and after, who advocated reducing the role of government through privatization, deregulation, deficit cutting, and elimination of social programs. Sometimes distinguished from neoliberalism in advocating a continuing role for government to promote certain traditional social values. (2, 14)

Neoliberalism. An ideological term, generally similar to neoconservatism, characterizing parties or politicians who advocate the government's withdrawal from the economy to allow it to operate on the pre-1900 capitalist principles of laissez-faire. (2, 14)

New middle class. A term from class analysis describing salaried professionals, such as teachers, public servants, nurses, and so on. (5, 8)

New Public Management (NPM). A movement within public administration after 1990 that involved downsizing government, encouraging technological change, finding new ways to provide public services, and forming partnerships with private-sector agencies. (22)

News management. A variety of techniques used by politicians and governments to ensure positive media coverage. (12)

Nomination. The act of becoming a candidate in an election, normally entailing being selected to represent a party at a nomination meeting and then completing official nomination forms. (13, 15)

Nonconfidence motion. A periodic motion in the House of Commons, moved by the opposition, inviting the House to demonstrate its lack of confidence in the government; if successful, such a motion would require the Cabinet's resignation or the calling of an election. (23)

North American Free Trade Agreement (NAFTA). The 1994 extension of the Canada–U.S. Free Trade Agreement to Mexico. (10)

Notwithstanding clause. Section 33 of the Charter of Rights and Freedoms, which allows federal or provincial governments to pass laws that violate certain sections of the Charter. (19)

Nunavut. The eastern half of the Northwest Territories, which was established as a separate, Inuit territory in 1999. (3, 4)

Oakes test. The strategy outlined in the *Oakes* case for interpreting the reasonable limits clause of the Charter of Rights and Freedoms. (19)

Official Languages Act. A law passed in 1969 giving citizens the right to deal with head offices as well as certain local offices of the federal government in either official language, and necessitating the hiring and promotion of francophone public servants. (5, 22)

One member-one vote (OMOV). A means of electing a party leader in which every member of the party is given a ballot, as opposed to a delegate convention. (14)

One-party dominance. A party system characterized by the dominance of a single party, usually related to Conservative Party dominance before 1900 and Liberal Party dominance since. (14)

Open federalism. The approach to federal-provincial relations adopted by Stephen Harper based on flexibility, decentralization, and increased federal-provincial transfers. (18)

Opposition. Those members of Parliament who do not support the government of the day. (23)

Opposition days. Twenty-two days per session set aside in the House of Commons for the opposition to determine the topic of debate and for the government to respond. (23)

Order in Council. A formal, legal decision made by the prime minister and Cabinet (Governor in Council), including regulations and appointments. (21)

Pacific scandal. A party finance scandal involving John A. Macdonald's Conservative Party and a group of businessmen who sought the contract to build the Canadian Pacific Railway. (13)

Padlock Law. An infamous law passed by Premier Maurice Duplessis in Quebec in the late 1930s that allowed him to place a padlock on any building that was being used for purposes of opposing the government. (19)

Parliament of Canada. Theoretically, the Queen, the House of Commons, and the Senate functioning collectively, such as in the approval of legislation, but often used to refer to the Commons alone or sometimes the Commons and Senate. (23)

Parliamentary party. That wing of a political party made up of its elected members—that is, its MPs or its parliamentary caucus. (14)

Parliamentary press gallery. Those members of the media who are registered to sit in the press gallery in the House of Commons and who report on its proceedings or on government in general. (12, 23)

Parliamentary privileges. Historic privileges that adhere to members of Parliament, the most important residual one being the freedom from prosecution for anything said in the Commons chamber. (23)

Parliamentary secretaries. Government MPs who have been given additional responsibilities to assist a Cabinet minister. (21)

Party caucus. The whole body of MPs of any party, who hold a regular weekly closed meeting, together with such senators as choose to attend, to discuss parliamentary strategy and policy. (14, 23)

Party discipline. The convention that all MPs within any party vote together on every occasion, as predetermined in the party caucus meeting, ordered by the prime minister in the case of the government party, and enforced by the party whip. (23)

Party identity. A psychological attachment to a single political party that is relatively stable over time. (15)

Party whip. An official of each party in the House of Commons whose function is to enforce party discipline, in part by relying on the incentives of drawing up speaking lists, committee assignments, office allocations, and official parliamentary travel plans. (23)

Pay equity. An element of employment equity programs designed to ensure that all employees are paid equally for work of equal value and are not discriminated against on the basis of gender or other factors. (7)

Peace, Order, and Good Government clause (POGG). The opening words of section 91 of the Constitution Act, 1867, describing the residual powers of the federal government (as well as the essence of the Canadian political culture), but often misinterpreted by the courts as an emergency power only. (18)

Persons case. The decision by the Judicial Committee of the Privy Council that determined that women were persons for the purposes of appointment to the Senate. (7, 23)

Petite bourgeoisie. A Marxist term to describe self-employed professionals, affluent farmers, and those operating small businesses. (8)

Pipeline debate. The heated House of Commons debate in the mid-1950s regarding the construction of the Trans-Canada Pipeline in which the Liberals treated Parliament in a particularly arrogant way. (14, 23)

Policy community. The notion that government policy is made in a series of discrete and specialized clusters of government departments and agencies, advocacy groups, politicians, corporations, and interested individuals. (16, 20)

Policy instruments. The devices chosen by the government to effect public policy that are commonly categorized according to the degree of intervention, intrusiveness, or coerciveness they represent. (20)

Policy network. The inner core of the policy community that is directly involved in the development and implementation of a government policy. (16, 20)

Political culture. The sum total of the politically relevant values, attitudes, beliefs, and orientations in any political system that constitute the context for government policymaking. (11)

Political efficacy. The feeling that one has political influence and that one's political participation can make an impact. (11)

Political equality. An element in the definition of democracy that entails the principle of "one person–one vote"—every citizen has a vote and each counts equally. (11)

Political freedom. An element in the definition of democracy that entails freedom of speech, press, assembly, association, and so on, such that people can organize and advocate in order to influence election results and public policy. (11)

Political party. An organized group that makes nominations and contests elections in the hope of influencing the personnel and policy of government. (14)

Political patronage. Making appointments to public offices or awarding government contracts on a partisan basis. (14, 22, 24)

Political socialization. The process whereby individuals acquire their political values, attitudes, beliefs, and orientations. (12)

Politics. The activity in which conflicting interests struggle for advantage or dominance in the making and execution of public policies. (1)

Popular sovereignty. An element in the definition of democracy that entails periodically allowing the public at large to exert its will—to have the final say—normally through general elections. (11)

Popular vote. The percentage of all votes cast won by a candidate or party, regardless of who was elected. (13)

Poverty line. An amount of income such that anyone who received less would be living in poverty. (8)

Power. The ability of one actor to impose its will on another to get its own way, or to do or get what it wants, usually considered to be the essence of politics and government. (1)

Prerogative powers. That small residual of powers of the Crown—the Queen or governor general—that remain from the era of an all-powerful monarch and that the Crown can still exercise at its own discretion. (21)

Pressure group. *See* Advocacy, interest, or pressure group. (16)

Prime ministerial government. The notion that the prime minister is now so pre-eminent that the label "Cabinet government" no longer accurately describes how decisions are made in the political executive. (21)

Prime Minister's Office (PMO). The office that supports and advises the prime minister in partisan terms. (21)

Private bill. A bill introduced in Parliament that only affects a specific individual, company, organization, or group. (23)

Private members' bill. A public bill introduced in the House of Commons or Senate by a member who is not in the Cabinet. (23)

Private sector. The profit-oriented, nongovernmental part of the economy. (1, 20)

Privatization. Transferring a government program, agency, or Crown corporation to the private sector, such as by selling shares in a Crown corporation to the public at large or to a private firm. (20, 22)

Privy Council Office (PCO). The office that supports and advises the prime minister, Cabinet, and Cabinet committees in nonpartisan terms on such matters as overall government policy, the machinery of government, and senior bureaucratic appointments. (21)

Proletariat. A Marxist term referring to those who sell their labour for an undervalued price to the bourgeoisie; the working class. (8)

Province-building. The converse of "nation-building," the notion of developing strong provincial governments, especially after 1960 or so, whether through provincial bureaucracies, Crown corporations, or central planning agencies, and their capacity to intervene in the process of industrial development. (18)

Public Accounts Committee. *See* Standing Committee on Public Accounts. (22)

Public bill. A bill introduced in Parliament dealing with public policy and that affects society in general. (23)

Public opinion. The sum total of opinions held by members of the public on any subject. (12)

Public ownership. A policy instrument involving government purchase ("nationalization") of a private corporation or the creation of a Crown corporation. (20)

Public policy. A course of action or inaction chosen by public authorities to address a given problem or interrelated set of problems. (20)

Public policy purpose. The point of creating a Crown corporation or other government program or agency—that is, to achieve the objectives of a public policy or to serve some public interest. (3, 22)

Public sector. That part of the economy operated or financed by government. (1, 20)

Public Service Commission. The central personnel agency of government designed to police the merit system and ensure that partisanship is kept out of the regular public service. (22)

Quasi-judicial. Court-like functions, powers, and procedures often possessed by regulatory tribunals (e.g., CRTC licence-issuing powers). (22)

Quasi-legislative. Functions and powers of regulatory agencies to make law-like regulations (e.g., CRTC Canadian-content regulations). (22)

Quebec Act. The British law passed in 1774 that provided for a system of government for the colony of Quebec (Canada) and that provided certain privileges to the French-speaking, Roman Catholic majority. (2, 5)

Question Period. The daily 45-minute period in the House of Commons in which opposition members spar with the prime minister and Cabinet ministers. (23)

Quiet Revolution. The dramatic change of values, attitudes, and behaviour of French-Canadian Quebeckers, a new collective self-confidence, a new brand of nationalism, and an enormous expansion of the role of the provincial state that characterized Quebec in the 1960s. (5, 17)

Reasonable limits clause. Section 1 of the Charter of Rights and Freedoms, which allows the courts to find that even though a law violates a Charter right, it is a reasonable limit on such and is therefore allowed to stand. (19)

Recall. A populist device in which a certain proportion of the electorate signing a petition could cause an elected member of a legislature to resign. (11)

Red Tories. A minority faction within the Canadian Progressive Conservative Party with collectivist leanings akin to many British and European conservatives, stressing order, tradition, stability, and a paternalistic concern for the condition of the working class. (14)

Redistribution. The process of reallocating seats in the House of Commons among the provinces after each decennial census and then redrawing constituency boundaries within each province. (13)

Reference cases. Cases referred to the courts by provincial or federal cabinets in order to obtain a ruling on their constitutionality. (24)

Referendum. A populist device in which certain public policy proposals are submitted directly to the electorate. (5, 11, 17)

Regional economic development programs. Government programs designed to improve employment prospects in have-not parts of the country, usually by means of giving loans or grants to companies to establish or expand operations in such areas. (3)

Regulations. The detailed rules drafted by the bureaucracy under the authority of laws passed by Parliament that are too voluminous and technical to put into the legislation itself. (20, 22, 23)

Regulatory tribunals. Government agencies established to regulate an area of public policy, such as transportation or communications, that operate at arm's length from the Cabinet and often have quasi-legislative and/or quasi-judicial powers. (22, 24)

Representative bureaucracy. A public service that reflects the composition of the population, with the most usual concerns being gender, ethnicity, and region. (22)

Representative government. A form of government including an assembly elected by the citizens, but one that does not necessarily incorporate the principle of responsible government. (2)

Reservation. An obsolete power of the federally appointed lieutenant governor of each province to refrain from giving royal assent to provincial legislation and instead to s[e]_ to the federal Cabinet for its consideration. (18)

Residual powers. Those powers not explicitly given to the provinces in the [C]_ Act, 1867, that were assigned to the federal government under the openin[g] 91. (18)

Responsible government. A form of government in which the political executive must retain the confidence of the elected legislature or assembly and must resign or call an election if and when it is defeated on a vote of nonconfidence. (2, 23)

Right. That part of the ideological spectrum that cherishes individualism and believes in leaving the private sector to operate with minimal government intervention. (14)

Rowell–Sirois Commission. The Royal Commission appointed in 1937 to examine federal–provincial relations and whose 1940 report eventually led to many changes in the federal–provincial financial relationship. (18)

Royal commission. An elaborate investigation set up by the Cabinet to research a significant policy problem, to listen to and educate the public, and to make recommendations to the government. (16, 22)

Royal Commission on Aboriginal Peoples. The Royal Commission appointed in the wake of the defeat of the Meech Lake Accord and the Oka standoff to provide a blueprint for addressing the long-standing needs of the Aboriginal community. (4)

Royal Commission on Bilingualism and Biculturalism. The Royal Commission established in reaction to the Quiet Revolution in Quebec in the 1960s that recommended official bilingualism as a way of keeping the country together. (5)

Royal Commission on Electoral Reform and Party Financing. The Royal Commission established in the wake of the controversial 1988 federal election, with the objective of enhancing the democratic character of Canadian elections. (13, 15)

Royal Commission on the Status of Women. The Royal Commission that reported in 1970 and helped to inspire the women's movement in its demands for policy changes over the following decades. (7)

Royal Proclamation of 1763. The British policy enunciated after Britain won Quebec from France that in a large area called Indian Territory the purchase or settlement of land was forbidden without a treaty between the Crown and the Indian people concerned. (2, 4)

Rule of law. The constitutional principle that all government action must be based on law and that governments and government officials must obey the law. (2, 19)

Rural alienation. The widespread feeling among people living in rural areas that their _____ of little interest to the majority of urban-based politicians and policymakers. (9)

gle party can be assured of winning election after results in a high turnover rate in the Canadian House

ference, usually either heterosexual or homosexual, a courts now prohibit discrimination. (7)

t programs whose cost is shared by the federal and

l ideology that emphasizes the principle of equality and vernment to intervene in society and the economy via , and public ownership. (14)

Social movements. An informal network of organizations and individuals who on the basis of a collective identity and shared values engage in political struggle intended to expand the boundaries of the existing system, such as the women's and environmental movements. (16)

Social safety net. The conglomeration of social programs developed over the years by federal and provincial governments, individually and jointly, and designed to help those who could not otherwise care for their own basic needs or those of their family. (8)

Social Union Framework Agreement (SUFA). An overall framework of federal–provincial relations, agreed to by the federal government and all provinces except Quebec in 1999, that sought to clarify where and how either level of government could act unilaterally or engage in joint programs. (18)

Sovereignty. Ultimate control or independence, whether in terms of Canadian national sovereignty vis-à-vis other countries or of Quebec sovereignty vis-à-vis the federal government. (5, 10)

Sovereignty-association. The Parti Québécois proposal in which Quebec would be sovereign while maintaining an economic association with the rest of Canada. (5, 17)

Speaker. The presiding officer of the House of Commons. (23)

Special committee. A committee of the House of Commons appointed for a special, temporary purpose, such as to investigate a problem before the government has prepared legislation on the subject. (23)

Special operating agencies (SOAs). An aspect of the New Public Management movement, SOAs are units that function with relative autonomy within government departments and that aim to deliver a service along private-sector lines. (22)

Specific claims. Aboriginal land claims arising from the alleged nonfulfillment of Indian treaties and other lawful obligations, as opposed to those based on traditional occupancy and use. (4)

Speech from the throne. The document prepared by the prime minister and Cabinet and read by the governor general at the opening of each session of Parliament outlining the government's legislative proposals for the session to follow. (21, 23)

Spending power. The unofficial power of the federal government to spend money on any subject, including those within provincial jurisdiction, and even to attach conditions to such grants to the provinces. (18)

Spin doctors. Party officials and ministerial aides who talk to the media and try to influence media coverage by putting the best face on an event from their party's poin[t] view. (12, 15)

Split-run magazines. American magazines directed at Canadians by adding a [   ] amount of Canadian editorial material and a maximum number of Canadia[n] advertisements. (10)

Spoils system. Hiring public servants on the basis of political partis[an   ]

Stakeholders. Those individuals, groups, corporations, or other organizations who have a stake in any issue; the principal players involved in any policy community. (20)

Standing committee. A committee of the House of Commons set up semi-permanently and often parallel to a government department. (23)

Standing Committee on Public Accounts. The House of Commons committee that examines the Auditor General's Report and criticizes government officials for illegal or unwise expenditures. (22, 23)

Standing Joint Committee on Scrutiny of Regulations. The joint parliamentary committee appointed to wade through the voluminous regulations issued by government departments under the authority of legislation and that has the power to recommend rescinding such regulations. (23)

Standing Orders. The written rules of the House of Commons. (23)

Staples theory. The notion that Canadian economic development has gone through a series of stages based on the exploitation and export of one natural resource or another without the development of a secondary or tertiary sector. (3)

Stare decisis. The legal principle that judicial precedents are binding on similar subsequent cases, which forms the basis of the common law system. (24)

State of emergency. A policy instrument that involves the greatest degree of intrusion and coercion on the part of the state, now based on the Emergencies Act rather than the War Measures Act. (20)

Status Indians. Those Aboriginal Canadians registered with the federal government according to the terms of the Indian Act who have not had their status removed for any reason, or those who have regained it. (4)

Statute of Westminster. The 1931 British law that declared Canada and the other Dominions to be fully independent. (2, 17)

Subcultures or limited identities. Clusters of people who share basic political values and attitudes based on common regional, ethnic, class, or other characteristics. (11)

'e that no other organ of government can overrule
ied to some extent in 1982 with an expanded power
harter of Rights and Freedoms. (2, 19, 23, 24)

he Canadian Parliament that provided for the
es as a legal base for the institution in the absence
(17, 24)

that raises revenue for Ottawa and protects domestic
ds more expensive to buy. (3)

ial agreements, especially with respect to personal
, under which Ottawa collects the taxes if provinces
portion of the tax. (18)

Tax expenditures. A policy instrument that provides a tax credit or tax deduction if taxpayers spend money in a desired way. (20)

Terrorism. An act intended to cause death or serious bodily harm to civilians with the purpose of intimidating a population or compelling a government to do or abstain from doing any act. (10, 19)

Third-party advertising. Advertising by advocacy groups, as opposed to political parties, during an election campaign. (13)

Three-party system. A party system characterized by three main parties, all with approximately similar levels of support, as in Canada during the 1980s. (14)

Trade and Commerce clause. Subsection 2 of section 91 of the Constitution Act, 1867, which was intended to provide a broad base for federal jurisdiction in this field but which was whittled away by judicial interpretation. (18)

Transnational corporations. Corporations operating simultaneously in many countries throughout the world that often take orders from company headquarters and that individual states find difficult to control. (10)

Treasury Board. A Cabinet committee whose primary responsibility is to restrain government spending. (21)

Treasury Board Secretariat. The government department that advises the Treasury Board in its deliberations, that functions as a restraining influence on departmental spending, and has general authority over the operations of the public service. (21, 22)

Treaty power. Section 132 of the Constitution Act, 1867, which speaks of Empire treaties and was intended to provide the federal government with a broad power to sign and implement treaties, but whose scope was limited by judicial interpretation. (18)

Triple-E Senate. A proposal for Senate reform in which each province would have an equal number of senators, who would be elected and who would be given effective powers. (17, 23)

Two-party system. A type of party system in which two main parties are of approximately equal strength and alternate in office, as in Canada between 1896 and 1921. (14)

Two-plus or two-and-a-half party system. A type of party system in which two main parties are of approximately equal strength and alternate in office, but which are accompanied by one or more minor parties of significant strength, as in Canada between 1921 and 1980. (14)

Union Government. The coalition government from 1917 to the end of the First World War made up of Conservatives and English-speaking Liberals whose aim was to maintain national unity while enforcing conscription and conducting the war in a vigorous manner. (5, 14)

Victoria Charter. The 1971 package of constitutional amendments including an amending formula, a charter of rights, and provisions designed to respond to demands emanating from the Quiet Revolution in Quebec. (17)

Visible minorities. Members of minority ethnocultural groups, other than Aboriginals, whose skin colour is not white. (6)

Voluntary sector. The non-profit sector of the economy, as opposed to the public sector (government) and the profit-oriented private sector. (1, 16, 20)

Voters' list. The list of eligible voters now called the National Register of Electors and maintained on a permanent basis. (13)

Wage and price controls. A controversial proposal put forward by the Conservatives in the 1974 election campaign to put a cap on wage and price increases to reduce inflationary pressures. (14)

War Measures Act. The law invoked during both world wars and during the 1970 FLQ crisis under which the federal Cabinet was given emergency powers to deal with a crisis; later replaced by the Emergencies Act. (5, 20)

Welfare state. The characterization of most Western democracies from about 1950 to 1985 in which governments functioned as provider and protector of individual security and well-being through the implementation of a wide array of social programs and income transfers to individuals. (2, 8, 14, 18)

Western alienation. The feeling shared by many Western Canadians that their interests are not taken seriously in the national policymaking process. (3, 11)

Westminster model. The model of government developed in Britain in which the political executive is given extensive power to provide effective leadership. (2, 23)

White Paper on Indians. The 1969 Trudeau–Chrétien policy proposal to do away with the Indian Act and fully integrate Aboriginals into Canadian society. (4)

Women's movement. The collection of women's groups that mushroomed across the country starting about 1970 and demanding complete equality for women. (7)

World Trade Organization (WTO). An international organization to which Canada and most other countries belong that has the power to disallow national policies and practices that it deems discriminatory against companies from other states. (10)

Index

Abella, Rosalie, 155
Aberhart, William, 342
Aboriginal peoples, 77–99, 79F,
    see also status Indians
  advocacy groups, 97
  Charter and rights, 92,
      504–505, 508
  corporations, 98–99
  demographic profile, 79–82
  discrimination against, 99
  federal-provincial relations,
      480–81
  gambling revenue, 95
  globalization, 99
  governance, 85, 87, 89–90
  history, 82–85
  hunting and fishing rights, 88
  integration of, 80
  land claims, 86–89
  languages, 80
  police forces, 95
  political action by, 85, 90
  poverty among, 81–82
  reserves, 96
  rights, 83, 90, 91
  as subculture, 268
  treaties with, 83–85, 84F
  urban, 78, 80
  voting and the Charter,
      504–505
Aboriginal self-government, 79,
    88, **90**, 92–96
Aboriginal title, **86**
abortion, 159
  Charter and, 500
absent mandate, **388**–89
Access to Information Act, **603**
Accountability Act, 299
Act of Union, **107**–108
Adams, Michael, 266
adjournment proceeding, 623–24
adjournment, of Parliament, 521
adjudication (rule), definition,
    659
administrative agencies, **598**

advertising
  during elections, 331–32
  elections, 375–77, 376T
  tobacco, and the Charter, 497
advocacy advertising, **285,** 409
advocacy groups, 12, 285,
    395–412, 419, 457, 533, 534
  and Aboriginals, 97
  active vs. categoric, 401
  alliances, 403, 412
  bureaucracy, 412, 405, 594
  business, 398T, 399–400, 412
  characteristics/categories,
      400–401
  definition, **395**
  ethnocultural, 400
  feminist legal challenges,
      157–58
  functions, 411, 3406
  funding, 412
  and government, 403,
      406–408, 410, 411
  House of Commons
      committees and, 636–37
  influence, 409
  intervenor status, 670
  labour, and, 400, 408, 411
  and language, 408
  methods, 404–10
  policymaking, 529F, 530
  poor and, 185
  public opinion, and, 409, 412
  rural Canadians, 200–201
  seniors, 210, 213
  structures, 403–404
  success, 410–12, 412
  targets, 404–10
  types, 397–401
  for veterans, 400
  women and, 150, 151–52,
      408
affirmative action programs,
    155, **505**–506
agencies
  administrative, 598–600, 598T

  central, 589–90
  regulatory, 598, 599
  special operating, 606
aging
  digital divide, 293, 294
  mandatory retirement, 212–13
Agreement on Internal Trade
    (1995), **476**–77
agriculture, 201. See also farmers
Air Canada, 55
Alaska Boundary dispute
    (1903), 29
Alaska Highway, 55
Alberta, 60, 64, 68
  Charter, 493
  health care in, 479, 480
  political culture, 64, 70–71
  and Senate reform, 71,
      651–52
Alberta Press Bill case, 493
alienation, regional, 71–72
  western, 70–71, 267–68
Allaire Report, 442
Alliance Quebec, 119
Allmand, Warren, 626
Alternative Service Delivery
    (ASD), **605**–606
Angus, David, 417
Anthony, Nancy Hughes, 399
anti-terrorism, 141
  policies, 505–504
APEC (Asia-Pacific Economic
    Cooperation), 219–20
Arctic Islands, 429
armed forces, 149, 217, 222,
    223, 262
arrest/detention, Charter and, 502
Asbestos Strike (1949), 180
Asian Canadians, 128, 321
Asper, David and family,
    287–88, 290, 375
Assemblée de la francophonie
    de l'Ontario (AFO), 119
Assembly of First Nations, **85,**
    97, 400

asymmetrical federalism, 120
Atlantic Canada Opportunities
　Agency (ACOA), **69**–70
Atlantic provinces, 57–58,
　58–59, 65. *See also* individual
　provinces
Aucoin, Peter, 607
Auditor General, **601,**
　603–604**,** 635–36
Auto Pact, **232**
Axworthy, Lloyd, 226

backbenchers, **618,** *see also*
　Parliament, members of
　(MPs)
　planted questions by, 623
bandwagon effect, **301**
banks, 63–64
　foreign corporations, 227–28
Baxter-Moore, Nicolas, 535, 539
Beaudoin-Edwards
　Committee, 443
Beauharnois scandal (1930), 326
Bégin, Monique, 152
Bell, David, 250
Bennett, R.B., 186, 342, 560
Berton, Pierre, 256, 262
bilingualism, 507
　in government, 591, 619
　in Manitoba, 109, 118
　official, 112, 255, 282, 506,
　　591
　in Ontario, 109, 118
Bill 22, **113**
Bill 86 (Que.), 86, **115**
Bill 101 (Que.), 114
Bill 178 (Que.), **115**
Bill of Rights, 157, 492, 494–95
bills, 530, 531
　amendments to, 629
　committee stage, 629, 630
　debates, 630
　defeat of, 628
　government, 627
　legitimation, 530–31
　private, 628
　private members', 627–28
　public, 627
　Report stage, 629–30
　Senate role, 647, 648–49
　whipped, 628
Black, Conrad, 176, 287

Black, Ed, 297
Black, Martha, 150
Blair, Tony, 354
Bloc Québécois, 116, 344
block grants, **467**–69
blogs, 294
Bombardier family, 174, 175, 176
Borden, Robert, 39, 110, 340
border policy, 226–27
　Smart Border Declaration, 226
Bouchard, Lucien, 116, 445, 447
Bourassa, Henri, 298, 443
Bourassa, Robert, 113, 440
bourgeoisie, 16, **169**. *See also*
　petite bourgeoisie
Bourgon, Jocelyn, 154
branch plants, 227, 228, 229
Britain
　and Canada, 27–30, 492
　civil liberties in, 493
　fundamental rights, 492
　immigration from, 131
　parliamentary system, 32, 33
British Columbia, 30, 61, 87
　economy, 61
　land claims and, 87
　referendum re: Aboriginal
　　issues, 92
　treaties, 83, 84F, 87
　treaty, modern urban, 97
　union, 429
British Columbia Treaty
　Commission Agreement, 87
British North America (BNA)
　Act, 31,112. *See also*
　Constitution Act (1867)
Broadbent, Ed, 326
Broadcast News (BN), 295
broadcasting, 289–92
broadcasting industry, 237, 238
　regulation, 238
broker parties, 338
brokerage politics, 14
brokerage theory, **346**–47
Brown, George, 297
budget, **565**, 621. *See also*
　Estimates
bureaucracy, 33, 405–406,
　583–612. *See also* government,
　　departments;
　government, employees
　and advocacy groups, 594

Alternative Service Delivery
　(ASD), 605–606
control of, 600–604
dysfunctions of, 604
elections, and the Charter,
　497–98
elite influence on, 611
executive federalism, 475–76
functions, 583–84
merit system, 590, 591
opinion polls, 300–301,
　303–304
party decline and, 349
policymaking role, 530, 584
power of, 19, 20, 21, 584
Program Review, 605
provincial, 457–58
red tape in, 604
reform of, 605–608
regulations, 531
representative, 591–92
scandals in, 608–609
staff, 587–88, 588–89, 592
women in federal, 154
Bush, George W., 224, 235
Business. *See also* crown corpo-
　rations; lobbying influence
　of, 18, 175–76
　infrastructure and, 177
Business Development Bank of
　Canada, 230
"Buy American" program, 233
Byng, Lord, 549

Cabinet, 406–408, 530, 552–54
　administration of the bureau-
　　cracy, 554
　committees, 567, 568–69
　composition, 562–65
　ethnic representation,
　　563–64
　meetings, 555–56
　Memorandum to, 569, 569B–
　　570B, 571
　operation of, 565–71
　powers, 29
　prime-minister centred,
　　567–68
　priority-setting role, 534, 535
　Privy Council Office, 573
　provincial representation in,
　　562, 563T

regulations, 554
spending approval, 592
types, 566–68
Cabinet government, **554**
Cabinet ministers
accountable, as, 586, 609
House leader, 632
staff, 587–88
cabinet secrecy, **565**–66
cabinet solidarity, **565**
Cable Public Affairs Channel
(CPAC), 289
Cadman, Chuck, 642B
cadre parties, 338
Cairns, Alan C., 97–98, 466
Calgary Declaration (1997), 437,
446
Campagnolo, Iona, 152
Campbell, Colin, 351, 647
Campbell, Gordon, 92
Campbell, Kim, 153, 585, 605
Canada, 32F. *See also* Canadians;
federal-provincial
relations; government; regions
aging Canadians, 210–12, 211T
and Britain, 33–34, 38–41
cabinet government, 554
as constitutional monarchy,
37–38
core *vs.* periphery, 199
democratic values, 256–62
division of powers, **459**
ethnic conflict, 108–13
as federation, 35–37
flag/anthem, 41
foreign governments and, 218
foreign investment, 227–31
foreign policy, 225–26
free trade, 231, 232, 233
global economic influences,
227–34
international agreements,
220–21
international organizations,
218–20
international unions, 236
language, 103–5, 108–13
Lower- *vs.* Upper- separation,
107
as mosaic, 258
national characteristics
(values), 255–63

national deficits, 219–20
physiographic regions, 53, 54F
pluralism and, 258, 259
political system, 3–10, 27–30,
510–15
province-building, **458**
rule of law, 38
rural, 199–201
security, 222
television-dependency, 297
trade, 231–34
U.S. influence on, 223–27
U.S. ownership, 236
Canada Act (U.K.), **430,** 439
Canada Assistance Plan (CAP),
161, 467
Canada Border Services Agency,
226
Canada Child Tax Credit, 160
Canada Clause, **263,** 443
Canada Council for the Arts,
241
Canada East (Quebec), 30
Canada Economic Development
for Quebec Regions (CED),
69–70
Canada Elections Act, 302, **321**
Canada Family Action Coalition,
208
Canada Health Act (1984), **468**
Canada Health and Social
Transfer (CHST), **188,** 469
Canada Mortgage and Housing
Corporation, 213
Canada Post, 155
Canada Revenue Agency (CRA),
478
Canada West (Ontario), 30
Canada-U.S. Free Trade
Agreement, 63, 65–66,
187, 220
Canada-U.S. Permanent Joint
Board on Defence, 223
Canadian Advisory Council on
the Status of Women
(CACSW), 161
Canadian Alliance, 70, 345
Canadian Bill of Rights, **494,**
see also Bill of Rights
Canadian Broadcasting
Corporation (CBC), 56, 236,
289

Canadian Charter of Rights and
Freedoms (1982), 135, 156,
157, 158, 251–52, 253, 255,
431, 495–510, 659
application to government,
509
collective bargaining and, 183
courts and politics, 507–508,
510–15
democratic/voting rights, 499
discrimination, as protection
against, 135
health care system, 500–501,
514–15
legislation and the judiciary,
513, 514
notwithstanding clause, 495
official languages, 506–507
political freedom, 253
public interest, 513, 514
reasonable limits clause, 496
and reverse onus, 502–503
right to life cases, 500
self-incrimination, 502–503
trial delays, 502
Canadian Centre for Policy
Alternatives, 18
Canadian Council of Chief
Executives (CCCE), **177,** 399
Canadian Council on Social
Development (CCS), 185
Canadian Democracy and
Corporation Accountability
Commission, 176
Canadian Ethnocultural Council,
135, 137
Canadian Federation of
Agriculture, 201
Canadian Federation of Students
(CFS), 14, **395**
Canadian Human Rights Act, 97
Canadian Human Rights
Commission, 155
Canadian Judicial Council, **677**
Canadian Labour Congress
(CLC), 183, 284, **183,** 4
Canadian Manufacturers
Exporters (CME),
Canadian Medical
(CMA), 400
Canadian M
Commit

Canadian Multiculturalism Act (1988), 135
Canadian National (CN), 54
Canadian Nuclear Safety Commission, 230
Canadian Pacific Railway (CPR), 53
Canadian Poverty Fact Book, 184
Canadian Press, 295
Canadian Radio-television and Telecommunications Commission (CRTC) 56, 238, 289, 291, 292, **598**
Canadian Transportation Agency, 55, 230
Canadian Wheat Board, 62, 201, 202
Canadians
 collective responsibility notions, 265
 and deference to authority, 259, 260
 diffidence of, 261–62
 government intervention, 265
 political activity, 272F
 political participation, 382–88
 political values, 385–86, 385F
 trust in public figures/professions, 265F
 viewing habits, 291–92, 291F
Canadian Television Fund, 239
candidates. *See also* elections
 secret contributions, 328
CanWest Global, 287, 293
capitalism, 16, *see also* class; individualism
Carty, Ken, 339, 363

Charlottetown Conference, 31
chief electoral officer, **318**
child care, 481
children, poverty among, 183–84, 184F
child welfare legislation, 149
Chinese Exclusion Act of 1923, 132
Chinese immigrants, head tax, 132
Chrétien, Jean, 21, 114, 224, 286, 325, 358
 Clarity Act, 447
 commercials mocking, 376
 lame-duck prime minister, as, 558–59
 and party discipline, 626
 and Senate, 65—51
Chrétien government, 354, 476–77
 1995 referendum, 447
 and Aboriginals, 93
 lobbying, 415, 416, 417
 Liberal Red Book, 373
 policy conference, 359
Christian, William, 351
Churchill Falls hydroelectric project, 66
cities, 481–82. *See also* municipalities
 Aboriginal peoples in, 78, 80
 provinces and, 458
civil liberties, **491**. *See also* rights
 arrest and the Charter, 502
 division of powers decisions, 493, 494
Clarity Act, **117, 447**
Clark, Joe, 206, 343, 345, 354, 358, 443, 568
 party policy, 359
 on, Adrienne, 153, 551
 on, Stephen, 22, 221, –37
 169–96
 Charter and individualism/ collectivism, 516
 cleavages and social safety net, 190
 consciousness, 170–71, 258–59, 348, 384–85
 consciousness and egalitarianism, 261

consciousness of the poor, 190
corporate elite and bureaucracy, 611
corporate elite and federalism, 485
definition, 169–72
discrimination *vs.* Aboriginals, 99
elections/party financing, 333
ethnicity and, 143–44
multinationals, 243
new Quebec middle class, 123
ownership of media, 305
politics and, 16–19, 384–85
rural residents, 214
seniors, 214
social impact of Charter, 515–16
class-consciousness, **170,** 384–85
cleavages, 9
 age, 209–13
 ethnic, 121
 religion, 203–209
 religious denominations, 207, 208
 urban vs. rural, 198–203
clerk of the House, 632
Clerk of the Privy Council and secretary to the Cabinet, **573**
clientele relationship, **405–406, 594–95**
climate change
 environment policy, case study, 540
closure, **628**
CN, 54
Coates, Michael, 417
Code Civil du Québec, 663
coercion, 5, 17, **169**
Coleman, William, 399
collective responsibility, **565**
collectivism, **256, 258,** 352
Commissioner for Federal Judicial Affairs, **672**
committee of the whole, 636
committee system, 633–37, 643
committees, standing, 634
common law, **660**
communications, 55–56
comprehensive claims, **86**
Comuzzi, Joe, 626
conditional grants, **466,** 467–69

and
Association
403
ticultural Advisory
tee, 135

Confederation, 29–32, 32F
Confederation Settlement, the,
  459–61. *See also* Constitution
  Act of Canada
  components, 459
  cultural guarantees, 461
Conflict of Interest Code, 638
Congress of Aboriginal
  Peoples, 97
conscription crisis, 340, **342**
conservatism, **351**–55
Conservative Party of Canada,
  339, 342
  business/liberal agenda, 353
  Canadian Alliance merger,
    353
  election strategy, 373
  federal/provincial organiza-
    tion, 362
  leadership, 343
  Liberals vs., 339–46
  majority government
    (Diefenbaker), 343
  Progressive, 342
  rebirth, 345
  red Tories, 352
  union of Canadian Alliance/
    PC parties, 345
constituencies (political), 315–17
constituency associations, 363,
  380, 382
Constitution Act, 1867, 203,
  255, 428–30
  amendments to, 429
  British amendments, 41
  cultural guarantees, **108**
  distribution of powers, 428
  domestic amendments, 41
  language guarantees, 108
  obsolete federal controls,
    472–73
  religious minorities
    protection, 109
  school systems, 203–204
  Senate and, 645
Constitution Act, 1982, **41**, 78,
  88, 90–92, 115, 430–31,
  437–40, 495
  aboriginal rights and, 90
  amending formula, 434–35
  distinct society clause, **440**
  language, 439

language education rights, 117
  section 35 Aboriginal rights, 88
Constitutional Act (1791),
  107
Constitution of Canada, 35–37,
  427– 51, 432–48. *See also*
  Confederation Settlement
  alternatives to amendment,
    449B
  amending formula, 433–35,
    439
  amendments, 462
  components, 429
  composition, 431
  concurrent powers, **459,**
    459–61
  Constitutional Amendment
    Act (1996), 446
  constitutional amendments
    since 1982, 448B
  declaratory power, 472
  development, 35–41
  disallowance power, 472
  division of powers, 460–61,
    460B, 461–66
  enumerated powers, **459**–61
  judicial interpretation, 462–64
  language and, 435
  major developments,
    1960-2010, 436–37
  notwithstanding clause, 440
  organic statutes, 430
  post-Charlottetown develop-
    ments, 445–48
  public opinion polls, 444–45
  reservation power, 472
  residual powers, **459**–61
constitutional amending
  formula, **433**–35, 434B–435B
constitutional conventions,
  431–32**,** 433, 439
constitutional law, 662–62
constitutional monarchy, **37,**
  38, 54
  definition, 38
cooperative federalism, 474–76
core-periphery analysis, 56–57
core-periphery system, **199**
corporate elite, *see* elite,
  corporate
corporations
  advocacy advertising, **285**

Charter and, 501, 513, 513F
  election campaigns, 177, 329T
  and environment, 77–78
  foreign-owned, 174
  hollowing out of Canada, 231
  lobbying, 417, 418, 418T
  media convergence, 292, 293T
  power of, 16–19
  transnationals, 221
Council of Canadians, 234, 402
Council of the Federation, **478**
Court Challenges Program, 154,
  157–58
Courtney, John, 317
courts, 6
  Canadian Bill of Rights, 494
  Charter invalidation of laws
    by, 507–508
  civil liberties/rights, 493
  implied bill of rights, **493**
  political system and the
    Charter, 510–15
  provincial, 664–66
  structure of, 663–67, 664F
  trial delays and the Charter,
    502
  trial, superior, 665–66
Coutu, Jean, 175
Coyne, James, 649
CPAC, 289
CPR, 53, 54
Cree-Naskapi (of Quebec) Act
  (1984), 91
Criminal Code, 117–18, 151,
  158, **662**
  aboriginal offender
    provisions, 95
  abortion, 205
  women, and, 151
criminal law, **662**
Crow Rate, 63
Crow's Nest Pass Act, 63
Crown, 545–52
  advantages/disadvantages,
    551–52
  ceremonial/symbolic fu
    tions, **546**–47
  definition, 545–4
  powers, 547–5
crown corpor
  595–98
  publi

CRTC, 56, 238, 289, 291, 292, **598**
CTVglobemedia, 287, 293T
cultural industries, 237–41
  arts funding, 241
culture, political, 249–75
  Canada *vs.* U.S., 255–62
  changing Canadian, 263–66
  definition, 249–51
  postmaterialism, 265–66
Canadian Wheat Board (CWB), 67

d'Aquino, Thomas, 399, 420
Dahl, Robert, 14
Davis, Bill, 204
day care. *See* child care
Day, Stockwell, 345
debates, bills, 630
decentralization, 259
Declaration of Independence, 255–56
declaratory power, federal, **460**
defence, 223–25
deference to authority, **259**–60
  historical, 260
democracy, **38,** 251–55, 253
  backbencher freedom, 264
  deference decline, 264–65
  direct participation/initiative, **264**
  majority rule, **255**
  quality of life values, 266–67
Democratic Representative Caucus, 345
democratic rights, **499**
Department of Finance, 590

no party policy, 359
Diefenbaker government, 111
Dion, Stéphane, 154, 358–59, 447, 550
  commercials mocking, 376–77
  Green shift, 373–74, 379
  nomination of women candidates, 380, 381
direct taxation, 466, 470–72
direct taxes, **460**
disabled
  social programs and, 186–87
disallowance power, federal, **460**
discrimination
  Aboriginal peoples and, 82
  Aboriginal women' status, 97
  anti-semitism, 205, 206
  blacks and civil rights abuse, 494
  Canadian foreign policy, 205–206
  Charter and, **505**–506
  Duplessis government and Jehovah's Witnesses, 493
  ethnocultural minorities, 140
  immigrants and, 132–34
  legislation re same-sex unions, 163
  mandatory retirement, 212–13
  multiculturalism policy and, 134–35
  racism vs. immigrants, 133
  separate school system, 497
  women and equality rights, 504–505
    -settlement mechanism,

    t society, **115**
    t society clause, **440**
    n, **633**
    e Act, 151, 205, 401
    wolsky, Alexandra, 354
    s, T.C. (Tommy), 186, 342
    P leader, 343
    es, Anthony, 14
    atent protection,
    bying, 414
    rafficking
    arter and, 503

Dryden, Ken, 481
Duceppe, Gilles, 377, 378
Dumont, Mario, 445
Dunn, Christopher, 568
Duplessis, Maurice, 106, 254, 299, 342, 493
  as leader of Unione Nationale, 324
Durham, Lord, 29, 30, 107
Durham Report (1839), 29–30

e-democracy, 264
e-government, 607
Early Learning and Child Care Initiative, 189
Easton, David, 10
economics, Keynesian, 475, **476**
education, 507
egalitarianism, 260–**261**
election campaigns, 372–79
  local, 381–82, 381T
  recent, 378–79
election day, 319–20
elections, 313–21
  absent mandate, **388–89**
  advocacy groups, 401
  candidates, 330, 372, 380–81
  Charter and voting, 497, 499
  dissolution of Parliament and, **621**
  financing for, 327–32, 372–73
  issues. 386-87
  leadership, 388
  media coverage, 374–77
  party identification, **386**
  political parties, 324–25, 324T
  popular sovereignty and, 252
  religious groups, 208, 209
  scandals, 327
  seats vs. votes in, 323–25, 324T
electoral map, 314–17, 315T
  Charter and, 499
  public hearings, 316
  redistribution of seats, **314**
electoral system
  dissolve Parliament, **317**
  first-past-the-post aspect, **320,** 322, 325
  photo-ID, 321
  proportionality of, 322–27
  reform, 325–27

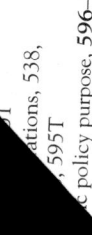

inc-
ations, 538,
595T
policy purpose, **596–97**

elite(s)
    judiciary and, 678–79
    policy/implementation, 541
    and minorities, 143
    and political executive, 576
    election candidates, 389
elite accommodation, 24, **407**
elite, corporate, 16–19
    banks, and, 174
    comprador, 174
    tobacco companies fined, 178
    as upper class, 172–78
    wealth, 176T
Elizabeth II, Queen, 545
embedded state, 24
Emergencies Act, 299
emergency doctrine, **462**–63
employment
    discrimination/mandatory
        retirement, 505
    equity in government, 592,
        593T
    mobility rights, 499–500
    women and, 155–56
    women and equality, 504–505
employment equity, **155**–56
    ethnic groups and, 141
Employment Equity Act (1986,
    1995), **136, 155**
employment insurance, *see*
    unemployment insurance
energy issues, 235–36
English Canada, 103–5
    allophones, 120
    ethnic groups and, 30
environment
    corporate lobbying, 177–78
    federal government jurisdic-
        tion, 465
    Kyoto Protocol, 234–35
    natural, 234–35
    policymaking case study,
        539–40
environmental protection
    corporations and, 177–78
equality, political, 260, 261
equality rights, **504**–506
equalization payments, 68,
    469–70, 470T, 480
Erasmus, Georges, 91
Eskimo, *see* Inuit
Estimates, 592–94, 601, **621**

ethics commissioner, 608, 638
ethnic groups
    gang crime and, 140
ethnic minorities
    political parties and, 141–42
ethnicity, 128–29, 384
    racial profiling, 139
European Free Trade
    Association, 234
European Union, 218
evangelicalism, **208**
Eves, Ernie, 206
Executive Council, 457
executive federalism, **474**–76,
    484
    definition, 474
exempt staff, **587**–88
exhortation, 536
extraterritoriality, **229**

Fairclough, Ellen, 151
Family Allowances Act (1944),
    151
farmers, 341
    political activity, 201
Federal Accountability Act,
    318, 417, 588, 638
Federal Court of Canada,
    666–67, 667F
Federal Economic Development
    Initiative in Northern
    Ontario (FedNor) 69–70
Federal Election Finance Act,
    328–31
federal provincial conference,
    474
federal-provincial agreements,
    449B, 477
federal-provincial powers
    division of, 461–66
    finance, 466–72
    judicial interpretation, 462–66
federal-provincial relations, 483
    Aboriginals, 480–81
    bureaucracy and, 594–95
    Charter groups, effect of, 512
    obsolete federal powers,
        472–73
federal-provincial transfer pay-
    ments, 469, 471T
federalism, 475–76, 476–77
    Canadian, 36–37

civil liberties/rights and free-
    doms, 493
    definition, 455
    evolution, 462–77
    federal-provincial relations,
        473–77, 484
    fiscal imbalance, **483**
    Harper *vs.* Martin, 120
    phases, 473–77
    in the 21st century, 477–83
federation, 35
Federation of Canadian
    Municipalities, 202, 483
feminism, women's movement
    progress and, **152**
feminization of poverty, **184**
fetal rights, 500
filibuster, **628**
film industry, 239
Filmon, Gary, 441
finance
    federal-provincial powers,
        466–72
Finkel, Alvin, 177
FIRA, 230
first ministers' conference, **474,**
    475
First Nations, 79F, 82
First Nations Governance Act
    (Bill C-61), 93
fishing, 234
FLQ, 113
Ford strike (1945), 180
foreign investment, 227–31,
    228F
Foreign Investment Review
    Agency (FIRA), 230
foreign ownership, 228
    assets in Canada, 230F
    government regulation, 230
foreign policy, 225–26
formative events theory, 250
Forsey, Eugene, 550, 641
fragment theory, 250
franchise, **320**–21
Fraser, Sheila, 603
free trade, 231–33
    election issue, 38
    policy, 243
Free Trade A
free votes,
freedom

freedom of expression, 497
  reasonable limits, 497–98
freedom of religion, 496–98
French Canada, 103–5
  cultural guarantees, 108
  current issues, 119
  English Canada and, 103–5,
    107–8, 108–13
  Quebec compared, 105T
  Quebec/Bill 22 language
    laws, 113
French Canadians, 28–30
Front de libération du Québec
  (FLQ), 113
FTA (Canada-U.S. Free Trade
  Agreement), 220
Fugère, René, 415
Fulton-Favreau formula (1964),
  433
fundamental freedoms, 253,
  496–98
fundamental justice, *see* legal
  rights

GATT, 231
gays/lesbians
  civil rights, 162–63
  couples, 162–63
  employment, 162
  marriage, 163
GDP (Provincial), 67T
gender, 147–65. *See also* women
  equality, and, 148
  gays and lesbians, 162–63
  identity and, 147, 148
Gender Equality, Federal Plan
  (1995), 152

Canadian policymaking
  and, 242
characteristics, 222
Charter and government
  restriction, 516
corporations, 221
cultural industries, 241
immigration diversity, 144
influence on values, 275
international organizations/
  the Constitution, 451
international political movements, 365
neoliberalism, 365
neoliberalism and federalism,
  486
policymaking and implementation, 541–42
political executive and, 577
prime minister and, 557
Quebec language policy, 123
religious diversity, 214–15
transnational corporations/
  social programs, 191–92
women's movement and, 165
Globe and Mail, 287, 290, 297
Golden Horseshoe, 69
Gomery Inquiry, **117, 588**
Gomery Report, 286, **286,** 417,
  608–609
Gomery, John, 117
governance, Aboriginal, 85, 87,
  89–90
  creation of Nunavut, 93
  incarceration, 94
  justice system, 94–95
  self-government, 90–92
government, **528,** 552. *See also*
  icies; government,
  ral; Parliament
  rtising and, 285–86
  cacy groups, 530, 532
  ness, and role of,
  76–77
  cit spending/economic
  ollapse, 43
  nition, 5
  egulation, 43, **538**
  nsizing, 43
  cutive branch, 29, 30
  cutive power *vs.* rule
  of law, 493

federation, 35
foreign ownership, 229–30
formation post election, 553
global economic crisis, 526
globalization and, 21, 43
health care system, 213
minority, 558–60
municipal, 458–59
new public management,
  532, 533
ownership and policy, 538
policy instruments, 535–39
provincial, 36, 457
regulation, 537–38
revenue vs. expenditures, and
  GDP, 257T
role of, 525–27
spending, 526, 527F, 537
transition team, 555
government bills, **627**
government regulation
  corporate elite and, 175
government, departments,
  585–95, 585T, 588F, 589–90,
  594–95
government, federal, *see also*
  bureaucracy; equalization
  payments; Parliament;
  transfer payments
  accountability,608–609
  as accountable, 608–609
  deregulation, **599**
  downsizing, 607
  employees, 585T, 588–89
  exempt staff, **587**–88
  French language schools, 118
  gender equality initiative, 152
  health/social programs, 186
  housing, 213
  immigrant mistreatment, 133
  nonprofit corporations,
    606–607
  partnerships, 606
  privatization, 597, 597T
  provinces and, 112–13,
    594–95
  religious issues, 205, 206
  spending by, 468, 536, 537,
    592, 594
  spending power, **468**
  transfers to provinces, 469
  treaty jurisdiction, 465

urban issues, 202, 203
governor general, 40, 547. *See also* Crown
    advisory role, 551
    controversial, 549
    selection, 547
    senate appointments, 645
governor, colonial, 29–30
Gray Report (1972), **228**
Great Depression, 42
green issues
    Blue Planet Project, 402
Green Paper, 530
Greene, Ian, 504
Gregg, Allan, 263, 300
gun amnesty, 202
gun control, 21

Halpern case (Ontario Court of Appeal), 163
Harper, Elijah, 85, 91, 441
Harper, Stephen, 95, 120, 268, 294, 345, 354, 358, 482–83, 556, 609. *See also* Harper government
    2006 campaign, 374, 379
    moderate approach, 373
    perceived as extreme, 378
    Stand Up for Canada, 389
Harper government, 69, 224, 231, 317–18, 482–83
    cabinet meetings, 568
    environmental protection, 482–83
    fiscal imbalance, 483
    lobbyists and, 417
    minority, 641–43
    open federalism, **482**
    prorogation of Parliament, 2008, 550–51
Harris, Mike, 353, 354
Hartz, Louis, 250, 251, 351
Hawthorn Report (1966), 89–90
head tax, 132
health care, 478–80
    Charter and, 500–501, 514–15
health care programs, 467–69
Heard, Andrew, 651
hegemony, 10–11, 250, 338–39, 397

Hiebert, Jane, 514
homosexuals, 162–63, 504–505
horizontal management, **589**
Horowitz, Gad, 250, 351
horse-race effect, **302**
House leader, **632**
House of Commons, 295, 338, 407, 408. *See also* bills; legislation; Parliament
    advocacy groups, 403, 406–408, 410, 411
    in Britain, 625, 627, 632, 634
    budgetary procedure, 592, 594
    bureaucratic control and, 601–602
    closure, **628**
    committees, 629, 633–37
    composition, 619–20
    confidence, 432
    functions, 618–44
    legislation, 530–31, 627–30, 629F
    minority government, **640–43**
    officers of, 630–32
    Opposition, 623, 641
    policymaking role, 530–31
    press gallery, 623
    prime minister's role, 557
    procedures, 632–33
    proportional representation, 433
    Question Period, 601–602, **623**
    reform of, 643–44
    rural representation, 201–202
    sessions, 621–24
    speeches, 633
    Standing Orders, **630**
    supremacy of Parliament principle, **618**
    timetable, 620–24
    voting, 632–33
    Westminster model of, 33
    women representatives, 153T
House of Commons Chamber, 631F
Howe, C.D., 55
Howe, Joseph, 297
Hudson's Bay Company, 27
Hudson's Bay company lands, 429

Human Development Index, 187
Human Poverty Index, 187, 188
human rights, 492
Human Rights Act, 162
Hurtig, Mel, 377
Hyder, Goldy, 417

Iacobucci, Frank, 95
identity(ies), 10. *See also* subcultures
    ethnocultural, 140, 142, 268–69
    gay and lesbian, 162
    Quebec Francophones, 105
    regional, 267–68
    religious, 207–209
    seniors, 209–13
    significance, 197–98
ideology
    1980s spectrum shift, 353
Ignatieff, Michael, 356, 357, 358, 359
immigrants
    dual citizenship, 141
    poverty levels, 140
    racism and bias, 133
immigration, 129–32, 131F
    Charter and refugees, 501
    discrimination, 132–34
    ministerial powers, 139
    opposition to, 137–39
    provinces and, 139–40
    sources of immigrants, 132F
    terrorism/Charter, 503–504
    visible minority levels, 129T
Immigration Act, 131, 163
Immigration and Refugee Protection Act (2002), 139
Imperial War Cabinet, 39
implied bill of rights, **493**
Income Tax Act, 158
Indian Act, 158
    amendment re native women status, 90
Indian Act (1876), 77, 82, 83, 86
Indian Remission Order, 95
Indian Territory, 83
indigenous elite, 174
indirect taxes, **460**
Individual Rights Protection Act (Alta), 162
individualism, **256,** 351

Information Commissioner, **603**
informed vote, 271
initiative, **264**
Innis, Harold, 58
institutionalism, 20
institutionalized cabinet, **566**
institutionalized groups, **401**
Intercolonial Railway, 53
interest groups, **395**. *See also*
   advocacy groups
International Institute for
   Democracy and Electoral
   Assistance (IDEA), 270
International Monetary Fund
   (IMF), 219
internet, 201, 294
   online government, 607
   rural provision of, 201
interstate federalism, 461
intervenor status, 670
intrastate federalism, 461
Inuit, 78, 79, 84–85
   Regional Government of
      Nunavik, 96
Inuit Tapiriit Kanatami, 97
Investment Canada, 230
Irvine, William, 325
Irving family, 174, 177
issue-oriented groups, **401**

James Bay and Northern
   Quebec Agreement (1975),
   87
James, Matt, 450
Japanese Canadians, 133
Japanese Redress Agreement
   (1988), 136
Judicial Committee of the Privy
   Council (JCPC), **41**, 431, 668
   federal-provincial powers,
      462–64
Jean, Michaëlle, 141, 153, 550,
   551
Jehovah's Witnesses
   discrimination, 493
Jenson, Jane 250
   ̲ees, **636**
   ̲, 319
   ̲7
   judiciary
   ̲ 672–76
   ̲76, 677

judicial discretion, **492,** 661
judicial independence, **34,** 676
judicial interpretation
   equality rights, 504
judicial review, **34,** 492, 661
judiciary, 602, 659–80. *See also*
   judges
   independence, 676–78
   policymaking role, 660–61
   review powers, 34, 492, 661
   rule adjudication function,
      659–61
justice, access to, 661–62
justice system, 6

Kelowna Accord, 96–97
Kennedy, John F., 223
Kenny, Colin, 648
Kent Royal Commission on
   Newspapers, **287**
Keynes, John Maynard, 42
Keynesian economics, **42,** 475,
   610
Kilgour, David, 642, 642B
King, William Lyon Mackenzie,
   40, 53, 110, 458
   Beauharnois Dam scandal,
      326
   Byng dispute, 341, 549
   farm and labour votes, 347
   leader of Liberal party, 340,
      341, 342
King-Byng dispute, 341, **549**
Klein, Ralph, 353
Knopf, Rainer, 513, 514
Kunz, F.A., 647, 648
Kymlicka, Will, 258
Kyoto Accord, 66
Kyoto Protocol, 234–35, 480

La Relève, 607
labour movement, 180, 183
   Charter, and the, 497, 498
   unions, and U.S., 236
Labour Party (Canada), 341–42
Labrador
   Innu land claims/self-
      government, 88
LaMarsh, Judy, 151
land claims/issues, 86–89
Landry, Bernard, 116
language, 205. *See also* bilin-

gualism, education
   Charter, 512
   minorities, 115, 507
   official, 506–507
   trials/Charter and, 503
Lapointe, Ernest, 561
Laporte, Pierre, 113
Latimer, Robert, 500
Laurier, Wilfrid, 39, 62, 110,
   204, 339, 340, 549
   leader of Liberal party, 340
   separate school issue, 204
laws, role of, 662–63, *see also*
   legislation
Layton, Jack, 378, 379
lead agency, 532
   policy implementation and,
      534
Leader of the Opposition, **623**
leaders' debates, 296–97, 377
leadership review, **358**
League of Nations, 39
LeBlanc, Dominic, 359
left, the, **352**
Legal Education and Action
   Fund (LEAF), 157
legal rights, **500–504**
legislation, 627–30. *See also*
   specific acts; bills; laws; policymaking; Quebec; regulations
   advocacy groups and, 636–37
   Cabinet and, 530–31, 627–30
   civil rights cases, 494, 495
   double majority, 30
   House of Commons and,
      530–31, 627–30
   judicial review, 37
   Senate and, 647, 648–49
   unions and Charter protec-
      tions, 498
   whistle-blowing, 601
legitimation, 534
Lesage, Jean, 111
Lesage government, 433
Lévesque, René, 113, 344
Lewis, David, 176
Liberal Party of Canada vs.
   Conservatives, 339–46
   dominance, 342, 345, 346,
      349
   election strategy, 373
   green shift, 379, 387

history, post-Pearson, 343–46
Keynesian economics, 352
leaders, 356
leadership, 358, 359
platform, 373–74
provincial and federal parts, 363
liberalism, **351,** 352
lieutenant governor, 457
limited identities, 267–69
Lipset, Seymour Martin, 250, 251, 255–56
lobbying, **396,** 412–19
Lobbying Act, 414, 415, **417**
lobbyists, 413, 414, 417, 418
Lobbyists Registration Act (1989), 413–14 *see also* Lobbying Act
London Conference (1866), 31
Loney, Martin, 49
Lord's Day Act, 206
Lord, Bernard, 118
Lortie, Pierre, 332
Lower Canada, 29, 30, 107

MacAdams, Roberta, 149
Macdonald Royal Commission on the Economic Union and Development Prospects for Canada, 232
MacDonald, Flora, 152, 153
Macdonald, John A., 339, 549, 644
Confederation and, 35–37
federalism and, 431, 459, 465, 473
Pacific scandal, 327
regional conflicts and, 62, 63
Riel rebellions and, 108–109
MacKay, Peter, 345, 354, 562
MacKay, R.A., 647, 648, 649
Mackell case (1917), 109
Mackenzie Valley Gas Pipeline, 55
Mackenzie, Alexander, 340
Mackenzie, William Lyon, 29
Macphail, Agnes, 150
Macpherson, C. B., 350
MacRae, Kenneth, 351
mad cow crisis, 202
magazines, 238–29
majority government, **33,** 558, 640

majority rule, **255**
mandatory retirement, 212–13
Mandel, Michael, 511–12
Manitoba
French-English conflict, 109
language legislation (1890), 109
language rights and, 118
separate school abolition, 204
Manitoba Act (1870), 109
Manley, John, 420
Manning, E. C., 342
Manning, Preston, 344, 354
Maritimes, *see* Atlantic provinces
marriage, 163.
Marshall, Donald, 94
Martin, Paul, 416
Aboriginal issues, 96, 481
as Finance minister, 354, 469, 558–59
Liberal Party leader, 345, 378, 626
minority government, 264, 559–60
Martin government, 96, 224
asymmetrical federalism, **483**
appointments, 90
equalization payments, 480
lobbying, 416, 417
minority, as, 559–60, 642B
New Deal for Cities and Communities, 459
privatization, 597–98
Quebec and, 120
Martin, Paul, Sr., 354
Marx, Karl, 16, 169, 170
mass parties, 338
Massey Royal Commission on National Development in the Arts, Letters and Sciences, 241
Massey, Vincent, 547
May, Elizabeth, 377, 379
McCain family, 174
McClelland and Stewart, 240
McClung, Nellie, 149
McCormick, Peter, 661
McDonough, Alexa, 153
McIvor, Heather, 338
McKinney, Louise, 149

McLaughlin, Audrey, 153
McQuaig, Linda, 175
McRoberts, Kenneth, 119
media, 281–307, 286–99
agents of socialization, 284
bias and style, 296
budget cuts/recession, 292
Canadian content, 289, 290
control, 305
convergence, 292
elections, 374–77
faith-based group television, 207
framing events, 295
freedom and expression and, 498
freedom of the press, 299
government and, 6–7, 298–99
news leaks, 298–99
party decline and, 349–50
political agenda, 295
political role, 305
politicians and, 297–99
public and, 294–95, 295F
search and seizure/ Charter protection, 501, 502
visual/sound bites influence, 296–97
Meech Lake Accord, 85, 90–92, 91, 115–16, **115**–16, 344, 440–41
reaction/objections to, 440–41
Senate, 440, 441
women and, 440
Meighen, Arthur, 340
Meisel, John, 349–50, 350
Memorandum to Cabinet (MC), 530, **569,** 569B–570B, 571
Mercier, Honoré, 108–109
merit system, **590,** 591
Métis, 78, 79, 79F, 84
Charter and, 508
distinct Aboriginal group, 95
hunting/fishing rights, 88
Métis National Council, 97
Mi'kmaq, 93, 95
fishing rights, 88
middle class, 178–80. *See also* petite bourgeoisie
new-, and unions, 178

two fractions of, 178–79
vs. upper class, 179
Milewski, Terry, 299
Miliband, Ralph, 420
Milliken, Peter, 631, 632
ministerial responsibility, **554,**
586
ministers, 406–408, *see also*
Cabinet; Cabinet ministers
junior, 561
portfolios, 564
without portfolio, 561
minorities, 592
Charter rights, 508
civil rights abuse, 493, 494
discrimination, *see*
discrimination
elites and, 143
ethnocultural, 127–44
judicial appointments, 674
multicultural policy and, 134,
135
religious, 206
rights, 255
use of Courts and Charter, 512
visible, 128
minority government, **33,** 559,
640–43
minority-language education
rights, **115,** 507
missionary parties, 338
mobility rights, **499**–500
Mohawks, Oka protest, 89
monarchy, 430. *See also* Crown;
governor general
Moores, Frank, 414
Morgentaler, Henry, 158, 205
Morton, F.L., 513, 514
Mulroney, Brian, 115, 152, 174,
232, 319, 358, 441, 476, 556
1992 referendum, 445
Conservative Party leader,
356
debating John Turner, 377
Meech Lake Accord,
440–41
policy guidance, 359
Mulroney government, 344, 599
advertising free trade, 286
business and, 399
Charlottetown Accord,
442–43

federal-provincial relations,
476
multiculturalism and,
135–36, 442
reform of House of
Commons, 643–44
Senate, 650
multiculturalism, 258, 442
as government policy, 130,
134–36, 138
Charter rights, 508
Liberal Party and, 135, 137
official, 138
opposition to, 137–38
policy, 130, 139, 219
multilateralism, **218**–20
multinationals
foreign ownership in Canada,
228
municipalities. See also cities
political activity, 202
provinces, 458
Muslims, 140, 141, 206, 207

National Action Committee on
the Status of Women
(NAC), **158,** 161, 402
policy participation, 158
National Advisory Council on
Aging, 210
National Anti-Poverty
Organization (NAPO), 185
National Capital Region, 464
National Citizens' Coalition
(NCC), **409**
National Council of Welfare
(NCW), 185
National Council of Women of
Canada (NCWC), 161
National Energy Board, 230,
235–36
National Energy Program
(NEP), 64, 65, 232, 236, 344
National Farmers Union
(NFU), 412
National Film Board (NFB), 239
National Hockey League, 241
National Pensioners and Senior
Citizens Federation, 213
National Policy (1879), 63, **227**
National Register of Electors,
318–19

national security, 222
terrorism and the Charter,
503–504
national values, Canada,
255–63
nationalism
Parti Québécois and, 113–14
Quebec, 105–6, 116, 120
Native Women's Association of
Canada, 97
NATO (North Atlantic Treaty
Organization), 223
natural resources. *See also* oil
and gas industry
ownership of, 61, 227, 228
taxation/regulation, 63, 65
NAVCanada, 606–607
Near, Harry, 417
Nelson Education, 240
neo-institutionalism, 20
neoconservatism, **43,** 353
neoliberalism, **43,** 181, 266, 353
Nevitte, Neil, 264–65
New Brunswick, 28, 31
bilingualism, 118
cultural equality, 118
language education, 118
New Democratic Party (NDP),
180
integrated party, as, 362
recent agenda/influence, 355
new middle class, **170**
New Public Management
(NPM), **605**–608
criticisms, 607–608
Newfoundland and Labrador
offshore petroleum, 69
school system, 205
Newman, Peter, 175, 177, 420
news. *See* media; newspapers
news management, **298**–99
newspapers, 240, 287–88
agenda-setting, 297
coverage fairness, 297
ownership, 287, 287T, 288T,
298
Nisga'a, 86, 87
Nisga'a Treaty, 98
self-governance/land claims
model, 98
nomination, **380**
nomination papers, **319**

non-status Indians, 83
nonconfidence motion, **641**
nonprofit corporations,
606–607
NORAD (North American
Aerospace Defence
Command), 223, 224
Nordlinger, Eric, 19
North, 61, 69. *See also individual
territories*
North American Free Trade
Agreement (NAFTA),
220–21, 264
North American Indians, 78,
79, 82, 86, *see also* Aboriginal
peoples
North-Western Territory, 31F
Northwest Territories, 32F
Nunavut creation, 93
notwithstanding clause,
509–10. *See also* Canadian
Charter of Rights and
Freedoms
Nova Scotia, 31
Nunavut, 32F, 61, 93
new territory of, 84F, 93
Nunziata, John, 319, 626

Obama, Barack, 23, 235
obscenity, *see* pornography
official bilingualism, 105, 112,
115, 122. *See also* bilingualism
Official Language Act (1890)
(Manitoba), 109
Official Languages Act (1969),
112–13, 118, **591**
Official Secrets Act, 299
offshore petroleum revenue, 69
Ogdensburg Agreement, 223
oil and gas industry, *see also*
National Energy Program
ownership, 236
Oka standoff, 89
Old Age Pensions Act, 150
Old Age Security (OAS), 210
ombudsman, 602
one-party dominance, **340**
Ontario, 29, 56, 60
economy, 60
French language schools, 109,
118
private schools, 206–207

public funded separate
schools, 204
religious courts, 207
treaties, 83
Ontario Coalition Against
Poverty, 189
opinion polls, 7, 13, 299–304,
444–45
elections, 301–303
opposition, **618**
Order of Business, 622F
Order of Canada, 548
orders-in-council, **552**
Organisation of Petroleum
Exporting Countries (OPEC),
65, 220
Ostry, Sylvia, 154

Pacific scandal (1827), **327**
Padlock Law (Que.), **493**
Page, Christopher, 304
Pal, Leslie, 527
Panitch, Leo, 178, 420
Papineau, Louis-Joseph, 29
Paris Peace Conference
(1919), 39
Parizeau government, 116
Parizeau, Jacques, 116, 445
sovereign Quebec proposals,
445–46
Parlby, Irene, 149
Parliament, 32–33, 617–54.
See also Cabinet; House of
Commons; Parliament,
members of; Senate
advocacy groups, 407–408
agents of, 599–600, 600T
budget debate, 521
Charter and legislation, 502
Charter decisions impact, 514
committees, 629, 633–37
dissolution of, **621**–22
legislation, 627–30
monarch (crown) and, 32–33
opposition days, **621**
Parliament, members of (MPs),
620T
as backbenchers, 624, 637, 638
benefits, salary, 637, 637T
roles, 638–39
speeches, 633
typical day, 639F

parliamentary press gallery, **295,**
623
parliamentary secretaries,
564–65
parliamentary supremacy,
492–93
Parrish, Carolyn, 642B
Parti Québécois (PQ)
government,113–14. *See also*
Quebec
Charter of the French
Language (Bill 101), 114
independence referendum, **114**
particularism, cultural, **258**
parties, political, 337–63,
344–45, 348, 356–59. *See also
specific parties*; elections;
patronage appointments
caucus, 626–27
class-based (ideological),
347–48
collectiveness, 353
control of, 362
conventions, 360
decline of, 349
discipline, 628
elections, 371–82, 372–79
elites in, 389
evolution, 339–46
federal-provincial links,
362–63
funding for, 328–32, 331T
headquarters, 361, 372–73
ideology, 351–55
leadership, 339–40, 342, 343,
374
membership, 272, 355–56
operations, 360–63
parliamentary wing, 362
party discipline, **624**–26
policymaking, 359–60
recent party positions, 354–55
religious affiliation, 208
structure, 355–63
support, 382–85, 383F
three-party system, 344
urban vs. rural support, 203
party caucus, **626**–27
party identification, **386**
party whips, **632**
party, political, 6. *See also*
parties, political

patronage
    government agencies, in,
        590, 591
    judicial appointments, 672
    political, 590, 672
Pauktuutit Inuit Women's
    Association, 97
pay equity, **155,** 591
Peace, Order, and Good
    Government (POGG) clause,
    462–66
    leading cases, 463B–464B
peaceful assembly, *see* freedom
    of association
Pearson Education, 240
Pearson government, 238, 468
Pearson, Lester, 224, 343, 475,
    646
Péladeau family, 287
Péladeau, Pierre-Karl, 175
Penner Report (1983), 90–91
Pépin-Robarts Task Force on
    Canadian Unity (1979), 438
Persons case, **150**–51, **646**
Peterson, David, 118
petite bourgeoisie, 17, 18, **170**
Pettipas, Randy, 417
pipeline debate, **343,** 628
pluralism, 11–14. *See also*
    multiculturalism; subcultures
    Aboriginal integration, 98
    advocacy groups, 419
    brokerage politics of
        accommodation, 364
    bureaucracy and, 610
    Charter protection of civil
        liberties, 515
    cleavages and, 73
    election platforms, groups
        and, 389
    ethnocultural groups inclu-
        siveness, 142
    federalism and, 484–85
    franchise restrictions, 333
    French-English relations and,
        122
    House of Commons, 653
    labour movement and, 191
    ᵈⁱa diversity, 306
        ⁻alism, 142–43
            nce in judi-
        ⁻80

redistribution of seats, 333
referenda on the constitu-
    tion, 450
religious groups, 214
representation in Cabinet,
    576
subcultures, 274
women's groups and, 164
policy advocacy, 406
policy communities, 21, **404,**
    532–35, 533F
policy instruments, **535**–39
policy networks, **404**–405,
    532–35
policymaking, 396, 525–40
    advocacy groups and,
    cabinet role, 528
    courts using the Charter, 511,
        512
    formulation phase/consulta-
        tions, 530
    implementation phase, 529F,
        531, 534
    initiation phase, 528, 529F,
        534
    judicial interpretation phase,
        531, 535
    legitimation phase, 529F,
        530–31
    parliamentary/extraparlia-
        mentary organizations, 362
    political parties, 359–62
    polls and, 303–304
    prime minister and, 556–57
    priority-setting phase, 530
    stakeholders, **535**
political efficacy, **269**
political elite
    newspapers, 297
political equality, **252**–53
political freedom, **253**–54
    breaches of, 253–54
    provincial violations, 254
political participation, 269–73
political party(ies), *see* parties,
    political
    definition, **337**
political patronage, **590,** 672
    definition, 338
political system
    aging/mandatory retirement,
        212–13

media influence, 294–95
poor and, 185
political values, families and,
    282
politicians, 298–99. See also
    Parliament, members of;
    senators
    and bureaucracy, 610–11
    as elites, 389
    journalists and, 298
    media, 297–99
politics, *see also* parties, polit-
    ical; politicians
    approaches to, 10–21
    brokerage, 346–47
    class, 347–48
    definition, 7
    globalization and, 22–23
    legalized/ Charter and,
        511–12
    minor parties and, 350
    pluralist approach, 11–14
    political action participation,
        272–73, 272F
    populism, 354
    public and, 7–8
    public choice approach,
        14–15
    state and (state-centred
        approach), 19–21
    structural analysts and, 10
polls, *see* opinion polls
pollsters, 300–301
pollution, *see* environment
poor, 183–86, *see also* poverty
    class-consciousness of, 190
    housing, 184–85
    minimum wage, 185
    social programs, 187–88, 189
    welfare, social assistance, 183
popular sovereignty, **252**
popular vote, **322,** 322T
population
    aging, 210–12, 211T
    urban vs. rural, 198–203,
        198F
pornography
    Charter and, 497, 498
poverty, *see also* poor
    Aboriginals, among, 81–82
    advocacy groups, 185
    children and, 183–84, 184F

education, 184
federal social programs, 186
feminization of, 184
reform, 191
social expenditure/GDP, 188
welfare cuts effect, 189
poverty line, **183**
power, 5
declaratory, 472
of disallowance, 472
executive, 493
of reservation, 460
Prairie provinces, 60–61. *See also* individual provinces
economy, 60–61
Prentice, Jim, 231
prerogative powers, **548**-50
pressure groups, **395**, *see also* advocacy groups
Presthus, Robert, 24
prime minister, 406–407, 554–60. *See also* Cabinet; government; House of Commons
advisor to governor general, 557
agenda setting, 558
appointments power, 557
chief policymaker, as, 556–57
minority governments, 558–60
party leader, 556
powers, 552–54, 555
styles of recent, 560, 560T
Prime Minister's Office (PMO), **572**
prime ministerial government, **554**
Prince Edward Island, 28, 31
union, 429
privacy, media and politicians, 298
private (civil) law, 662–63
private bills, **628,** 647
private medical insurance, 189
private members' bills, **623,** 627
private sector, 3–4, **532**–33. *See also* business; elite(s)
privatization, **535,** 538, 597
Privy Council, 552. *See also* Judicial Committee of the Privy Council

Privy Council Office (PCO), **572**–73, 587
bureaucracy and, 601
cabinet committees, 571
clerk's role, 573, 574
composition, 573
role, 573–74
professions
mobility rights and, 500
Progressive Conservative Party, 344, 345. *See also* Conservative Party of Canada
leadership, 358
proletariat, **169**
Pross, Paul, 12, 396, 397, 404, 532, 533F
protests, 409–10
provinces, *see also* equalization payments; federalism; federal-provincial powers; transfer payments
Charter groups, 512
confederation culture/language guarantees, 108
constitutional amendment veto, 439
constitutions of, 435
courts, 458, 664–66
direct taxation, 470–72, 472T
electoral reforms, 326–27
federal cabinet representation, 562, 563T
federal grants, and, 467–69
federal powers over, 460
foreign states, and, 482
language rights, 118–19
legislatures, 457, 459
linguistic minorities, 119
multiculturalism, and, 136–37
POGG and powers of, 465
political systems, 456–59
powers and the Charter, 513
responsibilities, 458
revenue, 466, 470–72
seat allocation, 314–15
Southern land claims and, 86
trade and, 476–77
welfare and, 187
welfare and Canada Assistance Plan, 467–68
workfare, 188

Public Accounts Committee, **601**
public allowances, 331T
public bills, **627**
public choice approach, 14–15
bureaucracy and politicians, 610–11
Cabinet and political power, 576–77
election laws/representation, 333
electoral aspects of federalism, 485–86
electoral/policymaking, 364
farmers, 214
French Canadian prominence, 122
gender-consciousness, 164–65
House of Commons, 653
marginal groups and policy, 540
media and politicians, 306
multiculturalism, 143
religion, 214
voter interest, 274
voting and elections, 389
working class and, 191
public expenditures, *see* government, spending/expenditures
public health insurance, 468, 469
public law cases, 670
public opinion, **299**–300
public opinion polls. *See* opinion polls
public ownership, **538**
public policy purpose, 55
public policy, **527**-28, *see also* policymaking
Public Safety Canada, 222
public sector, 3–4, **532**–33
Public Service Commission, **589,** 590
Public Service Modernization Act, 590
public service, *see* bureaucracy; government, federal
publishing industry, 240
punishment, cruel and unusual, 503

quasi-judicial decisions, **598**
quasi-legislative rules/regulations, 598
Quebec, 28, 56, 57, 58–59, *See also* Quiet Revolution
    Aboriginal land claims and, 87
    Bill 101, **114**
    conscription crises, 110
    constitutional amendment and, 440, 442–44
    current issues, 110
    discrimination, ethnic immigrants, 140–41
    distinct society and Meech Lake Accord, 115–16, 120
    economy, 58–60
    equalization payments, 68–69
    ethnic minorities, 120–21
    federal government and, 111–12
    federal politics, post-1990, 344–45
    federal relations, post-1995, 477
    Francophonie, **115**
    French-only signs, 115
    globalization and language, 123
    history, 107–108
    immigrant integration, 208
    James Bay project, 87
    mother tongue, 104T
    multiculturalism, and, 137
    nationalism, 105–6, 116, 120
    new middle class, 111
    notwithstanding clause, **509**
    population of, 104
    power companies nationalization, 111
    private law system, 663
    religion and, 205
    separatists, 113
    sovereignty-association, 114–15, **438**
    subculture, as, 268
    urban issues, 202–203
    veto re constitutional amendment, 440
Quebec Act (1774), 28, 107
Quebec *independantistes*, 116
Quebecor, 290, 293T

Question Period, 295, 601–602, **623**
    members' statements, 623
Quiet Revolution, 106, 110–13, 117, 205, **432**, 436

radio industry, 240
Radio-Canada, 238, 289
Rae, Bob, 359
RCMP (Royal Canadian Mounted Police), 154
    Sikhs, turban issue, 206
REAL Women, 161
reasonable limits clause
    Oakes and *Sharpe* cases/guidelines, **496**
reference cases, **667**, 668T
referendums, **114**, 444
    sovereign Quebec (1995), re, 446
Reform Party, 344–45, 354. *See also* Canadian Alliance
refugees, 140, *see also* immigrants; immigration
regional economic development programs, **69–70**
regionalism, 51–73
    approaches to, 51–53
    climate change, 66
    and economy. 58–62
    geography, 53–57
    identities and, 70–72
    and party system, 72
    population distribution, 56–57
    regions and, 53–58
regions
    disparities between, 67–70
    economy and, 62, 65–67
    federal funding, 68–69
    free trade, 65–66
    party support in, 382–85
RRSPs and income, 179F
regulation, 537–38. *See also* agencies
regulations (statutory instruments), **363**, 531, 554, 584. *See also* legislation
    quasi-legislative, 598–99
    review by Senate, 648
regulatory tribunals, **598**–99
    appeals, 666

Reisman, Heather, 155, 156
religion(s), 203–209, 204T, 384, 385. *See also* specific religious groups
    freedom of, 496–97
    globalization and diversity of, 214–15
religiosity, 197–98
representation by population, 252
representative bureaucracy, **591**
representative government, 29
reservation power, federal, **460**
reserves, 78–79, 81, 96
residential schools, 95
responsible government, 29, 30, **623**
ridings, *see* constituencies (political)
Riel, Louis, 32, 84, 108–109, 340
Riel Rebellions, 10, 108–109
right to strike
    labour and the Charter, 498
right, the, **352**
rights and freedoms, 492
    Charter of Rights and Freedoms, 495–510
    nature of, 492
    pre-Charter in Canada, 492–95
    rule of law and executive power, 493
Rivard, Lucien, 327
Roach, Kent, 514
Robinson Treaties (1850), 83
Robinson, Michael, 417
Rock, Allan, 21, 162, 416
Rogers, Ted, 174
Roman Catholic Church, 268, 285
    influence of, 285
Rose, Vanessa, 402
Rosenberg case (Ontario Court of Appeal), 162
Rothstein, Marshall, 659
Rowell-Sirois Commission, **466**–67
royal assent, 630
    new procedures, 630
Royal Canadian Mounted Police, *see under* RCMP

royal commissions, **408**–409, **600**
on Aboriginal Peoples
(1996), 92, **92**–93
on Bilingualism and
Biculturalism (1963), 85,
111, 134
on Electoral Reform and
Party Financing, **377**
on Equality in Employment
(1984), 155
on New Reproductive
Technologies (1993), 159
on Newspapers, 287
on the Status of Women
(1967–70), 152
royal prerogative, *see* prerogative powers
Royal Proclamation (1763), **83**,
90, 508
rule of law, **38**, 493
Rupert's Land, 27, 31, 31F, 32,
429
Russell, Peter, 512, 659, 673

Sable Island Offshore Energy
Project, 59
safe seats, **386**, 620
St. Laurent, Louis, 341, 342,
561
St. Lawrence Seaway, 53
Sandra Lovelace case, 90, 158
Saskatchewan, *see* Prairie provinces
language rights, 118–19
Saul, John Ralston, 251
Sauvé, Jeanne, 152, 153
Savoie, Donald J., 528, 554, 558
Sawatsky, John, 414
school(s). *See also* education
political socialization by,
282–84
residential, 95
separate, 203–205
schools, 306
Schreiber, Karlheinz, 631
Schreyer, Edward, 550
scrums, 623
search and seizure
Charter rights, 501
evidence and Charter,
507–508
secession, Quebec, 447

Sechelt Indian Band Self-
Government Act (1984), 91
security, 222
Security of Information Act, 299
security of the person
as Charter right, 500, 501
Senate, 338, 408
composition of, 645–46
crown power to appoint, 547
functions of, 646–51
government bills and, 630
powers and role, 644–45
powers and selection, 435
reform, 651–52
regional equality, 461
timetable, 648
Triple-E, 443, **651**–52
veto, 649
seniors, 209–13
dependency ratio, 211
grey power, 210
housing, 213
long-term care, 213
sentences, criminal
Charter and, 503
sexual orientation, **162**, 505
Sgro, Judy, 139
shared-cost programs, **467**–68
Sikh RCMP members and turbans, 206
Skelton, O.D., 40
Smart Border Declaration, 226
Smith, David, 339, 342, 546
Smith, Mary Ellen, 149
Smith, Miriam, 397
Sniderman, Paul, 256
social assistance, *see* provinces,
welfare
social conservatives, *see* neo-
conservativism
Social Credit Party, 64, 254,
342
social democracy, **351**, 352
social movements, **395**,
402–403
social programs, 186–90. *See
also* welfare state
corporate elite and, 177
cuts to, 187–90
dependency, 211–12
disabled, 186–87
seniors, 210, 212

Social Reconstruction, 342
social program spending, 468
social safety net, **186**–87
Social Sciences and Humanities
Research Council (SSHRC),
241
Social Union Framework
Agreement (SUFA), **477**
socialization, political, 282–86
business and, 284–85
political parties and, 284
sponsorship scandal, 286
think tanks, 285
softwood lumber, 23˙
Southern Ontario Development
Agency, 70
sovereignty, Aboriginal, 79
sovereignty association
(Quebec), **114**–15, 120
Speaker, **630**–32
special committees, **636**
special operating agencies
(SOAs), **606**
specific claims, **886**
Specific Claims Tribunal Act
(2008), 88
specific land claims, 88
speech from the throne, **553**–54
spending power, **468**
Spicer, Keith, 442
spin doctors, 298–99, 377
split-run editions, **238**
spoils system, **590**
sponsorship scandal, 417,
608–609
stakeholders, **535**
Standing Committee on Public
Accounts, **635**
standing committees, **634**–35
Standing Joint Committee on
the Scrutiny of Regulations,
636
Standing Orders, **630**
Stanfield, Robert, 319, 343
staples theory, 58
stare decisis, **660**
state-centred approach, 19–21
bureaucratic government
policy, 365
bureaucratic power/
mandarins, 610
changing role, 41–43

Charter as government restraint, 516
constitutional change, 450
continental economic policies, 243
embedded, 24
House of Commons, 654
information manipulation, 306
judiciary and, 679
liberalism, 352
paternalism to Aboriginals, 98
popular participation, 273–74
post-election policy innovation, 389
prime minister and cabinet, 575–76
public consultation in policymaking, 541
redistribution process/ election funding, 334
schools, 306
state of emergency
as policy instrument, **539**
status Indians, 83, 95. *See also* Aboriginal peoples
Status of Women Canada, 152
Statute of Westminster (1931), 40, 429
statutory appropriations, 592, 594
Stevens, Sinclair, 319
Stillman case (SCC), 502
Stowe, Emily, 148
strategic voting, 388
statutes, *see* legislation
Stronach, Belinda, 642B
structuralism, 397
subcultures
ethnic, 268–69
regional/provincial, **267**–68
Suez Crisis (1956), 41
supremacy of Parliament, 33, **661**
Supreme Court of Canada (SCC), 88, 155, 441, 667–71, 669F. *See also*

Canadian Charter of Rights and Freedoms
appeals, 670F
appointment of judges, 674–76
constitutional reference, 439
Quebec separation decision, 1998, 446–47
reference cases, 667–68, 668T
unilateral federal constitutional amendment, 439
Supreme court cases, 506
(*a partial list*)
Andrews, 504
Askov, 502
Borowski, 500
Broyles, 502
Calder, 86, 87
Chaoulli, 189, 479–80, 500–501
Charkaoui, 503–504
Corbière, 93, 504
Daigle, 500
Delgamuukw, 87
Donald Marshall, 88
Drybones, 494–95
Eldridge, 504–505
Gladue, 95
Godoy, 502
Hebert, 502
Khadr, 504
Lavell, 158
Law, 504
M. v. H., 162
Marshall, 508
Mercure, 118–19
Morgentaler, 158–59, 500
Munro, 464
Oakes, 502–503
Operation Dismantle, 500
R. v. Butler, 498
R. v. Kapp, 96–97
Reference re Same-Sex Marriage, 163
Reference re Quebec independence, 117
Sharon McIvor, 97
Sharpe Sharon McIvor, 97
Sharpe, 497, 498
Sioui, 88, 508
Sparrow, 88, 508

Symes, 158
Thibaudeau, 158
Valente, 502
Vriend, 162
symbolic response, 535–36

tariffs, 63
dispute-settlement mechanism, 220
trade agreements and, 220
Task Force on Canadian Unity (1979), 51
Tax Court of Canada, 667
tax expenditures, **536**–37
taxation, 460, 538
RRSPs and income, 179F
taxation agreements, **467,** 478
Telefilm Canada, 239
Teleglobe Canada, 56
Telesat, 56
television, 237–38, 292
Territorial Formula Financing (TTF), 69
Territories, *see also* individual territories
revenue, 470–72
terrorism, **222**
Charter and, 503–504
international, 222
Thatcher, Margaret, 558
think tanks, 285
third-party advertising, **331,** 332, 409
Thompson, John, 549
Thomson family, 174
Thomson media, 287
Thomson, Ken, 174
three-party system, **344**
throne speech, **553**–54
Tobin, Brian, 205
tolerance, *see* discrimination
Toronto-Ottawa-Montreal, 56–57
trade, 231–34
Canada- U.S., 220
Canada-North American, 220–21
globalization, 221, 222
trade and commerce clause, **465**
trade unions, *see* unions
Trading with the Enemy Act (U.S.), 229

Trans-Canada Airlines, 55
Trans-Canada Highway, 55
Trans-Canada Pipeline, 55
transfer payments
  federal-provincial, 469,
    471T
transnational corporations,
  221
transnationals, 174
  globalization and policy,
    542
transportation, 53–56, 63
Treasury Board, **571**
Treasury Board Secretariat
  (TBS), **575**, 590
treaties
  Aboriginal peoples and,
    83–85, 84F
  broken promises, 96
  modern urban British
    Columbia, 97
Treaty of Washington, 39
treaty power, **465**
treaty rights, 88
tribunals, regulatory, *see*
  regulation
Triple-E Senate, 443,
  651–52
Trudeau, Pierre Elliott, 112,
  205, 224, 441, 495, 507, 509,
  556
  constitutional reform propo-
    sals, 438–40
  Liberal Party leader, 342
  opposition to Meech Lake,
    441
  and party organization,
    361–62
  and unilateral constitutional
    amendment, 438–39
Trudeau government, 86, 343
  War Measures Act, 113
Trudeau-Chrétien White Paper
  (1969), 78, 85
Tsawwassen First Nation Final
  Agreement, 97
TTF (Territorial Formula
  Financing), 69
Turner, Garth, 626
Turner, John, 296, 317, 344
  debating Brian Mulroney, 377
Twitter, 294

unemployment insurance, 182,
  185
UNESCO, 483
Union Government (1917),
  110
Union Nationale, 342
unions,
  Charter and, 498
  International, 236
  United Auto Workers
    (UAW), 236
  United Steelworkers, 236
United Empire Loyalists,
  28–29, 107, 256
United Nations, 219
United Nations Human
  Development Index, 81
United Nations Human Rights
  Commission, 81
United Nations Human Rights
  Committee, 90
United States of America, 28, 30
  American political values,
    255–56
  "Buy American" program,
    233
  civil rights, 492
  enemy list and branch plants,
    229
  influence on Canadian poli-
    tics, 241–42
  international unions, 236
  magazine industry and, 238,
    239
  oil and gas industry owner-
    ship, 236
  political system, 34–35, 35F
  protectionism, 233
  separation of powers doc-
    trine, 34–35, 35F
  softwood lumber dispute,
    233
  television industry, 237,
    238
United Steelworkers, 236
Universal Declaration on
  Human Rights (U.N.), 494
Upper Canada, 29, 30
upper class, 172–78

values, *see* democracy
VIA Rail, 54

Victoria, Queen, 33
Victoria Charter, 437
visible minorities, **128,** 129.
  See also minorities
  racial animosity, 134
Voice of Women (VOW), 161
voluntary cession, 83
voluntary sector, 3–4, **532**–33
Voluntary Sector Initiative,
  534
voters, 382–88. *See also*
  elections; franchise; voting
  economy and, 386
  election campaign involve-
    ment, 271
  inmates' rights, 321
  knowledge, 270–71
  politicians and, 14, 15
  religions, 208–209
  secret ballot, 320
  youth, 270
voters' list, **318**–19
voting
  democratic rights and the
    Charter, 499
  election day, 319–20
  rural-urban split, 384
  turnout rate, 269–72, 270T,
    271T
voting (House of Commons)
  formal recorded vote, 633
  pairing, 633

Waddell, Christopher, 297
wage and price controls, **343**
War Measures Act, **113,** 299
war veterans, 187
watchdog agencies, 602–604
welfare state, **42**–43, 186, 352
Wells, Clyde, 205
Western alienation, **70,** 71,
  267–68
Western Economic
  Diversification Canada
  (WD), 69–70
Westerners, 267–68
Westminster model, 33, **617**
Weston, Galen, 174
White Paper, 85, 90, 530
White Paper on Indians, **78,**
  85, 90
Williams, Danny, 69

Wilson, Bertha, 153, 498
Winnipeg General Strike
(1919), 180
Women, 164. *See also* feminism;
gender
Aboriginal women's issues,
155
and abortion laws, 158–59
in business, 155–56
and the Charter, 501, 508
child care, 160
employment issues, 155–56
enfranchisement, 149–50,
149T
equality rights, 15657, 504,
505
family issues, 149, 150, 160
feminization of poverty, 160
in government, 150, 151,
152–53, 153T, 591
improved legislation, 151

in labour force, 156
legal challenges by, 157–58
participation, 151
pay equity, 154–55
politics, in, 150, 151, 152–55
pro-life groups, 161
prostitution laws, 159
rights, 148–52
in Senate, 646
social legislation and,
149–50
unpaid work, 156, 157T
violence, and, 159–60
as voters, 154 *see also infra*
enfranchisement
women legislators, 149
women's groups, 160–61
women's movement, 148,
152–62
working class, 180–83
CCF support, 348

globalization, 182
politics, and, 347–48
unions and, 180, 181,
182
voting and, 384–85
World Trade Organization
(WTO), **219**, 231, 239
WWII (World War II)
conscription, 110
immigration and, 132
Japanese Canadians, 136
Wylie, Torrence, 417

young people, 665
Youth Criminal Justice Act,
665
YouTube, 294
Yukon, 32F

Ziegel, Jacob, 675